Crime and Punishment

THE JONES AND BARTLETT SERIES IN PHILOSOPHY
Robert Ginsberg, General Editor

Ayer, A. J., *Metaphysics and Common Sense,* 1994 reprint with corrections and new introduction by Thomas Magnell, Drew University

Beckwith, Francis J., University of Nevada, Las Vegas, Editor, *Do the Right Thing: A Philosophical Dialogue on the Moral and Social Issues of Our Time*

Caws, Peter, George Washington University, *Ethics from Experience*

Cooper, Jane, The Pennsylvania State University, Delaware County Campus, *A Comparitive Primer for Ethics: With Applications in Biology and Medicine*

DeMarco, Joseph P., Cleveland State University, *Moral Theory: A Contemporary View*

Devine, Phillip E., Providence College, and Celia Wolf-Devine, Stonehill College, Editors, *Sex and Gender*

Edgar, Stacey L., State University of New York, Geneseo, *Computer Ethics*

Gorr, Michael, Illinois State University, and Sterling Harwood, San Jose State University, Editors, *Crime and Punishment: Philosophic Explorations*

Harwood, Sterling, San Jose State University, Editor, *Business as Ethical and Business as Usual, Text and Readings*

Heil, John, Davidson College, *First-Order Logic: A Concise Introduction*

Jason, Gary, San Diego State University, *Introduction to Logic*

Jason, Gary, San Diego State University, *Critical Thinking: Plain Speaking and Clear Understanding*

Merrill, Sarah A., Purdue University/Calumet, *Ethical Challenges in Construction, Engineering and Contracting, Text and Case Studies*

Moriarity, Marilyn, Hollins College, *The Conceptual Handbook to Scientific Writing: Critical Thinking Through Writing*

Pauling, Linus and Daisaku Ikeda, *A Lifelong Quest for Peace: A Dialogue,* Translator and Editor, Richard L. Gage

Pojman, Louis P., University of Mississippi, and Francis J. Beckwith, University of Nevada, Las Vegas, Editors, *The Abortion Controversy: A Reader*

Pojman, Louis P., The University of Mississippi, *Environmental Ethics: Readings in Theory and Application*

Pojman, Louis P., The University of Mississippi, *Life and Death: Grappling with the Moral Dilemmas of Our Time*

Pojman, Louis P., The University of Mississippi, *Life and Death: A Reader in Moral Problems*

Rolston, Holmes, III, Colorado State University, *Biology, Ethics, and the Origins of Life*

Townsend, Dabney, The University of Texas at Arlington, Editor, *Readings in Aesthetics*

Veatch, Robert M., The Kennedy Institute of Ethics, Georgetown University, *Cross-Cultural Perspectives in Medical Ethics: Readings*

Veatch, Robert M., The Kennedy Institute of Ethics, Georgetown University, *Medical Ethics*

Verene, Donald P., Emory University, Editor, *Sexual Love and Western Morality: A Philosophical Anthology*

Williams, Clifford, Trinity College, Illinois, Editor, *On Love and Friendship: Philosophical Readings*

Crime and Punishment

Philosophic Explorations

Edited by

Michael J. Gorr

Illinois State University

Sterling Harwood

San Jose State University

JONES AND BARTLETT PUBLISHERS

BOSTON LONDON

Editorial, Sales, and Customer Service Offices
Jones and Bartlett Publishers
One Exeter Plaza
Boston, MA 02116
1–800–832–0034
617–859–3900

Jones and Bartlett Publishers International
7 Melrose Terrace
London W6 7RL
England

Library of Congress Cataloging-in-Publication Data

Crime and punishment : philosophic explorations / edited by Michael J. Gorr,
Sterling Harwood.
p. cm. -- (The Jones and Bartlett series in philosophy)
Includes bibliographical references and index.
ISBN 0–86720–955–0
1. Criminal law--United States--Philosophy. 2. Criminal law--Philosophy 3. Punishment--Philosophy. I. Gorr, Michael J.
II. Harwood, Sterling. III. Series.
KF9223.A75C745 1995
345.73'001--dc20
[347.30501] 94–25385
CIP

Acquisitions Editor: Arthur C. Bartlett and Nancy E. Bartlett
Production Editor: Anne S. Noonan
Manufacturing Buyer: Dana L. Cerrito
Editorial Production Service: Wordcrafters Editorial Services, Inc.
Typesetting: Sunrise Composition
Cover Design: Marshall Henrichs
Printing and Binding: Hamilton Printing
Cover Printing: Henry N. Sawyer Co.

Printed in the United States of America
98 97 96 95 94 10 9 8 7 6 5 4 3 2 1

Contents

Preface

The purpose of this book is to provide the student with a set of essays that addresses the two fundamental philosophical questions concerning criminal law:

1. What sort of behavior should society criminalize?
2. What should society do with those who engage in such behavior?

While numerous anthologies focus on one or the other of these questions, no other anthology treats *both* in the systematic and comprehensive fashion found in this book.

It is important to explore these two questions together because they are intimately connected. If there are justifications for punishing criminals (as almost everyone believes), then they will surely be closely related to the criteria society should use to determine what sorts of activities should be subject to criminal sanctions. If, for example, one believes that the state should prohibit only behavior which in some way *harms* others, then it seems reasonable to suppose that the rationale for punishment will in some way be closely connected to the prevention of such harm. At the very least, anyone who would claim otherwise has some serious explaining to do. An assumption that informs this book is that there is a *unity of purpose* to the system of criminal law and that its fundamental features are significantly connected to each other.

In deciding what to include in this volume, we tried to choose essays that would

- Provide coverage of a wide range of issues, approaches, and perspectives.
- Be intelligible to beginning students with no prior knowledge of either philosophy or law.
- Avoid both the extreme of focusing exclusively on abstract philosophical issues and the opposite extreme of immersing the student in concrete legal issues without providing an appreciation of their philosophical significance and ramifications.
- Clarify, exemplify, and motivate an interest in the philosophical study of criminal law: the *moral appraisal* of the principles and institutions that comprise the basic elements of the system of criminal law.
- Explore some subjects often neglected (e.g., white-collar crime, hate crimes, blackmail, and the extent to which it is appropriate to show mercy to the guilty).

Hence, we have chosen to include selections from both classical and contemporary writers, as well as carefully edited case excerpts that serve to raise or illuminate such important and diverse issues as the legalization of drugs, the permissibility of "hate speech" regulations, and the justification of the death penalty.

We have also included several special features designed to help make the book more "user friendly." First, the Introduction both gives the students some understanding of the nature of the inquiry and motivates their interest in exploring these controversial issues in criminal law. Second, each selection begins with a brief summary sketching the main arguments and conclusions of the essay selected. Third, at the end of each of the book's many subsections, we have included a set of study questions designed to stimulate critical thinking and discussion about the arguments and issues of the subsection. Fourth, at the end of each of the two main parts of the book, we have included a list of additional readings on the relevant topics. Finally, we have included four appendices: the first gives students guidelines on how to write a paper in philosophy; the second gives brief summaries of some basic moral theories and principles that are relevant to the issues discussed in the book. The third appendix gives students reasons to take morality seriously by analyzing the pros and cons of moral relativism (a view many students bring to their first class dealing with moral values). Appendix D brings this book up to date with the views of many experts in a wide-ranging and penetrating discussion of the so-called "abuse excuse" and the recent cases of Lorena Bobbitt (who mutilated her husband), Tonya Harding (who was involved in the attack on skater Nancy Kerrigan), the Menendez brothers (who killed their parents), and Damian Williams (who was sentenced to 10 years for mayhem surrounding the beating of trucker Reginald Denny during the riots in Los Angeles in 1992).

Appendix D concerns the national debate about whether compassion and justice are compatible (see also S. Harwood, "Is Mercy Inherently Unjust?"). Alan Dershowitz, for example, discusses the Bobbitt case and the plight of battered women more generally. He urges battered women simply to call 911 and leave home rather than strike back. But others discuss how ineffective and even counterproductive Dershowitz's strategy is. Dershowitz's remarks should be read in light of the famous O. J. Simpson case, which has captivated America. Dershowitz joined Simpson's defense team. Nicole Brown, Simpson's murdered ex-wife, called 911 at least eight times to report domestic emergencies, and she ultimately left Simpson. If Simpson were found guilty, then the Simpson case would be a spectacular counterexample to Dershowitz's strategy for women.

Though one should rely on verifiable statistics rather than making a hasty generalization from one case or a few anecdotes, Christina Hoff Sommers' recent book *Who Stole Feminism?* casts some doubt on the reliability of the statistics now available on domestic violence, and many have noted that the case of Nicole Brown has raised consciousness on the issue of domestic violence just as the case of Anita Hill (alleging that now-Supreme Court Justice Clarence Thomas had sexually harrassed her) raised consciousness on the issue of sexual harrassment. The Simpson case can play such an educational role because it is not just a "whodunit"; the case raises such basic issues as, "Can the rich buy more justice than the poor by hiring the best lawyers?" "Can the rich literally get away with murder?" "Should murderers be executed, at least in cases where there are special circumstances such as the double murder of Nicole Brown and Ronald Goldman?" "Has the news media's pervasive technology and bias (for example, *Time* magazine's racist portrayal of Simpson on its cover) made getting a fair trial in a high-profile case too difficult or even impossible?" and "Has the courts' dependence on technological experts made arguing over literally splitting hairs a necessity?" This text gives the reader a strong basis for answering such key questions (for example, see McCloskey's article on convicting the innocent and the entire section on capital punishment).

Criminal cases such as the O. J. Simpson case have recently captivated America. We hope *Crime and Punishment: Philosophic Explorations* will not only succeed in exposing the student to what it is like to think in a rigorous and critical way about some important issues in criminal law, but will also communicate a sense of how fascinating it can be to explore the way the law confronts, and should confront, what it considers "the criminal mind."

Introduction

Although criminal law constitutes only a relatively small part of our overall legal system, it is the part that the average person is most familiar with (if only from films and television shows such as *Perry Mason*). This is not surprising, given how comparatively dramatic so many crimes are. For example, if someone successfully brings a civil suit against a company on the grounds that one of the company's products was defective and injured someone, the court will often order the company to pay a considerable sum of money to the injured person. While such an order is hardly a trivial matter (particularly if it is *your* company), it certainly seems less serious than suffering a conviction for a crime, the sentence for which is often years in prison—or even death! Under the civil law, courts often require people to compensate others for losses, and civil courts sometimes make people pay punitive (sometimes called treble) damages, but it is primarily the institutions of the system of criminal justice that impose punishments. Since punishing people characteristically involves doing very nasty and unpleasant things to them, things it would ordinarily be very wrong to do to anyone, the act of punishment calls for the closest moral scrutiny. Providing that scrutiny is a central purpose of the philosophy of criminal law, and it is what the readings in this book are all about.

Our concern here is not with providing a detailed *description* of the system of criminal law. Pure description is a job for a lawyer or criminologist. Rather, the philosopher of criminal law is interested in providing a *moral assessment* or *evaluation* of the criminal law system. That is, the philosopher is keen to inquire into what the criminal law *ought* to be like rather than merely what the criminal law *is* like. Fortunately, not everything about such evaluations is controversial. Few of us, for instance, would question the decision to criminalize the sort of actions generally classified as murder, rape, assault, or robbery. But, for example, whether the law should allow people generally to own and possess dangerous firearms is indeed controversial. The now famous David Koresh and his now dead followers apparently thought the law should have permitted them to own many dangerous weapons. Armed federal agents from the Bureau of Alcohol, Tobacco, and Firearms (BATF) and from the Federal Bureau of Investigation (FBI) thought otherwise. The result was the obviously tragic "massacre at Waco." The moral issue of whether or not gun control laws are strict enough is but one of a series of controversial issues that we discuss in Part I of this book.

A second, closely related issue concerns how we are entitled to treat those who are convicted of crimes. Some scholars claim that punishment is permissible only to the extent that it serves to protect society by incapacitating the criminal (that is, removing the criminal from the public) or by deterring the criminal and others from committing similar crimes in the future. But is this an adequate position? If so, then where should law draw the line? Is it, in general, morally right to harm people simply to provide benefits for others? Before you answer you should consider the following passage from Fyodor Dostoyevsky's classic novel *Crime and Punishment* (whose title we have borrowed, in tribute, for this anthology):

". . . I'll tell you what: I swear I could kill that damned old woman and rob her, without a single twinge of conscience," exclaimed the student hotly.

. . . "Let me ask you a serious question," went on the student, even more heatedly. "I was joking just now, of course, but look here: on the one hand you have a stupid, silly, utterly unimportant, vicious, sickly old woman, no good to anybody, but in fact quite the opposite, who doesn't know herself why she goes on living, and will probably die tomorrow without any assistance. Do you understand what I am saying?"

"Oh, I follow you," answered the officer, earnestly studying his companion's vehemence.

"Listen, then. On the other hand you have new, young forces running to waste for want of backing, and there are thousands of them, all over the place. A hundred, a thousand, good actions and promising beginnings might be forwarded and directed aright by the money that old woman destines for a monastery; hundreds, perhaps thousands, of existences might be set on the right path, scores of families saved from beggary, from decay, from ruin and corruption, from the lock hospitals—and all with her money! Kill her, take her money, on condition that you dedicate yourself with its help to the service of humanity and the common good: don't you think that thousands of good deeds will wipe out one little, insignificant transgression? For one life taken, thousands saved from corruption and decay! One death, and a hundred lives in exchange—why, it's simple arithmetic! What is the life of that stupid, spiteful, consumptive old woman weighed against the common good? No more than the life of a louse or a cockroach—less, indeed, because she is actively harmful. She battens on other people's lives, she is evil; not long since she bit Lizaveta's finger, out of sheer malice, and it almost had to be amputated!"

"She doesn't deserve to live, certainly," remarked the officer, "but there you are, that's nature."

"But don't you see, man, nature must be guided and corrected, or else we should all be swamped. . . .*

*From Fyodor Dostoevsky, *Crime and Punishment*, translated by Jessie Coulson. Oxford, England: Oxford University Press, 1953. By permission of Oxford University Press.

However, if benefiting society is an inadequate reason for punishing people, then what would be a good enough reason to do so? In Part II of this book, scholars analyze and debate many different answers to this question, including the view that *nothing* justifies punishment and that society should deal with criminals in an entirely different way. Whether it could ever make sense to show mercy to a duly convicted criminal and the conditions—if any—under which we would be justified in imposing the ultimate penalty of death are two further issues scholars discuss in the final two sets of essays in Part II.

What you can expect to get out of a philosophical study of the criminal law is, in large part, a function of *how* you go about studying. The selections in this book are all *argumentative* essays. This means that their objective is not simply to supply you with facts or to express the author's feelings but to provide you with convincing *reasons* to accept the author's position on the issue in question. For example, Jean Hampton, in her essay "The Moral Education Theory of Punishment," tries to convince the reader that the primary justification for punishing criminals is to morally educate them so that they will come to believe that their behavior was wrong and *for that reason* will choose not to repeat their offenses. She then attempts to show that this approach will provide us with satisfactory answers to a host of related questions (such as *how much* punishment is appropriate for a given crime) and has clear advantages over alternative theories. You will get the most out of the essays in this book if, while reading them, you make a special effort to determine each of the following:

1. *What position* the author is taking on the issue in question.
2. *What reasons* the author uses to support his or her position.
3. *How convincing* those reasons are (particularly in comparison with the reasons that support alternative positions).

The result will *not* be that you will necessarily arrive at exactly the same view as everyone else who follows this procedure. For better or worse, reasonable people sometimes disagree about moral—and nonmoral (e.g., purely scientific)—matters even after they have thought long, hard, and rationally about them. The history of scholarship in moral matters and in all other subjects (art, science, history, etc.), is largely the history of disagreement among reasonable people. So the goal of this book is not to get you to adopt a particular position on any of these controversial issues in the criminal law but only to help you to think about them in a more critical, systematic, and informed way than before. This book's goal is to help you to become as well informed, open minded, and rational (logical in presenting and believing ideas) as possible when thinking about these matters. The rest must be up to you as you actually embark on your own exploration of the fascinating issues of crime and punishment.

Your individual responsibility to study and evaluate the arguments carefully is one you should take seriously. The recent rioting in Los Angeles, with its record amount of casualties and damage to property, is a striking reminder of how costly a breakdown in our system of criminal law can be. The epilogue of this book is an essay about those riots. Ordinary citizens are often called upon to play a role in supporting the American system of criminal law, whether it is a matter of reporting a crime, serving as a juror in a criminal trial (such as the trial of the officers who beat Rodney King in Los Angeles), or simply a matter of rejecting bad examples and resisting peer pressure to commit crime. We are all in this society together, after all. So we all have a great personal interest in having the best and most reasonable system of criminal law to govern our society. The philosophical study of law will give you significant help in finding reasons and justifications to defend your own decisions and to rationally evaluate the conduct of others.

Crime and Punishment

PART I

What Are the Proper Subject Matters for Criminalization?

A Areas of Liberty and Privacy

On Liberty

John Stuart Mill

John Stuart Mill (1806–1873) was one of the founders of the moral theory called *utilitarianism*. Mill's *On Liberty*, first published in 1859, is such a widely discussed and influential classic that any educated person should become familiar with it. Utilitarianism commands each of us to produce the maximum amount of happiness we can for everybody over the long run. Since Mill is a utilitarian, the principle he defends in *On Liberty* is calculated to maximize happiness. Mill's principle has several names. Some scholars label it the Harm Principle, since it does explicitly mention harm, which is the opposite of happiness. Other scholars prefer to label it the Harm-to-Others Principle, since the principle explicitly allows criminalization of adult behavior only to prevent harm to *others* who do not consent to the behavior in question. Still other scholars label Mill's principle the Liberty Principle, since it puts a limit on when people may limit the liberty of others. Indeed, even though Mill is a utilitarian, libertarians also accept Mill's principle. Libertarianism is a moral theory that endorses a laissez faire approach of minimal governmental regulation of economic activity and permits any activity between consenting adults, whether or not these activities maximize happiness or maximize liberty. So Mill's principle is an area of common ground that utilitarians and libertarians agree upon, though others will disagree and point out conflicts between utilitarianism and libertarianism.

From *On Liberty*, Excerpts from Chapters I and II, and all of Chapter IV. First published in 1859.

The object of this Essay is to assert one very simple principle, as entitled to govern absolutely the dealings of society with the individual in the way of compulsion and control, whether the means used be physical force in the form of legal penalties, or the moral coercion of public opinion. That principle is, that the sole end for which mankind are warranted, individually or collectively, in interfering with the liberty of action of any of their number, is self-protection. That the only purpose for which power can be rightfully exercised over any member of a civilized community, against his will, is to prevent harm to others. His own good, either physical or moral, is not a sufficient warrant. He cannot rightfully be compelled to do or forbear because it will be better for him to do so, because it will make him happier, because, in the opinions of others, to do so would be wise, or even right. There are good reasons for remonstrating with him, or reasoning with him, or persuading him, or entreating him, but not for compelling him, or visiting him with any evil, in case he do otherwise. To justify that, the conduct from which it is desired to deter him must be calculated to produce evil to some one else. The only part of the conduct of any one, for which he is amenable to society, is that which concerns others. In the part which merely concerns himself, his independence is, of right, absolute. Over himself, over his own body and mind, the individual is sovereign.

It is, perhaps, hardly necessary to say that this doctrine is meant to apply only to human beings in the maturity of their faculties. We are not speaking of children, or of young persons below the age which the law may fix as that of manhood or womanhood. Those who are still in a state to require being taken care of by others, must be protected against their own actions as well as against external injury. For the same reason, we may leave out of consideration those backward states of society in which the race itself may be considered as in its nonage. The early difficulties in the way of spontaneous progress are so great, that there is seldom any choice of means for overcoming them; and a ruler full of the spirit of improvement is warranted in the use of any expedients that will attain an end, perhaps otherwise unattainable. Despotism is a legitimate mode of government in dealing with barbarians, provided the end be their improvement, and the means justified by actually effecting that end. Liberty, as a principle, has no application to any state of things anterior to the time when mankind have become capable of being improved by free and equal discussion. Until then, there is nothing for them but implicit obedience to an Akbar or a Charlemagne, if they are so fortunate as to find one. But as soon as mankind have attained the capacity of being guided to their own improvement by conviction or persuasion (a period long since reached in all nations with whom we need here concern ourselves), compulsion, either in the direct form or in that of pains and penalties for non-compliance, is no longer admissible as a means to their own good, and justifiable only for the security of others.

It is proper to state that I forego any advantage which could be derived to my argument from the idea of abstract right, as a thing independent of utility. I regard utility as the ultimate appeal on all ethical questions; but it must be utility in the largest sense, grounded on the permanent interests of man as a progressive being. Those interests, I contend, authorize the subjection of individual spontaneity to external control, only in respect to those actions of each, which concern the interest of other people. If any one does an act hurtful to others, there is a *primâ facie* case for punishing him, by law, or, where legal penalties are not safely applicable, by general disapprobation. There are also many positive acts for the benefit of others, which he may rightfully be compelled to perform; such as, to give evidence in a court of justice; to bear his fair share in the common defence, or in any other joint work necessary to the interest of the society of which he enjoys the protection; and to perform certain acts of individual beneficence, such as saving a fellow creature's life, or interposing to protect the defenceless against ill-usage, things which whenever it is obviously a man's duty to do, he may rightfully be made responsible to society for not doing. A person may cause evil to others not only by his actions but by his inaction, and in either case he is justly accountable to them for the injury. The latter case, it is true, requires a much more cautious exercise of compulsion than the former. To make any one answerable for doing evil to others, is the rule; to make him answerable for not preventing evil, is, comparatively speaking, the exception. Yet there are many cases clear enough and grave enough to justify that exception. In all things which regard the external relations of the individual, he is *de jure* amenable to those whose interests are concerned, and if need be, to society as their protector. There are often good reasons for not holding him to the responsibility; but these reasons must arise from the special expediencies of the case: either because it is a kind of case in which he is on the whole likely to act better, when left to his own discretion, than when controlled in any way in which society have it in their power to control him; or because the attempt to exercise control would produce other evils, greater than those which it would prevent. When such reasons as these preclude the enforcement of responsibility, the conscience of the agent himself should step into the vacant judgment-seat, and protect those interests of others which have no external protection; judging himself all the more rigidly, because the case does not admit of his being made accountable to the judgment of his fellow-creatures.

But there is a sphere of action in which society, as distinguished from the individual, has, if any, only an indirect interest; comprehending all that portion of a person's life and conduct which affects only himself, or, if it also affects others, only with their free, voluntary, and undeceived consent and participation. When I say only himself, I mean directly, and in the first instance: for whatever affects himself, may affect others *through* himself; and the objection which may be grounded on this contingency, will receive consideration in the sequel. This, then, is the appropriate region of human liberty. It comprises, first, the inward domain of consciousness: demanding liberty of conscience, in the most comprehensive sense; liberty of thought and feeling; absolute freedom of opinion and sentiment on all subjects, practical or speculative, scientific, moral, or theological. The liberty of expressing and publishing opinions may seem to fall under a different principle, since it belongs to that part of the conduct of an individual which concerns other people; but, being almost of as much importance as the liberty of thought itself, and resting in great part on the same reasons, is practically inseparable from it. Secondly, the principle requires liberty of tastes and pursuits; of framing the plan of our life to suit our own character: of doing as we like, subject to such consequences as may follow; without impediment from our fellow-creatures, so long as what we do does not harm them, even though they should think our conduct foolish, perverse, or wrong. Thirdly, from this liberty of each individual, follows the liberty, within the same limits, of combination among individuals; freedom to unite, for any purpose not involving harm to others: the persons combining being supposed to be of full age, and not forced or deceived.

No society in which these liberties are not, on the whole, respected, is free, whatever may be its form of government; and none is completely free in which they do not exist absolute and unqualified. The only freedom which deserves the name, is that of pursuing our own good in our own way, so long as we do not attempt to deprive others of theirs, or impede their efforts to obtain it. Each is the proper guardian of his own health, whether bodily, or mental and spiritual. Mankind are greater gainers by suffering each other to live as seems good to themselves, than by compelling each to live as seems good to the rest. . . .

We have now recognized the necessity to the mental well-being of mankind (on which all their other well-being depends) of freedom of opinion, and freedom of the expression of opinion, on four distinct grounds; which we will now briefly recapitulate.

First, if any opinion is compelled to silence, that opinion may, for aught we can certainly know, be true. To deny this is to assume our own infallibility.

Secondly, though the silenced opinion be an error, it may, and very commonly does, contain a portion of truth; and since the general or prevailing opinion on any subject is rarely or never the whole truth, it is only by the collision of adverse opinions that the remainder of the truth has any chance of being supplied.

Thirdly, even if the received opinion be not only true, but the whole truth; unless it is suffered to be, and actually is vigorously and earnestly contested, it will, by most of those who receive it, be held in the manner of a prejudice, with little comprehension or feeling of its rational grounds. And not only this, but, fourthly, the meaning of the doctrine itself will be in danger of being lost, or enfeebled, and deprived of its vital effect on the character and conduct: the dogma becoming a mere formal profession, inefficacious for good, but cumbering the ground, and preventing the growth of any real and heartfelt conviction from reason or personal experience. . . .

Of the Limits to the Authority of Society over the Individual

What, then, is the rightful limit to the sovereignty of the individual over himself? Where does the authority of society begin? How much of human life should be assigned to individuality, and how much to society?

Each will receive its proper share, if each has that which more particularly concerns it. To individuality should belong the part of life in which it is chiefly the individual that is interested; to society, the part which chiefly interests society.

Though society is not founded on a contract, and though no good purpose is answered by inventing a contract in order to deduce social obligations from it, every one who receives the protection of society owes a return for the benefit, and the fact of living in society renders it indispensable that each should be bound to observe a certain line of conduct towards the rest. This conduct consists, first, in not injuring the interests of one another; or rather certain interests, which, either by express legal provision or by tacit understanding, ought to be considered as rights; and secondly, in each person's bearing his share (to be fixed on some equitable principle) of the labors and sacrifices incurred for defending the society or its members from injury and molestation. These conditions society is justified in enforcing, at all costs to those who endeavor to withhold fulfillment. Nor is this all that society may do. The acts of an individual may be hurtful to others, or wanting in due consideration for their welfare, without going the length of violating any of their constituted rights. The offender may then be justly punished by opinion, though not by law. As soon as any part of a person's conduct affects prejudicially the interests of others, society has jurisdiction over it, and the question whether the general welfare will or will not be promoted by interfering with it, becomes open to discussion. But there is no room for entertaining any such question when a person's conduct affects the interests of no persons besides himself, or needs not affect them unless they like (all the persons concerned being of full age, and the ordinary amount of understanding). In all such cases there should be perfect freedom, legal and social, to do the action and stand the consequences.

It would be a great misunderstanding of this doctrine, to suppose that it is one of selfish indifference, which pretends that human beings have no business with each other's conduct in life, and that they should not concern themselves about the well-doing or well-being of one another, unless their own interest is involved. Instead of any diminution, there is need of a great increase of disinterested exertion to promote the good of others. But disinterested benevolence can find other instruments to persuade people to their good, than whips and scourges, either of the literal or the metaphorical sort. I am the last person to undervalue the self-regarding virtues; they are only second in importance, if even second, to the social. It is equally the business of education to cultivate both. But even education works by conviction and persuasion as well as by compulsion, and it is by the former only that, when the period of education is past, the self-regarding virtues should be inculcated. Human beings owe to each other help to distinguish the better from the worse, and encouragement to choose the former and avoid the latter. They should be forever stimulating each other to increased exercise of their higher faculties, and increased direction of their feelings and aims towards wise instead of foolish, elevating instead of degrading, objects and contemplations. But neither one person, nor any number of persons, is warranted in saying to another human creature of ripe years, that he shall not do with his life for his own benefit what he chooses to do with it. He is the person most interested in his own well-being: the interest which any other person, except in cases of strong personal attachment, can have in it, is trifling, compared with that which he himself has; the interest which society has in him individually (except as to his conduct to others) is fractional, and altogether indirect: while, with respect to his own feelings and circumstances, the most ordinary man or woman has means of knowledge immeasurably surpassing those that can be possessed by anyone else. The interference of society to overrule his judgment and purposes in what only regards himself, must be grounded on general presumptions; which may be altogether wrong, and even if right, are as likely as not to be misapplied to individual cases, by persons no better acquainted with the circumstances of such cases than those are who look at them merely from without. In this department, therefore, of human affairs, Individuality has its proper field of action. In the conduct of human beings towards one another, it is necessary that general rules should for the most part be observed, in order that people may know what they have to expect; but in each person's own concerns, his individual spontaneity is entitled to free exercise. Considerations to aid his judgment, exhortations to strengthen his will, may be offered to him, even obtruded on him, by others; but he, himself, is the final judge. All errors which he is likely to commit against advice and warning, are far outweighed by the evil of allowing others to constrain him to what they deem his good.

I do not mean that the feelings with which a person is regarded by others, ought not to be in any way affected by his self-regarding qualities or deficiencies. This is neither possible nor desirable. If he is eminent in any of the qualities which conduce to his own good, he is, so far, a proper object of admiration. He is so much the nearer to the ideal perfection of human nature. If he is grossly deficient in those qualities, a sentiment the opposite of admiration will follow. There is a degree of folly, and a degree of what may be called (though the phrase is not unobjectionable) lowness or depravation of taste, which, though it cannot justify doing harm to the person who manifests it, renders him necessarily and properly a subject of distaste, or, in extreme cases, even of contempt: a person would not have the opposite qualities in due strength without entertaining these feelings. Though doing no wrong to anyone, a person may so act as to compel us to judge him, and feel to him, as a fool, or as a being of an inferior order: and since this judgment and feeling are a fact which he would prefer to avoid, it is doing him a service to warn him of it beforehand, as of any other disagreeable consequence to which he exposes himself. It would be well, indeed, if this good office were much more freely rendered than the common notions of politeness at present permit, and if one person could honestly point out to another that he thinks him in fault, without being considered unmannerly or presuming. We have a right, also, in various ways, to act upon our unfavorable opinion of any one, not to the oppression of his individuality, but in the exercise of ours. We are not bound, for example, to seek his society; we have a right to avoid it (though not to parade the avoidance), for we have a right to choose the society most acceptable to us. We have a right, and it may be our duty to caution others against him, if we think his example or conversation likely to have a pernicious effect on those with whom he associates. We may give others a preference over him in optional good offices, except those which tend to his improvement. In these various modes a person may suffer very severe penalties at the hands of others, for faults which directly concern only himself; but he suffers these penalties only in so far as they are the natural, and, as it were, the spontaneous consequences of the faults themselves, not because they are purposely inflicted on him for the sake of punishment. A person who shows rashness, obstinacy, self-conceit—who cannot live within moderate means—who cannot restrain himself from hurtful indulgences—who pursues animal pleasures at the expense of those of feelings and intellect—must expect to be lowered in the opinion of others, and to have a less share of their favorable sentiments, but of this he has no right to complain, unless he has merited their favor by special excellence in his social relations, and has thus established a title to their good offices, which is not affected by his demerits towards himself.

What I contend for is, that the inconveniences which are strictly inseparable from the unfavorable judgment of others, are the only ones to which a person should ever be subjected for that portion of his conduct and character which concerns his own good, but which does not affect the interests of others in their relations with him. Acts injurious to others require a totally different treatment. Encroachment on their rights; infliction on them of any loss or damage not justified by his own rights; falsehood or duplicity in dealing with them; unfair or ungenerous use of advantages over them; even selfish abstinence from defending them against injury—these are fit objects of moral reprobation, and, in grave cases, of moral retribution and punishment. And not only these acts, but the dispositions which lead to them, are properly immoral, and fit subjects of disapprobation which may rise to abhorrence. Cruelty of disposition; malice and ill-nature; that most anti-social and odious of all passions, envy; dissimulation and insincerity; irascibility on insufficient cause, and resentment disproportioned to the provocation; the love of domineering over others; the desire to engross more than one's share of advantages (the πλε νεξτα of the Greeks); the pride which derives gratification from the abasement of others; the egotism which thinks self and its concerns more important than everything else, and decides all doubtful questions in his own favor—these are moral vices, and constitute a bad and odious moral character: unlike the self-regarding faults previously mentioned, which are not properly immoralities, and to whatever pitch they may be carried, do not constitute wickedness. They may be proofs of any amount of folly, or want of personal dignity and self-respect; but they are only a subject or moral reprobation when they involve a breach of duty to others, for whose sake the individual is bound to have care for himself. What are called duties to ourselves are not socially obligatory, unless circumstances render them at the same time duties to others. The term duty to oneself, when it means anything more than prudence, means self-respect or self-development; and for none of these is any one accountable to his fellow-creatures, because for none of them is it for the good of mankind that he be held accountable to them.

The distinction between the loss of consideration which a person may rightly incur by defect of prudence or of personal dignity, and the reprobation which is due to him for an offence against the rights of others, is not a merely nominal distinction. It makes a vast difference both in our feelings and in our conduct towards him, whether he displeases us in things in which we think we have a right to control him, or in things in which we know that we have not. If he displeases us, we may express our distaste, and we may stand aloof from a person as well as from a thing that displeases us; but we shall not therefore feel called on to make his life uncomfortable. We shall reflect that he already bears, or will bear, the whole penalty of his error; if he spoils his life by mismanagement, we shall not, for that reason, desire to spoil it still further: instead of wishing to punish him, we shall rather endeavor to alleviate his punishment, by showing him how he may avoid or cure the evils his conduct tends to bring upon him. He may be to us an object of pity, perhaps of dislike, but not of anger or resentment; we shall not treat him like an enemy of society: the worst we shall think ourselves justified in doing is leaving him to himself, if we do not interfere benevolently by showing interest or concern for him. It is far otherwise if he has infringed the rules necessary for the protection of his fellow-creatures, individually or collectively. The evil consequences of his acts do not then fall on himself, but on others; and society, as the protector of all its members, must retaliate on him; must inflict pain on him for the express purpose of punishment, and must take care that it be sufficiently severe. In the one case, he is an offender at our bar, and we are called on not only to sit in judgment on him, but, in one shape or another, to execute our own sentence: in the other case, it is not our part to inflict any suffering on him, except what may incidentally follow from our using the same liberty in the regulation of our own affairs, which we allow to him in his.

The distinction here pointed out between the part of a person's life which concerns only himself, and that which concerns others, many persons will refuse to admit. How (it may be asked) can any part of the conduct of a member of society be a matter of indifference to the other members? No person is an entirely isolated being; it is impossible for a person to do anything seriously or permanently hurtful to himself, without mischief reaching at least to his near connections, and often far beyond them. If he injures his property, he does harm to those who directly or indirectly derived support from it, and usually diminishes, by a greater or less amount, the general resources of the community. If he deteriorates his bodily or mental faculties, he not only brings evil upon all who depended on him for any portion of their happiness, but disqualifies himself for rendering the services which he owes to his fellow-creatures generally; perhaps becomes a burden on their affection or benevolence; and if such conduct were very frequent, hardly any offence that is committed would detract more from the general sum of good. Finally, if by his vices or follies a person does no direct harm to others, he is nevertheless (it may be said) injurious by his example; and ought to be compelled to control himself, for the sake of those whom the sight or knowledge of his conduct might corrupt or mislead.

And even (it will be added) if the consequences of misconduct could be confined to the vicious or thoughtless individual, ought society to abandon to their own guidance those who are manifestly unfit for it? If protection against themselves is confessedly due to children and persons under age, is not society equally bound to afford it to persons of mature years who are equally incapable of self-government? If gambling, or drunkenness, or incontinence, or idleness, or uncleanliness, are as injurious to happiness, and as great a hindrance to improvement, as many or most of the acts prohibited by law, why (it may be asked) should not law, so far as is consistent with practicability and social convenience, endeavor to repress these also? And as a supplement to the unavoidable imperfections of law, ought not opinion at least to organize a powerful police against these vices, and visit rigidly with social penalties those who are known to practise them? There is no question here (it may be said) about restricting individuality, or impeding the trial of new and original experiments in living. The only things it is sought to prevent are things which have been tried and condemned from the beginning of the world until now; things which experience has shown not to be useful or suitable to any person's individuality. There must be some length of time and amount of experience, after which a moral or prudential truth may be regarded as established; and it is merely desired to prevent generation after generation from falling over the same precipice which has been fatal to their predecessors.

I fully admit that the mischief which a person does to himself, may seriously affect, both through their sympathies and their interests, those nearly connected with him, and in a minor degree, society at large. When, by conduct of this sort, a person is led to violate a distinct and assignable obligation to any other person or persons, the case is taken out of the self-regarding class, and becomes amenable to moral disapprobation in the proper sense of the term. If, for example, a man, through intemperance or extravagance, becomes unable to pay his debts, or, having undertaken the moral responsibility of a family, becomes from the same cause incapable of supporting or educating them, he is deservedly reprobated, and might be justly punished; but it is for the breach of duty to his family or creditors, not for the extravagance. If the resources which ought to have been devoted to them, had been diverted from them for the most prudent investment, the moral culpability would have been the same. George Barnwell murdered his uncle to get money for his mistress, but if he had done it to set himself up in business, he would equally have been hanged. Again, in the frequent case of a man who causes grief to his family by addiction to bad habits, he deserves reproach for his unkindness or ingratitude; but so he may for cultivating habits not in themselves vicious, if they are painful to those with whom he passes his life, or who from personal ties are dependent on him for their comfort. Whoever fails in the consideration generally due to the interests and feelings of others, not being compelled by some more imperative duty, or justified by allowable self-preference, is a subject of moral disapprobation for that failure, but not for the cause of it, nor for the errors, merely personal to himself, which may have remotely led to it. In like manner, when a person disables himself, by conduct purely self-regarding, from the performance of some definite duty incumbent on him to the public, he is guilty of a social offence. No person ought to be punished simply for being drunk; but a soldier or a policeman should be punished for being drunk on duty. Whenever, in short, there is a definite damage, or a definite risk of damage, either to an individual or to the public, the case is taken out of the province of liberty, and placed in that of morality or law.

But with regard to the merely contingent, or, as it may be called, constructive injury which a person causes to society, by conduct which neither violates any specific duty to the public, nor occasions perceptible hurt to any assignable individual except himself; the inconvenience is one which society can afford to bear, for the sake of the greater good of human freedom. If grown persons are to be punished for not taking proper care of themselves, I would rather it were for their own sake, than under pretence of preventing them from impairing their capacity of rendering to society benefits which society does not pretend it has a right to exact. But I cannot consent to argue the point as if society had no means of bringing its weaker members up to its ordinary standard of rational conduct, except waiting till they do something irrational, and then punishing them, legally or morally, for it. Society has had absolute power over them during all the early portion of their existence: it has had the whole period of childhood and nonage in which to try whether it could make them capable of rational conduct in life. The existing generation is master both of the training and the entire circumstances of the generation to come; it cannot indeed make them perfectly wise and good, because it is itself so lamentably deficient in goodness and wisdom; and its best efforts are not always, in individual cases, its most successful ones; but it is perfectly well able to make the rising generation, as a whole, as good as, and a little better than, itself. If society lets any considerable number of its members grow up mere children, incapable of being acted on by rational consideration of distant motives, society has itself to blame for the consequences. Armed not only with all the powers of education, but with the ascendancy which the authority of a received opinion always exercises over the minds who are least fitted to judge for themselves; and aided by the *natural* penalties which cannot be prevented from falling on those who incur the distaste or the contempt of those who know them; let not society pretend that it needs, besides all this, the power to issue commands and enforce obedience in the personal concerns of individuals, in which, on all principles of justice and policy, the decision ought to rest with those who are to abide the consequences. Nor is there anything which tends more to discredit and frustrate the better means of influencing conduct, than a resort to the worse. If there be among those whom it is attempted to coerce into prudence or temperance, any of the material of which vigorous and independent characters are made, they will infallibly rebel against the yoke. No such person will ever feel that others have a right to control him in his concerns, such as they have to prevent him from injuring them in theirs; and it easily comes to be considered a mark of spirit and courage to fly in the face of such usurped authority, and do with ostentation the exact opposite of what it enjoins; as in the fashion of grossness which succeeded, in the time of Charles II, to the fanatical moral intolerance of the Puritans. With respect to what is said of the necessity of protecting society from the bad example set to others by the vicious or the self-indulgent; it is true that bad example may have a pernicious effect, especially the example of doing wrong to others with impunity to the wrongdoer. But we are now speaking of conduct which, while it does no wrong to others, is supposed to do great harm to the agent himself; and I do not see how those who believe this, can think otherwise than that the example, on the whole, must be more salutary than hurtful, since, if it displays the misconduct, it displays also the painful or degrading consequences which, if the conduct is justly censured, must be supposed to be in all or most cases attendant on it.

But the strongest of all the arguments against the interference of the public with purely personal conduct, is that when it does interfere, the odds are that it interferes wrongly, and in the wrong place. On questions of social morality, of duty to others, the opinion of the public, that is, of an overruling majority, though often wrong, is likely to be still oftener right; because on such questions they are only required to judge of their own interests; of the manner in which some mode of conduct, if allowed to be practised, would affect themselves. But the opinion of a similar majority, imposed as a law on the minority, on questions of self-regarding conduct, is quite as likely to be wrong as right; for in these cases public opinion means, at the best, some people's opinion of what is good or bad for other people; while very often it does not even mean that; the public, with the most perfect indifference, passing over the pleasure or convenience of those whose conduct they censure, and considering only their own preference. There are many who consider as an injury to themselves any conduct which they have a distaste for, and resent it as an outrage to their feelings; as a religious bigot, when charged with disregarding the religious feelings of others, has been known to retort that they disregard his feelings, by persisting in their abominable worship or creed. But there is no parity between the feeling of a person for his own opinion, and the feeling of another who is offended at his holding it; no more than between the desire of a thief to take a purse, and the desire of the right owner to keep it. And a person's taste is as much his own peculiar concern as his opinion or his purse. It is easy for any one to imagine an ideal public, which leaves the freedom and choice of individuals in all uncertain matters undisturbed, and only requires them to abstain from modes of conduct which universal experience has condemned. But where has there been seen a public which set any such limit to its censorship? or when does the public trouble itself about universal experience? In its interferences with personal conduct it is seldom thinking of anything but the enormity of acting or feeling differently from itself; and this standard of judgment, thinly disguised, is held up to mankind as the dictate of religion and philosophy, by nine tenths of all moralists and speculative writers. These teach that things are right because they are right; because we feel them to be so. They tell us to search in our own minds and hearts for laws of conduct binding on ourselves and on all others. What can the poor public do but apply these instructions, and make their own personal feelings of good and evil, if they are tolerably unanimous in them, obligatory on all the world?

The evil here pointed out is not one which exists only in theory; and it may perhaps be expected that I should specify the instances in which the public of this age and country improperly invests its own preferences with the character of moral laws. I am not writing an essay on the aberrations of existing moral feeling. That is too weighty a subject to be discussed parenthetically, and by way of illustration. Yet examples are necessary, to show that the principle I maintain is of serious and practical moment, and that I am not endeavoring to erect a barrier against imaginary evils. And it is not difficult to show, by abundant instances, that to extend the bounds of what may be called moral police, until it encroaches on the most unquestionably legitimate liberty of the individual, is one of the most universal of all human propensities.

As a first instance, consider the antipathies which men cherish on no better grounds than that persons whose religious opinions are different from theirs, do not practise their religious observances, especially their religious abstinences. To cite a rather trivial example, nothing in the creed or practice of Christians does more to envenom the hatred of Mahomedans against them, than the fact of their eating pork. There are few acts which Christians and Europeans regard with more unaffected disgust, than Mussulmans regard this particular mode of satisfying hunger. It is, in the first place, an offence against their religion; but this circumstance by no means explains either the degree or the kind of their repugnance; for wine also is forbidden by their religion, and to partake of it is by all Mussulmans accounted wrong, but not disgusting. Their aversion to the flesh of the "unclean beast" is, on the contrary, of that peculiar character, resembling an instinctive antipathy, which the idea of uncleanness, when once it thoroughly sinks into the feelings, seems always to excite even in those whose personal habits are anything but scrupulously cleanly, and of which the sentiment of religious impurity, so intense in the Hindoos, is a remarkable example. Suppose now that in a people, of whom the majority were Mussulmans, that majority should insist upon not permitting pork to be eaten within the limits of the country. This would be nothing new in Mahomedan countries.[1] Would it be a legitimate exercise of the moral authority of public opinion? and if not, why not? The practice is really revolting to such a public. They also sincerely think that it is forbidden and abhorred by the Deity. Neither could the prohibition be censured as religious persecution. It might be religious in its origin, but it would not be persecution for religion, since nobody's religion makes it a duty to eat pork. The only tenable ground of condemnation would be, that with the personal tastes and self-regarding concerns of individuals the public has no business to interfere.

To come somewhat nearer home: the majority of Spaniards consider it a gross impiety, offensive in the highest degree to the Supreme Being, to worship him in any other manner than the Roman Catholic; and no other public worship is lawful on Spanish soil. The people of all Southern Europe look upon a married clergy as not only irreligious, but unchaste, indecent, gross, disgusting. What do Protestants think of these perfectly sincere feelings, and of the attempt to enforce them against non-Catholics? Yet, if mankind are justified in interfering with each other's liberty in things which do not concern the interests of others, on what principle is it possible consistently to exclude these cases? or who can blame people for desiring to suppress what they regard as a scandal in the sight of God and man? No stronger case can be shown for prohibiting anything which is regarded as a personal immorality, than is made out for suppressing these practices in the eyes of those who regard them as impieties; and unless we are willing to adopt the logic of persecutors, and to say that we may persecute others because we are right, and that they must not persecute us because they are wrong, we must beware of admitting a principle of which we should resent as a gross injustice the application to ourselves.

The preceding instances may be objected to, although unreasonably, as drawn from contingencies impossible among us: opinion, in this country, not being likely to enforce abstinence from meats, or to interfere with people for worshipping, and for either marrying or not marrying, according to their creed or inclination. The next example, however, shall be taken from an interference with liberty which we have by no means passed all danger of. Wherever the puritans have been sufficiently powerful, as in New England, and in Great Britain at the time of the Commonwealth, they have endeavored, with considerable success, to put down all public, and nearly all private, amusements: especially music, dancing, public games, or other assemblages for purposes of diversion, and the theatre. There are still in this country large bodies of persons by whose notions of morality and religion these recreations are condemned; and those persons belonging chiefly to the middle class, who are the ascendant power in the present social and political condition of the kingdom, it is by no means impossible that persons of these sentiments may at some time or other command a majority in Parliament. How will the remaining portion of the community like to have the amusements that shall be permitted to them regulated by the religious and moral sentiments of the stricter Calvinists and Methodists? Would they not, with considerable peremptoriness, desire these intrusively pious members of society to mind their own business? This is precisely what should be said to every government and every public, who have the pretension that no person shall enjoy any pleasure which they think wrong. But if the principle of the pretension be admitted, no one can reasonably object to its being acted on in the sense of the majority, or other preponderating power in the country; and all persons must be ready to conform to the idea of a Christian commonwealth, as understood by the early settlers in New England, if a religious profession similar to theirs should ever succeed in regaining its lost ground, as religions supposed to be declining have so often been known to do.

To imagine other contingency, perhaps more likely to be realized than the one last mentioned. There is confessedly a strong tendency in the modern world towards a democratic constitution of society, accompanied or not by popular political institutions. It is affirmed that in the country where this tendency is most completely realized—where both society and the government are most democratic—the United States—the feeling of the majority, to whom any appearance of a more showy or costly style of living than they can hope to rival is disagreeable, operates as a tolerably effectual sumptuary law, and that in many parts of the Union it is really difficult for a person possessing a very large income to find any mode of spending it, which will not incur popular disapprobation. Though such statements as these are doubtless much exaggerated as a representation of existing facts, the state of things they describe is not only a conceivable and possible, but a probable result of democratic feeling, combined with the notion that the public has a right to a veto on the manner in which individuals shall spend their incomes. We have only further to suppose a considerable diffusion of Socialist opinions, and it may become infamous in the eyes of the majority to possess more property than some very small amount, or any income not earned by manual labor. Opinions similar in principle to these, already prevail widely among the artisan class, and weigh oppressively on those who are amenable to the opinion chiefly of that class, namely, its own members. It is known that the bad workmen who form the majority of the operatives in many branches of industry, are decidedly of opinion that bad workmen ought to receive the same wages as good, and that no one ought to be allowed, through piecework or otherwise, to earn by superior skill or industry more than others can without it. And they employ a moral police, which occasionally becomes a physical one, to deter skilful workmen from receiving, and employers from giving, a larger remuneration for a more useful service. If the public have any jurisdiction over private concerns, I cannot see that these people are in fault, or that any individual's particular public can be blamed for asserting the same authority over his individual conduct, which the general public asserts over people in general.

But, without dwelling upon suppositious cases, there are, in our own day, gross usurpations upon the liberty of private life actually practised, and still greater ones threatened with some expectation of success, and opinions proposed which assert an unlimited right in the public not only to prohibit by law everything which it thinks wrong, but in order to get at what it thinks wrong, to prohibit any number of things which it admits to be innocent.

Under the name of preventing intemperance, the people of one English colony, and of nearly half the United States, have been interdicted by law from making any use whatever of fermented drinks, except for medical purposes: for prohibition of their sale is in fact, as it is intended to be, prohibition of their use. And though the impracticability of executing the law has caused its repeal in several of the States which had adopted it, including the one from which it derives its name, an attempt has notwithstanding been commenced, and is prosecuted with considerable zeal by many of the professed philanthropists, to agitate for a similar law in this country. The association, or "Alliance" as it terms itself, which has been formed for this purpose, has acquired some notoriety through the publicity given to a correspondence between its Secretary and one of the very few English public men who hold that a politician's opinions ought to be founded on principles. Lord Stanley's share in this correspondence is calculated to strengthen the hopes already built on him, by those who know how rare such qualities as are manifested in some of his public appearances, unhappily are among those who figure in political life. The organ of the Alliance, who would "deeply deplore the recognition of any principle which could be wrested to justify bigotry and persecution," undertakes to point out the "broad and impassable barrier" which divides such principles from those of the association. "All matters relating to thought, opinion, conscience, appear to me," he says, "to be without the sphere of legislation; all pertaining to social act, habit, relation, subject only to a discretionary power vested in the State itself, and not in the individual, to be within it." No mention is made of a third class, different from either of these, viz., acts and habits which are not social, but individual; although it is to this class, surely, that the act of drinking fermented liquors belongs. Selling fermented liquors, however, is trading, and trading is a social act. But the infringement complained of is not on the liberty of the seller, but on that of the buyer and consumer; since the State might just as well forbid him to drink wine, as purposely make it impossible for him to obtain it. The Secretary, however, says, "I claim, as a citizen, a right to legislate whenever my social rights are invaded by the social act of another." And now for the definition of these "social rights." "If anything invades my social rights, certainly the traffic in strong drink does. It destroys my primary right of security, by constantly creating and stimulating social disorder. It invades my right of equality, by deriving a profit from the creation of a misery, I am taxed to support. It impedes my right to free moral and intellectual development, by surrounding my path with dangers, and by weakening and demoralizing society, from which I have a right to claim mutual aid and intercourse." A theory of "social rights," the like of which probably never before found its way into distinct language—being nothing short of this—that it is the absolute social right of every individual, that every other individual shall act in every respect exactly as he ought; that whosoever fails thereof in the smallest particular, violates my social right, and entitles me to demand from the legislature the removal of the grievance. So monstrous a principle is far more dangerous than any single interference with liberty; there is no violation of liberty which it would not justify; it acknowledges no right to any freedom whatever, except perhaps to that of holding opinions in secret, without ever disclosing them; for the moment an opinion which I consider noxious, passes any one's lips, it invades all the "social rights" attributed to me by the Alliance. The doctrine ascribes to all mankind a vested interest in each other's moral, intellectual, and even physical perfection, to be defined by each claimant according to his own standard.

Another important example of illegitimate interference with the rightful liberty of the individual, not simply threatened, but long since carried into triumphant effect, is Sabbatarian legislation. Without doubt, abstinence on one day in the week, so far as the exigencies of life permit, from the usual daily occupation, though in no respect religiously binding on any except Jews, it is a highly beneficial custom. And inasmuch as this custom cannot be observed without a general consent to that effect among the industrious classes, therefore, in so far as some persons by working may impose the same necessity on others, it may be allowable and right that the law should guarantee to each, the observance by others of the custom, by suspending the greater operations of industry on a particular day. But this justification, grounded on the direct interest which others have in each individual's observance of the practice, does not apply to the self-chosen occupations in which a person may think fit to employ his leisure; nor does it hold good, in the smallest degree, for legal restrictions on amusements. It is true that the amusement of some is the day's work of others; but the pleasure, not to say the useful recreation, of many, is worth the labor of a few, provided the occupation is freely chosen, and can be freely resigned. The operatives are perfectly right in thinking that if all worked on Sunday seven days' work would have to be given for six days' wages; but so long as the great mass of employments are suspended, the small number who for the enjoyment of others must still work, obtain a proportional increase of earnings: and they are not obliged to follow those occupations, if they prefer leisure to emolument. If a further remedy is sought, it might be found in the establishment by custom of a holiday on some other day of the week for those particular classes of persons. The only ground, therefore, on which restrictions on Sunday amusements can be defended, must be that they are religiously wrong; a motive of legislation which never can be too earnestly protested again. "Deorum injuriæ Diis curæ." It remains to be proved that society or any of its officers holds a commission from on high to avenge any supposed offence to Omnipotence, which is not also a wrong to our fellow-creatures. The notion that it is one man's duty that another should be religious, was the foundation of all the religious persecutions ever perpetrated, and if admitted, would fully justify them. Though the feeling which breaks out in the repeated attempts to stop railway travelling on Sunday, in the resistance to the opening of Museums, and the like, has not the cruelty of the old persecutors, the state of mind indicated by it is fundamentally the same. It is a determination not to tolerate others in doing what is permitted by their religion, because it is not permitted by the persecutor's religion. It is a belief that God not only abominates the act of the misbeliever, but will not hold us guiltless if we leave him unmolested.

I cannot refrain from adding to these examples of the little account commonly made of human liberty, the language of downright persecution which breaks out from the press of this country, whenever it feels called on to notice the remarkable phenomenon of Mormonism. Much might be said on the unexpected and instructive fact, that an alleged new revelation, and a religion founded on it, the product of palpable imposture, not even supported by the *prestige* of extraordinary qualities in its founder, is believed by hundreds of thousands, and has been made the foundation of a society, in the age of newspapers, railways, and the electric telegraph. What here concerns us is, that this religion, like other and better religions, has its martyrs; that its prophet and founder was, for his teaching, put to death by a mob; that others of its adherents lost their lives by the same lawless violence; that they were forcibly expelled, in a body, from the country in which they first grew up; while, now that they have been chased into a solitary recess in the midst of a desert, many of this country openly declare that it would be right (only that it is not convenient) to send an expedition against them, and compel them by force to conform to the opinion of other people. The article of the Mormonite doctrine which is the chief provocative to the antipathy which thus breaks through the ordinary restraints of religious tolerance, is its sanction of polygamy; which, though permitted to Mahomedans, and Hindoos, and Chinese, seems to excite unquenchable animosity when practised by persons who speak English, and profess to be a kind of Christian. No one has a deeper disapprobation than I have of this Mormon institution; both for other reasons, and because, far from being in any way countenanced by the principle of liberty, it is a direct infraction of that principle, being a mere riveting of the chains of one half of the community, and an emancipation of the other from reciprocity of obligation towards them. Still, it must be remembered that this relation is as much voluntary on the part of the women concerned in it, and who may be deemed the sufferers by it, as is the case with any other form of the marriage institution; and however surprising this fact may appear, it has its explanation in the common ideas and customs of the world, which teaching women to think marriage the one thing needful, make it intelligible that many a woman should prefer being one of several wives, to not being a wife at all. Other countries are not asked to recognize such unions, or release any portion of their inhabitants from their own laws on the score of Mormonite opinions. But when the dissentients have conceded to the hostile sentiments of others, far more than could justly be demanded; when they have left the countries to which their doctrines were unacceptable, and established themselves in a remote corner of the earth, which they have been the first to render habitable to human beings; it is difficult to see on what principles but those of tyranny they can be prevented from living there under what laws they please, provided they commit no aggression on other nations, and allow perfect freedom of departure to those who are dissatisfied with their ways. A recent writer, in some respects of considerable merit, proposes (to use his own words) not a crusade, but a *civilizade,* against this polygamous community, to put an end to what seems to him a retrograde step in civilization. It also appears so to me, but I am not aware that any community has a right to force another to be civilized. So long as the sufferers by the bad law do not invoke assistance from other communities, I cannot admit that persons entirely unconnected with them ought to step in and require that a condition of things with which all who are directly interested appear to be satisfied, should be put an end to because it is a scandal to persons some thousands of miles distant, who have no part or concern in it. Let them send missionaries, if they please, to preach against it; and let them, by any fair means (of which silencing the teachers is not one), oppose the progress of similar doctrines among their own people. If civilization has got the better of barbarism when barbarism had the world to itself, it is too much to profess to be afraid lest barbarism, after having been fairly got under, should revive and conquer civilization. A civilization that can thus succumb to its vanquished enemy must first have become so degenerate, that neither its appointed priests and teachers, nor anybody else, has the capacity, or will take the trouble, to stand up for it. If this be so, the sooner such a civilization receives notice to quit, the better. It can only go on from bad to worse, until destroyed and regenerated (like the Western Empire) by energetic barbarians.

NOTES

1. The case of the Bombay Parsees is a curious instance in point. When this industrious and enterprising tribe, the descendants of the Persian fire-worshippers, flying from their native country before the Caliphs, arrived in Western India, they were admitted to toleration by the Hindoo sovereigns, on condition of not eating beef. When those regions afterwards fell under the dominion of Mahomedan conquerors, the Parsees obtained from them a continuance of indulgence, on condition of refraining from pork. What was at first obedience to authority became a second nature, and the Parsees to this day abstain both from beef and pork. Though not required by their religion, the double abstinence has had time to grow into a custom of their tribe; and custom, in the East, is a religion.

The Enforcement of Morals

Patrick Devlin

Devlin, a contemporary British jurist, disagrees with Mill's harm principle. In this excerpt from *The Enforcement of Morals* (1965), Devlin defends a society's right to impose or defend particular values even upon consenting adults who reject those values. Laws against prostitution, homosexuality, sodomy, drugs, and gambling are examples of the sort of criminalization Devlin has in mind.

The Report of the Committee on Homosexual Offences and Prostitution, generally known as the Wolfenden Report, is recognized to be an excellent study of two very difficult legal and social problems. But it has also a particular claim to the respect of those interested in jurisprudence; it does what law reformers so rarely do; it sets out clearly and carefully what in relation to its subjects it considers the function of the law to be. Statutory additions to the criminal law are too often made on the simple principle that "there ought to be a law against it." The greater part of the law relating to sexual offences is the creation of statute and it is difficult to ascertain any logical relationship between it and the moral ideas which most of us uphold. Adultery, fornication, and prostitution are not, as the Report points out, criminal offences: homosexuality between males is a criminal offence, but between females it is not. Incest was not an offence until it was declared so by statute only fifty years ago. Does the legislature select these offences haphazardly or are there some principles which can be used to determine what part of the moral law should be embodied in the criminal? . . . What is the connexion between crime and sin and to what extent, if at all, should the criminal law of England concern itself with the enforcement of morals and punish sin or immorality as such?

Maccabaean Lecture in Jurisprudence read at the British Academy on 18 March 1959 and printed in the *Proceedings of the British Academy*, vol. xiv, under the title "The Enforcement of Morals."

The statements of principle in the Wolfenden Report provide an admirable and modern starting-point for such an inquiry. . . .

Early in the Report the Committee put forward:

> our own formulation of the function of the criminal law so far as it concerns the subjects of this enquiry. In this field, its function, as we see it, is to preserve public order and decency, to protect the citizen from what is offensive or injurious, and to provide sufficient safeguards against exploitation and corruption of others, particularly those who are specially vulnerable because they are young, weak in body or mind, inexperienced, or in a state of special physical, official or economic dependence.

It is not, in our view, the function of the law to intervene in the private lives of citizens, or to seek to enforce any particular pattern of behaviour, further than is necessary to carry out the purposes we have outlined.

The Committee preface their most important recommendation:

> that homosexual behaviour between consenting adults in private should no longer be a criminal offence, [by stating the argument] which we believe to be decisive, namely, the importance which society and the law ought to give to individual freedom of choice and action in matters of private morality. Unless a deliberate attempt is to be made by society, acting through the agency of the law, to equate the sphere of crime with that of sin, there must remain a realm of private morality and immorality which is, in brief and crude terms, not the law's business. To say this is not to condone or encourage private immorality.

Similar statements of principle are set out in the chapters of the Report which deal with prostitution. No case can be sustained, the

Report says, for attempting to make prostitution itself illegal. The Committee refer to the general reasons already given and add: "We are agreed that private immorality should not be the concern of the criminal law except in the special circumstances therein mentioned." They quote with approval the report of the Street Offences Committee, which says: "As a general proposition it will be universally accepted that the law is not concerned with private morals or with ethical sanctions." It will be observed that the emphasis is on *private* immorality. By this is meant immorality which is not offensive or injurious to the public in the ways defined or described in the first passage which I quoted. In other words, no act of immorality should be made a criminal offence unless it is accompanied by some other feature such as indecency, corruption, or exploitation. This is clearly brought out in relation to prostitution: "It is not the duty of the law to concern itself with immorality as such . . . it should confine itself to those activities which offend against public order and decency or expose the ordinary citizen to what is offensive or injurious." . . .

Morals and religion are inextricably joined—the moral standards generally accepted in Western civilization being those belonging to Christianity. Outside Christendom other standards derive from other religions. None of these moral codes can claim any validity except by virtue of the religion on which it is based. Old Testament morals differ in some respects from New Testament morals. Even within Christianity there are differences. Some hold that contraception is an immoral practice and that a man who has carnal knowledge of another woman while his wife is alive is in all circumstances a fornicator; others, including most of the English-speaking world, deny both these propositions. Between the great religions of the world, of which Christianity is only one, there are much wider differences. It may or may not be right for the State to adopt one of these religions as the truth, to found itself upon its doctrines, and to deny to any of its citizens the liberty to practise any other. If it does, it is logical that it should use the secular law wherever it thinks it necessary to enforce the divine. If it does not, it is illogical that it should concern itself with morals as such. But if it leaves matters of religion to private judgement, it should logically leave matters of morals also. A State which refuses to enforce Christian beliefs has lost the right to enforce Christian morals.

If this view is sound, it means that the criminal law cannot justify any of its provisions by reference to the moral law. It cannot say, for example, that murder and theft are prohibited because they are immoral or sinful. The State must justify in some other way the punishments which it imposes on wrongdoers and a function for the criminal law independent of morals must be found. This is not difficult to do. The smooth functioning of society and the preservation of order require that a number of activities should be regulated. The rules that are made for that purpose and are enforced by the criminal law are often designed simply to achieve uniformity and convenience and rarely involve any choice between good and evil. Rules that impose a speed limit or prevent obstruction on the highway have nothing to do with morals. Since so much of the criminal law is composed of rules of this sort, why bring morals into it at all? Why not define the function of the criminal law in simple terms as the preservation of order and decency and the protection of the lives and property of citizens, and elaborate those terms in relation to any particular subject in the way in which it is done in the Wolfenden Report? The criminal law in carrying out these objects will undoubtedly overlap the moral law. Crimes of violence are morally wrong and they are also offences against good order; therefore they offend against both laws. But this is simply because the two laws in pursuit of different objectives happen to cover the same area. Such is the argument. . . .

I think it is clear that the criminal law as we know it is based upon moral principle. In a number of crimes its function is simply to enforce a moral principle and nothing else. The law, both criminal and civil, claims to be able to speak about morality and immorality generally. Where does it get its authority to do this and how does it settle the moral principles which it enforces? Undoubtedly, as a matter of history, it derived both from Christian teaching. But I think that the strict logician is right when he says that the law can no longer rely on doctrines in which citizens are entitled to disbelieve. It is necessary therefore to look for some other source.

In jurisprudence, as I have said, everything is thrown open to discussion and, in the belief that they cover the whole field, I have framed three interrogatories addressed to myself to answer:

1. Has society the right to pass judgement at all on matters of morals? Ought there, in other words, to be a public morality, or are morals always a matter for private judgement?
2. If society has the right to pass judgement, has it also the right to use the weapon of the law to enforce it?
3. If so, ought it to use that weapon in all cases or only in some; and if only in some, on what principles should it distinguish?

I shall begin with the first interrogatory and consider what is meant by the right of society to pass a moral judgement, that is, a judgement about what is good and what is evil. The fact that a majority of people may disapprove of a practice does not of itself make it a matter for society as a whole. Nine men out of ten may disapprove of what the tenth man is doing and still say that it is not their business. There is a case for a collective judgement (as distinct from a large number of individual opinions which sensible people may even refrain from pronouncing at all if it is upon somebody else's private affairs) only if society is affected. Without a collective judgement there can be no case at all for intervention. . . .

The language used in the passages I have quoted from the Wolfenden Report suggests the view that there ought not to be a collective judgement about immorality *per se*. Is this what is meant by "private morality" and "individual freedom of choice and action"? Some people sincerely believe that homosexuality is neither immoral nor unnatural. Is the "freedom of choice and action" that is offered to the individual, freedom to decide for himself what is moral or immoral, society remaining neutral; or is it freedom to be immoral if he wants to be? The language of the Report may be open to question, but the conclusions at which the Committee arrive answer this question unambiguously. If society is not prepared to say that homosexuality is morally wrong, there would be no basis for a law protecting youth from "corruption" or punishing a man for living on the "immoral" earnings of a homosexual prostitute, as the Report recommends. This attitude the Committee make even clearer when they come to deal with prostitution. In truth, the Report takes it for granted that there is in existence a public morality which condemns homosexuality and prostitution. What the Report seems to mean by private morality might perhaps be better described as private behaviour in matters of morals.

This view—that there is such a thing as public morality—can also be justified by *a priori* argument. What makes a society of any sort is community of ideas, not only political ideas but also ideas about the way its members should behave and govern their lives; these latter ideas are its morals. Every society has a moral structure as well as a political one: or rather, since that might suggest two independent systems, I should say that the structure of every society is made up both of politics and morals. . . .

[W]ithout shared ideas on politics, morals, and ethics no society can exist. Each one of us has ideas about what is good and what is evil; they cannot be kept private from the society in which we live. If men and women try to create a society in which there is no fundamental agreement about good and evil they will fail; if, having based it on common agreement, the agreement goes, the society will disintegrate. For society is not something that is kept together physically; it is held by the invisible bonds of common thought. If the bonds were too far relaxed the members would drift apart.

A common morality is part of the bondage. The bondage is part of the price of society; and mankind, which needs society, must pay its price. . . .

But if society has the right to make a judgement and has it on the basis that a recognized morality is as necessary to society as, say, a recognized government, then society may use the law to preserve morality in the same way as it uses it to safeguard anything else that is essential to its existence. If therefore the first proposition is securely established with all its implications, society has a *prima facie* right to legislate against immorality as such.

The Wolfenden Report, notwithstanding that it seems to admit the right of society to condemn homosexuality and prostitution as immoral, requires special circumstances to be shown to justify the intervention of the law. I think that this is wrong in principle and that any attempt to approach my second interrogatory on these lines is bound to break down. . . .

I think . . . that it is not possible to set theoretical limits to the power of the State to legislate against immorality. It is not possible to settle in advance exceptions to the general rule or to define inflexibly areas of morality into which the law is in no circumstances to be allowed to enter. Society is entitled by means of its laws to protect itself from dangers, whether from within or without. Here again I think that the political parallel is legitimate. The law of treason is directed against aiding the king's enemies and against sedition from within. The justification for this is that established government is necessary for the existence of society and therefore its safety against violent overthrow must be secured. But an established morality is as necessary as good government to the welfare of society. Societies disintegrate from within more frequently than they are broken up by external pressures. There is disintegration when no common morality is observed and history shows that the loosening of moral bonds is often the first stage of disintegration, so that society is justified in taking the same steps to preserve its moral code as it does to preserve its government and other essential institutions. The suppression of vice is as much the law's business as the suppression of subversive activities; it is no more possible to define a sphere of private morality than it is to define one of private subversive activity. It is wrong to talk of private morality or of the law not being concerned with immorality as such or to try to set rigid bounds to the part which the law may play in the suppression of vice. There are no theoretical limits to the power of the State to legislate against treason and sedition, and likewise I think there can be no theoretical limits to legislation against immorality. You may argue that if a man's sins affect only himself it cannot be the concern of society. If he chooses to get drunk every night in the privacy of his own home, is any one except himself the worse for it? But suppose a quarter or a half of the population got drunk every night, what sort of society would it be? You cannot set a theoretical limit to the number of people who can get drunk before society is entitled to legislate against drunkenness. . . .

In what circumstances the State should exercise its power is the third of the interrogatories I have framed. But before I get to it I must raise a point which might have been brought up in any one of the three. How are the moral judgements of society to be ascertained? . . . English law has evolved and regularly uses a standard which does not depend on the counting of heads. It is that of the reasonable man. He is not to be confused with the rational man. He is not expected to reason about anything and his judgement may be largely a matter of feeling. It is the viewpoint of the man in the street—or to use an archaism familiar to all lawyers—the man in the Clapham omnibus. He might also be called the right-minded man. For my purpose I should like to call him the man in the jury box, for the moral judgement of society must be something about which any twelve men or women drawn at random might after discussion be expected to be unanimous. This was the standard the judges applied in the days before Parliament was as active as it is now and when they laid down rules of public policy. They did not think of themselves as making law but simply as stating principles which every right-minded person would accept as valid. It is what Pollock called "practical morality," which is based not on theological or philosophical foundations but "in the mass of continuous experience half-consciously or unconsciously accumulated and embodied in the morality of common sense." He called it also "a certain way of thinking on questions of morality which we expect to find in a reasonable civilized man or a reasonable Englishman, taken at random'.[1] . . .

Nothing should be punished by the law that does not lie beyond the limits of tolerance. It is not nearly enough to say that a majority dislike a practice; there must be a real feeling of reprobation. Those who are dissatisfied with the present law on homosexuality often say that the opponents of reform are swayed simply by disgust. If that were so it would be wrong, but I do not think one can ignore disgust if it is deeply felt and not manufactured. Its presence is a good indication that the bounds of toleration are being reached. Not everything is to be tolerated. No society can do without intolerance, indignation, and disgust; they are the forces behind the moral law, and indeed it can be argued that if they or something like them are not present, the feelings of society cannot be weighty enough to deprive the individual of freedom of choice. I suppose that there is hardly anyone nowadays who would not be disgusted by the thought of deliberate cruelty to animals. No one proposes to relegate that or any other form of sadism to the realm of private morality or to allow it to be practised in public or in private. It would be possible no doubt to point out that until a comparatively short while ago nobody thought very much of cruelty to animals and also that pity and kindliness and the unwillingness to inflict pain are virtues more generally esteemed now than they have ever been in the past. But matters of this sort are not determined by rational argument. Every moral judgement, unless it claims a divine source, is simply a feeling that no right-minded man could behave in any other way without admitting that he was doing wrong. It is the power of a common sense and not the power of reason that is behind the judgements of society. But before a society can put a practice beyond the limits of tolerance there must be a deliberate judgement that the practice is injurious to society. There is, for example, a general abhorrence of homosexuality. We should ask ourselves in the first instance whether, looking at it calmly and dispassionately, we regard it as a vice so abominable that its mere presence is an offence. If that is the genuine feeling of the society in which we live, I do not see how society can be denied the right to eradicate it. . . .

The last and the biggest thing to be remembered is that the law is concerned with the minimum and not with the maximum; there is much in the Sermon on the Mount that would be out of place in the Ten Commandments. We all recognize the gap between the moral law and the law of the land. No man is worth much who regulates his conduct with the sole object of escaping punishment, and every worthy society sets for its members standards which are above those of the law. We recognize the existence of such higher standards when we use expressions such as "moral obligation" and "morally bound." The distinction was well put in the judgement of African elders in a family dispute: "We have power to make you divide the crops, for this is our law, and we will see this is done. But we have not power to make you behave like an upright man."[2] . . .

This then is how I believe my third interrogatory should be answered—not by the formulation of hard and fast rules, but by a judgement in each case taking into account the sort of factors I have been mentioning. The line that divides the criminal law from the moral is not determinable by the application of any clear-cut principle. It is like a line that divides land and sea, a coastline of irregularities and indentations. There are gaps and promontories, such as adultery and fornication, which the law has for centuries left substantially untouched. Adultery of the sort that breaks up marriage seems to me to be just as harmful to the social fabric as homosexuality or bigamy. The only ground for putting it outside the criminal law is that a law which made it a crime would be too difficult to enforce; it is too generally regarded as a human weakness not suitably punished by imprisonment. All that the law can do with fornication is to act against its worst manifestations; there is a general abhorrence of the commercialization of vice, and that sentiment gives strength to the law against brothels and immoral earnings. There is no logic to be found in this. The boundary between the criminal law and the moral law is fixed by balancing in the case of each particular crime the pros and cons of legal enforcement in accordance with the sort of considerations I have been outlining. The fact that adultery, fornication, and lesbianism are untouched by the criminal law does not prove that homosexuality ought not to be touched. The error of jurisprudence in the Wolfenden Report is caused by the search for some single principle to explain the division between crime and sin. The Report finds it in the principle that the criminal law exists for the protection of individuals; on this principle fornication in private between consenting adults is outside the law and thus it becomes logically indefensible to bring homosexuality between consenting adults in private within it. But the true principle is that the law exists for the protection of society. It does not discharge its function by protecting the individual from injury, annoyance, corruption, and exploitation; the law must protect also the institutions and the community of ideas, political and moral, without which people cannot live together. Society cannot ignore the morality of the individual any more than it can his loyalty; it flourishes on both and without either it dies.

I have said that the morals which underly the law must be derived from the sense of right and wrong which resides in the community as a whole; it does not matter whence the community of thought comes, whether from one body of doctrine or another or from the knowledge of good and evil which no man is without. If the reasonable man believes that a practice is immoral and believes also—no matter whether the belief is right or wrong, so be it that it is honest and dispassionate—that no right-minded member of his society could think otherwise, then for the purpose of the law it is immoral. This, you may say, makes immorality a question of fact—what the law would consider as self-evident fact no doubt, but still with no higher authority than any other doctrine of public policy. I think that that is so, and indeed the law does not distinguish between an act that is immoral and one that is contrary to public policy. . . . It seems to me . . . that the freethinker and the non-Christian can accept, without offence to his convictions, the fact that Christian morals are the basis of the criminal law and that he can recognize, also without taking offence, that without the support of the churches the moral order, which has its origin in and takes its strength from Christian beliefs, would collapse. . . .

I return now to the main thread of my argument and summarize it. Society cannot live without morals. Its morals are those standards of conduct which the reasonable man approves. A rational man, who is also a good man, may have other standards. If he has no standards at all he is not a good man and need not be further considered. If he has standards, they may be very different; he may, for example, not disapprove of homosexuality or abortion. In that case he will not share in the common morality; but that should not make him deny that it is a social necessity. A rebel may be rational in thinking that he is right but he is irrational if he thinks that society can leave him free to rebel.

A man who concedes that morality is necessary to society must support the use of those instruments without which morality cannot be maintained. The two instruments are those of teaching, which is doctrine, and of enforcement, which is the law. If morals could be taught simply on the basis that they are necessary to society, there would be no social need for religion; it could be left as a purely personal affair. But morality cannot be taught in that way. Loyalty is not taught in that way either. No society has yet solved the problem of how to teach morality without religion. So the law must base itself on Christian morals and to the limit of its ability enforce them, not simply because they are the morals of most of us, nor simply because they are the morals which are taught by the established Church—on these points the law recognizes the right to dissent—but for the compelling reason that without the help of Christian teaching the law will fail.

NOTES

1. *Essays in Jurisprudence and Ethics* (1882), Macmillan, pp. 278 and 353.
2. A case in the Saa-Katengo Kuta at Lialiu, August 1942, quoted in *The Judicial Process among the Barotse of Northern Rhodesia* by Max Gluckman, Manchester University Press, 1955, p. 172.

Immorality and Treason

H. L. A. Hart

Hart, the most influential legal philosopher in contemporary Anglo-American jurisprudence, rebuts what he calls Devlin's "curious logic" and defends the liberal view that a democratic majority does not always have the right to impose its views on minorities or individuals.

The most remarkable feature of Sir Patrick's lecture is his view of the nature of morality—the morality which the criminal law may enforce. Most previous thinkers who have repudiated the liberal point of view have done so because they thought that morality consisted either of divine commands or of rational principles of human conduct discoverable by human reason. Since morality for them had this elevated divine or rational status as the law of God or reason, it seemed obvious that the state should enforce it, and that the function of human law should not be merely to provide men with the opportunity for leading a good life, but actually to see that they lead it. Sir Patrick does not rest his repudiation of the liberal point of view on these religious or rationalist conceptions. Indeed much that he writes reads like an abjuration of the notion that reasoning or thinking has much to do with morality. English popular morality has no doubt its historical connection with the Christian religion: "That," says Sir Patrick, "is how it got there." But it does not owe its present status or social significance to religion any more than to reason.

What then, is it? According to Sir Patrick it is primarily a matter of feeling. "Every moral judgment," he says, "is a feeling that no right-minded man could act in any other way without admitting that he was doing wrong." Who then must feel this way if we are to have what Sir Patrick calls a public morality? He tells us that it is "the man in the street," "the man in the jury box," or (to use the phrase so familiar to English lawyers) "the man on the Clapham omnibus." For the moral judgments of society so far as the law is concerned are to be ascertained by the standards of the reasonable man, and he is not to be confused with the rational man. Indeed, Sir Patrick says "he is not expected to reason about anything and his judgment may be largely a matter of feeling."

Reprinted from "Immorality and Treason" by H. L. A. Hart in *The Listener*, July 30, 1959. By permission.

Intolerance, Indignation, and Disgust

But what precisely are the relevant feelings, the feelings which may justify use of the criminal law? Here the argument becomes a little complex. Widespread dislike of a practice is not enough. There must, says Sir Patrick, be "a real feeling of reprobation." Disgust is not enough either. What is crucial is a combination of intolerance, indignation, and disgust. These three are the forces behind the moral law, without which it is not "weighty enough to deprive the individual of freedom of choice." Hence there is, in Sir Patrick's outlook, a crucial difference between the mere adverse moral judgment of society and one which is inspired by feeling raised to the concert pitch of intolerance, indignation, and disgust.

This distinction is novel and also very important. For on it depends the weight to be given to the fact that when morality is enforced individual liberty is necessarily cut down. Though Sir Patrick's abstract formulation of his views on this point is hard to follow, his examples make his position fairly clear. We can see it best in the contrasting things he says about fornication and homosexuality. In regard to fornication, public feeling in most societies is not now of the concert-pitch intensity. We may feel that it is tolerable if confined: only its spread might be gravely injurious. In such cases the question whether individual liberty should be restricted is for Sir Patrick a question of balance between the danger to society in the one scale, and the restriction of the individual in the other. But if, as may be the case with homosexuality, public feeling is up to concert pitch, if it expresses a "deliberate judgment" that a practice as such is injurious to society, if there is "a genuine feeling that it is a vice so abominable that its mere presence is an offence," then it is beyond the limits of tolerance, and society may eradicate it. In this case, it seems, no further balancing of the claims of individual liberty is to be done, though as a matter of prudence the legislator should remember that the popular limits of tolerance may shift: the concert-pitch feeling may subside. This may produce a dilemma for the law; for the law may then be left without the full moral backing that it needs, yet it cannot be altered without giving the impression that the moral judgment is being weakened.

✦ ✦ ✦

If this is what morality is—a compound of indignation, intolerance, and disgust—we may well ask what justification there is for taking it, and turning it as such, into criminal law with all the misery which criminal punishment entails. Here Sir Patrick's answer is very clear and simple. A collection of individuals is not a society; what makes them into a society is among other things a shared or public morality. This is as necessary to its existence as an organized government. So society may use the law to preserve its morality like anything else essential to it. "The suppression of vice is as much the law's business as the suppression of subversive activities." The liberal point of view which denies this is guilty of "an error in jurisprudence": for it is no more possible to define an area of private morality than an area of private subversive activity. There can be no "theoretical limits" to legislation against immorality just as there are no such limits to the power of the state to legislate against treason and sedition.

Surely all this, ingenious as it is, is misleading. Mill's formulation of the liberal point of view may well be too simple. The grounds for interfering with human liberty are more various than the single criterion of "harm to others" suggests: cruelty to animals or organizing prostitution for gain do not, as Mill himself saw, fall easily under the description of harm to others. Conversely, even where there is harm to others in the most literal sense, there may well be other principles limiting the extent to which harmful activities should be repressed by law. So there are multiple criteria, not a single criterion, determining when human liberty may be restricted. Perhaps this is what Sir Patrick means by a curious distinction which he often stresses between theoretical and practical limits. But with all its simplicities the liberal point of view is a better guide than Sir Patrick to clear thought on the proper relation of morality to the criminal law: for it stresses what he obscures—namely, the points at which thought is needed before we turn popular morality into criminal law.

No doubt we would all agree that a consensus of moral opinion on certain matters is essential if society is to be worth living in. Laws against murder, theft, and much else would be of little use if they were not supported by a widely diffused conviction that what these laws forbid is also immoral. So much is obvious. But it does not follow that everything to which the moral vetoes of accepted morality attach is of equal importance to society; nor is there the slightest reason for thinking of morality as a seamless web: one which will fall to pieces carrying society with it, unless all its emphatic vetoes are enforced by law. Surely even in the face of the moral feeling that is up to concert pitch—the trio of intolerance, indignation, and disgust—we must pause to think. We must ask a question at two different levels which Sir Patrick never clearly enough identifies or separates. First, we must ask whether a practice which offends moral feeling is harmful, independently of its repercussion on the general moral code. Secondly, what about repercussion on the moral code? Is it really true that failure to translate this item of general morality into criminal law will jeopardize the whole fabric of morality and so of society?

We cannot escape thinking about these two different questions merely by repeating to ourselves the vague nostrum: "This is part of public morality and public morality must be preserved if society is to exist." Sometimes Sir Patrick seems to admit this, for he says in words which both Mill and the Wolfenden Report might have used, that there must be the maximum respect for individual liberty consistent with the integrity of society. Yet this, as his contrasting examples of fornication and homosexuality show, turns out to mean only that the immorality which the law may punish must be generally felt to be intolerable. This plainly is no adequate substitute for a reasoned estimate of the damage to the fabric of society likely to ensue if it is not suppressed.

Nothing perhaps shows more clearly the inadequacy of Sir Patrick's approach to this problem than his comparison between the suppression of sexual immorality and the suppression of treason or subversive activity. Private subversive activity is, of course, a contradiction in terms because "subversion" means overthrowing government, which is a public thing. But it is grotesque, even where moral feeling against homosexuality is up to concert pitch, to think of the homosexual behaviour of two adults in private as in any way like treason or sedition either in intention or effect. We can make it *seem* like treason only if we assume that deviation from a general moral code is bound to affect that code, and to lead not merely to its modification but to its destruction. The analogy could begin to be plausible only if it was clear that offending against this item of morality was likely to jeopardize the whole structure. But we have ample evidence for believing that people will not abandon morality, will not think any better of murder, cruelty, and dishonesty, merely because some private sexual practice which they abominate is not punished by the law.

Because this is so the analogy with treason is absurd. Of course 'No man is an island': what one man does in private, if it is known, may affect others in many different ways. Indeed it may be that deviation from general sexual morality by those whose lives, like the lives of many homosexuals, are noble ones and in all other ways exemplary will lead to what Sir Patrick calls the shifting of the limits of tolerance. But if this has any analogy in the sphere of government it is not the overthrow of ordered government, but a peaceful change in its form. So we may listen to the promptings of common sense and of logic, and say that though there could not logically be a sphere of private treason there is a sphere of private morality and immorality.

Sir Patrick's doctrine is also open to a wider, perhaps a deeper, criticism. In his reaction against a rationalist morality and his stress on feeling, he has I think thrown out the baby and kept the bath water; and the bath water may turn out to be very dirty indeed. When Sir Patrick's lecture was first delivered *The Times* greeted it with these words: "There is a moving and welcome humility in the conception that society should not be asked to give its reason for refusing to tolerate what in its heart it feels intolerable." This drew from a correspondent in Cambridge the retort: "I am afraid that we are less humble than we used to be. We once burnt old women because, without giving our reasons, we felt in our hearts that witchcraft was intolerable."

This retort is a bitter one, yet its bitterness is salutary. We are not, I suppose, likely, in England, to take again to the burning of old women for witchcraft or to punishing people for associating with those of a different race or colour, or to punishing people again for adultery. Yet if these things were viewed with intolerance, indignation, and disgust, as the second of them still is in some countries, it seems that on Sir Patrick's principles no rational criticism could be opposed to the claim that they should be punished by law. We could only pray, in his words, that the limits of tolerance might shift.

It is impossible to see what curious logic has led Sir Patrick to this result. For him a practice is immoral if the thought of it makes the man on the Clapham omnibus sick. So be it. Still, why should we not summon all the resources of our reason, sympathetic understanding, as well as critical intelligence, and insist that before general moral feeling is turned into criminal law it is submitted to scrutiny of a different kind from Sir Patrick's? Surely, the legislator should ask whether the general morality is based on ignorance, superstition, or misunderstanding; whether there is a false conception that those who practice what it condemns are in other ways dangerous or hostile to society; and whether the misery to many parties, the blackmail and the other evil consequences of criminal punishment, especially for sexual offences, are well understood. It is surely extraordinary that among the things which Sir Patrick says are to be considered before we legislate against immorality these appear nowhere; not even as "practical considerations," let alone "theoretical limits." To any theory which, like this one, asserts that the criminal law may be used on the vague ground that the preservation of morality is essential to society and yet omits to stress the need for critical scrutiny, our reply should be: "Morality, what crimes may be committed in thy name!"

As Mill saw, and de Tocqueville showed in detail long ago in his critical but sympathetic study of democracy, it is fatally easy to confuse the democratic principle that power should be in the hands of the majority with the utterly different claim that the majority with power in their hands need respect no limits. Certainly there is a special risk in a democracy that the majority may dictate how all should live. This is the risk we run, and should gladly run; for it is the price of all that is so good in democratic rule. But loyalty to democratic principles does not require us to maximize this risk; yet this is what we shall do if we mount the man in the street on the top of the Clapham omnibus and tell him that if only he feels sick enough about what other people do in private to demand its suppression by law no theoretical criticism can be made of his demand.

Bowers v. Hardwick
478 U.S. 186 (1986)
United States Supreme Court

This is a case in which the United States Supreme Court recently decided that criminal bans on sodomy are constitutional. The case was so controversial that it provoked four Justices to dissent from the majority opinion of the Court. The Court's majority opinion was written by Justice Byron White, who, incidentally, was an All-American football player in college before he led the National Football League in rushing for the Detroit Lions and joined the NFL's Hall of Fame.

The opinion was so controversial, in part, because it focused on the issue of whether states may constitutionally punish *homosexual* acts as crimes even though the statute in question also banned *heterosexual* acts of oral and anal sex. But the more general issue concerns the privacy of the bedroom, and whether sexual acts between consenting adults in private should be beyond the state's coercive power to punish. As writer and wit Gore Vidal put it, given that so many of us want government off our backs, should we not, by parity of reasoning, want government "off our fronts," too?

Justice White delivered the opinion of the Court.

In August 1982, respondent Hardwick (hereafter respondent) was charged with violating the Georgia statute criminalizing sodomy by committing that act with another adult male in the bedroom of respondent's home. After a preliminary hearing, the District Attorney decided not to present the matter to the grand jury unless further evidence developed.

Respondent then brought suit in the Federal District Court, challenging the constitutionality of the statute insofar as it criminalized sodomy. He asserted that he was a practicing homosexual, that the Georgia sodomy statute, as administered by the defendants, placed him in imminent danger of arrest, and that the statute for several reasons violates the Federal Constitution. The District Court granted the defendants' motion to dismiss for failure to state a claim. . . .

A divided panel of the Court of Appeals for the Eleventh Circuit reversed.

. . . Relying on our decisions in *Griswold v. Connecticut*, . . . (1965); and *Roe v. Wade*,. . . (1973), the court went on to hold that the Georgia statute violated respondent's fundamental rights because his homosexual activity is a private and intimate association that is beyond the reach of state regulation by reason of the Ninth Amendment and the Due Process Clause of the Fourteenth Amendment.

. . . We agree with petitioner that the Court of Appeals erred, and hence reverse its judgment.

. . . This case does not require a judgment on whether laws against sodomy between consenting adults in general, or between homosexuals in particular, are wise or desirable. It raises no question about the right or propriety of state legislative decisions to repeal their laws that criminalize homosexual sodomy, or of state-court decisions invalidating those laws on state constitutional grounds. The issue presented is whether the Federal Constitution confers a fundamental right upon homosexuals to engage in sodomy and hence invalidates the laws of the many States that still make such conduct illegal and have done so for a very long time. The case also calls for some judgment about the limits of the Court's role in carrying out its constitutional mandate.

We first register our disagreement with the Court of Appeals and with respondent that the Court's prior cases have construed the Constitution to confer a right of privacy that extends to homosexual sodomy and for all intents and purposes have decided this case. The reach of this line of cases was sketched in *Carey v. Population Services International* . . . (1977). . . . *Griswold v. Connecticut*, . . . *Eisenstadt v. Baird*,. . . and *Roe v. Wade*. . . . (1973), . . . The latter three cases were interpreted as construing the Due Process Clause of the Fourteenth Amendment to confer a fundamental individual right to decide whether or not to beget or bear a child. . . .

Accepting the decisions in these cases and the above description of them, we think it evident that none of the rights announced in those cases bears any resemblance to the claimed constitutional right of homosexuals to engage in acts of sodomy that is asserted in this case. No connection between family, marriage, or procreation on the one hand and homosexual activity on the other has been demonstrated, either by the Court of Appeals or by respondent. Moreover, any claim that these cases nevertheless stand for the proposition that any kind of private sexual conduct between consenting adults is constitutionally insulated from state proscription is unsupportable. Indeed, the Court's opinion in *Carey* twice asserted that the privacy right, which the *Griswold* line of cases found to be one of the protections provided by the Due Process Clause, did not reach so far. . . .

Precedent aside, however, respondent would have us announce, as the Court of Appeals did, a fundamental right to engage in homosexual sodomy. This we are quite unwilling to do. It is true that despite the language of the Due Process Clauses of the Fifth and Fourteenth Amendments, which appears to focus only on the processes by which life, liberty, or property is taken, the cases are legion in which those Clauses have been interpreted to have substantive content, subsuming rights that to a great extent are immune from federal or state regulation or proscription. Among such cases are those recognizing rights that have little or no textual support in the constitutional language. *Meyer, Prince,* and *Pierce* fall in this category, as do the privacy cases from *Griswold* to *Carey*.

Striving to assure itself and the public that announcing rights not readily identifiable in the Constitution's text involves much more than the imposition of the Justices' own choice of values on the States and the Federal Government, the Court has sought to identify the nature of the rights qualifying for heightened judicial protection. In *Palke v. Connecticut,* . . . (1937), it was said that this category includes those fundamental liberties that are "implicit in the concept of ordered liberty," such that "neither liberty nor justice would exist if [they] were sacrificed." A different description of fundamental liberties appeared in *Moore v. East Cleveland,* . . . (1977) (opinion of Powell, J.), where they are characterized as those liberties that are "deeply rooted in this Nation's history and tradition." . . .

It is obvious to us that neither of these formulations would extend a fundamental right to homosexuals to engage in acts of consensual sodomy. Proscriptions against that conduct have ancient roots. . . . Sodomy was a criminal offense at common law and was forbidden by the laws of the original thirteen States when they ratified the Bill of Rights. In 1868, when the Fourteenth Amendment was ratified, all but 5 of the 37 States in the Union had criminal sodomy laws. In fact, until 1961, all 50 States outlawed sodomy, and today, 24 States and the District of Columbia continue to provide criminal penalties for sodomy performed in private and between consenting adults. . . . Against this background, to claim that a right to engage in such conduct is "deeply rooted in this Nation's history and tradition" or "implicit in the concept of ordered liberty" is, at best, facetious.

. . . Nor are we inclined to take a more expansive view of our authority to discover new fundamental rights imbedded in the Due Process Clause. The Court is most vulnerable and comes nearest to illegitimacy when it deals with judge-made constitutional law having little or no cognizable roots in the language or design of the Constitution. That this is so was painfully demonstrated by the face-off between the Executive and the Court in the 1930's, which resulted in the repudiation of much of the substantive gloss that the Court had placed on the Due Process Clauses of the Fifth and Fourteenth Amendments. There should be, therefore, great resistance to expand the substantive reach of those Clauses, particularly if it requires redefining the category of rights deemed to be fundamental. Otherwise, the Judiciary necessarily takes to itself further authority to govern the country without express constitutional authority. The claimed right pressed on us today falls far short of overcoming this resistance.

Respondent, however, asserts that the result should be different where the homosexual conduct occurs in the privacy of the home. He relies on *Stanley v. Georgia,* . . . (1969), where the Court held that the First Amendment prevents conviction for possessing and reading obscene material in the privacy of one's home: "If the First

Amendment means anything, it means that a State has no business telling a man, sitting alone in his house, what books he may read or what films he may watch." . . .

Stanley did protect conduct that would not have been protected outside the home, and it partially prevented the enforcement of state obscenity laws; but the decision was firmly grounded in the First Amendment. The right pressed upon us here has no similar support in the text of the Constitution, and it does not qualify for recognition under the prevailing principles for construing the Fourteenth Amendment. Its limits are also difficult to discern. Plainly enough, otherwise illegal conduct is not always immunized whenever it occurs in the home. Victimless crimes, such as the possession and use of illegal drugs, do not escape the law where they are committed at home. *Stanley* itself recognized that its holding offered no protection for the possession in the home of drugs, firearms, or stolen goods. . . . And if respondent's submission is limited to the voluntary sexual conduct between consenting adults, it would be difficult, except by fiat, to limit the claimed right to homosexual conduct while leaving exposed to prosecution adultery, incest, and other sexual crimes even though they are committed in the home. We are unwilling to start down that road.

. . . Even if the conduct at issue here is not a fundamental right, respondent asserts that there must be a rational basis for the law and that there is none in this case other than the presumed belief of a majority of the electorate in Georgia that homosexual sodomy is immoral and unacceptable. This is said to be an inadequate rationale to support the law. The law, however, is constantly based on notions of morality, and if all laws representing essentially moral choices are to be invalidated under the Due Process Clause, the courts will be very busy indeed. Even respondent makes no such claim, but insists that majority sentiments about the morality of homosexuality should be declared inadequate. We do not agree, and are unpersuaded that the sodomy laws of some 25 States should be invalidated on this basis.

Accordingly, the judgment of the Court of Appeals is

Reversed.

Justice Blackmun, with whom Justice Brennan, Justice Marshall, and Justice Stevens join, dissenting.

This case is no more about "a fundamental right to engage in homosexual sodomy," as the Court purports to declare, than *Stanley v. Georgia*. . . was about a fundamental right to watch obscene movies, or *Katz v. United States*, 389 U.S. 347 . . . (1967), was about a fundamental right to place interstate bets from a telephone booth. Rather, this case is about "the most comprehensive of rights and the right most valued by civilized men," namely, "the right to be let alone." *Olmstead v. United States*, . . . (1928) (Brandeis, dissenting).

The statute at issue, Ga. Code Ann. § 16-6-2 (1984), denies individuals the right to decide for themselves whether to engage in particular forms of private, consensual sexual activity. The Court concludes that § 16-6-2 is valid essentially because "the laws of . . . many States . . . still make such conduct illegal and have done so for a very long time." . . . But the fact that the moral judgments expressed by statutes like § 16-6-2 may be " 'natural and familiar . . . ought not to conclude our judgment upon the question whether statutes embodying them conflict with the Constitution of the United States' " *Roe v. Wade*, . . . (1973), . . . (Holmes, J., dissenting). Like Justice Holmes, I believe that "[i]t is revolting to have no better reason for a rule of law than that so it was laid down in the time of Henry IV. It is still more revolting if the grounds upon which it was laid down have vanished long since, and the rule simply persists from blind imitation of the past." Holmes, The Path of the Law, 10 Harv. L. Rev. 457, 469 (1897). I believe we must analyze Hardwick's claim in the light of the values that underlie the constitutional right to privacy. If that right means anything, it means that, before Georgia can prosecute its citizens for making choices about the most intimate aspects of their lives, it must do more than assert that the choice they have made is an "abominable crime not fit to be named among Christians." . . .

I

In its haste to reverse the Court of Appeals and hold that the Constitution does not "confe[r] a fundamental right upon homosexuals to engage in sodomy," . . . the Court relegates the actual statute being challenged to a footnote and ignores the procedural posture of the case before it. A fair reading of the statute and of the complaint clearly reveals that the majority has distorted the question this case presents.

First, the Court's almost obsessive focus on homosexual activity is particularly hard to justify in light of the broad language Georgia has used. Unlike the Court, the Georgia Legislature has not proceeded on the assumption that homosexuals are so different from other citizens that their lives may be controlled in a way that would not be tolerated if it limited the choices of those other citizens. . . . Rather, Georgia has provided that "[a] person commits the offense of sodomy when he performs or submits to any sexual act involving the sex organs of one person and the mouth or anus of another." . . . The sex or status of the persons who engage in the act is irrelevant as a matter of state law. In fact, to the extent I can discern a legislative purpose for Georgia's 1968 enactment of § 16-6-2, that purpose seems to have been to broaden the coverage of the law to reach heterosexual as well as homosexual activity. I therefore see no basis for the Court's decision to treat this case as an "as applied" challenge to § 16-6-2 . . . or for Georgia's attempt, both in its brief and at oral argument, to defend § 16-6-2 solely on the grounds that it prohibits homosexual activity. Michael Hardwick's standing may rest in significant part on Georgia's apparent willingness to enforce against homosexuals a law it seems not to have any desire to enforce against heterosexuals. . . . But his claim that § 16-6-2 involves an unconstitutional intrusion into his privacy and his right of intimate association does not depend in any way on his sexual orientation.

Second, I disagree with the Court's refusal to consider whether § 16-6-2 runs afoul of the Eighth or Ninth Amendments or the Equal Protection Clause of the Fourteenth Amendment. . . . Respondent's complaint expressly invoked the Ninth Amendment . . . and he relied heavily before this Court on *Griswold v. Connecticut* . . . (1965), which identifies that Amendment as one of the specific constitutional provisions giving "life and substance" to our understanding of privacy.

II

"Our cases long have recognized that the Constitution embodies a promise that a certain private sphere of individual liberty will be kept largely beyond the reach of government." *Thornburgh v. American College of Obstetricians & Gynecologists,* . . . (1986). In construing the right to privacy, the Court has proceeded along two somewhat distinct, albeit complementary, lines. First, it has recognized a privacy interest with reference to certain *decisions* that are properly for the individual to make. . . . Second, it has recognized a privacy interest with reference to certain *places* without regard for the particular activities in which the individuals who occupy them are engaged. . . . The case before us implicates both the decisional and the spatial aspects of the right to privacy.

A

The Court concludes today that none of our prior cases dealing with various decisions that individuals are entitled to make free of governmental interference "bears any resemblance to the claimed constitutional right of homosexuals to engage in acts of sodomy that is asserted in this case." . . . While it is true that these cases may be characterized by their connection to protection of the family, . . . the Court's conclusion that they extend no further than this boundary ignores the warning in *Moore v. East Cleveland* . . . (1977) (plurality opinion), against "clos[ing] our eyes to the basic reasons why certain rights associated with the family have been accorded shelter under the Fourteenth Amendment's Due Process Clause." We protect those rights not because they contribute, in some direct and material way, to the general public welfare, but because they form so central a part of an individual's life. "[T]he concept of privacy embodies the 'moral fact that a person belongs to himself and not others nor to society as a whole.' " *Thornburgh v. American College of Obstetricians & Gynecologists* . . . (Stevens, concurring), quoting Fried, Correspondence, 6 Phil. & Pub. Affairs 288–289 (1977). And so we protect the decision whether to marry precisely because marriage "is an association that promotes a way of life, not causes; a harmony in living, not political faiths; a bilateral loyalty, not commercial or social projects." *Griswold*. . . . We protect the decision whether to have a child because parenthood alters so dramatically an individual's self-definition, not because of demographic considerations or the Bible's command to be fruitful and multiply. . . . And we protect the family because it contributes so powerfully to the happiness of individuals, not because of a preference for stereotypical households. . . . The Court recognized in *Roberts* . . . that the "ability independently to define one's identity that is central to any concept of liberty" cannot truly be exercised in a vacuum; we all depend on the "emotional enrichment from close ties with others." . . .

Only the most willful blindness could obscure the fact that sexual intimacy is "a sensitive, key relationship of human existence, central to family life, community welfare, and the development of human personality," *Paris Adult Theatre I v. Slaton*, (1973) . . . The fact that individuals define themselves in a significant way through their intimate sexual relationships with others suggests, in a Nation as diverse as ours, that there may be many "right" ways of conducting those relationships, and that much of the richness of a relationship will come from the freedom an individual has to *choose* the form and nature of these intensely personal bonds.

In a variety of circumstances we have recognized that a necessary corollary of giving individuals freedom to choose how to conduct their lives is acceptance of the fact that different individuals will make different choices. For example, in holding that the clearly important state interest in public education should give way to a competing claim by the Amish to the effect that extended formal schooling threatened their way of life, the Court declared: "There can be no assumption that today's majority is 'right' and the Amish and others like them are 'wrong.' A way of life that is odd or even erratic but interferes with no rights or interests of others is not to be condemned because it is different." *Wisconsin v. Yoder*, (1972). The Court claims that its decision today merely refuses to recognize a fundamental right to engage in homosexual sodomy; what the Court really has refused to recognize is the fundamental interest all individuals have in controlling the nature of their intimate associations with others.

B

The behavior for which Hardwick faces prosecution occurred in his own home, a place to which the Fourth Amendment attaches special significance. The [C]ourt's treatment of this aspect of the case is symptomatic of its overall refusal to consider the broad principles that have informed our treatment of privacy in specific cases. Just as the right to privacy is more than the mere aggregation of a number of entitlements to engage in specific behavior, so too, protecting the physical integrity of the home is more than merely a means of protecting specific activities that often take place there. Even when our understanding of the contours of the right to privacy depends on "reference to a 'place,' " . . . "the essence of a Fourth Amendment violation is 'not the breaking of doors, and the rummaging of his drawers,' but rather is 'the invasion of his indefeasible right of personal security, personal liberty and private property.' " *California v. Ciraolo,* . . . (1986) (Powell, dissenting), (1986).

The Court's interpretation of the pivotal case of *Stanley v. Georgia* . . . (1969) . . . is entirely unconvincing. *Stanley* held that Georgia's undoubted power to punish the public distribution of constitutionally unprotected, obscene material did not permit the State to punish the private possession of such material. According to the majority here, *Stanley* relied entirely on the First Amendment, and thus, it is claimed, sheds no light on cases not involving printed materials. . . . But that is not what *Stanley* said. Rather, the *Stanley* Court anchored its holding in the Fourth Amendment's special protection for the individual in his home:

"The makers of our Constitution undertook to secure conditions favorable to the pursuit of happiness. They recognized the significance of man's spiritual nature, of his feelings and of his intellect. They knew that only a part of the pain, pleasure and satisfactions of life are to be found in material things. They sought to protect Americans in their beliefs, their thoughts, their emotions and their sensations."

"These are the rights that appellant is asserting in the case before us. He is asserting the right to read or observe what he pleases—the right to satisfy his intellectual and emotional needs in the privacy of his own home." 89 S.Ct., at 1248, quoting *Olmstead v. United States,* . . . (Brandeis, J., dissenting).

The central place that *Stanley* gives Justice Brandeis'[s] dissent in *Olmstead,* a case raising *no* First Amendment claim, shows that *Stanley* rested as much on the Court's understanding of the Fourth Amendment as it did on the First. Indeed, in *Paris Adult Theatre I v. Slaton,* . . . the Court suggested that reliance on the Fourth Amendment not only supported the Court's outcome in *Stanley* but actually was *necessary* to it: "If obscene material unprotected by the First Amendment in itself carried with it a 'penumbra' of constitutionally protected privacy, this Court would not have found it necessary to decide *Stanley* on the narrow basis of the 'privacy of the home,' which was hardly more than a reaffirmation that 'a man's home is his castle.' " . . . "The right of the people to be secure in their . . . houses," expressly guaranteed by the Fourth Amendment, is perhaps the most "textual" of the various constitutional provisions that inform our understanding of the right to privacy, and thus I cannot agree with the Court's statement that "[t]he right pressed upon us here has no . . . support in the text of the Constitution." . . . Indeed, the right of an individual to conduct intimate relationships in the intimacy of his or her own home seems to me to be the heart of the Constitution's protection of privacy.

III

The Court's failure to comprehend the magnitude of the liberty interests at stake in this case leads it to slight the question whether petitioner, on behalf of the State, has justified Georgia's infringement on these interests. I believe that neither of the two general justifications for § 16-6-2 that petitioner has advanced warrants dismissing respondent's challenge for failure to state a claim.

First, petitioner asserts that the acts made criminal by the statute may have serious adverse consequences for "the general public health and welfare," such as spreading communicable diseases or fostering other criminal activity. Inasmuch as this case was dismissed by the District Court on the pleadings, it is not surprising that the record before us is barren of any evidence to support petitioner's claim.

. . . Nothing in the record before the Court provides any justification for finding the activity forbidden by § 16-6-2 to be physically dangerous, either to the persons engaged in it or to others.[1]

The core of petitioner's defense of § 16-6-2, however, is that respondent and others who engage in the conduct prohibited by § 16-6-2 interfere with Georgia's exercise of the "right of the Nation and of the States to maintain a decent society."

. . . Essentially, petitioner argues, and the Court agrees, that the fact that the acts described in § 16-6-2 "for hundreds of years, if not thousands, have been uniformly condemned as immoral" is a sufficient reason to permit a State to ban them today. . . .

I cannot agree that either the length of time a majority has held its convictions or the passions with which it defends them can withdraw legislation from this Court's scrutiny.

. . . As Justice Jackson wrote so eloquently for the Court in *West Virginia Board of Education v. Barnette* (1943), "we apply the limitations of the Constitution with no fear that freedom to be intellectually and spiritually diverse or even contrary will disintegrate the social organization. . . . [F]reedom to differ is not limited to things that do not matter much. That would be a mere shadow of freedom. The test of its substance is the right to differ as to things that touch the heart of the existing order." . . . It is precisely because the issue raised by this case touches the heart of what makes individuals what they are that we should be especially sensitive to the rights of those whose choices upset the majority.

The assertion that "traditional Judeo-Christian values proscribe" the conduct involved . . . cannot provide an adequate justification for § 16-6-2.

. . . That certain, but by no means all, religious groups condemn the behavior at issue gives the State no license to impose their judgments on the entire citizenry. The legitimacy of secular legislation depends instead on whether the State can advance some justification for its law beyond its conformity to religious doctrine.

. . . Thus, far from buttressing his case, petitioner's invocation of Leviticus, Romans, St. Thomas Aquinas, and sodomy's heretical status during the Middle Ages undermines his suggestion that § 16-6-2 represents a legitimate use of secular coercive power. A State can no more punish private behavior because of religious intolerance than it can punish such behavior because of racial animus.

. . . No matter how uncomfortable a certain group may make the majority of this Court, we have held that "[m]ere public intolerance or animosity cannot constitutionally justify the deprivation of a person's physical liberty." *O'Connor v. Donaldson* (1975).

Nor can § 16-6-2 be justified as a "morally neutral" exercise of Georgia's power to "protect the public environment." . . . Certainly, some private behavior can affect the fabric of society as a whole. Reasonable people may differ about whether particular sexual acts are moral or immoral, but "we have ample evidence for believing that people will not abandon morality, will not think any better of murder, cruelty, and dishonesty, merely because some private sexual practice which they abominate is not punished by the law." H. L. A. Hart, Immorality and Treason, reprinted in The Law as Literature 220, 225 (L. Blom-Cooper ed. 1961). Petitioner and the Court fail to see the difference between laws that protect public sensibilities and those that enforce private morality. Statutes banning public sexual activity are entirely consistent with protecting the individual's liberty interest in decisions concerning sexual relations: the same recognition that those decisions are intensely private which justifies protecting them from governmental interference can justify protecting individuals from unwilling exposure to the sexual activities of others. But the mere fact that intimate behavior may be punished when it takes place in public cannot dictate how States can regulate intimate behavior that occurs in intimate places.

This case involves no real interference with the rights of others, for the mere knowledge that other individuals do not adhere to one's value system cannot be a legally cognizable interest . . . let alone an interest that can justify invading the houses, hearts, and minds of citizens who choose to live their lives differently.

IV

It took but three years for the Court to see the error in its analysis in *Minersville School District v. Gobitis,* 310 U.S. 586 . . . (1940), and to recognize that the threat to national cohesion posed by a refusal to salute the flag was vastly outweighed by the threat to those same values posed by compelling such a salute. See *West Virginia Board of Education v. Barnette* (1943). I can only hope that here, too, the Court soon will reconsider its analysis and conclude that depriving individuals of the right to choose for themselves how to conduct their intimate relationships poses a far greater threat to the values most deeply rooted in our Nation's history than tolerance of nonconformity could ever do. Because I think the Court today betrays those values, I dissent.

NOTES

1. Although I do not think it necessary to decide today issues that are not even remotely before us, it does seem to me that a court could find simple, analytically sound distinctions between certain private, consensual sexual conduct, on the one hand, and adultery and incest (the only two vaguely specific "sexual crimes" to which the majority points . . .), on the other. For example, marriage, in addition to its spiritual aspects, is a civil contract that entitles the contracting parties to a variety of governmentally provided benefits. A State might define the contractual commitment necessary to become eligible for these benefits to include a commitment of fidelity and then punish individuals for breaching that contract. Moreover, a State might conclude that adultery is likely to injure third persons, in particular, spouses and children of persons who engage in extramarital affairs. With respect to incest, a court might well agree with respondent that the nature of familial relationships renders true consent to incestuous activity sufficiently problematical that a blanket prohibition of such activity is warranted. . . . Notably, the Court makes no effort to explain why it has chosen to group private, consensual homosexual activity with adultery and incest rather than with private, consensual heterosexual activity by unmarried persons or, indeed, with oral or anal sex within marriage.

The Right to Privacy

JUDITH JARVIS THOMSON

Thomson, a leading philosopher who teaches at M. I. T., is struck by the fact that, for all the importance attached to the right to privacy, "nobody seems to have any very clear idea what it is." Thomson sets out to remedy this defect in our understanding, showing the traditional concern philosophers have for creating and refining the definition of fundamental concepts. The essay uses her characteristic approach of relying heavily on the analysis of a few fascinating examples. Her main contention is that there is no right to privacy over and above the rights we have over our person and our property. She thus

Judith Jarvis Thomson, "The Right to Privacy," *Philosophy & Public Affairs* 4(4) (Summer):295–314, 1975.

tries to reduce the right to privacy to these two other kinds of right. This type of reductionism is opposed in Ruth Gavison's article, which follows Thomson's.

I

Perhaps the most striking thing about the right to privacy is that nobody seems to have any very clear idea what it is. Consider, for example, the familiar proposal that the right to privacy is the right "to be let alone." On the one hand, this doesn't seem to take in enough. The police might say, "We grant we used a special X-ray device on Smith, so as to be able to watch him through the walls of his house: we grant we trained an amplifying device on him so as to be able to hear everything he said; but we let him strictly alone: we didn't touch him, we didn't even go near him—our devices operate at a distance." Anyone who believes there is a right to privacy would presumably believe that it has been violated in Smith's case; yet he would be hard put to explain precisely how, if the right to privacy is the right to be let alone. And on the other hand, this account of the right to privacy lets in far too much. If I hit Jones on the head with a brick I have not let him alone. Yet, while hitting Jones on the head with a brick is surely violating some right of Jones', doing it should surely not turn out to violate his right to privacy. Else, where is this to end? Is *every* violation of a right a violation of the right to privacy?

It seems best to be less ambitious, to begin with at least. I suggest, then, that we look at some specific, imaginary cases in which people would say, "There, in that case, the right to privacy has been violated," and ask ourselves precisely why this would be said, and what, if anything, would justify saying it.

II

But there is a difficulty to be taken note of first. What I have in mind is that there may not be so much agreement on the cases as I implied. Suppose that my husband and I are having a fight, shouting at each other as loud as we can; and suppose that we have not thought to close the windows, so that we can easily be heard from the street outside. It seems to me that anyone who stops to listen violates no right of ours; stopping to listen is at worst bad, Not Nice, not done by the best people. But now suppose, by contrast, that we are having a quiet fight, behind closed windows, and cannot be heard by the normal person who passes by; and suppose that someone across the street trains an amplifier on our house, by means of which he can hear what we say; and suppose that he does this in order to hear what we say. It seems to me that anyone who does this does violate a right of ours, the right to privacy, I should have thought.

But there is room for disagreement. It might be said that in neither case is there a violation of a right, that both are cases of mere bad behavior—though no doubt worse behavior in the second case than in the first, it being very much naughtier to train amplifiers on people's houses than merely to stop in the street to listen.

Or, alternatively, it might be said that in both cases there is a violation of a right, the right to privacy in fact, but that the violation is less serious in the first case than in the second.

I think that these would both be wrong. I think that we have in these two cases, not merely a difference in degree, but a difference in quality: that the passerby who stops to listen in the first case may act badly, but violates no one's rights, whereas the neighbor who uses an amplifier in the second case does not merely act badly but violates a right, the right to privacy. But I have no argument for this. I take it rather as a datum in this sense: it seems to me there would be a mark against an account of the right to privacy if it did not yield the conclusion that these two cases do differ in the way I say they do, and moreover explain why they do.

But there is one thing perhaps worth drawing attention to here: doing so may perhaps diminish the inclination to think that a right is violated in both cases. What I mean is this.

There is a familiar account of rights—I speak now of rights generally, and not just of the right to privacy—according to which a man's having a right that something shall not be done to him just itself consists in its being the case that anyone who does it to him acts badly or wrongly or does what he ought not do. Thus, for example, it is said that to have a right that you shall not be killed or imprisoned just itself consists in its being the case that if anyone does kill or imprison you, he acts badly, wrongly, does what he ought not do. If this account of rights were correct, then my husband and I would have a right that nobody shall stop in the street and listen to our loud fight, since anyone who does stop in the street and listen acts badly, wrongly, does what he ought not do. Just as we have a right that people shall not train amplifiers on the house to listen to our quiet fights.

But this account of rights is just plain wrong. There are many, many things we ought not do to people, things such that if we do them to a person, we act badly, but which are not such that to do them is to violate a right of his. It is bad behavior, for example to be ungenerous and unkind. Suppose that you dearly love chocolate ice cream but that, for my part, I find that a little of it goes a long way. I have been given some and have eaten a little, enough really, since I don't care for it very much. You then, looking on, ask, "May I have the rest of your ice cream?" It would be bad indeed if I were to reply, "No, I've decided to bury the rest of it in the garden." I ought not do that; I ought to give it to you. But you have no right that I give it to you, and I violate no right of yours if I do bury the stuff.

Indeed, it is possible that an act which is not a violation of a right should be a far worse act than an act which is. If you did not merely want the ice cream but needed it, for your health perhaps, then my burying it would be monstrous, indecent, though still, of course, no violation of a right. By contrast, if you snatch it away, steal it, before I can bury it, then while you violate a right (the ice cream is mine, after all), your act is neither monstrous nor indecent—if it's bad at all, it's anyway not very bad.

From the point of view of conduct, of course, this doesn't really matter: bad behavior is bad behavior, whether it is a violation of a right or not. But if we want to be clear about *why* this or that bit of bad behavior is bad, then these distinctions do have to get made and looked into.

III

To return, then, to the two cases I drew attention to, and which I suggest we take to differ in this way: in one of them a right is violated, in the other not. It isn't, I think, the fact that an amplifying device is used in the one case, and not in the other, that is responsible for this difference. On the one hand, consider someone who is deaf: if he passes by while my husband and I are having a loud fight at an open window and turns up his hearing-aid so as to be able to hear us, it seems to me he no more violates our right to privacy than does one who stops to listen and can hear well enough without a hearing-aid. And on the other hand, suppose that you and I have to talk over some personal matters. It is most convenient to meet in the park, and we do so, taking a bench far from the path since we don't want to be overheard. It strikes a man to want to know what we are saying to each other in that heated fashion, so he creeps around in the bushes behind us and crouches back of the bench to listen. He thereby violates the right to privacy—fully as much as if he had stayed a hundred yards away and used an amplifying device to listen to us.

IV

The cases I drew attention to are actually rather difficult tc deal with, and I suggest we back away from them for a while and look at something simpler.

Consider a man who owns a pornographic picture. He wants that nobody but him shall ever see the picture—perhaps because he wants that nobody shall know that he owns it, perhaps because he feels that someone else's seeing it would drain it of power to please. So he keeps it locked in his wall-safe, and takes it out to look at only at night or after pulling down the shades and closing the curtains. We have heard about his picture, and we want to see it, so we train our X-ray device on the wall-safe and look in. To do this is, I think, to violate a right of his—the right to privacy. I should think.

No doubt people who worry about violations of the right to privacy are not worried about the possibility that others will look at their *possessions*. At any rate, this doesn't worry them very much. That it is not nothing, however, comes out when one thinks on the special source of discomfort there is if a burglar doesn't go straight for the TV set and the silver, and then leave, but if he stops for a while just to look at things—e.g. at your love letters or at the mound of torn socks on the floor of your closet. The trespass and the theft *might* swamp everything else; but they might not: the burglar's merely looking around in that way might make the episode feel worse than it otherwise would have done.

So I shall suppose that we do violate this man's right to privacy if we use an X-ray device to look at the picture in his wall-safe. And now let us ask how and why.

To own a picture is to have a cluster of rights to respect of it. The cluster includes, for example, the right to sell it to whomever you like, the right to give it away, the right to tear it, the right to look at it. These rights are all "positive rights": rights to do certain things to or in respect of the picture. To own a picture is also to have certain "negative rights" in respect of it, that is, rights that others shall not do certain things to it—thus, for example, the right that others shall not sell it or give it away or tear it.

Does owning a picture also include having the negative right that others shall not look at it? I think it does. If our man's picture is good pornography, it would be pretty mingy of him to keep it permanently hidden so that nobody but him shall ever see it—a nicer person would let his friends have a look at it too. But he is within his rights to hide it. If someone is about to tear his picture, he can snatch it away: it's his, so he has a right that nobody but him shall tear it. If someone is about to look at his picture, he can snatch it away or cover it up: it's his, so he has a right that nobody but him shall look at it.

It is important to stress that he has not merely the right to snatch the picture away in order that nobody shall tear it, he has not merely the right to do everything he can (within limits) to prevent people from tearing it, he has also the right that nobody *shall* tear it. What I have in mind is this. Suppose we desperately want to tear his picture. He locks it in his wall-safe to prevent us from doing so. And suppose we are so eager that we buy a penetrating long-distance picture-tearer: we sit quietly in our apartment across the street, train the device on the picture in the wall-safe, press the button—and lo! we have torn the picture. The fact that he couldn't protect his picture against the action of the device doesn't make it all right that we use it.

Again, suppose that there was a way in which he could have protected his picture against the action of the device: the rays won't pass through platinum, and he could have encased the picture in platinum. But he would have had to sell everything else he owns in order to pay for the platinum. The fact he didn't do this does not make it all right for us to have used the device.

We all have a right to do what we can (within limits) to secure our belongings against theft. I gather, however, that it's practically impossible to secure them against a determined burglar. Perhaps only hiring armed guards or sealing the house in solid steel will guarantee that our possessions cannot be stolen; and perhaps even these things won't work. The fact (if it's a fact) that we can't guarantee our belongings against theft; the fact (if it's a fact) that though we can, the cost of doing so is wildly out of proportion to the value of the things, and therefore we don't; neither of these makes it all right for the determined burglar to walk off with them.

Now I said that if a man owns a picture he can snatch it away or he can cover it up to prevent anyone else from *looking* at it. He can also hide it in his wall-safe. But I think he has a right, not merely to do what he can (within limits) to prevent it from being looked at: he has a right that it shall not be looked at—just as he has a right that it shall not be torn or taken away from him. That he has a right that it shall not be looked at comes out, I think, in this way: if he hides it in his wall-safe, and we train our X-ray device on the wall-safe and look in, we have violated a right of his in respect of it, and the right is surely the right that it shall not be looked at. The fact that he couldn't protect his picture against the action of an X-ray device which enables us to look at it doesn't make it all right that we use the X-ray device to look at it—just as the fact that he can't protect his picture against the action of a long-distance picture-tearing device which enables us to tear his picture doesn't make it all right that we use the device to tear it.

Compare, by contrast, a subway map. You have no right to take it off the wall or cover it up: you haven't a right to do whatever you can to prevent it from being looked at. And if you do cover it up, and if anyone looks through the covering with an X-ray device, he violates no right of yours: you do not have a right that nobody but you shall look at it—it's not *yours*, after all.

Looking at a picture doesn't harm it, of course, whereas tearing a picture does. But this doesn't matter. If I use your toothbrush I don't harm it; but you, all the same, have a right that I shall not use it.

However, to have a right isn't always to claim it. Thus, on any view to own a picture is to have (among other rights) the right that others shall not tear it. Yet you might want someone else to do this and therefore (1) invite him to, or (2) get him to whether he wants to or not—e.g. by carefully placing it where he'll put his foot through it when he gets out of bed in the morning. Or again, while not positively wanting anyone else to tear the picture, you might not care whether or not it is torn, and therefore you might simply (3) let someone tear it—e.g. when, out of laziness, you leave it where it fell amongst the things the children are in process of wrecking. Or again still, you might positively want that nobody shall tear the picture and yet in a fit of absent-mindedness (4) leave it in some place such that another person would have to go to some trouble if he is to avoid tearing it, or (5) leave it in some place such that another person could not reasonably be expected to know that it still belonged to anybody.

Similarly, you might want someone else to look at your picture and therefore (1) invite him to, or (2) get him to whether he wants to or not. Or again, while not positively wanting anyone else to look at the picture, you might not care whether or not it is looked at, and therefore you might simply (3) let it be looked at. Or again still, you might positively want that nobody shall look at the picture, and yet in a fit of absent-mindedness (4) leave it in some place such that another person would have to go to some trouble if he is to avoid looking at it (at least, avert his eyes) or (5) leave it in some place such that another person could not reasonably be expected to know that it still belonged to anybody.

In all of these cases, it is permissible for another person on the one hand to tear the picture, on the other to look at it: no right of the owner's is violated. I think it fair to describe them as cases in which, though the owner had a right that the things not be done, he *waived* the right: in cases (1), (2), and (3) intentionally, in cases (4) and (5) unintentionally. It is not at all easy to say under what conditions a man has waived a right—by what acts of commission or omission and in what circumstances. The conditions vary, according as the right is more or less important; and while custom and convention, on the one hand, and the cost of securing the right, on the other hand, play very important roles, it is not clear precisely what roles. Nevertheless there plainly is such a thing as waiving a right; and given a man has waived his right to a thing, we violate no right of his if we do not accord it to him.

There are other things which may bring about that although a man had a right to a thing, we violate no right of his if we do not accord it to him: he may have transferred the right to another or he may have forfeited the right or he may still have the right, though it is overridden by some other, more stringent right. (This is not meant to be an exhaustive list.) And there are also some circumstances in which it is not clear what should be said. Suppose someone steals your picture and invites some third party (who doesn't know it's yours) to tear it or look at it; or suppose someone takes your picture by mistake, thinking it's his, and invites some third party (who doesn't know it's yours) to tear it or look at it; does the *third* party violate a right of yours if he accepts the invitation? A general theory of rights should provide an account of all of these things.

It suffices here, however, to stress one thing about rights: a man may have had a right that we shall not do a thing, he may even still have a right that we shall not do it, consistently with its being the case that we violate no right of his if we go ahead.

If this is correct, we are on the way to what we want. I said earlier that when we trained our X-ray device on the man's wall-safe in order to have a look at his pornographic picture, we violate a right of his, the right to privacy, in fact. It now turns out (if I am right) that we violated a property right of his, specifically the negative right that others shall not look at the picture, this being one of the (many) rights which his owning the picture consists of. I shall come back a little later to the way in which these rights interconnect.

V

We do not, of course, care nearly as much about our possessions as we care about ourselves. We do not want people looking at our torn socks; but it would be much worse to have people watch us make faces at ourselves in the mirror when we thought no one was looking or listen to us while we fight with our families. So you might think I have spent far too much time on that pornographic picture.

But in fact, if what I said about pornographic pictures was correct, then the point about ourselves comes through easily enough. For if we have fairly stringent rights over our property, we have very much more stringent rights over our own persons. None of you came to possess your knee in exactly the way in which you came to possess your shoes or your pornographic pictures: I take it you neither bought nor inherited your left knee. And I suppose you could not very well sell your left knee. But that isn't because it isn't yours to sell—some women used to sell their hair, and some people nowadays sell their blood—but only because who'd buy a used left knee? For if anyone wanted to, you are the only one with a right to sell yours. Again, it's a nasty business to damage a knee; but you've a right to damage yours, and certainly nobody else has—its being your left knee includes your having the right that nobody else but you shall damage it. And, as I think, it also includes your having the right that nobody else shall touch it or look at it. Of course you might invite somebody to touch or look at your left knee; or you might let someone touch or look at it; or again still, you might in a fit of absent-mindedness leave it in some place such that another person would have to go to some trouble if he is to avoid touching or looking at it. In short, you might waive your right that your left knee not be touched or looked at. But that is what doing these things would be: waiving a right.

I suppose there are people who would be deeply distressed to learn that they had absent-mindedly left a knee uncovered, and that somebody was looking at it. Fewer people would be deeply distressed to learn that they had absent-mindedly left their faces uncovered. Most of us wouldn't, but Moslem women would; and so might a man whose face had been badly disfigured, in a fire, say. Suppose you woke up one morning and found that you had grown fangs or that you no longer had a nose; you might well want to claim a right which most of us so contentedly waive: the right that your face not be looked at. That we have such a right comes out when we notice that if a man comes for some reason or another to want his face not to be looked at, and if he therefore keeps it covered, and if we then use an X-ray device in order to be able to look at it through the covering, we violate a right of his in respect of it, and the right we violate is surely the right that his face shall not be looked at. Compare again, by contrast, a subway map. No matter how much you may want a subway map to not be looked at, if we use an X-ray device in order to be able to look at it through the covering you place over it, we violate no right of yours: you do not have a right that nobody but you shall look at it—it is not *yours,* after all.

Listening, I think, works in the same way as looking. Suppose you are an opera singer, a great one, so that lots of people want to listen to you. You might sell them the right to listen. Or you might invite them to listen or let them listen or absent-mindedly sing where they cannot help but listen. But if you have decided you are no longer willing to be listened to; if you now sing only quietly, behind closed windows and carefully soundproofed walls; and if somebody trains an amplifier on your house so as to be able to listen, he violates a right, the right to not be listened to.

These rights—the right to not be looked at and the right to not be listened to[1]—are analogous to rights we have over our property. It sounds funny to say we have such rights. They are not mentioned when we give lists of rights. When we talk of rights, those that come to mind are the grand ones: the right to life, the right to liberty, the right to not be hurt or harmed, and property rights. Looking at and listening to a man do not harm him, but neither does stroking his left knee harm him, and yet he has a right that it shall not be stroked without permission. Cutting off all a man's hair while he's asleep will not harm him, nor will painting his elbows green; yet he plainly has a right that these things too shall not be done to him. These un-grand rights seem to be closely enough akin to be worth grouping together under one heading. For lack of a better term, I shall simply speak of "the right over the person," a right which I shall take to consist of the un-grand rights I mentioned, and others as well.

When I began, I said that if my husband and I are having a quiet fight behind closed windows and cannot be heard by the normal person who passes by, then if anyone trains an amplifier on us in order to listen he violates a right, the right to privacy, in fact. It now turns out (if I am right) that he violates our right to not be listened to, which is one of the rights included in the right over the person.

I had said earlier that if we use an X-ray device to look at the pornographic picture in a man's wall-safe, we violate his right to privacy. And it then turned out (if I was right) that we violated the right that others shall not look at the picture, which is one of the rights which his owning the picture consists in.

It begins to suggest itself, then, as a simplifying hypothesis, that the right to privacy is itself a cluster of rights, and that it is not a distinct cluster of rights but itself intersects with the cluster of rights which the right over the person consists in and also with the cluster of rights which owning property consists in. That is, to use an X-ray device to look at the picture is to violate a right (the right that others shall not look at the picture) which is both one of the rights which the right to privacy consists in and also one of the rights which property-ownership consists in. Again, that to use an amplifying device to listen to us is to violate a right (the right to not be listened to) which is both one of the rights which the right to privacy consists in and also one of the rights which the right over the person consists in.

Some small confirmation for this hypothesis comes from the other listening case. I had said that if my husband and I are having a loud fight, behind open windows, so that we can easily be heard by the normal person who passes by, then if a passerby stops to listen, he violates no right of ours, and so in particular does not violate our right to privacy. Why doesn't he? I think it is because, though he listens to us, we have *let* him listen (whether intentionally or not), we have waived our right to not be listened to—for we took none of the conventional and easily available steps (such as closing the windows and lowering our voices) to prevent listening. But this would only be an explanation if waiving the right to not be listened to were waiving the right to privacy, or if it were at least waiving the only one among the rights which the right to privacy consists in which might plausibly be taken to have been violated by the passerby.

But for further confirmation, we shall have to examine some further violations of the right to privacy.

VI

The following cases are similar to the ones we have just been looking at. (a) A deaf spy trains on your house a bugging device which produces, not sounds on tape, but a typed transcript, which he then reads. (Cf. footnote 1.) (b) A blind spy trains on your house an X-ray device which produces, not views of you, but a series of bas-relief panels, which he then feels. The deaf spy doesn't listen to you, the blind spy doesn't look at you, but both violate your right to privacy just as if they did.

It seems to me that in both cases there is a violation of that same right over the person which is violated by looking at or listening to a person. You have a right, not merely that you not be looked at or listened to but also that you not have your words transcribed, and that you not be modeled in bas-relief. These are rights that the spies violate, and it is these rights in virtue of the violation of which they violate your right to privacy. Of course, one may waive these rights: a teacher presumably waives the former when he enters the classroom, and a model waives the latter when he enters the studio. So these cases seem to present no new problem.

VII

A great many cases turn up in connection with information.

I should say straightaway that it seems to me none of us has a right over any fact to the effect that that fact shall not be known by others. You may violate a man's right to privacy by looking at him or listening to him; there is no such thing as violating a man's right to privacy by simply knowing something about him.

Where our rights in this area do lie is, I think here: we have a right that certain steps shall not be taken to find out facts, and we have a right that certain uses shall not be made of facts. I shall briefly say a word about each of these.

If we use an X-ray device to look at a man in order to get personal information about him, then we violate his right to privacy. Indeed, we violate his right to privacy whether the information we want is personal or impersonal. We might be spying on him in order to find out what he does all alone in his kitchen at midnight; or we might be spying on him in order to find out how to make puff pastry, which we already know he does in the kitchen all alone at midnight; either way his right to privacy is violated. But in both cases, the simplifying hypothesis seems to hold: in both cases we violate a right (the right to not be looked at) which is both one of the rights which the right to privacy consists in and one of the rights which the right over the person consists in.

What about torturing a man in order to get information? I suppose that if we torture a man in order to find out how to make puff pastry, then though we violate his right to not be hurt or harmed, we do not violate his right to privacy. But what if we torture him to find out what he does in the kitchen all alone at midnight? Presumably in that case we violate both his right to not be hurt or harmed and his right to privacy—the latter, presumably, because it was personal information we tortured him to get. But here too we can maintain the simplifying hypothesis: we can take it that to torture a man in order to find out personal information is to violate a right (the right to not be tortured to get personal information) which is both one of the rights which the right to privacy consists in and one of the rights which the right to not be hurt or harmed consists in.

And so also for extorting information by threat: if the information is not personal, we violate only the victim's right to not be coerced by threat; if it is personal, we presumably also violate his right to privacy—in that we violate his right to not be coerced by threat to give personal information, which is both one of the rights which the right to privacy consists in and one of the rights which the right to not be coerced by threat consists in.

I think it a plausible idea, in fact, that doing something to a man to get personal information from him is violating his right to privacy only if doing that to him is violating some right of his not identical with or included in the right to privacy. Thus writing a man a letter asking him where he was born is no violation of his right to privacy: writing a man a letter is no violation of any right of his. By contrast, spying on a man to get personal information is a violation of the right to privacy, and spying on a man for any reason is a violation of the right over the person, which is not identical with or included in (though it overlaps) the right to privacy. Again, torturing a man to get personal information is presumably a violation of the right to privacy, and torturing a man for any reason is a violation of the right not to be hurt or harmed, which is not identical with or included in (though it overlaps) the right to privacy. If the idea is right, the simplifying hypothesis is trivially true for this range of cases. If a man has a right that we shall not do such and such to him, then he has a right that we shall not do it to him in order to get personal information from him. And his right that we shall not do it to him in order to get personal information from him is included in both his right that we shall not do it to him, and (if doing it to him for this reason is violating his right to privacy) his right to privacy.

I suspect the situation is the same in respect of uses of information. If a man gives us information on the condition we shall not spread it, and we then spread it, we violate his right to confidentiality, whether the information is personal or impersonal. If the information is personal, I suppose we also violate his right to privacy—by virtue of violating a right (the right to confidentiality in respect of personal information) which is both one of the rights which the right to privacy consists in and one of the rights which the right to confidentiality consists in. The point holds whether our motive for spreading the information is malice or profit or anything else.

Again, suppose I find out by entirely legitimate means (e.g., from a third party who breaks no confidence in telling me) that you keep a pornographic picture in your wall-safe; and suppose that, though I know it will cause you distress, I print the information in a box on the front page of my newspaper, thinking it newsworthy: Professor Jones of State U. Keeps Pornographic Picture in Wall-Safe! Do I violate your right to privacy? I am, myself, inclined to think not. But if anyone thinks I do, he can still have the simplifying hypothesis: he need only take a stand on our having a right that others shall not cause us distress, and then add that what is violated here is the right to not be caused distress by the publication of personal information, which is one of the rights which the right to privacy consists in, and one of the rights which the right to not be caused distress consists in. Distress, after all, is the heart of the wrong (if there is a wrong in such a case): a man who positively wants personal information about himself printed in newspapers, and therefore makes plain he wants it printed, is plainly not wronged when newspapers cater to his want.

(My reluctance to go along with this is not due to a feeling that we have no such right as the right to not be caused distress:

that we have such a right seems to me a plausible idea. So far as I can see, there is nothing special about physical hurts and harms; mental hurts and harms are hurts and harms too. Indeed, they may be more grave and long-lasting than the physical ones, and it is hard to see why we should be thought to have rights against the one and not against the other. My objection is, rather, that even if there is a right to not be caused distress by the publication of personal information, it is mostly, if not always, overridden by what seems to me a more stringent right, namely the public's right to a press which prints any and all information, personal or impersonal, which it deems newsworthy; and thus that in the case I mentioned no right is violated, and hence, a fortiori, the right to privacy is not violated.)[2]

VIII

The question arises, then, whether or not there are *any* rights in the right to privacy cluster which aren't also in some other right cluster. I suspect there aren't any, and that the right to privacy is everywhere overlapped by other rights. But it's a difficult question. Part of the difficulty is due to it's being (to put the best face on it) unclear just what is in this right to privacy cluster. I mentioned at the outset that there is disagreement on cases; and the disagreement becomes even more stark as we move away from the kinds of cases I've so far been drawing attention to which seem to me to be the central, core cases.

What should be said, for example, of the following?

(a) The neighbors make a terrible racket every night. Or they cook foul-smelling stews. Do they violate my right to privacy? Some think yes, I think not. But even if they do violate my right to privacy, perhaps all would be well for the simplifying hypothesis since their doing this is presumably a violation of another right of mine, roughly, the right to be free of annoyance in my house.

(b) The city, after a city-wide referendum favoring it, installs loudspeakers to play music in all the buses and subways. Do they violate my right to privacy? Some think yes, I think not. But again perhaps all is well: it is if those of us in the minority have a right to be free of what we (though not the majority) regard as an annoyance in public places.

(c) You are famous, and photographers follow you around, everywhere you go, taking pictures of you. Crowds collect and stare at you. Do they violate your right to privacy? Some think yes, I think not: it seems to me that if you do go out in public, you waive your right to not be photographed and looked at. But of course you, like the rest of us, have a right to be free of (what anyone would grant was) annoyance in public places; so in particular, you have a right that the photographers and crowds not press in too closely.

(d) A stranger stops you on the street and asks, "How much do you weigh?" Or an acquaintance, who has heard of the tragedy, says, "How terrible you must have felt when your child was run over by that delivery truck!"[3] Or a cab driver turns around and announces, "My wife is having an affair with my psychoanalyst." Some think that your right to privacy is violated here; I think not. There is an element of coercion in such cases: the speaker is trying to force you into a relationship you do not want, the threat being your own embarrassment at having been impolite if you refuse. But I find it hard to see how we can be thought to have a right against such attempts. Of course the attempt may be an annoyance. Or a sustained series of such attempts may become an annoyance. (Consider, for example, an acquaintance who takes to stopping at your office *every morning* to ask if you slept well.) If so, I suppose a right *is* violated, namely, the right against annoyances.

(e) Some acquaintances of yours indulge in some very personal gossip about you.[4] Let us imagine that all of the information they share was arrived at without violation of any right of yours, and that none of the participants violates a confidence in telling what he tells. Do they violate a right of yours in sharing the information? If they do, there is trouble for the simplifying hypothesis, for it seems to me there is no right not identical with, or included in, the right to privacy cluster which they could be thought to violate. On the other hand, it seems to me they *don't* violate any right of yours. It seems to me we simply do not have rights against others that they shall not gossip about us.

(f) A state legislature makes it illegal to use contraceptives. Do they violate the right to privacy of the citizens of that state? No doubt certain techniques for enforcing the statute (e.g., peering into bedroom windows) would be obvious violations of the right to privacy; but is there a violation of the right to privacy in the mere enacting of the statute—in addition to the violations which may be involved in enforcing it? I think not. But it doesn't matter for the simplifying hypothesis if it is: making a kind of conduct illegal is infringing on a liberty, and we all of us have a right that our liberties not be infringed in the absence of compelling need to do so.

IX

The fact, supposing it a fact, that every right in the right to privacy cluster is also in some other right cluster does not by itself show that the right to privacy is in any plausible sense a "derivative" right. A more important point seems to me to be this: the fact that we have a right to privacy does not explain our having any of the rights in the right to privacy cluster. What I have in mind is this. We have a right to not be tortured. Why? Because we have a right to not be hurt or harmed. I have a right that my pornographic picture shall not be torn. Why? Because it's mine, because I own it. I have a right to do a somersault now. Why? Because I have a right to liberty. I have a right to try to preserve my life. Why? Because I have a right to life. In these cases we explain the having of one right by appeal to the having of another which includes it. But I don't have a right to not be looked at because I have a right to privacy; I don't have a right that no one shall torture me in order to get personal information about me because I have a right to privacy; one is inclined, rather, to say that it is because I have *these* rights that I have a right to privacy.

This point, supposing it correct, connects with what I mentioned at the outset: that nobody seems to have any very clear idea what the right to privacy is. We are confronted with a cluster of rights—a cluster with disputed boundaries—such that most people think that to violate at least any of the rights in the core of the cluster is to violate the right to privacy; but what have they in common other than their being rights such that to violate them is to violate the right to privacy? To violate these rights is to not let someone alone? To violate these rights is to visit indignity on someone? There are too many acts in the course of which we do not let someone alone, in the course of which we give affront to dignity, but in the performing of which we do not violate anyone's right to privacy. That we feel the need to find something in common to all of the rights in the cluster and, moreover, feel we haven't yet got it in the very fact that they *are* all in the cluster, is a consequence of our feeling that one cannot explain our having any of the rights in the cluster in the words: "Because we have a right to privacy."

But then if, as I take it, every right in the right to privacy cluster is also in some other right cluster, there is no need to find the that-which-is-in-common-to-all rights in the right to privacy cluster and no need to settle disputes about its boundaries. For if I am right, the right to privacy is "derivative" in this sense: it is possible to explain in the case of each right in the cluster how come we have it without ever once mentioning the right to privacy. Indeed, the wrongness of every violation of the right to privacy can be explained without ever once mentioning it. Someone tortures you to get personal information from you, and you have that right because you have the right to not be hurt or harmed—and it is because you have this right that what he does is wrong. Someone looks at your pornographic picture in your wall-safe? He violates your right that your belongings not be looked at, and you have that right because you have ownership rights—and it is because you have them that what he does is wrong. Someone uses an X-ray device to look at you through the walls of your house? He violates your right to not be looked at, and you have that right because you have rights over your person analogous to the rights you have over your property—and it is because you have these rights that what he does is wrong.

In any case, I suggest it is a useful heuristic device in the case of any purported violation of the right to privacy to ask whether or not the act is a violation of any other right, and if not whether the act *really* violates a right at all. We are still in such deep dark in respect of rights that any simplification at all would be well worth having.[5]

NOTES

I am grateful to the members of the Society for Ethical and Legal Philosophy for criticisms of the first draft of this paper. Alan Sparer made helpful criticisms of a later draft.

1. In "A Definition of Privacy," *Rutgers Law Review*, 1974, p. 281, Richard B. Parker writes:

   > The definition of privacy defended in this article is that *privacy is control over when and by whom the various parts of us can be sensed by others*. By "sensed," is meant simply seen, heard, touched, smelled, or tasted. By "parts of us," is meant the parts of our bodies, our voices, and the products of our bodies. "Parts of us" also includes objects very closely associated with us. By "closely associated" is meant primarily what is spatially associated. The objects which are "parts of us" are objects we usually keep with us or locked up in a place accessible only to us.

   The right to privacy, then, is presumably the right to this control. But I find this puzzling, on a number of counts. First, why *control?* If my neighbor invents an X-ray device which enables him to look through walls, then I should imagine I thereby lose control over who can look at me: going home and closing the doors no longer suffices to prevent others from doing so. But my right to privacy is not violated until my neighbor actually does train the device on the wall of my house. It is the actual looking that violates it, not the acquisition of power to look. Second, there *are* other cases. Suppose a more efficient bugging device is invented: instead of tapes, it produces neatly typed transcripts (thereby eliminating the middlemen). One who reads those transcripts does not *hear* you, but your right to privacy is violated just as if he does.

   On the other hand, this article is the first I have seen which may be taken to imply (correctly, as I think) that there are such rights as the right to not be looked at and the right to not be listened to. And in any case, Professor Parker's interest is legal rather than moral: he is concerned to find a definition which will be useful in legal contexts. (I am incompetent to estimate how successful he is in doing this.)

   I am grateful to Charles Fried for drawing my attention to this article.
2. It was Warren and Brandeis, in their now classic article, "The Right to Privacy," *Harvard Law Review*, 1890, who first argued that the law ought to recognize wrongs that are (they thought) committed in cases such as these. For a superb discussion of this article, see Harry Kalven, Jr., "Privacy in Tort Law—Were Warren and Brandeis Wrong?" *Law and Contemporary Problems*, Spring 1966.
3. Example from Thomas Nagel.
4. Example from Gilbert Harman.
5. Frederick Davis' article, "What Do We Mean by 'Right to Privacy'?" *South Dakota Law Review*, Spring 1959, concludes, in respect of tort law, that

   > If truly fundamental interests are accorded the protection they deserve, no need to champion a right to privacy arises. Invasion of privacy is, in reality, a complex of more fundamental wrongs. Similarly, the individual's interest in privacy itself, however real, is derivative and a state better vouchsafed by protecting more immediate rights [p.20]. . . . Indeed, one can logically argue that the concept of a right to privacy was never required in the first place, and that its whole history is an illustration of how well-meaning but impatient academicians can upset the normal development of the law by pushing it too hard [p. 230].

I am incompetent to assess this article's claims about the law, but I take the liberty of warmly recommending it to philosophers who have an interest in looking further into the status and nature of the right to privacy.

Privacy and the Limits of the Law

Ruth Gavison

Gavison attempts "to vindicate the way most of us think and talk about privacy issues." She challenges those who argue that legal claims to a "right to privacy" are merely rhetoric. She denies that rights to privacy can be usefully reduced to protection of interests. Gavison argues that rights to privacy are distinct, coherent, and useful in three contexts: (1) when identifying a loss of privacy; (2) when identifying the value of privacy; and (3) when identifying occasions calling for legal protection of privacy. Gavison claims to find evidence of the coherence and usefulness of the concept of privacy by observing everyday speech.

Anyone who studies the law of privacy today may well feel a sense of uneasiness. On one hand, there are popular demands for increased protection of privacy, discussions of new threats to privacy, and an intensified interest in the relationship between privacy and other values, such as liberty, autonomy, and mental health. These demands have generated a variety of legal responses. Most states recognize a cause of action for invasions of privacy. The Supreme Court has declared a constitutional right to privacy, a right broad enough to protect abortion and the use of contraceptives. Congress enacted the Privacy Act of 1974 after long hearings and debate. These activities seem to imply a wide consensus concerning the distinctness and importance of privacy.

On the other hand, much of the scholarly literature on privacy is written in quite a different spirit. Commentators have argued that privacy rhetoric is misleading: when we study the cases in which the law (or our moral intuitions) suggest that a "right to privacy" has been violated, we always find that some other interest has been involved. Consequently, they argue, our understanding of privacy will be improved if we disregard the rhetoric, look behind the decisions, and identify the real interests protected. When we do so, they continue, we can readily see why privacy itself is never protected: to the extent that there is something distinct about claims for privacy, they are either indications of hypersensitivity or an unjustified wish to manipulate and defraud. Although these commentators disagree on many points, they are united in denying the utility of thinking and talking about privacy as a legal right, and suggest some form of reductionism.

This article is an attempt to vindicate the way most of us think and talk about privacy issues: unlike the reductionists, most of us consider privacy to be a useful concept. To be useful, however, the concept must denote something that is distinct and coherent. Only then can it help us in thinking about problems. Moreover, privacy must have a coherence in three different contexts. First, we must have a neutral concept of privacy that will enable us to identify when a loss of privacy has occurred so that discussions of privacy and claims of privacy can be intelligible. Second, privacy must have coherence as a value, for claims of legal protection of privacy are compelling only if losses of privacy are sometimes undesirable and if those losses are undesirable

Reprinted by permission of The Yale Law Journal Company and Fred B. Rothman & Company from *Yale Law Journal*, Vol. 89, pp. 421–471. Notes omitted.

for similar reasons. Third, privacy must be a concept useful in legal contexts, a concept that enables us to identify those occasions calling for legal protection, because the law does not interfere to protect against every undesirable event.

Our everyday speech suggests that we believe the concept of privacy is indeed coherent and useful in the three contexts, and that losses of privacy (identified by the first), invasions of privacy (identified by the second), and actionable violations of privacy (identified by the third) are related in that each is a subset of the previous category. Using the same word in all three contexts reinforces the belief that they are linked. Reductionist analyses of privacy—that is, analyses denying the utility of privacy as a separate concept—sever these conceptual and linguistic links. This article is an invitation to maintain those links, because an awareness of the relationships and the larger picture suggested by them may contribute to our understanding both of legal claims for protection, and of the extent to which those claims have been met.

I begin by suggesting that privacy is indeed a distinct and coherent concept in all these contexts. Our interest in privacy, I argue, is related to our concern over our accessibility to others: the extent to which we are known to others, the extent to which others have physical access to us, and the extent to which we are the subject of others' attention. This concept of privacy as a concern for limited accessibility enables us to identify when losses of privacy occur. Furthermore, the reasons for which we claim privacy in different situations are similar. They are related to the functions privacy has in our lives: the promotion of liberty, autonomy, selfhood, and human relations, and furthering the existence of a free society. The coherence of privacy as a concept and the similarity of the reasons for regarding losses of privacy as undesirable support the notion that the legal system should make an explicit commitment to privacy as a value that should be considered in reaching legal results. This analysis does not require that privacy be protected in all cases; that result would require consideration of many factors not discussed here. I argue only that privacy refers to a unique concern that should be given weight in balancing values.

My analysis of privacy yields a better description of the law and a deeper understanding of both the appeal of the reductionist approach and its peril. The appeal lies in the fact that it highlights an important fact about the state of the law—privacy is seldom protected in the absence of some other interest. The danger is that we might conclude from this fact that privacy is not an important value and that losses of it should not feature as considerations for legal protection. In view of the prevalence of the reductionist view, the case for an affirmative and explicit commitment to privacy—vindicating the antireductionist perspective—becomes compelling.

I. The Meaning and Functions of Privacy

"Privacy" is a term used with many meanings. For my purposes, two types of questions about privacy are important. The first relates to the *status* of the term: is privacy a situation, a right, a claim, a form of control, a value? The second relates to the *characteristics* of privacy: is it related to information, to autonomy, to personal identity, to physical access? Support for all of these possible answers, in almost any combination, can be found in the literature.

The two types of questions involve different choices. Before resolving these issues, however, a general distinction must be drawn between the concept and the value of privacy. The concept of privacy identifies losses of privacy. As such, it should be neutral and descriptive only, so as not to preempt questions we might want to ask about such losses. Is the loser aware of the loss? Has he consented to it? Is the loss desirable? Should the law do something to prevent or punish such losses?

This is not to imply that the neutral concept of privacy is the most important, or that it is only legitimate to use "privacy" in this sense. Indeed, in the context of legal protection, privacy should also indicate a value. The coherence and usefulness of privacy as a value is due to a similarity one finds in the reasons advanced for its protection, a similarity that enables us to draw principles of liability for invasions. These reasons identify those aspects of privacy that are considered desirable. When we claim legal protection for privacy, we mean that only those aspects should be protected, and we no longer refer to the "neutral" concept of privacy. In order to see which aspects of privacy are desirable and thus merit protection as a value, however, we must begin our inquiry in a nonpreemptive way by starting with a concept that does not make desirability, or any of the elements that may preempt the question of desirability, part of the notion of privacy. The value of privacy can be determined only at the conclusion of discussion about what privacy is, and when—and why—losses of privacy are undesirable.

In this section I argue that it is possible to advance a neutral concept of privacy, and that it can be shown to serve important functions that entitle it to prima facie legal protection. The coherence of privacy in the third context—as a legal concept—relies on our understanding of the functions and value of privacy: discussion of the way in which the legal system should consider privacy is therefore deferred until later sections.

A. The Neutral Concept of Privacy

I. The Status of Privacy

The desire not to preempt our inquiry about the value of privacy by adopting a value-laden concept at the outset is sufficient to justify viewing privacy as a situation of an individual vis-á-vis others, or as a condition of life. It also requires that we reject attempts to describe privacy as a claim, a psychological state, or an area that should not be invaded. For the same reasons, another description that should be rejected is that of privacy as a form of control.

This last point requires some elaboration, because it may appear that describing privacy as a form of control does not preempt important questions. Were privacy described in terms of control, for example, we could still ask whether *X* has lost control, and whether such loss is desirable. The appearance of a nonpreemptive concept is misleading, however, and is due to an ambiguity in the notion of control. Hyman Gross, for example, defines privacy as "control over acquaintance with one's personal affairs." According to one sense of this definition, a voluntary, knowing disclosure does not involve loss of privacy because it is an exercise of control, not a loss of it. In another, stronger sense of control, however, voluntary disclosure is a loss of control because the person who discloses loses the power to prevent others from further disseminating the information.

There are two problems here. The weak sense of control is not sufficient as a description of privacy, for *X* can have control over whether to disclose information about himself, yet others may have information and access to him through other means. The strong sense of control, on the other hand, may indicate loss of privacy when there is only a threat of such loss. More important, "control" suggests that the important aspect of privacy is the ability to choose it and see that the choice is respected. All possible choices are consistent with enjoyment of control, however, so that defining privacy in terms of control relates it to the power to make certain choices rather than to the way in which we choose to exercise this power. But individuals may choose to have privacy or to give it up. To be nonpreemptive, privacy must not depend on choice. We need a framework within which privacy may be the result of a specific exercise of control, as when *X* decides not to disclose certain information about himself, or the result of something imposed on an individual against his wish, as when the law prohibits the performance of sexual intercourse in a public place. Furthermore, the reasons we value privacy may have nothing to do with whether an individual has in fact chosen it. Sometimes we may be inclined to criticize an individual for not choosing privacy, and other times for choosing it. This criticism cannot be made if privacy is defined as a form of control.

Insisting that we start with a neutral concept of privacy does not mean that wishes, exercises of choice, or claims are not important elements in the determination of the aspects of privacy that are to be deemed desirable or of value. This insistence does mean, however, that we are saying something meaningful, and not merely repeating the implications of our concept, if we conclude that only choices of privacy should be protected by law.

Resolving the status of privacy is easier than resolving questions concerning the characteristics of privacy. Is privacy related to secrecy, freedom of action, sense of self, anonymity, or any specific combination of these elements? The answers here are not constrained by methodological concerns. The crucial test is the utility of the proposed concept in capturing the tenor of most privacy claims, and in presenting coherent reasons for legal protection that will justify grouping these claims together. My conception of privacy as related to secrecy, anonymity, and solitude is defended in these terms.

2. *The Characteristics of Privacy*

In its most suggestive sense, privacy is a limitation of others' access to an individual. As a methodological starting point, I suggest that an individual enjoys *perfect* privacy when he is completely inaccessible to others. This may be broken into three independent components: in perfect privacy no one has any information about *X*, no one pays any attention to *X*, and no one has physical access to *X*. Perfect privacy is, of course, impossible in any society. The possession or enjoyment of privacy is not an all or nothing concept, however, and the total loss of privacy is as impossible as perfect privacy. A more important concept, then, is *loss* of privacy. A loss of privacy occurs as others obtain information about an individual, pay attention to him, or gain access to him. These three elements of secrecy, anonymity, and solitude are distinct and independent, but interrelated, and the complex concept of privacy is richer than any definition centered around only one of them. The complex concept better explains our intuitions as to when privacy is lost, and captures more of the suggestive meaning of privacy. At the same time, it remains sufficiently distinctive to exclude situations that are sometimes labeled "privacy," but that are more related to notions of accountability and interference than to accessibility.

a. Information Known about an Individual

It is not novel to claim that privacy is related to the amount of information known about an individual. Indeed, many scholars have defined privacy exclusively in these terms, and the most lively privacy issue now discussed is that related to information-gathering. Nevertheless, at least two scholars have argued that there is no inherent loss of privacy as information about an individual becomes known. I believe these critics are wrong. If secrecy is not treated as an independent element of privacy, then the following are only some of the situations that will not be considered losses of privacy: (a) an estranged wife who publishes her husband's love letters to her, without his consent; (b) a single databank containing all census information and government files that is used by all government officials; and (c) an employer who asks every conceivable question of his employees and yet has no obligation to keep the answers confidential. In none of these cases is there any intrusion, trespass, falsification, appropriation, or exposure of the individual to direct observation. Thus, unless the amount of information others have about an individual is considered at least partly determinative of the degree of privacy he has, these cases cannot be described as involving losses of privacy.

To talk of the "amount of information" known about an individual is to imply that it is possible to individuate items or pieces of information, to determine the number of people who know each item of information about *X*, and thus to quantify the information known about *X*. In fact, this is impossible, and the notion requires greater theoretical elaboration than it has received until now. It is nevertheless used here because in most cases its application is relatively clear. Only a few of the many problems involved need to be mentioned.

The first problem is whether we should distinguish between different kinds of knowledge about an individual, such as verbal as opposed to sensory knowledge, or among different types of sensory knowledge. For example, assume *Y* learns that *X* is bald because he reads a verbal description of *X*. At a later time, *Y* sees *X* and, naturally, observes that *X* is bald. Has *Y* acquired any further information about *X*, and if so, what is it? It might be argued that even a rereading of a verbal description may reveal to *Y* further information about *X*, even though *Y* has no additional source of information.

A related set of problems arises when we attempt to compare different "amounts" of knowledge about the same individual. Who has more information about *X*, his wife after fifteen years of marriage, his psychiatrist after seven years of analysis, or the biographer who spends four years doing research and unearths details about *X* that are not known either to the wife or to the analyst?

A third set of problems is suggested by the requirement that for a loss of privacy to occur, the information must be "about" the individual. First, how specific must this relationship be? We know that most people have sexual fantasies and sexual relationships with others. Thus, we almost certainly "know" that our new acquaintances have sexual fantasies, yet they do not thereby suffer a loss of privacy. On the other hand, if we have detailed information about the sexual lives of a small number of people, and we are then introduced to one of them, does the translation of the general information into personal information about this person involve a loss of privacy? Consider the famous anecdote about the priest who was asked, at a party, whether he had heard any exceptional stories during confessionals. "In fact," the priest replied, "my first confessor is a good example, since he confessed to a murder." A few minutes later, an elegant man joined the group, saw the priest, and greeted him warmly. When asked how he knew the priest, the man replied: "Why, I had the honor of being his first confessor."

The priest gave an "anonymous" piece of information, which became information "about" someone through the combination of the anonymous statement with the "innocent" one made by the confessor. Only the later statement was "about" a specific individual, but it turned what was previously an anonymous piece of information into further information "about" the individual. The translation here from anonymous information to information about *X* is immediate and unmistakable, but the process is similar to the combination of general knowledge about a group of people and the realization that a certain individual is a member of that group.

Problems of the relationship between an individual and pieces of information exist on another level as well. Is information about *X*'s wife, car, house, parents, or dog information about *X*? Clearly, this is information about the other people, animals, or things involved, but can *X* claim that disclosure of such information is a loss of his privacy? Such claims have often been made. Their plausibility in at least some of the cases suggests that people's notions of themselves may extend beyond their physical limits.

A final set of problems concerns the importance of the truth of the information that becomes known about an individual. Does dissemination of false information about *X* mean that he has lost privacy? The usual understanding of "knowledge" presupposes that the information is true, but is this sense of "knowledge" relevant here? In one sense, *X* has indeed lost privacy. People now believe they know more about him. If the information is sufficiently spectacular, *X* may lose his anonymity and become the subject of other people's attention. In another sense, however, *X* is not actually "known" any better. In fact, he may even be known less, because the false information may lead people to disregard some correct information about *X* that they already had. Another difficulty is revealed when we consider statements whose truth is not easily determinable, such as "*X* is beautiful" or "*X* is dumb and irresponsible." Publication of such statements clearly leads to some loss of privacy: listeners now know what the speaker thinks about *X*, and this itself is information about *X* (as well as about the speaker). But does the listener also know that *X* is indeed beautiful? This is hard to tell.

b. Attention Paid to an Individual

An individual always loses privacy when he becomes the subject of attention. This will be true whether the attention is conscious and purposeful, or inadvertent. Attention is a primary way of acquiring information, and sometimes is essential to such acquisition, but attention alone will cause a loss of privacy even if no new information becomes known. This becomes clear when we consider the effect of calling, "Here is the President," should he attempt to walk the streets incognito. No further information is given, but none is necessary. The President loses whatever privacy his temporary anonymity could give him. He loses it because attention has focused on him.

Here too, however, some elaboration is needed. *X* may be the subject of *Y*'s attention in two typical ways. First, *Y* may follow *X*, stare at him, listen to him, or observe him in any other way. Alternatively, *Y* may concentrate his thoughts on *X*. Only the first way of paying attention is directly related to loss of privacy. Discussing, imagining, or thinking about another person is related to privacy in a more indirect way, if at all. Discussions may involve losses of privacy by communicating information about a person or by creating an interest in the person under discussion that may itself lead to more attention. Thinking about a person may also produce an intensified effort to recall or obtain information about him. This mental activity may in turn produce a loss of privacy if new information is obtained. For the most part, however, thinking about another person, even in the most intense way, will involve no loss of privacy to the subject of this mental activity. The favorite subject of one's sexual fantasies may have causes for complaint, but it is unlikely that these will be related to loss of privacy.

c. Physical Access to an Individual

Individuals lose privacy when others gain physical access to them. Physical access here means physical proximity—that *Y* is close enough to touch or observe *X* through normal use of his senses. The ability to watch and listen, however, is not in itself an indication of physical access, because *Y* can watch *X* from a distance or wiretap *X*'s telephone. This explains why it is much easier for *X* to know when *Y* has physical access to him than when *Y* observes him.

The following situations involving loss of privacy can best be understood in terms of physical access: (a) a stranger who gains entrance to a woman's home on false pretenses in order to watch her giving birth; (b) Peeping Toms; (c) a stranger who chooses to sit on "our" bench, even though the park is full of empty benches; and (d) a move from a single-person office to a much larger one that must be shared with a colleague. In each of these cases, the essence of the complaint is not that more information about us has been acquired, nor that more attention has been drawn to us, but that our spatial aloneness has been diminished.

d. Relations among the Three Elements

The concept of privacy suggested here is a complex of these three independent and irreducible elements: secrecy, anonymity, and solitude. Each is independent in the sense that a loss of privacy may occur through a change in any one of the three, without a necessary loss in either of the other two. The concept is nevertheless coherent because the three elements are all part of the same notion of accessibility, and are related in many important ways. The three elements may coexist in the same situation. For example, the psychiatrist who sits next to his patient and listens to him acquires information about the patient, pays attention to him, and has physical access to him. At the same time, none of the three elements is the necessary companion of the other two.

Information about *X* may of course be acquired by making *X* the subject of *Y*'s attention. When *Y* follows, watches, or observes *X* in any way, he increases the likelihood of acquiring information about *X*. Similarly, when *Y* is in physical proximity to *X*, he has an opportunity to observe and thus obtain information about *X*. Nevertheless, information about *X* may be obtained when *Y* has no physical access to *X*, and when *X* is not the subject of *Y*'s attention. It is possible to learn information about an individual by questioning his friends and neighbors, and thus without observing the individual or being in his physical proximity. It is also possible to learn information about an individual entirely by accident, when the individual is not even the subject of attention.

Attention may be paid to *X* without learning new information about him. The mother who follows her child in order to make sure the child does not harm himself is not interested in gaining new information about the child, nor will she necessarily obtain any new information. Pointing *X* out in a crowd will increase the attention paid to *X*, even in the absence of any physical proximity.

Finally, an individual can be in physical proximity to others without their paying attention or learning any new information about him. Two people may sit in the same room without paying any attention to each other, and yet each will experience some loss of privacy.

The interrelations between the three elements may be seen when we consider the different aspects of privacy that may be involved in one situation. For instance, police attempt to learn of plans to commit crimes. Potential criminals may raise a privacy claim concerning this information, but are unlikely to gain much support. The criminal's desire that information about his plans not be known creates a privacy claim, but not a very convincing one. We might be more receptive, however, to another privacy claim that criminals might make concerning attention and observation, or the opportunity to be alone. If constant surveillance were the price of efficient law enforcement, we might feel the need to rethink the criminal law. The fact that these are two independent claims suggests that concern for the opportunity to have solitude and anonymity is related not only to the wish to conceal some kinds of information, but also to needs such as relaxation, concentration, and freedom from inhibition.

Yet another privacy concern emerges when we talk about the right against self-incrimination. Again, the essence of the concern is not simply the information itself; we do not protect the suspect against police learning the information from other sources. Our concern relates to the way the information is acquired: it is an implication of privacy that individuals should not be forced to give evidence against themselves. Similarly, evidentiary privileges that may also be defended in terms of privacy do not reflect concern about the information itself. The concern here is the existence of relationships in which confidentiality should be protected, so that the parties know that confidences shared in these relationships will not be forced out. In some cases, disclosure will not be sought, and in others the law may even impose a duty against disclosure.

The irreducibility of the three elements may suggest that the complex concept of privacy lacks precision, and that we would do better to isolate each of the different concerns and discuss separately what the law should do to protect secrecy, anonymity, and solitude. Such isolation may indeed be fruitful for some purposes. At present, however, the proposed concept suggests a coherent concern that is generally discussed in extra-legal contexts as "privacy." It therefore seems justified to prefer the complex notion of accessibility to the loss of richness in description that would result from any more particularistic analysis.

e. What Privacy Is Not

The neutral concept of privacy presented here covers such "typical" invasions of privacy as the collection, storage, and computerization of information; the dissemination of information about individuals; peeping, following, watching, and photographing individuals; intruding or entering "private" places; eavesdropping, wiretapping, reading of letters; drawing attention to individuals; required testing of individuals; and forced disclosure of information. At the same time, a number of situations sometimes said to constitute invasions of privacy will be seen not to involve losses of privacy per se under this concept. These include exposure to unpleasant noises, smells, and sights; prohibitions of such conduct as abortions, use of contraceptives, and "unnatural" sexual intercourse; insulting, harassing, or persecuting behavior; presenting individuals in a "false light"; unsolicited mail and unwanted phone calls; regulation of the way familial obligations should be discharged; and commercial exploitation. These situations are all described as "invasions of privacy" in the literature, presumably indicating some felt usefulness in grouping them under the label of "privacy," and thus an explanation of the reasons for excluding these cases from my argument seems appropriate. Such an explanation may also clarify the proposed analysis and its methodological presuppositions.

The initial intuition is that privacy has to do with accessibility to an individual, as expressed by the three elements of information-gathering, attention, and physical access, and that this concept is distinct. It is part of this initial intuition that we want and deem desirable many things, and that we lose more than we gain by treating all of them as the same thing. If the concepts we use give the appearance of differentiating concerns without in fact isolating something distinct, we are likely to fall victims to this false appearance and our chosen language will be a hindrance rather than a help. The reason for excluding the situations mentioned above, as well as those not positively identified by the proposed analysis, is that they present precisely such a danger.

There is one obvious way to include all the so-called invasions of privacy under the term. Privacy can be defined as "being let alone," using the phrase often attributed—incorrectly—to Samuel Warren and Louis Brandeis. The great simplicity of this definition gives it rhetorical force and attractiveness, but also denies it the distinctiveness that is necessary for the phrase to be useful in more than a conclusory sense. This description gives an appearance of differentiation while covering almost any conceivable complaint anyone could ever make. A great many instances of "not letting people alone" cannot readily be described as invasions of privacy. Requiring that people pay their taxes or go into the army, or punishing them for murder, are just a few of the obvious examples.

For similar reasons, we must reject Edward Bloustein's suggestion that the coherence of privacy lies in the fact that all invasions are violations of human dignity. We may well be concerned with invasions of privacy, at least in part, because they are violations of dignity. But there are ways to offend dignity and personality that have nothing to do with privacy. Having to beg or sell one's body in order to survive are serious affronts to dignity, but do not appear to involve loss of privacy.

To speak in privacy terms about claims for noninterference by the state in personal decisions is similar to identifying privacy with "being let alone." There are two problems with this tendency. The first is that the typical privacy claim is not a claim for noninterference by the state at all. It is a claim *for* state interference in the form of legal protection against other individuals, and this is obscured when privacy is discussed in terms of noninterference with personal decisions. The second problem is that this conception excludes from the realm of privacy all claims that have nothing to do with highly personal decisions, such as an individual's unwillingness to have a file in a central databank. Moreover, identifying privacy as noninterference with private action, often in order to avoid an explicit return to "substantive due process," may obscure the nature of the legal decision and draw attention away from important considerations. The limit of state interference with individual action is an important question that has been with us for centuries. The usual terminology for dealing with this question is that of "liberty of action." It may well be that some cases pose a stronger claim for noninterference than others, and that the intimate nature of certain decisions affects these limits. This does not justify naming this set of concerns "privacy," however. A better way to deal with these issues may be to treat them as involving questions of liberty, in which enforcement may raise difficult privacy issues.

Noxious smells and other nuisances are described as problems of privacy because of an analogy with intrusion. Outside forces that enter private zones seem similar to invasions of privacy. There are no good reasons, however, to expect any similarity between intrusive smells or noises and modes of acquiring information about or access to an individual.

Finally, some types of commercial exploitation are grouped under privacy primarily because of legal history: the first cases giving a remedy for unauthorized use of a name or picture, sometimes described as invasions of privacy, usually involved commercial exploitation. The essence of privacy is not freedom from commercial exploitation, however. Privacy can be invaded in ways that have nothing to do with such exploitation, and there are many forms of exploitation that do not involve privacy even under the broadest conception. The use of privacy as a label for protection against some forms of commercial exploitation is another unfortunate illustration of the confusions that will inevitably arise if care is not taken to follow an orderly conceptual scheme.

B. The Functions of Privacy

In any attempt to define the scope of desirable legal protection of privacy, we move beyond the neutral concept of "loss of privacy," and seek to describe the positive concept that identifies those aspects of privacy that are of value. Identifying the positive functions of privacy is not an easy task. We start from the obvious fact that both perfect privacy and total loss of privacy are undesirable. Individuals must be in some intermediate state—a balance between privacy and interaction—in order to maintain human relations, develop their capacities and sensibilities, create and grow, and even to survive. Privacy thus cannot be said to be a value in the sense that the more people have of it, the better. In fact, the opposite may be true. In any event, my purpose here is not to determine the proper balance between privacy and interaction; I want only to identify the positive functions that privacy has in our lives. From them we can derive the limits of the value of privacy, and then this value can be balanced against others.

The best way in which to understand the value of privacy is to examine its functions. This approach is fraught with difficulties, however. These justifications for privacy are instrumental, in the sense that they point out how privacy relates to other goals. The strength of instrumental justifications depends on the extent to which other goals promoted by privacy are considered important, and on the extent to which the relationship between the two is established. In most cases, the link between the enjoyment of privacy and other goals is at least partly empirical, and thus this approach raises all the familiar problems of social science methodology.

Two possible ways to avoid these difficulties should be discussed before I proceed further. One approach rests the desirability of privacy on a want-satisfaction basis, and the other argues that privacy is an ultimate value. The want-satisfaction argument posits the desirability of satisfying wishes and thus provides a reason to protect all wishes to have privacy. It does not require empirical links between privacy and other goals. Moreover, the notion that choice should be respected is almost universally accepted as a starting point for practical reasoning. The want-satisfaction argument cannot carry us very far, however. It does not explain why we should prefer *X*'s wish to maintain his privacy against *Y*'s wish to pry or acquire information. Without explaining why wishes for privacy are more important than wishes to invade it, the want-satisfaction principle alone cannot support the desirability of privacy. Indeed, some wishes to have privacy do not enjoy even prima facie validity. The criminal needs privacy to complete his offense undetected, the con artist needs it to manipulate his victim; we would not find the mere fact that they wish to have privacy a good reason for protecting it. The want-satisfaction principle needs a supplement that will identify legitimate reasons for which people want and need privacy. This is the task undertaken by an instrumental inquiry. These reasons will identify the cases in which wishes to have privacy should override wishes to invade it. They will also explain why in some cases we say that people need privacy even though they have not chosen it. Thus, these instrumentalist reasons will explain the distinctiveness of privacy.

The attractiveness of the argument that privacy is an ultimate value lies in the intuitive feeling that only ultimate values are truly important, and in the fact that claims that a value is ultimate are not vulnerable to the empirical challenges that can be made to functional analyses. But these claims also obscure the specific functions of privacy. They prevent any discussion with people who do not share the intuitive belief in the importance of privacy. Given the current amount of skeptical commentary, such claims are bound to raise more doubts than convictions about the importance and distinctiveness of privacy.

Thus it appears that we cannot avoid a functional analysis. Such an analysis presents an enormous task, for the values served by privacy are many and diverse. They include a healthy, liberal, democratic, and pluralistic society; individual autonomy; mental health; creativity; and the capacity to form and maintain meaningful relations with others. These goals suffer from the same conceptual ambiguities that we have described for privacy, which makes it difficult to formulate questions for empirical research and very easy to miss the relevant questions. More important, the empirical data is not only scant, it is often double-edged. The evaluation of links between privacy and other values must therefore be extremely tentative. Nevertheless, much can be gained by identifying and examining instrumental arguments for privacy; this is the indispensable starting point for any attempt to make sense of our concern with privacy, and to expose this concern to critical examination and evaluation.

It is helpful to start by seeking to identify those features of human life that would be impossible—or highly unlikely—without some privacy. Total lack of privacy is full and immediate access, full and immediate knowledge, and constant observation of an individual. In such a state, there would be no private thoughts, no private places, no private parts. Everything an individual did and thought would immediately become known to others.

There is something comforting and efficient about total absence of privacy for all. A person could identify his enemies, anticipate dangers stemming from other people, and make sure he was not cheated or manipulated. Criminality would cease, for detection would be certain, frustration probable, and punishment sure. The world would be safer, and as a result, the time and resources now spent on trying to protect ourselves against human dangers and misrepresentations could be directed to other things.

This comfort is fundamentally misleading, however. Some human activities only make sense if there is some privacy. Plots and intrigues may disappear, but with them would go our private diaries, intimate confessions, and surprises. We would probably try hard to suppress our daydreams and fantasies once others had access to them. We would try to erase from our minds everything we would not be willing to publish, and we would try not to do anything that would make us likely to be feared, ridiculed, or harmed. There is a terrible flatness in the person who could succeed in these attempts. We do not choose against total lack of privacy only because we cannot attain it, but because its price seems much too high.

In any event, total lack of privacy is unrealistic. Current levels of privacy are better in some ways, because we all have some privacy that cannot easily be taken from us. The current state is also worse in some ways, because enjoyment of privacy is not equally distributed and some people have more security and power as a result. The need to protect privacy thus stems from two kinds of concern. First, in some areas we all tend to have insufficient amounts of privacy. Second, unequal distribution of privacy may lead to manipulation, deception, and threats to autonomy and democracy.

Two clusters of concerns are relevant here. The first relates to our notion of the individual, and the kinds of actions we think people should be allowed to take in order to become fully realized. To this cluster belong the arguments linking privacy to mental health, autonomy, growth, creativity, and the capacity to form and create meaningful human relations. The second cluster relates to the type of society we want. First, we want a society that will not hinder individual attainment of the goals mentioned above. For this, society has to be liberal and pluralistic. In addition, we link a concern for privacy to our concept of democracy.

Inevitably, the discussion of functions that follows is sketchy and schematic. My purpose is to point out the many contexts in which privacy may operate, not to present full and conclusive arguments.

1. Privacy and the Individual

Functional arguments depend on a showing that privacy is linked to the promotion of something else that is accepted as desirable. In order to speak about individual goals, we must have a sense of what individuals are, and what they can and should strive to become. We do not have any one such picture, of course, and certainly none that is universally accepted. Nonetheless, privacy may be linked to goals such as creativity, growth, autonomy, and mental health that are accepted as desirable by almost all such theories, yet in ways that are not dictated by any single theory. This may give functional arguments for privacy an eclectic appearance, but it may also indicate the strength of these arguments. It appears that privacy is central to the attainment of individual goals under every theory of the individual that has ever captured man's imagination. It also seems that concern about privacy is evidenced in all societies, even these with few opportunities for physical privacy. Because we have no single theory about the nature of the individual and the way in which individuals relate to others, however, it should be recognized that the way in which we perceive privacy contributing to individual goals will itself depend on the theory of the individual that we select.

In the following discussion, I will note where a difference in perspective may dictate different approaches or conclusions. These different perspectives relate to theories of human growth, development, and personality. It is easy to see that different answers to questions such as the following may yield different arguments for privacy: Is there a "real self" that can be known? If there is, is it coherent and always consistent? If not, can we identify one that is better, and that we should strive to realize? Are human relations something essential, or a mere luxury? Should they ideally be based on full disclosure and total frankness? Or is this a misguided ideal, not only a practical impossibility?

a. Contextual Arguments

Some arguments for privacy do not link it empirically with other goals. These arguments contend that privacy, by limiting access, creates the necessary context for other activities that we deem essential. Typical of these contextual arguments is the one advanced by Jeffrey Reiman that privacy is what enables development of individuality by allowing individuals to distinguish between their own thoughts and feelings and those of others. Similarly, Charles Fried advanced a contextual argument that privacy is necessary for the development of trust, love, and friendship. Contextual arguments are instrumental, in that they relate privacy to another goal. They are strengthened by the fact that the link between privacy and the other goal is also conceptual.

A similar argument can be made about the relationship between privacy and intimacy.

Here too, it is not simply the case that intimacy is more likely with increasing amounts of privacy. Being intimate in public is almost a contradiction in terms. Such contextual arguments highlight an important goal for privacy, similar to that indicated by examining the possible consequences of a total loss of privacy. We can now move to a detailed examination of more specific functions of privacy.

b. Freedom From Physical Access

By restricting physical access to an individual, privacy insulates that individual from distraction and from the inhibitive effects that arise from close physical proximity with another individual. Freedom from distraction is essential for all human activities that require concentration, such as learning, writing, and all forms of creativity. Although writing and creativity may be considered luxuries, learning—which includes not only acquiring information and basic skills but also the development of mental capacities and moral judgment—is something that we all must do. Learning, in turn, affects human growth, autonomy, and mental health.

Restricting physical access also permits an individual to relax. Even casual observation has an inhibitive effect on most individuals that makes them more formal and uneasy. Is relaxation important? The answer depends partially upon one's theory of the individual. If we believe in one coherent "core" personality, we may feel that people should reflect that personality at all times. It could be argued that relaxation is unimportant—or undesirable—because it signals a discrepancy between the person in public and in private. The importance that all of us place on relaxation suggests that this theory is wrong, however, or at least overstated. Whatever the theory, people seem to need opportunities to relax, and this may link privacy to the ability of individuals to maintain their mental health. Furthermore, freedom from access contributes to the individual by permitting intimacy. Not all relationships are intimate, but those that are tend to be the most valued. Relaxation and intimacy together are essential for many kinds of human relations, including sexual ones. Privacy in the sense of freedom from physical access is thus not only important for individuals by themselves, but also as a necessary shield for intimate relations.

Because physical access is a major way to acquire information, the power to limit it is also the power to limit such knowledge. Knowledge and access are not necessarily related, however. Knowledge is only one of the possible consequences of access, a subject to which we now turn.

c. Promoting Liberty of Action

An important cluster of arguments for privacy builds on the way in which it severs the individual's conduct from knowledge of that conduct by others. Privacy thus prevents interference, pressures to conform, ridicule, punishment, unfavorable decisions, and other forms of hostile reaction. To the extent that privacy does this, it functions to promote liberty of action, removing the unpleasant consequences of certain actions and thus increasing the liberty to perform them.

This promotion of liberty of action links privacy to a variety of individual goals. It also raises a number of serious problems, both as to the causal link between privacy and other goals, and as to the desirability of this function.

Freedom From Censure and Ridicule. In addition to providing freedom from distractions and opportunities to concentrate, privacy also contributes to learning, creativity, and autonomy by insulating the individual against ridicule and censure at early stages of groping and experimentation. No one likes to fail, and learning requires trial and error, some practice of skills, some abortive first attempts before we are sufficiently pleased with our creation to subject it to public scrutiny. In the absence of privacy we would dare less, because all our early failures would be on record. We would only do what we thought we could do well. Public failures make us unlikely to try again.

Promoting Mental Health. One argument linking privacy and mental health, made by Sidney Jourard, suggests that individuals may become victims of mental illness because of pressures to conform to society's expectations. Strict obedience to all social standards is said inevitably to lead to inhibition, repression, alienation, symptoms of disease, and possible mental breakdown. On the other hand, disobedience may lead to sanctions. Ironically, the sanction for at least some deviations is a social declaration of insanity. By providing a refuge, privacy enables individuals to disobey in private and thus acquire the strength to obey in public.

Mental health is one of the least well-defined concepts in the literature. It appears that Professor Jourard's argument for privacy uses the term in a minimalistic sense: avoiding mental breakdown. Whether mental breakdown is always undesirable is questionable. More serious problems are raised when we examine the link between mental health and privacy. Must chronic obedience always lead to mental breakdown? This is plausible if individuals obey social norms only because of social pressures and fear of sanctions, but this is not the case. Professor Jourard identifies a need for privacy that applies only to those who do not accept the social norms. The strength of his argument thus depends on the likelihood that people reject some norms of their society, and may be adequate only for extremely totalitarian societies. It will probably also depend on the nature of the norms and expectations that are not accepted. Moreover, even if pressures to conform to social norms contribute to mental breakdown, the opposite may also be true. It could be argued that too much permissiveness is at least as dangerous to mental health as too much conformity. One of the important functions of social norms is to give people the sense of belonging to a group defined by shared values. People are likely to lose their sanity in the absence of such norms and the sense of security they provide. Nevertheless, some individuals in institutions do complain that the absence of privacy affects their mental state, and these complaints support Jourard's argument.

Promoting Autonomy. Autonomy is another value that is linked to the function of privacy in promoting liberty. Moral autonomy is the reflective and critical acceptance of social norms, with obedience based on an independent moral evaluation of their worth. Autonomy requires the capacity to make an independent moral judgment, the willingness to exercise it, and the courage to act on the results of this exercise even when the judgment is not a popular one.

We do not know what makes individuals autonomous, but it is probably easier to be autonomous in an open society committed to pluralism, toleration, and encouragement of independent judgment rather than blind submissiveness. No matter how open a society may be, however, there is a danger that behavior that deviates from norms will result in harsh sanctions. The prospect of this hostile reaction has an inhibitive effect. Privacy is needed to enable the individual to deliberate and establish his opinions. If public reaction seems likely to be unfavorable, privacy may permit an individual to express his judgments to a group of like-minded people. After a period of germination, such individuals may be more willing to declare their unpopular views in public.

It might be argued that history belies this argument for privacy in terms of autonomy: societies much more totalitarian than ours have always had some autonomous individuals, so that the lack of privacy does not mean the end of autonomy. Even if we grant that privacy may not be a necessary condition for autonomy for all, however, it is enough to justify it as a value that most people may require it. We are not all giants, and societies should enable all, not only the exceptional, to seek moral autonomy.

Promoting Human Relations. Privacy also functions to promote liberty in ways that enhance the capacity of individuals to create and maintain human relations of different intensities. Privacy enables individuals to establish a plurality of roles and presentations to the world. This control over "editing" one's self is crucial, for it is through the images of others that human relations are created and maintained.

Privacy is also helpful in enabling individuals to continue relationships, especially those highest in one's emotional hierarchy, without denying one's inner thoughts, doubts, or wishes that the other partner cannot accept. This argument for privacy is true irrespective of whether we deem total disclosure to be an ideal in such relations. It is built on the belief that individuals, for reasons that they themselves do not justify, cannot emotionally accept conditions that seem threatening to them. Privacy enables partners to such a relationship to continue it, while feeling free to endorse those feelings in private.

Each of these arguments based on privacy's promotion of liberty shares a common ground: privacy permits individuals to do what they would not do without it for fear of an unpleasant or hostile reaction from others. This reaction may be anything from legal punishment or compulsory commitment to threats to dissolve an important relationship. The question arises, then, whether it is appropriate for privacy to permit individuals to escape responsibility for their actions, wishes, and opinions.

It may be argued that we have rules because we believe that breaches of them are undesirable, and we impose social sanctions to discourage undesirable conduct. People are entitled to a truthful presentation and a reasonable consideration of their expectations by those with whom they interact. Privacy frustrates these mechanisms for regulation and education; to let it do so calls for some justification. In general, privacy will only be desirable when the liberty of action that it promotes is itself desirable, or at least permissible. It is illuminating to see when we seek to promote liberty directly, by changing social norms, and when we are willing to let privacy do the task.

Privacy is derived from liberty in the sense that we tend to allow privacy to the extent that its promotion of liberty is considered desirable. Learning, practicing, and creating require privacy, and this function is not problematic. Similarly, because we usually believe that it is good for individuals to relax and to enjoy intimacy, we have no difficulty allowing the privacy necessary for these goals.

The liberty promoted by privacy also is not problematic in contexts in which we believe we should have few or no norms; privacy will be needed in such cases because some individuals will not share this belief, will lack the strength of their convictions, or be emotionally unable to accept what they would like to do. Good examples of such cases are ones involving freedom of expression, racial tolerance, and the functioning of close and intimate relations. The existence of official rules granting immunity from regulation, or even imposing duties of nondiscrimination, does not guarantee the absence of social forces calling for conformity or prejudice. A spouse may understand and even support a partner's need to fantasize or to have other close relations, but may still find knowing about them difficult to accept. In such situations, respect for privacy is a way to force ourselves to be as tolerant as we know we should be. We accept the need for privacy as an indication of the limits of human nature.

A related but distinct situation in which privacy is permitted is that in which we doubt the desirability of norms or expectations, or in which there is an obvious absence of consensus as to such desirability. Treatment of homosexual conduct between consenting adults in private seems to be a typical case of this sort. Another context in which we sometimes allow privacy to function in this way is when privacy would promote the liberty of individuals not to disclose some parts of their past, in the interest of rehabilitation or as a necessary protection against prejudice and irrationality.

Privacy works in all these cases to ameliorate tensions between personal preferences and social norms by leading to nonenforcement of some standards. But is this function desirable? When the liberty promoted is desirable, why not attack the norms directly? When it is not, why allow individuals to do in private what we would have good reasons for not wanting them to do at all?

Conceptually, this is a strong argument against privacy, especially because privacy perpetuates the very problems it helps to ease. With mental health, autonomy, and human relations, the mitigation of surface tensions may reduce incentives to face the difficulty and deal with it directly. When privacy lets people act privately in ways that would have unpleasant consequences if done in public, this may obscure the urgency of the need to question the public regulation itself. If homosexuals are not prosecuted, there is no need to decide whether such conduct between consenting adults in private can constitutionally be prohibited. If people can keep their independent judgments known only to a group of like-minded individuals, there is no need to deal with the problem of regulating hostile reactions by others. It is easier, at least in the short run and certainly for the person making the decision, to conceal actions and thoughts that may threaten an important relationship. Thus, privacy reduces our incentive to deal with our problems.

The situation is usually much more complex, however, and then the use of privacy is justified. First, there are important limits on our capacity to change positive morality, and thus to affect social pressures to conform. This may even cause an inability to change institutional norms. When this is the case, the absence of privacy may mean total destruction of the lives of individuals condemned by norms with only questionable benefit to society. If the chance to achieve change in a particular case is small, it seems heartless and naive to argue against the use of privacy. Although legal and social changes are unlikely until individuals are willing to put themselves on the line, this course of action should not be forced on any one. If an individual decides that the only way he can maintain his sanity is to choose private deviance rather than public disobedience, that should be his decision. Similarly, if an individual prefers to present a public conformity rather than unconventional autonomy, that is his choice. The least society can do in such cases is respect such a choice.

Ultimately, our willingness to allow privacy to operate in this way must be the outcome of our judgment as to the proper scope of liberty individuals should have, and our assessment of the need to help ourselves and others against the limited altruism and rationality of individuals. Assume that an individual has a feature he knows others may find objectionable—that he is a homosexual, for instance, or a communist, or committed a long-past criminal offense—but that feature is irrelevant in the context of a particular situation. Should we support his wish to conceal these facts? Richard Posner and Richard Epstein argue that we should not. This is an understandable argument, but an extremely harsh one. Ideally, it would be preferable if we could all disregard prejudices and irrelevancies. It is clear, however, that we cannot. Given this fact, it may be best to let one's ignorance mitigate one's prejudice. There is even more to it than this. Posner and Epstein imply that what is behind the wish to have privacy in such situations is the wish to manipulate and cheat, and to deprive another of the opportunity to make an informed decision. But we always give only partial descriptions of ourselves, and no one expects anything else. The question is not whether we should edit, but how and by whom the editing should be done. Here, I assert, there should be a presumption in favor of the individual concerned.

It is here that we return to contextual arguments and to the specter of a total lack of privacy. To have different individuals we must have a commitment to some liberty—the liberty to be different. But differences are known to be threatening, to cause hate and fear and prejudice. These aspects of social life should not be overlooked, and oversimplified claims of manipulation should not be allowed to obscure them.

The only case in which this is less true is that of human relationships, where the equality between the parties is stronger and the essence of the relationship is voluntary and intimate. A unilateral decision by one of the parties not to disclose in order to maintain the relationship is of questionable merit. The individual is likely to choose what is easier for him, rather than for both. His decision denies the other party an understanding of the true relationship and the opportunity to decide whether to forgive, accommodate, or leave. Although we cannot rely on the altruism and willingness to forgive of employers or casual acquaintances, to deny a life partner the opportunity to make informed decisions may undermine the value of the relationship. This is another point at which our theories about human relations become relevant. The extent to which paternalistic protection should be a part of relationships between adults, and the forms such concern may appropriately take, are relevant in deciding this issue.

Limiting Exposure. A further and distinct function of privacy is to enhance an individual's dignity, at least to the extent that dignity requires nonexposure. There is something undignified in exposure beyond the fact that the individual's choice of privacy has been frustrated. A choice of privacy is in this sense distinct from a choice to interact. Rejection of the latter frustrates *X*'s wish, but there is no additional necessary loss of dignity and selfhood. In exposure, there is. It is hard to know what kind of exposures are undignified, and the effect such unwanted exposures have on individuals. The answer probably depends on the culture and the individual concerned, but this is nonetheless an important function of privacy.

2. *Privacy and Society*

We desire a society in which individuals can grow, maintain their mental health and autonomy, create and maintain human relations, and lead meaningful lives. The analysis above suggests that some privacy is necessary to enable the individual to do these things, and privacy may therefore both indicate the existence of and contribute to a more pluralistic, tolerant society. In the absence of consensus concerning many limitations of liberty, and in view of the limits on our capacity to encourage tolerance and acceptance and to overcome prejudice, privacy must be part of our commitment to individual freedom and to a society that is committed to the protection of such freedom.

Privacy is also essential to democratic government because it fosters and encourages the moral autonomy of the citizen, a central requirement of a democracy. Part of the justification for majority rule and the right to vote is the assumption that individuals should participate in political decisions by forming judgments and expressing preferences. Thus, to the extent that privacy is important for autonomy, it is important for democracy as well.

This is true even though democracies are not necessarily liberal. A country might restrict certain activities, but it must allow some liberty of political action if it is to remain a democracy. This liberty requires privacy, for individuals must have the right to keep private their votes, their political discussions, and their associations if they are to be able to exercise their liberty to the fullest extent. Privacy is crucial to democracy in providing the opportunity for parties to work out their political positions, and to compromise with opposing factions, before subjecting their positions to public scrutiny. Denying the privacy necessary for these interactions would undermine the democratic process.

Finally, it can be argued that respect for privacy will help a society attract talented individuals to public life. Persons interested in government service must consider the loss of virtually all claims and expectations of privacy in calculating the costs of running for public office. Respect for privacy might reduce those costs.

II. The Limits of Law

One of the advantages of this analysis is that it draws attention to—and explains—the fact that legal protection of privacy has always had, and will always have, serious limitations. In many cases, the law cannot compensate for losses of privacy, and it has strong commitments to other ideals that must sometimes override the concern for privacy. Consequently, one cannot assume that court decisions protecting privacy reflect fully or adequately the perceived need for privacy in our lives.

Part of the reason for this inadequate reflection is that in many cases actions for such invasions are not initiated. The relative rarity of legal actions might be explained by expectations that such injuries are not covered by law, by the fact that many invasions of privacy are not perceived by victims, and by the feeling that legal remedies are inappropriate, in part because the initiation of legal action itself involves the additional loss of privacy. When these factors are forgotten, it is easy to conclude that privacy is not such an important value after all. This conclusion is mistaken, however, as the proposed analysis stresses. Understanding the difficulty of legal protection of privacy will help us resist the tendency to fall victim to this misperception.

It is obvious that privacy will have to give way, at times, to important interests in law enforcement, freedom of expression, research, and verification of data. The result is limits on the scope of legal protection of privacy. I shall concentrate on less obvious reasons why the scope of legal protection is an inadequate reflection of the importance of privacy.

To begin, there are many ways to invade an individual's privacy without his being aware of it. People usually know when they have been physically injured, when their belongings have been stolen, or when a contractual obligation has not been honored. It is more difficult to know when one's communications have been intercepted, when one is being observed or followed, or when others are reading one's dossier. This absence of awareness is a serious problem in a legal system that relies primarily on complaints initiated by victims. In some cases, victims learn of invasions of their privacy when information acquired about them is used in a public trial, as was the case with Daniel Ellsberg. In most situations, however, there is no need to use the information publicly, and the victim will not be able to complain about the invasion simply because of his ignorance. The absence of complaints is thus no indication that invasions of privacy do not exist, or do not have undesirable consequences. Indeed, because deterrence depends at least partly on the probability of detection, these problems of awareness may encourage such invasions.

Ironically, those invasions of privacy that pose no problem of detection, such as invasions through publication, have different features that make legal proceedings unattractive and thus unlikely for the prospective complainant. Legal actions are lengthy, expensive, and involve additional losses of privacy. In the usual case, plaintiffs do not wish to keep the essence of their action private. In a breach of contract suit, for example, the plaintiff may not seek publicity, but usually does not mind it. This is not true, however, for the victim of a loss of privacy. For him, a legal action will further publicize the very information he once sought to keep private, and will thus diminish the point of seeking vindication for the original loss.

Moreover, for the genuine victim of a loss of privacy, damages and even injunctions are remedies of despair. A broken relationship, exposure of a long-forgotten breach of standards, acute feelings of shame and degradation, cannot be undone through money damages. The only benefit may be a sense of vindication, and not all victims of invasions of privacy feel sufficiently strongly to seek such redress.

The limits of law in protecting privacy stem also from the law's commitment to interests that sometimes *require* losses of privacy, such as freedom of expression, interests in research, and the needs of law enforcement. In some of these cases, we would not even feel sympathy for the complainant: the criminal does not need privacy for his autonomy, mental health, or human relations. In other situations, however, the injury is real but legal vindication is considered too costly. Victims realize these facts, and this in turn reduces the tendency to seek vindication through law.

Finally, perhaps the most serious limit of legal protection is suggested by the instrumentalist analysis of privacy above. Privacy is important in those areas in which we want a refuge from pressures to conform, where we seek freedom from inhibition, the freedom to explore, dare, and grope. Invasions of privacy are hurtful because they expose us; they may cause us to lose our self-respect, and thus our capacity to have meaningful relations with others. The law, as one of the most public mechanisms society has developed, is completely out of place in most of the contexts in which privacy is deemed valuable.

These factors indicate that it is neither an accident nor a deliberate denial of its value that the law at present does not protect privacy in many instances. There are simply limits to the law's effectiveness. On the other hand, this does not indicate that there is nothing distinct behind claims for privacy. Emphasis of this point is important, for we must resist the temptation to see privacy as adequately reflected in the law or in reductive accounts. This is also an important reason to seek an explicit commitment to privacy as part of the law.

III. Privacy as a Legal Concept

My analysis has shown that privacy is a coherent and useful concept in the first two contexts: losses of privacy may be identified by reference to the central notion of accessibility, and the reasons for considering it desirable are sufficiently similar to justify adopting it as a value. Most reductionists do not deny these facts; they assert, however, that privacy is not a useful *legal* concept because analysis of actual legal protection, and claims for protection, suggests that it is not and is not likely to be protected simply for its own sake. I believe this denial of the utility of privacy as a legal concept is misleading and has some unfortunate results. To counteract that view, I therefore argue that the law should make an explicit commitment to privacy.

A. The Poverty of Reductionism

One way to think about "the law of privacy" is to start by asking what privacy is, and proceed to question to what extent the law protects it. This approach raises questions as to why people want privacy, why it is that although they want it they do not make claims for legal protection, and, if they do, why the law is reluctant to respond. Answering these questions gives us a fuller understanding of the scope of actual legal protection and the way the law reflects social needs, the limits of the law in protecting human aspirations, and the need for further legal protection created by changes in social and technological conditions. In contrast, another approach to privacy starts from the legal decisions—or moral intuitions—that define the scope of legal protection for privacy. The practical benefit of this approach is obvious: by reducing decisions to a small number of principles of liability, lawyers and judges are able to rely on legal tradition without having to consult all the cases anew each time a privacy claim is made.

In principle, the starting point should not affect the results of our attempt to find an adequate description of the scope of actual legal protection of privacy. It should not be surprising, however, that these starting from judicial decisions tend to conclude with a reductionist account. First, despite the common use of the term "privacy," the two starting points define different data to be explained. Those scholars who start from decisions, without an external concept of privacy, are led to rely on the concept that may be derived from the decisions themselves. One of the advantages of their enterprise is that their account seeks to explain *all* those cases in which the courts have explicitly invoked the concept of privacy. There is no guarantee that the concepts arising from adjudication will be coherent, however, especially when the theoretical basis for the concept is not settled. An attempt to impose coherence on the use of a single concept in judicial decisions is bound to be misleading when such a coherence does not in fact exist. The reductionists have perceived this lack of coherence in the case of privacy, and have concluded that the best way to describe existing law is with several separate categories of recovery, all designed to protect interests other than privacy and having little else in common.

It is here that the reductionists' starting point has blinded them to other ways to deal with the lack of coherence in judicial decisions. In some cases, the label of privacy has indeed been used to protect interests other than privacy because of the promise and limits of legal categories. In most cases in which a claim of privacy has been made, however, a loss of privacy has been involved. It is for this reason that there are many common features to liability in privacy cases despite the disparate principles that are used as an adequate account of the law. The reductionists cannot explain this unity, and their account obscures it. On the other hand, dealing only with explicit privacy decisions blinds the reductionists to those cases in which the law is in fact used to protect privacy, albeit under a different label.

A second problem with reliance on actual decisions is that the data-base is narrow. We deal only with claims that have actually been made, and primarily with cases in which the court has granted recovery. This may be misleading, particularly in areas such as privacy, because there are numerous disincentives for invoking legal protection. Finally seeking to explain the scope of legal protection in order to identify when courts are likely to give a remedy can obscure the reasons why a remedy is not given, which may be crucial for understanding the larger issues.

Starting from the extra-legal concept of privacy enables us to avoid these pitfalls. The account of legal protection resulting from this approach is at least as helpful to practitioners, and also has additional advantages over the reductionist account: it brings to the fore many important observations about privacy and its legal protection, and helps to draw attention to privacy costs.

The primary advantage the approach advocated here exhibits over even the best reductionist account is that it will include within it all legal protection of one coherent value—privacy—in all branches of the law, and under any label. Limited disclosures about individuals, breaches of confidence, the reasons behind testimonial privileges, the right against self-incrimination, and privacy legislation—which have all been discussed in privacy terms but excluded by Prosser's reductionism—will be included. So will be the exclusionary rule and rules of trespass and defamation to the extent they have been used to protect privacy. At the same time, this approach excludes those cases that explicitly refer to privacy in which the concept is invoked misleadingly. Some claims of appropriation, and some claims of immunity from interference, will be excluded. This description thus provides a better picture of current legal protection than does the reductionist account.

The reductionist approach fails even on its strongest claim to adequacy—the exposure of the limits of legal protection of privacy. The primary insight of these accounts is that the law never protects privacy per se, as is indicated by the fact that whenever a remedy for invasion of privacy is given, there is another interest such as property or reputation that is invaded as well. This insight, in general, is quite true, and is certainly important. It reflects the limits of law discussed above. It is nonetheless misleading. It may be true that the law tends to protect privacy only when another interest is also invaded, whereas invasions of other interests may compel protection on their own. It does not follow from this that the presence of privacy in a situation does not serve as an additional reason for protection. Privacy, property, and reputation are all interests worthy of protection. The law grants none of them absolute protection. When two of them are invaded in one situation, recovery may be compelled even though neither alone would suffice. In such cases, the plaintiff would not have recovered had not his privacy been invaded. This operation of privacy is completely obscured by the reductionists.

Besides obscuring the extent of current legal protection, reductionist accounts obscure the continuity of legal protection over time. They give the erroneous impression that the concern with privacy is modern, whereas in fact both the wish to invade privacy and the need to control such wishes have been features of the human condition from antiquity. The common-law maxim that a person's home is his castle; early restrictions on the power of government officials to search, detain, or enter; strict norms of confidence; and prohibition of Peeping Toms or eavesdropping all attest to this early concern. Even when the explicit label of privacy has not been invoked, the law has been used to protect privacy in a variety of ways. Warren and Brandeis, in their famous plea for explicit legal protection of privacy, traced much of this earlier protection by the law of contract, trespass, defamation, and breach of confidence. They offered this tradition of protection as a ground for arguing that the courts could provide remedies for invasion of privacy without legislating a new cause of action in tort. Awareness of this continuity helps us to understand the functions of privacy in our lives, and the changes in circumstances that have led to new claims or protection.

There is nothing in reductionist accounts to suggest insights into why new claims for privacy arise. Nevertheless, understanding what has caused these new claims may be helpful in deciding what to do about them. Despite the tradition of legal protection, it is true that growing concern with losses of privacy is a modern phenomenon. This need not be because of any change in people's awareness, sensitivity, or conception of the essential components of the good life, as Warren and Brandeis implied. Indeed, my analysis of privacy suggests that the functions of privacy are too basic to human life to be so sensitive to changes in perception, and it is in any event doubtful whether modern man is more sensitive or morally sophisticated than his predecessors. Moreover, most individuals today have more opportunities for privacy than our ancestors ever did, as well as a greater ability to regain anonymity after any loss of privacy occurs.

The main reason for this modern concern appears to be a change in the nature and magnitude of threats to privacy, due at least in part to technological change. The legal protection of the past is inadequate not because the level of privacy it once secured is no longer sufficient, but because that level can no longer be secured. Advances in the technology of surveillance and the recording, storage, and retrieval of information have made it either impossible or extremely costly for individuals to protect the same level of privacy that was once enjoyed. "Overstepping" by the press, cited by Warren and Brandeis, gives the old invasions of privacy via publication and gossip a new dimension through the speed and scope of the modern mass media. We can dramatize this point by noting that the loss of anonymity of public figures is of a new order of magnitude. Many old stories could not plausibly be written today: Victor Hugo's rehabilitated mayor, Shakespeare's disguised dukes, the benevolent great people who do charity in disguise, are all extremely unlikely in our modern culture.

The identification of technological developments as a major source of new concern may be supported by the fact that modern claims concerning the secrecy and anonymity aspects of privacy have not been accompanied by new claims concerning physical access: technological advances have affected the acquisition, storage, and dissemination of information, but gaining physical access is a process that has not changed much. On the other hand, the increase in the number of people whose profession it is to observe and report, the intensified activity in search of publishable information, and the changes in the equipment that enables such enterprises, make it more likely that events and information will in fact be recorded and published.

Technology is not the whole story, however. The privacy concerns created by the mass media go beyond the fact that the development of scandal magazines and investigative journalism lets more people acquire more information more quickly. An additional problem is that journalism is crude, and may not do justice to the situation exposed. Partial truths are unsettling because they present a one-dimensional image of the subject, often without compassion or benevolence. This may be not unlike scandal journalism's old sister, gossip. The most important difference is that gossip usually concerns people who are already known in their other facets, and thus partial truths are less misleading. In contrast, there is no way that most readers of newspapers can correct for the one-dimensional images they receive through print.

The new concern with privacy may also be explained, at least in part, as a tendency to put old claims in new terms. From this perspective, part of the new interest in privacy is not caused by new needs, but rather by new doctrinal moves or hopes for legal change. Privacy has been used to overcome the limitations of defamation; it has been used to avoid such historically loaded legal terms as "substantive due process" and "liberty", and it has been used to avoid basing all entitlements, without differentiation, on the notion of property.

Finally, and perhaps most importantly, reductive accounts reinforce the tendency to overlook the privacy costs that may be involved in a case. Because these accounts suggest that privacy is only a label used to protect other interests, logic would dictate that whenever a privacy question is discussed, the balancing should be among the "real" interests involved. Consequently, privacy is made redundant despite its usage. Although we talk in terms of privacy, the reductionist suggests, what we actually take into consideration are the interests to which privacy is reducible. It is this quality of reductionism that threatens to undermine our belief in the distinctness and importance of privacy, and to have an adverse effect on our policy decisions. The proposed analysis, by clarifying the distinctness and importance of privacy through a functional analysis, enables us to challenge such reductionism.

B. The Case for an Explicit Commitment to Privacy

There is much to be said for making an explicit legal commitment to privacy. Such a commitment would affirm that privacy is not just a convenient label, but a central value. An explicit commitment would put reductionist accounts in their correct perspective, as attempts to give lawyers and judges a guide to identify cases in which recovery is likely under a given heading. The legal protection of privacy is more than a mere by-product of the protection of other, more "respectable" values. An explicit commitment to privacy would recognize that losses of privacy are undesirable, at least in the circumstances in which such losses frustrate the functions and goals described above. It would recognize that such losses should be taken into account by the legal system, and that we should strive to minimize them.

Clearly, an explicit commitment to privacy does not mean that privacy deserves absolute protection. It does not mean that privacy is the one value we seek to promote, or even the most important among a number of values to which we are committed. This is true for all our values, however. None is protected absolutely, not even those to which a commitment is made in unequivocal terms in the Constitution. Nor would making such a commitment suggest that invasions of privacy would generally be actionable. I have indicated many of the reasons why it is unlikely to expect the law to protect privacy extensively. Making an explicit commitment could not be understood to deny the need for balancing; it would simply identify the factors that should be considered by the legal system.

In positive terms, the case for an explicit commitment to privacy is made by pointing out the distinctive functions of privacy in our lives. Privacy has as much coherence and attractiveness as other values to which we have made a clear commitment, such as liberty. Arguments for liberty, when examined carefully, are vulnerable to objections similar to the arguments we have examined for privacy, yet this vulnerability has never been considered a reason not to acknowledge the importance of liberty, or not to express this importance by an explicit commitment so that any loss will be more likely to be noticed and taken into consideration. Privacy deserves no less.

Further insight about the need for an explicit commitment to privacy comes from study of the arguments made against this approach. First, it may be argued that the

American legal system has already made this commitment, and that we should concentrate on answering questions of the scope of legal protection rather than spend time arguing for commitments that have already been made. Questions of scope are no doubt important, and had a commitment to privacy been made and its implications internalized, there would indeed be no further need for an explicit affirmation. But the reductionist literature is at least as influential as that which affirms the distinctness and importance of privacy, and although it is true that some parts of the legal system are informed by an affirmation of privacy, it is equally clear that others are not. For the latter, an explicit commitment to privacy could make an important difference.

A more substantive argument, and one inconsistent with the first, is that we should not make a commitment to privacy because there is no need for further legal protection: we already have all the privacy we could possibly want or need. In those areas in which invasions of privacy are undesirable, the law already provides a remedy. If anything, this argument goes, we need less legal protection today because rising standards of living mean that individuals enjoy more privacy than ever before. Critics emphasize the relatively small number of difficult cases in which we sympathize with the person complaining about invasion of his privacy. In the hundred years of the tort remedy's existence, there as been only one Sidis, one Melvin, one Barber.

It is here that understanding the reasons for the new concern with privacy becomes crucial. It is true that individuals today enjoy more opportunities for privacy in some areas, but this observation, taken alone, is misleading. The rarity of actions is not a good indication of the need for privacy, or of the extent to which invasions are undesirable. We enjoy our privacy not because of new opportunities for seclusion or because of greater control over our interactions, but because of our anonymity, because no one is interested in us. The moment someone becomes sufficiently interested, he may find it quite easy to take all that privacy away. He may follow us all the time, obtain information about us from a host of data systems, record our conversations, and intrude into our bedrooms. What protects privacy is not the difficulty of invading it, but the lack of motive and interest of others to do so. The important point, however, is that if our privacy is invaded, it may be invaded today in more serious and more permanent ways than ever before. Thus, although most of us are unlikely to experience a substantial loss of privacy, we have an obligation to protect those who lose their anonymity. In this sense, privacy is no different from other basic entitlements. We are not primarily concerned with the rights of criminal suspects because we have been exposed to police brutality ourselves. We know that we may be exposed to it in the future, but, more generally, we want to be part of a society that is committed to minimizing violations of due process.

Even if the law had already dealt with all the situations in which privacy should be legally protected, however, an explicit commitment to privacy would still be significant. It is significant in ways that no specific, localized legal protection can be. It would serve to remind us of the importance of privacy, and thus to color our understanding of protection in specific contexts.

The result of this awareness would not necessarily or even primarily be more legal rules to protect privacy. For example, such an explicit commitment to privacy might focus attention on ways to ameliorate the difficulties resulting from the inappropriateness of current legal remedies and legal proceedings. Some thought could go into whether limits on the publicity of judicial proceedings that involve privacy claims could be established without paying too high a price in terms of freedom of expression or fair trials. Moreover, an explicit commitment could increase individual sensitivity to losses of privacy and thus encourage people to prevent invasions of privacy without reliance on law at all. It may lead to increased efforts to make it possible to minimize losses of privacy without invoking the law, through such efforts as development of technological devices to make leaks from data systems more difficult. It would also draw the attention of those whose occupations involve systematic breaches of others' privacy, such as journalists, doctors, detectives, policemen, and therapists, to the fact that although some invasions of privacy are inevitable, a loss of sensitivity about such losses may corrupt the invader as well as harm the victim.

An explicit commitment to privacy is not vulnerable to the charge that the law should not protect privacy because its efficacy in doing so is limited. It might be argued that the contexts within which privacy has functional value are those in which the law is traditionally reluctant to interfere. This reluctance stems, at least in part, from an awareness that some questions cannot and should not be dealt with by the law. It is unlikely, for example, that the law will ever impose an obligation on parents to give their children some privacy in order to grow, develop autonomy, and explore others. We would probably find such a law an unpalatable interference with liberty. An explicit legal commitment to privacy might make such specific protection of privacy unnecessary, however. Parents might then realize more fully that privacy is important for their children, and this would lead them to respect their children's privacy without any direct legal obligation to do so.

The general commitment would also help in administering the laws. It could serve as a principle of interpretation, pointing out the need to balance losses of privacy, perhaps with a presumption in favor of protecting privacy. It might also supplement existing privacy laws by identifying improper conduct and invoking the general sense of obligation to obey the laws. A general commitment may thus lead to a reduction of invasions of privacy even in situations in which the victims would not have sued had the invasions occurred, either because of ignorance or for other reasons discussed above.

The functions of a general commitment to the value of privacy as a part of the law are varied, and cannot be reduced to the amount of protection actually given to that value in the legal system. Here again, the commitment to privacy is no different than the commitment to other values, such as freedom of expression or liberty. As I have argued before, a commitment to privacy as a legal value may help to raise awareness of its importance and thus deter reckless invasions. Most importantly, however, an explicit commitment to privacy will have an educational impact. This function is of special importance, because most of us enjoy privacy without the need for legal protection. For the most part, what we should learn is how to appreciate our available privacy and use it well. A clear statement in the law that privacy is a central value could make us more aware of the valuable functions privacy can serve. Ultimately, the wish to have privacy must be in our hearts, not only in our laws. But this does not mean that a commitment to the value of privacy should not be in our laws as well.

The Phenomenon of Stalking: Do Existing State Statutes Provide Adequate Protection?

KAREN S. MORIN*

Introduction

In 1990, California responded to four brutal stalking deaths by enacting a revolutionary statute aimed at deterring such incidents. Each of the stalking victims had been murdered despite the presence of temporary restraining orders that were issued for their protection.

Reprinted with permission from *San Diego Justice Journal,* vol. 1:123, pp. 123–152.

*Candidate for J.D., Western State University College of Law (San Diego), May 1994.

The author wishes to express her gratitude to the editorial staff for their assistance and guidance. Special thanks are extended to Lorraine Harris, Miranda Franks, Gregory Schneider and Dr. Meloy. Last but not least, sincerest appreciation is expressed to Professor Kenneth Vandevelde and The Honorable Patricia Benke for their time and highly respected comments.

Stalking is a phenomenon that has existed for years, but has only recently gained notoriety through movies such as *"Fatal Attraction."* Situations exist throughout the nation in which police are unable or unwilling to provide assistance.

One such horror story involved 11-year-old Caty Thayer, who ten years ago, was stalked for a period of nineteen months. One day Caty was found sorting her dolls and, when asked about this, told her mother she was deciding which dolls would go to whom after she was killed. Caty was kidnapped and subsequently found dead—she had been repeatedly stabbed and raped.

Cases abound in which restraining orders have proven ineffective in protecting victims against further crimes. One victim, twenty-one-year-old Kristen Lardner, was killed by an ex-boyfriend despite the fact that she had recently obtained a restraining order against him. She procured the order after he was charged with assault and battery for beating and kicking her unconscious. At the time he killed her, Ms. Lardner's ex-boyfriend was on probation, having served six months in prison for battering another girlfriend. A protective order was in place prior to that incident as well.

Another victim, Tereasa Bean, lives in constant fear that her estranged husband will break into her home and either beat or kill her. She sleeps with a loaded shotgun and keeps dog repellent spray and a knife near her bed. Her estranged husband previously inflicted serious injuries upon her by fracturing her skull and stabbing her in the breast with a coat hanger. He was once imprisoned for violating a restraining order, but was subsequently released by a different judge who cited due process violations.

In Maryland, a Baltimore woman obtained a court order that was intended to keep her abusive husband out of their home. He then stalked her and set her on fire when he trapped her in a laundromat. After that episode, he was sentenced to thirty years imprisonment. The permanently disfigured victim spoke out in favor of changing existing laws; she made every effort to protect herself by obtaining the court order, but it had failed to protect her.

Prior to Virginia's enactment of a stalking law, Loretta Hill testified before the House Committee that for more than six years she and her three children were stalked by her former husband. She had been shot at, abducted, beaten and raped by him as he repeatedly violated court orders to stay away. She finally shot him when he broke through her living room window. He survived the incident and she has since seen him in passing.

Additional impetus for the California stalking bill resulted from public awareness of cases involving Hollywood celebrities. The highly publicized cases of Rebecca Schaeffer and Theresa Saldana are but a few. Rebecca Schaeffer was killed by Robert John Bardo, an obsessed fan, who hired a private investigator to find her address after searching for her for two years. Similarly, Arthur Richard Jackson hired a private investigator to find the home address of Theresa Saldana. He then went to her home and stabbed her repeatedly in the chest and thigh. Jackson was finally stopped by a passer-by who held him until police arrived. Other celebrity victims include David Letterman, Michael Jackson, Cher, Sharon Gless and Katarina Witt.

At some point in their lives, about five percent of women in the general populace will become victims of stalking. The majority of stalking cases involve females as the targets with former spouses or lovers as the perpetrators. When women do seek to protect themselves against this type of abuse, there are no guarantees the abuse will stop. Such violence has generally been treated by the judicial system as "domestic disputes." The Attorney General's Task Force on Domestic Violence reported that in 1987, boyfriends and husbands perpetrated thirty-one percent of murders in which women were the victims. These men are responsible for causing nearly 1,500 deaths each year. When encounters by husbands or boyfriends turn deadly, reports indicate that up to ninety percent of the victims were initially stalked. Based on these figures, it can be estimated that approximately 1,350 deaths each year are preceded by episodes of stalking. Statistical information from Kansas City and Detroit reveals that ninety percent of these women made police contact at least once for assistance. Over fifty percent called a minimum of five times.

Since California initiated the first stalking statute, twenty-eight other states have adopted similar legislation. Stalking legislation is currently pending in Michigan, New Jersey, and Pennsylvania. States preparing legislation for introduction in 1993 include Texas and Indiana. States regulating stalking through the use of other laws include Maine (terrorizing), Minnesota (trespass, terroristic threats, and harassment), and Arizona (through misdemeanor classifications of harassment).

Although no appellate court has yet addressed a stalking case, an interesting issue arises in anticipation of such review: will state statutes meet federal constitutional challenges? Federal legislation has recently been passed that requires the National Institute of Justice to draft a constitutional and enforceable anti-stalking statute within one year. This prototype may then serve as a model for those states desiring to formulate their own statute or to amend existing legislation.

This paper will first identify psychological features commonly associated with stalking and note possible legal implications. Then traditional remedies will be evaluated to ascertain their overall effect on stalking. Next, state statutes will be summarized, followed by an analysis of potential constitutional issues that may arise through their interpretation. Finally, recommendations aimed at developing a constitutional, enforceable and effective stalking statute will be presented.

I. Psychological Factors

Several different behaviors are encompassed within the concept of "stalking." Some of these behaviors are potentially more dangerous than are others. Victims may be targeted for a variety of reasons. Depending on the circumstances, measures taken to deter stalking may or may not result in the desired effect. These factors must be considered in evaluating the practical impact of existing statutes on the total incidence of stalking.

Studies of stalking behavior remain in their infancy and may be limited to individual aspects of the overall phenomenon. This section will begin with a general discussion of identified categories of stalkers, and then focus on available information regarding celebrity stalkers.

Dr. Michael A. Zona and colleagues recently conducted a study using seventy-four case files taken from the Los Angeles Police Department's Threat Management Unit.[1] They identified three distinct groups from this sample which they categorized under the headings of "Erotomania," "Love Obsessional," and "Simple Obsessional." All of the subjects exhibited a pattern of harassment deemed obsessional in nature. Less than ten percent met criteria for "Erotomania" classification where the "[s]talker falsely believes that the target, usually someone famous or rich, is in love with the stalker." Forty-three percent were classified as "Love Obsessional" where the "[s]talker is a stranger to the target but is obsessed and mounts a campaign of harassment to make the target aware of the stalker's existence." Forty-seven percent were classified as "Simple Obsessional," in which the "[s]talker, usually male, knows [sic] target as an ex-spouse, ex-lover, or former boss, and begins a campaign of harassment."

Thirty-eight percent of the victims will be ordinary citizens, thirty-two percent lesser known entertainment figures, seventeen percent highly recognized celebrities, and thirteen percent will be former employers or other professionals.

Further insight into the syndrome of Erotomania is provided in a recent book by forensic psychologist Dr. J. Reid Meloy, Ph.D.[2] Dr. Meloy distinguishes between delusional erotomania and nondelusional or what he terms "borderline" erotomania. Individuals belonging to the delusional category will steadfastly believe they are passionately loved by the object of their delusion; even significant refuting evidence will not deter this belief. Usually no prior "attachment" with the targeted individual exists but rather, an "object concept" in the erotomanic's mind, distorted with emotions and meaning that are not supported in reality. In extreme cases, the subject may believe he or she has merged with the love object and may lose distinction between self and others.

The "borderline" erotomanic usually has some prior "emotional engagement" with the object, varying in degree from a congenial glance to an emotional and sexual relationship that has dissolved. Separation is viewed as abandonment or rejection. There are no "clear delusion[s] of love," but rather an "enduring, intense attachment to a love object that no longer reciprocates the feeling."

The distinction between delusional and "borderline" erotomania

> [I]s clinically significant and also *has legal implications concerning pleas of insanity*. The former implies the presence of psychosis; the latter indicates a gross disturbance of attachment or bonding but not necessarily a loss of reality testing.[3]

The behavior of the erotomanic will not be overtly bizarre or odd and rarely will symptoms be accompanied by hallucinations. The delusions of erotomania will usually focus on spiritual union or idealized romance, rather than on sexual attraction. The object of the delusion will frequently be of higher economic or social status.

Generally the erotomanic will not be violent, but if they are, they will direct the violence toward the one they desire or a third party presumed to be interfering with the relationship. While historically erotomania was envisioned as a female delusional disorder, recent reports suggest that men also develop the syndrome and in fact are more likely to act out violently when they do. Erotomanic symptoms may accompany other psychiatric disorders, and diagnosis of these as well as other personality factors will be important in determining the risk of future violent actions.

> [L]egal interventions to protect the erotomanic person's love object must be carefully weighed. In some cases they will work, but in other cases judicial sanction may only enrage the erotomanically disturbed patient, spurring the person on to more intrusive and violent behavior.[4]

Returning to the study by Dr. Zona, information regarding contact efforts is now presented. All of the erotomanic subjects in the study wrote letters to their victims; eighty-five percent achieved telephone contact and seventy-one percent actually found the victim's home. The erotomanics were twice as likely to stalk their victims, but rarely pursued person-to-person contact even when presented with opportunities to do so. Despite contact efforts and numerous threats, there were no attempts to harm either the victim's person or property.

Individuals in the "love obsessional" group "simply love[d] their object." They were extremely fanatical and unwilling or unable to stop their activities. There was generally an absence of preexisting personal knowledge of the victim who initially was known only through the media. The victim was usually a sexy actress or "bombshell." The authors of this study report that this category coincides with what others have referred to as "borderline erotomania." The primary contacts made by this category were via phone or letter and threats were infrequent. Only one person damaged property of a victim, and there were no reports of physical injury.

Subjects in the "simple obsessional" group knew their victim, sometimes to the point of having had intimate knowledge of them. Their behaviors were usually precipitated by a love gone sour. This group exhibited a high index of person-to-person confrontation. Two subjects from this group actually harmed their victims and five destroyed property. This group was responsible for the majority of threats, which were acted upon in thirty percent of cases. Only twenty-eight percent of this group exhibited stalking behavior, compared to forty-three percent of the erotomanic group and twenty-one percent of the "love obsessional" group.

Celebrity Victims

A 1991 study examined the characteristics of threatening and otherwise inappropriate letters that were sent to Hollywood celebrities.[5] Based on the number of written communications and whether the subject actually approached the celebrity, the study group estimated that the lowest approach rate was by those who had written just once. The peak rate was among those who had written 10–14 times.

At least twelve percent used means other than letters in their endeavors to contact the celebrity. Celebrities were significantly more likely to have been approached if the subject telephoned in addition to writing. Fifty-five percent of the subjects enclosed items along with their communications ranging from business cards to blood, semen, and a coyote's head. The most common enclosures were pictures of, or poetry by, the contacting party. Subjects commonly cast themselves in the role of friend, advisor, acquaintance, spouse, or other intimate associate. Only five percent depicted themselves as enemies of the celebrity.

Threats were identified in twenty-three percent of the cases. Subjects sometimes made more than one type of threat but the majority, seventy-one percent, were conditional threats. Thirty-nine percent were veiled threats, and twenty-six percent were direct threats. The celebrity was the most frequent target of the threat, followed by the subject who had targeted himself or herself for suicide or self-mutilation. Occasionally, threats were made concerning property, other persons, or other public figures.

There appears to be no association between approaching and verbal threats.

> This finding contradicts a vast body of assumptions that is relied on each day in judging whether harassing communications warrant concern, notification of the police, security precautions or investigation. With respect to inappropriate communications to entertainment celebrities, the presence or absence of a threat in the communications is no indication whatsoever of whether a subject is going to pursue an encounter. Those who rely on the presence or absence of threats in making judgments about what to do are making a serious mistake. *Unfortunately, this error is codified in the criminal law, which recognizes various types of verbal threats as unlawful but does not accord equal recognition to harassment without threats, even though the latter often poses an equal or greater danger of harm to persons or property.*[6]

Dr. Park Elliot Dietz, a leading expert on celebrity stalking, criticizes the way in which "threat" is defined by some of the laws. "A direct threat—'I'm going to kill you'—is covered, but a veiled or conditional threat—'If you don't do as I say something bad might happen to you'—is excluded."[7]

Dr. Dietz further cautions that "arresting but failing to prosecute or imprison the stalker always worsens the situation for the victim." This confirms the relationship to the stalker who is mentally ill and presents an "angering challenge" to the stalker who is less ill.

Dr. Dietz, who co-authored the above article regarding letters to celebrities, evaluated Robert John Bardo before his trial for the murder of Rebecca Schaeffer. As a teenager, Bardo was briefly institutionalized until his mother removed him from treatment saying there was nothing wrong with him. A school counselor became worried when Bardo said "his mission from the devil was to kill."

Prior to his pursuit of Rebecca Schaeffer, Bardo tried to approach Samantha Smith, the young girl who had written to Soviet President Yuri Andropov regarding world peace. In addition, he focused on singer Debbie Gibson during a period when his interest in Schaeffer dimmed. Research has shown that those who pursue one public figure will often pursue another.

"Nice" celebrities attract more pursuers than those perceived as less friendly, possibly a factor in Bardo's attraction to Rebecca Schaeffer. Women with strong personalities rarely become targets.

Before he attacked Schaeffer, Bardo indicated to his sister that he was about to do something drastic. He wrote her a letter, illustrated with a tombstone, in which he said he was going to do something of which she would not approve. When she thought she knew what he planned, he refused to discuss it further.

Letters mailed by Bardo to Schaeffer were platonic, containing no blatant hints of violence. This fact did not surprise Dr. Dietz who said that those who make overt sexual propositions are much less likely to approach.

At trial, Bardo was described as suffering from many symptoms of schizophrenia, but was not pronounced insane. He engaged a mechanism called "splitting" in which the victim is seen as being all good or all bad. Bardo could love and hate at the same time and switch in an instant, thus allowing for Bardo's ability to love and adore Schaeffer at the same time he planned to kill her. Bardo was found guilty under California state law of first-degree murder while lying in wait.

II. Traditional Remedies: Restraining Orders

Previously, restraining orders were the only weapons available for use against stalking. Unfortunately, these orders often failed to provide the anticipated protection. As evidenced in the introduction, some of the most brutal acts of violence occur despite the presence of court orders.

In addition to compliance problems, difficulties may arise when attempts are made to procure restraining orders. For example, an abused woman was found ineligible for a protective order because at the time of the attack she did not live with her abuser. The victim had been abducted by her estranged husband who then tied a rope around her neck and threatened to drag her to death from behind his truck. On a previous occasion, her abuser taped her mouth closed and terrorized her with a razor blade.

A similar lack of protection was afforded another victim who requested a second protective order. She was violated twice after the original order expired, once resulting in a broken jaw, the other in sexual assault, beating, and the degradation of having her assailant urinate upon her.

While incidents of abuses are all too frequent, success stories in related situations do exist. For example, a comprehensive effort aimed at providing adequate protection for abused women was undertaken in Quincy, Massachusetts. Judge Albert Kramer worked with police, women's groups, prosecutors, and probation officers to establish an early intervention program that today serves as a national model. There were no domestic homicides in his district in 1991, while in a neighboring district there were fifteen.

Other Remedies

Common-law tort actions such as assault, trespass, nuisance, defamation, invasion of privacy, and intentional infliction of emotional distress are available for victims of harassment. These actions may prove applicable in some instances of stalking. For example, an Illinois man was charged with stalking following a series of incidents directed at a former girlfriend. He made threatening comments, exhibited assaultive and battering behaviors, and even forced her car off the road. He was seen near her home, her place of employment, and had "buzzed" her house while flying a small aircraft. In addition to the assault and battery charges, there may well have been an action for trespass. Further, he falsely claimed she had AIDS by passing out letters to this effect at the college she attended. This action could constitute defamation.

Invasion of privacy actions may lie where there are repeated, undesired, and persistent phone calls to the victims. Actual infliction of emotional distress may occur and is also sometimes an element of the stalking statute itself.

> Criminal statutes against harassment range from slightly to grossly inadequate. Every state has a statute criminalizing at least some types of telephone misuse. Several states also proscribe physical or postal abuse, but only a few have enacted criminal statutes directed at the broad forms of harassment.[8]

Occasionally, federal charges may be instituted. For example, Harry Veltman III, a California resident, was charged under federal law for mailing obscene and threatening materials to figure-skating gold medalist

Katarina Witt. After sending marriage proposals, a Bible, over 100 obscene love letters, and nude photos of himself, he began sending death threats. At this point, the FBI intervened.

As illustrated, many of the aforementioned actions are applicable only in very specific circumstances. Therefore, they will rarely be useful in situations involving stalking. Stalking laws enable victims to press charges before the behaviors escalate to the point of causing injury or death. Previously, a victim could take action only when confrontation or contact amounting to a battery resulted.

III. State Statutes

Existing state statutes possess both basic similarities and striking differences. This section will outline popular trends, highlight unique provisions, and identify common modes in penalties, treatments and exclusions.

General Findings

"States typically have defined 'stalking' as willful, malicious, and repeated following and harassing of another person." Some include reference to conduct that alarms, harasses, or annoys. Many statutes require that a credible threat be made. Some define "credible" for this purpose as causing a reasonable person to fear for his or her life or safety. Occasionally, statutes do not qualify the threat as "credible," yet seem to apply the same standard. Some demand that there be intent and apparent ability to carry out the threat. Others require that the threat be made in a manner warning of the infliction of death or great bodily injury upon the victim. Some require the intent to inflict substantial emotional distress and some require that it actually occur. Few additionally provide protection against property damage.

Although most statutes require that the threat be made to the victim personally, a few specify that it may include the immediate family. Oklahoma is the only state to specifically define "immediate family." Included are victims up to the third degree of consanguinity, or those who regularly reside in the household or who did reside there within the prior six months.

Uniquely, the West Virginia statute provides that the victim must have formerly resided, cohabitated, or formerly engaged in a sexual or intimate relationship with the perpetrator. Even though many cases involve estranged relationships, West Virginia provides no protection for victims of unknown or minimally known stalkers.

Initial Action

Only one statute imposes a duty upon a police officer to respond as soon as possible and to cooperate with the alleged victim of a stalking. One state requires that its residents give a reasonable warning or a request to desist to the stalker, made by or on behalf of the victim, before proceedings will be initiated.

Preventive Detention

Bail may be denied in certain situations involving stalking. For example, Illinois allows preventive detention after a hearing if,

1. The proof is evident or the presumption great that the defendant committed the offense of stalking or aggravated stalking; and
2. The defendant poses a real and present threat to the physical safety of the alleged victim of the offense; and
3. The denial of release on bail or personal recognizance is necessary to prevent fulfillment of the threat upon which the charge is based; and
4. The court finds that no condition or combination of conditions set forth in subsection (b) of Section 110-10 of this code, including mental health treatment at a community mental health center, hospital, or facility of the Department of Mental Health and Developmental Dis-

abilities, can reasonably assure the physical safety of the alleged victim of the offense.

Illinois further requires presence of clear and convincing evidence of the offense. The defendant cannot be held longer than ninety days if not brought to trial during that time.

One state may, in certain circumstances, deny a defendant bail while he or she is awaiting judgment of conviction and sentencing following a plea or guilty verdict, or while awaiting appeal. Another state allows preventive detention to extend to misdemeanors, including stalking, when a firearm is involved or a restraining order has been violated.

Penalties and Treatment

Penalties and classifications for the crime of stalking vary greatly from state to state. Some are classed as misdemeanors, others as felonies, and some depend on whether there were prior incidents of stalking or violations of protective orders.

One state, while generally treating first offenses as a misdemeanor, will classify the offense as a felony if the victim is less than sixteen years of age.

Most states require that before classification as a subsequent conviction, any prior conviction must have been for an offense toward the same person. One state allows charges to be made whether or not the act was toward the same or a separate individual, and three states allow charges even if the conviction occurred in another jurisdiction.

One state requires that there be no suspending or reducing of sentences below the mandatory minimum, and that there be no allocation of parole or probation until the minimum sentence is served. Very few states specify that counseling may be required for persons convicted of stalking.

Exclusions

Some states specifically exclude "constitutionally protected" activities without giving further definition, while others provide an exception for lawful labor picketing. A few have exclusions for private investigative businesses or activities in furtherance of law enforcement.

IV. Potential Constitutional Issues

Some stalking statutes may encounter successful constitutional challenge either due to the nature of the right affected, or due to statutory construction that allows for unconstitutional interpretation. This section will examine potential issues as they relate to freedom of expression, preventive detention, and unconstitutional vagueness.

Freedom of Expression

"Congress shall make no law . . . abridging the freedom of speech."

Stalking behavior usually includes repeated harassing or threatening behavior such as following an individual, showing up at the victim's house or work place, making harassing phone calls, vandalizing property, or leaving written messages for the targeted victim. Some actions will consist of behavior that can be classed as pure conduct, some as pure speech and some as conduct combined with verbal expression. Regulation of pure conduct will not be violative of the freedom of speech provision of First Amendment, nor will regulation of pure speech containing "true threats." Threats of violence remain outside First Amendment protection because they protect individuals from a fear of violence and the disruption it engenders, and from a fear the threatened behavior will occur. The Court in *Watts v. United States,* a case involving threats against the President, required that the government prove a "true" threat rather than mere political hyperbole. The definition was expanded in *United States v. Kelner,* where the court determined that when a threat affronted an important social interest, it was punishable even absent proof of specific intent to carry it through if "on its face and in the circumstances in which it is made is so unequivocal, unconditional, immediate and specific as to the person threatened, as to convey a gravity of purpose and imminent prospect of execution."[9]

In certain circumstances words may violate laws directed at conduct rather than against speech, perhaps only incidentally sweeping up proscribable speech. For example, a statute against telephone harassment that included a provision prohibiting threats to commit crimes against persons or property was interpreted as constitutional in *Thorne v. Bailey*. The court held that harassment was not communication even though it took the form of speech, and was thus not protected merely because it involved the use of a telephone. Phone calls were not prohibited if made with the intent to communicate, only if made with the intent to harass. The court reasoned that the requirement of a specific intent to harass clearly indicated which actions the statute sought to criminalize.

Many of the stalking statutes target harassing or following behaviors in combination with "threats." Thus, if the threats take the form of speech, they may be incorporated incidentally into the statute. In order to clearly manifest an intention to proscribe the stalking behavior, statutes should include provisions of intent describing the behavior or the effects of the behavior they are attempting to target. For example, since the reason threats of violence are not considered protected speech is because of the fear element they produce, statutes directed at preventing this harm will be acceptable.

Stalkers sometimes send frequent letters, which may or may not contain explicit threats. If the letters are platonic or not otherwise proscribable, the tendency may be to view the speech as protected. However, it is the action of sending the letters that stalking statutes wish to target, not the speech contained therein. Since it makes no difference what the letters actually say, the restrictions are not based on content. Further, it may be argued that whether or not letters contain express threats, they may in fact become threatening by nature of persistent attempts at unwelcome contact. As discussed above, nonthreatening letters to celebrities were noted to be equally, if not more, dangerous than threatening letters.

Vagueness

> A criminal statute must be sufficiently definite to give fair notice of the required conduct to one who would avoid its penalties, and to guide the judge in its application and the lawyer in defending one charged with its violation.[10]

The forbidden conduct must be clearly defined so that people of average intelligence will not have to guess its meaning or its applicability. The statute must "give fair notice" of which acts are punishable.

Some statutes specifically denote the prohibited behavior. For example, they may require that there be repeated following or harassment of another along with a "credible threat" that is made with the intent of placing that person in reasonable fear of death or great bodily injury. As specific as these provisions are, it is unlikely they will be stricken for vagueness. In fact, the problem will likely be that these statutes are too specific to be of much benefit. For example, since the repeated following or harassing must be accompanied by the threat of death or serious bodily harm, it would appear that one may stalk and follow a victim without repercussion as long as one does not make verbal threats to the victim.

Some statutes are constructed in such a manner that they may be interpreted to prohibit simply following another person. These statutes are probably too vague in that they may be interpreted to proscribe behaviors that are constitutionally protected or not otherwise illegal, such as picketing or the employment duties of police, reporters, or television camera crews. No definition of "to follow" is provided, which leads to unanswered questions regarding the context and extent of limitations. Since no distinction is made between innocent and harmful conduct, erratic and arbitrary arrests or convictions may result.

In a situation involving loitering, the court noted that statutes of this type additionally "implicate[] consideration of the constitutional right to freedom of movement."[11] Freedom of movement across and inside frontiers is a basic aspect of this country's heritage. This right to travel entails liberty interests of which deprivation without due process of law is not allowed.

If an individual is detained under vague circumstances, Fourth Amendment issues may also arise. In *Terry v. Ohio,* police interruption of Terry's freedom of movement and invasion of privacy "arose only because circumstances warranted forcing an encounter with Terry in an effort to prevent or investigate a crime."[12] In order to detail individuals, police are required to possess a reasonable suspicion based on specific and articulable facts. Merely being in the vicinity of another will not meet this requirement.

Inclusion of the phrase "for no legitimate purpose" into the statute may be a basis for its determination as unconstitutionally vague by injecting uncertainty into the statute and inviting subjective evaluation of proscribed behaviors.

For the above reasons, stalking statutes must be specific enough to place the offender on notice as to prohibited acts, and to place police on notice as to acts that will satisfy reasonable suspicion. Statutory construction must be carefully considered to avoid possible unconstitutional interpretations.

Preventive Detention

Most state constitutions include a bail provision. In response to societal concerns for public safety following release of those persons considered dangerous, some states have adopted preventive detention statutes, as has Congress.

Only Illinois specifically outlines preventive detention measures as applied to stalking. A few others reference stalking in conjunction with general provisions for bail denial, or provide limited provisions under differing circumstances.

The federal preventive detention statute has received thorough constitutional analysis.

V. Recommendations

The most important aspect of developing a model stalking statute is to perfect a symmetry between the safety needs of the victim and the constitutional requirements of the defendant. Compounding this difficulty is the fact that there are many different types of behaviors associated with "stalking." Some stalkers will follow but not attempt person-to-person contact. Some will make direct threats and follow them through while others will not. Some may kill without apparent warning. Some stalkers will be considered delusional, others will not.

Many of the statutes target only stalking behavior that is combined with a "credible threat." Problems arise in the attempt to define which actions will constitute a "credible" threat. The prevailing attitude seems to be that unless an individual makes a direct and specific threat, the threatening behavior is not "credible" and the victim is not in sufficient danger to warrant protection. This attitude prevails despite clear evidence to the contrary. Studies discussed above report varying degrees of follow-through on threats and indicate that with reference to celebrities, veiled threats can be more dangerous than explicit ones. Therefore, clauses that specifically require a "credible" threat will likely be underinclusive in their protection of victims and should not be included.

Clauses that can be interpreted as proscribing "following" behavior alone should also be avoided to prevent being stricken as unconstitutionally vague.

To avoid First Amendment problems, clauses must include an intention to proscribe the threatening or offending stalking behavior or the fear it engenders, rather than targeting speech itself. Most criminal statutes interpret an "intent" requirement to include actions that a reasonable person would be aware of as having the prohibited effect. Depending on the interpretation of intent, "mentally disturbed" stalkers who are simply attracted to their victims may avoid prosecution. Therefore, statutes should include provisions for coverage on a "knew, or should have known" standard.

It is clear that one will never be able to predict with absolute certainty another's future behavior. However, preventive detention in certain circumstances must be considered. The danger that stalkers represent to victims is too compelling to continue to ignore or minimize. Since there are so many different types of stalking behavior and psychological features to be considered, the determination of who amongst the stalkers is most likely to commit future injurious acts may be difficult. The decision to release or detain cannot be made simply by determining how specific and detailed a threat appears of its face. To that end, psychological assessment is indicated prior to release or detention, even when behaviors seem insignificant. The Illinois provision, together with the added proviso that psychological assessment by professionals be required, will serve as a helpful model to those states who choose to include such a provision.

Penalties must be thoughtfully considered. Minor fines and sentences are unlikely to deter the behavior. If it is deemed through psychological evaluation that counseling is appropriate, provision for treatment should be made available.

A sample definition of stalking is outlined below. Specifics such as penalties, counseling, preventive detention and other contemplated provisions should be carefully weighed by the state before a decision is made to include or exclude such clauses. The sample provision reads as follows:

> A person commits the offense of stalking if, with the intent to harass, alarm, or annoy, or if the person knew or should have known of the risk thereof, he or she engages in a repeated course of conduct directed at a specific individual or his or her immediate family, that would cause a reasonable person to suffer significant emotional distress, and that individual subsequently suffers significant emotional distress.
>
> Course of conduct is defined as implicit or explicit acts that under the circumstances can be interpreted as amounting to a threat, such as, but not limited to: repeated and unwanted attempts at physical, verbal or written contact, or threats or innuendo that physical injury will occur.
>
> Repeated is defined as having occurred on two or more occasions.

VI. Conclusion

"Stalking" is a phenomenon that has only recently become a focus of nationwide attention. In an attempt to tackle the stalking issue, various statutory formulations have been created. Several of these, unfortunately, will probably not adequately protect victims, while others are so inclusive in the behaviors targeted that they will likely face successful constitutional challenge. The serious implications this result poses to victims of stalkers demands that careful consideration be given towards resolving these inconsistencies.

NOTES

1. Michael A. Zona, M.D., Kaushal K. Sharma, M.D., Lt. John Lane, *A Comparative Study of Erotomanic and Obsessional Subjects in a Forensic Sample,* at 7.
2. J. Reid Meloy, Ph.D., *Violent Attachments* (1992).
3. *Id.* at 25 (emphasis added).
4. *Id.* at 189.
5. Dietz, P.E., M.D., M.P.H., Ph.D., Matthews, D.B., M.D., Ph.D., Van Duyne, C., M.A., Martell, D.A., Ph.D., Perry, C.D.H., Ph.D., Stewart, T., M.A., Warren, J., D.S.W., and Crowder, J.D., M.D., *Threatening and Otherwise Inappropriate Letters to Hollywood Celebrities,* 36 JFSCA, No. 1, Jan. 1991.
6. *Id.* at 208 (emphasis added).
7. Maria Puente, Legislators Tackling the Terror of Stalking, *USA Today,* July 21, 1992 at 9A (quoting Dr. Dietz).

8. A Remedial Approach to Harassment, 70 Va.L.Rev. 507, 522–523 (1984).
9. United States v. Kelner, 534 F.2d 1020, 1027 (2nd Cir. 1976), *cert. denied,* Kelner v. United States, 429 U.S. 1022 (1976).
10. State v. Marley, 54 Haw. 450, 460, 509 P.2d 1095, 1103 (1973).
11. Kolender v. Lawson, 461 U.S. 352, 358 (1983).
12. Terry v. Ohio, 392 U.S. 1, 34 (1968).

Study Questions

1. Can utilitarianism (see Appendix B for its definition) support Mill's absolute ban on paternalism against adults and still remain sensitive enough to the changing circumstances and consequences of our actions? Is there any disagreement between libertarianism and Mill's view here?
2. Does Devlin commit the *ad populum* fallacy, the error of thinking that whatever most people in a community believe is for the best really must be for the best?
3. Who won the Hart/Devlin debate? Explain why one of them had the better of the argument overall. Identify specific problems in each of their views. Where should we draw the line or strike the balance between majority rule and minority (and individual) rights?
4. Did the Supreme Court make the morally best ruling in *Bowers* v. *Hardwick?* Explain your answer using moral principles defined in Appendix B.
5. Does Thomson support a right to privacy? If so, why? If not, why not? What is the best definition of privacy? Does Thomson rely on any false analogies? If so, which ones are false? If not, explain why a few of her analogies are sensible comparisons. Is anything between consenting adults morally permissible, as libertarianism insists? Can you think of any counterexamples to libertarianism's sweeping claim here?
6. Is Gavison's understanding of the meaning of privacy an improvement over Thomson's understanding? If so, why? If not, why not? Does Gavison support a legal right to privacy? Does she vindicate the way most of us think and talk about issues of privacy? If so, how? If not, where does she go wrong?
7. What is Morin's answer to the question, "Do existing state statutes provide adequate protection against stalkers?" Do you agree with Morin's answer to this question? If so, why? If not, why not? Further, do you think stalking is so inherently vague conceptually that constitutional protection from stalkers is impossible? What reasons do you have to support your answer?

B Blackmail

The Paradox of Blackmail

Joel Feinberg

Feinberg analyzes what he calls "the paradox of blackmail." Blackmail is illegal and generally viewed as immoral. Yet, paradoxically, the blackmailer apparently threatens to do only what he or she has a right to do in the first place, namely, turn in a wrongdoer. So Feinberg seeks the best explanation for why we should criminalize an act between consenting adults—the blackmailed person's purchase of the blackmailer's silence.

Without closer examination it will seem that blackmail certainly should be a crime, and also that it should be a crime precisely because it severely harms and wrongs its victims. As blackmail is currently defined in our penal codes, however, it is disconcertingly difficult to show that its prohibition satisfies the requirements of the harm principle.[1] It is more clear, at least at first sight, that the criminalization of blackmail does satisfy the exploitation principle[2] and perhaps other forms of legal moralism. In its most egregious instances, blackmail is unfair advantage-taking for great profit. The blackmailer in those cases is an unproductive parasite who sells relief from a danger that would not exist but for his having created it. His opportunistic profiteering may tend to discourage crime and other wrongdoing (or at least to make the wrongdoer more careful) but only by "threatening to capture its fruits for himself" (Block and Gordon 1985, 40). It is an inherent evil, many people would judge, that *he* should make a big gain as a byproduct of someone else's crime or indiscretion, that he should profit unproductively from others' wrongdoing. That his gain is unjust seems clear.

Why is it not equally clear that the party from whom he extracts his gain is wronged as well as adversely affected by his conduct? His choice to pay the blackmailer is considerably less than fully voluntary since it was produced by the blackmailer's coercive threat to disclose information to others that will be at the least severely embarrassing, and at the most damaging to his (the blackmailee's) interests. The question is whether the threats are coercive enough in the circumstances to vitiate the blackmailee's consent, as a threat to kill him for example would be, or whether his consent, even though given under coercion, might yet be voluntary enough to provide the threatener with an exculpating defense. When we compare the blackmailer's threat with threats that do invalidate a victim's consent to money demands, we see one striking difference. The blackmailer threatens only to do what he has an independent legal right to do anyway, namely, exercise his free speech in truthfully communicating information about his victim to interested third parties. The robber, on the other hand, when *he* demands money, threatens to commit a criminal act, namely, to conflict immediate bodily

Reprinted with permission from *Ratio Juris*, Vol. 1 No. 1, March 1988, pp. 83–95.

harm or death (battery or murder) on his victim, something he has neither moral nor legal right to do, and extortionists (other types of extortionists) threaten bodily harm in the future, or harm to other parties, harm to property, or even harm to reputation through *false* accusations, all of which are independently prohibited by the criminal or civil law. The robber and other extortionists, in short, threaten to do what they have no legal right to do, and then demand money for not doing it, while the blackmailer threatens only to do what he has a legal right to do, and then offers to refrain from doing so for a fee.

The complex fact that the blackmailer's threatened act would be legal, and an unconditional threat to perform that act would also be legal, and yet it would be illegal for him to demand money in exchange for *not* doing it is now standardly called "the paradox of blackmail."[3] "The heart of the problem," as James Lindgren sees it, "is that two separate acts, each of which is a moral and legal right, can combine to make a moral and legal wrong." For example, "If I threaten to expose a sexual affair unless I am given a job . . . I have committed blackmail. I have a legal right to expose or threaten to expose the . . . affair, and I have a legal right to seek a job or money, but if I combine these rights, it is blackmail." However, "If a person's ends—seeking a job or money—and his means—threatening to expose—are both otherwise legal," Lindgren asks, "why is it illegal to combine them?" (Lindgren, 1984, 702).

The legal moralist who uses the exploitation principle has a ready answer to Lindgren's question. The whole is equal to more than the sum of its independently innocent parts in these blackmail cases, he may argue, because combining the innocent components in the blackmailer's fashion creates the new element of *wrongful gain*. The "victim," he continues, is not wronged any more than he is by any hard commercial bargain which puts an exorbitant price tag on a much desired service (in this case, the service of silence), and his consent, even though subject to coercive pressure, would normally be voluntary enough to defeat the charge that the blackmailer has wronged him. But the chemistry of the combination of innocent components has produced an unjust gain for the parasitic interloper that the State, so the argument concludes, cannot tolerate. The blackmailer (*A*), by taking money for not doing what he has a perfect right to do otherwise (reveal the truth about *B*), seems to be punished for making an unjust gain off of *B* rather than for wronging *B*.

Thus, the exploitation principle provides a rationale for blackmail laws where the liberal's unsupplemented harm principle finds only a "paradox." If the liberal cannot resolve his paradox by finding a harm principle rationale for blackmail that leaves the criminal law a coherent whole, then either he must grant validity to the exploitation principle, which as a form of legal moralism would be repugnant to his liberalism, or he must abandon the initial assumption of this paper, deeply rooted though it seems to be in common sense, that blackmail should be a crime. The best hope of escaping this dilemma is to begin by making some distinctions. It may well be that once we distinguish the various types of threats and demands, it will turn out that only some types of blackmail are "paradoxical," and that only the nonparadoxical types fit the common sense expectation of criminalization. In that event the liberal might be able to advocate decriminalization of some types of blackmail without embarrassment while offering a consistent liberal rationale for maintaining the prohibition on other types.

We can now distinguish five categories of informational blackmail corresponding to the types of secrets the blackmailer threatens to reveal.

Category 1. Threats to Expose Criminal Wrongdoing

In the first category are threats to reveal to the police (truly) that the blackmailee has committed a crime and/or to present evidence or testimony in support of that allegation. This is a special case of blackmail, critically different from the threat to reveal merely embarrassing truths, for example, in that the blackmailer does not merely have a "right" to do what he threatens to do; he has a *duty* to do it which he would violate if he kept his silence, as he offers to do. Like all his fellow citizens, he has a duty to cooperate with the police in the enforcement of the law, a duty also owed to all the rest of us insofar as we are potential victims of the sorts of crime the blackmailee has committed. No citizen can be allowed to barter away his duties for personal advantage, or even to offer to do so (the offer in this case being very much like an *attempt* at crime, itself punishable).[4] If the blackmailer has a duty to report the crime, he cannot claim that he is merely proposing an ordinary business deal when he offers to be derelict in that duty in exchange for money. The "paradox of blackmail" does not apply to his crime, because he is not simply charging a fee for "not doing what he has a perfect right to do." Rather he proposes not to do what he has a duty to do; he has no "perfect right" not to do his duty. And if the paradox of blackmail does not apply to category 1 blackmail proposals, there is no further difficulty for the liberal defense of their criminal prohibition, for the harm principle provides ample reason for such prohibitions. Category 1 blackmail is a practice that causes public harm. Like contempt of court, bribery of policemen, subornation of jurors, obstruction of justice, and deliberate concealment of evidence, it impedes the efficient operation of the criminal justice system in which we all have a stake. The "harm" incidentally caused to the not-so-innocent "victim"—the money that is periodically extracted from him by extortionate threat—is not the relevant "harm" here. From the public point of view, the category 1 blackmailer benefits his "victim" as much as he harms him, by enabling him to stay free of the police, and their joint agreement is detrimental to the public.

There is admittedly a problem about the precise status of the duty to report crimes to the police. In the Anglo-American system, it is not clear that this duty is enforced by the criminal law. There was a common law crime called "misprision of felony" committed by a person who knows of the commission of a crime and does not disclose it to the proper authorities. Perkins reports a "tendency for misprision of felony to be ignored at the present time," (Perkins, 1957, 563) and even where misprision of felony is still found in American statutes, according to Perkins, "the words 'whoever . . . conceals' have been held to require something more than a negative failure to report the felony, some affirmative act of concealment."[5] Another common law crime that might be thought to impose a legal duty to report crimes (and not merely not to "conceal" them) was called "compounding crime," and is committed by anyone who accepts money under an agreement not to "prosecute," i.e., bring charges against a person he knows to have committed a crime. Compounding was usually the settling out of court of a claim that was really the state's to make, since it involved criminal not merely civil violations. As such, it was not clear whether it could be committed by third parties, but modern statutes now make clear that a crime can be compounded by someone other than its victim.[6] If, however, there is no prior legal duty to report a crime as such, then the category 1 blackmailer who compounds another's crime by accepting money for not reporting it, might invoke the paradox of blackmail, and complain that he is merely taking payment for what he has a legal right to do (no legal duty not to do), namely, refrain from reporting a crime.

Partly because of such difficulties, two recent writers of libertarian persuasion, Walter Block and David Gordon, have argued that there is no legal duty, in any sense, to report a crime, and that therefore the law creates an incoherence by criminalizing the blackmailer-compounder. They go too far, however, when they argue not only that the law does not (always) in fact impose duties to report crimes, but that morally speaking the law *cannot* impose such duties: "Just as the law cannot properly compel the individual to be a good samaritan, so can it not compel him to acquaint the legal authorities with the facts concerning crimes he knows to have taken place. Turning in the criminal may be an act over and above the call of duty, but it is not an act of duty itself" (Block and Gordon, 1985, 40). In response I should point out, first of all, that even if a given penal code imposes no duty to reveal criminals to the authorities, or no duty to be a good samaritan even when there is no unreasonable risk in being one, it does not follow that there is some inherent difficulty in principle with such provisions. Several American states and most continental European nations have "bad samaritan" criminal statutes, and misprision statutes are far from unknown. Moreover, the argument that there is something wrong or morally illegitimate in such statutes, that we *ought* not to have legal duties to rescue or to inform on felons, has not been persuasively made.[7] Very likely, in fact, misprision of felony statutes have passed into desuetude, not because of moral misgivings, but because of practical difficulties in enforcement, especially fear of underworld revenge.

In any event, even if there is no *legal* duty to reveal criminals in the form of criminal statutes that require it or grounds for civil liability for failing to do it, it remains deeply misleading to say that the category 1 blackmailer is merely taking payment for not doing what he has a right not to do anyway. For many democratic political systems themselves, defined not only by civil and penal codes, but by constitutional documents and traditions, clearly impose a *civic duty,* a duty of citizenship, to cooperate with law enforcement, even when that duty is not specifically enforced by the criminal or civil law. It is to assert a false proposition in most democracies to say that a citizen is morally free, with a "perfect right" to cooperate with law enforcement or not, as he sees fit, unless under direct threat of legal punishment. The requirement to report criminals is a civic duty presupposed by our legal system and implicitly recognized by it in many ways.

Category 2. Threats to Reveal that the Victim Has Engaged in, and Continues to Engage in, Perfectly Legal but Devious Trickery or Underhanded Dealing

Blackmail threats in this second category concern truly discreditable behavior, the exposure of which to the general public would quite justly damage the "victim's" reputation. The blackmailee may be a wily womanizer whose reputation is undeservedly good. If he is exposed to the group that contains possible future victims of his harmful but legally innocent exploitation, then his mischief will be more difficult to produce. Or the blackmailee may be a merchant whose underhandedness falls short of outright fraud (which of course is illegal) but misleads unwary customers into purchasing inferior products for inflated prices, or a doctor who strings patients along, collecting high fees for unnecessary office calls, before confessing his inability to provide the assistance the patients seek. The state provides no remedy for these wrongs, relying instead on the marketplace to set things straight. A bad reputation, after all, is bad for business.

Morally speaking, a person who is aware of someone's continuing practice of underhanded dealing may very well have not only the right but a duty of public spiritedness to warn others. Such a duty would be analogous to the civic duty imposed by the political system to report criminals to the police, except that it is *merely* moral, having no quasi-official status or tacit recognition by the law. At the very least, people have the legal *right* to expose noncriminal trickery, the option to expose or not as they please. A sufficient reason for not imposing a legal *duty* to do so, is that it is practically difficult to draw the line between the public-spirited exposer and the officious intermeddler. What seems clear, in any event, is that there are cases in which the exposure of perfectly legal wrongdoing would be a socially useful thing and something that ought to be done. If the personal risks in such a case are minimal, then the would-be blackmailer is blameworthy for taking money not to do it.

Despite the lack of moral justification for category 2 blackmail, the attempt to justify its criminalization stumbles over the paradox of blackmail. The difference between category 2 and category 1 in this respect is slight but critical. The legal system tacitly recognizes a civic duty to report criminals even when, for practical reasons, it does not threaten liability for not doing so, whereas the duty to report legally innocent wrongdoing is one that it does not officially endorse. It does, on the contrary, recognize a legal right (liberty) to expose legal trickery or not as one sees fit, provided of course, that the accusations are true. Therefore, to criminalize category 2 blackmail would indeed be to prohibit the extraction of money by a threat to do what it would be legally permissible to do, namely speak the truth about a wrongdoer. To preserve the coherence of a criminal code, *either* the threatened disclosure should be made independently illegal, that is, illegal in its own right quite antecedent to any blackmail threat, in which case the threat, to make that disclosure unless one is paid hush money could be unparadoxically prohibited, *or* the disclosure as such should continue to be independently permissible (a valid exercise of free speech), in which case blackmail could be unparadoxically permitted. In other words, if we make disclosure independently illegal then we can ban blackmail because it uses the threat to do something illegal to extract a gain, and if we legalize the disclosure as such, then we must legalize blackmail too since it only uses a threat to do what is legally permitted, in order to extract a gain. We cannot on liberal grounds independently criminalize category 2 disclosures since they do not wrongfully harm anyone, and indeed may indirectly work to prevent wrongful harms by putting potential victims on warning. Therefore, we cannot on liberal grounds punish category 2 blackmail either.

Category 3. Threats to Expose Some Innocent Characteristic or Activity That Is Not Objectively Discreditable but Would in Fact Damage the Victim's Reputation in Some Benighted Group If It Were Disclosed

In this third category are various threats to expose matters that the victim should not feel ashamed of—an adult's bed-wetting problem, a southern white's black grandmother, a sensitive or troubled person's continuing psychoanalysis, an ambitious person's humble or "illegitimate" origins, an otherwise respectable person's homosexual orientation. (Some instances of marital infidelity might belong in this category also, but because it is usually impossible for an outsider to know which, moral judgment is hazardous.) The number of traits and activities that could be the basis for category 3 threats was much larger in Victorian times and was itself a symptom, I have suggested, of a cultural disorder—the grotesque overvaluation of respectability (see Hepworth, 1975, esp. chap. 4).

Neither third parties nor the public in general need to be warned about category 3 activities for their own protection. Otherwise an informed person might have a duty, morally speaking, to expose them. But exposure would only embarrass or hurt them without "protecting" anyone else. There is then no plausible ground for positing a moral duty to disclose the embarrassing information. In fact there is good reason for affirming a moral duty *not* to make the disclosures, which is to say that one does not have a moral right to do so. Thus it would appear, morally speaking at least, that one may not in this way extract money by threatening to do what one has no right to do.

Legally speaking, however, the situation is less clear, and the paradox of blackmail looms menacingly again. A person has no independent duty imposed by the criminal law either to disclose information or not to disclose information of the category 3 kind. One is therefore at liberty, so far as the criminal law is concerned, to disclose or not disclose as one sees fit, and no doubt that is as it should be. Nor it is plausible, in these cases, to posit an implicit "duty as a citizen" either to disclose or not to disclose, analogous to the civic duty to report crime. If there is any duty of citizens at all, then, in respect to these private matters, it must find its source in the private law. After all, the law of torts too can be said to impose duties, though it does not enforce them with criminal sanctions. The law of negligence, for example, imposes a duty—a *legal* duty—of care, and sanctions it by the prospect of civil liability. One does not have "a perfect legal right" to be negligent, or defamatory, or a nuisance. If there is a similar duty to be found in the law of torts to refrain from revealing the intimate secrets of category 3—even secrets that are not truly discreditable—then category 3 blackmail would involve forcing money payments from a victim by threatening to do something one has no legal right to do, and its criminalization would not be paradoxical. Such a duty will not be found in the civil law of defamation because a defamatory statement must be *false* in order to be actionable, and category 3 revelations are perfectly truthful. The most plausible place to look for such a duty, I think, is in the law of tortious *privacy* invasions.

In the United States "Violation of privacy" is a general term for at least four quite distinct torts (Keeton et al., 1984, 581), but the one that is clearly most relevant to our purposes is the public disclosure of private information about the plaintiff, "even though it is true and no action would lie for defamation" (Keeton et al., 1984, 856). The disclosure must be a public disclosure and not merely a private one,[8] and that would leave private disclosures to the spouse of an adulterer within the protection of the law, but the damage of the *clearly* third category revelations does consist of the facts getting on to a more general audience. Another requirement of our present law is that the public not have "a legitimate interest in having the information made available" (Keeton et al., 1984, 857), a requirement that would serve to mark off category 3 from category 2 disclosures. A third requirement is that the disclosed true information "would be highly offensive and objectionable to a reasonable person of ordinary sensibilities" (Keeton et al., 1984, 857). This obscure phrase, I think, refers to a hypothetical plaintiff who is not hypersensitive to what others may know and think of him, and whose upset state of mind on learning of his "exposure" is quite understandable. He may find the information highly embarrassing in its own right or he may understandably fear that it will damage his standing in some group with power over him, even though it is not truly discreditable (i.e., not such that a reasonable person would think less of him for it).

We can now begin to unravel the paradox of blackmail as applied to category 3 threats. If a certain factual disclosure would lead to civil liability for privacy invasion, then there is a clear sense in which that disclosure is not permitted by law even though it is not subject to criminal sanction.[9] (That the criminal law is silent about some kind of conduct does not imply that it gives a person some sort of tacit license to do what is elsewhere in the law forbidden.) The category 3 threats in large part *are* threats to invade privacy and therefore to do something prohibited by law. The category 3 blackmailer's threat in support of a money demand is often, therefore, a threat to do something he has no legal right to do, which is to say that he threatens to do what he has a legal duty *not* to do. There is therefore no "paradoxical" incoherence in a law that criminally prohibits category 3 blackmail.

An advocate of decriminalization, however, might still not be satisfied. He may admit that complete legal permissiveness toward category 3 blackmail would not coherently fit in a legal system that allowed civil damages for privacy invasions. But he may point out that there is a middle way between total permissiveness and criminalization, namely, providing a tort remedy for the blackmail itself. He may be driven to this ingenious proposal by a lurking suspicion that it is not yet *fully* coherent to *criminally prohibit* the support of money demands by threats to do what is *criminally permitted.* It would make better sense, he insists to "civilly prohibit" the supporting of money demands by threats to do what is civilly prohibited.

I agree that this would be a tidier, more symmetrical solution, although I don't agree that it would be more coherent. Let us pause for a moment to imagine how it might work. The blackmail victim would already have the counterthreat of a privacy suit with which to confront his blackmailer, so an additional cause of action, the projected civil blackmail suit, would be redundant except perhaps for establishing aggravation for punitive damages. The blackmailer *A* tells *B:* "I will publicly reveal *X* unless you pay me $10,000." *B* then can reply: "I welcome the opportunity to keep *X* secret by making this payment, but I would much prefer to have both my privacy and my money. Therefore I refuse to pay you, and I threaten you, in turn, that if you reveal *X* I will sue *you* for $10,000 for invading my privacy, and furthermore I will cite evidence of this blackmail attempt and claim $100,000 more in punitive damages." One thing *B* is unlikely to do is to threaten an immediate suit for damages for an independent blackmail tort even before there is any release of information, since that would lead to an unnecessary revelation of his secret during the trial. The privacy suit, on the other hand, would take place only after the beans have been spilled anyway. An independent tort of blackmail shares this problem with the remedy of criminal prosecution for blackmail. The victim would have to initiate the legal action in both cases, and he might be deterred by fear that his secret will become public during the proceedings. The civil action would have the advantage in some instances, at least, of providing him with ample pecuniary compensation for his embarrassment, although his persecutor may have inadequate funds for this purpose.

Whatever we decide about the desirability of allowing this new civil action, however, there is no real reason why we should not keep the blackmail threat a crime, since in theory the victim's rights could be protected by either or both sanctions. When a blackmailer backs up a money demand with a threat to do something that is legally prohibited (if only by tort law) his conduct is legally recognizable as extortive, that is, as a coercive use of a threat to do something that one has no legal right to do, as a way of forcing a victim to relinquish his property. It is therefore an attempt at *theft* (by extortion), and there is no "paradox" in treating it as a crime.

Category 4. Threats to Expose Past Mistakes of a Currently Reformed Person

The more common threats in this category include threats to expose past membership in a radical political party, or to reveal that a person is an ex-convict, or to disclose that as a teenager she bore a child out of wedlock and gave it up for adoption. These examples are much like those in category 3 in an important respect. The revelations can not only embarrass a person but also damage her reputation in certain benighted circles in a way that could be harmful to her interests. Given that the person has outgrown her youthful errors and is now genuinely reformed, she does not deserve to have her past held against her; she has paid her bill and her slate is clean. Still, the threat of exposure may force her to pay a blackmailer for his silence. The blackmailer in these cases can truthfully argue that he threatens nothing illegal. He does seem to have a legal right to make the disclosures if he chooses. He would certainly not incur criminal liability if he did. Nor would he incur civil liability for defamation since what he says is true. Nor would a civil action for invasion of privacy lie since what he reports is part of the public record (you could look it up), and so, in a relevant sense, consists of public rather than private facts.

It is open to the liberal, however, to argue that there *ought* to be a civil remedy for such moral wrongs, so that he can argue for criminalization of category 4 blackmail without being thwarted by the paradox of blackmail. To avoid that paradox a person must argue that either category 4 blackmail should be legalized (since the blackmailer threatens to do only what it is legal to do), or else the threatened disclosures should be made independently contrary to law, in this case to the law of torts. The liberal who advocates preservation of the criminal status of category 4 blackmail then has strong motive to make a case, if he can, for imposing an independent duty through tort law to refrain from all purely malicious disclosures (revelations serving no proper public purpose).

The introduction of such a tort is by no means a new idea. Various commentators, over the years, have considered modifying the truth defense to defamation charges in such a way as to protect reformed persons, among others, from maliciously motivated harmful revelations. In an earlier article I favorably summarized the case for a new "malicious truth" remedy with rather more optimism than was justified by subsequent events:

> Most of the historical rationales for the truth defense worked out in the courts and in legal treatises will not stand scrutiny. They all founder, I think, on the following kind of case. A New York girl supports her drug addiction by working as a prostitute in a seedy environment of crime and corruption. After a brief jail sentence, she decides to reform, and travels to the far west to begin her life anew. She marries a respectable young man, becomes a leader in civic and church affairs, and raises a large and happy family. Then twenty years after her arrival in town, her neurotically jealous neighbor learns of her past, and publishes a lurid but accurate account of it for the eyes of the whole community. As a consequence, her "friends" and associates snub her; she is asked to resign her post as church leader; gossipmongers prattle ceaselessly about her; and obscene inscriptions appear on her property and in her mail. She cannot sue her neighbor for defamation since the defamatory report is wholly true. She has been wronged, but she has no legal remedy. . . . (Feinberg, 1986, 220)

With this kind of case in mind, I concluded that

> when the personal interest in reputation outweighs the dilute public interest in truth (and there is no doubt that this is sometimes the case) then it must be protected even at some cost to our general knowledge of the truth. . . . A growing number of American states have now modified the truth defense so that it applies only when the defamatory statement has been published with good motives, or is necessary for some reasonable public purpose, or (in some cases) both. The change is welcome. (Feinberg, 1986b, 221)

The welcome I expressed in this passage was premature, and for practical reasons the changes I described might be difficult to implement, but from the moral point of view, I still think they would be desirable. Were they made, the category 4 blackmailer could no longer say in his own defense that he is threatening to do only what he has a perfect legal right to do, since the new laws would impose a legal duty on him, civilly sanctioned, to refrain from malicious or spiteful revelations. And if his threatened revelation has as its sole purpose to extract money from the reluctant victim, that alone would argue for its malice, and if the harmful truths were actually revealed because of the victim's refusal to pay, that would argue quite conclusively for their spitefulness.

Category 5. Threats in Any of the Other Categories to Make Accusations that Are Known to Be False

It would surely be criminal blackmail without paradox for *A* to demand money from *B* under threat of denouncing him as a Communist, and making the threat credible by showing or implying the existence of fabricated and perjured evidence. Lest this seems farfetched, the reader should consult the history of blackmail prosecutions, from which he may learn that category 5 is prominently represented in the record and may even be the most common species.

In the Victorian period, the heyday of blackmail, one of the most common forms of the crime involved the *false* accusation of "sodomitical practice" supported by trumped-up evidence and fraudulent manipulation. In a typical case the blackmailers hired a teenage boy to accost a well-dressed man (a hairdresser by trade) as he was emerging from a public lavatory and to request money from him. Two men then came up and caught the hairdresser by the arm. They posed as plainclothes policemen and listened while the well-coached youth recited his accusation. On the way to the police station the phoney policemen offered to "settle" with the hairdresser (for a price), threatening that things would go very badly for him otherwise (see Hepworth, 1975, 37).

This typical blackmail scheme involved more than the threat to publish information. It also had elements of perjury, fraud, and impersonation of police officers. It was in fact an elaborate confidence swindle. Not a trace of "paradox" remains in cases of this sort. But even without the more egregious manipulation involved in the example, category 5 blackmail is unproblematic and unparadoxical. A person has no legal right to falsely accuse another of a crime. To do so is itself in some circumstances to commit a crime. Nor is there a legal right to publish false and defamatory allegations of disreputable conduct, or of disreputable characteristics, no right at least that will protect one from civil liability. It follows that the criminalization of category 5 blackmail does not mean that one is prohibited from taking money by threatening to do what the law considers an innocent exercise of free speech. Hence, there is no paradox in the prohibition, and since the prohibited conduct is of a kind that violates the rights and sets back the interests of its victims, its criminal prohibition is, on liberal grounds, morally legitimate.

In summary, I have argued that only category 2 blackmail involving threats to warn the public of legally innocent underhanded dealing need be legalized in order to preserve the overall coherence of a legal system. Coherence could be preserved otherwise only by the independent criminalization of disclosures of the category 2 type, or by making such disclosures civilly actionable, and the harm principle would not warrant that. The other four categories, however, are instances of attempts to force payments by threats that are legally extortive since they threaten to do what is contrary either to the criminal law or to the civil law, or to what *ought* to be forbidden by a legal rule of one kind or another, or would be forbidden but for theoretically irrelevant practical difficulties. Admittedly, the five categories are not finely drawn, and there are many cases that will be hard to classify without further refinements. So the fivefold classification is not a practical model for legislative draftsmanship, but it does reveal, in a rough way, how in principle one can resolve the paradox of blackmail without being committed either to the exploitation principle and its legitimization of the punishment of wrongful gain as such, or to the complete decriminalization of informational blackmail.

REFERENCES

Block, Walter, and David Gordon. 1985. Blackmail, Extortion, and Free Speech: A Reply to Posner, Epstein, Nozick, and Lindgren. *Loyola of Los Angeles Law Review* 19.

Feinberg, Joel. 1984. *Harm to Others*. New York: Oxford University Press.

———. 1986a. Harm to Others: A Rejoinder. *Criminal Justice Ethics* 5.

———. 1986b. Limits to the Freedom of Opinion. In *Philosophy of Law*. 3rd ed. Ed. Joel Feinberg and H. Gross. Belmont, Cal.: Wadsworth.

Hepworth, Mike. 1975. *Blackmail: Publicity and Secrecy in Everyday Life*. London: Routledge & Kegan Paul.

Keeton, W. Page, Dan B. Dobbs, Robert E. Keeton, and David G. Owen, eds. 1984. *Prosser and Keeton on the Law of Torts*. 5th ed. St. Paul, Minn.: West Publishing Co.
Lindgren James. 1984. Unraveling the Paradox of Blackmail. *Columbia Law Review* 84.
Perkins, Rollin M. 1957. *Criminal Law*. Brooklyn: The Foundation Press.
Williams, Glanville. 1954. Blackmail. *The Criminal Law Review* 1: 79–92, 162–172., 240–46.

NOTES

1. I define the harm principle as the principle that it is always a good reason in support of penal legislation that it will prevent harm (setback to interest plus violation of rights) to people other than the actor (the one prohibited from acting). "Liberalism" is sometimes defined as the view that the harm principle is the only valid liberty-limiting principle.
2. I define the exploitation principle as the principle that it is always a good reason in support of penal legislation that it will prevent wrongful (unjust) gain even when there is no corresponding wrongful loss (harm).
3. The phrase was originally coined by Glanville Williams, 1954. The paradox, according to Williams, is that "two things that taken separately are moral and legal whites together make a moral and legal black" (Williams, 1954, 163).
4. Lord Mansfield, speaking of the similar crime of bribery, declared: "Whatever is a crime to take is a crime to give. They are reciprocal. And the attempt is a crime: it is complete on the side who offers it." Rex v. Vaughan, 4 Burr. 2494, 2500, 98 Eng. Rep. 308, 311, 1769.
5. Perkins, 1957, 563n cites Neal v. United States, 102F. 2d 643 (8th Cir. 1939).
6. Cf. West's Ann. Cal. Pen. Code, 153: "Every person who having knowledge of the actual commission of a crime, takes money . . . upon any agreement to abstain from prosecution thereof, or withhold any evidence of. . . ."
7. Indeed, I have argued emphatically on liberal grounds that bad samaritan statutes are morally legitimate. See Feinberg, 1984, chap 4.
8. Santiesteban v. Goodyear Tire and Rubber Co., 5th Cir., 1962, 306 F. 2d 9.
9. To those readers who think it is incorrect to speak of tort law as "not permitting," "prohibiting," "requiring," and the like, I can only repeat what I have written elsewhere: Our civil law does not [characteristically] tell us that we *may* inflict harmful or offensive bodily contacts on our neighbor, falsely defame him, eavesdrop on him, or collide into his vehicle, provided only that we are willing to pay just compensation to him afterwards. I think it is closer to the truth to say that the law of torts, no less than the criminal law, *prohibits* such harmful and annoying behavior. After all, we do speak of "civil *sanctions,*" as well as criminal ones, for enforcing legal requirements. And the law of torts holds us to certain *standards,* even—in the case of inadvertent torts—to standards of due care. All legal commentators speak of the law of torts as imposing *duties* on citizens and cite the defendant's "breach of duty" to the plaintiff as one of the conditions of civil liability. Moreover, the traditional tort procedure issues judgments of *fault,* and requires determination of which party was to *blame* for a harm. The damages paid by the defendant to the plaintiff are not just the price he pays for an already consumed benefit . . . it is thought also to be a *penalty* paid by a *law* violator, even though paid to the victim of his wrongdoing rather than to an independent authority representing the state. . . . (Feinberg, 1986a, 20).

Liberalism and the Paradox of Blackmail

MICHAEL J. GORR

Gorr argues that the key to resolving the paradox of blackmail is to determine why blackmailers are legally permitted to do what they threaten. He tries to establish both that (1) there are *practical* reasons why such acts should be legally optional and (2) such practical considerations do not pose an obstacle to the criminalization of the corresponding blackmail proposals. Hence the prohibition of blackmail is not incompatible with the principles of a liberal society.

Earlier versions of this article were read before philosophy colloquia at Illinois State University and

Blackmail is usually regarded as a particularly sleazy business. As legal theorists have long been aware, however, this consensus as to its moral status does not seem enough to explain why blackmail has also been made a *criminal* offense (and a quite serious one at that).[1] For in sharp contrast to crimes such as robbery, it is generally the case that what the blackmailer threatens to *do* if her demands are not met is something that it is perfectly legal for her to do (e.g., inform your spouse that you have been having an affair or turn you over to the IRS for failing to disclose all of your taxable income). But since it is also the case that the blackmailer is legally free to *refrain* from performing the threatened act, it is unclear why it should be wrong for her to propose to make this refraining conditional upon receiving a consideration of some sort from the person whose interests are most at stake. If, to deal with this problem, one argues that blackmail ought to be outlawed not because it constitutes a wrong to the victim but only because it involves an *undeserved gain* for the blackmailer, then it becomes an open question whether its proscription is compatible with the principles of a liberal political order, at least if we follow Joel Feinberg in defining liberalism as "the view that the harm and offense principles, duly clarified and qualified, exhaust the class of morally relevant reasons for criminal prohibitions."[2]

I believe there are at least two fundamental reasons why what has become known as the "paradox of blackmail" has seemed so intractable. First, there has sometimes been a failure to appreciate fully the important ways in which blackmail proposals can differ from one another.[3] Recognition of such differences, I shall argue, is crucial to providing a full and comprehensive account of why blackmail warrants criminalization. The explanation of why it is wrong to blackmail someone by threatening to reveal his homosexuality, for example, will be shown to differ significantly from the explanation of why it is wrong to blackmail someone by threatening to reveal that he is embezzling money from his employer. Second, and more important, most theorists have also tended to suppose that there is nothing especially problematic about the fact that we permit blackmailers to *do* what they threaten, and that all that really needs explaining is how, in light of this, it could ever make sense to prohibit the threats themselves. My contention, however, is that this is precisely the wrong way to view the matter and that the key to resolving the paradox of blackmail (and to meeting some of the other important objections to its continued criminalization) is to determine just *why* blackmailers are given the liberty to do the acts that they threaten. What I shall try to show is (1) that, in general, we would not make such acts legally optional were it not for practical considerations having to do primarily with the costs and difficulties of enforcement and (2) that such considerations fail to pose a similar obstacle to the criminalization of the corresponding blackmail proposals. In the process I shall try to make clear why I believe the success of this strategy demonstrates that liberals need have no qualms about supporting the continued prohibition of blackmail.

I. The Paradox of Blackmail

A typical blackmail proposal is a proposition that can be expressed in the following form:

I will refrain from bringing about (aversive) consequence *C* if and only if you do act *A*.[4]

Such a proposition is logically equivalent to the conjunction of the following *conditional offer*[5] and *conditional threat:*

If you do act *A*, then I will refrain from bringing about consequence *C* and

If you fail to do act *A*, then I will bring about consequence *C*.

In many cases (though not in all, as we shall see), the propriety or impropriety of the proposal as a whole depends primarily on the moral status of the threat component. The content of such threats can vary considerably; according to a widely used legal encyclopedia,

> a person is guilty of blackmail who either verbally, or by any letter or writing or any written

> or printed communication, demands of any person, with menaces of personal injury, any chattel, money, or other valuable security; or who accuses or threatens to accuse, or knowingly sends or delivers any letter or writing or any written or printed communication accusing or threatening to accuse, any person of any crime punishable by law, or of any immoral conduct, which if true, would tend to degrade and disgrace such person, or in any way to subject him to the ridicule or contempt of society; or who threatens injury to the person or property of anyone, with intent to extort or gain from such person any chattel, money, or valuable security, or any pecuniary advantage whatsoever, or with any intent to compel the person threatened to do any act against his will.[6]

As this passage suggests, statutes often fail to draw any clear distinction between blackmail and extortion, though there is some informal precedent (which I shall follow here) for confining the latter term to conditional threats to do unjustified physical harm to person or property and the former to conditional threats to *disclose information* that would be damaging in some way to the victim's reputation. The criminalization of extortion (so understood) would seem relatively unproblematic. If it is wrong for me to harm you or your property, then it is generally[7] wrong for me to seek advantage by threatening such harm.[8] In this article I shall therefore consider only cases in which advantage is sought by means of blackmail in the narrower sense, that is, by means of threats to make disclosures that would damage another person's reputation.

Threats of the sort with which we are concerned can differ with respect to (1) *how* the damaging information was acquired by the blackmailer, (2) the *nature* of that information, and (3) *what* the blackmailer demands in return for his silence. Each of these factors is surely relevant to the question of the moral status of the corresponding blackmail proposal, which is in turn relevant to the question of what its legal status should be. Furthermore, as will become clear as we proceed, the moral status of a blackmail proposal will be a function of both the moral status of the blackmailer's unilateral disclosure of the information in question and the moral status of whatever activity of the victim that serves as the basis for the blackmail.

Let us then consider some of the different forms a blackmail proposal can take. If the blackmailer has learned what he knows in an illicit way (e.g., by a prior violation of the victim's right to privacy),[9] then he would ordinarily lack any right to communicate that knowledge to anyone else.[10] Hence there could hardly be any question of his having a right to threaten to use it to the detriment of his victim. Even if the blackmailer comes by the information innocently, there may be some additional characteristic of the way it was acquired that would support a legal prohibition on its disclosure. For example, he may have been made privy to the information only because he agreed to keep it confidential. Again, so long as the communication itself is illegitimate, there is no paradox in forbidding the corresponding blackmail proposal. The morally problematic cases, then, are ones in which the information is innocently acquired and where its disclosure would not breach any prior valid agreements.

There are also important differences with respect to the nature of the damaging information that the blackmailer threatens to disclose. First, there is the question of whether or not the alleged information is true. If what the blackmailer proposes is to make a *false* claim about the victim, then she is threatening to do what would ordinarily make her civilly liable for defamation. But, as Feinberg has pointed out, there is nothing obviously incoherent or otherwise inappropriate about attaching criminal sanctions to a threat to perform a tort.[11] Assuming, then, that we are confining our attention to threats to disclose some truth about the victim, there is a further question about the content of the damaging information. Feinberg claims that there are four principal categories to consider: threats to reveal that the victim (1) has committed a crime, (2) has participated in legal but "underhanded" practices, (3) has engaged in a perfectly innocent activity that, nevertheless, would discredit him in the eyes of some "benighted" group, or (4) has in the past committed some serious indiscretion even though he is now completely reformed.[12] Feinberg goes on to argue that a blackmail statute is paradoxical only with respect to category 2 cases (to which we will return shortly). Concerning the others, he maintains both that (1) disclosure (or, in some cases, *non*-disclosure) would generally constitute a violation of some sort of legal requirement, and (2) there is no legal right to threaten to perform an illegal act. For example, a threat to reveal intimate and embarrassing details about a person's sexual proclivities (an instance of category 3 blackmail) would normally be a violation of that person's right to privacy.[13] Since, again, there should be no right to threaten to engage in tortious activity, there is nothing paradoxical about criminalizing the corresponding blackmail proposal. On the other hand, what is objectionable about a category 1 blackmail proposal is not the conditional threat to reveal criminal wrongdoing but the conditional offer *not* to do so in return for money. Feinberg claims that although such offers are generally not forbidden by either the criminal or civil law, they are nevertheless not "perfectly" legal because failure to report a crime would violate "a *civic* duty presupposed by our legal system and implicitly recognized by it."[14] Finally, cases of category 4 blackmail would usually present no problems if we were to recognize a new tort (as Feinberg thinks we should)[15] that would impose a legal duty to refrain from making purely malicious disclosures. Though I shall have more to say about the matter later on, Feinberg's strategy for dissolving the paradox in these cases seems a plausible one and I shall generally assume its correctness in what follows.

The third dimension of a blackmail proposal that needs to be considered is the nature of the blackmailer's demand. Obviously he cannot insist that his victim commit a criminal (or otherwise illegal) act since that would make the blackmailer guilty of criminal coercion (and perhaps inducement as well). But suppose, to go to the opposite extreme, that what the blackmailer demands is that the victim perform some morally or legally *required* act. Eric Mack suggests that this would be unobjectionable: "[I]magine a case in which one party, by legally permissible trickery and underhanded dealing, acquired what another party truly deserves. Wouldn't it be perfectly moral for the morally deserving party to blackmail the first party into transferring that valued good—especially if what was threatened was precisely the revelation of the trickery and underhandedness?"[16] While I suspect such high-minded blackmail is considerably less common than that which is engaged in simply to line one's undeserving pockets, I am willing to concede that there are undoubtedly some cases where it should be permitted.[17]

It seems, therefore, that the criminalization of blackmail remains clearly paradoxical only in cases where the blackmailer (1) obtains her information innocently, (2) is under no special obligation to maintain confidentiality, (3) demands, in return for her silence, that the victim perform an act that is not itself either legally required or legally forbidden, and (4) threatens that, if her demands go unmet, she will perform an act that is not itself either legally required or legally forbidden. The paradigm example of this sort of blackmail is a proposal that fits in Feinberg's category 2, namely, a threat "to reveal that the victim has engaged in, and continues to engage in, perfectly legal but devious trickery or underhanded dealing." Feinberg maintains that in such cases the victim's activity must be "truly discreditable" (otherwise revealing it would be a violation of his right to privacy), not a part of his past that he has since disavowed (otherwise revealing it would constitute "malicious disclosure"), yet not itself illegal (otherwise failing to reveal it would be a violation of one of the blackmailer's civic duties). As examples of the sort of person whose behavior he has in mind, Feinberg lists the following: a "wily womanizer," a "merchant whose underhandedness falls short of outright fraud (which of course is illegal) but misleads unwary customers into purchasing inferior products for inflated prices," and a "doctor who strings patients along, collecting high fees for unnecessary office calls, before confessing his inability to provide the assistance the patients seek."[18] He argues that criminalizing blackmail threats to reveal information of this sort creates an incoherence in the system of criminal law, an incoherence that can be eliminated only by either criminalizing the disclosure itself or permitting the blackmail proposal. Since he thinks that the former alternative is incompatible with the form of liberalism that he supports (on the grounds that such disclosures "do not wrongfully harm anyone and indeed may indirectly work to prevent harms by putting potential victims on warning"),[19] Feinberg reluctantly concludes that we can avoid incoherence only by decriminalizing this form of blackmail.

This, I submit, is a rather astonishing concession. If Feinberg is right, consistent liberals must be willing to permit someone who (say) discovers that a physician has been "misleading" and "stringing along" his patients to pressure that physician into paying money in order to prevent his reprehensible conduct from being brought to the attention of the public (including, of course, potential future victims)! Previously only libertarians even more radical than Robert Nozick and Richard Epstein (both of whom generally *support* prohibiting blackmail in such cases)[20] have been willing to defend such a view. It must be conceded, however, that the argument on which Feinberg presumably relies here is a seductive one. It appears to run something like this:

1. If an act is legal, then attempting to influence someone's behavior by conditionally threatening to perform that act should also be legal.[21]
2. It is legal to reveal that another person is guilty of ongoing trickery or underhanded dealing that is itself legal.[22]
3. Thus, it should be legal to attempt to influence another's behavior by blackmail threats to reveal ongoing trickery or underhanded dealing that is itself legal.

In the next section I shall try to show that the plausibility of the first premise is considerably diminished once we make clear just *why* it is sometimes proper to tolerate instances of genuine trickery and underhanded dealing. In the process I shall call into question Feinberg's strong and rather conservative assumption that liberals can consistently support the criminalization of blackmail only in cases where the threatened disclosure would itself be either legally required or legally forbidden.

II. Resolving the Paradox

The principal strategy that I shall follow here will require identifying the moral relationships that obtain between the three possible actions that must be considered in the assessment of any blackmail transaction: (1) the act of the victim that serves to motivate the blackmail, (2) the blackmailer's disclosure of the supposedly damaging information that the victim has performed that act, and (3) the blackmailer's conditional threat to make such a disclosure unless he is paid not to do so. Consider first the status the victim's act has with respect to the criminal law. There are, of course, only three possibilities: either it will be *forbidden, required,* or *optional.* Any case in which an act is forbidden by the criminal law (at least where such a prohibition is morally justified) is a case in which, if Feinberg is correct, anyone aware of this has at least a civic duty to disclose this information, in which case there is nothing puzzling about prohibiting the corresponding blackmail proposal. On the other hand, any case in which that act is required by the criminal law is a case in which there would be nothing for which the victim could be blackmailed (except, perhaps, in very odd situations that I think we can safely ignore here). Clearly the cases that are most relevant to the blackmail controversy are those in which the victim's act is what I shall term "c-optional," that is, such that it is neither required nor forbidden by the criminal law.

What about the *moral* status of c-optional acts? Again, there would seem to be three possibilities: the act could be morally forbidden, morally required, or morally optional. We can safely disregard the second of these since it is extremely unlikely that the disclosure that someone had done something he was morally obligated to do could prove sufficiently damaging to his reputation to be of concern.[23] Suppose, then, that the c-optional act were also morally optional. There would then be at least two importantly different possibilities to consider. First, it might be the case that the act is morally optional because there are simply no significant reasons that would support morally prohibiting it and no significant reasons that would support morally requiring it. The disclosure of such morally indifferent actions could discredit the person only in the eyes of the "benighted" (as Feinberg puts it), in which case such a disclosure would usually constitute a violation of his right to privacy, a fact that would again remove any obstacle to the criminalization of the corresponding blackmail proposal. On the other hand, the act might be morally optional because there are good reasons for morally forbidding it and *equally* good reasons for morally permitting (or even requiring) it. I shall assume that blackmail situations involving such actions are sufficiently rare that we may disregard them. If blackmail laws are ever problematic, then, it will nearly always be in cases where the victim's act is morally wrong.[24]

It is sometimes said that a necessary condition for justifiably criminalizing an act is that it be immoral.[25] Actually I think a stronger claim is warranted: a prerequisite for criminalizability should be *other-regarding* immorality, that is, immorality that involves some sort of significant *harm* (or at least *offense*) to another person. While this is certainly a more controversial thesis, it is plainly implied by the sort of liberalism Feinberg endorses. Hence we may conclude that the most important cases in which there is likely to be a serious question about the legal permissibility of blackmail are those in which the act that would motivate the blackmail (1) is morally wrong, (2) involves some significant harm to another person, and (3) is (justifiably) c-optional.

But how are cases of this sort possible? If the victim's act is an immoral one that harms another person, that fact would by itself be a reason for criminalizing it. Where acts of this sort (rightly) qualify as c-optional, therefore, there must be some countervailing reason for *not* criminalizing them. But what could this be? One obvious possibility is that an immoral, harm-causing act may be tolerated by the criminal law solely for pragmatic reasons having to do with the dangers of abuse and the difficulty and costs of enforcement. For example, laws against a certain kind of wrongful activity might be inadvisable because they would be difficult to implement without unacceptable intrusions on personal privacy.[26] Alternatively, effective enforcement of a given statute might be possible only by making demands on the criminal justice system that would significantly compromise its ability to deal with more serious offenses. In at least some cases of this sort it is plausible to suppose that the reasons for criminalizing the activities in question are outweighed by the reasons for not doing so.

But if a particular activity neither is nor should be a criminal offense, it is difficult to see what purpose would be served by legally requiring knowledgeable persons to report its occurrence. What, after all, could the authorities legitimately *do* with such information that would compensate for the disadvantages of attempting to enforce legal sanctions for concealing it? Even if all of this is granted, however, the crucial point is that it does not follow that there are grounds for drawing a similar conclusion with respect to the sort of blackmail proposals that would be made possible by the knowledge of such activities. To see this, consider two of Feinberg's examples of category 2 blackmail: the doctor who strings along his patients and the businessman who misleads his customers. Surely these are both activities that would warrant criminalization were it not for purely practical difficulties concerning enforcement costs and the like. Even if we concede that similar practical considerations would justify a decision not to criminalize the failure of a third party to report such activities, there is no reason to suppose that such considerations would also apply in the case of the corresponding blackmail proposals. For one thing, the effort needed to enforce statutes outlawing all forms of minor immorality would surely be vastly greater than what would be required to outlaw the comparatively few blackmail proposals that are likely to arise out of another person's knowledge of such immorality. In addition, there is a special reason for wanting to prevent blackmail: it involves an attempt by the blackmailer to acquire significant *resources* belonging to his victim. While the latter may well deserve retribution of some sort, his debt is to those he has wronged, not to the blackmailer. If my argument thus far has been correct, it follows that to permit blackmailers in these category 2 cases to gain at the expense of their victims would be to legitimize a form of *theft*.[27]

The blackmail of an adulterer (Feinberg's third example of category 2 blackmail) requires separate treatment. Let us make the conventional assumption that, leaving aside cases of "open marriage" and the like where there would normally be no basis for a blackmail threat, adultery is a serious wrong to the adulterer's spouse because it involves an act of betrayal or promise-breaking (and often deception as well).[28] If so, it might initially seem that it should be treated on a par with Feinberg's other examples, in which case we would again conclude that, were it not for practical difficulties concerning implementation, it would be a crime to commit such an act and that there would be an attendant obligation on the part of knowing third parties to report its occurrence.

In fact, adultery *is* still a statutory crime in certain jurisdictions (in some of which it even constitutes a felony).[29] These laws are no longer seriously enforced, however, and most respected legal commentators (including the American Law Institute)[30] have urged that they be abolished. The considerations most commonly cited in support of this recommendation include not only practical ones having to do with the allocation of limited resources and the dangers posed by invasive enforcement techniques but, more importantly, the belief that it is inappropriate to criminalize mere "private" immorality.[31] Indeed, I suspect that few liberals would favor criminalizing adultery even if doing so were entirely costless. Assuming their view to be correct, we cannot employ the strategy we used in dealing with Feinberg's other two examples of category 2 blackmail, for this would involve arguing that it is permissible to prohibit blackmailing an adulterer because both adultery and the failure to report it *would be* criminal offenses save for practical difficulties that are not present (at least to the same extent) in the case of the blackmail proposal itself.

A more plausible position is that adultery should be subject only to *civil* sanctions. There are in fact two closely related tort actions based on adultery—criminal[32] conversation and alienation of affections—which, if successful, entitle the plaintiff to "recover substantial damages for the adultery itself. . . . The plaintiff may also recover for all direct and proximate losses occasioned by the tort, including loss of love and consortium, and may recover for any physical pain, mental agony, lacerated feelings, wounded sensibilities, or the like."[33] Since this is not the place for a detailed analysis of the laws concerning adultery, I shall provisionally assume that at least some of these sanctions are morally defensible. If so, the question we must now address concerns what *ought* to be the legal status of the act of reporting the adulterer's activities. Lindgren argues that criminalization would be inappropriate because "society has not reached . . . a consensus about the act of hiding or revealing [such information]."[34] The suggestion, I take it, is either that there is fundamental moral disagreement as to the propriety of disclosure or that most people do not have any strong view one way or another and simply find the whole issue problematic. While one or the other of these assessments may be correct, I am inclined to think the lack of consensus is not primarily a reflection of any *moral* disagreement or uncertainty but, rather, arises out of a recognition that the likely *effects* of such a disclosure will vary considerably from case to case. *Sometimes* telling the cheated spouse would be a way of bringing about the morally best state of affairs, whereas in other cases it would only cause unnecessary misery for everyone concerned.[35] Since in most circumstances it will be difficult if not impossible to determine which of these outcomes is more likely, it seems reasonable to hold, on purely practical grounds, that there could be no justification for criminalizing either the disclosure or the failure to disclose, and that the only plausible solution would be to leave the choice entirely up to the judgment of the person who has the information.

Feinberg apparently endorses a position something like this, as can be seen in the criticism he makes of the following important argument for prohibiting adultery-blackmail:

> Either the cheated spouse has a right to know, the argument begins, or he does not. If he does have such a right then a third-party observer has a duty to transmit the unhappy news to him, and it would be wrong to conceal it in exchange for money. If he does not have such a right, the argument continues, then it would be wrong to violate the adulterer's privacy by revealing her secrets spitefully if the blackmail threat fails. If the blackmailer has a duty to the husband (in this example) to inform him, then he does not have a duty to the wife to keep silent, and vice-versa, so once he undertakes the path of blackmail, he is bound to default a duty to one or the other.[36]

Feinberg complains that the argument fails because there is good reason to think that "the third-party observer may *neither* have a duty to inform the spouse *nor* a duty not to."[37] But what is this reason? Although Feinberg does not elaborate further, presumably what he has in mind are both *practical* considerations of the sort that we identified above and epistemic worries (particularly "doubt . . . about the prior distribution of moral rights and duties among the related parties").[38] But even if these are compelling, it is a *non sequitur* to suppose that they would also block the criminalization of the corresponding blackmail proposals. To see this, consider the following amended version of the argument Feinberg rejects:

> In the absence of practical and epistemic difficulties, there would be a morally conclusive reason for imposing on third-party observers a legal requirement either to report the occurrence of adultery or (depending upon the circumstances) to refrain from reporting its occurrence. It follows that, in the absence of such concerns, there would also be a morally conclusive reason for prohibiting the corresponding blackmail proposals since these would constitute attempts to acquire some of the adulterer's assets either by offering to conceal what ought morally to be disclosed or by threatening to disclose what ought morally to be concealed. But, *ex hypothesi,* although such difficulties do serve to inhibit us from imposing duties with respect to the mere disclosure or nondisclosure of the adulterer's activities, they do not prevent us from imposing duties not to engage in the blackmailing of such persons.

Assuming this reasoning is sound, we have shown, contrary to the first premise of the argument at the end of Section I, that there *can* be grounds for disallowing certain kinds of threats to perform acts that themselves warrant legal tolerance. It follows, therefore, that the so-called paradox of blackmail need not discourage liberals from supporting the prohibition even of those forms of blackmail that fall in category 2. Whether there are any other grounds for permitting blackmail of this sort is a matter we shall take up in the next section.

III. Three Additional Arguments for Legalizing Blackmail

In a recent column discussing the widespread use of boycotts to achieve economic and political objectives, one of the editors of *The New Republic* wrote: "Any boycott is a form of blackmail."[39] Interestingly enough, he did not go on to draw the conclusion that all boycotts should be outlawed but only that there ought to be certain restrictions on their use.[40] But then what distinguishes the sort of "blackmail" involved in boycotting, which most of us agree should generally be permitted, from the other sort, which most of us think should generally be forbidden? Eric Mack has suggested that there is really *no* morally significant difference and that consistency requires that we call either for the banning of boycotts (which, of course, he rejects as absurd) or for the legalization of blackmail (which he favors because he thinks the latter is just another instance of a hard economic transaction).[41]

It might be thought that this argument breaks down because it overlooks at least one significant difference between boycotts and blackmail. What a blackmailer threatens is to *do* something that will *cause* his victim's reputation to suffer. A boycotter, on the other hand, is someone who offers her patronage on the condition (and only on the condition) that the retailer accede to her demands. What she "threatens,"[42] in other words, is only to *refrain* from buying from the retailer at the price *he* prefers. So long, then, as we are willing to accord some significance to the distinction between *causing harm* to someone and *failing to benefit* him, it might seem that there are grounds for making a principled distinction between boycott proposals and blackmail threats.[43]

But this response is inadequate since the most it can demonstrate is that there is a morally significant difference between blackmailing someone and threatening one's *own* participation in a boycott.[44] In the usual and more interesting case, however, what is threatened is the *organization* of a boycott that will involve *other* persons in addition to the threatener (e.g., Martin Luther King's sponsorship of a boycott of the municipal bus system in Montgomery, Alabama, in the late 1950s). Since such organization would involve persuading those others to join the boycott, the corresponding threat is clearly a threat to *cause* harm to the object of the boycott in a way that seems analogous to the way in which the blackmailer threatens to cause harm to his victim.[45]

A better answer would be this. The clearest example of a legally permissible boycott (and, judging by the examples he uses, the sort that Mack is primarily concerned with) is one that involves an appeal to consumers to refrain from purchasing the products or services of a particular employer, company, or industry (e.g., the boycott of California grapes in the early 1970s). Not only is it legal to organize and participate in such a boycott, it is also legal to threaten to do so, even though the economic harm that would thereby be caused seems fully comparable to the harm that would typically be caused by a blackmailer's disclosures. I suggest that what distinguishes the boycotter from the blackmailer is that what the former proposes to do is something that is and *ought to be* legally optional *regardless* of whether or not it would be impractical to prohibit it; namely, attempting to *persuade* other persons to refuse to give their patronage to whoever is the target of the boycott.[46] No doubt the arguments offered by boycott organizers may often be found wanting, but that can hardly serve, at least for liberals, as grounds for restricting their activities. Here we need do no more than invoke the familiar but powerful case for recognizing a robust right to freedom of expression with respect to matters of public interest and concern, a right that could hardly play a similar role in justifying the activities of the typical blackmailer.[47]

A second objection to the criminalization of blackmail is that in some cases such a policy appears to make both the blackmailer *and* his potential victim worse off than they would otherwise be by preventing each of them from choosing his most preferred alternative (for the victim, the blackmailer's silence, and for the blackmailer, his victim's money). One might attempt to answer this objection by pointing out that very similar things could be said about the "transaction" between a traveler and a highwayman who demands, "Your money or your life!" After all, the highwayman prefers getting the traveler's money to killing him, and the traveler prefers surrendering his money to surrendering his life, yet no one finds anything remotely objectionable about prohibiting exchanges of this sort. But such a response fails because there is a fundamental difference between this case and one involving ordinary blackmail—the highwayman, unlike the blackmailer, threatens to do what it would be legally wrong for him to do. His act, therefore, is one of robbery or extortion, not blackmail.

An alternative response would be to argue that permitting blackmail would be objectionable because it would compromise the interests of *third parties*. James Lindgren has defended a view of this sort, which he summarizes as follows: "When a blackmailer threatens to expose damaging but noncriminal behavior unless paid money, he is . . . turning third-party leverage to his own benefit. What makes his conduct blackmail is that he interposes himself parasitically in an actual or potential dispute in which he lacks a sufficiently direct interest. What right has he to make money by settling other people's claims? . . . The blackmailer is negotiating for his own gain with someone else's leverage or bargaining chips."[48] If we suppose that the metaphorical talk about bargaining with someone else's "chips" is just a picturesque way of referring to a violation of that person's legal rights, the principal difficulty with this proposal is that Lindgren never explains just what third-party rights are violated by a category 2 blackmail proposal.[49] In the case where the object of the proposal is a philandering husband threatened with exposure, for example, Lindgren's theory would apparently commit him to holding that the aggrieved spouse has some sort of legal entitlement to be informed about the philanderer's activities (as a corollary, perhaps, of her right to "settle her own claims"). If this were so, then the blackmailer's offering to maintain silence in return for money would be a proposal to act contrary to his obligation to inform her, in which case there would of course be nothing paradoxical in prohibiting such a proposal. But it is simply not true that the spouse is legally entitled to be provided with such information.

A third response would begin by pointing out that the "who's being harmed?" objection is indeterminate until we specify the appropriate baseline with respect to which the two parties to a blackmail transaction are alleged to be worse off if it is prohibited. Clearly the objector is assuming that the blackmailer, if thwarted by the law in her attempt to extract blackmail payments, would go ahead and reveal the damaging information about the other person (either out of maliciousness or for some other reason). In that case, of course, the prohibition on blackmail *would* work to the detriment of both parties. But why isn't it just as legitimate to suppose that the blackmailer has no interest whatever in disclosing what she knows and would threaten to do so only in order to sell her abstention? We could then safely assume that she would do nothing with this information if blackmail were illegal (and if she were unwilling to disregard the threat of sanctions for engaging in such activity). In that case the blackmailer would continue to be worse off than she would be if blackmail were permitted (and her demands were met) but the potential victim would be better off since he would not have to choose between his reputation and his money.

Unfortunately, the only assumption about blackmailers' motives that it would be legitimate to make here is that they are likely to be quite varied. *Some* potential blackmailers would no doubt reveal their information if they were legally prevented from seeking blackmail payments while others would not. Of course, if we suppose that (1) *most* potential blackmailers would choose to reveal their information if their proposals were declined, (2) *most* potential blackmailers would choose not to reveal their information if legally prevented from charging for their silence, and (3) the cost to the average potential blackmailer of being unable to make his proposal would be *less* than the cost to his potential victim of either complying or not complying with it, then we would appear to have fairly strong consequentialist reasons for supporting the prohibition on blackmail. Unfortunately, it is not clear that we are entitled to make any of these assumptions. Furthermore, even if we were so entitled, the case would not be closed unless we also had good reason both to discount the possible benefits of legalizing blackmail (e.g., the creation of an additional deterrent to committing the sort of genuinely discreditable behavior that often serves to motivate blackmail threats)[50] and to embrace consequentialist moral principles (at least across this range of cases). Otherwise those potential blackmail victims who would be harmed by revelations that they could have prevented had blackmail been legal might well have grounds for complaining that their interests were being unjustly sacrificed. While this is hardly as powerful as the original objection, it is better insulated from criticism. Anyone who is not a consequentialist and who favors the continued criminalization of blackmail should find it disturbing.

Fortunately, there are good reasons for dismissing even this more qualified objection. It must be conceded, of course, that some potential victims *will* be made worse off by a ban on blackmail since the information they would have preferred to pay to keep hidden will be revealed instead. I shall argue that what nevertheless justifies prohibiting blackmail in such cases is that either their being made worse off in this way is not morally undeserved or, where it is undeserved, there is no feasible alternative that would produce a lesser amount of injustice.

Cases of category 1 blackmail (threats to expose criminal wrongdoing) would seem to present little difficulty. For the information the potential blackmailer would offer to conceal is information that we *want* revealed and that the blackmailer has a legal duty to reveal. That the "victim" might be made worse off by the prohibition of blackmail is irrelevant for the obvious reason that *crimes* do not ordinarily deserve to be concealed. In cases of category 3 blackmail (threats to reveal perfectly innocent activities that would damage the victim's reputation only among the benighted), the disclosure will normally constitute an actionable invasion of privacy. But the existence of appropriate civil sanctions will provide potential blackmailers with a powerful motive not to make the disclosures that they would like to be able to threaten to make, in which case their potential victims should rarely if ever be disadvantaged by an effective ban on blackmail. Much the same can be said about category 4 blackmail (threats to reveal past mistakes of the currently reformed), unless we credit Feinberg's concern that there may be compelling practical reasons for not introducing a malicious disclosure tort. Although in the latter case we would have to acknowledge that there are likely to be some regrettable instances in which the victim will be disadvantaged by a ban on blackmail, such a ban is still justified since permitting blackmail would almost certainly produce far more injustice. In any event, whatever harm occurs in such cases would seem to be primarily the responsibility of the person who makes the disclosures rather than of those who support and enact laws proscribing blackmail. Finally, category 2 blackmail would seem relatively unproblematic in this respect since, as is the case with category 1 blackmail, disclosure is in fact the morally preferred state of affairs. We did concede, however, that there may be some situations, such as those involving adultery, in which, because disclosure would serve no useful purpose, morality would support nondisclosure. But even if, in some of these cases, the combination of a ban on blackmail and a legal liberty to disclose would work to the disadvantage of (say) an adulterer, it hardly seems likely that *he* is morally entitled to complain. The suffering of his spouse and family, on the other hand, while genuinely undeserved, might have to be chalked up as an unavoidable cost of an unavoidably imperfect legal system. Only if we had reason to believe that present policies would cause more undeserved suffering than would occur if blackmail were permitted would we have a compelling argument for changing them.

Murray Rothbard offers yet a third objection to the criminalization of blackmail contracts: "Suppose that, . . . instead of Smith going to Jones with an offer of silence, Jones had heard of Smith's knowledge and his intent to print it, and went to Smith to offer to purchase the latter's silence? Should *that* contract be illegal? And if so, why?"[51] Of course, as Rothbard is no doubt fully aware, there would normally be nothing legally objectionable about either Jones's making such an offer or Smith's accepting it.[52] His point is that it seems arbitrary to criminalize blackmail proposals but not activities of this sort unless some principled reason can be found for distinguishing between "payment for silence" transactions that are proposed by the prospective payee and those that are proposed by the prospective payer.

Defenders of blackmail law need not hesitate in agreeing that, where we are dealing with a category 3 or category 4 case, the mere *making* of this preemptive offer is morally unproblematic and should not be criminalized. For in that case all Jones is trying to do is defend himself against an immoral action that he believes Smith would perform unless paid not to do so. If there is nothing wrong or criminalizable about paying someone not to harm you unjustifiably, then it is hard to see what could be discreditable about offering to make such a payment. The real objection must be to *Smith's agreeing* to such a proposal and accepting money in return for keeping quiet. If that action is legitimate in this situation, then it does seem strange that it should become illegitimate in situations where Smith is the one to suggest the exchange.

I would argue, however, that there is no real puzzle here. For either Smith intended to blackmail Jones or he did not. If he did intend this, then he is just as culpable as someone who actually made a blackmail threat even though, for obvious reasons, it will normally be impossible to prove the existence of such an intention (and hence impossible to actually impose liability).[53] If he did not intend this, then his case is different from that of the blackmailer and it is not at all clear that he has done anything more reprehensible than take advantage of Jones's mistaken beliefs, which seems at least a less serious offense.

If, on the other hand, Jones is trying to induce Smith to conceal his knowledge of some crime Jones committed (a category 1 case), then Jones is guilty of obstructing justice by tampering with a witness.[54] Should Smith accept such a payment, then he would be guilty of compounding a felony, an alternative form of obstructing justice.[55] Rothbard's objection thus has no force in these situations since, if Smith were the one to make the proposal and Jones the one to accept it, both parties would again be guilty of serious offenses (in Smith's case, blackmail, and in Jones's case, obstructing justice). Where we are dealing with a category 2 concern, however, things are a bit more complicated. Recall Feinberg's example of the sleazy doctor. If I threaten to reveal the doctor's questionable methods unless he pays me off, I am guilty of blackmail. Should the doctor comply and make the payment demanded, he is presumably not legally guilty of anything. On the other hand, should the doctor be the one to suggest paying me for my silence, he would again appear not to be legally guilty of anything. If under such circumstances I go ahead and accept the payment, then there are two possibilities to consider. If I had intended to blackmail the doctor, then, as in the category 3 and category 4 cases, I would be just as blameworthy as I would have been had I actually made the blackmail proposal, and only practical considerations would block the imposition of liability. If I had no such intention, then I have done nothing more than accept money for doing what I have a legal right to do, namely, keep silent about the doctor's practices. In each of these cases, then, Rothbard's objection can be answered since either (1) it does *not* make a significant legal difference whether it is the payer or the payee who proposes a payment for silence transaction, or (2) where it *does* make such a difference, a plausible explanation can be provided as to why this is the case.

IV. Conclusion

I am aware, of course, that I have made a number of important and not wholly uncontroversial assumptions in the course of my argument. In particular, I have supposed the correctness of certain principles concerning defamation, privacy, malicious disclosure, criminal liability, freedom of expression, and civic obligation, not all of which would command universal assent, even among liberals. Those with an exceptionally strong commitment to First Amendment values, for example, might object to the creation of a malicious disclosure tort on the grounds that *any* expression of the truth should be afforded a stronger degree of protection than is allowed under Feinberg's proposal.[56] Others may argue that, even under ideal circumstances in which implementation problems were negligible, a third party's obligation to disclose the activities of an adulterer should be "enforced" only by means of *private,* nonlegal sanctions such as public criticism or the like.[57] Finally, considerations of personal autonomy and well-being might be thought to place serious constraints on the imposition of some of the affirmative obligations that we have discussed in conjunction with these principles.

But even if these complaints have merit (as I suspect most of them do), they fail to undermine the defense of blackmail law that I have undertaken here. For all they show is that there may sometimes be reasons for not requiring disclosure (or nondisclosure, as the case may be) *in addition to* the purely practical ones concerning implementation that I have emphasized in this article. The existence of such reasons, however, does not in any way mitigate the wrongness of seeking to acquire the resources of another either by threatening to disclose what ought to be concealed or by offering to conceal what ought to be disclosed. If, for example, I would be relieved of an obligation to reveal someone else's adultery, even under ideal circumstances in which enforcement would not be a problem, solely because requiring this would involve an unacceptable imposition on *my* time and energy, that fact would hardly provide me with a warrant to threaten such a disclosure simply to effect a personal gain *at the adulterer's expense*. Insofar as the adulterer has a debt, it is surely owed not to me but to his or her spouse. It remains the case, therefore, that the propriety of something very close to the traditional law of blackmail can be established on the basis of plausible and relatively weak assumptions that are entirely compatible with liberalism.

NOTES

1. Blackmail threats that involve a demand for money or property are classified as a form of *theft by extortion,* while those that involve a demand that the victim act in some way against his will (without transferring resources) are considered a form of *criminal coercion* (see the *Model Penal Code,* arts. 223.4 and 212.5 [Official Draft and Revised Comments, 1980]). For an excellent overview of both the law of blackmail and the extensive critical commentary on it, see James Lindgren, "Unraveling the Paradox of Blackmail," *Columbia Law Review* 84 (1984): 670–717.
2. Joel Feinberg, *Harmless Wrongdoing* (New York: Oxford University Press, 1990), p. x. Feinberg's discussion of the difficulties of reconciling blackmail law with liberalism is found primarily in Chapter 32.
3. See, e.g., most of the theories that are discussed and evaluated in Lindgren, "Unraveling the Paradox of Blackmail."
4. For the sake of simplicity I shall ignore cases where the blackmailer is trying to coerce his victim into *omitting* to do something.
5. Actually I think the first of these is not, strictly speaking, an *offer* since it is a proposal not to do something to *improve* the situation of the offeree but only to *refrain from worsening* it. Elsewhere I have suggested that proposals of this sort would be more accurately termed "neutral conditional proposals"; see my *Coercion, Freedom, and Exploitation* (New York: Peter Lang, 1989), Chap. I, sec. 2.
6. "Extortion, Blackmail, and Threats," in *American Jurisprudence,* 2d ed. (Rochester, N.Y.: The Lawyers Co-operative Publishing Co., 1967), sec. 8, p. 906.
7. One possible exception would be a case in which this were the only way to deter the occurrence of some serious evil. For a fuller discussion of when it may be justifiable to threaten to do what it would be wrong to actually do, see Gregory Kavka, "Some Paradoxes of Deterrence," *Journal of Philosophy* 75 (1978): 285–302.
8. Though it is clear *that* this is generally wrong, it turns out to be not so easy to explain *why*. For one attempt, see my *Coercion, Freedom, and Exploitation,* Chap. 3.
9. Unless otherwise stated, all references to rights in this paper should be understood as references to *legal* rights.
10. I am assuming, of course, that we are considering only cases where such a disclosure would be harmful to the victim. Even so, there are obviously cases where the presumption against nondisclosure would be overridden (e.g., cases where I eavesdrop and discover that you are planning to murder someone).
11. Feinberg, *Harmless Wrongdoing,* pp. 250–54.
12. Ibid., pp. 241–56.
13. As the Editors of *Philosophy & Public Affairs* have pointed out, this is not so for every case of category 3 blackmail. If, for example, you threaten to reveal to my bigoted neighbors that I have just hired a black person to fill a responsible position in my company, it does not appear that you are in any way threatening my *privacy*. This, I think, is a problem for Feinberg, who, so far as I can

tell, would have to allow this sort of blackmail. My view would call for its prohibition on grounds similar to those on which I later argue for the criminalization of category 2 blackmail (except that here I would claim that, were it not for practical problems concerning implementation and abuse, the malicious unilateral *disclosure* of the information would be prohibitable).

14. *Harmless Wrongdoing,* p. 245 (author's emphasis).
15. Actually Feinberg waffles a bit on this, acknowledging that the creation of such a new tort "might be difficult to implement" (ibid., p. 256). Though he does not explain just what these difficulties might be, they are presumably connected with (among other things) showing that such a disclosure would be wholly or primarily motivated by *malice.* If such practical difficulties proved insurmountable, then, in order to avoid incoherence and remain a liberal, Feinberg would have to concede that category 4 blackmail should also be legalized. The solution I propose later in the paper would not be open to such an objection.
16. Eric Mack, "In Defense of Blackmail," *Philosophical Studies* 41 (1982): 277.
17. These, presumably, would be cases where, for some reason, the blackmailer's grievance cannot be settled through more acceptable means (such as a civil suit). For useful discussions of what have been termed "claim-of-right" defenses to blackmail, see Lindgren, "Unraveling the Paradox of Blackmail," pp. 676–80, and Feinberg, *Harmless Wrongdoing,* pp. 262–71.
18. Feinberg, *Harmless Wrongdoing,* p. 245.
19. Ibid., p. 246.
20. See Robert Nozick, *Anarchy, State and Utopia* (New York: Basic Books, 1974), pp. 84–86, and Richard Epstein, "Blackmail, Inc.," *University of Chicago Law Review* 50 (1983): 553–66. For libertarian defenses of the decriminalization of blackmail see, in addition to Mack's essay, Walter Block, "Trading Money for Silence," in *Economic Imperialism: The Economic Approach Applied Outside the Field of Economics,* ed. Gerard Radnitzky and Peter Bernholz (New York: Paragon House, 1987), pp. 157–217, and Murray Rothbard, *The Ethics of Liberty* (Atlantic Highlands, N.J.: Humanities Press, 1982), pp. 240–43.
21. Two points should be noted here. First, I use the term "legal" to refer only to acts that are legally *optional,* not to those that are legally *required.* Second, the behavior that the threatener is attempting to bring about must itself be legal (otherwise he would ordinarily be guilty of some form of criminal coercion).
22. I am ignoring cases where one has a *special* reason not to make such disclosures (e.g., where doing so would be life-threatening).
23. Situations where there is serious and widespread disagreement as to whether or not a given act is morally obligatory raise special difficulties which I am unable to discuss here. On the other hand, I would argue that those rare cases in which the disclosure of a morally required act could prove damaging to a person's reputation (e.g., a case in which I try to blackmail you by threatening to reveal to your racist neighbors that you once prevented a lynching) should be handled like the bigotry example discussed in note 13.
24. See, e.g., the standard definition of blackmail quoted in Section I.
25. See, e.g., Jeffrie Murphy. "Blackmail: A Preliminary Inquiry," *Monist* 63 (1980): 163.
26. This, for example, would be one (though hardly the only) important reason for objecting to laws prohibiting the possession and sale of drugs. For a harrowing account of how efforts to enforce drug laws have involved what the author terms an "assault on civil liberties," see Steven Wisotsky, *Beyond the War on Drugs* (Buffalo, N.Y.: Prometheus Books, 1990), Chap. 7.
27. Which, of course, is how blackmail is legally classified; see note 1.
28. See, e.g., Richard Wasserstrom's "Is Adultery Immoral?" in *Today's Moral Problems,* ed. Richard Wasserstrom, 3d ed. (New York: Macmillan, 1985).
29. See "Adultery and Fornication," in *American Jurisprudence,* sec. 2.
30. See *Model Penal Code,* art. 213.6 ("Note on Adultery and Fornication").
31. Ibid., p. 435.
32. The term "criminal" refers to the fact that this was at one time an ecclesiastical crime; see Jacob Lippman, "The Breakdown of Consortium," *Columbia Law Review* 30 (1930): 651–73.
33. "Husband and Wife," in *American Jurisprudence,* sec. 482, pp. 407–08. See also Jeremy D. Weinstein (Note), "Adultery, Law and the State: A History." *Hastings Law Journal* 38 (1986): 195–238, and *Second Restatement of Torts* (American Law Institute, 1986), secs. 683–92.
34. Lindgren, "Unraveling the Paradox of Blackmail," p. 681, n. 58.
35. I am assuming that there are cases in which justice can be "trumped" by other moral considerations such as mercy or benevolence.
36. Feinberg, *Harmless Wrongdoing,* pp. 248–49.
37. Ibid., p. 249.
38. Ibid., p. 248.

39. "Sour Grapes," *The New Republic,* 10 December 1990, p. 45.
40. There are, of course, certain sorts of boycotts that are illegal (e.g., secondary and group boycotts, which are prohibited by the National Labor Relations Act). For further details see Douglas L. Leslie, *Labor Law,* 2d ed. (St. Paul, Minn.: West Publishing, 1986), Chap. 6.
41. Mack, "In Defense of Blackmail," pp. 281–83.
42. I have put scare quotes here because I believe that, strictly speaking, one can *threaten* a person only by proposing (at least conditionally) to take active steps to *worsen* his situation. For further discussion see my *Coercion, Freedom, and Exploitation,* Chap. 1, sec. 2.
43. It should be noted that making such a distinction also allows us to differentiate blackmail from hard bargains since the blackmailer threatens to cause harm while someone who proposes a hard bargain is someone who "threatens" only to fail to confer a benefit. In his essay, "Blackmail: A Preliminary Inquiry," Jeffrie Murphy has argued that the harming/nonbenefiting distinction is not only unclear but also morally too insignificant to bear such weight. His argument, however, confuses cases of nonbenefit with cases of *preventing* someone from receiving a benefit that she would *otherwise* have received (which are really cases of *causing* harm, not merely failing to benefit). For more on the significance of the basic distinction between causing harm and failing to prevent it, see my "Some Reflections on the Difference between Positive and Negative Duties," *Tulane Studies in Philosophy* 33 (1985): 93–100.
44. I am grateful to Sterling Harwood for helping me to see this.
45. Note that it will not do to argue that boycotts are permissible because, unlike blackmail, they are motivated by considerations of morality rather than personal gain. Perfectly legal boycotts can be (and have been) directed to morally questionable ends while criminal acts of blackmail can be (and have been) intended to advance worthwhile objectives.
46. I am aware, of course, that boycott organizers sometimes resort to threats when their arguments prove insufficiently persuasive. Obviously nothing in my paper supports the view that activities of *that* sort should be afforded legal protection.
47. See Hugh Evans, "Why Blackmail Should Be Banned," *Philosophy* 65 (1990): 93–94.
48. Lindgren, "Unraveling the Paradox of Blackmail," p. 702.
49. This objection is raised by Walter Block and David Gordon in their article "Blackmail, Extortion and Free Speech: A Reply to Posner, Epstein, Nozick and Lindgren," *Loyola of Los Angeles Law Review* 19 (1985): 53. For Lindgren's reply see "In Defense of Keeping Blackmail a Crime: Responding to Block and Gordon," *Loyola of Los Angeles Law Review* 20 (1986): 35–44.
50. For a further discussion of these possible benefits see Block, "Trading Money for Silence," pp. 185–87.
51. Rothbard, *The Ethics of Liberty,* p. 125 (emphasis in original).
52. Except, of course, in cases where the activity being covered up was a crime.
53. I realize that this is a somewhat controversial claim. For a rigorous defense of such an "internalist" account of moral appraisability, see Michael Zimmerman, *An Essay on Moral Responsibility* (Totowa, N.J.: Rowman and Littlefield, 1988), Chap. 3.
54. See *Model Penal Code,* art. 241.6.
55. See *Model Penal Code,* art. 242.5. (The code categorizes this offense as a misdemeanor unless there is an impending police investigation or judicial inquiry, in which case it is upgraded to a felony.)
56. For an interesting discussion of some of the less apparent disadvantages of attempting to suppress embarrassing truths, see Richard Epstein, "Privacy, Property Rights, and Misrepresentations," *Georgia Law Review* 12 (1978): 469–74.
57. Indeed, doubts about the propriety of subjecting adultery itself to legal sanctions of any sort have led many states to abolish or severely restrict civil actions for criminal conversation and alienation of affections; see W. Page Keeton, Dan B. Dobbs, Robert E. Keeton, and David G. Owen, eds., *Prosser and Keeton on the Law of Torts,* 5th ed. (St. Paul, Minn.: West Publishing, 1984), sec. 124.

Study Questions

1. What is the paradox of blackmail? How does Feinberg try to resolve this paradox? Does he succeed? If so, how? If not, why not?
2. Does Gorr succeed in showing that a ban on blackmail is compatible with liberal principles? If so, how? If not, why not? Would libertarianism (as defined in Appendix B) support a ban on blackmail? Explain your answer.

C Corporate and White-Collar Crime

"YOU ROBBED AN S&L WITH A GUN?"

The Neglected Victims and Unexamined Costs of White-Collar Crime

ELIZABETH MOORE AND
MICHAEL MILLS

For decades the victims of crime were all but ignored by researchers, criminal justice professionals, and policymakers. Recent years have seen a dramatic reversal of this situation. As public officials and a victims' movement focused unprecedented attention on the financial loss, physical injuries, and suffering caused by street crimes, victim-rights legislation and assistance programs were developed across the nation. Although this victims' movement has spawned significant policy reforms, white-collar crime victims have been ignored and what was true 15 years ago remains true today: "The subject of victims of [white-collar] crime has scarcely been addressed [by investigators and policymakers]" (Vaughan and Carlo 1976, p. 154). This article

Reprinted with permission from *Crime & Delinquency,* Vol. 36 No. 3, July 1990 408–418.

The authors are graduate students, Department of Sociology, University of Tennessee, Knoxville.

begins with brief comments on the problems of crime victims, the development of programs for victims, and the nature of these programs. We then discuss the costs of white-collar crime to victims and some reasons why the victims' movement has ignored them. We conclude with a call for more research and policy attention to the costs of white-collar crime.

Victims' Problems, Progress, and Programs

Research has documented the disruptive and sometimes devastating effects of street crime on its victims. Victims often report psychological and somatic problems triggered by their victimization, including stress, diminished self-esteem, and helplessness. Many alternate between intense anger and increased feelings of vulnerability and fear (Burt and Katz 1985; Fischer 1984; Janoff-Bulman 1985; Leyman 1985; Maguire 1980; Wortman 1983). These reactions can be trivial or devastating, transitory or enduring.

The problems faced by crime victims do not end once their plight becomes known to authorities. Victims who come to criminal justice officials expecting protection and remedy often find something very different:

> They discover . . . that they [are] treated as appendages of a system appallingly out of balance. They learn that somewhere along the way the system has lost track of the simple truth that it is supposed to be fair and to protect those who obey the law while punishing those who break it. Somewhere along the way, the system began to serve lawyers and judges and defendants, treating the victim with institutionalized disinterest. (President's Task Force on Victims of Crime 1982, p. vi)

The past 15 years have seen increasing official attention to the problems faced by victims. The first action came in the form of 1964 federal legislation establishing guidelines for victim compensation programs. The following year, California created the first state program (U.S. Department of Justice 1988a). By 1974 the Law Enforcement Assistance Administration was contributing $50 million to eight victim/witness assistance programs.

Ronald Reagan's victory in the 1980 presidential election boosted the visibility and political strength of the victims' movement. In 1980 he appointed a Victims of Crime Task Force to investigate the problems of crime victims and to recommend new policies. The task force report led to passage of the Victim and Witness Protection Act of 1982. This act protects and assists victims and witnesses of federal crimes by (1) making it a felony to threaten or intimidate a victim or witness, (2) providing for inclusion of a victim impact statement in presentence reports, (3) furnishing explicit authority for federal trial courts to order offenders to make restitution to victims, and (4) requiring judges to state on the record the reasons for not ordering restitution (Finn n.d.). Also in 1982, California voters amended the state constitution to incorporate a victim's bill of rights. In the next 5 years, 28 states followed California's lead and enacted similar bills of rights (Viano 1987, pp. 440–41).

The Victims of Crime Act of 1984 (VOCA) authorized the U.S. Attorney General to make grants to states to establish programs for victim compensation and assistance. By 1987, 38 states had done so (U.S. Department of Justice 1988b; Finn n.d.). These programs offer monetary compensation and other assistance; for example, counseling for victims of crime who suffer physical injury, emotional injury, or lost wages (U.S. Code 1983–1985, p. 1102).

VOCA also established a Crime Victims Fund that is replenished through revenues collected from criminal fines, penalty assessments, and sales of property seized from convicted federal defendants. The principal crimes for which victims are compensated by state programs are assault, homicide, "other," sexual offenses, and child sexual abuse. In 1987, $55 million was paid to victims of assaults and other violent crimes, $6.1 million was paid to families of homicide victims, and $5 million was paid to victims of sexual offenses. The average compensation award was $1,864 (U.S. Department of Justice 1988a, p. i). The 1984 VOCA also made available grants to states for programs to assist victims of designated crimes, including sexual assault, spouse abuse, and child abuse.

Victims of White-Collar Crime

Whereas street crimes disproportionately victimize the poor and marginal, white-collar crime is more democratic in its impact. It harms not only well-heeled financial speculators but couples and individual citizens with few if any assets beyond a modest savings account. We know little or nothing about its impacts on victims. The type of victimization surveys that have enhanced our knowledge of street crime victimization do not lend themselves easily to studies of white-collar crime, and the National Crime Survey (NCS) does not collect data on incidents of white-collar or corporate victimization. These and other aspects of the problem of white-collar crime present obstacles to research that are absent or attenuated where street crimes are concerned. As a result, what was true a decade ago remains true today: "Little systematic attention has been paid to the white-collar crime victim" (Duncan and Caplan 1980; National Institute 1977; Walsh and Schram 1980). Although statistical data are scarce, many excellent case studies of corporate and white-collar crime document the sufferings of their victims (collections include Douglas and Johnson 1977; Ermann and Lundman 1987; Heilbroner 1972; Hills 1987; Hochstedler 1984; Johnson and Douglas 1978). Much of what we have learned about the costs and victim impacts of white-collar crime come from these very important investigations.

Neglect of white-collar crime victims seems particularly unfortunate in light of its enormous physical, economic, and social toll. No one disputes that it "produce[s] far more destruction and cost than conventional crime" (Elias 1986, p. 115). Victims of some white-collar crime suffer death; others sustain serious injuries, or exposure to unsafe working conditions that cause long-term, progressively debilitating illness; and financial losses may leave still others with a lowered standard of living. Oftentimes the victims include those now "past their prime working years, with perhaps very small savings to piece out the submarginal existence afforded by social security payments. Such victims have just about worked out their life schemes to avoid becoming public charges in their old age" (Edelhertz 1970, p. 10). Aside from its emotional impact, loss of modest savings or retirement funds virtually impoverishes victims such as these. They may be forced to make do with less frequent medical checkups, to forgo elective surgery, to eat out less often or to purchase less, and less nutritious, food. The *primary* costs of white-collar crimes appear in the physical, psychological, and monetary suffering of its victims.

Like victims of street crimes, there is reason to believe that white-collar crime victims who seek redress by notifying public officials of their apparent victimization receive less than a satisfactory response (Geis 1975; McGuire and Edelhertz 1980). It may be necessary for them to negotiate a maze of agencies and institutions, most of uncertain jurisdiction and commitment. Often the process produces little beyond frustration and, eventually, angry resignation. Vaughan and Carlo (1975) discovered that a group of citizens victimized by an appliance repairman, hardly the most serious of white-collar offenders, "repeatedly expressed their indignation at being cheated and their frustration at being unable to get satisfaction from the offender, or from anyplace else" (p. 158). A study of fraud in California that victimized many elderly citizens pointed to the "callous indifference that the system demonstrates toward those whom it is particularly charged with assisting" (Geis 1976, p. 14):

> Many [victims] . . . feel their needs have extremely low priority and that, at best, they are tolerated and then often with ill humor. Their role, they say, seems much like that of the

> expectant father in the hospital at delivery time: necessary for things to have gotten underway in the past but at the moment rather superfluous and mildly bothersome. . . . the offender, at least, is regarded by criminal justice functionaries as a doer, an antagonist, someone to be wary of. . . . The victim, on the other hand, is part of the background scenery. (Geis 1976, p. 15)

Interviews with a sample of 42 individuals who filed complaints with the consumer fraud bureau of the Illinois Attorney General's office revealed that "dissatisfaction with and even hostility toward the Bureau were widespread." The Bureau was seen as "too slow, unaggressive, biased, disorganized, and 'bureaucratic' " (Steele 1975, p. 1179). In short, "just as the criminal-justice system has been termed a 'nonsystem,' the approach taken by the criminal-justice system to white-collar crime containment might be considered a 'nonapproach' " (Edelhertz and Rogovin 1980, p. 78). The fact that white-collar crime victims have been ignored by the justice system is only the latest example of this.

Undeserving Victims

Like the post-1975 wave of criminal sentencing reform that swept over the nation, the victims' movement drew support from diverse sources. By focusing attention on women as targets of violence, the women's movement promoted a new definition of their plight as victims. Angered by liberal U.S. Supreme Court decisions expanding the rights of the accused, politically conservative citizens and public officials seized the opportunity to redress this perceived imbalance by promoting *victims'* rights. This was not extended to victims of white-collar crime.

For conservative politicians, the victims' rights movement offered an opportunity to do something positive about crime, thereby undercutting criticisms that their crime control policies amount to nothing more than repression. By establishing restitution and compensation programs, conservatives could show they were willing to fund programs that would benefit women and minorities, groups typically not part of the conservative constituency. These political gains could be achieved at limited political cost and the only group not benefiting from expanded victim rights was street criminals.

The politics of government programs may explain the failure of the victim rights legislation to take explicit account of white-collar crime victims. Compensation and restitution programs for victims of street crime seem a natural extension of the traditional government responsibility to preserve public order. Innocent victims of street crime deserve to be compensated, if only because the state has failed in its responsibility to protect them. Street criminals, however, typically are poor and have few prospects of ever being able to repay their victims. Hence it follows that the state should help make good victims' losses.

This reasoning is harder to apply in the case of white-collar crime. Whereas its victims may or may not be poor, the offenders may, but need not, be part of the wealthy and powerful business establishment. In this situation, the argument that the state owes it to victims to defray the costs of victimization is not persuasive. If the offenders are not poor, why not have them pay for the costs of victimization? Why not set up programs requiring that perpetrators of consumer fraud, bank scams, securities fraud, and other such crimes automatically pay restitution to their victims? But at this point, we confront certain political and economic realities.

New programs facilitating victims' ability to recover from corporate white-collar offenses would necessarily impose costs on the business community. Attempts to legislate such programs will encounter resistance. The business community will point to the existing network of laws, regulations, and agencies and argue that mechanisms for redressing the wrongs suffered by white-collar crime victims are already in place; no new ones are needed. Given the antiregulation, probusiness sentiments increasingly evidenced by public officials, these arguments likely would be well received by many state and federal legislators. Ironically, the conservative political philosophy underpinning the original victims' rights movement may be responsible in part for its continued failure to address white-collar crime victimization.

Other reasons for continued neglect are rooted in prevailing notions about white-collar crime and its victims. Walsh and Schram (1980) suggested that white-collar crime, like the crime of rape, raises "double standard issues." Both crimes are characterized by widespread ambivalence toward the proscribed conduct, victim involvement, and victims' claims for redress. As a result, many white-collar victims do not "arouse the general sympathy reserved for those who have suffered harm, loss, or injury. Instead, these victims often are viewed with a mixture of skepticism, suspicion, and disbelief" and they are seen as "unworthy of society's protection" (pp. 46–47). Little wonder that simply reporting white-collar crime and seeing one's complaint through to resolution can be both exhausting and disillusioning.

Beyond the Primary Costs of Crime

Although the primary costs of white-collar crime are obvious, its *secondary* costs may be equally harmful. Sutherland (1949) noted, some 40 years ago, that white-collar crime is harmful to the social fabric in ways uniquely its own. Because most white-collar offenses violate trust, they breed distrust, lower social morale, and "attack the fundamental principles of the American institutions" (p. 13). These secondary costs

> are far more significant than mere dollar losses—no matter how great—because they go to the very heart of the issue of integrity of our society and to that confidence in our private and public institutions that is essential to their usefulness and effectiveness in serving the public. (Edelhertz 1980, p. 124)

Three areas of potentially significant secondary impact have been identified: (1) diminished faith in a free economy and in business leaders, (2) loss of confidence in political institutions, processes, and leaders, and (3) erosion of public morality.

Many have expressed fears about the potential impact of white-collar crime on our nation's economic life. They reason that restraint of trade, for example,

> tends to undermine the principles of free enterprise that the antitrust laws are intended to protect. [Thus,] the damage from the price-fixing conspiracy in the electrical equipment industry was not limited to the direct extra costs imposed. As Judge T. Cullen Ganey declared in sentencing a defendant: "This is a shocking indictment of a vast section of our economy, for what is really at stake here is the survival of the kind of economy under which this country has grown great, the free enterprise system." (President's Commission 1967, p. 48)

American citizens must have faith and confidence that corporate and business leaders are motivated by an ethic of responsible concern for others and for the common good. To the extent citizens believe otherwise, believe that business decisions are motivated by greed and selfishness, they may withhold financial support and economic investment.

Another secondary cost is the effect of white-collar crime on faith in and support for political institutions, public officials, and governmental processes. Citizens, for the most part, expect public officials to be honest themselves and also to deal unflinchingly with those who employ deceit and exploitation to prey on the public. In a word,

> [citizens] want to see evidence that the criminal-justice system will treat deception and abuses of institutional position as harshly as stealth and physical attack and that it is willing to punish privileged and powerful offenders as well as those who are relatively powerless. (Moore 1980, p. 44)

This is true especially in the U.S., whose economy is based largely on trust in the honesty and legitimacy of agencies that regulate financial markets and activities. The Internal Revenue Service, for example, depends greatly on voluntary, honest compliance by American citizens. The viability of banks and thrifts greatly depends on citizens' confidence in regulatory officials and agencies. Whenever citizens see corrupt public officials and other white-collar offenders violate the law with impunity they inevitably must question official integrity and commitment to fairness. In many ways, the greatest harm to the victims of white-collar crime may be this loss of faith in the very possibility of fair, impartial government. Surely this problem is exacerbated and cynicism intensified when victims' efforts to enlist the aid of political officials in the pursuit of simple justice lead only to frustration. The result may be increased citizen apathy and feelings of *delegitimation.* In one of the few empirical investigations of this hypothesized relationship, Peters and Welch (1980) found that charges of corruption apparently had little effect on net voter turnout and election outcomes in five Congressional elections from 1968 to 1978. They suggested, however, that individual-level studies would be more appropriate for examining whether official corruption or other forms of white-collar crime cause delegitimation.

The state's failure to mete out swift and appropriately severe punishment to white-collar criminals may erode not only victims' confidence in and support for American political and social institutions but also their commitment to and willingness to play by "the rules." Thus, the final secondary impact of white-collar crime is its potentially deleterious effect on public morality. As the President's Commission on Law Enforcement and Administration put it:

> It is reasonable to assume that prestigious companies that flout the law set an example for other businesses and influence individuals, particularly young people, to commit other kinds of crime on the grounds that everyone is taking what he can get. If businessmen who are respected as leaders of the community can do such things as break the antitrust laws or rent dilapidated houses to the poor at high rents, it is hard to convince the young that they should be honest. (1967, p. 48)

In other words, by violating citizens' sense of equity, lenient treatment of white-collar criminals may provide them with easy rationalizations for personal misconduct. This reaction may be understandable particularly among poor and minority citizens who see the stark contrast between our harsh response to street criminals and our limp response to white-collar criminals. Moore (1980) suggests that, "given the intensity of our attack on street crime, there seems to be a *special* obligation to prosecute respectable people who use their position and reputation to steal through deception and exploitation" (p. 30).

White-Collar Crime Victims and Public Policy

Many times, official response to white-collar crime includes agencies that play little or no part in responding to street crimes. For example, use of bankruptcy proceedings to distribute any remaining defendants' assets is a common occurrence in white-collar crime cases (Kusic 1989). We do not know if the complex of agencies, personnel, and legal processes set in motion by white-collar crimes present obstacles and problems for victims that are different from those experienced by street crime victims. Currently, victim assistance programs in the United States work almost exclusively with *individual* victims of interpersonal criminal violence and street property crimes. Because these street crimes usually harm individuals and their immediate social networks, this is a reasonable policy response. By contrast, some white-collar crimes victimize thousands of individuals.

This important difference between street crime and white-collar crime victimization constrains investigation, prosecution, and settlement of the latter. There is reason to believe that it constrains intelligent and reasoned responses to victims as well (Edelhertz and Rogovin, 1980). Nonetheless, the absence of systematic data on these matters means that we do not know if existing procedures and programs could be modified or new ones developed to provide assistance to white-collar crime victims.

It does seem clear that lack of concern for white-collar crime victims is not cost free. As a former federal prosecutor suggests, the "inadequate concern to provide remedies for the victims of white-collar crime" undermines efforts to control it (Edelhertz 1980, p. 123).

REFERENCES

Burt, Martha R. and Bonnie L. Katz. 1985. "Rape, Robbery, and Burglary: Responses to Actual and Feared Victimization, with Special Focus on Women and the Elderly." *Victimology* 10:325–58.

Douglas, Jack D. and John M. Johnson, eds. 1977. *Official Deviance.* Philadelphia: J. B. Lippincott.

Duncan, J. T. Skip and Marc Caplan. 1980. *White-Collar Crime: A Selected Bibliography.* Washington, DC: U. S. Department of Justice, National Institute of Justice.

Edelhertz, Herbert. 1970. *The Nature, Impact and Prosecution of White-Collar Crime.* Washington, DC: U.S. Department of Justice, National Institute of Law Enforcement and Criminal Justice.

———. 1980. "Appendix B: White-Collar Crime." Pp. 119–31 in *A National Strategy for Containing White-Collar Crime,* edited by H. Edelhertz and C. Rogovin. Lexington, MA: D. C. Heath.

Edelhertz, Herbert and Charles Rogovin, eds. 1980. *A National Strategy for Containing White-Collar Crime.* Lexington, MA: D. C. Heath.

Elias, Robert. 1986. *The Politics of Victimization.* New York: Oxford University Press.

Ermann, M. David and Richard J. Lundman, eds. 1987. *Corporate and Governmental Deviance,* 3rd ed. New York: Oxford University Press.

Finn, Peter. n.d. *Victims.* Washington, DC: U.S. Department of Justice, Bureau of Justice Statistics.

Fischer, Constance T. 1984. "A Phenomenological Study of Being Criminally Victimized: Contributions and Constraints of Qualitative Research." *Journal of Social Issues* 40: 161–78.

Geis, Gilbert. 1975. "Victimization Patterns in White-Collar Crime." Pp. 89–105 in *Victimology: A New Focus. Exploiters and Exploited.* Vol. 5, edited by I. Drapkin and E. Viano. Lexington, MA: D. C. Heath.

———. 1976. "Defrauding the Elderly." Pp. 7–19 in *Crime and the Elderly,* edited by J. Goldsmith and S. Goldsmith. Lexington, MA: D. C. Heath.

Heilbroner, Robert L., ed. 1972. *In the Name of Profit.* New York: Warner.

Hills, Stuart L., ed. 1987. *Corporate Violence.* Totowa, NJ: Rowman & Littlefield.

Hochstedler, Ellen, ed. 1984. *Corporations as Criminals.* Beverly Hills, CA: Sage.

Janoff-Bulman, Ronnie. 1985. "Criminal vs. Non-criminal Victimization: Victims' Reactions." *Victimology* 10:498–511.

Johnson, John M. and Jack D. Douglas, eds. 1978. *Crime at the Top.* Philadelphia: J. B. Lippincott.

Kusic, Jane Y. 1989. *White Collar Crime 101 Prevention Handbook.* Vienna, VA: White Collar Crime 101.

Leymann, Heinz. 1985. "Somatic and Psychological Symptoms after the Experience of Life Threatening Events: A Profile Analysis." *Victimology* 10:512–538.

Maguire, Mike. 1980. "The Impact of Burglary upon Victims." *British Journal of Criminology* 20:261–275.

McGuire, Mary and Herbert Edelhertz. 1980. "Consumer Abuse of Older Americans: Victimization and Remedial Action in Two Metropolitan Areas." Pp. 266–292 in *White-Collar Crime: Theory and Research,* edited by G. Geis and E. Stotland. Beverly Hills, CA: Sage.

Moore, Mark H. 1980. "Notes toward a National Strategy to Deal with White-Collar Crime." Pp. 21–53 in *A National Strategy for Containing White-Collar Crime,* edited by H. Edelhertz and C. Rogovin. Lexington, MA: D. C. Heath.

National Institute of Law Enforcement and Criminal Justice. 1977. *White Collar Crime: A Selected Bibliography.* Washington, DC: U.S. Department of Justice.

Peters, John G. and Susan Welch. 1980. "The Effects of Charges of Corruption on Voting Behavior in Congressional Elections." *American Political Science Review* 74:697–708.

President's Commission on Law Enforcement and Administration of Justice. 1967. *The Challenge of Crime in a Free Society.* Washington, DC: U.S. Government Printing Office.

President's Task Force on Victims of Crime. 1982. *Final Report.* Washington, DC: U.S. Government Printing Office.

Steele, Eric H. 1975. "Fraud, Dispute, and the Consumer: Responding to Consumer Complaints." *University of Pennsylvania Law Review* 123:1107–1186.

Sutherland, Edwin H. 1949. *White Collar Crime.* New York: Holt, Rinehart & Winston.

United States Code. 1983–1985. *Containing the General and Permanent Laws of the United*

States, Enacted During the 98th Congress Vol. 3, Title 28-Title 42. Washington DC: U.S. Government Printing Office.
U.S. Department of Justice. 1988a. *Report to Congress.* Washington, DC: Office for Victims of Crime.
________. 1988b. *Report to the Nation on Crime and Justice.* 2nd ed. Washington, DC: Bureau of Justice Statistics.
Vaughan, Diane and Giovanna Carlo. 1975. "The Appliance Repairman: A Study of Victim Responsiveness and Fraud." *Journal of Research in Crime and Delinquency* 12: 153–161.
________. 1976. "Victims of Fraud: Victim-Responsiveness, Incidence, and Reporting." Pp. 79–95 in *Victims, Criminals and Society,* edited by E. Viano. Leiden, the Netherlands: A. W. Sijthoff.
Viano, Emilio. 1987. "Victim's Rights and the Constitution: Reflections on a Bicentennial." *Crime and Delinquency* 33:438–451.
Walsh, Marilyn E. and Donna D. Schram. 1980. "The Victim of White-Collar crime: Accuser or Accused?" Pp. 32–51 in *White-Collar Crime: Theory and Research,* edited by G. Geis and E. Stotland. Beverly Hills, CA: Sage.
Wortman, Camille B. 1983. "Coping with Victimization: Conclusions and Implications for Future Research." *Journal of Social Issues* 39:195–221.

Computer Crimes

STEVEN L. MANDELL

Mandell usefully defines his key terms before beginning his analysis. He profiles the computer criminal, estimates the prevalence of computer crime, gauges the effect of media publicity on computer crime, explains the vulnerability of the computer to abuse, and describes four types of computer crimes, giving some concrete examples of each.

Reprinted by permission from *Computers, Data Processing, and the Law* by Steven L. Mandell, pp. 154–62.

Definitions

What is meant by the term "computer crime"? There is no consensus on this question although the legal community has been focusing more attention on it through legislation and court opinions. Some authors prefer the term "computer abuse" to computer crime because it encompasses a broader range of illicit activity and because existing laws are not equipped to provide adequate guidance in this emerging area of criminal activity.[1] Others may take the view that computer crime should be defined very narrowly to exclude crimes in which the criminal conduct is the same as that used in noncomputer crimes.[2] According to this view, for example, obtaining money by impersonating a bank officer over the phone and giving a secret code number would not be a pure "computer crime," since the real essence of the wrongful conduct by which the crime was perpetrated was an *impersonation,* not a computer manipulation. According to this view, true computer crimes are so rare that they are almost mythical.

This [article] takes a broad but pragmatic view toward defining computer crime: A computer crime is simply a criminal act that poses a greater threat to a computer user than to an otherwise similarly situated nonuser. Computer crime, as defined here, consists of two kinds of activity:

1. the use of a computer to perpetrate acts of deceit, theft, or concealment that are intended to provide financial, business-related, property, or service advantages; and

2. threats to the computer itself, such as theft of hardware or software, sabotage, and demands for ransom.

Because computer crimes seldom involve acts of physical violence, they are generally classified as white-collar crimes.

Profile of the Computer Criminal

The popular view of the successful computer criminal is interesting and somewhat unsettling. Most companies would be eager to hire personnel who fit this description. Often such people are young and ambitious with impressive educational credentials. They tend to be technically competent and come from all levels of employees, including technicians, programmers, managers, and high-ranking executives. These people are often viewed as heroes challenging an impersonal computer as an opponent in a game. In contrast, the corporate victim of computer crime is not a sympathetic figure. The victim is often seen as one who is caught in a trap of the victim's own creation. Perhaps most unnerving, a commonly held belief is that many computer criminals have been discovered by chance, not by established detection techniques.

Prevalence of Computer Crime

Because so many computer crimes are discovered accidentally, there has been much speculation, and little consensus, about the actual extent of computer crime. Two of the more reputable studies diverge widely in their estimates.

The Stanford Research Institute (SRI) study was funded by grants from the National Science Foundation, the Atomic Energy Commission, and various private organizations. Data for the study on computer abuse were gathered over a four-year period, and results were published beginning in 1973.[3] By far the most ambitious study of its kind ever undertaken, the study initially identified 381 computer abuse cases from official sources, magazines, and newspapers. Admittedly, the accuracy of some stories printed in the popular media is questionable, both with regard to the exact nature of the crime and the amount of money involved. Despite these drawbacks, the study has generally been well received, since imperfect information may be better than none. Even fictitious accounts have some value as they allow us to study the feasibility of such a crime.

Some of the conclusions drawn by the study illustrate the potential dangers of computer abuse. It found that the average loss per crime was $450,000 and speculated that the crimes reported represented only a fraction of the actual total. However, this finding should be balanced by the fact that the number of cases compiled by the Stanford Research Institute was an insignificant percentage of the 100,000 computers in use at the time.

The Government Accounting Office (GAO) made a search among ten federal agencies for incidents of computer crime.[4] Its findings were much more modest than those of the SRI study. The search generated a list of 69 cases. Nine of these were privacy invasion cases that involved no monetary loss. The average dollar loss for those crimes that did involve money was $44,110, a far cry from the SRI's $450,000 figure. In addition, the GAO report stated that 50 of the crimes were committed by technically naive users.

The large differences in the findings of these two reports does not necessarily reflect biases on the part of those collecting data but rather reflects the more fundamental problems of defining computer abuse, estimating unknown incidents, and allowing for inconsistency in media coverage. Simply stated, there is a great deal of mystery surrounding computer crime that defies quantification with any degree of accuracy. What is certain, however, is that computer crime is real, it involves potentially large sums of money, and it is not likely to decrease as use of computers continues to spread rapidly.

The Effect of Media Publicity

Part of the difficulty in assessing the extent and impact of computer crime is due to its widespread and occasionally inaccurate exposure in the media. Newspapers and magazines have focused on incidents of computer abuse for several reasons. The average person (and perhaps the average newspaper reporter) understands little about the complexities of modern computers and therefore is easily intimidated by them. This lack of understanding is often reflected in media reports, which at times tend to exaggerate the severity of a crime. For instance, a story that appeared in the *San Francisco Chronicle* reported how one computer technician was able to gain access to a computer, resulting in unauthorized use of computer time worth "possibly millions." When the case was brought to court, expert testimony put the value of stolen services at $2,000. Of course, the exaggerated version makes the headlines, while the true version often does not get publicized at all.

As we noted, computer abuse also tends to be glamorized. Often the perpetrator is portrayed as an eccentric genius engaged in a Robin Hood–type operation, stealing from a large, impersonal machine, the epitome of the "establishment." Such a point of view, by fostering sympathy for the lone bandit, leads the public to ignore the high cost to society that such crimes exact.

The Vulnerability of the Computer

There are several factors that make a computer an attractive target for criminals. Among them are the speed with which the computer does its work, making many small thefts of a few cents potentially profitable; the invisibility of records stored in a computer's memory; and the use of programmed processing controls, which can be manipulated or bypassed altogether.

Often overlooked is the fact that although the computer is itself a complex machine, many of the processes used with it are relatively simple. There are five key areas in the operation of a computer, all of which are subject to abuse:

1. Input operations may be manipulated to avoid legitimate charges to a user or to cause the computer to print a check in payment for nonexistent services. Fictitious accounts, and even whole companies, have been created in this way.
2. A program controls the computer's operations and if tampered with can benefit the criminal at the expense of the entity that owns the computer. Also, programs themselves are valuable items that are subject to theft.
3. The central processing unit (CPU) may be exposed to vandalism or destruction. A user's exclusive reliance on it for vital functions makes it a prime target for vandalism or ransom demands.
4. Output, though the least likely target for criminal attack, can still present serious criminal problems. Valuable data, such as mailing lists, can be stolen. The computer output, such as checks, is usually the goal of the criminal who manipulates the system.
5. The communication process is vital to all information flowing in and out of the computer. This data can be intercepted from the lines of communication through wiretapping or the communication facilities themselves can be destroyed.

Types of Computer Crimes

The variety of computer crimes is quite extensive and can be classified into four broad categories: sabotage, theft of services, property crimes, and financial crimes. This section examines each of these categories and gives examples drawn from actual crimes.

Sabotage

This type of computer crime is usually, though not exclusively, directed against computer hardware. Sabotage of computers often resembles traditional sabotage because a computer facility's unique capabilities would not typically be used to carry out the destruction, although sabotage may require some sophistication if computer-assisted security systems must be thwarted or the system is manipulated to do harm to itself.

Computers are targets of sabotage and vandalism especially during times of political activism. Dissident political groups during the 1960s, for instance, conducted assaults on computer installations, often causing extensive damage. Other forms of physical violence have included shooting a computer with a revolver and flooding the computer room. One fired employee simply walked through the data storage area with an electromagnet, thereby erasing valuable company records. A computer's power source can also be the target of a saboteur.

Obviously, these acts of violence do not require any special expertise on the part of the criminal. Sabotage may, however, be conducted by dissatisfied former employees who may put to use some of their knowledge of company operations to gain access to and destroy both hardware and software.

Though computer sabotage is not the type of computer crime that people see as threatening in the same way as if the secrets of the computer were manipulated by a misguided genius, its potential threat should not be taken lightly. The degree of sophistication in a computer crime does not necessarily correlate with the cost of rectifying the damage.

Theft of Services

Computer services may be abused in a variety of ways, depending upon the individual system. Some examples of theft of computer services have involved politicians using a city's computer to conduct campaign mailings or employees conducting unauthorized free-lance services on a company computer after working hours.

Time-sharing systems have been exposed to great amounts of abuse due to inadequate or nonexistent security precautions. It is much easier to gain unauthorized access to a time-sharing system than to a closed system. Though most require passwords to gain access, such a system is only as good as the common sense and caution of its users. A time-sharing system that does not require regular changing of access codes is inviting the theft of valuable computer time. The amazing lack of care exercised by supposedly sophisticated users in this regard made national headlines . . . when it was discovered that a group of high school computer buffs in Milwaukee had accessed numerous information systems, including those of banks, hospitals, and even the defense research center in Los Alamos, New Mexico. The students reportedly gained access by using each system's password, some of which had not been changed for years and many of which were obtained from public sources.

Wiretapping is another technique used to gain unauthorized access to a time-sharing system. By "piggybacking" onto a legitimate user's line, one can have free use of the user's privileges whenever the line is not being used by the authorized party.

One of the prime examples of computer services theft took place at the University of Alberta. In 1976, a student at the university undertook an independent study under the supervision of a professor to investigate the security of the university's computer system, a time-sharing system with more than 5,000 users, some as far away as England. After discovering several gaps in the system's security, he was able to develop a program that reduced the possibility for unauthorized use as well as for other tampering. He brought this program to the attention of the computer center, which took no action on the student's recommendations because it was assumed that planned changes in the system would remove security shortcomings. However, the changes were not implemented for another nine months, and during this period, the program was leaked to several students on campus. "Code Green," as the program was nicknamed, was eventually invoked several thousand times.

The university attempted to crack down on the unauthorized users and revoked several students' access privileges. Among these students were two who had been able to manipulate the program to get the computer to display the complete listing of all user passwords, including those at the highest privilege levels. In essence, this gave them unlimited access to the computer's files and programs. These students retaliated against the university administration by occasionally rendering the system inoperable, as well as less harmful acts such as periodically inserting an obscenity into the payroll file. With an unlimited supply of IDs, they were able to escape detection, compiling a library of the computer's programs and even monitoring the implementation of the new security system. The desperate university computer personnel focused exclusively on this situation, keeping a detailed log of all terminal dialogues. This effort led them to a terminal in the geology department one evening, and the students were apprehended.

Though an extreme example, the situation at the University of Alberta shows the extent to which the theft of computer services can be committed in the absence of adequate security measures. Perhaps a more difficult problem exists in dealing with the theft of computer services by employees who are authorized to use the computer for employment purposes. Recent court cases have dealt with the issue of whether an employee's unauthorized use of the employer's computer for personal use constitutes a crime, with varying results.

In *United States* v. *Sampson,*[5] for example, an employee of a computer service company under contract with NASA was charged with theft of a "thing of value" belonging to the United States[6] after he was discovered using the company computer for his own personal gain. The federal court held that computer time did qualify as a thing of value within the scope of the relevant federal criminal statute.

In *People* v. *Weg,*[7] a computer programmer employed by a board of education was charged with a misdemeanor of theft of services for allegedly using the board's computer without permission for various personal projects, including calculating a racehorse handicapping system and tracing the genealogy of horses that he owned. The statute provided that a defendant had committed a "theft of services" when

> obtaining or having control over labor in the employ of another person, or of business, commercial, or industrial equipment or facilities of another person, knowing that he is not entitled to the use thereof, and with intent to derive a commercial or other substantial benefit for himself or a third person, he uses or diverts to the use of himself or a third person such labor, equipment, or facilities.

The judge dismissed the case, finding that since the computer was owned by the public school board, no "business, commercial, or industrial equipment or facilities of another person" were involved; that is, a school board was not considered to be a business. In addition, the judge ruled that the charges failed to include any factual allegation that the defendant intended to derive a commercial benefit from the services.

Property Crimes

The most obvious computer crime that comes to mind in crimes of property is the theft of computer equipment itself. This has been more common with the increasing miniaturization of computer components and the advent of home computers. Such crimes, like acts of vandalism, are easily absorbed into traditional concepts of crime and present no unique legal problems.

Computer crimes of property theft frequently involve merchandise of a company whose orders are processed by computers. These crimes are usually committed by internal personnel who have a thorough knowledge of the operation. By manipulating records, dummy accounts can be created causing orders to be shipped to an accomplice outside the organization. Similarly, one can cause checks to be paid out for receipt of nonexistent merchandise.

Theft of property need not be limited to actual merchandise but may also extend to software. Those with access to a system's program library can easily obtain copies for their own use or, more frequently, for resale to a competitor. Technical security measures in a computer installation are of little use when dishonest personnel take advantage of their positions of responsibility.

Commission of property theft is by no means limited to those within the company structure, however. A computer service having specialized programs but poor security may open itself up to unauthorized access by a competitor. All that is necessary is that the outsider gain access to proper codes. This can be done in a number of ways, including clandestine observation of a legitimate user logging on from a remote terminal or use of a remote minicomputer to test for possible access codes.

Financial Crimes

Although not the most common, financial computer crimes are perhaps the most serious in terms of monetary loss. With the projected increasing dependence on electronic fund transfers, implications for the future are indeed ominous.

A common method of committing a financial computer crime involves checks. These mass-produced negotiable instruments can be manipulated in a number of ways. An employee familiar with a firm's operations can cause multiple checks to be made out to the same person. Checks can also be rerouted to a false address or to an accomplice. Such crimes do not seem so incredible when one realizes the scope of *unintentional* mistakes that have been made with computerized checks. For example, the Social Security Administration once accidentally sent out 100,000 checks to the wrong addresses while the system's files were being consolidated.

A form of financial computer crime that has captured the attention of many authors, but has probably been used much less frequently than one would expect from media discussion, is known as the "round-off fraud." In this crime, the thief, perhaps a bank employee, collects the fractions of cents in customers' accounts that are created when the applicable interest rates are applied. These fractions are then stored in an account created by the thief. The theory is that fractions of cents collected from thousands of accounts on a regular basis will yield a substantial amount of money. It has been suggested that in reality, however, round-off schemes may not yield enough money to make all the manipulations and risks worthwhile.[8]

Another type of financial crime involves juggling confidential information within a computer, both personal and corporate. Once appropriate access is gained to records, the ability to alter them can be highly marketable. At least one group operating in California engaged in the business of creating favorable credit histories to clients seeking loans.

By far the most massive fraud of this nature that ever occurred was the Equity Funding fraud, involving $2 billion over a period of ten years. This fraud, too complex to explain briefly in any detail, occurred in three distinct stages. Much of the criminal activity did not involve the company's computer per se, but there is no doubt that the speed of its data-processing facilities made possible the theft of this exorbitant amount of money.

The Equity Funding Corporation of America (EFCA) had four main activities: the sale of investment programs to the public, the financing of its operations, the purchase of mutual fund shares, and the issuing of insurance. The initial phase of the fraud began in 1964 and involved inflating the company's reported earnings, which made its funded life insurance plan more attractive to investors. An individual bought mutual fund shares, then borrowed on them to pay life insurance premiums over a ten-year period. The hope was that the income generated by the mutual funds would cover the cost of borrowing the money and pay for part of the insurance premium. This phase of the fraud emphasized sales appeal at the expense of profitability, and required only manual entries into company books. It involved about $85 million.

The second phase was known as the foreign phase. It consisted of borrowing funds from foreign subsidiaries without recording the borrowing as liabilities on the company records. Between 1968 and 1970 this scheme allowed the apparently fast-growing organization to acquire several banks, insurance companies, and other financial institutions.

Equity Funding had thus grown from a marketing organization to an insurance conglomerate, bringing into play the third phase of the fraud, carried out with the assistance of a computer. To generate short-term cash flow, Equity Funding sold many of its insurance policies to a co-insurer, Pennsylvania Life Insurance Company. By this time, the company was losing substantial amounts of money due to the necessity of servicing fraudulent policies already in existence, so it created wholly fictitious insurance policies and resold them immediately to co-insurers. To maintain profitability, Equity Funding would have had to sell vast amounts of new insurance, which it failed to do.

The company used its computer to create the new policies, mainly in the form of mass-marketing policies not using individual billing. Eventually, 64,000 fraudulent policies were issued. The fact that many of Equity Funding's subsidiaries were audited by unconnected auditing firms made it possible to shift assets from company to company as the need arose. For instance, an asset on the books of one company would not appear as a liability on another.

At the same time, the computer was programmed to fabricate the appropriate number of deaths, cancellations, and lapses that were to be expected from actual policies. Whenever individual audits were requested, the company would claim that the file was temporarily in service, instruct a programmer to prepare a false file overnight, and have it delivered the next morning. Obviously, the computer's speed and great capacity were central to the success of this phase of the fraud.

The fraud, long suspected by some, was finally exposed in 1973 by a surprise audit by examiners sent by the Illinois Insurance Commission. The company officers were caught off-guard and were unable to manipulate financial records quickly enough to perpetuate their massive fraud.

Twenty-two people were convicted of federal crimes in this $2 billion fraud and at least 50 civil suits were filed in connection with the ongoing crime. The computer, though instrumental only in the final stages of the fraud, was the means by which Equity Funding was able to obtain most of its illicit funds. Obviously, a fraud of this proportion is not the result of a breach in the security system of a computer but rather was made possible by deliberate corporate policy.[9] The only bodies capable of exposing fraud of this degree are external entities, such as private securities investigators or governmental regulatory agencies, and the process took ten years in this case.

Another celebrated computer crime was that perpetrated by Stanley Mark Rifkin, a computer consultant retained by the Seattle Pacific Bank. Rifkin was able to penetrate the bank's computerized system and transferred $10.2 million to a numbered Swiss bank account. In this case, the media worked both for and against the criminal. Although somewhat glamorizing the criminal as a clever loner swindling a corporate giant, the substantial publicity given to his subsequent attempt to steal an additional $50 million while his case was awaiting trial was also widely reported in the press, quite likely contributing to the judge's uncharacteristically stiff sentence at the end of his trial: eight years in a federal penitentiary.[10]

Finally, one of the more ingenious financial crimes perpetrated through the use of a computer occurred in 1977 at Florida's Flagler Dog Track. The dog-racing odds were figured by computer, and often the races were conducted so quickly that the odds would not be figured completely until after the race was over. A conspiracy was developed whereby an operator of the computer received the race results from an accomplice observing the race. He then stopped the computer program in progress, deducted a number of losers and added a corresponding number to the pool of winners in computer storage. The program was restarted and shortly finished its run. False winning tickets were then printed, also by computer, and were cashed in the next day. Since winners were paid from a pool formed by the losers' money, there was no way to detect the loss. Rather, each winner's share was somewhat less than it should have been.

The examples cited in this section represent some main areas in which computer crime can occur. It is by no means comprehensive, because the possibilities are nearly limitless for one with computer expertise and a fertile imagination. It should also be noted, however, that most of these crimes, many involving extremely large sums of money, could have been prevented or detected earlier through adequate security measures.

NOTES

1. See, e.g., Kling, "Computer Abuse and Computer Crime as Organizational Activities," 2 Comp. L. J. 403 (1980); D. Parker, S. Nycum, & S. Aura, "Computer Abuse" (Stan. Research Inst. Rep. 1973).
2. See, e.g., Taber, *A Survey of Computer Crime Studies,* 2 Comp. L.J. 275 (1980).
3. D. Parker, S. Nycum, & S. Aura, "Computer Abuse" (Stan. Research Inst. Rep. 1973). *See* Parker, "Computer Abuse Research Update," 2 Comp. L.J. 329, 351 (1980) for a bibliography of the SRI project for 1975–1980. See also D. Parker, *Crime by Computer* (1976).
4. General Accounting Office, *Computer Related Crimes in Federal Programs* (1976), reprinted in Problems Associated with Computer Technology in Federal Programs and Private Industry, Computer Abuses, Sen. Comm. on Gov't Operations, 94th Cong. 2d Sess. 71–91 (Comm. Print 1976).
5. 6 CLSR 879 (N.D. Cal. 1978).
6. 18 USC 641 (1976).
7. 113 Misc.2d 1017, 450 N.Y.S.2d 957 (N.Y. City Crim. Ct. 1982). See also "Using Computer Time No Crime, Judge Says," 68 ABA J. 671 (1982).
8. Taber, supra note 2.
9. See Kling, "Computer Abuse and Computer Crime as Organizational Activities," 2 Comp. L.J. 403 (1980).
10. See Becker, "Rifkin, A Documentary History," Comp. L.J. 471 (1980).

Crime and Not Much Punishment

JOHN ROTHCHILD

Rothchild compares the military-industrial complex, President Eisenhower's famous phrase, with General Noriega concerning the treachery each has displayed in conspiring against the government of the United States. Rothchild contrasts, however, the harsh treatment of Noriega with the forgiving treatment of corporate criminals.

What famous general pleaded guilty last summer to fraud, conspiracy and violations of the Money Laundering Control Act?

General Noriega comes to mind, but no. It was General Electric.

Last July 22, General Electric, a highly regarded *Fortune* 500 company, admitted to a major felony: padding the bills for a shipment of jet engines to the government.

It was a spectacular confession that somehow didn't make big headlines. Nowhere in the tabloids did we see: "GE Says 'I Did It!' in Uncle Sam Bilk."

Uncle Sam used to do business with General Noriega, then sent troops to Panama to snatch him away and prove once and for all that you can't make a fool of the most powerful country on Earth.

Uncle Sam was considerably more relaxed about having been made a fool of by GE, which paid only a $9.5 million fine plus $59.5 million in restitution for its ill-gotten gain on the fraud.

For a company that earns $2.6 billion in after-tax dollars, a $9.5 million fine has about the same sting as a $1,000 fine levied by the Chicago Bulls against Michael Jordan for missing a team meeting.

Seven months after GE's admission of guilt, nobody even remembers that the company has a criminal record.

Besides General Electric, several other major companies accused of cheating the government have gotten off easy—mostly in the defense area, where you'd figure that stealing from the government would not be tolerated.

Textron, for instance, was accused of producing faulty engine parts for Coast Guard helicopters and then finagling the bills so the government had to pay for the transgression. The company was allowed to settle the case (for $17.9 million) without admitting any wrongdoing.

While Textron was settling its case, seven other defense contractors got caught up in Operation Illwind, a name that has helped keep the investigation out of polite dinner conversation.

Striking as it did at the core of the military-industrial complex, Illwind was arguably more important than Operation Just Cause, which resulted in the capture of General Noriega.

After months of dogged investigating by the U.S. attorney's office in Alexandria, Virginia, the seven confessed to criminal charges ranging from fraud, bribery, conspiracy and false claims to the illegal use of inside information.

Illwind is not only a military scandal. It is potentially a stock market scandal as well, since the shares of at least five of the seven—Emerson Electric, Teledyne, Unisys, Loral and United Technologies—are widely held by institutions.

Naturally, the public heard very little about any of this. The seven guilty parties quietly paid GE-style fines, averaging $5 million per company, and went back to the business of getting lucrative government contracts.

An individual with a felony record can never again legally purchase a firearm, a prohibition that even the NRA accepts as sensible. But the guilty parties in Illwind continue to make bombs, fighter planes and other sophisticated weaponry with the blessing of the client they bilked.

Loral Corp., a manufacturer of military electronic systems, confessed to conspiracy, conversion of government property, and false statements. Yet its relationship with the Pentagon continues.

Sundstrand Corp., a maker of aerospace parts, admitted it used taxpayer funds to finance European revelry, including the upkeep on a French chalet. The government initially suspended the company's Pentagon contracts but restored them after Sundstrand's chairman resigned and the company promised to stay on a budget.

Knowing of the government's policy of rehabilitation rather than punishment in these cases, Wall Street learned long ago not to overreact. The market's initial reaction to the Illwind pleas ranged from a loss of 88 cents a share for Teledyne to a gain of $1.38 for Loral.

In two other recent cases—Salomon Brothers' settlement with the SEC for falsifying records and Rockwell International's admission of environmental felonies—the market reaction was within the same limited range.

No matter how damning the confession or plea, the stock price always seems to hold up nicely on the day it is announced. And six months after each event, the stocks of Salomon, Rockwell, and the Illwind defendants were up an average of 11 percent.

Thus you can be a socially unconscious investor and do very well, as long as you pick your villains carefully and avoid the small-timers, such as Cascade International and ZZZZ Best, which lack government connections.

Here's a rule for stock pickers: If the company bilks investors and fools the analysts, it's a sell. If it bilks and fools Uncle Sam, it's a hold or a buy.

Operation Illwind went beyond the fines paid by corporations. Fifty-two unincorporated individuals were also prosecuted, including 13 consultants, nine government officials and 30 executives who hatched the corporate plots. Two stood trial and were acquitted. The other 50 were either convicted or pleaded guilty.

Of the 50 felons, 14 got community service and/or suspended sentences and never saw the inside of a prison cell. Another 11 were installed in halfway houses or community facilities and avoided hard time. For the 25 who got prison terms, the sentences averaged about 16 months. Noriega has a chance of doing more time than those sentences combined, if he manages to live that long.

In fact, most of the Illwind defendants who went to jail are already out by now.

In the Rockwell International case, where illegal dumping of radioactive waste at its Rocky Flats plant may cost $1 billion to clean up, not a single corporate executive was charged with any crime, even though a grand jury pushed to indict numerous individuals.

Indeed, not incorporating may be the great failing of organized crime. John Gotti, the unincorporated mobster, is in jail, and Rockwell International is still making parts for nuclear bombs for the Pentagon.

Why do we even call it organized crime, when the real organized criminals have stock symbols and are incorporated in Delaware, and those who pass for organized are just a bunch of guys having dinner at a trattoria—and they can't even write it off as a business expense?

Study Questions

1. Do you think that white-collar crime (for example, pollution and embezzlement) is usually more serious, less serious or about as serious as blue-collar crime (purse snatching, mugging)? Do you agree with Moore and Mills that the victims of white-collar crime are neglected and that the costs of such crimes are largely unexamined? Explain your answer.
2. Do you agree with Mandell's definition of a computer crime? Should the law take computer crimes more seriously than it does now? If so, why? If not, why not?
3. Is Rothchild's comparison of corporate crimes and General Noriega's actions a good comparison or a false analogy? What relevant similarities and differences do you see between these two sets of actions? Explain why they are morally relevant based on some moral principle (see Appendix B). Is Rothchild right to conclude that the law is not taking the military industrial complex's crimes seriously enough? If so, why? If not, why not?

D Drugs

Against the Legalization of Drugs

James Q. Wilson*

James Q. Wilson is a recognized veteran of the so-called "drug war." He notes that prominent politicians have been calling for a war on drugs at least as far back as 1972, when President Nixon appointed Wilson as chairman of the National Advisory Council for Drug Abuse Prevention. Wilson focuses his analysis on heroin and cocaine, asks why we treat alcohol so differently from heroin and cocaine, and discusses other drugs such as PCP and marijuana. Finally, he describes a role for science in the drug war.

In 1972, the President appointed me chairman of the National Advisory Council for Drug Abuse Prevention. Created by Congress, the Council was charged with providing guidance on how best to coordinate the national war on drugs. (Yes, we called it a war then, too.) In those days, the drug we were chiefly concerned with was heroin. When I took office, heroin use had been increasing dramatically. Everybody was worried that this increase would continue. Such phrases as "heroin epidemic" were commonplace.

That same year, the eminent economist Milton Friedman published an essay in *Newsweek* in which he called for legalizing heroin. His argument was on two grounds: as a matter of ethics, the government has no right to tell people not to use heroin (or to drink or to commit suicide); as a matter of economics, the prohibition of drug use imposes costs on society that far exceed the benefits. Others, such as the psychoanalyst Thomas Szasz, made the same argument.

We did not take Friedman's advice. (Government commissions rarely do.) I do not recall that we even discussed legalizing heroin, though we did discuss (but did not take action on) legalizing a drug, cocaine, that many people then argued was benign. Our marching orders were to figure out how to win the war on heroin, not to run up the white flag of surrender.

That was 1972. Today, we have the same number of heroin addicts that we had then—half a million, give or take a few thousand. Having that many heroin addicts is no trivial matter; these people deserve our attention. But not having had an increase in that number for over fifteen years is also something that deserves our attention. What happened to the "heroin epidemic" that many people once thought would overwhelm us?

The facts are clear: a more or less stable pool of heroin addicts has been getting older, with relatively few new recruits. In 1976 the average age of heroin users who appeared in hospital emergency rooms was about twenty-seven; ten years later it was thirty-two. More

Reprinted from *Commentary*, February 1990, by permission;

*James Q. Wilson, Collins Professor of Management and Public Policy at UCLA, is the author of *Thinking About Crime* and co-author (with Richard Hernstein) of *Crime and Human Nature*. His latest book, *Bureaucracy*, has recently been published by Basic Books.

than two-thirds of all heroin users appearing in emergency rooms are now over the age of thirty. Back in the early 1970's, when heroin got onto the national political agenda, the typical heroin addict was much younger, often a teenager. Household surveys show the same thing—the rate of opiate use (which includes heroin) has been flat for the better part of two decades. More fine-grained studies of inner-city neighborhoods confirm this. John Boyle and Ann Brunswick found that the percentage of young blacks in Harlem who used heroin fell from 8 percent in 1970–71 to about 3 percent in 1975–76.

Why did heroin lose its appeal for young people? When the young blacks in Harlem were asked why they stopped, more than half mentioned "trouble with the law" or "high cost" (and high cost is, of course, directly the result of law enforcement). Two-thirds said that heroin hurt their health; nearly all said they had had a bad experience with it. We need not rely, however, simply on what they said. In New York City in 1973–75, the street price of heroin rose dramatically and its purity sharply declined, probably as a result of the heroin shortage caused by the success of the Turkish government in reducing the supply of opium base and of the French government in closing down heroin-processing laboratories located in and around Marseilles. These were short-lived gains for, just as Friedman predicted, alternative sources of supply—mostly in Mexico—quickly emerged. But the three-year heroin shortage interrupted the easy recruitment of new users.

Health and related problems were no doubt part of the reason for the reduced flow of recruits. Over the preceding years, Harlem youth had watched as more and more heroin users died of overdoses, were poisoned by adulterated doses, or acquired hepatitis from dirty needles. The word got around: heroin can kill you. By 1974 new hepatitis cases and drug-overdose deaths had dropped to a fraction of what they had been in 1970.

Alas, treatment did not seem to explain much of the cessation in drug use. Treatment programs can and do help heroin addicts, but treatment did not explain the drop in the number of *new* users (who by definition had never been in treatment) nor even much of the reduction in the number of experienced users.

No one knows how much of the decline to attribute to personal observation as opposed to high prices or reduced supply. But other evidence suggests strongly that price and supply played a large role. In 1972 the National Advisory Council was especially worried by the prospect that U.S. servicemen returning to this country from Vietnam would bring their heroin habits with them. Fortunately, a brilliant study by Lee Robins of Washington University in St. Louis put that fear to rest. She measured drug use of Vietnam veterans shortly after they had returned home. Though many had used heroin regularly while in Southeast Asia, most gave up the habit when back in the United States. The reason: here, heroin was less available and sanctions on its use were more pronounced. Of course, if a veteran had been willing to pay enough—which might have meant traveling to another city and would certainly have meant making an illegal contact with a disreputable dealer in a threatening neighborhood in order to acquire a (possibly) dangerous dose—he could have sustained his drug habit. Most veterans were unwilling to pay this price, and so their drug use declined or disappeared.

Reliving the Past

Suppose we had taken Friedman's advice in 1972. What would have happened? We cannot be entirely certain, but at a minimum we would have placed the young heroin addicts (and, above all, the prospective addicts) in a very different position from the one in which they actually found themselves. Heroin would have been legal. Its price would have been reduced by 95 percent (minus whatever we chose to recover in taxes). Now that it could be sold by the same people who make aspirin, its quality would have been assured—no poisons, no adulterants. Sterile hypodermic needles would have been readily available at the neighborhood drugstore, probably at the same counter where the heroin was sold. No need to travel to big cities or unfamiliar neighborhoods—heroin could have been purchased anywhere, perhaps by mail order.

There would no longer have been any financial or medical reason to avoid heroin use. Anybody could have afforded it. We might have tried to prevent children from buying it, but as we have learned from our efforts to prevent minors from buying alcohol and tobacco, young people have a way of penetrating markets theoretically reserved for adults. Returning Vietnam veterans would have discovered that Omaha and Raleigh had been converted into the pharmaceutical equivalent of Saigon.

Under these circumstances, can we doubt for a moment that heroin use would have grown exponentially? Or that a vastly larger supply of new users would have been recruited? Professor Friedman is a Nobel Prize–winning economist whose understanding of market forces is profound. What did he think would happen to consumption under his legalized regime? Here are his words: "Legalizing drugs might increase the number of addicts, but it is not clear that it would. Forbidden fruit is attractive, particularly to the young."

Really? I suppose that we should expect no increase in Porsche sales if we cut the price by 95 percent, no increase in whiskey sales if we cut the price by a comparable amount—because young people only want fast cars and strong liquor when they are "forbidden." Perhaps Friedman's uncharacteristic lapse from the obvious implications of price theory can be explained by a misunderstanding of how drug users are recruited. In his 1972 essay he said that "drug addicts are deliberately made by pushers, who give likely prospects their first few doses free." If drugs were legal it would not pay anybody to produce addicts, because everybody would buy from the cheapest source. But as every drug expert knows, pushers do not produce addicts. Friends or acquaintances do. In fact, pushers are usually reluctant to deal with non-users because a non-user could be an undercover cop. Drug use spreads in the same way any fad or fashion spreads: somebody who is already a user urges his friends to try, or simply shows already-eager friends how to do it.

But we need not rely on speculation, however plausible, that lowered prices and more abundant supplies would have increased heroin usage. Great Britain once followed such a policy and with almost exactly those results. Until the mid-1960's, British physicians were allowed to prescribe heroin to certain classes of addicts. (Possessing these drugs without a doctor's prescription remained a criminal offense.) For many years this policy worked well enough because the addict patients were typically middle-class people who had become dependent on opiate painkillers while undergoing hospital treatment. There was no drug culture. The British system worked for many years, not because it prevented drug abuse, but because there was no problem of drug abuse that would test the system.

All that changed in the 1960's. A few unscrupulous doctors began passing out heroin in wholesale amounts. One doctor prescribed almost 600,000 heroin tablets—that is, over thirteen pounds—in just one year. A youthful drug culture emerged with a demand for drugs far different from that of the older addicts. As a result, the British government required doctors to refer users to government-run clinics to receive their heroin.

But the shift to clinics did not curtail the growth in heroin use. Throughout the 1960's the number of addicts increased—the late John Kaplan of Stanford estimated by fivefold—in part as a result of the diversion of heroin from clinic patients to new users on the streets. An addict would bargain with the clinic doctor over how big a dose he would receive. The patient wanted as much as he could get, the doctor wanted to give as little as was needed. The patient had an advantage in this conflict because the doctor could not be certain how much was really needed. Many patients would use some of their "maintenance" dose and sell the remaining part to friends, thereby recruiting new addicts. As the clinics learned of this, they began to shift their treatment away from heroin and toward methadone, an addictive drug that, when taken orally, does not produce a "high" but will block the withdrawal pains associated with heroin abstinence.

Whether what happened in England in the 1960's was a mini-epidemic or an epidemic depends on whether one looks at numbers or at rates of change. Compared to the United States, the numbers were small. In 1960 there were 68 heroin addicts known to the British government; by 1968 there were 2,000 in treatment and many more who refused treatment. (They would refuse in part because they did not want to get methadone at a clinic if they could get heroin on the street.) Richard Hartnoll estimates that the actual number of addicts in England is five times the number officially registered. At a minimum, the number of British addicts increased by thirtyfold in ten years; the actual increase may have been much larger.

In the early 1980's the numbers began to rise again, and this time nobody doubted that a real epidemic was at hand. The increase was estimated to be 40 percent a year. By 1982 there were thought to be 20,000 heroin users in London alone. Geoffrey Pearson reports that many cities—Glasgow, Liverpool, Manchester, and Sheffield among them—were now experiencing a drug problem that once had been largely confined to London. The problem, again, was supply. The country was being flooded with cheap, high-quality heroin, first from Iran and then from Southeast Asia.

The United States began the 1960's with a much larger number of heroin addicts and probably a bigger at-risk population than was the case in Great Britain. Even though it would be foolhardy to suppose that the British system, if installed here, would have worked the same way or with the same results, it would be equally foolhardy to suppose that a combination of heroin available from leaky clinics and from street dealers who faced only minimal law-enforcement risks would not have produced a much greater increase in heroin use than we actually experienced. My guess is that if we had allowed either doctors or clinics to prescribe heroin, we would have had far worse results than were produced in Britain, if for no other reason than the vastly larger number of addicts with which we began. We would have had to find some way to police thousands (not scores) of physicians and hundreds (not dozens) of clinics. If the British civil service found it difficult to keep heroin in the hands of addicts and out of the hands of recruits when it was dealing with a few hundred people, how well would the American civil service have accomplished the same tasks when dealing with tens of thousands of people?

Back to the Future

Now cocaine, especially in its potent form, crack, is the focus of attention. Now as in 1972 the government is trying to reduce its use. Now as then some people are advocating legalization. Is there any more reason to yield to those arguments today than there was almost two decades ago?[1]

I think not. If we had yielded in 1972 we almost certainly would have had today a permanent population of several million, not several hundred thousand, heroin addicts. If we yield now we will have a far more serious problem with cocaine.

Crack is worse than heroin by almost any measure. Heroin produces a pleasant drowsiness and, if hygienically administered, has only the physical side effects of constipation and sexual impotence. Regular heroin use incapacitates many users, especially poor ones, for any productive work or social responsibility. They will sit nodding on a street corner, helpless but at least harmless. By contrast, regular cocaine use leaves the user neither helpless nor harmless. When smoked (as with crack) or injected, cocaine produces instant, intense, and short-lived euphoria. The experience generates a powerful desire to repeat it. If the drug is readily available, repeat use will occur. Those people who progress to "bingeing" on cocaine become devoted to the drug and its effects to the exclusion of almost all other considerations—job, family, children, sleep, food, even sex. Dr. Frank Gawin at Yale and Dr. Everett Ellinwood at Duke report that a substantial percentage of all high-dose, binge users become uninhibited, impulsive, hypersexual, compulsive, irritable, and hyperactive. Their moods vacillate dramatically, leading at times to violence and homicide.

Women are much more likely to use crack than heroin, and if they are pregnant, the effects on their babies are tragic. Douglas Besharov, who has been following the effects of drugs on infants for twenty years, writes that nothing he learned about heroin prepared him for the devastation of cocaine. Cocaine harms the fetus and can lead to physical deformities or neurological damage. Some crack babies have for all practical purposes suffered a disabling stroke while still in the womb. The long-term consequences of this brain damage are lowered cognitive ability and the onset of mood disorders. Besharov estimates that about 30,000 to 50,000 such babies are born every year, about 7,000 in New York City alone. There may be ways to treat such infants, but from everything we now know the treatment will be long, difficult, and expensive. Worse, the mothers who are most likely to produce crack babies are precisely the ones who, because of poverty or temperament, are least able and willing to obtain such treatment. In fact, anecdotal evidence suggests that crack mothers are likely to abuse their infants.

The notion that abusing drugs such as cocaine is a "victimless crime" is not only absurd but dangerous. Even ignoring the fetal drug syndrome, crack-dependent people are, like heroin addicts, individuals who regularly victimize their children by neglect, their spouses by improvidence, their employers by lethargy, and their coworkers by carelessness. Society is not and could never be a collection of autonomous individuals. We all have a stake in ensuring that each of us displays a minimal level of dignity, responsibility, and empathy. We cannot, of course, coerce people into goodness, but we can and should insist that some standards must be met if society itself—on which the very existence of the human personality depends—is to persist. Drawing the line that defines those standards is difficult and contentious, but if crack and heroin use do not fall below it, what does?

The advocates of legalization will respond by suggesting that my picture is overdrawn. Ethan Nadelmann of Princeton argues that the risk of legalization is less than most people suppose. Over 20 million Americans between the ages of eighteen and twenty-five have tried cocaine (according to a government survey), but only a quarter million use it daily. From this Nadelmann concludes that at most 3 percent of all young people who try cocaine develop a problem with it. The implication is clear: make the drug legal and we only have to worry about 3 percent of our youth.

The implication rests on a logical fallacy and a factual error. The fallacy is this: the percentage of occasional cocaine users who become binge users *when the drug is illegal* (and thus expensive and hard to find) tells us nothing about the percentage who will become dependent when the drug is legal (and thus cheap and abundant). Drs. Gawin and Ellinwood report, in common with several other researchers, that controlled or occasional use of cocaine changes to compulsive and frequent use "when access to the drug increases" or when the user switches from snorting to smoking. More cocaine more potently administered alters, perhaps sharply, the proportion of "controlled" users who become heavy users.

The factual error is this: The federal survey Nadelmann quotes was done in 1985, *before* crack had become common. Thus the probability of becoming dependent on cocaine was derived from the responses of users who snorted the drug. The speed and potency of cocaine's action increases dramatically when it is smoked. We do not yet know how greatly the advent of crack increases the risk of dependency, but all the clinical evidence suggests that the increase is likely to be large.

It is possible that some people will not become heavy users even when the drug is readily available in its most potent form. So far there are no scientific grounds for predicting who will and who will not become dependent. Neither socio-economic background nor personality traits differentiate between casual and intensive users. Thus, the only way to settle the question of who is correct about the effect of easy availability on drug use. Nadelmann or Gawin and Ellinwood, is to try it and see. But that social experiment is so risky as to be no experiment at all, for if cocaine is legalized and if the rate of its abusive use increases dramatically, there is no way to put the genie back in the bottle, and it is not a kindly genie.

Have We Lost?

Many people who agree that there are risks in legalizing cocaine or heroin still favor it because, they think, we have lost the war on drugs. "Nothing we have done has worked" and the current federal policy is just "more of the same." Whatever the costs of greater drug use, surely they would be less than the costs of our present, failed efforts.

That is exactly what I was told in 1972—and heroin is not quite as bad a drug as cocaine. We did not surrender and we did not lose. We did not win, either. What the nation accomplished then was what most efforts to save people from themselves accomplish: the problem was contained and the number of victims minimized, all at a considerable cost in law enforcement and increased crime. Was the cost worth it? I think so, but others may disagree. What are the lives of would-be addicts worth? I recall some people saying to me then, "Let them kill themselves." I was appalled. Happily, such views did not prevail.

Have we lost today? Not at all. High-rate cocaine use is not commonplace. The National Institute of Drug Abuse (NIDA) reports that less than 5 percent of high-school seniors used cocaine within the last thirty days. Of course this survey misses young people who have dropped out of school and miscounts those who lie on the questionnaire, but even if we inflate the NIDA estimate by some plausible percentage, it is still not much above 5 percent. Medical examiners reported in 1987 that about 1,500 died from cocaine use; hospital emergency rooms reported about 30,000 admissions related to cocaine abuse.

These are not small numbers, but neither are they evidence of a nationwide plague that threatens to engulf us all. Moreover, cities vary greatly in the proportion of people who are involved with cocaine. To get city-level data we need to turn to drug tests carried out on arrested persons, who obviously are more likely to be drug users than the average citizen. The National Institute of Justice, through its Drug Use Forecasting (DUF) project, collects urinalysis data on arrestees in 22 cities. As we have already seen, opiate (chiefly heroin) use has been flat or declining in most of these cities over the last decade. Cocaine use has gone up sharply, but with great variation among cities. New York, Philadelphia, and Washington, D.C., all report that two-thirds or more of their arrestees tested positive for cocaine, but in Portland, San Antonio, and Indianapolis the percentage was one-third or less.

In some neighborhoods, of course, matters have reached crisis proportions. Gangs control the streets, shootings terrorize residents, and drug-dealing occurs in plain view. The police seem barely able to contain matters. But in these neighborhoods—unlike at Palo Alto cocktail parties—the people are not calling for legalization, they are calling for help. And often not much help has come. Many cities are willing to do almost anything about the drug problem except spend more money on it. The federal government cannot change that; only local voters and politicians can. It is not clear that they will.

It took about ten years to contain heroin. We have had experience with crack for only about three or four years. Each year we spend perhaps $11 billion on law enforcement (and some of that goes to deal with marijuana) and perhaps $2 billion on treatment. Large sums, but not sums that should lead anyone to say, "We just can't afford this any more."

The illegality of drugs increases crime, partly because some users turn to crime to pay for their habits, partly because some users are stimulated by certain drugs (such as crack or PCP) to act more violently or ruthlessly than they otherwise would, and partly because criminal organizations seeking to control drug supplies use force to manage their markets. These also are serious costs, but no one knows how much they would be reduced if drugs were legalized. Addicts would no longer steal to pay black-market prices for drugs, a real gain. But some, perhaps a great deal, of that gain would be offset by the great increase in the number of addicts. These people, nodding on heroin or living in the delusion-ridden high of cocaine, would hardly be ideal employees. Many would steal simply to support themselves, since snatch-and-grab, opportunistic crime can be managed even by people unable to hold a regular job or plan an elaborate crime. Those British addicts who get their supplies from government clinics are not models of law-abiding decency. Most are in crime, and though their per-capita rate of criminality may be lower thanks to the cheapness of their drugs, the total volume of crime they produce may be quite large. Of course, society could decide to support all unemployable addicts on welfare, but that would mean that gains from lowered rates of crime would have to be offset by large increases in welfare budgets.

Proponents of legalization claim that the costs of having more addicts around would be largely if not entirely offset by having more money available with which to treat and care for them. The money would come from taxes levied on the sale of heroin and cocaine.

To obtain this fiscal dividend, however, legalization's supporters must first solve an economic dilemma. If they want to raise a lot of money to pay for welfare and treatment, the tax rate on the drugs will have to be quite high. Even if they themselves do not want a high rate, the politicians' love of "sin taxes" would probably guarantee that it would be high anyway. But the higher the tax, the higher the price of the drug, and the higher the price the greater the likelihood that addicts will turn to crime to find the money for it and that criminal organizations will be formed to sell tax-free drugs at below-market rates. If we managed to keep taxes (and thus prices) low, we would get that much less money to pay for welfare and treatment and more people could afford to become addicts. There may be an optimal tax rate for drugs that maximizes revenue while minimizing crime, bootlegging, and the recruitment of new addicts, but our experience with alcohol does not suggest that we know how to find it.

The Benefits of Illegality

The advocates of legalization find nothing to be said in favor of the current system except, possibly, that it keeps the number of addicts smaller than it would otherwise be. In fact, the benefits are more substantial than that.

First, treatment. All the talk about providing "treatment on demand" implies that there is a demand for treatment. That is not quite right. There are some drug-dependent people who genuinely want treatment and will remain in it if offered; they should receive it. But there are far more who want only short-term help after a bad crash; once stabilized and bathed, they are back on the street again, hustling. And even many of the addicts who enroll in a program honestly wanting help drop out after a short while when they discover that help takes time and commitment. Drug-dependent people have very short time horizons and a weak capacity for commitment. These two groups—those looking for a quick fix and those unable to stick with a long-term fix—are not easily helped. Even if we increase the number of treatment slots—as we should—we would have to do something to make treatment more effective.

One thing that can often make it more effective is compulsion. Douglas Anglin of UCLA, in common with many other researchers, has found that the longer one stays in a treatment program, the better the chances of a reduction in drug dependency. But he, again like most other researchers, has found that drop-out rates are high. He has also found, however, that patients who enter treatment under legal compulsion stay in the program longer than those not subject to such pressure. His research on the California civil-commitment program, for example, found that heroin users involved with its required drug-testing program had over the long term a lower rate of heroin use than similar addicts who were free of such constraints. If for many addicts compulsion is a useful component of treatment, it is not clear how compulsion could be achieved in a society in which purchasing, possessing, and using the drug were legal. It could be managed, I suppose, but I would not want to have to answer the challenge from the American Civil Liberties Union that it is wrong to compel a person to undergo treatment for consuming a legal commodity.

Next, education. We are now investing substantially in drug-education programs in the schools. Though we do not yet know for certain what will work, there are some promising leads. But I wonder how credible such programs would be if they were aimed at dissuading children from doing something perfectly legal. We could, of course, treat drug education like smoking education: inhaling crack and inhaling tobacco are both legal, but you should not do it because it is bad for you. That tobacco is bad for you is easily shown; the Surgeon General has seen to that. But what do we say about crack? It is pleasurable, but devoting yourself to so much pleasure is not a good idea (though perfectly legal)? Unlike tobacco, cocaine will not give you cancer or emphysema, but it will lead you to neglect your duties to family, job, and neighborhood? Everybody is doing cocaine, but you should not?

Again, it might be possible under a legalized regime to have effective drug-prevention programs, but their effectiveness would depend heavily, I think, on first having decided that cocaine use, like tobacco use, is purely a matter of practical consequences; no fundamental moral significance attaches to either. But if we believe—as I do—that dependency on certain mind-altering drugs is a moral issue and that their illegality rests in part on their immorality, then legalizing them undercuts, if it does not eliminate altogether, the moral message.

That message is at the root of the distinction we now make between nicotine and cocaine. Both are highly addictive; both have harmful physical effects. But we treat the two drugs differently, not simply because nicotine is so widely used as to be beyond the reach of effective prohibition, but because its use does not destroy the user's essential humanity. Tobacco shortens one's life, cocaine debases it. Nicotine alters one's habits, cocaine alters one's soul. The heavy use of crack, unlike the heavy use of tobacco, corrodes those natural sentiments of sympathy and duty that constitute our human nature and make possible our social life. To say, as does Nadelmann, that distinguishing morally between tobacco and cocaine is "little more than a transient prejudice" is close to saying that morality itself is but a prejudice.

The Alcohol Problem

Now we have arrived where many arguments about legalizing drugs begin: Is there any reason to treat heroin and cocaine differently from the way we treat alcohol?

There is no easy answer to that question because, as with so many human problems, one cannot decide simply on the basis either of moral principles or of individual consequences; one has to temper any policy by a common-sense judgment of what is possible. Alcohol, like heroin, cocaine, PCP, and marijuana, is a drug—that is, a mood-altering substance—and consumed to excess it certainly has harmful consequences: auto accidents, barroom fights, bedroom shootings. It is also, for some people, addictive. We cannot confidently compare the addictive powers of these drugs, but the best evidence suggests that crack and heroin are much more addictive than alcohol.

Many people, Nadelmann included, argue that since the health and financial costs of alcohol abuse are so much higher than those of cocaine or heroin abuse, it is hypocritical folly to devote our efforts to preventing cocaine or drug use. But as Mark Kleiman of Harvard has pointed out, this comparison is quite misleading. What Nadelmann is doing is showing that a *legalized* drug (alcohol) produces greater social harm than *illegal* ones (cocaine and heroin). But of course. Suppose that in the 1920's we had made heroin and cocaine legal and alcohol illegal. Can anyone doubt that Nadelmann would now be writing that it is folly to continue our ban on alcohol because cocaine and heroin are so much more harmful?

And let there be no doubt about it—widespread heroin and cocaine use are associated with all manner of ills. Thomas Bewley found that the mortality rate of British heroin addicts in 1968 was 28 times as high as the death rate of the same age group of nonaddicts, even though in England at the time an addict could obtain free or low-cost heroin and clean needles from British clinics. Perform the following mental experiment: suppose we legalized heroin and cocaine in this country. In what proportion of auto fatalities would the state police report that the driver was nodding off on heroin or recklessly driving on a coke high? In what proportion of spouse-assault and child-abuse cases would the local police report that crack was involved? In what proportion of industrial accidents would safety investigators report that the forklift or drill-press operator was in a drug-induced stupor or frenzy? We do not know exactly what the proportion would be, but anyone who asserts that it would not be much higher than it is now would have to believe that these drugs have little appeal except when they are illegal. And that is nonsense.

An advocate of legalization might concede that social harm—perhaps harm equivalent to that already produced by alcohol—would follow from making cocaine and heroin generally available. But at least, he might add, we would have the problem "out in the open" where it could be treated as a matter of "public health." That is well and good, *if* we knew how to treat—that is, cure—heroin and cocaine abuse. But we do not know how to do it for all the people who would need such help. We are having only limited success in coping with chronic alcoholics. Addictive behavior is immensely difficult to change, and the best methods for changing it—living in drug-free therapeutic communities, becoming faithful members of Alcoholics Anonymous or Narcotics Anonymous—require great personal commitment, a quality that is, alas, in short supply among the very persons—young people, disadvantaged people—who are often most at risk for addiction.

Suppose that today we had, not 15 million alcohol abusers, but half a million. Suppose that we already knew what we have learned from our long experience with the widespread use of alcohol. Would we make whiskey legal? I do not know, but I suspect there would be a lively debate. The Surgeon General would remind us of the risks alcohol poses to pregnant women. The National Highway Traffic Safety Administration would point to the likelihood of more highway fatalities caused by drunk drivers. The Food and Drug Administration might find that there is a non-trivial increase in cancer associated with alcohol consumption. At the same time the police would report great difficulty in keeping illegal whiskey out of our cities, officers being corrupted by bootleggers, and alcohol addicts often resorting to crime to feed their habit. Libertarians, for their part, would argue that every citizen has a right to drink anything he wishes and that drinking is, in any event, a "victimless crime."

However the debate might turn out, the central fact would be that the problem was still, at that point, a small one. The government cannot legislate away the addictive tendencies in all of us, nor can it remove completely even the most dangerous addictive substances. But it can cope with harms when the harms are still manageable.

Science and Addiction

One advantage of containing a problem while it is still containable is that it buys time for science to learn more about it and perhaps to discover a cure. Almost unnoticed in the current debate over legalizing drugs is that basic science has made rapid strides in identifying the underlying neurological processes involved in some forms of addiction. Stimulants such as cocaine and amphetamines alter the way certain brain cells communicate with one another. That alteration is complex and not entirely understood, but in simplified form it involves modifying the way in which a neurotransmitter called dopamine sends signals from one cell to another.

When dopamine crosses the synapse between two cells, it is in effect carrying a message from the first cell to activate the second one. In certain parts of the brain that message is experienced as pleasure. After the message is delivered, the dopamine returns to the first cell. Cocaine apparently blocks this return, or "reuptake," so that the excited cell and others nearby continue to send pleasure messages. When the exaggerated high produced by cocaine-influenced dopamine finally ends, the brain cells may (in ways that are still a matter of dispute) suffer from an extreme lack of dopamine, thereby making the individual unable to experience any pleasure at all. This would explain why cocaine users often feel so depressed after enjoying the drug. Stimulants may also affect the way in which other neurotransmitters, such as serotonin and noradrenaline, operate.

Whatever the exact mechanism may be, once it is identified it becomes possible to use drugs to block either the effect of cocaine or its tendency to produce dependency. There have already been experiments using desipramine, imipramine, bromocriptine, carbamazpine, and other chemicals. There are some promising results.

Tragically, we spend very little on such research, and the agencies funding it have not in the past occupied very influential or visible posts in the federal bureaucracy. If there is one aspect of the "war on drugs" metaphor that I dislike, it is its tendency to focus attention almost exclusively on the troops in the trenches, whether engaged in enforcement or treatment, and away from the research-and-development efforts back on the home front where the war may ultimately be decided.

I believe that the prospects of scientists in controlling addiction will be strongly influenced by the size and character of the problem they face. If the problem is a few hundred thousand chronic, high-dose users of an illegal product, the chances of making a difference at a reasonable cost will be much greater than if the problem is a few million chronic users of legal substances. Once a drug is legal, not only will its use increase but many of those who then use it will prefer the drug to the treatment: they will want the pleasure, whatever the cost to themselves or their families, and they will resist—probably successfully—any effort to wean them away from experiencing the high that comes from inhaling a legal substance.

If I Am Wrong . . .

No one can know what our society would be like if we changed the law to make access to cocaine, heroin, and PCP easier. I believe, for reasons given, that the result would be a sharp increase in use, a more widespread degradation of the human personality, and a greater rate of accidents and violence.

I may be wrong. If I am, then we will needlessly have incurred heavy costs in law enforcement and some forms of criminality. But if I am right, and the legalizers prevail anyway, then we will have consigned millions of people, hundreds of thousands of infants, and hundreds of neighborhoods to a life of oblivion and disease. To the lives and families destroyed by alcohol we will have added countless more destroyed by cocaine, heroin, PCP, and whatever else a basement scientist can invent.

Human character is formed by society; indeed, human character is inconceivable without society, and good character is less likely in a bad society. Will we, in the name of an abstract doctrine of radical individualism, and with the false comfort of suspect predictions, decide to take the chance that somehow individual decency can survive amid a more general level of degradation?

I think not. The American people are too wise for that, whatever the academic essayists and cocktail-party pundits may say. But if Americans today are less wise than I suppose, then Americans at some future time will look back on us now and wonder, what kind of people were they that they could have done such a thing?

NOTES

1. I do not here take up the question of marijuana. For a variety of reasons—its widespread use and its lesser tendency to addict—it presents a different problem from cocaine or heroin. For a penetrating analysis, see Mark Kleiman, *Marijuana: Costs of Abuse, Costs of Control* (Greenwood Press).

Recreational Drugs and Paternalism

DOUGLAS N. HUSAK

Husak initially notes that the drug war is apparently endless. In an age where about seven million Americans are unemployed and at least 33 million live in poverty, Husak attempts what he calls "a modest step toward placing the 'drug problem' in its proper perspective," rather than uncritically accept public opinion polls identifying drugs as America's greatest problem. He also questions the drug war's paternalism, the restriction of a person's freedom, allegedly for that person's own good.

I.

Whenever this paper is read, America will doubtless be waging yet another round of its apparently endless "war on drugs." Any of the approximately seven million unemployed Americans, or thirty-three million Americans living in poverty, might be skeptical of polls that identify drug use as our nation's greatest problem. How should a philosopher respond to their skepticism?

In this paper I will take a modest step toward placing the "drug problem" in its proper perspective by critically examining whether and under what conditions criminal legislation against the use of recreational drugs (henceforth abbreviated as CLAURD) can be supported on paternalistic grounds.[1] My point is not merely to encourage philosophers to resist the hysteria and hyperbole that has accompanied past and present "wars on drugs." My larger project is to reveal the complexity in attempts to identify and apply criteria for the legitimate use of paternalistic criminal legislation. I conclude that the most plausible arguments offered by the paternalist on behalf of CLAURD depend upon unarticulated and controversial empirical assumptions to a much greater extent than is generally acknowledged. These arguments make unwarranted generalizations from a "worst case" scenario that seldom conforms to the reality of typical drug use.

Among the more noteworthy aspects of this issue is its almost total neglect among philosophers.[2] This omission is unfortunate. Drug laws are among the most frequently enforced criminal statutes in America. Approximately one out of every four arrests in the United States is directly related to the use of a drug.[3] Nor are punishments trivial. Prisons in metropolitan areas are strained by unprecedented over-crowding as a result of "get tough" policies enacted by legislatures against drug offenders. The judiciary has acquiesced in these efforts. The Supreme Court has held that the sentence of two consecutive twenty-year terms in prison for the offense of possession and distribution of approximately $200 worth of marijuana is not unconstitutional as disproportionate to the seriousness of the crime.[4] And matters may get worse, for much of the public believes that sentences are too lenient. President Reagan reserved judgment when asked whether "drug dealers" should be executed, but was quick to add, "I know they deserve it."[5] "Get-tough" policies are not reserved for so-called drug "kingpins," for a major part of "drug czar" William

Law and Philosophy 8: 353–381, 1989. © 1989 *Kluwer Academic Publishers,* the Netherlands.

Bennett's strategy in the war on drugs is to increase the penalties for casual drug users. If drug laws are unwarranted, they represent among the most serious legal injustices in American history. Yet philosophers have remained strangely silent about any maltreatment suffered by drug offenders.

Legal philosophers have been interested in the general issue of paternalism since the publication of Gerald Dworkin's pioneering essay.[6] Those theorists who provide examples of legal paternalism invariably mention CLAURD as a paradigm case.[7] But disappointment follows. Although these philosophers are anxious to apply their abstract principles to actual instances of legislation, they fail to explicitly identify the implications of their arguments upon CLAURD. Perhaps CLAURD represents a taboo that even philosophers are reluctant to address. The public in general, and philosophical community in particular, are prepared to take seriously an argument against mandatory use of seat belts or motorcycle helmets. But society seems unreceptive to an argument against CLAURD. Few public figures who hope to preserve credibility within "the establishment" have taken a principled stance against CLAURD.[8] The proposals to decriminalize drug use, when not dismissed out of hand, are generally motivated either by a fear that law enforcement jeopardizes civil liberties, or by a utilitarian concern to protect the innocent public upon whom addicts prey, or by an economic objective to raise tax revenues. The decriminalization movement is seldom motivated by a desire to safeguard any supposed "rights of drug users."

John Kleinig's excellent discussion of paternalism devotes several pages to the topic of seat belts, but barely touches the issue of drugs.[9] Donald VanDeVeer's exhaustive treatent of paternalism does not address drugs, beyond listing CLAURD as a paradigm case.[10] The fourteen essays in Rolf Sartorious's otherwise comprehensive anthology hardly mention drugs, and none of the contributors examines them extensively.[11] Joel Feinberg deserves credit for stating that laws proscribing voluntary drug use constitute an "easy case" that "is in fact the litmus test example for distinguishing the paternalist from the liberal."[12] But his discussion of drugs, as I hope he would agree, is somewhat superficial and unresponsive to the real concerns of the paternalist.

I will describe opposition to CLAURD as the pro-choice position on recreational drug use. Those who argue that abortion should be permitted have good reason to describe their position as pro-choice; on similar grounds, this characterization is also preferable in the context of CLAURD. The judgment that conduct is morally permissible, and should be legally tolerated, must not be confused with advocacy of that conduct.

For a number of reasons, my topic may appear to be somewhat ill-chosen. I will address several possible reservations in Part II. I will examine some of the general arguments in favor of a pro-choice position in Part III. In Part IV, I will discuss the attempt to justify paternalistic interferences with nonvoluntary conduct, and I will continue this analysis in Part V by considering how the phenomenon of addiction bears on CLAURD. I will conclude in Part VI by evaluating attempts to justify paternalistic interferences with decisions that are voluntary. Throughout my discussion, I will focus primarily on the work of Joel Feinberg, whose *Harm to Self* provides the most thoughtful and detailed approach to paternalism among contemporary philosophers. My perspective fits comfortably within the general framework about paternalism that Feinberg has constructed.

II.

For several reasons, a discussion of the paternalistic case for CLAURD must remain tentative and inconclusive. In this section I will briefly comment upon six of these difficulties.

(1.) I begin with the mildly controversial assumption that some instances of criminal paternalism are legitimate exercises of state authority over sane adults. Libertarians and others who apparently reject this supposition may believe that there is no point in reading further. Nonetheless, they should find the ensuing discussion worthwhile. Even those philosophers who categorically denounce all examples of criminal paternalism[13] must believe that some such laws are more or less objectionable than others. In this paper I will describe a number of factors that help to distinguish acceptable from unacceptable criminal paternalism. Those who resist all paternalism are invited to construe these criteria as distinguishing bad from worse paternalism.

(2.) I have little to say about whether CLAURD can be supported under the less controversial "harm to others" rationale. For two reasons, this narrow focus may appear to be artificial and unduly restrictive. First, the very task of distinguishing paternalistic from nonpaternalistic rationales for a given law is suspect. It is a truism that virtually any piece of criminal legislation may be supported by both paternalistic and nonpaternalistic considerations. Many theorists express this point by denying the existence of examples of "pure" or "unmixed" paternalism.[14] Second, inasmuch as the two rationales can be separated, many of the familiar arguments for CLAURD emphasize how drug use is indirectly harmful to others.[15] Perhaps my discussion neglects the more compelling defense of CLAURD; arguably the nonpaternalistic basis for drug proscription is sufficient. Thus little of practical significance may follow from a refutation of the paternalistic case in favor of CLAURD.

Nonetheless, my inquiry is not merely of theoretical interest. Any conclusion can be supported by more than one argument, but the evaluation of each argument is not thereby rendered unimportant. Although CLAURD can be defended by more than one rationale, each rationale should be examined on its own merits. Virtually all commentators who have discussed paternalism cite CLAURD among their paradigm examples, and paternalistic arguments in favor of drug legislation are frequently voiced. If these arguments are unsound, it is important to understand why. Careful thought about one class of paternalistic laws is bound to produce insight about others. Moreover, suppose *arguendo* that support for CLAURD from nonpaternalistic sources is forceful although ultimately inconclusive. If so, it would be crucial to understand the strengths and weaknesses of the paternalistic case in some detail. It is seldom discussed whether a plausible though insufficient paternalistic basis for a law might combine with a plausible though insufficient nonpaternalistic basis for a law to produce a compelling case overall. The issue of when two insufficient justifications, one paternalistic and the other nonpaternalistic, combine to become sufficient, is unchartered philosophical territory.

(3.) It is also essential, although difficult, to distinguish paternalistic arguments for CLAURD from those of the legal moralist. According to legal moralism, the immorality of an activity may be a sufficient reason to prohibit it, quite apart from whether it produces harm to oneself or to others. Although support for legal moralism among philosophers is minimal, there can be little doubt that much of the public sympathy for CLAURD rests upon it. The activity of using drugs for recreational purposes is widely depicted as wrongful and degrading. It would be fascinating to explore these attitudes in detail,[16] but I confine myself to a single observation here. Society is tolerant of the moderate use of many nonprescription drugs to calm (alcohol), to invigorate (caffeine), or to relieve minor discomfort (aspirin). Unless the legal moralist is content to enforce social prejudice,[17] he must explain why some of these purposes are legitimate, while others are allegedly wrongful and degrading.

(4.) An analysis of the paternalistic case for CLAURD must be regarded as tentative for yet another reason. No one doubts that substantial support for the paternalistic case against given drugs derives from the fact that use of these substances is already illegal. Controversy surrounds the question of how much strength is added to the paternalistic case from this source. But surely a large part of the reason why some drugs are so harmful stems from their illegality. At the very least, much of the economic hardship that illegal drug users suffer is a function of the fact that drugs are expensive, which in turn is a consequence of their proscription.[18] The same point can be made about a number of medical problems.[19]

Thus it is crucial to assess the harmfulness of various drugs without tainting that investigation by including the harm that would not be caused were they not illegal. Unfortunately, there is no firm basis for making precise estimates about how the degree of harm to users would be affected by decriminalization. Would the incidence of drug abuse increase because of the absence of deterrence and the reduction in price? Or would the incidence of drug abuse decrease because the mystique and glamor of drugs would erode? How would the immediate effects differ from the long-term effects? Philosophers should have little confidence in the accuracy of their conjectures about these questions.

(5.) It may seem fantastic to address the issue of drug use *simpliciter*. Surely the arguments against caffeine differ so markedly from those against heroin that it may seem preposterous to examine them together.[20] A single discussion of both legal and illegal drugs is bound to blur distinctions and to produce results that will strike many persons as counterintuitive.

But it is important to identify the general conditions that any activity, including use of a given drug, must satisfy if the paternalistic case against it is compelling. What properties must a drug possess so that sound paternalistic principles justify its prohibition? What properties must a drug possess so that there could be no reasonable basis for criminalizing or even discouraging its use? These inquiries may have some surprising results in that the arguments for criminalization of some legal substances might be more persuasive than those for some illegal substances.[21] But the fact that these results are surprising is surely not a good reason to disqualify the theory or principle that gives rise to them. It cannot be emphasized too strongly that our so-called intuitions about the acceptability or unacceptability of the results to which a theory or principle gives rise are greatly influenced by our familiarity with those results. A principle or theory that calls for punishment for the use of alcohol will immediately be dismissed; our national experience with criminalization is widely recognized as disastrous. Similarly, a principle or theory that calls for the decriminalization of hallucinogens will offend many people's "common sense." But are these attitudes defensible? Perhaps few of our opinions about CLAURD will withstand critical scrutiny.

(6.) Finally, incredible complexities surround the phenomenon Feinberg describes as the "garrison threshold." At some point, conduct that would initially be categorized as private and self-regarding may become so pervasive and widespread that it poses a threat to society. Any community can tolerate self-indulgent conduct that is harmful to the agent unless and until it is practiced by a significant percentage of the population, and crosses the threshold into serious public harm. The difficulty, of course, is to identify the "significant" point at which initially private conduct becomes an epidemic of public concern. Arguably, this threshold has been crossed by the use of alcohol and tobacco products. Whether it would be crossed if illegal drugs were decriminalized depends once again upon controversial predictions of how patterns of drug use would be affected by various legal reforms.

In addition, there are any number of "garrison threshold" phenomena that plague a principled discussion of CLAURD. I will mention only one further difficulty here, although several more will be encountered shortly. A great deal of anti-drug rhetoric focuses on the effects of drug use upon children. It is tempting to believe that a compelling case against drug use by juveniles has no implications whatever for the case against drug use by adults. No one seriously proposes that alcohol and tobacco products should be criminalized because they are especially harmful when used by children. But suppose that juveniles consume a very high percentage of a given recreational drug. Is there any point at which this percentage becomes so significant that the state is warranted in prohibiting that drug altogether as part of the most effective strategy to reduce its use by children? If this question is answered affirmatively, yet a second threshold must be identified in a comprehensive examination of CLAURD.

For the above reasons, an examination of the paternalistic case for CLAURD must remain tentative and inconclusive. But despite these formidable obstacles, I am hopeful that some progress in assessing CLAURD can be made.

III.

Arguably there exists a "presumption of freedom," such that interferences with liberty are illegitimate in the absence of a justification.[22] This presumption places the burden of proof on those who would criminalize drug use. Despite this presumption, the overwhelming consensus in contemporary America is that most controlled substances should remain illegal. Perhaps CLAURD can be supported by a "presumption in favor of the status quo." In light of these conflicting presumptions, it is probably unfair to begin an evaluation of CLAURD by supposing that either side of this dispute bears the onus of proof.

Pro-choice arguments are essentially of two kinds. The first is consequentialist. It might be contended that the decriminalization of drug use will produce better effects than criminalization. John Stuart Mill, as is well known, objected to all paternalistic legislation on this basis.[23] The central problems in evaluating this consequentialist strategy are to estimate and balance the benefits and evils that would follow from a pro-choice position. The second kind of argument is deontological. A principle of autonomy that protects the right to use drugs might be defended. This is Feinberg's strategy, and it may fail for either of two reasons. The initial characterization of autonomy might be defective, or the importance of autonomy might be overestimated when weighed against competing values.

In this section I will briefly discuss both consequentialist and deontological pro-choice arguments. For two reasons, I will concentrate more heavily upon deontological considerations. First, as indicated above, consequentialist discussions of paternalism involve tremendous speculation. The long-term consequences of decriminalization cannot be estimated precisely. Second and more importantly, consequentialist arguments about paternalism are less widely accepted among contemporary philosophers, and for good reason. Questions about whether personal freedom should yield to state authority are more properly addressed within a philosophical framework that affords special protection to the rights of individuals. Legislation that violates personal rights should be treated with skepticism regardless of the beneficial consequences it promotes. Since I am primarily concerned with whether a right to use drugs can withstand an attack by the paternalist, I will focus almost entirely upon deontological arguments.

Consequentialists who support CLAURD on paternalistic grounds believe that legal proscriptions create more utility than disutility. Presumably these benefits are achieved because CLAURD deters drug use. Of course, whatever reservations one may have about the deterrent effect of legislation in general apply more forcefully to CLAURD in particular, since the likelihood of apprehension and conviction is especially low for drug offenders. Here, however, I want to raise an additional difficulty for consequentialists. When the effects of prohibiting some activity are assessed, it is crucial to take into account both the satisfaction and the dissatisfaction produced by deterring people from that activity. For this reason, no one would take seriously a proposal to prohibit television, for example, despite the wealth of data about its deleterious effects. This evidence is not dispositive, it is said, because it neglects the fact that consumers want television, they enjoy it, they derive satisfaction from it. The prohibition of alcohol ultimately failed because of the public demand, and only a morality unresponsive to personal wants and desires could be blind to this consideration.

Conspicuous by its absence, however, is a similar response to CLAURD. Why are consumer preferences not given comparable weight here? Most of the many millions of

Americans who use illegal drugs annually derive (at least) short-term pleasure from their experience. Once their pleasure is placed on the utilitarian scales, no one has any clear idea whether drug use produces more utility than disutility. It is simple prejudice to insist without evidence that the use of any given drug must create more harm than good. Proponents of CLAURD might avoid the uncertainties of a utilitarian balancing by denying that the pleasures of drug use belong on the scales in the first place. But on what basis might they be excluded? Two possible reasons will be discussed; neither deserves to be taken very seriously.

First, it might be contended that consumers do not really want, enjoy, or derive satisfaction from recreational drug use. This strategy will be dismissed by economists who take wants as given and make policy recommendations designed to maximize the satisfaction of existing consumer preferences. And it is almost certain to be rejected by philosophers familiar with the sleight-of-hand that results from positing an alleged "rational will," and then supposing that a person's "true wants" can be identified apart from his expressed desires.[24] But this position remains extraordinarily common among nonusers. Persons who do not consume a particular drug (e.g., tobacco) find it almost impossible to fathom how users could possibly enjoy it. Critics of paternalism have cautioned that "where we disapprove of an activity, or cannot appreciate it, we tend to think that the agent himself derives little benefit from it. In these ways the practice of paternalism easily becomes a cloak for the imposition of our values on those who are coerced."[25] Drug use is almost invariably depicted as leading to ruin, such that the vast majority of candid users, with hindsight, would admit to a preference that they had never been exposed to illegal substances in the first place. The use of illegal drugs is widely explained by peer pressure, boredom, alienation, ignorance, depression, or some other human weakness.

But such weaknesses could not begin to account for the high incidence of drug use. Insofar as it is possible to generalize, the initial decision to experiment with a drug is probably best explained by simple curiosity. But curiosity could hardly explain the decision to persist in drug use. Heretical though it may sound, a great many persons continue to use drugs because they enjoy their experience. "Educational" policies to combat drugs will inevitably fail as long as the pleasures of use are discounted, and consumption is explained solely in terms of some personality deficiency. The model of the drug user who would like to quit but cannot overcome his addiction applies only to a small percentage of individuals.[26] This model is distorted even when applied to the most addictive drugs.[27] And even if the true motivations for drug use could be explained by the above factors, further argument is required to show why it is legitimate to invoke the criminal law to protect persons from succumbing to these influences. Many consumer choices, e.g., a taste for expensive, fashionable clothes, are shaped by such weaknesses; why dismiss them as inappropriate and in need of paternalistic intervention when they lead to drug use?

A second and somewhat more sophisticated strategy for ignoring consumer preferences is to contend that the pleasure derived from drug use, although genuine, is pathological. Arguably, the pleasure derived from pathological activities should not count in a utilitarian calculus. To cite an extreme example, no one would seriously attempt to balance the pleasure of rapists against the pain of their victims in order to assess the justifiability of laws against rape. There is a parallel (but mysterious and unexplained) tendency to label as pathological and thus dismiss the pleasure of the experience of altering consciousness.

The chief difficulty here, of course, is to defend a theory to distinguish pathological from nonpathological pleasures. This obstacle is formidable. In the example of rape, it is evident that the pleasure derived from violating rights, from inflicting suffering upon another, qualifies as pathological. But there is less promise that a theory of pathological pleasures for self-regarding conduct can be constructed and applied.

The pleasure of drug use might be condemned as pathological if it were believed to be immoral to experience. As it stands, however, this belief is a conclusion in search of an argument. Moreover, this support for CLAURD depends on legal moralism rather than paternalism: Drug use is condemned not because of its harmful effects on the user, but because it is wrong notwithstanding its effects. In light of this realization, it might be desirable to move beyond consequentialist reasoning at this point. Instead of trying to determine how the pleasures of drug use might be discounted, it is preferable (as most philosophers have realized) to reject theories that approach these sorts of issues by balancing aggregate utility against disutility. Henceforth I will confine my attention almost exclusively to deontological pro-choice arguments against CLAURD.

The principle of autonomy as explicated by Feinberg clearly protects drug use.[28] He writes:

> The kernel of the idea of autonomy is the right to make choices and decisions—what to put into my body, what contacts with my body to permit, where and how to move my body through public space, how to use my chattels and physical property, what personal information to disclose to others, what information to conceal, and more.[29]

The first and foremost of these alleged rights —the choice or decision to put a substance into one's body—is incompatible with CLAURD.

Has the principle of autonomy been correctly interpreted?[30] One way to assess Feinberg's principle of autonomy is to evaluate alternatives to it. Surely some decisions are "personal" and beyond state interference; some principle(s) distinguish the realm of the private from the public.[31] Can a version of the autonomy principle be formulated that would protect a person's right to make those harmful decisions that most everyone would agree to be a matter of personal choice, while not also protecting the use of drugs?[32] This is the challenge that must by overcome by a philosopher who concedes that personal autonomy would be violated by a law prohibiting, e.g., the eating of fried foods, or by a law requiring, e.g., regular cardiovascular exercise, but not by a law prohibiting, e.g., the use of cocaine.

How might this challenge be met? Feinberg discusses only one reservation about his principle of autonomy.[33] He questions whether autonomy should be construed to protect "the myriad options of lesser significance, the choice of whether or not to fasten a seat belt, for example."[34] He might have responded, quite plausibly, that the decision about which choices are of greater or lesser significance is itself encompassed by the principle of autonomy. But even if this response is mistaken, and the principle of autonomy protects only important decisions, criteria for distinguishing the important from the unimportant must be provided. Needless to say, this task is difficult, and it is doubtful that the decision to use drugs will fall on the unimportant side of whatever distinction is drawn. Decisions about what to put into one's body seemingly qualify as important.

An autonomy principle might fail to protect the use of recreational drugs for several additional reasons; I will mention only one. Perhaps such a principle could effectively distinguish between the use of unhealthy foods and dangerous drugs by reference to the degree of harm risked by the user. According to this interpretation, the principle of autonomy protects both important and unimportant decisions from state interference, but only if a given amount of harm (which I will describe as "*h*") is not risked. Admittedly, the perception that drugs are especially harmful probably explains much of the public hostility toward them.[35] Nonetheless, this basis for distinguishing acceptable from unacceptable paternalism does not seem especially promising. Since many philosophers hold that the autonomy principle protects the decision to commit suicide, it seems disingenuous to prohibit the use of even the most dangerous recreational drugs because of the extent of the harm they might cause.

Even if a principle of autonomy did not allow persons to exceed a risk of harm *h*, it is unlikely that its application would prohibit all illegal drugs. Here again, empirical "threshold" questions must be confronted. Which drugs cause *h*, and with what frequency? It is coherent to concede that the use of some possible substance might cause *h* with sufficient regularity to be criminalized by sound paternalistic principles, while denying that the use of any existing recreational drug does so. Moreover, it is difficult to devise a common standard that would allow comparisons between the risk of drug use and the dangers of unhealthy foods, sky diving, driving without a seat belt, boxing, mountain climbing, and similar recreational activities.

If the decision to use drugs is indeed protected by a principle of autonomy, it still can be argued that this principle is outweighed by competing considerations. If the likelihood of harm to self were always or usually sufficient to outweigh the principle of autonomy, the door would be open to a wider scope of paternalism than almost anyone would accept. In order to exclude some paternalism, autonomy must occasionally prevail when its exercise produces harm to oneself. How is respect for autonomy to be balanced against protection from harm to oneself? Feinberg's position on this issue is uncompromising. He holds that "a person's right of self-determination, being sovereign, takes precedence even over his own good."[36] He rejects the alternative that "we must balance the person's right against his good and weigh them intuitively" on the ground that it "is hard enough to do in individual cases, [and] may raise even more difficult problems for the legislator who must reason intuitively about whole classes of cases."[37] Feinberg does not, however, claim to provide a decisive argument for this "absolutist" position about the priority of the right over the good, and many philosophers will find his views to be extreme. Further argument is required to decide whether and under what conditions a principle of autonomy that provides initial protection to drug use can be overridden by paternalistic considerations.

IV.

Under what conditions would a deontologist who defends a principle of autonomy that protects drug use allow an interference with choice on paternalistic grounds? Feinberg's general position is that only soft paternalism[38] is warranted, i.e., "the state has the right to prevent self-regarding harmful conduct when but only when that conduct is substantially nonvoluntary."[39] According to Feinberg, if an agent's choice is nonvoluntary, it is not truly his, and an interference with it does not violate his autonomy. Clearly, applications of this important exception to the general rule against paternalism require an explication of the concept of voluntariness.

Feinberg recognizes that any number of existing models of voluntariness are unhelpful and unrealistic, creating an "impossibly difficult ideal standard, one that would hardly ever be satisfied."[40] Few decisions are the product of dispassionate, fully informed, rational calculation; they do not conform to a conception of "perfect voluntariness," but neither are they completely nonvoluntary. Feinberg's model of voluntariness is responsive to this fact. He construes voluntariness as a " 'variable concept,' determined by higher and lower cut-off points depending on the nature of the circumstances, the interests at stake, and the moral or legal purpose to be served."[41] It is at this point, in applying his insights about the "variability" of the concept of voluntariness, that Feinberg provides his most detailed discussion of drug use.

In explicating his views about nonvoluntariness, Feinberg describes three scenarios in which Mr. Roe discusses with Dr. Doe his decision to use a dangerous recreational drug, *X*. In the first example, Roe mistakenly believes that *X* does not cause physical harm.

Feinberg concludes that Roe's decision to use X is substantially nonvoluntary, because he does not intend to ingest a substance that will in fact harm him.[42] In the second example, Roe is aware that X is harmful, but indicates that he actually intends to harm himself. Feinberg concludes that Roe's odd decision is probably nonvoluntary; it is likely that he has somehow lost the full use of his faculties. If further examination does not reveal independent evidence of incapacitation, however, Roe should be allowed to proceed. In the final example, Roe understands the risks of X, has no desire to harm himself, and states: "I don't care if it causes me physical harm. I'll get a lot of pleasure first, so much pleasure in fact, that it is well worth the risk."[43] Feinberg concludes that this case is "easy." There is no reason to believe Roe's decision is nonvoluntary; an interference with his choice would unjustly violate his autonomy.

Feinberg's imaginary conversations between Mr. Roe and Dr. Doe provide insight into the permissibility of paternalism in interpersonal relationships, but it is difficult to see how they advance our understanding of when legislation in general, and CLAURD in particular, are warranted. A defense of paternalism in inter-personal relationships may not lead to a defense of paternalistic legislation. Dr. Doe can inquire about why Roe decides to engage in risky behavior, and assess whether his answers betray evidence of nonvoluntariness. But the state can hardly engage in a private dialogue with each of its citizens.[44] Feinberg acknowledges that the law must be couched in general terms,[45] but fails to explain how this concession makes it possible to apply his hypothetical conversations to arguments for or against CLAURD.

How might this bridge be crossed? It is tempting to believe that the law, necessarily expressed in general terms, should be responsive to the most frequent, typical reason individuals run given risks. If so, it is crucial to notice that the overwhelming majority of drug use seems to correspond to Feinberg's third example. Although mistakes about the effects of drug use come in all shapes and sizes, it is relatively rare for an adult user to believe that consumption involves no appreciable risk of harm. Drug users who labor under misconceptions about the risks of harm should be educated rather than permanently restrained; if they persist after having been warned, their behavior corresponds more closely to Feinberg's third example than to his first.[46] And almost never does a person take drugs in order to harm himself. Most persons consume drugs for much the same reason as they eat ice cream, hang glide, or ride motorcycles; they believe that the likelihood of immediate pleasure outweighs the risk of eventual harm. It would be preposterous to prohibit drugs to the vast majority who share this rationale because a small minority are unaware of the risks, or are deprived of their faculties and actually desire to harm themselves. To base legal policy on this small minority is to generalize from a "worst case" scenario. If I am correct that the overwhelming majority of drug use corresponds to Feinberg's third example,[47] there is little reason to believe that paternalistic interferences with drug consumption can be justified on the ground that such use is nonvoluntary.[48]

But a consistent deontologist should not base legal policy upon the most frequent, typical reason that individuals run given risks. It is crucial to realize that generalizations from any particular scenario, worst or otherwise, are incompatible with a commitment to preserve the moral autonomy of persons. Consequentialists encounter well-known difficulties in protecting individual rights, since they allow increases in the welfare of some to compensate for losses in the welfare of others. But these sorts of trade-offs are alien to a deontological moral perspective that takes seriously a commitment to the autonomy of persons. The fear that some individuals, perhaps even a majority, will use a drug nonvoluntarily, is simply not a persuasive ground to deny that drug to those whose use is voluntary. For this reason, deontologists should be much more likely to oppose CLAURD than consequentialists. Arguments in support of CLAURD are much more compelling in a consequentialist framework that downplays the significance of the moral rights of persons, and allows the good of some to be enhanced by sacrificing the moral autonomy of others.[49]

It should be pointed out that Feinberg's position on the connection between mistake, nonvoluntariness, and drug use provides less reason to prohibit recreational drugs than medicinal drugs of dubious efficacy. Consider the debate about whether cancer patients should have access to laetrile, despite FDA findings that laetrile is unhelpful and perhaps harmful.[50] Here the consumer is simply wrong about the factual properties of the drug; his desperation makes him vulnerable to wishful thinking. His case corresponds most closely to the first of Feinberg's three conversations between Roe and Doe.[51] One might endorse the judgment that "the patient's appeal to the principle of autonomy in . . . cases of ineffective drug usage seems to amount to nothing but an appeal to the right to be wrong which is no right at all."[52] The adult recreational drug user, by way of contrast, is less likely to be factually mistaken; he is almost certain to be aware of health risks, but is prepared to undertake them for the sake of the short-term pleasure he is confident will result. His disagreement with the supporters of CLAURD is not about facts, but rather about what might be called his priorities in life. It is exactly these kinds of interferences that opponents of paternalism have feared.

V.

It is peculiar that Feinberg does not discuss what is surely a familiar and serious argument for CLAURD: Persons who use drugs run substantial risks of addiction. Once a person becomes addicted to a harmful drug, the argument continues, proscriptions can be justified under a "soft" paternalist strategy, for addiction renders drug use nonvoluntary. This argument seems to me to be the most promising basis to support CLAURD on soft paternalistic grounds. As the discussion in Part IV indicates, it is difficult to fathom how typical drug use could be construed as nonvoluntary unless users undertook risks of addiction.

The claim that a substance is addictive has proved to be incredibly elusive, with at least three distinct interpretations.[53] First, a drug might be addictive if users develop a *tolerance,* requiring progressively greater dosages to produce the same effect. Second, a drug might be addictive if users afford it a *psychological centrality* relative to their other interests. Third, a drug might be addictive if users develop *physical dependence,* and undergo withdrawal symptoms when the drug becomes unavailable. My project here is not to unravel the extraordinarily complicated questions about how these three interpretations of addiction might be clarified and related, but to understand how they bear on the paternalistic case for CLAURD.

Neither of the first two of these interpretations of addiction can support the conclusion that drug use is nonvoluntary. Clearly the fact that greater dosages of a substance are required to attain the same effect cannot render use of that substance less than fully voluntary. Nor is it easy to comprehend how the fact that users elevate drugs to a significant status relative to their other interests differentiates them from many other pursuits (e.g., wealth, sex, soap operas) that are not candidates for paternalistic intervention.[54] But the phenomenon of physical dependence is more troubling for pro-choice advocates. If the difficulties of overcoming withdrawal are too great, persons will lose their ability to choose to discontinue their use of a drug, which then will be said to become nonvoluntary. Drug addiction is commonly portrayed as a kind of slavery, and the potential addict might require paternalistic legislation to prevent him from succumbing to this sorry state.

A serious attempt to apply this argument to CLAURD would begin by sorting drugs into two categories: those that are addicting, and those that are not. This strategy would not yield results that coincide with existing laws, for some legal drugs (e.g., caffeine) create a physical dependency among users, while some illegal drugs (e.g., LSD) do not. This fact should make many paternalists uneasy about relying on the phenomenon of addiction as the sole basis for continuing to support CLAURD.

In any event, this ground for CLAURD suffers from several difficulties. First, despite initial appearances, it is not obvious that nonvoluntariness is a consequence of the physical dependency of addiction.[55] Nonvoluntariness has long been recognized as a criminal law defense. Yet it is important to note that no jurisdiction allows addiction to constitute a defense to a charge of drug use.[56] Admittedly, the concept of voluntariness is "variable," so that the criterion for deciding whether paternalistic interferences are warranted may differ from the criterion for deciding whether a criminal law defense should be recognized. But an explanation of this discrepancy in the criteria of voluntariness is clearly required. The fact that the drug use of addicts is deemed voluntary for purposes of imposing criminal liability should at least give pause to those who would conclude without hesitation that addiction renders drug use nonvoluntary, and thus justifies interference under a "soft paternalist" strategy.

Second, the concession that the sustained use of an addictive substance is nonvoluntary does not entail that its proscription is legitimate. Nonvoluntariness is a necessary, not a sufficient condition for paternalistic interference; a law is not justified simply because it protects persons from harm brought about by their nonvoluntary choices. Reconsider Feinberg's "easy" case in which Mr. Roe concludes that the pleasure of drug *X* outweighs its harmful effects. Roe's calculation does not automatically become so misguided as to warrant intervention simply because *X* is addictive. It is surely conceivable that a rational person could continue to believe that the pleasure of a drug outweighs its harm notwithstanding the fact that he will become addicted to it.[57]

Feinberg implicitly acknowledges that a person should be allowed to follow his preferences about the use of addictive drugs in his insightful discussion of laws that prevent persons from voluntarily becoming slaves.[58] Many philosophers who are generally critical of paternalism, such as Mill, have strained to allow an exception in this kind of case. Feinberg, to his credit, remains consistent here. The fact that a decision to become a slave is permanent and irrevocable is not a sufficient reason to label it as nonvoluntary or to prohibit it. He writes: "If one is not in principle 'free not to be free' then he does not enjoy de jure autonomy."[59] Analogously, the fact that a decision to use an addictive drug may be permanent and irrevocable is not a sufficient reason to prohibit it.

For at least four reasons, moreover, the case for prohibiting use of an addictive drug is infinitely weaker than the case for prohibiting a person from voluntarily becoming a slave. First, unlike the slavery example in which the contract becomes binding immediately upon agreement, no one becomes addicted to a drug upon his initial use. The fact that the addictive process is gradual leaves an opportunity for reconsideration that is unavailable in the slavery example. How quickly must use of a drug lead to addiction before its prohibition can be justified on soft paternalist principles? Second, contrary to the many myths that surround the phenomenon of addiction, not all users of addictive drugs become addicts.[60] What percentage of users of an addictive drug must become addicts before its prohibition can be justified on soft paternalist principles? Third, addiction is almost never continuous or permanent.[61] Many illegal substances are consumed by the young, who voluntarily decrease and eventually abandon their use with age. What percentage of users of a given drug would have to become continuously and permanently addicted before its prohibition could be justified on soft paternalist principles? Finally, there is a tendency to grossly exaggerate the pains of withdrawal from the nonavailability of a drug to which a user is addicted. One author compares the pain of heroin withdrawal to a case of a one-week flu.[62] John Kaplan writes:

"Despite our image of the heroin slave, addicts commonly go through withdrawal and undergo considerable periods of voluntary—or semi-voluntary—abstinence."[63] How terrible must withdrawal be before persons who cannot overcome addiction can be said to use drugs nonvoluntarily? These several questions illustrate once again the extent to which many arguments for CLAURD depend upon controversial empirical assumptions that are seldom explicitly articulated, raise "threshold" questions uncongenial to deontological moral philosophy, and generalize from "worst case" scenarios that fail to conform to the reality of typical drug use. Even if the autonomy principle does not protect a person's "freedom to be unfree," the fact that a drug is addictive is hardly a decisive reason to embrace CLAURD.

VI.

Not all philosophers have accepted Feinberg's soft paternalist position that conduct harmful to oneself may be prohibited only when it is nonvoluntary. Some have embraced a wider scope of paternalism. It is important to determine whether their willingness to allow a greater degree of paternalism is defensible in general, and, if so, whether it warrants the state in enacting CLAURD.

The most thoughtful alternative to Feinberg's rejection of hard paternalism is proposed by John Kleinig.[64] He notes, quite correctly, that "our lives do not always display the cohesion and maturity of purpose that exemplifies the liberal ideal of individuality, but instead manifest a carelessness, unreflectiveness, short-sightedness, or foolishness that . . . represents a departure from some of our own more permanent and central commitments and dispositions."[65] In light of this phenomenon, Kleinig cautiously endorses what he calls "the Argument from Personal Integrity." He writes:

> Where our conduct or choices place our more permanent, stable, and central projects in jeopardy, and where what comes to expression in this conduct or these choices manifests aspects of our personality that do not rank highly in our constellation of desires, dispositions, etc., benevolent interference will constitute no violation of integrity. Indeed, if anything, it helps to preserve it.[66]

Of course, this "Argument from Personal Integrity" would hardly win universal assent among philosophers. Those who resist hard paternalism would forcefully object that it ultimately undermines personal integrity, the very value it is designed to protect. It is exceedingly difficult, even in inter-personal relationships, to correctly distinguish "more permanent, stable, and central projects" from those that are less significant to the agent overall. Any procedure to allow interference under this rationale would be susceptible to extraordinary abuse and mistake.

Nonetheless, Kleinig's basis for allowing hard paternalism seems attractive. Circumstances exist in which it is relatively certain that an individual's refusal to act in his own best interest is simply incompatible with his own priorities. Interference in such cases does not substitute another's preferences for those of the agent, but actually helps the agent to pursue his own goals. If hard paternalism ever is justified, it is here. Thus it is worthwhile to tentatively accept Kleinig's strategy as sound, and to assess its implications upon CLAURD.

In attempting to identify these implications, two difficulties emerge that are comparable to problems in applying Feinberg's views about voluntariness. First, what kind of general law can be warranted under this limited concession to hard paternalism? It is telling that Kleinig does not provide a single example of legislation that he believes his principle would justify. Is the legislator instructed to generalize from the "standard" case? The projects deemed worthy, the importance attached to them, and the extent to which drug use interferes with their pursuit, vary so radically from individual to individual that no generalization seems possible. The promising lives of some people are perhaps ruined by drugs; the lives of others are not hampered in any apparent way; the lives of still others are probably enriched. Much the same can be said about virtually any other recreational activity. Most such pursuits (e.g., spectator sports) do not promote a person's more significant interests, but can hardly be said to interfere with them. No doubt the more permanent projects of some individuals suffer because of their failure to keep a given activity in perspective. At what point does a person devote so much time and effort to the pursuit of short-term pleasure that he jeopardizes his more fundamental objectives? Here again is a kind of "threshold" problem. What percentage of users of given drugs exceed this threshold, as compared with comparable percentages for other pastimes, e.g., video games? I have little confidence that answers to these difficult questions are forthcoming.

More importantly, the attempt to defend CLAURD by appeals to an "Argument from Personal Integrity" is vulnerable to a second defect noted in the discussion of addiction. The fact that the use of drugs interferes with the more important projects of many individuals, perhaps a majority, is not a sufficient reason to withhold drugs from those persons whose important projects are not hampered by drug use. A legal philosophy that protects autonomy will be reluctant to allow gains for some to justify prohibitions upon others whose good is not enhanced. Only consequentialists who allow such trade-offs can be comfortable in translating their concern for "personal integrity" into an argument for CLAURD.

I conclude that Kleinig's limited concession to "hard paternalism" offers little support to CLAURD. Unless some other plausible basis for interfering with voluntary choices can be defended, the prospects for constructing a paternalistic rationale for criminal laws against the use of recreational drugs appear to be bleak. I hope to have shown that a more definitive assessment of this question awaits (*inter alia*) the arrival of reliable data about a number of disputed empirical issues.

NOTES

1. Five brief comments on the criminalization of "recreational drug use" are in order:

First, I will make no serious effort to define "drugs." A commonly cited definition is any substance other than food which by its chemical nature affects the structure or function of the living organism." See "Drug Abuse in America: Problem in Perspective," (Second Report, National Commission on Marijuana and Drug Abuse, 1973). It is noteworthy that many legislative schemes have abandoned the concept altogether in favor of "controlled substances" or "controlled dangerous substances." All controlled substances would commonly be classified as drugs, but nothing in these legislative schemes precludes listing water as a controlled substance, since "controlled substances" or "controlled dangerous substances" are typically defined as whatever substances appear in the statutory schedules. See *New Jersey Code of Criminal Justice,* sec. 24: 21–2 (1987). Courts will rarely entertain challenges that a substance is not a "drug," is not "dangerous," or does not belong on a schedule of controlled substances. See *NORML v. Bell,* 488 F. Supp. 123 (D.C.C. 1980). The Dangerous Drug Diversion Control Act of 1984 gives the Attorney General authority to add a substance to Schedule I, and the statute provides that such an order "is not subject to judicial review."

Second, I will not attempt to refine the distinction between recreational and medicinal (or therapeutic) drugs. I hope that this elusive distinction can be drawn in practice without serious difficulty. I do not suppose the distinction to be exhaustive. Steroid use by athletes, for example, does not fit comfortably into either category.

Third, I will confine my attention to laws against drug use, even though most drug offenses involve possession, distribution, or "being under the influence." I barely discuss whether criminal penalties are appropriate for related offenses that do not involve drug use.

Fourth, I will not examine the reasonable distinctions that a legal system might draw between various classes of drug users. Most significantly, the decriminalization of drug use does not require that children should be permitted to use drugs.

Finally, I will discuss only criminal penalties. I do not address whether it is legitimate to discourage drug use by education, taxation, warnings about health hazards, etc. Nor do I discuss the collateral consequences of drug use, for example, whether the use of illegal drugs should preclude confirmation of a nominee to the Supreme Court. Thus I do not look "beyond decriminalization" to describe the kinds of regulations of drug use that might be appropriate.

2. A striking exception is David Richards, *Sex, Drugs, Death, and the Law* (Totowa: Rowman and Littlefield, 1982). See also F. A. Whitlock, *Drugs, Morality, and the Law* (St. Lucia: University of Queensland Press, 1975).
3. "Drug Abuse in America," *supra* note 1, p. 13. Most authors caution that statistics about drugs should be regarded with skepticism.
4. *Hutto v. Davis,* 454 U.S. 370 (1982). Of course, this punishment is hardly the norm. But the fact that the treatment of drug offenders is so varied, ranging from a mere police warning to several years in prison, is itself a major problem. Few offenses give rise to such a wide latitude in punishment.
5. *Newsweek* (Aug. 11, 1986): p. 18.
6. "Paternalism," *Monist* 56 (1972): 64.
7. "The current defence of the prohibition [against marijuana use] is that [it] causes harm, not so much to society, but to the individual who uses it." Naomi Overend, "Marijuana Possession: A Criminal Act or Compliance Problem?," *U. Toronto Faculty Law Rev.* 42 (1984): 114, 118. On the other hand, when the severity of punishment exceeds the harm risked by the offender, it is difficult to construe the law as designed to protect the user.
8. When Lefty Driessel, basketball coach at the University of Maryland, claimed that under very limited conditions cocaine use might actually improve athletic performance, he had little subsequent choice but to "clarify" his remarks.
9. *Paternalism* (Totowa: Rowman & Alanheld, 1983).
10. *Paternalistic Intervention* (Princeton: Princeton University Press, 1986).
11. *Paternalism* (Minneapolis: University of Minnesota Press, 1983).
12. *Harm to Self* (New York: Oxford U. Press, 1986), p. 133.
13. Michael Bayles, although not a libertarian, claims to identify a "moral inconsistency" in all cases of criminal paternalism. See "Criminal Paternalism," in J. Roland Pennock and John Chapman, eds., *Nomos XV: The Limits of Law* (New York: Lieber-Atherton, 1974), p. 174.
14. Feinberg, *supra* note 12, p. 8, provides good reason to prefer the label "mixed" to "pure" in describing cases in which the "law is justified partly by the aim of preventing people from suffering harm at their own hands . . . and partly for other reasons." Donald Regan seemingly denies the existence of cases of unmixed paternalism in "Justifications for Paternalism," *Nomos XV, supra* note 13, p. 189.
15. Drug use is frequently condemned on two nonpaternalistic grounds. First, drug use creates a public health hazard, with consequent costs to society, most notably the loss of productivity among workers. In a televised speech, President Reagan stated that drug abuse costs nondrug-using Americans at least $60 billion a year. See Julie Bach, ed., *Drug Abuse: Opposing Viewpoints* (St. Paul: Greenhaven Press, 1988), p. 13.

    Second, drug use is said to be related to criminal activity in a least four ways: (1) Those who violate drug laws, and become labeled as criminals, are more likely to commit other crimes. (2) Those who violate drug laws associate with criminals, making it easier for them to commit other crimes. (3) Those who violate drug laws frequently steal to support their habits. (4) Those who are under the influence of drugs have reduced inhibitions against committing other crimes.
16. See Richards, *supra* note 2, pp. 169–77, Whitlock, *supra* note 2, pp. 32–37, and Feinberg, *Harmless Wrongdoing* (New York: Oxford U. Press, 1988).
17. See Ronald Dworkin's response to Lord Devlin in "Liberty and Moralism," in his *Taking Rights Seriously* (Cambridge: Harvard University Press, 1977), Chapter Ten.
18. Although estimates vary widely, one commentator believes that the price of heroin is approximately two hundred times greater than under a free market of supply and demand. See Mark Deininger, "The Economics of Heroin: Key to Optimizing the Legal Response," *Georgia Law Review* 10(1976): 583.
19. See the sanguine discussion of the " 'heroin overdose' mystery" in Consumer Reports, *Licit and Illicit Drugs* (Boston: Little, Brown and Co., 1972), Chapter 12. Supervision by the Food and Drug Agency would reduce the impurities presently detected in "street drugs," and thereby lessen the hazards of drug use.

    AIDS has spread throughout the population of heroin addicts by the sharing of unsterilized needles. Decriminalization of heroin and drug paraphernalia might reduce the likelihood that addicts will share needles.

20. It is easy to forget that some substances qualify as drugs according to medical definitions. In one survey, less than 25% of the public identified tobacco as a drug. See Gerald Uelmen and Victor Haddox, eds., *Drug Abuse and the Law Sourcebook* (New York: Clark Boardman Co., 1985), pp. 1–3.
21. "By any standard of measurement, the more pervasive national drug problem is the abuse of alcohol, tobacco, and legal prescription and over-the-counter drugs." See James Felman and Christopher Petrini, "Drug Testing and Public Employment: Toward a Rational Application of the Fourth Amendment," *Law and Contemporary Problems* 51 (1989): 253, 259.
22. See Douglas Husak, "The Presumption of Freedom," *Nous* XVII (1983), p. 345.
23. More accurately, Mill claims to pursue this strategy. He is frequently accused of incorporating deontological considerations into his argument. See Dworkin, *supra* note 6.
24. Thus Feinberg disassociates his conception of moral autonomy from that of Kant. *Supra* note 12, pp. 94–97.
25. C. L. Ten, *Mill on Liberty* (Oxford: Clarendon Press, 1980), p. 116.
26. See the discussion of alcohol in Herbert Fingarette, *Heavy Drinking* (Berkeley: University of California Press, 1988).
27. See John Kaplan, *The Hardest Drug: Heroin and Public Policy* (Chicago: University of Chicago Press, 1983).
28. Donald VanDeVeer's "principle of autonomy-respecting paternalism" (PARP) would seem to protect drug use as well, with possible complications raised by addiction. *Supra* note 10, p. 88. See also the conception of privacy defended in Richards, *supra* note 2.
29. Feinberg, *supra* note 12, p. 54.
30. At some points, Feinberg appears less interested in *defending* his understanding of the principle of autonomy than in "sketching as coherent a doctrine as [he] can of sovereign self-rule as applied to individuals" that "makes sense [and] stands ready for use as a tool of our moral judgments if we want it." *Id.*, p. 52.
31. Apparently some legal philosophers are skeptical that theoretical limits to state power can be identified, at least with respect to "private immorality." Typically they are worried about the "garrison threshold" problem mentioned in Part II (F). See Patrick Devlin, *The Enforcement of Morality* (New York: Oxford University Press, 1965).
32. Although he does not propose an alternative formulation of an autonomy principle, Mark Sagoff contends that "the desire to take a particular drug not approved as safe and efficacious, lacks the connection with autonomy, freedom, or justice that might give it standing as a right," "Paternalism and the Regulation of Drugs," *International Journal of Applied Philosophy* 2 (1984): 43, 54.
33. For additional difficulties with the connection between autonomy and paternalism, see Douglas Husak, "Autonomy and Paternalism," *Philosophy and Public Affairs* 10 (1981): 27.
34. *Supra* note 12, p. 54.
35. Advocates of drug testing for athletes frequently attempt to justify the sacrifice of civil liberties by pointing out the alleged magnitude of the drug problem. According to Red Auerbach, General Manager of the Boston Celtics, "there comes a time when you have to put this altruistic civil rights stuff down the toilet." See Bach, *supra* note 15, p. 147.
36. *Supra* note 12, p. 61.
37. *Id.*, p. 61.
38. In *supra* note 12, pp. 15–16, Feinberg protests that protecting people from the harmful consequences of their nonvoluntary choices probably should not qualify as paternalism at all. But see Kleinig, *supra* note 9, p. 9.
39. *Id.*, p. 12.
40. *Id.*, p. 116.
41. *Id.*, p. 117.
42. It is ultimately unimportant whether ignorance renders a decision nonvoluntary. What is significant is that Feinberg (and most anyone else) would allow at least a temporary interference with Roe's choice. But see Richard Arenson, "Mill versus Paternalism," *Ethics* 90 (1980): 471.
43. *Supra* note 12, p. 133.
44. It is possible to imagine a legal system in which a license is required to allow persons to engage in activities that risk harm to themselves. A license would be obtained by demonstrating to experts that the agent appreciates the likelihood of harm. Such a system would be costly and cumbersome. More importantly, philosophers should be suspicious of the assumption that persons should not be allowed to engage in given kinds of activities without first demonstrating their awareness to appropriate officials. What is the justification for placing this burden of proof on prospective drug users? How can this placement be reconciled with a commitment to moral autonomy?
45. See Feinberg, *Harm to Others* (New York: Oxford University Press, 1986), p. 188.

46. There is evidence that the less persons know about the effects of recreational drugs, the more dangerous they consider them to be. See James Bakalar and Lester Grinspoon, *Drug Control in a Free Society* (New York: Cambridge University Press, 1984), p. 17.
47. I discuss the connection between addiction and nonvoluntariness in Part V.
48. One possible reason to support CLAURD concedes that drug use per se is rarely nonvoluntary, but contends that persons under the influence of drugs are more inclined to commit subsequent nonvoluntary acts that harm themselves.
49. Yet almost certainly there is some point at which it becomes reasonable to make a drug unavailable to Smith because Jones will abuse it. It is here that the "garrison threshold" phenomenon requires a compromise of personal autonomy for the sake of utilitarian objectives. In order to keep this problem in its proper perspective, it should be noticed that the difficulty of locating this threshold is common to any number of debates about both paternalistic and nonpaternalistic legislation. It has been argued, for example, that a society should ban pornography altogether because a few perverted individuals might be more inclined to commit sex crimes after exposure to obscene materials. Liberal and conservative legal philosophies differ radically in locating the point at which individual liberties must yield to social interests. This point will become more distant to the extent that personal autonomy is valued.
50. See, for example, *People v. Privitera,* 74 Cal. App. 3d 936 (1977).
51. There might be an important difference, however. In the case of laetrile, the user is mistaken about whether the drug is helpful, and probably not mistaken about whether it is potentially harmful.
52. Tal Scriven, "Utility, Autonomy, and Drug Regulation," *International Journal of Applied Philosophy* 2 (1984): 27, 31.
53. See Robert Byck, "Cocaine, Marijuana, and the Meaning of Addiction," in Ronald Hamony, ed., *Dealing With Drugs* (Lexington: D. C. Heath and Co., 1987), p. 221.
54. But see the discussion of Kleinig's "Argument from Personal Integrity" in Part VI.
55. "The experience or fear of drug withdrawal cannot render addictive conduct legally involuntary." Herbert Fingarette and Ann Hasse, *Mental Disabilities and Criminal Responsibility* (Berkeley: University of California Press, 1979), p. 166.
56. See the discussion of "pharmacological coercion" in *Castle v. U.S.*, 492 F.2d 492 (1965). See also *U.S. v. Moore,* 486 F.2d 1139 (1973).
57. See Richards, *supra* note 2, p. 183.
58. Feinberg, *supra* note 12, pp. 71–81.
59. *Id.*, p. 77.
60. It is noteworthy that tobacco is the drug for which the greatest percentage of users become addicts. There is evidence that 9 of 10 persons who try cigarettes become addicted, while only 1 in 6 who try crack become addicted. See "Treatment for Crack Addicts: Drug Experts Report Finding Clues to a Cure," *New York Times* (August 24, 1989), p. B7: 1.
61. See Kaplan's discussion of heroin, *supra* note 27, p. 34.
62. See Mansky, "Opiates: Human Psychopharmacology," in Iversen, Iversen, and Snyder, eds., *Handbook of Psychopharmacology* (New York: Plenum Press, 1978), p. 158.
63. *Supra* note 27, p. 34. See also Bruce Johnson, "Once an Addict, Seldom an Addict," *Contemporary Drug Problems* 7 (1978): 48.
64. *Supra* note 9. Although Kleinig contends that his approach "finds a toe hold" for "strong, no less than weak paternalism," (p. 68) he later indicates that the "character deficiencies" in virtue of which a larger scope of paternalism is permitted "represent a falling short of full voluntariness" (p. 69).
65. *Id.*, p. 67.
66. *Id.*, p. 68.

Study Questions

1. Would Wilson's arguments oppose even the temporary legalization of drugs in experimental states or counties? Should he oppose such collection of empirical data on the effects of legalization?
2. Is the distinction between recreational drugs (which are usually illegal) and therapeutic drugs (which are usually legal) broad enough to support the law here? Isn't recreation a form of therapy that, for example, will relieve stress? Do you agree with Husak's priorities regarding drugs and other social problems? If so, why? If not, why not?

E Euthanasia and Suicide

Cruzan v. Director, Missouri Department of Health

UNITED STATES SUPREME COURT

The United States Supreme Court decided this controversial case in 1990. A tragic automobile accident left Nancy Cruzan in a permanent vegetative state. Is death better than this quality of life? Even if it is, can we trust others with this great power to decide when life is worth living? Or have we already been living with this great power in the hands of others all along? These issues and more arise in the *Cruzan* case. The case seems influential because many have filled out so-called "living wills" since the case was decided.

Chief Justice Rehnquist delivered the opinion of the Court.

Petitioner Nancy Beth Cruzan was rendered incompetent as a result of severe injuries sustained during an automobile accident. Co-petitioners Lester and Joyce Cruzan, Nancy's parents and co-guardians, sought a court order directing the withdrawal of their daughter's artificial feeding and hydration equipment after it became apparent that she had virtually no chance of recovering her cognitive faculties. The Supreme Court of Missouri held that because there was no clear and convincing evidence of Nancy's desire to have life-sustaining treatment withdrawn under such circumstances, her parents lacked authority to effectuate such a request. We granted certiorari, and now affirm.

On the night of January 11, 1983, Nancy Cruzan lost control of her car as she traveled down Elm Road in Jasper County, Missouri. The vehicle overturned, and Cruzan was discovered lying face down in a ditch without detectable respiratory or cardiac function. Paramedics were able to restore her breathing and heartbeat at the accident site, and she was transported to a hospital in an unconscious state. An attending neurosurgeon diagnosed her as having sustained probable cerebral contusions compounded by significant anoxia (lack of oxygen). The Missouri trial court in this case found that permanent brain damage generally results after 6 minutes in an anoxic state; it was estimated that Cruzan was deprived of oxygen from 12 to 14 minutes. She remained in a coma for approximately three weeks and then progressed to an unconscious state in which she was able to orally ingest some nutrition. In order to ease feeding and further the recovery, surgeons implanted a gastrostomy feeding and hydration tube in Cruzan with the consent of her then husband. Subsequent rehabilitative efforts proved unavailing. She now lies in a Missouri state hospital in what is commonly referred to as a persistent vegetative state: generally, a condition in which a person exhibits motor reflexes but evinces no indications of significant cognitive function. The State of Missouri is bearing the cost of her care.

After it had become apparent that Nancy Cruzan had virtually no chance of regaining her mental faculties her parents asked hospital employees to terminate the artificial nutrition and hydration procedures. All agree that such a removal would cause her death. The employees refused to honor the request without court approval. The parents then sought and received authorization from the state trial court for termination. The court found that a person in Nancy's condition had a fundamental right under the State and Federal Constitutions to refuse or direct the withdrawal of "death prolonging procedures." The court also found that Nancy's "expressed thoughts at age twenty-five in somewhat serious conversation with a housemate friend that if sick or injured she would not wish to continue her life unless she could live at least halfway normally suggests that given her present condition she would not wish to continue on with her nutrition and hydration."

The Supreme Court of Missouri reversed by a divided vote. The court recognized a right to refuse treatment embodied in the common-law doctrine of informed consent, but expressed skepticism about the application of that doctrine in the circumstances of this case. The court also declined to read a broad right of privacy into the State Constitution which would "support the right of a person to refuse medical treatment in every circumstance," and expressed doubt as to whether such a right existed under the United States Constitution. It then decided that the Missouri Living Will statute embodied a state policy strongly favoring the preservation of life. The court found that Cruzan's statements to her roommate regarding her desire to live or die under certain conditions were "unreliable for the purpose of determining her intent, and thus insufficient to support the co-guardians' claim to exercise substituted judgment on Nancy's behalf." It rejected the argument that Cruzan's parents were entitled to order the termination of her medical treatment, concluding that "no person can assume that choice for an incompetent in the absence of the formalities required under Missouri's Living Will statutes or the clear and convincing, inherently reliable evidence absent here." The court also expressed its view that "[b]road policy questions bearing on life and death are more properly addressed by representative assemblies" than judicial bodies.

We granted certiorari to consider the question of whether Cruzan has a right under the United States Constitution which would require the hospital to withdraw life-sustaining treatment from her under these circumstances.

At common law, even the touching of one person by another without consent and without legal justification was a battery. Before the turn of the century, this Court observed that "[n]o right is held more sacred, or is more carefully guarded, by the common law, than the right of every individual to the possession and control of his own person, free from all restraint or interference of others, unless by clear and unquestionable authority of law." This notion of bodily integrity has been embodied in the requirement that informed consent is generally required for medical treatment. Justice Cardozo, while on the Court of Appeals of New York, aptly described this doctrine: "Every human being of adult years and sound mind has a right to determine what shall be done with his own body; and a surgeon who performs an operation without his patient's consent commits an assault, for which he is liable in damages." The informed consent doctrine has become firmly entrenched in American tort law.

The logical corollary of the doctrine of informed consent is that the patient generally possesses the right not to consent, that is, to refuse treatment. Until about 15 years ago and the seminal decision in *In re Quinlan* . . . (1976), the number of right-to-refuse-treatment decisions were relatively few. Most of the earlier cases involved patients who refused medical treatment forbidden by their religious beliefs, thus implicating First Amendment rights as well as common law rights of self-determination. More recently, however, with the advance of medical technology capable of sustaining life well past the point where natural forces would have brought certain death in earlier times, cases involving the right to refuse life-sustaining treatment have burgeoned.

In the *Quinlan* case, young Karen Quinlan suffered severe brain damage as the result of anoxia, and entered a persistent vegetative state. Karen's father sought judicial approval to disconnect his daughter's respirator. The New Jersey Supreme Court granted the relief, holding that Karen had a right of privacy grounded in the Federal Constitution to terminate treatment. Recognizing that this right was not absolute, however, the court balanced it against asserted state interests. Noting that the State's interest "weakens and the individual's right to privacy grows as the degree of bodily invasion increases and the prognosis dims," the court concluded that the state interests had to give way in that case. The court also concluded that the "only practical way" to prevent the loss of Karen's privacy right due to her incompetence was to allow her guardian and family to decide "whether she would exercise it in these circumstances."

After *Quinlan,* however, most courts have based a right to refuse treatment either solely on the common law right of informed consent or on both the common law right and a constitutional privacy right. In *Superintendent of Belchertown State School v. Saikewicz* (1977), the Supreme Judicial Court of Massachusetts relied on both the right of privacy and the right of informed consent to permit the withholding of chemotherapy from a profoundly-retarded 67-year-old man suffering from leukemia. Reasoning that an incompetent person retains the same rights as a competent individual "because the value of human dignity extends to both," the court adopted a "substituted judgment" standard whereby courts were to determine what an incompetent individual's decision would have been under the circumstances. Distilling certain state interests from prior case law—the preservation of life, the protection of the interests of innocent third parties, the prevention of suicide, and the maintenance of the ethical integrity of the medical profession—the court recognized the first interest as paramount and noted it was greatest when an affliction was curable, "as opposed to the State interest where, as here, the issue is not whether, but when, for how long, and at what cost to the individual [a] life may be briefly extended."

In *In re Storar,* (1981), the New York Court of Appeals declined to base a right to refuse treatment on a constitutional privacy right. Instead, it found such a right "adequately supported" by the informed consent doctrine. In *In re Eichner* (decided with *In re Storar)* an 83-year-old man who had suffered brain damage from anoxia entered a vegetative state and was thus incompetent to consent to the removal of his respirator. The court, however, found it unnecessary to reach the question of whether his rights could be exercised by others since it found the evidence clear and convincing from statements made by the patient when competent that he "did not want to be maintained in a vegetative coma by use of a respirator." In the companion *Storar* case, a 52-year-old man suffering from bladder cancer had been profoundly retarded during most of his life. Implicitly rejecting the approach taken in *Saikewicz, supra,* the court reasoned that due to such life-long incompetency, "it is unrealistic to attempt to determine whether he would want to continue potentially life-prolonging treatment if he were competent." As the evidence showed that the patient's required blood transfusions did not involve excessive pain and without them his mental and physical abilities would deteriorate, the court concluded that it should not "allow an incompetent patient to bleed to death because someone, even someone as close as a parent or sibling, feels that this is best for one with an incurable disease."

Many of the later cases build on the principles established in *Quinlan, Saikewicz,* and *Storar/Eichner.* For instance, in *In re Conroy,* (1985), the same court that decided *Quinlan* considered whether a nasogastric feeding tube could be removed from an 84-year-old incompetent nursing-home resident suffering irreversible mental and physical ailments. While recognizing that a federal right of privacy might apply in the case, the court, contrary to its approach in *Quinlan,* decided to base its decision on the common-law right to self-determination and informed consent. "On balance, the right to self-determination ordinarily outweighs any countervailing state interests, and competent persons generally are permitted to refuse medical treatment, even at the risk of death. Most of the cases that have held otherwise, unless they involved the interest in protecting innocent third parties, have concerned the patient's competency to make a rational and considered choice."

Reasoning that the right of self-determination should not be lost merely because an individual is unable to sense a violation of it, the court held that incompetent individuals retain a right to refuse treatment. It also held that such a right could be exercised by a surrogate decisionmaker using a "subjective" standard when there was clear evidence that the incompetent person would have exercised it. Where such evidence was lacking, the court held that an individual's right could still be invoked in certain circumstances under objective "best interest" standards. Thus, if some trustworthy evidence existed that the individual would have wanted to terminate treatment, but not enough to clearly establish a person's wishes for purposes of the subjective standard, and the burden of a prolonged life from the experience of pain and suffering markedly outweighed its satisfactions, treatment could be terminated under a "limited-objective" standard. Where no trustworthy evidence existed, and a person's suffering would make the administration of life-sustaining treatment inhumane, a "pure-objective" standard could be used to terminate treatment. If none of these conditions obtained, the court held it was best to err in favor of preserving life.

The court also rejected certain categorical distinctions that had been drawn in prior refusal-of-treatment cases as lacking substance for decision purposes: the distinction between actively hastening death by terminating treatment and passively allowing a person to die of a disease; between treating individuals as an initial matter versus withdrawing treatment afterwards; between ordinary versus extraordinary treatment; and between treatment by artificial feeding versus other forms of life-sustaining medical procedures. As to the last item, the court acknowledged the "emotional significance" of food, but noted that feeding by implanted tubes is a "medical procedur[e] with inherent risks and possible side effects, instituted by skilled health-care providers to compensate for impaired physical functioning" which analytically was equivalent to artificial breathing using a respirator.

In contrast to *Conroy*, the Court of Appeals of New York recently refused to accept less than the clearly expressed wishes of a patient before permitting the exercise of her right to refuse treatment by a surrogate decisionmaker; in *In re Westchester County Medical Center on behalf of O'Connor* (1988) (*O'Connor*). There, the court, over the objection of the patient's family members, granted an order to insert a feeding tube into a 77-year-old woman rendered incompetent as a result of several strokes. While continuing to recognize a common-law right to refuse treatment, the court rejected the substituted judgment approach for asserting it "because it is inconsistent with our fundamental commitment to the notion that no person or court should substitute its judgment as to what would be an acceptable quality of life for another. Consequently, we adhere to the view that, despite its pitfalls and inevitable uncertainties, the inquiry must always be narrowed to the patient's expressed intent, with every effort made to minimize the opportunity for error." The court held that the record lacked the requisite clear and convincing evidence of the patient's expressed intent to withhold life-sustaining treatment.

Other courts have found state statutory law relevant to the resolution of these issues. In *Conservatorship of Drabick* (1988), the California Court of Appeal authorized the removal of a nasogastric feeding tube from a 44-year-old man who was in a persistent vegetative state as a result of an auto accident. Noting that the right to refuse treatment was grounded in both the common law and a constitutional right of privacy, the court held that a state probate statute authorized the patient's conservator to order the withdrawal of life-sustaining treatment when such a decision was made in good faith based on medical advice and the conservatee's best interests. While acknowledging that "to claim that [a patient's] 'right to choose' survives incompetence is a legal fiction at best," the court reasoned that the respect society accords to persons as individuals is not lost upon incompetence and is best preserved by allowing others "to make a decision that reflects [a patient's] interests more closely than would a purely technological decision to do whatever is possible."

In *In re Estate of Longeway,* 133 Ill.2d 33, 139 Ill.Dec. 780, 549 N.E.2d 292 (1989), the Supreme Court of Illinois considered whether a 76-year-old woman rendered incompetent from a series of strokes had a right to the discontinuance of artificial nutrition and hydration. Noting that the boundaries of a federal right of privacy were uncertain, the court found a right to refuse treatment in the doctrine of informed consent. The court further held that the State Probate Act impliedly authorized a guardian to exercise a ward's right to refuse artificial sustenance in the event that the ward was terminally ill and irreversibly comatose. Declining to adopt a best interests standard for deciding when it would be appropriate to exercise a ward's right because it "lets another make a determination of a patient's quality of life." The court opted instead for a substituted judgment standard. Finding the "expressed intent" standard utilized in *O'Connor, supra,* too rigid, the court noted that other clear and convincing evidence of the patient's intent could be considered. 133 Ill.2d, at 50–51, 139 Ill.Dec., at 787, 549 N.E.2d, at 300. The court also adopted the "consensus opinion [that] treats artificial nutrition and hydration as medical treatment." *Id.,* at 42, 139 Ill.Dec., at 784, 549 N.E.2d, at 296. Cf. *McConnell v. Beverly Enterprises-Connecticut, Inc.,* 209 Conn. 692, 705, 553 A.2d 596, 603 (1989) (right to withdraw artificial nutrition and hydration found in the Connecticut Removal of Life Support Systems Act, which "provid[es] functional guidelines for the exercise of the common law and constitutional rights of self-determination"; attending physician authorized to remove treatment after finding that patient is in a terminal condition, obtaining consent of family, and considering expressed wishes of patient).

As these cases demonstrate, the common-law doctrine of informed consent is viewed as generally encompassing the right of a competent individual to refuse medical treatment. Beyond that, these decisions demonstrate both similarity and diversity in their approach to decision of what all agree is a perplexing question with unusually strong moral and ethical overtones. State courts have available to them for decision a number of sources—state constitutions, statutes, and common law—which are not available to us. In this Court, the question is simply and starkly whether the United States Constitution prohibits Missouri from choosing the rule of decision which it did. This is the first case in which we have been squarely presented with the issue of whether the United States Constitution grants what is in common parlance referred to as a "right to die." We follow the judicious counsel of our decision in *Twin City Bank v. Nebeker,* 167 U.S. 196, 202. 17 S.Ct. 766, 769, 42 L.Ed. 134 (1897), where we said that in deciding "a question of such magnitude and importance . . . it is the [better] part of wisdom not to attempt, by any general statement, to cover every possible phase of the subject."

The Fourteenth Amendment provides that no State shall "deprive any person of life, liberty, or property, without due process of law." The principle that a competent person has a constitutionally protected liberty interest in refusing unwanted medical treatment may be inferred from our prior decisions. In *Jacobson v. Massachusetts,* 197 U.S. 11, 24–30 (1905), for instance, the Court balanced an individual's liberty interest in declining an unwanted smallpox vaccine against the State's interest in preventing disease. Decisions prior to the incorporation of the Fourth Amendment into the Fourteenth Amendment analyzed searches and seizures involving the body under the Due Process Clause and were thought to implicate substantial liberty interests. See, e.g., *Breithaupt v. Abram,* 352 U.S. 432, 439, 77 S.Ct. 408, 412, 1 L.Ed.2d 448 (1957) ("As against the right of an individual that his person be held inviolable . . . must be set the interests of society. . . .").

Just this Term, in the course of holding that a State's procedures for administering antipsychotic medication to prisoners were sufficient to satisfy due process concerns, we recognized that prisoners possess "a significant liberty interest in avoiding the unwanted administration of antipsychotic drugs under a the Due Process Clause of the Fourteenth Amendment." *Washington v. Harper,* 110 S.Ct. 1028, 1036, (1990); see also *id.,* at . . . 110 S.Ct., at 1041 ("The forcible injection of medication into a nonconsenting person's body represents a substantial interference with that person's liberty"). Still other cases support the recognition of a general liberty interest in refusing medical treatment. *Vitek v. Jones,* 445 U.S. 480, 494, 100 S.Ct. 1254, 1264, 63 L.Ed.2d 552 (1980) (transfer to mental hospital coupled with mandatory behavior modification treatment implicated liberty interests); *Parham v. J.R.,* 442 U.S. 584, 600 . . . (1979) ("a child, in common with adults, has a substantial liberty interest in not being confined unnecessarily for medical treatment").

But determining that a person has a "liberty interest" under the Due Process Clause does not end the inquiry; "whether respondent's constitutional rights have been violated must be determined by balancing his liberty interests against the relevant state interests." *Youngberg v. Romeo,* 457 U.S. 307, 321, 102 S.Ct. 2452, 2461, 73 L.Ed.2d 28 (1982). See also *Mills v. Rogers,* 457 U.S. 291, 299, 102 S.Ct. 2442, 2448, 73 L.Ed.2d 16 (1982).

Petitioners insist that under the general holdings of our cases, the forced administration of life-sustaining medical treatment, and even of artificially-delivered food and water essential to life, would implicate a competent person's liberty interest. Although we think the logic of the cases discussed above would embrace such a liberty interest, the dramatic consequences involved in refusal of such treatment would inform the inquiry as to whether the deprivation of that interest is constitutionally permissible. But for purposes of this case, we assume that the United States Constitution would grant a competent person a constitutionally protected right to refuse lifesaving hydration and nutrition.

Petitioners go on to assert that an incompetent person should possess the same right in this respect as is possessed by a competent person. They rely primarily on our decisions in *Parham v. J.R., supra,* and *Youngberg v. Romeo,* 457 U.S. 307, 102 S.Ct. 2452, 73 L.Ed.2d 28 (1982). In *Parham,* we held that a mentally disturbed minor child had a liberty interest in "not being confined unnecessarily for medical treatment," 442 U.S., at 600, 99 S.Ct., at 2503, but we certainly did not intimate that such a minor child, after commitment, would have a liberty interest in refusing treatment. In *Youngberg,* we held that a seriously retarded adult had a liberty interest in safety and freedom from bodily restraint, 457 U.S., at 320, 102 S.Ct., at 2460. *Youngberg,* however, did not deal with decisions to administer or withhold medical treatment.

The difficulty with petitioners' claim is that in a sense it begs the question: an incompetent person is not able to make an informed and voluntary choice to exercise a hypothetical right to refuse treatment or any other right. Such a "right" must be exercised for her, if at all, by some sort of surrogate. Here, Missouri has in effect recognized that under certain circumstances a surrogate may act for the patient in electing to have hydration and nutrition withdrawn in such a way as to cause death, but it has established a procedural safe-guard to assure that the action of the surrogate conforms as best it may to the wishes expressed by the patient while competent. Missouri requires that evidence of the incompetent's wishes as to the withdrawal of treatment be proved by clear and convincing evidence. The question, then, is whether the United States Constitution forbids the establishment of this procedural requirement by the State. We hold that it does not.

Whether or not Missouri's clear and convincing evidence requirement comports with the United States Constitution depends in part on what interests the State may properly seek to protect in this situation. Missouri relies on its interest in the protection and preservation of human life, and there can be no gainsaying this interest. As a general matter, the States—indeed, all civilized nations—demonstrate their commitment to life by treating homicide as serious crime. Moreover, the majority of States in this country have laws imposing criminal penalties on one who assists another to commit suicide. We do not think a State is required to remain neutral in the face of an informed and voluntary decision by a physically able adult to starve to death.

But in the context presented here, a State has more particular interests at stake. The choice between life and death is a deeply personal decision of obvious and overwhelming finality. We believe Missouri may legitimately seek to safeguard the personal element of this choice through the imposition of heightened evidentiary requirements. It cannot be disputed that the Due Process Clause protects an interest in life as well as an interest in refusing life-sustaining medical treatment. Not all incompetent patients will have loved ones available to serve as surrogate decision-makers. And even where family members are present, "[t]here will, of course, be some unfortunate situations in which family members will not act to protect a patient." A State is entitled to guard against potential abuses in such situations. Similarly, a State is entitled to consider that a judicial proceeding to make a determination regarding an incompetent's wishes may very well not be an adversarial one, with the added guarantee of accurate factfinding that the adversary process brings with it. Finally, we think a State may properly decline to make judgments about the "quality" of life that a particular individual may enjoy, and simply assert an unqualified interest in the preservation of human life to be weighed against the constitutionally protected interests of the individual.

In our view, Missouri has permissibly sought to advance these interests through the adoption of a "clear and convincing" standard of proof to govern such proceedings. "The function of a standard of proof, as that concept is embodied in the Due Process Clause and in the realm of factfinding, is to 'instruct the factfinder concerning the degree of confidence our society thinks he should have in the correctness of factual conclusions for a particular type of adjudication.' " . . . "This Court has mandated an intermediate standard of proof—'clear and convincing evidence'—when the individual interests at stake in a state proceeding are both 'particularly important' and 'more substantial than mere loss of money.' " Thus, such a standard has been required in deportation proceedings, in denaturalization proceedings, in civil commitment proceedings, and in proceedings for the termination of parental rights. Further, this level of proof, "or an even higher one, has traditionally been imposed in cases involving allegations of civil fraud, and in a variety of other kinds of civil cases involving such issues as . . . lost wills, oral contracts to make bequests, and the like."

We think it self-evident that the interests at stake in the instant proceedings are more substantial, both on an individual and societal level, than those involved in a run-of-the-mill civil dispute. But not only does the standard of proof reflect the importance of a particular adjudication, it also serves as "a societal judgment about how the risk of error should be distributed between the litigants." The more stringent the burden of proof a party must bear, the more that party bears the risk of an erroneous decision. We believe that Missouri may permissibly place an increased risk of an erroneous decision on those seeking to terminate an incompetent individual's life-sustaining treatment.

An erroneous decision not to terminate results in a maintenance of the status quo; the possibility of subsequent developments such as advancements in medical science, the discovery of new evidence regarding the patient's intent, changes in the law, or simply the unexpected death of the patient despite the administration of life-sustaining treatment, at least create the potential that a wrong decision will eventually be corrected or its impact mitigated. An erroneous decision to withdraw life-sustaining treatment, however, is not susceptible of correction. In *Santosky,* one of the factors which led the Court to require proof by clear and convincing evidence in a proceeding to terminate parental rights was that a decision in such a case was final and irrevocable. The same must surely be said of the decision to discontinue hydration and nutrition of a patient such as Nancy Cruzan, which all agree will result in her death.

It is also worth noting that most, if not all, States simply forbid oral testimony entirely in determining the wishes of parties in transactions which, while important, simply do not have the consequences that a decision to terminate a person's life does. At common law and by statute in most States, the parole evidence rule prevents the variations of the terms of a written contract by oral testimony. The statute of frauds makes unenforceable oral contracts to leave property by will, and statutes regulating the making of wills universally require that those instruments be in writing. There is no doubt that statutes requiring wills to be in writing, and statutes of frauds which require that a contract to make a will be in writing, on occasion frustrate the effectuation of the intent of a particular decedent, just as Missouri's requirement of proof in this case may have frustrated the effectuation of the not-fully-expressed desires of Nancy Cruzan. But the Constitution does not require general rules to work faultlessly; no general rule can.

In sum, we conclude that a State may apply a clear and convincing evidence standard in proceedings where a guardian seeks to discontinue nutrition and hydration of a person diagnosed to be in a persistent vegetative state. We note that many courts which have adopted some sort of substituted judgment procedure in situations like this, whether they limit consideration of evidence to the prior expressed wishes of the incompetent individual, or whether they allow more general proof of what the individual's decision would have been, require a clear and convincing standard of proof for such evidence.

The Supreme Court of Missouri held that in this case the testimony adduced at trial did not amount to clear and convincing proof of the patient's desire to have hydration and nutrition withdrawn. In so doing, it reversed a decision of the Missouri trial court which had found that the evidence "suggest[ed]" Nancy Cruzan would not have desired to continue such measures, App. to Pet. for Cert. A98, but which had not adopted the standard of "clear and convincing evidence" enunciated by the Supreme Court. The testimony adduced at trial consisted primarily of Nancy Cruzan's statements made to a housemate about a year before her accident that she would not want to live should she face life as a "vegetable," and other observations to the same effect. The observations did not deal in terms with withdrawal of medical treatment or of hydration and nutrition. We cannot say that the Supreme Court of Missouri committed constitutional error in reaching the conclusion that it did.

Petitioners alternatively contend that Missouri must accept the "substituted judgment" of close family members even in the absence of substantial proof that their views reflect the views of the patient. They rely primarily upon our decisions in *Michael H. v. Gerald D.* (1989), and *Parham v. J.R.* (1979). But we do not think these cases support their claim. In *Michael H.,* we *upheld* the constitutionality of California's favored treatment of traditional family relationships; such a holding may not be turned around into a constitutional requirement that a State *must* recognize the primacy of those relationships in a situation like this. And in *Parham,* where the patient was a minor, we also *upheld* the constitutionality of a state scheme in which parents made certain decisions for mentally ill minors. Here again petitioners would seek to turn a decision which allowed a State to rely on family decisionmaking into a constitutional requirement that the State recognize such decisionmaking. But constitutional law does not work that way.

No doubt is engendered by anything in this record but that Nancy Cruzan's mother and father are loving and caring parents. If the State were required by the United States Constitution to repose a right of "substituted judgment" with anyone, the Cruzans would surely qualify. But we do not think the Due Process Clause requires the State to repose judgment on these matters with anyone but the patient herself. Close family members may have a strong feeling—a feeling not at all ignoble or unworthy, but not entirely disinterested, either—that they do not wish to witness the continuation of the life of a loved one which they regard as hopeless, meaningless, and even degrading. But there is no automatic assurance that the view of close family members will necessarily be the same as the patient's would have been had she been confronted with the prospect of her situation while competent. All of the reasons previously discussed for allowing Missouri to require clear and convincing evidence of the patient's wishes lead us to conclude that the State may choose to defer only to those wishes, rather than confide the decision to close family members.

The judgment of the Supreme Court of Missouri is

Affirmed.

The Right to Death

Ronald Dworkin

T. M. Scanlon, reviewing Dworkin's *Life's Dominion* for The New York Review of Books, recently wrote "Ronald Dworkin is our leading public philosopher." Dworkin, a leader in contemporary Anglo-American jurisprudence who holds positions at both New York University and Oxford University, analyzes the *Cruzan* case and argues forcefully against the majority opinion Chief Justice Rehnquist wrote in that case. Dworkin draws some lessons from *Cruzan* for other currently controversial issues, such as abortion and a so-called "suicide machine."

1.

The tragedy of Nancy Cruzan's life is now part of American constitutional law. Before her automobile accident in 1983, she was an energetic twenty-four-year-old recently married woman. Her injuries deprived her brain of oxygen for fourteen minutes, and left her in what doctors describe as a permanent vegetative state. Only the lower part of her brain stem continued to function. She was unconscious and oblivious to the environment, though she had reflexive responses to sound and perhaps to painful stimuli. She was fed and hydrated through tubes implanted in her stomach, and other machines performed her other bodily functions. She was washed and turned regularly, but all of her limbs were contracted and her fingernails cut into her wrists.

For months after the accident her parents and her then husband pressed doctors to do everything possible to restore her to some kind of life. But when it became plain that she would remain in a vegetative state until she died, which might mean for thirty more years, her parents, who had become her legal guardians, asked the state hospital to remove the tubes and allow her to die at once. Since the hospital refused to do so without a court order, the parents petitioned a Missouri court, which appointed a guardian *ad litem* (a special guardian appointed to represent her in these proceedings) to offer arguments why it should not grant that order. After a hearing the court granted the order on the ground that it was in Cruzan's best interests to be permitted to die with some dignity now rather than to live on in an unconscious state.

The guardian *ad litem* felt it his duty to appeal the order to the Missouri supreme court, though he told that court that he did not disagree with the decision. But the supreme court reversed the lower court's decision: it held that Cruzan's legal guardians had no power to order feeding stopped without "clear and convincing" evidence that she herself had decided, when competent, not to be fed in her present circumstances. Though a friend had testified that Cruzan had said, in a conversation soon after the death of her grandmother, that she would not want to be kept alive if she could not really live, the supreme court held that this testimony was not adequate evidence of the necessary decision.

Cruzan's parents appealed to the United States Supreme Court: their lawyers argued that the Missouri decision violated her right not to be subjected to unwanted medical treatment. The Court had not previously ruled on the question how far states must respect that right. Last June 25, by a five-to-four vote, the Court refused to reverse the Missouri decision: it denied that Cruzan had a constitutional right that could be exercised by her parents in these circumstances.

The main opinion was written by Chief Justice Rehnquist, and was joined by Justices Kennedy and White. Many newspaper reports and comments on the case declared that, although the Court had refused the Cruzan family's request, it had nevertheless endorsed a general constitutional right of competent people to decide that they should not be kept alive through medical technology. *The New York Times,* for example, said that the Court had decided that "the Constitution protects a person's liberty to reject life-sustaining technology," and congratulated the Court for a "monumental example of law adjusting to life." *The Washington Post* headline read, "Court Rules Patient's Wishes Must Control 'Right to Die.' "

It is important to notice, however, that Rehnquist took care to say that he and the two justices who joined his opinion were not actually deciding that people have a right to die. He said they were assuming such a right only *hypothetically,* "for-purposes-of-this-case," and he emphasized that he thought it still an open question whether even a competent person's freedom to die with dignity could be overridden by a state's own constitutional right to keep people alive.[1] Although the logic of past cases would embrace a "liberty interest" of a competent person to refuse artificially delivered food and water, he said, "the dramatic consequences involved in refusal of such treatment would inform the inquiry as to whether the deprivations of that interest is constitutional."

Even if we do assume that people have a constitutional right to refuse to be kept alive if they become permanently vegetative, Rehnquist said, Missouri did not infringe that right. It only insisted that people must exercise the right for themselves, while still competent, and do so in a formal and unmistakable way, by executing a "living will," for example. The United States Constitution does not prohibit states from adopting strict evidentiary requirements of that sort, he said. The Constitution does not require Missouri to recognize what most people would think was very strong evidence of Cruzan's convictions, that is, her serious and apparently well-considered statements to a close friend soon after a relative's death.

Justices O'Connor and Scalia, though they agreed to uphold the Missouri supreme court's decision, filed separate concurring opinions. O'Connor made an important practical point: that instead of drafting a living will describing precisely what should not be done to keep them alive, many people would prefer to designate someone else—a relative or close friend—to make those decisions for them when the need arises.[2] She stated her own view that the Constitution gave people that right, and emphasized that the Court's decision against Cruzan's parents was not to the contrary, since Cruzan had made no formal designation.

Scalia's concurring opinion was of a very different character. He repeated his extraordinarily narrow view of constitutional rights: that the Constitution, properly interpreted, allows the states to do anything that it does not expressly forbid. Since, he said, the Constitution "says nothing" about people's rights to control their own deaths, there is no question of any constitutional right of that sort, and state legislatures are free to make any decision they wish about what can be done to people to keep them technically alive. Scalia left little doubt about his own views of what a sensible state legislature would decide; he said that no reasonable person would wish to inhabit a body that was only technically alive. But, he said, the Constitution does not require state legislatures to be either reasonable or humane.

Justice Brennan dissented in an opinion joined by Justices Marshall and Blackmun. Brennan's opinion, one of the last he delivered before his retirement, was a valedictory address that made even plainer how much his humanity and intelligence will be missed. He pointed out the main fallacy in Rehnquist's opinion: It is inconsistent to assume that people have a constitutional right not to be given medical care contrary to their wishes, but yet for the state to be allowed to impose evidentiary rules that make it unlikely that an incompetent person's past wishes will actually be discovered. "Even someone with a resolute determination to avoid life-support under circumstances such as Nancy's," he said, "would still need to know that such things as living wills exist and how to execute one. . . . For many, the thought of an ignoble end, steeped in decay, is abhorrent. A quiet, proud death, bodily integrity intact, is a matter of extreme consequence."

Justice Stevens dissented separately. He criticized the majority for not having enough regard for Cruzan's best interests, and stressed the religious basis of Missouri's case. "[N]ot much may be said with confidence about death," he wrote, "unless it is said from faith, and that alone is reason enough to protect the freedom to conform choices about death to individual conscience."

Last August Cruzan's parents petitioned the lower court that had initially decided in their favor with what they called new evidence: three more friends of Cruzan had come forward prepared to testify that she had told them, too, that she would not want to live as a vegetable. Though this evidence was of the same character as that which the Missouri Supreme Court had earlier said was not sufficiently "clear and convincing," the state attorney general decided this time not to oppose the parents' petition. On December 14, the lower court granted the parents' petition. Within a few days feeding and hydration were stopped, and Cruzan was given medication to prevent pain. She died on December 26.

2.

When competent people refuse medical treatment that is necessary to save their lives, doctors and legal officials may face a dilemma. They have an ethical and legal obligation both to act in the patient's best interests and to respect his autonomy, his right to decide for himself what will be done with or to his body. These obligations may be in conflict, because a patient may refuse treatment the doctors think essential. Rehnquist introduced a third consideration into the constitutional issue. He contrasted the patient's autonomy not just with his or her own best interests but also with the *state's* interest in "protecting and preserving life." In most cases when a competent person refuses life-saving aid—for example, when he refuses an essential blood transfusion on religious grounds—there is no difference between what most people would regard as his best interests and the state's interest in keeping him alive, because it is assumed that it is in his best interests to live. But in some cases—when the patient is in great pain, for example, and cannot live very long even with treatment—then the state's supposed interest in keeping him alive may conflict with his own best interests, not only as he but as most people would judge these.

If we accept that some state policy might be served by prolonging life even in such cases, then two constitutional issues are presented. Does a state have the constitutional power to impose life-saving medical treatment on a person against his will, that is, in defiance of his autonomy, when it believes that treatment is in his own best interests? Does it have the constitutional power to impose such treatment for its own purposes, even when it concedes that this is *against* his best interests, that is, in defiance of the normal rule that patients should not be given medical treatment that is bad for them?

The law of most American states seems settled that the autonomy of a competent patient will be decisive in all such cases, and that doctors may not treat him against his will either for his sake or for the sake of some social interest in keeping him alive. The Supreme Court had never explicitly decided that the Constitution compels states to take that position, though in the present case, as I said, Rehnquist assumed hypothetically that it does.

In the case of people who are unconscious or otherwise incompetent, however, and who did not exercise their right of self-determination when they were able to do so, the distinction between their own best interests and the alleged interest of the state in keeping them alive is of great importance, as Rehnquist's opinion, carefully examined, makes clear. He offered two different, though not clearly distinct, arguments why Missouri has a right to tip the scales in favor of keeping comatose people alive by demanding "clear and convincing" evidence that they had decided they would rather die. His first argument appealed to the best interests of incompetent people. He said that a rule requiring evidence of a formal declaration of a past decision to die, before life support can be terminated, benefits people who have become comatose because it protects them against guardians who abuse their trust, and because a decision not to terminate is always reversible if documented evidence of a formal past decision emerges later. His second argument is very different: it appeals not to the interests of comatose patients but to Missouri's supposed independent interests in keeping such patients alive. He said that a state has its own legitimate reasons for protecting and preserving life, which "no one can gainsay," and that Missouri is therefore entitled for its own sake to tip the evidentiary scales against termination.

He treats these as cumulative arguments: he thinks that taken together they justify Missouri's evidentiary rule. I shall consider them separately, however, because they raise very different issues, and because, though Rehnquist mentions the second only obliquely and in passing, it has important implications for other constitutional issues, including the abortion controversy, and so deserves separate study.

Rehnquist devotes most of his opinion to the first argument: that the Missouri rule is in the best interests of most of the thousands of people who live in a permanent vegetative state and did not sign living wills when they could. That seems implausible. Many people who are now in that position talked and acted in ways that make it very likely that they would have signed a living will had they anticipated their own accidents, as Nancy Cruzan did in conversations with her friends. The Missouri rule flouts rather than honors their autonomy. Many others, at least in the opinions of their family and others who know them best, almost certainly would have decided that way if they had ever considered the matter. The Missouri rule denies them what they probably would have chosen. Why is so indiscriminate a rule necessary? Why would it not be better to allow lower courts to decide each case on the balance of probabilities, so that a court might decide that on the best evidence Nancy Cruzan would have chosen to die, as the initial Missouri court in fact did decide?

While Rehnquist concedes that Missouri's rigid rule may sometimes lead to a "mistake," he says that the Constitution does not require states to adopt procedures that work perfectly. But his arguments that the Missouri rule would even in general work to the benefit of incompetent people are question-begging: they reflect a presumption that it is normally in the best interests of permanently comatose people to live, so that they should be kept alive unless there is decisive evidence that they have actually decided to the contrary. It is true that in some situations a presumption of that kind is sensible. A state need not accept the judgment of devout Jehovah's Witnesses, for example, that it would be in the best interests of an unconscious relative not to have a blood transfusion that would bring him back to conscious life, even if the state would accept his own decision not to be treated were he conscious. But we think the presumption sensible in that case because we believe that life and health are fundamentally so important that no one should be allowed to reject them on behalf of someone else.

No such assumption is plausible when the life in question is only the insensate life of the permanently vegetative. That kind of life is not valuable to anyone. Some people, no doubt, would want to be kept alive indefinitely in such a state out of religious convictions: they might think that failing to prolong life as long as possible is insulting to God, for example. But even they do not think that it is in *their* interests to live on; most such people would hope, I think, for an early death in that situation, though one in which everything had been done to prolong life. They would regard an early death as an instance of God's mercy.

But Rehnquist is so far in the grip of the presumption that life is of great importance even to people in a vegetative state that he argues, at times, as if the Cruzan family's petition was a proceeding *against* their daughter. He says that the state is entitled to act as a "shield" for the incompetent, and he cites cases in which the Supreme Court required that government have "clear and convincing" evidence of fault before deporting someone, or depriving him of citizenship, or terminating his parental rights. In such cases constitutional law properly tips the scales against punitive action, because, as in an ordinary criminal trial, a mistake on one side, against the defendant, is much more serious than a mistake on the other. Cruzan's case is not an adversary proceeding, however. Her own parents are seeking relief on her *behalf*, and fairness argues for only one thing: the most accurate possible identification of what Nancy Cruzan's wishes were and where her interests now lie.

Some of Rehnquist's arguments depend not on the assumption that it is primarily in the interests of a permanently comatose person to continue living but on the equally implausible assumption that continued life in those circumstances is never against such a person's interests. This is the premise of his argument, for example, that it is better to keep a comatose patient alive than to allow her to die, even if the chances of recovery are infinitesimal, because the latter decision is irreversible. He assumes that someone in Nancy Cruzan's position suffers no disadvantage in continuing to live, so that if there is only the barest conceivable possibility of some extraordinary medical discovery in the future, however remote that may seem now, it must be on balance in their interests to continue living as long as possible.

If the only things people worried about, or wanted to avoid, were pain and other unpleasant physical experiences, then of course they would be indifferent about whether, if they became permanently comatose, their bodies continued to live or not. But people care about many other things as well. They worry about their dignity and integrity, and about the view other people have of them, how they are conceived and remembered. Many of them are anxious that their relatives and friends not have to bear the burdens, whether emotional or financial, of keeping them alive. Many are appalled by the thought of resources being wasted on them that might be used for the benefit of other persons who have genuine, conscious lives to lead.

These various concerns explain the horror so many people feel at the idea of existing pointlessly for years as a vegetable. They think that a bare biological existence, with no intelligence or sensibility or sensation, is not a matter of indifference, but something bad for them, something that damages their lives considered as a whole. This was the view Nancy Cruzan expressed to her friend after her grandmother's death. Rehnquist seems depressingly insensitive to all these concerns.

In any case his assumption—that people lose nothing when permission to terminate their lives is refused—ignores them. A great many people, at least, believe the contrary; that a decision to keep them alive would cheat them forever of a chance to die with both dignity and consideration for others, and that to be deprived of that chance would be a great and irreversible loss.

Of course, given the devastating importance of the decision to terminate life support, a state may impose strenuous procedural constraints on any doctor's or guardian's decision to do so. The state may require them to show, for example, in an appropriate hearing before a judge or hospital committee or some other suitable body, and with appropriate medical support, that there is no genuine hope that the victim will ever become competent again. It may require guardians to show, moreover, that there is no persuasive reason to think the patient would have preferred to have life support continued. It may also adopt suitable precautions to insure that the decision is made by people solely concerned with the patient's wishes and interests; it may specify, for example, that the decision not be made by guardians who would gain financially by the patient's early death. Though these and other procedural constraints may somewhat increase the chance that a patient who would have wished to die is kept alive, they can plausibly be described as in the best interests of patients overall, or in the interests of protecting their autonomy.

The Cruzan family satisfied all such requirements, however. There is no evidence that Nancy Cruzan had any religious beliefs that would have led her to prefer mere biological life to death. On the contrary, the evidence of her serious conversations strongly suggested—to put it at its weakest—that she would vigorously oppose being kept alive. Since Missouri itself paid the full cost of her treatment, the family had no financial incentive to allow her to die. So the state's evidentiary procedures cannot reasonably be said to have been in Cruzan's best interests, or in the best interests of vegetative patients generally. If Missouri's rule is constitutional, it must be for some other reason.

3.

We must therefore turn to Rehnquist's second, much less developed, argument: that Missouri can impose evidentiary requirements, even if that is against Cruzan's interests and those of other permanently incompetent people, in order to protect its own interests in preserving life. He said that "societal" and "institutional" issues are at stake, as well as individual ones, that no one can "gainsay" Missouri's "interest in the protection and preservation of human life."

No doubt Missouri pressed this agreement, and perhaps Rehnquist adopted it, with an eye to the abortion controversy. In 1989's abortion case, *Webster v. Missouri Reproductive Services,* Missouri cited its own sovereign interest in preserving all human life as justification for refusing to allow abortions to be performed in state-financed medical facilities. Even *Roe* v. *Wade,* the 1973 decision that established a woman's limited right to an abortion, acknowledged that a state has a legitimate concern with protecting the life of a fetus. Though Justice Blackmun said, in that case, that a state's right to protect a fetus is outweighed by a woman's right of privacy during the first two trimesters of pregnancy, he held that the state's right was sufficiently strong thereafter to allow a state to make most third-trimester abortions illegal. In the *Webster* decision, several justices said that the state's legitimate interest in protecting human life is more powerful than Blackmun recognized, and justifies more sweeping regulation of abortion than he allowed.

Nevertheless, in spite of the crucial part that the idea of a legitimate state interest in preserving all human life now plays in constitutional law, there has been remarkably little attention, either in Supreme Court opinions or in the legal literature, to the question of what that supposed interest is or why it is legitimate for a state to pursue it. It is particularly unclear how the supposed state interest bears on the questions that were at stake in the *Cruzan* case. Of course government is properly concerned with the welfare and well-being of its citizens, and it has the right, for that reason, to try to prevent them from being killed or put at risk of death from disease or accident. But the state's obvious and general concern with its citizen's well-being does not give it a reason to preserve someone's life when his or her welfare would be better served by being permitted to die in dignity. So the state interest that Rehnquist has in mind, as justifying Missouri's otherwise unreasonable evidentiary rule, must be a different, less familiar, one: it must supply a reason for forcing people to accept medical treatment when they or their guardians plausibly think they would be better off dead.

Scalia, in his concurring opinion, said that we must assume that states are constitutionally entitled to preserve people's lives, even against their own interests, because otherwise familiar laws making either suicide or aiding suicide a crime, which no one doubts are valid, would be unconstitutional. As I said, he disagreed with Rehnquist's hypothetical assumption that, at least, competent people have a constitutional right to refuse life-saving medical treatment. But Scalia's argument is doubly suspect.

First, his assumption that states have the constitutional power to prevent suicide in all circumstances is too broad and it is premature. It is true that both suicide and assisting suicide were crimes according to common law, and Scalia relies heavily on the views of William Blackstone, the famous and influential eighteenth-century legal commentator, who declared that it was a crime even for someone suffering a terminal illness and in terrible pain to take his own life. But there are many examples in constitutional history of constraints on liberty that were unquestioned for long periods of history but were then reexamined and found unconstitutional because lawyers and the public as a whole had developed a more sophisticated understanding of the underlying ethical and moral issues.[3] That is particularly likely when the historical support for the constraint has been mainly religious. It was long unquestioned that states have the power to outlaw contraception, for example, before the Supreme Court held otherwise in 1965 in *Griswold* v. *Connecticut*.

Longstanding practice is an even worse guide to constitutional law when technological change has created entirely new problems or exacerbated old ones. Doctors can now keep people alive in terminal illness for long periods that would have seemed incredible in the recent past, and their new abilities have made the position of people who would rather die than continue living in pain both more tragic and more common. So when the Supreme Court is next asked to rule on whether states can constitutionally forbid someone in that position from taking his own life, or can make it criminal for a doctor to assist him, even if the doctor takes every precaution to be sure that the person has freely decided to do so, the Court will face a very different situation from that in which the common law principles about suicide developed. It seems premature for Scalia simply to declare that the power of states to forbid suicide has no exceptions at all. Government is entitled to try to prevent people from killing themselves in many circumstances—in periods of severe but transient depression, for example. But it does not follow that it has the power to prolong the suffering of someone in terrible and pointless pain.

In any case, it is bizarre to classify as suicide someone's decision to reject treatment that would keep him alive but at a cost he and many other people think too great. Many people whose lives could be lengthened through severe amputations or incapacitating operations decide to die instead, and they are not thought to have taken their own lives for that reason. It seems plain that states have no constitutional power to direct doctors to perform such operations without the consent and against the wishes of the patient. People imagining themselves as permanently comatose are in the same position: their biological lives could then be prolonged only through medical treatment they would think degrading, and only in a form they would think worse than death. So it is a mistake, for that reason, to describe someone who signs a living will as committing hypothetical suicide. It seems a mistake for another reason as well. Even if Scalia were right, that a conscious and competent patient who refuses an amputation that would prolong his life should be treated as a suicide, it would still not follow that someone who decides to die if he were to become a permanent vegetable is in fact taking his own life, because it is at least a reasonable view that a permanently comatose person is, for all that matters, dead already.

4.

Scalia's argument is therefore a red herring, and in spite of Rehnquist's confident remark that no one can "gainsay" Missouri's interest in protecting and preserving life, we still lack an explanation of what that interest is and why it is proper for Missouri to pursue it. It might be said that keeping people alive, even when they would be better off dead, helps to protect the community's sense of the importance of life. I agree that society is better and more secure when its members share a sense that human life is sacred, and that no effort should be spared to save lives. People who lack that sense may themselves be more ready to kill, and will be less anxious to make sacrifices to protect the lives of others. That seems to me the most powerful available argument why states should be permitted to outlaw elective abortion of very late-stage fetuses, for example.[4] But it is extremely implausible that allowing a permanently comatose patient to die, after a solemn proceeding devoted only to her wishes and interests, will in any way erode a community's sense of the importance of life.

So a state cannot justify keeping comatose people alive on the instrumental ground that this is necessary to prevent murder or to encourage people to vote for famine relief. If Rehnquist is right that a state has a legitimate interest in preserving all human life, then this must be in virtue not of any instrumental argument but of the *intrinsic* value of such life, its importance for its own sake. Most people do believe that human life has intrinsic importance, and perhaps Rehnquist thinks it unnecessary either to clarify or to justify that idea.[3] It is unclear, however, that they accept the idea on any ground, or in any sense, that supports his case. For some people, for example, life has intrinsic value because it is a gift of God; they believe, as I said, that it is wrong not to struggle to prolong life, because this is an insult to Him, who alone should decide when life ends. But the Constitution does not allow states to justify policy on grounds of religious doctrine; some more secular account of the intrinsic value of life would be needed to support Rehnquist's second argument.

It will be helpful to distinguish two forms that a more secular version of the claim might take. The first supposes that a human life, in any form or circumstance, is a unique and valuable addition to the universe, so that the stock of value is needlessly diminished when any life is shorter than it might be. That does not seem a convincing view. Even if we think that a conscious, reflective, engaged human life is inherently valuable, we might well doubt that an insensate, vegetative life has any value at all.

The view that all forms of life are inherently valuable is also disqualified for a different reason. On that view we would have as much reason to bring new lives into being, increasing the population, as for prolonging lives already in progress. After all, people who think that great art is inherently valuable have the same reason for encouraging the production of more masterpieces as for preserving art that now exists. But most people who think life has intrinsic significance do not think that they therefore have any general duty to procreate or to encourage procreation. In any case, the Supreme Court's decision in *Griswold,* which is now accepted by almost everyone, holds that the states have no power to prohibit contraception.

People who think that life has intrinsic value or importance, but do not think that this fact offers any reason for increasing the population, understand life's value in a second and more conditional way. They mean, I think, that once a human life has begun it is terribly important that it go well, that it be a good rather than a bad life, a successful rather than a wasted one. Most people accept that human life has inherent importance in that sense. That explains why they try not just to make their lives pleasant but to give them worth and also why it seems a tragedy when people decide, late in life, that they can take neither pride nor satisfaction in the way they have lived.[6] Of course nothing in the idea that life has intrinsic importance in this second sense can justify a policy of keeping permanently comatose people alive. The worth of their lives—the character of the lives they have led—cannot be improved just by keeping the bodies they used to inhabit technically alive. On the contrary, that makes their lives worse, because it is a bad thing, for all the reasons I described earlier, to have one's body medicated, fed, and groomed, as an object of pointless and degrading solicitude, after one's mind is dead. Rehnquist's second argument is therefore a dramatic failure: Missouri's policy is not supported but condemned by the idea that human life is important for its own sake, on the only understanding of that idea that is available in our constitutional system.

5.

It is a relatively new question how the medical technology that now allows doctors to keep wholly incompetent people alive for decades should be used. Of course the Constitution leaves considerable latitude to the state legislatures in fixing detailed schemes for regulating how and what doctors and guardians decide. But the Constitution does limit a state's power in certain ways, as it must in order to protect the autonomy and the most fundamental interests of the patient.

In the *Cruzan* case the Supreme Court recognized, even if only hypothetically, an important part of that constitutional protection: that in principle a state has no right to keep a comatose patient alive against his previously expressed wish that he be allowed to die in the circumstances he has now reached. But the Court undercut the full value of that principle by allowing Missouri to impose an evidentiary rule that substantially decreases the chance a patient will receive only the treatment he or she would have wanted. Even worse, the justification the Chief Justice offered for the Court's decision put forward two principles that, unless they are soon rejected, will damage the rest of the law as it develops. It is therefore worth summarizing the argument I have made against these principles.

Rehnquist assumed that it is in the best interests of at least most people who become permanent vegetables to remain alive in that condition. But there is no way in which continued life can be good for such people, and several ways in which it might well be thought bad. He also assumed that a state can have its own legitimate reasons for keeping such people alive even when it concedes that this is against their best interests. But that judgment rests on a dangerous misunderstanding of the irresistible idea that human life has intrinsic moral significance. We do not honor that idea—on the contrary we insult it—when we waste resources in prolonging a bare, technical, insensate form of life.

More than just the right to die, or even the right to abortion, is at stake in these issues. In the next decades the question of why and how human life has intrinsic value is likely to be debated, by philosophers, lawyers, and the public, not just with respect to those issues but others as well, including genetic engineering, for example. Constitutional law will both encourage and reflect the debate, and though it is far too early to anticipate what form that law will take, Rehnquist's unreasoned opinion was a poor beginning.

NOTES

1. In fact five justices—Justice O'Connor and the four dissenters—did declare that people have that right. But one of the dissenters, Justice Brennan, has retired, and it is not known whether Justice Souter, who took his place, agrees.
2. On July 1, 1990, the New York state legislature enacted a law, the "health care proxy bill," that provides for such delegation. Governor Cuomo said that the *Cruzan* decision helped to break a logjam on the bill. See *The New York Times*, July 2, 1990.

3. The recent, well-publicized case of Janet Adkins, who killed herself using Dr. Jack Kevorkian's suicide machine in the back of his Volkswagen van, suggests the moral complexity of suicide provoked by illness, and the degree to which Americans are divided about the issues raised by such suicide. Adkins was fifty-three and in the relatively early stages of Alzheimer's disease. Her mental capacity had begun to diminish—she found tennis scoring and the foreign languages she used to speak too difficult, for example, though she had lost little physical capacity, and had recently beaten her thirty-three-year-old son at tennis. She was still alert and intelligent, and had retained her sense of humor. But she wanted to die before the irreversible disease worsened; the life she would soon lead, she said, "is not the way I wanted it at all. . . ." She telephoned Kevorkian, whom she had seen on television discussing his device. They met in Michigan, chosen because assisting suicide is not a crime there, in a motel room where he taped a forty-minute conversation which recorded her competence and her wish to die. Two days later he inserted a needle into her vein as she lay in the back of his van, and told her which button to push for a lethal injection. Michigan prosecutors charged Kevorkian with murder, but the judge acquitted him after listening to the tape.

   The case raises serious moral issues that the Cruzan case does not. Janet Adkins apparently had several years of meaningful life left, and Kevorkian's examination may not have been long or substantial enough to rule out the possibility that she was in a temporary depression from which she might recover while still competent. It is of interest that about half of the 250 doctors who wrote in response to a critical article in a medical journal approved of what Kevorkian did, while the rest disapproved.
4. See my article "The Great Abortion Case," in *The New York Review*, June 29, 1989.
5. I do not mean to deny that animal life might have intrinsic importance, too.
6. I do not mean that many people often reflect on their lives as a whole, or live according to some overall theory about what makes their lives good or bad. Most people define living well in much more concrete terms: living well means having a good job, a successful family life, warm friendships, and time and money for recreation or travel, for example. But I believe that people take pride as well as pleasure in these concrete achievements and experiences, and have a sense of failure as well as displeasure when a job goes wrong or a friendship sours. Very few of them, perhaps, except those for whom religion is important, self-consciously think of their lives as an opportunity that they may either waste or make into something worthwhile. But most people's attitudes toward successes and failures do seem to presuppose that view of life's importance. Most of us think it is important that the lives of other people, as well as our own, be worthwhile: we think it is a central role of government to encourage people to make something of their lives rather than just survive, and to provide some of the institutions, including the schools, necessary for them to do so. These assumptions are premises of liberal education, and also of the limited paternalism involved in stopping people from using drugs or wasting their lives in other ways, and in trying to prevent or discourage people who are depressed or despondent from killing themselves when they could in fact lead lives worth living.

   That human life has intrinsic value in this sense—that it is important that a life go well once it has begun—obviously has important though complex implications for the abortion issue. In a recent Holmes Lecture at Harvard Law School I explored these implications. I argued that the idea that life has intrinsic value in the sense I described does explain many of our attitudes about abortion, including the opinion many people have that abortion even in an early stage poses moral problems. It does not follow that abortion is always wrong; indeed it sometimes follows that abortion is morally recommended or required. I argued, moreover, that understanding our moral notions about abortion as flowing from respect for the inherent value of life reinforces the Supreme Court decision in *Roe* v. *Wade* that the state has no business coercing pregnant women to take a particular view about what the principle of respect for the inherent value of life requires.

Of Suicide

David Hume

David Hume (1711–1776), a Scot who was one of the greatest and most influential philosophers of the Western world, addresses the sensitive and important topic of suicide with his characteristically elegant prose. Ironically, his "Of Suicide" was withdrawn from publication and published only posthumously. Publishing "Of Suicide" during Hume's lifetime was thought to be itself suicidal or at least unduly risky given the intolerant religious attitudes prevailing in Britain in his day. Of course, such intolerant reactions to some philosophies—and even fiction (e.g., reaction to Salmon Rushdie's *The Satanic Verses* forced him to go into hiding in Britain)—occur even today. Hume attempts to develop a surprisingly commonsensical counterexample to the views of those who oppose suicide on religious grounds.

One considerable advantage, that arises from philosophy, consists in the sovereign antidote, which it affords to superstition and false religion. All other remedies against that pestilent distemper are vain, or, at least, uncertain. Plain good-sense, and the practice of the world, which alone serve most purposes of life, are here found ineffectual: History, as well as daily experience, affords instances of men, endowed with the strongest capacity for business and affairs, who have all their lives crouched under slavery to the grossest superstition. Even gaiety and sweetness of temper, which infuse a balm into every other wound, afford no remedy to so virulent a poison; as we may particularly observe of the fair sex, who, tho' commonly possessed of these rich presents of nature, feel many of their joys blasted by this importunate intruder. But when sound philosophy has once gained possession of the mind, superstition is effectually excluded; and one may safely affirm, that her triumph over this enemy is more compleat than over most of the vices and imperfections, incident to human nature. Love or anger, ambition or avarice, have their root in the temper and affections, which the soundest reason is scarce ever able fully to correct. But superstition, being founded on false opinion, must immediately vanish, when true philosophy has inspired juster sentiments of superior powers. The contest is here more equal between the distemper and the medicine: And nothing can hinder the latter from proving effectual, but its being false and sophisticated.

It will here be superfluous to magnify the merits of philosophy, by displaying the pernicious tendency of that vice, of which it cures the human mind. The superstitious man, says Tully,[1] is miserable in every scene, in every incident of life. Even sleep itself, which banishes all other cares of unhappy mortals, affords to him matter of new terror; while he examines his dreams, and finds in those visions of the night, prognostications of future calamities. I may add, that, tho' death alone can put a full period to his misery, he dares not fly to this refuge, but still prolongs a miserable existence, from a vain fear, lest he offend his maker, by using the power, with which that beneficent being has endowed him. The presents of God and Nature are ravished from us by this cruel enemy; and notwithstanding that one step would remove us from the regions of pain and sorrow, her menaces still chain us down to a hated being, which she herself chiefly contributes to render miserable.

'Tis observed of such as have been reduced by the calamities of life to the necessity of employing this fatal remedy, that, if the unseasonable care of their friends deprive them of that species of death, which they proposed to themselves, they seldom venture upon any other, or can summon up so much resolution, a second time, as to execute their purpose. So great is our horror of death, that when it presents itself under any form, besides that to which a man has endeavoured to reconcile his imagination, it acquires new terrors, and overcomes his feeble courage. But when the menaces of superstition are joined to this natural timidity, no wonder it quite deprives men of all power over their lives; since even many pleasures and enjoyments, to which we are carried by a strong propensity, are torn from us by this inhuman tyrant. Let us here endeavour to restore men to their native liberty, by examining all the common arguments against Suicide, and shewing, that That action may be free from every imputation of guilt or blame; according to the sentiments of all the antient philosophers.

If Suicide be criminal, it must be a transgression of our duty, either to God, our neighbour, or ourselves.

To prove, that Suicide is no transgression of our duty to God, the following considerations may perhaps suffice. In order to govern the material world, the almighty creator has established general and immutable laws, by which all bodies, from the greatest planet to the smallest particle of matter, are maintained in their proper sphere and function. To govern the animal world, he has endowed all living creatures with bodily and mental powers; with senses, passions, appetites, memory, and judgment; by which they are impelled or regulated in that course of life, to which they are destined. These two distinct principles of the material and animal world continually encroach upon each other, and mutually retard or forward each other's operation. The powers of men and of all other animals are restrained and directed by the nature and qualities of the surrounding bodies; and the modifications and actions of these bodies are incessantly altered by the operation of all animals. Man is stopped by rivers in his passage over the surface of the earth; and rivers, when properly directed, lend their force to the motion of machines, which serve to the use of man. But tho' the provinces of the material and animal powers are not kept entirely separate, there result from thence no discord or disorder in the creation: On the contrary, from the mixture, union, and contrast of all the various powers of inanimate bodies and living creatures, arises that surprizing harmony and proportion, which affords the surest argument of supreme wisdom.

The providence of the deity appears not immediately in any operation, but governs every thing by those general and immutable laws, which have been established from the beginning of time. All events, in one sense, may be pronounced the action of the almighty: They all proceed from those powers, with which he has endowed his creatures. A house, which falls by its own weight, is not brought to ruin by his providence more than one destroyed by the hands of men; nor are the human faculties less his workmanship than the laws of motion and gravitation. When the passions play, when the judgment dictates, when the limbs obey; this is all the operation of God; and upon these animate principles, as well as upon the inanimate, has he established the government of the universe.

Every event is alike important in the eyes of that infinite being, who takes in, at one glance, the most distant regions of space and remotest periods of time. There is no one event, however important to us, which he has exempted from the general laws that govern the universe, or which he has peculiarly reserved for his own immediate action and operation. The revolutions of states and empires depend upon the smallest caprice or passion of single men; and the lives of men are shortened or extended by the smallest accident of air or diet, sunshine or tempest. Nature still continues her progress and operation; and if general laws be ever broke by particular volitions of the deity, 'tis after a manner which entirely escapes human observation. As on the one hand, the elements and other inanimate parts of the creation carry on their action without regard to the particular interest and situation of men; so men are entrusted to their own judgment and discretion in the various shocks of matter, and may employ every faculty, with which they are endowed, in order to provide for their ease, happiness, or preservation.

What is the meaning, then, of that principle, that a man, who, tired of life, and hunted by pain and misery, bravely overcomes all the natural terrors of death, and makes his escape from this cruel scene; that such a man, I say, has incurred the indignation of his creator, by encroaching on the office of divine providence, and disturbing the order of the universe? Shall we assert, that the Almighty has reserved to himself, in any peculiar manner, the disposal of the lives of men, and has not submitted that event, in common with others, to the general laws, by which the universe is governed? This is plainly false. The lives of men depend upon the same laws as the lives of all other animals; and these are subjected to the general laws of matter and motion. The fall of a tower or the infusion of a poison will destroy a man equally with the meanest creature: An inundation sweeps away every thing, without distinction, that comes within the reach of its fury. Since therefore the lives of men are for ever dependent on the general laws of matter and motion; is a man's disposing of his life criminal, because, in every case, it is criminal to encroach upon these laws, or disturb their operation? But this seems absurd. All animals are entrusted to their own prudence and skill for their conduct in the world, and have full authority, as far as their power extends, to alter all the operations of nature. Without the exercise of this authority, they could not subsist a moment. Every action, every motion of a man innovates in the order of some parts of matter, and diverts, from their ordinary course, the general laws of motion. Putting together, therefore, these conclusions, we find, *that* human life depends upon the general laws of matter and motion, and *that* 'tis no encroachment on the office of providence to disturb or alter these general laws. Has not every one, of consequence, the free disposal of his own life? And may he not lawfully employ that power with which nature has endowed him?

In order to destroy the evidence of this conclusion, we must shew a reason, why this particular case is excepted. Is it because human life is of so great importance, that it is a presumption for human prudence to dispose of it? But the life of man is of no greater importance to the universe than that of an oyster. And were it of ever so great importance, the order of nature has actually submitted it to human prudence, and reduced us to a necessity, in every incident, of determining concerning it.

Were the disposal of human life so much reserved as the peculiar province of the almighty that it were an encroachment on his right for men to dispose of their own lives; it would be equally criminal to act for the preservation of life as for its destruction. If I turn aside a stone, which is falling upon my head, I disturb the course of nature, and I invade the peculiar province of the almighty, by lengthening out my life, beyond the period, which, by the general laws of matter and motion, he had assigned to it.

A hair, a fly, an insect is able to destroy this mighty being, whose life is of such importance. Is it an absurdity to suppose, that human prudence may lawfully dispose of what depends on such insignificant causes?

It would be no crime in me to divert the *Nile* or *Danube* from its course, were I able to effect such purposes. Where then is the crime of turning a few ounces of blood from their natural chanels!

Do you imagine that I repine at providence or curse my creation, because I go out of life, and put a period to a being, which, were it to continue, would render me miserable? Far be such sentiments from me. I am only convinced of a matter of fact, which you yourself acknowledge possible, that human life may be unhappy, and that my existence, if farther prolonged, would become uneligible. But I thank providence, both for the good, which I have already enjoyed, and for the power, with which I am endowed, of escaping the ill that threatens me.[2] To you it belongs to repine at providence, who foolishly imagine that you have no such power, and who must still prolong a hated being, tho' loaded with pain and sickness, with shame and poverty.

Do you not teach, that when any ill befalls me, tho' by the malice of my enemies, I ought to be resigned to providence; and that the actions of men are the operations of the almighty as much as the actions of inanimate beings? When I fall upon my own sword, therefore, I receive my death equally from the hands of the deity, as if it had proceeded from a lion, a precipice, or a fever.

The submission, which you require to providence, in every calamity, that befalls me, excludes not human skill and industry; if possibly, by their means, I can avoid or escape the calamity. And why may I not employ one remedy as well as another?

If my life be not my own, it were criminal for me to put it in danger, as well as to dispose of it: Nor could one man deserve the appellation of *Hero,* whom glory or friendship transports into the greatest dangers, and another merit the reproach of *Wretch* or *Miscreant,* who puts a period to his life, from the same or like motives.

There is no being, which possesses any power or faculty, that it receives not from its creator; nor is there any one, which, by ever so irregular an action, can encroach upon the plan of his providence, or disorder the universe. Its operations are his work equally with that chain of events, which it invades; and which ever principle prevails, we may, for that very reason, conclude it to be most favoured by him. Be it animate or inanimate, rational or irrational, 'tis all a case: Its power is still derived from the supreme creator, and is alike comprehended in the order of his providence. When the horror of pain prevails over the love of life: When a voluntary action anticipates the effect of blind causes; it is only in consequence of those powers and principles, which he has implanted in his creatures. Divine providence is still inviolate, and placed far beyond the reach of human injuries.

It is impious, says the old *Roman* superstition,[3] to divert rivers from their course, or invade the prerogatives of nature. 'Tis impious, says the *French* superstition, to inoculate for the small-pox, or usurp the business of providence, by voluntarily producing distempers and maladies. 'Tis impious, says the modern *European* superstition, to put a period to our own life, and thereby rebel against our creator. And why not impious, say I, to build houses, cultivate the ground, and sail upon the ocean? In all these actions, we employ our powers of mind and body to produce some innovation in the course of nature; and in none of them do we any more. They are all of them, therefore, equally innocent or equally criminal.

But you are placed by providence, like a sentinel, in a particular station; and when you desert it, without being recalled, you are guilty of rebellion against your almighty sovereign, and have incurred his displeasure. I ask, why do you conclude, that Providence has placed me in this station? For my part, I find, that I owe my birth to a long chain of causes, of which many and even the principal, depended upon voluntary actions of men. *But Providence guided all these causes, and nothing happens in the universe without its consent and co-operation.* If so, then neither does my death, however voluntary, happen without its consent; and whenever pain and sorrow so far overcome my patience as to make me tired of life, I may conclude, that I am recalled from my station, in the clearest and most express terms.

It is providence, surely, that has placed me at present in this chamber: But may I not leave it, when I think proper, without being liable to the imputation of having deserted my post or station? When I shall be dead, the principles, of which I am composed, will still perform their part in the universe, and will be equally useful in the grand fabric, as when they composed this individual creature. The difference to the whole will be no greater than between my being in a chamber and in the open air. The one change is of more importance to me than the other; but not more so to the universe.

It is a kind of blasphemy to imagine, that any created being can disturb the order of the world, or invade the business of providence. It supposes, that that being possesses powers and faculties, which it received not from its creator, and which are not subordinate to his government and authority. A man may disturb society, no doubt; and thereby incur the displeasure of the almighty: But the government of the world is placed far beyond his reach and violence. And how does it appear, that the almighty is displeased with those actions, that disturb society? By the principles which he has implanted in human nature, and which inspire us with a sentiment of remorse, if we ourselves have been guilty of such actions, and with that of blame and disapprobation, if we ever observe them in others. Let us now examine, according to the method proposed, whether Suicide be of this kind of actions, and be a breach of our duty to our *neighbour* and to society.

A man, who retires from life, does no harm to society. He only ceases to do good; which, if it be an injury, is of the lowest kind.

All our obligations to do good to society seem to imply something reciprocal. I receive the benefits of society, and therefore ought to promote it's interest. But when I withdraw myself altogether from society, can I be bound any longer?

But allowing, that our obligations to do good were perpetual, they have certainly some bounds. I am not obliged to do a small good to society, at the expence of a great harm to myself. Why then should I prolong a miserable existence, because of some frivolous advantage, which the public may, perhaps, receive from me? If upon account of age and infirmities, I may lawfully resign any office, and employ my time altogether in fencing against these calamities, and alleviating, as much as possible, the miseries of my future life: Why may I not cut short these miseries at once by an action, which is no more prejudicial to society?

But suppose, that it is no longer in my power to promote the interest of the public: Suppose, that I am a burthen to it: Suppose, that my life hinders some person from being much more useful to the public. In such cases my resignation of life must not only be innocent but laudable. And most people, who lie under anm temptation to abandon existence, are in some such situation. Those, who have health, or power, or authority, have commonly better reason to be in humour with the world.

A man is engaged in a conspiracy for the public interest; is seized upon suspicion; is threatened with the rack; and knows, from his own weakness, that the secret will be extorted from him: Could such a one consult the public interest better than by putting a quick period to a miserable life? This was the case of the famous and brave *Strozzi* of *Florence*.

Again, suppose a malefactor justly condemned to a shameful death; can any reason be imagined, why he may not anticipate his punishment, and save himself all the anguish of thinking on its dreadful approaches? He invades the business of providence no more than the magistrate did, who ordered his execution; and his voluntary death is equally advantageous to society, by ridding it of a pernicious member.

That Suicide may often be consistent with interest and with our duty to *ourselves,* no one can question, who allows, that age, sickness, or misfortune may render life a burthen, and make it worse even than annihilation. I believe that no man ever threw away life, while it was worth keeping. For such is our natural horror of death, that small motives will never be able to reconcile us to it. And tho' perhaps the situation of a man's health or fortune did not seem to require this remedy, we may at least be assured, that any one, who, without apparent reason, has had recourse to it, was curst with such an incurable depravity or gloominess of temper, as must poison all enjoyment, and render him equally miserable as if he had been loaded with the most grievous misfortunes.

If Suicide be supposed a crime, 'tis only cowardice can impel us to it. If it be no crime, both prudence and courage should engage us to rid ourselves at once of existence, when it becomes a burthen. 'Tis the only way, that we can then be useful to society, by setting an example, which, if imitated, would preserve to every one his chance for happiness in life, and would effectually free him from all danger of misery.[4]

NOTES

1. *De Divin.* lib. ii. [Cicero, *On Divination* 2.72 (150).]
2. *Agamus Deo gratias, quod nemo in vita teneri potest.* Seneca, *Epist.* xii. [Seneca, *Epistles,* no. 12: "On Old Age," sec. 10: "And let us thank God that no man can be kept in life" (Loeb translation by Richard M. Gummere).]
3. *Tacit. Ann.* lib. i.
4. It would be easy to prove, that Suicide is as lawful under the *christian* dispensation as it was to the heathens. There is not a single text of scripture, which prohibits it. That great and infallible rule of faith and practice, which must controul all philosophy and human reasoning, has left us, in this particular, to our natural liberty. Resignation to providence is, indeed, recommended in scripture; but that implies only submission to ills, which are unavoidable, not to such as may be remedied

by prudence or courage. *Thou shalt not kill* is evidently meant to exclude only the killing of others, over whose life we have no authority. That this precept like most of the scripture precepts, must be modified by reason and common sense, is plain from the practice of magistrates, who punish criminals capitally, notwithstanding the letter of this law. But were this commandment ever so express against Suicide, it could now have no authority. For all the law of *Moses* is abolished, except so far as it is established by the law of nature; and we have already endeavoured to prove, that Suicide is not prohibited by that law. In all cases, *Christians* and *Heathens* are precisely upon the same footing; and if *Cato* and *Brutus, Arria* and *Portia* acted heroically, those who now imitate their example ought to receive the same praises from posterity. The power of committing Suicide is regarded by *Pliny* as an advantage which men posses even above the deity himself. *Deus non sibi potest mortem consciscere, si velit, quod homini dedit optimum in tantis vitoe poenis*. Lib. ii. Cap. 7. [Pliny, *Natural History* 2.5.27 in the Loeb edition: "(God cannot) even if he wishes, commit suicide, the supreme boon that he has bestowed on man among all the penalties of life" (Loeb translation by H. Rackham).]

Study Questions

1. Did the Supreme Court make the morally best ruling in *Cruzan v. Director, Missouri Department of Health?* Explain your answer using moral principles defined in Appendix B. Does Justice Rehnquist defer too much to legislatures in determining an individual's "right to die"? How do you balance majority rule with individual rights here?

2. What are Dworkin's main arguments for a right to death? Does a right to death make sense, since we will all die sooner or later anyway? If "right to die" or "right to death" are poor phrases, how would you phrase the right at issue here?

3. Do you think suicide can ever be rational? If so, why? If not, why not? Is Hume's comparison of suicide with deflecting a falling stone a false analogy or an accurate comparison?

F Feminism, The First Amendment, and Pornography

American Booksellers Association v. Hudnut (1985)

UNITED STATES COURT OF APPEALS, SEVENTH CIRCUIT

The United States Court of Appeals, Seventh Circuit, recently decided this case on the popular issue of pornography and obscenity. The case concerned an Indianapolis ordinance containing four prohibitions. One central idea of the ordinance was to prohibit the depiction of women as sexual objects who enjoy pain or humiliation or who experience sexual pleasure in being raped or physically hurt generally. Judge Easterbrook wrote the court's opinion that the ordinance unconstitutionally violated the right of free speech. The famous rock musician John Lennon, a feminist, rejected the old sexist saying that "Women should be seen and not heard" when he mocked it as "Women should be obscene and not heard." By the 1980s other feminists claimed a link between obscenity and ordinary sexism, and actively led the effort to pass the ordinance because they believed pornography and obscenity reinforced sexist attitudes toward women. Many think it is unfair to criminalize pornography because it cannot be defined precisely enough. Supreme Court Justice Potter Steward once said that he could not define pornography but that he knew it when he saw it. It was probably the most memorable sentence of his professional life, but Stewart later said it was the sentence he most regretted of all those in his career.

Easterbrook, Circuit Judge.

Indianapolis enacted an ordinance defining "pornography" as a practice that discriminates against women. "Pornography" is to be redressed through the administrative and judicial methods used for other discrimination. The City's definition of "pornography" is considerably different from "obscenity," which the Supreme Court has held is not protected by the First Amendment.

. . . To be "obscene" under *Miller v. California,* . . . (1973), "a publication must, taken as a whole, appeal to the prurient interest, must contain patently offensive depictions or descriptions of specified sexual conduct, and on the whole have no serious literary, artistic, political, or scientific value." . . . Offensiveness must be assessed under the standards of the community. Both offensiveness and an appeal to something other than "normal, healthy sexual desires" . . . are essential elements of "obscenity."

"Pornography" under the ordinance is "the graphic sexually explicit subordination of women, whether in pictures or in words, that also includes one or more of the following:

1. Women are presented as sexual objects who enjoy pain or humiliation; or

2. Women are presented as sexual objects who experience sexual pleasure in being raped; or
3. Women are presented as sexual objects tied up or cut up or mutilated or bruised or physically hurt, or as dismembered or truncated or fragmented or severed into body parts; or
4. Women are presented as being penetrated by objects or animals; or
5. Women are presented in scenarios of degradation, injury, abasement, torture, shown as filthy or inferior, bleeding, bruised, or hurt in a context that makes these conditions sexual; or
6. Women are presented as sexual objects for domination, conquest, violation, exploitation, possession, or use, or through postures or positions of servility or submission or display."

The Indianapolis ordinance does not refer to the prurient interest, to offensiveness, or to the standards of the community. It demands attention to particular depictions, not to the work judged as a whole. It is irrelevant under the ordinance whether the work has literary, artistic, political, or scientific value. The City and many *amici* point to these omissions as virtues. They maintain that pornography influences attitudes, and the statute is a way to alter the socialization of men and women rather than to vindicate community standards of offensiveness. And as one of the principal drafters of the ordinance has asserted, "if a woman is subjected, why should it matter that the work has other value?" Catherine A. MacKinnon, *Pornography, Civil Rights, and Speech,* 20 Harv.Civ.Rts.—Civ.Lib.L. Rev. 1, 21 (1985).

Civil rights groups and feminists have entered this case as *amici* on both sides. Those supporting the ordinance say that it will play an important role in reducing the tendency of men to view women as sexual objects, a tendency that leads to both unacceptable attitudes and discrimination in the workplace and violence away from it. Those opposing the ordinance point out that much radical feminist literature is explicit and depicts women in ways forbidden by the ordinance and that the ordinance would reopen old battles. It is unclear how Indianapolis would treat works from James Joyce's *Ulysses* to Homer's *Iliad:* both depict women as submissive objects for conquest and domination.

We do not try to balance the arguments for and against an ordinance such as this. The ordinance discriminates on the ground of the content of the speech. Speech treating women in the approved way—in sexual encounters "premised on equality" (MacKinnon, *supra,* at 22)—is lawful no matter how sexually explicit. Speech treating women in the disapproved way—as submissive in matters sexual or as enjoying humiliation—is unlawful no matter how significant the literary, artistic, or political qualities of the work taken as a whole. The state may not ordain preferred viewpoints in this way. The Constitution forbids the state to declare one perspective right and silence opponents.

The ordinance contains four prohibitions. People may not "traffic" in pornography, "coerce" others into performing in pornographic works, or "force" pornography on anyone. Anyone injured by someone who has seen or read pornography has a right of action against the maker or seller.

Trafficking is defined in § 16–3(g)(4) as the "production, sale, exhibition, or distribution of pornography." The offense excludes exhibition in a public or educational library, but a "special display" in a library may be sex discrimination. Section 16–3(g)(4)(C) provides that the trafficking paragraph "shall not be construed to make isolated passages or isolated parts actionable."

"Coercion into pornographic performance" is defined in § 16–3(g)(5) as "[c]oercing, intimidating or fraudulently inducing any person . . . into performing for pornography. . . ." The ordinance specifies that proof of any of the following "shall not constitute a defense: I. That the person is a woman; . . . VI. That the person has previously posed for sexually explicit pictures . . . with anyone . . . ; . . . VIII. That the person actually consented to a use of the performance that is changed into pornography; . . . IX. That the person knew that the purpose of the acts or events in question was to make pornography; . . . XI. That the person signed a contract, or made statements affirming a willingness to cooperate in the production of pornography; XII. That no physical force, threats, or weapons were used in the making of the pornography; or XIII. That the person was paid or otherwise compensated."

"Forcing pornography on a person," according to § 16–3(g)(5), is the "forcing of pornography on any woman, man, child, or transsexual in any place of employment, in education, in a home, or in any public place." The statute does not define forcing, but one of its authors states that the definition reaches pornography shown to medical students as part of their education or given to language students for translation. MacKinnon, *supra,* at 40–41.

Section 16–3(g)(7) defines as a prohibited practice the "assault, physical attack, or injury of any woman, man, child, or transsexual in a way that is directly caused by specific pornography."

For purposes of all four offenses, it is generally "not . . . a defense that the respondent did not know or intend that the materials were pornography. . . ." Section 16–3(g)(8). But the ordinance provides that damages are unavailable in trafficking cases unless the complainant proves "that the respondent knew or had reason to know that the materials were pornography." It is a complete defense to a trafficking case that all of the materials in question were pornography only by virtue of category (6) of the definition of pornography. In cases of assault caused by pornography, those who seek damages from "a seller, exhibitor or distributor" must show that the defendant knew or had reason to know of the material's status as pornography. By implication, those who seek damages from an author need not show this.

A woman aggrieved by trafficking in pornography may file a complaint "as a woman acting against the subordination of women" with the office of equal opportunity. Section 16–17(b). A man, child, or transsexual also may protest trafficking "but must prove injury in the same way that a woman is injured. . . ." *Ibid,* Subsection (a) also provides, however, that "any person claiming to be aggrieved" by trafficking, coercion, forcing, or assault may complain against the "perpetrators." We need not decide whether § 16–17(b) qualifies the right of action in § 16–17(a).

The office investigates and within 30 days makes a recommendation to a panel of the equal opportunity advisory board. The panel then decides whether there is reasonable cause to proceed (§ 16–24(2)) and may refer the dispute to a conciliation conference or to a complaint adjudication committee for a hearing (§§ 16–24(3), 16–26(a)). The committee uses the same procedures ordinarily associated with civil rights litigation. It may make findings and enter orders, including both orders to cease and desist and orders "to take further affirmative action . . . including but not limited to the power to restore complainant's losses. . . ." Section 16–26(d). Either party may appeal the committee's decision to the board, which reviews the record before the committee and may modify its decision.

Under Indiana law an administrative decision takes effect when rendered, unless a court issues a stay. . . . The board's decisions are subject to review in the ordinary course. . . . Judicial review in pornography cases is to be de novo . . . , which provides a second complete hearing. When the board finds that a person has engaged in trafficking or that a seller, exhibitor, or distributor is responsible for an assault, it must initiate judicial review of its own decision, . . . and the statute prohibits injunctive relief in these cases in advance of the court's final decision. . . .

The district court held the ordinance unconstitutional. . . . The court concluded that the ordinance regulates speech rather than the conduct involved in making pornography. The regulation of speech could be justified, the court thought, only by a compelling interest in reducing sex discrimination, an interest Indianapolis had not established. The ordinance is also vague and overbroad, the court believed, and establishes a prior restraint of speech.

. . . "If there is any fixed star in our constitutional constellation, it is that no official, high or petty, can prescribe what shall be orthodox in politics, nationalism, religion, or other matters of opinion or force citizens to confess by word or act their faith therein." *West Virginia State Board of Education v. Barnette*, . . . (1943). Under the First Amendment the government must leave to the people the evaluation of ideas. Bold or subtle, an idea is as powerful as the audience allows it to be. A belief may be pernicious—the beliefs of Nazis led to the death of millions, those of the Klan to the repression of millions. A pernicious belief may prevail. Totalitarian governments today rule much of the planet, practicing suppression of billions and spreading dogma that may enslave others. One of the things that separates our society from theirs is our absolute right to propagate opinions that the government finds wrong or even hateful. . . .

Under the ordinance graphic sexually explicit speech is "pornography" or not depending on the perspective the author adopts. Speech that "subordinates" women and also, for example, presents women as enjoying pain, humiliation, or rape, or even simply presents women in "positions of servility or submission or display" is forbidden, no matter how great the literary or political value of the work taken as a whole. Speech that portrays women in positions of equality is lawful, no matter how graphic the sexual content. This is thought control. It establishes an "approved" view of women, of how they may react to sexual encounters, of how the sexes may relate to each other. Those who espouse the approved view may use sexual images; those who do not, may not.

Indianapolis justifies the ordinance on the ground that pornography affects thoughts. Men who see women depicted as subordinate are more likely to treat them so. Pornography is an aspect of dominance. It does not persuade people so much as change them. It works by socializing, by establishing the expected and the permissible. In this view pornography is not an idea; pornography is the injury.

There is much to this perspective. Beliefs are also facts. People often act in accordance with the images and patterns they find around them. People raised in a religion tend to accept the tenets of that religion, often without independent examination. People taught from birth that black people are fit only for slavery rarely rebelled against that creed; beliefs coupled with the self-interest of the masters established a social structure that inflicted great harm while enduring for centuries. Words and images act at the level of the subconscious before they persuade at the level of the conscious. Even the truth has little chance unless a statement fits within the framework of beliefs that may never have been subjected to rational study. . . .

Yet this simply demonstrates the power of pornography as speech. All of these unhappy effects depend on mental intermediation. Pornography affects how people see the world, their fellows, and social relations. If pornography is what pornography does, so is other speech. Hitler's orations affected how some Germans saw Jews. Communism is a world view, not simply a *Manifesto* by Marx and Engels or a set of speeches. Efforts to suppress communist speech in the United States were based on the belief that the public acceptability of such ideas would increase the likelihood of totalitarian government. Religions affect socialization in the most pervasive way. The opinion in *Wisconsin v. Yoder*, . . . (1972), shows how a religion can dominate an entire approach to life, governing much more than the relation between the sexes. Many people believe that the existence of television, apart from the content of specific programs, leads to intellectual laziness, to a penchant for violence, to many other ills. The Alien and Sedition Acts passed during the administration of John Adams rested on a sincerely held belief that disrespect for the government leads to social collapse and revolution—a belief with support in the history of many nations. Most governments of the world act on this empirical regularity, suppressing critical speech. In the United States, however, the strength of the support for this belief is irrelevant. . . .

Racial bigotry, anti-semitism, violence on television, reporters' biases—these and many more influence the culture and shape our socialization. None is directly answerable by more speech, unless that speech too finds its place in the popular culture. Yet all is protected as speech, however insidious. Any other answer leaves the government in control of all of the institutions of culture, the great censor and director of which thoughts are good for us.

Sexual responses often are unthinking responses, and the association of sexual arousal with the subordination of women therefore may have a substantial effect. But almost all cultural stimuli provoke unconscious responses. Religious ceremonies condition their participants. Teachers convey messages by selecting what not to cover; the implicit message about what is off limits or unthinkable may be more powerful than the messages for which they present rational argument. Television scripts contain unarticulated assumptions. People may be conditioned in subtle ways. If the fact that speech plays a role in a process of conditioning were enough to permit governmental regulation, that would be the end of freedom of speech.

It is possible to interpret the claim that the pornography is the harm in a different way. Indianapolis emphasizes the injury that models in pornographic films and pictures may suffer. The record contains materials depicting sexual torture, penetration of women by red-hot irons and the like. These concerns have nothing to do with written materials subject to the statute, and physical injury can occur with or without the "subordination" of women. . . . [A] state may make injury in the course of producing a film unlawful independent of the viewpoint expressed in the film.

The more immediate point, however, is that the image of pain is not necessarily pain. In *Body Double,* a suspense film directed by Brian DePalma, a woman who has disrobed and presented a sexually explicit display is murdered by an intruder with a drill. The drill runs through the woman's body. The film is sexually explicit and a murder occurs—yet no one believes that the actress suffered pain or died. In *Barbarella* a character played by Jane Fonda is at times displayed in sexually explicit ways and at times shown "bleeding, bruised, [and] hurt in a context that makes these conditions sexual"—and again no one believes that Fonda was actually tortured to make the film. In *Carnal Knowledge* a woman grovels to please the sexual whims of a character played by Jack Nicholson; no one believes that there was a real sexual submission, and the Supreme Court held the film protected by the First Amendment. . . . And this works both ways. The description of women's sexual domination of men in *Lysistrata* was not real dominance. Depictions may affect slavery, war, or sexual roles, but a book about slavery is not itself slavery, or a book about death by poison a murder.

Much of Indianapolis's argument rests on the belief that when speech is "unanswerable," and the metaphor that there is a "marketplace of ideas" does not apply, the First Amendment does not apply either. The metaphor is honored; Milton's *Aeropagitica* and John Stuart Mill's *On Liberty* defend freedom of speech on the ground that the truth will prevail, and many of the most important cases under the First Amendment recite this position. The Framers undoubtedly believed it. As a general matter it is true. But the Constitution does not make the dominance of truth a necessary condition of freedom of speech. To say that it does would be to confuse an outcome of free speech with a necessary condition for the application of the amendment.

A power to limit speech on the ground that truth has not yet prevailed and is not likely to prevail implies the power to declare truth. At some point the government must be able to say (as Indianapolis has said): "We know what the truth is, yet a free exchange of speech has not driven out falsity, so that we must now prohibit falsity." If the government may declare the truth, why wait for the failure of speech? Under the First Amendment, however, there is no such thing as a false idea, *Gertz v. Robert Welch, Inc.* . . . (1974), so the government may not restrict speech on the ground that in a free exchange truth is not yet dominant.

Liberalism and Pornography

Lorenne M. G. Clark

Clark reexamines the moral underpinnings of women's liberation. She notes that "the fight for women's rights has largely been fought under the banner of liberalism." This is fascinating, since in American politics "liberalism" has recently become something of a dirty word (the "L-word", as some call it) even as "the year of the woman" has seen a historic increase in the number of women elected to Congress in 1992. Clearly a reexamination of liberalism is warranted. Clark says we must ask the fundamental question, "Is the moral theory of liberalism consistent with equality?" And a related question is, "To what degree, if any, does pornography promote inequality between the sexes?" Her answer to the first question is that only a liberalism that modifies its distinction between public and private and that expands its concept of harm to include pornography's harm to women is consistent with full equality for women. Her answer to the second question is that pornography significantly promotes inequality between the sexes because it harms women.

Since at least the mid-nineteenth century, the fight for women's rights has largely been fought under the banner of liberalism. The ethical principles of people like John Stuart Mill formed the moral justification for these struggles, and many of these individuals were themselves committed to the cause of women's equality.[1] Thus, the cause of women's liberation has much thanks to give both to the theory and to its proponents. But it is, I believe, time to take another look at the moral underpinnings we have until now accepted, though I am by no means suggesting that utilitarianism, or more popular versions of liberal, or libertarian ethics, have been the only moral touchstones upon which the demand for sexual equality has rested. This has been fed by other moralities as well, notably that deriving from the work of Marx and Engels. But at least insofar as both of these moral systems acknowledged that the historical position of women had been an oppressed and exploited one, it was possible to present a united front on many issues, particularly those most clearly related to the achievement of legal and social reform. Most of these fights were publicly defended on liberal principles, and the most famous one, the fight for the right to vote, certainly was.

The reason for this is clear. The central value of liberalism is the freedom, or liberty, of the individual. Thus, demands by women for greater participation in public life were straightforward demands for greater liberty. The demands made in the name of sexual equality were, first, to establish that women ought to be entitled to the same rights as men, and, second, to ensure that these rights could be practically and effectively exercised. But there is a central difficulty with liberalism in this respect. The central value of liberalism is freedom, or what has been termed more specifically "negative liberty."[2] "Negative" liberty or freedom is the freedom to do or get what you want unimpeded by interference from others. It is contrasted with "positive" liberty, which entails not only that other persons refrain from interference, but that the person with the freedom in fact has the means or ability to get what he or she wants. Thus one is free in the negative sense when one is not prohibited or prevented from entering a restaurant to obtain a meal even if one lacks the money to pay for it. One is free in the positive sense only if one has both the

A version of this article appeared under the title "Sexual Equality and the Problem of an Adequate Moral Theory" in Mary Kathryn Shirley and Rachel Emma Vigier, ed, *In Search of the Feminist Perspective: The Changing Potency of Women. Resources for Feminist Research Special Publication* #5, Toronto (Spring 1979). Reprinted by permission of the author and *Resources for Feminist Research.*

means to get what is wanted and is not prevented from using those means to get what he or she wants. Negative freedom can be seen therefore to consist merely in the *absence of restraint*. Thus, while liberals could accept that it was wrong to prevent women from voting, they have more difficulty accepting that effective exercise of the right to reproductive autonomy necessitates providing publicly financed clinics for the provision of safe, cheap abortion. Achieving the right to vote was a good cause for liberal support, because all that it required was the removal of a legal impediment which would result in greater liberty. But fights which necessitate not the removal of legal restraints, but the creation of legal duties on others in order to give persons the means needed to do what they want, are not good causes on which to seek liberal support, because these necessarily involve a reduction in negative liberty. Reproductive autonomy requires not only the removal of legal restraints on one's ability to get an abortion but providing the means whereby women who cannot afford expensive medical and hospital care can nonetheless obtain an abortion if they want one. But providing safe, publicly financed clinics to perform abortions regardless of the woman's ability to pay places restraints on doctors and hospitals as to whom they can choose to treat, and on the government's choices as to which social service programmes it will support. Thus, promoting reproductive autonomy as a positive as well as a negative freedom reduces the negative freedoms that some persons and legal bodies currently enjoy. It places restraints on their freedom of choice and therefore infringes their negative freedom.

Since a central tenet of liberalism is that one can be said to be free, or to have a right to something merely from the fact that there is no statute or other legal limitation which prohibits the doing of the thing in question, the absence of a prohibition is itself enough to generate the idea that one has a right. Legally speaking, the right that one has is what is properly termed a "privilege" or "liberty" right,[3] and does not entail that anything or anyone has a correlative duty to do anything, or provide anything, which would facilitate one in actually getting that to which the right entitled one. A "privilege" or "liberty" right is a right which arises from the absence of restraint, like one's right to use a public park or to vote. It entails simply that one has no duty to refrain from doing the thing in question. But it also entails that no one else is under a duty to see that we do or get the thing we are not duty-bound to refrain from. Thus, if the right we have is a privilege right, we can do it if we want to, since we are under no duty not to do it; but if we lack the means to do it, no one has an obligation to see that we can do it, our lack of resources notwithstanding. Rights of this sort are contrasted with "claim" rights, rights which arise out of the fact that others have a duty to see that we get that to which we are said to have the right, things such as the right to an education up to at least a certain minimum age or standard. Claim rights do not therefore depend for their effective exercise on our having the means to utilize them. They are things to which we are entitled regardless of our other resources. Thus, if a right is a claim, this entails that someone or something necessarily has a duty with respect to providing us with the thing, or the means to the thing, in question, whereas if the right is a privilege, no such correlative obligation exists on others.

As is obvious, there are more impediments to human endeavor than legal impediments, and there is more to having rights than simply not being prohibited from doing something, at least if the having of rights is to mean anything to those who do not have the other means needed to get what they want. In the face of pre-existing social inequality, the effective exercise of rights can be assured only by creating a legal *claim*-right which *does* entail obligations on the part of someone or something else to provide the thing, or the means to the thing, guaranteed by the right. Thus, mere privilege rights must be *converted into claim rights* if those who have the rights are to be ensured the effective exercise of their rights. They can only get what the right gives them if someone else has an obligation to provide them with it, independent of the recipient's ability to pay and things of that sort. But the conversion of privileges into claims involves creating obligations on others. And the creation of legal obligations on others is one of the most important ways of limiting a person's ability to do what he or she wants. Thus, the establishment of claim rights is itself an *infringement* of liberty, or negative freedom, since it makes it mandatory to do what it was before permissible either to do or not to do. The history of social reform is largely the history of first establishing that some previously disenfranchised group ought to have rights that have already been accorded to others, then removing legal or other social and institutional impediments to their getting what they want, and then fighting further to have these privileges converted into claims. But this involves liberalism in a fundamental contradiction, because it means that, during the third stage, the libertarian has to argue for the *limitation* of the freedom of some in the name of promoting greater equality among all those nominally said to be in possession of the right. On the face of it, utilitarianism has no difficulty with this, since its principle is that it is best to do whatever promotes the greatest happiness of the greatest number, where each individual counts as one. But utilitarianism thus parts company with the central tenet of liberalism in those cases in which the greater positive liberty of all demands diminished negative liberty for some. Worse, it is powerless as a moral tool in just those cases in which the loss to some is evenly balanced by the gains to others, because it does not have a principle of justice independent of the principle of utility which would justify such a redistribution even in cases where the original distribution occurs within a domain characterized by inequality. While the promoters of utilitarianism, and many of their followers, have been dedicated social reformers, there are some aspects of our continuing historical reality which they either take for granted, or about which they are at any rate unaware or unaffected by the fact, that the application of their principles within these contexts perpetrates, and indeed reinforces, fundamental inequalities.

The fundamental question we have to ask is: Is the moral theory of liberalism consistent with equality? If it is, then we must be able to show how the mistakes it has made can be explained without throwing out the theory, and hence, how it must be revised in order to prevent similar errors from occurring in future. And if it isn't, then it is time we turned our attention to looking for or developing moral alternatives which are.

One of the fundamental principles endorsed by a liberal ethic is that there must be some areas of one's life in which one has the freedom to do what one wants, free from interference by others. It has been argued that there simply are some areas of life which are none of the law's business. For those familiar with the Wolfenden Report on Homosexuality in England, and the subsequent debate that this started both within and outside academic circles, this phrase, "none of the law's business," will have a familiar ring. Philosophically, this is reflected in debates about which areas of one's life should be essentially characterized by negative freedom, the ability to act free of the restraints and scrutiny of others. Legally, it is reflected in debates about privacy, about the areas of one's life into which others should be legally prohibited from interfering.[4] Among the areas often said to be protected by a right to privacy are those parts of a person's life designated as "personal," his or her home and family, or interpersonal, particularly emotional and sexual, life. Other areas dealt with in the same way are freedom of speech and of the press. The right to use pornography relates to both these broad areas and has been justified both because it is personal, related solely to one's individual private sexual proclivities and preferences, and because it has to do with freedom of the press, or more broadly speaking, freedom of information, the right to read and to see what one wants and to the need to promote a wide divergence in the range of available materials.

There is virtually no one who would want to say that we should have no negative liberty or no privacy, but the debate still rages as to which areas of one's life should be guaranteed as areas of negative liberty through the creation of a legal right to privacy. The difficulty is that no one has found a satisfactory method of drawing the boundaries between the private and other areas of life. In the past, the boundary was thought to be a *natural* one, based on the traditional distinction between the public and the private. The private just *was* "the private," and, as such, should be guaranteed as an area of negative liberty and fully protected by means of a legally enforceable right to privacy. This was one of the bases of the argument in the Wolfenden Report. Here it was alleged that sexual relations between consenting adults are simply none of the law's business. It was further argued that such behavior should justifiably be left to the absolute discretion of individuals, because it has effects on no one other than the participants. This was the rationale provided by John Stuart Mill in "On Liberty," which was reiterated and defended by Herbert Hart in *Law, Liberty, and Morality*.[5] The best defence of this liberal tenet is the view developed by Mill that the law is justified in prohibiting actions if and only if doing them results in the inability of others to exercise rights of a similar kind. The underlying view is that rights should be distributed equally, which entails that no one can have rights the exercise of which would prevent others from exercising similar rights. The difficulty is that liberals have all too often assumed that the area of life traditionally thought to be "private," and hence immune from regulation and control, conforms to the rules Mill laid down as to what should be left as an area of negative freedom.

But as is now abundantly clear, it is indefensible to draw the legal boundary between public and private on the basis of the historical division between these spheres of human activity. Privacy functioned historically to protect those who were privileged to begin with. Privacy was a consequence of the ownership of private property and, hence, a commodity purchased with property. It has been a privilege accorded those of wealth and high social status. More important from a feminist perspective, it protected not only the dominant economic class in the Marxist sense, but the dominant sex-class as well. The traditionally "private" was the sphere of the personal, home and hearth. And that area was the area within which women and children were forms of private property under the exclusive ownership and control of males. As the person in whom the absolute personality of the family vested, male heads of households had virtually absolute rights over their wives and children. The family, clearly, was not and is not a partnership of equals. There is no mutuality in the marital relation, and the rights and duties are decidedly one-sided.

Of course it is not the concept of privacy which is responsible for this state of affairs. But in drawing the boundary between the historically private and public, for the purpose of entrenching a legal right to privacy in the area of the traditionally private, it certainly functioned to condone and encourage the abusive and unjustified practices which were possible within this unequal relation. As is now clear, the family has been characterized by a great deal of physical violence. The legitimate basis of authority in the family is physical coercion, and it is and has been regularly relied on to secure to the male head of the house the attitudes and behaviors he wants. Women, much less children, had no right to protest such behavior but were expected to suffer it, willingly or otherwise. Thus, the last place feminists want to see a right to privacy is in the family. What possible sense can be made of the notion of being a *consenting adult* when one is in a relation in which one has no right to say no? Clearly, if we want privacy at all, where we do not want it is in the home, at least as that has been institutionalized historically.

The area of life most in need of regulation and control in the interest of creating more liberty and equality for women is the area of the traditionally private and personal. Greater liberty and equality for women can be purchased only at the cost of less liberty, and a loss of status, for men. To the extent that women are given more rights within marriage, men are less able to do as they please. What was before permissible would now be either mandatory, as, for example, in making it a duty for men to share in housework and child-care; or prohibited, as for example in allowing a charge of rape between spouses. Within terms of the basic principle, such changes are justified. The past operation of the law has permitted many forms of behavior which in fact caused physical and other direct and tangible harms to others, and which certainly prevented the effective exercise of like rights on the part of others. On the principle of like liberties for all, marriage must be turned into a relation of mutuality, and the relationships within it must be subject to regulation and control.

Why, then, has the demand for privacy centered so exclusively on preserving the traditional domain of male privilege? And why do the staunchest defenders of that view fail to see that in invoking these principles within a domain characterized by fundamental sexual inequality they are in fact both reinforcing that inequality and sanctioning its worst abuses? At the very least, adherents of the liberal ethic must acknowledge that there is no *natural* basis for deciding on what is private and what public for the purpose of entrenching a legal right to privacy, and that the traditional area of the private is the area most in need of loss of privacy in the name of promoting greater positive liberty and greater equality. How this fares on a purely utilitarian principle is of course problematic, for since men and women each make up roughly half the population, we cannot be sure that the benefits to women will in fact outweigh the losses to men.

Equality cannot flourish without limiting the privileges some already have in both the private and the public spheres, because the inequalities of the present system were a product of the unequal attribution of rights in the first instance; thus greater equality and liberty for those least advantaged under the present system necessitates placing restrictions on the privilege rights of those who are presently most advantaged. And since this must be done by creating obligations either to do or to forbear actions previously permitted, it can be accomplished only at the expense of negative liberty. While the principles of the liberal ethic itself do not require the historical division between public and private, it has certainly been presupposed in liberal thinking about these issues. Recognition of the extent to which this has played a role must lead to a reappraisal of what it is that people should be at liberty to do, and it must find a basis for this which does not rest on traditional views of the different spheres of life, and the different roles of the sexes.

What is needed, at base, is a reappraisal of what is *harmful*. That, too, has historically been defined in terms of what the dominant sex and the dominant economic class find "harmful." An analysis of rape law demonstrates that point as well as anything could. Physically coerced sexual intercourse has been regarded as constituting a redressable harm if and only if the female victim was a dependent female living under either parental or matrimonial control, and in possession of those qualities which made her desirable as a piece of sexual reproductive property available for the exclusive use of a present or future husband, and only if the perpetrator was someone other than the victim's lawful husband.[6] Physically coerced intercourse between husband and wife was not regarded as harmful, much less as redressable. It was regarded as "normal," a privilege of the head of the household, the bearer of the legal personality of the family unit; it was a hallmark of the essential legal relation of husband and wife, which was a species of the master-servant relationship in which the wife had the status of a chattel. The right that husbands had with respect to access to their wives' sexuality and reproductivity was a claim right, since wives had a legal duty to honor the conjugal demands of their husbands. It goes without saying that no similar right was accorded to wives and no similar duty devolved on husbands. Husbands also had a privilege right with respect to the use of physical coercion in pursuance of their exercise of their claim right to sexual access, since they had no legal duty to refrain from its use in this content (or indeed in others, since this was sanctioned as legitimate "discipline"). Thus, the structure of marriage with respect to sexuality and reproductivity represents a clear violation of Mill's approach to the private, since it accords rights to some which prohibit the exercise of like rights by others. Despite that, liberals have persistently seen the family as the paradigm of the private and have seen attempts to rectify its injustices and abuses as unwarranted infringements of liberty. The strength of Mill's position is that it does *not* depend on drawing a boundary between the public and the private and indeed lays down principles which can themselves be invoked to justify enforcing the same principles within the traditionally private as well as within the traditionally public sphere.

But liberals have been unwilling to apply these principles in evaluating the matrimonial relationship in particular, and sexual relations between men and women in general. Their unwillingness to see that male privileges relating to access to female sexuality and to being able to use physical coercion to effect this is a fundamental inequality, a violation of women's rights and clear harm to women, can only reflect their unwillingness to give up their advantaged position. It is this same unwillingness to acknowledge that men have been advantaged in what they have been legally permitted to do in their sexual relationships with women which makes them intransigent about the pornography issue, because pornography stands as a living testament to men's ability to use physical coercion within the sexual context. And they can rely on liberalism's central commitment to negative liberty in opposing feminist views on this and related issues precisely because rectifying the fundamental injustices which have historically characterized male-female sexual relations necessarily infringes negative liberties, both by creating obligations to refrain which previously did not exist and by abolishing previously existing privilege rights. While the basic principles Mill enunciated certainly do not commit liberals to continuing to uphold this inequality, it remains to be seen whether or not liberalism can survive and transcend the limitations of its own historical perspective. In so far as it must renounce much of its accepted thinking about what sorts of actions individuals ought to be free to do, and must recognize that negative liberty must at least temporarily take a back seat to the promotion of equality, I cannot say I am hopeful about the outcome. But the ethics of liberalism will not do as the moral framework for the achievement of sexual equality unless it can meet this challenge.

But it is clear from a consideration of the issue of pornography that so far at least the ethic of liberalism has been unable to rethink its concept of harm in a way which is consistent with sexual equality. Feminists and civil libertarians are now at complete loggerheads over this issue. The trend among feminists is clear. More and more of them are coming to see pornography as a species of hate literature.[7] Hate literature seeks to make one dislike and despise the people depicted, to make those persons seem inferior and unworthy of our respect. It seeks to set them apart and to show them as relevantly different from "us" in a way which justifies "us" in treating them differently, or it shows them as deserving to be treated badly because they have no respect for "us" or "our" values. What it must do to succeed is enforce a radical sense of their difference, their non-identity, with "us," a difference which is either utterly distasteful to "us," or one utterly opposed to "our" shared goals and values. It may also revel in their misery in an attempt to encourage feelings of wishing to contribute to that misery by doing things to them we would not think of doing to those we perceive to be relevantly similar to ourselves. So too with pornography. To achieve its impact, it relies on depicting women in humiliating, degrading, and violently abusive situations. To make matters worse, it frequently depicts them willingly, even avidly, suffering and inviting such treatment. As is obvious to even the naivest of eyes, such re-creations of heterosexual behavior and relationships feed traditional male phantasies about both themselves and women, and glorify the traditional advantages men have enjoyed in relation to exploitation of female sexuality.

Pornography is a method of socialization; it is the tangible, palpable embodiment of the imposition of the dominant sexual system which is a part of the dominant sex-class system. It is a vivid depiction of how to deploy male sexuality in just the way that will achieve maximum effect in maintaining the *status quo*. Pornography would be neither desired nor tolerated within any system other than one which sprang from the differential attribution of rights of ownership in which women and children are forms of sexual property, and in which they must either like it or quite literally lump it. It is a morality which stresses female passivity and submissiveness, and it encourages the actualization of such states through active aggression and violence. Pornography has very little to do with sex, certainly with any conception of egalitarian sexual relations between the sexes, but it has everything to do with showing how to use sexuality as an instrument of active oppression, and that is why it is wrong. Some allege that it also feeds female phantasies about themselves and men, but that is certainly being questioned, at least in so far as it can be said that there is any hard empirical data to support it.

That there should be no laws prohibiting the manufacture, sale, and distribution of pornography has traditionally and increasingly been defended as a freedom of speech, and freedom of press, issue. It is alleged that the reading or viewing of such material does not cause any harm, or that if it does, it is harm only to those who willingly consent to it. The premise that it doesn't cause harm is defended by arguing that it relates only to the phantasy level and does not translate itself into interpersonal behavior. And it goes further than this to argue that, indeed, it provides a healthy outlet, a cathartic effect, for those who might otherwise be tempted to act out their phantasies. Those who oppose pornography, particularly those who advocate its prohibition, are treated as Victorian prudes with sexual hangups. Women who object to it are seen as up-tight, unliberated, and just not "with it," sexually speaking.

The general principle underlying the liberal view is of course that expressed by Mill in "On Liberty," who argued against any form of censorship on the ground that it was only through the free flow of information that the true and the false could be separated. Prohibitions against the dissemination of any form of information function to preserve the *status quo* and to prevent the development of a critically reflective morality which is itself necessary to pave the way for needed social change. The principle has much to be said for it. But that cannot change the fact that when it is uncritically made to apply within a domain characterized by inequality and by frankly abusive behavior, a domain which is fundamentally shaped by a framework of social relations and institutions which makes all sexual relationships between men and women fundamentally coercive in nature,[8] it is bound to produce results which will be unacceptable because harmful to those who are in the preexisting inferior position and who stand to be most affected by the attitudes and beliefs, as well as the practices, of those who use it.

The liberal argument has been that such material isn't harmful at all, and certainly cannot be seen as harmful because it functions merely to inflame male sexual desire. What is the harm if all it does is give a guy a bit of a rush? And it is right here that we must begin our critique. Surely we must acknowledge at least two things. First, it is not "normal" to get one's rushes from just anything. Second, if one gets desirable reactions from things which create a clear and substantial risk to others, then one can justifiably be prohibited from getting them that way. Persons who get their sexual stimulation from watching the atrocities perpetrated against the Jews during the holocaust are not regarded as "normal," and rightly so. Furthermore, we do not feel that we are infringing any legitimate rights of others in preventing them access to material designed to provide sexual stimulation by this means. And the reasons for that are at least two-fold. First, as history has made all too clear, actions of this particular species do not remain at the level of mere phantasy. They have been acted out on the grand scale, so grand as to make any rational and reflective person aware that the possibility of a correlation between thought and action is at least strong enough to justify the imposition of prohibitions against material of this sort. Second, it stems from recognizing that even if the actual actions themselves are not acted out, the attitudes and beliefs of the persons enjoying it reflect attitudes toward the objects of the actions which are bad in themselves and which are bound to produce practical effects in real life, if only to be expressed in bigoted and racist attitudes. All of the same arguments apply to material which depicts black people in degrading, humiliating, and abusive circumstances. Such material is, in itself, an affront to the dignity of the objects depicted, not least because they *are* being depicted purely as objects, dehumanized and depersonalized instruments for the satisfaction of someone else's perverted tastes.

The same case can be made with respect to heterosexual pornography.[9] As Camille Le Grand puts it, "pornography teaches society to view women as less than human. It is this view which keeps women as victims."[10] The typical way in which women are depicted in pornography certainly reflects a view of them as inferior to men, as inherently masochistic, and as primarily of value as instruments for the satisfaction of male lust. That is, in itself, offensive to women, and is a straightforward objective affront to their dignity as equal persons. So on that ground alone, pornography ought to be prohibited, just as we prohibit material depicting other social groups in such a fashion.

Of course, we could hardly argue within the parameters of our present culture that it is abnormal for males to react as they do to pornography. It is, unfortunately, all too normal, at least where we have any notion of statistical normality in mind. But neither is it unusual for rape victims to feel shamed, humiliated, and degraded by being raped; this is "normal" in the culture, but from any more rational perspective, it certainly is not "normal" in any normative sense. Much of recent efforts around the issue of rape have been designed specifically to change the perspective which rape victims have on that experience. Rape victims can come to see the assaultive behavior perpetrated against them as legitimizing the anger which is appropriate to the nature of the attack. In short, it is possible both to identify the specific effects of socialization within a male supremacist and sexually coercive society, and to offset these effects with appropriate reconceptualization of the event. Women can come to identify the masochism and victimization into which they have been socialized, and can then act both to counteract it, and to be sublimely angry at a culture which socialized them into that mode. So, too, it should be possible for men to identify the sadism and attitudes of sexual aggressivity into which they are socialized and so act both to counteract them, and to be angry at a social system that produced that response. In short, *it is not a mark of personal depravity or immorality to be aroused by such material.* Given the cultural pattern of which it is a manifestation, that is not at all surprising. Indeed, it is just what we would expect. But what must be recognized is that it *is* a socialized response, and that it is a response about which men as well as women should be both concerned and angry. And certainly, once its cultural roots are exposed, it is a response which should not be seen as needing or justifying the sale and distribution of the material which elicited it. Women must object to pornography because it both reflects and reinforces the patterns of socialization appropriate to a system based on the unequal status of the sexes, in which women are consistently regarded and treated as the inferiors, and the sexual property, of men. The socialization it brings about is *in itself* a limitation of the autonomy of women. Men ought to object to it for the same reason, and they ought to recognize that the socialization it brings about in terms of their self-images and internalized standards of conduct is also undesirable, given any commitment to the notion of sexual equality.

To the extent that men are able to internalize the conviction that women and men are equal persons, and that men are not justified in using physical coercion to force women into sexual servitude, they must recognize that the pleasurable responses they get from pornography are inappropriate to that conviction and are destructive to their ability to form self-images consistent with it. But that does not entail that they are in any sense to blame for those responses: they had as little choice about that as they did about their names. But we have, then, given strong arguments in support of the view that the eliciting of a pleasurable response is not in itself any reason to condone the sale and distribution of pornography, and that a proper understanding of the nature and causes of that response gives men as well as women solid grounds for objecting to the material which occasioned it. I believe that many more men would be able to understand and accept the feminist perspective on pornography if they could come to realize that they are not responsible for their sexual responses to it given the pattern of socialization which exists to mould us all into a set of social relations which institutionalizes male aggression and female passivity.

Thus, pornography is harmful, both to women and to men, because it encourages men to combat feelings of inadequacy and low self-esteem by being aggressive and sadistic and women to feel shamed and humiliated just for being women. It encourages just that radical difference between men and women which allows men to see women as deserving of treatment they would refrain from subjecting someone to whom they perceived to be like themselves. To the extent that it also encourages women to combat insecurity and low self-esteem by becoming passive and masochistic, it presents even clearer dangers to them than it does to men, since it creates the conditions for their own victimization, but the damage it does to men who do not identify themselves as aggressive and superior to women cannot be under-estimated either. However, that does not end the argument with defenders of liberalism, because their argument then moves on to the assertion that the harm to women is not direct enough to justify the legal prohibition of pornography. Frankly, I think that the argument that pornography is intrinsically offensive to the dignity of women ought to carry the day, but in the interests of completeness I want to go on to consider the other arguments that are brought to pornography's defence.

Apart from this notion of being intrinsically offensive and an infringement of the rights of women, it will be argued that even if pornography is harmful to the user, it does not lead to direct harm to women, because the phantasies it supports remain phantasies, and it in fact prevents direct harm to women through its cathartic effect. I may say at the outset that I'm not at all impressed with either of these arguments. So far as the first is concerned, there is plenty of hard evidence available which supports the contention that role modeling has a powerful effect on human behavior. Studies of wife and child abuse consistently attest to the fact that there is a strong correlation between those who are abusers and those who come from family situations which were themselves abusive. The battered child becomes the battering parent; the son who witnessed his father battering his mother, and who was himself battered, becomes a battering husband.[11] Also, the evidence about the effect of violence depicted on television on the behavior of children also points strongly in this direction.[12] People tend to act out and operationalize the behavior that they see typically acted out around them. And surely that is hardly surprising. It is what has kept civilization going. If we weren't able to perpetuate the patterns of behavior developed through cultural organization we wouldn't have come very far. So far as I know, however, there is no hard data to support the catharsis theory. It is a theory espoused by those who are looking for a rationale, though doubtless it has its roots in their awareness that they read pornography but don't rape and brutalize women. But raping and brutalizing women isn't the only harm that can be perpetrated against women. But so far there is little empirical support offered for the view that pornography feeds only the phantasy. Most psychiatric literature dealing with the "perversions" asserts that some people remain content with the phantasy while others do not.[13] But no one knows what differentiates the one who does actualize it from the one who doesn't. If this argument is going to be effective, it must be empirically demonstrated that this is so, and surely we cannot predict until the data is in that those who don't so outnumber those who do that we should, in the interests of an open society, tolerate the risk that some will. And since we are all imprisoned by the cultural stereotypes and the patterns of socialization appropriate to a society based on the sexual coercion of one sex by the other, how can those who do read it assert with certainty that they do not cause harm to women? They are hardly the best judges. As rape makes clear again, there is nowhere greater difference in perception than there is in the confusion surrounding rape and seduction. The men believe they are merely seducing, but the women perceive it as rape. And who is to judge? Certainly it is unfair to permit only those who are the perpetrators of such behavior to have a say in its interpretation.

While the liberal principle behind opposition to censorship is based on a recognition that desirable social change requires public access to information which challenges the beliefs and practices of the *status quo,* what it does not acknowledge is that information which supports the *status quo* through providing role models which advocate the use or threat of coercion as a technique of social control directed at a clearly identifiable group depicted as inferior, subordinate, and subhuman, works against the interest both of desirable social change and of the members of the subgroup so identified. This has been clearly acknowledged in the case of violently anti-semitic and other forms of racist literature. The same principles apply with respect to violently anti-female literature, and the same conclusion should follow. But this cannot come about until it is recognized and acknowledged that the dissemination of such material is itself a harm to the members of the group involved. It remains to be seen whether liberalism can accomplish this, but until it does, we cannot hope for its support on this issue.

In refusing to count as "harms" actions and practices which serve the interest of the dominant sex by reinforcing the patterns and effects of modes of socialization which support a sexist system, it renders itself incapable of changing that system and of promoting greater equality and positive liberty for women. Liberalism serves the interest of the dominant sex and the dominant class, though it contains within itself the potential for promoting greater equality and greater positive liberty for all. It can realize this potential, however, only by reconceptualizing harm in a way consistent with sex and class equality, and by recognizing that negative liberty must take second place to the promotion of equality, at least until we have achieved a framework of enforceable rules which guarantees equality within both the public and the private spheres.

When no one is allowed to do what is harmful to others, and/or what prevents them from effectively exercising liberty rights to autonomy and equality consistent with the equal attribution and effective exercise of like rights on the part of others, then we will have achieved a state in which liberty is concrete, and not a chimera which upholds the liberty of some at the expense of inequality to the rest. As women we are members of the disadvantaged sex. We are thus acting contrary to the interests of our sex in accepting any position which does not place the achievement of legally enforceable sexual equality at the forefront of its programme, particularly in relation to sexual and reproductive relations between the sexes.

That entails that we have to challenge traditional concepts of harm, and of liberty as the absence of restraint. We have been successful in removing many of the legal restraints which made both equality and liberty impossible, and that was the stage at which the ethics of liberalism served our purpose well. But unless it can extend its own principles into the sphere of interpersonal relations between the sexes, it not only cannot be relied on to serve our interests but must be confronted as adverse to those interests. The achievement of real rather than merely possible equality and liberty now depends on placing effective, enforceable restraints on those who have in the past enjoyed advantages which made both our equality and our liberty impossible. Liberalism may be prepared to scrap its reliance on the traditional division into public and private, and it may be prepared to acknowledge that the negative liberty and the privilege rights which men have traditionally been accorded, and which legitimize the use of physical coercion in their sexual and reproductive relations with women, constitute a harm and an infringement of the rights of women to reproductive and sexual autonomy and to protection from physical assault. Unless it is so prepared, we can expect little support from liberals on the issue of pornography or any other issues which reflect that basic and fundamental inequality between the sexes.

NOTES

1. This is, of course, true of John Stuart Mill himself, as is clear from his essay, "The Subjection of Women," written in 1860 and first published in 1869.
2. After the distinction between "negative" and "positive" liberty made current by Isaiah Berlin in "Two Concepts of Liberty," in *Four Essays on Liberty,* O.U.P., London, 1969.
3. I am relying here on the distinctions first made by W. N. Hohfeld, *Fundamental Legal Conceptions,* Yale U.P., 1932.
4. A more detailed account of the relationship between these philosophical and legal debates, as well as a discussion of the complexity of the legal issue of privacy itself, is found in Clark, Lorenne M. G., "Privacy, Property, Freedom, and the Family," *Philosophical Law,* (Ed.) R. Bronaugh, Greenwood Press, Conn., and London, U.K., 1978, and *Towards a Feminist Political Theory,* University of Toronto Press, Toronto, forthcoming.
5. Hart, H. L. A., *Law, Liberty, and Morality,* O.U.P., London, 1963. This was Hart's answer to the objections raised by Lord Devlin to the recommendations and theory expressed in the Wolfenden Report. Devlin's position on this and other related matters is found in Devlin, Lord Patrick, *The Enforcement of Morals,* O.U.P., London, 1965.
6. For a discussion of the way in which the historical evolution and conception of rape law functioned to maintain the sexual status quo,and indeed continues to produce just the results we should expect to find with respect to the treatment and handling of rape cases within the criminal justice system, see Clark, Lorenne M. G., and Lewis, Debra J., *Rape: The Price of Coercive Sexuality,* Canadian Women's Educational Press, Toronto, 1977.
7. Among the articles that spring readily to mind are Morgan, Robin, "Theory and Practice: Pornography and Rape," *Going Too Far,* Random House, N.Y., 1977, Ch. IV, pp. 163–69; Russell, Diana, "Pornography: A Feminist Perspective," unpublished paper; Brownmiller, Susan, *Against Our Will,* Simon & Schuster, N.Y., 1975, pp. 394–6; and Shear, Marie, "Free Meat Talks Back," *J. of Communication,* Vol. 26, No. 1, Winter, 1976, pp. 38–9.
8. Clark and Lewis, *Rape: The Price of Coercive Sexuality, op. cit.,* Chs. 7 and 8 in particular.
9. Indeed, it is true of male homosexual pornography as well. But in the interest of not legislating in the interest of others, I am not advocating that we should prohibit this species of pornography. If men object to it, as in my view they should, whether homo- or heterosexual, it is up to them to express their opposition. Certainly I do not wish to infringe the rights homosexuals have to look at what they like, even though I cannot say with certainty that I am not adversely affected by it.
10. Quoted in Russell, Diana, "Pornography: A Feminist Perspective," *op. cit.,* p. 7, no reference given.
11. See, for example, Martin, Del, *Battered Wives,* Glide Publications, San Francisco, 1976, pp. 22–3; Pizzey, Erin, *Scream Quietly or the Neighbours Will Hear,* Penguin Books, England, 1974, Ch. 4; Van Stolk, Mary, *The Battered Child in Canada,* McClelland & Stewart, Toronto, 1972, pp. 23–7.
12. Bandura, A., Ross, D., and Ross, S. A., "Transmission of Aggression Through Imitation of Aggressive Models," *J. Abnormal and Social Psychology,* 63, No. 3, 575–82.
13. Kraft-Ebbing, Richard von, *Psychopathia Sexualis,* 11th ed. rev. and enlarged, Stuttgard, 1901, pp. 94–5; Freud, S., *Introductory Lectures on Psycho-Analysis,* Standard Edition, 16:306.

Pornography, Feminism and Liberalism

Joel Feinberg

Feinberg, a leading philosopher who teaches at the University of Arizona, presents a careful and detailed analysis of the feminist case against the "porno industry." He notes that the feminist case comes not from "prudes and bluenoses, but from women who have been in the forefront of the sexual revolution." He explores the distinction between pornography and what Gloria Steinem and others call "erotica." Feinberg then considers whether and how pornography causes harm or offense, ending his essay with an analysis of some interesting cases. His main conclusion is that pornography as such need not be degrading to women.

1. The Feminist Case Against Pornography[1]

In recent years a powerful attack on pornography has been made from a different quarter and on different, but often shifting grounds. Until 1970 or so, the demand for legal restraints on pornography came mainly from "sexual conservatives," those who regarded the pursuit of erotic pleasure for its own sake to be immoral or degrading, and its public depiction obscene. The new attack, however, comes not from prudes and bluenoses, but from women who have been in the forefront of the sexual revolution. We do not hear any of the traditional complaints about pornography from this group—that erotic states in themselves are immoral, that sexual titillation corrupts character, and that the spectacle of "appeals to prurience" is repugnant to moral sensibility. The new charge is rather that pornography degrades, abuses, and defames women, and contributes to a general climate of attitudes toward women that makes violent sex crimes more frequent. Pornography, they claim, has come to pose a threat to public safety, and its legal restraint can find justification either under the harm principle, or, by analogy with Nazi parades in Skokie and K.K.K. rallies, on some theory of profound (and personal) offense.

It is somewhat misleading to characterize the feminist onslaught as a new argument, or new emphasis in argument, against the same old thing. By the 1960s pornography itself had become in large measure a new and uglier kind of phenomenon. There had always been sado-masochistic elements in much pornography, and a small minority taste to be served with concentrated doses of it. There had also been more or less prominent expressions of contemptuous attitudes toward abject female "sex objects," even in much relatively innocent pornography. But now a great wave of violent pornography appears to have swept over the land, as even the mass circulation porno magazines moved beyond the customary nude cheesecake and formula stories, to explicit expressions of hostility to women, and to covers and photographs showing "women and children abused, beaten, bound, and tortured" apparently "for the sexual titillation of consumers."[2] When the circulation of the monthly porn magazines comes to 16 million and the porno industry as a whole does 84 billion a year in business, the new trend cannot help but be alarming.[3]

There is no necessity, however, that pornography *as such* be degrading to women. First of all, we can imagine easily enough an ideal pornography in which men and women are depicted enjoying their joint sexual pleasures in ways that show not a trace of dominance or humiliation of either party by the other.[4] The materials in question might clearly satisfy my previous definition of "pornography" as materials designed entirely and effectively to induce erotic excitement in ob-

From *Offense to Others* (New York: Oxford University Press, 1985), pp. 143–164.

servers, without containing any of the extraneous sexist elements. Even if we confine our attention to actual specimens of pornography—and quite typical ones—we find many examples where male dominance and female humiliation are not present at all. Those of us who were budding teenagers in the 1930s and '40s will tend to take as our model of pornography the comic strip pamphlets in wide circulation among teenagers during that period. The characters were all drawn from the popular legitimate comic strips—The Gumps, Moon Mullins, Maggie and Jiggs, etc.—and were portrayed in cartoons that were exact imitations of the originals. In the pornographic strips, however, the adventures were all erotic. Like all pornography, the cartoons greatly exaggerated the size of organs and appetites, and the "plot lines" were entirely predictable. But the episodes were portrayed with great good humor, a kind of joyous feast of erotica in which the blessedly unrepressed cartoon figures shared with perfect equality. Rather than being humiliated or dominated, the women characters equalled the men in their sheer earthy gusto. (That feature especially appealed to teenage boys who could only dream of unrestrained female gusto.) The episodes had no butt at all except prudes and hypocrites. Most of us consumers managed to survive with our moral characters intact.

In still other samples of actual pornography, there is indeed the appearance of male dominance and female humiliation, but even in many of these, explanations of a more innocent character are available. It is in the nature of fantasies, especially adolescent fantasies, whether erotic or otherwise, to glorify imaginatively, in excessive and unrealistic ways, the person who does the fantasizing. When that person is a woman and the fantasy is romantic, she may dream of herself surrounded by handsome lovesick suitors, or in love with an (otherwise) magnificent man who is prepared to throw himself at her feet, worship the ground she walks on, go through hell for her if necessary—the clichés pile up endlessly. If the fantasizing person is a man and his reverie is erotic, he may dream of women who worship the ground *he* walks on, etc., and would do anything for the honor of making love with him, and who having sampled his unrivaled sexual talents would grovel at his feet for more, etc., etc. The point of the fantasy is self-adulation, not "hostility" toward the other sex.

Still other explanations may be available. "Lust," wrote Norman Mailer, "is a world of bewildering dimensions. . . ."[5] When its consuming fire takes hold of the imagination, it is likely to be accompanied by almost any images suggestive of limitlessness, any natural accompaniments of explosive unrestrained passion. Not only men but women too have been known to scratch or bite (like house cats) during sexual excitement, and the phrase "I could hug you to pieces"—a typical expression of felt "limitlessness"—is normally taken as an expression of endearment, not of homicidal fury. Sexual passion in the male animal (there is as yet little but conjecture on this subject) may be associated at deep instinctive or hormonal levels with the states that capture the body and mind during aggressive combat. Some such account may be true of a given man, and explain why a certain kind of pornography may arouse him, without implying anything at all about his settled attitudes toward women, or his general mode of behavior toward them. Then, of course, it is a commonplace that many "normal" people, both men and women, enjoy sado-masochistic fantasies from time to time, without effect on character or conduct. Moreover, there are pornographic materials intended for men, that appeal to their masochistic side exclusively, in which they are "ravished" and humiliated by some grim-faced amazon of fearsome dimensions. Great art these materials are not, but neither are they peculiarly degrading to women.

It will not do then to isolate the most objectionable kinds of pornography, the kinds that are most offensive and even dangerous to women, and reserve the label "pornographic" for them alone. This conscious redefinition is what numerous feminist writers have done, however, much to the confusion of the whole discussion. Gloria

Steinem rightly protests against "the truly obscene idea that sex and the domination of women must be combined"[6] (*there* is a proper use of the word "obscene"), but then she manipulates words so that it becomes true by definition (hence merely trivially true) that *all* pornography is obscene in this fashion. She notes that "pornography" stems from the Greek root meaning "prostitutes" or "female captives," "thus letting us know that the subject is not mutual love, or love at all, but domination and violence against women."[7] Steinem is surely right that the subject of the stories, pictures, and films that have usually been called "pornographic" is not love, but it doesn't follow that they are all without exception about male domination over women either. Of course Steinem doesn't make that further claim as a matter of factual reporting, but as a stipulated redefinition. Her proposal can lead other writers to equivocate, however, and find sexist themes in otherwise innocent erotica that have hitherto been called "pornographic"—simply because they *are* naturally called by that name. Steinem adopts "erotica" as the contrasting term to "pornography" as redefined. Erotica, she concludes, is about sexuality, but "pornography is about power, and sex-as-a-weapon," conquerors dominating victims. The distinction is a real one, but better expressed in such terms as "degrading pornography" (Steinem's "pornography") as opposed to "other pornography" (Steinem's "erotica").

At least one other important distinction must be made among the miscellany of materials in the category of degrading pornography. Some degrading pornography is also violent, glorifying in physical mistreatment of the woman, and featuring "weapons of torture or bondage, wounds and bruises."[8] "One frightening spread from *Chic Magazine* showed a series of pictures of a woman covered with blood, masturbating with a knife. The title was 'Columbine Cuts Up.' "[9] A movie called "Snuff" in which female characters (and, it is alleged, the actresses who portrayed them) are tortured to death for the sexual entertainment of the audiences, was shown briefly in a commercial New York theatre. The widely circulated monthly magazine *Hustler* once had a cover picture of a nude woman being pushed head first into a meat grinder, her shapely thighs and legs poised above the opening to the grinder in a sexually receptive posture, while the rest comes out of the bottom as ground meat. The exaggeration of numbers in Kathleen Barry's chilling description hardly blunts its horror: "In movie after movie women are raped, ejaculated on, urinated on, anally penetrated, beaten, and, with the advent of snuff films, murdered in an orgy of sexual pleasure."[10] The examples, alas, are abundant and depressing.

There are other examples, however, of pornography that is degrading to women but does not involve violence. Gloria Steinem speaks of more subtle forms of coercion: "A physical attitude of conqueror and victim, the use of race or class difference to imply the same thing, perhaps a very unequal nudity with one person exposed and vulnerable while the other is clothed."[11] As the suggested forms of coercion become more and more subtle, obviously there will be very difficult line-drawing problems for any legislature brave enough to enter this area.

Yet the most violent cases at one end of the spectrum are as clear as they can be. They all glory in wanton and painful violence against helpless victims and do this with the extraordinary intention (sometimes even successful) of causing sexual arousal in male viewers. One could give every other form of pornography, degrading or not, the benefit of the doubt, and still identify with confidence all members of the violent extreme category. If there is a strong enough argument against pornography to limit the liberty of pornographers, it is probably restricted to this class of materials. Some feminist writers speak as if that would not be much if any restriction, but that may be a consequence of their *defining* pornography in terms of its most revolting specimens.[12] A pornographic story or film may be degrading in Steinem's subtle sense, in that it shows an intelligent man with a stupid woman, or a wealthy man with a chambermaid, and intentionally exploits the inequality for the sake of the special sexual tastes of the presumed male consumer, but if that were the *only* way in which the work degraded women, it would fall well outside the extreme (violent) category. All the more so, stories in which the male and female are equals—and these materials too can count as pornographic—would fall outside the objectionable category.

May the law legitimately be used to restrict the liberty of pornographers to produce and distribute, and their customers to purchase and use, erotic materials that are violently abusive of women? (I am assuming that no strong case can be made for the proscription of materials that are merely degrading in one of the relatively subtle and nonviolent ways.) Many feminists answer, often with reluctance, in the affirmative. Their arguments can be divided into two general classes. Some simply invoke the harm principle. Violent pornography wrongs and harms women, according to these arguments, either by defaming them as a group, or (more importantly) by inciting males to violent crimes against them or creating a cultural climate in which such crimes are likely to become more frequent. The two traditional legal categories involved in these harm-principle arguments, then, are *defamation* and *incitement*. The other class of arguments invoke[s] the offense principle, not in order to prevent mere "nuisances," but to prevent profound offense analogous to that of the Jews in Skokie or the blacks in a town where the K.K.K. rallies.

2. Violent Pornography, the Cult of Macho, and Harm to Women

I shall not spend much time on the claim that violent and other extremely degrading pornography should be banned on the ground that it *defames* women. In a skeptical spirit, I can begin by pointing out that there are immense difficulties in applying the civil law of libel and slander as it is presently constituted in such a way as not to violate freedom of expression. Problems with *criminal* libel and slander would be even more unmanageable, and *group* defamation, whether civil or criminal, would multiply the problems still further. The argument on the other side is that pornography is essentially propaganda—propaganda against women. It does not slander women in the technical legal sense by asserting damaging falsehoods about them, because it *asserts* nothing at all. But it spreads an image of women as mindless playthings or "objects," inferior beings fit only to be used and abused for the pleasure of men, whether they like it or not, but often to their own secret pleasure. This picture lowers the esteem men have for women, and for that reason (if defamation is the basis of the argument) is sufficient ground for proscription even in the absence of any evidence of tangible harm to women caused by the behavior of misled and deluded men.

If degrading pornography defames (libels or slanders) women, it must be in virtue of some beliefs about women—false beliefs—that it conveys, so that in virtue of those newly acquired or reinforced false beliefs, consumers lower their esteem for women in general. If a work of pornography, for example, shows a woman (or group of women) in exclusively subservient or domestic roles, that may lead the consumer to *believe* that women, in virtue of some inherent female characteristics, are only fit for such roles. There is no doubt that much pornography does portray women in subservient positions, but if that is defamatory to women in anything like the legal sense, then so are soap commercials on TV. So are many novels, even some good ones. (A good novel may yet be about some degraded characters.) That some groups are portrayed in unflattering roles has not hitherto been a ground for the censorship of fiction or advertising. Besides, it is not clearly the *group* that is portrayed at all in such works, but only one individual (or small set of individuals) and fictitious ones at that. Are fat men defamed by Shakespeare's picture of Falstaff? Are Jews defamed by the characterization of Shylock? Could any writer today even hope to write a novel partly about a fawning corrupted black, under group defamation laws, without risking censorship or worse? The chilling effect on the practice of fiction-writing would amount to a near freeze.

Moreover, as Fred Berger points out,[13] the degrading images and defamatory beliefs pornographic works are alleged to cause are not produced in the consumer by explicit statements asserted with the intent to convince the reader or auditor of their truth. Rather they are caused by the stimulus of the work, in the context, on the expectations, attitudes, and beliefs the viewer brings with him to the work. That is quite other than believing an assertion on the authority or argument of the party making the assertion, or understanding the assertion in the first place in virtue of fixed conventions of language use and meaning. Without those fixed conventions of language, the work has to be interpreted in order for any message to be extracted from it, and the process of interpretation, as Berger illustrates abundantly, is "always a matter of judgment and subject to great variation among persons."[14] What looks like sexual subservience to some looks like liberation from sexual repression to others. It is hard to imagine how a court could provide a workable, much less fair, test of whether a given work has sufficiently damaged male esteem toward women for it to be judged criminally defamatory, when so much of the viewer's reaction he brings on himself, and viewer reactions are so widely variable.

It is not easy for a single work to defame successfully a group as large as 51 percent of the whole human race. (Could a misanthrope "defame" the whole human race by a false statement about "the nature of man"? Would every human being then be his "victim"?) Perhaps an unanswered barrage of thousands of tracts, backed by the prestige of powerful and learned persons without dissent might successfully defame any group no matter how large, but those conditions would be difficult to satisfy so long as there is freedom to speak back on the other side. In any case, defamation is not the true gravamen of the wrong that women in general suffer from extremely degrading pornography. When a magazine cover portrays a woman in a meat grinder, *all* women are insulted, degraded, even perhaps endangered, but few would naturally complain that they were *libeled* or *slandered*. Those terms conceal the point of what has happened. If women are harmed by pornography, the harm is surely more direct and tangible than harm to "the interest in reputation."[15]

The major argument for repression of violent pornography under the harm principle is that it promotes rape and physical violence. In the United States there is a plenitude both of sexual violence against women and of violent pornography. According to the F.B.I. Uniform Crime Statistics (as of 1980), a 12-year-old girl in the United States has one chance in three of being raped in her lifetime; studies only a few years earlier showed that the number of violent scenes in hard-core pornographic books was as high as 20 percent of the total, and the number of violent cartoons and pictorials in leading pornographic magazines was as much as 10 percent of the total.[16] This has suggested to some writers that there must be a direct causal link between violent pornography and sexual violence against women; but causal relationships between pornography and rape, if they exist, must be more complicated than that. The suspicion of direct connection is dissipated, as Aryeh Neier points out,

> . . . when one looks at the situation in other countries. For example, violence against women is common in . . . Ireland and South Africa, but pornography is unavailable in those countries. By contrast violence against women is relatively uncommon in Denmark, Sweden, and the Netherlands, even though pornography seems to be even more plentifully available than in the United States. To be sure, this proves little or nothing except that more evidence is needed to establish a causal connection between pornography and violence against women beyond the fact that both may exist at the same time. But this evidence . . . simply does not exist.[17]

On the other hand, there is evidence that novel ways of committing crimes are often suggested (usually inadvertently) by bizarre tales in films or TV . . . , and even factual newspaper reports of crimes can trigger the well-known "copy-cat crime" phenomenon. But if the possibility of copy-cat cases, by itself, justified censorship or punishment, we would have grounds for suppressing films of *The Brothers Karamozov* and the TV series *Roots* (both of which have been cited as influences on imitative crimes). "There would be few books left on our library shelves and few films that could be shown if every one that had at some time 'provoked' bizarre behavior were censored."[18] A violent episode in a pornographic work may indeed be a causally necessary condition for the commission of some specific crime by a specific perpetrator on a specific victim at some specific time and place. But for his reading or viewing that episode, the perpetrator may not have done precisely what he did in just the time, place, and manner that he did it. But so large a part of the full causal explanation of his act concerns his own psychological character and predispositions, that it is likely that some similar crime would have suggested itself to him in due time. It is not likely that nonrapists are converted into rapists *simply* by reading and viewing pornography. If pornography has a serious causal bearing on the occurrence of rape (as opposed to the trivial copy-cat effect) it must be in virtue of its role (still to be established) in implanting the appropriate cruel dispositions in the first place.

Rape is such a complex social phenomenon that there is probably no one simple generalization to account for it. Some rapes are no doubt ineliminable, no matter how we design our institutions. Many of these are the product of deep individual psychological problems, transferred rages, and the like. But for others, perhaps the preponderant number, the major part of the explanation is sociological, not psychological. In these cases the rapist is a psychologically normal person well adjusted to his particular subculture, acting calmly and deliberately rather than in a rage, and doing what he thinks is expected of him by his peers, what he must do to acquire or preserve standing in his group. His otherwise inexplicable violence is best explained as a consequence of the peculiar form of his socialization among his peers, his pursuit of a prevailing ideal of manliness, what the Mexicans have long called *machismo,* but which exists to some degree or other among men in most countries, certainly in our own.

The macho male wins the esteem of his associates by being tough, fearless, reckless, wild, unsentimental, hard-boiled, hard drinking, disrespectful, profane, willing to fight whenever his honor is impugned, and fight without fear of consequences no matter how extreme. He is a sexual athlete who must be utterly dominant over "his" females, who are expected to be slavishly devoted to him even though he lacks gentleness with them and shows his regard only by displaying them like trophies; yet he is a hearty and loyal companion to his "teammates" (he is always on a "team" of some sort.) Given the manifest harm the cult of macho has done to men,[19] women, and to relations between men and women, it is difficult to account for its survival in otherwise civilized nations. Perhaps it is useful in time of war, and war has been a preoccupation of most generations of young men, in most nations, up to the present. If so, then the persistence of *machismo* is one of the stronger arguments we have (among many others) for the obsolescence of war.

The extreme character of macho values must be understood before any sense can be made of the appeal of violent pornography. The violent porn does not appeal to prurience or lust as such. Indeed, it does not appeal at all to a psychologically normal male who is not in the grip of the macho cult. In fact these pictures, stories, and films have no other function but to express and reenforce the macho ideology. "Get your sexual kicks," they seem to say, "but make sure you get them by humiliating the woman, and showing her who's boss. Make sure at all costs not to develop any tender feelings toward her that might give her a subtle form of control over you and thus destroy your standing with the group. Remember to act in the truly manly manner of a 'wild and crazy guy.' "

In her brilliant article on this subject, Sarah J. McCarthy cites some horrible examples from *Penthouse* Magazine of the macho personality structure which is peculiarly receptive to, and a necessary condition for, the appeal of violent porn:

> . . . There's still something to be said for bashing a woman over the head, dragging her off behind a rock, and having her," said one of the guys in the February 1980 *Penthouse* . . . "Women Who Flirt With Pain" was the cover hype for a *Penthouse* interview with an assortment of resident Neanderthals (a name that would swell them with pride).
>
> "We're basically rapists because we're created that way," proclaims Dale. "We're irrational, sexually completely crazy. Our sexuality is more promiscuous, more immediate, and more fleeting, possibly less deep. We're like stud bulls that want to mount everything in sight. . . ."
>
> The letters-to-the-editor in the February *Penthouse* contains an ugly letter from someone who claims to be a sophomore at a large midwestern university and is "into throat-fucking." He writes of Kathy and how he was "ramming his huge eleven-inch tool down her throat." [Sexual bragging, pornography style.] Kathy "was nearly unconscious from coming." [Deceit and self-deception, pornography style.] Gloria Steinem writes in the May 1980 *Ms.*: "Since *Deep Throat,* a whole new genre of pornography has developed. Added to the familiar varieties of rape, there is now an ambition to rape the throat. . . ."
>
> Another issue of *Penthouse* contains an article about what they have cleverly called "tossing." A college student from Albuquerque, who drives a 1974 Cadillac and who is "attracted to anything in a skirt," tells how it's done. "How did you get into tossing?" the *Penthouse* interviewer asks. "It just happened," says Daryl. "I was doing it in high school two years ago and didn't know what it was. I'd date a chick once, fuck her in my car, and just dump her out. Literally."[20]

These repugnant specimens are not examples of make-believe violent pornography. Rather, they are examples of the attitudes and practices of persons who are antecedently prone to be appreciative consumers of violent pornography. These grisly sentiments are perhaps found more commonly among working class youths in military barracks and factories but they are only slightly more familiar than similar bravado heard by middle-class Americans in fraternity houses and dormitories. These remarks are usually taken as meant to impress their male auditors; they are uttered with a kind of aggressive pride. The quotations from *Penthouse* capture the tone exactly. These utterly outrageous things are said publicly and casually, not in passion, not in hate, not in lust. They seem to say "That's just the way we machos are—for better or worse." Sarah McCarthy understands it perfectly—

> Though I'm sure male rage exists, just as female rage exists, it is probably not the main cause of rape. What we may be dealing with is the banality of rape, the sheer ordinariness of it as the logical end of macho, the ultimate caricature of our sexual arrangements. Some men may think that rape is just the thing to do. Its source could, in large part, be due to something as mundane as faulty sex education, rather than a wellspring of rage of mythic proportions. In many subcultures within the United States, violence against women has become acceptable, expected, even trendy. . . .[21]

There is probably no more typical pure macho enterprise than gang rape, a kind of group rite among cultish "individualists," in some ways like a primitive puberty ritual in which insecure males "prove themselves" to one another, and the victim is but an incidental instrument to that end. In a chapter on rape and war in her *Against Our Will,*[22] Susan Brownmiller discusses the behavior of American troops in Vietnam. Various veterans are quoted to the effect that rape was widespread but rarely reported. One veteran, who denied his own participation, had a terse explanation of the behavior of others: "They only do it when there are a lot of guys around. You know, it makes them feel good. They show each other what they can do. They won't do it by themselves."[23] Macho values thrive and spread in wartime battle zones. They become part of the process by which soldiers celebrate their cynical toughness and try to convince themselves and one another that they truly have it.

Would it significantly reduce sexual violence if violent pornography were effectively banned? No one can know for sure, but if the cult of macho is the main source of such violence, as I suspect, then repression of violent pornography, whose function is to pander to the macho values already deeply rooted in society, may have little effect. Pornography does not cause normal decent chaps, through a single exposure, to metamorphoze into rapists. Pornography-reading machos commit rape, but that is because they already have macho values, not because they read the violent pornography that panders to them. Perhaps then *constant* exposure to violent porn might turn a decent person into a violence-prone macho. But that does not seem likely either, since the repugnant violence of the materials could not have any appeal in the first place to one who did not already have some strong macho predispositions, so "constant exposure" could not begin to become established. Clearly, other causes, and more foundational ones, must be at work, if violent porn is to have any initial purchase. Violent pornography is more a symptom of *machismo* than a cause of it, and treating symptoms merely is not a way to offer protection to potential victims of rapists. At most, I think there may be a small spill-over effect of violent porn on actual violence. Sometimes a bizarre new sadistic trick (like "throat-fucking"?) is suggested by a work of violent pornography and taken up by those prone to cruel violence to begin with. More often, perhaps, the response to an inventive violent porno scene may be like that of the college *Penthouse* reader to "tossing": "I was doing it in high school two years ago, and I didn't know what it was." He read *Penthouse* and learned "what it was," but his conduct, presumably, was not significantly changed.

If my surmise about causal connections is correct they are roughly as shown:

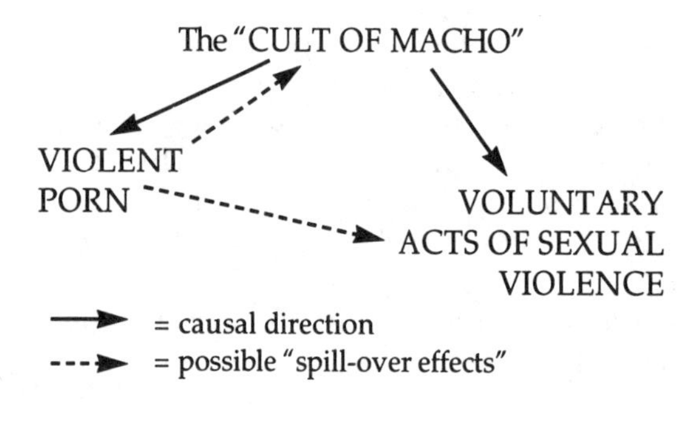

The primary causal direction is not from violent pornography to violent real-life episodes. Neither is it from violent pornography to the establishment and reenforcement of macho values. Rather, the cult of macho expectations is itself the primary cause *both* of the existence of violent porn (it provides the appreciative audience) and of the real-life sexual violence (it provides the motive). The dotted arrows express my acknowledgement of the point that there might be some small spill-over effect from violent pornography back on the macho values that spawn it, in one direction, and on real-life violence in the other, but the pornography cannot be the primary causal generator. Sexual violence will continue to fester so long as the cult of macho flourishes, whether or not we eliminate legal violent pornography.

How then can we hope to weaken and then extirpate the cultish values at the root of our problem? The criminal law is a singularly ill-adapted tool for that kind of job. We might just as well legislate against entrepreneurship on the grounds that capitalism engenders "acquisitive personalities," or against the military on the grounds that it produces "authoritarian personalities," or against certain religious sects on the ground that they foster puritanism, as criminalize practices and institutions on the grounds that they contribute to *machismo*. But macho values are culturally, not instinctively, transmitted, and the behavior that expresses them is learned, not inherited, behavior. What is learned can be unlearned. Schools should play a role. Surely, learning to see through machismo and avoid its traps should be as important a part of a child's preparation for citizenship as the acquisition of patriotism and piety. To be effective, such teaching should be frank and direct, not totally reliant on general moral platitudes. It should talk about the genesis of children's attitudes toward the other sex, and invite discussion of male insecurity, resentment of women, cruelty, and even specific odious examples. Advertising firms and film companies should be asked (at first), then pressured (if necessary) to cooperate, as they did in the successful campaign to deglamorize cigarette smoking. Fewer exploitation films should be made that provide attractive models of youths flashing knives, playing chicken or Russian roulette, or "tossing" girls. Materials (especially films) should be made available to clergymen as well as teachers, youth counselors, and parole officers. A strong part of the emphasis of these materials should be on the harm that bondage to the cult of macho does to men too, and how treacherous a trap *machismo* can be. The new moral education must be careful, of course, not to preach dull prudence as a preferred style for youthful living. A zest for excitement, adventure, even danger, cannot be artificially removed from adolescent nature. Moreover, teamwork, camaraderie, and toughness of character need not be denigrated. But the cult of macho corrupts and distorts these values in ways that can be made clear to youths. The mistreatment of women, when its motivation is clearly revealed and understood, should be a sure way of eliciting the contempt of the group, not a means to greater prestige within it.

Rape is a harm and a severe one. Harm prevention is definitely a legitimate use of the criminal law. Therefore, if there is a clear enough causal connection to rape, a statute that prohibits violent pornography would be a morally legitimate restriction of liberty. But it is not enough to warrant suppression that pornography as a whole might have some harmful consequences to third parties, even though most specific instances of it do not. "Communications from other human beings are among the most important causes of human behavior," Kent Greenawalt points out, "but criminal law cannot concern itself with every communication that may fortuitously lead to the commission of a crime. It would, for example, be ludicrous to punish a supervisor for criticizing a subordinate, even if it could be shown that the criticism so inflamed the subordinate that he assaulted a fellow worker hours later."[24] An even stronger point can be made. Even where there is statistical evidence that a certain percentage of communications of a given type will predictably lead the second party to harm third parties, so that in a sense the resultant harms are not "fortuitous," that is not sufficient warrant for prohibiting all communications of that kind. It would be even more ludicrous, for example, for a legislature to pass a criminal statute against the criticism of subordinates, on the ground that inflamed employees sometimes become aggressive with their fellow workers.

A more relevant example of the same point, and one with an ironic twist, is provided by Fred Berger:

> A journal that has published studies often cited by the radical feminists . . . has also published an article that purports to show that the greater emancipation of women in western societies has led to great increases in criminal activity *by* women. Such crimes as robbery, larceny, burglary, fraud, and extortion have shown marked increase, as have arson, murder, and aggravated assault. But freedom of expression would mean little if such facts could be taken as a reason to suppress expression that seeks the further liberation of women from their secondary, dependent status with respect to men.[25]

Of course, one can deny that violent porn is a form of valuable free expression analogous to scholarly feminist articles, but the point remains that indirectly produced harms are not by themselves sufficient grounds for criminalizing materials, that some further conditions must be satisfied.

Those instances of sexual violence which may be harmful side-effects of violent pornography are directly produced by criminals (rapists) acting voluntarily on their own. We already have on the statute books a firm prohibition of rape and sexual assault. If, in addition, the harm principle permits the criminalization of actions only indirectly related to the primary harm, such as producing, displaying or selling violent pornography, then there is a danger that the law will be infected with unfairness; for unless certain further conditions are fulfilled, the law will be committed to punishing some parties for the entirely voluntary criminal conduct of other parties. . . . Suppose that *A* wrongfully harms (e.g. rapes) *B* in circumstances such that (1) *A* acts fully voluntarily on his own initiative, and (2) nonetheless, but for what *C* has communicated to him, he would not have done what he did to *B*. Under what further conditions, we must ask, can *C* be rightfully held criminally responsible along with *A* for the harm to *B*? Clearly *C* can be held responsible if the information he communicated was helpful assistance to *A* and intended to be such. In that case *C* becomes a kind of collaborator. Under traditional law, *C* can also incur liability if what he communicated to *A* was some kind of encouragement to commit a crime against *B*. The clearest cases are those in which *C* solicits *A*'s commission of the criminal act by offering inducements to him. "Encouragement" is also criminal when it takes the form of active urging. Sometimes mere advice to commit the act counts as an appropriate sort of encouragement. When the encouragement takes a general form, and the harmful crime is recommended to "the general reader" or an indefinite audience, then the term "advocacy" is often used. Advocating criminal conduct is arguably a way of producing such conduct, and is thus often itself a crime. An article in a pornographic magazine advocating the practice of rape (as opposed to advocating a legislative change of the rape laws) would presumably be a crime if its intent were serious and its audience presumed to be impressionable to an appropriately dangerous degree.[26]

Violent pornography, however, does not seem to fit any of these models. Its authors and vendors do not solicit rapes; nor do they urge or advise rapes; nor do they advocate rape. If some of their customers, some of the time, might yet "find encouragement" in their works to commit rapes because rape has been portrayed in a way that happens to be alluring to them, that is their own affair, the pornographer might insist, and their own responsibility. The form of "encouragement" that is most applicable (if any are) to the pornography case is that which the common law has traditionally called "incitement." Sir Edward Coke wrote in 1628 that "all those that incite . . . set on, or stir up any other" to a crime are themselves accessories.[27] Thus, haranguing an angry crowd on the doorsteps of a corn dealer, in Mill's famous example,[28] might be the spark that incites the mob's violence against the hated merchant, even though the speaker did not explicitly urge, advise, or advocate it. Yet, a similar speech, twenty-four hours earlier, to a calmer audience in a different location, though it may have made a causal contribution to the eventual violence, would not have borne a close enough relation to the harm to count as an "incitement," or "positive instigation" (Mill's term) of it.

Given that "communication" is a form of expression, and thus has an important social value, obviously it cannot rightly be made criminal simply on the ground that it may lead some others on their own to act harmfully. Even if works of pure pornography are *not* to be treated as "communication," "expression" or "speech" in the sense of the First Amendment), but as mere symbolic aphrodisiacs or sex aids without further content[29] . . . , they may yet have an intimate personal value to those who use them, and a social value derived from the importance we attach to the protection of private erotic experience. By virtue of that significance, one person's liberty can be invaded to prevent the harm other parties might cause to *their* victims only when the invaded behavior has a specially direct connection to the harm caused, something perhaps like direct "incitement." Fred Berger suggests three necessary conditions that expected harms must satisfy if they are to justify censorship or prohibition of erotic materials, none of which, he claims, is satisfied by pornography, even violent pornography.

1. There must be strong evidence of a very likely and serious harm. [I would add— "that would not have occurred otherwise."]
2. The harms must be clearly and directly linked with the expression.
3. It must be unlikely that further speech or expression can be used effectively to combat the harm.[30]

Berger suggests that the false shout of "fire" in a crowded theatre is paradigmatically the kind of communication that satisfies these conditions. If so, then he must interpret the second condition to be something like the legal standard of incitement—setting on, stirring up, inflaming the other party (or mob of parties) to the point of hysteria or panic, so that their own infliction of the subsequent damage is something less than deliberate and fully voluntary. Their inciter in that case is as responsible as they are, perhaps even more so, for the harm that ensues. Surely, the relation between pornographers and rapists is nowhere near that direct and manipulative. If it were, we would punish the pornographers proportionately more severely, and blame the actual rapist (poor chap; he was "inflamed") proportionately less.

It may yet happen that further evidence will show that Berger's conditions, or some criteria similar to them, are satisfied by violent pornography. In that case, a liberal should have no hesitation in using the criminal law to prevent the harm. In the meantime, the appropriate liberal response should be a kind of uneasy skepticism about the harmful effects of pornography of third party victims, conjoined with increasingly energetic use of "further speech or expression" against the cult of macho, "effectively to combat the harm."

3. Violent Pornography and Profound Offense

The harm principle grounds for legally banning pornography do not appear sufficient. Does the offense principle do any better? Pornographic displays *can* be public nuisances, of course, and when the balancing tests tip in the nuisance direction, the offending activities may fairly be prohibited, or redirected to less offensive channels. The manner in which degrading and violent pornography offends women (and men who support women's rights) is substantially different from that in which erotica as such offend the prudish. The shame, embarrassment, shock, disgust, and irritation of the latter group can be effectively avoided if the erotic displays are concealed from their view. The offense to a woman's sensibilities when her whole sex is treated as grist for the meat grinder, however, is deeply repugnant to her moral sensibilities whether out of view or not. Feminist writers often make this point by means of analogies to racist literature and films.

Suppose some unscrupulous promoters decide that they can make large profits by pandering to the latent hatred against blacks which they suppose to be endemic in a substantial minority of the white community. Since explicitly racist remarks and overt racist behavior are no longer widely acceptable in American society, many secret black-haters might enjoy an occasional night at the movies where they can enjoy to their heart's content specially made films that lampoon minstrel-style "darkies" "with wide eyes as white as moons, hair shot straight in the air like Buchwheat's, afraid of everything—spiders, [their] own shadows, ghosts."[31] So much for comic openers. The main features could be stories of uppity blacks put in their place by righteous whites, taunted and hounded, tarred and feathered, tortured and castrated, and in the climactic scenes, hung up on gallows to the general rejoicing of their betters. The aim of the films would be to provide a delicious catharsis of pent-up hatred. It would be prudent, on business grounds, to keep advertisements discreet, and to use euphemistic descriptions like "folk films" (analogous to "adult films").

I don't imagine that many blacks would be placated by the liberal lawmaker who argues in support of his refusal to enact prohibitive legislation that there is little evidence of actual harm done to blacks by the films, that they do not advocate violence to blacks or incite mobs to fury, and that for all we know they will make the racists less dangerous by providing a harmless outlet for their anti-social impulses. Neither would many blacks be assuaged by the liberal assurance that we should all be wary of possible harmful effects anyway, continue to look for evidence thereof, and use educational campaigns as a more effective means of exposing the evils of racism. "That is all well and good," the blacks might reply, "but first we must lance this painful boil on our sensibilities. The 'folk films,' whether we are in the audience or not, are morally abominable affronts to us. Their very existence in our midst is a perpetual laceration of our feelings. We aren't present to be humiliated, but they degrade the very atmosphere in which we breathe and move."

The analogy to violent pornographic films is close though not perfect. (It is an interesting fact to ponder that although there undoubtedly is a large racist underground in this country, no promoter has yet found a way of exploiting it in the manner of our example.) The pornographic films do serve an erotic interest of their customers, and that gives them, *ceteris paribus,* a personal value greater perhaps than that of the "folk films." The racist films, on the other hand, may be easier to disguise as genuine works of drama, thus making it much more difficult for a line to be drawn between them and genuine attempts at dramas about odious people and their victims. The bare-knowledge offense in the two cases seems almost equally profound, going well beyond anything called "mere nuisance," to touch the chord of moral sensibility.

It does not express an unsympathetic attitude toward the offended parties, however, to deny a basis in either the harm or offense principles for the use of legal force to "lance the boil." Profound offense . . . , is either an impersonal and disinterested moral outrage or else an aggrieved response on one's own behalf because of the unpleasant mental states one has been forced to experience. If it is an impersonal response, then it can warrant legal force against its cause only on the basis of the principle of legal moralism which is unacceptable to liberals. We would have to argue in that case that the very showing of violent films to appreciative audiences is an evil in itself and one of such magnitude that it can be rightly prevented by legal force if necessary, even though it is not the kind of evil that *wrongs* any one. . . . If, on the other hand, the profound offense is a felt personal wrong voiced on one's own behalf as its "victim," then the complaint is that the offending materials cause one to suffer unpleasant states that are a nuisance to avoid. But that offense will not have much weight on the scales if one is not forced to witness the showings, or lurid announcements of the showings, and is not forced to take irritating and inconveniencing detours to avoid them. The offense principle, in short, will not warrant legal prohibition of the films unless the offense they cause is not reasonably avoidable, and bare-knowledge offense, insofar as it is mere offensive nuisance, is reasonably avoidable. It is only in its character as disinterested moral outrage that it is not reasonably avoidable, but we cannot ban everything that is thought to be outrageous, whether right-violating or not, without recourse to legal moralism.

This argument, I conceded, is subject to two strong qualifications. . . . It may be possible in certain untypical situations to go between its horns and thus escape its dilemma. A profoundly offended state of mind may be both disinterested moral outrage and also involve a sense of personal grievance, as when the offending cause is an affront to the offended party himself or a group to which he belongs. To feel personally degraded or insulted before others may well be to feel personally *wronged,* even though one's interests are unaffected and one's unpleasant states easily avoidable. The more difficult question is whether one truly *is* personally wronged when this happens, whether one's own rights have in fact been violated. The difficult cases I have in mind fall in between more extreme cases on either side that are easier to make judgments about. Consider hypothetical Cases 1, 2 (A and B), and 3. Cases 2A and B are the difficult ones I have in mind.

Case 1

A desecrates in private an icon that *B* regards as inherently sacred. *B* is morally outraged later when he learns about it. We can assume for the sake of the argument that *A*'s action was morally wrong, but that it caused no harm to *B* (or anyone else). Neither was it, in any sense, directed at *B*. (*A* and *B* are total strangers.) Nevertheless, *B* suffers deep offense, as well as moral outrage, whenever he thinks about it. But *B* does not feel personally wronged. *A* did not violate *his* rights simply because he did something *B* morally disapproved of. *B* is neither the "target" of *A*'s morally wrongful action, nor its victim.

Case 2A

B is morally outraged (in at least the disinterested way) when he learns that *A* and his friends, all of whom resent *B* for no good reason, frequently insult him when they gather together in private, and maliciously ridicule him behind his back. *A* and his friends act wrongly, but not in a manner that harms *B* (there is, for example, no incitement or defamation against him), but their conduct is, in a sense, directed at *B*, and *B* is deeply offended to learn about it. He *feels* personally wronged, but is he in fact wronged? Have his rights been violated? He was the "target" of morally wrongful behavior, but was he its *victim?* *A* and his friends might rebut his grievance by saying: "We all happen to dislike you (whether or not for good reason is beside the point), and we get great collective pleasure from sharing that dislike. How does that violate your rights? Do you have a right not to be disliked or not to have that dislike shared by those who have it? In fact, our little private party, while understandably not to your liking, was none of your business."

Case 2B

A and his friends are anti-semitic Nazi sympathizers who gather together privately and in secret in *A*'s apartment, and spend an evening regaling themselves with abusive and mocking stories about Jews, and top off their evening of fun by showing old Nazi propaganda films against Jews, and even newsreels of Jewish corpses discovered in the newly liberated concentration camps. The latter cause general hilarity except for one odd chap in a corner who masturbates excitedly at depictions of torture instruments. We can safely assume that all of this is morally wrongful though not necessarily harmful behavior, and that it has Jews, as a class, as its "target." *B* is a Jew who learns of the party later, and is morally outraged, deeply offended, and in his estimation personally wronged by the immoral activities. But again we can admit that he was (part of) the target of those activities so that his offense was in a clear sense "personal," while doubting that he was the victim of those activities, one whose own rights were violated.

Case 3

This is an easier case. *A* and his friends include at their party (in 2A) *C*, *D*, and *E*, who know nothing about *B*. *A* then deliberately lies to *C*, *D*, and *E* by telling them that *B* is an exconvict, a child molester, and bad check passer. This utterly destroys *B*'s reputation for probity with *C*, *D*, and *E*, who eventually spread the libel widely among many other persons, including *B*'s customers. *B*'s business declines and his economic interests as well as his interest in his good name are harmed by the defamation. *B* later learns what has happened and is outraged. He was not only the target of wrongful behavior; he was its victim, the one whose rights were violated. He not only feels personally wronged; he clearly was personally wronged.

The moral I draw from these stories is that the targets of abuse in 2A and B were not in fact its victims, so that their profound offense, while both moral and personal, is not the sort of "wrongful offense" (a right-violating offense) that is a reason for criminal prohibition. I am realistic enough to expect that many readers will not share my "intuition," and that the matter is not easily settled by argument. Even if I concede, however, for the sake of the argument, that *B*'s rights *were* violated in 2A and B as well as 3 (though not in 1), there will be little gain for those who would invoke legal action against *A* (without resorting to legal moralism) in those cases. It would be an extraordinary extension of the offense principle to punish such activities even on the supposition that some parties' rights were violated by their bare-knowledge offense. That would be to consider the quite avoidable offended feelings of those parties to have more weight on the balancing scales than the freedom of others to speak their minds to one another in private. *B* may be even more offended to learn that his enemies have insulted or ridiculed him to other parties who may not even know him, and this case, I admit, is a more plausible if not entirely convincing example of a violated right, even without defamation. But all that is conveyed by these comments to the strangers who hear them is that *A* has a low regard for *B* (which is his right). They may also infer from this that *B* has low regard for *A*. *B* surely will not be reluctant to express that disregard to any of *A*'s auditors who inquire, which, I should think, would also be *his* right.

Racist and porno films do not directly insult specific individuals, but rather large groups, thus diluting the impact of the insult, or at least its directed personal character, proportionately. The "folk films" might be more serious affronts in this respect than the porno films since their target is a much smaller group than half of the human race, and one which has historically been brutalized by slavery and cruel repression. A black man might be more likely to feel a *personal* grievance at the folk film he does not witness than a woman would to a porno film she does not witness, for these reasons.[32] This personal aspect of his offense would overlay the more general disinterested moral indignation he shares with the women who are offended by their bare knowledge of the existence of violent pornographic displays. Nonetheless, understandable as the black's felt grievance may be, the insulting film shown to a willing audience in a private or commercial theatre is in the same boat as the insulting conversations among willing friends in a private home or club. In both cases the conduct is morally execrable, but in neither case do liberal principles warrant state intervention to punish the mischief. If, however, I concede for the sake of the argument what seems to me to be dubious, namely that undeserved insults *wrong* the insulted party (violate his rights), and further (what is not doubtful) that he can be inflamed by the bare knowledge of them even though they occur behind his back, then I must make the further concession that these are relevant reasons under the offense principle in support of criminal prohibition. They cite, after all, a wrongful offense of the appropriate kind. But unless the balancing tests that mediate the offense principle are satisfied (and in these cases that would require that the offending conduct be of a kind that has virtually no redeeming personal and social value whatever), that relevant consideration can never be a sufficient reason.

The second accommodation our theory must make for profound offense is to acknowledge that severe restrictions should be made on announcements and advertisements. A black need not suffer the direct humiliation and stinging affront to his dignity and self-respect that would come from his being forced into the audience for a "folk film." He can simply stay away, and avoid the worst of it. But if the city is blanketed with garish signs announcing the folk films, or worse than that, signs that dispense with euphemisms and advertise "shows that put niggers in their place," then the affronts are no longer private; the offense is no longer avoidable; and its nature no less profound. The signs . . . can be expected to inflame the blacks, who are the direct object of their insult, in the manner of fighting words, further frustrating them since violent response cannot be permitted. The offense of conspicuous advertisements, even nongraphic ones (though graphic ones are the worst), is so great that any restriction of them short of interference with the minimum basic right of communication is warranted.

In this and the preceding chapter we have distinguished three types of activities the bare knowledge of which can be profoundly offensive. The first category is illustrated by private desecration of cherished symbols like religious icons and national flags, and by the mistreatment in private of dead bodies. We are to think of these "private" activities as unwitnessed by others or witnessed only voluntarily by other participants or spectators. In the second category are the "Skokie-type cases," for example, a Nazi demonstration in Skokie or a K.K.K. march in Harlem. Spectators are deliberately sought out and taunted by the display of hated symbols of racial cruelty known to offend deeply those they insult. In the third category are racist "folk films" and violent porno films shown in privately owned and secluded places for the pleasure of anyone in the general public who wishes to buy a ticket. All three categories can cause bare-knowledge offense as well as equally "profound" offense to unwilling observers (if any). But they differ subtly in various other important respects.

The bare-knowledge offense taken at "private desecrations" is not personal; that is, the offense is not taken because the offended party thinks of *himself* as wronged. (In fact he may admit that no one is personally wronged by the conduct he finds odious.) If he demands that legal force be used to prevent the outrageous behavior (anyway), the offending party might challenge him thus: "What concern is my behavior to you? You are morally outraged at what I have done, but I've done nothing *to* you except to morally outrage you. The outrage may or may not be justifiable, but it's no business of *yours* (or of anyone else's for that matter) to intervene, either to enforce your moral judgment (which implies legal moralism) or simply because you find your own intense moral aversion unpleasant. You can always escape *that* unpleasantness by ceasing to dwell in your imagination upon unseen things. If you can't escape the annoyance that way, then you are suffering from a severe neurotic obsession and should seek help." The offense produced by the sacrilegious private conduct, in short, cannot be thought to be a wrong *to* anyone, even if it is morally wrong in itself. Hence, it cannot be rightly banned on liberal principles, no matter how repugnant it might be to think about.

In the other two categories, however, the bare-knowledge offense, while equally profound, is also personal. The folk film promoter's challenge "What concern is that to you?" can be answered by some people—"I am black. Your film mocks and insults blacks, and therefore mocks and insults me, my family, and my dear ones. That's how it concerns me." If it is plausible to think of a person as truly wronged by abusively insulting materials shown to others behind his back, (and I have doubted this) then the black person's bare-knowledge offense, and the woman's bare-knowledge offense at violent porn films, are not only profound, they are also wrongful (to them) in the sense required by the offense principle. There is then a reason of the appropriate kind for banning them, but that reason is not likely to be decisive in most cases when the actual offensive materials are not thrust upon any unwilling observers or advertised in prominent places and obtrusive ways. The offending materials usually have very little personal or social value, it is true, but they are instances of a general category (films or books) which we all have a very great stake in keeping free. The porno films, in addition, service certain erotic tastes, which kinky though they may be, are a source of important personal value to some, and an area of personal experience that has a strong claim to noninterference. Whatever minimal value the porno film may have, it is not nullified by any spiteful or malicious motives of its displayers. The theatre owner would prefer that women were never in the neighborhood to be offended. It is no part of his purpose to offend women; his whole aim is to make money from men. Indeed, it is in his commercial interest not to arouse the wrath of organized women's groups, for their unrelentingly pesky campaigns against him could in the end drive him out of business in search of a less stressful way of making money. If that happens in time to all violent porn displayers, the whole genre will be as empty as racial folk films are now, and for similar reasons. Even without the help of legislatures, the black community would make such a fuss about folk film theatres, that customers would prefer to stay at home with their own videotaped materials, and theatre owners would throw in the towel. But then the home films would be as clearly immune from criminal prohibition as insulting private conversations (no matter how abusive of third parties) and private voluntary sexual activity (no matter how kinky).

The third category, which includes the examples of Nazis in Skokie and Klansmen in Harlem, differ in two important respects from the second category. The offending behavior deliberately seeks out the audience that will be most intensely, most profoundly, and most personally offended, and imposes its offense on them as its sole motivating purpose. It is therefore spiteful and malicious through and through, thus lacking measurable social value. In the purest hypothetical cases, at least, where for some people the offense cannot possibly be avoided, and the menacing abuse of the displayed symbols is the sole "message" communicated, the offense principle clearly justifies prohibition, whether by preliminary injunction, by on the spot "cease and desist orders," or by general prohibitory statute. The difference between these cases and the violent porn cases are subtle; but small differences in mode and manner of offense can be the basis of large differences in the form of political response, and in the realm of criminal law policy, must inevitably be so. Wherever a line is drawn between permission and prohibition, there will be cases close to the line on both sides of it.

NOTES

1. I do not wish to imply that there is one position about the punishability or censorship of pornography that all writers called "feminists" hold. Some, like Ann Garry in "Pornography and Respect for Women" (*Social Theory and Practice,* vol. 4, 1978) deny that pornography is necessarily by its very nature degrading to women. Others, like Wendy Kaminer in "Pornography and the First Amendment: Prior Restraints and Private Actions" in *Take Back the Night: Women on Pornography,* ed. Laura Lederer (New York: William Morrow and Co., Inc., 1980), accept the analysis of pornography that I discuss in the text, but deny that it provides a sufficient ground for censorship. The view I attribute to "feminists" is simply one held by many leading radical feminists, and most frequently and plausibly defended by feminist writers in the 1970s and '80s.
2. Lisa Lehrman, Preface to the Colloquium on Violent Pornography: "Degradation of Women Versus Right of Free Speech," *New York University Review of Law and Social Change* 8 (1978–79), p. 181.
3. The figure estimates are from Sarah J. McCarthy, "Pornography, Rape, and the Cult of Macho," *The Humanist,* Sept./Oct. 1980, p. 11.
4. Ann Garry, *op. cit.* (footnote 1) is persuasive on this point:

   Imagine the following situation, which exists only rarely today: Two fairly conventional people who love each other enjoy playing tennis and bridge together, and having sex together. In all these activities they are free from hang-ups, guilt, and tendencies to dominate or objectify each other. These two people like to watch tennis matches and old romantic movies on TV, like to watch Julia Child cook, like to read the bridge column in the newspaper, and like to watch pornographic movies. Imagine further that this couple is not at all uncommon in society and that nonsexist pornography is as common as this kind of nonsexist relationship. The situation sounds fine and healthy to me. I see no reason to think that an interest in pornography would disappear in the circumstances. People seem to enjoy watching others experience or do (especially do well) what they enjoy experiencing, doing, or wish they could do themselves. We do not morally object to people watching tennis on TV: why would we object to these hypothetical people watching pornography? (p. 419)

   I would qualify Garry's account in two ways. First, it is not essential to her point that the two people "love each other," provided only that they like and respect each other. Second, their pleasures will be possible only if the film is well done, in particular keeping at least minimal photographic distance from what is depicted. Otherwise it might arouse anti-erotic repugnance.
5. Norman Mailer, *The Prisoner of Sex* (New York: New American Library, 1971), p. 82.
6. Gloria Steinem, "Erotica and Pornography, A Clear and Present Difference," *Ms.,* November, 1978, p. 53.
7. *Ibid.,* p. 54. Susan Wendell proposes a similar definition according to which depictions of "unjustified physical coercion of human beings" with some exceptions will count as pornographic even if they are not in any way *sexual.* See David Copp and Susan Wendell, eds., *Pornography and Censorship, Scientific, Philosophical, and Legal Studies* (Buffalo, N.Y.: Prometheus Books, 1983), p. 167. Pornography [all pornography] is to Susan Brownmiller "the undiluted essence of anti-female propaganda"—*Against Our Will: Men, Women, and Rape* (New York: Simon and Schuster, 1975), p. 394. Lorenne Clark takes it to be essential to pornography that it portrays women "in humiliating, degrading,

and violently abusive situations," adding that "it frequently depicts them willingly, even avidly, suffering and inviting such treatment." See her "Liberalism and Pornography" in the Copp-Wendell volume, *supra.*

8. Steinem, *op. cit.* (footnote 6), p. 54.
9. Lisa Lehrman, *op. cit* (footnote 2), pp. 181–82.
10. Kathleen Barry, *Female Sexual Slavery* (New York: Avon Books, 1979), p. 206.
11. Steinem, *op. cit.* (footnote 6), p. 54.
12. The most extreme of these definitions is that of Andrea Dworkin in her "Pornography and Grief" in *Take Back the Night: Women on Pornography,* ed. Laura Lederer (New York: William Morrow and Co., 1980), p. 288—"The eroticization of murder is the essence of pornography. . . ."
13. Fred R. Berger, "Pornography, Feminism, and Censorship," (Unpublished paper, Philosophy Department, University of California, Davis), pp. 17ff. I am greatly indebted to this scholarly and well-argued essay.
14. *Ibid.,* p. 18.
15. "Defamation [libel or slander] is an invasion of the interest in reputation and good name, by communications to others which tend to diminish the esteem in which the plaintiff is held, or to excite adverse feelings or opinions against him."—William L. Prosser, *Handbook of the Law of Torts* (St. Paul: West Publishing Co., 1955), p. 572.
16. The studies are cited by Berger, *op. cit.* (footnote 13), p. 38.
17. Aryeh Neier, "Expurgating the First Amendment," *The Nation,* June 21, 1980, p. 754.
18. *Loc. cit.*
19. The former major league baseball pitcher Ryne Duren had a brief but distinguished career despite his constant heavy drinking and rowdiness off the field. Only when he was nearing forty did he manage to reform himself with the help of a rehabilitation center. Why did he behave so irrationally—playing, for example, with a constant hangover? "The problem is the image of the macho man who defies everything," he says. "Most of the guys I played with admired anyone who could drink all night and play baseball the next afternoon." *Newsweek,* June 20, 1983, p. 13.
20. Sarah J. McCarthy, "Pornography, Rape, and the Cult of Macho," *The Humanist,* Sept., Oct., 1980, p. 15.
21. *Ibid.,* p. 17.
22. Susan Brownmiller, *Against Our Will: Men, Women, and Rape* (New York: Macmillan, 1975).
23. Quoted by McCarthy, *op. cit.* (footnote 20), p. 17.
24. Kent Greenawalt, "Speech and Crime," *American Bar Foundation Research Journal,* no. 4 (1980), p. 654.
25. Berger, *op. cit.* (footnote 13), pp. 23–24. The study cited by Berger is: Freda Adler, "The Interaction Between Women's Emancipation and Female Criminality: A Cross-cultural Perspective," *International Journal of Criminology and Penology,* 5 (1977):101–12.
26. The Supreme Court's standards of seriousness and dangerousness have been so extraordinarily high, however, that even a magazine article advocating (in a general way) rape might escape constitutionally valid punishment unless it urged *imminent* action against precise victims. In the landmark case *Brandenburg* v. *Ohio,* 395 U.S. 444 (1969), the court ruled that advocacy of illegal violence may be proscribed only when the advocacy amounts to *incitement* of imminent lawless action. Two conditions must be satisfied for liability. The advocacy must be (1) "directed to inciting or producing imminent lawless action," and (2) likely to succeed in inciting or producing such action.
27. Edward Coke, Second Part of the *Institutes of the Laws of England,* p. 182.
28. John Stuart Mill, *On Liberty,* chap. 3, para. 1. Mill writes: "An opinion that corn dealers are starvers of the poor, or that private property is robbery, ought to be unmolested when simply circulated through the press, but may justly incur punishment when delivered orally to an excited mob assembled before the house of a corn dealer, or when handed about among the same mob in the form of a placard."
29. This interpretation is persuasively argued by Frederick Schauer in his article "Speech and 'Speech'—Obscenity and 'Obscenity': An Exercise in the Interpretation of Constitutional Language," *Georgia Law Review* 67 (1979).
30. Fred L. Berger, *op. cit.* (footnote 13), p. 28.
31. Sarah J. McCarthy, *op. cit.* (footnote 20), p. 11.
32. On the other hand, it is hard to know how typical is Andrea Dworkin's highly personal response to other people's pornography—" . . . pornography silences me . . . pornography makes me sick every day of my life." Panel Discussion, "Effects of Violent Pornography" in "Colloquium on Violent Pornography," *op. cit.* (footnote 2), p. 239.

Study Questions

1. Did the court make the morally best ruling in *American Booksellers v. Hudnut*? Explain your answer based on the moral principles defined in Appendix B. What is the best definition of pornography? Can pornography be adequately defined? If not, is it fair to try to punish those who produce or sell pornography?
2. Is Clark a liberal? What is liberalism's position regarding the legalization of pornography? What is Clark's position?
3. Is Feinberg a feminist? What is the main feminist position on pornography? What is Feinberg's position?

G Gun Control and the Control of Crime

Why We Should Ban Handguns in the United States

Nicholas Dixon*

Dixon, who teaches philosophy at Alma College in Michigan, writes about a topic that philosophers neglect far too often, namely, gun control. Dixon's paper is, to our knowledge, the most thorough and detailed study any philosopher has yet published on gun control. Dixon's essay is characteristic of the new approach many contemporary philosophers take to applied ethics, since he relies heavily on statistics and empirical data—rather than only on conceptual analysis—to support his conclusions. Dixon also bases his conclusion on the moral principle of utilitarianism, the view that each of us must maximize net happiness for all in the long run. Dixon argues at length that gun control will do just that.

Readers of this review are likely to be familiar with the controversy over whether restrictions on gun ownership are compatible with the Second Amendment's guarantee of "the right to bear arms."[1] There would be little point in discussing the complex question of the constitutionality of gun restrictions, however, unless there were good reasons for implementing them in the first place. The purpose of this paper, which will be confined to *handguns,* is to argue that there *are* good reasons for the most stringent restriction—an outright handgun ban. This paper can thus be

Reprinted with permission from St. Louis University *Public Law Review,* Vol. 12, No. 2. © 1991 by St. Louis University.

*Associate Professor of Philosophy, Alma College, Alma, Michigan.

viewed as motivating and setting the stage for the constitutional debate.

My argument for banning handguns is utilitarian: the likely good consequences of my proposal, I argue, far outweigh the possible bad consequences. My main focus will be on homicide, but I will also sometimes discuss robbery and assault in connection with handguns. Aside from my detailed discussion of existing literature and evidence, I hope to advance the debate over gun control in two main ways. First, I have gathered original data, strongly supporting my hypothesis, on the correlation between handgun ownership and handgun homicide rates in various countries. Second, I have placed the discussion of rival interpretations of the evidence in the context of an elementary discussion of the nature of confirmation of hypotheses in the social sciences, and of the burden of proof that falls on their proponents and opponents. While the points I make in this regard are indeed elementary, they have been persistently ignored by opponents of gun control. In keeping with the utilitarian nature of my argument, the majority of my paper is devoted to a discussion of empirical data. However, the theoretical key to my argument is my brief account of confirmation and the burden of proof in section one, to which I will refer throughout the paper.

I. Initial Argument

A. Introduction

In 1990 there were 23,438 homicides in the United States, 9,923 of which are known to have been committed with handguns.[2] Of the 639,271 robberies in the United States in 1990, 36.6% involved firearms,[3] while 23.1% of the 1,054,863 aggravated assaults were made with guns.[4]

> *THESIS* There are strong reasons for believing that one of the major causes of these 9,923 murders is the extremely high rate of private ownership of handguns in the United States. Similarly, this high rate is also a major cause of the 233,973 firearms robberies and 243,673 firearms assaults. Reducing the handgun ownership rate will reduce handgun violence, and hence the overall number of violent crimes. The most effective way to achieve such a reduction is a ban on the private ownership of handguns, with exceptions narrowly confined to the armed forces, the police, private security guards, and licensed gun collectors.

A ban on the private ownership of handguns will restrict the freedom of United States citizens and require an adjustment in the way that some of them spend their leisure time. I accept that the burden of proof is on me to demonstrate that the benefits of my proposal outweigh its costs. I discharge this burden in the rest of section I and reinforce my response throughout section II. Having shifted the burden of proof to opponents of gun control, in section II I discuss responses that have been given to arguments for a handgun ban. My argument is primarily a utilitarian discussion of the beneficial consequences of a handgun ban (a reduction in the murder rate and a general decrease in violent crime, especially robbery and aggravated assault). The pleasure and additional self-defense which is alleged to result from owning and using handguns is trivial compared to the death and misery that is caused by their misuse. However, my thesis could be equally well expressed in terms of rights (the right to life, freedom from assault, and property of victims of handgun crimes). The restriction of the alleged right to bear arms is minor compared to the violations of the rights of the victims of handgun crimes that occur every day.

I have focused on a handgun ban primarily because handguns are the weapon of choice of violent criminals. In 1990 handguns were used in 77.2% of murders involving firearms and 49.5% of all murders in the United States. More recent figures are not available, but in 1967 96% of firearms used in robberies and 86% of those used in aggravated assaults were handguns.[5] These numbers are almost certainly attributable to their relative cheapness, their small size (and hence greater concealability), and the fact that they are easy to use. At the same time, long guns (shot guns and rifles) are used more than handguns in recreational pursuits, which, *ceteris paribus*, it would be desirable to allow to go unhindered. Consequently, and in view of their minimal criminal use, I see no pressing need for a ban on long guns. Because of the high percentage of violent crimes that are committed with handguns, and because they are uniquely suited to such use, a handgun ban will result in a reduction in *overall* rates of violent crime.[6]

Many recreational uses of handguns are compatible with a ban on private ownership. For instance, target shooting can still be enjoyed at licensed facilities. Shooters would be allowed to own or rent handguns that would be permanently stored at the shooting ranges.[7]

Licensed gun collectors would be allowed to keep handguns of recognized antique value—say fifty years old or more—on the strict condition that no ammunition be kept. Another cost of a ban would be that gun dealers would lose the profits they currently make from the sale of handguns and their ammunition. However, they would be able to recoup some of these losses by diversifying their stock of long guns, which would be unaffected by my proposal. The reduction in violent crime that would result outweighs whatever loss of profits may occur for this relatively affluent sector of our society.

James B. Jacobs has raised serious questions about handgun bans that allow for exceptions.[8] Since I advocate exceptions, I will consider and respond to his arguments. He points out that the widely-publicized handgun prohibitions in San Francisco and Morton Grove, Illinois, allow for extensive exceptions. In addition to the exceptions I allow, these prohibitions permit people such as prison guards, campus police, sheriffs, police chiefs, and retired law enforcement personnel to keep handguns at home and at work, and San Francisco allows business owners or employees to carry handguns on business premises.[9] Such exceptions, argues Jacobs, call into question the fairness of denying guns to other people who may feel that they have an equally good reason to own handguns. Moreover, "the exceptions reinforce the apparently widely held feeling that handguns are valuable, even necessary, for personal security."[10] Jacobs even goes so far as to suggest that we cannot even allow the police to use handguns "without letting loose tremendous pressure to recognize other self-defense and safety claims that could ultimately swallow up the prohibition."[11] As a result, such bans will lack credibility in the eyes of the public, who will freely disobey them."[12] A credible, effective handgun ban must be total and include the police, whose leadership will be crucial in changing people's attitudes towards guns. It is even more important to disarm private security guards.

> If policymakers acknowledge the value of handguns for self-defense and crime prevention by allowing private security personnel to carry handguns, however, the moral coherence of handgun prohibition is seriously, perhaps fatally, weakened. Large numbers of private citizens remain unshakably convinced that they need handguns in their stores and in their homes to deter or thwart criminal predators.[13]

My strategy in responding to Jacobs' slippery slope argument is to show that there are relevant differences between those people whom I would allow to use handguns and the rest of the population. I consider first the police. Like Jacobs, I would welcome the day when the United States police, like the British police, do not need to routinely carry guns. I also appreciate his efforts to explore ways that police could protect themselves, carry out arrests, and deter crime without carrying guns.[14] However, because long guns will still be legal and widely owned, and some criminals can be expected to keep their handguns until caught even if my ban is enacted, police will have to remain armed for the foreseeable future in order to adequately enforce the law. It will take many generations, maybe centuries, before we achieve the same situation as in countries like England, which do not have a tradition of private handgun ownership. The moral legitimacy of allowing the police a deadly force which is denied to the general population is easily established by reference to the special role of the police. Since the police are entrusted with the protection of society and the prevention and deterrence of crime, it is only to be expected and indeed encouraged that they be given force superior to the rest of society. Since they are subject to extensive training and strict discipline, police are less likely to abuse handguns than the private citizen, including both criminals and law-abiding citizens who own guns for self-defense.

Private security guards would be allowed to use handguns while on duty and keep them at home, safely locked and unloaded. The justification for distinguishing between ordinary citizens and private security guards is again the nature of their work. Security guards are entrusted with the protection of large amounts of cash or other valuables, and by virtue of their uniforms and their place of work, they are visible targets for attack. Consequently, they need to be at least as well armed as potential attackers. A further distinction between ordinary citizens and private security guards is the training that the guards would undergo. Furthermore, private security companies would have to be licensed, and a condition of such licenses would be precisely that they give adequate training to their employees.

Owners of convenience stores, gas stations, and other small businesses, which are the target of an increasing number of armed robberies, can also reasonably claim a need for handguns on their premises for self-protection. However, the danger of over-zealous use of firearms in response to perceived threats of robbery,[15] and the general undesirability of adding to the pool of privately owned guns that may fall into the wrong hands, argue against this exception. Security guards are specialists in the protective use of firearms and are far less likely to abuse their weapons. It is reasonable to expect business owners who feel they need such protection to hire private security guards. These guards can transport cash takings to the bank and provide permanent protection at the place of business. Hiring such protection would be one of the expenses taken into account by those contemplating going into business and desiring armed protection.

B. An International Comparison

In 1988 Interpol reported the following number of handgun homicides for these countries:

	Handgun Homicides	*Population*[16]	*Rate per 100,000*
Australia	13	16,538,000 (1988)	0.07
Canada	8	25,857,000 (1987)	0.031
Great Britain	7	57,376,000 (1990)	0.012
Israel	25	4,614,000 (1990)	0.542
Sweden	19	8,332,000 (1984)	0.228
Switzerland	53	6,473,000 (1985)	0.819
United States	8,915	250,410,000 (1990)	3.560

It was this astounding disparity between the United States and other developed countries which first drew my attention to the issue of handgun control.

My contention is that a major cause of this disparity is the much higher rate of handgun ownership among private citizens in the United States compared to other countries. More generally, I argue that any country's handgun ownership rate is a major determinant of its handgun homicide rate. The following table is based on information from government agencies, including police departments, in the respective countries. Any systematic bias, which may result from a government agency's desire to minimize or exaggerate gun ownership levels, can reasonably be assumed to apply equally to all of the countries studied. Since my interest is in comparative ownership rates rather than the absolute numbers, any such bias is irrelevant. The numbers refer to estimates of the total number of handguns owned by civilians in each country, both legally and illegally.

	Handguns	Handguns per 100,000	Handgun Homicides per 100,000
United States	56,833,000[17]	22,696	3.56
Israel	171,448[18]	3,716	0.542
Sweden	308,261[19]	3,700	0.228
Canada	595,000[20]	2,301	0.031
Australia	263,900[21]	1,596	0.07
Great Britain	480,000[22]	837	0.012

(The Swiss government was unable to provide any handgun ownership estimates.)

My handgun ownership estimates (except the number for Great Britain) are the result of *independent* inquiries to government agencies in each country. The close coincidence between the rank ordering of handgun ownership and handgun homicide rates in these six diverse countries is most plausibly explained by the causal connection I assert. The multiplicity of causes of handgun homicide which opponents of handgun control are eager to assert, and which I accept, make a perfect correlation most unlikely. The one anomaly is the relative position of Australia and Canada; but the actual handgun homicide numbers (13 and 8, respectively) are so small as to make the difference in homicide rate of little importance.

Of more interest than the rank ordering of individual nations, which is more sensitive to "interference" from other causal factors, is the emergence of three clear categories in which handgun ownership and handgun homicide rates coincide: low (Canada, Australia, and Great Britain), moderate (Israel and Sweden), and high (United States). The most significant fact of all is the vast disparity between the United States and all the comparison countries in both the handgun ownership and handgun homicide rates. I conclude that a dramatic reduction in the handgun ownership rate in this country would substantially reduce handgun homicide rates.

I am assuming that the number of handguns in a country depends on (1) the permissiveness of its handgun laws, and (2) the demand for handguns. Handgun laws in the United States are far more permissive than in any of the comparison countries.[23] Since the law is much more easily controlled than the people's wishes, by far the easiest way to reduce handgun ownership is to pass more restrictive laws. My proposal, then, is that the best way to reduce handgun homicides is to pass maximally restrictive laws—a handgun ban.

Two interesting points concerning the demand for handguns are worth noting. First, it is probable that, doubtless due in part to the long history of private gun ownership in this country, there is more demand for them in the United States than in the other countries.[24] In order to achieve the same levels of gun ownership in the United States as in other countries, therefore, it is likely that even more restrictive handgun laws will be required. Second, a reduction in the number of handguns in this country (by means of a handgun ban) can reasonably be expected to result in a reduction in demand, which will in turn cause a further reduction in ownership levels. This result is because a major reason for handgun ownership at present is to defend oneself against the huge number of people who already have handguns. (See *infra* section II.E for a discussion of the defensive efficacy of handguns.) I propose stemming this spiral of gun ownership at its source rather than simply acquiescing in the unlimited proliferation of handguns.

Two important clarifications need to be made at this point. First, it is not being claimed that the high rate of gun ownership in the United States is the *only*, or even the main, cause of its exceptionally high handgun homicide rate. What is being claimed is that its handgun ownership rate is *one* of the causes. Furthermore, it is the easiest to control of all of the probable causes. Consequently, reducing ownership of handguns is the most realistic way to start reducing murder and handgun-related crime in the United States. Second, I am fully cognizant of the error of assuming that a correlation implies a causal connection. In order to avoid this error, anyone who posits a causal connection based on a correlation must do at least two things. One must first show that there are no other variables which correlate better with the effect, and which would account for the effect better than, or in place of, the posited cause. Take, for instance, the view that AIDS was a punishment for homosexuality, which, in the early 1980s, did seem to correlate very closely with the syndrome of diseases. As heterosexual AIDS cases emerged, the "punishment" hypothesis lost credibility. What finally destroyed the credibility of that hypothesis was the discovery of a 100% correlation between AIDS symptoms and the presence of HIV, along with the emergence of an increasing number of heterosexuals with AIDS. The second requirement is the provision of a probable theoretical explanation of *how* the causation occurred. The second requirement is also illustrated by the case of AIDS. What made the HIV hypothesis increasingly convincing was the development of a detailed biochemical explanation of exactly how the virus attacks the immune system and leads to the symptoms of AIDS. Both the 100% correlation and the detailed theoretical account make the HIV hypothesis practically certain. In the case of causal hypotheses in the social sciences, where the web of causation is much more complex and causes much harder to distinguish, a more modest correlation and a less rigorous theoretical explanation are sufficient to establish the plausibility of a causal connection.

Since I do not claim that handguns are the only cause of murder, I do not need to rule out the existence of other causes. Consequently, to try to refute my position by pointing out these other causes is to commit a straw man fallacy. All I need to show is that there is no other cause that correlates so well with handgun murder as to rule out my own causal hypothesis. I undertake this task in the next subsection and on various occasions throughout this paper. While the evidence does indeed suggest a *prima facie* case for several other causal factors, none of them is nearly strong enough to be considered as the *only* cause, and hence, to disprove my hypothesis. As for a theoretical explanation of why high rates of handgun ownership correlate with high rates of handgun related murder, one need not go beyond common sense. Assuming human nature to be relatively similar in different developed democratic countries (i.e. those represented in the Interpol statistics quoted above), one would expect people to be subject to roughly similar amounts of stress, provocation, jealousy, anger, desperation, resentment of other people's affluence, and whatever other factors are liable to lead some people to violence. If one of these nations has a vastly higher rate of private ownership of handguns, one would expect that the similar provocations to violence would spill over into handgun murder far more often than in the other nations. This low-level theoretical explanation is sufficient to show that my handgun hypothesis is more than an accidental coincidence and, unlike the "AIDS as punishment" hypothesis, is not based on prejudice and superstition.

C. The Burden of Proof

I have presented evidence of a striking correlation between the rate of private ownership of handguns and the rate of handgun murder in six different countries. I have given a theoretical account of why this correlation is a causal one. Throughout the rest of my paper, I will show that none of the other alleged causes of the high homicide rate in the United States comes even close to disproving my hypothesis that the high ownership rate of handguns is one of its significant causes. By the end of my paper I will have amply met the burden of proof that I set for myself above—namely, showing that a ban on handguns will reduce our homicide and violent crime rates, thus justifying the minor restriction on liberty that it will involve.

I now wish to go on the offensive and suggest that I have already written enough to issue a different burden of proof challenge to opponents of a ban on handguns, in light of the strong *prima facie* case I have made for my causal hypothesis. In the case of my comparative international homicide statistics, and of the other statistics that I will adduce throughout my paper, it is incumbent on them to produce an alternative causal account proving that the United States' high handgun murder rate is caused by factors unrelated to its high rate of handgun ownership. They must specify what these causes are, quantify their relative presence in the United States as compared to the countries with lower homicide rates, demonstrate that variations in these factors correlate with variations in the murder rate, and provide a plausible theory explaining the causal mechanisms at work. I contend that they have utterly failed to even approach a satisfactory response to this burden of proof.

A strategy commonly used by opponents of gun control is to construct thought experiments in which the evidence gathered by advocates of gun control can be attributed to factors other than guns. Except in the case of deductively valid arguments, it will always be possible to describe scenarios in which the premises are true and the conclusion false. When dealing with the highly complex webs of causation that are at work in crime and violence, the best we can hope for is arguments that offer reasonably high degrees of inductive support for their conclusions. The counter examples offered by opponents of gun control certainly show that the arguments in favor of gun control are not deductively valid; but no one has ever claimed that they are.[25] Scenarios unsupported by statistical evidence and theoretical explanations of the causal mechanisms do not even address the burden of proof I have asserted. The only way opponents can disprove my hypothesis is to provide such evidence and explanations and show that they are more probable than the causal explanations I provide.

D. Comparison with Capital Punishment

In order to illustrate the burden of proof which I place on opponents of a handgun ban, I turn briefly to the criteria by which we decide whether the effectiveness of capital punishment (CP) as a deterrent to murder has been established. The available evidence indicates that there is no significant correlation between a jurisdiction's murder rate and whether or not it has the death penalty. This lack of correlation is strong *prima facie* evidence against the main utilitarian argument for capital punishment: that it will reduce the murder rate.

Proponents of CP have responded that its superior deterrent effect is "masked" by a complex of other factors. For instance, the similar murder rates in states with and without CP is explained by CP's "general deterrent" effect, which allegedly operates even in those states that do not have CP.[26] Sociopolitical differences between these states may also serve to mask CP's superior deterrence. Without CP, some states would likely have a far greater than average murder rate that is currently kept in check precisely because of the operation of CP. *Prima facie* support for these contentions is provided by considerations such as the "Preference Argument," according to which it is clear that, given the choice, nearly everyone would choose life imprisonment rather than execution.[27] Together, these considerations are used to argue that CP is indeed the best deterrent to murder, even though various other factors combine to obscure this deterrent effect.

This brief discussion of the deterrent effect of CP illustrates how the burden of proof principles which I outline above apply to a concrete situation that is in some ways analogous to the handgun control debate. First, given the strong empirical evidence that CP is not a superior deterrent, the burden of proof is on those who believe that it is. They need to produce plausible explanations of why CP is the best deterrent, even though the evidence fails to bear this out. It is fair to say that supporters of CP have been reasonably successful in suggesting causal hypotheses that account for the lack of empirical support for their belief. However, they have fallen short of showing that these causal hypotheses are in fact correct. In other words, showing that the evidence is *compatible with* CP's superiority as a deterrent fails to meet the burden of proving that it *is in fact* a superior deterrent. This, I contend, is the situation in which those who deny my causal hypothesis concerning the prevalence of handguns and the handgun murder rate find themselves. Opponents have shown that it is *possible* that my hypothesis is false (which I have never denied, since it is not claimed to be a deductively valid argument); but they have failed to give any good reason to believe that it *is in fact* false.

Second, if, on the other hand, there were a substantially lower murder rate in states and countries that have CP, the burden of proof would shift. It would then be encumbent on opponents of CP to explain why, appearances to the contrary, CP is not a better deterrent than other punishments for murder. It seems very likely that many of those who currently oppose CP on utilitarian grounds would abandon their opposition in the face of such hypothetical evidence. The evidentiary situation with regard to the connection between the ownership of firearms and the murder rate is, on the surface, more clear-cut than in the case of CP. When comparing the United States with most other developed countries, there is an astounding disparity with regard to both the handgun homicide rate and the handgun ownership rate. By parity of reasoning, then, it is fair to insist that opponents of a handgun ban abandon their view unless they can explain why their view is correct in spite of the evidence.

II. Responses to the Burden of Proof Challenge

To be fair to opponents of gun control, there is a substantial literature addressing the burden of proof challenge that I have issued. Defenders of private handgun ownership have written extensively on why, appearances notwithstanding, a ban on handguns will not reduce the homicide rate in the United States. This section will be devoted to the analysis of such defenses.

A. Comparisons with Other Countries

Since comparisons with the far lower murder rates in countries that have stricter handgun control were the main impetus for gun control, it is wise to start with this issue. The overall strategy of handgun supporters is to argue that the higher murder rate in the United States compared to other developed countries is attributable to factors other than the higher prevalence of handguns in the United States.[28] For example, Don Kates, one of the most prolific and articulate opponents of banning handguns, argues: "The determinants of violence are . . . fundamental economic, sociocultural, and institutional differences. . . . Since gun laws, by definition, do not focus on these kinds of fundamental determinants, their potential benefits can be no more than marginal."[29] Disappointingly, neither Kates nor any of the other contributors to his volume give any analysis of what exactly these "deeper" causes are and how one might hope to remedy them. Such vague hypotheses fail to meet the evidentiary burden of proof that I have placed on opponents of gun control.[30]

Other opponents of gun control try to show that international comparisons actually *weaken* the case for gun control. Though I could not obtain any handgun ownership statistics from the Swiss government, it is often claimed that the rate of gun ownership in Switzerland is higher than that in the United States.[31] This is alleged to disprove any causal connection between firearm ownership and homicide rates. However, there are two crucial differences between this country and the United States. First, the guns owned in Switzerland are primarily long guns.[32] Long guns are not the issue in this paper, which advocates a ban on handguns only. Second, all male citizens in Switzerland are required to retain the gun that they were given during their military service.[33] The context of their gun ownership is, then, mandatory service in a citizens' militia, with its attendant training and discipline, which bears no comparison with the minimally controlled private handgun ownership in the United States. In fact, this comparison was most ill-advised on the part of handgun supporters. The handgun homicide rate in Switzerland, though less than that in the United States, is almost four times higher than that in Sweden and is on average over ten times higher than that in Sweden and is on average over ten times higher than that in other countries with restrictive handgun laws (Australia, Canada, and Britain). The factors to which opponents of gun control appeal in order to explain the high rate of handgun homicide in the United States—e.g. extensive poverty, high unemployment, a minimal welfare system, and racial tension—cannot plausibly be asserted of Switzerland.[34] The United States' alleged high rate of firearms ownership remains the most plausible explanation of its comparatively high handgun homicide rate.

More importantly, it is not necessary for me to respond to these and other attempts to discredit my international comparison by reference to causes of crime that are unrelated to gun laws. I have already made clear that I do not deny that factors other than the prevalence of handguns may influence the rate of violent crime. It should be no surprise that these factors prevent a uniform correspondence in all countries between levels of gun ownership and violent crime. Advocating a ban on handguns is perfectly compatible with recognizing that a concerted attack on unemployment, homelessness, huge disparities in wealth and real opportunity, racial inequality, and other sources of injustice are of much greater importance in the attempt to reduce homicide and violence.

My central thesis is that *a* major cause of the high handgun homicide rate in the United States is its huge arsenal of privately owned guns, and a handgun ban would be the best way to reduce this arsenal. I have presented striking empirical data to support my causal hypothesis. The burden of proof that I have charged to opponents of gun control is certainly not met by pointing out the existence of some causes of murder and violent crime that are not addressed by gun control. In view of the fact that the deeper socio-economic causes of violent crime are very difficult to control, we need to address other causes that *are* amenable to control. The availability of firearms is one such factor that can be controlled by legislation. It is ironic that opponents of a handgun ban point out these deeper, more institutional causes of violence in the United States, as if they somehow show the pointlessness of remedial measures. On the contrary, they only serve to underline the need for strict handgun control measures.

Scepticism as to the value of international comparisons concerning gun control and gun related crime is even less plausible in light of a study done in 1988.[35] In order to isolate the key variable—the impact of gun control on violent crime in general and on firearm violence in particular—the authors studied two cities that are very similar in most other respects: Seattle and Vancouver, Canada.[36] The two cities have a similar population, geography, climate, level of schooling, unemployment rate, median annual household income, and cultural values.[37] Of particular interest, however, is the great similarity in their overall crime statistics. Vancouver had a very slightly higher burglary rate, and in other types of crime, Seattle had a slightly higher relative risk: robbery (1.09:1), simple assault (1.18:1), and aggravated assault (1.16:1).[38] With regard to the weapons used in aggravated assaults, both cities reported almost identical rates of assaults with knives, other dangerous weapons, and hands and feet.[39] These similarities are in precisely the same factors to which gun control opponents usually appeal in order to account for the higher rate of gun violence in the United States. At this point the similarities in crime patterns end. In the period studied, Seattle had 11.3 homicides per 100,000 person-years, whereas Vancouver had 6.9 per 100,000 person-years.[40] Consequently, the relative risk of being murdered in Seattle as compared to Vancouver was 1.63:1.[41] The relative risk of homicide excluding those committed with firearms was very similar (1.08:1), but the risk of being murdered with a firearm in Seattle as compared to Vancouver was 4.8:1.[42] Eighty-five percent of the firearms homicides in both cities were committed with handguns.[43] It will be difficult to deny that the almost fivefold difference in the frequency of homicides committed with firearms is responsible for the substantially higher homicide rate in Seattle.[44]

One marked difference between the two cities is that Vancouver, like all of Canada, has significantly stricter gun control laws.[45] The most important difference is that Vancouver does not allow concealed weapons and grants handgun permits for sporting and collecting purposes only.[46] Handguns may be transported by car only if they are stored in the trunk in a locked box.[47] In Seattle, concealed weapons are allowed with a permit.[48] This has resulted in a disparity in the rates of gun ownership in the two cities. In the 1984–88 period, the total number of handgun permits issued in Vancouver was 4137.[49] In the same time span, Seattle issued 15,289 concealed-weapons permits; in addition, no permit at all was needed for handguns kept at home.[50] An independent measure of gun ownership is provided by "Cook's gun prevalence index," which is based on surveys and the number of suicides, assaults, and homicides involving firearms in forty-nine cities in the United States. The index assigns a 41% gun ownership rate to Seattle, and only 12% to Vancouver.[51] To summarize, we have two cities which closely resemble each other in terms of sociology, population, economics, culture, and overall crime patterns, including non-homicidal violent crime. However, there is a noticeable disparity in their rates of homicide and a huge difference in their rates of gun-related homicide. The city with the lower homicide rates has far stricter gun control laws (especially for handguns, which were responsible for 85% of the firearms-related murders in both cities), and, not surprisingly, a far lower rate of gun ownership. The burden is on opponents of gun control to show why this study does not demonstrate the link between rates of gun ownership and homicide rates.

It is to the credit of opponents of gun control that they have taken on the challenge presented by the Seattle-Vancouver study. James Wright has criticized it on two main grounds. First, it fails to prove that guns are more widely available in Seattle than in Vancouver. Second, the difference in murder rate is attributable to racial factors, not to differences in gun laws.[52] To establish the first criticism, Wright points out that the study's reason for believing that there are more guns in Seattle than in Vancouver is based on the number of gun permits handed out in the two cities. He discounts these numbers on the ground that the cities have different permit regulations.[53] However, the very difference between permit regulations indicates that the figures vastly *under*-estimate the number of handguns in Seattle, since Seattle, unlike Vancouver, requires neither permits nor registration for handguns kept at home.

Wright's second main line of objection is based on a comparison of the homicide rates of Seattle and Vancouver by ethnic groups. While they have similar percentages of white residents (Seattle:79.2%, and Vancouver: 75.6%), the makeup of their non-white populations is very different. Vancouver is dominated by Asians (22.1%), whereas Seattle has a higher percentage of blacks (9.5–0.3%) and Hispanics (2.6–0.5%).[54] Revealingly, despite its overall substantially lower murder rate, Vancouver's annual homicide rate for its white non-hispanic population is slightly *higher* than Seattle's (6.4 to 6.2 per 100,000.)[55] If the alleged difference in gun ownership were the cause of the difference in overall murder rate, one would expect this effect to be reflected among all racial groups, whites included. Since the difference appears only among racial minorities, the evidence indicates racial differences, not differences in gun laws, as the cause of the difference in murder rates.

However, the existence of these racial variations does not invalidate the Seattle-Vancouver study. Its authors are perfectly well aware of these differences and suggest that the usual socio-economic disadvantages of these groups are part of the cause.[56] These disadvantages make members of racial minorities more likely to commit murders, and the vast majority of murders are committed by someone of the same ethnic group as the victim.[57] Their own statistics show that, with the exception of Asians in Vancouver, all non-white groups in both cities suffer from a higher murder rate than whites.[58] No one in the gun control movement ever claims that the availability of guns is the *only* cause of murder. The point is that it is *one* of the causes that exacerbates the other causes such as socio-economic deprivation. In support of this hypothesis is the fact that the non-white/white disparity in murder rate is much more pronounced in Seattle (5.78:1) than in Vancouver (3.63:1).[59] The difference in the white/non-white disparity is plausibly explained by the far greater prevalence of handguns in Seattle. It is among those elements of the population who, by virtue of disadvantages linked to race (discrimination, lack of economic opportunity, poverty, unemployment, and so forth), are more likely to kill that we should expect the homicide-increasing influence of handguns to be most pronounced. It is, as it were, "the straw that breaks the camel's back" in the case of violence-prone sectors of society.[60] It is less surprising that there is no perceptible influence of guns on white people who, statistically, are less prone to be murdered in the first place.[61] Moreover, Seattle and Vancouver are anomalous in this regard. Nationwide, "the homicide rate among whites alone is almost three times higher in the U.S. than in Canada."[62] The "racial differences" hypothesis is of no use in explaining this disparity.

It is worth noting that the burden of proof issue is again relevant with regard to the Seattle-Vancouver study. The study provides a documented correlation between gun availability and homicide rates, which is, furthermore, supported by a theory explaining why the easy availability of guns is a major cause of a high murder rate. The critics assert that the real cause of the difference in homicide rate may be unrelated to guns, and related instead to differences between the situation of non-white populations in the two cities. They do not specify exactly what these differences are, nor do they quantify these differences and provide empirical evidence to support their numbers. In any event, then, they have failed to provide serious reasons to doubt that the study provides strong support for banning handguns.

B. Inter-State and Inter-City Comparisons

Further support for gun control would be provided by statistics demonstrating higher gun-related homicides and other violent crime rates in those states with more permissive gun laws. However, it is widely agreed in the anti-control literature that the evidence fails to provide any such support.[63] In response, advocates of gun control suggest that the genuine deterrent effect of a state's strict gun control laws may be "masked" by the easy availability of guns in other states (especially adjacent ones) that have permissive gun laws, or none at all. Such guns can be easily "imported" from one state to another. What is called for, then, is a *national* gun control policy, not the abandonment of all gun control. Indeed, a plausible causal story would see it as no coincidence that states with strict gun control have high crime rates, since it is precisely in response to these high crime rates that gun control is more likely to be introduced in the first place. It is perverse to assume the contrary—namely, that gun control is itself the cause of increased crime.

However plausible such responses on behalf of gun control may be, Kates and Benenson dismiss them as the "adjacent state" excuse.[64] They argue that these responses do indeed sketch possible scenarios, but they fail to meet the burden of proof that falls on advocates of gun control. Given that they are proposing a restriction on liberty, and that violators of a handgun ban would be subject to severe punishment, it is encumbent on advocates of such a ban to prove that these burdens would be outweighed by even more substantial benefits. I accept this burden of proof as applicable to those who would restrict ownership of handguns. However, the starting point of this paper is precisely that handgun ban advocates have met this burden by producing statistics showing an overwhelming disparity in the murder rate between the United States and developed countries with far stricter gun controls. This, in combination with the powerful Seattle-Vancouver study, has, I argue, turned the burden of proof over to opponents of gun control. They must now respond to the immensely plausible argument that posits the easy availability of handguns as a major cause of violent crime.

To make the burden more onerous, and to further respond to the "adjacent state excuse" argument given by Kates and Benenson, I refer to the results of a May 1976 study done by the Bureau of Alcohol, Tobacco and Firearms.[65] The study traced the origin of all handguns seized by police in sixteen cities from July to December 1973, in order to determine the last retail dealer who sold the gun. Seizures would result from such causes as arrests for crimes in which the gun was used, other arrests resulting in the discovery of illegal gun possession, or from sting operations in which undercover police agents purchased guns from illegal dealers. The results strongly confirm the hypothesis that there is indeed a causal connection, which is hidden by an influx of out of state guns, between strict gun controls and the use of guns in crime. "The strength of firearm regulations or enforcement of those regulations in the differing project cities is directly proportional to the percentage of crime guns that were purchased in another State."[66]

The most striking results come from "Phase 1" of the study comparing Atlanta, Detroit, New York City, and New Orleans. Atlanta had no requirements to register and obtain licenses for handguns, and 81% of all the guns seized by the police were from Georgia.[67] (The only restriction in Atlanta was a ban on some "Saturday Night Specials.") The New Orleans Municipal Code, unlike Atlanta, does require handgun permits; but Louisiana does not, and 63% of the handguns seized in that city were from Louisiana.[68] In sharp contrast, both Detroit and New York City, and their states of Michigan and New York, have strict gun controls. Only 8% of the guns seized in Detroit were from Michigan,[69] and only 4% of the New York City guns were from New York State.[70] The conclusion that criminals in these two cities were deterred by strong gun controls, and they were forced to go out of state to get their handguns, is hard to resist. While gun controls operate only on the state or local level, they will constantly be undercut by the possibility of gun importation from states with more permissive gun laws. In order to prevent this, and to maximize the evident benefits of strict gun control laws, a nationwide gun control law is the obvious policy.[71]

There is always the danger, of course, that strict national gun controls will increase the number of handguns illegally imported into the United States. This is indeed a disturbing possibility, but it hardly justifies the abandonment of any attempt to control guns in the United States. An effective *reductio ad absurdum* of this argument can be made by considering a parallel argument which could be given against any attempt to control, for example, the manufacture of LSD, amphetamines, or barbiturates in this country. After all, it seems likely that any success we achieve would be accompanied by an increased demand for and supply of illegally imported drugs. This possibility would not be seriously entertained as a reason for giving up the fight against dangerous drugs made in the United States. What is called for is an assault on *both* domestic and imported drugs. In exactly the same way, attempts to control the handguns made and sold in this country in no way preclude a crackdown on illegal imports of firearms, by means of devoting more resources to detection, and of heavier penalties for those apprehended.[72]

C. Handguns, Criminals, and Law-Abiding Citizens

A more troubling argument, however, concerns the different impact that a handgun ban is likely to have on criminal and law-abiding citizens. It seems plausible to suggest that law-abiding citizens are more likely than criminals to voluntarily comply with gun control laws, including outright bans on handguns, which will require owners to turn in their guns to the police. Criminal gun-owners have already committed felonies or intend to use their guns for the commission of felonies in the future, and the fact that they are committing a further felony by keeping their guns will not force compliance with handgun control laws. Indeed, the penalty for possessing an illegal gun is likely to be minimal compared to penalties that criminals face should they be apprehended for the more serious crimes that they intend to commit with the help of their guns. The very fact that they have bought guns for this purpose indicates that they are *not* deterred by the heavier penalties for the felonies that they plan to commit. Furthermore, drying up legal access to handguns will effectively prevent normally law-abiding citizens from becoming new handgun owners. In contrast, criminals are likely to have access to illegal black market guns and will not hesitate to avail themselves of it. The very success of a handgun ban in reducing the existing "pool" of handguns will thus result in a higher percentage of them being owned by criminals.[73] The likely result of gun control, then, especially an outright ban on handguns, is to disarm the general population, while criminals remain just as heavily armed as they are today.[74] No matter how effective a gun ban is in reducing the number of handguns in circulation, "the number of potential misusers is so small that the number of firearms legally or illegally available to its members will always be ample for their needs, regardless of how restrictive gun laws are or how strenuously they are enforced."[75] In the light of these plausible projections, some people who oppose a handgun ban do support measures which are targeted at precisely those criminal elements who will be most resistant to bans on guns and are most likely to abuse their guns.[76] Kleck, for instance, supports a ban on gun ownership for those with prior criminal convictions, which would leave the law-abiding gun owner undisturbed.[77]

Underlying the effort to target gun control at those who have prior convictions is the belief that it is these people who are most likely to misuse firearms in the future, especially in the case of homicide. However, in the case of homicides, this belief is vigorously challenged by advocates of gun control. Murder, the argument goes, is not confined to the ranks of those with criminal records. It is an act of terrible violence of which we are all capable if sufficiently provoked. Only 21% of murders occur during the commission of another felony.[78] In at least 48.8% of 1990 homicides, the victim was either a relative or an acquaintance of the murderer.[79] In 1990, 34.5% of all murders resulted from domestic or other kinds of argument.[80] Since we are all capable of heated arguments, we are all, in the wrong circumstances, capable of losing control and killing our opponent. There, but for the grace of God, we all go. Given the ease with which homicide can be committed with a handgun as opposed to other more primitive methods (e.g. clubs or knives), the ease of availability of handguns may well be the factor which transforms a heated argument into a lethal attack. The simple option of running away—which is very seldom mentioned in the anti-gun control literature—will be available far more often in the case of these other kinds of attacks than in the case of a handgun attack. Gun control measures that are targeted solely at those with criminal records fail to protect us from the most likely source of handgun murder: ordinary citizens.

Such arguments are dismissed by Kleck and Bordua as "the myth of the noncriminal killer."[81] The fact that in most homicides the victim is known to the murderer does not prove that murder is in general a temporary aberration on the part of otherwise peaceful citizens. It merely reflects the fact that one is most likely to argue and fight with people one knows.[82] Criminals are just as likely to have relatives, friends, and acquaintances as law-abiding citizens. Evidence indicates that a disproportionate number of murders are committed by people with an arrest record. The number of convicted murderers with prior felony *convictions* is less impressive, but Kleck and Bordua's "conservative estimate" of 25% is still far more than one would expect given the presumably smaller percentage of the population with convictions.[83] "The myth of the noncriminal killer" is further weakened by a study in Kansas City of family homicides, a category one would expect to be unconnected with other criminal activity. In 90% of these cases, the police had been called to the same address at least once within the previous five years in response to domestic quarrels, and in 50% of the cases, police had been called in five or more times.[84] These statistics appear to indicate that gun control measures geared specifically at those with criminal records are necessary. Across the board bans would have at best a minimal impact on reducing the homicide rate, while restricting the freedom of huge numbers of peaceful gun owners.

How are we to evaluate these arguments? To begin with, the Kansas City study indicates a connection between family homicide and prior brushes with the law *short of* convictions. However, to deny someone access to handguns on the ground that she has been arrested (but not convicted), or that the police visited her house because of a domestic disturbance, may be unconstitutional in the light of the "equal protection" clause of the Fourteenth Amendment. A selective ban will have to focus on the 25% of convicted handgun murderers with prior felony records. This means, then, that the other 75%[85] will have the same access to handguns as they do today. Only a comprehensive ban would inhibit the access to handguns of this majority of handgun murderers. And, of course, since the ban will be comprehensive, it will include the 25% of potential handgun murderers who have been convicted for felonies. Thus my proposal *includes* the minor benefits of narrowly targeted gun control measures.

Another reason why a general ban is preferable to a targeted restriction is that, by virtue of reducing the overall "pool" of guns, it will reduce the real number of guns in the hands of criminals, even if it does increase the percentage of gun owners who are felons. The illegal means by which criminals would have to obtain guns—for instance buying them from unlicensed pawnbrokers, illegal transfers, buying them from friends who originally bought them legally, and outright theft—are all dependent on the presence of a substantial supply of legally purchased handguns on the market. My proposal would shrink this supply, and hence make it increasingly difficult for criminals to obtain handguns. It would also help to keep guns out of the hands of lawbreakers who have so far eluded conviction, and would hence qualify for gun ownership under a "targeted" ban. The "cost" of my proposal is that it does restrict many gun owners who never would have used their guns to commit homicide or any other crime. However, this price is more than justified by its far greater effectiveness than felons-only bans in reducing the number of murders, as it gradually and over the years reduces the number of handguns in circulation in the United States and chips away at the "gun culture" that encourages their use.

At this point it will be useful to delineate the differences between my view and other positions on gun control. I agree with all those groups that advocate stricter enforcement of laws against firearms crimes, and "sentence enhancement" to further punish firearms felons.[86] The fact that I advocate *any* gun control is enough to distinguish me from extreme opponents of handgun ownership restrictions. More importantly, I differ from both moderate opponents of gun control such as Kleck, and organizations such as Handgun Control, Inc., who are united in supporting handgun restrictions targeted at felons, such as the handgun control component of the Crime Bill debated by the Senate in July 1991.[87] I welcome such modest proposals as a step in the right direction. However, for the reasons explained above, I believe that only a *general* ban on handguns (with strictly limited exceptions) will effectively reduce handgun violence.

D. Substitution of Other Weapons for Handguns

Let us suppose for the sake of argument that a ban on handguns would indeed be effective in reducing the number of handgun murders and violent crime. In the pro-gun literature it is widely denied that this would result in an *overall* reduction in murder and violence, for the simple reason that would-be criminals will substitute other weapons for handguns. Let us first consider the effect of such substitution on robberies.

Let us suppose that robbers turn to knives, clubs, other instruments, and their hands and feet to threaten and perhaps injure their victims. This is exactly what gun control advocates want, since these weapons are far less lethal than handguns.[88] While it is true that stabbings and beatings are horribly lethal in their own right, a crucial difference is that running away will at least sometimes be an option for the victim, whereas this tactic will be of little use in the face of a loaded gun. A reduction in robberies and in their degree of violence is a likely result of such a substitution.

Hardy and Kates deny this conclusion. The destructive power of handguns makes them particularly effective in intimidating robbery victims into handing over their belongings or cash. As a result, robbers with guns only use their weapons to injure their victims in 17% of robberies, and can usually rely on threats alone. In contrast, robbers with knives injure 32% of their victims, and those using clubs and other weapons injure fifty-three percent of their victims.[89] In the case of blunt instruments, a blow is sometimes used to *initiate* the crime. Another likely consequence of the substitution of non-firearm weapons is, ironically, that there will be more robberies and hence more attendant violence. This follows for the simple reason that handgun robberies are the most efficient. In order to reap the same profits using other weapons, several robberies will be needed.[90] If gun control leads to an increase in number of robberies and injuries, one of its main purposes is clearly defeated.

However, it is strange logic indeed that would welcome the use of more lethal weapons on the ground that they will reduce the incidence and violence of robberies. This view leads to absurd consequences. If the reduction of the number of robberies is regarded as the *summum bonum,* then we should distribute not just handguns but assault-style automatic weapons to criminals, who will be able to use them to become rich by means of rare, but highly efficient and relatively bloodless heists.

Opponents of a handgun ban are on firmer ground when they discuss the danger that robbers, assaulters, and other criminals will "upgrade" to *long guns* in the event of a ban on handguns. According to Kates and Benenson, "at a minimum, a shot fired from a long gun is four times as likely to kill as one fired from a handgun."[91] Widespread substitution of long guns for handguns in the commission of crimes would dramatically increase the number of homicides and violent crimes. They calculate that if only 30% of those who attempt homicide were to switch from handguns to long guns, while the other 70% "downgrade" to knives, there would still be a "substantial increase" in homicide. If the ratio were instead 50:50, the number of homicides would double, even if none of those who used knives succeeded in killing their victims.[92] Kleck asserts that an even higher substitution rate is likely. He quotes a survey by Wright and Rossi, in which prisoners who had committed several crimes with guns were asked whether they would carry a sawed-off shotgun (which would be much easier to conceal than a regular shotgun) if they were denied access to handguns. Seventy-two percent said they would, and Kleck feels justified in concluding that such a rate of long gun substitution would in fact occur.[93]

One has to doubt the reliability of the statements of prisoners as to what firearms they *would* carry in certain circumstances. Macho bragging and outright lying are very likely in such situations, and relegate Kleck's projections to the status of unsupported conjecture. In view of the fact that such a small percentage of the actual murders in the United States in 1990 were committed with long guns,[94] the burden on Kleck to prove his hypothetical speculation is even heavier. As for Kates and Benenson, their projections are based on the unsupported assertion that the 70% of handgun killers who do not turn to long guns would instead use knives, the most lethal weapon other than firearms. It is more probable that at least some potential murderers would turn to less lethal weapons or their bare hands, and that some would be deterred from assaults altogether. Since Kates and Benenson ignore these probable scenarios, and since their substitution predictions are in any case purely speculative, it is safe to conclude that their estimate of the increase in the homicide rate in the event of a handgun-only ban is inflated. The conjectures offered in support of the substitution hypothesis are inadequate and fail to meet the burden of proof encumbent on opponents of my proposal.

Another reason to doubt that long guns would be used in great numbers to replace handguns in robberies, assaults, and homicides is that long guns are obviously much more difficult to conceal. A potential mugger roaming the streets wielding a long gun will cause everyone in sight to flee, and is likely to be quickly arrested when alarmed people call the police. Similarly, a bank robber carrying a long gun will be immediately detected by security guards, alarm systems will be triggered, and the chances of a successful robbery greatly diminished. Handguns are obviously much more convenient for the commission of such crimes. Kates and Benenson point out that most homicides occur in the home, where concealability is "irrelevant."[95] However, concealability would seem to be an important factor even in the home. Since the victim may well be unaware that the killer is carrying a concealed weapon, the "surprise factor" which is peculiar to handguns can still apply even in the home. In contrast, people can hardly be unaware that the person they are with is carrying a shotgun or rifle. Moreover, in *any* argument or domestic quarrel, regardless of whether the potential victim knows that the assaulter is carrying a handgun, the ease of pulling out the gun and shooting makes such arguments more likely to spill over into murder. In contrast, by the time the assaulter has gone into another room to retrieve their long gun and loaded it, the potential victim has crucial seconds in which to escape.

Another reason that the concealability of handguns is not a good reason for a handgun-only ban is proposed by Hardy and Kates in their discussion of the impact of handgun control on robberies. They point out that "[t]he difference between a long gun and a handgun is ten minutes and a hacksaw."[96] Even robberies, then, would not be diminished by a handgun ban. However, this contention runs directly counter to the evidence collected by the Bureau of Alcohol, Tobacco and Firearms' *Project Identification*.

> Seventy-one percent, or 7,538, of the handguns submitted for tracing, had a barrel length of 3 inches or less. Sixty-one percent, or 6,476, had a caliber of .32 or less. Since both of these factors relate to the size of the weapon, these figures indicate that concealability is an overriding factor in selecting a handgun for use in crime.[97]

Sawed-off shotguns will be much longer and much bulkier than any of these short and small-caliber handguns, especially "Saturday Night Specials," which combine a caliber of .32 or less with a barrel length of three inches or less, comprised 44% of all the weapons successfully traced, and fit into the palm of an average sized hand. We may conclude, then, that because of the difficulty of concealment, neither long guns nor sawed-off versions of the same are likely to be used in great numbers to replace handguns in the commission of crimes. The difficulty of concealment factor will outweigh the greater lethalness of long gun shots. Consequently, a ban on handguns will indeed result in a decrease in firearms-related homicide and other violent crimes. Since firearms are the most lethal weapons, and they were used in 64.1% of homicides in the United States in 1990,[98] such a ban is, therefore, likely to result in a reduction in the overall murder rate.[99]

E. Defensive Uses of Handguns

1. General Crime Reduction

The anti-ban literature which I have so far discussed tries to show that permissive handgun laws do not increase homicide and violent crime. I have argued that these arguments fail. Opponents of a handgun ban are at their strongest, however, when they discuss alleged positive benefits of handgun ownership. They focus, in particular, on the value of guns in self-defense, and in defending property against robbery and theft. Any benefits of my proposal in reducing crime would have to be weighed against the reduction in defensive uses of handguns that would presumably result from a handgun ban.[100] These arguments are based on common sense observations about the likely effectiveness of handguns (as opposed to other weapons, or no weapons at all) in self-defense, and the deterrent effect that this is likely to have on potential assaulters, robbers, and burglars. Situations in which guns would be useful would be assaults and robbery attempts on the street, as well as assault and burglary attempts in the home. This deterrence is over and above any deterrence that may be exerted by the fear of apprehension and arrest by the police.

An often-quoted study intended to establish this deterrent effect was done by Wright and Rossi.[101] They interviewed over 1800 prisoners in ten States concerning their attitude toward the possibility of armed victims. 34% said that they had been "scared off, shot at, wounded, or captured by an armed victim"; another 34% said that they were concerned that they might be shot by their victim (interestingly, the same percentage feared being shot by the police); 57% said that "most criminals are more worried about meeting an armed victim than they are about running into the police"; and 59% agreed that "a store owner who is known to keep a gun on the premises is not going to get robbed very often."[102] While no one would deny that firearms do have a deterrent effect on potential felons, the reliability of a survey conducted among felons is very dubious. Referring to a similar survey done by Wright and Rossi, a *supporter* of the defensive use of firearms pointed out

> the difficulties in relying on surveys of convicted criminals (who, as a group, are remarkable neither for honesty nor acute introspection). Then there are the difficulties in extrapolating from their answers to the attitudes of fellow criminals who, perhaps because of distinguishing characteristics such as greater shrewdness, have not been caught.[103]

Another widely-quoted study was performed by Gary Kleck.[104] Based on six surveys, he estimates that handguns are used 645,000 times per year in defensive response to crimes or attempted crimes. This allegedly compares with 580,000 "criminal misuses" of handguns per year.[105] Moreover, he estimates that "gun wielding civilians in self-defense or some other legally justified cause" kill between 1,527 and 2,819 felons in 1980.[106] To be fair, Kleck does stress that the most common defensive use of handguns is achieved without firing a shot. Merely waving a gun at the aggressor or intruder is often enough to scare him off. Moreover, he envisages a generalized deterrent effect of handguns, whereby the well-known, widespread ownership of guns makes a criminal hesitate before committing *any* assault, robbery, or burglary, for fear of retaliation.

Kleck's estimate of the number of self-defensive uses of guns is a projection based on surveys, and is subject to a serious criticism. The respondents were gun owners who have a vested interest in exaggerating both the need for self-defense, and the effectiveness of their guns in providing it. What gun owner, for instance, is going to admit that he fired his gun at a false alarm, or that he used more force than necessary in repelling an intruder who turned out to be harmless? Such nuances are likely to be left out of responses to surveys, and the incidents in question will be recorded as successful defenses of self and property. Even more likely than deliberate dishonesty among respondents to surveys is self-deception and outright error concerning the need to use a gun in self-defense. A chilling example of this trigger-happy attitude is provided by an incident involving Bernard Goetz *before* he achieved notoriety as the "subway vigilante." At 8 p.m. one evening he was asked for money by "a crazy kid on drugs" who was walking behind him on Sixth Avenue. Even though he admits that there were many other ways to deal with the situation, Goetz pulled his gun on the youth.[107] In apparent support of his advocacy of the defensive efficacy of handguns, Kleck cites the infamous subway shootings of 1984, by referring to the sharp decrease in subway crime which followed them.[108] Not only must unjustifiable uses of firearms, when less force would have been sufficient to escape the real or perceived danger, be subtracted from the benefits that Kleck claims for the defensive use of guns; they must be added to the long list of *bad* consequences of handgun ownership around which this paper is based.

Kleck's estimate of 1,527 to 2,819 self-defensive killings in 1980 is based on his claim that the official number of justifiable gun homicides by civilians reported to the FBI (379) vastly underestimates the real number. His projection is based on an extrapolation from data from Detroit and Miami. One assumes that the vast majority of these justifiable homicides were responses to the threat of murder. Let us generously assume that all 2,819 of Kleck's self-defensive killings did indeed prevent killings. In the same year, there were at least 13,650 murders with firearms.[109] Kleck has failed to prove that the self-defensive use of firearms outweighs their abuse in homicide.

The most impressive evidence quoted by Kleck consists of statistics indicating that resisting robbery and assault with firearms is the best way to minimize the chances of being injured or robbed. Only 30.9% of robberies are completed against armed victims, of whom only 17.4% are injured; and only 12.1% of armed victims are injured in assaults. Interestingly, the next best strategy is non-resistance. While 88.5% of robberies are completed against them, only 24.7% of non-resistors are injured; and only 27.3% of non-resistors are injured in assaults.[110] Armed victims, then, appear to be less likely to be robbed or injured than nonresistors. However, it must be remembered that Kleck's source is another survey, this time of victims of attempted assaults and robberies, and that, as pointed out above, gun owners are likely to exaggerate the defensive value of their weapons.

More generally, a substantial number of the crimes of the kind that Kleck alleges are prevented by the defensive use of firearms are themselves committed with guns (64.1% of homicides, 36.6% of robberies, and 23.1% of aggravated assaults.)[111] Even if Kleck is right that a ban on handguns would reduce people's ability to defend themselves, it would also reduce the *need* for self-defense in the first place. A heavily-armed citizenry might be a rational response if heavily-armed criminals were inevitable; but far more rational would be a society that strives to disarm *all* private citizens, thus obviating the need to use firearms in self-defense.

The reasoning that seeks safety in the profileration of privately owned firearms is precisely the rationale that supported nuclear proliferation under the strategy of mutual assured destruction (MAD). This policy rested the survival of the human race on the hope that mutual fear of retaliation would prevent a first strike. It has been heavily criticized on the ground that an unspeakable catastrophe could follow an accidental firing of a nuclear missile, or a deliberate attack by a fanatical nation that did not care about retaliation. These criticisms parallel those that I have leveled at the argument for handguns as self-defense, with the difference that lethal accidents with and aggressive abuse of handguns are an everyday reality, rather than a feared possibility. A further parallel is that the high rate of handgun ownership in this country is self-perpetuating. First, it is *in response* to the proliferation of handguns that an increasing number of people believe they need to buy a handgun for self-defense (though, as I have argued, it is an illusion that more widespread ownership of guns will decrease gun crime). Second, while some potential criminals may be deterred by a heavily-armed citizenry, others will arm themselves with more and more powerful firearms in order to outgun resisters. Trading gunfire or playing chicken with increasingly heavily-armed criminals is a tenuous basis for the defense of society.

A study by Arthur Kellermann and Donald Reay undercuts the central factual claim made by Kleck in his study.[112] Unlike Kleck's projections, this study is based on an analysis of the *actual* homicide figures for King's County, Washington (population 1,270,000) from 1978 to 1983. Kellermann and Reay focused on the 398 shooting deaths that occurred in the residence where the lethal firearm was kept. Thus their study gives a useful measure of the value of handguns (which comprised over 70% of the firearms involved) as defensive weapons when kept in the home. The authors conclude somewhat misleadingly that there were "53 suicides, criminal homicides, or accidental gunshot deaths involving a gun kept in the home for every case of homicide for self-protection."[113] They achieve this startling 53:1 by confining their attention to only "self-protection homicide." When other kinds of defensive homicide are also considered, the ratio between suicides, criminal homicides, and accidental deaths and, on the other hand, defensive killings, becomes 21:1.

As Kellermann and Reay themselves note, the defensive efficacy of guns is not exhausted by the number of people killed in this way. As noted above, people with guns are most successful when they frighten off the would-be criminal before he even attempts a crime; and the study measures only defensive homicides, not defensive uses of firearms which prevented crimes by causing nonlethal injuries or by causing the criminal to flee. They also recognize the limitations of a study which focuses on just one county, which might turn out to be a freakish, unrepresentative case.

Another qualification which is in order is to point out the key role played by suicides in producing the outlandish ratio quoted in the study.[114] Suicide rates throughout the world are far higher than homicide rates, and it would be unfair to lay the blame for these deaths at the doorstep of handguns. The suicide rate in many countries with stricter handgun control than the United States is higher than that in the United States.[115] Nonetheless, Kellermann and Reay are justified in asserting "given the high case-fatality rate associated with suicide attempts involving firearms, it seems likely that easy access to guns increases the probability that an impulsive suicide attempt will end in death."[116] A more pertinent comparison which can be drawn from their evidence about firearms deaths is that alongside the eighteen defensive homicides that occurred in King County during the six year period, there were fifty-three criminal homicides and accidental deaths. Instead of Kellermann and Reay's ratio of 53:1, we have one of 2.94 criminal homicides and accidental deaths for every defensive homicide resulting from firearms. It must be remembered, moreover, that any number of these defensive homicides may themselves have been precipitated by the *offensive* use of firearms.

The value of their study is to provide concrete evidence, based on actual gunshot wounds, of the startling disparity between the *proven* lethal abuses of firearms and the proven defensive uses. It does not preclude the kind of defensive efficacy of handguns asserted by Kleck, and indeed it is hard to deny that the threat of deadly retaliation will sometimes be a powerful deterrent to crime. However, it certainly puts the burden of proof on him to produce more evidence, beyond his projections from statistics and extrapolations based on surveys, that the positive effects of permissive handgun laws outweigh the negative effects demonstrated by the study. Kleck himself claims only that the evidence he adduces is "compatible with" his hypothesis.[117] A major theme of this paper, reinforced by Kellerman's and Reay's study, is that the onus is on defenders of handguns to show that their thesis is in fact true, not that it *may* be true. In the meantime, it is fair to conclude that Kellermann and Reay provide strong reason to doubt whether the defensive value of handguns kept in the home outweighs their dangers.

It cannot be denied that owning handguns may make people *feel* secure in their homes and on the streets. However, if my arguments in this section are sound, this feeling is illusory, and an illusory feeling of security cannot seriously be advanced as more important than a substantial reduction in murder and violent crime.

Taking handguns from law-abiding citizens does not deprive them of many methods of self-defense. They still have the option of escaping or calling for help, using weapons other than handguns, using their bare hands, reasoning with the criminal, or simply not resisting (which, as I pointed out above, is the next best way to avoid being injured.) It is possible that in some cases a victim would have been able to avoid theft, injury, or even death had she been armed with a handgun. This "cost" of my proposal needs to be weighed against the likely negative results of the defensive use of handguns described above: unnecessary and excessive use of handguns in self-defense; and the deaths shown by Kellermann and Reay to result from the abuse of handguns in the home.

An even more important set of objections to the defensive use of handguns is beyond the scope of the largely utilitarian argument of this paper. Can allowing private citizens to effectively become both the arbiter of law and the administrator of justice be reconciled with the rule of law in a civilized society? Don Kates traces a long history of private law enforcement in both Britain and the United States,[118] and Bruce Benson argues for its effectiveness.[119] However, neither of them consider the serious moral issues concerning the extent to which force may *justifiably* be used defensively, and the propriety of allowing private citizens to act as law enforcers.

It should be remembered that these drawbacks pertain to the defensive use of handguns, which is put forward by opponents of a handgun ban as one of the strongest reasons *for* allowing private citizens to own handguns. Elsewhere in my paper I have detailed the many other reasons for banning handguns. This section has given little reason to believe that any lives saved through the defensive use of handguns would outweigh the reduction in the current annual handgun murder toll of 9,923, and in the number of handgun assaults and robberies, that would be effected by a handgun ban.

2. *Handguns and Violence against Women*

The case for self-defensive ownership becomes stronger, however, in the context of violent crimes against women.[120] Guns take on special significance in the case of crimes committed by men against women because they enable women to compensate for the greater physical strength of men.[121] A woman armed with a handgun will be able to repel an attack by a much stronger male, unless he too is carrying a firearm. As was claimed in the previous section on self-defense in general, the value of handgun possession by women is not to be measured in terms of the number of assailants whom they kill, wound, or repel by shooting at them. Instead it manifests itself in the deterrent effect produced by the knowledge that a particular woman owns a gun, and the general deterrence created by widespread female ownership of handguns. Both kinds of deterrence would minimize the number of women who have to actually use their guns. Silver and Kates approvingly cite the slogan, "God didn't make men and women equal, Colonel Colt did."[122] While one may want to avoid basing women's moral equality on their possession of lethal firepower, anything which offers even *prima facie* promise of reducing violence against women deserves serious consideration.

Unless it was clear that she could have escaped without killing the assailant, the use of lethal force by a woman in order to protect herself from murder, rape or aggravated assault will rarely be criticized. The apparent inability of the police to protect women from threats of violence is illustrated by graphic cases in which police have insisted that they cannot arrest an assailant unless he has actually initiated aggression, thus strengthening the case for private self-protection.[123] The fact that women are responsible for such a small percentage of violent crime[124] indicates that the protection afforded women by handguns is unlikely to be accompanied by an increase in handgun crime.

A major theme of this paper has been that the benefits of self-defense from handguns are in general outweighed by the danger of handgun abuse. Since the vast majority of handgun abuse is by men, a suggested policy is a ban on male handgun ownership, while allowing women with a proven need for self-protection to own handguns. (In light of the high rate of violence against women, perhaps *all* women have this proven need.) However, such a sex-based ban would not be feasible. First, men could easily solicit women to "buy for" them. Second, a policy that discriminates against males would be subject to constitutional challenge. It appears, then, that the only way to allow women the defensive benefits of handguns is to make handguns available to both women and men.

The case for female ownership of handguns is highlighted by an examination of spousal homicide. From 1977 until 1984, just over one half of spousal homicides were committed by husbands,[125] and this number had increased to 70.6% by 1991.[126] More important, a significant proportion of wife-husband homicides are committed by abused wives who are defending themselves or their children.[127] More widespread ownership of handguns appears likely to reduce the number of wives killed by their husbands. While it would be preferable for women to protect themselves without killing their husbands, there can be little objection to their doing so if this is the only way for them to save their own lives. To eliminate handguns altogether may reduce the number of wife-husband killings, but it "would only change the sex of the decedents by ensuring that, in virtually every case, it would be the abused wife, not the murderous husband" who died.[128] Other things being equal, it seems fair that the aggressive husband, and not the victimized wife, be the one to forfeit his life. While it is true that a woman's handgun will be of less defensive value against an armed assailant, the fact is that women's assailants rarely use firearms.

> In 89.6% of the violent crimes directed against women during the 10 years of 1973–82, the offender did not have a gun; only ten percent of rapists used guns and only twenty-five percent of nonstrangers who attacked victims (whether male or female) had any weapon whatever.[129]

After an extensive study of the "spouse abuse literature", Howard concedes that reducing ownership of firearms may actually decrease spousal homicide:

> To the extent it is a crime of passion, spousal homicide should respond to enforced legislation banning all guns . . . If a [handgun only] ban removed handguns from the reach of angry husbands and wives, many of these individuals would simply grasp the most conveniently available alternative weapon, as the data on spousal homicide suggests they are already doing. The substituted weapon would probably be a knife and increased use of knives might decrease the number of fatalities, given the lower lethality of knives as compared with guns.[130]

However, Howard recommends "increasing the options available to battered wives" (e.g. tougher laws against spouse abuse, more shelters for victims of domestic violence) as a better method of protecting women than gun control. She advocates attacking the psychological roots of violence against women, instead of focussing on handguns, which are simply one of the exacerbating factors. Because of the argument that physically weaker women need handguns to protect themselves against whatever violence would still occur, she opposes a handgun ban.

The case for allowing women to own handguns, then, hinges on their role as an "equalizer" to compensate for men's superior strength. I do not dispute that they are sometimes *sufficient* for doing so. My point is that they are not *necessary*, since there are alternative ways to protect women.[131] With regard to current or former husbands or boyfriends who threaten violence, restraining orders and police protection *can* make a difference, though the latter will require substantial public funding. Changing locks, and installing secure doors and burglar alarms can make homes more secure. Martial arts and other forms of unarmed self-defense can be highly effective against an assailant without a firearm, yet these options are dismissed summarily by Silver and Kates, on the grounds that guns are (1) "less arduous," and (2) more effective.[132]

Few would dispute that guns are more effective; but if unarmed self-defense is *sufficiently* effective in warding off attacks, using a more lethal method of defense would be gratuitous violence. Nor need we confine our attention to unarmed resistance. Mace is a very effective weapon which can be used to immobilize an assailant, without causing serious injury. It also has the advantages of being even easier to conceal and use than a handgun, and of being far less likely than handguns to be used in the commission of crimes. Being neither lethal nor capable of causing permanent injuries, it will be less effective in intimidating victims into submission. Against the 10% or so of women's assailants who do carry firearms, mace would be less effective, but it has to be realized that handguns are also of less use against an assailant with firearms. Moreover, my proposed handgun ban would make it less likely that he would be armed in the first place. In contrast, a likely result of women carrying handguns is the same proliferation described in the previous section: more of their assailants would carry guns, in order to ensure the success of their attack.

Let us concede for the sake of argument that the combination of all of the alternative methods of self-defense that I have proposed would still be marginally less effective than handguns in protecting women against violence in the 10% or so of assaults that involve firearms. The inference to the conclusion that a handgun ban would decrease protection for women results from a comparison between a world in which handguns are banned, and an imaginary world in which most women arm themselves with handguns. In the actual world women may now legally own handguns, but the vast majority choose *not* to do so.

The relevant comparison is between the actual world, in which handguns are used in hundreds of thousands of violent crimes every year, yet in which few women own handguns; and, on the other hand, a world in which a handgun ban substantially reduced the number of handguns owned by both women and their potential assaulters. Whatever protection would be lost by disarming the small number of women who currently own handguns is outweighed by the reduction in violence against women that would be effected by a handgun ban, which would take one of the most potent weapons out of the hands of many potential assaulters.

It is true that 50% of those who own guns solely for defense are female.[133] However, far more men than women own guns.[134] Given women's extra vulnerability, and the fact that there are now many more female-headed households than in the mid-sixties, one would expect more women to own guns. In fact, a Harris poll showed that gun ownership in female-headed households was less than a half of that in homes in which an adult male lived.[135] The indications are that women themselves, whatever their extra vulnerability may be, are generally unconvinced of the need to own handguns for self-defense.

The alleged protection for women resulting from the defensive ownership of handguns, then, fails to provide a serious objection to a handgun ban. In contrast, throughout my paper I have detailed the substantial reduction in murder and violent crime that is likely to result from a handgun ban. Women, too, are the beneficiaries in a society in which far fewer of their loved ones are killed and maimed.

V. Conclusion

After a detailed analysis of the literature that opposes a handgun ban, I have shown that none of these arguments seriously respond to the "burden of proof" challenge which I present in section IC. I have established a strong *prima facie* case for my hypothesis, justifying at least an *experimental* handgun ban, for, say, twenty-five years.[136]

If my hypothesis is wrong, a minor restriction on people's behavior will have been needlessly imposed, and whatever self-defense handguns may have provided will have been lost. This loss is minimal in comparison with the many *harmful* uses of handguns which, if I am correct, would be prevented by a handgun ban. Consequently, even assuming that there is only a 50% chance that my hypothesis is true (though I have argued that the probability is far higher), a handgun ban is justified on the ground of its greater expected utility.

I have not addressed what may be considered the strongest objection to a handgun ban: the Second Amendment, and its guarantee of the right to bear arms. What I *have* shown is that there is a strong utilitarian case for banning handguns, and that the constitutionality of such a ban therefore merits careful consideration.[137]

NOTES

1. *See, e.g.*, Don B. Kates, Jr., "Handgun Prohibition and the Original Meaning of the Second Amendment," 82 *Mich. L. Rev.* 204–73 (1983); Sanford Levinson, "The Embarrassing Second Amendment," 99 *Yale L.J.* 637–59 (1989–90); Wendy Brown, "Guns, Cowboys, Philadelphia Mayors, and Civic Republicanism: On Sanford Levinson's 'The Embarrassing Second Amendment', *id.* at 661–67.
2. *Federal Bureau of Investigation, Uniform Crime Reports 12* (1990). The actual number of handgun murders is higher, since 9,923 is the number that emerged from an analysis of just 85.5% of the total murders.
3. *Id.* at 21.
4. *Id.* at 24.
5. *Id.* at 12; Franklin E. Zimring & Gordon Hawkins, *The Citizen's Guide to Gun Control 38* (1987).
6. The danger that long guns will be substituted for handguns in the event of a handgun ban will be discussed *infra.* section II.D.
7. In Canada, handgun owners are allowed to keep their weapons at home, and then transport them to shooting ranges only in a locked box. "Criminal Code of Canada, Firearms and Other Offensive Weapons," *Martin's Criminal Code of Canada,* § 81–016.9 (1982). Because of the far greater rate of handgun violence in the United States (*see infra* text at 248 for comparative handgun homicide rates), target shooters must not be allowed to keep handguns at home in this country.
8. James J. Jacobs, "Exceptions to a General Prohibition on Handgun Possession: Do They Swallow Up the Rule?," in *Law and Contemporary Problems 49,* (Don B. Kates, Jr. ed., 1986).
9. *Id.* at 7–13.
10. *Id.* at 7.
11. *Id.* at 18.
12. *Id.* at 6.
13. Jacobs, *supra* note 8, at 33.
14. *Id.* at 14–22. His arguments are, incidentally, very damaging to those who oppose a handgun ban. If even the police can do their job without the use of guns, then the claim of the average citizen to need a handgun for self-defense is greatly weakened.
15. A tragic instance involved a store owner who shot and killed a 13 year-old intruder whom he had already immobilized by hitting him on the head. See "Owner Charged in Slaying at Store," *Detroit Free Press,* Sept. 2, 1991, at A1.
16. *The New Encyclopedia Britannica* (1990); except for Australia's figure, which was supplied by the Australian Institute of Criminology. Correspondence from Dr. J.M. Herlihy, Australian Institute of Criminology (Nov. 25, 1991).
17. A press release from the Bureau of Alcohol, Tobacco and Firearms, May 22, 1991, estimates the number of handguns either privately owned or else "available for sale" at 66,666,000. Gary Kleck, a supporter of private handgun ownership, estimates that by 1978 there were 47 million privately owned handguns. Gary Kleck, "Guns and Self-Defense: Crime Control Through the Use of Force in the Private Sector," in *Social Problems* 35:1, 4 (Feb. 1988). Since the data for other countries that I use concerns not handguns available for sale, but those actually privately owned, taking the average of these numbers seems a reasonable compromise, which if anything *under*estimates the number of handguns actually owned by now.

18. The Office of Information Services and International Relations of the Israeli Police Department reports that in 1990 there were 171,448 licensed handguns owned by civilians in Israel. Correspondence from Naomi Shapira, Information Services of International Relations (Dec. 15, 1991). Since all of the other estimates in my table refer to the *total* number of handguns, legal and illegal, (a figure that the Israeli Police Department was unable to supply), the number which I have quoted for Israel is almost certainly an under estimate.
19. The Swedish Central Police Agency (Rikspolisstyrelsen) estimates that there are 2.5 million firearms owned by civilians in Switzerland. Correspondence from Staffan Thunqvist, National Swedish Police Board (Nov. 25, 1992). I arrived at my estimate of the number of handguns by dividing this number by 8.11, which is the average ratio of total firearms to handguns in the countries for which I have this information (Australia, Canada, Great Britain, and the United States).
20. A Canadian Justice Department study estimates that there are 5.9 million privately owned firearms in Canada. See generally Angus Reid Group, Inc., *Firearms Ownership in Canada* 4 (1991). Of this number, the Justice Department estimated that 440,000 were handguns. James Hayes, the Coordinator of the Canadian Department of Justice Firearms Control Task Group, now estimates the number of handguns at 750,000. Telephone Interview with James Hayes, Canadian Justice Department (Feb. 22, 1993). I have used the mid-point of these two estimates of the number of handguns in Canada.
21. In 1987 the Australian Institute of Criminology estimated that there were at least 3.5 million guns of all kinds in Australia, legal and illegal. To estimate what number of these guns are handguns, I refer to the results of an International Crime Victims Survey (1990), which included Australia. It found that 20.7% of Australian households own a gun of some kind, while 1.6% own a handgun. Thus 7.72% of gun-owning households own handguns. *See Duncan Chappell, A National Gun Control Strategy: The Recommendations of the National Committee on Violence, Address Before the Australian Crime Prevention Council National Conference, Wollongong (Sept. 4, 1991).*

    An independent measure of the total firearms to handguns ratio can be obtained by comparing the number of licensed handguns and long guns in the four states/territories for which these numbers are available from the Australian Institute of Criminology (Victoria, South Australia, Tasmania, and Northern Territory). Handguns on average comprise 7.36% of the licensed firearms in these jurisdictions. See Anita Scandia, "Numbers of Licensed Firearms and Shooters by State and Territory," Australian Institute of Criminology document (Aug. 29, 1991). My estimate of the total number of handguns privately owned in Australia is obtained by applying the mean of these two very similar, but independently derived measures (7.54% of all firearms are handguns) to the estimated total of 3.5 million firearms.
22. Michael Black reports that there are 160,000 licensed holders of "firearms" (handguns) in Britain. "Gun Law in Britain: How Hard Is It to Buy a Gun?" *Illustrated London News*, Aug. 1988 at 24. He cites estimates that the actual number of handguns "in legitimate circulation" is three times higher, (i.e. 480,000.)
23. For details on handgun and other firearms laws in other countries, see *Law Library of Congress, Firearms Regulations in Various Foreign Countries* (1990).
24. The historical interest in gun ownership in the United States is evidenced by the Second Amendment's guarantee of the right to bear arms. Further evidence of the high demand for handguns is provided by current ownership rates.
25. This elementary point is persistently ignored by the Tobacco Institute. The institute still uses thought experiments to deny that smoking tobacco causes lung cancer despite the overwhelming evidence in favor of this hypothesis. A causal hypothesis is not refuted by showing that it is not logically true, which is a condition that *no* informative hypothesis can meet.
26. *See* Ernest van der Haag, "On Deterrence and the Death Penalty," 60 *Journal of Criminal Law, Criminology, and Political Science* (1969), reprinted in "Raziel Abelson & Marie-Louise Friquegnon, Ethics for Modern Life" 208 (1982).
27. For a discussion of this argument, *see* David Conway, "Capital Punishment and Deterrence: Some Considerations in Dialogue Form," 3 *Philosophy and Public Affairs* (1974), reprinted in "John Arthur and William H. Shaw," *Readings in Philosophy of Law* 258–59 (1984).
28. This strategy is the same as that used by capital punishment advocates in order to

explain the recalcitrant evidence. *See supra* text section I.D.

29. *Firearms and Violence: Issues of Public Policy* 529 (Don B. Kates, Jr. ed., 1984).
30. An exception is Gary Kleck, who devotes one and one-fourth pages to advocating renewed emphasis on social programs such as the Job Corps. Kleck claims such measures help address some of the underlying causes of crime. *See* Gary Kleck, "Policy Lessons From Recent Gun Control Research," in *Law and Contemporary Problems* 49, 61–62 (Don B. Kates, Jr. ed., 1986).
31. See *Restricting Handguns: The Liberal Skeptics Speak Out* 31–32 (Don B. Kates, Jr. ed., 1979); Bruce L. Benson, "Guns for Protection and Other Private Sector Responses to the Fear of Rising Crime," in *Firearms and Violence: Issues of Public Policy* 351–52 (Don B. Kates, Jr. ed., 1984).
32. See Zimring and Hawkins, *supra* note 5 at 8–9.
33. See *Restricting Handguns: The Liberal Skeptics Speak Out* 38 (Don B. Kates, Jr. ed., 1979).
34. *26 Encyclopedia Americana* 148 (1991).
35. John Henry Sloan, Arthur L. Kellermann, Donald T. Reay, James A. Ferris, Thomas Koepsell, Frederick P. Rivara, Charles Rice, Laurel Gray, and James LoGerfo, "Handgun Regulations, Crime, Assaults, and Homicide: A Tale of Two Cities" 319 *New Eng. J. Med.* 1256–62 (1988).
36. These two cities are particularly well chosen to eliminate any bias due to the generally higher level of violence, especially homicide, in the United States as compared with Canada. Seattle's homicide rate is only 50–70% that of other major United States cities, while Vancouver's homicide rate is two to three times higher than that of Ottawa, Toronto, and Calgary. *Id.* at 1259.
37. *Id.* at 1256–7.
38. *Id.* at 1259.
39. *Id.*
40. *Id.*
41. John Henry Sloan, et al., "Handgun Regulations, Crime, Assaults, and Homicide: A Tale of Two Cities" 319 *New Eng. J. Med.* 1256, 1259 (1988).
42. *Id.* at 1259.
43. *Id.*
44. If one excludes those homicides committed by the police in the line of duty, and all those homicides done in self-defense or otherwise deemed justifiable (32 in total), the relative risk of being murdered in Seattle is still 1.57 that in Vancouver. *Id.*
45. *Id.* at 1257.
46. John Henry Sloan et al., "Handgun Regulations, Crime, Assaults, and Homicide: A Tale of Two Cities" 319 *New Eng. J. Med.* 1256, 1257 (1988).
47. *Id.*
48. *Id.*
49. *Id.* at 1258.
50. *Id.*
51. John Henry Sloan et al., "Handgun Regulations, Crime, Assaults, and Homicide: A Tale of Two Cities" 319 *New Eng. J. Med.* 1256, 1258 (1988).
52. James Wright, "Guns and Sputter," *Reason,* 46–47 (July 1989). *See also* Paul H. Blackman, "Medical Journal's Article Seriously Flawed, NRA Says," *New England Journal of Medicine,* reprinted in *NRA Official Journal,* 55–56 (Jan. 1989). *See also* 320 *The New England Journal of Medicine,* 1214–17 (May 4, 1989). In order to keep discussion manageable, I will focus on the two objections I have listed, which I consider to be the most telling.
53. James Wright, "Guns and Sputter," *Reason,* 46–7 (July 1989).
54. *Id.*
55. *Id.*
56. Sloan et al., *supra* note 35 at 1260.
57. *Id.*
58. *Id.*
59. *Id.*
60. Support for this hypothesis is provided by a study that is *favorable* to the view that race is a major determinant of the homicide rates in American and Canadian cities. *See* Robert J. Mundt, A Tale of Four Cities: Firearms and Violence in the U.S. and Canada, Remarks at the Annual Meeting of the American Political Science Association, (Aug. 29, 1991). Mundt concludes (23-6) that race alone does *not* account for the higher rate of crime in the American cities he studies and that the greater availability of firearms may also be a causal factor.
61. In 1991, 51% of murder victims and 55% of known murderers in the United States were black. *Uniform Crime Reports* 16 (1991). Only 12.3% of the population is black. *Statistical Abstract* 16 (1992).
62. Mundt, *supra* note 60 at 25.
63. *See, e.g.,* Mark K. Benenson and David T. Hardy, "Critiquing the Case for Handgun Prohibition," in *Restricting Handguns: The Liberal Skeptics Speak Out* 81–82 (Don B. Kates, Jr. ed., 1979). See also Don B. Kates, Jr. and Mark K. Benenson, who conclude that "tested over a wide spectrum of demographically, culturally, and geographically diverse states, handgun

prohibition laws nowhere appear to have had any reductive effect upon any type of violent crime." "Handgun Prohibition and Homicide: A Plausible Theory Meets the Intractible Facts," in *Restricting Handguns: The Liberal Skeptics Speak Out* 94 (Don B. Kates, Jr. ed., 1979).

64. *Id.* at 96–100.
65. *The Department of Treasury, Project Identification: A Study of Handguns Used in Crime* (May 1976).
66. *Id.* at 19.
67. *Id.* at 14.
68. *Id.* at 14–15.
69. *Id.* at 14.
70. *The Department of Treasury, Project Identification: A Study of Handguns Used in Crime* (May 1976).
71. The results of the study done by the Bureau of Alcohol, Tobacco and Firearms also serve as a response to the objection that gun laws are unenforceable.
72. A similar response applies to another utilitarian objection that refers to the likelihood of illegal and "homemade" gun production in this country in the event of a handgun ban. Restrictions on when guns may be owned legally are quite compatible with a crackdown on *illegally* made guns. Moreover, the fact that such guns are inaccurate and dangerous to the user will also act as a restraint on illegal gun production.
73. *See* David Hardy and Don Kates, "Handgun Availability and the Social Harm of Robbery: Recent Data and Some Projections, in *Restricting Handguns: The Liberal Skeptics Speak Out* 129–30 (Don B. Kates, Jr. ed., 1979).
74. *See* Kleck, *supra* note 30 at 41.
75. Kates, *supra* note 29 at 528.
76. However, it should be noted that the very arguments raised against a general prohibition on handguns (i.e. that criminals are unlikely to respond to it) also make it unlikely that a restriction targeted at felons will fare any better.
77. Kleck, *supra* note 30 at 41–43.
78. Uniform Crime Reports 13 (1990).
79. *Id.*
80. *Id.* at 14.
81. Gary Kleck and David J. Bordua, "The Assumptions of Gun Control," in *Firearms and Violence: Issues of Public Policy* 34–43 (Don B. Kates, Jr. ed. 1984).
82. James D. Wright, "Second Thoughts About Gun Control," 91 *The Public Interest* 31 (Spring 1988).
83. Kleck and Bordua, *supra* note 81 at 42.
84. *Id.* at 43.
85. 7442 per annum, based on the FBI's handgun homicide numbers. *Uniform Crime Reports* 12 (1990).
86. Sentence enhancement adds a mandatory prison term onto the sentence of any felon convicted of a crime that involves the use of a firearm. *See* Alan Lizotte and Marjorie S. Zatz, "The Use and Abuse of Sentence Enhancement for Firearms Offenses in California," *Law and Contemporary Problems* 49, 199–221 (Don B. Kates, Jr. ed., 1986).
87. This bill, which resulted from amendments to the proposed Brady Bill, requires a five day waiting period during which a background check is conducted. The applicant may then purchase a handgun if and only if this check shows that he has no criminal record. The waiting period will be phased out when a national computerized instant background check system becomes available.
88. Zimring and Hawkins have shown that approximately five times as many gun assaults as knife assaults result in death. *See* Zimring and Hawkins, *supra* note 5 at 15. In response, Hardy and Kates argue that criminals will likely substitute ice picks and butcher knives, which are almost as lethal as handguns. Handy and Kates, *supra* note 73 at 123–25. The mind boggles at how such weapons are supposed to be concealed before robberies. Also in response, Gary Kleck has argued that the death rates found by Newton and Zimring may be due not to the intrinsic lethalness of the guns themselves, but "the greater seriousness of intent to injure or kill among users of guns." Kleck, *supra.*, note 30 at 38. Both the "ice pick and butcher knife" and the "serious intent" conjectures are *compatible with* Zimring's and Hawkings' evidence. However, no evidence is given to show that either of these intuitively implausible hypotheses is actually *true. See generally* Zimring and Hawkins, *supra* note 5 at 13–21.
89. Hardy and Kates, *supra* note 73 at 121–22.
90. *Id.*at 122–23.
91. Don B. Kates and Mark K. Beneson, "Handgun Prohibition and Homicide: A Plausible Theory Meets the Intractable Facts," in *Restricting Handguns: The Liberal Skeptics Speak Out* 111 (Don B. Kates, Jr., ed., 1979).
92. *Id.*
93. Kleck, *supra* note 30 at 49.
94. 9.88%, according to the *Uniform Crime Reports* 12 (1990).
95. Kates and Beneson, *supra* note 91 at 114.
96. Hardy and Kates, *supra* note 73 at 127.
97. *Project Identification, supra* note 65 at 2.

98. *Uniform Crime Reports* at 12.
99. Despite my scepticism about the "long gun substitution theory" which is given in objection to handgun bans, I fully support one proposal that is made in the light of this theory: we need to restrict long guns in order to minimize criminal substitution of such guns in the event of handgun restrictions. *See,* Gary Kleck, "Handgun-Only Gun Control: A Policy Disaster in the Making," in *Firearms and Violence: Issues of Public Policy* 197–99 (Don B. Kates, Jr., ed., 1984). A background check on purchasers of long guns (of the kind recently proposed for handgun purchasers) could be profitably *combined* with a ban on handguns.
100. James D. Wright, "The Ownership of Firearms for Reasons of Self-Defense," in *Firearms and Violence: Issues of Public Policy* 301–27 (Don B. Kates, Jr., Ed., 1984); Kleck, *Supra* note 30 at 43–48; Don B. Kates, Jr., "Guns, Murder, and the Constitution" 17–36 (Pacific Research Institute for Public Policy) (1990).
101. Kleck, *supra* note 30 at 46.
102. *Id.*
103. Daniel D. Polsby, "Reflections on Violence, Guns, and the Defensive Use of Lethal Force" in *Law and Contemporary Problems* 49, 97 (Don B. Kates, Jr. ed., 1986).
104. Gary Kleck, "Guns and Self-Defense: Crime Control Through the Use of Force in the Private Sector, 35 *Social Problems* 4 (Feb. 1988).
105. *Id.* at 4.
106. *Id.* at 5.
107. George P. Fletcher, *A Crime of Self Defense: Bernhard Goetz and The Law on Trial,* 104–5 (1988).
108. Kleck, *supra* note 104 at 15.
109. *Uniform Crime Reports* 12 (1980).
110. Kleck, *supra* note 104 at 7–9.
111. *Uniform Crime Reports* 12,21,24 (1990).
112. Arthur Kellerman and Donald Reay, "Protection or Peril? An Analysis of Firearm-Related Deaths in the Home," 314 *New England Journal of Medicine,* 1557–60 (1986).
113. *Id.* at 1560.
114. 37 of the alleged 43 deaths for every self-defensive killing are suicides.
115. *See* Don B. Kates, Jr., *Guns, Murder, and the Constitution* 42 (Pacific Research Institute for Public Policy) (1990).
116. Kellerman and Reay, *supra* note 112 at 1559.
117. *Supra* note 104 at 17.
118. Kates, *supra* note 115, at 19.
119. Bruce L. Benson, "Guns for Protection and Other Private Sector Responses to the Fear of Rising Crime" in *Firearms and Violence: Issues of Public Policy* (Don B. Kates, Jr. ed., 1984)
120. *See* Carol Ruth Silver and Don B. Kates, "Self-Defense, Handgun Ownership, and the Independence of Women in a Violent, Sexist Society" in *Restricting Handguns: The Liberal Skeptics Speak Out* 139–69 (Don B. Kates, Jr. ed., 1979); Kates, *supra* note 115 at 24–32; Margaret Howard, "Husband-Wife Homicide: An Essay From a Family Law Perspective" in *Law and Contemporary Problems* 49, 63–88 (Don B. Kates, Jr. ed., 1986).
121. For instance, Kates quotes the finding that "men who batter [their mates] average 45 pounds heavier and 4 to 5 inches taller than the women they attack." Kates, *supra* note 115 at 24.
122. *See* Carol Ruth Silver and Don B. Kates, "Self-Defense, Handgun Ownership, and the Independence of Women in a Violent, Sexist Society" in *Restricting Handguns: The Liberal Skeptics Speak Out* 169 (Don B. Kates, Jr. ed., 1979).
123. *Id.* at 144–47.
124. In 1991, women committed 10% of homicides, 9% of robberies, and 14% of aggravated assaults, *Uniform Crime Reports,* 16, 29, 34 (1991).
125. Margaret Howard, "Husband and Wife Homicide: An Essay From a Family Law Perspective" in *Law and Contemporary Problems* 49, 67 (Don B. Kates, Jr. ed., 1986).
126. *Uniform Crime Reports* 19 (1991).
127. Kates claims this to be the case in "the overwhelming majority" of wife-husband homicides, without quoting specific evidence giving the percentage. Kates, *supra* note 115 at 25. Howard is more specific, quoting a survey of husband killers in the Cook County, Illinois jail. 40% of these women had been abused by their victims. She also refers to an earlier study by Wolfgang, in which nearly 60% of the murdered husbands had abused their wives. *See* Howard, *supra* note 125 at 74–5.
128. Kates, *supra* note 115 at 26.
129. *Id.* at 29.
130. Howard, *supra* note 125 at 88.
131. As indicated above, Howard suggests several excellent measures to reduce violence against women without using firearms. Howard, *supra* note 125 at 86–87.
132. Silver and Kates, *supra* note 122 at 161.
133. Kates, *supra* note 115 at 11–12.
134. In the 1960s, only 7% of the people who bought handguns were women. Zimring and Hawkins, *supra* note 5 at 186.
135. *Id.* at 187.

136. Such a lengthy trial period is necessary in order for a gradual decrease in the vast number of handguns *already* in circulation to take effect. To this end, I support the "buyback" schemes currently operated by some police departments.

137. An early draft of this paper was researched and written at a National Endowment for the Humanities Summer Seminar at the University of Maryland in 1991. I am grateful to seminar members and director David Luban for helpful suggestions, and especially to Sterling Harwood for extensive written comments and discussion.

Defensive Gun Ownership as a Response to Crime

DON KATES

Don Kates is probably the most prolific writer of material opposing gun control, though among his many writings one can also find some proposals he makes *for* gun control. Here Kates is concerned to show the disadvantages of gun-control proposals that would prevent defensive gun ownership as a response to crime. Kates's approach might have special appeal to students who, agreeing with the rap group Public Enemy, believe that 911 is a joke. Kates considers cases and statistics which show the problems police are having in stopping crime in a timely way. Some politicians (e.g., President Clinton) have proposed increasing the number of police by at least 100,000 officers nationwide. An alternative or additional approach is self-protection with a gun. A fascinating element of Kates's argument is his emphasis on women using guns in self-defense. Feminism against gun control reminds us of feminism against pornography. Feminism has traditionally supported and been supported by liberalism; that feminism might join conservatism in opposing pornography and gun control shows that politics makes for some strange coalitions.

Reprinted with permission of Pacific Research Institute for Public Policy, San Francisco, CA.

The impossibility of the police preventing endemic crime, or protecting every victim, has become tragically evident over the past quarter century. The issues are illustrated by the ongoing phenomenon of pathological violence against women by their mates or former mates:[1]

Maryland. Daonna Barnes was forced into hiding with her children because, since making threats is not a crime, police could not arrest her former boyfriend for his threats to kill her. On August 11, 1989, he discovered the location of her new apartment, broke in, and shot and stabbed her and her new boyfriend. Released on bail while awaiting trial on charges of attempted murder, the former boyfriend continues to harass Ms. Barnes, who says: "I feel like there is nobody out there to help me. It's as if [I'll have to wait until he kills me] for anyone to take this seriously. . . ."

Indiana. Finally convicted of kidnapping and battery against Lisa Bianco, her husband was sentenced to 7 years imprisonment. On March 4, 1989, he took advantage of release on an 8-hour pass to break into her house and beat her to death.

California. On August 27, 1989, Maria Navarro called the sheriff's office to report that her former husband was again threatening to kill her, despite a restraining order she had obtained against him. The dispatcher instructed her, "If he comes over, don't let him in. Then call us." Fifteen minutes later he burst in on her twenty-seventh birthday party and shot her and three others dead. Noting that Ms. Navarro's call was part of a perennial overload of 2,000 or more 911 calls that the sheriff's office receives daily, a spokesman frankly admitted, "Faced with the same situation again, in all probability, the response would be the same."

Colorado. On February 16, 1989, a mere 9 days after she filed for divorce, Lois Lende's husband broke into her home, beat and stabbed her to death, and then shot himself to death.

Connecticut. Late last year Anthony "Porky" Young was sentenced to a year in prison for stripping his girlfriend naked and beating her senseless in front of her 4-year-old son. "He says next time he's going to make my kids watch while he kills me," she says. Despite scores of death threats he has written to her while in prison, the prison authorities will have to release him when his year is up.

Literally dozens of such newspaper stories appear each week around the United States. Even extreme anti-gun advocates must wonder if a society that cannot protect its innocent victims should not leave them free to choose to own a handgun for defense.[2] This section of the paper is devoted to analyzing the arguments offered for denying that choice.

1. Police Protection vs. the Capacity to Defend Oneself

Perhaps the single most common argument against freedom of choice is that personal self-defense has been rendered obsolete by the existence of a professional police force.[3] For decades, anti-gun officials in Chicago, San Francisco, New York, and Washington, D.C., have admonished the citizenry that they don't need guns for self-defense because the police will defend them. This advice is mendacious: when those cities are sued for failure to provide police protection, those same officials send forth their city attorneys to invoke

> [the] fundamental principle of American law that a government and its agents are under no general duty to provide public services, such as police protection, to any individual citizen.[4]

Even as a matter of theory (much less in fact), the police do *not* exist to protect the individual citizen. Rather their function is *to deter crime in general* by patrol activities and by apprehension after the crime has occurred. If circumstances permit, the police should and will protect a citizen in distress. But they are not legally duty-bound even to do that nor to provide any direct protection—no matter how urgent a distress call they may receive. *A fortiori* the police have no duty to, and do not, protect citizens who are under death threat (e.g., women threatened by former boyfriends or husbands).

An illustrative case is *Warren* v. *District of Columbia* in which three rape victims sued the city under the following facts. Two of the victims were upstairs when they heard the other being attacked by men who had broken in downstairs. Half an hour having passed and their roommate's screams having ceased, they assumed the police must have arrived in response to their repeated phone calls. In fact, their calls had somehow been lost in the shuffle while the roommate was being beaten into silent acquiescence. When the roommates went downstairs to see to her, as the court's opinion graphically describes it, "For the next fourteen hours the women were held captive, raped, robbed, beaten, forced to commit sexual acts upon each other, and made to submit to the sexual demands" of their attackers.

Having set out these facts, the District of Columbia's highest court exonerated the District and its police, because it is "fundamental [in] American law" that the police do not exist to provide personal protection to individual citizens.[5] In addition to the case law I have cited, this principle has been expressly enunciated over and over again in statute law.[6]

The fundamental principle that the police have no duty to protect individuals derives equally from practical necessity and from legal history. Historically, there were no police, even in large American or English cities, before the mid-19th century. Citizens were not only expected to protect themselves (and each other), but also legally required in response to the hue and cry to chase down and apprehend criminals. The very idea of a police was anathema, American and English liberalism viewing any such force as a form of the dreaded "standing army."[7] This view yielded only grudgingly to the fact that citizens were unwilling to spend their leisure hours patrolling miles of city streets and were incapable even of chasing fleeing criminals down on crowded city streets—much less tracing and apprehending them or detecting surreptitious crimes.

Eventually, police forces were established to *augment* citizen self-protection by systematic patrol to deter crime and to detect and apprehend criminals if a crime should occur. Historically, there was no thought of the police displacing the citizen's right of self-protection. Nor, as a practical matter, is that displacement remotely feasible in light of the demands a high-crime society makes on the limited resources available to police it. Even if all 500,000 American police officers were assigned to patrol, they could not protect 240 million citizens from upwards of 10 million criminals who enjoy the luxury of deciding when and where to strike. But we have nothing like 500,000 patrol officers: to determine how many police are actually available for any one shift, we must divide the 500,000 by four (three shifts per day, plus officers who have days off, are on sick leave, etc.). The resulting number must be cut in half to account for officers assigned to investigations, juvenile, records, laboratory, traffic, etc., rather than patrol.[8]

Doubtless the deterrent effect of the police helps ensure that many Americans will never be so unfortunate as to live in circumstances requiring personal protection. But for those who do need such protection, police do not and cannot function as bodyguards for ordinary citizens (though in New York and other major cities police may perform bodyguard services for the mayor and other prominent officials). Consider just the number of New York City women who each year seek police help, reporting threats by ex-husbands, ex-boyfriends, etc. To bodyguard just those women would exhaust the resources of the nation's largest police department, leaving no officers available for street patrol, traffic control, crime detection, apprehension of perpetrators, responses to emergency calls and so forth.[9]

Given what New York courts have called "the crushing nature of the burden,"[10] the police cannot be expected to protect the individual citizen. Individuals remain responsible for their own personal safety, with police providing only an auxiliary general deterrent. The issue is whether those individuals should be free to choose gun ownership as a means of protecting themselves, their homes, and their families.

2. The Defensive Utility of Victim Firearms Ownership—Pre-1980s Analysis

Until recently a combination of problematic data, lacunae, and legerdemain allowed anti-gun advocates to claim "the handgun owner seldom even gets the *chance* to use his gun" and "guns purchased for protection are rarely used for that purpose."[11] The evidence to support this view came from a selective and manipulative rendition of pre-1980s city-level figures on the number of violent felons whom civilians lawfully kill. Because of a lack of any better data, these lawful homicide data were the best available before the 1980s. But anti-gun discussions should have mentioned the major defect in judging how many defense uses there were on the basis of defensive killings alone. That excludes as much as 96 percent of all defensive gun uses which did not involve killing criminals but only scaring them off or capturing them without death. This omission speciously minimizes the extent of civilian defensive gun use. Data now available show that gun-armed civilians capture or rout upwards of 30 times more criminals than they kill.[12]

Exacerbating the minimization problem was the highly misleading way opponents of handgun ownership selected and presented pre-1980s lawful homicide data. Some big cities had kept lawful homicide data since the

1910s. Naturally, many more felons were killed by victims in high crime eras like the 1970s and 1980s, or the 1920s and 1930s (when victims tended to buy and keep guns loaded and ready), than in the low crime era of 1945–65. For instance, Chicago figures starting in the 1920s show that lawful civilian homicide constituted 31.4 percent of all homicides (including fatal automobile accidents), that for decades the number of felons killed by civilians roughly equaled those killed by police, and that by the 1970s civilians were lawfully killing about three times as many felons as were police. Yet no mention of Chicago or these data (or comparable Washington, D.C., figures) are found in the anti-gun literature.[13]

Instead, that literature concentrates on Detroit. Even so, the data somehow omit these pertinent facts. In the 1920s, felons killed by civilians constituted 26.6 percent of all homicides in Detroit.[14] As crime rose after 1965, civilian killings of felons rose 1,350 percent (by 1971) and continued rising so that, by the late 1970s, twice as many felons were being lawfully killed by civilians than by police.[15]

Without mentioning any of this, even the most scrupulous of the anti-gun analysts, George Newton and Franklin Zimring, advanced the highly misleading claim that in the 5 years 1964–68 only "seven *residential* burglars were shot and killed by" Detroit householders, and there were only "three cases of the victim killing a *home* robber."[16] This claim is highly misleading because Newton and Zimring have truncated the lawful homicide data without informing readers that they are omitting the two situations in which most lawful defensive homicides occur: robbers killed by shopkeepers, and the homicidal assailant shot by his victim (e.g., the abusive husband shot by the wife he is strangling). Had these two categories not been surreptitiously omitted, Newton and Zimring's Detroit figure of lawful civilian homicide would have been 27 times greater—not 10 deaths, but rather 270 in the 1964–68 period.[17]

3. 1980's Data on the Defensive Efficacy of Handguns

All pre-1980's work has been eclipsed by more recent data, which allow estimation not only of how many felons are killed annually by armed citizens but also of those captured or scared off. This evidence derives from private national surveys on gun issues. Though sponsored by pro- or anti-gun groups, the polls were conducted by reputable independent polling organizations and have all been accorded credibility by social scientists analyzing gun issues.[18] Further evidence of the polls' accuracy is that their results are consistent (particularly their results on defensive gun use), regardless of their sponsorship.[19] Moreover, because the different surveys' data are mutually consistent, any suspicion of bias or falsification may be precluded by simply not using data from NRA-sponsored polls.

Therefore, on the basis of only anti-gun polls, it is now clear that handguns are used as or more often in repelling crimes annually as in committing them, approximately 645,000 defense uses annually versus about 580,000 criminal misuses.[20] Handguns are used another 215,000 times annually to defend against dangerous snakes and animals. As to their effectiveness, handguns work equally well for criminals and victims: in about 83 percent of the cases in which a victim faces a handgun, he (or she) submits; in 83 percent of the cases in which a victim with a handgun confronts a criminal, the criminal flees or surrenders.

These victim survey data are confirmed by complementary data from a survey among felons in state prisons across the country. Conducted under the auspices of the National Institute of Justice, the survey found that 34 percent of the felons said that

> they had been "scared off, shot at, wounded, or captured by an armed victim," [quoting the actual question asked] and about two-thirds (69 percent) had at least one acquaintance who had had this experience.[21]

In response to two other questions, 34 percent of the felons said that in contemplating a crime they either "often" or "regularly" worried that they "might get shot at by the victim," and 57 percent agreed that "most criminals are more worried about meeting an armed victim than they are about running into the police."[22]

In sum, the claim that "guns purchased for protection are rarely used for that purpose" could not have been maintained by a full and accurate rendition of pre-1980s data; that claim is definitively refuted by the comprehensive data collected in the 1980s under the auspices of the National Institute of Justice and both pro- and anti-gun groups.

4. Anti-Gun Obliviousness to Women's Defensive Needs

(a) The Case of Domestic and Spousal Homicide

My point is not that opponents of precautionary handgun ownership are oblivious to domestic homicide, but only that they are oblivious (or worse) to the situation of women in such homicides. That obliviousness is epitomized by the failure to differentiate men from women in the ubiquitous anti-gun admonition that "the use of firearms for self-protection is more likely to lead to . . . *death among family and friends* than to the death of an intruder."[23] This admonition misportrays domestic homicide as if it were all murder and ignores the fact that around 50 percent of interspousal homicides are committed by abused wives.[24] To understand domestic homicide, we must distinguish unprovoked murder from lawful self-defense against homicidal attack—a distinction that happens in these cases to correlate closely with the distinction between husband and wife.

Not surprisingly when we look at *criminal* violence between spouses, we find that "91 percent were *victimizations of women* by their husbands or ex-husbands. . . ."[25] Thus, the 50 percent of interspousal homicides in which husband kills wife are real murders—but in the overwhelming majority of cases where wife kills husband, she is defending herself or the children.[26] In Detroit, for instance, husbands are killed by wives more often than vice versa, yet men are far more often convicted for killing a spouse—because three-quarters of wives who killed were not even charged, prosecutors having found their acts lawful and necessary to preserve their lives or their children's.[27]

When a woman kills a man, she requires a weapon (most often a handgun) to do so. Eliminating handguns from American life would not decrease the total number of killings between spouses. (If anything, the number would increase because, as we have seen, gun-armed victims may ward off attacks without killing 25–30 times more often than the few times they have to kill). To eliminate handguns would only change the sex of the decedents by ensuring that, in virtually every case, it would be the abused wife, not the murderous husband. After all, a gun is of far more use to the victim than her attacker. "Husbands, due to size and strength advantages, do not need weapons to kill."[28] Having a gun is not necessary to attack a

> victim who is unarmed, alone, small, frail. . . . [But e]ven in the hands of a weak and unskilled assailant a gun can be used . . . without much risk of effective counterattack . . . [and] because everyone knows that a gun has these attributes, the mere display of a gun communicates a highly effective threat.[29]

Of course, it is tragic when an abused woman has to kill a current or former mate. But such killings cannot be counted as if they were costs of precautionary handgun ownership; rather they are palpable benefits from society's and the woman's point of view, if not from the attacker's. Thus, it is misleading (to the point of willful falsehood) for critics of handgun ownership to misrepresent such lawful defensive killings as what they prevented—domestic murder.

A final tangential, but significant, point emerges from statistics on using guns in domestic self-defense: those statistics strongly support the defensive efficacy of firearms. As noted "men who batter [wives] average 45 pounds heavier and 4 to 5 inches taller than" their victim.[30] If guns were not effective for defense, a homicidal attack by a husband upon his wife would almost invariably end in the wife's death rather than in his about 50 percent of the time.

---

5. Anti-Gun Obliviousness to Women's Defensive Needs

(b) Attacks by Male Acquaintances

In arguing against precautionary handgun ownership, anti-gun authors purport to comprehensively refute the defensive value of guns (i.e., to every kind of victim). Yet, *without exception* (and without mentioning the omission), those authors omit any mention of the acquaintance crime to which women are most often subjected. The empirical evidence establishes that "women are more likely to be assaulted, more likely to be injured, more likely to be raped, and more likely to be killed by a male partner than by any other type of assailant."[31] Yet, to a man (and, invariably, they are men), anti-gun authors treat self-defense in terms of the gun owner's fears "that a hostile *stranger* will invade *his* home."[32]

Only by turning a blind eye to acquaintance crime could the Chairman of Handgun Control Inc. claim that "the handgun owner rarely even gets the *chance* to use his gun." That assertion restates the argument of Newton and Zimring and the Handgun Control Staff. They emphasized the unexpectedness of stranger attacks—from which they characterized it as "ludicrous" to think a victim "will have sufficient time to retrieve" her handgun.[33]

As discussed above, even in cases of crime by strangers, this view is supported only by Newton and Zimring's inaccurate and misleading rendition of pre-1980s data, which is further discredited by the data available today. Moreover, in relation to violence against women, the assertion that women would invariably be too surprised by violent attack to use a handgun in self-defense is insupportable. On the contrary, in most instances, the man who beats or murders a woman (often even the rapist) is an acquaintance who has previously assaulted her on one or more occasions.[34] Such crimes commonly occur after a protracted and bellicose argument over a long simmering dispute. The women's defensive homicide literature shows that such a victim is almost uniquely positioned for self-defense. Knowing the mannerisms and circumstances that triggered or preceded her attacker's earlier attacks, she has

> "a hypervigilance to cues of any kind of impending violence. . . . [She is] a little bit more responsive to situations than somebody who has not been battered might be." A woman who has [previously] been battered and then is threatened with more abuse is more likely to perceive the danger involved faster than one who has not been abused.[35]

In this connection consider a point that anti-gun crusaders make in another context but ignore in this one. They (rightly) warn victims that a defense gun may be of little use if a person is attacked by a robber who is himself using a gun. The fact is that a gun is so dangerous a weapon that it is extremely risky for a victim to resist—even if the victim has a gun. A basic dictum of police and martial arts training is that even a trained professional should never attack a gun-armed assailant unless convinced that the assailant is about to shoot (in which case there is nothing to lose).[36]

This strong point about the overwhelming power of the person wielding a gun should have provoked academic anti-gun crusaders into at least considering a correlative question: Where does the balance of power lie between a victim who has a gun and an attacker armed only with a knife or some lesser weapon? Under those circumstances the victim will usually have the clear advantage (remember Kleck's finding that in 83 percent of cases in which a victim has a handgun, the criminal surrenders or flees). But anti-gun crusaders avoid the embarrassment of admitting that a victim with a gun might have an advantage over a lesser-armed attacker; they either ignore the issue or assume it away. Anti-gun analyses that expressly deal with a situation in which a victim tries to use a gun against an attacker wantonly assumes that the attacker will also have a gun.[37] In fact, however, in 89.6 percent of the violent crimes directed against women during the 10 years of 1973–82, the offender did not have a gun;[38] only 10 percent of rapists used guns[39] and only 25 percent of nonstrangers who attacked victims (whether male or female) had any weapon whatever.[40] In sum, the same strong arguments that anti-gun analysts offer against the wisdom of a victim resisting a gun-armed attacker suggest that women with handguns will have the advantage because most rapists and other attackers do not have guns.[41]

At this point it may be appropriate to address the old bugaboo that a woman who seeks to resist a male attacker will have her gun taken away and used against her. I emphasize that this is only a *theoretical* bugaboo: the rape literature contains no example of such an occurrence.[42] Moreover, police instructors and firearms experts strongly reject its likelihood. Not only do they aver that women are capable of gun-armed self-defense,[43] they find women much easier to properly train than men, because women lack the masculine ego problems that cause men to stubbornly resist accepting instruction. Thus, a police academy instructor who simultaneously trained a male police academy class and a class of civilian women "most of [whom] had never held a revolver, much less fired one" found that after one hour on the range and two hours of classroom instruction in the Chattanooga Police Academy's combat pistol course, the women consistently outshot police cadets who had just received eight times as much formal instruction and practice.[44]

6. Anti-Gun Obliviousness to Women's Defensive Needs

(c) Rape

Anti-gun academics necessarily neglect analyzing the gun's value in defending against rape because they eschew any mention of rape.[45] This surprising omission cannot be explained as a mere side effect of ignoring acquaintance crimes. After all, many rapists are strangers rather than acquaintances; indeed, many rapes are committed in the course of crimes that anti-gun literature does address, such as robbery and burglary.[46] But, almost invariably, the "intruder" whom anti-gun authors discuss is not a rapist but a "robber" whom they represent as "confront[ing] too swiftly" for rape or a "burglar" whom they represent as only breaking into unoccupied homes.[47]

This obliviousness to women's self-defense in general, and to rape in particular, leaves anti-gun authors free to deprecate the defensive utility of guns on grounds that don't apply to most circumstances in which women use guns defensively. Anti-gun writings correctly stress that it is illegal to shoot to prevent mere car theft, shoplifting, or trespass that does not involve entry into the home itself.[48] In contrast, the law allows a woman to shoot a rapist or homicidal attacker.[49] Also, in some cases a man attacked by another man of comparable size and strength may be hard put to justify his need to shoot, which is far less of a problem for a female victim of male attack.[50]

In short, to the extent academic anti-gun crusaders have made valid points about armed self-defense, these points do not apply to women. The anti-gun crusaders avoid acknowledging attacks on women by the simple device of never mentioning rape, or women's armed self-defense, at all. One anti-gun writer, Robert Drinan, did discuss rape, albeit not entirely voluntarily; he was responding to an article in which I highlighted the issue as justifying women's freedom to choose guns for self-defense. Drinan responded, in essence, that women detest guns and don't want to own them for self-defense.[51] This response is both factually and conceptually erroneous. It is factually erroneous because evidence shows that currently (though not necessarily when Drinan wrote) women constitute one-half of purely precautionary gun owners. It is conceptually erroneous because freedom of choice is a residual value even for things that many or most people do not now—and may not ever—want to choose.

Newton and Zimring's chapter on self-defense dismisses women's concerns about rape (or, presumably, other kinds of attack) in one contemptuous sentence to the effect that "women generally are less capable of self-defense [than men] and less knowledgeable about guns."[52] Feminist outrage about this derisive comment may account for the fact that Prof. Zimring's subsequent writings, including his self-defense chapter in a 1987 book, prudently eschew any attempt to deal with women's rights to, or capacity for, self-defense with guns.[53]

Other anti-gun treatments do not specifically address rape beyond their general position that victims should always submit to criminals unless flight is possible: the best way to "keep you alive [is to] put up no defense—give them what they want or run" advises Handgun Control Inc.[54] However unacceptable that advice may be to feminists, at least it avoids the confusion that marks the discussion of gun-armed defense against rape in a pamphlet by the Handgun Control Staff of the U.S. Conference of Mayors. For the first 31 of its 36 pages, the pamphlet harps on the prohibitive dangers of any physical resistance to crime. Throughout, the Handgun Control Staff's argument against precautionary gun ownership consists of warning against handguns or *any other* form of physical resistance—the risk of *any kind* of physical resistance is so high that victims should always submit to attackers.[55]

But when they finally got to rape, the Staff offers a startling *volte face*—all the more startling because the pamphlet lacks an explanation, much less a justification, of its contradicting all that preceded it. The Handgun Control Staff blithely announces that women don't need handguns to resist rape because of "the effectiveness of other means of resistance such as verbal and physical resistance."[56] Yet, if the authors believe their own prior warnings, "physical resistance" is prohibitively dangerous. For example, the pamphlet twice repeated its point (each time in italics) that *"a victim is more than eight times as likely to be killed when using a self-protective measure"* of any kind,[57] and it contained a more general admonition (again in italics) that *"victims who resist experience much higher rates of fatality and injury"*[58]

The Handgun Control Staff's pamphlet also points out that many rapes do not occur in the victim's home but in places where she presumably would not be legally entitled to carry a gun. However, this highlights the fact that most rapes *do* occur in the victim's home where she is entitled to have a gun (in all but a few jurisdictions like Washington, D.C., where victims are not permitted guns for self-defense). In short, most rapes occur where a woman may legally have a gun, and the empirical evidence is that in 83 percent of the cases it will protect her from being raped.

7. Incidence of Injury to Handgun-Armed Victims Who Resist Criminal Attack

Some readers may object that the preceding section of this paper shirks the crucial issue of victim injury by veering onto the side issue of intellectual honesty. Yes (they may say), the Handgun Control Staff's discussion of rape is inconsistent to the point of dishonesty; nevertheless, the pamphlet does marshall impressive data that victims who resist are often seriously hurt or killed.[59] Do those data not validate Zimring, Hawkins, and Handgun Control Inc., in teaching that victims ought to submit to rapists, robbers, or other violent criminals?: the best way to "keep you alive [is to] put up no defense—give them what they want or run."[60]

The short answer is the Handgun Control Staff's pamphlet presents data that are irrelevant to the risk of injury to victims who resist with a handgun. The pre-1980s data do not deal with guns specifically. The information gives only a conglomerate figure for the percentage of victims injured or killed when resisting physically in any way. This conglomerate figure includes some few victims who resisted with a gun; many more who used knives, clubs, or some makeshift weapon; and many who resisted totally unarmed. It is crucial to distinguish resistance with a gun from all other kinds of resistance, because a gun differs *qualitatively* in its defensive value. Criminals generally select victims who are weaker than themselves. Only a gun gives weaker, older, less-aggressive victims equal or better chances against a stronger attacker. As even Zimring and Hawkins state, guns empower "persons [who are] physically or psychologically unable to overpower [another] through violent physical contact."[61]

The difference is evident in post-1978 National Crime Survey data, which do allow us to distinguish victim injury in cases of gun-armed resistance from victim injury in cases where resistance was with lesser weapons, and from victim injury in cases of nonresistance. Ironically, the results validate the anti-gun critics' danger-of-injury concerns for every form of resistance *except* a gun. The gun-armed resister was actually much less likely to be injured than the nonresister who was, in turn, much less likely to be injured than those who resisted without a gun. Only 12 to 17 percent of gun-armed resisters were injured. Those who submitted to the felons' demands were twice as likely to be injured (gratuitously). Those resisting without guns were three times as likely to be injured as those with guns.[62]

I emphasize that these results do *not* mean that a gun allows victims to resist regardless of circumstances. In many cases submission will be the wiser course. Indeed, what the victim survey data suggest differs startlingly from both pro- and anti-gun stereotypes: keeping a gun for defense may induce sober consideration of the dangers of reckless resistance. The low injury rate of these victims may show that gun owners are not only better able to resist, but to evaluate *when* to submit, than are nonowners who, having never seriously contemplated those choices, must suddenly decide between them.

8. The "Submission Position" Advocated by White, Male Academia

By the "submission position," I mean, of course, the view embraced by various anti-gun scholars that victims should submit to felons rather than offering forcible resistance *of any kind.* If an attacker cannot be "talked out" of his crime, the victim should comply to avoid injury.[63] Not insignificantly, academic proponents of the submission position are all white males.[64]

This white male's viewpoint is significant insofar as the submission position is conditioned by the relative immunity to crime that its proponents enjoy because of their racial, sexual, and economic circumstances. In general, the submission position literature does not even mention rape. Equally significant, it treats robbery as the once-in-a-lifetime danger it is for a salaried, white, male academic. His risk of meeting a robber is so low that he is unlikely to keep a gun ready for that eventuality. Moreover, submitting once in his life to losing the money in his wallet may well be "the better part of valor" for a victim who can replace that money at his bank's automatic teller machine and can minimize the loss by taking it off his taxes. A very different calculus of costs and benefits of resisting may apply either to

> an elderly Chicano whom the *San Francisco Examiner* reports has held onto his grocery by outshooting fifteen armed robbers [while]

nearby stores have closed because thugs have either bankrupted them or have casually executed their unresisting proprietors . . . [or to] welfare recipients whom robbers target, knowing when their checks come and where they cash them . . . [or to] the elderly trapped in deteriorating neighborhoods (such as the Manhattan couple who in 1976 hanged themselves in despair over repeatedly losing their pension checks and furnishings to robbers).[65]

Regrettably, for many victims, crime is not the isolated happenstance it is for white male academics.[66] Let us imagine a black shopkeeper, perhaps a retired Marine master sergeant who has invested his life savings in the only store he can afford following his "20-years-and-out" career. Not coincidentally, the store is in an area where robbery insurance is prohibitively high or unobtainable at any price. In deciding whether to submit to robbery or resist, he and others who live or work in such areas must weigh a factor that finds no place in the submission position literature: that to survive they may have to establish a reputation for not being easily victimized.[67] The submission position literature is equally oblivious to special factors that are important to rape victims; even one rape—much less several—may cause catastrophic psychological injury that may be worsened by submission and may be mitigated by even an unsuccessful attempt at resistance.[68]

By no means am I arguing that resistance with guns (or without) is optimum for crime victims in any or all situations. I am just adding factors that really ought to be considered by well-salaried, white, male intellectuals who presume (as I certainly would not) to tell people who are most often crime victims what is best for them. Scholars, however learned, are presumptuous to pontificate on what is best for a victim whose values and situation they may not share. Consider the reflections of a woman who (without a gun) successfully resisted rape:

> I believed he would kill me if I resisted. But the other part was that I would try to kill him first because I guess that for me, at that time in my life, it would have been better to have died resisting rape than to have been raped. I decided I wasn't going to die. It seemed a waste to die on the floor of my apartment so I decided to fight.[69]

NOTES

1. As exemplified by the examples given in the text, I use the terms "husband," "wife," "mate," and "spousal" to include not only actual, ongoing, and legal marriages, but also "common law" marriage (which is legal in some states, but not others) and "boyfriend-girlfriend," as well as estranged and former versions of all these relationships.
2. All discussion of gun-armed self-defense in this paper is directed to handguns because they are infinitely more efficacious for defense than rifles or shotguns. In contrast to the unwieldy long gun, the short-barrelled handgun is much easier to bring into play at close quarters and much harder for an assailant to wrest away. Consider the situation of a woman holding an intruder at bay while trying to dial the police. With a rifle, this is difficult and hazardous at best. Given only the two-inch barrel of a snub-nosed handgun to grasp, not even the strongest man can lever it from a woman's grip before she shoots him. M. Ayoob, *The Truth About Self-Protection* (N.Y.: Bantam, 1983) 332–33, 341–42, 345–55.
3. Thus Ramsey Clark denounces precautionary gun ownership as an atavistic insult to American government: "A state in which a citizen needs a gun to protect himself from crime has failed to perform its first purpose"; it is "anarchy, not order under law—a jungle where each relies on himself for survival," R. Clark, *Crime in America* 88 (1971). For similar views, see also Wills, "Handguns that Kill," *Washington Star*, Jan. 18, 1981; "John Lennon's War," *Chicago Sun Times*, Dec. 12, 1980; and "Or Worldwide Gun Control," *Philadelphia Inquirer*, May 17, 1981; editorial: "Guns and the Civilizing Process," *Washington Post*, Sept. 26, 1972.
4. *Warren* v. *District of Columbia*, 444 A.2d 1 (D.C. Ct. of Ap. 1981). For similar cases from New York and Chicago, see *Riss* v. *City of New York*, 22 N.Y. 2d 579, 293 NYS2d 897, 240 N.E. 2d 860 (N.Y. Ct. of Ap. 1958); *Keane* v. *City of Chicago*, 98 Ill. App.2d 460, 240 N.E.2d 321 (1968). See also the cases cited in the next two footnotes and *Bowers* v. *DeVito*, 686 F.2d 61 (7 Cir. 1982) (no federal constitutional requirement that state or local agencies provide sufficient police protection).

5. 444 A.2d at 6; see also *Morgan* v. *District of Columbia,* 468 A.2d 1306 (D.C. Ct. of Ap. 1983). To the same effect, see *Calogrides* v. *City of Mobile,* 475 So. 2d 560 (S.Ct. Ala. 1985); *Morris* v. *Musser,* 478 A.2d 937 (1984); *Davidson* v. *City of Westminster,* 32 C.3d 197, 185 Cal. Rptr. 252, 649 P.2d 894 (S. Ct. Cal. 1982); *Chapman* v. *City of Philadelphia,* 434 A.2d 753 (Sup. Ct. Penn. 1981); *Weutrich* v. *Delia,* 155 N.J. Super. 324, 326, 382 A.2d 929, 930 (1978); *Sapp* v. *City of Tallahassee,* 348 So.2d 363 (Fla. Ct. of Ap. 1977); *Simpson's Food Fair* v. *Evansville,* 272 N.E. 2d 871 (Ind. Ct. of Ap.); *Silver* v. *City of Minneapolis,* 170 N.W.2d 206 (S. Ct. Minn. 1969); and the other authorities cited in the notes preceding and following this one.
6. See Cal. Govt. Code §§ 821, 845, 846, and 85 Ill. Rev. Stat. 4–102, construed in *Stone* v. *State,* 106 C.A.3d 924, 165 Cal. Rptr. 339 (Cal. Ct. of Ap. 1980); and *Jamison* v. *City of Chicago,* 48 Ill. App. 567 (Ill. Ct. of Ap. 1977) respectively; see generally 18 *McQuillen on Municipal Corporations,* sec. 53.80.
7. See generally 82 *Mich. L. Rev.* above at 214–16. and F. Morn, "Firearms Use and the Police: A Historic Evolution of American Values," in D. Kates (ed.), *Firearms and Violence* (1984).
8. See the extended discussion in Bowman, "An Open Letter," *Police Marksman,* July–Aug. 1986.
9. Silver and Kates, "Handgun Ownership, Self-Defense and the Independence of Women in a Violent, Sexist Society," in D. Kates (ed.), *Restriction Handguns* at 144–47. Prof. Leddy, formerly a N.Y. officer, cites personal experience:

   The ability of the state to protect us from personal violence is limited by resources and personnel shortages [in addition to which] the state is usually unable to know that we need protection until it is too late. By the time that the police can be notified and then arrive at the scene, the violent criminal has ample opportunity to do serious harm. *I once waited 20 minutes for the New York City Police to respond to an "officer needs assistance" call which has their highest priority.* On the other hand, a gun provides immediate protection. Even where the police are prompt and efficient, the gun is speedier.

   From "The Ownership and Carrying of Personal Firearms," forthcoming in *Int'l. J. Victimol.* (Emphasis added). Cf. the Riss and Silver cases cited above, as well as *Wong* v. *City of Miami,* 237 So.2d 132 (Fla., 1970). All emphasize the need for judicial deference to administrators' allocation of scarce police resources as a reason for denying liability for failure to protect.
10. *Wiener* v. *Metropolitan Transit Authority,* 433 N.E. 2d 124, 127, 55 N.Y. 2d 175, 498 N.Y.S. 2d 141 (N.Y. App. Div. 1982).
11. The first quotation is from a book by Nelson "Pete" Shields, the founder of Handgun Control, Inc., *Guns Don't Die, People Do* 49 (1981) (emphasis in original); the second is from Meredith, "The Murder Epidemic," *Science,* Dec. 1986, at p. 46. The point appears as a *leit motif* throughout the Handgun Control Staff pamphlet). To the same effect, please see Newton & Zimring above at 68 and F. Zimring & G. Hawkins, *The Citizen's Guide to Gun Control* (1987) (hereinafter Zimring & Hawkins, 1987) at 31.
12. In 68–75 percent of instances, the attacker is scared off without being shot at all. See *Social Problems* above at 4. See results reported and analyzed in NIJ Evaluation above at 146; and Hardy, "Firearms Ownership and regulation: Tackling an Old Problem with Renewed Vigor," 20 *Wm. & M. L. Rev* 235 (1978). See generally "Policy Lessons" above at 44. Even where attackers are shot, in more than five out of six instances they are wounded rather than killed. Id., Cook, "The Case of the Missing Victims: Gunshot Wounds in the National Crime Survey," 1 *J. Quan. Crim. 91,* 94–96.
13. For the civilian–police comparisons, Silver & Kates, "Handgun Ownership, Self-Defense and the Independence of Women in a Violent, Sexist Society," in D. Kates (ed.), *Restricting Handguns* (1979) at 156. Robin, "Justifiable Homicide by Police Officers," at p. 295, n. 3, of M. Wolfgang, *Studies in Homicide* (1967) notes that 1920s justifiable civilian homicides composed 26.6 percent and 31.4 percent of all homicides in Detroit and Chicago, respectively, and 32 percent of the total homicides in Washington, D.C., in the period 1914–18.
14. Zahn, "Homicide in the 20th Century," in T. Gurr (ed.), 1 *Violence in America* 221–22 (1989).
15. M. Dietz, *Killing For Profit: The Social Organization of Felony Homicide* (Chicago: Nelson-Hall, 1983), Table A.1 at 202–203.
16. Newton & Zimring above at p. 63 (author's emphasis).
17. Computation from the yearly Detroit homicide figures for "Excusable" and "Justifiable: Civilian" homicides in Dietz above. Because about 10 percent of excusable homicides are nonculpable accidental killings, in computing from the excusable column I have reduced its

total by 10 percent. See discussion of justifiable and excusable homicide in *Policy Lessons* above at 44.

18. See for example, *Social Problems* at 7–9; Wright, "Public Opinion and Gun Control: A Comparison of Results from Two Recent National Surveys," 455 *Annals Amer. Acad. Pol. & Soc. Sci.* 24 (1981); Hardy above and Bordua, "Adversary Polling and the Construction of Social Meaning," 5 *Law & Pol. Q.* 345 (1983).
19. *Social Problems* at 7–9.
20. Id.
21. The survey was released by the National Institute of Justice in summary form only. The entire survey with exhaustive analysis has been privately published by Aldine de Guyter Press as J. Wright & P. Rossi, *Armed and Considered Dangerous: A Survey of Felons and Their Firearms* (1986). The survey question and results cited appear at 154.
22. Id. at 145 and Table 7.2.
23. Emphasis added. This particular wording derives from the Handgun Control Staff pamphlet at 1 and from the other Handgun Control Staff publication Alviani & Drake above at 8. But the same theme, often expressed in virtually identical language, will be found in almost all critical treatments of precautionary gun ownership. See, for example, Rushforth et al., "Violent Death in a Metropolitan County," 297 *N. Eng. J. Med.* 531, 533 (1977); Drinan, "Gun Control: The Good Outweighs the Evil," 3 *Civil Liberties Rev.* 44, 49 (1976); and Shields above at 49–53 and 124–25.
24. U.S. Bureau of Justice Statistics release "Family Violence" (April 1984), table 1. See generally Straus, "Domestic Violence and Homicide Antecedents," 62 *Bull. N.Y. Acad. Med.* 446 (1986); "Current Research" at 203–204 and sources there cited.
25. Figures reported for the period 1973–81 in U.S. Bureau of Justice Statistics release "Family Violence" (April, 1984) at 4 (emphasis added).
26. See for example, Straus, above Saunders, "When Battered Women Use Violence: Husband Abuse or Self-Defense?" 1 *Violence and Victims* 47, 49 (1986) (hereinafter cited as Saunders-1); Barnard et al., "Till Death Do Us Part: A Study of Spouse Murder," 10 *Bull. Am. Acad. Psych. & Law* 271 (1982); D. Lunde, *Murder and Madness* (San Francisco, 1976) 10 (in 85 percent of cases of decedent-precipitated interspousal homicides, the wife is the killer and the husband precipitated his own death by abusing her); M. Daly & M. Wilson, *Homicide* (N.Y.: Aldine, 1988) at 278 ("when women kill, their victims are . . . most typically men who have assaulted them"); E. Benedek, "Women and Homicide," in B. Danto et al., *The Human Side of Homicide* (N.Y.: Columbia, 1982).

    It must be noted, however, that not all female defensive killings of husbands are legal. The legality depends on whether the wife reasonably anticipated that the husband's beating would cause her death or great bodily harm. Even where the statutes classify wife beating as a felony her proper resort is to seek prosecution; unless she was in imminent danger of death or great bodily harm, she must submit to beating rather than resist with deadly force. *People* v. *Jones*, 191 C.A.2d 478 (Cal. Ct. of Ap., 1961); see generally Kates & Engberg, "Deadly Force Self-Defense Against Rape," 15 *U.C.-Davis L. Rev.* 873, 876–7 (1982). When a wife kills only after surviving numerous prior beatings, it may be particularly difficult to convince police or jury that she reasonably believed this time was different—even though the pattern of men who eventually kill their wives is generally one of progressively more severe beatings until the final one. See Howard above.
27. Daly & Wilson above at 15 and table 9.1 at 200.
28. Howard above at 82–83; see also Saunders-1, above: "Men who batter [wives] average 45 pounds heavier and 4 to 5 inches taller than" their victims.
29. Cook, "The Role of Firearms in Violent Crime: An Interpretative Review of the Literature," in M. Wolfgang & N. Weiler (ed.), *Criminal Violence* 269 (1982) 247; Wright, "Second Thoughts About Gun Control," 91 *The Public Interest* 3, 32 (1988) ("Analysis of the family homicide data reveals an interesting pattern. When women kill men, they often use a gun. When men kill women, they usually do it in some more degrading or brutalizing way—such as strangulation or knifing"); and Saunders, "Who Hits First and Who Suffers Most?
    Evidence for the Greater Victimization of Women in Intimate Relationships," a paper presented at the 1989 Annual Meeting of the American Society of Criminology (available from Daniel Saunders, M.D., Department of Psychiatry, U. of Wisconsin).
30. Saunders-1 above at 94.
31. Browne & Williams above.
32. Zimring & Hawkins (1987) at 32 (emphasis added); Rushforth, Hirsch, Ford, & Adelson, "Accidental Firearm Fatalities in a Metropolitan County (1958–73)," 100 *Am. J. Epidem.* 499, 502 (1975) (depreciating value

of gun-armed self-defense, based only on analysis expressly limited to shootings of "burglars, robbers, or intruders *who were not relatives or acquaintances*"—emphasis added); Conklin & Seiden, "Gun Deaths: Biting the Bullet on Effective Control," 22 *Pub. Affairs Rep.* (U. Cal. Inst. of Govt. Studies, 1981) 1, 4 (same: "burglars or thieves" entering home); J. Spiegler & J. Sweeney, *Gun Abuse in Ohio* 41 (same: "burglars, robbers, or intruders"). See also two publications by the National Coalition to Ban Handguns: its undated, unpaginated pamphlet, "A Shooting Gallery Called America," and Fields, "Handgun Prohibition and Social Necessity," 23 *St. Louis U. L. J.* 35, 39–42 (1979); Handgun Control Staff (Alviani & Drake, above at 5–7 considering defense only against the "robber or burglar"); and Shields, *Guns Don't Die, People Do,* as well as Teret & Wintemute, "Handgun Injuries: The Epidemiologic Evidence for Assessing Legal Responsibility," 6 *Hamline L. Rev.* 341, 349–50 (1983); Riley, "Shooting to Kill the Handgun: Time to Martyr Another American[6] 'Hero,' " 51 *J. Urb. L.* 491, 497–99 (1974); I. Block, *Gun Control: One Way to Save Lives* 10–12 (pamph. issued by Public Affairs Committee, 1976); and Drinan above.

33. Handgun Control Staff pamphlet at 35 and Alviani & Drake above at 6 (paraphrasing almost identically Newton & Zimring at 68):

    The handgun is rarely an effective instrument for protecting the home against either the *burglar* or the *robber* because the former avoids confrontation [by striking only unoccupied premises] and the latter confronts too swiftly [for the victim to get his gun].

    Compare Zimring & Hawkins (1987) at 31 (emphasis added): "it is rare indeed that a household handgun actually stops the *burglar* [because he strikes when the home is unoccupied], or the home *robber* who counts on surprise and a weapon of his own." See also Riley and I. Block above.
34. Saunders-1 at 51, 56; Saunders-2; Benedek, "Women and Homicide" at 155–56, 162; Browne & Williams; Browne & Flewelling; and sources there cited.
35. *People* v. *Aris,* C.A.3d [89 Cal. Daily Op. Serv. 8505, 8509 (Cal. Ct. of Ap., Nov. 17, 1989)] (citing and adopting the testimony of expert witness, Dr. Lenore Walker, the leading American authority on battered wife syndrome). See also *State* v. *Kelly,* 478 A.2d 364, 378 (1984); Schneider, "Describing and Changing: Women's Self-Defense Work and the Problem of Expert Testimony on Battering," 9 *Women's Rts. L. R.* 195 (1986); and authorities there cited.
36. This is particularly true against a handgun whose short barrel makes it both much harder to wrest away than a long gun and much easier to bring into play at close quarters. See note 68.
37. For instance, although fewer than 10 percent of burglars carry guns, Riley conceptualizes what will ensue if householders with guns confront burglars in terms of 'bedroom shootouts' [which will be] won by alert desperadoes with drawn guns rather than the usually unwarned, sleepy-eyed residents," "Shooting to Kill the Handgun: Time to Martyr Another American 'Hero,' " 51 *J. Urb. L.* 491, 497–98; see also Zimring & Hawkins (1987) at 31; I. Block, *Gun Control: One Way to Save Lives* 10–12 (pamph. issued by Public Affairs Committee, 1976). Neither these nor any other anti-gun treatment ever consider the possibility of a victim with a gun being attacked by a felon without a gun.
38. U.S. Bureau of Justice Statistics release, "The Use of Weapons in Committing Offenses" (Jan. 1986), Table 6.
39. U.S. Bureau of Justice Statistics release, "The Crime of Rape" (March, 1985).
40. U.S. Bureau of Justice Statistics release, "Violent Crime by Strangers and Non-Strangers" (Jan. 1987). Note that this is a different sample (covering the period 1982–84) and that the figure for armed victimizations applies to all victims, not just women.
41. Kleck & Bordua, "The Factual Foundation for Certain Key Assumptions of Gun Control," 5 *L. & Pol. Q.* 271, 290 (1983).
42. Silver & Kates above at 159–61.
43. P. Quigley, *Armed and Female* (1988); M. Ayoob, *In the Gravest Extreme* 38 (1980). Cf.J. Carmichel, *The Women's Guide to Handguns* (N.Y.: Bobbs-Merrill, 1982) 3–4: ". . . when it comes to shooting, women are not the weaker sex," noting that the leading woman's score equalled the leading man's in recent Olympic handgun competition and that in college shooting where "no distinction is made between men and women," women are coming more and more to dominate . . . because women have certain physical and mental characteristics that give them an edge over men"—viz. patience, "excellent hand-eye coordination," and the concentration to perform delicate motor functions time after time.
44. Hicks, "Point Gun, Pull Trigger," *Police Chief,* May 1975. See also Quigley, Carmichel, & Ayoob above.

45. See for example Riley, "Shooting to Kill the Handgun: Time to Martyr Another American 'Hero,' " 51 *J. Urb. L.* 491, 497–99 (1974); Fields, "Handgun Prohibition," 23 *St. Louis U. L. J.* 35, 39–42 (1979); Teret & Wintemute, "Handgun Injuries: The Epidemiologic Evidence for Assessing Legal Responsibility," 6 *Hamline L. Rev.* 341, 349–50 (1983).
46. See generally the U.S. Bureau of Criminal Justice releases, "The Crime of Rape" (March 1985), "Robbery Victims" (April 1987), and "Household Burglary" (January 1985).
47. Handgun Control Staff pamphlet at 35; and Alviani & Drake above at 6 (paraphrasing almost identically Newton & Zimring at 68):

    The handgun is rarely an effective instrument for protecting the home against either the *burglar* or the *robber* because the former avoids confrontation [by only striking unoccupied premises] and the latter confronts too swiftly [for the victim to get his gun].

    Compare Zimring & Hawkins-1987 at 31.
48. Newton & Zimring at 68.
49. Cf. Kates & Engberg, "Deadly Force Self-Defense Against Rape," 15 *U.C.-Davis L. Rev.* 873, 877–78ff.
50. Id. at 879 and 890–94. See also Saunders, "When Battered Women Use Violence: Husband-Abuse or Self-Defense?" 1 *Victims and Violence* 47, 49 (1986)—("men who batter [their mates] average 45 pounds heavier and 4 to 5 inches taller than" the victim).
51. Drinan, "Gun Control: The Good Outweighs the Evil," 3 *Civil Liberties Rev.* 44, 50–51 (1976).
52. Newton & Zimring above at 64.
53. Zimring & Hawkins (1987), chap. 4.
54. Shields, *Guns Don't Die, People Do* at 124–25. To the same effect see Riley, "Shooting to Kill the Handgun: Time to Martyr Another American 'Hero,' " 51 *J. Urb. L.* 491, 497–98 (1972); Zimring & Hawkins (1987); Newton & Zimring; and the Handgun Control Staff pamphlet above.
55. As discussed *infra,* the primary problem with the Handgun Control Staff pamphlet is that the evidence, upon which it posits the rate of injury to gun-armed resisters, is fundamentally flawed because it applies to resistance with all kinds of weapons and does not break out gun-armed resistance.
56. Handgun Control Staff pamphlet at 33. The pamphlet cites no statistics to show that rapists are less likely than robbers or burglars to injure or kill victims who resist, nor could they be since rapist, robber, and burglar are often one and the same. See for example, Bureau of Justice Statistics releases *Household Burglary* (January 1985) and *Robbery Victims* (1987).
57. Handgun Control Staff pamphlet at 18; also at p. 2 (also in italics).
58. Handgun Control Staff pamphlet at 17. See also pp. 16 and 18, respectively, for the admonitions (again in original italics) that *"victims who take self-protective measures are more likely to be injured than victims not using such measures"* and that *"a victim is three times more likely to be injured when taking a self-protection measure than when not."* See also p. 11 ("the likelihood of being seriously injured during a robbery is directly related to taking a measure of self-protection" rather than submitting); p. 14 ("running away or reasoning with the offender . . . [is] less likely to result in injury to the victim"); p. 19 ("those taking a self-protective measure accounted for 58 percent of the emergency room treatments and their injuries were twice as serious, judged by the mean days of hospitalization"); and again on p. 19 (of victims hospitalized after rape, mugging, or assault, compared to nonresisters, "the seriousness of injury was five times as great for those using a weapon for self-protection"); and p. 30 (injuries in aggravated assault are "more likely to be serious if the victim physically resists the offender").
59. A point that the pamphlet never makes—but that emerges quite forcefully from neutral evaluations of the evidence—is that submission does not ensure that the victim will escape injury or death. Felons may injure victims at the outset to ensure compliance with the demands and to foreclose resistance, or felons may execute victims gratuitously. See for example, Cook, "The Relationship Between Victim Resistance and Injury in Noncommercial Robbery," 15 *J. Legal Stud.* 405, 406 (1986).
60. To avoid confusion, we should note that (a) Handgun Control Inc., currently the most important organization in the anti-gun lobby, has no direct link to the Handgun Control Staff, a nonlobbying "research" organization that fell into desuetude in the 1970s, and that (b) Professors Zimring and Hawkins are academic gun control advocates with no direct link to either organization. The "give them what they want" language is from Shields, *Guns Don't Die, People Do* (at 124–25), which relies heavily on the Handgun Control Staff's research. Zimring, Hawkins, and Newton take the same position; see also Riley, "Shooting to Kill the Handgun: Time to Martyr Another American 'Hero,' " 51 *J. Urb. L.* 491, 497–98 (1972).

61. Zimring & Hawkins (1987) above at 15. Curiously, they make this point in discussing how guns aid weaker people to victimize stronger ones—a crime pattern that is comparatively rare, to say the very least. The point is unaccountably missing from their later chapter on "Guns for Self Defense" to which it is far more relevant.
62. *Social Problems* at 7–9. The National Crime Surveys are conducted under auspices of the National Institute of Justice (NIJ). Census Bureau interviewers contact a nationally representative sample of about 60,000 households every 6 months and record information from personal interviews concerning the crime victimization experience of all household members aged 12 or older. Cook, "The Relationship between Victim Resistance and Victim Resistance and Injury in Noncommercial Robbery," 15 *J. Legal Stud.* 405, 406 (1986).
63. The preeminent submission exponents include Zimring & Zuehl, "Victim Injury and Death in Urban Robbery: A Chicago Study," 15 *J. Legal Stud.* 1 (1986); Skogan & Block, "Resistance and Injury in Nonfatal Assaultive Violence," 8 *Victimology* 215 (1983) and Wolfgang, "Victim Intimidation, Resistance, and Injury: A Study of Robbery" (paper presented at the Fourth International Symposium on Victimology, Tokyo, 1982). Prof. Wolfgang's ethically based support for banning guns is detailed in Benenson, "A Controlled Look at Gun Controls," 14 *N. Y. L. For.* 718, 723 (1968). As to Prof. Zimring's pragmatically based anti-gun views (which Prof. Block shares), see generally Newton & Zimring & Zuehl at 37–38.
64. Their views have been strongly criticized by a female criminologist (who is, nevertheless, *not pro-gun*) on the ground that for victims to submit encourages crime. Ziegenhagen & Brosnan, "Victim Responses to Robbery and Crime Control Policy," 23 *Criminology* 675, 677–78 (1985).
65. "Gun Control," 84 *The Public Interest* above at 45 and 46.
66. A recent U.S. Department of Justice study concludes that, over their lifetimes, 83 percent of American children now aged 12 will be victims of some kind of violent felony, 52 percent will suffer two or more such offenses, and 87 percent will have property stolen on three or more occasions. In all these crime categories, blacks will be much more frequently victimized than whites. *New York Times,* March 9, 1987, n. above 13. Cf. Sherman, "Free Police from the Shackles of 911," *Wall Street Journal,* March 20, 1987. Minneapolis police records show that in 1986 "23 percent of all the robberies, 15 percent of all the rapes, and 19 percent of all the assaults and disturbances" occurred repeatedly at only 3 percent of the city's commercial and residential addresses; "a mere 5 percent of all the addresses . . . produced 64 percent of all the calls for police service." Needless to say, it is unlikely that any of those who have to live or work at those repeatedly victimized addresses are white male academics.
67. See for example, "There's This Place in the Queens It's Not Such a Good Idea to Rob'" *Wall Street Journal,* October 20, 1971 (Puerto Rican shopkeeper reported to have shot more violent criminals in a year than had any New York City police officer in an entire career).
68. Kates and Engberg, "Deadly Force Self-Defense Against Rape," 15 *U.C. Davis L. Rev.* 873, 879–80, n. 20, and 898ff. (1982).
69. Quoted in Silver & Kates above at 139.

Study Questions

1. Do you agree with Dixon that banning handguns in the United States will in the long run maximize happiness for all concerned?

2. Is defensive gun ownership an adequate or sensible response to crime? Do statistics show that gun owners are more likely to shoot themselves, a loved one, or a friend than to shoot an intruder? Would feminists agree with Kates that guns are great equalizers in the battle of the sexes? Should the feminists agree with him?

H Hate Crimes

R. A. V. v. *City of St. Paul*

United States Supreme Court

Justice Antonin Scalia wrote the majority opinion, which ruled that the St. Paul ordinance banning such acts as burning crosses (which is associated with the Ku Klux Klan) and writing Nazi graffiti was unconstitutional because it violated the First Amendment's protection of speech.

Justice Scalia delivered the opinion of the Court.

In the predawn hours of June 21, 1990, petitioner and several other teenagers allegedly assembled a crudely made cross by taping together broken chair legs. They then allegedly burned the cross inside the fenced yard of a black family that lived across the street from the house where petitioner was staying. Although this conduct could have been punished under any of a number of laws, one of the two provisions under which respondent city of St. Paul chose to charge petitioner (then a juvenile) was the St. Paul Bias-Motivated Crime Ordinance, St. Paul, Minn. Legis. Code § 292.02 (1990), which provides:

> "Whoever places on public or private property a symbol, object, appellation, characterization or graffiti, including, but not limited to, a burning cross or Nazi swastika, which one knows or has reasonable grounds to know arouses anger, alarm or resentment in others on the basis of race, color, creed, religion or gender commits disorderly conduct and shall be guilty of a misdemeanor."

Petitioner moved to dismiss this count on the ground that the St. Paul ordinance was substantially overbroad and impermissibly content-based and therefore facially invalid under the First Amendment. The trial court granted this motion, but the Minnesota Supreme Court reversed. That court rejected petitioner's overbreadth claim because, as construed in prior Minnesota cases, see, *e.g.*, *In re Welfare of S. L. J.* (Minn. 1978), the modifying phrase "arouses anger, alarm or resentment in others" limited the reach of the ordinance to conduct that amounts to "fighting words," *i.e.*, "conduct that itself inflicts injury or tends to incite immediate violence . . .," *In re Welfare of R. A. V.* (Minn. 1991), and therefore the ordinance reached only expression "that the first amendment does not protect." The court also concluded that the ordinance was not impermissibly content-based because, in its view, "the ordinance is a narrowly tailored means toward accomplishing the compelling governmental interest in protecting the community against bias-motivated threats to public safety and order." We granted certiorari.

I

In construing the St. Paul ordinance, we are bound by the construction given to it by the Minnesota court. *Posadas de Puerto Rico Associates* v. *Tourism Co. of Puerto Rico* (1986). Accordingly, we accept the Minnesota Supreme Court's authoritative statement that the ordinance reaches only those expressions that constitute "fighting words" within the meaning of *Chaplinsky*. Petitioner and his *amici* urge us to modify the scope of the *Chaplinsky* formulation, thereby invalidating the ordinance as "substantially overbroad," *Broadrick* v. *Oklahoma* (1973). We find it unnecessary to consider this issue. Assuming, *arguendo,* that all of the expression reached by the ordinance is proscribable under the "fighting words" doctrine, we nonetheless conclude that the ordinance is facially unconstitutional in that it prohibits otherwise permitted speech solely on the basis of the subjects the speech addresses.

The First Amendment generally prevents government from proscribing speech, see, *e.g., Cantwell* v. *Connecticut* (1940) or even expressive conduct, see, *e.g., Texas* v. *Johnson* (1989), because of disapproval of the ideas expressed. Content-based regulations are presumptively invalid. *Simon & Schuster, Inc.* v. *Members of N. Y. State Crime Victims Bd.* (1991). From 1791 to the present, however, our society, like other free but civilized societies, has permitted restrictions upon the content of speech in a few limited areas, which are "of such slight social value as a step to truth that any benefit that may be derived from them is clearly outweighed by the social interest in order and morality." *Chaplinsky*. We have recognized that "the freedom of speech" referred to by the First Amendment does not include a freedom to disregard these traditional limitations. Our decisions since the 1960s have narrowed the scope of the traditional categorical exceptions for defamation, see *New York Times Co.* v. *Sullivan* (1964); *Gertz* v. *Robert Welch, Inc.* (1974); see generally *Milkovich* v. *Lorain Journal Co.* (1990), and for obscenity, see *Miller* v. *California* (1973), but a limited categorical approach has remained an important part of our First Amendment jurisprudence.

We have sometimes said that these categories of expression are "not within the area of constitutionally protected speech," *Roth, Beauharnais, Chaplinsky,* or that the "protection of the First Amendment does not extend" to them, *Bose Corp.* v. *Consumers Union of United States, Inc.* (1984); *Sable Communications of Cal., Inc.* v. *FCC* (1989). Such statements must be taken in context, however, and are no more literally true than is the occasionally repeated shorthand characterizing obscenity "as not being speech at all," Sunstein, Pornography and the First Amendment. What they mean is that these areas of speech can, consistently with the First Amendment, be regulated *because of their constitutionally proscribable content* (obscenity, defamation, etc.)—not that they are categories of speech entirely invisible to the Constitution, so that they may be made the vehicles for content discrimination unrelated to their distinctively proscribable content. Thus, the government may proscribe libel; but it may not make the further content discrimination of proscribing *only* libel critical of the government. We recently acknowledged this distinction in *Ferber,* where, in upholding New York's child pornography law, we expressly recognized that there was no "question here of censoring a particular literary theme. . . ."

Our cases surely do not establish the proposition that the First Amendment imposes no obstacle whatsoever to regulation of particular instances of such proscribable expression, so that the government "may regulate [them] freely," *post* (White, J., concurring in judgment). That would mean that a city council could enact an ordinance prohibiting only those legally obscene works that contain criticism of the city government or, indeed, that do not include endorsement of the city government. Such a simplistic, all-or-nothing-at-all approach to First Amendment protection is at odds with common sense and with our jurisprudence as well. It is not true that "fighting words" have at most a *"de minimis"* expressive content, *ibid.,* or that their content is *in all respects* "worthless and undeserving of constitutional protection," *post,* sometimes they are quite expressive indeed. We have not said that they constitute "*no* part of the expression of ideas," but only that they constitute "no *essential* part of any exposition of ideas." *Chaplinsky* (emphasis added).

The proposition that a particular instance of speech can be proscribable on the basis of one feature (*e.g.*, obscenity) but not on the basis of another (*e.g.*, opposition to the city government) is commonplace, and has found application in many contexts. We have long held, for example, that nonverbal expressive activity can be banned because of the action it entails, but not because of the ideas it expresses—so that burning a flag in violation of an ordinance against outdoor fires could be punishable, whereas burning a flag in violation of an ordinance against dishonoring the flag is not. Similarly, we have upheld reasonable "time, place, or manner" restrictions, but only if they are "justified without reference to the content of the regulated speech." *Ward* v. *Rock Against Racism* (1989) (internal quotation marks omitted); see also *Clark* v. *Community for Creative Non-Violence* (1984) (noting that the *O'Brien* test differs little from the standard applied to time, place, or manner restrictions). And just as the power to proscribe particular speech on the basis of a noncontent element (*e.g.*, noise) does not entail the power to proscribe the same speech on the basis of a content element; so also, the power to proscribe it on the basis of *one* content element (*e.g.*, obscenity) does not entail the power to proscribe it on the basis of *other* content elements.

In other words, the exclusion of "fighting words" from the scope of the First Amendment simply means that, for purposes of that Amendment, the unprotected features of the words are, despite their verbal character, essentially a "nonspeech" element of communication. Fighting words are thus analogous to a noisy sound truck: Each is, as Justice Frankfurter recognized, a "mode of speech," *Niemotko* v. *Maryland* (1951) (Frankfurter, J., concurring in result); both can be used to convey an idea; but neither has, in and of itself, a claim upon the First Amendment. As with the sound truck, however, so also with fighting words: The government may not regulate use based on hostility—or favoritism—towards the underlying message expressed. Compare *Frisby* v. *Schultz* (1988) (upholding, against facial challenge, a content-neutral ban on targeted residential picketing) with *Carey* v. *Brown* (1980) (invalidating a ban on residential picketing that exempted labor picketing).

The concurrences describe us as setting forth a new First Amendment principle that prohibition of constitutionally proscribable speech cannot be "underinclusiv[e]," *post* (White, J., concurring in judgment)—a First Amendment "absolutism" whereby "within a particular 'proscribable' category of expression, . . . a government must either proscribe *all* speech or no speech at all," *post* (Stevens, J., concurring in judgment). That easy target is of the concurrences' own invention. In our view, the First Amendment imposes not an "underinclusiveness" limitation but a "content discrimination" limitation upon a State's prohibition of proscribable speech. There is no problem whatever, for example, with a State's prohibiting obscenity (and other forms of proscribable expression) only in certain media or markets, for although that prohibition would be "underinclusive," it would not discriminate on the basis of content.

Even the prohibition against content discrimination that we assert the First Amendment requires is not absolute. It applies differently in the context of proscribable speech than in the area of fully protected speech. The rationale of the general prohibition, after all, is that content discrimination "rais[es] the specter that the Government may effectively drive certain ideas or viewpoints from the marketplace," *Simon & Schuster*. But content discrimination among various instances of a class of proscribable speech often does not pose this threat.

When the basis for the content discrimination consists entirely of the very reason the entire class of speech at issue is proscribable, no significant danger of idea or viewpoint discrimination exists. Such a reason, having been adjudged neutral enough to support exclusion of the entire class of speech from First Amendment protection, is also neutral enough to form the basis of distinction within the class. To illustrate: A

State might choose to prohibit only that obscenity which is the most patently offensive *in its prurience—i.e.,* that which involves the most lascivious displays of sexual activity. But it may not prohibit, for example, only that obscenity which includes offensive *political* messages. And the Federal Government can criminalize only those threats of violence that are directed against the President, see 18 U. S. C. § 871—since the reasons why threats of violence are outside the First Amendment (protecting individuals from the fear of violence, from the disruption that fear engenders, and from the possibility that the threatened violence will occur) have special force when applied to the person of the President. See *Watts* v. *United States* (1969) (upholding the facial validity of § 871 because of "the overwhelmin[g] interest in protecting the safety of [the] Chief Executive and in allowing him to perform his duties, without interference from threats of physical violence"). But the Federal Government may not criminalize only those threats against the President that mention his policy on aid to inner cities. And to take a final example (one mentioned by Justice Stevens, *post,* at 6–7), a State may choose to regulate price advertising in one industry but not in others, because the risk of fraud (one of the characteristics of commercial speech that justifies depriving it of full First Amendment protection, see *Virginia Pharmacy Bd.* v. *Virginia Citizens Consumer Council, Inc.* (1976)) is in its view greater there. But a State may not prohibit only that commercial advertising that depicts men in a demeaning fashion, see, *e.g.*, L. A. Times, Aug. 8, 1989, section 4, p. 6, col. 1.

Another valid basis for according differential treatment to even a content-defined subclass of proscribable speech is that the subclass happens to be associated with particular "secondary effects" of the speech, so that the regulation is "*justified* without reference to the content of the . . . speech," *Renton* v. *Playtime Theatres, Inc.* A State could, for example, permit all obscene live performances except those involving minors. Moreover, since words can in some circumstances violate laws directed not against speech but against conduct (a law against treason, for example, is violated by telling the enemy the nation's defense secrets), a particular content-based subcategory of a proscribable class of speech can be swept up incidentally within the reach of a statute directed at conduct rather than speech. Thus, for example, sexually derogatory "fighting words," among other words, may produce a violation of Title VII's general prohibition against sexual discrimination in employment practices, 42 U. S. C. § 2000e-2; 29 CFR § 1604.11 (1991). Where the government does not target conduct on the basis of its expressive content, acts are not shielded from regulation merely because they express a discriminatory idea or philosophy.

These bases for distinction refute the proposition that the selectivity of the restriction is "even arguably 'conditioned upon the sovereign's agreement with what a speaker may intend to say.' " *Metromedia, Inc.* v. *San Diego* (1981) (Stevens, J., dissenting in part) (citation omitted). There may be other such bases as well. Indeed, to validate such selectivity (where totally proscribable speech is at issue) it may not even be necessary to identify any particular "neutral" basis, so long as the nature of the content discrimination is such that there is no realistic possibility that official suppression of ideas is afoot. (We cannot think of any First Amendment interest that would stand in the way of a State's prohibiting only those obscene motion pictures with blue-eyed actresses.) Save for that limitation, the regulation of "fighting words," like the regulation of noisy speech, may address some offensive instances and leave other, equally offensive, instances alone.

II

Applying these principles to the St. Paul ordinance, we conclude that, even as narrowly construed by the Minnesota Supreme Court, the ordinance is facially unconstitutional. Although the phrase in the ordinance, "arouses anger, alarm or resentment in others," has been limited by the Minnesota Supreme

Court's construction to reach only those symbols or displays that amount to "fighting words," the remaining, unmodified terms make clear that the ordinance applies only to "fighting words" that insult, or provoke violence, "on the basis of race, color, creed, religion or gender." Displays containing abusive invective, no matter how vicious or severe, are permissible unless they are addressed to one of the specified disfavored topics. Those who wish to use "fighting words" in connection with other ideas—to express hostility, for example, on the basis of political affiliation, union membership, or homosexuality—are not covered. The First Amendment does not permit St. Paul to impose special prohibitions on those speakers who express views on disfavored subjects.

In its practical operation, moreover, the ordinance goes even beyond mere content discrimination, to actual viewpoint discriminations. Displays containing some words—odious racial epithets, for example—would be prohibited to proponents of all views. But "fighting words" that do not themselves invoke race, color, creed, religion, or gender—aspersions upon a person's mother, for example—would seemingly be usable *ad libitum* in the placards of those arguing *in favor* of racial, color, etc., tolerance and equality, but could not be used by that speaker's opponents. One could hold up a sign saying, for example, that all "anti-Catholic bigots" are misbegotten; but not that all "papists" are, for that would insult and provoke violence "on the basis of religion." St. Paul has no such authority to license one side of a debate to fight freestyle, while requiring the other to follow Marquis of Queensbury Rules.

What we have here, it must be emphasized, is not a prohibition of fighting words that are directed at certain persons or groups (which would be *facially* valid if it met the requirements of the Equal Protection Clause); but rather, a prohibition of fighting words that contain (as the Minnesota Supreme Court repeatedly emphasized) messages of "bias-motivated" hatred and in particular, as applied to this case, messages "based on virulent notions of racial supremacy." One must wholeheartedly agree with the Minnesota Supreme Court that "[i]t is the responsibility, even the obligation, of diverse communities to confront such notions in whatever form they appear," *ibid.*, but the manner of that confrontation cannot consist of selective limitations upon speech. St. Paul's brief asserts that a general "fighting words" law would not meet the city's needs because only a content-specific measure can communicate to minority groups that the "group hatred" aspect of such speech "is not condoned by the majority." Brief for Respondent 25. The point of the First Amendment is that majority preferences must be expressed in some fashion other than silencing speech on the basis of its content.

Despite the fact that the Minnesota Supreme Court and St. Paul acknowledge that the ordinance is directed at expression of group hatred, Justice Stevens suggests that this "fundamentally misreads" the ordinance. *Post.* It is directed, he claims, not to speech of a particular content, but to particular "injur[ies]" that are "qualitatively different" from other injuries. *Post.* This is word-play. What makes the anger, fear, sense of dishonor, etc., produced by violation of this ordinance distinct from the anger, fear, sense of dishonor, etc., produced by other fighting words is nothing other than the fact that it is caused by a distinctive idea, conveyed by a distinctive message. The First Amendment cannot be evaded that easily. It is obvious that the symbols which will arouse "anger, alarm or resentment in others on the basis of race, color, creed, religion or gender" are those symbols that communicate a message of hostility based on one of these characteristics. St. Paul concedes in its brief that the ordinance applies only to "racial, religious, or gender-specific symbols" such as "a burning cross, Nazi swastika or other instrumentality of like import." Brief for Respondent. Indeed, St. Paul argued in the Juvenile Court that "[t]he burning of a cross does express a message and it is, in fact, the content of that message which the St. Paul Ordinance attempts to legislate." Memorandum from the Ramsey County Attorney to the Honorable Charles A. Flinn, Jr., dated July 13, 1990, in *In re Welfare of R. A. V.*

The content-based discrimination reflected in the St. Paul ordinance comes within neither any of the specific exceptions to the First Amendment prohibition we discussed earlier, nor within a more general exception for content discrimination that does not threaten censorship of ideas. It assuredly does not fall within the exception for content discrimination based on the very reasons why the particular class of speech at issue (here, fighting words) is proscribable. As explained earlier, see *supra,* at 8, the reason why fighting words are categorically excluded from the protection of the First Amendment is not that their content communicates any particular idea, but that their content embodies a particularly intolerable (and socially unnecessary) *mode* of expressing *whatever* idea the speaker wishes to convey. St. Paul has not singled out an especially offensive mode of expression—it has not, for example, selected for prohibition only those fighting words that communicate ideas in a threatening (as opposed to a merely obnoxious) manner. Rather, it has proscribed fighting words of whatever manner that communicate messages of racial, gender, or religious intolerance. Selectivity of this sort creates the possibility that the city is seeking to handicap the expression of particular ideas. That possibility would alone be enough to render the ordinance presumptively invalid, but St. Paul's comments and concessions in this case elevate the possibility to a certainty.

St. Paul argues that the ordinance comes within another of the specific exceptions we mentioned, the one that allows content discrimination aimed only at the "secondary effects" of the speech, see *Renton* v. *Playtime Theatres, Inc.* (1986). According to St. Paul, the ordinance is intended, "not to impact on [sic] the right of free expression of the accused," but rather to "protect against the victimization of a person or persons who are particularly vulnerable because of their membership in a group that historically has been discriminated against." Brief for Respondent 28. Even assuming that an ordinance that completely proscribes, rather than merely regulates, a specified category of speech can ever be considered to be directed only to the secondary effects of such speech, it is clear that the St. Paul ordinance is not directed to secondary effects within the meaning of *Renton.* As we said in *Boos* v. *Barry* (1988), "[l]isteners' reactions to speech are not the type of 'secondary effects' we referred to in *Renton.*" *Id.,* at 321. "The emotive impact of speech on its audience is not a 'secondary effect.' " *Ibid.*

It hardly needs discussion that the ordinance does not fall within some more general exception permitting *all* selectivity that for any reason is beyond the suspicion of official suppression of ideas. The statements of St. Paul in this very case afford ample basis for, if not full confirmation of, that suspicion.

Finally, St. Paul and its *amici* defend the conclusion of the Minnesota Supreme Court that, even if the ordinance regulates expression based on hostility towards its protected ideological content, this discrimination is nonetheless justified because it is narrowly tailored to serve compelling state interests. Specifically, they assert that the ordinance helps to ensure the basic human rights of members of groups that have historically been subjected to discrimination, including the right of such group members to live in peace where they wish. We do not doubt that these interests are compelling, and that the ordinance can be said to promote them. But the "danger of censorship" presented by a facially content-based statute, *Leathers* v. *Medlock* (1991) requires that that weapon be employed only where it is "*necessary* to serve the asserted [compelling] interest," *Burson* v. *Freeman* (1992) (plurality) (emphasis added): The existence of adequate content-neutral alternatives thus "undercut[s] significantly" any defense of such a statute, *Boos* v. *Barry,* casting considerable doubt on the government's protestations that "the asserted justification is in fact an accurate description of the purpose and effect of the law," *Burson.* The dispositive question in this case, there-for example, would have precisely the same beneficial effect. In fact the only interest distinctively served by the content limitation is that of displaying the city council's special hostility towards the particular biases thus singled out. That is precisely what the First Amendment forbids. The politicians of St. Paul are entitled to express that hostility—but not through the means of imposing unique limitations upon speakers who (however benightedly) disagree.

Let there be no mistake about our belief that burning a cross in someone's front yard is reprehensible. But St. Paul has sufficient means at its disposal to prevent such behavior without adding the First Amendment to the fire.

The judgment of the Minnesota Supreme Court is reversed, and the case is remanded for proceedings not inconsistent with this opinion.

It is so ordered.

Justice White, with whom Justice Blackmun and Justice O'Connor join, and with whom Justice Stevens joins except as to Part I(A), concurring in the judgment.

I agree with the majority that the judgment of the Minnesota Supreme Court should be reversed. However, our agreement ends there.

This case could easily be decided within the contours of established First Amendment law by holding, as petitioner argues, that the St. Paul ordinance is fatally overbroad because it criminalizes not only unprotected expression but expression protected by the First Amendment. See Part II, *infra*. Instead, "find[ing] it unnecessary" to consider the questions upon which we granted review, *ante*, the Court holds the ordinance facially unconstitutional on a ground that was never presented to the Minnesota Supreme Court, a ground that has not been briefed by the parties before this Court, a ground that requires serious departures from the teaching of prior cases and is inconsistent with the plurality opinion in *Burson* v. *Freeman* (1992), which was joined by two of the five Justices in the majority in the present case.

This Court ordinarily is not so eager to abandon its precedents. Twice within the past month, the Court has declined to overturn longstanding but controversial decisions on questions of constitutional law. See *Allied Signal, Inc.* v. *Director, Division of Taxation* (1992); *Quill Corp.* v. *North Dakota* (1992). In each case, we had the benefit of full briefing on the critical issue, so that the parties and amici had the opportunity to apprise us of the impact of a change in the law. And in each case, the Court declined to abandon its precedents, invoking the principle of *stare decisis*. *Allied Signal, Inc.*

But in the present case, the majority casts aside long-established First Amendment doctrine without the benefit of briefing and adopts an untried theory. This is hardly a judicious way of proceeding, and the Court's reasoning in reaching its result is transparently wrong.

I

A

This Court's decisions have plainly stated that expression falling within certain limited categories so lacks the values the First Amendment was designed to protect that the Constitution affords no protection to that expression. *Chaplinsky* v. *New Hampshire* (1942), made the point in the clearest possible terms:

> There are certain well-defined and narrowly limited classes of speech, the prevention and punishment of which have never been thought to raise any Constitutional problem. . . . It has been well observed that such utterances are no essential part of any exposition of ideas, and are of such slight social value as a step to truth that any benefit that may be derived from them is clearly outweighed by the social interest in order and morality.

See also *Bose Corp.* v. *Consumers Union of United States, Inc.* (1984).

Thus, as the majority concedes, see *ante,* at 5, this Court has long held certain discrete categories of expression to be proscribable on the basis of their content. For instance, the Court has held that the individual who falsely shouts "fire" in a crowded theatre may not claim the protection of the First Amendment. *Schenck* v. *United States* (1919). The Court has concluded that neither child pornography, nor obscenity, is protected by the First Amendment. *New York* v. *Ferber* (1982). And the Court has observed that, "[l]eaving aside the special considerations when public officials [and public figures] are the target, a libelous publication is not protected by the Constitution." *Ferber* (citations omitted).

All of these categories are content based. But the Court has held that First Amendment does not apply to them because their expressive content is worthless or of *de minimis* value to society. *Chaplinsky*. We have not departed from this principle, emphasizing repeatedly that, "within the confines of [these] given classification[s], the evil to be restricted so overwhelmingly outweighs the expressive interests, if any, at stake, that no process of case-by-case adjudication is required." *Ferber*. This categorical approach has provided a principled and narrowly focused means for distinguishing between expression that the government may regulate freely and that which it may regulate on the basis of content only upon a showing of compelling need.

Today, however, the Court announces that earlier Courts did not mean their repeated statements that certain categories of expression are "not within the area of constitutionally protected speech." *Roth*. The present Court submits that such clear statements "must be taken in context" and are not "literally true." *Ante*.

To the contrary, those statements meant precisely what they said: The categorical approach is a firmly entrenched part of our First Amendment jurisprudence. Indeed, the Court in *Roth* reviewed the guarantees of freedom of expression in effect at the time of the ratification of the Constitution and concluded, "[i]n light of this history, it is apparent that the unconditional phrasing of the First Amendment was not intended to protect every utterance."

In its decision today, the Court points to "[n]othing . . . in this Court's precedents warrant[ing] disregard of this longstanding tradition." *Burson* (Scalia, J., concurring in judgment). Nevertheless, the majority holds that the First Amendment protects those narrow categories of expression long held to be undeserving of First Amendment protection—at least to the extent that lawmakers may not regulate some fighting words more strictly than others because of their content. The Court announces that such content-based distinctions violate the First Amendment because "the government may not regulate use based on hostility—or favoritism—towards the underlying message expressed." *Ante*. Should the government want to criminalize certain fighting words, the Court now requires it to criminalize all fighting words.

To borrow a phrase, "Such a simplistic, all-or-nothing-at-all approach to First Amendment protection is at odds with common sense and with our jurisprudence as well." *Ante*. It is inconsistent to hold that the government may proscribe an entire category of speech because the content of that speech is evil, *Ferber,* but that the government may not treat a subset of that category differently without violating the First Amendment; the content of the subset is by definition worthless and undeserving of constitutional protection.

The majority's observation that fighting words are, "quite expressive indeed," *ante,* is no answer. Fighting words are not a means of exchanging views, rallying supporters, or registering a protest; they are directed against individuals to provoke violence or to inflict injury. *Chaplinsky*. Therefore, a ban on all fighting words or on a subset of the fighting words category would restrict only the social evil of hate speech, without creating the danger of driving viewpoints from the marketplace. See *ante*.

Therefore, the Court's insistence on inventing its brand of First Amendment underinclusiveness puzzles me. The overbreadth doctrine has the redeeming virtue of attempting to avoid the chilling of protected expression, *Broadrick* v. *Oklahoma* (1973); but the Court's new "underbreadth" creation serves no desirable function. Instead, it permits, indeed invites, the continuation of expressive conduct that in this case is evil and worthless in First Amendment terms, see *Ferber, Chaplinsky,* until the city of St. Paul cures the underbreadth by adding to its ordinance a catch-all phrase such as "and all other fighting words that may constitutionally be subject to this ordinance."

Any contribution of this holding to First Amendment jurisprudence is surely a negative one, since it necessarily signals that expressions of violence, such as the message of intimidation and racial hatred conveyed by burning a cross on someone's lawn, are of sufficient value to outweigh the social interest in order and morality that has traditionally placed such fighting words outside the First Amendment. Indeed, by characterizing fighting words as a form of "debate," *ante,* the majority legitimates hate speech as a form of public discussion.

Furthermore, the Court obscures the line between speech that could be regulated freely on the basis of content (*i.e.*, the narrow categories of expression falling outside the First Amendment) and that which could be regulated on the basis of content only upon a showing of a compelling state interest (*i.e.*, all remaining expression). By placing fighting words, which the Court has long held to be valueless, on at least equal constitutional footing with political discourse and other forms of speech that we have deemed to have the greatest social value, the majority devalues the latter category. See *Burson* v. *Freeman.*

B

In a second break with precedent, the Court refuses to sustain the ordinance even though it would survive under the strict scrutiny applicable to other protected expression. Assuming, *arguendo,* that the St. Paul ordinance is a content-based regulation of protected expression, it nevertheless would pass First Amendment review under settled law upon a showing that the regulation " 'is necessary to serve a compelling state interest and is narrowly drawn to achieve that end.' " *Simon & Schuster, Inc.* v. *New York Crime Victims Board* (1991). St. Paul has urged that its ordinance, in the words of the majority, "helps to ensure the basic human rights of members of groups that have historically been subjected to discrimination. . . ." *Ante.* The Court expressly concedes that this interest is compelling and is promoted by the ordinance. *Ibid.* Nevertheless, the Court treats strict scrutiny analysis as irrelevant to the constitutionality of the legislation:

> The dispositive question . . . is whether content discrimination is reasonably necessary in order to achieve St. Paul's compelling interests; it plainly is not. An ordinance not limited to the favored topics would have precisely the same beneficial effect. *Ibid.*

Under the majority's view, a narrowly drawn, content-based ordinance could never pass constitutional muster if the object of that legislation could be accomplished by banning a wider category of speech. This appears to be a general renunciation of strict scrutiny review, a fundamental tool of First Amendment analysis.

This abandonment of the doctrine is inexplicable in light of our decision in *Burson* v. *Freeman,* which was handed down just a month ago. In *Burson,* seven of the eight participating members of the Court agreed that the strict scrutiny standard applied in a case involving a First Amendment challenge to a content-based statute. The statute at issue prohibited the solicitation of votes and the display or distribution of campaign materials within 100 feet of the entrance to a polling place. The plurality concluded that the legislation survived strict scrutiny because the State had asserted a compelling interest in regulating electioneering near polling places and because the statute at issue was narrowly tailored to accomplish that goal. *Id.*, (9+17–18).

Significantly, the statute in *Burson* did not proscribe all speech near polling places; it restricted only political speech. *Id.*, at 5. The *Burson* plurality, which included The Chief Justice and Justice Kennedy, concluded that the distinction between types of speech required application of strict scrutiny, but it squarely rejected the proposition that the legislation failed First Amendment review because it could have been drafted in broader, content-neutral terms:

> States adopt laws to address the problems that confront them. *The First Amendment does not require States to regulate for problems that do not exist. Id.*, at 16). (emphasis added).

This reasoning is in direct conflict with the majority's analysis in the present case, which leaves two options to lawmakers attempting to regulate expressions of violence: (1) enact a sweeping prohibition on an entire class of speech (thereby requiring "regulat[ion] for problems that do not exist); or (2) not legislate at all.

Had the analysis adopted by the majority in the present case been applied in *Burson*, the challenged election law would have failed constitutional review, for its content-based distinction between political and nonpolitical speech could not have been characterized as "reasonably necessary," *ante*, to achieve the State's interest in regulating polling place premises.

As with its rejection of the Court's categorical analysis, the majority offers no reasoned basis for discarding our firmly established strict scrutiny analysis at this time. The majority appears to believe that its doctrinal revisionism is necessary to prevent our elected lawmakers from prohibiting libel against members of one political party but not another and from enacting similarly preposterous laws. *Ante*. The majority is misguided.

Although the First Amendment does not apply to categories of unprotected speech, such as fighting words, the Equal Protection Clause requires that the regulation of unprotected speech be rationally related to a legitimate government interest. A defamation statute that drew distinctions on the basis of political affiliation or "an ordinance prohibiting only those legally obscene works that contain criticism of the city government," *ante*, would unquestionably fail rational basis review.

Turning to the St. Paul ordinance and assuming *arguendo*, as the majority does, that the ordinance is not constitutionally overbroad (but see Part II, *infra*), there is no question that it would pass equal protection review. The ordinance proscribes a subset of "fighting words," those that injure "on the basis of race, color, creed, religion or gender." This selective regulation reflects the City's judgment that harms based on race, color, creed, religion, or gender are more pressing public concerns than the harms caused by other fighting words. In light of our Nation's long and painful experience with discrimination, this determination is plainly reasonable. Indeed, as the majority concedes, the interest is compelling. *Ante*.

C

The Court has patched up its argument with an apparently nonexhaustive list of ad hoc exceptions, in what can be viewed either as an attempt to confine the effects of its decision to the facts of this case, see *post*, at 1–2 (Blackmun, J., concurring in judgment), or as an effort to anticipate some of the questions that will arise from its radical revision of First Amendment law.

For instance, if the majority were to give general application to the rule on which it decides this case, today's decision would call into question the constitutionality of the statute making it illegal to threaten the life of the President. 18 U. S. C. § 871. Surely, this statute, by singling out certain threats, incorporates a content-based distinction; it indicates that the Government especially disfavors threats against the President as opposed to threats against all others. See *ante*. But because the Government could prohibit all threats and not just those directed against the President, under the Court's theory, the compelling reasons justifying the enactment of special legislation to safeguard the President would be irrelevant, and the statute would fail First Amendment review.

To save the statute, the majority has engrafted the following exception onto its newly announced First Amendment rule: Content-based distinctions may be drawn within an unprotected category of speech if the basis for the distinctions is "the very reason the entire class of speech at issue is proscribable." *Ante*. Thus, the argument goes, the statute making it illegal to threaten the life of the President is constitutional, "since the reasons why threats of violence are outside the First Amendment (protecting individuals from the fear of violence, from the disruption that fear engenders, and from the possibility that the threatened violence will occur) have special force when applied to the person of the President." *Ante*.

The exception swallows the majority's rule. Certainly, it should apply to the St. Paul ordinance, since "the reasons why [fighting words] are outside the First Amendment . . . have special force when applied to [groups that have historically been subjected to discrimination]."

To avoid the result of its own analysis, the Court suggests that fighting words are simply a mode of communication, rather than a content-based category, and that the St. Paul ordinance has not signaled out a particularly objectionable mode of communication. *Ante*. Again, the majority confuses the issue. A prohibition on fighting words is not a time, place, or manner restriction; it is a ban on a class of speech that conveys an overriding message of personal injury and imminent violence, *Chaplinsky*, a message that is at its ugliest when directed against groups that have long been the targets of discrimination. Accordingly, the ordinance falls within the first exception to the majority's theory.

As its second exception, the Court posits that certain content-based regulations will survive under the new regime if the regulated subclass "happens to be associated with particular 'secondary effects' of the speech. . ." *ante*, at 10, which the majority treats as encompassing instances in which "words can . . . violate laws directed not against speech but against conduct . . ." *Ante*. Again, there is a simple explanation for the Court's eagerness to craft an exception to its new First Amendment rule: Under the general rule the Court applies in this case, Title VII hostile work environment claims would suddenly be unconstitutional.

Title VII makes it unlawful to discriminate "because of [an] individual's race, color, religion, sex, or national origin," 42 U. S. C. § 2000e–2(a)(1), and the regulations covering hostile workplace claims forbid "sexual harassment," which includes "[u]nwelcome sexual advances, requests for sexual favors, and other verbal or physical conduct of a sexual nature" which creates "an intimidating, hostile, or offensive working environment." 29 CFR § 1604.11(a) (1991). The regulation does not prohibit workplace harassment generally; it focuses on what the majority would characterize as the "disfavored topi[c]" of sexual harassment. *Ante*. In this way, Title VII is similar to the St. Paul ordinance that the majority condemns because it "impose[s] special prohibitions on those speakers who express views on disfavored subjects." *Ibid*. Under the broad principle the Court uses to decide the present case, hostile work environment claims based on sexual harassment should fail First Amendment review; because a general ban on harassment in the workplace would cover the problem of sexual harassment, any attempt to proscribe the subcategory of sexually harassing expression would violate the First Amendment.

Hence, the majority's second exception, which the Court indicates would insulate a Title VII hostile work environment claim from an underinclusiveness challenge because "sexually derogatory 'fighting words' . . . may produce a violation of Title VII's general prohibition against sexual discrimination in employment practices." *Ante,* at 11. But application of this exception to a hostile work environment claim does not hold up under close examination.

First, the hostile work environment regulation is not keyed to the presence or absence of an economic *quid pro quo, Meritor Savings Bank* v. *Vinson* (1986), but to the impact of the speech on the victimized worker. Consequently, the regulation would no more fall within a secondary effects exception than does the St. Paul ordinance. *Ante.* Second, the majority's focus on the statute's general prohibition on discrimination glosses over the language of the specific regulation governing hostile working environment, which reaches beyond any "incidental" effect on speech. *United States* v. *O'Brien* (1968). If the relationship between the broader statute and specific regulation is sufficient to bring the Title VII regulation within *O'Brien,* then all St. Paul need do to bring its ordinance within this exception is to add some prefatory language concerning discrimination generally.

As the third exception to the Court's theory for deciding this case, the majority concocts a catchall exclusion to protect against unforeseen problems, a concern that is heightened here given the lack of briefing on the majority's decisional theory. This final exception would apply in cases in which "there is no realistic possibility that official suppression of ideas is afoot." *Ante.* As I have demonstrated, this case does not concern the official suppression of ideas. The majority discards this notion out-of-hand. *Ante.*

As I see it, the Court's theory does not work and will do nothing more than confuse the law. Its selection of this case to rewrite First Amendment law is particularly inexplicable, because the whole problem could have been avoided by deciding this case under settled First Amendment principles.

II

Although I disagree with the Court's analysis, I do agree with its conclusion: The St. Paul ordinance is unconstitutional. However, I would decide the case on overbreadth grounds.

We have emphasized time and again that overbreadth doctrine is an exception to the established principle that "a person to whom a statute may constitutionally be applied will not be heard to challenge that statute on the ground that it may conceivably be applied unconstitutionally to others, in other situations not before the Court." *Broadrick* v. *Oklahoma.* A defendant being prosecuted for speech or expressive conduct may challenge the law on its face if it reaches protected expression, even when that person's activities are not protected by the First Amendment. This is because "the possible harm to society in permitting some unprotected speech to go unpunished is outweighed by the possibility that protected speech of others may be muted." *Broadrick.*

However, we have consistently held that, because overbreadth analysis is "strong medicine," it may be invoked to strike an entire statute only when the overbreadth of the statute is not only "real, but substantial as well, judged in relation to the statute's plainly legitimate sweep," *Broadrick,* and when the statute is not susceptible to limitation or partial invalidation. *Id.,* at 613; *Board of Airport Comm'rs of Los Angeles* v. *Jews for Jesus, Inc.* (1987). "When a federal court is dealing with a federal statute challenged as overbroad, it should . . . construe the statute to avoid constitutional problems, if the statute is subject to a limiting construction." *Ferber.* Of course, "[a] state court is also free to deal with a state statute in the same way." *Ibid.*

Petitioner contends that the St. Paul ordinance is not susceptible to a narrowing construction and that the ordinance therefore should be considered as written, and not as construed by the Minnesota Supreme Court. Petitioner is wrong. Where a state court has interpreted a provision of state law, we cannot ignore that interpretation, even if it is not one that we would have reached if we were construing the statute in the first instance. *Ibid.*

Of course, the mere presence of a state court interpretation does not insulate a statute from overbreadth review. We have stricken legislation when the construction supplied by the state court failed to cure the overbreadth problem. But in such cases, we have looked to the statute as construed in determining whether it contravened the First Amendment. Here, the Minnesota Supreme Court has provided an authoritative construction of the St. Paul antibias ordinance. Consideration of petitioner's overbreadth claim must be based on that interpretation.

I agree with petitioner that the ordinance is invalid on its face. Although the ordinance as construed reaches categories of speech that are constitutionally unprotected, it also criminalizes a substantial amount of expression that—however repugnant—is shielded by the First Amendment.

In attempting to narrow the scope of the St. Paul antibias ordinance, the Minnesota Supreme Court relied upon two of the categories of speech and expressive conduct that fall outside the First Amendment's protective sphere: words that incite "imminent lawless action," *Brandenburg* v. *Ohio* (1969), and "fighting" words, *Chaplinsky* v. *New Hampshire.* The Minnesota Supreme Court erred in its application of the *Chaplinsky* fighting words test and consequently interpreted the St. Paul ordinance in a fashion that rendered the ordinance facially overbroad.

In construing the St. Paul ordinance, the Minnesota Supreme Court drew upon the definition of fighting words that appears in *Chaplinsky*—words "which by their very utterance inflict injury or tend to incite an immediate breach of the peace." *Id.*, at 572. However, the Minnesota court was far from clear in identifying the "injur[ies]" inflicted by the expression that St. Paul sought to regulate. Indeed, the Minnesota court emphasized (tracking the language of the ordinance) that "the ordinance censors only those displays that one knows or should know will create anger, alarm or resentment based on racial, ethnic, gender or religious bias." *In re Welfare of R. A. V.* (1991). I therefore understand the court to have ruled that St. Paul may constitutionally prohibit expression that "by its very utterance" causes "anger, alarm or resentment."

Our fighting words cases have made clear, however, that such generalized reactions are not sufficient to strip expression of its constitutional protection. The mere fact that expressive activity causes hurt feelings, offense, or resentment does not render the expression unprotected.

In the First Amendment context, "[c]riminal statutes must be scrutinized with particular care; those that make unlawful a substantial amount of constitutionally protected conduct may be held facially invalid even if they also have legitimate application." *Houston* v. *Hill* (1987) (citation omitted). The St. Paul anti-bias ordinance is such a law. Although the ordinance reaches conduct that is unprotected, it also makes criminal expressive conduct that causes only hurt feelings, offense, or resentment, and is protected by the First Amendment. The ordinance is therefore fatally overbroad and invalid on its face.

III

Today, the Court has disregarded two established principles of First Amendment law without providing a coherent replacement theory. Its decision is an arid, doctrinaire interpretation, driven by the frequently irresistible impulse of judges to tinker with the First Amendment. The decision is mischievous at best and will surely confuse the lower courts. I join the judgment, but not the folly of the opinion.

Justice Blackmun, concurring in the judgment.

I regret what the Court has done in this case. The majority opinion signals one of two possibilities: it will serve as precedent for future cases, or it will not. Either result is disheartening.

In the first instance, by deciding that a State cannot regulate speech that causes great harm unless it also regulates speech that does not (setting law and logic on their heads), the Court seems to abandon the categorical approach, and inevitably to relax the level of scrutiny applicable to content-based laws. As Justice White points out, this weakens the traditional protections of speech. If all expressive activity must be accorded the same protection, that protection will be scant. The simple reality is that the Court will never provide child pornography or cigarette advertising the level of protection customarily granted political speech. If we are forbidden from categorizing, as the Court has done here, we shall reduce protection across the board. It is sad that in its effort to reach a satisfying result in this case, the Court is willing to weaken First Amendment protections.

In the second instance is the possibility that this case will not significantly alter First Amendment jurisprudence, but, instead, will be regarded as an aberration—a case where the Court manipulated doctrine to strike down an ordinance whose premise it opposed, namely, that racial threats and verbal assaults are of greater harm than other fighting words. I fear that the Court has been distracted from its proper mission by the temptation to decide the issue over "politically correct speech" and "cultural diversity," neither of which is presented here. If this is the meaning of today's opinion, it is perhaps even more regrettable.

I see no First Amendment values that are compromised by a law that prohibits hoodlums from driving minorities out of their homes by burning crosses on their lawns, but I see great harm in preventing the people of St. Paul from specifically punishing the race-based fighting words that so prejudice their community.

I concur in the judgment, however, because I agree with Justice White that this particular ordinance reaches beyond fighting words to speech protected by the First Amendment.

Justice Stevens, with whom Justice White and Justice Blackmun join as to Part I, concurring in the judgment.

Conduct that creates special risks or causes special harms may be prohibited by special rules. Lighting a fire near an ammunition dump or a gasoline storage tank is especially dangerous; such behavior may be punished more severely than burning trash in a vacant lot. Threatening someone because of her race or religious beliefs may cause particularly severe trauma or touch off a riot, and threatening a high public official may cause substantial social disruption; such threats may be punished more severely than threats against someone based on, say, his support of a particular athletic team. There are legitimate, reasonable, and neutral justifications for such special rules.

This case involves the constitutionality of one such ordinance. Because the regulated conduct has some communicative content—a message of racial, religious or gender hostility—the ordinance raises two quite different First Amendment questions. Is the ordinance "overbroad" because it prohibits too much speech? If not, is it "underbroad" because it does not prohibit enough speech?

In answering these questions, my colleagues today wrestle with two broad principles: first, that certain "categories of expression [including 'fighting words'] are 'not within the area of constitutionally protected speech,' " *ante* (White, J., concurring in judgment); and second, that "[c]ontent-based regulations [of expression] are presumptively invalid." *Ante.* (Opinion of the Court). Although in past opinions the Court has repeated both of these maxims, it has—quite rightly—adhered to neither with the absolutism suggested by my colleagues. Thus, while I agree that the St. Paul ordinance is unconstitutionally overbroad for the reasons stated in Part II of Justice White's opinion, I write separately to suggest how the allure of absolute principles has skewed the analysis of both the majority and concurring opinions.

I

Fifty years ago, the Court articulated a categorical approach to First Amendment jurisprudence.

> There are certain well-defined and narrowly limited classes of speech, the prevention and punishment of which have never been thought to raise any Constitutional problem. . . . It has been well observed that such utterances are no essential part of any exposition of ideas, and are of such slight social value as a step to truth that any benefit that may be derived from them is clearly outweighed by the social interest in order and morality. *Chaplinsky* v. *New Hampshire* (1942).

We have, as Justice White observes, often described such categories of expression as "not within the area of constitutionally protected speech." *Roth* v. *United States* (1957).

The Court today revises this categorical approach. It is not, the Court rules, that certain "categories" of expression are "unprotected," but rather that certain "elements" of expression are wholly "proscribable." To the Court, an expressive act, like a chemical compound, consists of more than one element. Although the act may be regulated because it contains a proscribable element, it may not be regulated on the basis of another (nonproscribable) element it also contains. Thus, obscene antigovernment speech may be regulated because it is obscene, but not because it is antigovernment. *Ante*. It is this revision of the categorical approach that allows the Court to assume that the St. Paul ordinance proscribes *only* fighting words, while at the same time concluding that the ordinance is invalid because it imposes a content-based regulation on expressive activity.

As an initial matter, the Court's revision of the categorical approach seems to me something of an adventure in a doctrinal wonderland, for the concept of "obscene anti-government" speech is fantastical. The category of the obscene is very narrow; to be obscene, expression must be found by the trier of fact to "appea[l] to the prurient interest, . . . depic[t] or describ[e], in a patently offensive way, sexual conduct, [and] taken as a whole, *lac[k] serious literary, artistic, political or scientific value.*" *Miller* v. *California* (1973) (emphasis added). "Obscene antigovernment" speech, then, is a contradiction in terms: If expression is antigovernment, it does not "lac[k] serious . . . political . . . value" and cannot be obscene.

The Court attempts to bolster its argument by likening its novel analysis to that applied to restrictions on the time, place, or manner of expression or on expressive conduct. It is true that loud speech in favor of the Republican Party can be regulated because it is loud, but not because it is pro-Republican; and it is true that the public burning of the American flag can be regulated because it involves public burning and not because it involves the flag. But these analogies are inapposite. In each of these examples, the two elements (*e.g.*, loudness and pro-Republican orientation) can coexist; in the case of "obscene antigovernment" speech, however, the presence of one element ("obscenity") by definition means the absence of the other. To my mind, it is unwise and unsound to craft a new doctrine based on such highly speculative hypotheticals.

I am, however, even more troubled by the second step of the Court's analysis—namely, its conclusion that the St. Paul ordinance is an unconstitutional content-based regulation of speech. Drawing on broadly worded *dicta*, the Court establishes a near-absolute ban on content-based regulations of expression and holds that the First Amendment prohibits the regulation of fighting words by subject matter. Thus, while the Court rejects the "all-or-nothing-at-all" nature of the categorical approach, *ante*, at 6, it promptly embraces an absolutism of its own: within a particular "proscribable" category of expression, the Court holds, a government must either proscribe *all* speech or no speech at all. This aspect of the Court's ruling fundamentally misunderstands the role and constitutional status of content-based regulations on speech, conflicts with the very nature of First Amendment jurisprudence, and disrupts well-settled principles of First Amendment law.

Although the Court has, on occasion, declared that content-based regulations of speech are "never permitted," *Police Dept. of Chicago* v. *Mosley* (1972), such claims are overstated. Indeed, in *Mosley* itself, the Court indicated that Chicago's selective proscription of nonlabor picketing was not *per se* unconstitutional, but rather could be upheld if the City demonstrated that nonlabor picketing was "clearly more disruptive than [labor] picketing." *Id.*, at 100. Contrary to the broad *dicta* in *Mosley* and elsewhere, our decisions demonstrate that content-based distinctions, far from being presumptively invalid, are an inevitable and indispensable aspect of a coherent understanding of the First Amendment.

This is true at every level of First Amendment law. In broadest terms, our entire First Amendment jurisprudence creates a regime based on the content of speech. The scope of the First Amendment is determined by the content of expressive activity: Although the First Amendment broadly protects "speech," it does not protect the right to "fix prices, breach contracts, make false warranties, place bets with bookies, threaten, [or] extort." Schauer, Categories and the First Amendment: A Play in Three Acts, 34 Vand. L. Rev. 265, 270 (1981). Whether an agreement among competitors is a violation of the Sherman Act or protected activity under the *Noerr-Pennington* doctrine hinges upon the content of the agreement. Similarly, "the line between permissible advocacy and impermissible incitation to crime or violence depends, not merely on the setting in which the speech occurs, but also on exactly what the speaker had to say." *Young* v. *American Mini Theatres, Inc.* (1976) (plurality opinion).

Likewise, whether speech falls within one of the categories of "unprotected" or "proscribable" expression is determined, in part, by its content. Whether a magazine is obscene, a gesture a fighting word, or a photograph child pornography is determined, in part, by its content. Even within categories of protected expression, the First Amendment status of speech is fixed by its content. *New York Times Co.* v. *Sullivan* (1964) and *Dun & Bradstreet, Inc.* v. *Greenmoss Builders, Inc.* (1985), establish that the level of protection given to speech depends upon its subject matter: speech about public officials or matters of public concern receives greater protection than speech about other topics. It can, therefore, scarcely be said that the regulation of expressive activity cannot be predicated on its content: much of our First Amendment jurisprudence is premised on the assumption that content makes a difference.

Consistent with this general premise, we have frequently upheld content-based regulations of speech. For example, in *Young* v. *American Mini Theatres,* the Court upheld zoning ordinances that regulated movie theaters based on the content of the films shown. In *FCC* v. *Pacifica Foundation* (1978) (plurality opinion), we upheld a restriction on the broadcast of specific indecent words. In *Lehman* v. *City of Shaker Heights* (1974) (plurality opinion), we upheld a city law that permitted commercial advertising, but prohibited political advertising, on city buses. In *Broadrick* v. *Oklahoma* (1973), we upheld a state law that restricted the speech of state employees, but only as concerned partisan political matters. We have long recognized the power of the Federal Trade Commission to regulate misleading advertising and labeling, see, *e.g.*, *Jacob Siegel Co.* v. *FTC* (1946), and the National Labor Relations Board's power to regulate an employer's election-related speech on the basis of its content. See, *e.g.*, *NLRB* v. *Gissel Packing Co.* (1969). It is also beyond question that the Government may choose to limit advertisements for cigarettes, see 15 U. S. C. § 1331–1340, but not for cigars; choose to regulate airline advertising, see *Morales* v. *Trans World Airlines* (1992), but not bus advertising; or choose to monitor solicitation by lawyers, see *Ohralik* v. *Ohio State Bar Assn.* (1978), but not by doctors.

All of these cases involved the selective regulation of speech based on content—precisely the sort of regulation the Court invalidates today. Such selective regulations are unavoidably content based, but they are not, in my opinion, "presumptively invalid." As these many decisions and examples demonstrate, the prohibition on content-based regulations is not nearly as total as the *Mosley* dictum suggests.

Disregarding this vast body of case law, the Court today goes beyond even the overstatement in *Mosley* and applies the prohibition on content-based regulation to speech that the Court had until today considered wholly "unprotected" by the First Amendment—namely, fighting words. This new absolutism in the prohibition of content-based regulations severely contorts the fabric of settled First Amendment law.

Our First Amendment decisions have created a rough hierarchy in the constitutional protection of speech. Core political speech occupies the highest, most protected position; commercial speech and nonobscene, sexually explicit speech are regarded as a sort of second-class expression; obscenity and fighting words receive the least protection of all. Assuming that the Court is correct that this last class of speech is not wholly "unprotected," it certainly does not follow that fighting words and obscenity receive the *same* sort of protection afforded core political speech. Yet in ruling that proscribable speech cannot be regulated based on subject matter, the Court does just that. Perversely, this gives fighting words *greater* protection than is afforded commercial speech. If Congress can prohibit false advertising directed at airline passengers without also prohibiting false advertising directed at bus passengers and if a city can prohibit political advertisements in its buses while allowing other advertisements, it is ironic to hold that a city cannot regulate fighting words based on "race, color, creed, religion or gender" while leaving unregulated fighting words based on "union membership or homosexuality." *Ante.* The Court today turns First Amendment law on its head: Communication that was once entirely unprotected (and that still can be wholly proscribed) is now entitled to greater protection than commercial speech—and possibly greater protection than core political speech. See *Burson* v. *Freeman* (1992).

Perhaps because the Court recognizes these perversities, it quickly offers some ad hoc limitations on its newly extended prohibition on content-based regulations. First, the Court states that a content-based regulation is valid "[w]hen the content discrimination is based upon the very reason the entire class of speech . . . is proscribable." In a pivotal passage, the Court writes

> the Federal Government can criminalize only those physical threats that are directed against the President, see 18 U. S. C. § 871—since the reasons why threats of violence are outside the First Amendment (protecting individuals from the fear of violence, from the disruption that fear engenders, and from the possibility that the threatened violence will occur) have special force when applied to the . . . President. *Ante,* at 10.

As I understand this opaque passage, Congress may choose from the set of unprotected speech (all threats) to proscribe only a subset (threats against the President) because those threats are particularly likely to cause "fear of violence," "disruption," and actual "violence."

Precisely this same reasoning, however, compels the conclusion that St. Paul's ordinance is constitutional. Just as Congress may determine that threats against the President entail more severe consequences than other threats, so St. Paul's City Council may determine that threats based on the target's race, religion, or gender cause more severe harm to both the target and to society than other threats. This latter judgment—that harms caused by racial, religious, and gender-based invective are qualitatively different from that caused by other fighting words—seems to me eminently reasonable and realistic.

Next, the Court recognizes that a State may regulate advertising in one industry but not another because "the risk of fraud (one of the characteristics that justifies depriving [commercial speech] of full First Amendment protection . . .)" in the regulated industry is "greater" than in other industries. *Ante*. Again, the same reasoning demonstrates the constitutionality of St. Paul's ordinance. "[O]ne of the characteristics that justifies" the constitutional status of fighting words is that such words "by their very utterance inflict injury or tend to incite an immediate breach of the peace." *Chaplinsky*. Certainly a legislature that may determine that the risk of fraud is greater in the legal trade than in the medical trade may determine that the risk of injury or breach of peace created by race-based threats is greater than that created by other threats.

Similarly, it is impossible to reconcile the Court's analysis of the St. Paul ordinance with its recognition that "a prohibition of fighting words that are directed at certain persons or groups . . . would be facially valid." *Ante* (emphasis deleted). A selective proscription of unprotected expression designed to protect "certain persons or groups" (for example, a law proscribing threats directed at the elderly) would be constitutional if it were based on a legitimate determination that the harm created by the regulated expression differs from that created by the unregulated expression (that is, if the elderly are more severely injured by threats than are the nonelderly). Such selective protection is no different from a law prohibiting minors (and only minors) from obtaining obscene publications. See *Ginsberg* v. *New York* (1968). St. Paul has determined—reasonably in my judgment—that fighting-word injuries "based on race, color, creed, religion or gender" are qualitatively different and more severe than fighting-word injuries based on other characteristics. Whether the selective proscription of proscribable speech is defined by the protected target ("certain persons or groups") or the basis of the harm (injuries "based on race, color, creed, religion or gender") makes no constitutional difference: what matters is whether the legislature's selection is based on a legitimate, neutral, and reasonable distinction.

In sum, the central premise of the Court's ruling—that "[c]ontent-based regulations are presumptively invalid"—has simplistic appeal, but lacks support in our First Amendment jurisprudence. To make matters worse, the Court today extends this overstated claim to reach categories of hitherto unprotected speech and, in doing so, wreaks havoc in an area of settled law. Finally, although the Court recognizes exceptions to its new principle, those exceptions undermine its very conclusion that the St. Paul ordinance is unconstitutional. Stated directly, the majority's position cannot withstand scrutiny.

II

Although I agree with much of Justice White's analysis, I do not join Part I-A of his opinion because I have reservations about the "categorical approach" to the First Amendment. These concerns lead me to find Justice White's response to the Court's analysis unsatisfying.

Admittedly, the categorical approach to the First Amendment has some appeal: either expression is protected or it is not—the categories create safe harbors for governments and speakers alike. But this approach sacrifices subtlety for clarity and is, I am convinced, ultimately unsound. As an initial matter, the concept of "categories" fits poorly with the complex reality of expression. Few dividing lines in First Amendment law are straight and unwavering, and efforts at categorization inevitably give rise only to fuzzy boundaries. Our definitions of "obscenity" and "public forum," illustrate this all too well. The quest for doctrinal certainty through the definition of categories and subcategories is, in my opinion, destined to fail.

Moreover, the categorical approach does not take seriously the importance of *context*.

The meaning of any expression and the legitimacy of its regulation can only be determined in context. Whether, for example, a picture or a sentence is obscene cannot be judged in the abstract, but rather only in the context of its setting, its use, and its audience. Similarly, although legislatures may freely regulate most nonobscene child pornography, such pornography that is part of "a serious work of art, a documentary on behavioral problems, or a medical or psychiatric teaching device," may be entitled to constitutional protection; the "question whether a specific act of communication is protected by the First Amendment always requires some consideration of both its content and its context." *Ferber* (Stevens, J., concurring in judgment). The categorical approach sweeps too broadly when it declares that all such expression is beyond the protection of the First Amendment.

Perhaps sensing the limits of such an all-or-nothing approach, the Court has applied its analysis less categorically than its doctrinal statements suggest. The Court has recognized intermediate categories of speech (for example, for indecent nonobscene speech and commercial speech) and geographic categories of speech (public fora, limited public fora, nonpublic fora) entitled to varying levels of protection. The Court has also stringently delimited the categories of unprotected speech. While we once declared that "[l]ibelous utterances [are] not . . . within the area of constitutionally protected speech, *Beauharnais* v. *Illinois* (1952), our rulings in *New York Times Co.* v. *Sullivan* (1964); *Gertz* v. *Robert Welch, Inc.* (1974), and *Dun & Bradstreet, Inc.* v. *Greenmoss Builders, Inc.* (1985), have substantially qualified this broad claim. Similarly, we have consistently construed the "fighting words" exception set forth in *Chaplinsky* narrowly. In the case of commercial speech, our ruling that "the Constitution imposes no . . . restraint on government [regulation] as respects purely commercial advertising," *Valentine* v. *Chrestensen* (1942), was expressly repudiated in *Virginia Bd. of Pharmacy* v. *Virginia Citizens Consumer Council, Inc.* (1976). In short, the history of the categorical approach is largely the history of narrowing the categories of unprotected speech.

This evolution, I believe, indicates that the categorical approach is unworkable and the quest for absolute categories of "protected" and "unprotected" speech ultimately futile. My analysis of the faults and limits of this approach persuades me that the categorical approach presented in Part I-A of Justice White's opinion is not an adequate response to the novel "underbreadth" analysis the Court sets forth today.

III

As the foregoing suggests, I disagree with both the Court's and part of Justice White's analysis of the constitutionality St. Paul ordinance. Unlike the Court, I do not believe that all content-based regulations are equally infirm and presumptively invalid; unlike Justice White, I do not believe that fighting words are wholly unprotected by the First Amendment. To the contrary, I believe our decisions establish a more complex and subtle analysis, one that considers the content and context of the regulated speech, and the nature and scope of the restriction on speech. Applying this analysis and assuming *arguendo* (as the Court does) that the St. Paul ordinance is *not* overbroad, I conclude that such a selective, subject-matter regulation on proscribable speech is constitutional.

Not all content-based regulations are alike; our decisions clearly recognize that some content-based restrictions raise more constitutional questions than others. Although the Court's analysis of content-based regulations cannot be reduced to a simple formula, we have considered a number of factors in determining the validity of such regulations.

First, as suggested above, the scope of protection provided expressive activity depends in part upon its content and character. We have long recognized that when government regulates political speech or "the expression of editorial opinion on matters of public importance," *FCC* v. *League of Women Voters of California* (1984), "First Amendment protectio[n] is 'at its zenith.' " *Meyer* v. *Grant* (1988). In comparison, we have recognized that "commercial speech receives a limited form of First Amendment protection," *Posadas de Puerto Rico Associates* v. *Tourism Co. of Puerto Rico* (1986), and that "society's interest in protecting [sexually explicit films] is of a wholly different, and lesser magnitude than [its] interest in untrammeled political debate." *Young* v. *American Mini Theatres*. The character of expressive activity also weighs in our consideration of its constitutional status. As we have frequently noted, "[t]he government generally has a freer hand in restricting expressive conduct than it has in restricting the written or spoken word." *Texas* v. *Johnson* (1989).

The protection afforded expression turns as well on the context of the regulated speech. We have noted, for example, that "[a]ny assessment of the precise scope of employer expression, of course, must be made in the context of its labor relations setting . . . [and] must take into account the economic dependence of the employees on their employers." *NLRB* v. *Gissel Packing Co.* Similarly, the distinctive character of a university environment, see *Widmar* v. *Vincent* (1981) (Stevens, J., concurring in judgment), or a secondary school environment, see *Hazelwood School Dist.* v. *Kuhlmeier* (1988), influences our First Amendment analysis. The same is true of the presence of a " 'captive audience[, one] there as a matter of necessity, not of choice.' " *Lehman* v. *City of Shaker Heights* (citation omitted). Perhaps the most familiar embodiment of the relevance of context is our "fora" jurisprudence, differentiating the levels of protection afforded speech in different locations.

The nature of a contested restriction of speech also informs our evaluation of its constitutionality. Thus, for example, "[a]ny system of prior restraints of expression comes to this Court bearing a heavy presumption against its constitutional validity." *Bantam Books, Inc.* v. *Sullivan* (1963). More particularly to the matter of content-based regulations, we have implicitly distinguished between restrictions on expression based on *subject matter* and restrictions based on *viewpoint,* indicating that the latter are particularly pernicious. "If there is a bedrock principle underlying the First Amendment, it is that the Government may not prohibit the expression of an idea simply because society finds the idea itself offensive or disagreeable." *Texas* v. *Johnson*. "Viewpoint discrimination is censorship in its purest form," *Perry Education Assn.* v. *Perry Local Educators' Assn.* (1983) (Brennan, J., dissenting), and requires particular scrutiny, in part because such regulation often indicates a legislative effort to skew public debate on an issue. "Especially where . . . the legislature's suppression of speech suggests an attempt to give one side of a debatable public question an advantage in expressing its views to the people, the First Amendment is plainly offended." *First National Bank of Boston* v. *Bellotti* (1978). Thus, although a regulation that on its face regulates speech by subject matter may in some instances effectively suppress particular viewpoints, in general, viewpoint-based restrictions on expression require greater scrutiny than subject-matter based restrictions.

Finally, in considering the validity of content-based regulations we have also looked more broadly at the scope of the restrictions. For example, in *Young* v. *American Mini Theatres,* we found significant the fact that "what [was] ultimately at stake [was] nothing more than a limitation on the place where adult films may be exhibited." Similarly, in *FCC* v. *Pacifica Foundation,* the Court emphasized two dimensions of the limited scope of the FCC ruling. First, the ruling concerned only broadcast material which presents particular problems because it "confronts the citizen . . . in the privacy of the home"; second, the ruling was not a complete ban on the use of selected offensive words, but rather merely a limitation on the times such speech could be broadcast.

All of these factors play some role in our evaluation of content-based regulations on expression. Such a multi-faceted analysis cannot be conflated into two dimensions. Whatever the allure of absolute doctrines, it is just too simple to declare expression "protected" or "unprotected" or to proclaim a regulation "content-based" or "content-neutral."

In applying this analysis to the St. Paul ordinance, I assume *arguendo*—as the Court does—that the ordinance regulates *only* fighting words and therefore is *not* overbroad. Looking to the content and character of the regulated activity, two things are clear. First, by hypothesis the ordinance bars only low-value speech, namely, fighting words. By definition such expression constitutes "no essential part of any exposition of ideas, and [is] of such slight social value as a step to truth that any benefit that may be derived from [it] is clearly outweighed by the social interest in order and morality." *Chaplinsky*. Second, the ordinance regulates "expressive conduct [rather] than . . . the written or spoken word." *Texas* v. *Johnson*.

Looking to the context of the regulated activity, it is again significant that the statute (by hypothesis) regulates *only* fighting words. Whether words are fighting words is determined in part by their context. Fighting words are not words that merely cause offense; fighting words must be directed at individuals so as to "by their very utterance inflict injury." By hypothesis, then, the St. Paul ordinance restricts speech in confrontational and potentially violent situations. The case at hand is illustrative. The cross-burning in this case—directed as it was to a single African-American family trapped in their home—was nothing more than a crude form of physical intimidation. That this cross-burning sends a message of racial hostility does not automatically endow it with complete constitutional protection.

Significantly, the St. Paul ordinance regulates speech not on the basis of its subject matter or the viewpoint expressed, but rather on the basis of the *harm* the speech causes. In this regard, the Court fundamentally misreads the St. Paul ordinance. The Court describes the St. Paul ordinance as regulating expression "addressed to one of [several] specified disfavored *topics*," *ante* (emphasis supplied), as policing "disfavored *subjects*," *ibid.* (emphasis supplied), and as "prohibit[ing] . . . speech solely on the basis of the *subjects* the speech addresses." *Ante* (emphasis supplied). Contrary to the Court's suggestion, the ordinance regulates only a subcategory of expression that causes *injuries* based on "race, color, creed, religion or gender," not a subcategory that involves *discussions* that concern those characteristics. The ordinance, as construed by the Court, criminalizes expression that "one knows . . . [by its very utterance inflicts injury on] others on the basis of race, color, creed, religion or gender." In this regard, the ordinance resembles the child pornography law at issue in *Ferber*, which in effect singled out child pornography because those publications caused far greater harms than pornography involving adults.

Moreover, even if the St. Paul ordinance did regulate fighting words based on its subject matter, such a regulation would, in my opinion, be constitutional. As noted above, subject-matter based regulations on commercial speech are widespread and largely unproblematic. As we have long recognized, subject-matter regulations generally do not raise the same concerns of government censorship and the distortion of public discourse presented by viewpoint regulations. Thus, in upholding subject-matter regulations we have carefully noted that viewpoint-based discrimination was not implicated. Indeed, some subject-matter restrictions are a functional necessity in contemporary governance: "The First Amendment does not require States to regulate for problems that do not exist." *Burson* v. *Freeman*.

Contrary to the suggestion of the majority, the St. Paul ordinance does *not* regulate expression based on viewpoint. The Court contends that the ordinance requires proponents of racial intolerance to "follow the Marquis of Queensbury Rules" while allowing advocates of racial tolerance to "fight freestyle." The law does no such thing.

The Court writes:

> One could hold up a sign saying, for example, that all "anti-Catholic bigots" are misbegotten: but not that all "papists" are, for that would insult and provoke violence "on the basis of religion" *Ante.*

This may be true, but it hardly proves the Court's point. The Court's reasoning is asymmetrical. The response to a sign saying that "all [religious] bigots are misbegotten" is a sign saying that "all advocates of religious tolerance are misbegotten." Assuming such signs could be fighting words (which seems to me extremely unlikely), neither sign would be banned by the ordinance for the attacks were not "based on . . . religion" but rather on one's beliefs about tolerance. Conversely (and again assuming such signs are fighting words), just as the ordinance would prohibit a Muslim from hoisting a sign claiming that all Catholics were misbegotten, so the ordinance would bar a Catholic from hoisting a similar sign attacking Muslims.

The St. Paul ordinance is evenhanded. In a battle between advocates of tolerance and advocates of intolerance, the ordinance does not prevent either side from hurling fighting words at the other on the basis of their conflicting ideas, but it does bar *both* sides from hurling such words on the basis of the target's "race, color, creed, religion or gender." To extend the Court's pugilistic metaphor, the St. Paul ordinance simply bans punches "below the belt"—*by either party*. It does not, therefore, favor one side of any debate.

Finally, it is noteworthy that the St. Paul ordinance is, as construed by the Court today, quite narrow. The St. Paul ordinance does not ban all "hate speech," nor does it ban, say, all cross-burnings or all swastika displays. Rather it only bans a subcategory of the already narrow category of fighting words. Such a limited ordinance leaves open and protected a vast range of expression on the subjects of racial, religious, and gender equality. As construed by the Court today, the ordinance certainly does not " 'raise the specter that the Government may effectively drive certain ideas or viewpoints from the marketplace.' " *Ante.* Petitioner is free to burn a cross to announce a rally or to express his views about racial supremacy, he may do so on private property or public land, at day or at night, so long as the burning is not so threatening and so directed at an individual as to "by its very [execution] inflict injury." Such a limited proscription scarcely offends the First Amendment.

In sum, the St. Paul ordinance (as construed by the Court) regulates expressive activity that is wholly proscribable and does so not on the basis of viewpoint, but rather in recognition of the different harms caused by such activity. Taken together, these several considerations persuade me that the St. Paul ordinance is not an unconstitutional content-based regulation of speech. Thus, were the ordinance not overbroad, I would vote to uphold it.

Words Which Wound: Burning Crosses and the R. A. V. Case

MARI J. MATSUDA
AND CHARLES R. LAWRENCE III

This essay is the insightful epilogue to the book *Words That Wound: Critical Race Theory, Assaultive Speech, and the First Amendment.* Matsuda and Lawrence argue that Supreme Court Justice Scalia's opinion in the R. A. V. case is exactly the sort of judicial opinion they oppose. They argue that Scalia ignores history and fails to appreciate adequately the plight of those victimized by hate crimes.

In the early morning hours of June 21, 1990, long after they had put their five children to bed, Russ and Laura Jones were awakened by voices outside their house. Russ got up, went

"Words Which Wound: Burning Crosses and the R. A. V. Case," Mari Matsuda and Charles Lawrence, 1990, by permission of Westview Press, Boulder, Colorado.

to his bedroom window, and peered into the dark. "I saw a glow," he recalled. There, in the middle of his yard, was a burning cross. The Joneses are African Americans. In the spring of 1990 they had moved into their four-bedroom, three-bathroom dream house in St. Paul, Minnesota. They were the only Black family on the block. Two weeks after they had settled into their predominantly white neighborhood, the tires on both of their cars were slashed. A few weeks later one of their car windows was shattered, and a group of teenagers walked past their house and shouted "nigger" at their nine-year-old son. And now this burning cross. Russ Jones did not have to guess at the meaning of this symbol of racial hatred. There is no Black person in America who has not learned the significance of this instrument of persecution and intimidation, who has not had emblazoned on his or her mind the image of Black men's scorched bodies hanging from trees.

The assailant who burned the makeshift cross in the fenced yard of the Jones home was identified and prosecuted under a local hate crime ordinance. Following the predictable pattern identified in the introduction to this book, the defendant claimed the assaultive act was protected by the First Amendment: Burning a cross is political speech, and any ordinance directed against such speech is thus unconstitutional. The Minnesota Supreme Court rejected this argument. Citing Mari Matsuda's work, the court found:

> Burning a cross in the yard of an African American family's home is deplorable conduct that the City of St. Paul may without question prohibit. The burning cross is itself an unmistakable symbol of violence and hatred based on virulent notions of racial supremacy. It is the responsibility, even the obligation, of diverse communities to confront such notions in whatever form they appear.

The Minnesota judges thus adopted a perspective urged by critical race theorists. They looked to history and context to understand the effect of a cross-burning. Unlike ordinary trespassing or littering on someone's front lawn, the burning cross is inextricably tied to violence, to lynching, and to exclusion. Crosses burn to warn newcomers out of segregated neighborhoods, to silence whites who speak up in favor of racial tolerance, to draw upon and promote the fear that began with the nightriders of the Reconstruction era and continues to this day in the rituals of skinheads, Klansmen, and local thugs. Attackers use this symbol precisely because of the extreme and concrete distress it causes. Their aim is to cause harm, to silence and to exclude. As with death threats and fraud, the goal of cross-burning is accomplished through speech. As we have argued throughout this book, however, ending the analysis at the determination that hate speech *is* speech is simplistic and doctrinally unworkable. It is also an affirmative harm to those whose injury goes unredressed by law.

In a climate of media attention focused on right-wing claims that a powerful "politically correct movement" was overrunning the nation, disempowering and silencing conservative white men, the Supreme Court of the United States agreed in June 1991 to review the Minnesota cross-burning case. Critical race theorists were immediately concerned that the Reagan-Bush court took on the case in order to further dismantle civil rights gains. We were thus not surprised at Justice Antonin Scalia's opinion declaring the anti–cross-burning ordinance unconstitutional. Local governments, Scalia held, may prohibit littering or arson on peoples' lawns, but they may not single out racially motivated acts, such as cross-burning, for criminalization. The decision thus limits the ability to treat the racist assault of cross-burning as a particularly serious crime.

Justice Scalia's opinion in the *R. A. V.* case, as the cross-burning case is now known, was a clear example of exactly the kind of legal analysis this book is intended to counter. It is completely ahistorical and acontextual. The Jones family's terror at finding a cross burning in their yard in the middle of the night is nowhere described. We are told that a "crudely made cross" was burned in the yard of a Black family, but we are told nothing about that family or the hostility they experienced upon moving into the neighborhood. The Ku Klux Klan, lynching, nightriders, the Reconstruction, continuing patterns of hate crimes and racial violence in this country are never mentioned. Hate crime statistics and social science evidence showing increasing use of burning crosses and swastikas to harass ethnic and religious minorities are not mentioned. The many reported cases in which state and federal courts have struggled to protect schoolchildren, voters, homeowners, workers, and other citizens from ethnic intimidation by cross-burners are neither discussed nor cited. In effect, the opinion proceeds as though we know nothing about the origins of the practice of cross-burning or about the meaning that a burning cross carries both for those who use it and those whom it terrorizes.

What we do learn from the opinion is that cross-burning is not a "majority preference" and that the ordinance reflects inappropriate "special hostility" against "particular biases." The cross-burners are portrayed as an unpopular minority that the Supreme Court must defend against the power of the state. The injury to the Jones family is appropriated and the cross-burner is cast as the injured victim. The reality of ongoing racism and exclusion is erased and bigotry is redefined as majoritarian condemnation of racist views. The powerful impact of the burning cross—the assault, the terror—is also inverted. The power is replaced in the hands of those who oppose racism. The powerful antiracists have captured the state and will use the state to oppress powerless racists. As a final element to this upside-down story, the Reagan-Bush judges are cast as the defenders of the down-trodden, the courageous upholders of the Bill of Rights.

This inverted story will no doubt surprise the many local lawmakers and law-enforcement officials who are struggling daily to keep the lid on the pressure cooker of racial animosity. Hate crime ordinances came about not because local legislators were bent on oppressing a tiny minority of unpopular racists, but because hate crimes had reached such an epidemic proportion that no one concerned with keeping the peace could ignore them. Civil rights organizations struggled mightily to raise public consciousness about the prevalence of hate crimes and to show how the targets of hate crimes were disempowered, silenced, and disenfranchised. None of this is mentioned in the Scalia opinion, however. Instead, local legislators dealing responsibly with local problems are painted as group-think imposers of orthodoxy.

Concurring Justices Byron White, Harry Blackmun, Sandra Day O'Connor, and John Paul Stevens would also overturn the St. Paul ordinance for overbreadth, but they would not prohibit all local efforts to prevent cross-burnings and other forms of bigoted intimidation. Two of these Justices condemn the Scalia opinion for turning First Amendment doctrine "on its head." While the critique is intended as a doctrinal one, for the Scalia opinion both misstates and revises existing doctrine in confusing and astonishing ways, it also echoes the political critique made by critical race theorists. Judges from Oliver Wendell Holmes to Harry Blackmun have not had to be radicals to recognize the simple truth that doing justice requires more than manipulating doctrine in a vacuum. The concurring opinions explicitly discuss the harm of cross-burnings and respect the determination of local lawmakers that the threat to society from burning crosses is greater than the threat from burning trash.

Where does the *R. A. V.* decision leave us? It provides little guidance for legislators, school administrators, and community activists who are attempting to deal with the racism that—Supreme Court erasures notwithstanding—still plagues our neighborhoods and institutions. The *R. A. V.* decision will not outlive the problem of racism, and, indeed, its incoherence and illogic are unlikely to withstand the test of even a few years' time. We urge those concerned about racism to continue their creative efforts to respond to assaultive speech, guided by the reality of racism's concrete harms. This requires listening carefully to the stories of families who spend the night imprisoned by fear while crosses burn and linking that to the broad gulfs that separate, still, the life chances of haves and have-nots in America. As critical race theorists, we do not separate cross-burning from police brutality nor epithets from infant mortality rates. We believe there are systems of culture, of privilege, and of power that intertwine in complex ways to tell a sad and continuing story of insider/outsider. We choose to see and to struggle against a world made by burning crosses.

In this book we have argued for an antisubordination interpretation of the First Amendment. The First Amendment goal of maximizing public discourse is not attained in a marketplace of ideas distorted by coercion and privilege. Burning crosses do not bring to the table more ideas for discussion, and the Court's failure to see this is part of a long history of not seeing what folks on the bottom see. We hold faith that a critical view of law can reconstruct the First Amendment to bring the voices of the least to the places of power. In arguing against existing law, we argue not against law but for a legal world worthy of democracy's name.

Liberalism and Campus Hate Speech: A Philosophical Examination

ANDREW ALTMAN

Altman argues for particular narrowly drawn rules banning hate speech. He attempts to steer a middle course between those who reject all regulations of hate speech on campus and those who support comparatively sweeping regulations of hate speech. He agrees with those who support sweeping legislation that hate speech sometimes causes serious psychological harm. But he also agrees with those who reject all regulation that regulation of hate speech fails to maintain neutrality between conflicting views on campus. He argues that hate speech should be regulated based on its wrongfulness rather than merely on the psychological harm it causes.

For valuable comments and criticisms on earlier drafts of this article, I am grateful to Steven Lee, Kent Greenawalt, Peter Caws, David DeGrazia, the members of the Human Sciences Seminar at George Washington University, and an anonymous reviewer for this journal and its associate editors.

Reprinted with permission from *Ethics* 103 (January 1993): 302–317.

Introduction

In recent years a vigorous public debate has developed over freedom of speech within the academic community. The immediate stimulus for the debate has been the enactment by a number of colleges and universities of rules against hate speech. While some have defended these rules as essential for protecting the equal dignity of all members of the academic community, others have condemned them as intolerable efforts to impose ideological conformity on the academy.

Liberals can be found on both sides of this debate. Many see campus hate-speech regulation as a form of illegitimate control by the community over individual liberty of expression. They argue that hate-speech rules violate the important liberal principle that any regulation of speech be viewpoint-neutral. But other liberals see hate-speech regulation as a justifiable part of the effort to help rid society of discrimination and subordination based on such characteristics as race, religion, ethnicity, gender, and sexual preference.

In this article, I develop a liberal argument in favor of certain narrowly drawn rules prohibiting hate speech. The argument steers a middle course between those who reject all forms of campus hate speech regulation and those who favor relatively sweeping forms of regulation. Like those who reject all regulation, I argue that rules against hate speech are not viewpoint-neutral. Like those who favor sweeping regulation, I accept the claim that hate speech can cause serious psychological harm to those at whom it is directed. However, I do not believe that such harm can justify regulation, sweeping or otherwise. Instead, I argue that some forms of hate-speech inflict on their victims a certain kind of wrong, and it is on the basis of this wrong that regulation can be justified. The kind of wrong in question is one that is inflicted in virtue of the performance of a certain kind of speech-act characteristic of some forms of hate speech, and I argue that rules targeting this speech-act wrong will be relatively narrow in scope.[1]

Hate Speech, Harassment, and Neutrality

Hate-speech regulations typically provide for disciplinary action against students for making racist, sexist, or homophobic utterances or for engaging in behavior that expresses the same kinds of discriminatory attitudes.[2] The stimulus for the regulations has been an apparent upsurge in racist, sexist, and homophobic incidents on college campuses over the past decade. The regulations that have actually been proposed or enacted vary widely in the scope of what they prohibit.

The rules at Stanford University are narrow in scope. They require that speech meet three conditions before it falls into the proscribed zone: the speaker must intend to insult or stigmatize another on the basis of certain characteristics such as race, gender, or sexual orientation; the speech must be addressed directly to those whom it is intended to stigmatize; and the speech must employ epithets or terms that similarly convey "visceral hate or contempt" for the people at whom it is directed.[3]

On the other hand, the rules of the University of Connecticut, in their original form, were relatively sweeping in scope. According to these rules, "Every member of the University is obligated to refrain from actions that intimidate, humiliate or demean persons or groups or that undermine their security or self-esteem." Explicitly mentioned as examples of proscribed speech were "making inconsiderate jokes . . . stereotyping the experiences, background, and skills of individuals, . . . imitating stereotypes in speech or mannerisms [and] attributing objections to any of the above actions to 'hyper-sensitivity' of the targeted individual or group."[4]

Even the narrower forms of hate-speech regulation, such as we find at Stanford, must be distinguished from a simple prohibition of verbal harassment. As commonly understood, harassment involves a pattern of conduct that is intended to annoy a person so much as to disrupt substantially her activities.[5] No one questions the authority of universities to enact regulations that prohibit such conduct, whether the conduct be verbal or not. There are three principal differences between hate-speech rules and rules against harassment. First, hate-speech rules do not require a pattern of conduct: a single incident is sufficient to incur liability. Second, hate-speech rules describe the offending conduct in ways that refer to the moral and political viewpoint it expresses. The conduct is not simply annoying or disturbing; it is racist, sexist, or homophobic.

The third difference is tied closely to the second and is the most important one: rules against hate speech are not viewpoint-neutral. Such rules rest on the view that racism, sexism, and homophobia are morally wrong. The liberal principle of viewpoint-neutrality holds that those in authority should not be permitted to limit speech on the ground that it expresses a viewpoint that is wrong, evil, or otherwise deficient. Yet, hate-speech rules rest on precisely such a basis. Rules against harassment, on the other hand, are not viewpoint-based. Anyone in our society could accept the prohibition of harassment because it would not violate their normative political or moral beliefs to do so.[6] The same cannot be said for hate-speech rules because they embody a view of race, gender, and homosexuality contrary to the normative viewpoints held by some people.[7]

If I am correct in claiming that hate-speech regulations are not viewpoint-neutral, this will raise a strong prima facie case against them from a liberal perspective. Contrary to my claim, however, Thomas Grey, author of Stanford's hate-speech policy, argues that his regulations are viewpoint-neutral. He claims that the policy "preserves practical neutrality—that is, it does not differentially deprive any significant element in American political life of its rhetorical capital. . . . The Right has no special stake in the free face-to-face use of epithets that perform no other function except to portray whole classes of Americans as subhuman and unworthy of full citizenship."[8]

I cannot agree with Grey's contentions on this score. The implicit identification of groups such as the neo-Nazis and the KKK as insignificant presupposes a value judgment that is not viewpoint-neutral, namely, that the views of such groups have no significant merit. If Grey claims that he is simply making the factual judgment that the influence of these groups on the political process is nil, it is not clear why that is relevant (even assuming its truth—which is debatable). Certainly, such groups aim to become significant influences on the process, and their use of language that would violate Stanford's rules is a significant part of their rhetoric. In fact, I will argue later that the use of such language is tied in an especially close way to their substantive moral and political views.

Grey might be suggesting that our public political discourse does not tolerate the sorts of slurs and epithets his rules proscribe: public debate proceeds with an unwritten prohibition on that kind of language. Such a suggestion is certainly correct, as can be seen by the fact that racists who enter the public arena must rely on "code words" to get their message across. But from the racists' point of view, this is just further evidence of how our public political discourse has been captured by "liberals" and is biased against their view.

Viewpoint-neutrality is not simply a matter of the effects of speech regulation on the liberty of various groups to express their views in the language they prefer. It is also concerned with the kinds of justification that must be offered for speech regulation. The fact is that any plausible justification of hate-speech regulation hinges on the premise that racism, sexism, and homophobia are wrong. Without that premise there would be no basis for arguing that the viewpoint-neutral proscription of verbal harassment is insufficient to protect the rights of minorities and women. The liberal who favors hate-speech regulations, no matter how narrowly drawn, must therefore be prepared to carve out an exception to the principle of viewpoint-neutrality.

The Harms of Hate Speech

Many of the proponents of campus hate-speech regulation defend their position by arguing that hate-speech causes serious harm to those who are the targets of such speech. Among the most basic of these harms are psychological ones. Even when it involves no direct threat of violence, hate speech can cause abiding feelings of fear, anxiety, and insecurity in those at whom it is targeted. As Mari Matsuda has argued, this is in part because many forms of such speech tacitly draw on a history of violence against certain groups.[9] The symbols and language of hate speech call up historical memories of violent persecution and may encourage fears of current violence. Moreover, hate speech can cause a variety of other harms, from feelings of isolation, to a loss of self-confidence, to physical problems associated with serious psychological disturbance.[10]

The question is whether or not the potential for inflicting these harms is sufficient ground for some sort of hate-speech regulation. As powerful as these appeals to the harms of hate speech are, there is a fundamental sticking point in accepting them as justification for regulation, from a liberal point of view. The basic problem is that the proposed justification sweeps too broadly for a liberal to countenance it. Forms of racist, sexist, or homophobic speech that the liberal is committed to protecting may cause precisely the kinds of harm that the proposed justification invokes.

The liberal will not accept the regulation of racist, sexist, or homophobic speech couched in a scientific, religious, philosophical, or political mode of discourse. The regulation of such speech would not merely carve out a minor exception to the principle of viewpoint-neutrality but would, rather, eviscerate it in a way unacceptable to any liberal. Yet, those forms of hate speech can surely cause in minorities the harms that are invoked to justify regulation: insecurity, anxiety, isolation, loss of self-confidence, and so on. Thus, the liberal must invoke something beyond these kinds of harm in order to justify any hate-speech regulation.

Liberals who favor regulation typically add to their argument the contention that the value to society of the hate speech they would proscribe is virtually nil, while scientific, religious, philosophical, and political forms of hate speech have at least some significant value. Thus, Mary Ellen Gale says that the forms she would prohibit "neither advance knowledge, seek truth, expose government abuses, initiate dialogue, encourage participation, further tolerance of divergent views, nor enhance the victim's individual dignity or self respect."[11] As an example of such worthless hate speech Gale cites an incident of white students writing a message on the mirror in the dorm room of blacks: "African monkeys, why don't you go back to the jungle."[12] But she would protect a great deal of racist or sexist speech, such as a meeting of neo-Nazi students at which swastikas are publicly displayed and speeches made that condemn the presence of Jews and blacks on campus.[13]

Although Gale ends up defending relatively narrow regulations, I believe liberals should be very hesitant to accept her argument for distinguishing regulable from nonregulable hate speech. One problem is that she omits from her list of the values that valuable speech serves one which liberals have long considered important, especially for speech that upsets and disturbs others. Such speech, it is argued, enables the speaker to "blow off steam" in a relatively nondestructive and nonviolent way. Calling particular blacks "African monkeys" might serve as a psychological substitute for harming them in a much more serious way, for example, by lynchings or beatings.

Gale could respond that slurring blacks might just as well serve as an encouragement and prelude to the more serious harms. But the same can be said of forms of hate speech that Gale would protect from regulation, for example, the speech at the neo-Nazi student meeting. Moreover, liberals should argue that it is the job of legal rules against assault, battery, conspiracy, rape, and so on to protect people from violence. It is, at best, highly speculative that hate speech on campus contributes to violence against minorities or women. And while the claim about blowing off steam is also a highly speculative one, the liberal tradition clearly puts a substantial burden of proof on those who would silence speech.

There is a more basic problem with any effort to draw the line between regulable and nonregulable hate speech by appealing to the value of speech. Such appeals invariably involve substantial departures from the principle of viewpoint-neutrality. There is no way to make differential judgments about the value of different types of hate speech without taking one or another moral and political viewpoint. Gale's criteria clearly illustrate this as they are heavily tilted against the values of racists and sexists, and yet she does not adequately address the question of how a liberal position can accommodate such substantial departures from viewpoint-neutrality.

Gale contends that existing legal rules and regulations against sexual and racial harassment in the workplace should serve as the model in terms of which campus hate-speech regulations can be justified.[14] Those rules are based on an interpretation of Title VII of the Civil Rights Act of 1964, outlawing discrimination in the terms and conditions of employment, and they prohibit a hostile or offensive work environment. But there are three problems with appealing to these harassment rules. First, almost all legal cases involving claims of a hostile work environment have required more than simply hostile verbal conduct for a finding of a violation.[15]

Second, it is doubtful that the context of a student at a university is sufficiently similar to that of a worker in the workplace to assume that the exact same rules should apply for both settings. Freedom of expression is far more vital to the role of the university than it is to that of the typical workplace, and so it is reasonable to think that university rules should be less restrictive of expression. Third, even if the university context is sufficiently similar to that of the typical workplace, Gale's invocation of the existing rules covering workplace harassment begs the crucial question of whether the current interpretation of Title VII itself involves an unjustifiably sweeping departure from viewpoint-neutrality.[16]

I do not assume that the principle of viewpoint-neutrality is an absolute or ultimate one within the liberal framework. Liberals do defend some types of speech regulation that seem to rely on viewpoint-based claims. For example, they would not reject copyright laws, even if it could be shown—as seems plausible—that those laws are biased against the views of people who regard private property as theft.[17] Moreover, the viewpoint-neutrality principle itself rests on deeper liberal concerns which it is thought to serve. Ideally, a liberal argument for the regulation of hate speech would show that regulations can be developed that accommodate these deeper concerns and that simultaneously serve important liberal values. I believe that there is such a liberal argument. In order to show this, however, it is necessary to examine a kind of wrong committed by hate speakers that is quite different from the harmful psychological effects of their speech.

Subordination and Speech Acts

Some proponents of regulation claim that there is an especially close connection between hate speech and the subordination of minorities. Thus, Charles Lawrence contends, "all racist speech constructs the social reality that constrains the liberty of nonwhites because of their race."[18] Along the same lines, Mari Matsuda claims, "racist speech is particularly harmful because it is a mechanism of subordination."[19]

The position of Lawrence and Matsuda can be clarified and elaborated using J. L. Austin's distinction between perlocutionary effects and illocutionary force.[20] The perlocutionary effects of an utterance consist of its causal effects on the hearer: infuriating her, persuading her, frightening her, and so on. The illocutionary force of an utterance consists of the kind of speech act one is performing in making the utterance: advising, warning, stating, claiming, arguing, and so on. Lawrence and Matsuda are not simply suggesting that the direct perlocutionary effects of racist speech constitute harm. Nor are they simply suggesting that hate speech can persuade listeners to accept beliefs that then motivate them to commit acts of harm against racial minorities. That again is a matter of the perlocutionary effects of hate speech. Rather, I believe that they are suggesting that hate speech can inflict a wrong in virtue of its illocutionary acts, the very speech acts performed in the utterances of such speech.[21]

What exactly does this speech-act wrong amount to? My suggestion is that it is the wrong of treating a person as having inferior moral standing. In other words, hate speech involves the performance of a certain kind of illocutionary act, namely, the act of treating someone as a moral subordinate.[22]

Treating persons as moral subordinates means treating them in a way that takes their interests to be intrinsically less important, and their lives inherently less valuable, than the interests and lives of those who belong to some reference group. There are many ways of treating people as moral subordinates that are natural as opposed to conventional: the status of these acts as acts of subordination depend solely on universal principles of morality and not on the conventions of a given society. Slavery and genocide, for example, treat people as having inferior moral standing simply in virtue of the affront of such practices to universal moral principles.

Other ways of treating people as moral subordinates have both natural and conventional elements. The practice of racial segregation is an example. It is subordinating because the conditions imposed on blacks by such treatment violate moral principles but also because the act of separation is a convention for putting the minority group in its (supposedly) proper, subordinate place.

I believe that the language of racist, sexist, and homophobic slurs and epithets provides wholly conventional ways of treating people as moral subordinates. Terms such as 'kike', 'faggot', 'spic', and 'nigger' are verbal instruments of subordination. They are used not only to express hatred or contempt for people but also to "put them in their place," that is, to treat them as having inferior moral standing.

It is commonly recognized that through language we can "put people down," to use the vernacular expression. There are many different modes of putting people down: putting them down as less intelligent or less clever or less articulate or less skillful. Putting people down in these ways is not identical to treating them as moral subordinates, and the ordinary put-down does not involve regarding someone as having inferior moral standing.[23] The put-downs that are accomplished with the slurs and epithets of hate speech are different from the ordinary verbal put-down in that respect, even though both sorts of put-down are done through language.

I have contended that the primary verbal instruments for treating people as moral subordinates are the slurs and epithets of hate speech. In order to see this more clearly, consider the difference between derisively calling someone a "faggot" and saying to that person, with equal derision, "You are contemptible for being homosexual." Both utterances can treat the homosexual as a moral subordinate, but the former accomplishes it much more powerfully than the latter. This is, I believe, because the conventional rules of language make the epithet 'faggot' a term whose principal purpose is precisely to treat homosexuals as having inferior moral standing.

I do not believe that a clean and neat line can be drawn around those forms of hate speech that treat their targets as moral subordinates. Slurs and epithets are certainly used that way often, but not always, as is evidenced by the fact that sometimes victimized groups seize on the slurs that historically have subordinated them and seek to "transvalue" the terms. For example, homosexuals have done this with the term 'queer,' seeking to turn it into a term of pride rather than one of subordination.

Hate speech in modes such as the scientific or philosophical typically would not involve illocutionary acts of moral subordination. This is because speech in those modes usually involves essentially different kinds of speech acts: describing, asserting, stating, arguing, and so forth. To assert or argue that blacks are genetically inferior to whites is not to perform a speech act that itself consists of treating blacks as inferior.[24] Yet, language is often ambiguous and used for multiple purposes, and I would not rule out a priori that in certain contexts even scientific or philosophical hate speech is used in part to subordinate.

The absence of a neat and clean line around those forms of hate speech that subordinate through speech acts does not entail that it is futile to attempt to formulate regulations that target such hate speech. Rules and regulations rarely have an exact fit with what they aim to prevent: over- and under-inclusiveness are pervasive in any system of rules that seeks to regulate conduct. The problem is to develop rules that have a reasonably good fit. Later I argue that there are hate-speech regulations that target subordinating hate speech reasonably well. But first I must argue that such speech commits a wrong that may be legitimately targeted by regulation.

Speech-Act Wrong

I have argued that some forms of hate speech treat their targets as moral subordinates on account of race, gender, or sexual preference. Such treatment runs counter to the central liberal idea of persons as free and equal. To that extent, it constitutes a wrong, a speech-act wrong inflicted on those whom it addresses. However, it does not follow that it is a wrong that may be legitimately targeted by regulation. A liberal republic is not a republic of virtue in which the authorities prohibit every conceivable wrong. The liberal republic protects a substantial zone of liberty around the individual in which she is free from authoritative intrusion even to do some things that are wrong.

Yet, the wrongs of subordination based on such characteristics as race, gender, and sexual preference are not just any old wrongs. Historically, they are among the principal wrongs that have prevented—and continue to prevent—Western liberal democracies from living up to their ideals and principles. As such, these wrongs are especially appropriate targets of regulation in our liberal republic. Liberals recognize the special importance of combating such wrongs in their strong support for laws prohibiting discrimination in employment, housing, and public accommodations. And even if the regulation of speech-act subordination on campus is not regarded as mandatory for universities, it does seem that the choice of an institution to regulate that type of subordination on campus is at least justifiable within a liberal framework.

In opposition, it may be argued that subordination is a serious wrong that should be targeted but that the line should be drawn when it comes to subordination through speech. There, viewpoint-neutrality must govern. But I believe that the principle of viewpoint-neutrality must be understood as resting on deeper liberal concerns. Other things being equal, a departure from viewpoint-neutrality will be justified if it can accommodate these deeper concerns while at the same time serving the liberal principle of the equality of persons.

The concerns fall into three basic categories. First is the Millian idea that speech can promote individual development and contribute to the public political dialogue, even when it is wrong, misguided, or otherwise deficient.[25] Second is the Madisonian reasons that the authorities cannot be trusted with formulating and enforcing rules that silence certain views: they will be too tempted to abuse such rules in order to promote their own advantage or their own sectarian viewpoint.[26] Third is the idea that any departures from viewpoint-neutrality might serve as precedents that could be seized upon by would-be censors with antiliberal agendas to further their broad efforts to silence speech and expression.[27]

These concerns that underlie viewpoint-neutrality must be accommodated for hate-speech regulation to be justifiable from a liberal perspective. But that cannot be done in the abstract. It needs to be done in the context of a particular set of regulations. In the next section, I argue that there are regulations that target reasonably well those forms of hate speech that subordinate, and in the following section I argue that such regulations accommodate the concerns that underlie the liberal endorsement of the viewpoint-neutrality principle.

Targeting Speech-Act Wrong

If I am right in thinking that the slurs and epithets of hate speech are the principal instruments of the speech-act wrong of treating someone as a moral subordinate and that such a wrong is a legitimate target of regulation, then it will not be difficult to formulate rules that have a reasonably good fit with the wrong they legitimately seek to regulate. In general, what are needed are rules that prohibit speech that (1) employs slurs and epithets conventionally used to subordinate persons on account of their race, gender, religion, ethnicity, or sexual preference, (2) is addressed to particular persons, and (3) is expressed with the intention of degrading such persons on account of their race, gender, religion, ethnicity, or sexual preference. With some modification, this is essentially what one finds in the regulations drafted by Grey for Stanford.[28]

Restricting the prohibition to slurs and epithets addressed to specific persons will capture many speech-act wrongs of subordination. But it will not capture them all. Slurs and epithets are not necessary for such speech acts, as I conceded earlier. In addition, it may be possible to treat someone as a moral subordinate through a speech act, even though the utterance is not addressing that person. However, prohibiting more than slurs and epithets would run a high risk of serious over-inclusiveness, capturing much speech that performs legitimate speech acts such as stating and arguing. And prohibiting all use of slurs and epithets, whatever the context, would mandate a degree of intrusiveness into the private lives of students that would be difficult for liberals to license.

The regulations should identify examples of the kinds of terms that count as epithets or slurs conventionally used to perform speech acts of subordination. This is required in order to give people sufficient fair warning. But because the terms of natural languages are not precise, univocal, and unchanging, it is not possible to give an exhaustive list, nor is it mandatory to try. Individuals who innocently use an epithet that conventionally subordinates can plead lack of the requisite intent.

The intent requirement is needed to accommodate cases in which an epithet or slur is not used with any intent to treat the addressee as a moral subordinate. These cases cover a wide range, including the efforts of some minorities to capture and trans-value terms historically used to subordinate them. There are several different ways in which the required intent could be described: the intent to stigmatize or to demean or to insult or to degrade and so on. I think that 'degrade' does the best job of capturing the idea of treating someone as a moral subordinate in language the average person will find familiar and understandable. 'Insult' does the poorest job and should be avoided. Insulting someone typically does not involve treating the person as a moral subordinate. Rather, it involves putting someone down in other ways: as less skillful, less intelligent, less clever, and the like.

The regulations at some universities extend beyond what I have defended and prohibit speech that demeans on the basis of physical appearance. I do not believe that such regulations can be justified within the liberal framework I have developed here. Speech can certainly be used to demean people based on physical appearance. 'Slob', 'dog', 'beast', 'pig': these are some examples of terms that are used in such verbal put-downs.[29] But I do not believe that they are used to treat people as moral subordinates, and thus the terms do not inflict the kind of speech-act wrong that justifies the regulation of racist, sexist, or homophobic slurs and epithets.

It should not be surprising that terms which demean on the basis of appearance do not morally subordinate, since the belief that full human moral standing depends on good looks is one that few people, if any, hold.[30] The terms that put people down for their appearance are thus fundamentally different from racist, sexist, or homophobic slurs and epithets. The latter terms do reflect beliefs that are held by many about the lower moral standing of certain groups.

Accommodating Liberal Concerns

I have argued that regulations should target those forms of hate speech that inflict the speech-act wrong of subordination on their victims. This wrong is distinct from the psychological harm that hate speech causes. In targeting speech-act subordination, the aim of regulation is not to prohibit speech that has undesirable psychological effects on individuals but, rather, to prohibit speech that treats people as moral subordinates. To target speech that has undesirable psychological effects is invariably to target certain ideas, since it is through the communication of ideas that the psychological harm occurs. In contrast, targeting speech-act subordination does not target ideas. Any idea would be free from regulation as long as it was expressed through a speech act other than one which subordinates: stating, arguing, claiming, defending, and so on would all be free of regulation.[31]

Because of these differences, regulations that target speech-act subordination can accommodate the liberal concerns underlying viewpoint-neutrality, while regulations that sweep more broadly cannot. Consider the important Millian idea that individual development requires that people be left free to say things that are wrong and to learn from their mistakes. Under the sort of regulation I endorse, people would be perfectly free to make racist, sexist, and homophobic assertions and arguments and to learn of the deficiencies of their views from the counterassertions and counterarguments of others. And the equally important Millian point that public dialogue gains even through the expression of false ideas is accommodated in a similar way. Whatever contribution a racist viewpoint can bring to public discussion can be made under regulations that only target speech-act subordination.

The liberal fear of trusting the authorities is somewhat more worrisome. Some liberals have argued that the authorities cannot be trusted with impartial enforcement of hate-speech regulations. Nadine Strossen, for example, claims that the hate-speech regulations at the University of Michigan have been applied in a biased manner, punishing the racist and homophobic speech of blacks but not of whites.[32] Still, it is not at all clear that the biased application of rules is any more of a problem with rules that are not viewpoint-neutral than with those that are. A neutral rule against harassment can also be enforced in a racially discriminatory manner. There is no reason to think a priori that narrowly drawn hate-speech rules would be any more liable to such abuse. Of course, if it did turn out that there was a pervasive problem with the biased enforcement of hate-speech rules, any sensible liberal would advocate rescinding them. But absent a good reason for thinking that this is likely to happen—not just that it could conceivably happen—the potential for abusive enforcement is no basis for rejecting the kind of regulation I have defended.

Still remaining is the problem of precedent: even narrowly drawn regulations targeting only speech-act subordination could be cited as precedent for more sweeping, antiliberal restrictions by those at other universities or in the community at large who are not committed to liberal values.[33] In response to this concern, it should be argued that narrowly drawn rules will not serve well as precedents for would-be censors with antiliberal agendas. Those who wish to silence socialists, for example, on the ground that socialism is as discredited as racism will find scant precedential support from regulations that allow the expression of racist opinions as long as they are not couched in slurs and epithets directed at specific individuals.

There may be some precedent-setting risk in such narrow regulations. Those who wish to censor the arts, for example, might draw an analogy between the epithets that narrow hate-speech regulations proscribe and the "trash" they would proscribe: both forms of expression are indecent, ugly, and repulsive to the average American, or so the argument might go.

Yet, would-be art censors already have precedents at their disposal providing much closer analogies in antiobscenity laws. Hate-speech regulations are not likely to give would-be censors of the arts any additional ammunition. To this, a liberal opponent of any hate-speech regulation might reply that there is no reason to take the risk. But the response will be that there is a good reason, namely, to prevent the wrong of speech-act subordination that is inflicted by certain forms of hate speech.

Conclusion

There is a defensible liberal middle ground between those who oppose all campus hate-speech regulation and those who favor the sweeping regulation of such speech. But the best defense of this middle ground requires the recognition that speech acts of subordination are at the heart of the hate-speech issue. Some forms of hate speech do wrong to people by treating them as moral subordinates. This is the wrong that can and should be the target of campus hate-speech regulations.

NOTES

1. In a discussion of the strictly legal issues surrounding the regulation of campus hate speech, the distinction between private and

public universities would be an important one. The philosophical considerations on which this article focuses, however, apply both to public and private institutions.

2. In this article I will focus on the restriction of racist (understood broadly to include anti-Semitic), sexist, and homophobic expression. In addition to such expression, regulations typically prohibit discriminatory utterances based on ethnicity, religion, and physical appearance. The argument I develop in favor of regulation applies noncontroversially to ethnicity and religion, as well as to race, gender, and sexual preference. But in a later section I argue against the prohibition of discriminatory remarks based on appearance. I understand 'speech' as whatever has nonnatural meaning according to Grice's account, i.e., any utterances or actions having the following nested intentions behind them: the intention to produce a certain effect in the audience, to have the audience recognize that intention, and to have that recognition be the reason for the production of the effect. See Paul Grice, "Meaning," in his *Studies in the Way of Words* (Cambridge, Mass.: Harvard University Press, 1989), pp. 220–21. On this Gricean account, not only verbal utterances but also the display of symbols or flags, gestures, drawings, and more will count as speech. Although some commentators have produced counterexamples to this account of speaker's meaning, I do not believe that they pose insurmountable problems. See Robert Fogelin, "Review of Grice, *Studies in the Way of Words*," *Journal of Philosophy* 88 (1991): 217.
3. The full text of the Stanford regulations is in Thomas Grey, "Civil Rights v. Civil Liberties: The Case of Discriminatory Verbal Harassment," *Social Philosophy and Policy* 8 (1991): 106–7.
4. The University of Connecticut's original regulations are found in the pamphlet "Protect Campus Pluralism," published under the auspices of the Department of Student Affairs, the Dean of Students Office, and the Division of Student Affairs and Services. The regulations have since been rescinded in response to a legal challenge and replaced by ones similar to those in effect at Stanford. See *University of Connecticut Student Handbook* (Storrs: University of Connecticut, 1990–91), p. 62.
5. Kingsley Browne points out that the legal understanding of harassment as conceived under current interpretations of Title VII of the Civil Rights Act of 1964 departs from the ordinary understanding in important ways. See Kingsley Browne, "Title VII as Censorship: Hostile Environment Harassment and the First Amendment," *Ohio State Law Journal* 52 (1991): 486.
6. Laws against the defamation of individuals are essentially viewpoint-neutral for the same reason: anyone in society can accept them, regardless of their moral or political viewpoint.
7. Compare Kent Greenawalt, "Insults and Epithets," *Rutgers Law Review* 24 (1990): 306–7.
8. Grey. pp. 103–4.
9. Mari Matsuda, "Legal Storytelling: Public Response to Racist Speech; Considering the Victim's Story," *Michigan Law Review* 87 (1989): 2329–34, 2352.
10. See Richard Delgado, "Words That Wound: A Tort Action for Racial Insults, Epithets and Name-Calling," *Harvard Civil Rights—Civil Liberties Law Review* 17 (1982): 137, 146.
11. Mary Ellen Gale, "Reimagining the First Amendment: Racist Speech and Equal Liberty," *St. John's Law Review* 65 (1991): 179–80.
12. Ibid., p. 176.
13. Ibid.
14. Ibid., pp. 174–75.
15. See Browne, p. 483.
16. Ibid., pp. 491–501, 547.
17. I think liberals could argue that the deviation of copyright laws from viewpoint-neutrality is both minor and reasonable, given the extreme rarity of the antiproperty view in our society and given the great social value that such laws are seen as serving.
18. Charles Lawrence, "If He Hollers Let Him Go: Regulating Racist Speech on Campus," *Duke Law Journal* (1990), p. 444.
19. Matsuda, p. 2357.
20. J. L. Austin, *How to Do Things with Words* (New York: Oxford University Press, 1962), pp. 98 ff. The concept of an illocutionary act has been refined and elaborated by John Searle in a series of works starting with "Austin on Locutionary and Illocutionary Acts," *Philosophical Review* 77 (1968): 420–21. Also see his *Speech Acts* (New York: Cambridge University Press, 1969), p. 31, and *Expression and Meaning* (New York: Cambridge University Press, 1979): and John Searle and D. Vanderveken, *Foundations of Illocutionary Logic* (New York: Cambridge University Press, 1985).
21. Both Lawrence and Matsuda describe racist speech as a unique form of speech in its internal relation to subordination. See Lawrence, p. 440, n. 42; and Matsuda, p. 2356. I do not think that their view is correct.

Homophobic and sexist speech, for example, can also be subordinating. In fact, Lawrence and Matsuda are applying to racist speech essentially the same idea that several feminist writers have applied to pornography. These feminists argue that pornography does not simply depict the subordination of women; it actually subordinates them. See Melinda Vadas, "A First Look at the Pornography/Civil Rights Ordinance: Could Pornography Be the Subordination of Women?" *Journal of Philosophy* 84 (1987): 487–511.

22. Lawrence and Matsuda argue that all racist speech is subordinating. I reject their argument below and claim that the speech act of treating someone as a moral subordinate is not characteristic of all forms of racist speech. They also describe the wrong of speech-act subordination as a "harm." But the wrong does not in itself interfere with a person's formulation and pursuit of her plans and purposes. On that basis, I have been persuaded by my colleague Peter Caws that it is better to avoid the term 'harm' when describing speech-act subordination. Why such speech acts are, from a liberal perspective, wrongs is explained below.

23. The distinction which I am drawing between putting someone down as a moral subordinate and putting him down in other ways is an instance of a more general moral distinction. That general distinction is described in different ways: as one between respect and esteem, or between two forms of respect, or between worth and merit. See, e.g., Gregory Vlastos, "Human Worth, Merit, and Equality," in *Moral Concepts,* ed. Joel Feinberg (New York: Oxford University Press, 1969); Larry Thomas, "Morality and Our Self-Concept," *Journal of Value Inquiry* 12 (1978): 258–68; and David Sachs, "How to Distinguish Self-Respect from Self-Esteem," *Philosophy and Public Affairs* 10 (1981): 346–60. I do not believe that liberal claims about the equal moral status of persons can make sense without presupposing some such distinction.

24. Thus I agree with Marcy Strauss's claim that there is a viable distinction between speech that discriminates and speech that advocates discrimination, but I reject the way she draws the distinction. She attempts to do it by appealing to differences in what amounts to perlocutionary effects, failing to realize that the essential difference lies in the illocutionary act. See Marcy Strauss, "Sexist Speech in the Workplace," *Harvard Civil Rights—Civil Liberties Law Review* 25 (1990): 39–40.

25. See Robert Post, "Racist Speech, Democracy, and the First Amendment," *William and Mary Law Review* 32 (1991): 290–91.

26. See Frederick Schauer, "The Second-Best First Amendment," *William and Mary Law Review* 31 (1989): 1–2.

27. Peter Linzer, "White Liberal Looks at Racist Speech," *St. John's Law Review* 65 (1991): 219.

28. Stanford describes the intent that is needed for a hate speaker to be liable as the intent to insult or stigmatize. My reservations about formulating the requisite intent in terms of 'insult' are given below.

29. Most such terms are conventionally understood as applying to women and not to men, a clear reflection of our culture's way of perceiving men and women.

30. Some people believe that being overweight is the result of a failure of self-control and thus a kind of moral failing. But that is quite different from thinking that the rights and interests of overweight people are morally less important than those of people who are not overweight. See n. 23 above.

31. A similar argument was made by some supporters of a legal ban on desecrating the American flag through such acts as burning it: to the extent that the ban would prohibit some people from expressing their political viewpoints, it was only a minor departure from viewpoint-neutrality, since those people had an array of other ways to express their views. But the critical difference between the flag-burning case and the hate-speech case is that flag burning is not an act that treats anyone as a moral subordinate.

32. Nadine Strossen, "Regulating Racist Speech on Campus: A Modest Proposal?" *Duke Law Journal* (1990), pp. 557–58. Eric Barendt argues that the British criminal law against racist speech "has often been used to convict militant black spokesmen" (Eric Barendt, *Freedom of Speech* [Oxford: Clarendon, 1985], p. 163).

33. This concern should be distinguished from the idea that any hate-speech regulation is a step down the slippery slope to the totalitarian control of ideas. That idea is difficult to take seriously. Even for nations that have gone much farther in regulating hate speech than anything envisioned by liberal proponents of regulation in the United States, countries such as England, France, and Germany, the idea that they are on the road to totalitarianism is preposterous. A summary of the laws against racist speech in Britain, France, and Germany can be found in Barendt, pp. 161–66.

Study Questions

1. Did the Supreme Court make the morally best ruling in *R. A. V. v. City of St. Paul?* Explain your answer based on the moral principles defined in Appendix B. What is the best definition of a hate crime?

2. Are Matsuda and Lawrence right that the Supreme Court neglected history and victims of hate crimes in the *R.A.V.* case?

3. Does Altman successfully steer a middle course between extreme positions on both sides of the issue here? What problems exist for Altman's view? Do these problems have adequate solutions?

Suggestions for Further Reading

Anonymous, ed., *Would Gun Control Reduce Crime?* (San Diego, CA: Greenhaven Press, 1984).

Baird, Robert M., and Rosenbaum, Stuart E., eds., *Pornography: Private Right or Public Menace?* (Buffalo, NY: Prometheus Books, 1991).

Bakal, Carl, *No Right To Bear Arms* (Paperback Library, 1968).

Bayefsky, Anne, ed., *Legal Theory Meets Legal Practice* (Academic Printing & Publishing, 1988), Part Four "Consent in Criminal Law."

Bayles, Michael D. and High, Dallas M., eds., *Medical Treatment of the Dying: Moral Issues* (Rochester, VT: Schenkman, 1978).

Beauchamp, Tom L., and Perlin, Seymour, eds., *Ethical Issues in Death and Dying* (Englewood Cliffs, NJ: Prentice-Hall, 1978).

Beauchamp, Tom L., and Davidson, Arnold I., "The Definition of Euthanasia," 4 *Journal of Medicine and Philosophy* 294–312 (1979).

Beauchamp, Tom L., "The Moral Justification for Withholding Heroic Procedures," in Bell, Nora K., ed., *Who Decides? Conflicts of Rights in Health Care* (Clifton, NJ: Humana Press, 1982).

Beauchamp, Tom L., "A Reply to Rachels on Active and Passive Euthanasia," 316–323 in Tom L. Beauchamp and LeRoy Walters, eds., *Contemporary Issues in Bioethics,* 2nd ed. (1982).

Beauchamp, Tom L., and Childress, James F., *Principles of Biomedical Ethics,* 3rd ed. (New York: Oxford University Press, 1989), esp. Chaps. 4 and 5.

Berger, Fred R., ed., *Freedom of Expression* (Belmont, CA: Wadsworth, 1980).

Black, C.L., Jr., *Capital Punishment: The Inevitability of Caprice and Mistake.* (New York: W. W. Norton, 1974).

Bronaugh, Richard, ed., *Philosophical Law* (Greenwood Press, 1978), Part IV, "Privacy."

Childress, James F., "To Live or Let Die," in Copp, David, and Wendell, Susan, eds., *Pornography and Censorship* (Buffalo, NY: Prometheus Books, 1983).

Dworkin, Ronald, *Taking Rights Seriously,* revised ed. (Cambridge, MA: Harvard University Press, 1977), Chap. 10 "Liberty and Moralism," and Chap. 11 "Liberty and Liberalism."

Dworkin, Ronald, *A Matter of Principle* (Cambridge, MA: Harvard University Press, 1985), Chap. 17 "Do We Have a Right to Pornography?"

Dworkin, Ronald, *Life's Dominion* (New York: Knopf, 1993).

Fisse, Brent, and French, Peter A., eds. *Corrigible Corporations and Unruly Law* (Trinity University Press, 1985).

Fletcher, George P., *Rethinking Criminal Law* (Boston, MA: Little, Brown, 1978), Chap. 5 "The Jurisprudence of Homicide."

Gould, Carol C., ed., *Beyond Domination: New Perspectives on Women and Philosophy* (Lanham, MD: Rowman & Littlefield, 1983).

Kamisar, Yale, "Some Non-Religious Objections To Euthanasia," 42 *Minnesota Law Review* (1958).

Kipnis, Kenneth, ed., *Philosophical Issues in Law: Cases and Materials* (Englewood Cliffs, NJ: Prentice-Hall, 1977), Section Two "The Enforcement of Community Standards."

Mahowald, Mary Briody, ed., *Philosophy of Woman,* 2nd ed. (Indianapolis, IN: Hackett, 1983).

Narveson, Jan, ed., *Moral Issues.* (Cambridge, MA: Oxford University Press, 1983).

Nisbet, Lee, ed., *The Gun Control Debate: You Decide* (Buffalo, NY: Prometheus Books, 1990).

Rachels, James, "Active and Passive Euthanasia," 292 *The New England Journal Of Medicine* 78–80 (1975).

Shields, Pete, *Guns Don't Die—People Do* (Priam Books, 1981).

Smith, Patricia, ed., *Feminist Jurisprudence* (Cambridge, MA: Oxford University Press, 1993).

Stone, Christopher D., *Where the Law Ends: The Social Control of Corporate Behavior* (Prospect Heights, IL: Waveland Press, 1991).

Veatch, Robert M., "Death and Dying: The Legislative Options," 7 *Hastings Center Report* 5–8 (1977).

Vetterling-Braggin, Mary; Elliston, Frederick A.; and English, Jane, eds., *Feminism and Philosophy* (Lanham, MD: Littlefield, Adams, 1981).

Williams, Glanville, *The Sanctity of Life and the Criminal Law.*

Williams, Glanville, " 'Mercy-Killing' Legislation—A Rejoinder," 42 *Minnesota Law Review* (1958).

PART II

How Can Punishment Be Morally Justified?

A Utilitarianism

The Origin of Punishment

Cesare Beccaria

Beccaria, the great eighteenth-century Italian penal reformer, argues for a broadly utilitarian approach to punishment. People, he maintains, formed governments in order to escape from the insecurity of anarchy. Punishment is justified only to the extent that it serves to protect such societies from collapsing back into this lawless state.

No lasting advantage is to be hoped for from political morality if it is not founded upon the ineradicable feelings of mankind. Any law that deviates from these will inevitably encounter a resistance that is certain to prevail over it in the end—in the same way that any force, however, small, if continuously applied, is bound to overcome the most violent motion that can be imparted to a body.

Let us consult the human heart, and we shall find there the basic principles of the true right of the sovereign to punish crimes.

No man ever freely sacrificed a portion of his personal liberty merely in behalf of the common good. That chimera exists only in romances. If it were possible, every one of us would prefer that the compacts binding others did not bind us; every man tends to make himself the center of his whole world.

The continuous multiplication of mankind, inconsiderable in itself yet exceeding by far the means that a sterile and uncultivated nature could offer for the satisfaction of increasingly complex needs, united the earliest savages. These first communities of necessity caused the formation of others to resist the first, and the primitive state of warfare thus passed from individuals to nations.

Laws are the conditions under which independent and isolated men united to form a society. Weary of living in a continual state of war, and of enjoying a liberty rendered useless by the uncertainty of preserving it, they sacrificed a part so that they might enjoy the rest of it in peace and safety. The sum of all these portions of liberty sacrificed by each for his own good constitutes the sovereignty of a nation, and their legitimate depositary and administrator is the sovereign. But merely to have established this deposit was not enough; it had to be defended against private usurpations by individuals each of whom always tries not only to withdraw his own share but also to usurp for himself that of others. Some tangible motives had to be introduced, therefore, to prevent the despotic spirit, which is in every man, from plunging the laws of society into its original chaos. These tangible motives are the punishments established against infractors of the laws. I say "tangible motives" because experience has shown that the multitude adopt no fixed principles of conduct and will not be released from the sway of that universal principle of dissolution which is seen to operate both in the physical and the moral universe, except for motives that directly strike the senses. These motives, by dint of repeated representation to the mind, counterbalance the powerful impressions of the private passions that oppose the common good. Not eloquence, not declamations, not even the most sublime truths have sufficed, for any considerable length of time, to curb passions excited by vivid impressions of present objects.

It was, thus, necessity that forced men to give up part of their personal liberty, and it is certain, therefore, that each is willing to place in the public fund only the least possible portion, no more than suffices to induce others to defend it. The aggregate of these least possible portions constitutes the right to punish; all that exceeds this is abuse and not justice; it is fact but by no means right.

Punishments that exceed what is necessary for protection of the deposit of public security are by their very nature unjust, and punishments are increasingly more just as the safety which the sovereign secures for his subjects is the more sacred and inviolable, and the liberty greater.

The Utilitarian Theory of Punishment

JEREMY BENTHAM

Bentham (1748–1832) was a British legal reformer who provided the first systematic statement of utilitarianism, the view which holds that the fundamental principle of morality requires us always to maximize net happiness for all in the long run. In this excerpt he develops, in considerable detail, a set of rules to be followed to ensure that a system of punishment will satisfy this principle. In particular, he identifies the factors that need to be taken into account by the legislator (a) in determining when punishment should be inflicted and when it should not be, and (b) in establishing how much punishment is appropriate for a given crime.

Reprinted with permission from *An Introduction to the Principles of Morals and Legislation* by Jeremy Bentham (J. H. Burns and H. L. A. Hart, eds.). London: Methuen, Inc., 1970.

The Principle of Utility

1. Nature has placed mankind under the governance of two sovereign masters, *pain* and *pleasure*. It is for them alone to point out what we ought to do, as well as to determine what we shall do. On the one hand the standard of right and wrong, on the other the chain of causes and effects, are fastened to their throne. They govern us in all we do, in all we say, in all we think: every effort we can make to throw off our subjection, will serve but to demonstrate and confirm it. In words a man may pretend to abjure their empire: but in reality he will remain subject to it all the while. The *principle of utility** recognises this subjection, and assumes it for the foundation of that system, the object of which is to rear the fabric of felicity by the hands of reason and of law. Systems which attempt to ques-

*Note by the author, July 1822.

To this denomination has of late been added, or substituted, the *greatest happiness* or *greatest felicity* principle: this for shortness, instead of saying at length *that principle* which states the greatest happiness of all those whose interest in in question, as being the right and proper, and only right and proper and universally desirable, end of human action: of human action in every situation, and in particular in that of a functionary or set of functionaries exercising the powers of Government. The word *utility* does not so clearly point to the ideas of *pleasure* and *pain* as the words *happiness* and *felicity* do: nor does it lead us to the consideration of the *number,* of the interests affected; to the *number,* as being the circumstance, which contributes, in the largest proportion, to the formation of the standard here in question; the *standard of right and wrong,* by which alone the propriety of human conduct, in every situation, can with propriety be tried. This want of a sufficiently manifest connexion between the ideas of *happiness* and *pleasure* on the one hand, and the idea of *utility* on the other, I have every now and then found operating, and with but too much efficiency, as a bar to the acceptance, that might otherwise have been given to this principle.

tion it, deal in sounds instead of sense, in caprice instead of reason, in darkness instead of light.

But enough of metaphor and declamation: it is not by such means that moral science is to be improved.

2. The principle of utility is the foundation of the present work: it will be proper therefore at the outset to give an explicit and determinate account of what is meant by it. By the principle of utility is meant that principle which approves or disapproves of every action whatsoever, according to the tendency which it appears to have to augment or diminish the happiness of the party whose interest is in question: or, what is the same thing in other words, to promote or to oppose that happiness. I say of every action whatsoever; and therefore not only of every action of a private individual, but of every measure of government.

3. By utility is meant that property in any object, whereby it tends to produce benefit, advantage, pleasure, good, or happiness, (all this in the present case comes to the same thing) or (what comes again to the same thing) to prevent the happening of mischief, pain, evil, or unhappiness to the party whose interest is considered: if that party be the community in general, then the happiness of the community: if a particular individual, then the happiness of that individual.

4. The interest of the community is one of the most general expressions that can occur in the phraseology of morals: no wonder that the meaning of it is often lost. When it has a meaning, it is this. The community is a fictitious *body*, composed of the individual persons who are considered as constituting as it were its *members*. The interest of the community then is, what?—the sum of the interests of the several members who compose it.

5. It is in vain to talk of the interest of the community, without understanding what is the interest of the individual. A thing is said to promote the interest, or to be *for* the interest, of an individual, when it tends to add to the sum total of his pleasures: or, what comes to the same thing, to diminish the sum total of his pains.

6. An action then may be said to be conformable to the principle of utility, or, for shortness sake, to utility (meaning with respect to the community at large) when the tendency it has to augment the happiness of the community is greater than any it has to diminish it.

7. A measure of government (which is but a particular kind of action, performed by a particular person or persons) may be said to be conformable to or dictated by the principle of utility, when in like manner the tendency which it has to augment the happiness of the community is greater than any which it has to diminish it.

8. When an action, or in particular a measure of government, is supposed by a man to be conformable to the principle of utility, it may be convenient, for the purposes of discourse, to imagine a kind of law or dictate, called a law or dictate of utility: and to speak of the action in question, as being conformable to such law or dictate.

9. A man may be said to be a partisan of the principle of utility, when the approbation or disapprobation he annexes to any action, or to any measure, is determined by, and proportioned to the tendency which he conceives it to have to augment or to diminish the happiness of the community: or in other words, to its conformity or unconformity to the laws or dictates of utility. . . .

Of the Four Sanctions or Sources of Pain and Pleasure

1. It has been shown that the happiness of the individuals, of whom a community is composed, that is their pleasures and their security, is the end and the sole end which the legislator ought to have in view: the sole standard, in conformity to which each individual ought, as far as depends upon the legislator, to be *made* to fashion his behaviour. But whether it be this or any thing else that is to be *done*, there is nothing by which a man can ultimately be *made* to do it, but either pain or pleasure. Having taken a general view of these two grand objects (*viz.*,

pleasure, and what comes to the same thing, immunity from pain) in the character of *final* causes; it will be necessary to take a view of pleasure and pain itself, in the character of *efficient* causes or means.

2. There are four distinguishable sources from which pleasure and pain are in use to flow: considered separately, they may be termed the *physical*, the *political*, the *moral*, and the *religious*: and inasmuch as the pleasures and pains belonging to each of them are capable of giving a binding force to any law or rule of conduct, they may all of them be termed *sanctions*.

3. If it be in the present life, and from the ordinary course of nature, not purposely modified by the interposition of the will of any human being, nor by any extraordinary interposition of any superior invisible being, that the pleasure or the pain takes place or is expected, it may be said to issue from or to belong to the *physical sanction*.

4. If at the hands of a *particular* person or set of persons in the community, who under names correspondent to that of *judge*, are chosen for the particular purpose of dispensing it, according to the will of the sovereign or supreme ruling power in the state, it may be said to issue from the *political sanction*.

5. If at the hands of such *chance* persons in the community, as the party in question may happen in the course of his life to have concerns with, according to each man's spontaneous disposition, and not according to any settled or concerted rule, it may be said to issue from the *moral* or *popular sanction*.

6. If from the immediate hand of a superior invisible being, either in the present life, or in a future, it may be said to issue from the *religious sanction*.

Of Human Actions in General

1. The business of government is to promote the happiness of the society, by punishing and rewarding. That part of its business which consists in punishing, is more particularly the subject of penal law. In proportion as an act tends to disturb that happiness, in proportion as the tendency of it is pernicious, will be the demand it creates for punishment. What happiness consists of we have already seen: enjoyment of pleasures, security from pains.

2. The general tendency of an act is more or less pernicious, according to the sum total of its consequences: that is, according to the difference between the sum of such as are good, and the sum of such as are evil.

3. It is to be observed, that here, as well as henceforward, wherever consequences are spoken of, such only are meant as are *material*. Of the consequences of any act, the multitude and variety must needs be infinite: but such of them only as are material are worth regarding. Now among the consequences of an act, be they what they may, such only, by one who views them in the capacity of a legislator, can be said to be material, as either consist of pain or pleasure, or have an influence in the production of pain or pleasure. . . .

Cases Unmeet for Punishment

§ i. General View of Cases Unmeet for Punishment

1. The general object which all laws have, or ought to have, in common, is to augment the total happiness of the community; and therefore, in the first place, to exclude, as far as may be, every thing that tends to subtract from that happiness: in other words, to exclude mischief.

2. But all punishment is mischief: all punishment in itself is evil. Upon the principle of utility, if it ought at all to be admitted, it ought only to be admitted in as far as it promises to exclude some greater evil.

3. It is plain, therefore, that in the following cases punishment ought not to be inflicted.

1. Where it is *groundless;* where there is no mischief for it to prevent; the act not being mischievous upon the whole.

2. Where it must be *inefficacious:* where it cannot act so as to prevent the mischief.
3. Where it is *unprofitable,* or too *expensive;* where the mischief it would produce would be greater than what it prevented.
4. Where it is *needless:* where the mischief may be prevented, or cease of itself, without it: that is, at a cheaper rate.

§ ii. Cases in Which Punishment Is Groundless

These are,

4. (1) Where there has never been any mischief: where no mischief has been produced to any body by the act in question. Of this number are those in which the act was such as might, on some occasions, be mischievous or disagreeable, but the person whose interest it concerns gave his *consent* to the performance of it. This consent, provided it be free, and fairly obtained, is the best proof that can be produced, that, to the person who gives it, no mischief, at least no immediate mischief, upon the whole, is done. For no man can be so good a judge as the man himself, what it is gives him pleasure or displeasure.

5. (2) Where the mischief was *outweighed:* although a mischief was produced by that act, yet the same act was necessary to the production of a benefit which was of greater value than the mischief. This may be the case with any thing that is done in the way of precaution against instant calamity, as also with any thing that is done in the exercise of the several sorts of powers necessary to be established in every community, to wit, domestic, judicial, military, and supreme.

6. (3) Where there is a certainty of an adequate compensation: and that in all cases where the offence can be committed. This supposes two things: 1. That the offence is such as admits of an adequate compensation; 2. That such a compensation is sure to be forthcoming. Of these suppositions, the latter will be found to be a merely ideal one: a supposition that cannot, in the universality here given to it, be verified by fact. It cannot, therefore, in practice, be numbered amongst the grounds of absolute impunity. It may, however, be admitted as a ground for an abatement of that punishment, which other considerations, standing by themselves, would seem to dictate.

§ iii. Cases in Which Punishment Must be Inefficacious

These are,

7. (1) Where the penal provision is *not established* until after the act is done. Such are the cases, 1. Of an *ex-post-facto* law; where the legislator himself appoints not a punishment till after the act is done; 2. Of a sentence beyond the law; where the judge, of his own authority, appoints a punishment which the legislator had not appointed.

8. (2) Where the penal provision, though established, is *not conveyed* to the notice of the person on whom it seems intended that it should operate. Such is the case where the law has omitted to employ any of the expedients which are necessary, to make sure that every person whatsoever, who is within the reach of the law, be apprized of all the cases whatsoever, in which (being in the station of life he is in) he can be subjected to the penalties of the law.

9. (3) Where the penal provision, though it were conveyed to a man's notice, *could produce no effect* on him, with respect to the preventing him from engaging in any act of the *sort* in question. Such is the case, 1. In extreme *infancy;* where a man has not yet attained that state or disposition of mind in which the prospect of evils so distant as those which are held forth by the law, has the effect of influencing his conduct; 2. In *insanity;* where the person, if he has attained to that disposition, has since been deprived of it through the influence of some permanent though unseen cause; 3. In *intoxication;* where he has been deprived of it by the transient influence of a visible cause: such as the use of wine, or opium, or other drugs, that act in this manner on the nervous system: which condition is indeed neither more nor

less than a temporary insanity produced by an assignable cause.

10. (4) Where the penal provision (although, being conveyed to the party's notice, it might very well prevent his engaging in acts of the sort in question, provided he knew that it related to those acts) could not have this effect, with regard to the *individual* act he is about to engage in: to wit, because he knows not that it is of the number of those to which the penal provision relates. This may happen, 1. In the case of *unintentionality;* where he intends not to engage, and thereby knows not that he is about to engage, in the *act* in which eventually he is about to engage; 2. In the case of *unconsciousness;* where, although he may know that he is about to engage in the *act* itself, yet, from not knowing all the material *circumstances* attending it, he knows not of the *tendency* it has to produce that mischief, in contemplation of which it has been made penal in most instances; 3. In the case of *mis-supposal;* where, although he may know of the tendency the act has to produce that degree of mischief, he supposes it, though mistakenly, to be attended with some circumstance, or set of circumstances, which, if it had been attended with, it would either not have been productive of that mischief, or have been productive of such a greater degree of good, as has determined the legislator in such a case not to make it penal.

11. (5) Where, though the penal clause might exercise a full and prevailing influence, were it to act alone, yet by the *predominant* influence of some opposite cause upon the will, it must necessarily be ineffectual; because the evil which he sees himself about to undergo, in the case of his *not* engaging in the act, is so great, that the evil denounced by the penal clause, in case of his engaging in it, cannot appear greater. This may happen, 1. In the case of *physical danger;* where the evil is such as appears likely to be brought about by the unassisted powers of *nature;* 2. In the case of a *threatened mischief;* where it is such as appears likely to be brought about through the intentional and conscious agency of *man.*

12. (6) Where (though the penal clause may exert a full and prevailing influence over the *will* of the party) yet his *physical faculties* (owing to the predominant influence of some physical cause) are not in a condition to follow the determination of the will insomuch that the act is absolutely *involuntary.* Such is the case of physical *compulsion* or *restraint,* by whatever means brought about; where the man's hand, for instance, is pushed against some object which his will disposes him *not* to touch; or tied down from touching some object which his will disposes him to touch.

§ iv. Cases Where Punishment Is Unprofitable

These are,

13. (1) Where, on the one hand, the nature of the offence, on the other hand, that of the punishment, are, *in the ordinary state of things,* such, that when compared together, the evil of the latter will turn out to be greater than that of the former.

14. Now the evil of the punishment divides itself into four branches, by which so many different sets of persons are affected. 1. The evil of *coercion* or *restraint:* or the pain which it gives a man not to be able to do the act, whatever it be, which by the apprehension of the punishment he is deterred from doing. This is felt by those by whom the law is *observed;* 2. The evil of *apprehension:* or the pain which a man, who has exposed himself to punishment, feels at the thoughts of undergoing it. This is felt by those by whom the law has been *broken,* and who feel themselves in *danger* of its being executed upon them; 3. The evil of *sufferance:* or the pain which a man feels, in virtue of the punishment itself, from the time when he begins to undergo it. This is felt by those by whom the law is broken, and upon whom it comes actually to be executed; 4. The pain of sympathy, and the other *derivative* evils resulting to the persons who are in *connection* with the several classes of original sufferers just mentioned. Now of these four lots of evil, the first will be greater or less, according to the nature of the act from which the party is restrained: the second and third according to the nature of the punishment which stands annexed to that offence.

15. On the other hand, as to the evil of the offence, this will also, of course, be greater or less, according to the nature of each offence. The proportion between the one evil and the other will therefore be different in the case of each particular offence. The cases, therefore, where punishment is unprofitable on this ground, can by no other means be discovered, than by an examination of each particular offence; which is what will be the business of the body of the work.

16. (2) Where, although in the *ordinary state* of things, the evil resulting from the punishment is not greater than the benefit which is likely to result from the force with which it operates, during the same space of time, towards the excluding the evil of the offence, yet it may have been rendered so by the influence of some *occasional circumstances.* In the number of these circumstances may be, 1. The multitude of delinquents at a particular juncture; being such as would increase, beyond the ordinary measure, the *quantum* of the second and third lots, and thereby also of a part of the fourth lot, in the evil of the punishment; 2. The extraordinary value of the services of some one delinquent; in the case where the effect of the punishment would be to deprive the community of the benefit of those services; 3. The displeasure of the *people;* that is, of an indefinite number of the members of the *same* community, in cases where (owing to the influence of some occasional incident) they happen to conceive, that the offence or the offender ought not to be punished at all, or at least ought not to be punished in the way in question; 4. The displeasure of *foreign powers;* that is, of the governing body, or a considerable number of the members of some *foreign* community or communities, with which the community in question, is connected.

§ v. Cases Where Punishment Is Needless

These are,

17. (1) Where the purpose of putting an end to the practice may be attained as effectually at a cheaper rate: by instruction, for instance, as well as by terror: by informing the understanding, as well as by exercising an immediate influence on the will. This seems to be the case with respect to all those offences which consist in the disseminating pernicious principles in matters of *duty;* of whatever kind the duty be; whether political, or moral, or religious. And this, whether such principles be disseminated *under,* or even *without,* a sincere persuasion of their being beneficial. I say, even *without:* for though in such a case it is not instruction that can prevent the writer from endeavoring to inculcate his principles, yet it may the readers from adopting them: without which, his endeavouring to inculcate them will do no harm. In such a case, the sovereign will commonly have little need to take an active part: if it be the interest of *one* individual to inculcate principles that are pernicious, it will as surely be the interest of *other* individuals to expose them. But if the sovereign must needs take a part in the controversy, the pen is the proper weapon to combat error with, not the sword.

Of the Proportion Between Punishments and Offences

1. We have seen that the general object of all laws is to prevent mischief; that is to say, when it is worth while; but that, where there are no other means of doing this than punishment, there are four cases in which it is *not* worth while.

2. When it *is* worth while, there are four subordinate designs or objects, which, in the course of his endeavours to compass, as far as may be, that one general object, a legislator, whose views are governed by the principle of utility, comes naturally to propose to himself.

3. (1) His first, most extensive, and most eligible object, is to prevent, in as far as it is possible, and worth while, all sorts of offences whatsoever: in other words, so to manage, that no offence whatsoever may be committed.

4. (2) But if a man must needs commit an offence of some kind or other, the next object

is to induce him to commit an offence *less* mischievous, *rather* than one *more* mischievous: in other words, to choose always the *least* mischievous, of two offences that will either of them suit his purpose.

5. (3) When a man has resolved upon a particular offence, the next object is to dispose him to do *no more* mischief than is *necessary* to his purpose: in other words, to do as little mischief as is consistent with the benefit he has in view.

6. (4) The last object is, whatever the mischief be, which it is proposed to prevent, to prevent it at as *cheap* a rate as possible.

7. Subservient to these four objects, or purposes, must be the rules or canons by which the proportion of punishments to offences is to be governed.

8. The first object, it has been seen, is to prevent, in as far as it is worth while, all sorts of offences; therefore,

The value of the punishment must not be less in any case than what is sufficient to outweigh that of the profit of the offence.

If it be, the offence (unless some other considerations, independent of the punishment, should intervene and operate efficaciously in the character of tutelary motives) will be sure to be committed notwithstanding: the whole lot of punishment will be thrown away: it will be altogether *inefficacious.*

9. The above rule has been often objected to, on account of its seeming harshness: but this can only have happened for want of its being properly understood. The strength of the temptation, *caeteris paribus,* is as the profit of the offence: the quantum of the punishment must rise with the profit of the offence: *caeteris paribus,* it must therefore rise with the strength of the temptation. This there is no disputing. True it is, that the stronger the temptation, the less conclusive is the indication which the act of delinquency affords of the depravity of the offender's disposition. So far then as the absence of any aggravation, arising from extraordinary depravity of disposition, may operate, or at the utmost, so far as the presence of a ground of extenuation, resulting from the innocence or beneficence of the offender's disposition, can operate, the strength of the temptation may operate in abatement of the demand for punishment. But it can never operate so far as to indicate the propriety of making the punishment ineffectual, which it is sure to be when brought below the level of the apparent profit of the offence.

The partial benevolence which should prevail for the reduction of it below this level, would counteract as well those purposes which such a motive would actually have in view, as those more extensive purposes which benevolence ought to have in view: it would be cruelty not only to the public, but to the very persons in whose behalf it pleads: in its effects, I mean, however opposite in its intention. Cruelty to the public, that is cruelty to the innocent, by suffering them, for want of an adequate protection, to lie exposed to the mischief of the offence: cruelty even to the offender himself, by punishing him to no purpose, and without the chance of compassing that beneficial end, by which alone the introduction of the evil of punishment is to be justified.

10. But whether a given offence shall be prevented in a given degree by a given quantity of punishment, is never any thing better than a chance; for the purchasing of which, whatever punishment is employed, is so much expended in advance. However, for the sake of giving it the better chance of outweighing the profit of the offence,

The greater the mischief of the offence, the greater is the expence, which it may be worth while to be at, in the way of punishment.

11. The next object is, to induce a man to choose always the least mischievous of two offences; therefore

Where two offences come in competition, the punishment for the greater offence must be sufficient to induce a man to prefer the less.

12. When a man has resolved upon a particular offence, the next object is, to induce him to do no more mischief than what is necessary for his purpose: therefore

The punishment should be adjusted in such manner to each particular offence, that for every part of the mischief there may be a motive to restrain the offender from giving birth to it.

13. The last object is, whatever mischief is guarded against, to guard against it at as cheap a rate as possible: therefore

The punishment ought in no case to be more than what is necessary to bring it into conformity with the rules here given.

14. It is further to be observed, that owing to the different manners and degrees in which persons under different circumstances are affected by the same exciting cause, a punishment which is the same in name will not always either really produce, or even so much as appear to others to produce, in two different persons the same degree of pain: therefore,

That the quantity actually inflicted on each individual offender may correspond to the quantity intended for similar offenders in general, the several circumstances influencing sensibility ought always to be taken into account.

15. Of the above rules of proportion, the four first, we may perceive, serve to mark out the limits on the side of diminution; the limits *below* which a punishment ought not to be *diminished:* the fifth, the limits on the side of increase; the limits *above* which it ought not to be *increased.* The five first are calculated to serve as guides to the legislator: the sixth is calculated, in some measure, indeed, for the same purpose; but principally for guiding the judge in his endeavours to conform, on both sides, to the intentions of the legislator.

16. Let us look back a little. The first rule, in order to render it more conveniently applicable to practice, may need perhaps to be a little more particularly unfolded. It is to be observed, then, that for the sake of accuracy, it was necessary, instead of the word *quantity* to make use of the less perspicuous term *value.* For the word *quantity* will not properly include the circumstances either of certainty or proximity: circumstances which, in estimating the value of a lot of pain or pleasure, must always be taken into the account. Now, on the one hand, a lot of punishment is a lot of pain; on the other hand, the profit of an offence is a lot of pleasure, or what is equivalent to it. But the profit of the offence is commonly more *certain* than the punishment, or, what comes to the same thing, *appears* so at least to the offender. It is at any rate commonly more *immediate.* It follows, therefore, that, in order to maintain its superiority over the profit of the offence, the punishment must have its value made up in some other way, in proportion to that whereby it falls short in the two points of *certainty* and *proximity.* Now there is no other way in which it can receive any addition to its *value,* but by receiving an addition in point of *magnitude.* Wherever then the value of the punishment falls short, either in point of *certainty,* or of *proximity,* of that of the profit of the offence, it must receive a proportionable addition in point of *magnitude.*

17. Yet farther. To make sure of giving the value of the punishment the superiority over that of the offence, it may be necessary, in some cases, to take into the account the profit not only of the *individual* offence to which the punishment is to be annexed, but also of such *other* offences of the *same sort* as the offender is likely to have already committed without detection. This random mode of calculation, severe as it is, it will be impossible to avoid having recourse to, in certain cases: in such, to wit, in which the profit is pecuniary, the chance of detection very small, and the obnoxious act of such a nature as indicates a habit: for example, in the case of frauds against the coin. If it be *not* recurred to, the practice of committing the offence will be sure to be, upon the balance of the account, a gainful practice. That being the case, the legislator will be absolutely sure of *not* being able to suppress it, and the whole punishment that is bestowed upon it will be thrown away. In a word (to keep to the same expressions we set out with) that whole quantity of punishment will be *inefficacious.*

18. These things being considered, the three following rules may be laid down by way of supplement and explanation to Rule 1.

To enable the value of the punishment to outweigh that of the profit of the offence, it must be increased, in point of magnitude, in proportion as it falls short in point of certainty.

19. Punishment must be further increased in point of magnitude, in proportion as it falls short in point of proximity.

20. Where the act is conclusively indicative of a habit, such an encrease must be given to the punishment as may enable it to outweigh the profit not only of the individual offence, but of such other like offences as are likely to have been committed with impunity by the same offender.

21. There may be a few other circumstances or considerations which may influence, in some small degree, the demand for punishment: but as the propriety of these is either not so demonstrable, or not so constant, or the application of them not so determinate, as that of the foregoing, it may be doubted whether they be worth putting on a level with the others.

22. When a punishment, which in point of quality is particularly well calculated to answer its intention, cannot exist in less than a certain quantity, it may sometimes be of use, for the sake of employing it, to stretch a little beyond that quantity which, on other accounts, would be strictly necessary.

23. In particular, this may sometimes be the case, where the punishment proposed is of such a nature as to be particularly well calculated to answer the purpose of a moral lesson.

24. The tendency of the above considerations is to dictate an augmentation in the punishment: the following rule operates in the way of diminution. There are certain cases (it has been seen) in which, by the influence of accidental circumstances, punishment may be rendered unprofitable as to a part only. Accordingly,

In adjusting the quantum of punishment, the circumstances, by which all punishment may be rendered unprofitable, ought to be attended to.

25. It is to be observed, that the more various and minute any set of provisions are, the greater the chance is that any given article in them will not be borne in mind: without which, no benefit can ensue from it. Distinctions, which are more complex than what the conceptions of those whose conduct it is designed to influence can take in, will even be worse than useless. The whole system will present a confused appearance: and thus the effect, not only of the proportions established by the articles in question, but of whatever is connected with them, will be destroyed. To draw a precise line of direction in such case seems impossible. However, by way of memento, it may be of some use to subjoin the following rule.

Among provisions designed to perfect the proportion between punishments and offences, if any occur, which, by their own particular good effects, would not make up for the harm they would do by adding to the intricacy of the Code, they should be omitted.

26. It may be remembered, that the political sanction, being that to which the sort of punishment belongs, which in this chapter is all along in view, is but one of four sanctions, which may all of them contribute their share towards producing the same effects. It may be expected, therefore, that in adjusting the quantity of political punishment, allowance should be made for the assistance it may meet with from those other controlling powers. True it is, that from each of these several sources a very powerful assistance may sometimes be derived. But the case is, that (setting aside the moral sanction, in the case where the force of it is expressly adopted into and modified by the political) the force of those other powers is never determinate enough to be depended upon. It can never be reduced, like political punishment, into exact lots, nor meted out in number, quantity, and value. The legislator is therefore obliged to provide the full complement of punishment, as if he were sure of not receiving any assistance whatever from any of those quarters. If he does, so much the better: but lest he should not, it is necessary he should, at all events, make that provision which depends upon himself.

27. It may be of use, in this place, to recapitulate the several circumstances, which, in establishing the proportion betwixt punishments and offences, are to be attended to. These seem to be as follows:

I. *On the part of the offence:*

1. The profit of the offence;
2. The mischief of the offence;

3. The profit and mischief of other greater or lesser offences, of different sorts, which the offender may have to choose out of;
4. The profit and mischief of other offences, of the same sort, which the same offender may probably have been guilty of already.

II. *On the part of the punishment:*
5. The magnitude of the punishment: composed of its intensity and duration;
6. The deficiency of the punishment in point of certainty;
7. The deficiency of the punishment in point of proximity;
8. The quality of the punishment;
9. The accidental advantage in point of quality of a punishment, not strictly needed in point of quantity;
10. The use of a punishment of a particular quality, in the character of a moral lesson.

III. *On the part of the offender:*
11. The responsibility of the class of persons in a way to offend;
12. The sensibility of each particular offender;
13. The particular merits or useful qualities of any particular offender, in case of punishment which might deprive the community of the benefit of them;
14. The multitude of offenders on any particular occasion.

IV. *On the part of the public,* at any particular conjuncture:
15. The inclinations of the people, for or against any quantity or mode of punishment;
16. The inclinations of foreign powers.

V. *On the part of the law:* that is, of the public for a continuance:
17. The necessity of making small sacrifices, in point of proportionality, for the sake of simplicity.

28. There are some, perhaps, who, at first sight, may look upon the nicety employed in the adjustment of such rules, as so much labour lost: for gross ignorance, they will say, never troubles itself about laws, and passion does not calculate. But the evil of ignorance admits of cure: and as to the proposition that passion does not calculate, this like most of these very general and oracular propositions, is not true. When matters of such importance as pain and pleasure are at stake, and these in the highest degree (the only matters, in short, that can be of importance) who is there that does not calculate? Men calculate, some with less exactness, indeed, some with more: but all men calculate. I would not say, that even a madman does not calculate. Passion calculates, more or less, in every man: in different men, according to the warmth or coolness of their dispositions: according to the firmness or irritability of their minds: according to the nature of the motives by which they are acted upon. Happily, of all passions, that is the most given to calculation, from the excesses of which, by reason of its strength, constancy, and universality, society has most to apprehend: I mean that which corresponds to the motive of pecuniary interest: so that these niceties, if such they are to be called, have the best chance of being efficacious, where efficacy is of the most importance.

Arguments Against the Utilitarian Theory

IGOR PRIMORATZ

Primoratz argues that a pure utilitarian view such as Bentham's would involve injustice in that (a) it would not allow for mercy, (b) it would sometimes call for disproportionately harsh—or disproportionately lenient—punishments, and (c) it would sometimes countenance the deliberate punishment of innocent people. The root of these (and other) difficulties, he maintains, is that utilitarians pay no attention to what an offender *deserves* but only to what will bring about the best consequences for society as a whole.

1. Ends and Means in Punishing

Seen from a utilitarian point of view, punishment, like any other social practice, is a means to an end: society has to defend itself against crime. It can never realistically hope to eradicate it completely, but it has to keep on doing its best to keep it under control, to reduce it as much as possible. Punishment is a means to this end; for a utilitarian, this is its main purpose and its true justification. An evil in itself, it is justified because it helps achieve a socially vital objective.

Or does it? In the face of the high rates of criminality in most modern societies, the tendency of these rates to go up, or at least not to go down, despite all attempts at improvement of punitive practices and institutions, and the phenomenon of widespread recidivism, many have come to doubt both the deterrent and reformatory effectiveness of punishment as we know it. Many have come to the conclusion that it simply does not work, or at least not in a reasonably efficient and economical way. This belief has motivated various proposals for dismantling the institution of punishment and replacing it by a completely different social response to crime—by restitution of the victim, or by therapy provided for the offender. This is the first and most obvious objection to the utilitarian theory of punishment: that it is predicated on an empirically false belief. Punishment cannot be justified in terms of its utility, for, as a matter of fact, it is not useful.

Reprinted with permission from *Justifying Legal Punishment* by Igor Primoratz. Atlantic Highlands, NJ: Humanities Press, 1989.

It is true that, whatever their doubts and reservations regarding various specific punishments or the practice of punishment in general at certain times or in certain jurisdictions, adherents of the utilitarian theory normally believe that punishment is basically sound: that it does, or can be made to, work efficiently and economically, and that it is a socially necessary institution. They normally believe, as Bentham has it, that

> we should never be able to subjugate, however imperfectly, the vast empire of evil, had we not learned the method of combating one evil by another. It has been necessary to enlist auxiliaries among pains, to oppose other pains which attack us on every side. So, in the art of curing pains of another sort, poisons well applied have proved to be remedies.[1]

Still, the empirical objection to the utilitarian view of punishment is not very weighty. For the utilitarian can retort that even if it were shown, to the satisfaction of all concerned, that punishment does not work, that would not mean that his theory has been refuted. This conclusion would follow only if it were assumed that punishment *is* justified, and that the only question is, Just what is it that justifies it? But he can refuse to make this assumption. The utilitarian claim is that only utility can justify punishment. Even if it turns out that, contrary to what people have thought for centuries or even millennia, punishment is not useful, or not useful enough, the theory will stand; the conclusion will be that punishment is *not* justified, and that we should replace it by whatever seems to be the most promising alternative.

There is another, non-empirical objection that can be brought forward against the view that punishment is to be morally justified as a means to an end. This view is a corollary of a view of humanity characteristic of utilitarianism in general. The confrontation between the utilitarian and retributive views of punishment is rooted in a confrontation at a deeper level, between two very different, even irreconcilable views of human beings. As we shall see in the following chapter in some detail, the retributive theory insists on justice and desert as *the* moral criteria of punishment. Talk of justice and desert makes sense when we relate to a being who decides and acts freely, and therefore carries responsibility for its decisions and actions; when dealing with animals, or with the insane, or with children, we normally go by other standards. Retributivism approaches the problem of punishment from the standpoint of a conception of humans as free, mature, responsible, self-determining beings. It sees and respects the offender as such a being, and relates to his act as to an act of such a being. The punishment is then viewed as a reaction that is fully determined—with regard to the right to punish, the duty to punish, and the proper measure of punishment—by the free action of the offender, an action for which he is responsible and by which he has accordingly deserved to be punished. By viewing both offense and punishment in these terms, retributivism affirms the conception of human beings as persons; for we relate to another as a person when the way *we* treat him is determined by his *own* decisions and actions.

From the utilitarian point of view, on the other hand, the offense as such is not essential for the justification of punishment; what counts are the objectives secured through punishment. Punishment, and *ipso facto* the person punished, is but a means for attaining the aims of society. If the objective of punishment is reformation of the offender, he is being treated as an unfree, immature being, whose behavior may legitimately be reshaped by others in accordance with their notions of what is good, desirable, and socially acceptable. If the punishment aims at exerting an educative influence on the public at large, that public is treated as a collectivity of such beings. If the aim of punishment is to intimidate the offender or potential offenders in the public at large, both the offender and everyone else whom punishment is meant to deter are treated in a way that ignores their basic human dignity. As Hegel puts it, "to base a justification of punishment on threat is to liken it to the act of a man who lifts his stick to a dog. It is to treat a man like a dog instead of with freedom and respect due to him as a man."[2] In the view of humanity that is the basis of the utilitarian theory of punishment and utilitarianism in general, there is no room for the idea of the dignity of every human being as *human being*, and the individual is not seen first and foremost as a person, that is a being whose freedom and responsibility are to be respected and who, to a considerable extent, shapes his own fate. He is rather seen as a being who may legitimately be used for attaining the objectives of others, and whose destiny is not crucially determined by his own free decisions and actions, but by the aims for which he will be used as a means; this, again, is determined by circumstances which he cannot control and very often cannot even predict.

All this is rather general. What it amounts to will become clearer in the next section, where I take up various types of punishment that might turn out to be useful, and therefore also justified from the utilitarian point of view.

2. Utilitarianism and Justice

In addition to the general point about the view of man which is the basis of the utilitarian theory of punishment, there are a number of more specific arguments against this theory. All of them have to do with the distinctively utilitarian view of justice.

For a utilitarian, justice—as all other moral concepts, ideals, principles—is but a particular facet of utility, a particular way of promoting the common good. To be sure, a utilitarian, no less than anyone else, accepts a concept of justice which could be termed legal justice pure and simple, and which means the application of law in an impartial, objective manner, with no regard to individual or group interest. In this sense, a judge who enforces an unjust law will be acting justly as long as she enforces it without any regard to either personal interest or the interest of a particular social group, in a consistent and impartial way. But this notion of justice is of no great philosophical interest; philosophical questions about justice are for the most part posed and discussed at another, higher level, at which it makes sense to inquire about the justice or injustice of a particular law, or even of a whole system of law, as well as other social rules and institutions. At this level the utilitarian will view justice as "an imaginary personage, feigned for the convenience of discourse, whose dictates are the dictates of utility, applied to certain particular cases . . . nothing more than an imaginary instrument, employed to forward on certain occasions, and by certain means, the purposes of benevolence. The dictates of justice are nothing more than a part of the dictates of benevolence."[3] Consequently, within a utilitarian theory of punishment there is no need, and no room, for the idea of desert, which is logically connected with that of justice, so that, as J. Plamenatz has neatly put it, from a utilitarian perspective "no one can deserve punishment; it can merely be right that he should be punished."[4] This is the root of a whole series of difficulties that plague the utilitarian view of punishment.

One of them has to do with mercy and pardon. It may be claimed that every theory of punishment should be able to allow for the application of the ideal of mercy in certain cases, and make some room for the institution of pardon as the legal embodiment of this ideal. The utilitarian theory is unable to do this. It makes sense to say that we have shown mercy to the offender only if we have reduced, or completely repealed, the punishment which he has *deserved* by his act and which is consequently *just*. Acts of mercy shown to offenders are logically possible only against the background of a conflict of two considerations: the principle of just, deserved punishment, and the ideal of mercy.[5] But within utilitarianism such a conflict cannot take place, for "desert" and "justice" have no standing of their own, independent of utility; the latter is the sole criterion of our choices. Therefore, if a punishment

> served no good purpose, then the question of imposing it wouldn't come up at all; nor consequently would the question of mercy. The utilitarian has no choice; he must recommend the course of action that produces most good, and if this means a certain penalty he cannot act mercifully and impose less than that penalty. Real mercy is never a possibility for him because he must always impose what is, according to his ethic, the fully justifiable penalty. Even where there is a serious conflict of interests, and punishment is suspended because the harm it would do to others is greater than the good it will do, this cannot properly be called mercy, because there is no significant sense in which the utilitarian can say "I *ought* to do such and such, but special considerations persuade me to act differently on this occasion." For him, the statement "I shall act mercifully" can *only* mean "I shall impose a penalty less than the one which will produce most good," which in turn can *only* mean "I shall impose a penalty less than the one which will produce most good because this action is the one which will produce most good."[6]

Bentham's account of punishment bears this out: it allows for pardon only when that is the way to correct a law or a sentence that is not fully justified in utilitarian terms—that is, as a way of ensuring that the option most desirable from the utilitarian point of view is taken after all. This, of course, is not mercy properly speaking; mercy proper remains beyond the scope of the utilitarian theory. Bentham explicitly states this: "In a Penal Code, having for its first principle the greatest-happiness principle—no such word would have place."[7]

Further difficulties in the utilitarian theory arise in connection with the question of the proper measure of punishment. It has been claimed that the utilitarian is committed to draconian penalties: "Why stop at the minimum, why not be on the safe side and penalise [the offender] in some pretty spectacular way—wouldn't that be more likely to deter others? Let him be whipped to death, publicly of course, for a parking offence; that would certainly deter *me* from parking on the spot reserved for the Vice-Chancellor!"[8] This objection, as it stands, is obviously misguided, for preventing parking offenses in such a spectacular manner would mean preventing an evil by inflicting an incomparably greater one. Utilitarians would want punishments to be effective, but at a reasonable price. Still, the argument points in the right direction: utilitarianism *would* justify disproportionately harsh punishments, as long as they satisfied the condition of economy at the same time. For instance, if a certain not particularly grave offense such as shoplifting became extremely widespread, and the usual, comparatively short prison term was no longer efficient in preventing it, it might be useful to prescribe very stiff prison sentences for it. If we managed to prevent shoplifting almost completely for a very long period of time by giving, say, two-year terms to a few offenders, these punishments would be effective but economical, and accordingly justified from the utilitarian point of view. But they would be out of all proportion to the gravity of the offenses committed, and thereby clearly undeserved and unjust.

On the other hand, the utilitarian would also be committed to injustice in punishment in the opposite direction. If it turned out, for example, that six months in prison were deterrent enough for rape, or that a year's term were enough with regard to murder, these would be punishments she would consider right and proper for the crimes of rape and murder, respectively. Depending on the circumstances, the utilitarian would be meting out punishments that are way beyond, or below, what is proportionate to the gravity of the offenses committed, and consequently deserved and just.

Another kind of injustice the utilitarian would be committing when measuring out punishments has to do with offenses committed under provocation or in a passion. A retributivist would say that in such cases the guilt is reduced, and consequently the punishment should be less severe than otherwise. This is also the view accepted in criminal court practice. As we have seen in the preceding chapter, however, a utilitarian sees things quite differently: for her, punishments for offenses committed in a passion or under provocation should be especially severe.[9] That is, the very same factors that are normally taken for extenuating circumstances within the utilitarian theory become aggravating ones. For, if prevention of offenses is the main objective of punishment and its basic justification, then, as E. Westermarck says,

> the heaviest punishment should be threatened where the strongest motive is needed to restrain. Consequently, an injury committed under great temptation, or in a passion, should be punished with particular severity; whereas a crime like parricide might be treated with more indulgence than other kinds of homicide, owing to the restraining influence of filial affection. Could the moral consciousness approve of this?[10]

Another difficulty the utilitarian theory meets, even more compromising, arises with regard to the mentally ill. It is generally held that offenders proven to be mentally ill ought not to be punished, and that the state should respond to their offenses in some other way, most likely by compulsory therapy or hospitalization. Could a utilitarian subscribe to this view as well? Bentham thinks so. To be sure, he does not believe that such offenders must not be punished because of the lack of guilt or desert on their part, and the injustice that will consequently be involved in having them punished; from the utilitarian point of view such considerations are irrelevant. Bentham's explanation is that such punishments could not be efficient, for their deterrent efficiency—and human nature being what it is, it is mainly by deterring people that we prevent them from offending against the law—presupposes the very rationality and ability to control one's actions that the mentally ill lack.[11]

This explanation is not convincing. True, we cannot hope to influence the behavior of the mentally ill by punishment: we cannot deter the actual mentally ill offender from breaking the law again by punishing him, nor will his punishment deter those mentally ill in the public at large who might break the law. But it does not follow that such punishments have to be inefficient. For they could have a strong deterrent effect on *normal* potential offenders. If the insanity defense were abolished and the law provided for the mentally ill offenders to be punished in the same way as normal offenders, the perspective faced by a sane would-be offender would be considerably graver than the one he faces now in an important respect: he could entertain no hope of getting himself declared not responsible for his action and evading punishment for it by convincingly simulating mental illness.[12]

A utilitarian could deny that her theory commits her to punishing the mentally ill. She could claim that the final balance of consequences would go against it after all. The common moral consciousness views this matter in a completely nonutilitarian way, and could not possibly reconcile itself to what it would consider a grave violation of justice. Therefore, such punishments would bring about very unfavorable reactions from the public, which would come to think that the whole criminal law system is unjust and would accordingly deny it support and cooperation. This would undermine the system in a serious way. Such consequences, obviously, would be so bad that they would override any preventive effects that could possibly be secured by punishing mentally ill offenders along with the sane. In Bentham's terminology, such punishments would be so unpopular that they would become unprofitable.[13]

This defense, however, is not plausible. Our refusal to accept punishment of the mentally ill is not a concession to nonutilitarian prejudices of the common moral consciousness; it follows from a clear and deeply rooted moral conviction which is part of our understanding of justice. We would consider such punishment no less morally wrong for a society in which the common moral opinion would not object to it than for a society in which it would be very unpopular.[14]

Another possible response of the utilitarian to the argument on punishment of the mentally ill would refer to the distinction presupposed by the argument, between a normal and a mentally ill offender. If it is possible to formulate the criteria for applying the distinction in practice in an adequate and reasonably precise way, normal offenders will have no reason to hope that they will manage to deceive the court into thinking that they are mentally ill and not responsible for their misdeeds, and thus get away with them; therefore there is no need for punishing the mentally ill so as to prevent the sane from counting on this. On the other hand, if such criteria cannot be established, we cannot differentiate between the two groups of offenders, and the whole issue of punishing the mentally ill cannot arise at all.[15]

This defense is no more successful than the previous one. It is a fact that courts have at their disposal certain criteria for distinguishing between offenders who are sane and responsible and those who are not. These criteria, though not perfect, are reasonably good. The dilemma posed with regard to these criteria simplifies the matter by ignoring the question of the degree to which the public is informed and enlightened and the way it relates to these criteria and the use of psychiatry in criminal courts in general. This is crucial for any good assessment of the utility of applying the criteria and desisting from punishing mentally ill offenders. H. J. McCloskey has nicely reviewed the possibilities and the corresponding implications of the utilitarian theory of punishment:

> In an ignorant community it might well be useful to punish as responsible moral agents "criminals" who in fact were not responsible for their actions but who were generally believed to be responsible agents. The experts suggest that many sex offenders and others who commit the more shocking crimes, are of this type, but even in reasonably enlightened communities the general body of citizens do not always accept the judgements of the experts. Thus, in communities in which enlightened opinion generally prevails (and these are few) punishment of mentally deranged "criminals" would have little if any deterrent value, whereas in most communities some mentally deranged people may usefully be punished, and in ignorant, backward communities very useful results may come from punishing those not responsible for their actions. Similarly, very undesirable results may come from not punishing individuals generally believed to be fully responsible moral agents. Yet, clearly, the morality of punishing such people does not depend on the degree of the enlightenment of the community. Util-

> itarian theory suggests that it does, that such punishment is right and just in ignorant, prejudiced communities, unjust in enlightened communities. The utility of such punishment varies in this way, but not its justice.[16]

We have seen that from the utilitarian theory it follows that under certain circumstances it would be morally justified to mete out punishments that are considerably more, or considerably less, severe than those that would be deserved and just in view of the gravity of the offenses committed and the measure of responsibility with which they were committed, and also to punish those whose punishment is wholly undeserved and hence unjust—the mentally ill offenders. On the other hand, it also follows from the theory that sometimes the guilty should not be punished at all. From the utilitarian point of view, only consequences constitute good reason for punishing or abstaining from punishment; desert and justice do not count in their own right. Punishment is an evil which a utilitarian considers morally justified only when it is the means for securing a greater good, which is usually but not always the case. Sometimes the opposite is to be expected: punishing the offender would have worse consequences than were he to get away with his misdeed; punishment would prove unprofitable. And according to utilitarianism, every unprofitable punishment is *ipso facto* morally unjustified: as Bentham puts it, "it is cruel to expose even the guilty to useless sufferings."[17]

When would punishing an offender be unprofitable? As we have seen in the preceding chapter, Bentham has in mind cases such as the following: when the punishment would cause such a great displeasure of the public, or a foreign power, that in the final account it would have worse consequences than abstaining from punishing; or when an offender, if not punished, could render a service to the community which outweighs the utility of his punishment. In such cases punishing the guilty would "cost society too dear" and therefore would be morally unjustified.[18] From a nonutilitarian point of view, on the other hand, a criminal law system guided by calculations of this kind would thereby gravely compromise itself; and the implication of the utilitarian theory of punishment that such calculations are morally relevant and even binding goes to compromise the theory. "What then are we to think of the proposal," asks Kant, "that the life of a condemned criminal should be spared if he agrees to let dangerous experiments be carried out on him in order that the doctors may gain new information of value to the commonwealth, and is fortunate enough to survive?" His answer is that "a court of justice would dismiss with contempt any medical institution which made such a proposal; for justice ceases to be justice if it can be bought at a price."[19]

Another kind of situation in which it would be morally justified not to punish the guilty is when the desirable effects of punishment can be secured without actually punishing—by producing an illusion of punishment. In cases when the utilitarian cannot or need not count on the effects of punishment in the way of particular prevention and when, accordingly, the decision depends solely on the contribution of punishment to its most important purpose, the general prevention, a crucial role in her deliberation will have to be accorded to Bentham's distinction between real and apparent punishment—punishment which is actually inflicted on someone, and the idea of that punishment formed in the minds of others—and to the rule that the proportion between the two should be as favorable as possible to the latter. Punishment works as a means of general prevention by its apparent aspect; real infliction of punishment is needed only to produce the apparent effect. Whenever the deterrent effects of punishment on the general public can be attained by having the offender punished only apparently, without actually inflicting punishment, this will be the best option from the utilitarian point of view. Really to inflict punishment in such cases would mean to be unreasonably and unjustifiably cruel.[20]

A telling example of this kind of utilitarian economy is recounted by Bentham from a report published in *Lloyd's Evening Post* in 1776:

> At the Cape of Good Hope, the Dutch made use of a stratagem which could only succeed among Hottentots. One of their officers having killed an individual of this inoffensive tribe, the

> whole nation took up the matter, and became furious and implacable. It was necessary to make an example to pacify them. The delinquent was therefore brought before them in irons, as a malefactor: he was tried with great form, and was condemned to swallow a goblet of ignited brandy. The man played his part—he feigned himself dead, and fell motionless. His friends covered him with a cloak, and bore him away. The Hottentots declared themselves satisfied. "The worst we should have done with the man," said they, "would have been to throw him into the fire; but the Dutch have done better—they have put the fire into the man."[21]

According to the utilitarian theory of punishment, whenever this would be the alternative with the best possible consequences, a feigned punishment would be staged instead of a real one, and the public should be put in a position analogous to that of the innocent Hottentots.

The arguments on non-punishment of the guilty demonstrate how the utilitarian theory of punishment would, in certain circumstances, transform the criminal law system into a market for trading in justice, or a stage on which, instead of doing justice, shows of its being done are performed. On the other hand, under different circumstances still, this theory would imply that it is morally justified to punish the innocent.

Bentham holds that whenever punishment of the innocent is the option with the best consequences, such punishment "not only may, but ought to be introduced." As an example of such punishment, he cites collective punishment in cases when it is impossible to differentiate between the innocent and the guilty.[22] But if we take the view that it is morally right to punish the innocent whenever that is the course of action with the best consequences, the situation mentioned by Bentham will by no means be the only one in which we shall decide on such punishment. Collective punishment might be the thing to do from the point of view of the consequences of alternative options, even when we know who is the offender: punishing him *and* his family, or all the inhabitants of his village, or a group of his compatriots can sometimes have a much greater deterrent effect than punishing only the offender, and at the same time satisfy the condition of economy, the evil of offenses prevented still outweighing the evil inflicted by such collective punishment.[23]

Again, punishing a single scapegoat will sometimes be the course of action with the best consequences under the circumstances. Suppose there is a country where, due to the incompetence of the police and the courts, criminal behavior has become widespread, and popular trust in the legal order has been seriously undermined. The only expeditious and efficient way out of this situation, and of preventing many offenses from being committed, as they assuredly will be if things remain the way they are, is finally to punish an offender. This punishment, with proper publicity, will have a strong preventive effect on a large number of potential offenders, and will help a great deal toward restoring popular confidence in the ability of the legal order and the police to provide the necessary protection. However, precisely because the police are so incompetent, the opportunity never arises. Once again they have got the wrong person—a person innocent of the crime he is charged with, that is. His acquittal will have good consequences as far as he is concerned, but an opportunity to ensure consequences that are far more desirable from the standpoint of the common good will be lost. On the other hand, to punish him, his innocence notwithstanding, will have bad consequences for him, but overwhelmingly good consequences for the common good. From the utilitarian point of view, it would be morally unjustified and wrong to do the former, and morally justified and even obligatory to do the latter.

I think that the case against the utilitarian theory of punishment can be strengthened at this point by adding an argument complementary to the previous one, which might be termed the argument of self-sacrifice of the innocent. From Kant, who seems to have been the first to suggest the punishment-of-the-innocent argument, onwards, critics of utilitarianism have always viewed the situation described in the argument from the point of view of the *judge,* pointing out the unacceptable implication of utilitarianism as to what the judge would be obligated to do. But the situation could profitably be examined from another angle, that of the *innocent person accused.* If the circumstances are such that punishing an innocent will have the best possible effects and is, therefore, according to utilitarianism, the morally right thing to do, this provides moral guidance not only for the judge, but for all those on whose conduct the outcome depends. The accused is, obviously, one of them: in such cases, cooperation on the part of the accused can only make the trial more convincing, and thereby render the positive effects expected from it and from the punishment which is to follow—the effects that provide the moral justification of such a course of action—much more likely than they otherwise would be. Thus the same premises which, according to the utilitarian view of punishment, make it incumbent upon the judge to pronounce an innocent person guilty and to sentence him, and imply that it would be morally wrong for her to act otherwise, also make it incumbent upon the innocent defendant to cooperate in passing and carrying out the sentence. Regardless of the fact that he is innocent, and that he knows that the judge is aware of his innocence, he ought to collaborate assiduously in his own condemnation and punishment by "confessing" to the false charge and perhaps by pretending to be repentant as well. From the utilitarian standpoint, any insistence on his innocence and any attempt to change the outcome of the trial would be morally impermissible. The only morally right thing for him to do under the circumstances is to sacrifice himself for the common good.

These are some of the implications of the uutilitarian theory of punishment. Each one of them suggests as the morally right course an action which is obviously and seriously unjust and will therefore be found by most of us to be morally unacceptable. If they were to be graded in terms of their moral reprehensibility, I believe that the last two—that it is sometimes right to punish an innocent person, and that in such cases the innocent should collaborate in their own sentence and punishment—would be placed on top of the list.

NOTES

1. J. Bentham, *Theory of Legislation,* trans. from the French of E. Dumont by R. Hildreth, 2d ed. (London: Trübner, 1871), p. 54.
2. G. W. F. Hegel, *Philosophy of Right,* trans T.M. Knox (Oxford: Oxford University Press, 1965), p. 246.
3. J. Bentham, *An Introduction to the Principles of Morals and Legislation,* ed. W. Harrison (Oxford: Basil Blackwell, 1960), pp. 240–241, n. 2. For a discussion of the utilitarian approach to justice, see H. A. Bedau, "Justice and Classical Utilitarianism," in C. J. Friedrich and J. W. Chapman (Eds.), *Justice,* "Nomos" 6 (New York: Atherton Press, 1963).
4. J. Plamenatz, *The English Utilitarians,* 2d ed. (Oxford: Basil Blackwell, 1966), p. 80.
5. For an analysis of the concept of mercy, see A. Smart, "Mercy," in H. B. Acton (ed.), *The Philosophy of Punishment* (London: Macmillan, 1969).
6. Ibid., pp. 224–225.
7. J. Bentham, *Principles of Penal Law, The Works of Jeremy Bentham,* ed. J. Bowring (New York: Russell & Russell, 1962), vol. 1, p. 529.
8. K. G. Armstrong, "The Retributivist Hits Back," in Acton, *Philosophy of Punishment,* p. 152.
9. *Supra,* pp. 27–28.
10. E. Westermarck, *The Origin and Development of the Moral Ideas,* 2d ed. (London: Macmillan, 1912), vol. 1, p. 83. See A. C. Ewing, *The Morality of Punishment* (London: Kegan Paul, Trench, Trubner & Co., 1929), p. 53. For an attempt at a (partial) defense of utilitarianism on this point, see F. W. Maitland, "The Relation of Punishment to Temptation," *Mind* 5 (1880).
11. Cf. *supra,* p. 23. This rationale of excusing the mentally ill is not consistent with Bentham's claim that would-be offenders always calculate the desirable and undesirable effects of what they consider doing, and that even the insane do so (*supra,* p. 21).
12. Cf. H. L. A. Hart, *Punishment and Responsibility* (Oxford: Oxford University Press, 1973), pp. 19–20, 40–44; O. S. Walker, "Why Should Irresponsible Offenders Be Excused?," *Journal of Philosophy* 66 (1969), p. 280; J.J.C. Smart, "Utilitarianism and Criminal Justice," *Bulletin of the Australian Society of Legal Philosophy* (Special Issue, 1981), 12–14.
13. Cf. D. F. Thomson, "Retribution and the Distribution of Punishment," *Philosophical Quarterly* 16 (1966), p. 59.

14. Cf. H. L. A. Hart, *Punishment and Responsibility*, pp. 20–21.
15. T. L. S. Sprigge, "A Utilitarian Reply to Dr. McCloskey," in M. D. Bayles (Ed.), *Contemporary Utilitarianism* (Garden City, N.Y.: Doubleday, 1968), pp. 290–291.
16. H. J. McCloskey, "A Non-Utilitarian Approach to Punishment," in Bayles, *Contemporary Utilitarianism*, p. 252.
17. J. Bentham, *Theory of Legislation*, p. 345.
18. Supra, p. 23.
19. I. Kant, "The Metaphysics of Morals," *Kant's Political Writings*, ed. H. Reiss, trans. H. B. Nisbet (Cambridge: Cambridge University Press, 1970), p. 155.
20. See *supra*, pp. 28–29.
21. J. Bentham, *Principles of Penal Law*, p. 398.
22. See *supra*, pp. 24–26.
23. Cf. H. J. McCloskey, "Non-Utilitarian Approach," p. 250.

Convicting the Innocent

JAMES MCCLOSKEY

If the utilitarian approach is correct, then whether or not a given system of punishment is justified will depend on both its overall benefits and its overall costs. McCloskey tries to show that various features of the U.S. system of criminal justice produce very significant costs indeed. These include various forms of misconduct and incompetence on the part of police, prosecutors, defense attorneys, and juries. He estimates that, as a result, "at least 10 percent of those convicted of serious and violent crimes are completely innocent."

On most occasions when it has been discovered that the wrong person was convicted for another's crime, the local law enforcement community, if it has commented at all, has assured the public that such instances are indeed rare and isolated aberrations of a criminal justice system that bats nearly 1,000 percent in convicting the guilty and acquitting the innocent. And this view is shared, I think, not only by the vast majority of the public but also by almost all of the professionals (lawyers and judges) whose work comes together to produce the results.

I realize that I am a voice crying in the wilderness, but I believe that the innocent are convicted far more frequently than the public cares to believe, and far more frequently than those who operate the system dare to believe. An innocent person in prison, in my view, is about as rare as a pigeon in the park. The primary purpose of this article is to delineate why and how I have come to believe that this phenomenon of the "convicted innocent" is so alarmingly widespread in the United States. Although no one has any real idea of what proportion it has reached, it is my perception that at least 10 percent of those convicted of serious and violent crimes are completely innocent. Those whose business it is to convict or to defend would more than likely concede to such mistakes occurring in only 1 percent of cases, if that. Regardless of where the reader places his estimate, these percentages, when converted into absolute numbers, tell us that thousands and even tens of thousands of innocent people languish in prisons across the nation.

Allow me to outline briefly the ground of experience on which I stand and speak. For the past eight years I have been working full time on behalf of the innocent in prison. To date, the nonprofit organization I founded to do this work has freed and vindicated eleven innocent lifers and another from Texas's death row. Currently we are working on ten cases across the country (New Jersey, Pennsylvania, Virginia, Washington D.C., Texas, Missouri, and California). We have received well over 3,000 requests for assistance and have developed extensive files on more than 1,000 of these requests which come to us daily from every state of the nation from

James McCloskey is Director of Centurion Ministries, Inc., Princeton, N.J.

From James McCloskey, "Convicting the Innocent," (as appeared in *Criminal Justice Ethics* Vol. 8, No. 1, [Winter/Spring, 1989] pp. 54–59). Reprinted by permission of *The Institute for Criminal Justice Ethics*, 899 Tenth Avenue, New York, NY, 10019.

those who have been convicted, or from their advocates, proclaiming their innocence. We serve as active advisers on many of those cases.

Besides being innocent and serving life or death sentences, our beneficiaries have lost their legal appeals. Their freedom can be secured only by developing new evidence sufficient to earn a retrial. This new evidence must materially demonstrate either that the person is not guilty or that the key state witnesses lied in critical areas of their testimony. We are not lawyers. We are concerned only with whether the person is in fact completely not guilty in that he or she had nothing whatsoever to do with the crime. When we enter the case it is usually five to fifteen years after the conviction. Our sole focus is to reexamine the factual foundation of the conviction—to conduct an exhaustive investigation of the cast of characters and the circumstances in the case, however long that might take.

We find and interview as often as necessary anyone who has knowledge about the case and/or the people who are related to the case. We search for documentation and employ whatever forensic scientific tests are available that in any way shed light on, point to, or establish the truth of the matter. While developing this new information, we retain and work with the most suitable attorney in seeking judicial relief for our clients. We raise and disburse whatever funds are required to meet the legal, investigative, and administrative costs of seeking justice for these otherwise forgotten and forsaken souls buried in our prisons all across the land.

Appellate Relief for the Convicted Innocent

As all lawyers and jurists know, but most lay people do not, innocence or guilt is irrelevant when seeking redress in the appellate courts. As the noted attorney F. Lee Bailey observed, "Appellate courts have only one function, and that is to correct legal mistakes of a serious nature made by a judge at a lower level. Should a jury have erred by believing a lying witness, or by drawing an attractive but misleading inference, there is nothing to appeal." So, if the imprisoned innocent person is unable to persuade the appellate judges of any legal errors at trial, and generally he cannot, even though he suffered the ultimate trial error, he has no recourse. Nothing can be done legally to free him unless new evidence somehow surfaces that impeaches the validity of the conviction. Commonly, the incarcerated innocent are rubber-stamped into oblivion throughout the appeals process, both at the state and at the federal level.

So where does that leave the innocent person once he is convicted? Dead in the water, that's where! He is screaming his head off that he is innocent, but no one believes him. One of our beneficiaries standing before his sentencing judge told him, "Your Honor . . . I will eat a stone, I will eat dust, I will eat anything worse in the world for me to prove my innocence. I am not the man. I am innocent. I am not the man." The jury didn't believe him. The judge didn't. Certainly the prosecutor didn't, and more important than all of these put together, neither did his trial attorney nor his appellate lawyer. And so it goes for the convicted innocent. Their cries of innocence will forever fall on deaf ears and cynical minds.

Once he is convicted, no one in whose hands his life is placed (his lawyer and the appellate judges) either believes him or is concerned about his innocence or guilt. It is no longer an issue of relevance. The only question remaining that is important or material is whether he "legally" received a fair trial, not whether the trial yielded a result that was factually accurate. Appellate attorneys are not expected to, nor do they have the time, inclination, and resources to, initiate an investigation designed to unearth new evidence that goes to the question of a false conviction. Such an effort is simply beyond the scope of their thinking and beyond the realm of their professional responsibility. It is a rare attorney indeed who would dare go before any American appellate court and attempt to win a retrial for his client based on his innocence. That's like asking an actor in a

Shakespearian tragedy to go on stage and pretend it's a comedy. It is simply not done.

Causes of Wrongful Conviction

But enough of this post-conviction appellate talk. That's putting the cart before the horse. Let's return to the trial and discuss those elements that commonly combine to convict the innocent. Let me state at the outset that each of these ingredients is systemic and not peculiar to one part of the country or one type of case. We see these elements as constant themes or patterns informing the cases that cross our desks. They are the seeds that sow wrongful convictions. After one has reflected on them individually and as a whole, it becomes readily apparent, I think, how easy it is and how real the potential is in every courthouse in America for wrongful convictions to take place.

(a) Presumption of Guilt

The first factor I would like to consider is the "presumption-of-innocence" principle. Although we would all like to believe that a defendant is truly considered innocent by those who represent and judge him, this is just not so. Once accusations have matured through the system to the point at which the accused is actually brought to trial, is it not the tendency of human nature to suspect deep down or even believe that the defendant probably did it? Most people are inclined to believe that where there is smoke, there is fire. This applies to professional and lay people alike albeit for different reasons perhaps.

The innate inclinations of the average American law-abiding citizen whose jury experience is that person's first exposure to the criminal justice system is to think that law enforcement people have earnestly investigated the case and surely would not bring someone to trial unless they had bona fide evidence against the person. That is a strong barrier and a heavy burden for the defense to overcome. And how about judges and defense lawyers? These professionals, like members of any profession, have a natural tendency to become somewhat cynical and callous with time. After all, isn't it true that the great majority of the defendants who have paraded before them in the past have been guilty? Why should this case be any different? As far as defense attorneys are concerned, if they really believe in their clients' innocence, why is it that in so many instances they are quick to urge them to take a plea for a lesser sentence than they would get with a trial conviction? So, by the time a person is in the trial docket, the system (including the media) has already tarnished him with its multitude of prejudices, which, of course, would all be denied by those who entertain such prejudices.

(b) Perjury by Police

Another reason for widespread perversions of justice is the pervasiveness of perjury. The recent District Attorney of Philadelphia once said, "In almost any factual hearing or trial, someone is committing perjury; and if we investigate all of those things, literally we would be doing nothing but prosecuting perjury cases." If he is guilty, the defendant and his supporters would lie to save his skin and keep him from going to prison. That is assumed and even expected by the jury and the judge. But what would surprise and even shock most jury members is the extent to which police officers lie on the stand to reinforce the prosecution and not jeopardize their own standing within their own particular law enforcement community. The words of one twenty-five-year veteran senior officer of a northern New Jersey police force still ring in my ears: "They [the defense] lie, so we [police] lie. I don't know one of my fellow officers who hasn't lied under oath." Not too long ago a prominent New York judge, when asked if perjury by police was a problem, responded, "Oh, sure, cops often lie on the stand."

(c) False Witnesses for the Prosecution

What is more, not only do law officers frequently lie, but the primary witnesses for the prosecution often commit perjury for the state, and do so under the subtle guidance of the prosecutor. Inveterately, common criminals who are in deep trouble themselves with the same prosecutor's office or local police authority are employed as star state witnesses. In exchange for their false testimony, their own charges are dismissed, or they are given noncustodial or greatly reduced prison sentences. In other words a secret deal is struck whereby the witness is paid for his fabricated testimony with that most precious of all commodities—freedom!

Such witnesses are usually brought forward by the state to say either that the defendant confessed the crime to them or that they saw the defendant near the crime scene shortly before it happened, or they saw him flee the scene of the crime as it was occurring. If I have seen one, I have seen a hundred "jailhouse confessions" spring open the prison doors for the witness who will tell a jury on behalf of the state that the defendant confessed the crime to him while they shared the same cell or tier. When the state needs important help, it goes to its bullpen, the local county jail, and brings in one of the many ace relievers housed there to put out the fire. As several of these "jailhouse priests" have told me, "It's a matter of survival: either I go away or he [the defendant] goes away, and I'm not goin'." Jailhouse confessions are a total perversion of the truth-seeking process. Amazingly enough, they are a highly effective prosecutorial means to a conviction. Part and parcel of a jailhouse confession is the witness lying to the jury when he assures them that he expects nothing in return for his testimony, that he is willing to swallow whatever pill he must for his own crimes.

(d) Prosecutorial Misconduct

The right decision by a jury depends largely on prosecutorial integrity and proper use of prosecutorial power. If law enforcement officers, in their zeal to win and convict, manipulate or intimidate witnesses into false testimony, or suppress evidence that impeaches the prosecution's own witnesses or even goes to the defendant's innocence, then the chances of an accurate jury verdict are greatly diminished. Sadly, we see this far too often. It is frightening how easily people respond to pressure or threats of trouble by the authorities of the law. Our insecurities and fears as well as our desires to please those who can punish us allow all of us to be far more malleable than we like to think.

Few of us have the inner strength we think we have to resist such overreaching by the law. This applies to mainline citizenry as well as to those living on the margins. However, the underclasses are particularly vulnerable and susceptible to police pressure because they are powerless; and both they and the police know it. A few examples will illustrate.

In 1981 three white high school janitors were threatened by the Texas Rangers into testifying that they had seen Clarence Brandley, their black custodial supervisor, walking into the restroom area of the high school where the victim had entered only minutes before she had disappeared. Brandley was convicted and sentenced to death based on the inferential testimony that since he was the last person seen near her, then he must have killed her. Eight years later Brandley was exonerated by the judge who conducted his evidentiary hearing when one of these janitors came forward and told how they had lied in implicating Brandley because of coercion by the investigating law officer.

On the eve of the Rene Santana trial in Newark, New Jersey, which was a year and a half after the crime, the prosecutors produced a surprise "eyewitness" who said he saw Mr. Santana flee the scene of the crime. A decade later that same witness visited Mr. Santana at New Jersey's Rahway State Prison and asked for his forgiveness after admitting to him that he had concocted the "eyewitness" testimony in response to intense pressure from the prosecutor's investigator. Since this "eyewitness" was from Trujillo's Dominican Republic police state, his innate fear of the police made him vulnerable to such police coercion.

Or how about the *Wingo* case in white, rural northwestern Louisiana? Wingo's common-law wife came forward on the eve of his execution and admitted that she had lied at his trial five years earlier because the deputy sheriff had threatened to put her in jail and forever separate her from her children unless she regurgitated at trial what he wanted her to say.

And in the *Terry McCracken* case in the suburbs of Philadelphia, a fellow high school student of the caucasian McCracken testified that he saw McCracken flee the convenience store moments after a customer was shot to death during the course of a robbery. The teenager was induced to manufacture this false eyewitness account after three visits to the police station. Among the evidence that vindicates McCracken are the confessions by the real robber/killers. So, you see, it not only can happen anywhere, it does happen everywhere; and it does happen to all different people, regardless of race and background.

Another common trait of wrongful convictions is the prosecutor's habit of suppressing or withholding evidence which he is obliged to provide to the defendant in the interests of justice and fairness. Clarence Darrow was right when he said, "A courtroom is not a place where truth and innocence inevitably triumph; it is only an arena where contending lawyers fight not for justice but to win." And so many times this hidden information is not only "favorable" to the defendant but it clears him. In Philadelphia's *Miguel Rivera* case the district attorney withheld the fact that two shopkeepers had seen the defendant outside their shop when the art museum murder was actually in progress. And in the *Gordon Marsh* case near Baltimore, Maryland, the state failed to tell the defendant that its main witness against him was in jail when she said she saw him running from the murder scene. One has to wonder what the primary objective of prosecutors is. Is it to convict, regardless of the factual truth, or is it to pursue justice?

The prosecution is the "house" in the criminal justice system's game of poker. The cards are his, and he deals them. He decides whom and what to charge for crimes, and if there will be a trial or whether a plea is acceptable. He dominates. Unfortunately, his power is virtually unchecked because he is practically immune from punishment for offenses, no matter how flagrant or miscreant. According to many state and federal courts, prosecutorial misbehavior occurs with "disturbing frequency." When the "house" cheats, the innocent lose. Lamentably, we see prosecutors throughout the nation continually violating the standards set for them by the U.S. Supreme Court in 1935 when it said that the prosecutor's

> interest in a criminal prosecution is not that it shall win a case, but that justice shall be done. . . . He is in a peculiar and very definite sense the servant of the law, the twofold arm of which is that guilt shall not escape or innocence suffer. . . . While he may strike hard blows, he is not at liberty to strike foul ones. It is as much his duty to refrain from improper methods calculated to produce a wrongful conviction as it is to use every legitimate means to bring about a just one.

It is human nature to resist any information that indicates that we have made a grievous mistake. This is particularly true of prosecutors when presented with new evidence that impeaches a conviction and goes to the innocence of a person convicted by their office at a prior time, whether it occurred four months or forty years before. Not only are they coldly unresponsive to such indications but they quickly act to suppress or stamp them out. New evidence usually comes in the form of a state witness who, plagued with a guilty conscience, admits that he lied at the trial; or from a person completely new to the case who comes forward with his exculpatory knowledge. Without exception, in my experience, the prosecutor's office will treat that person with total contempt in its usually successful attempt to force the person to retreat into silence. If that doesn't work, it will dismiss such testimony as somehow undeserving of any credibility and blithely ignore it. This prosecutorial impishness reminds me of a little boy holding his hands to his ears on hearing an unpleasant sound.

The *Joyce Ann Brown* case is a poignant illustration of this kind of prosecutorial posturing. One year after Joyce's 1980 conviction for being one of two black women who had robbed a Dallas, Texas, furrier and killed one of the proprietors, the admitted shooter was captured and pleaded guilty while accepting a life sentence. She also told her attorney that the district attorney had convicted the wrong woman (Joyce Brown) as her partner in the crime. She had never known or even heard of that Joyce Brown. Despite the district attorney fighting her with all of his might, we managed to develop enough new evidence to win her release.

(e) Shoddy Police Work

The police work of investigating crimes, when done correctly and thoroughly, is indeed a noble profession. Law and order are essential to a cohesive and just society. Because police work is fraught with so many different kinds of pressures, it is rather easy for an investigation to go awry. The high volume of violent crime plagues every urban police department. Skilled detectives are few, and their caseloads are overwhelming. The "burnout" syndrome is a well-documented reality within police ranks. Interdepartmental politics and the bureaucracy stifle initiative and energy. The pressure to "solve" a case is intensely felt by the line detective and comes both from his superiors and the community and from his own ambitious need for recognition and advancement. If today's climate of "burn or bury" them puts more pressure on the detective to resolve, it also gives him more license to do so by whatever means.

Too often, as a result of the above factors, police officers take the easy way out. Once they come to suspect someone as the culprit, and this often occurs early within the investigation and is based on rather flimsy circumstantial information, then the investigation blindly focuses in on that adopted "target." Crucial pieces of evidence are overlooked and disregarded. Some witnesses are not interviewed who should be, while others are seduced or coerced into telling the police what they want to hear. Evidence or information that does not fit the suspect or the prevailing theory of the crime is dismissed as not material or is changed to implicate the suspect. Good old-fashioned legwork is replaced by expediency and shortcuts. Coercive confessions are extracted and solid leads are ignored.

Before too long, momentum has gathered, and the "project" now is to put it on the suspect. Any information that points to the suspect, no matter how spuriously secured, is somehow obtained; and anything that points away from him is ridiculed and twisted into nothingness. The task is made much easier if the suspect has a police record because he should be "taken off the streets" anyhow. That kind of person is not only a prime suspect but also a prime scapegoat. An example of this is Clarence Brandley, who was mentioned earlier. He was arrested in late August four days after the crime and on the weekend before school was to begin. The high school where the rape and murder took place was flooded with telephone calls by scared parents who refused to send their children to school until the murderer was caught. The arrest of Brandley calmed the community, and school started as scheduled. It was after Brandley's arrest that the investigation then spent five hundred hours building the case against him.

(f) Incompetent Defense Counsel

The wrongly convicted invariably find themselves between the rock of police/prosecutorial misconduct and the hard place of an incompetent and irresponsible defense attorney. While the correct decision by a jury hinges on a fair prosecution, it also depends on dedicated and skilled defendant lawyering. And there is such a paucity of the latter. Not only are there very few highly competent defense lawyers but there are very few criminal defense lawyers, period. They are rapidly becoming an extinct species.

The current Attorney General of New Jersey not too long ago told the New Jersey State Bar Association that finding quality private defense attorneys "may be the most crying need that we have." He also told this same assemblage that unless there is an adequate number of well-trained private defense lawyers, there will be little hope for justice. Of the 30,000 lawyers in New Jersey, the number of those doing primarily criminal defense work is only in the hundreds. At this same conference the First Assistant Attorney General pointed out that 85 percent of New Jersey's criminal cases are handled by the public defender system; and he wondered if there would be a private defense bar by the year 2000.

This means, of course, that 85 percent of those charged with a crime cannot afford an attorney, so they are forced to use the public defender system. As competent as New Jersey's full-time salaried public defenders generally are, their resources (budget and people) are vastly inadequate and are dwarfed by those of their adversaries (the local prosecutor's office). Moreover, they are so overwhelmed by the sheer volume of caseload that no defender can give quality attention to any one of his cases, let alone all of them. So, in response to this shortage, public defender cases are farmed out to "pooled" attorneys, who are paid a pittance relative to what they earn from other clients who retain them privately.

The experience of these pooled attorneys in criminal matters is often limited and scanty. In addition, they do not bring to their new-found indigent client the desired level of heart and enthusiasm for their cases. All of these conditions leave the defendant with an attorney somewhat lacking in will, effort, resources, and experience. Thus, the defendant goes to trial with two strikes against him.

What we have discovered as a common theme among those whose cases we have studied from all over the country is that their trial attorney, whether from the public domain or privately retained, undertakes his work with an appalling lack of assiduity. Communication with the defendant is almost nonexistent. When it does take place, it is carried on in a hurried, callous, and dismissive manner. Attempts at discovery are made perfunctorily. Prosecutors are not pressed for this material. Investigation is shallow and narrow, if conducted at all. Preparation meets minimal standards. And advocacy at trial is weak. Cross-examination is superficial and tentative.

Physical evidence is left untested, and forensic experts are not called to rebut whatever scientific evidence the state introduces through its criminalists. I cannot help thinking of the *Nate Walker* case, where, at Nate's 1976 trial for rape and kidnapping, the doctor who examined the victim the night of her ordeal testified that he found semen in her vaginal cavity. Walker's privately retained attorney had no questions for the doctor when it came time for cross-examination, nor did he even ask anyone to test the vaginal semen for blood type. Twelve years later, that test was performed at our request, and Walker was exonerated and immediately freed.

This is not to say, however, that we have not encountered some outstanding examples of vigorous and thorough defense lawyering that left no stones unturned. What a rare but inspiring sight! We could not do our work without the critically important services of the extremely able and dedicated attorneys with whom we team up. If only the preponderance of attorneys would heed the admonition of Herbert Stern, a former U.S. Attorney and U.S. District Court judge in Newark, New Jersey, when he addressed a new crop of attorneys who had just been sworn in. He told them that they were free to choose their own clients. "But," he continued, "once that choice is made, once a representation is undertaken, then that responsibility is as sacred to us as the one assumed by a surgeon in the operating room. You must be as committed and as selfless as any surgeon." He further challenged them to "be an advocate. Represent your clients—all of them—fearlessly, diligently, unflinchingly. . . . Withhold no proper legal assistance from any client. And when you do that, you thereby preserve, protect, and defend the Constitution of the United States, just as you have this day sworn to."

(g) Nature of Convicting Evidence

The unschooled public largely and erroneously believes that convictions are mostly obtained through the use of one form of tangible evidence or another. This naive impression is shaped by watching too many TV shows like Perry Mason or Matlock. The reality is that in most criminal trials the verdict more often than not hinges on whose witnesses—the state's or defendant's—the jury chooses to believe. It boils down to a matter of credibility. There is no "smoking gun" scientific evidence that clearly points to the defendant. This puts an extremely heavy burden on the jury. It must somehow ferret out and piece together the truth from substantially inconsistent and contradictory testimony between and within each side. The jury is forced to make one subjective call after another in deciding whom to believe and what inferences to draw from conflicting statements.

For example, how can a jury accept a victim's positive identification at trial of the defendant as her assailant when she had previously described her attacker in physical terms that were very different from the actual physical characteristics of the defendant, or when the defense has presented documented information that precludes the defendant from being the assaulter? Several cases come to mind. Boy was convicted of robbing a convenience store in Georgia. The clerk initially told the police that since she was 5 feet 3 inches, was standing on a 3-inch platform, and had direct eye contact with the robber, he must have been about 5 feet 6 inches tall. Boy is 6 feet 5 inches tall. Four teenage girls identified Russell Burton as their rapist on a particular day in Arkansas. Burton introduced evidence that on that day his penis was badly blistered from an operation two days before for removal of a wart. And a Virginia woman was certain that Edward Honaker was her rapist even though her rapist had left semen with sperm within her, and Honaker had had a vasectomy well in advance of the assault.

Criminal prosecutions that primarily or exclusively depend on the victim's identification of the defendant as the perpetrator must be viewed with some skepticism unless solid corroborating evidence is also introduced. Traumatized by a crime as it occurs, the victim frequently is looking but not seeing. Victims are extremely vulnerable and can easily be led by the police, through unduly suggestive techniques, into identifying a particular person. The victim in Nate Walker's case, for example, was with her abductor/rapist for two and a half hours with ample opportunity to clearly view him. She told the jury without hesitation eighteen months later that "he's the man." Nate had an ironclad alibi. The jury struggled for several days but in the end came in with a guilty verdict. As mentioned earlier, he was scientifically vindicated twelve years later.

When juries are confronted with a choice between a victim's ringing declaration that "that's the man" and solid evidence that "it couldn't be him," they usually cast their lot with the victim. I suggest that this can be a very dangerous tendency and practice. And this is particularly so when identification crosses racial lines, that is, when a white victim says it was that black person. Future jurors should be aware that identifications can be very unreliable forms of evidence.

Another type of evidence that can be misleading and even confusing to jurors is that offered by laboratory scientists. Results of laboratory tests that are presented by the forensic scientists are not always what they appear to be, although they strongly influence jury decisions. A recent *New York Times* article pointed out that there is a "growing concern about the professionalism and impartiality of the laboratory scientists whose testimony in court can often mean conviction or acquittal." This article went on to say that the work of forensic technicians in police crime laboratories is plagued by uneven training and questionable objectivity.

We share this mounting concern because we see instance after instance where the prosecutor's crime laboratory experts cross the line from science to advocacy. They exaggerate the results of their analysis of hairs, fibers, blood, or semen in such a manner that it is absolutely devastating to the defendant. To put the defendants at a further disadvantage, the defense attorneys do not educate themselves in the forensic science in question, and therefore conduct a weak cross-examination. Also, in many cases, the defense does not call in its own forensic experts, whose testimony in numerous instances could severely damage the state's scientific analysis.

One case profoundly reflects this common cause of numerous unjust convictions. Roger Coleman sat on Virginia's death row primarily because the Commonwealth's Bureau of Forensic Science expert testified that the two foreign pubic hairs found on the murdered victim were "consistent" with Mr. Coleman's, and that it was "unlikely" that these hairs came from someone other than Mr. Coleman. The defense offered nothing in rebuttal, so this testimony stood unchallenged. In a post-conviction hearing Mr. Coleman's new lawyer introduced the testimony of a forensic hair specialist who had twenty-five years of experience with the F. B. I. He testified that "it is improper to conclude that it is likely that hairs came from a particular person simply because they are consistent with that person's hair because hairs belonging to different people are often consistent with each other, especially pubic hairs."

Another problem that we continually observe within the realm of forensic evidence is the phenomenon of lost and untested physical evidence. Often, especially in cases up to the early 1980s, the specimens that have the potential to exclude the defendant have not been tested and eventually get misplaced. At best this is gross negligence on the part of both the police technician and the defense attorney in not ensuring that the tests be done.

Conclusion

We agree with a past president of the New Jersey Division of the Association of Trial Lawyers of America who said that "juries are strange creatures. Even after taking part in many, many trials, I still find them to be unpredictable. The jury system isn't perfect, but it does represent the best system to mete out justice. They're right in their decisions more often than not." Remember when I quoted a former district attorney who said that "in almost any factual hearing or trial someone is committing perjury." So, a wide margin of error exists when earnest but all too fallible juries are only right "more often than not" and when trial testimony is so frequently and pervasively perjurious. My contention is that at least 10 percent of those convicted for serious, violent crimes are incorrectly convicted because some combination of the trial infirmities described in this article results in mistaken jury determinations.

Everyone will agree that the system is not perfect, but the real question is this: To what extent do its imperfections prevail? I contend that for all the reasons detailed above the system is a far leakier cistern than any among us has ever imagined. Untold numbers of innocents have tumbled into the dark pit of prison. Some of them have eventually gained their freedom, but a majority remain buried in prison, completely forsaken and forgotten by the outside world.

Other than my own wholly inadequate organization, no person or agency, private or public, exists anywhere that works full time and serves exclusively as an advocate and arm for the innocent in prison. The body of justice that has evolved over the centuries has many members. But not one part that functions within this whole has been created or is properly equipped specifically to secure the freedom of the incarcerated innocent.

The Effects of Punishment

C. L. Ten

In this reading, Ten summarizes some recent empirical evidence as to the actual effects of our institutions of punishment. He concludes that at present there is no particularly strong evidence that punishment rehabilitates or deters the criminal, though there are some grounds for thinking that it may have a deterrent effect on potential offenders.

The utilitarian theory justifies punishment solely in terms of the good consequences produced. There are disagreements among utilitarians about the nature of the good consequences which punishment is supposed to produce. Some utilitarians may even believe that the harm done by punishment outweighs the good, and hence punishment is not justified. But many utilitarians see the main beneficial effects of punishment in terms of the reduction of crime, and believe that punishing offenders will have at least some, if not all, of the following good effects. First, punishment acts as a deterrent to crime. The deterrent effects can be both individual and general. Punishment deters the offender who is punished from committing similar offences in future, and it also deters potential offenders. The offender who is punished is supposed to be deterred by his experience of punishment and the threat of being punished again if he re-offends and is convicted. This is the individual deterrent effect. The general deterrent effect of punishment on potential offenders works through the threat of their being subjected to the same kind of punishment that was meted out to the convicted offender.

Secondly, punishment is supposed to have reformative or rehabilitative effects.[1] This is confined to the offender who is punished. He is reformed in the sense that the effect of punishment is to change his values so that he will not commit similar offences in future because he believes such offences to be wrong. But if he abstains from criminal acts simply because he is afraid of being caught and punished again, then he is deterred rather than reformed and rehabilitated by punishment. So the effects of individual deterrence and rehabilitation are the same. What distinguishes them is the difference in motivation.

The third good consequence of punishment is its incapacitative effect. When an offender is serving his sentence in prison, he is taken out of general social circulation and is therefore prevented from committing a variety of offences, even though he may neither be deterred nor reformed by punishment. Of course punishment would not have an overall incapacitative effect if the offender would not have re-offended even if he were free, or if his incarceration led someone else, who would not otherwise have done so, to engage in criminal activity, perhaps as his replacement in a gang. While in prison, the offender might still commit certain offences: he might assault a fellow prisoner or a prison guard. But his opportunities are generally reduced. In some cases, however, his contacts with other prisoners would create opportunities for further involvement in crime when he is released. The incapacitative effect, though perhaps most likely in the case of imprisonment, may also be present in other forms of punishment. For example, parole may have some incapacitative effect in that although the offender is free, the fact that he is under supervision may restrict his opportunities for criminal activities.

The empirical evidence of the effects of punishment is very complex, but a brief survey will be of some use.

It looks as if the present state of our knowledge provides no basis for claiming that punishment by imprisonment reforms or rehabilitates the criminal, or that it is an individual deterrent. The position is well summed up by the Report of the Panel of the National Research Council in the United States on Research on Deterrent and Incapacitative Effects, hereafter referred to as the Panel:

> The available research on the impact of various treatment strategies both in and out of prison seems to indicate that, after controlling for initial selection differences, there are generally no statistically significant differences between the subsequent recidivism of offenders, regardless of the form of "treatment." This suggests that neither rehabilitative nor criminogenic effects operate very strongly. Therefore, at an aggregate level, these confounding effects are probably safely ignored.[2]

By "criminogenic effects" the Panel refers to the undesirable effects of imprisonment in either increasing the criminal's propensity to commit crimes or to extend the duration of his criminal career. Such effects are the opposite of the rehabilitative effects. So the present evidence seems to suggest that in general the effect of imprisonment, or of the various programmes for rehabilitation which accompany imprisonment, is neither to make the criminal a better nor a worse person with respect to the standards of behaviour set by the criminal law.

The evidence also suggests that in general punishment has no individual deterrent effect. Daniel Nagin points out that at the observational level it is difficult to distinguish between individual (or what he calls special) deterrence and rehabilitation. He concludes that, "The figures suggest that recidivism rates cannot be affected by varying the severity of the punishment, at least within acceptable limits."[3] But Nagin cautiously adds that the evidence is only preliminary.

In a few specific cases there is indeed some evidence of the individual deterrent effect of punishment. Thus Johannes Andenaes draws attention to a study of amateur shoplifters which shows that detection and arrest, even without prosecution, produces serious shock. There is little or no recidivism among those who are apprehended and interrogated by the store police and then set free without being formally charged.[4] A study of drunk driving in Sweden also shows that those drivers who had been arrested estimated the risk of being arrested as many times higher than other drivers.[5]

There is disagreement about the general deterrent effects of punishment. Johannes Andenaes believes that, "In general terms it can only be stated that general deterrence works well in some fields and works poorly or not at all in other fields."[6] But in 1974 Gordon Tullock published an article, "Does Punishment Deter Crime?", in which he surveyed the work done by economists and sociologists.[7] Tullock points out that economists began their work under the impression that punishment would deter crime because demand curves slope downwards showing that if the cost of a good is increased then less of it will be consumed. So if the cost of committing crime is increased by more severe punishment, then there will be fewer crimes. Sociologists, on the other hand, started out with the intention of confirming what was then the accepted view in their discipline that punishment would not deter crime. But Tullock argues that, although their starting points and assumptions were radically different, both economists and sociologists, after analysing the evidence, came to the same conclusion that punishment did indeed deter crime. After surveying their studies Tullock himself is convinced that "the empirical evidence is clear," and he states his conclusion unequivocally: "Even granting the fact that most potential criminals have only a rough idea as to the frequency and severity of punishment, multiple regression studies show that increasing the frequency or severity of the punishment does reduce the likelihood that a given crime will be committed."[8]

However, Tullock's confidence about the clarity of the empirical evidence is not shared by the Panel. The Panel argues that although the evidence consistently establishes a negative association between crime rates and sanctions (as measured by the risks of apprehension, conviction, or imprisonment), that is, higher crime rates are associated with lower sanctions and vice versa, this does not necessarily show the general deterrent effect of sanctions. The negative association may be partly or wholly explained in terms of lower sanctions being the effect rather than the cause of higher crime rates. Higher crime rates may so overburden the resources of the criminal justice system that they reduce its ability to deal with new offenders. Overburdened judges and prosecutors may use their discretion to dismiss or reduce charges, or to offer attractive plea bargains.[9] Overcrowding of prisons may lead to a reduction in the time served in prison as more prisoners are released early on parole. The sanctions imposed on certain crimes may be reduced. So unless one can separate out the effect of higher crime rates on sanctions from the deterrent effect of sanctions on crime, one cannot interpret the evidence as establishing the presence of the general deterrent effect of punishment. The Panel's cautious assessment of the evidence is summed up in its remark that "we cannot yet assert that the evidence warrants an affirmative conclusion regarding deterrence," but the Panel adds that "the evidence certainly favours a proposition supporting deterrence more than it favours one asserting that deterrence is absent."[10] On the other hand, the Panel believes that the evidence does not even show a significant negative association between crime rates and the severity of punishment as measured by the time served in prison, but suggests that this may partly be accounted for in terms of various distortions.[11]

Moving from the analysis of statistics to the experimental evidence, the Panel identifies three studies which are not methodologically flawed. Of these, two show that the level of crime decreased significantly with increases in the level of sanctions, while one showed that the removal of criminal sanctions for abortions in Hawaii did not affect the incidence of abortions.[12] So it looks as if the present experimental evidence does not permit the drawing of general conclusions. But much of the experimental evidence is consistent with the operation of deterrence, as has been noted by Nigel Walker.[13]

Finally, we turn to the incapacitative effect of punishment. In her review of the literature for the Panel, Jacqueline Cohen suggests that disagreements about the magnitude of that effect can be attributed almost entirely to the different estimates of the average crime rate of prisoners.[14] The estimate of the increase in crime if current prison use were reduced or eliminated has been as low as five percent.[15] Estimating the incapacitative effect of present prison policies is one thing. There is also the different question as to what we can expect the incapacitative effect to be if present policies are changed. Here one estimate is of a five-fold decrease in crime, but Cohen points out that this can only be achieved by increasing the prison population by between 355 percent and 567 percent.[16] The incapacitative effect will not be the same for all crimes. Cohen points out that using the assumptions made by the available models, the increase in prison population required to reduce violent crimes is much less than the increases needed for similar reductions in other crimes. Violent crimes can be reduced by 10 percent with less than 30 percent increase in prison population.[17] This kind of consideration has led to an increasing interest in the use of selective incapacitation in which the focus of imprisonment is on certain types of offenders who are identified as having a high rate of committing crimes.[18]

We see that the evidence is perhaps more hospitable to the claim that punishment has some general deterrent effect and some incapacitative effect than it is to the claim that it has individual deterrent effect or that it rehabilitates offenders. This will no doubt be puzzling to some, but it provides a basis for caution in responding to a high rate of recidivism. Where there is such a high rate, it shows that punishment does not deter those who are punished. But it does not show that potential offenders are not in fact deterred by punishment, or that punishment does not incapacitate.

NOTES

1. Jack P. Gibbs distinguishes between "rehabilitation" and "reformation." An offender is "rehabilitated" if he ceases to violate the law as a result of non-punitive means, whereas he is "reformed" if he ceases to violate the law as a result of punishment, but for reasons independent of the fear of punishment. See *Crime, Punishment, and Deterrence* (New York, 1975), p. 72. I use the two terms interchangeably and broadly to refer to cases in which the offender, after serving a sentence, no longer commits crimes because he believes that criminal behaviour is wrong and not because he fears punishment. His changed values can be brought about by punishment itself or by non-punitive means. Jean Hampton develops a sophisticated version of the moral education view of punishment according to which punishment communicates a moral message aimed at educating both the wrongdoer and the rest of society about the immorality of the offence. She is eager to distinguish her view from rehabilitative theories of punishment both in terms of the different ends to be achieved and the methods used to attain those ends.

According to her, the aim of rehabilitation is to make the offender accept society's mores and operate successfully in society, and the pursuit of these goals is not constrained by respect for the autonomy of the wrongdoer. See 'The Moral Education Theory of Punishment', *Philosophy & Public Affairs,* 13 (1984).

2. Alfred Blumstein, Jacqueline Cohen, and Daniel Nagin (eds), *Deterrence and Incapacitation: Estimating the Effects of Criminal Sanctions on Crime Rates,* National Academy of Sciences, Panel on Research on Deterrent and Incapacitative Effects (Washington, 1978), p. 66. Hereafter this book will be referred to as *The Panel.*
3. Daniel Nagin, "General Deterrence: A Review of the Empirical Evidence," in *The Panel,* p. 96.
4. Johannes Andenaes, 'Does Punishment Deter Crime?', in Gertrude Ezorsky (ed.), *Philosophical Perspectives on Punishment* (Albany, 1972), p. 354.
5. Ibid., p. 354.
6. Ibid., p. 346.
7. Gordon Tullock, "Does Punishment Deter Crime?", *The Public Interest* (1974), pp. 103–11.
8. Ibid., p. 109.
9. *The Panel,* p. 39.
10. Ibid., p. 7.
11. Ibid., pp. 37–8.
12. Ibid., p. 55.
13. Nigel Walker, *Punishment, Danger and Stigma* (Oxford, 1980), pp. 77–80.
14. Jacqueline Cohen, 'The Incapacitative Effect of Imprisonment: A Critical Review of the Literature', in *The Panel,* p. 209.
15. Ibid., p. 188.
16. Ibid., p. 218.
17. Ibid., p. 227.
18. See Mark H. Moore, Susan R. Estrich, Daniel McGillis, and William Spelman, *Dangerous Offenders: The Elusive Target of Justice* (Cambridge, 1984). I discuss the problem of dangerous offenders in Ch. 6.

Study Questions

1. How do you think Bentham would respond to Primoratz's objections?
2. If McCloskey and Ten are correct in their estimates of the actual consequences of our system of punishment, do you think such a system could be justified on utilitarian grounds?
3. What exactly does Primoratz mean when he claims that utilitarianism would "transform the criminal law system into a market for trading in justice"? How convincing are his reasons for claiming this?
4. Is anything of importance left out if we evaluate institutions of punishment solely in terms of their net social benefits?

B Retributivism

Punishment as Retribution

David Lyons

Lyons provides a brief survey of some of the more important traditional versions of retributivism, particularly that associated with the great eighteenth-century German philosopher, Immanuel Kant. According to retributivists, people should be punished only to the extent that they *deserve* to be in virtue of the seriousness of their offense. As Lyons notes, defenders of such a view have often had difficulty in explaining (a) what legitimate moral purpose is served by punishment, (b) how punishments are to be fitted to offenses, and (c) why only the state is justified in imposing punishment.

The desire for retribution is familiar. We are accustomed to thinking that someone who acts badly deserves bad treatment in return—or at least forfeits some part of his claim to good treatment by others. If someone who is seeking personal gain or is simply careless of others' interests causes injury, we form an unfavorable judgment of that person's character. Such judgments can be triggered, not only when harm is actually done, but also by someone's failure to satisfy minimal standards of decency and consideration for others. And so we may think that a person deserves punishment for negligent acts, and even for bungled attempts to hurt others which cause no actual harm.

Retributive theories of punishment maintain that retributive attitudes can be translated responsibly into practice. They do not celebrate vengeance or call for blind, unreflective revenge. They call for justice—the justice of treating people as they *deserve* to be treated by virtue of their conduct and the attitudes that conduct represents.

One difficulty that we face in evaluating the retributive approach to punishment is that it often seems to be inadequately developed and limited to the recitation of catchphrases. A brief survey of some retributive suggestions will illustrate this point and the problems that result.

One of the ideas sometimes advanced is that punishment is justified as a means of "restoring the moral balance." This presumably means that a wrongdoer should be deprived of any advantage he secured through his wrongdoing and his victim should be compensated for his loss. A difficulty facing the application of this theory is that it could not clearly justify requiring compensation of a victim by a wrongdoer, unless the original positions of the affected parties could themselves be judged to reflect justice. More important, the aim of restoring a moral balance between wrongdoer and victim is not generally served by systems of *punishment,* which concentrate on making wrongdoers suffer and typically show little concern for compensating victims.

The problem here is, not that our penal practices may need reform, but rather that punishment is precisely the wrong primary

From *Ethics and the Rule of Law* by David Lyons. New York: Cambridge University Press, © 1984, pp. 146–54. Reprinted with the permission of Cambridge University Press.

means of achieving the end that this theory assumes. Penal law imposes punishments for specific offenses. Remedial law seeks just compensation for victims from those responsible for their losses. If compensation is what we should require, because justice demands it, then we should concentrate our efforts on providing remedies, not penalties. This type of theory therefore does not help us understand how punishment itself, without compensation for victims, might be justified.

A different traditional idea seems more to the point. The *lex talionis,* which demands "an eye for an eye," seems to have clear implications for at least some cases of wrongdoing. One who takes a life should have his own life taken; one who beats another should be beaten in return; and so on. But, once we go beyond a few simple cases like these, the requirements of the formula are either unpalatable, uncertain, or impossible to satisfy. It is unclear, for example, that we would always be justified in treating wrongdoers as they have treated others, since this would mean torturing those who have tortured others and raping those who are guilty of rape. It is unclear how the formula requires us to punish people for acts that cause no actual harm but only create danger or express irresponsible attitudes, as in drunken driving and tax evasion for personal gain. If punishments can be justified in such cases, the formula seems incomplete. And it is unclear that we can possibly treat wrongdoers as they have treated others, when the acts for which they might be punished cannot be duplicated in penalties. How can we follow the formula to determine punishments for those who lie, cheat, defraud, blackmail, or bribe others? So the *lex talionis* does not seem an adequate basis for justifying punishment. It is at best incomplete, and it seems to imply objectionable instructions in some cases.

Another problem facing the *lex talionis* is that it seems unfaithful to some important retributive ideas. Retributive theories are usually understood to say that punishment must be dispensed in accordance with a wrongdoer's deserts. But our judgments of desert are not tied so tightly, as the "eye for an eye" formula is, to overt behavior and the harm that results. We distinguish between harmful behavior, on the one hand, and the blameworthiness of the individual, on the other. To intend harm is one thing; to cause it unintentionally but carelessly is another; to bring about harm by accident or because one's bodily movements are not entirely under one's control is something else again. It is widely believed that a system of punishment should deal with such cases differently, just as it is believed that punishments can be justified even when no harm is done. The *lex talionis* seems to ignore this vital aspect of personal desert.

A more promising retributive approach to punishment is suggested by Kant's moral theory, which takes into account the attitude of the wrongdoer. Kant's theory has the further merit of providing a basis for the requirements violation of which justifies punishment. Retributive theories usually take for granted that punishment may or must be given for wrongdoing, but they typically fail to provide any clear account of the standards that may justifiably be enforced. Kant's theory offers a basis for determining the standards of morally responsible conduct as well as a justification for punishing violations of those standards.

According to Kant,[1] people are not mere cogs in a mechanistic universe, but "rational agents." We understand what we are doing (at least when we can be held responsible for our behavior). Though we do not always articulate them consciously, we act for reasons. We have some ends, purposes, or goals and we conceive of what we are doing in relation to them. To interpret a person's behavior accurately, therefore, is to attribute to that person a "subjective principle" of conduct or a "maxim" of action which represents how that person truly directs his own behavior. These maxims, not overt bodily movements, are the basis for moral judgments of conduct.

Because we are rational agents, Kant maintains, we are committed to "universalizing" the maxims of our actions. We regard them as principles which any rational agent may properly follow. We "legislate" for all humanity; that is, we are committed to regarding our maxims as principles that should become universal laws of human nature. If I see myself as helping another person in need, for example, then the maxim of my action is to help others who are in need, and I am committed to the view that people should generally help others who are in need. By the same token, if I am really taking advantage of another person's helplessness, the maxim of my action is to take advantage of others' helplessness, and I am committed to the view that people may generally take advantage of others' helplessness.

The Kantian theory applies this notion so as to generate principles of duty. My fundamental duty is to act only on maxims that I as a rational agent could "consistently will" to become a universal law of human nature. Kant believed that a rational agent could consistently will some maxims to become universal laws of human nature, but not all. He believed, for example, that I could not consistently will the universalization of the maxim involved in making a false promise—a promise that I have no intention of keeping. If I act on such a maxim, then I act wrongly. Principles of duty thus negate maxims of action that cannot be universalized in this special sense.

The Kantian theory also uses this notion to justify punishment for breaches of duty. If, in acting on a maxim, I am committed to willing that my maxim become a universal law of human nature, then I am committed to the principle that others may treat me as I treat them. If I am prepared to help others, I authorize others to help me. If I am prepared to take advantage of others' helplessness, I authorize others to take advantage of me when I am helpless.

This seems to provide a theoretical rationale for familiar retributive ideas. It explains what lies behind the "eye for an eye" formula, but qualifies it accordingly. It also explains the retributive idea that a wrongdoer "wills his own punishment." In acting well or badly towards others, one is committed to willing that others treat one in similar ways. If one treats others badly, and they reciprocate in kind, then one can be understood to have "brought the punishment on himself."

The Kantian theory of punishment has questionable theoretical underpinnings, but we shall not concentrate on them here. What needs to be seen is the gap between even such a relatively well-developed retributive theory such as Kant's and the justification of legal punishment.

To suggest the magnitude of the problem, let us first consider a different but more familiar notion, that justice is satisfied when the virtuous prosper and the wicked suffer, which we might call cosmic justice. It rests on a theory of cosmic desert: Good people deserve to fare well and bad people deserve to fare badly. Such a theory does not translate into prescriptions for punishment of the sort that humans can satisfy, or perhaps any prescriptions for punishment at all. First, the punishments that are imposed by human beings are meted out for specific actions, not for the sake of cosmic justice. And the practice of dispensing punishments for specific acts cannot be relied on to insure that the wicked will eventually suffer according to their cosmic deserts (nor does it begin to insure that the virtuous will prosper). We could not hope to establish a system that dispensed justice according to cosmic deserts. Second, it is not clear that we ought to try. The doctrine of cosmic justice does not explain how anyone can acquire the right to "play God." From the premise that someone deserves to suffer because he is wicked, it does not follow that I or anyone else has the right to impose punishments in order to insure that result. So it is unclear how considerations of cosmic justice could justify acts of punishing, which are part of what must be justified by a normative theory of punishment.

Similar problems face retributive theories of punishment, including Kant's. If these theories are supposed to justify anything like our usual practices of punishing, then they seek to justify the measured allocation of officially authorized punishments in accordance with prescribed procedures. But traditional retributive theories do not begin to address the institutional aspects of legal punishment.

Thus, a theory of legal punishment should presumably show how officially authorized penalties may be imposed for wrongdoing, to the exclusion of private retribution. It must provide, in other words, a *differential* justification for punishing acts, reserving it generally for established authorities. But retributive theories generally fail to do this. They give us no idea how one person acquires the right to punish another or, if they do, they give us no idea why the state should have a special role in punishment. They ignore the political context within which legal punishment occurs.

Similar problems face other theories of punishment. It is sometimes suggested, for example, that the legal use of coercion can be justified if private individuals "transfer" to the state the right to punish those who violate their rights.[2] This assumes not only that individuals have rights that are independent of law, but also that they as individuals are morally permitted to protect and enforce those rights by their own private acts. But it is by no means clear that private individuals are morally entitled to use force in order to protect whatever rights they have. If they lack the right to punish, no such general transfer could take place.

If I have a right, another person may have a corresponding obligation. This is true of some rights, and it can be true outside as well as inside of law, as when others have promised me to act in certain ways, owe me compensation for injuries they have done, or have other debts to me. Not all promises are enforceable in a court of law, for example, but they can give rise to rights and obligations that are recognized as binding from a moral point of view. If others fail to respect my rights or threaten to infringe them, I can be justified in complaining, demanding compensation, and acting in other ways that would not ordinarily be warranted. It does not follow, however, that I may use force whenever my rights are threatened or infringed, either to protect them or to secure an appropriate remedy. That would seem to depend on further circumstances, including the importance of the right and what else may be at stake. If so, we cannot assume that I am in a position to authorize others to act on my behalf by enforcing my rights.

One would also expect that state action is more difficult to justify than private enforcement, even when the latter could be justified. State action does not merely substitute for private initiative, since the state claims in such cases to act on behalf of the entire community. It does not merely enforce my rights, but treats the matter as one of public concern. My rights and disputes concerning them are not automatically a matter of public concern in this respect, however, and I cannot make them such just by willing it. Therefore, the question persists, under what conditions a public authority, which *claims* the right to govern the entire community, can *acquire* the moral right to use coercive means.

To justify the legal practice of punishment is to defend the use of penal sanctions to enforce behavioral guidelines. Although punishment is imposed retrospectively, for acts already done (at least in the standard cases), it is authorized beforehand, when standards for conduct are laid down. So, even if retributive theories say that punishment can be justified by reference to what a wrongdoer has done, what they seek to justify is part of a system that includes the establishment of standards concerning future conduct and the legal consequences of compliance. Any theory hoping to justify legal punishment must take this into account.

This is relevant in two ways. First, a theory of legal punishment should presumably limit such justifications, at least normally, to acts that violate established standards. Even if punishment could not be justified except for acts that are wrong in themselves *(mala in se)*, that an act is wrong in itself is not usually taken as a *sufficient* justification for legal punishment. Retributivism seems to demand punishment for all moral wrongs, and many would regard this as excessive. Some derelictions do not warrant public intervention, which might violate further rights or be too costly. More important, it is generally assumed that punishment should be restricted to the enforcement of standards that are laid down in advance. The retributive theory of punishment does not seem to acknowledge this restriction on legal punishment, but it gives no reason for regarding it as wrong. It seems to condone the use of *ex post facto* criminal laws.

Second, the retributive theory provides no clear justification for punishing acts that are *not* wrong in themselves, but that *may* be punished because enforcement of the regulations that prohibit such acts is required to serve some reasonable legislative purpose (*mala prohibita*). Legislation governing traffic and economic competition, for example, is not designed exclusively to prevent immoral acts or to give individuals their just deserts, but is aimed at serving some further purposes—perhaps safety and convenience in the former case, efficiency and fairness in the latter. To serve such purposes effectively, coercive measures may be needed. Legal sanctions are believed justified because they are a necessary means of establishing needed practices and enforcing the required regulations. If these regulations can be justified, and if people have an obligation to abide by such rules, then the imposition of punishment under them might accord with moral guilt and desert, but the justification of such punishments would include a non-retributive element. Traffic regulations, for example, are somewhat arbitrary. They do not mirror moral principles. No Kantian argument is available to show that driving on an arbitrarily determined side of the road or stopping at a light of a certain color is a breach of moral duty and thus subject to punishment. We seem to need a more comprehensive theory of legislation to explain how the enforcement of such regulations can be justified.

According to traditional retributive theories, punishment is required by considerations of justice. The *only* good reason for punishing is the guilt of the individual, and the guilty must be punished as they deserve. Our discussion suggests, however, that moral guilt and desert are not the only relevant considerations. Retributive theories appear to fail because they justify too much or too little. If they justify any punishment at all, they seem to justify punishments in too many cases, and by too many people. But it is unclear that they succeed in justifying any punishment at all, especially by legally constituted authorities, because they either do not show why anyone has the right to punish or why the right to punish should be reserved to the state. They also fail to acknowledge some of the reasons that seem to justify coercive legal rules, reasons that accordingly seem to play an essential role in the justification of punishment under those rules.

These comments on traditional retributive ideas should not be taken, however, as disposing of retributive principles concerning punishment. That is because the notion of a "retributive principle," as it is used in moral theory, includes any standard that would not be counted as utilitarian. Some retributive principles which have been proposed would avoid the criticisms we have noted. Many retributivists, for example, would insist that punishment should be restricted to offenses that have been established in advance, and should not be imposed for all moral wrongs. Similarly, retributive principles may be incorporated into a general theory which provides a justification for restrictions on behavior that is not wrong in itself.

We have so far ignored limited retributive principles like these because it is unclear that they can be said to have any general, underlying rationale, except as placing moral limits on practices that might be condoned by utilitarians.

NOTES

1. For Kant's ethical theory, summarized in the following four paragraphs, see his *Groundwork of the Metaphysics of Morals;* for its application to punishment, see his *Metaphysical Elements of Justice* (1797), trans. John Ladd (New York: Bobbs-Merrill, 1965). This reading of Kant is suggested by Edmund Pincoffs, *The Rationale of Legal Punishment* (New York: Humanities Press, 1966), chap. I.
2. See Robert Nozick, *Anarchy, State, and Utopia* (New York: Basic Books, 1974), pp. 137–42.

Punishment and Fairness

HERBERT MORRIS

The central point of Morris's elegant version of retributivism is to explain *how* punishing an offender serves a legitimate moral purpose. His argument, very briefly, is as follows. A society in which everyone obeys the law is a society in which, in return for the burden of one's own compliance, one obtains the benefits of everyone else's compliance. Under such circumstances, the distribution of social benefits and burdens is *fair*. A criminal is one who, by his or her act, obtains these benefits without assuming such a burden. This is unfair. Hence, justice requires that we restore a proper distribution of social benefits and burdens by punishing the criminal in order to remove an unfair advantage.

Let us first turn attention to the institutions in which punishment is involved. The institutions I describe will resemble those we ordinarily think of as institutions of punishment; they will have, however, additional features we associate with a system of just punishment.

Let us suppose that men are constituted roughly as they now are, with a rough equivalence in strength and abilities, a capacity to be injured by each other and to make judgments that such injury is undesirable, a limited strength of will, and a capacity to reason and to conform conduct to rules. Applying to the conduct of these men are a group of rules, ones I shall label "primary," which closely resemble the core rules of our criminal law, rules that prohibit violence and deception and compliance with which provides benefits for all persons. These benefits consist in noninterference by others with what each person values, such matters as continuance of life and bodily security. The rules define a sphere for each person, then, which is immune from interference by others. Making possible this mutual benefit is the assumption by individuals of a burden. The burden consists in the exercise of self-restraint by individuals over inclinations that would, if satisfied, directly interfere or create a substantial risk of interference with others in proscribed ways. If a person fails to exercise self-restraint even though he might have and gives in to such inclinations, he renounces a burden which others have voluntarily assumed and thus gains an advantage which others, who have restrained themselves, do not possess. This system, then, is one in which the rules establish a mutuality of benefit and burden and in which the benefits of noninterference are conditional upon the assumption of burdens.

Connecting punishment with the violation of these primary rules, and making public the provision for punishment, is both reasonable and just. First, it is only reasonable that those who voluntarily comply with the rules be provided some assurance that they will not be assuming burdens which others are unprepared to assume. Their disposition to comply voluntarily will diminish as they learn that others are with impunity renouncing burdens they are assuming. Second, fairness dictates that a system in which benefits and burdens are equally distributed have a mechanism designed to prevent a maldistribution in the benefits and burdens. Thus, sanctions are attached to noncompliance with the primary rules so as to induce compliance with the primary rules among those who may be disinclined to obey. In this way the likelihood of an unfair distribution is diminished.

Third, it is just to punish those who have violated the rules and caused the unfair distribution of benefits and burdens. A person

*Reprinted with permission from "Persons and Punishment," by Herbert Morris, *The Monist,* 52:4. La Salle, IL: 1968, pp. 476–79.

who violates the rules has something others have—the benefits of the system—but by renouncing what others have assumed, the burdens of self-restraint, he has acquired an unfair advantage. Matters are not even until this advantage is in some way erased. Another way of putting it is that he owes something to others, for he has something that does not rightfully belong to him. Justice—that is punishing such individuals—restores the equilibrium of benefits and burdens by taking from the individual what he owes, that is, exacting the debt. It is important to see that the equilibrium may be restored in another way. Forgiveness—with its legal analogue of a pardon—while not the righting of an unfair distribution by making one pay his debt is, nevertheless, a restoring of the equilibrium by forgiving the debt. Forgiveness may be viewed, at least in some types of cases, as a gift after the fact, erasing a debt, which had the gift been given before the fact, would not have created a debt. But the practice of pardoning has to proceed sensitively, for it may endanger in a way the practice of justice does not, the maintenance of an equilibrium of benefits and burdens. If all are indiscriminately pardoned less incentive is provided individuals to restrain their inclinations, thus increasing the incidence of persons taking what they do not deserve.

There are also in this system we are considering a variety of operative principles compliance with which provides some guarantee that the system of punishment does not itself promote an unfair distribution of benefits and burdens. For one thing, provision is made for a variety of defenses, each one of which can be said to have as its object diminishing the chances of forcibly depriving a person of benefits others have if that person has not derived an unfair advantage. A person has not derived an unfair advantage if he could not have restrained himself or if it is unreasonable to expect him to behave otherwise than he did. Sometimes the rules preclude punishment of classes of persons such as children. Sometimes they provide a defense if on a particular occasion a person lacked the capacity to conform his conduct to the rules. Thus, someone who in an epileptic seizure strikes another is excused. Punishment in these cases would be punishment of the innocent, punishment of those who do not voluntarily renounce a burden others have assumed. Punishment in such cases, then, would not equalize but rather cause an unfair distribution in benefits and burdens.

Along with principles providing defenses there are requirements that the rules be prospective and relatively clear so that persons have a fair opportunity to comply with the rules. There are, also, rules governing, among other matters, the burden of proof, who shall bear it and what it shall be, the prohibition on double jeopardy, and the privilege against self-incrimination. Justice requires conviction of the guilty, and requires their punishment, but in setting out to fulfill the demands of justice we may, of course, because we are not omniscient, cause injustice by convicting and punishing the innocent. The resolution arrived at in the system I am describing consists in weighing as the greater evil the punishment of the innocent. The primary function of the system of rules was to provide individuals with a sphere of interest immune from interference. Given this goal, it is determined to be a greater evil for society to interfere unjustifiably with an individual by depriving him of good than for the society to fail to punish those that have unjustifiably interfered.

Finally, because the primary rules are designed to benefit all and because the punishments prescribed for their violation are publicized and the defenses respected, there is some plausibility in the exaggerated claim that in choosing to do an act violative of the rules an individual has chosen to be punished. This way of putting matters brings to our attention the extent to which, when the system is as I have described it, the criminal "has brought the punishment upon himself" in contrast to those cases where it would be misleading to say "he has brought it upon himself," cases, for example, where one does not know the rules or is punished in the absence of fault.

Is Punishment Fair?

C. L. TEN

Ten summarizes some of the more important objections that have been raised against Morris's "fairness" version of retributivism. In particular, he emphasizes those having to do with (a) the precise nature of the unfair advantage gained by the criminal, (b) the appropriateness of *punishment* as a way of restoring the social equilibrium, and (c) the extent to which Morris's theory depends upon unrealistic assumptions about people and societies.

We come now to that version of the retributive theory which justifies punishment in terms of the claim that the offender has taken an unfair advantage of the law-abiding citizens. The most well-known attempt to develop this type of retributive theory is that of Herbert Morris in his richly illuminating paper, "Persons and Punishment."[1] Similar theories are also independently presented by John Finnis and Jeffrie Murphy.[2]

Morris maintains that "the core rules of the criminal law," which prohibit violence and deception, confer benefits on all persons in a society. The benefits consist in the non-interference by others with a certain protected area of a person's life. But these benefits are only possible if a burden of self-restraint is accepted, and people do not seek to satisfy their inclinations to engage in activities which interfere with the protected area of the lives of others. When the criminal violates the law, he or she renounces the burden which the law-abiding citizens accept. At the same time the criminal continues to enjoy the benefits of the law. The criminal has therefore taken an unfair advantage of the law-abiding citizens.

Punishment is justified because, by removing the unfair advantage of the criminal, it restores the just equilibrium of benefits and burdens which was upset by the criminal's act. Morris goes on to argue that only those who have voluntarily renounced the relevant burden should be punished as only they have taken the unfair advantage. This provides a basis for the recognition of various legal excuses. The failure to recognize such excuses would itself produce an unfair distribution of benefits and burdens by punishing those who, although they broke the law, did so in circumstances in which they could not be said to have taken an unfair advantage.

This specifically retributive reason for punishment must be distinguished from the other reasons which Morris also mentions. Thus he claims that punishment is also justified because it prevents the weakening of the disposition to obey the law among the law-abiding citizens. If they know that offenders can renounce with impunity the burden that they have accepted, then they will be less inclined to go on accepting this burden. This reason points to the good consequences of punishment in reducing crime. So also does Morris's other reason that punishment induces compliance with the rules. The specifically retributive reason, on the other hand, does not refer to the restoration of the equilibrium of the benefits and burdens as something that is distinct from, and caused by, punishment. Instead the act of punishment, by removing the unfair advantage taken by the offender, is itself the act restoring the equilibrium of benefits and burdens.

In his paper, "The Return to Retribution in Penal Theory," D. J. Galligan distinguishes between two versions of the retributive argument for punishment.[3] The first and stronger version of the argument maintains that punishment removes the illicit advantage gained by the crime and thereby restores the equilibrium. This argument is rejected by Galligan on the ground that it fails to give an adequate explanation of how punishment restores the social equilibrium. Obviously punishment does not restore the equilibrium in the way that the repayment of a debt restores the original position. For the injury done by the crime is not removed or cancelled out by the infliction of punishment of the offender. But the second version of the argument gets round this by making no reference to the restoration of the social equilibrium as a further end to be achieved by punishment. Instead, punishment is justified simply because it removes the unfair advantage which the offender has gained.

However, in Morris's account of punishment, the notion of restoring the equilibrium of benefits and burdens is not separable from the notion of removing the unfair advantage gained, or of preventing the offender from continuing to enjoy his or her illicit advantage over the law-abiding citizens. There is no further sense in which punishment is supposed to restore the social equilibrium. In other words, the equilibrium is restored not by the impossibility of wiping out what the offender has done in the past but in the very process of removing the unfair advantage gained by the offender while allowing law-abiding citizens to continue in the enjoyment of their benefits.

For Morris then the unfair advantage taken by the offender does not consist in the material benefits which the offender might have gained, for those benefits cannot be taken back if the offender has consumed them, and has no comparable resources with which to replace them. Punishment therefore does not restore the equilibrium in the way that a tax imposed on an offender and transferred as compensation to the victim might be said to restore the equilibrium.[4] Compensation is something that is owed to victims, whereas in Morris's argument the unfairness of the offender is an unfairness to the law-abiding citizens. This means that the unfair benefit is something which the offender has, and which all the law-abiding citizens have voluntarily forgone. This benefit is the voluntary renunciation of the burden of restraining oneself from violating the law. It is this benefit which other defenders of theories similar to Morris's have identified as the relevant benefit unfairly taken by the offender. Thus Finnis speaks of the offender as having illicitly "indulged his will," and as exercising "self-will or free choice."[5] And Murphy talks about the offender renouncing the burden of self-restraint.[6] So punishment removes the offender's advantage of freely indulging his or her will or of renouncing self-restraint. But it should be remembered that the indulgence of one's will or the renunciation of self-restraint only constitutes the taking of unfair advantage when it is done in the context of enjoying benefits made possible by the willingness of others to assume burdens that one has renounced.

Morris's theory of punishment seems to be a version of the more general theory of political obligation known as "the principle of fair play" or "the principle of fairness." This principle, expounded in slightly different forms by Hart and Rawls, maintains that when people engage in a just and mutually beneficial joint enterprise according to rules which restrict their liberty, then those who have benefited from the submission of others to these restrictions, have a duty to submit themselves to the same restrictions.[7]

It is sometimes thought that this theory of political obligation has been so decisively refuted that any version of it which shares its central features cannot be taken seriously. The most well-known objections to the principle are those put forward by Nozick in *Anarchy, State, and Utopia*.[8] These objections have been subjected to detailed scrutiny by others.[9] I shall not be concerned with the merits of Nozick's objections, but I shall briefly indicate that his arguments do not affect the version of the principle of fairness that Morris needs in order to justify punishment.

Nozick gives an example of a group of people who start a public address system giving benefits in the form of playing records, telling amusing stories, and giving news bulletins. There are 365 adults in the neighbourhood, and the arrangement made by the group is that each person should spend one day running the system. If you have benefited by occasionally opening your window and listening to the entertainment, does it follow that you have a duty to play your part in running the system? Nozick argues that you have not. "Though you benefit from the arrangement, you may know all along that 364 days of entertainment supplied by others will not be worth your giving up *one* day."[10] You have also not consented to the scheme.

But the criminal's renunciation of the burden of self-restraint is very different from your refusal to help in the running of the public address system. In renouncing his burden, the criminal deprives law-abiding citizens of some of the benefits which he himself enjoys. Nozick's example would come closer to the case of the criminal's conduct if one supposes that for some peculiar reason your enjoyment of the public address system is enhanced by your shutting your neighbour's window thereby depriving her of the entertainment, even though, unlike you, she has already taken her turn to run the system. It is not unreasonable to claim that you have a duty to refrain from shutting her window. So Morris's theory depends on the much narrower principle that one who accepts the benefits of a just scheme of social co-operation must accept the burden of co-operation where this involves restraining oneself from depriving co-operating members of some of their benefits.

In a recent detailed criticism of Morris's theory, Richard Burgh first attributes to him the view that the offender's benefit is the sphere of non-interference resulting from general obedience to the particular law he or she violated.[11] Burgh then points out that the offender might not have benefited from the existence of that particular law. For example, embezzlers might not be in a position to be embezzled, and hence the law prohibiting embezzlement gives them no benefit. Hence they cannot be said to have taken unfair advantage of those law-abiding citizens who are in positions to be embezzled. If we shift the relevant benefit to that given by obedience to laws in general, then Burgh points out that this is a benefit which is enjoyed equally by all offenders. The murderer enjoys this benefit just as much as the embezzler. So if both of them are deserving of punishment because of the unfair benefits they have enjoyed, then both deserve punishment to the same degree. On this view there would be no basis for punishing different offenders to different degrees.

Finally, Burgh argues that the theory cannot be rescued by treating the unfair benefit of the offender as the renunciation of the burden of self-restraint. Since the extent of benefit now depends on the weight of the burden of self-restraint renounced, and the burden of self-restraint is to be measured by the strength of the inclination to commit the crime, it follows that the stronger the inclination to commit the crime, the greater is the benefit derived from the offence. But the degree of punishment suggested by this account is highly counter-intuitive, for it means that if there is a stronger inclination to evade taxes than to murder, then the punishment for tax evasion would have to be more severe than that for murder.

In fact Morris's theory combines two elements that Burgh keeps apart—the benefit of renouncing self-restraint and the benefit of obedience to laws in general. The renunciation of the burden of self-restraint is only regarded as an unfair advantage when it is done in the context of enjoying the benefits of having a protected sphere made possible by the obedience of others to laws in general. But does this interpretation still make Morris's theory vulnerable to the objections raised by Burgh that the theory either fails to account for the differential punishment to be meted out to various offenders, or that it gives a wrong account of which offender should be punished more severely?

We should recall that the offender's unfair benefits are relative to the benefits and burdens of law-abiding citizens. Any measure of the extent of the offender's benefits is a measure of the degree of unfair advantage taken, and must therefore take account of the value to both the offender and to the law-abiding citizens of the law that has been violated. For example, a petty thief, no matter what the strength of his inclination to commit the crime, still obeys the rest of the laws conferring considerable benefits on himself and the law-abiding citizens. These benefits include the protection of life which is highly valued by all parties. The murderer, on the other hand, again irrespective of the strength of his inclination to murder, violates a law which makes a far greater contribution than does the law prohibiting petty theft to the benefits enjoyed by both the murderer and law-abiding citizens. So in this sense it can be said that the unfair advantage taken by the petty thief is much less than that of the murderer. The petty thief invades a less important part of the protected sphere of others.

Morris's theory does not spell out the basis on which one is to determine the extent of punishment which each offender deserves, for it is primarily concerned with establishing a case for punishing all offenders who voluntarily invade the protected sphere. But it looks as if, contrary to Burgh's argument, it is possible to interpret the theory in a manner which makes it compatible with some proportionality principle which states that the degree of punishment should vary with the gravity of the offence committed. . . . Morris's theory survives so far. But there are other problems to be faced.

In the legal systems with which we are familiar, the violation of the core rules of the criminal law are met with punishments usually in the form of imprisonment and fines. But given that Morris's theory establishes the case for restoring the equilibrium of benefits and burdens by removing the unfair benefits of offenders, why is it that only these forms of punishment can remove the unfair benefits? As Galligan points out, the theory "requires at most that the offender be singled out, condemned and subjected to some form of disadvantage; but just what manner and form the disadvantage must take is left open."[12] Here Morris's theory needs some help from external considerations before it can provide a full justification of punishment.

The appeal to external considerations is also necessary at another point, for there are circumstances in which even offenders who have voluntarily renounced their burdens should not be punished. Finnis recognizes this when he argues that the restoration via punishment of fairness in distribution is not the only component of the social good, and so need not be pursued regardless of consequences.[13] But if utilitarian considerations enter into the final decision as to whether punishment should be inflicted, then these considerations form part of the complete theory of punishment.

For a moral pluralist, who believes in several values, each not reducible to any of the others, it makes sense to say that although fairness dictates that one should punish on a particular occasion, the requirement of fairness is overridden by other values which dictate that one should not punish. Fairness is a moral principle for guiding one's actions, and it can provide a reason for acting even when one acts against it in the light of competing reasons for action. But if fairness is only one of the considerations relevant to the determination of whether punishment should be inflicted, then fairness is not the only component of a complete theory of punishment.

So far we have acknowledged that there are considerations external to Morris's theory which count against punishing offenders who have voluntarily renounced the burden of self-restraint. But it would appear that there are also considerations internal to the theory which sometimes urge against punishment. Morris's theory treats the offender's violation of the law as the taking of an unfair advantage which punishment removes. But although punishment restores the equilibrium of benefits and burdens between the particular offender and the law-abiding citizens, it can also have various effects on others. Suppose that it somehow causes others to commit crimes. This would appear to be a relevant consideration for *not* inflicting punishment. As Finnis acknowledges, if punishment causes more crime, it creates greater unfairness to law-abiding citizens and this is surely precisely what the theory wishes to avoid.[14] Indeed it would be odd for the theory to insist on punishment in such a case since the people on whose behalf punishment is exacted, namely the law-abiding citizens, would presumably prefer a situation in which there are fewer crimes.

But now suppose that punishment deters potential offenders from committing crimes. Then by the same token it reduces the unfairness to law-abiding citizens, and so the deterrent effects of punishment should count as a reason for punishment. In a particular case, it is possible that the punishment of an offender will encourage some potential offenders to commit crimes while it deters other potential offenders. If the former effect is a reason for not punishing the offender, then the latter effect should be a reason in favour of punishment.

But through these moves, the character of Morris's retributive theory is in danger of changing radically to the extent that it now appears to be a type of consequentialist doctrine which seeks to minimize unfairness or to maximize fairness. Of course this does not mean that the doctrine collapses into utilitarianism. Whereas utilitarianism takes into account all the consequences of actions which affect happiness or the satisfaction of desires, the doctrine limits the relevant consequences to those which bear on the removal of unfairness. But on the interpretation there is now nothing in the doctrine which blocks the punishment of the innocent if such punishment is conducive to the minimization of unfairness. Suppose that by punishing an innocent person we will minimize the violations of the law and therefore the amount of unfairness. If the goal is to minimize unfairness, then it appears that there would be no reason to avoid such punishment. There will be no special unfairness in punishing the innocent, for the State's punishment of the innocent is on a par with, and to be weighed on the same scale as, the unfairness of the actions of criminals.

To meet this objection, it is necessary to re-examine the motivation behind Morris's theory. In fact the theory cannot be accurately represented as one which seeks to minimize unfairness by any means whatever. It starts with the assumption that it is possible to have a situation in which there is a fair distribution of benefits and burdens for everyone. Any departure from this state through the voluntary actions of individuals in renouncing their burdens while still accepting benefits is unfair, and punishment restores the initial equilibrium. So the only people who are to be punished are those who have acted unfairly. The theory is compatible with not punishing those who have acted unfairly if punishment will produce even greater unfairness. And so long as the punishment of the offender is not disproportionate to the degree of unfairness of his or her act, an appeal to other considerations can be made in order to determine the exact amount of punishment. But punishing the innocent, who have not acted unfairly, is a different matter. It strikes at the very root of the system of co-operation designed to confer equal mutual benefits on all. It means that the system itself is unfair. The system is designed to maintain fairness by punishing unfair behaviour, and not to prevent unfairness by itself sanctioning unfair acts. The aim of establishing a system of rules is to provide each person with a protected sphere in which he or she can proceed free of interference from others. The punishment of the innocent is an interference with the very area of their lives that it was the purpose of the system to protect. The system seeks to guarantee that a person will only be interfered with by the law if he or she voluntarily invades the protected sphere of others.

So in fact Morris's theory erects a barrier against punishing the innocent which resembles Nozick's idea of moral side-constraints which we are forbidden to violate even in the pursuit of desirable goals.[15] Nozick distinguishes the theory of individual rights as side-constraints from what he calls "utilitarianism of rights." According to the latter view, one would be required to violate a person's rights when by so doing one minimizes the total amount of violations of rights in society. So, for example, one may violate an innocent man's right by punishing him if this will prevent a mob from rampaging through the town, killing and burning and thereby violating the rights of others. On the other hand, if rights are side-constraints, then they may not be violated even in the cause of preventing greater violations of similar rights.

There are of course also considerations external to Morris's theory which explain why it is wrong to punish the innocent. One argument deserves special mention because it relies on a feature of punishment to which we have referred earlier. Punishment expresses moral disapproval. We normally express moral disapproval for what a person has done or failed to do. But in punishing the innocent we express moral disapproval of them when there is no basis for such disapproval. All cases of punishing the innocent share this feature of unjustly attributing blame to someone who is in fact blameless. That is why such punishment is a serious wrong even when the actual suffering of deprivation inflicted by punishment may not be great in a particular case. This does not mean that it is absolutely wrong to punish the innocent. Even the idea of rights as moral side-constraints does not require that these constraints must never be violated. But it does mean that such punishment cannot be justified simply in utilitarian terms.

The scope of Morris's theory is restricted to punishment for violations of those "core rules" of the criminal law which are necessary for the survival of society. All those living in society have a common interest in having such rules for regulating their social relations, and it is only from the application of these rules that people with otherwise very diverse interests can in principle gain equal benefits and share equal burdens. The general content of these rules depends on facts about human nature and the natural world. Morris himself draws attention to some of these facts in the following remark: "Let us suppose that men are constituted roughly as they now are, with rough equivalence in strength and abilities, a capacity to be injured by each other and to make judgements that such injury is undesirable, a limited strength of will, and a capacity to reason and to conform conduct to rules.[16] Hart has a more detailed discussion in his account of "the minimum content of natural law."[17] The additional features on which Hart focuses are limited resources, and the need for division of labour to ensure efficient production. The vulnerability of human beings to injury means they require protection by rules prohibiting assault and killing. Limited resources mean that if individuals are to have incentives to cultivate these resources for food, there must be rules protecting food from being taken while it is in the process of cultivation. Rules protecting property are therefore necessary, although the exact content of these rules will vary from society to society. Division of labour leads to exchange of goods and thus calls for rules regulating such exchanges. There will be a common interest in protection against fraud.

Morris's theory will not therefore be relevant to all the cases in which punishment may be thought to be justified. One such case, cited by Burgh, is the law prohibiting cruelty to animals.[18] This limitation in its scope is not fatal to the theory, but it shows, what should by now be obvious, that there are other reasons for justifying the punishment which are not captured by the theory. Even within the area of its application the theory cannot possibly tell the full story about the wrongness of, for example, murder and assault. For the theory locates the wrongness of such acts in the unfairness to law-abiding citizens, and not in the harm inflicted on victims.

There is a more general problem about the application of Morris's theory to societies in the real world which all deviate in varying degrees from the ideal of a just society. Finnis makes explicit his supposition that "the legal system and social order in question are substantially just. . . ."[19] But Murphy points out that the theory is largely inapplicable to contemporary societies where there are vast inequalities of income, wealth, and opportunities.[20] In these societies most criminals come from economically and socially disadvantaged groups which cannot be said to derive much benefit from the operation of the rules of society. Morris's theory presupposes a just equilibrium of benefits and burdens which the criminal's act upsets, and which is then restored by punishment. But if Murphy is right, then the distribution of social benefits and burdens is in the first place unfair, and punishment does not therefore restore fairness. Even if we confine the relevant burden to self-restraint, it is quite clear that the economically and socially favoured groups in society will find it much easier to accept the burden of self-restraint than disadvantaged groups.

So if criminals were all the victims of a broader social injustice in the distribution of society's resources, and the victims of crime were all the beneficiaries of the injustice, then Morris's theory would have no application. But the situation is in fact more complex. Many of the victims of crime come from the same economically and socially deprived groups as those who offend against them and there is also a substantial number of offenders who belong to the favoured groups in society. So even in societies in which the distribution of benefits and burdens is quite unfair, the argument that crime involves the taking of an unfair advantage from law-abiding citizens still has some residual force. Of course the problems of general social injustice cannot be solved by punishment.

Secondly, not to punish offenders will very likely result in even greater injustice. It will encourage more crime and lead to attempts at private enforcement of rules. The passion for revenge will remain unchecked. There will be a profusion of vigilante groups whose attitudes towards criminals will be quite brutal. And those most likely to suffer will be the poor and disadvantaged who are unable to protect themselves as well as others.

But Morris's theory runs into further difficulties because it seems to rest on dubious psychological assumptions. Self-restraint, exercised in conforming to the law, is seen as a burden which some accept for the benefit of all, while others reject it. However, many, and perhaps most, law-abiding citizens lack the desire to violate the core rules of the criminal law in the first place. For them conformity with the law does not involve the acceptance of the burden of self-restraint. Other law-abiding citizens have to exercise self-restraint in not breaking the law, but they refrain from breaking the law out of the fear of punishment rather than out of a desire to maintain the system of mutually beneficial social co-operation. Offenders cannot be said to have taken unfair advantage of these law-abiding citizens who would themselves be offenders but for the deterrent effect of punishment.[21]

Our discussion of retributive theories suggests that on their own these theories provide inadequate justifications of punishment. For even when they succeed in showing that some form of action should be taken against offenders, they do not explain why such action should take the specific form of punishment. There are a number of options open of which punishment is only one. The selection of punishment itself, or a particular form of punishment, from the available options is based on the utilitarian consideration that the practice of punishment is in general most effective in reducing crime. But once punishment is chosen as the preferred general response to crime, retributive considerations can provide further support for the punishment of offenders in particular cases. Retributive considerations also shape the practice of punishment by imposing strong constraints on the punishment of the innocent.

NOTES

1. Herbert Morris, "Persons and Punishment," in Jeffrie G. Murphy (ed.), *Punishment and Rehabilitation* (Belmont, 1973). In a more recent essay, Morris argues that "a principal justification for punishment is the potential and actual wrongdoer's good." See Herbert Morris, "A Paternalistic Theory of Punishment," in Rolf Sartorius (ed.), *Paternalism* (Minneapolis, 1983).
2. For John Finnis's contributions, see: "Old and New in Hart's Philosophy of Punishment," *The Oxford Review* 8 (1968); "The Restoration of Retribution," *Analysis,* 52 (1971–2); "Meaning and Ambiguity in Punishment (and Penology)," *Osgooge Hall Law Journal,* 10 (1972); *Natural Law and Natural Rights* (Oxford, 1980), pp. 262–66: *Fundamentals of Ethics* (Oxford, 1983), pp. 128–32. Jeffrie G. Murphy's best-known contribution is "Marxism and Retribution" which is reprinted with other relevant essays in Jeffrie G. Murphy, *Retribution, Justice, and Therapy* (Dodrecht, 1979).
3. D. J. Galligan, "The Return to Retribution in Penal Theory," in C. Tapper (ed.), *Crime,*

Proof and Punishment (London, 1981), pp. 154–57.

4. See Richard Wasserstrom's discussion of his interpretation of Morris in "Capital Punishment as Punishment: Some Theoretical Issues and Objections." *Midwest Studies in Philosophy* 7 (1982), p. 498.
5. The quotations are from "The Restoration of Retribution," p. 134, and *Natural Law and Natural Rights*, p. 263.
6. "Marxism and Retribution," p. 100.
7. See: H. L. A. Hart, "Are There Any Natural Rights?," *Philosophical Review*, 64 (1955), p. 185; and John Rawls, *A Theory of Justice* (Oxford, 1972), pp. 108–14.
8. Robert Nozick, *Anarchy, State, and Utopia* (Oxford, 1974), pp. 90–95.
9. See: A. John Simmons, *Moral Principles and Political Obligations* (Princeton, 1981), pp. 118–36; and Richard J. Arneson, "The Principle of Fairness and Free-Rider Problems," *Ethics* 92 (1982).
10. *Anarchy, State and Utopia*, p. 93.
11. Richard W. Burgh, "Do the Guilty Deserve Punishment?," *The Journal of Philosophy*, 79 (1982), p. 203.
12. "The Return to Retribution in Penal Theory," p. 158.
13. "The Restoration of Retribution," p. 135.
14. Ibid., p. 135.
15. *Anarchy, State, and Utopia*, pp. 28–30.
16. "Persons and Punishment," p. 42.
17. H. L. A. Hart, *The Concept of Law* (Oxford, 1961), pp. 189–95.
18. "Do the Guilty Deserve Punishment?," p. 205.
19. *Natural Law and Natural Rights*, p. 264.
20. "Marxism and Retribution."
21. I owe these points to discussion with H. L. A. Hart but he is not responsible for the manner in which I have formulated or used them.

Can Retributivists Support Legal Punishment?*

GEORGE SCHEDLER

Schedler's provocative essay is intended to undermine the traditional view that, whatever else can be said about it, retributivism has one clear advantage over utilitarianism in that it could never countenance punishing the innocent. He points out that human imperfection guarantees that any feasible system of punishment will occasionally "misfire" and impose sanctions on those who are not guilty of the offenses with which they have been charged. Hence, like their utilitarian counterparts, retributivists who support legal punishment support an institution that they *know* will involve the punishing of innocent people.

In the first half of this century, Anglo-American moral philosophers concerned themselves with the vexing question of whether legal officials could deliberately "punish" the innocent and whether a utilitarian justification for such a practice is possible. Interest in this topic waned after Rawls drew a crucial distinction in his article, "Two Concepts of Rules," between two kinds of systems for dealing with wrongdoing.[1] One was legal punishment, as we understand it; the other was the practice of "telishment," in which the officials, as Rawls said, "have authority to arrange a trial for the condemnation of an innocent man whenever they are of the opinion that doing so would be in the best interests of society."[2] A utilitarian justification for such an arrangement is most unlikely, Rawls claimed, because of the very great risks that such an institution might misfire.[3]

Perhaps because it is obvious that retributivists must condemn such a practice, not much attention has been devoted to the question of what, if any, problems are raised for retributivists when this distinction is drawn. In this essay, I intend to show that the retributivist cannot coherently and consistently condemn telishment as unjust without also condemning all systems of legal punishment as unjust. Due to the fact that retributivists have failed to note that legal punishment is really the moral equivalent of

Reprinted with permission from "Can Retributivists Support Legal Punishment" by George Schedler, *The Monist* (April 1980).

*The central point of this paper first occurred to me during conversations with Professor Matthew J. Kelly. Revisions of this paper have been greatly improved by his comments, as well as those of Professors Herbert Morris, Ramon M. Lemos, and David S. Clarke, Jr.

telishment, their premises justify punishment only as it might take place in certain narrowly defined, non-legal contexts. (Unless I indicate otherwise, however, the term, *punishment* should be construed as being synonymous with *legal punishment*.) . . .

Let us now turn to the basis for the retributivist objections to telishment, as well as the retributivist case for punishment. Retributivists from Kant to McCloskey, and even non-retributivists such as Rawls, are agreed that the following proposition is central to the retributivist doctrine: It is unjust to punish those who have done no moral wrong nor committed any crime.[4] We will call this "weak retributivism" or the "weak version" of retributivism, and we will always use the term, "innocent," in this way, to refer to one who is innocent of crime and moral wrongdoing. Many retributivists have asserted that justice requires more than this. Kant insisted that, with few exceptions, everyone guilty of a crime should be punished in accordance with the principle of *lex talionis*. (Indeed, he called the sovereign's right to pardon "the most slippery of all rights of the sovereign.")[5] St. Augustine felt that justice requires that everyone suffer in proportion to the degree of moral wrongdoing of which one is guilty.[6] Even these retributivists seem to agree that, in addition to the proposition that the innocent should never be punished, it is also true that justice requires that all who are guilty of crimes which constitute serious moral wrongdoing should be punished in accordance with the principle of *lex talionis*.[7] We shall call the joint assertion of these propositions, "strong retributivism" or the "strong version" of retributivism. (Our shorthand expression for the additional principle will be: all those guilty of crimes should be punished. Similarly, the terms "criminal," "wrongdoer," "guilty," and "guilty of a crime" will be used interchangeably to refer to someone guilty of a crime that constitutes serious moral wrongdoing.) We should note that the strong and weak versions are not being interpreted here as merely elucidating logical points about the use of the term, "punishment," nor are we construing retributivism as a doctrine that offers advice only for judges dealing with individual cases that fall under the rules of a system of punishment.[8] Clearly, Kant was not making a linguistic point, nor merely advising judges when he insisted that all murderers should be punished with death.[9] He was stating a moral requirement for a system, or what Rawls calls a "practice."[10] Accordingly, we shall consider retributivism in both its forms as recommendations about the design of systems of legal punishment, though we shall devote most of our attention to the weak version, since there seems to be more agreement that it is really what is essential to retributivism.

In spite of the fact that both these versions are faithful to the views of classical retributivists, as they stand, neither the strong nor the weak version could be used as the basis for any moral objection to the practice of telishment, since each object only to punishment of the innocent. Therefore, we shall interpret retributivists as holding to a more general principle (from which weak retributivism would follow) that systems in which officials knowingly inflict suffering on the innocent are unjust. Furthermore, since justice is an overriding value for retributivists, they must also be willing to hold that it is immoral to support systems which we know will inflict suffering on the innocent. These claims, then, will be viewed as part of weak (and strong) retributivism.

Let us now turn our attention to the justification for systems of punishment. We know all too well that a system of legal punishment will on occasion convict and punish by mistake individuals who are innocent in the sense just discussed. To admit this is merely to admit that well-intentioned human beings are fallible and imperfect and that, as a consequence, their legal systems will reflect these characteristics. Now, we can understand that retributivists (and apparently Kant was one of these) might not be cognizant of this fact and support a system of punishment, believing (naively) that no innocent person would ever suffer at the hands of the system.[11] But, once a retributivist fully appreciates the significance of human imperfection, such a thinker cannot consistently advocate the establishment of systems of legal punishment and yet condemn the establishment of systems of telishment. The principle that it is wrong to support systems which are known to inflict suffering on innocent people requires that we support neither. Thus, retributivists who would support systems of legal punishment are subject to the same moral criticism that they lodge against utilitarians who would administer a system of telishment: such people support systems that they know will condemn innocent people. Let us now consider some ways that retributivists might avoid this charge.

It might be thought that our conclusion is too hastily drawn, since systems of punishment and systems of telishment are different in important respects: Officials in the former system believe that the individuals who are convicted under the system are guilty, while, in the latter, officials sentence individuals they know to be innocent. But this difference only shows that the systems are unjust in different ways, for we must not forget that officials in a system of legal punishment believe that convicted criminals are guilty only in a very narrow sense of "believe." Officials can say only that those convicted under the system are believed guilty insofar as the courtroom procedures, the rules of evidence, and so forth show that such persons must be declared guilty of certain crimes. But, since these same officials are also aware of the fallibility of human nature and the incompleteness of human knowledge, they cannot truly say that they believe all persons convicted under the system are really guilty. They could maintain that they do not know the identities of the innocent individuals who have been convicted under the system. And they might also correctly say that they do not know how many innocent people are condemned to such fates. But they do know what is morally relevant in this context: the price for the maintenance of a system of legal punishment is paid by those innocents who are convicted under it. Indeed, legal systems of punishment are by their very nature designed to cope with human imperfection, not only in the sense that they provide a way for dealing with those who are prone to prey on others, but also in the sense that they are arrangements designed to be operated by beings prone to error. The officials administer the system knowing that suffering will be inflicted on innocent people. To be sure, the officials do not select out the innocent people themselves, as they might in a system of telishment, but it is easy to show that this is not a morally relevant difference. Let us suppose that a system of telishment were designed much like a firing squad, ignoring for now how the former might operate in its details. The members of the firing squad share the responsibility for executing the prisoner, but no one knows which member of the squad fired live ammunition. Now, suppose that a system of telishment were so bureaucratized and individual tasks so highly specialized that only the highest officials knew that innocent people were being convicted, but no one knew the identities of the innocents or exactly how many there were. This complex arrangement would surely not make the system any more just in the eyes of retributivists than a system in which the highest officials personally selected the victims of the system. All those who are aware of the nature of the system and who consciously support it are as responsible for what they do as are the members of the firing squad.

Of course, it will be said that, in spite of the similarities between officials in systems of punishment and those in systems of telishment, there is the important difference that the former officials never intend to inflict suffering on the innocent, while the latter do intend this result. Even though this is one way of differentiating the officials, the moral significance of this difference is quite minimal. For officials in both systems, although their intentions are different, are willing to support arrangements that they know will result in suffering do innocents. Similarly, retributivists who advocate punishment are relevantly like utilitarians who will sacrifice the welfare of innocents for the greater good, since retributivists are willing to trade the welfare of the innocents who are punished by mistake for the greater good of the punishment of the guilty. While never intending to punish the innocent, they nonetheless do not choose to withdraw their support for arrangements that have this result. The difference, then, between punishment officials and telishment officials is that the latter directly intend an objectionable result, while the former voluntarily perform actions they know will have the objectionable result. The relevant question here is why retributivists should choose punishment in the first place.

It might be said in response that those who support telishment have a choice: they can choose between punishment and telishment. But those who support, it might be thought, punishment have no choice: they must either support a system of punishment or refuse to protect innocent people at all. Thus, it seems that punishment is the only alternative to the approval of criminal behavior by inaction. There is no such case, it might be concluded, for telishment, and hence there is a morally relevant difference between advocating one and advocating the other.

If we examine this argument with care, however, we will discover that the situation is not nearly as simple as it seems. Those who support telishment are advocating that we do one kind of injustice so we may discourage worse people (namely, criminals and potential criminals) from doing an even worse injustice. This reasoning is repulsive to retributivists because it would justify even the most barbarous acts provided those acts cause less misery to innocents than what others will very likely do unless preemptive action is taken. But the moral equivalent of this reasoning is being urged in support of legal punishment. We are being asked to protect some innocent people from potential criminals by maintaining a system of punishment under which other innocent people will suffer at the hands of the state. Nor can it be said that defenders of punishment have no choice in the matter. We can still choose to protect innocent people as best we can without supporting systems that cause suffering to other innocents. We could simply refuse to lend support to any system which we know will cause innocent people to suffer. To be sure, the number of innocent people who are victims of a system of punishment may be far smaller than the number of innocents who would suffer if there were no punishment. We do not know for certain that this is true, of course, but, if we assume it is, and we regard this as a morally relevant fact, we are reasoning in the same way as supporters of telishment. We are doing a balancing act by supporting a system that causes innocent people to suffer in order to avoid the far greater misery wrongdoers will inflict. We do all this when we have open to us the alternative of refusing to establish systems that cause innocent people to suffer.

We are thus caught in a dilemma. Either we must assert that it is always wrong to contribute to the suffering of innocents or it is not, provided we inflict the least amount any practical alternative allows, where "practical alternative" does not include inaction. Unfortunately, this latter principle would justify inflicting any amount of suffering whatever, provided we have assurance that someone else will inflict even more. If we are unwilling to adopt this position, however, we must conclude that (human) systems of punishment have no retributive justification. But it seems unreasonable to hold that even the fairest imaginable system of punishment has no moral justification simply because some innocent person will at some time (let us say, only once in a hundred years) suffer under it.

NOTES

1. John Rawls, "Two Concepts of Rules," *Philosophical Review,* vol. 64, no. 1 (January 1955).
2. Rawls, "Two Concepts of Rules," p. 11.
3. Rawls, ibid., p. 12.
4. Kant claims, for example, that judicial punishment "must in all cases be imposed on [the criminal] only on the ground that he has committed a crime. . . ." *(The Metaphysical Elements of Justice* (New York: Bobbs Merrill, 1965), p. 100). Rawls says that what "retributionists have rightly insisted upon is that no man can be punished unless he is guilty" ("Two Concepts of Rules," p. 7). See

also H. J. McCloskey, "Utilitarian and Retributive Punishment," *Journal of Philosophy*, vol. 64, no. 3 (February 16, 1967): 102–04.

5. Kant, *The Metaphysical Elements of Justice*, p. 108. Hegel also held that justice requires that all criminals be punished and seems to have supposed that actual legal systems accomplish this. See *Philosophy of Right*, Part I, para. 99; Part II, para. 22; Additions 63–65.
6. Augustine quotes Luke 6:38, "With the same measure that ye mete withal it shall be measured to you again," and observes that " 'the same measure' refers, not to an equal space of time, but to the retribution of evil, or, in other words, to the law by which he who has done evil suffers evil" (*The City of God*, trans. Marcus Dods, New York: Random House, 1950, p. 782). How it is possible for God to be both merciful and just is not explained, but Augustine says that on the day of final judgment God's justice will be clear to all. See *The City of God*, pp. 711–12.
7. I have formulated strong retributivism in such a way that it does not emcompass the full scope of views actually held by such thinkers as St. Augustine, who called for the punishment of all wrongdoers (even those who are not criminals). But strong retributivism does represent a common core of views on punishment that goes beyond weak retributivism. Similarly, a retributivist who insisted on the punishment of all criminals, regardless of their moral culpability, could still agree with the theses of strong retributivism.
8. See Anthony M. Quinton, "On Punishment," *Analysis*, vol. 14, no. 6 (June 1954): 134 and Rawls, "Two Concepts of Rules," pp. 6–7.
9. Kant, *The Metaphysical Elements of Justice*, pp. 104–05.
10. See p. 3, n.1 of Rawls's "Two Concepts of Rules." As I see it, a practice is a conceptual model of how a system of punishment ought to be designed. So there is a difference between a practice and a system. In other works, I have used the term "institution," instead of "practice." See Schedler, "On Telishing the Guilty," pp. 259–60 and George Schedler, *Behavior Modification and "Punishment" of the Innocent* (Amsterdam: B. R. Gruner, 1977), pp. 20–22.
11. Kant says "No one suffers punishment because he has willed the punishment, but because he has willed a punishable action," as though it could never happen that one might be punished without having willed a punishable action (*The Metaphysical Elements of Justice*, p. 105). It is curious that the only mistakes the sovereign might make which give Kant pause are the possible abuses of the right to pardon. He says that by exercising the right, the sovereign "can wreak injustice *[unrecht]* to a high degree" (*The Metaphysical Elements of Justice*, p. 108).

Study Questions

1. How does Morris's brand of retributivism differ from the more traditional versions discussed by Lyons?
2. Do you agree with Ten that retributivism is inadequate because "even when [defenders of this view] succeed in showing that some form of action should be taken against offenders, they do not explain why such action should take the specific form of punishment"?
3. Do you agree with Schedler that retributivists cannot consistently condemn telishment without at the same time condemning all systems of legal punishment?
4. Are there any advantages that a utilitarian theory (such as Bentham's) has over retributive theories of the sort discussed in this section?

C Compromise (Mixed Utilitarian/Retributivist) Theories

The Practice of Punishment

JOHN RAWLS

Rawls, one of the most important contemporary moral theorists, argues that any satisfactory account of punishment must include both retributivist and utilitarian features. More precisely, he maintains that while we must appeal to considerations of social utility in justifying the institution of punishment *as a whole* (i.e., from the standpoint of a *legislator* attempting to *formulate* basic rules and procedures), retributive considerations are decisive *within* that institution (i.e., from the standpoint of a *judge* attempting to *apply* rules to particular cases).

In this paper I want to show the importance of the distinction between justifying a practice[1] and justifying a particular action falling under it, and I want to explain the logical basis of this distinction and how it is possible to miss its significance. While the distinction has frequently been made,[2] and is now becoming commonplace, there remains the task of explaining the tendency either to overlook it altogether, or to fail to appreciate its importance.

From John Rawls, "Two Concepts of Rules," *The Philosophical Review* 44 (1955), intro., sec. 1. pp. 3–13. Reprinted by permission of the author and *The Philosophical Review*.

To show the importance of the distinction I am going to defend utilitarianism against those objections which have traditionally been made against it in connection with punishment and the obligation to keep promises. I hope to show that if one uses the distinction in question then one can state utilitarianism in a way which makes it a much better explication of our considered moral judgments than these traditional objections would seem to admit.[3] Thus the importance of the distinction is shown by the way it strengthens the utilitarian view regardless of whether that view is completely defensible or not.

To explain how the significance of the distinction may be overlooked, I am going to discuss two conceptions of rules. One of these conceptions conceals the importance of distinguishing between the justification of a rule or practice and the justification of a particular action falling under it. The other conception makes it clear why this distinction must be made and what is its logical basis.

The subject of punishment, in the sense of attaching legal penalties to the violation of legal rules, has always been a troubling moral question.[4] The trouble about it has not been that people disagree as to whether or not punishment is justifiable. Most people have held that, freed from certain abuses, it is an acceptable institution. Only a few have rejected punishment entirely, which is rather surprising when one considers all that can be said against it. The difficulty is with the justification of punishment: various arguments for it have been given by moral philosophers, but so far none of them has won any sort of general acceptance; no justification is without those who detest it. I hope to show that the use of the aforementioned distinction enables one to state the utilitarian view in a way which allows for the sound points of its critics.

For our purposes we may say that there are two justifications of punishment. What we may call the retributive view is that punishment is justified on the grounds that wrongdoing merits punishment. It is morally fitting that a person who does wrong should suffer in proportion to his wrongdoing. That a criminal should be punished follows from his guilt, and the severity of the appropriate punishment depends on the depravity of his act. The state of affairs where a wrongdoer suffers punishment is morally better than the state of affairs where he does not; and it is better irrespective of any of the consequences of punishing him.

What we may call the utilitarian view holds that on the principle that bygones are bygones and that only future consequences are material to present decisions, punishment is justifiable only by reference to the probable consequences of maintaining it as one of the devices of the social order. Wrongs committed in the past are, as such, not relevant considerations for deciding what to do. If punishment can be shown to promote effectively the interest of society it is justifiable, otherwise it is not.

I have stated these two competing views very roughly to make one feel the conflict between them: one feels the force of *both* arguments and one wonders how they can be reconciled. From my introductory remarks it is obvious that the resolution which I am going to propose is that in this case one must distinguish between justifying a practice as a system of rules to be applied and enforced, and justifying a particular action which falls under these rules; utilitarian arguments are appropriate with regard to questions about practices, while retributive arguments fit the application of particular rules to particular cases.

We might try to get clear about this distinction by imagining how a father might answer the question of his son. Suppose the son asks, "Why was *J* put in jail yesterday?" The father answers, "Because he robbed the bank at *B*. He was duly tried and found guilty. That's why he was put in jail yesterday." But suppose the son had asked a different question, namely, "Why do people put other people in jail?" Then the father might answer, "To protect good people from bad people," or "To stop people from doing things that would make it uneasy for all of us; for otherwise we wouldn't be able to go to bed at night and sleep in peace." There are two very different questions here. One question emphasizes the proper name: It asks why *J* was punished rather than someone else, or it asks what he was punished for. The other question asks why we have the institution of punishment: Why do people punish one another rather than, say, always forgiving one another?

Thus the father says in effect that a particular man is punished, rather than some other man, because he is guilty, and he is guilty because he broke the law (past tense). In his case the law looks back, the judge looks back, the jury looks back, and a penalty is visited upon him for something he did. That a man is to be punished, and what his punishment is to be, is settled by its being shown that he broke the law and that the law assigns that penalty for the violation of it.

On the other hand we have the institution of punishment itself, and recommend and accept various changes in it, because it is thought by the (ideal) legislator and by those to whom the law applies that, as a part of a system of law impartially applied from case to case arising under it, it will have the consequence, in the long run, of furthering the interests of society.

One can say, then, that the judge and the legislator stand in different positions and look in different directions: one to the past, the other to the future. The justification of what the judge does, qua judge, sounds like the retributive view; the justification of what the (ideal) legislator does, qua legislator, sounds like the utilitarian view. Thus both views have a point (this is as it should be since intelligent and sensitive persons have been on both sides of the argument); and one's initial confusion disappears once one sees that these views apply to persons holding different offices with different duties, and situated differently with respect to the system of rules that make up the criminal law.[5]

One might say, however, that the utilitarian view is more fundamental since it applies to a more fundamental office, for the judge carries out the legislator's will so far as he can determine it. Once the legislator decides to have laws and to assign penalties for their violation (as things are there must be both the law and the penalty) an institution is set up which involves a retributive conception of particular cases. It is part of the concept of the criminal law as a system of rules that the application and enforcement of these rules in particular cases should be justifiable by arguments of a retributive character. The decision whether or not to use law rather than some other mechanism of social control, and the decision as to what laws to have and what penalties to assign, may be settled by utilitarian arguments, but if one decides to have laws then one has decided on something whose working in particular cases is retributive in form.[6]

The answer, then, to the confusion engendered by the two views of punishment is quite simple: one distinguishes two offices, that of the judge and that of the legislator, and one distinguishes their different stations with respect to the system of rules which make up the law; and then one notes that the different sorts of considerations which would usually be offered as reasons for what is done under the cover of these offices can be paired off with the competing justifications of punishment. One reconciles the two views by the time-honored device of making them apply to different situations.

But can it really be this simple? Well, this answer allows for the apparent intent of each side. Does a person who advocates the retributive view necessarily advocate, as an *institution,* legal machinery whose essential purpose is to set up and preserve a correspondence between moral turpitude and suffering? Surely not.[7] What retributionists have rightly insisted upon is that no man can be punished unless he is guilty, that is, unless he has broken the law. Their fundamental criticism of the utilitarian account is that, as they interpret it, it sanctions an innocent person's being punished (if one may call it that) for the benefit of society.

On the other hand, utilitarians agree that punishment is to be inflicted only for the violation of law. They regard this much as understood from the concept of punishment itself.[8] The point of the utilitarian account concerns the institution as a system of rules: utilitarianism seeks to limit its use by declaring it justifiable only if it can be shown to foster effectively the good of society. Historically it is a protest against the indiscriminate and ineffective use of the criminal law.[9] It seeks to dissuade us from assigning to penal institutions the improper, if not sacrilegious, task of matching suffering with moral turpitude. Like others, utilitarians want penal institutions designed so that, as far as humanly possible, only those who break the law run afoul of it. They hold that no official should have discretionary power to inflict penalties whenever he thinks it for the benefit of society; for on utilitarian grounds an institution granting such power could not be justified.[10]

The suggested way of reconciling the retributive and the utilitarian justifications of punishment seems to account for what both sides have wanted to say. There are, however, two further questions which arise, and I shall devote the remainder of this section to them.

First, will not a difference of opinion as to the proper criterion of just law make the proposed reconciliation unacceptable to retributionists? Will they not question whether, if the utilitarian principle is used as the criterion, it follows that those who have broken the law are guilty in a way which satisfies their demand that those punished deserve to be punished? To answer this difficulty, suppose that the rules of the criminal law are justified on utilitarian grounds (it is only for laws that meet his criterion that the utilitarian can be held responsible). Then it follows that the actions which the criminal law specifies as offenses are such that, if they were tolerated, terror and alarm would spread in society. Consequently, retributionists can only deny that those who are punished deserve to be punished if they deny that such actions are wrong. This they will not want to do.

The second question is whether utilitarianism doesn't justify too much. One pictures it as an engine of justification which, if consistently adopted, could be used to justify cruel and arbitrary institutions. Retributionists may be supposed to concede that utilitarians intend to reform the law and to make it more humane; that utilitarians do not wish to justify any such thing as punishment of the innocent; and that utilitarians may appeal to the fact that punishment presupposes guilt in the sense that by punishment one understands an institution attaching penalties to the infraction of legal rules, and therefore that it is logically absurd to suppose that utilitarians in justifying *punishment* might also have justified punishment (if we may call it that) of the innocent. The real question, however, is whether the utilitarian, in justifying punishment, hasn't used arguments which commit him to accepting the infliction of suffering on innocent persons if it is for the good of society (whether or not one calls this punishment). More generally, isn't the utilitarian committed in principle to accepting many practices which he, as a morally sensitive person, wouldn't want to accept? Retributionists are inclined to hold that there is no way to stop the utilitarian principle from justifying too much except by adding to it a principle which distributes certain rights to individuals. Then the amended criterion is not the greatest benefit of society simpliciter, but the greatest benefit of society subject to the constraint that no one's rights may be violated. Now while I think that the classical utilitarians proposed a criterion of this more complicated sort, I do not want to argue that point here.[11] What I want to show is that there is *another* way of preventing the utilitarian principle from justifying too much, or at least of making it much less likely to do so: namely, by stating utilitarianism in a way which accounts for the distinction between the justification of an institution and the justification of a particular action falling under it.

I begin by defining the institution of punishment as follows: A person is said to suffer punishment whenever he is legally deprived of some of the normal rights of a citizen on the ground that he has violated a rule of law, the violation having been established by trial according to the due process of law, provided that the deprivation is carried out by the recognized legal authorities of the state, that the rule of law clearly specifies both the offense and the attached penalty, that the courts construe statutes strictly, and that the statute was on the books prior to the time of the offense.[12] This definition specifies what I shall understand by punishment. The question is whether utilitarian arguments may be found to justify institutions widely different from this and such as one would find cruel and arbitrary.

This question is best answered, I think, by taking up a particular accusation. Consider the following from Carritt:

> . . . the utilitarian must hold that we are justified in inflicting pain always and only to prevent worse pain or bring about greater happiness. This, then , is all we need to consider in so-called punishment, which must be purely preventive. But if some kind of very cruel crime becomes common, and none of the criminals can be caught, it might be highly expedient, as an example, to hang an innocent man, if a charge against him could be so framed that he were universally thought guilty; indeed this would only fail to be an ideal instance of utilitarian "punishment" because the victim himself would not have been so likely as a real felon to commit such a crime in the future; in all other respects it would be perfectly deterrent and therefore felicific.[13]

Carritt is trying to show that there are occasions when a utilitarian argument would justify taking an action which would be generally condemned; and thus that utilitarianism justifies too much. But the failure of Carritt's argument lies in the fact that he makes no distinction between the justification of the general system of rules which constitutes penal institutions and the justification of particular applications of these rules to particular cases by the various officials whose job it is to administer them. This becomes perfectly clear when one asks who the "we" are of whom Carritt speaks. Who is this who has a sort of absolute authority on particular occasions to decide that an innocent man shall be "punished" if everyone can be convinced that he is guilty? Is this person the legislator, or the judge, or the body of private citizens, or what? It is utterly crucial to know who is to decide such matters, and by what authority, for all of this must be written into the rules of the institution. Until one knows these things one doesn't know what the institution is whose justification is being challenged; and as the utilitarian principle applies to the institution one doesn't know whether it is justifiable on utilitarian grounds or not.

Once this is understood it is clear what the countermove to Carritt's argument is. One must describe more carefully what the institution is which his example suggests, and then ask oneself whether or not it is likely that having this institution would be for the benefit of society in the long run. One must not content oneself with the vague thought that, when it's a question of this case, it would be a good thing if somebody did something even if an innocent person were to suffer.

Try to imagine, then, an institution (which we may call "telishment") which is such that the officials set up by it have authority to arrange a trial for the condemnation of an innocent man whenever they are of the opinion that doing so would be in the best interests of society. The discretion of officials is limited, however, by the rule that they may not condemn an innocent man to undergo such an ordeal unless there is, at the time, a wave of offenses similar to that with which they charge him and telish him for. We may imagine that the officials having the discretionary authority are the judges of the higher courts in consultation with the chief of police, the minister of justice, and a committee of the legislature.

Once one realizes that one is involved in setting up an *institution*, one sees that the hazards are very great. For example, what check is there on the officials? How is one to tell whether or not their actions are authorized? How is one to limit the risks involved in allowing such systematic deception? How is one to avoid giving anything short of complete discretion to the authorities to telish anyone they like? In addition to these considerations, it is obvious that people will come to have a very different attitude towards their penal system when telishment is adjoined to it. They will be uncertain as to whether a convicted man has been punished or telished. They will wonder whether or not they should feel sorry for him. They will wonder whether the same fate won't at any time fall on them. If one pictures how such an institution would actually work, and the enormous risks involved in it, it seems clear that it would serve no useful purpose. A utilitarian justification for this institution is most unlikely.

It happens in general that as one drops off the defining features of punishment one ends up with an institution whose utilitarian justification is highly doubtful. One reason for this is that punishment works like a kind of price system: by altering the prices one has to pay for the performance of actions it supplies a motive for avoiding some actions and doing others. The defining features are essential if punishment is to work in this way; so that an institution which lacks these features, e.g., an institution which is set up to "punish" the innocent, is likely to have about as much point as a price system (if one may call it that) where the prices of things change at random from day to day and one learns the price of something after one has agreed to buy it.[14]

If one is careful to apply the utilitarian principle to the institution which is to authorize particular actions, then there is less danger of its justifying too much. Carritt's example gains plausibility by its indefiniteness and by its concentration on the particular case. His argument will only hold if it can be shown that there are utilitarian arguments which justify an institution whose publicly ascertainable offices and powers are such as to permit officials to exercise that kind of discretion in particular cases. But the requirement of having to build the arbitrary features of the particular decision into the institutional practice makes the justification much less likely to go through.

NOTES

1. I use the word "practice" throughout as a sort of technical term meaning any form of activity specified by a system of rules which defines offices, roles, moves, penalties, defenses, and so on, and which gives the activity its structure. As examples one may think of games and rituals, trials and parliaments.
2. The distinction is central to Hume's discussion of justice in *A Treatise of Human Nature,* bk. III, pt. 11, esp. secs. 2–4. It is clearly stated by John Austin in the second lecture of *Lectures on Jurisprudence* (4th ed.; London, 1873), I, 116ff. (1st ed., 1832). Also it may be argued that J. S. Mill took it for granted in *Utilitarianism;* on this point cf. J. O. Urmson, "The Interpretation of the Moral Philosophy of J. S. Mill," *Philosophical Quarterly,* Vol. III (1953). In addition to the arguments given by Urmson there are several clear statements of the distinction in *A System of Logic* (8th ed.; London, 1872), bk. VI, ch. xii pars. 2, 3, 7. The distinction is fundamental to J. D. Mabbott's important paper, "Punishment," *Mind,* n.s., vol. XLVIII (April, 1939). [And] the distinction has been stated with particular emphasis by S. E. Toulmin in *The Place of Reason in Ethics* (Cambridge 1950), see esp. ch. xi, where it plays a major part in his account of moral reasoning. Toulmin doesn't explain the basis of the distinction, nor how one might overlook its importance, as I try to in this paper, and in my review of his book (*Philosophical Review,* Vol. LX [October, 1951]), as some of my criticisms show, I failed to understand the force of it. See also H. D. Aiken, "The Levels of Moral Discourse," *Ethics,* vol. LXII (1952), A. M. Quinton, "Punishment," *Analysis,* vol. XIV (June 1954), and P. H. Nowell-Smith, *Ethics* (London, 1954), pp. 236–39, 271–73.
3. On the concept of explication see the author's paper *Philosophical Review,* Vol. LX (April 1951).
4. While this paper was being revised, Quinton's appeared; *supra* note 2. There are several respects in which my remarks are similar to his. Yet as I consider some further questions and rely on somewhat different arguments, I have retained the discussion of punishment and promises together as two test cases for utilitarianism.
5. Note the fact that different sorts of arguments are suited to different offices. One way of taking the differences between ethical theories is to regard them as accounts of the reasons expected in different offices.
6. In this connection see Mabbott, *op. cit.,* pp. 163–64.
7. On this point see Sir David Ross, *The Right and the Good* (Oxford 1930), pp. 57–60.
8. See Hobbes's definition of punishment in *Leviathan,* ch. xxviii; and Bentham's definition in *The Principle of Morals and Legislation,* ch. xii, par. 36, ch. xv, par. 28, and in *The Rationale of Punishment* (London 1830), bk. I, ch. i. They could agree with Bradley that: "Punishment is punishment only when it is deserved. We pay the penalty, because we owe it, and for no other reason; and if punishment is inflicted for any other reason whatever than because it is merited by wrong, it is a gross immorality, a crying injustice, an abominable crime, and not what it pretends to be." *Ethical Studies* (2nd ed.; Oxford 1927), 26–27. Certainly by definition it isn't what it pretends to be. The innocent can only be punished by mistake; deliberate "punishment" of the innocent necessarily involves fraud.
9. Cf. Leon Radzinowicz, *A History of English Criminal Law: The Movement for Reform* 1750–1833 (London 1948), esp. ch. xi on Bentham.
10. Bentham discusses how corresponding to a punitory provision of a criminal law there is another provision which stands to it as an antagonist and which needs a name as much as the punitory. He calls it, as one might expect, the *anaetiosostic,* and of it he says: "The punishment of guilt is the object of the former one: the preservation of innocence that of the latter." In the same connection he asserts that it is never thought fit to give the judge the option of deciding whether a thief (that is, a person whom he believes to be a thief, for the judge's belief is what the question must always turn upon) should hang or not, and so the law writes the provision: "The judge shall not cause a thief to be hanged unless he have been duly convicted and sentenced in course of law" (*The Limits of Jurisprudence Defined,* ed. C. W. Everett [New York 1945], pp. 238–39).
11. By the "classical utilitarians" I understand Hobbes, Hume, Bentham, J. S. Mill, and Sidgwick.

12. All these features of punishment are mentioned by Hobbes; cf. *Leviathan*, ch. xxviii.
13. *Ethical and Political Thinking* (Oxford 1947), p. 65.
14. The analogy with the price system suggests an answer to the question how utilitarian considerations insure that punishment is proportional to the offense. It is interesting to note that Sir David Ross, after making the distinction between justifying a penal law and justifying a particular application of it, and after stating that utilitarian considerations have a large place in determining the former, still holds back from accepting the utilitarian justification of punishment on the grounds that justice requires that punishment be proportional to the offense, and that utilitarianism is unable to account for this. Cf. *The Right and the Good* (Oxford: Clarendon Press, 1930), pp. 61–62. I do not claim that utilitarianism can account for this requirement as Sir David might wish, but it happens, nevertheless, that if utilitarian considerations are followed penalties will be proportional to offenses in this sense: the order of offenses according to seriousness can be paired off with the order of penalties according to severity. Also the absolute level of penalties will be as low as possible. This follows from the assumption that people are rational (i.e., that they are able to take into account the "prices" the state puts on actions), the utilitarian rule that a penal system should provide a motive for preferring the less serious offense, and the principle that punishment as such is an evil. All this was carefully worked out by Bentham in *The Principles of Morals and Legislation*, chs. xiii–xv.

The Paradox of Punishment

ALAN H. GOLDMAN

Goldman argues that it is not possible to design a system of punishment in which its social benefits outweigh its social costs (the minimal utilitarian constraint) and the degree of punishment inflicted upon an offender is proportional to the seriousness of his or her offense (the minimal retributivist constraint). This is because no feasible system of justice can achieve a conviction rate high enough to make its social costs worthwhile unless it threatens offenders with sanctions whose severity is sufficient to compensate for the infrequency with which they are applied, that is, with sanctions that would be disproportionately severe. Hence "mixed" views such as those of Rawls are unsatisfactory.

The paradox of punishment is that a penal institution somewhat similar to that in use in our society seems from a moral point of view to be both required and unjustified. Usually such a statement would be a confused way of saying that the practice is a necessary evil, hence it *is* justified, all things considered. But in the case of punishment this reduction does not appear so simple.

The paradox results from the intuitive plausibility of two theses: one associated with a retributivist point of view and another associated with a utilitarian justification of the institution of punishment. Some philosophers have thought that objections to these two theories of punishment could be overcome by making both retributive and utilitarian criteria necessary for the justification of punishment. Utilitarian criteria could be used to justify the institution, and retributive to justify specific acts within it; or utilitarian to justify legislative decisions regarding punishment, and retributive to justify enforcement decisions.[1] (These distinctions in levels of justification are matters of degree, since when justifying an institution, one must consider acts within it; and when justifying legislative decisions, one must consider their applications in the judicial

From Goldman, Alan; "The Paradox of Punishment," in *Philosophy and Public Affairs* 9:1, pp. 42–43, 45–51, 54–56, 58.

system.) The compromise positions, according to which punishment must be both deserved and beneficial, have considerable plausibility. But if I am right about the two theses to be assessed here, these criteria may be ultimately inconsistent. If so, then the mixed theory of justification, initially attractive, is at least as problematic as its rivals.

Let us consider the retributivist thesis first, since it is likely to be considered the more controversial. The thesis ultimately concerns the amount of punishment justifiable in particular cases. If we are to justify punishment of particular wrongdoers or lawbreakers, that is, if we are to show why *they* cannot legitimately complain of injustice done to them by the imposition of punishment, we must argue that they have forfeited those rights of which we are depriving them. We must say that by violating the rights of others in their criminal activities, they have lost or forfeited their legitimate demands that others honor all their formerly held rights. It seems clear that this is the only way we could convince criminals themselves that they are not being treated unjustly in being punished.[2] Appeal to the idea that the community benefits from a prisoner's role as an example for others would not be sufficient, in view of the severity of the impositions. Persons normally have rights not to be severely imposed upon in order to benefit others. If we are justifiably to ignore these rights, it could only be when they have been forfeited or alienated. And the only way in which this can be done involuntarily is by violation of the rights of others. Since having rights generally entails having duties to honor the same rights of others, it is plausible that when these duties are not fulfilled, the rights cease to exist. . . .

While violating the rights of others involves forfeiting rights oneself,[3] it is clear that violating specific rights of others does not entail losing *all* one's own rights. If *A* steals fifty dollars from *B*, this does not give *B* or anyone else, official or not, the right to impose all and any conceivable harms upon *A* in return. Nor does *A* thereby become available for any use to which the community then wants to put him. Just as an innocent person can complain if forced to make severe sacrifices for the benefit of others, so a guilty person may claim that violation of any rights beyond those forfeited or alienated in order to benefit others is an injustice. And if we ask which rights are forfeited in violating rights of others, it is plausible to answer just those rights that one violates (or an equivalent set). One continues to enjoy rights only as long as one respects those rights in others: violation constitutes forfeiture. But one retains those rights which one has continued to respect in others. Since deprivation of those particular rights violated is often impracticable, we are justified in depriving a wrongdoer of some equivalent set, or in inflicting harm equivalent to that which would be suffered in losing those same rights (for example, rights to fifty dollars of one's own and not to suffer the trauma of being a victim of theft). Equivalence here is to be measured in terms of some average or normal preference scale, much like the one used by the utilitarian when comparing and equating utilities and disutilities.

It would be difficult for a wrongdoer to complain of injustice when we treat him in a way equivalent to the way in which he treated his victim, provided that we also have a good (consequentialist) reason for imposing upon him in that way. If he cannot demonstrate a morally relevant difference between himself and his victim, then he cannot claim that he must enjoy all those rights that he was willing to violate. But if we deprive him not only of these or equivalent rights, but of ones far more important, whose loss results in far greater harm, then we begin to look like serious wrongdoers ourselves in multiplying violations of rights. It is at this point that the claim that two wrongs do not make a right begins to apply. A claim of injustice or victimization by the community made by the criminal begins to have merit, although in our anger at his wrongdoing, we are often unwilling to hear it. If a person can be said to deserve only so much punishment and no more, then any excess appears to be as objectionable as an equivalent harm imposed upon an innocent person. In fact the stronger thesis concerning the degree of justified imposition can be viewed as the source of the weaker thesis that the innocent should not be punished at all. The latter is implied as a special case of the former. Philosophers have been far more concerned with the thesis as applied to innocents than with its more general application, perhaps because of a supposed difficulty in judging when punishment is equivalent to crime. When we think in terms of forfeiting those rights one violates, or an equivalent set, there is no special difficulty here. One right or set of rights is equivalent to another for these purposes when an average preference scale registers indifference between the loss of either the one or the other. There are problems facing construction of the proper preference scale—for example, the loss of fifty dollars to which one has a right will mean more to a poor person than to a rich person—but these are problems facing any moral theory concerned with distribution. We also need to adjust our concept of deserved punishment to focus upon intention rather than actual harm, and to allow for excuses. I leave these complications to pursue our main topic.

To this retributivist premise might be raised an objection similar to one sometimes made against utilitarian theories of punishment. It might be claimed that our argument limiting the severity of justified punishments errs in calculating harm to the guilty and that to the innocent on the same scale. But, an objector might hold, the guilty do not deserve equal consideration or equal treatment. What they have forfeited in harming others and in violating others' rights is precisely the right to have their own interests considered equally. Society therefore has the right to impose greater harm upon wrongdoers than that done to innocent victims, if it finds it necessary or beneficial to do so. This counterargument rests upon a confusion. Treatment of wrongdoers equal to or the same as rightful treatment of the innocent would demand no harm or deprivation of rights at all. We are not, as this argument suggests, counting the interests of wrongdoers equally with those of the innocent, since we impose harm upon the former but not upon the latter. The prior wrongdoing of the guilty enables us to harm them without treating them unjustly, but only to the extent of treating them as they treated their victims. If we inflict greater harm than this, we become, like them, violators of rights not forfeited and hence wrongdoers ourselves. Their wrongdoing does not give us the right to do equal wrong, or any wrong, ourselves. It must be remembered also that punishment justly imposed is distinct from compensation owed to victims. Justice may well require wrongdoers to be liable for restoring their victims as far as possible to the level of well-being that they would have attained had no injustice occurred (compensation is a matter of restoring a balance or returning to a just status quo, while punishment is not). It requires *in addition* that they be made to suffer harm equivalent to that originally caused to the victims.

To bring out the paradox in the justification of punishment, we need to combine this premise regarding the limits of justly imposed punishments with one at least equally plausible from the utilitarian theory. It states that a political institution involving the administration of punishment by state officials can be justified only in terms of the goal of reducing crime and the harms caused by crime to a tolerable level. The state is not concerned to ensure that all its members receive their just positive and negative deserts in some abstract moral sense. It is concerned neither to proportion burdens to benefits in general, nor even to protect all moral rights. Certainly that someone deserves to be harmed in some way, or that he could not complain of injustice at being harmed in some way, does not in itself entail that the state ought to take it upon itself to harm him. At least one other condition is necessary for the state to be justified in adopting rules calling for such official imposition. The wrongs in question must be so grave that the social costs of official interference do not exceed the benefits in terms of reducing these wrongs. There are, for example, moral wrongs whose detection is so unsure that their official prohibition would involve costs too great to be worthwhile: betrayals of friendship, deceptions in love affairs, and so on. The social benefits from an institution of punishment must outweigh the costs, including the harms imposed, especially when these harms are undeserved (occasional punishment of the innocent and excessive punishments of the guilty). That our penal institution does deter crime is the primary source of its justification and social necessity. The state must seek to deter violations of its distributive rules if it is serious about their adoption, and it must seek to deter serious attacks upon persons; the sanctions which attach to these violations exist primarily for this deterrent effect.

Combining this justification for a social penal institution with the limit upon just impositions so that no one may be deprived of rights he has not forfeited, we derive the mixed theory of punishment advocated by Ross and Hart, and endorsed by other philosophers in recent years.[4] This theory views the social goal of punishment as deterrence, and yet recognizes that we are entitled to pursue this goal only when we restrict deprivation of rights to those forfeited through crime or wrongdoing. In actuality proponents of this theory usually state the limitation only as prohibiting punishment of the innocent. But, as argued above, in terms of the broader principle that no one is to be deprived of rights not forfeited, excessive punishment of the guilty is on a par with punishment of the innocent. Thus for officially imposed punishment to be justified, the person punished must have forfeited those rights of which he is deprived, and the state must be entitled to inflict the harm by appeal to the social benefit of deterrence. (This appeal may involve the need to have a rule calling for punishment of a particular type of wrongdoing and the need to apply the rule consistently.)

The problem is that while the mixed theory can avoid punishment of the innocent, it is doubtful that it can avoid excessive punishment of the guilty if it is to have sufficient deterrent effect to make the social costs worthwhile. In our society the chances of apprehension and punishment for almost every class of crime are well under fifty percent. Given these odds a person pursuing what he considers his maximum prospective benefit may not be deterred by the threat of an imposition of punishment equivalent to the violation of the rights of the potential victim. If threats of sanctions are not sufficient to deter such people, they would probably fail to reduce crime to a tolerable enough level to make the social costs of the penal institution worthwhile. On the other hand, in order to deter crime at all effectively, given reasonable assumptions about police efficiency at bearable costs, sanctions must be threatened and applied which go far beyond the equivalence relation held to be just. The limitation stipulated in our first premise then, in effect, annuls just and effective pursuit of the social goal stipulated in our second premise. And yet pursuit of this goal seems morally required and impossible without effective punitive threats. Hence the paradox, or, more strictly, the dilemma.

Caught in this dilemma, our society does not limit punishment to deprivation of rights forfeited, that is, rights of others which have been violated by the criminal. Especially in regard to crimes against property, punishments by imprisonment are far more severe, on the average, than the harm caused to victims of these crimes. Probably because such punishment is administered by officials of the state, cloaked in appropriate ritual and vested with authority, most of us systematically ignore its relative severity. If, however, we imagine an apolitical context, in which there is money and property, but no penal institution, would theft of several thousand dollars justify the victim's taking the perpetrator and locking him away in some small room for five to ten years? In our society such deprivation of freedom is a small portion of the harms likely to be suffered in prison as punishment for a felonious crime against property. The disproportion between violated or deprived rights of the victims and those of the criminals in these crimes is obvious.

It might be argued that we could lower penalties to make them equal to harms from crimes and yet still have a deterrent effect, since for most persons, the threat of official sanctions simply adds to internal moral sanctions against harmful or criminal acts. Furthermore, for people who enjoy a decent standard of living without turning to criminal activity, it will not be worth even minimal risk of public exposure to attempt to increase acquisitions by criminal means. For such persons, who are reasonably well-off and have much to lose if apprehended, the moral disapproval of the community might be felt as a more serious harm than an actual prison sentence or fine. The problem with these claims is that they do not apply to the typical criminal in our society, or to the potential criminal whom threats of punishment are intended to deter. We may assume the potential criminal has a fairly desperate economic situation, and therefore, at most, a neutral attitude toward risk. Thus suggestions to the community to sharply lower penalties for property crimes would be taken about as seriously as is epistemological skepticism outside philosophy classrooms and articles. Even suggestions to eliminate the more horrid aspects of prison life that are not officially part of the penalty of imprisonment are met with resistance. I am convinced that punishments, when administered at all, tend to be far more severe than harms suffered in those particular crimes against property for which these punishments are imposed. Yet, while this strikes me as seriously unjust, it does not appear that we can afford at present to lessen the deterrent force of sanctions for potential criminals to the point at which they stand to lose nothing by attempting further crimes. At stake is not only increased harm to innocent victims but our ability to put into effect those distributive rules we consider just. (Assuming that we do consider some such set of rules just, the problem that I am defining will be real.)

Others have noted conflicts between utilitarian criteria for proper amounts of punishment and what is called the retributive proportionality principle.[5] This states that more serious crimes should draw more severe penalties. It fails to match utilitarian criteria in application. This is because utilitarian criteria call for a deterrent threat sufficient to bring crimes of a given class down to a tolerable level; and deterrent threat varies not only with the severity of the punishment threatened but also with such factors as the comparative probability of apprehension and conviction for various types of crime, and the degree to which various crimes are normally preceded by unemotional prudential calculations. Crimes which are more difficult to prosecute call for more severe threats, while threats are wasted for crimes of passion. But these variables are irrelevant to moral rights violated and harm suffered by the victims of the crimes, the sole variables relevant according to retributive criteria of proportionality. The conflict I have noted above is, however, more fundamental, since the absolute limitation upon justified punishment in terms of equivalence to loss of rights violated is more basic than the proportionality principle. It is clear that we require absolute as well as proportionate limits, since without absolute limits all punishments might be too severe or the spread between them might be too great, even if they are arranged in correct order of severity.[6] It is plausible again, therefore, to view the proportionality principle as a particular implication of the absolute limits for various punishments, much as we viewed the prohibition against punishing the innocent. The absolute equivalence limitation, as we may call it, is the fundamental retributive principle; and it is this principle which appears to be fundamentally in conflict with the utilitarian goal of adequate deterrence.[7]

It might be thought that in the case of the guilty there is a relevant difference which we have not yet considered. Publicizing the penalties attached to each class of crime warns people in advance of the potential consequences of criminal activities. In this way they are able to control their own futures. If they choose to engage in criminal activity, they in a real sense "bring the punishment upon themselves." This is the sense to be made of the claim that criminals have chosen their penalties through their behavior, in contrast to the sense considered earlier: the Kantian claim that wrongdoers somehow will to be punished. That criminals have been warned may be thought to constitute an important difference between their situation, even when excessively punished, and that of innocent victims of crime. When penalties are made public, they can be avoided completely by those who choose not to take the risk of incurring them; whereas innocent victims of crime are helpless to avoid the harms imposed upon them by criminals. This again might be construed as legitimate grounds for society's choosing to protect potential victims at the expense of criminals, who could have avoided any punishment whatsoever if they had chosen to act within the law. It might even be said to create a kind of desert for the punishment imposed, much as an advance announcement of a prize or reward creates desert for those who fulfill the conditions stipulated. If positive desert can be created simply through the creation of a rule setting forth conditions for a reward, perhaps this is an element of negative desert as well, if in the latter case one can easily avoid fulfilling the conditions set forth in the rule. In any case, harm to innocent victims may be worse or more objectionable than harm to the guilty, since crimes against the innocent are unexpected and often unavoidable. Hence we can justifiably choose to protect the innocent at the additional expense of the guilty.

Again, however, this argument is flawed and cannot create the distinction we seek. While advance notice of penalties attached to various crimes may be a necessary condition for just imposition of punishment, it is never a sufficient condition justifying the imposition of any punishment that society chooses to inflict, no matter how severe. The case of rules creating positive entitlements to rewards is different. If someone has some benefit to give away, he normally can give it to whomever he chooses without wronging others. He also can create whatever frivolous rules or contests he likes for determining who is to receive his gift or prize. Those who satisfy the criteria in the rules, or those who win the contests, then become entitled to the benefits. (They will not *deserve* the benefits, however, if their qualifying acts are independently morally objectionable.) But in the case of imposing harm, one cannot justify doing so merely by giving adequate warning. My warning you that I will assault you if you say anything I believe to be false does nothing to justify my assaulting you, even if you could avoid it by saying nothing. A society's giving warning that it will cut off the hands of thieves does not justify its doing so. In general, having warned someone that he would be treated unjustly is no justification for then doing so, even if, once warned, he could have avoided the unjust treatment by acting in some way other than the way he acted. The harm imposed must be independently justified. Once we have determined the proper amount of punishment for wrongdoing (I have argued that it is determined by social utility up to the equivalence limitation), adequate warning is normally a further necessary condition for just imposition. That criminals could have avoided punishment by having acted differently is again one reason why we are justified in punishing them at all. It does not justify excessive punishment. As for harm causing less suffering when it is expected, I would think that often the opposite is the case. Even when awaiting expected punishment is not as bad as actually suffering it, it certainly adds to the suffering of being punished. It is true that the resentment against undeserved harm felt by victims of crime adds to their suffering; but then undeserved excessive punishment of the guilty will be resented also. Thus none of the points of the previous paragraph justify excessive punishment of the guilty. Since giving warning to criminals does not reduce the harm imposed upon them to less than the harm suffered by victims, on average in single cases, it does not give us grounds for imposing excessive punishment to prevent crimes.

There are, of course, ways of increasing deterrent effects of punishments without increasing their severity. Given the variables affecting deterrence mentioned earlier, one can, for example, increase the force of threats by improving chances of detection. One can add personnel to police forces and remove procedural constraints upon detection, apprehension, and conviction efforts. But there are social costs, not the least of which include possible abuses, convictions of innocent people, and invasions of privacy, which place limits upon the justified pursuit of this course. It has been suggested also in a recent article that penalties ought to be imposed more consistently and automatically, that inconsistent application of punishment resulting from extensive discretionary powers at all levels of enforcement significantly lowers effective deterrence.[8] It is not clear, first, that even fully automatic arrest, prosecution, and sentencing would enable us to reduce penalties to fit within the equivalence limitation and still have effective deterrence against property crimes. Second, the elimination of discretion on the part of enforcement officials undoubtedly would result in more unjust punishments in many cases, punishments which ought not to be imposed at all in the particular circumstances of particular cases. Third, there is the short-term problem of overcrowded courts and prisons, and this would have to be overcome before this suggestion could be at all capable of implementation.

The final, most fundamental, and most promising alternative would be (not surprisingly) to attack the social and economic causes of crime by reducing the great inequalities in our society. I have nothing to say against this, except that the means to accomplish it short of authoritarian political mechanisms have eluded us. But even were we to progressively achieve the egalitarian program and approach a just economic and social distribution, I believe that the moral problem defined here would remain, though perhaps in less acute form. Many would still be tempted to crime, and deterrence seemingly would still be required. It would still be true that genuinely just punishment would not suffice to deter avoidable harm to innocent members of the community, or to enforce genuinely just distributive rules.

NOTES

1. For classic statements of these mixed positions, see John Rawls, "Two Concepts of Rules," *Philosophical Review* 64, no. 1 (1955): 3–32; H. L. A. Hart, "Prolegomenon to the Principles of Punishment," in *Punishment and Responsibility* (Oxford: Clarendon Press, 1968), pp. 1–13.
2. Compare Herbert Morris, "Persons and Punishment," *The Monist* 52, no. 4 (1968): 475–501.
3. Violation of the rights of others may be only a necessary, but not a sufficient, condition for forfeiture if there are certain inalienable rights. The concept of forfeiture is best explained here in terms of a contract model of rights. See my "Rights, Utilities and Contracts," *Canadian Journal of Philosophy* 3, supplement (1977): 121–135.
4. See, for example, Michael Lessnoff, "Two Justifications of Punishment," *The Philosophical Quarterly* 21, no. 83 (1971): 141–48.
5. Michael Clark, "The Moral Gradation of Punishment," *The Philosophical Quarterly* 21, no. 83 (1971): 132–40; Alan Wertheimer, "Should the Punishment Fit the Crime?" *Social Theory & Practice* 3, no. 4 (1975): 403–423.
6. This is admitted by Wertheimer, "Should the Punishment Fit the Crime?", p. 410. But he fails to say more on this subject, again probably because he views it as impossible to calculate an equivalence between punishment and crime. See also John Kleinig, *Punishment and Desert* (The Hague: Martinus Nijhoff, 1973), pp. 118–119.
7. The one philosopher who notes a possible conflict here is Robert Nozick, in *Anarchy, State, and Utopia* (New York: Basic Books, 1974), pp. 59–63. Nozick does not defend both premises, however.
8. Alan Wertheimer, "Deterrence and Retribution," *Ethics* 86, no. 3 (1976): 181–199.

Punishment and Societal Defense

PHILLIP MONTAGUE

Montague claims that a system of punishment incorporating the strengths (but not the weaknesses) of both retributivist and utilitarian theories may be justified by appeal to a very general moral principle which also underlies the relatively uncontroversial right to self-defense. On his view, punishment is most usefully conceived of as a matter of *societal* defense.

Questions concerning the justifiability of legal punishment are commonly divided into two types: those concerned with the morality of individual acts of punishment, and those concerned with the morality of legal punishment as a general practice. I shall focus here on questions of the second type and will sketch an approach to answering them based on the concept of societal defense. On this approach, the morality of adopting systems of legal punishment depends, at least in part, on the conditions under which societies are justified in establishing practices aimed at protecting their members from being wrongfully harmed.[1]

Standard Defense Situations

In order to understand the moral status of defensive measures taken by societies, it will be helpful first to examine the morality of defensive actions performed by individuals.[2]

Let us refer to standard defense situations as those in which wrongful harm will culpably be done to some individual (henceforth known as Victim) by another (called Aggressor) unless the latter is himself harmed. For the sake of simplicity, we can focus for now on standard defense situations in which lives are at stake—situations in which Victim will be killed unless Aggressor is.

Standard defense situations have three noteworthy characteristics:

1. In such situations, harm is unavoidable from Victim's standpoint. Assuming that he is in a position to save himself, he must choose how to distribute this unavoidable harm: On one distribution, he will lose his life; on another distribution, Aggressor will lose his. And, of course, any Third Party who can defend Victim is faced with a similar choice.
2. Victim has a *right* to defend himself, and Third Party is required (at least ceteris paribus) to do so. Victim's right is not simply the absence of a duty to forbear. Rather, it is a right in the strong sense which implies a duty on the part of all others to refrain from interfering with him if he chooses to defend himself against Aggressor.
3. Victim's right and Third Party's obligation are unaffected by the number of Aggressors who jointly threaten Victim's life, and who must all be killed to save Victim.

Standard defense situations are, of course, not the only ones in which individuals must decide how to distribute harm* which they cannot prevent. For many of these situations, however, there are no analogs of the second and third conditions. Consider innocent threat cases, for example. These are cases in which one person will die if another does not, and where neither is an aggressor and both are the innocent victims of circumstances beyond their control.[3] In such cases, a person may be *permitted* to choose in his or her own favor, but that person surely has no *right* to do so. Similarly, a third party might be permitted to save one person at the other's expense, but there is nothing in the nature of innocent threat cases that dictates which individual should be favored. Moreover, in innocent threat cases numbers are relevant in a way they are not in standard defense situations. If a choice must be made between one innocent life and many, then this fact must certainly be taken into account when attempting to determine which choice is morally correct.

A more controversial class of cases involves innocent aggressors. We might, for example, have a case like the following:

> *A* suffers from a serious mental illness which causes him to believe that he is constantly the object of wrongful aggression on the part of others. He attacks *B* in the mistaken and totally irrational conviction that *B* will murder him if

From Phillip Montague, "Punishment and Societal Defense," (as appeared in *Criminal Justice Ethics*, Vol. 2, No. 1, [Winter/Spring, 1983] pp. 30–36). Reprinted by permission of *The Institute for Criminal Justice Ethics*, 899 Tenth Avenue, New York, NY 10019.

*The letters *DH* will be used in this paper to denote "distribution of harm" (Editor's note).

he does not. The only way *B*'s life can be saved is by killing *A*.[4]

There are those who would claim that *B* has a *right* to defend himself, and hence that others are required to refrain from interfering with any attempt he might make to do so. I doubt that this is true, however. If A is in fact *innocent*, then I see no reason why *B* should be favored over *A*—why a third party who is in a position to protect *A* from *B*'s defensive measures should be required to refrain from doing so. To insist that *B does* have a right to defend himself against *A*'s attack is to imply that innocent aggressor cases differ morally from innocent threat cases by virtue of the fact that aggression is involved in the former but not in the latter. It strikes me as unreasonable to regard the presence or absence of aggression as singly making this kind of moral difference.

The morally significant features of standard defense situations become apparent when we recognize that these situations can be subsumed under a broader class of cases satisfying the following conditions:

(i) some individual *x* can escape being harmed if and only if some other individual *y* is himself harmed;
(ii) *z* (who may be identical to *x*) is in a position to determine which of the two individuals will be harmed;
(iii) it is *y*'s fault that he and *x* are in a situation in which one of them will be harmed.

In these situations, *z* must decide how to distribute harm which is unavoidable from his standpoint. It seems clear that if *z* is identical to *x* (and if certain other things are equal) he has a right to protect himself at *y*'s expense; and if *z* is different from *x*, then he is obligated (again ceteris paribus) to choose in *x*'s favor. Furthermore, if a choice must be made between saving *x* and saving several others who are jointly to blame for the danger facing them all, then *x* still has a right to choose in his own favor, and third parties are obligated (ceteris paribus) to do so. Consider the following case, for example:

C is an experienced Alpine guide and *D* a novice climber. As a result of culpable negligence on *C*'s part, both are trapped on an exposed ledge without adequate clothing and with no shelter. A storm is approaching and both will die if not rescued before it arrives. *E* has a helicopter, but it can carry only one passenger, and there is only time for one trip to the ledge before the storm hits.

This case satisfies conditions (i), (ii), and (iii) (with *z* different from *x*), and it seems clear that *E* has an obligation to save *D* rather than *C*. Moreover, if we modify the case so that *D* is trapped on the ledge with *several* guides who are jointly at fault for their predicament; and if we assume that *D* is very heavy and the guides very light so that *E*'s helicopter can carry either *D* or the guides; then we must still conclude that *E*'s obligation is to save *D* rather than the others.

It should be readily apparent, I think, that standard defense situations are special instances of the cases defined by (i), (ii), and (iii). In the former situations it is Aggressor's fault that there is harm to be distributed—harm which is unavoidable from Victim's (and perhaps Third Party's) standpoint. Because the existence of harm is Aggressor's fault, it is quite appropriate—and appropriate as a matter of justice—that the harm should befall him rather than some innocent person. Implicit in this last claim is a principle which applies to standard defense situations and to the broader class of cases described above which defense situations instantiate:

DH: When unavoidable harm is being distributed among a group of individuals, and when some members of the group are to blame for the predicament of all, then justice requires (ceteris paribus) that the harm be distributed among those who are blameworthy.

Three major ceteris paribus conditions for DH are worth mentioning at this point. The first is a proportionality condition according to which the distribution of unavoidable harm among those who are to blame for the existence of that harm must be proportional to the harm that would be suffered by innocent persons under a different distribution. It is important to recognize that this condition concerns individual rather than collective harm. If a choice must be made between distributing harm to one person or to several, and if the several are jointly to blame for the existence of that harm; then, as was noted above in connection with standard defense situations and our example of the trapped climbers, the innocent person must be favored even if the *total* harm resulting from such a distribution is much greater than that which would result from a distribution favoring those who are blameworthy. But according to the proportionality condition, the harm suffered by each blameworthy individual under a given distribution must be proportional to that which would be suffered by an innocent person under a different distribution. Returning to our example of the trapped climbers, the proportionality condition would prevent DH from being used to justify doing major harm to *C* (or to any number of collectively blameworthy guides) in order to save *D* from suffering minor harm. If the only harm possible in a given situation is the loss of life (something we assumed when discussing standard defense situations), then the proportionality condition is automatically satisfied, and questions about the quantity of harm done do not arise unless *innocent* persons are affected differently by different distributions.

The proportionality condition places a maximum on the amount of unavoidable harm that may be done to individuals according to DH. There is also a minimization condition according to which those to blame for the existence of unavoidable harm may not themselves be harmed more than is necessary in order to protect innocent persons. Turning again to our mountain-climbing example, DH with this minimization condition cannot be used to justify a distribution of harm which results in *C*'s death if another distribution is possible which saves *D*'s life without killing *C*.

The third ceteris paribus condition for DH that I shall mention here concerns the harmful side effects for innocent persons that may result from distributions of harm aimed at protecting other innocent persons. The need for this condition can be illustrated by cases of the following sort: *x* is in a position to distribute harm that is unavoidable from his standpoint either to *y* or to *z*; it is *y*'s fault that either he or *z* must be harmed; if *x* distributes the harm to *y*, then some other innocent person will be harmed; the latter will be left untouched by a distribution which harms *z* rather than *y*. For example, we might have a defense case in which Third Party can defend Victim by harming Aggressor, but if he does, then some innocent bystander will also be harmed; while if Third Party does not act in Victim's defense, the bystander will not be harmed. Under these conditions, DH does not straightforwardly imply that Third Party should defend Victim.

Societal Defense

Let us now consider how the above remarks pertain to matters of *societal* defense. Here we shall be concerned with the conditions under which societies are justified in establishing institutions and practices aimed at defending some of their members against the wrongfully aggressive acts of others.

Imagine a society *S* which contains a subclass *S'* of individuals who will wrongfully harm innocent members of *S* if not directly prevented from doing so. Assume for now that *S* can protect its innocent members only by establishing a police force with powers of direct intervention in cases where those in *S'* attempt to harm innocent persons; and assume also that in some cases the police must harm those bent on wrongdoing in order to protect their intended victims. If we focus on the choice facing S as a society, then we have a situation exactly analogous to the cases of individual self- and other-defense described earlier. A certain amount of harm is unavoidable from the standpoint of S as a whole, but it can be distributed by S in different ways. Moreover, certain members of S (i.e., those in S') are to blame for the fact that there is unavoidable harm to be distributed. Thus, according to DH, justice requires (ceteris paribus) S to distribute the harm among those in S', and hence to establish a police force.

Let us now modify our example somewhat. Suppose that those in S' cannot be *prevented* from harming innocent persons no matter how large and diligent a police force S establishes, but that they can be deterred from doing so by credible threats to their own well-being. We will also assume that S can pose such threats in only one way—that is, by establishing and effectively implementing a system of legal punishment. Under these conditions harm is again unavoidable from the standpoint of S as a whole,[5] though S does have some control over how this harm is distributed. A distribution involving the use of punishment will favor innocent members of S over those in S', while a distribution not involving punishment will have the opposite result. And since those in S' are to blame for the fact that there is unavoidable harm to be distributed, DH requires S (ceteris paribus) to establish a system of legal punishment.

As is indicated here, this last condition follows only if other things are equal—that is, only if the proportionality, minimization, and side-effect conditions for DH are satisfied. These conditions must be met whether harm is being distributed by individuals among other individuals or by groups of individuals among other groups. Thus, for example, if we think of S as wishing to distribute unavoidable harm among groups of its members by establishing and implementing a system of legal punishment, then S must select a system the implementation of which results in harm to those in S' that is proportional to the wrongful harm that will be done by members of S' if the system is not implemented. In addition, S must select a system which results in the minimum harm to those in S' that is necessary to protect innocent persons, and must also be concerned with the harm that might be distributed to some innocent persons as side effects of protecting others.

If we regard S as at least approximating a real society, then the kinds of wrongful harm which those in S' do or wish to do might well include such widely varied activities as burglary, assault, and murder. If so, then the system of punishment selected by S must reflect these differences if the proportionality condition of DH is to be satisfied. Furthermore, if it is possible to deter those in S' from engaging in some category of wrongdoing by correlating with that class of wrongdoings a punishment *less* than proportionality permits, then the minimization condition of DH requires that the lesser punishment be adopted. And if implementing the punishments prescribed by a system of punishment for given offenses will have harmful side effects for innocent persons, then this must be taken into account when assessing the moral acceptability of that system. In this way, limits are placed on the kinds of punishments that may be correlated with different kinds of wrongdoing in a system of punishment. A system which stipulates the death penalty for burglary almost certainly violates the proportionality requirement; a system according to which premeditated murder is punishable by death may satisfy the proportionality requirement, but it may fail to meet the minimization requirement. And a system of punishment which prescribes the death penalty for certain offenses may have unacceptably harmful side effects for innocent persons. Whether a society fails to meet any of these requirements when it establishes a particular system of punishment depends on what conditions obtain in that society.

Among other things implicit in these remarks is the idea that punishments must fit crimes. This idea is commonly associated with retributivism, but it can now be seen to arise from basic and very general considerations of distributive justice having nothing to do with "getting even" or with correcting moral imbalances in the universe. Punishments must fit crimes in the same way and for the same reasons that any distribution of unavoidable harm satisfying the conditions mentioned in DH must meet proportionality requirements; and retributivist considerations clearly have no general bearing on these distributions. This is not to minimize the difficulties that can arise when attempting to answer questions about proportionality in particular cases. I do think, however, that there is a tendency to exaggerate these difficulties when the relationship between punishments and offenses is at issue.

In addition to the three general ceteris paribus conditions just discussed which qualify DH no matter how it is applied, there are conditions which are relevant primarily to the use of DH in the area of legal punishment. Two such conditions are worth some brief discussion here.

Let us continue to suppose that S cannot prevent those in S' from harming innocent members of S, but that S can deter the former from performing their wrongful acts by establishing a system of legal punishment. Although it follows (given our assumptions about S') that S is required (ceteris paribus) to establish a system of punishment, not every system will be morally acceptable. For example, S would not be justified in adopting a system which prescribes death by slow torture for certain offenses, no matter how grave those offenses might be. That is, for the system of punishment adopted by S to be morally acceptable, it must be humane. Moreover, if we think of systems of punishment as containing sets of rules which specify certain acts as offenses (ordered according to their gravity), and which correlate with these offenses certain punishments (ordered by severity), then for a system to be morally acceptable, it must satisfy the familiar requirement of justice that relevantly similar cases be treated similarly and relevantly dissimilar cases be treated dissimilarly.[6] This requirement would clearly be violated by a system which prescribes the death penalty for both murder and petty theft, or which prescribes twenty years in jail for burglary and six months in jail for embezzlement. Although I will not take the time to do so here, it is clear enough, I think, that by specifying in more detail the characteristics of systems of punishment (in the area of procedure, for example), we could generate additional restrictions on the use of DH in justifying the establishment of such systems.

A Comparison with Other Justifications of Punishment

The use of DH in justifying legal punishment satisfies at least one intuition underlying retributivism in requiring that systems of punishment satisfy proportionality conditions. It is also tempting to link DH with retributivism by claiming that on both views it is somehow *fitting* that wrongdoers suffer, simply by virtue of their having engaged in wrongdoing. Indeed, we may wish to express this relationship in terms that are even more closely associated with retributivism: We might say that one whose fault it is that either he or some innocent person will be harmed receives his just deserts when the harm is distributed to him rather than to the innocent person. The relationship between this use of *desert* and the retributivist's is rather tenuous and at any rate unclear, but it may provide some basis for regarding DH as containing a retributivist element.

These similarities between the two positions do not go very far, however. I think H. L. A. Hart is correct in maintaining that, according to retributivists, "the justification for punishing . . . is that the return of suffering for moral evil voluntarily done, is itself just or morally good."[7] If we accept Hart's characterization, however, then we must recognize that retributivists have a problem. For even if it is good that wrongdoers suffer, there is no reason to suppose that societies should promote this good by engaging in the practice of legal punishment. In order to maintain the retributivist position we must either take as given and absolutely fundamental the requirement that societies establish practices which inflict suffering on wrongdoers; or we must say that societies should establish practices aimed at the realization of all goods; or we must regard societies as required to seek after certain goods, and we must then provide plausible criteria according to which one of the goods at which societies must aim is that which results when wrongdoers suffer.

Only the third of these alternatives strikes me as reasonable; and while it might be accepted by a retributivist, doing so will almost certainly require adjustments in his position. These adjustments might well lead to a principle like DH, which *does* provide a basis for the societal requirements to engage in legal punishment under certain conditions, but which generates this requirement from considerations that are ultimately independent of retributivism. In particular, it is not possible by the use of DH (as it is by appealing to strictly retributivist considerations) to justify establishing the practice of legal punishment when doing so has no value as an instrument of societal defense and serves only to insure that wrongdoers suffer.

Because it places considerable emphasis on forward-looking considerations, DH has a certain affinity with utilitarianism. These two approaches to justifying legal punishment differ in several important respects, however. For one thing, it is unlikely that utilitarianism can comfortably accommodate criteria for determining the moral acceptability of systems of punishment—criteria such as those embodied in the requirement that relevantly similar cases be treated similarly and relevantly dissimilar cases be treated dissimilarly. Presumably, utilitarians will claim that systems of punishment which do not meet such requirements have low social utility relevant to those which do; or they might maintain that the requirements are somehow contained in the very notion of a system of punishment, and are therefore met as a matter of necessity by all such systems.[8] Although I shall not argue the point here, neither of these responses strikes me as particularly plausible.

Whatever utilitarians say about the moral acceptability of systems of punishment must obviously be consistent with their basic contention that societies are justified in establishing systems of punishment only if doing so is less harmful than alternative courses of action. Assuming that the harm referred to here is *collective* harm, the implications of utilitarianism for particular cases can differ significantly from those of DH. It might happen, for example, that if society S engages in legal punishment, its members will collectively suffer more harm than they will if no system of punishment is established. Presumably, a utilitarian must then conclude that S should not engage in legal punishment. Depending on how the harm in question is distributed, however, DH might yield a very different result. In particular, if, by establishing the practice of legal punishment, S distributes unavoidable harm among those whose fault it is that harm is unavoidable, then S should engage ceteris paribus in legal punishment even if, as a society, S suffers more collective harm than it would without legal punishment.[9]

This same point can be made in somewhat different terms.

We surely want societies to distribute burdens as well as benefits in a just manner. Utilitarians will judge these distributions (and the practices within which they occur) by their results. This idea has, of course, been criticized by a host of philosophies—but almost always in connection with distributions of benefits. It is claimed that certain kinds of non-utilitarian considerations are relevant to the justice of distributing benefits among members of societies—that, for example, an individual's contribution to producing the benefits should be taken into account. DH can be viewed as implying that certain non-utilitarian considerations are relevant to the just distribution of *burdens*—that, for example, one's blameworthiness for the existence of a situation can be relevant to whether he is justly burdened in that situation.

I realize that utilitarians have attempted in various ways to incorporate certain kinds of backward-looking considerations into their theories. What utilitarians cannot consistently maintain, however, is that such considerations are morally significant in and of themselves. Thus, for example, the fact that someone is at fault for the existence of a dangerous situation cannot be regarded by a utilitarian as relevant *in itself* to whether harm should be distributed to that individual rather than to someone else. The relevance of such considerations must be indirect, by way of their relation to appropriate forward-looking considerations, something which is certainly not the case when appeals are made to DH.

NOTES

1. Some reasons for thinking that neither retributivism nor utilitarianism is capable of dealing adequately with the concept of societal defense are implicit in the final section of this paper. I make no attempt here to argue explicitly for this point, though I think it would not be difficult to produce arguments that are quite compelling.
2. A particularly valuable treatment of individual self-defense is provided by Judith Thomson in "Self-defense and Rights," Findley Lecture, 1976 (Lawrence, KA: University of Kansas Press, 1977). I have also discussed the subject further in "Self-defense and Choosing Between Lives," *Philosophical Studies,* 40 (1981), pp. 207–219.
3. The now-familiar "runaway trolley" cases are examples of innocent threat cases. See Judith Thomson, "Killing, Letting-die, and the Trolley Problem," *The Monist* 59 (1976), pp. 204–217.
4. For an intriguing discussion of these cases, see George P. Fletcher, "Proportionality and the Psychotic Aggressor: A Vignette in Comparative Criminal Theory," *Israeli Law Review* 6 (1973), pp. 367–390.
5. We can assume that some members of *S* are bound to be punished if a system of punishment is established and implemented.
6. I have argued elsewhere that this requirement applies quite generally to what might be called "desert systems," which include systems of compensation, grading, and reward, as well as systems of punishment. See my "Comparative and Non-comparative Justice," *The Philosophical Quarterly* 30 (1980), pp. 130–140.
7. H. L. A. Hart, *Punishment and Responsibility* (Oxford: Oxford University Press, 1968), pp. 231. As it is being used here, "retributivism" refers to what is sometimes called "maximal" or "strong" retributivism.
8. John Rawls seems to have something of the latter sort in mind when he makes this statement: "Now, that similar particular cases, as described by a practice, should be treated similarly as they arise, is part of the very concept of a practice; it is involved in the notion of an activity in accordance with rules." ("Justice as Fairness," *The Philosophical Review,* 67 (1958), pp. 164 194.
9. This point about societal defense appears to have been missed by a number of writers. For example, Hugo Adam Bedau claims that there is no reasonable way to compare the value of innocent lives with that of guilty lives, and concludes from this that decisions regarding the morality of capital punishment "will probably have to be made on some basis other than societal defense." ("Capital Punishment" in Tom Regan (ed.), *Matters of Life and Death* (New York: Random House, 1980), p. 173).

Study Questions

1. How does Rawls deal with the objection that utilitarianism would permit punishing the innocent?
2. Is Goldman successful in showing that the retributivist insistence on proportionality is "fundamentally in conflict with the utilitarian goal of adequate deterrence"? How might Rawls respond to Goldman's criticisms?
3. Is Montague successful in showing that punishment can be justified on the basis of the very principle which justifies ordinary cases of self-defense?
4. In what respects does Montague believe that his theory is an improvement over traditional utilitarian and retributivist theories? Do you agree with him? Why or why not?

D Rehabilitation and Education

The Moral Education Theory of Punishment

JEAN HAMPTON

Hampton defends the view that the proper objective of punishment is the moral education of the offender (and of potential offenders). In her view, punishment should communicate a moral message aimed at educating the offender (and the rest of society) about the wrongness of what he has done with the hope of persuading him to mend his ways and to freely adopt correct moral values. She argues that the educative function of punishment can provide a complete and comprehensive justification of punishment that is superior to that provided by either retributivist or utilitarian theories.

> We ought not to repay injustice with injustice or to do harm to any man, no matter what we may have suffered from him.
>
> Plato, *Crito,* X, 49

There are few social practices more time-honored or more widely accepted throughout the world than the practice of punishing wrongdoers. Yet if one were to listen to philosophers discussing this practice, one would think punishment impossible to justify and difficult even to understand. However, I do not believe that one should conclude that punishment as a practice is morally unjustifiable or fundamentally irrational. Instead I want to explore the promise of another theory of punishment which incorporates certain elements of the deterrence, retributivist, and rehabilitation views, but whose justification for punishment and whose formula for determining what punishment a wrongdoer deserves are distinctive and importantly different from the reasons and formulas characterizing the traditional rival theories.

This view, which I call the moral education theory of punishment, is not new. There is good reason to believe Plato and Hegel accepted something like it,[1] and more recently, Herbert Morris and Robert Nozick have maintained that the moral education which punishment effects is at least part of punishment's justification.[2] I want to go further, however, and suggest that by reflecting on the educative character of punishment we can provide a full and complete justification for it. Hence my discussion of the moral education theory in this paper is meant to de-

Hampton, Jean; "The Moral Education Theory of Punishment," *Philosophy and Public Affairs* 13:3, pp. 208–38.

I have many people to thank for their help in developing the ideas in this paper, among them: Warren Quinn, Thomas Hill, Judith DeCew, Marilyn Adams, Robert Adams, Richard Healey, Christopher Morris, Norman Dahl, Julie Heath, George Fletcher, Robert Gerstein, David Dolinko, and especially Herbert Morris. I also want to thank the Editors of *Philosophy & Public Affairs* for their incisive comments, and members of my seminar on punishment at UCLA in the Spring of 1983 for their lively and helpful discussions of the theory. Portions of the article were also read, among other places, at the 1982 Pacific Division APA Meeting, at C.S.U. Northridge, and at the University of Rajasthan, Jaipur, India.

velop it as a complete justification of punishment and to distinguish it from its traditional rivals. Most of my discussion will focus on the theory's application to the state's punishment of criminal offenders, but I will also be looking at the theory's implications for punishment within other societal institutions, most notably the family.

I will not, however, be able to give an adequate development of the theory in this paper. It is too complex, and too closely connected to many difficult issues, including the nature of law, the foundation of ethical reasoning, and the way human beings develop ethical concepts. Hence what I shall do is simply to *introduce* the theory, sketching its outlines in the first half, and suggesting what seem to be certain advantages and drawbacks of the view in the second half. Much more work needs to be done before anyone is in a position to embrace the view wholeheartedly, hence I won't even attempt to argue in any detailed way here that it is superior to the three traditional views. But I hope my discussion will show that this theory is promising, and merits considerably more discussion and study by the larger intellectual community.

I. The Justification

Philosophers who write about punishment spend most of their time worrying about whether the *state*'s punishment of criminals is justifiable, so let us begin with that particular issue.

When does punishment by the state take place? The answer to this question seems simple: the state carries out punishment upon a person when he or she has broken a *law*. Yet the fact that the state's punishment always follows the transgression of a law is surely neither coincidental nor irrelevant to the understanding and justification of this practice. What is the nature of law? This is a thorny problem which has vexed philosophers for hundreds of years. For the purposes of this article, however, let us agree with Hart that there are (at least) two kinds of law, those which are power-conferring rules, for example, rules which specify how to make a contract or a will, and those which are "rules of obligation."[3] We are concerned with the latter kind of rule, and philosophers and legal theorists have generally analyzed the structure of this sort of law as "orders backed by threats" made by the state.

What is the subject matter of these orders? I will contend (consistent with a positivist account of law) that the subject matter *ought* to be (although it might not always be) drawn either from ethical imperatives, of the form "don't steal," or "don't murder," or else from imperatives made necessary for moral reasons, for example, "drive on the right"—so that the safety of others on the road is insured, or "advertise your university job in the professional journals"—so that blacks and women will not be denied an opportunity to secure the job.[4] The state makes these two kinds of commands not only to define a minimal set of duties which a human being in that community must follow in his or her dealings with others, but also to designate actions which, when followed by all members of the society, will solve various problems of conflict and coordination.[5]

And the threat? What role does it play? In the end, this is the central question for which we must have an adequate answer if we are to construct a viable theory of punishment.

The threat, which specifies the infliction of pain if the imperative is not obeyed, gives people a nonmoral incentive, that is, the avoidance of pain, to refrain from the prohibited action. The state hopes this incentive will block a person's performance of the immoral action whenever the ethical incentive fails to do so. But insofar as the threat given in the law is designed to play this kind of "deterring" role, carrying out the threat, that is, punishing someone when he or she has broken the law, is, at least in part, a way of "making good" on the threat. The threat will only deter the disobedience of the state's orders if people believe there is a good chance the pain will be inflicted upon them after they commit the crime. But if the state punishes in order to make good on its threats, then the deterrence of future crime cannot be wholly irrelevant to the justification of punishment. And anyone, including Kant, who analyzes laws as orders backed by threats must recognize that fact.[6]

Moreover, I believe we must accept the deterrence theorist's contention that the justification of punishment is connected with the fact that it is a necessary tool for preventing future crime and promoting the public's well-being. Consider standard justifications of the state: philosophers from Plato to Kant to Hart have argued that because a community of people cannot tolerate violent and destructive behavior in its midst, it is justified in establishing a state which will coercively interfere in people's lives for publicly announced and agreed-upon reasons so that an unacceptable level of violence and harm can be prevented. Whereas we normally think the state has to respect its citizens' choices about how to live, certain choices, for example, choices to rape, to murder, or to steal, cannot be respected by a community which is committed to preserving and pursuing the well-being of its members. So when the state annexes punishment to these damaging activities, it says that such activities are not a viable option for anyone in that community.

But to say that the state's punishment is needed to prevent crime is not to commit oneself to the deterrence justification of punishment—it all depends on what one takes prevention to entail. And, as Hegel says, if we aimed to prevent wrongdoing only by deterring its commission, we would be treating human beings in the same way that we treat dogs.[7] Consider the kind of lesson an animal learns when, in an effort to leave a pasture, it runs up against an electrified fence. It experiences pain and is conditioned, after a series of encounters with the fence, to stay away from it and thus remain in the pasture. A human being in the same pasture will get the same message and learn the same lesson—"if you want to avoid pain, don't try to transgress the boundary marked by this fence." But, unlike the animal in the pasture, a human being will also be able to reflect on the reasons for that fence's being there, to theorize about *why* there is this barrier to his freedom.

Punishments are like electrified fences. At the very least they teach a person, via pain, that there is a "barrier" to the action she wants to do, and so, at the very least, they aim to deter. But because punishment "fences" are marking *moral* boundaries, the pain which these "fences" administer (or threaten to administer) conveys a larger message to beings who are able to reflect on the reasons for these barriers' existence: they convey that there is a barrier to these actions *because* they are morally wrong. Thus, according to the moral education theory, punishment is not intended as a way of conditioning a human being to do what society wants her to do (in the way that an animal is conditioned by an electrified fence to stay within a pasture); rather, the theory maintains that punishment is intended as a way of teaching the wrongdoer that the action she did (or wants to do) is forbidden because it is morally wrong and should not be done for that reason. The theory also regards that lesson as public, and thus as directed to the rest of society. When the state makes its criminal law and its enforcement practices known, it conveys an educative message not only to the convicted criminal but also to anyone else in the society who might be tempted to do what she did.

Comparing punishments to electrical fences helps to make clear how a certain kind of deterrent message is built into the larger moral point which punishment aims to convey. If one wants someone to understand that an offense is immoral, at the very least one has to convey to him or her that it is prohibited—that it ought not to occur. Pain is the way to convey that message. The pain says "Don't!" and gives the wrongdoer a reason for not performing the action again; an animal shocked by a fence gets the same kind of message and the same kind of incentive. But the state also wants to use the pain of punishment to get the human wrongdoer to reflect on the moral reasons for that barrier's existence, so that he will make the decision to reject the prohibited action for *moral* reasons, rather than for the self-interested reason of avoiding pain.

If those who are punished (or who watch the punishment take place) reject the moral message implicit in the punishment, at least they will learn from it that there is a barrier to the actions they committed (or are tempted to commit). Insofar as they choose to respond to their punishment (or the punishment of others) merely as a threat, it can keep them within moral boundaries in the same way that fences keep animals in a pasture. This deterrent effect of punishment is certainly welcome by the state whose role is to protect its citizens, and which has erected a "punishment barrier" to certain kinds of actions precisely because those actions will seriously harm its citizens. But on the moral education view, it is incorrect to regard simple deterrence as the aim of punishment; rather, to state it succinctly, the view maintains that punishment is justified as a way to prevent wrongdoing insofar as it can teach both wrongdoers and the public at large the moral reasons for *choosing* not to perform an offense.

I said at the outset that one of the reasons any punishment theory is complicated is that it involves one in taking stands on many difficult ethical and legal issues. And it should be quite clear already that particular positions on the nature of morality and human freedom are presupposed by the moral education view which distinguish the theory from its traditional rivals. Given that the goal of punishment, whether carried out by the state on criminals or by parents on children, is the offender's (as well as other potential offenders') realization of an action's wrongness, the moral education view naturally assumes that there is a fact of the matter about what is right and what is wrong. That is, it naturally rests on ethical objectivism. Perhaps certain sophisticated subjectivists could adapt the theory to accommodate their ontological commitments (punishment, they might say, teaches what society defines as right and wrong). But such an accommodation, in my view, does real damage to the theory, which purports to explain punishment as a way of conveying when an action *is* wrong. Given that the theory holds that punishment is a way of teaching ethical *knowledge,* if there is no such thing, the practice seems highly suspect.

The theory also takes a strong stand on human freedom. It rests on the idea that we can act freely in a way that animals cannot. If we were only like animals, attempts at punishment would affect us in the way that electrical fences affect animals—they would deter us, nothing more. But this theory assumes that we are autonomous, that we can choose and be held accountable for our actions. Thus it holds that punishments must attempt to do more than simply deter us from performing certain offenses; they must also, on this view, attempt to provide us with moral reasons for our *choosing* not to perform these actions. Only creatures who are free to determine their lives according to their moral values can choose not to do an action because it is wrong. Insofar as the moral education view justifies punishment as a way of promoting that moral choice, it assumes that punishment is (and ought only to be) inflicted on beings who are free in this sense.[8] It might be that human beings who have lost their autonomy and who have broken a law can be justifiably treated in a painful way so as to deter them (even as we would deter dangerous animals) from behaving similarly in the future, but this theory would not call such treatment punishment.

Thus one distinction between the moral education view and the deterrence justification of punishment is that on the moral education view, the state is not concerned to use pain coercively so as to progressively eliminate certain types of behavior; rather, it is concerned to educate its citizens morally so that they choose not to engage in this behavior. Moreover, there is another important difference between the two views. On the deterrence view, the infliction of pain on certain individuals is justified as a way of promoting a larger social end. But critics of the deterrence view have pointed out that this is just to say that it is all right to *use* certain individuals to achieve a desirable social goal. The moral education theory, however, does not sanction the use of a criminal for social purposes; on the contrary, it attempts to justify punishment as a way to benefit the person who will experience it, a way of helping him to gain moral knowledge if he chooses to listen. Of course other desirable social goals will be achieved through his punishment, goals which include the education of the larger community about the immorality of the offense, but none of these ends is to be achieved at the expense of the criminal. Instead the moral good which punishment attempts to accomplish within the wrongdoer makes it something which is done *for* him, not *to* him.

There are also sharp differences between the moral education view and various rehabilitative theories of criminal "treatment." An advocate of the moral education view does not perceive punishment as a way of treating a "sick" person for a mental disease, but rather as a way of sending a moral message to a person who has acted immorally and who is to be held responsible for her actions.[9] And whereas both theorists are concerned with the good which punishment can do for the wrongdoer, they disagree about what that good is, one defining it as moral growth, the other as the wrongdoer's acceptance of society's mores and her successful operation in the community. In addition, as we shall discuss in Section II, they disagree about what methods to use to achieve these different ends.

Some readers might wonder how close the moral education view is to the old retribution theory. Indeed references in the literature to a view of this type frequently characterize it as a variant of retribution.[10] Nonetheless, there are sharp and important differences between the two views, which we will explore in more detail in Section II. Suffice to say now that whereas retributivism understands punishment as performing the rather metaphysical task of "negating the wrong" and "reasserting the right," the moral education theorist argues that there is a concrete moral goal which punishment should be designed to accomplish, and that goal includes the benefiting of the criminal himself. The state, as it punishes the lawbreaker, is trying to promote his moral personality; it realizes that "[h]is soul is in jeopardy as his victim's is not."[11] Thus, it punishes him as a way of communicating a moral message to him, which he can accept or not, as he chooses.

Certain retributivists have also been very attracted to the idea that punishment is a kind of speech act. For example, Robert Nozick in his book *Philosophical Explanations* has provided a nice nine-point analysis of punishment which presents it as a kind of communication and which fits the account of meaning put forward by H. P. Grice.[12] Yet if punishment is a way of (morally) speaking with a wrongdoer, then why doesn't this show that it is fundamentally justified *as a communication,* in virtue of what it is trying to communicate, rather than, in Nozick's view, as some kind of symbolic "linkage" of the criminal with "correct values"?[13]

Indeed, I would maintain that regarding punishment as a kind of moral communication is intuitively very natural and attractive. Consider, for example, what we say when we punish others: a father who punishes his child explains that he does so in order that the child "learn his lesson"; someone who has been physically harmed by another demands punishment "so that she will understand what she did to me"; a judge recently told a well-known user of cocaine that he was receiving a stiff sentence because his "matter-of-fact dabbling in cocaine . . . tells the whole world it is all right to use it."[14] These kinds of remarks accompanying our punishment efforts suggest that our principal concern as we punish is to get the wrongdoer to stop doing the immoral action by communicating to her that her offense was immoral. And the last remark by the judge to the cocaine user shows that when the state punishes it is important that these communications be public, so that other members of society will hear the same moral message. Even people who seem to be seeking revenge on wrongdoers behave in ways which show that they too want to make a moral point not only to the wrongdoer, but to anyone else who will listen. The hero seeking revenge in a Western movie, for example, never simply shoots the bad guy in the back when he finds him—he always confronts the bad guy first (usually in the presence of other people) and tells him *why* he is about to die. Indeed, the movie would be unsatisfying if he didn't make that communication. And surely, the hero's desire to explain his actions is linked with his desire to convey to the bad guy and to others in society that the bad guy had "done him wrong."[15]

Moreover, if one understands punishment as a moral message aimed at educating both the wrongdoer and the rest of society about the immorality of the offense, one has a powerful explanation (at least as powerful as the one offered by retributivism) of why victims so badly want their assailants punished. If the point of punishment is to convey to the criminal (and others) that the criminal *wronged* the victim, then punishment is implicitly recognizing the victim's plight, and honoring the moral claims of that individual. Punishment affirms as a *fact* that the victim has been wronged, and as a *fact* that he is owed a certain kind of treatment from others. Hence, on this view, it is natural for the victim to demand punishment because it is a way for the community to restore his moral status after it has been damaged by his assailant.

Thus far, I have concentrated on how the state's punishment of criminals can be justified as an attempt at moral education. But I want to contend that punishment efforts by *any* institution or individual should be perceived as efforts at moral education, although the nature and extensiveness of the legitimate educative roles of these institutions and individuals might differ sharply. For example, I believe it is quite clear that parents want to make such a moral communication through their punishments.[16] Suppose for example, that a mother sees her daughter hitting another child. After stepping in to stop this violent behavior, the mother will reflect on what she can do to prevent its reoccurrence[sic]. If the mother chooses to try to do this by punishing her daughter, one of the things she "says" through the punishment is, "if you do this again, you will experience the same unpleasantness," and this message is directed at any other children in the family, as well as at this daughter. Hence, one of the things the mother is doing is introducing the incentive of avoiding pain into the children's "calculations" about how to act if and when they are tempted in the future to hurt each other. If a genuine concern for each other's well-being is absent from the children's minds, at least this incentive (as well as fear of losing her approval) might be strong enough to prevent them from hurting each other in the future.[17] But clearly the mother is also trying to get her children to appreciate that there is a *moral* reason for prohibiting this action. The punishment is supposed to convey the message, "Don't do this action again because it is *wrong;* love and not hatred or unwarranted violence is what one should display towards one another." The ultimate goal of the punishment is not merely to deter the child from performing the bad action in the future, but to deter her *by convincing her* (as well as the other children) to renounce the action because it is wrong. And the older and more ethically mature the child becomes, the less the parent will need to resort to punishment to make her moral point, and the more other techniques, like moral suasion, discussion, or debate, will be appropriate.

However, although both state and parental punishment should, according to this theory, be understood as efforts at moral communication and education, the theory does not regard the two kinds of punishment as exactly the same. While punishment should always be regarded as moral education, the "character" of that education can vary enormously, depending in particular on the nature of the institution or individual charged with inflicting the punishment. For example, a parent who is responsible for the full maturation and moral development of her child is naturally thought to be entitled to punish her children for many more offenses and in very different ways, than the children's schoolteacher, or the neighbor down the street. We also think of a university as having punishment rights over its students, but we certainly reject the idea that this sort of institution acts *in loco parentis* towards its students generally. Hence, the theory would not have us understand the punishment role of all institutions, and particularly governments, as the *same* as punishment by parents.[18] None of us, I believe, thinks that the state's role is to teach its citizens the entire content of morality—a role we might characterize as "moral paternalism." A variety of considerations are important in limiting the mode and extent of the state's punishment.

Nonetheless, some readers still might think the moral education theory implies a paternalistic theory of the state—after all, doesn't it maintain that the state can interfere in people's lives for their own good? But when such philosophers as John Stuart Mill have rejected paternalism, what they have rejected is a certain position on what should be law; specifically, they have rejected the state's passing any law which would restrict what an individual can do to *himself* (as opposed to what he can do to another). They have not objected to the idea that when the state justifiably interferes in someone's life *after* he has broken a law (which prohibited harm to another), it should intend good rather than evil towards the criminal. Now it is possible they might call this theory paternalistic anyway, not because it takes any stand on what should be law, but because it views the state's punishment as interference in his life plans without his consent for his own good. But why should paternalism in this sense be offensive? It would be strange indeed if philosophers insisted that the state should only try to prevent further harm to the community by actively intending to harm, or use, or at least be indifferent to, the people it punishes!

But, Mill might complain, if you are willing to allow the state to morally educate those who harm others, why not allow it to morally educate those who harm themselves? This is a good question, but one the moral education theory cannot answer. Indeed, answering it is the same as answering the question: What ought to be made law? Or, alternatively, what is the appropriate area for legislation? Though central to political theory, these questions are ones to which the moral education theory can give no answer, for while the theory maintains that punishment of a certain sort should follow the transgression of a law, it is no part of the theory to say *what* ethical reasons warrant the imposition of a law. Indeed, one of the advantages of the theory is that one can adopt it no matter what position one occupies on the political spectrum.

But, critics might insist, isn't this theory arguing that the state should be in the business of deciding and enforcing morality, overriding the autonomous moral decisions of its citizens? Yes, that is exactly the theory's point, the state *is* in that business in a very limited way. Imagine a murderer saying: "You, the state, have no right to tell me that my murder of this man is wrong," or a rapist protesting: "Who is the state to tell me that my rape of this woman is immoral?" These statements sound absurd, because we believe not merely that such actions are wrong, but that they are also heinous and morally appalling. The state is justified in punishing rapists and murderers because their choices about what to do betray a serious inability to make decisions about immoral and moral actions, which has resulted in substantial harm to some members of that community. And while some readers might find it offensive to contemplate the state presuming to morally educate anyone but serious felons, is this not exactly the kind of sentiment behind the libertarians' call for extensive constraints on the state's role and power?

Moreover, I wonder whether, by calling this theory paternalistic, one might not be irritated more by the thought of being governed than by the thought of what this particular theory says being governed involves. Yet, unless one is prepared to be an anarchist, one must admit that being governed is necessary as long as we, as human beings, are prone to immoral acts. We do not outgrow cruelty, or meanness, or the egoistic disregard for others when we reach the age of majority. On this view, the state exists because even adults need to be governed, although not in the way that children require governing by their parents. (Indeed, these ideas suggested by the theory form a germ of an argument against anarchism, which I can only pursue in another place.)

But, critics might insist, it is this theory's view of what governing involves that is objectionable. Who and what is the state, that it can presume to teach us a moral lesson? Yet I regard this question not as posing a challenge to the moral education view itself, but rather as posing a challenge *by* that theory to any existing state. Not only does the theory offer a partial explanation of the state's role, but it also proposes a view of what the state *ought* to be like if its punishment activities have any legitimacy. For example, insofar as the state should be morally educating when it punishes, this theory implies that the state's laws should be arrived at by reflection on what is right or wrong, and not on what is in the best interest of a particular class, or race, or sex. That this is not always true of the laws of our society is an indictment of our state, and punishments inflicted as a way of enforcing these biased laws cannot be justified. Moreover, if we accept the idea that the state is supposed to morally educate its citizens, it is natural to argue that all of its citizens should participate either directly or through representatives in the legislative branch of that institution in order to control and supervise its moral enforcement so that the resulting laws reflect the moral consensus of the community rather than the views of one class. Hence the moral education view can underlie an argument for the democratic structure of a state.

Finally, I would contend that the moral education theory illuminates better than any of its theoretical rivals the strategy of those who are civilly disobedient. Martin Luther King, Jr. wrote that it is critical for anyone who wants to be civilly disobedient to accept the penalty for his or her lawbreaking, not only to express "the very highest respect for law" but also "to arouse the conscience of the community over its injustice."[19] The moral education theory explains how both these objectives are achieved. The civilly disobedient person, when she accepts the penalty for law-breaking, is respecting the state's right to punish transgressors of its laws, but she is also forcing the state to commit itself, in full view of the rest of society, to the idea that her actions show she needs moral education. And when that person is protesting, as Gandhi or King did, offensive and unjust laws, she knows the state's punishment will appear morally outrageous and will arouse the conscience of anyone sensitive to the claims of justice. Therefore, the civilly disobedient person is, on this view, using the idea of what the state and its laws ought to be like if its punishment activities have legitimacy in order to effect moral improvement in the legal system.

II. Questions and Criticisms

Although I will not fully develop and defend the moral education view in this article, I now want to put some flesh on the skeletal presentation of the view just given by considering some questions which spring naturally to mind as one reflects on the theory.

1. What Is This Theory's Punishment Formula?

Punishment formulas always follow directly from punishment justifications. If punishment is justified as a deterrent, then it follows from that justification that particular punishments should be structured so as to deter. But if punishment is justified as a way of morally educating the wrongdoer and the rest of society about the immorality of the act, then it follows that one should punish in ways that promote this two-part goal. But how do we go about structuring punishments that morally educate? And would this way of determining punishments yield intuitively more just punishments than those yielded by the formulas of the traditional theories?

One reason these formulas of all the traditional theories have been attacked as unjust is that all of them fail to incorporate an acceptable upper bound on what punishments can be legitimately inflicted on an offender. Consider that, once the deterrence theorist has defined his deterrence goal, any punishment that will achieve this goal is justified, including the most brutalizing. Similarly, the retributivist's *lex talionis* punishment formula (dictating that punishments are to be somehow equal to the crime) would seem to recommend, for example, torturing the torturer, murdering *all* murderers, and such recommendations cast serious doubt on the formula's moral adequacy.[20] Even the rehabilitation theory does not place strict limits on the kinds of "treatments" which can legitimately be given to offenders. If the psychiatric "experts" decide that powerful drugs, shock treatments, lobotomies or other similar medical procedures are legitimate and necessary treatments of certain criminals, why shouldn't they be used? The only upper bound on the treatments inherent in this theory derives from the consciences of psychiatrists and their consensus about what constitutes "reasonable" treatment, and many contend that history has shown such an upper bound to be far too high.[21]

The moral education theory, however, does seem to have the resources to generate a reasonable upper limit on how much punishment the state can legitimately administer. Because part of the goal of punishment is to educate the criminal, this theory insists that as he is educated, his autonomy must be respected. The moral education theorist does not want "education" confused with "conditioning." Shock treatments or lobotomies that would damage or destroy the criminal's freedom to choose are not appropriate educative techniques. On this view the goal of punishment is not to destroy the criminal's freedom of choice, but to persuade him to use his freedom in a way consistent with the freedom of others. Thus, any punishment that would damage the autonomy of the criminal is ruled out by this theory.

In addition, it is important to remember that, on this view, punishments should be designed to convey to the criminal and to the rest of society the idea that the criminal's act was wrong. And it seems difficult if not impossible for the state to convey this message if it is carrying out cruel and disfiguring punishments such as torture or maiming. When the state climbs into the moral gutter with the criminal in this way it cannot credibly convey either to the criminal or to the public its moral message that human life must always be respected and preserved, and such actions can even undercut its justification for existing. Note that both of these considerations indicate this theory rules out execution as punishment.[22] (Of course, the moral education theory says nothing about whether the execution of criminals might be justified not as punishment but as a method of "legitimate elimination" of criminals who are judged to have lost all of their essential humanity, making them wild beasts of prey on a community that must, to survive, destroy them. Whether such a justification of criminal execution can be morally tolerable is something I do not want to explore here.)

But, the reader might wonder, how can inflicting *any* pain upon a criminal be morally educational? And why isn't the infliction of mild sorts of pains and deprivations also climbing into the moral gutter with the criminal? The moral education theorist must provide an explanation of why certain sorts of painful experiences (whose infliction on others we would normally condemn) may legitimately be inflicted in order to facilitate moral growth. But is such an explanation possible? And even if it is, would the infliction of pain always be the right way to send a moral message? If a criminal's psychological make-up is such that pain would not reform him, whereas "inflicting" a pleasurable experience would produce this reform, are we therefore justified only in giving him that pleasurable experience? Retributivists like Robert Nozick think the answer to this last question is yes, and thus reject the view as an adequate justification of punishment by itself.[23]

All three of these worries would be allayed if the moral education theorist could show that only the infliction of pain of a certain sort following a wrongdoing is necessarily connected with the promotion of the goal of moral education. In order to establish this necessary connection between certain sorts of painful experiences and moral growth, the moral education theorist needs an account of what moral concepts are, and an account of how human beings come to acquire them (that is, what moral education is). I cannot even attempt to propose, much less develop, answers to these central ethical issues here. But I will try to offer reasons for thinking that painful experiences of a particular sort would seem to be necessary for the communication of a certain kind of moral message.

It is useful to start our discussion by getting a good understanding of what actions count as punishment. First, if we see punishment from the offender's standpoint, we appreciate that it involves the loss of her freedom. This is obviously true when one is locked up in a penitentiary, but it is also true when, for example, parents stop their child's allowance (money that had previously been defined as hers is withheld—whether she likes it or not) or when they force her to experience a spanking or a lecture. I would argue that this loss of freedom is why (autonomous) human beings so dislike punishment. Second, whereas it is very natural to characterize punishment as involving pain or other unpleasant consequences, the infliction of what we intuitively want to call punishment might involve the wrongdoer in performing actions which one would not normally describe as painful or unpleasant. For example, a doctor who cheated the Medicare system and who is sentenced to compulsory weekend service in a state-supported clinic would not be undergoing what one would normally describe as a painful or unpleasant experience (he isn't being incarcerated, whipped, fined). Nonetheless, insofar as some of his free time is being taken away from him, the state is depriving him of his freedom to carry out his own plans and to pursue the satisfaction of his own interests. In this case, the state is clearly punishing an offender, but it sounds distorted to say that it is inflicting pain on him. Thus we need a phrase to describe punishment which will capture better than "infliction of pain" all of the treatments which we intuitively want to call punishment. For this purpose I propose the phrase "disruption of the freedom to pursue the satisfaction of one's desires," a phrase which is suitably general and which fits a wide variety of experiences that we want to call experiences of *punishment*. (It may well be *too* general, but I do not want to pursue that issue here.)[24]

Thus I understand punishment as an experience which a wrongdoer is forced by an authority to undergo in virtue of the fact that he has transgressed (what ought to be) a morally derived rule laid down by that authority, and which disrupts (in either a major or a minor way) the wrongdoer's freedom to pursue the satisfaction of his desires. Given that punishment is understood in this way, how do coercion and the disruption of one's self-interested pursuits convey a *moral* message?

Before answering this question, it is important to make clear that punishment is only *one* method of moral education. Upon reflection, it is clear, I think, that we choose to employ this method only when we're trying to teach someone that an action is *wrong*, rather than when we are trying to teach someone what (imperfect) moral duties he or she ought to recognize. (We punish a child when he kicks his brother; we don't punish him in order to get him to give Dad a present on Father's Day.)

What is one trying to get across when one wants to communicate an action's wrongness? The first thing one wants to convey is that the action is forbidden, prohibited, "fenced off." Consider a mother who sees her child cheating at solitaire. She might say to the child, "You mustn't do that." Or if she saw her child putting his left shoe on his right foot, she would likely say, "No, you mustn't dress that way." In both cases it would be highly inappropriate for her to follow these words with punishment. She is communicating to her child that what he is doing in these circumstances is inadvisable, imprudent, not playing by the rules, but she is not communicating (and not trying to communicate) the idea that such actions violate one's moral duty to others (or, for that matter, one's moral duty to oneself). Now consider this mother seeing her son kick the neighbor's young daughter. Once again she might say, "You mustn't do that," to the child, but the "mustn't" in the mother's words here is unique. It is more than "you shouldn't" or "it isn't advisable" or "it's against the rules of the game." Rather, it attempts to convey the idea that the action is forbidden, prohibited, intolerable.

But merely telling the child that he "mustn't do that" will not effectively convey to the child that there is this profound moral boundary. Without punishment why shouldn't the child regard the "mustn't" in the parent's statement just as he did the "mustn't" in "You mustn't cheat at solitaire"? The mother needs to get across to the child the very special nature of the prohibition against this immoral act. How can she do this? Consider the fact that someone who (for no moral reason) violates a positive duty to others is not acting out of any interest in the other's well-being. A teenager who steals from a passer-by because she needs the money, a man who rapes a woman so that he can experience a sense of power and mastery—such people are performing immoral acts in order to satisfy their own needs and interests, insensitive to the needs and interests of the people they hurt. The way to communicate to such people that there is a barrier of a very special sort against these kinds of actions would seem to be to link performance of the actions with what such people care about most—the pursuit of their own pleasure. Only when disruption of that pursuit takes place will a wrongdoer appreciate the special force of the "mustn't" in the punisher's communication. So the only effective way to "talk to" such people is through the disruption of their own interests, that is, through punishment (which has been defined as just such a disruption).

What conclusions will a person draw from this disruption of his pleasure? At the very least he will conclude that his society (in the guise of the family, the state, the university, etc.) has erected a barrier to that kind of action, and that if he wants to pursue the satisfaction of his own desires, he won't perform that action again. So at the very least, he will understand his punishment as society's attempt to deter him from committing the action in the future. Such a conclusion does not have moral content. The person views his punishment only as a sign of society's condemnation of the act, not as a sign of the act's *wrongness*. But it is a start, and a *necessary first start*. If a wrongdoer has little or no conception of an action's wrongness, then the first thing one must do is to communicate to him that the action is prohibited. We must put up the electrical fence in an attempt to keep him out of a forbidden realm.

But given that we want the offender to understand the moral reasons for the action's condemnation, how can punishment communicate those reasons? The punisher wants the wrongdoer to move from the first stage of the educative process initiated by punishment—the realization that society prohibits the action—to a second stage, where the moral reasons for the condemnation of the action are understood and accepted. Can punishment, involving the disruption of a person's self-interested pursuits, help an offender to arrive at this final moral conclusion, to understand, in other words, why this fence has been erected?

What is it that one wants the wrongdoer to see? As we noted before, someone who (for no moral reason) violates her (perfect) moral duty to others is not thinking about the others' needs and interests, and most likely has little conception of, or is indifferent to, the pain her actions caused another to suffer. Hence, what the punisher needs to do is to communicate to the wrongdoer *that* her victims suffered and how much they suffered, so that the wrongdoer can appreciate the harmfulness of her action. How does one get this message across to a person insensitive to others? Should not such a person be made to endure an unpleasant experience designed, in some sense, to "represent" the pain suffered by her victim(s)? This is surely the intuition behind the *lex talionis* but it best supports the concept of punishment as moral education. As Nozick admits,[25] it is very natural to regard the pain or unpleasantness inflicted by the wrongdoer as the punisher's way of saying: "This is what you did to another. You hate it; so consider how your victim felt." By giving a wrongdoer something like what she gave to others, you are trying to drive home to her just how painful and damaging her action was for her victims, and this experience will, one hopes, help the wrongdoer to understand the immorality of her action.

Of course, the moral education formula does not recommend that punishments be specifically *equal* to the crime—in many instances this doesn't even make sense. But what does the "representation" of the wrongful act involve, if not actual equality? This is a terribly difficult question, and I find I can only offer tentative, hesitant answers. One way the moral education theorist can set punishments for crimes is to think about "fit." Irrespective of how severe a particular crime is, there will sometimes be a punishment that seems naturally suited to it; for example, giving a certain youth charged with burglarizing and stealing money from a neighbor's house the punishment of supervised compulsory service to this neighbor for a period of time, or giving a doctor charged with cheating a government medical insurance program the punishment of compulsory unremunerated service in a state medical institution. And probably such punishments seem to fit these crimes because they force the offender to compensate the victim, and thus help to heal more effectively the "moral wound" which the offense has caused. Another way the moral education theorist can make specific punishment recommendations is to construct an ordinal scale of crimes, going from most offensive to least offensive, and then to link determinate sentences to each crime, respecting this ordinal comparison, and insuring proportionality between crime and punishment. But it is not easy to use either method to fashion a tidy punishment table because it is not easy to determine which painful experiences will be educative but not cruel, both proportional to the offense committed and somehow relevant to that offense. Indeed, our society has been notoriously unsuccessful in coming up with punishments that are in any way morally educative. And I would argue that it speaks in favor of this theory that it rejects many forms of incarceration used today as legitimate punishments, insofar as they tend to make criminals morally worse rather than better.

But even if this theory can tell us how to represent wrongdoing in a punishment, it must still handle other questions which I do not have time to pursue properly in this article. For example, how does that representation help the wrongdoer to understand and *accept* the fact that she did wrong and should do otherwise in the future? And if we want to send the most effective message possible in order to bring about this acceptance, should we try to tailor punishments to the particular psychological and moral deficiencies of the wrongdoer, or must considerations of equal treatment and fairness override this? Finally, does the view justify the state's punishing people who are innocent of any illegal act but who seem to need moral education?

The theory has a very interesting and complicated response to this last question. We have said that punishment is not the appropriate method to teach every sort of moral lesson, but only the lesson that a certain action is wrong. But on whom is the state justified in imposing such a lesson?—clearly, a person who has shown she needs the lesson by committing a wrong which the state had declared illegal, and clearly *not* a person who has shown she already understands this lesson (at least in some sense) by conscientiously obeying that law. We also believe that the state is justified in imposing this lesson on a person who has not broken that law but who has *tried* to do so. She might, for example, be punished for "attempted murder" or "attempted kidnapping." (And do we make the punishments for such attempts at wrongdoing less than for successful wrongdoings because we're not sure the attempts provide conclusive evidence that such people would have carried through?) But what about a person who has not broken a law or even attempted to do so but who has, say, talked about doing so publicly? Is that enough evidence that she needs moral education? Probably—by *some* person or institution, but not by the state. The point is that we believe the state should refrain from punishing immoral people who have nonetheless committed no illegal act, not because they don't need moral education but because the state is not the appropriate institution to effect that education. Indeed, one of the reasons we insist that the state operate by enacting laws is that doing so defines when it may coercively interfere in the lives of its citizens and when it may not; its legislation, in other words, defines the extent of its educative role (and there might exist constitutional rules guiding this legislation). So if the state were to interfere with its citizens' lives when they had not broken its laws, it would exceed its own legitimate role. In the end, the state may not punish immoral people who are innocent of any crime not because they don't need moral education, but because the state is not justified in giving it to them.

However, there is another question relevant to the issue of punishing the innocent. Given that I have represented the moral education theory as having a two-part goal—the moral education of the criminal and the moral education of the rest of society—it might be that a punishment which would achieve one part of this goal would not be an effective way of realizing the other part. Must we choose between these two objectives, or is it possible to show that they are inextricably linked? And if they are not, could it be that in order to pursue the goal of morally educating *society*, it would be necessary to punish an innocent person? More generally, could it be justifiable on this view to punish a wrongdoer much more (or much less) severely than her offense (if any) would seem to warrant if doing so would further society's moral education? If this were true, the theory would not preserve proportionality between crime and punishments. However, there are reasons for thinking that educating the criminal and educating the community are inextricably linked. For example, if the state aims to convey a moral lesson to the community about how other human beings should be treated, it will completely fail to do so if it inflicts pain on someone innocent of any wrongdoing—indeed, it would send a message exactly contrary to the one it had intended. But even if we suppose, for the sake of argument, that these educational objectives could become disengaged, we can preserve proportionality between a person's crime and her punishment by making the moral education of the criminal lexically prior to the moral education of the community (after all, we *know* she needs the lesson, we're less sure about the community).[26]

However, giving adequate arguments for solutions to any of the problems I have posed in this section requires a much more fully developed account of what moral education is and of how punishment would help to effect it. Some readers might think that developing such an account is simply an empirical rather than a philosophical task. But before we can know how to morally educate, we need a better theoretical understanding of what moral knowledge is, and why human beings do wrong. (Is it because, as Kant insists, we choose to defy the power of the moral law or because, as Socrates argues, we are morally ignorant?) Moreover, we need a better appreciation of the source and extent of the state's authority if we are to understand its legitimate role as moral educator. Further work on this theory has to come to grips with these issues in moral and political philosophy before we can know whether to embrace it. But I have tried to suggest in my remarks in this section that certain kinds of approaches to these issues are at least promising.

2. Is the Moral Education of Most Criminals Just a Pipe Dream?

How can we really expect hard-core criminals convicted of serious offenses to be able to change and morally improve? In answer to this last question, the moral education theorist will admit that the state can predict that many of the criminals it punishes will refuse to accept the moral message it delivers. As I have stressed, the moral education theory rests on the assumption of individual autonomy, and thus an advocate of this theory must not only admit but insist that the choice of whether to listen to the moral message contained in the punishment belongs to the criminal. Thus it is very unlikely that society will be 100 percent successful in its moral education efforts, no matter how well it uses the theory to structure punishments.

But at least the punishment the state delivers can have a deterrent effect; even if the criminal refuses to understand the state's communication about why there is a barrier to his action, at least he will understand *that* the barrier exists. Hegel once wrote that if a criminal is coerced by a punishment, it is because he *chooses* to be so coerced; such a person rejects the moral message and accepts instead the avoidance of pain as his sole reason for avoiding the action.[27] In the end, punishments might only have deterrent effects because that is all wrongdoers will let them have.

However, neither the state nor anyone else can determine who the "losers" are. None of us can read another's mind, none of us knows the pressures, beliefs, and concerns motivating another's actions and decisions. The state cannot, even with the help of a thousand psychiatrists, *know for sure* who is a hopeless case and who isn't. Nor is this just a simple epistemological problem. Insofar as the state, on this view, should regard each person it punishes as autonomous, it is committed to the view that the choice of whether to reform or not is a free one, and hence one the state cannot hope to predict. Finally, the state's assumption that the people it is entitled to punish are free means it must never regard any one it punishes as hopeless, insofar as it is assuming that each of these persons still has the ability to choose to be moral. Thus, as Hegel puts it,[28] punishment is the criminal's "right" as a free person—to refuse to punish him on the grounds that he has been diagnosed as hopeless is to regard him as something other than a rational human being.

But even if it seems likely that punishing some criminals will not effect their moral growth, and may not even deter them, the moral education of the community about the nature of their crimes can still be promoted by their punishment. Indeed any victim of crime is going to be very sensitive to this fact, insofar as he has been the one against whom the wrong has been committed, and is the one who is most interested in having the community acknowledge that what happened to him *shouldn't* have happened. And as long as the person whom we punish is admitted to be an autonomous human being, we cannot be convicted of using her as we educate the community about the wrongness of her offense, because we are doing something to her which is *for* her, which can achieve a great deal of good for her, if she will but let it.

3. Shouldn't the Moral Education Theory Imply an Indeterminate Sentencing Policy?

Throughout your discussion, rehabilitationists might complain, you have been assuming that punishment by the state should proceed from determinate sentences for specific crimes. But isn't indeterminate sentencing fairer? Why keep a criminal who has learned his moral lesson in jail just because his sentence has not run out, and why release a criminal who is unrepentant and who will probably harm the public again, just because his sentence has run out?

However, the moral education theorist has very good reasons, provided by the foundations of the theory itself, for rejecting the concepts of indeterminate sentencing and parole boards. First, this theorist would strongly disagree with the idea that a criminal should continue to receive "treatment" until his reform has been effected. Recall that it is an important tenet of the view that the criminals we punish are free beings, responsible for their actions. And you can't *make* a free human being believe something. In particular, you can't coerce people to be just for justice's sake. Punishment is the state's attempt to teach a moral lesson, but whether or not the criminal will listen and accept it is up to the criminal himself.

The moral education theorist takes this stand not simply because she believes one ought to respect the criminal's autonomy, but also because she believes one has no choice but to respect it. The fact that parole boards in this country have tried to coerce repentance is, from the standpoint of this theorist, a grave and lamentable mistake. (Consider James McConnell's claim, in an article in *Psychology Today,* that "Somehow we've got to *force* people to love one another, to force them to want to behave properly.")[29] Indeed, critics of present parole systems in the United States maintain that these systems only open the way for manipulation.[30] The parole board uses the threat of the refusal of parole to get the kind of behavior it wants from the criminal, and the criminal manipulates back—playing the game, acting reformed, just to get out. In the process, no moral message is conveyed to the criminal, and probably no real reformation takes place. The high recidivism rate in the United States tells the tale of how successful parole boards have been in evaluating the rehabilitation of prisoners. As one prisoner put it: "If they ask if this yellow wall is blue, I'll say, of course it's blue. I'll say anything they want me to say if they're getting ready to let me go."[31]

The moral education theorist doesn't want the state to play this game. A sentence for a crime is set, and when the criminal breaks a law, the sentence is inflicted on him as a way of teaching him that what he did was wrong. When the sentence is up, the criminal is released. The state hopes its message was effective, but whether it was or not is largely up to the criminal himself.

There is another important reason why the moral education theorist does not want to insist on repentance before release. Even a good state can make mistakes when it enacts law. It is not just possible but probable that the state at one time or another will declare a certain action immoral which some of its citizens will regard as highly moral. These citizens will often decide to disobey this "immoral" law, and while being punished, will steadfastly refuse to repent for an action they believe was right. Martin Luther King, Jr., never repented for breaking various segregation laws in the South while he was in jail; few draft resisters repented for refusing to go to Vietnam when they were in prison. By not insisting on the repentance of its criminals, the state is, once again, respecting the freedom of its citizens—particularly each citizen's freedom of conscience, and their right, as free beings, to disagree with its rulings. Hence, the moral education theorist doesn't want the state to insist on repentance because it doesn't want Solzhenitsyns rotting in jail until they have "reformed."[32]

How can the moral education theorist justify the punishment of a criminal who is already repentant prior to his sentencing, or who repents before his sentence is completely served? The theorist's response to this question is complicated. Because it is difficult to be sure that a seemingly repentant criminal is *truly* repentant, and thus because a policy of suspending or shortening sentences for those who seem repentant to the authorities could easily lead the criminal to fake repentance before a court or a parole board, the moral education theorist would be very reluctant to endorse such a policy.

Moreover, it might well be the case that, prior to or during sentencing, a criminal's experience of repentance is produced in large part by the expectation of receiving the full punishment, so that the state's subsequent failure to inflict it could lead to a weakening of the criminal's renunciation of the action. Like a bad but repentant child who will conclude, if he is not punished by his parents, that his action must not have been so bad, the repentant criminal might well need to experience his complete sentence in order to "learn his lesson" effectively.

Finally, the lesson learning effected by punishment can also involve a purification process for a wrongdoer, a process of healing. As Herbert Morris has written, experiencing the pain of punishment can be a kind of catharsis for the criminal, a way of "burning out" the evil in his soul.[33] Novelists like Dostoevsky have explored the criminal's need, born of guilt and shame, to experience pain at the hands of the society he has wronged in order to be reconciled with them. Thus the rehabilitationist who would deny the criminal the experience of pain at the hands of the state would deny him what he may want and need to be forgiven—both by society and by himself. And punishment understood as moral education would explain how it could be perceived as a purification process. For how is it that one overcomes shame? Is it not by becoming a person *different* from the one who did the immoral action? The subsiding of shame in us seems to go along with the idea, "Given who I was, I did the action then, but I'm different now—I'm *better* now—and I wouldn't do the same act again." But how do we become different, how do we change, improve? Insofar as punishment is seen as a way of educating oneself about the offense, undergoing that experience is a way of changing for the better. It might well be the yearning for that change which drives a person like Raskolnikov towards his punishment.

Nonetheless, if there were clear evidence that a criminal was very remorseful for his action and had already experienced great pain because of his crime (had "suffered enough"), this theory would endorse a suspension of his sentence or else a pardon (*not* just a parole). His moral education would have already been accomplished, and the example of his repentance would be lesson enough for the general public. (Indeed, punishment under these circumstances would make the state appear vindictive.) In addition, because the state conceives itself to be punishing a wrong, it is appropriate for it to allow certain sorts of excuses and mitigating circumstances to lessen the penalty normally inflicted for the crime in question.

4. Does the Moral Education Theory Actually Presuppose the Truth of Retribution?

Retributivists have a very interesting criticism of the moral education theory available to them. Granted, they might maintain, that punishment is connected with moral education, still this only provides an additional reason for punishing someone—it does not provide the fundamental justification of punishment. That fundamental justification, they would argue, is retributive: wrongdoers simply *deserve* to experience pain for the sake of the wrong they have committed. As Kant has argued, however much good one intends one's punishment to effect,

> yet it must first be justified in itself as punishment, i.e., as mere harm, so that if it stopped there, and the person punished could get no glimpse of kindness hidden behind this harshness, he must yet admit that justice was done him, and that his reward was perfectly suitable to his conduct.[34]

Moreover, such modern retributivists as Walter Moberly have argued that it is only when the wrongdoer can assent to his punishment as already justified in virtue of his offense that the punishment can do him any good.[35]

In a certain sense, Moberly's point is simply that a criminal will perceive his punishment as vindictive and vengeful unless he understands or accepts the fact that it is justified. But should the justification of punishment be cashed out in terms of the retributive concept of desert, given that it has been difficult for retributivists to say what they mean by the criminal's "deserving" punishment simply in virtue of his offense? Robert Nozick tries to cash out the retributive link between crime and "deserved" punishment by saying that the punishment represents a kind of "linkage" between the criminal and "right values."[36] But why is inflicting pain on someone a way of effecting this linkage? Why isn't the infliction of a pleasurable experience for the sake of the crime just as good a way of linking the wrongdoer with these right values? And if Nozick explains the linkage of pain with crime by saying that the pain is necessary in order to communicate to the criminal that his action was wrong, he has answered the question but lost his retributive theory. Other philosophers, like Hegel,[37] speak of punishment as a way of "annulling" or "canceling" the crime and hence "deserved" for that reason. But although Hegel's words have a nice metaphorical ring to them, it is hard to see how they can be given a literal force that will explain the retributivist concept of desert. As J. L. Mackie has written, insofar as punishment occurs after the crime, it certainly cannot cancel it—past events are not eliminated by later ones.[38]

It is partly because retributivists have been at a loss to explain the notion of desert implicit in their theory of punishment that I have sought to propose and explore a completely nonretributivist justification of punishment. But my reasons for rejecting retributivism are deeper. The retributive position is that it is somehow morally appropriate to inflict pain for pain, to take an eye for an eye, a tooth for a tooth. But how is it ever morally appropriate to inflict one evil for the sake of another? How is the society that inflicts the second evil any different from the wrongdoer who has inflicted the first? He strikes first, they strike back; why is the second strike acceptable but the first not? Plato, in a passage quoted at the start of this article, insists that both harms are wrong; and Jesus attacks retributivism[39] for similar reasons:

> You have learned that they were told, "Eye for eye, tooth for tooth." But what I tell you is this: Do not set yourself against the man who wrongs you. . . . You have heard that they were told "Love your neighbor, hate your enemy." But what I tell you is this: Love your enemy and pray for your persecutors; only so can you be children of your heavenly father, who makes the sun rise on good and bad alike, and sends the rain on the honest and dishonest. [Matt. 5:38–9, 43–6]

In other words, both reject retributivism because they insist that the only thing human beings "deserve" in this life is *good,* that no matter what evil a person has committed, no one is justified in doing further evil to her.

But if one accepts the idea that no one can ever deserve ill, can we hope to justify punishment? Yes, if punishment can be shown to be a good for the wrongdoer. The moral education theory makes just such an attempt to explain punishment as a good for those who experience it, as something done *for* them, not to them, something designed to achieve a goal that includes their own moral well-being. This is the justification of punishment the criminal needs to hear so that he can accept it as legitimate rather than dismiss it as vindictive. Therefore, my interest in the moral education theory is connected with my desire to justify punishment *as a good* for those who experience it, and to avoid any theoretical justification of punishment that would regard it as a deserved evil.[40] Reflection on the punishment activities of those who truly love the people they punish, for example, the infliction of pain by a parent on a beloved but naughty child, suggests to me that punishment should not be justified as a deserved evil, but rather as an attempt, by someone who cares, to improve a wayward person.

Still, the moral education theory can incorporate a particular notion of desert which might be attractive to retributivists. Anyone who is punished according to this theory would know that his punishment is "deserved," that is, morally required, insofar as the community cannot morally tolerate the immoral lesson that his act conveys to others (for example, the message that raping a woman is all right if it gives one a feeling of self-mastery) and cannot morally allow that he receive no education about the evil of his act.

So the theory's point is this: Wrong occasions punishment not because pain deserves pain, but because evil deserves correction.

NOTES

1. See Hegel, *Philosophy of Right,* trans. T. Knox (Oxford: Clarendon Press, 1952), sections 90–104 (pp. 66–74); and see Plato, in particular the dialogues: *The Laws* (bks. 5 and 9), *Gorgias* (esp. pp. 474ff.), *Protagoras* (esp. pp. 323ff.) and Socrates's discussion of his own punishment in the *Apology,* and the *Crito.* I am not convinced that this characterization of either Hegel's or Plato's views is correct, but will not pursue those issues here. J. E. McTaggart has analyzed Hegel's position in a way that suggests it is a moral education view. See his "Hegel's Theory of Punishment," *International Journal of Ethics* 6 (1896), pp. 482–99; portions reprinted in *Philosophical Perspectives On Punishment,* ed. Gertrude

Ezorsky (Albany, NY: State University of New York Press, 1972). In her *Plato on Punishment,* M. M. Mackenzie's presentation of Plato's position suggests it is not a strict moral education view.

2. Recently Morris has been explicitly advocating this view in "A Paternalistic Theory of Punishment," *American Philosophical Quarterly* 18, no. 4 (October 1981), but only as *one aspect* of the justification of punishment. Morris argues that punishment is sufficiently complicated to require a justification incorporating all of the justificatory reasons offered by the traditional theories of punishment as well as by the moral education view. I do not think this sort of patchwork approach to punishment will work and, in this article, I explore the idea that the moral education view can, by itself, give an adequate justification of punishment.

   See also Nozick's book *Philosophical Explanations* (Cambridge: Harvard University Press, 1981), pp. 363–97.
3. See Hart, *The Concept of Law* (Oxford: Clarendon Press, 1961), chaps. 5 and 6.
4. As stated, this is a positivist definition of law. However, with John Chipman Gray I am maintaining that morality, although not the same as law, should be the source of law. (See Gray's *The Nature and Source of Law* [New York: Macmillan, 1921], p. 84.)
5. See Edna Ullman-Margalit, *The Emergence of Norms* (Oxford: Clarendon Press, 1977) for a discussion of how law can solve coordination and conflict problems.
6. Although Kant's position on punishment is officially retributive (see his *Metaphysical Elements of Justice,* trans. J. Ladd [Indianapolis: Bobbs-Merrill, 1965], p. 100, Academy edition, p. 331), his definition of law conflicts with his retributivist position. Note, for example, the deterrent flavor of his justification of law:

   > if a certain use of freedom is itself a hindrance to freedom according to universal laws (that is, unjust), then the use of coercion to counteract it, inasmuch as it is the prevention of a hindrance to freedom according to universal laws, is consistent with freedom according to universal laws; in other words, this use of coercion is just (p. 36, Academy edition, p. 231; see also *Metaphysical Elements of Justice,* pp. 18–9, 33–45; Academy edition, pp. 218–21, 229–39).
7. Hegel, *Philosophy of Right,* addition to par. 99, p. 246.
8. Kantians who see a close connection between autonomy and moral knowledge will note that this connection is suggested in these remarks.
9. Rehabilitationists disagree about exactly what disease criminals suffer from. See for example the various psychiatric diagnoses of Benjamin Karpman in "Criminal Psychodynamics: A Platform," reprinted in *Punishment and Rehabilitation,* ed. J. Murphy (Belmont, CA: Wadsworth, 1973) as opposed to the behaviorist analysis of criminal behavior offered by B. F. Skinner in *Science and Human Behavior* (New York: Macmillan, 1953). pp. 182–3 and 446–49.
10. See, for example, Nozick's characterization of the view as "teleological retributivism," pp. 370–74 and Gertrude Ezorsky's use of that term in *Philosophical Perspectives on Punishment.*
11. Morris, "The Paternalistic Theory of Punishment," p. 268.
12. In Nozick, pp. 369–80.
13. Ibid., pp. 374ff. The point is that if one is going to accept the idea that punishment is a communication, one is connecting it with human purposive activity, and hence the *purpose* of speaking to the criminal (as well as to the rest of society) becomes central to the justification of the communication itself. To deny this is simply to regard punishment as something fundamentally different from a species of communication (for example, to regard it as some kind of "value-linkage device") which Nozick seems reluctant to do.
14. *Los Angeles Times,* 30 July 1981, part 4. p. 1.
15. Nozick has also found the "communication" element in comic book stories about revenge; see *Philosophical Explanations,* pp. 368–69.
16. Parental punishment can take many forms; although spanking and various kinds of corporal punishment are usually what spring to mind when one thinks of parental punishment, many parents punish through the expression of anger or disapproval, which can be interpreted by the child as a withdrawal of love or as the (at least temporary) loss of the parent's friendship. Such deprivations are in many ways far more serious than the momentary experience of bodily pain or the temporary loss of certain privileges, and hence, although they seem to be mild forms of punishment, they can in actuality be very severe I am indebted to Herbert Morris for suggesting this point.
17. Because children are not completely responsible, rational beings, punishing them can also be justified as a way of encouraging in them certain kinds of morally desirable habits, insofar as it has "conditioning like"

effects. Aristotle seems to regard punishment of children as, at least in part, playing this role. See for example *Nicomachean Ethics,* bk. 1. chap. 4. I would not want to deny that aspect of parental punishment.

18. It is because I believe there are sharp and important differences between parental and state punishment that I eschew Herbert Morris's title for this type of punishment theory (that is, his title "the paternalistic theory of punishment").
19. Martin Luther King, Jr., "Letter from a Birmingham Jail," from *Civil Disobedience,* ed. H. A. Bedau (New York: Pegasus, 1969), pp. 78–9.
20. Some retributivists have tried to argue that the *lex talionis* needn't be regarded as a formula whose upper bound *must* be respected; see, for example, K. C. Armstrong, "The Retributivist Hits Back," *Philosophy of Punishment,* ed. H. B. Acton (London: Macmillan, 1969). However, critics can object that Armstrong's weaker retributivist position still does not *rule out* barbaric punishments (like torture) as permissible, nor does it explain why and when punishments which are less in severity than the criminal act can be legitimately inflicted.
21. Consider the START program used in a Connecticut prison to "rehabilitate" child molesters: electrodes were connected to the prisoner's skin, and then pictures of naked boys and girls were flashed on a screen while electric shocks were applied. The Federal Bureau of Prisons canceled this program just before they were about to lose a court challenge to the program's constitutionality (see David J. Rothman's discussion of this in "Behavior Modification in Total Institutions," *Hastings Center Report* 5, no. 1 [1975]: 22).
22. Apart from the fact that killing someone is hardly an appropriate technique for educating him, it is likely that this action sends a poor message to the rest of society about the value of human life. Indeed, in one of their national meetings, the Catholic bishops of the United States argued that repeal of capital punishment would send "a message that we can break the cycle of violence, that we need not take life for life, that we can envisage more human and more hopeful and effective responses to the growth of violent crime." ("Statement on Capital Punishment," *Origins* 10, no. 24 [27 November 1980]: 374.)
23. Nozick, pp. 373–74.
24. George Fletcher, in *Rethinking Criminal Law* (Boston: Little, Brown, 1978), p. 410, worries about defining punishment so that it doesn't include too much (for example, it should not include the impeachment of President Nixon, despite the fact that it would be a case of unpleasant consequences inflicted on Nixon by an authority in virtue of a wrongdoing). I do not . . . here consider how to hone my definition such that it will not encompass impeachments, deportation, tort damages, and so forth. Indeed, perhaps the only way one can do this is to bring into the definition of punishment its justification as moral education.
25. Compare Nozick's discussion of the content of the Gricean message of punishment, pp. 370–74.
26. I have profited from discussions with Katherine Shamey on this point.
27. See Hegel, *Philosophy of Right,* sec. 91.
28. Ibid., sec. 100, p. 70.
29. From "Criminals Can be Brainwashed—Now," *Psychology Today,* April 1970, p. 14; also quoted in Rick Carlson's *The Dilemma of Corrections* (Lexington, MA: Lexington Books, 1976), p. 35.
30. See "The Crime of Treatment," American Friends Service Committee, from *The Struggle for Justice,* chap. 6 (New York: Hill and Wang, 1971) reprinted in *Punishment: Selected Readings,* eds., Feinberg and Gross.
31. Quoted by Carlson, p. 161; from David Fogel, *We Are the Living Proof* (Cincinnati: W. H. Anderson, n.d.).
32. Jeffrie Murphy has argued that instituting a rehabilitationist penal system would deny prisoners many of their present due process rights. See "Criminal Punishment and Psychiatric Fallacies," especially pp. 207–209, in *Punishment and Rehabilitation,* ed. J. Murphy. The American Friends Service Committee has also charged that the California penal system, which was heavily influenced by the rehabilitation theory, has in fact done this. See "The Crime of Treatment," pp. 91–93, in Feinberg et al.
33. See Morris's discussion of certain wrongdoers' need to experience punishment in "The Paternalistic Theory of Punishment," p. 267.
34. Kant, *Critique of Practical Reason,* "The Analytic of Pure Practical Reason," Remark II. (Abbott trans. in *Kant's Theory of Ethics* [London: Longman, 1959], p. 127; Academy edition, p. 38.)
35. Walter Moberly, *The Ethics of Punishment* (London: Faber & Faber, 1968), p. 141.
36. Nozick, pp. 374ff.
37. For example, see Hegel, *The Philosophy of Right,* sec. 101–103.
38. J. L. Mackie, "Morality and the Retributive Emotions," in *Criminal Justice Ethics* 1, no. 1 (Winter/Spring 1982): 3–10. In the face of the retributivists' failure to explain why punishment is deserved, Mackie wants to argue that our retributive intuitions spring from fundamental retributive emotions, which

are part of a human being's fundamental moral make-up (and he gives a sketch of how our evolution as a species could have generated such emotions). But many retributivists, particularly the Kantian sort, would eschew such an explanation which, in any case, is hardly a *justification* of the retributive impulse itself.

39. Jesus rejected not only "negative retributivism," that is, the idea that we deserve bad for doing bad, but also "positive retributivism," that is, the idea that we deserve good for doing good.
40. Indeed, I believe that it is because retribution would justify punishment as a deserved evil that it strikes many as much too close to revenge.

Can Punishment Morally Educate?

RUSS SHAFER-LANDAU

Shafer-Landau criticizes moral education theories of the sort Hampton defends for failing to explain either how traditional forms of punishment can be morally educative or how the achievement of educative goals is compatible with showing proper respect for the autonomy of offenders. He also argues that it is unclear why we should be thought to have an obligation to expend scarce social resources to morally educate. Finally, he suggests that such a theory may require indeterminate sentencing, which many have thought to be a serious form of injustice.

I. The Theory and Its Benefits

Punishment is paternalistic if and only if it attempts to confer a benefit on the offender while limiting his liberty against his will. It is natural to ask, What benefit?, and different responses to this question will yield different paternalistic theories. The theory I wish to discuss has been developed recently in articles by Jean Hampton and Herbert Morris, and can trace its philosophical roots back to Plato.[1] The weaker version of the theory, held by Morris, states that moral education is but one of the main aims of justified punishment. Hampton holds a stronger view: a satisfactory theory of punishment can be developed which incorporates moral education as the exclusive general justifying aim.

An excellent picture of the end to which this education is to be directed (i.e., the benefit to be conferred) has been provided by Morris in his recent article. There, Morris claims that punishment should take the form of a moral education which yields a person who is "an autonomous individual freely attached to that which is good."[2] Morris glosses the contents of the good by claiming that it is composed of "those relationships with others that sustain and give meaning to a life."[3] The good also incorporates emotions of guilt and remorse for having done wrong, empathy for those who have suffered at one's hands, comprehension and endorsement of the moral standards one has violated, a commitment to behavioral reformation, and a conception of oneself as a responsible individual worthy of respect.[4] Hampton adds an additional condition: the educational effects are to extend not only to the criminal, but to the society at large.[5]

It's extremely important for both Morris and Hampton that the individual, as a result of punishment, be *freely* attached to the good. They believe that any form of conditioning, even that administered at the behest of the criminal, is improper and frustrates the goal that punishment is to serve.[6] The goal, then, is not simply the development of some settled moral dispositions on the part of the criminal, but the development of these dispositions in a manner that respects the criminal's moral autonomy.

This seems to me a very attractive and humane conception of the goals of punishment. Its emphasis on respect for autonomy

Reprinted with permission from "Can Punishment Morally Educate?" by Russ Shafer-Landau, *Law and Philosophy*, Vol. 10, 1991, pp. 189–219. The Netherlands: Kluwer Academic Publishers.

allows it to avoid many of the major objections that have often been leveled against paternalistic theories.[7] Indeed, this emphasis on autonomy, coming from an avowed paternalist, may seem puzzling at first. Aren't paternalists those who typically allow claims of autonomy to be overridden by the perceived need of the state to ensure a satisfactory level of personal welfare? The puzzle can be resolved by noticing at least two levels at which a paternalistic analysis can come into play.

As a comprehensive view about the legitimate limits of state power, paternalism holds that it is sometimes permissible for the state to infringe an individual's autonomy for purposes of benefitting, or preventing harm to, that individual. The much narrower claims about punishment made by moral educationists need not toe this comprehensive line. Theirs is a claim, not (primarily) about what the law should be, but about the acceptable treatment of individuals once they have broken the law.[8] Moral educationists place great weight on personal autonomy, and regard its continued respect as a precondition for justifiable punishment. Since a paternalistic theory of punishment can derive its justification from non-paternalistic comprehensive theories of the right and the good, attacks on the comprehensive theory needn't be damaging to the theory of punishment.

Attention to the restricted scope of moral education theories enables the theorist to counter one of the traditional problems in the philosophy of punishment. The narrow compass of the moral education view explains why its proponents are not committed to using punishment to morally educate those who haven't broken the law. If moral education were an overriding aim of a political theory, there would apparently be no bar to "educating," via hard treatment, those perceived to be in need of such treatment. But as the educationists have sketched it, the only claim made about fundamental political values has to do with the value of autonomy. They make no attempt to situate their views on punishment within a more comprehensive theory, thereby avoiding the "punishing the innocent" scenarios which so often plague consequentialist theorists.

In addition to nicely sidestepping these problems, the theory has many positive benefits as well. With its emphasis on autonomy, it adheres to the Kantian prohibition on treating others as mere means. Perhaps better than any of its alternatives, it satisfies the requirement that punishment serve a communicative purpose.[9] It also conforms to our considered judgments about the nature of most criminals; as opposed to most rehabilitative views, criminals are not viewed as diseased or unhealthy, but as free agents consciously engaging in bad actions for which they are to be punished, not "treated" or "cured."[10] The moral education theory also sets an upper boundary to the types of punishments that may be inflicted on a criminal, providing strong grounds for excluding the morally unacceptable punishment that a strict application of *lex talionis* might occasion. For these and other reasons set out in the papers by Morris and Hampton, the moral education theory has much to recommend it. I am nevertheless skeptical about the prospects of its success as a comprehensive justification of punishment. Even viewed as a major strand in an overall justification, the theory has serious difficulties.[11] I hope to present these difficulties in what follows, confident that the benefits of the theory will be obvious to those already familiar with Morris's and Hampton's work.

II. The Value of Autonomy

The central role given to autonomy by the moral education theory is bound to generate criticism. Some detractors will feel that legitimate deterrence and retributive aims will be sacrificed by continued respect for the convicted offender's autonomy. Others might consider the emphasis on autonomy to reflect an unjustified liberal bias in one of the basic social institutions. The first task for philosophers like Morris and Hampton is thus to show how and why the authorities are constrained by considerations of autonomy in meting out a criminal's punishment.

Let us grant an important role for personal autonomy in living a good life. What the paternalist must show is that the benefits of a punishment that undermines the offender's autonomy cannot justify the loss of autonomy itself.

The following is perhaps the most familiar route to this conclusion. We begin by attempting to demonstrate that average social utility would be decreased by a policy which allowed an offender's autonomy to be restricted. It is far from clear that this could be done. Even if we allow the success of such a demonstration, it is probably impossible to show that isolated, non-public instances of such treatment would be less than optimific. At this point, those not antecedently convinced of utilitarian conclusions will invoke rights claims as a means of protecting autonomy.

This is, in fact, what the moral educationists do. But they offer little more than hints about the justifications for the relevant rights, merely indicating a worthy research project to be undertaken, rather than providing the necessary arguments.

For now, let us grant that a perspicuous account of a "right to autonomy" can be provided.[12] Such an account must not only detail the content of the right (which claims it protects), but its strength or weight (how overriding it is when in conflict with other ethical claims). To make the moral educationist's argument even stronger, assume as well that such a right is the foundation of all other moral rights.[13] It remains unclear whether such a right would be sufficient to raise the desired barrier against autonomy-restricting punishment. For someone could accept that *if* a person has moral rights, then she has a right to be treated as an autonomous agent, but simply deny the antecedent. This is what Plato does with respect to the morally "incurable" (see note 6). For Plato, we have no moral obligations to those who have committed heinous crimes and are unwilling to submit to moral suasion.

Moral education theorists agree with Plato that the criminal has lost her right to freedom. Why hasn't she lost all of her moral rights? Why must we respect the unrepentant criminal's autonomy? One possibility is that failure to show such respect would result in harm to the character of the punishing authorities. While this may be true, it is not the kind of argument the moral educationist needs. That's because this argument focuses on the harm suffered by the punisher: what's needed is an argument to show that the criminal is wronged by such treatment. This justification for respecting an offender's autonomy loses sight of the paternalistic aim that any justifiable punishment must incorporate. As Hampton says, "The moral good which punishment attempts to accomplish within the wrongdoer makes it something which is done *for* him, not *to* him."[14]

Part of the present difficulty is rooted in the fact that neither Morris nor Hampton presents us with a clear conception of autonomy. This makes for a dilemma: either autonomy may sometimes be permissibly infringed, or it may not. A natural chain of reasoning leading to the first option might be the following: punishment is sometimes justified; punishment involves autonomy infringement; therefore autonomy infringement is sometimes justified. The difficulty now confronting the educationist is that of providing a principled distinction between those autonomy infringements which are morally permissible and those which are not.

Alternately, the educationist may wish to avoid a slippery slope by claiming that moral autonomy may never be justifiably infringed. This is the route Morris takes, stating that his theory "implies a nonwaivable, nonforfeitable, nonrelinquishable right—the right to one's status as a moral being."[15] If this is the case, then punishment, insofar as it is justified, is obviously viewed as compatible with complete respect for autonomy; the minor premise in the above paragraph would be rejected. Opting for this horn of the dilemma yields three requirements: 1. The moral educationist must explain why punishment is not a limitation on autonomy; 2. she must argue for the existence of an inalienable right to moral autonomy, for an exceptionless prohibition on autonomy infringement; and 3. she must dissolve the apparent tension between an attachment to autonomy and the belief in inalienable rights, since inalienable rights specify restrictions on the autonomy of rights-holders.[16]

Given the difficulty and the length of the task, it is not surprising that both Morris and Hampton refrain from clearly choosing among these alternatives. Nevertheless, a successful justification of the moral education theory requires a choice and a defense. This is the first argumentative burden that the educationist must assume.

III. The Efficacy of Incarceration

Should we expect punishment to effect a moral reformation among the criminals who represent the would-be beneficiaries? To answer this question, we must first be clear about what punishment is. There is general agreement that punishment involves the infliction of hard treatment (i.e., something over and above requiring the criminal to compensate the victim) by a recognized representative of the state, upon an individual for a legal offense, accompanied by an authoritative condemnation of the offender's activities in the name of the state.[17] Hampton offers us a simpler version: punishment is "the disruption of freedom to pursue the satisfaction of one's desires."[18] Punishment has, in our society, usually taken the form of incarceration. Why think that incarceration will provide a moral education?

Moral educationists are not necessarily committed to a belief that incarceration is an effective means of promoting their designated goal. They may believe that an alternative to incarceration provides the best method of punishing, thereby offering a radical critique of existing punitive practices. But punitive alternatives to incarceration are not easy to find. Exile is a possibility, but, aside from its impracticality in these times, there is no reason to suppose it any better than incarceration at achieving the educationist's goal.[19] Assessing punitive monetary damages is another possibility, but there is no reason to think that criminals will become benefited in the desired ways from having forked over large sums of money. Strong public censure or institutional shaming procedures might work in some cases, but there is the difficulty of determining whether that would count as hard treatment, and if so, how efficacious it would be on a large scale. Systems of forced labor will definitely mete out hard treatment in an authoritative fashion, but are not likely by themselves to confer much moral education. Coerced therapeutic measures, even if administered with the best intentions, will certainly count as punitive. But whatever benefits are achieved by such procedures will be vitiated, in the educationist's eyes, by the violations of autonomy that accompany them.

Perhaps the only alternative to incarceration that would satisfy the paternalist's conditions of justified punishment would be a system of punishments specially tailored to the characteristics of, and harms caused by, each offender. Thus we might require a rapist to work in a battered woman's shelter, or an arsonist to work in a burn victim ward. But this kind of sentencing program is problematic.

Tailoring sentences to the particular facts of each case is highly impractical. Judges lack the time to get sufficiently acquainted with an offender's history to make such individuated sentences. Even with adequate time on their hands, most judges will lack the creativity and ingenuity required of those who would hand down such punishments. Further, assuming both adequate information and a robust creativity, many offenses seem incapable of being correlated to such unconventional punishments. What, for instance, are we to do to a counterfeiter, a tax cheat, or a criminal trespasser? It seems doubtful whether there are any nonincarcerative punishments specially suited to effect a moral education for such offenders.

It might be objected that difficulties in practically implementing principles of sentencing do not undermine the principles themselves. Paternalists could claim that justice requires that we individually tailor nonincarcerative punishments to the offender's deeds and character. If we are unable to do so, that shows that punishment in such cases is unjustified, not that our sentencing principles must be abandoned. We can retain allegiance to individuated sentencing and thus criticize present punitive practices for failing to meet these standards, rather than abandon individuated sentencing because it is impractical.

While this is a possible response, I do not think it a good one, and I do not think that either Hampton or Morris would endorse it. Sentencing is an essentially practical affair, so the principles which set standards for sentencing policy must be made with an eye towards implementation. If they demand too much—more than any system of finite resources and fallible officials can possibly do—then it seems we have reason to amend or abandon the principles themselves. If that weren't so, we'd be forced to admit in advance that punishments could almost never be justified, a conclusion no one in the present debate wants to accept. Of course we needn't tailor our sentencing principles to ensure justification of the status quo. The moral educationist's goals, in fact, provide good grounds for criticizing many current punitive practices.[20] But without the prospect of implementation in moderately just societies, sentencing principles simply fail to fulfill the purpose for which they are constructed.

Further, a sentencing policy which individuates punishments in the manner just described will naturally incorporate an indeterminate sentencing policy. I discuss the merits of such a policy below, in Section VI. For now, it is important to note only that both Hampton and Morris are opposed in principle to indeterminate sentencing policies. Given such attitudes, a system of individually tailored punishments is not the one most likely to attract favorable reviews from the moral educationists.

Neither Morris nor Hampton ever questions the justification of an enlightened incarceration policy. This fact, taken in conjunction with the considerations just enumerated, lead me to attribute to the educationists the view that incarceration plays an important and possibly indispensable role in punishment.

Suppose, then, that we had a system of incarceration free from the present problems that beset our own prisons. It remains unlikely that being put behind bars in a respectable environment will bring about moral change. Incarceration, even under the best conditions, seems at most to provide only the setting in which the real moral education can take place. Incarceration *simpliciter* will not do the job, or, more realistically, it will do the job in only a handful of cases. What's required is some form of education that's to take place during incarceration. But this education is not punishment; the education is not any kind of hard treatment (unless it uses conditioning techniques that involve aversive stimuli of the kind already ruled out by the paternalist's concern with autonomy). The punishment itself—incarceration—is simply insufficient to attain the educationist's goal.

In anticipation of this skeptical challenge, Morris gives four reasons for thinking that punishment will render the criminal more morally sensitive.[21] First, it makes offenders aware of the socially-endorsed limits on behavior that members of a community expect one another to abide by. Second, a punitive response to wrongdoing conveys the extent to which society's members are attached to the values underlying the prohibitions that the criminal has violated. Third, punishment "rights the wrong," allowing the criminal to repay the debt he owes. Finally, punishment provides an opportunity for redemption and forgiveness, a chance to restore relationships to the *status quo ante.*

The first two reasons do not seem very persuasive grounds for thinking punishment an effective means of promoting moral reformation. These reasons appeal to sought-for changes in the cognitive states of the offender. They imply that the criminal, prior to her crime, was unaware of the prohibitions and the extent to which society endorsed them. But attributing such ignorance to most criminals is disingenuous at best. They know the rules, and they know that most people feel strongly about them. Criminals themselves no doubt feel very strongly about them, when another is threatening to violate the laws at the criminal's expense. The first two reasons, appealing as they do to a misguided conception of the typical criminal offender (as being a person who is simply ignorant of what is right and wrong), are unpersuasive.

Perhaps such dismissal is too quick. Isn't there anything a criminal learns behind bars? Isn't there an opportunity to experience a kind of empathy with one's victims which is not available without punishment? Being incarcerated doesn't add anything to one's knowledge of the relevant moral codes. It may, however, provide a different sort of knowledge—an appreciation of the harm that results from violating society's rules.

As an empirical matter, this seems clearly true for some criminals. But I retain my skepticism about incarceration's general ability to foster such an appreciation. If empathetic knowledge is so important, it seems that by far the best way to create it is to follow the retributivist's *lex talionis* principle, thereby placing the criminal in much the same situation as the victim. But application of this principle, when possible, would often involve clear violations of autonomy, thus blocking the most effective road to empathetic knowledge. Additionally, even if incarceration were generally successful in promoting empathetic knowledge, this is only a portion of the educationist's goal. The educationist wants a person freely attached to the good. Understanding another's suffering gets one only part of the way. Incarceration doesn't seem to provide any means of closing the gap between such understanding and the production of an autonomous individual freely attached to what is good.

The primary difficulty with Morris's third justification for punishment is that the sense in which punishment rights a wrong, involves a repayment of a debt, is obscure. Morris tried to make sense of the debt metaphor in his earlier, more retributivist paper "Persons and Punishment." Though I can't discuss it here, I think his attempts were unsuccessful.[22] In the absence of a clear and persuasive argument revealing the subtleties of the repayment metaphor, this third reason for thinking punishment a good means to moral education will fail. Further, even if it were to succeed, it is unclear how paternalistic this reason is, how repayment of a debt is supposed to yield educative benefits to the criminal.

The final reason for thinking punishment a good means to moral education is the most promising. Punishment, on this account, allows for the prospect of forgiveness and the restoration of old relationships. The thought is that only by suffering can an offender regain the trust and respect that he lost after his conviction.

I will restrict my comments to forgiveness, but very similar points can be made in the case of restoration of old relationships. First, many crimes are so awful that no amount of incarceration will absolve the guilt of the offending party. Forgiveness of the victim or the victim's family will, in very many cases, never be forthcoming, no matter how long one is put behind bars. Second, Morris may be speaking of communal, not the victim's, forgiveness. But here again it seems empirically false to say that a prison sentence will usually make a criminal more likely to garner communal forgiveness.

If the community to which the criminal returns after a prison stay is the community of the criminal underworld, then incarceration is obviously irrelevant to communal forgiveness, since this community is not likely to consider the offender deserving of sanctions in the first place. On the other hand, suppose the community is, in a broad sense, morally upright. In such a community, forgiveness is likely to come, if at all, primarily because of a manifest change of heart on the criminal's part. After all, if the criminal emerges from prison no different than he was when he went in, there seems little reason to accord him forgiveness.

Morris's strongest point, then, is that moral education may be had through forgiveness, and that forgiveness is predicated on the offender's incarceration. But this seems mistaken. What's important is not necessarily the incarceration, but the offender's change of heart. Further, Morris was committed to the idea that incarceration can produce this change of heart. But this leaves Morris with a circular argument: moral education will occur as a result of forgiveness, but forgiveness will occur only after the moral education has taken place. Claiming that incarceration will lead to moral education because leading to forgiveness is putting the cart before the horse. Morris needs an argument to show that the kind of moral education, independent of that which comes from forgiveness, and capable of grounding the forgiveness, will result from incarceration. He hasn't provided one.[23] I conclude that we have as yet no good reason for supposing incarceration an efficacious means of morally educating the criminal offender.

If we know in advance that the educationist's punitive goals will usually fail to be met, then one of three things follow: either the goals must be abandoned or modified, or incarceration must be abandoned, or practices in addition to incarceration must be employed. In the next section, I raise considerations opposing this last alternative.

IV. Why Should the State Confer a Benefit on Those Who Have Done Wrong?

Plato's answers to this question were always political; making a person morally better would make the state more just, tranquil, and cohesive. This is why he allows any means to be employed in order to secure the moral regeneration of an offender (see note 6). But contemporary paternalists cannot countenance Plato's approach. Plato condones treating people without respect for their autonomy, provided that doing so is instrumental to promoting the desired end.[24] Morris and Hampton, as we've seen in our discussion of the goal of punishment, require that any moral education be accomplished with complete respect for an individual's autonomy.

It would be silly to think that moral educationists have no concern for the social benefits that arise as a result of moral education. The point is that these social benefits are not the primary reason for conferring the benefit of moral education upon the criminal, and this can be seen by witnessing the disapproval of methods that might be more socially efficacious but less respectful of the offender's autonomy. For educationists, the primary reason to confer the benefit of moral education is that it is for the criminal's own good to do so; the resulting social goods are gladly accepted, but these are ancillary benefits.

Social resources are always limited, and a society must constantly consider how it is to allocate the wealth at its disposal. The question is, why spend money trying to benefit those who have violated the law, when so many innocents are in need? If one believes that no more is required for moral education than incarceration, then an answer is obvious. In our society, we have deemed it necessary to deal with certain offenders through incarceration, and consider it appropriate to allocate resources for the creation of institutions that will enable us to deal with those offenders accordingly. It is a happy coincidence that money already allocated for incarceration will also serve to morally educate, but we needn't spend any additional resources on the education, since incarceration is usually sufficient to effect the desired reform.

I have challenged the idea that incarceration alone will serve the purposes of moral education. If my doubts were well-founded, the educationist is faced with the following difficulty. Since moral education must take the form of a program that occurs in addition to incarceration, it will involve costs that exceed simple incarceration. The question now seems more pointed: Why spend scarce resources on those who have violated the primary rules as opposed to those who haven't, especially when we're already spending millions on incarcerating offenders?

There are really two argumentation debts to discharge here. The first is to show why we are obligated to benefit a criminal at all, even if we had unlimited resources.[25] The second is to show why, in the real world of scarce social resources, we ought to allocate money to the moral education of criminals, when doing so necessarily comes at the expense of allocating resources to help law-abiding citizens.

The latter question has not, to my knowledge, been addressed by moral education theorists. The second question arises only if we believe that moral education will involve costs additional to those associated with incarceration, and there is no reason to believe that unless one rejects (as I do) the claim that incarceration will effect the desired moral education. I will not, however, discuss this second question, because I am skeptical about whether an answer to the first can be provided. I don't believe the educationists can defend the weaker claim that we have obligations to morally educate criminals even in a world of limitless resources. If we have no such obligation, certainly we haven't any in the real world of scarce resources.

Morris begins his defense of the obligation to educate in the following passage:

> The evil—as Socrates long ago pointed out—that they [criminals] have done themselves by their wrongdoing is a moral evil greater than that which they have done others. Their souls are in jeopardy as their victims' are not. What could possibly justify an unconcern with this evil if the wrongdoer is one of us and if we sense, rightly I believe, that there but for the grace of God go we?[26]

It is easier to accept Morris's concern if we accept his picture of the evil that wrongdoers suffer. Suffering usually elicits a response of sympathy; if the criminal really suffers the evil Morris and Socrates says he does, perhaps our reluctance to help evildoers can (and should) be overcome. But does the criminal suffer so dread an evil? It seems unpersuasive to say, as Morris does, that the evil suffered by a criminal is usually greater than that of his victim. Take some typical criminal offenses: rape, murder, assault, robbery. Are we really so ready to elevate the criminal's suffering over that of his victim? To do so requires subscribing to a host of Socratic notions about the primacy of psychological harms and the relationship between wrongdoing and self-harm. These are extremely contentious positions.[27] Unless they can be satisfactorily made out, our concern for the criminal may well be greatly diminished.

Suppose we were convinced about the criminal's great suffering. Why should we exhibit any concern for her? Why not do the minimum required, consistent with continued respect for her autonomy? In the above passage, Morris appeals to our sense that the line dividing "us" from "them" is very slight, and even fortuitously drawn—there but for the grace of God go we. If it really is mostly a matter of luck that we ended up law-abiding citizens, we should refrain from making too harsh a judgment on the criminals, themselves victims of the worst moral evil that can befall a person. After all, we should certainly want the concern of others if we found ourselves in the criminal's position.

This line of reasoning seems to undercut the attribution of responsibility to the criminal that was the basis of our response to her in the first place. We "treat someone as a criminal"—prosecute her, authoritatively condemn her, subject her to hard treatment—only if we believe that she has passed a threshold of responsibility that allows us to properly attribute the criminal actions to her. To claim that the commission of a crime or the decision to refrain from such is mostly a matter of good or ill-fortune, a matter of divine whimsy, is to remove that aspect of responsibility that is so crucial to the justification of treating the criminal as we do.

Morris is claiming that our concern for the criminal is natural because she is greatly suffering and because we may easily have found ourselves in her shoes. This first claim is far from obvious. The second relies on the idea that we have much less control over, and hence are less responsible for, the direction of our lives than we believe. While this may be true, much argument is required concerning the problems of free will and responsibility. Further, if it is true, then much of the justification for punitive institutions in general may be undercut, taking with it particular justifications for the moral education theory.

Lastly, it is necessary to distinguish cases in which we might identify with the criminal from cases in which this is clearly preposterous. Most of us might be tempted to embezzle funds if the circumstances were propitious; identifying with such a person would not be too difficult for us. How many of us, on the other hand, could see an unfortunate twist of fate turning us into rapists or murderers? Our inability to envision this doesn't result simply from a lack of imagination. Morris owes us an account of natural sympathy which can maintain these apparently plausible distinctions in cases, or else reveal to us the justification for treating them alike.

In this section I have challenged the idea that, even in a world of limitless resources, our concern for the criminal offender requires us to confer upon him the benefit of a moral education. (Of course it might be nice or generous of us to spend the extra money—but is it really a *necessary condition* of justifiable punishment?)

The argument that we ought to be concerned with the moral welfare of the criminal stemmed from a picture of the criminal as one who greatly suffers. The benefit of moral education is designed specifically to remedy this suffering. It is now time to discuss whether the putative benefit of moral education is genuine; whether, that is, the suffering it is designed to alleviate is as profound and extensive as the paternalists believe.

V. Is Moral Education Really a Benefit?

Benefits advance interests. If moral education really is the benefit paternalists claim it is, it must advance a criminal's interests. Which interests? Presumably, the interest the criminal has in becoming a morally better person; as Morris says, the interest in being an autonomous individual freely attached to the good.

Why assume that criminals have such an interest? It is certainly not enough to show that criminals should have such an interest; moral education wouldn't be a benefit, after all, if it advanced none of the interests one actually has, but only those one ought to have.

It is clear that the defender of a paternalistic theory must argue that subjective interests do not exhaust the class of existing interests. Having a subjective interest is the same thing as wanting something; I have a subjective interest in doing philosophy just in case I want to do philosophy. Certainly there are some criminals who do not want to become morally better persons. If making them so really is a benefit, it must be because they have interests other than those represented by their actual wants.

Establishing the existence of objective interests in being a moral person is naturally related to showing how being immoral represents a harmful state. As we saw in Section IV, moral education will be a benefit only if being immoral is tantamount to being badly-off. Defense of this claim requires construction of a picture of human flourishing which must hold for all persons regardless of their subjective interests. Plato certainly believed in such a picture, which led him to devote much time trying to show how immoral behavior has to result from ignorance, since moral behavior is always in our interests, and we always act so as to promote our perceived interests. If we act immorally, we misperceive the situation, misidentify what is really in our interests.[28]

Whether or not we always act so as to fulfill our perceived interests, Plato's claim holds water only if he can show that morally good activity is always in our interests. This requires him (a) to provide a theory of objective interests, and (b) to show that among them is the interest in being a morally good person. This is of course a very tall order, and one cannot fault Morris and Hampton for not addressing the issue in their already wide-ranging essays. But the existence of an objective interest in becoming a morally better person must be successfully defended. Without this defense, it seems unrealistic to attribute serious self-harm to those who have greatly profited from their criminal misdeeds.

What Plato says to diffuse such an observation is to reduce the importance of the types of things capable of being gotten through immorality. The importance of political power, material goods, social influence is downplayed, while the health of one's soul is elevated to the status of all-important good. Unless one is willing to go along with Plato in diminishing the importance of ill-gotten gains, the claim that immorality necessitates serious personal harm is highly doubtful.

Moral educationists must do one of two things. They must either agree with Plato about the relative ranking of goods, diminishing the importance of those acquirable through immorality, or accept the importance of such goods but claim that even greater evils accompany their immoral acquisition. If they opt for the latter alternative, paternalists must show that an individual can be made better off by a moral education, even if this education does not further any of her existing wants. There appears to be no prima facie reason for thinking that immoral individuals are necessarily harmed by their immorality, that a moral education necessarily constitutes a benefit conferred. It seems we are justified in believing that immoral individuals may live successfully, until such time as we are given a persuasive account of how immorality necessarily impedes human flourishing. That account has yet to be provided.

VI. An Indeterminate Sentencing Policy?

Will a paternalistic theory allow an indeterminate sentencing policy? Morris clearly thinks not, as the following passage indicates:

> The practice of punishment . . . cannot permit open-ended punishments, repeated punishments, or punishments that are excessively severe. For the goal is not repentance at all costs, if that has meaning, but repentance freely arrived at, repentance that is not merely a disposition towards conformity with the norms. Also, the punishment provided for wrongdoing must reflect judgments of the seriousness of the wrong done; such punishment cannot focus on some end-state of the person and disregard the potential for moral confusion that would arise from repeated or excessive punishment.[29]

I think Morris is correct about excluding excessively severe punishments, where excessive severity implies treating an offender as less than a person. But if we are restricting the discussion simply to the duration of incarceration, I do not see any paternalistic grounds that would exclude an indeterminate sentencing policy.

It is unrealistic to think that we can bring about the autonomous moral reformation of offenders by meting out identical sentences to those who have committed like crimes. Some will be harder to educate than others, regardless of whether they have committed identical crimes. Further, judges will almost certainly be unable to specify, at the time of sentencing, the precise duration of the incarceration necessary to achieve the desired reeducation. Morris believes that giving disparate sentences to criminals who have committed like offenses will undercut the effects of moral education. This would be true only if we believed that those who commit like offenses are equally adaptable to moral education. That seems a rather implausible assumption.

Morris believes that individuals ought to be punished in proportion to their wrongdoing. This would lead us to like sentences for like offenses. This principle seems a natural component of a retributivist theory, and Morris, of course, is free to borrow it, since he holds that paternalism is only part of the overall justification for punishment. (Hampton is just as clearly not entitled to its use, since she claims that moral education can provide an exclusive justification for punishment.) Still, acceptance of a proportionality principle does not entail acceptance on paternalistic grounds, and that, after all, is what Morris wants to show.

It seems unlikely that imposing identical sentences for like crimes will always, or even usually, bring offenders closer to being autonomous persons freely attached to the good. We may have other reasons for applying a proportionality principle—equal treatment considerations, for example—but they derive no support from a paternalistic framework. Insofar as a theory is paternalistic, there is no bar to according longer sentences to the morally recalcitrant than to the morally repentant, even if they have committed like offenses.

Hampton agrees with Morris in rejecting a sentencing policy that shortens the repentant's stay and lengthens that of the unrepentant. We do not extend the sentences of the unrepentant because it makes no practical sense, and is in fact gratuitously cruel, to attempt to force a criminal to undertake moral reformation after his fixed sentence is up. Alternately, we do require the apparently repentant criminal to serve out her sentence in full. Not only that, but we also punish those who, prior to punishment, have exhibited clear signs of repentance. There are fallibilistic reasons for doing so; we can never be certain that the reform is sincere. Further, in suspending punishment, we remove what for many is a major source of repentance—the apprehension of the actual suffering through hard treatment—thereby undercutting our educational goals.

If our inability to know the real moral character of a convict precludes us from suspending her sentence, why doesn't it also enable us to extend the sentence of a criminal who is apparently unrepentant? Although it seems to us as if he'll remain unrepentant, we cannot foresee, given our limited knowledge of another's moral character, that he won't change his ways with further punishment (or perhaps just the prospect of further punishment). Additionally, extending the sentence of an unrepentant criminal needn't be seen as an attempt to force the criminal to moral reform. So long as the extended punishment is carried out respectfully, there is no reason to suppose that the extension is any more of a forcing than the original punishment.

Alternately, if we can adequately distinguish a criminal's true repentance from a faked one, there seems no possible educationist justification for requiring the repentant criminal to serve her sentence in its entirety. And if our knowledge extends this far, we will be able to identify at least some of those who are morally incurable. This is important, because if we know in advance of the futility of our educative efforts, it seems the moral educationist is unable to justify punishment. Punishment, in those circumstances, would seem nothing more than an exercise of gratuitous cruelty. But this has the unsavory consequence that those who are irremediably evil should be exempt from punishment. That's hardly what we'd expect from a plausible justification of punishment.[30]

A further problem arises when we ask what the educationist basis shall be for determining the length of sentences. Hampton speaks as if sentences were somehow fixed, and then proceeds to question whether they should be lengthened or shortened to correspond with apparent moral reformation or intransigence. But precisely how are educational goals to determine sentencing policies? Given the paternalists' emphasis on moral education, there appears to be no reason for determining the duration of a sentence by reference only to the class of crime committed.

The obvious response is that there is a correlation between type of crime committed and the need for moral education. But this answer fails, for two reasons. First, criminals committing similar crimes often exhibit wildly unequal needs for moral education. Second, some criminals who commit less severe crimes are in greater need of moral education than those with more serious offenses to their names.

The most promising avenue for the educationist is to claim that one of the moral truths we wish to provide our criminals is that equals ought to be treated equally. Thus part of the moral education will be devoted to showing why those in relevantly similar situations ought not to be treated differently. By employing an indeterminate sentencing policy, our practice would be antithetical to our preaching.

This is a powerful point for the educationist. But its importance is diminished, I think, by the following considerations. First, although it is important that the criminal subscribe to equal treatment principles, it is also important that the criminal develop the empathetic knowledge discussed earlier. While determinate sentencing policies would reinforce a commitment to equal treatment, there is no reason to think they assist in the development of empathetic knowledge. Quite the contrary: there is every reason to suppose that some will develop this knowledge more quickly than others. To the extent that educationist goals conflict, we must rank them and structure our sentencing practices accordingly. It seems plausible to suppose that the development of empathetic knowledge is as important as fostering subscription to equal treatment principles. If this is so, we have a prima facie case for indeterminate sentencing policies.

Second, it is not even clear that the goals of equal treatment and empathetic knowledge conflict. That's because equal treatment may not require identical sentencing for like crimes. There are always three questions to ask when discussing equal treatment: what treatment is being proposed, what makes this treatment equal, and what features must be equally possessed in order to justify extending equal treatment? It is the third question that interests me here. We have been assuming that equal treatment requires identical sentences, because we have also assumed that the only basis for equal sentencing is having committed like crimes. But equal punitive treatment need not be based solely on this feature. In fact, there seems every reason to include another feature in the educationist account of equal treatment, namely, the need for moral education. Thus, we would treat people equally if we meted out identical sentences to those who stand in similar need of moral education. But there is no reason to suppose that those who commit identical crimes equally possess the feature which triggers equal treatment considerations, namely, an equal need for moral education. On educationist grounds, it would thus seem permissible to extend different sentences to those committing similar crimes.[31]

VII. Partial or Comprehensive?

Morris and Hampton disagree about the types of justifications that can be offered on behalf of the moral educative theory. Morris believes that any plausible justification for punishment cannot be exclusive; it must incorporate strands from other prominent traditions of justification for punishment. Hampton, on the other hand, does believe an exclusive justification can be provided, although she acknowledges that her article represents only a first step for such a program.

The strongest criticism of an exclusive justification arises when considering instances in which the success of the attempted education is doomed from the start. The criticism, in brief, is this: a justification for punishment is implausible if it does not allow punishment for the criminal known to be irremediably evil; Hampton's proposal is such a justification; therefore her proposal is implausible.

If the justification for punishment is exclusively educationist, then the ends which justify punishment must be solely concerned with conferring moral benefits. If, by hypothesis, such benefits cannot be conferred, because the would-be recipient is known to be intransigent, then the possibility of justification apparently drops from view. The educationist cannot say that punishment is justified by its ancillary benefits, e.g., incapacitation or deterrence. So long as the paternalist's goals are being promoted through punishment, she is free to cite these ancillary benefits as valuable bonuses emerging from an application of her favored theory. If moral education purports to be an exclusive justification for punishment, however, it must be unsuccessful to the extent that its primary aim is incapable of being achieved. Thus punishment for the known moral intransigent would be unjustified. But this seems revolting—if punishment is ever justified, surely this person is the one to receive it!

This shows our very deep attachment to other punitive goals—among them, retribution, deterrence, and incapacitation. Of course, Hampton and others are free to claim that our attachments are misplaced. But the principled basis on which to make such a claim is unclear. For Hampton has apparently set out to justify the moral education theory by showing that it conforms to many of our most deeply-held intuitions about the proper treatment of others. She does not, for instance, attempt to justify the theory by deriving it from some more comprehensive ethical theory. But her methodological approach has yielded very counter-intuitive conclusions for a class of cases, thereby damaging the prospect of providing an exclusive justification.

Hampton might respond by claiming that punishment is justified just in case it attempts to morally educate the criminal. So the fact that some punishments will be ineffective doesn't undermine their justification. After all, no one can expect a perfect success rate. A criminal's intransigence doesn't eliminate the justification for punishing him; it simply means that his justified punishment will take place without conferring the desired benefit.

The weakness of this response may be seen when we look at the structure of attempts. In most cases, one attempts to perform an action only if one thinks the attempt capable of succeeding. We are likely to be puzzled by the person who antecedently knows of the futility of her attempts, yet proceeds in her endeavors. A known inability to attain one's goal will undercut the justification for the attempt. It seems no different in the case of punishment. If one knows antecedently of the futility of attaining one's goal—moral education of the criminal—what could justify such hard treatment? Such treatment should appear to the educationist as nothing more than the infliction of gratuitous suffering. Unless she is surreptitiously relying on retributivist or special deterrence positions, there seems no good reason to allow the deprivation that punishment entails, and reliance on such positions would effectively undercut the exclusive nature of the moral education justification.

I have no comprehensive theory of my own to offer as an alternative to the moral education theories I have criticized. Even if I did, this would not be the appropriate point at which to develop it. But since I did not intend my criticisms in this paper to rely on a particular theory of punishment, the absence of one should not undermine my conclusions. Nevertheless, I should say something about how a comprehensive theory of punishment should be structured.

I am sympathetic to Morris's view that an acceptable justification for punishment must meld together various strands of traditional justifications. This certainly is easier said than done. Mixed theories generate justificatory problems that do not beset theories, like Hampton's, which can be derived from a single principle. As a preliminary matter, any mixed theory must overcome the following hurdles. First, one must select and justify the strands that are to be entwined in the theory. Will the theory combine deterrence and retributive features? Rehabilitative and incapacitative and educationist goals? Given an absence of consensus both on the desiderata for a justification of punishment, and on the appropriate means of justifying a desideratum when disagreements about its merit arise, justifying the incorporation of one's favored elements is likely to be very difficult.

Second, and no less difficult, one must assign weights to the various strands. Perhaps all of the goals get equal billing in a conjunctive justification: punishment is justified, say, if and only if it deters and attempts to morally educate and punishes only the criminal proportionally to her guilt. Perhaps, on the other hand, we should place emphasis on some goals more than others: the primary goal, say, is to morally educate, but this cannot justifiably be done unless some deterrent effects accompany the education.

Third, some of the goals will invariably compete with one another, so that satisfaction of one comes at the expense of another. The theorist needs a principled way to adjudicate such practical and oftentimes theoretical conflicts. For instance, do we allow a criminal's moral education to be sacrificed in a well-publicized case with lots of deterrent capacity? What if punishing a popular brigand proportionally to his guilt reduces respect for the law? What if the only way to deter the criminal is to punish excessively? Problems of selection, justification, and weighting of the components in a comprehensive theory await any moral educationist who rejects, as Morris does, the possibility of exclusive justifications for punishment.

Conclusion

The paternalist's first argumentative burden involves defending the idea that moral education must be constrained by respect for autonomy. Doing this requires an examination of the concept of autonomy, and a defense of one of two theses: either that autonomy may never be permissibly infringed, in which case one must argue for inalienable rights, or that it may be permissibly infringed, and is so in the case of punishment. Second, one must rebut charges that incarceration is morally inefficacious in bringing about one's desired goal, either by showing that punishment will not take the form of incarceration, or by providing additional reasons, not subject to my criticisms, for attributing to it a role in moral education. Third, paternalists must show that scarce resources are justifiably allocated to the moral education of criminal offenders, rather than to addressing the needs of law-abiding citizens. They must also show that we are obligated to provide for a criminal's moral education, even in a world of limitless resources. Fourth, a theory of objective interests is needed, showing why immorality necessarily constitutes a harm to an individual. Fifth, educationists must either defend an indeterminate sentencing policy or show that there are good paternalistic reasons for excluding such a policy from the desired penal institutions. Lastly, my criticism of an exclusive educationist theory must be rebutted, or work must be undertaken to provide a justification which incorporates moral education as but one element among others.[32]

NOTES

1. Herbert Morris, "A Paternalistic Theory of Punishment," *American Philosophical Quarterly* 18 (1981): 263–71 [henceforth. Morris]; Jean Hampton, "The Moral Education Theory of Punishment," *Philosophy and Public Affairs* 13 (1984): 208–38 [henceforth, Hampton]. Robert Nozick and R. A. Duff have recently incorporated elements of the moral education approach into their justifications of punishment. For Nozick's views, see below, note 9. For Duff's account, see *Trials and Punishments* (New York: Cambridge University Press. 1985), esp. pp. 64–73, 254–62 and 268–77.

   Plato's thoughts on the subject can be found in the *Gorgias* 476a–479e and the *Laws* 860a–864b. The best extended account of Plato's thoughts on these matters can be found in M. M. Mackenzie's book *Plato on Punishment* (Berkeley: University of California, 1985), esp. pp. 170–206.
2. Morris, 265.
3. Ibid.
4. Ibid.
5. Hampton, 212.
6. Morris, 265, 269, 270; Hampton 212–13, 214, 222. At 265 Morris says "Unacceptable to this theory would be any response that sought the good of a wrongdoer in a manner that bypassed the human capacity for reflection, understanding and revision of attitude than may result from such efforts." At 269: "This theory would regard as morally unacceptable a response, conditioned or otherwise, that had as its goal not just aversion to wrongdoing, but obliteration of one's capacity to choose to do so." Hampton on the same point: "According to the moral education theory, punishment is not intended as a way of conditioning a human being to do what society wants her to do." (212) At 222: "This theory insists that as [the criminal] is educated, his autonomy must be respected. The moral education theorist does not want 'education' confused with 'conditioning.' " Contrast Plato on this point: "We may use absolutely *any* means to make him [the

criminal] hate injustice and embrace true justice—or at any rate not hate it" (*Laws* 862e). Plato also sounds an ominous note for those deemed incurable of their immorality: "Those who commit the ultimate injustices and because of such injustices become incurable, examples are made of them" (*Gorgias* 525b). See also *Laws* 735e: "Punishment is, ultimately, taken to the point of death or exile. That usually gets rid of the major criminals who are incurable and do the state enormous harm."

With Plato, the emphasis is on the end state of the criminal—what's important is that he ultimately be the kind of person who chooses good over evil. For Morris and Hampton, what's ultimately important is that we respect the criminal's right to be treated as a moral agent, even if this means that he rejects morality in the end.

7. Hampton dislikes the term "paternalistic" as a description of her theory, but I will nonetheless use it for purposes of simplicity, treating "paternalist" and "moral education theorist" as synonyms.
8. See Hampton, p. 219; Morris, p. 263. Moral education theorists must say something about the content of the criminal law, namely, that all of its prohibitions be moral offenses as well. For if it were not the case that a certain criminal act were immoral, there would be no basis for attempting moral education, and hence no justified basis for punishment. But this claim is compatible with rejecting the comprehensive paternalistic view that prevention of self-harm is in itself a (sometimes overriding) reason to enact criminal prohibitions.
9. Hampton aptly illustrates this (at p. 216) with a typical Wild West movie scenario, in which the good guy, before apprehending the bad guy, must first tell him why he's about to suffer his fate. We would find deeply dissatisfying a situation in which the good guy shot his opponent in the back without explanation. Hence the importance of communicating to the wrongdoer the reasons for his punishment. Robert Nozick provides a good discussion of this point in *Philosophical Explanations* (Cambridge: Harvard University Press, 1981) pp. 368–74, as does Joel Feinberg in "The Expressive Function of Punishment," found in *Doing and Deserving* (Princeton University Press, 1977), *passim*. See also Morris, p. 264.
10. Perhaps the most influential U.S. advocate of the therapeutic model of criminality is Karl Menninger. See *The Crime of Punishment* (Viking, 1969).
11. I agree with Morris when he says that "any justification [for punishment] proposed as an exclusive one must . . . be met with skepticism, if not scorn." *Morris*, p. 271. See also p. 265. However, the problems with even a non-exclusive moral education theory may be so great as to render it ineligible to play a justificatory role for punishment. See section VII of this paper, "Partial or Exclusive?"
12. This right most likely represents a kind of shorthand for a set of rights whose core, scope, and weight would be more precisely drawn.
13. Morris, in fact, makes just this point in a much-anthologized earlier article entitled "Persons and Punishment," in J. Feinberg and H. Gross, *Philosophy of Law* (Belmont, Ca: Wadsworth, 1981) pp. 667–670.
14. Hampton, 214.
15. Morris, 270.
16. Neither Morris nor Hampton makes any defense of the inalienability claim in their recent articles. Morris does try to argue for the claim in "Persons and Punishment," but fails. His descriptions there of the right to be treated as a person (which is identical to the right to moral autonomy) are very rich, but the argument for its inalienability reduces to mere assertion. He states that the right can be neither transferred nor waived. Why not? Because our agreeing to waive it would not morally permit another to treat us as less than human. But this is no explanation; only a restatement of the position to be defended. Morris provides no other justification for the alienability claim.

    Morris's difficulties are compounded because he believes that the right to be treated as a person is also a human right—a moral right possessed by all human beings. Inalienable and human rights needn't be coextensive: inalienability specifies what one can(not) do with one's right, being a human right specifies who can possess the right. If we have a human right to be treated as a moral agent—as a person—what is the feature(s) on the basis of which we are accorded this right? It must, presumably, be a moral characteristic; why, for instance, would we accord such a strong protection on the basis of having a particular genetic code or having a particular skin color? But if some (as yet unidentified) moral feature is to ground this inalienable right, why suppose that even the most hard-bitten criminals possess it?
17. This formulation borrows from those presented by J. Feinberg in "The Expressive Function of Punishment," op. cit., H. L. A. Hart in "Prologomenon to the Principles of

Punishment," from *Punishment and Responsibility* (New York: Oxford University Press, 1968), and Morris in "A Paternalistic Theory . . . ," p. 264.

18. Hampton, 224.
19. One need only read the first fifty pages of Robert Hughes's *The Fatal Shore* (New York: Knopf, 1987) to be convinced of this. See also Darwin's interesting and pessimistic account of the Australian penal colonies in *Voyage of the Beagle* (Boston: Harvard Classics, 1968), pp. 448–49.
20. "It speaks in favor of [the moral education] theory that it rejects many forms of incarceration used today as legitimate punishments, insofar as they tend to make criminals morally worse rather than better." (Hampton, 228.)
21. These are discussed in Morris, 266–67.
22. Morris's defense of punishment in the earlier article relies on his assumption that society is a cooperative scheme which equally distributes benefits and burdens. The burdens are those involved in restraining oneself from violating the primary social rules (those addressed to citizens dictating what's to count as legally permissible behavior). The benefits—social stability and cohesion—are derived from the citizen's assumption of this burden of self-restraint. When a citizen fails to assume this burden—when she violates the law—she has effectively accumulated the benefits of the cooperative scheme without contributing to the costs that allow the benefits to accrue in the first place. As a way of repaying these costs, and nullifying the undeserved benefits, society imposes costs on the offender in the form of lost liberty.

    I believe Morris is committed to picturing the burdens that are to be equally distributed as psychological burdens of self-restraint. This is because the existence of these burdens is supposed to explain the existence of the benefits. It does seem sensible to explain the accumulation of the benefits accruing from social cooperation as having resulted, at least in part, from the self-restraint of a society's members. But if the relevant burdens are seen in this way, it seems false to say that they are ever equally distributed, since some find obedience to the laws much more difficult than others. If the burdens are equally distributed, what's to count as a maldistribution of benefits and burdens will be much more difficult to ascertain, and this maldistribution is, after all, precisely the basis upon which a society acquires the right to punish, according to Morris's earlier article. For an interesting (but, I think, ultimately unsuccessful) attempt to defend Morris against these familiar charges, see W. Sadurski, *Moral Pluralism and Legal Neutrality* (Dordrecht: Kluwer Academic Press, 1990), pp. 153–60.

23. Analogous problems arise with the restoration of old relationships. If one's old friends are part of a criminal community, incarceration wasn't necessary to restore the interrupted friendships. If one is attempting to restore a relation with one's victim, it is unclear that being incarcerated will help matters much. If restoration with one's victim is possible at all, it will most likely come not as a result of incarceration, but as a result of compensation, or a change of heart, or both. But then we are left with the old problem of trying to show how incarceration will produce a change of heart (it certainly won't make one better able to pay compensation). We're saddled with another cart-before-the-horse problem. Punishment, claims Morris, can morally educate because it can lead to the restoration of old relationships. But moral education cannot *consist* in this restoration, since any restoration is predicated upon an offender's already having been morally educated.

24. It is a vexed question in *Republic* scholarship whether non-rulers can become just. If they can, however, it is clear that Plato approves of morally educating the non-rulers in ways which violate their autonomy. See, for a famous example, Socrates' discussion of the noble lie at *Republic* 414c–416a.

25. It may seem that I am requiring too much of the educationist when I say that she must defend the existence of a social obligation to confer benefits on the offender. In written comments, an anonymous reviewer suggested that the educationist need show only that society ought to confer educative benefits on the offender, not that there is an obligation to do so. But what is the force of this "ought"? If it means simply that "it would be better that" such benefits were conferred, or that "there is some moral reason" to confer such benefits, then the claim is too weak. Paternalists claim that a punishment not designed to render moral education is ipso facto unjustified. That means that there are overriding moral reasons to at least attempt to morally educate through punishments. But if that is so, then failure to make such an attempt represents a failure to do what one has overriding moral reason to do. And this is nothing more than a failure to fulfill one's moral obligations. Thus the fact that educationists deem knowingly uneducative punishments as unjustified entails the view that if one is to punish, one has a

moral obligation to at least attempt to confer benefits on the offender.

26. Morris, 268.
27. First, it may be the case that the criminal is well-off, since it is possible that the criminal's soul is internally harmonious, yet directed to the promotion of evil rather than good. Socrates wishes to deny this, and claims that a well-ordered soul must be directed toward promotion of the good. It's far from clear that Socrates succeeded in his aim. Callicles, in the *Gorgias* (481b–486d), argues that the primacy of reason over the emotions and appetites entails nothing about the ends to which one's reason is aimed. It remains to be shown why having a well-ordered soul precludes having its ruling element (reason) directed at certain immoral ends.

    Second, if psychic well-being is the all-important human good, as Socrates claims, then it is unclear why justice (represented by the soul's internal harmony) so strongly requires us to refrain from physically harming others. Claiming that the criminal suffers more than his victim makes sense only if 1. The criminal actually is suffering; 2. the most important kind of suffering is psychological suffering; and 3. the criminal's degree of psychological suffering is greater than that of his victim's. Unless we can show that the criminal's soul is necessarily internally disharmonious (led by unreasoning elements), and that this disharmony is of greater importance than physical impairment, Morris's and Socrates's claims fail.
28. See the discussions in *Meno,* 77b–78b; *Gorgias,* 467c–468e; and *Protagoras* 352a–358a.
29. Morris, 268.
30. This is discussed at greater length in the following section. For now, note that if Hampton argues that we can never be sure that an individual is immune from the moral message, then we return to the problem of the preceding paragraph. If we can't be sure that an apparently unrepentant criminal who has served his fixed time will remain unreceptive to the moral message, why can't we keep him longer than others who have accepted the moral benefits, in hopes that he will come to see the light? If the primary goal is education, why not extend the lesson? Hampton might claim that it is somehow violative of autonomy to do so, but to make this case, she must first present us with an account of autonomy and its limits (or an account of autonomy and inalienable rights). Additionally, adoption of this tactic may undercut her claim that the moral education theory can provide an exclusive justification of punishment. For it would then appear that whenever purely educational goals were insufficient to constrain punishment in desired ways, we could introduce autonomy-based constraints as an ad hoc catch-all means of tidying things up.
31. Actually, this paragraph does not impugn the idea of a determinate sentencing policy, for the educationist might adopt a series of fixed sentences based solely on the need of criminals to receive a moral education. In this case, those who possess the relevant feature—the need for a moral education—to a like degree will receive like sentences, even if they have committed vastly different crimes. Though a determinate sentencing policy, it is still quite different from the one envisioned by Hampton in her article.
32. I would like to thank Allen Buchanan, Joel Feinberg, Julia Annas, and Ron Milo for very helpful criticisms and discussions of earlier drafts of this paper.

Study Questions

1. Even if it is assumed that Hampton's proposal is theoretically sound, what difficulties would there be in putting it into practice?
2. What sort of response do you think Hampton could make to Shafer-Landau's objections?
3. Would a more plausible theory of punishment hold that moral education provides only a *partial* justification for punishment? If so, what would provide the remaining justification?

E Restitution

Restitution: A New Paradigm of Criminal Justice

Randy E. Barnett

In this selection, a radical alternative to conventional theories of punishment is proposed. Barnett claims that what is needed is a drastic reorientation in our thinking so that we will cease to regard crime as an offense against "society" and conceive of it instead as a wrong done to the individual victim of the criminal's act. Once this is done, we will see the plausibility of adopting a new paradigm of criminal justice—that of *restitution* by the criminal to his or her victim. He attempts to show that replacing punishment with such a system would have many advantages and is not open to any significant objections that are not also problems for traditional systems of punishment.

Outline of a New Paradigm

The idea of restitution is actually quite simple. It views crime as an offense by one individual against the rights of another. The victim has suffered a loss. Justice consists of the culpable offender making good the loss he has caused. It calls for a complete refocusing of our image of crime. Kuhn would call it a "shift of worldview." Where we once saw an offense against society, we now see an offense against an individual victim. In a way, it is a common-sense view of crime. *The armed robber did not rob society, he robbed the victim.* His debt, therefore, is not to society; it is to the victim. There are really two types of restitution proposals: a system of "punitive" restitution and a "pure" restitutional system.

1. Punitive Restitution. "Since rehabilitation was admitted to the aims of penal law two centuries ago, the number of penological aims has remained virtually constant. Restitution is waiting to come in."[1] Given this view, restitution should merely be added to the paradigm of punishment. Stephan Schafer outlines the proposal: "[Punitive] restitution, like punishment, must always be the subject of judicial consideration. Without exception it must be carried out by personal performance by the wrong-doer, and should even then be equally burdensome and just for all criminals, irrespective of their means, whether they be millionaires or labourers."[2]

Reprinted from *Ethics*, vol. 87, no. 4 (July 1977), pp. 279–301, by permission of The University of Chicago Press. Some footnotes are omitted.

This paper was made possible by a research fellowship from the Law and Liberty Project of the Institute for Humane Studies, Menlo Park, California. A somewhat expanded version of it appear in the book, *Assessing the Criminal: Restitution, Retribution and the Legal Process*, ed. Randy E. Barnett and John Hagel (Cambridge, Mass.: Ballinger Publishing Co.). Also, I wish to extend my appreciation to John V. Cody, Davis E. Keeler, Murray N. Rothbard, and Lloyd L. Weinreb for their invaluable criticism and comments. I am greatly in their debt and hope to be able at some future time to make suitable restitution.

There are many ways by which such a goal might be reached. The offender might be forced to compensate the victim by his own work, either in prison or out. If it came out of his pocket or from the sale of his property this would compensate the victim, but it would not be sufficiently unpleasant for the offender. Another proposal would be that the fines be proportionate to the earning power of the criminal. Thus, "A poor man would pay in days of work, a rich man by an equal number of days' income or salary."[3] Herbert Spencer made a proposal along similar lines in his excellent "Prison-Ethics," which is well worth examining.[4] Murray N. Rothbard and others have proposed a system of "double payments" in cases of criminal behavior.[5] While closer to pure restitution than other proposals, the "double damages" concept preserves a punitive aspect.

Punitive restitution is an attempt to gain the benefits of pure restitution, which will be considered shortly, while retaining the perceived advantages of the paradigm of punishment. Thus, the prisoner is still "sentenced" to some unpleasantness—prison labor or loss of *X* number of days' income. That the intention is to preserve the "hurt" is indicated by the hesitation to accept an out-of-pocket payment or sale of assets. This is considered too "easy" for the criminal and takes none of his time. The amount of payment is determined not by the *actual harm* but by the *ability of the offender to pay*. Of course, by retaining the paradigm of punishment this proposal involves many of the problems we raised earlier. In this sense it can be considered another attempt to salvage the old paradigm.

2. Pure Restitution. "Recompense or restitution is scarcely a punishment as long as it is merely a matter of returning stolen goods or money. . . . The point is not that the offender deserves to suffer; it is rather that the offended party desires compensation."[6] This represents the complete overthrow of the paradigm of punishment. No longer would the deterrence, reformation, disablement, or rehabilitation of the criminal be the guiding principle of the judicial system. The attainment of these goals would be incidental to, and as a result of, reparations paid to the victim. No longer would the criminal deliberately be made to suffer for his mistake. Making good that mistake is all that would be required. What follows is a possible scenario of such a system.

When a crime occurred and a suspect was apprehended, a trial court would attempt to determine his guilt or innocence. If found guilty, the criminal would be sentenced to make restitution to the victim.[7] If a criminal is able to make restitution immediately, he may do so. This would discharge his liability. If he were unable to make restitution, but were found by the court to be trustworthy, he would be permitted to remain at his job (or find a new one) while paying restitution out of his future wages. This would entail a legal claim against future wages. Failure to pay could result in garnishment or a new type of confinement.

If it is found that the criminal is not trustworthy, or that he is unable to gain employment, he would be confined to an employment project.[8] This would be an industrial enterprise, preferably run by a private concern, which would produce actual goods or services. The level of security at each employment project would vary according to the behavior of the offenders. Since the costs would be lower, inmates at a lower-security project would receive higher wages. There is no reason why many workers could not be permitted to live with their families inside or outside the facility, depending, again, on the trustworthiness of the offender. Room and board would be deducted from the wages first, then a certain amount for restitution. Anything over that amount the worker could keep or apply toward further restitution, thus hastening his release. If a worker refused to work, he would be unable to pay for his maintenance, and therefore would not in principle be entitled to it. If he did not make restitution he could not be released. The exact arrangement which would best provide for high productivity, minimal security, and maximum incentive to work and repay the victim cannot be determined in advance. Experience is bound to yield some plans superior to others. In fact, the experimentation has already begun.[9]

While this might be the basic system, all sorts of refinements are conceivable, and certainly many more will be invented as needs arise. A few examples might be illuminating. With such a system of repayment, victim *crime insurance* would be more economically feasible than at present and highly desirable. The cost of awards would be offset by the insurance company's right to restitution in place of the victim (right of subrogation). The insurance company would be better suited to supervise the offender and mark his progress than would the victim. To obtain an earlier recovery, it could be expected to innovate so as to enable the worker to repay more quickly (and, as a result, be released that much sooner). The insurance companies might even underwrite the employment projects themselves as well as related industries which would employ the skilled worker after his release. Any successful effort on their part to reduce crime and recidivism would result in fewer claims and lower premiums. The benefit of this insurance scheme for the victim is immediate compensation, conditional on the victim's continued cooperation with the authorities for the arrest and conviction of the suspect. In addition, the centralization of victim claims would, arguably, lead to efficiencies which would permit the pooling of small claims against a common offender.

Another highly useful refinement would be *direct arbitration* between victim and criminal. This would serve as a sort of healthy substitute for plea bargaining. By allowing the guilty criminal to negotiate a reduced payment in return for a guilty plea, the victim (or his insurance company) would be saved the risk of an adverse finding at trial and any possible additional expense that might result. This would also allow an indigent criminal to substitute personal services for monetary payments if all parties agreed.

Arbitration is argued for by John M. Greacen, deputy director of the National Institute for Law Enforcement and Criminal Justice. He sees the possible advantages of such reform as the ". . . development of more creative dispositions for most criminal cases; for criminal victims the increased use of restitution, the knowledge that their interests were considered in the criminal process; and an increased satisfaction with the outcome; increased awareness on the part of the offender that his crime was committed against another human being, and not against society in general; increased possibility that the criminal process will cause the offender to acknowledge responsibility for his acts."[10] Greacen notes several places where such a system has been tried with great success, most notably Tucson, Arizona, and Columbus, Ohio.[11]

Something analogous to the medieval Irish system of *sureties* might be employed as well.[12] Such a system would allow a concerned person, group, or company to make restitution (provided the offender agrees to this). The worker might then be released in the custody of the surety. If the surety had made restitution, the offender would owe restitution to the surety who might enforce the whole claim or show mercy. Of course, the more violent and unreliable the offender, the more serious and costly the offense, the less likely it would be that anyone would take the risk. But for first offenders, good workers, or others that charitable interests found deserving (or perhaps unjustly convicted) this would provide an avenue of respite.

Restitution and Rights

These three possible refinements clearly illustrate the flexibility of a restitutional system. It may be less apparent that this flexibility is *inherent* to the restitutional paradigm. Restitution recognizes rights in the victim, and this is a principal source of its strength. The nature and limit of the victim's right to restitution at the same time defines the nature and limit of the criminal liability. In this way, the aggressive action of the criminal creates a *debt* to the victim. The recognition of rights and obligations make possible many innovative arrangements. Subrogation, arbitration, and suretyship are three examples mentioned above. They are possible because this right to compensation[13] is considered the property of the victim and can therefore be delegated, assigned, inherited, or bestowed. One could determine in advance who would acquire the right to any restitution which he himself might be unable to collect.

The natural owner of an unenforced death claim would be an insurance company that had insured the deceased. The suggestion has been made that a person might thus increase his personal safety by insuring with a company well known for tracking down those who injure its policy holders. In fact, the partial purpose of some insurance schemes might be to provide the funds with which to track down the malefactor. The insurance company, having paid the beneficiaries would "stand in their shoes." It would remain possible, of course, to simply assign or devise the right directly to the beneficiaries, but this would put the burden of enforcement on persons likely to be unsuited to the task.

If one accepts the Lockean trichotomy of property ownership,[14] that is, acquiring property via exchange, gifts, and *homesteading* (mixing one's labor with previously unowned land or objects), the possibility arises that upon a person's wrongful death, in the absence of any heirs or assignees, his right to compensation becomes unowned property. The right could then be claimed (homesteaded) by anyone willing to go to the trouble of catching and prosecuting the criminal. Firms might specialize in this sort of activity, or large insurance companies might make the effort as a kind of "loss leader" for public relations purposes.

This does, however, lead to a potentially serious problem with the restitutional paradigm: what exactly constitutes "restitution"? What is the *standard* by which compensation is to be made? Earlier we asserted that any such problem facing the restitutional paradigm faces civil damage suits as well. The method by which this problem is dealt with in civil cases could be applied to restitution cases. But while this is certainly true, it may be that this problem has not been adequately handled in civil damage suits either.

Restitution in cases of crimes against property is a manageable problem. Modern contract and tort doctrines of restitution are adequate. The difficulty lies in cases of personal injury or death. How can you put a price on life or limb, pain or suffering? Is not any attempt to do so of necessity arbitrary? It must be admitted that a fully satisfactory solution to this problem is lacking, but it should also be stressed that this dilemma, though serious, has little impact on the bulk of our case in favor of a restitutional paradigm. It is possible that no paradigm of criminal justice can solve every problem, yet the restitutional approach remains far superior to the paradigm of punishment or any other conceivable rival.

This difficulty arises because certain property is unique and irreplaceable. As a result, it is impossible to approximate a "market" or "exchange" value expressed in monetary terms. Just as there is no rational relationship between a wrongfully taken life and ten years in prison, there is little relationship between that same life and $20,000. Still, the nature of this possibly insoluble puzzle reveals a restitutional approach theoretically superior to punishment. For it must be acknowledged that a real, tangible loss *has* occurred. The problem is only one of incommensurability. Restitution provides *some* tangible, albeit inadequate, compensation for personal injury. Punishment provides none at all.[15]

It might be objected that to establish some "pay scale" for personal injury is not only somewhat arbitrary but also a disguised reimplementation of punishment. Unable to accept the inevitable consequences of restitutional punishment, the argument continues, I have retreated to a pseudorestitutional award. Such a criticism is unfair. The true test in this instance is one of primacy of intentions. Is the purpose of a system to compensate victims for their losses (and perhaps, as a consequence, punish the criminals), or is its purpose to punish the criminals (and perhaps, as a consequence, compensate the victims for their losses)? The true ends of a criminal justice system will determine its nature. In short, arbitrariness *alone* does not imply a retributive motive. And while arbitrariness remains to some extent a problem for the restitutional paradigm, it is less of a problem for restitution than for punishment, since compensation has *some* rational relationship to damages and costs.

Advantages of a Restitutional System

1. The first and most obvious advantage is the assistance provided to victims of crime. They may have suffered an emotional, physical, or financial loss. Restitution would not change the fact that a possibly traumatic crime has occurred (just as the award of damages does not undo tortious conduct). Restitution, however, would make the resulting loss easier to bear for both victims and their families. At the same time, restitution would avoid a major pitfall of victim compensation/welfare plans: Since it is the criminal who must pay, the possibility of collusion between victim and criminal to collect "damages" from the state would be all but eliminated.

2. The possibility of receiving compensation would encourage victims to report crimes and to appear at trial. This is particularly true if there were a crime insurance scheme which contractually committed the policyholder to testify as a condition for payment, thus rendering unnecessary oppressive and potentially tyrannical subpoenas and contempt citations. Even the actual reporting of the crime to police is likely to be a prerequisite for compensation. Such a requirement in auto theft insurance policies has made car thefts the most fully reported crime in the United States. Furthermore, insurance companies which paid the claim would have a strong incentive to see that the criminal was apprehended and convicted. Their pressure and assistance would make the proper functioning of law enforcement officials all the more likely.

3. Psychologist Albert Eglash has long argued that restitution would aid in the rehabilitation of criminals. "Restitution is something an inmate does, not something done for or to him. . . . Being reparative, restitution can alleviate guilt and anxiety, which can otherwise precipitate further offenses."[16] Restitution, says Eglash, is an active effortful role on the part of the offender. It is socially constructive, thereby contributing to the offender's self-esteem. It is related to the offense and may thereby redirect the thoughts which motivated the offense. It is reparative, restorative, and may actually leave the situation better than it was before the crime, both for the criminal and victim.[17]

4. This is a genuinely "self-determinative" sentence.[18] The worker would know that the length of his confinement was in his own hands. The harder he worked, the faster he would make restitution. He would be the master of his fate and would have to face that responsibility. This would encourage useful, productive activity and instill a conception of reward for good behavior and hard work. Compare this with the current probationary system and "indeterminate sentencing" where the decision for release is made by the prison bureaucracy, based only (if fairly administered) on "good behavior"; that is, passive acquiescence to prison discipline. Also, the fact that the worker would be acquiring *marketable* skills rather than more skillful methods of crime should help to reduce the shocking rate of recidivism.

5. The savings to taxpayers would be enormous. No longer would the innocent taxpayer pay for the apprehension and internment of the guilty. The cost of arrest, trial, and internment would be borne by the criminal himself. In addition, since now-idle inmates would become productive workers (able, perhaps, to support their families), the entire economy would benefit from the increase in overall production.[19]

6. Crime would no longer pay. Criminals, particularly shrewd white-collar criminals, would know that they could not dispose of the proceeds of their crime and, if caught, simply serve time. They would have to make full restitution plus enforcement and legal costs, thereby greatly increasing the incentive

to prosecute. While this would not eliminate such crime it would make it rougher on certain types of criminals, like bank and corporation officials, who harm many by their acts with a virtual assurance of lenient legal sanctions.[20] It might also encourage such criminals to keep the money around for a while so that, if caught, they could repay more easily. This would make a full recovery more likely.

A restitutional system of justice would benefit the victim, the criminal, and the taxpayer. The humanitarian goals of proportionate punishment, rehabilitation, and victim compensation are dealt with on a *fundamental* level making their achievement more likely. In short, the paradigm of restitution would benefit all but the entrenched penal bureaucracy and enhance justice at the same time. What then is there to stop us from overthrowing the paradigm of punishment and its penal system and putting in its place this more efficient, more humane, and more just system? The proponents of punishment and others have a few powerful counterarguments. It is to these we now turn.

Objections to Restitution

1. Practical criticisms of restitution. It might be objected that "crimes disturb and offend not only those who are directly their victim, but also the whole social order."[21] Because of this, society, that is, individuals other than the victim, deserves some satisfaction from the offender. Restitution, it is argued, will not satisfy the lust for revenge felt by the victim or the "community's sense of justice." This criticism appears to be overdrawn. Today most members of the community are mere spectators of the criminal justice system, and this is largely true even of the victim.[22] One major reform being urged presently is more victim involvement in the criminal justice process.[23] The restitution proposal would necessitate this involvement. And while the public generally takes the view that officials should be tougher on criminals, with "tougher" taken by nearly everyone to mean more severe in punishing, one must view this "social fact" in light of the lack of a known alternative. The real test of public sympathies would be to see which sanction people would choose: incarceration of the criminal for a given number of years or the criminal's being compelled to make restitution to the victim: While the public's choice is not clearly predictable, neither can it be assumed that it would reject restitution. There is some evidence to the contrary.

This brings us to a second practical objection: that monetary sanctions are insufficient deterrents to crime. Again, this is something to be discovered, not something to be assumed. There are a number of reasons to believe that our *current* system of punishment does not adequately deter, and for the reasons discussed earlier an increase in the level of punishment is unlikely. In fact, many have argued that the deterrent value of sanctions has less to do with *severity* than with *certainty*, and the preceding considerations indicate that law enforcement would be more certain under a restitutional system. In the final analysis, however, it is irrelevant to argue that more crimes may be committed if our proposal leaves the victim better off. It must be remembered: *Our goal is not the suppression of crime; it is doing justice to victims.*

A practical consideration which merits considerable future attention is the feasibility of the employment project proposal. A number of questions can be raised. At first blush, it seems naively optimistic to suppose that offenders will be able or willing to work at all, much less earn their keep and pay reparations as well. On the contrary, this argument continues, individuals turn to crime precisely because they lack the skills which the restitutional plan assumes they have. Even if these workers have the skills, but refuse to work, what could be done? Would not the use of force to compel compliance be tantamount to slavery? This criticism results in part from my attempt to sketch an "ideal" restitution system; that is, I have attempted to outline the type toward which every criminal justice system governed by the restitution paradigm should strive. This is not to say that every aspect of the hypothetical system would, upon implementation, function smoothly. Rather, such a system could only operate ideally once the paradigm had been fully accepted and substantially articulated.

With this in mind, one can advance several responses. First, the problem as usually posed assumes the offender to be highly irrational and possibly mentally unbalanced. There is no denying that some segment of the criminal population fits the former description. What this approach neglects, however, is the possibility that many criminals are making rational choices within an irrational and unjust political system. Specifically I refer to the myriad laws and regulations which make it difficult for the unskilled or persons of transitory outlook to find legal employment. I refer also to the laws which deny legality to the types of services which are in particular demand in economically impoverished communities. Is it "irrational" to choose to steal or rob when one is virtually foreclosed from the legal opportunity to do otherwise? Another possibility is that the criminal chooses crime not because of foreclosure, but because he enjoys and obtains satisfaction from a criminal way of life. Though morally repugnant, this is hardly irrational.

Furthermore, it no longer can be denied that contact with the current criminal justice system is itself especially damaging among juveniles. The offenders who are hopelessly committed to criminal behavior are not usually the newcomers to crime but those who have had repeated exposure to the penal system. In Kuhn's words, "Existing institutions have ceased to meet the problems posed by an environment *they have in part created.*" While a restitutionary system might not change these hard-core offenders, it could, by the early implementation of sanctions perceived by the criminal to be just, break the vicious circle which in large part accounts for their existence.

Finally, if offenders could not or would not make restitution, then the logical and just result of their refusal would be confinement until they could or would. Such an outcome would be entirely in their hands. While this "solution" does not suggest who should justly pay for this confinement, the problem is not unique to a restitutionary system. In this and other areas of possible difficulty we must seek guidance from existing pilot programs as well as from the burgeoning research in this area and in victimology in general.

2. Distributionary criticisms of restitution. There remains one criticism of restitution which is the most obvious and the most difficult with which to deal. Simply stated, it takes the following form: "Doesn't this mean that rich people will be able to commit crimes with impunity if they can afford it? Isn't this unfair?" The *practical* aspect of this objection is that whatever deterrent effect restitution payments may have, they will be less for those most able to pay. The *moral* aspect is that whatever retributive or penal effect restitution payments may have they will be less for those who are well off. Some concept of equality of justice underlies both considerations.

Critics of restitution fail to realize that the "cost" of crime will be quite high. In addition to compensation for pain and suffering, the criminal must pay for the cost of his apprehension, the cost of the trial, and the legal expenditures of *both* sides. This should make even an unscrupulous wealthy person think twice about committing a crime. The response to this is that we cannot have it both ways. If the fines would be high enough to bother the rich, then they would be so high that a project worker would have no chance of earning that much and would, therefore, have no incentive to work at all. If, on the other hand, you lower the price of crime by ignoring all its costs, you fail to deter the rich or fully compensate the victim.

This is where the option of arbitration and victim crime insurance becomes of practical importance. If the victim is uninsured, he is unlikely to recover for all costs of a very severe crime from a poor, unskilled criminal, since even in an employment project the criminal might be unable to earn enough. If he had no hope of earning his release, he would have little incentive to work very hard beyond paying for his own maintenance. The victim would end up with less than if he had "settled" the case for the lesser amount which a project worker could reasonably be expected to earn. If, however, the victim had full-coverage criminal insurance, he would recover his damages in full, and the insurance company would absorb any disparity between full compensation and maximal employment project worker's output. This cost would be reflected in premium prices, enabling the insurance company which settled cases at an amount which increased the recovery from the criminal to offer the lowest rates. Eventually a "maximum" feasible fine for project workers would be determined based on these considerations. The "rich," on the other hand, would naturally have to pay in full. This arrangement would solve the practical problem, but it should not be thought of as an imperative of the restitutional paradigm.

The same procedure of varying the payments according to ability to pay would answer the moral considerations as well (that the rich are not hurt enough) and this is the prime motive behind *punitive* restitution proposals. However, we reject the moral consideration outright. The paradigm of restitution calls not for the (equal) hurting of criminals, but for restitution to victims. Any appeal to "inadequate suffering" is a reversion to the paradigm of punishment, and by varying the sanction for crimes of the same magnitude according to the economic status of the offender it reveals its own inequity. *Equality of justice means equal treatment of victims.* It should not matter to the victim if his attacker was rich or poor. His plight is the same regardless. Any reduction of criminal liability because of reduced earning power would be for practical, not moral, reasons.

Equality of justice derives from the fact that the rights of men should be equally enforced and respected. Restitution recognizes a victim's right to compensation for damages from the party responsible. Equality of justice, therefore, calls for equal enforcement of each victim's right to restitution. *Even if necessary or expedient, any lessening of payment to the victim because of the qualities of the criminal is a violation of that victim's rights and an inequality of justice.* Any such expedient settlement is only a recognition that an imperfect world may make possible only imperfect justice. As a practical matter, a restitutional standard gives victims an enormous incentive to pursue wealthy criminals since they can afford quick, full compensation. Contrast this with the present system where the preference given the wealthy is so prevalent that most victims simply assume that nothing will be done.

The paradigm of restitution, to reiterate, is neither a panacea for crime nor a blueprint for utopia. Panaceas and utopias are not for humankind. We must live in a less than perfect world with less than perfect people. Restitution opens the possibility of an improved and more just society. The old paradigm of punishment, even reformed, simply cannot offer this promise.

Other Considerations

Space does not permit a full examination of other, less fundamental, implications of such a system. I shall briefly consider five.

1. Civil versus criminal liability. If one accepts a restitutionary standard of justice, what sense does it make to distinguish between crime and tort, since both call for payment of damages? For most purposes I think the distinction collapses. Richard Epstein, in a series of brilliant articles, has articulated a theory of strict liability in tort.[24] His view is that since one party has caused another some harm and one of the parties must bear the loss, justice demands that it falls on the party who caused the harm. He argues that intention is only relevant as a "third-stage" argument; that notwithstanding some fault on the part of the plaintiff (a second-stage argument), the defendant intended the harm and is therefore liable.[25] With a restitutional system I see no reason why Epstein's theory of tort liability could not incorporate criminal liability into a single "system of corrective justice that looks to the conduct, broadly defined, of the parties to the case with a view toward the protection of individual liberty and private property."

There would, at least initially, be some differences, however. The calculation of damages under the restitutionary paradigm which includes cost of apprehension, cost of trial, and legal costs of both parties would be higher than tort law allows. A further distinction would be the power of enforcers to confine unreliable offenders to employment projects.[26]

2. Criminal responsibility and competency. Once a criminal sanction is based not on the offender's badness but on the nature and consequences of his acts, Thomas Szasz's proposal that the insanity plea be abolished makes a great deal of sense,[27] as does his argument that "all persons charged with offenses—except those grossly disabled—[are fit to stand trial and] should be tried."[28] On this view, Epstein's concept of fairness *as between the parties* is relevant. A restitution proceeding like a "lawsuit is always a comparative affair. The defendant's victory ensures the plaintiff's [or victim's] defeat. . . . Why should we prefer the injurer to his victim in a case where one may win and the other lose? . . . As a matter of fairness between the parties, the defendant should be required to treat the harms which he has inflicted upon another as though they were inflicted upon himself."[29]

3. Victimless crimes. The effect of restitutional standards on the legality of such crimes as prostitution, gambling, high interest loans, pornography, and drug use is intriguing. There has been no violation of individual rights, and consequently no damages and, therefore, no liability. While some may see this as a drawback, I believe it is a striking advantage of the restitutional standard of justice. So-called victimless crimes would in principle cease to be crimes. As a consequence, criminal elements would be denied a lucrative monopoly, and the price of these services would be drastically reduced. Without this enormous income, organized crime would be far less able to afford the "cost" of its nefarious activities than it is today.

4. Legal positivism. What is true for victimless crimes is true for the philosophy of legal positivism. On the positivist view, whatever the state (following all the correct political procedures) says is law, is law; hence, whatever the state makes a crime is a crime. A restitutional standard would hold the state to enforcing individual rights through the recovery of individual damages.

5. Legal process. Because the sanction for crime would no longer be punitive, the criminal process could explore less formal procedures for dispute settlement. Also, the voice of the victim would be added to the deliberations. One possible reform might be a three-tiered verdict: guilty, not proven, and not guilty. If found "guilty," the offender would pay all the costs mentioned above. If the charges are "not proven," then neither party would pay the other. If found "not guilty," the defendant would be reimbursed by the enforcement agency for his costs and inconvenience. This new interpretation of "not guilty" would reward those defendants who, after putting on a defense, convinced the trier of fact that they were innocent.

These and many other fascinating implications of restitution deserve a more thorough examination. As any new paradigm becomes accepted, it experiences what Kuhn calls a period of "normal research," a period characterized by continuous expansion and perfection of the new paradigm as well as a testing of its limits. The experimentation with restitutionary justice will, however, differ from the trial and error of the recent past since we will be guided by the principle that the purpose of our legal system is not to harm the guilty but to help the innocent—a principle which will above all restore our belief that our overriding commitment is to do justice.

NOTES

1. Gerhard O. W. Mueller, "Compensation for Victims of Crime: Thought before Action," *Minnesota Law Review* 50 (1965): 221.
2. Schafer, p. 127.
3. Ibid.
4. Herbert Spencer, "Prison-Ethics," in *Essays: Scientific, Political and Speculative* (New York: D. Appleton & Co., 1907), 3:152–91.
5. Murray N. Rothbard, *Libertarian Forum* 14, no. 1 (January 1972): 7–8.
6. Kaufmann, p. 55.
7. The nature of judicial procedure best designed to carry out this task must be determined. For a brief discussion of some relevant considerations, see Laster, pp. 80–98; Burt Galaway and Joe Hudson, "Issues in the Correctional Implementation of Restitution to Victims of Crime," in *Considering the Victim*, pp. 351–60. Also to be dealt with is the proper standard of compensation. At least initially, the problem of how much payment constitutes restitution would be no different than similar considerations in tort law. This will be considered at greater length below.
8. Such a plan (with some significant differences) has been suggested by Kathleen J. Smith in *A Cure for Crime: The Case for the Self-determinate Prison Sentence* (London: Gerald, Duckworth & Co., 1965), pp. 13–29; see also Morris and Linda Tannehill, *The Market for Liberty* (Lansing, Mich.: Privately printed, 1970), pp. 44–108.
9. For a recent summary report, see Burt Galaway, "Restitution as an Integrative Punishment" (paper prepared for the Symposium on Crime and Punishment: Restitution, Retribution, and Law, Harvard Law School, March 1977).
10. John M. Greacen, "Arbitration: A Tool for Criminal Cases?" *Barrister* (Winter 1975), p. 53; see also Galaway and Hudson, pp. 352–55; "Conclusions and Recommendations, International Study Institute on Victimology, Bellagio, Italy, July 1–12, 1975," *Victimology* 1 (1976): 150–51; Ronald Goldfarb, *Jails: The Ultimate Ghetto* (Garden City, N.Y.: Anchor Press/Doubleday, 1976), p. 480.
11. Greacen, p. 53.
12. For a description of the Irish system, see Joseph R. Peden, "Property Rights in Medieval Ireland: Celtic Law versus Church and State" (paper presented at the Symposium on the Origins and Development of Property Rights, University of San Francisco, January 1973); for a theoretical discussion of a similar proposal, see Spencer, pp. 182–86.
13. Or, perhaps more accurately, the compensation itself.
14. For a brief explanation of this concept and several of its possible applications, see Murray N. Rothbard, "Justice and Property Rights," in *Property in a Humane Economy*, ed. Samuel L. Blumenfeld (La Salle, Ill.: Open Court Publishing Co., 1974), pp. 101–22.
15. That the "spiritual" satisfaction which punishment may or may not provide is to be recognized as a legitimate form of "compensation" is a claim retributionists must defend.
16. Albert Eglash, "Creative Restitution: Some Suggestions for Prison Rehabilitation Programs," *American Journal of Correction* 40 (November–December 1958): 20.
17. Ibid.; see also Eglash's "Creative Restitution: A Broader Meaning for an Old Term," *Journal of Criminal Law and Criminology* 48 (1958): 619–22; Burt Galaway and Joe Hudson, "Restitution and Rehabilitation—Some Central Issues," *Crime and Delinquency* 18 (1972): 403–10.
18. Smith, pp. 13–29.
19. An economist who favors restitution on efficiency grounds is Gary S. Becker, although he does not break with the paradigm of punishment. Those interested in a mathematical "cost-benefit" analysis should see his "Crime and Punishment," *Journal of Political Economy* 76 (1968): 169–217.
20. This point is also made by Minocher Jehangirji Sethna in his paper, "Treatment and Atonement for Crime," in *Victims and Society*, p. 538.
21. Del Vecchio, p. 198.
22. William F. McDonald, "Towards a Bicentennial Revolution in Criminal Justice: The Return of the Victim," *American Criminal Law Review* 13 (1976): 659; see also his paper "Notes on the Victim's Role in the Prosecutional and Dispositional Stages of the Criminal Justice Process" (paper presented at the Second International Symposium on Victimology, Boston, September 1976); Jack M. Kress, "The Role of the Victim at Sentencing" (paper presented at the Second International Symposium on Victimology, Boston, September 1976).
23. McDonald, pp. 669–73; Kress, pp. 11–15. Kress specifically analyzes restitution as a means for achieving victim involvement.
24. Richard A. Epstein, "A Theory of Strict Liability in Tort," *Journal of Legal Studies* 2 (1973): 151–204.
25. Richard A. Epstein, "Intentional Harms," *Journal of Legal Studies* 3 (1975): 402–8; see also his article, "Defenses and Subsequent

Pleas in a System of Strict Liability," ibid., 3 (1974): 174–85.

26. It would seem that the only way to account for these differences would be an appeal to the *mens rea* or badness of the criminal as opposed to the unintentional tortfeasor. Yet such an approach, it might be argued, is not available to a restitutionary system which considers the moral outlook of an offender to be irrelevant to the determination of the proper criminal sanction. A possible response is that this overstates the restitutionist claim. That a criminal's mental state does not justify punishment does not imply that it is not relevant to *any* aspect of the criminal justice process. It may well be that it is relevant to the consideration of methods by which one is justified in extracting what, on other grounds, is shown to be a proper sanction, that is, restitution.
27. Szasz, pp. 228–30.
28. Ibid., pp. 228–29. "The emphasis here is on gross disability: it should be readily apparent or easily explicable to a group of lay persons, like a jury" (p. 229). But even the qualification of gross disablement might be unjustified (see Yochelson and Samenow, pp. 227–35).
29. Epstein, p. 398. In his article "Crime and Tort: Old Wine in Old Bottles," he takes exactly this approach with the insanity defense in tort law.

Punishment as Restitution: The Rights of the Community

MARGARET R. HOLMGREN

Holmgren agrees with Barnett that restitution is the appropriate paradigm of penal justice but maintains that criminal behavior harms not only the immediate or direct victim but also the community as a whole. She then attempts to show that "the members of the community are morally justified in instituting a practice of legal punishment in order to obtain restitution for the harm they suffer as a result of criminal violations."

Randy Barnett has recently argued that the traditional paradigm of criminal justice—punishment—is seriously flawed on both moral and practical grounds and ought to be replaced by a new paradigm—restitution. Instead of punishing the criminal, Barnett claims, we ought to exact restitution from him for the victim of his crime.[1]

From a moral point of view at least, Barnett's proposal has some appeal. Restitution is an intuitively plausible model of retributive justice, and it is free of some of the difficult moral problems that inhere in the traditional approaches to the justification of punishment. The purpose of exacting restitution from the criminal is not to make him suffer; it is to alleviate the suffering he has inflicted on another. This practice, then, is clearly compatible with the widely held conviction that it is wrong to make an individual suffer unless we must do so in order to secure an important interest for others (or perhaps for that individual himself).

Of course many writers have attempted to justify punishment on the grounds that it secures important benefits for everyone—benefits such as the protection of society and maintenance of respect for the law. But anyone who approaches the justification of punishment in this way must go on to show that the criminal is not being used as a mere means to secure these social benefits. This has been a notoriously difficult task. On the other hand, if we seek restitution from the criminal for the losses he has brought about, it seems clear that we are not using him as a mere means to promote social goals. Here, we only attempt to nullify the harmful effects of

From Margaret R. Holmgren, "Punishment as Restitution: The Rights of the Community," (as appeared in *Criminal Justice Ethics*, Vol. 2, No. 1, [Winter/Spring, 1983] pp. 36–49). Reprinted by permission of *The Institute for Criminal Justice Ethics*, 899 Tenth Avenue, New York, NY 10019.

I am indebted to Michael Churgin, William Galston, John Hodson, Robert Kane, and especially Edmund Pincoffs for helping me to develop the analysis suggested in this paper.

his own violation; we do not use him to produce a positive social benefit or to accomplish ends of our own. Once restitution has been made, those who have been harmed are, at best, in the same position they were in before the crime.

It seems reasonable to me to accept the claim that restitution is the appropriate paradigm of retributive justice, and, in the analysis that follows, I suggest that a practice of legal punishment can be justified in the context of this paradigm. My strategy is to show first that those who commit crimes bring about a significant loss for the members of their community in addition to harming the immediate victims of their crimes and, second, that a practice of legal punishment constitutes a means by which the members of the community can exact restitution for this loss. I argue, then, that the members of the community are morally justified in instituting a practice of legal punishment in order to obtain restitution for the harm they suffer as a result of criminal violations. After formulating this argument, I show that a restitutive analysis of punishment both captures and illuminates much of the retributivist position. Finally, I briefly consider some of the more specific implications of this approach to the justification of punishment and point out that it also diverges from the retributivist position in an important respect.

The concepts of punishment and restitution play a central role in the following discussion. For the purposes of this analysis, we can adopt the definition of punishment that Benn gives in *The Encyclopedia of Philosophy*: "Characteristically, punishment is unpleasant. It is inflicted on an offender because of an offense he has committed; it is deliberately imposed . . . and the unpleasantness is essential to it, not an accompaniment to some other treatment (like the pain of a dentist's drill)."[2]

The concept of restitution, as it is to be understood in the following analysis, contains two central components. I shall be concerned here only with situations in which one person, *A*, has brought about a loss for another person (or group of persons), *B*, in violation of the requirements of justice. In this context, I shall say that *B* has received (some) restitution for the loss he has suffered if and only if he has received a benefit of some sort *and* this benefit has been secured for him primarily at *A*'s expense. These two conditions constitute a weak form of the concept of restitution. They do not require that *A* play an active role in securing a benefit for *B*. When we speak of restitution, we often have in mind a stronger form of the concept, one which requires some kind of active (although perhaps compelled) participation by the wrongdoer. For instance, we might imagine *A* painting *B*'s house to make restitution for a loss he has unjustly inflicted on *B*. The weak sense of restitution encompasses cases in which the wrongdoer plays as active role, but it also allows for the possibility that he will simply be the recipient (willing or unwilling) of a particular type of treatment.

As I use the term *restitution*, it incorporates two different methods of making good *B*'s loss. First, *B* can be *restored* to his base line position—the position he would have been in, at the time restitution is made, if *A* had not performed the act in question. For example, if *A* steals *B*'s car, *B* will be restored to his base line position if *A* returns the car undamaged, provided *B* has not yet suffered any inconvenience in connection with this event. In some cases, however, restoration is impossible. If *A* gouges out *B*'s eye, the eye cannot be restored to *B*. In this case, though, *B* can obtain restitution from *A* by extracting some other benefit from him (perhaps a large sum of money) to *compensate* for the loss. If *B* is indifferent between his base line position and the position he would be in at the time of compensation, then he can be said to have received full compensation for his loss. Finally, when *A* brings about a loss for *B* in violation of the requirements of justice, I shall say that *B* has been harmed. Thus the term *harm* will denote this type of loss, and the terms *harm* and *loss* will be used interchangeably. Let us now consider the types of losses that result from criminal violations.

The Secondary Effects of Criminal Violations

The most obvious type of harm the criminal inflicts on others is that which is suffered by the immediate victim of the crime and often by his family or others who depend on him. The victim of an assault and battery, for example, typically suffers from the pain and incapacitating effects of his injuries, from having to pay medical bills, and, frequently, from being unable to work while he recuperates. The members of the victim's family may be forced to reduce their standard of living because of his financial setbacks. If the victim is the only doctor in the community, his patients may suffer while he is recovering. A criminal who incapacitates the president of a country, an important civil rights leader, or a scientist who is on the verge of discovering a cure for cancer may affect many persons in this way. I shall refer to the harm suffered by the immediate victim and by those who suffer directly because of his loss as *primary* harm.

Although primary harm is an important part of the harm criminals inflict on others, it does not exhaust the damaging effects of criminal violations. Central to the analysis of punishment presented here is the fact that those who commit crimes also inflict a loss on members of their community, regardless of whether these community members have experienced any primary harm as a result of a crime. Those who commit a particular type of criminal violation provide grounds for the members of the community to infer that they may become the victims of this type of violation in the future and that they therefore should take steps to protect themselves. As more and more crimes are committed, the members of the community suffer a substantial loss in this respect.[3] I shall refer to this type of harm, suffered by members of the community, as *secondary* harm.[4]

To gain a better understanding of secondary harm, let us first consider an example on a small scale. Suppose there is a quiet, peaceful neighborhood in which there have been no burglaries for a very long time. The neighbors all trust each other, never bother to lock their doors, and in general never think seriously about the possibility that someone might break into one of their homes. Then suppose that one night a burglary takes place. The residents may not be very concerned about one burglary, but if a second, third, and fourth burglary occur, it is only reasonable for them to take steps to protect themselves. Depending on how many burglaries have taken place (and on how many valuable possessions are in each household), the residents will pay for increased police protection, purchase theft insurance, install extra locks, hire house-sitters while they are on vacation, etc. Thus, after a certain number of burglaries have taken place, the neighbors can be said to have suffered a significant loss. They have been put in a position in which they have good grounds to believe they must either take a risk with their possessions or spend time and other resources to protect themselves.

To take a second example, suppose several rapes are committed in a given community. After these rapes have occurred, it becomes reasonable for the women in the community to take precautions to ensure that they do not become the victims of rape. They may refrain from walking anywhere alone at night; they may refuse to apply for highly paid jobs (such as unloading ships) located in areas in which it is especially likely that they will be raped; or they may spend a good deal of time and energy training themselves in a martial art. In any case, they are put at a distinct disadvantage in pursuing their own life plans by having to take such precautions.

These two examples should provide some indication of what is meant by secondary harm. Perhaps the clearest way to explicate this term is to consider a community that is governed by a set of just laws. These laws ensure that a just distribution of burdens, benefits, and opportunities is maintained, provided each person complies with the laws. Let us also suppose that, in this community, each person always does comply with the law, and that this state of affairs has obtained for a long period of time. In a just community, we are all *entitled* to this state of affairs. If anyone changes this situation for the worse, he has wrongfully harmed us.

In such a community, there would be little need for locks and keys, theft insurance, etc. Although there would be some danger of being attacked by persons who are not responsible for their behavior, in general, everyone would be free to go anywhere at any time. The community would have to devote only very minimal resources to maintaining a police force. Businesses and governmental institutions could operate much more efficiently because they would not need extensive safeguards against larceny, fraud, and embezzlement. In general, all the resources that are usually devoted to erecting defenses against crime could be channeled into positive pursuits, and no individual would have to curtail his activities to avoid becoming the victim of a crime.

When we consider the difference between this state of affairs and the one which would obtain in our just community after a large number of criminal violations have taken place, it becomes apparent that criminals inflict a significant loss on the members of their community. The fact that members of the community have to make substantial sacrifices to defend themselves against crime after these violations occur is clearly the fault of the persons who have committed them. We make these sacrifices to protect ourselves against crime because, on the basis of what has happened in the past, we believe we need to do so. The mere logical possibility of incurring a particular type of harm does not in itself bring about the need for a defense against it. There must also be some *probability* that the harm will materialize. And each person calculates the probability that he will become the victim of a crime on the basis of the crimes that have taken place in his community. Of course, no one knows that crimes will continue to be committed at the same rate in the future. Perhaps no crime will be committed again, and if this does prove to be the case, then there will have been no need to seek protection against crime. Past experience, however, constitutes the best basis available for making choices about the future.[5]

Thus there is a *historical connection* between our need to defend ourselves against crime and the criminal violations that have been committed. To use Nozick's phrase, the need to protect ourselves does not fall on us "like manna from heaven."[6] It is not a fixed feature of the universe that exists independently of the way in which persons have chosen to behave. Those who are guilty of criminal violations create this need, and they are responsible for the fact that we have to cope with it, at least insofar as they have violated just laws.

A number of points should be made to clarify the nature of the secondary harm and the way in which those who commit crimes are responsible for it. First, when we consider the impact of the secondary harm on each individual, we must remember that it accumulates over the course of his or her life. Ms. Smith may make only a small contribution to maintaining the police force each year; however, she makes this contribution forty or fifty times during her life. And although it may be a small sacrifice for her to refrain from walking alone at night on one occasion, over the years these sacrifices add up.

Second, it is important to recognize that a member of the community experiences secondary harm regardless of whether he or she is *afraid* of becoming the victim of a crime. For example, Mr. Smith may not be in the least bit afraid of having a burglar enter his home. But once a number of burglaries have occurred in his community, he has still been put in a position in which it is reasonable for him to take steps to protect his possessions. The secondary harm, then, is not to be equated with fear. On the other hand, many people do experience fear at the prospect of becoming the victim of a crime, and this anxiety constitutes part of the secondary harm provided it is based on an accurate conception of the harm anticipated and the probability of incurring that harm.[7]

Third, the account of secondary harm presented here does not depend on any particular view of the relationship between the individual and society. To take an extreme case, suppose that several hermits live in one geographical area. They have no legal system, no social structure, and they rarely communicate with one another. Each survives by fishing and growing his own vegetables. If a few of the hermits begin to steal from the others, then all of the hermits who are aware of this fact experience secondary harm. They now have reason to believe that they ought to take steps to protect themselves. Thus we may view individuals as highly atomistic and the analysis we have given still applies.

Fourth, it is important for our purposes to establish that each criminal contributes to secondary harm. It might be argued that once a certain number of crimes have been committed, the need for a defense has been established and subsequent violations do not contribute to the secondary harm. If this is the case, then some criminals cannot be held responsible for bringing about this type of loss. There are two points to be made in response to this line of argument. First, the need for a defense is not something that we either have or do not have; it admits of degrees. As more crimes are committed, this need becomes more substantial. Thus each criminal adds to the seriousness of the secondary harm. Second, although the need for a defense against crime has been established already by violations that have occurred in the past, each additional violation *sustains* that need. If each person would comply with all of his moral obligations from now on, the need for a defense against crime would gradually begin to dissipate. After a sufficient length of time, we could begin to discard some of the precautions we take to defend ourselves. With each additional violation, then, the community's need to defend itself is both strengthened and sustained.

Finally, the situation we are considering is somewhat unusual in that each criminal inflicts only a small quantity of secondary harm on the members of his community, but they suffer a substantial loss as a result of the cumulative effects of criminal violations. The situation is analogous to a stoning in which each person who participates throws one stone at the victim. The amount of damage done by any one of the participants is relatively minor. In fact, if he had been the only one to act, the damage might not have been worth worrying about. However, the cumulative effect of these individuals' actions is to bring about the death of the victim. In order to give an accurate description of what each participant has done, then, we must consider the final outcome of his actions. Rather than saying that he is responsible for the small amount of damage he would have done if he had been the only one to throw a stone, we should say that he and each of the others bear an equal share of the responsibility for the victim's death. Likewise, each criminal bears an equal share of the responsibility for the total secondary harm suffered by the community with respect to the type of violation he has committed.

To summarize, I have argued that when an individual commits a crime, he brings about primary harm for his immediate victim (and for others who depend on him) and secondary harm for the members of his community. Those who commit crimes put the members of their community in a position in which it is reasonable for the latter to sacrifice activities and expend resources in order to defend themselves against crime, and in which many community members experience anxiety in anticipating future criminal harm. Each criminal bears an equal share of the responsibility for the cumulative secondary harm that results from the type of crime he committed.

The Response to Criminal Violations

If we accept restitution as the appropriate paradigm of retributive justice, then those who commit crimes owe restitution for all the harm they wrongfully inflict on others. They owe restitution not only to their immediate victims for primary harm but also to members of their community for secondary harm. If enough crimes have been committed, the restitution for secondary harm will be substantial. A large number of individuals are adversely affected by this type of harm, and it is difficult to restore them to their base line positions. Once a person has lost security in the way we have described, it can be restored to him only if he is provided with a good form of protection. In most cases, however, it is very difficult to arrange adequate protection for one person, to say nothing of providing it for the hundreds of persons who need it. Those who commit crimes, then, face a large task in repairing the damage they have done.

It is not immediately obvious how members of the community can exact restitution from criminals for secondary harm. It would not be feasible to require each criminal to make restitution to each of the many persons he has affected. The vast majority of criminals simply would not be able to do this. However, it is possible for members of the community to obtain restitution for secondary harm by instituting a practice of legal punishment, provided that it functions with a reasonable degree of efficiency to prevent crimes. By instituting a practice of punishment, we provide some protection for each member of the community, largely at the expense of criminals. Thus we remove from each person at least part of the burden of defending himself and allow him greater freedom to pursue his own life plans. A practice of legal punishment, then, constitutes a means by which the members of the community can exact restitution for secondary harm they have suffered. They receive a benefit—protection—primarily at the expense of those who have harmed them. The persons who commit crimes deprive members of the community of the security they are entitled to, and part of that security is restored to them when those criminals are punished. In this way, members of the community are moved back toward their base line position.

There are two conditions under which we will not want to adopt a practice of legal punishment if our goal is to obtain restitution for secondary harm from those who are guilty of criminal violations. First, it might be the case that the community will receive more restitution, all things considered, if a different requirement is imposed on criminals. For example, if a practice of punishment and a practice of requiring criminals to undergo vocational training cost the community roughly the same amount of money to administer, and if the latter practice yields a greater degree of security for the community, then a practice of punishment will not be called for. The important point to remember here is that the community does not owe any benefits to the criminal (in a just society); the criminal owes restitution to the community. Thus any practice instituted is not instituted for the criminal's sake. It is instituted in order to restore the members of the community to their base line position, insofar as it is possible to do this.

Second if a practice of legal punishment does not constitute a reasonably efficient means of preventing crimes (or yield some other significant benefit for the community), then it does not provide restitution for the members of the community and they will have no justification for adopting this practice. In this case, however, the criminal is not yet off the hook. He still owes restitution for the secondary harm, and he may be required to pay a sum of money to the state, to pick up litter, to paint public buildings, etc., even if this type of requirement is of no use in the attempt to prevent crime, since the fulfillment of such a requirement does at least provide some benefit for the community, in compensation for the criminal's share of the secondary loss.

Thus, if we are justified in exacting restitution from those who wrongfully bring about losses for others, we have some justification for instituting a practice of punishment provided that neither of the two conditions just discussed obtains. A variety of moral theories, particularly rights-based moral theories, yield the conclusion that persons owe restitution for the losses they inflict on others in violation of the requirements of justice. Speaking very generally, there are at least two lines of argument that support this conclusion.

First, under a system of just law, each individual is guaranteed certain fundamental interests—bodily integrity, security, control over his property, etc. These are benefits to which a person is entitled in a just distribution of burdens and benefits: He has a right to them. Under a system of just law, each individual is also obligated to respect the rights of others. That is, a person is obligated to refrain from depriving others of the benefits to which they are entitled. Exacting restitution from an individual for losses he has brought about for others can be viewed as a logical extension of requiring him to respect their rights. *A* ought not deprive *B* of a benefit that is rightfully his, and if he does, we are permitted to extract a payment from *A* in order to restore that benefit to *B* (or to compensate *B* for the loss). In the long run, we do not allow *A* to succeed in depriving *B* of something he ought to have. *B*'s legitimate interests remain intact.

Second, a practice of obtaining restitution from persons for the losses they wrongfully inflict on others secures a fundamental benefit for everyone. It ensures that each person has the *opportunity* to live his own life to the fullest extent possible. Once *A* has brought about a loss for *B*, someone must make a sacrifice. Either *B* must absorb the loss, or *A* or some third party must take on the burden of making the loss good. If we institute a practice in which those who are responsible for bringing about the loss are the ones to bear the burden, then we create a situation in which each person has the opportunity to avoid making any sacrifice in this regard. Any individual who so chooses can avoid the sacrifice simply by complying with the law. On the other hand, if we adopt a practice in which those who suffer the losses are required to absorb them, or in which an innocent third party is required to make good the loss, then we create a situation in which persons have little or no control over whether they incur this type of harm. They have no opportunity to avoid the sacrifice they are required to make, and they are likely to be extensively hindered in the pursuit of their own life plans by other persons' wrong choices.

Certainly there are limits to what can be justifiably required of the person who brings about the loss. We cannot require the offender to sacrifice the major part of his life so that the members of the community can obtain restitution for a relatively small amount of damage. But as long as these limits are respected, it would seem to be morally legitimate to require persons to make restitution for the losses they wrongfully inflict on others. And as long as these limits are respected, the members of the community would seem to be justified in instituting a practice of punishment as a means by which they can exact restitution for the secondary harm they have suffered.

Finally, if we can establish that the criminal owes restitution for both the primary and the secondary harm, a third requirement arises for him. Since he has brought about a situation in which he owes restitution both to his immediate victim and to the members of his community, he ought to be required to pay the process costs of these two transactions.

The process costs include the expenses of apprehending the criminal, providing him with a fair trial, and exacting restitution from him. Under the current system of law, the claims of the immediate victim and the claims of the community are processed separately. The victim must pay for his own lawyer, court fees, and sheriff fees, and he can usually add these costs (or some of them) to the damages he claims.

The community incurs a greater expense in this regard in connection with most crimes. A significant amount of the taxpayers' money is spent to hire detectives to determine who the criminals are and what they have done, and to hire policemen to apprehend them and bring them to trial. The amount of money spent in such cases depends primarily on the individual criminal. For example, the criminal who hides from the law costs the community much more than the criminal who comes forward and confesses to his crime. It is incumbent on each criminal to repay the community for whatever costs are incurred in apprehending him, and he should know in advance that the more difficult he makes this job, the more he will have to pay.

Those who commit crimes also force the community to spend money on lawyers, judges, court facilities, etc., which are required to give them fair trials. The community spends some money on trying persons who are subsequently acquitted, and these individuals do not owe the members of the community any payment for these services. Those who are guilty, however, ought to repay the community for the expenses it incurs in this way. If it had not been for their wrong choices, the community would not have had these expenses.

Finally, those who commit crimes bring about the additional expense for the community of exacting restitution from them, and they also ought to repay the community for this expense. The cost of collecting restitution varies both with the individual and with the type of punishment (or other means of exacting restitution) the community inflicts. In general, the more cooperative and trustworthy the criminal is, the less it will cost to punish him. Again, we should make it clear in advance that those who produce greater costs will be required to pay more.

Thus, the complete response to the criminal contains three components, each of which is based on the claim that he owes restitution for the losses that he has wrongfully inflicted on others:

1. The immediate victim(s) of the crime (or his agent) may exact restitution from the criminal for primary harm.

2. The members of the community in which the crime took place (or their agents) may exact restitution from the criminal for secondary harm, either by punishing him, if this constitutes an efficient means of defending themselves against future criminal violations, or by requiring some other form of payment if punishment is inefficient in this respect.

3. The criminal is required to pay the process costs of these two transactions.

Retributivism

The account of punishment I have proposed incorporates aspects of both the utilitarian and the retributivist positions. The restitutive analysis of punishment is utilitarian in that it contains a strong *forward-looking* component. It looks forward from the crime to see what can be done in the future to restore to members of the community the security they have lost. Punishment is justified only if it can be expected to help restore this security (or to provide some other benefit for the community). If it fails to do so, then it is not justifiable and the community must look for some other way to exact restitution from the criminal.

The retributivist's position is not as well defined as that of the utilitarian, and more discussion is required to explain the sense in which a restitutive theory of punishment is retributive. There are three central components of retributivism that are captured by the account of punishment I have proposed. First, the restitutive theory contains a *backward-looking* component. In order to answer the question of who ought to bear the burden of protecting society against crime, we look backward to see who was responsible for bringing about the need for that protection. Second, the justification of punishment I have proposed cannot be logically extended to justify punishing the innocent. The innocent have not inflicted any secondary harm on the members of the community and do not owe them restitution. And third, as we mentioned before, it seems clear in the context of a restitutive justification of punishment that we are not using the criminal as a mere means to secure social benefits. Those who commit crimes are only required to make sacrifices so that the community can repair the damage that has been done.

The fact that our account incorporates these three components indicates that it captures an important part of the retributivist position. However, there are a number of other general tenets that are commonly associated with retributivism, although they are not asserted by every retributivist. If we accept the methodology of wide reflective equilibrium, we can test the adequacy of the theory we have proposed by examining the extent to which it captures the more firmly established retributive convictions or suggests good reason for revising them.

One widely held retributive tenet is that it is justifiable to punish an individual only if he is guilty of moral wrongdoing. As it turns out, a restitutive analysis yields this conclusion. In the context of this analysis, it is justifiable to punish an individual (or to force him to make some other kind of payment) because he has brought about a loss for the members of his community and owes them restitution for it. However, we cannot exact restitution from an individual for just any type of loss he brings about for others. Specifically, if we are going to claim that *A* owes *B* restitution, it must be the case that *B* was entitled to that which he lost as a result of *A*'s action. Consider a case in which *B* plans to open a used bicycle shop and, in order to obtain merchandise to start his business, he steals several bicycles. Then suppose that the police discover what *B* has done and return the bicycles to their proper owners. There is a sense in which the police have brought about a loss for *B* . They have made him worse off than he was when he had the bicycles and was ready to start business. But they do not owe *B* restitution for this loss because he was not entitled to the bicycles in the first place.

Similarly, if we are to claim that the criminal owes restitution to members of the community for reducing their confidence in their own security, it must be the case that they are entitled to that security. In other words, it must be the case that persons are justly required to refrain from performing the type of act in question. I am entitled to security from becoming the victim of a robbery because justice dictates that others ought not rob me. But if justice dictates that homosexuals are allowed to display affection in public, then I am not entitled to any assurances that I will not be exposed to this sort of scene. It follows that it is justifiable to punish an individual only if he has violated a requirement of justice. Whenever an individual violates a requirement of justice (without justification or excuse), he is guilty of moral wrongdoing. Therefore, it is justifiable to punish an individual in the context of a restitutive theory only if he is guilty of moral wrong-doing.

Another common retributive theme is that the criminal owes a debt to society, and that we are justified in punishing him on this account. Morris says that "punishing such individuals . . . restores the equilibrium of benefits and burdens by taking from the criminal what he owes, that is, exacting the debt."[8] Bradley claims that "we pay the penalty because we owe it, and for no other reason"[9] and, according to Murphy, Kant's analysis of punishment "regards it as a debt owed to the law-abiding members of one's community."[10] Again, a restitutive theory of punishment captures and explains this retributive thesis. In fact, it allows us to provide a very literal interpretation of the claim that in punishing the criminal we are exacting a debt from him.

In general, we say that *A* owes *B* a debt when he is obligated to make some kind of payment to *B*. If *A* accepts *B*'s services with the understanding that *B* will be paid for them, then *A* is obligated to pay *B* the sum of money they agreed on. In this case, we would say that *A* owes *B* the money, and *B* is entitled to exact the debt. Similarly, if *A* borrows *B*'s car and demolishes it, he is obligated to pay *B* for the damage. In other words, he *owes* *B* some kind of payment for the loss. On a restitutive theory of punishment, the criminal owes a debt to the members of his community in exactly this sense. He is obligated to make a payment for the secondary harm he has caused. The community can literally exact its debt by punishing the criminal in order to restore the security it has lost as a result of his violation.

One of the most obscure claims associated with the retributivist position is that punishment is required in order to annul or cancel out the crime and to remove the evil that results from it.[11] A restitutive theory of punishment allows us to make sense of this claim. We have argued that when persons commit crimes, they bring about losses both for their immediate victims and for the members of the victims' community. The evil that results from the crime, then, consists in the fact that these individuals have been deprived of benefits to which they were entitled. By exacting restitution from the criminal, we help to restore these individuals to the position they were in before the crime was committed (or to a comparable position). Thus, insofar as it is possible for us to do this, we annul or cancel out the criminal's transgression by removing the losses that he has brought about for others. In the context of the restitutive theory of punishment, then, punishment can be viewed as a means by which crimes are annulled.

Finally, some retributivists (including Kant) maintain that we ought to punish those who commit crimes even if no good consequences would result from the punishment. For example, suppose we were to find Adolf Hitler living alone on a beautiful desert island. Suppose also that punishing Hitler would do no good: No positive benefits would be produced for anyone in this way. Some retributivists would claim that we should punish him nevertheless. He deserves to suffer and should not be allowed to continue with his happy life.

In the context of the theory of punishment I have proposed, one could not justifiably imprison, kill, or torture Hitler if no real benefits could be provided for anyone by doing so. However, we would not be obligated to let him return to his life on the desert island. We would be justified in requiring him to work for the rest of his life to make restitution for the very serious secondary harm he has caused. In cases in which it is not justifiable to punish the guilty, it is always justifiable, in the context of this theory, to require them to make some other form of restitution for secondary harm. Further, the restitution Hitler owes to his immediate victims and their families is unfathomable. Thus, the restitutive theory as well as this kind of retributive theory dictate that we are justified in requiring Hitler to make extensive sacrifices. These theories differ only as to the *type* of sacrifice that he may be required to make. The restitutive theory insists that the sacrifice result in some benefit for others.

Moreover, on the theory I have proposed, we are not only justified in forcing Hitler to make restitution; we are required to do so. The individuals who have suffered losses as a result of his actions have a just claim against him. They have a right to whatever restitution he can provide. It would not be right for those in authority to disregard these just claims any more than it would be right for them to stand back and allow one individual to steal from another.

It thus seems that a restitutive theory of punishment captures a significant portion of the retributivist position, allowing us to interpret a number of the more abstract retributivist claims in such a way that they have a clear and plausible meaning.

Some Implications of a Restitutive Theory of Punishment

In the space that remains, I will attempt to work out some of the more specific implications of the theory of punishment I have proposed. First, let us consider the question of what is to count as a crime. For our purposes, we can consider a type of act to be a crime if one is morally justified in punishing those who perform it (or in requiring them to provide some other benefit for the community). In light of the argument given, it is clear that one is morally justified in punishing those who perform a particular type of act only if the two following conditions are met:

1. Justice must require that persons refrain from performing the type of act in question. Unless this condition is met, members of the community are not entitled to any assurances that they will not be affected by such acts in the future.
2. Members of the community must experience a significant amount of secondary harm as a result of this type of violation.

Analysis will show that most of the traditional crimes are captured by these criteria. Most of the violations designated as crimes in our legal system are acts in which the agent inflicts a substantial amount of harm on another person in violation of the requirements of justice. In connection with these violations, people have reason to believe that they ought to sacrifice activities and/or resources in order to defend themselves. For some types of crimes—rape and burglary, for example—the nature and extent of the secondary harm is fairly obvious to us. For other types of crimes it is not as obvious, largely because many of us are not affected by the type of secondary harm that results from them. We might use the crime of murder to illustrate this point. The average man on the street may not devote much time or energy preparing to defend himself against murder because he believes, and reasonably so, that it is unlikely anyone will attempt to kill him. Thus he does not experience much secondary harm as a result of this crime. However, those who have reason to believe that others wish to kill them will experience a significant amount of secondary harm as a result of this type of violation. And those who have committed murder in the past under similar conditions are responsible for the secondary harm that these individuals experience. If no one had ever committed murder in the past under these circumstances, then the individuals in question typically would not have reason to believe that they were in danger.

Further, these criteria provide a basis for excluding from the range of criminal violations certain acts which seem to produce some kind of secondary harm but which we would not necessarily want to classify as criminal. Examples of such acts are operating a nuclear power plant in compliance with all the feasible safety regulations or selling adulterated milk after having taken every precaution to avoid doing so. It might be argued that secondary harm is produced by each of these acts. However, on the analysis given, acts of this sort do not constitute criminal violations unless persons are justly required to refrain from engaging in the activity that creates the risk of harm.

There are several activities we find valuable (either in themselves or instrumentally) that create the risk of harm for others. In order to guarantee all individuals complete security from these risks, we would have to deny everyone the opportunity to engage in the activities that create them. Our lives would be greatly impoverished if we were to adopt such a policy. Certainly, we are justly permitted to engage in some of these activities, if the risk to others is relatively small and the activity itself is relatively valuable. We are morally permitted to drive cars at low speeds, for example, because this activity is important and the risk of harm to others is not too great.

We may be justly required to take certain precautions, however, while we are pursuing these potentially dangerous activities, either to reduce the risk of accident or to avoid making a mistake that will adversely affect others. Again, whether or not we are required to take a given precaution depends on the cost of taking this measure and the benefits others can be expected to derive if we do so. It is unjust to demand that excessive steps be taken. For example, we cannot require each person to have his car inspected once a week by a professional mechanic in order to avoid a small risk of harm.

When an individual is engaged in a legitimate activity and has taken all of the required precautions, then he is not violating a requirement of justice. It is still possible that he will bring about harm for others by accident or by mistake, but ex hypothese, members of the community are not entitled to security from the risk of harm that arises in this way. Thus the person who brings about harm (or the threat of harm) under these circumstances does not owe members of the community restitution for secondary harm and is not justifiably punished. His act does not constitute a criminal violation. If this line of reasoning is correct, it provides us with a method for determining when we must recognize the excuses of accident and mistake in the criminal law, and thus it also provides a method for determining which strict liability offense ought to be eliminated.

A further implication of the restitutive theory of punishment is that the punishment for criminal attempts ought to be equal to the punishment for successful crimes. An attempted robbery produces the same amount of secondary harm as a successful robbery. In either case the members of the community have been given grounds to infer that they may become the victims of robberies in the future and that they had better take steps to defend themselves. Thus the same amount of punishment is warranted in each case.[12] However, in the context of the complete practice proposed here, those who successfully carry out a crime will be faced with a much more substantial burden in making restitution for the primary harm.

In connection with this point, it is interesting to note that those who commit similar types of violations but bring about very different quantities of primary harm receive the same amount of punishment on a restitutive theory. For example, suppose that criminal *A* robs a jewelry store, stealing ten diamond necklaces. Criminal *B* robs another jewelry store and takes what he believes to be ten diamond necklaces but which he later discovers to be only cheap imitations. These two criminals have brought about very different quantities of primary harm, but their acts seem equally culpable. The theory proposed here dictates that each of these individuals receive the same amount of punishment because each has produced the same kind of secondary harm. In each case, the members of the community have been given grounds to infer that they need to protect themselves against serious thefts. Of course, criminal *A* again owes much more restitution for primary harm than criminal *B*.[13]

One of the most difficult questions one faces in working out the details of a practice of punishment is how to determine the severity of the punishment. I cannot give a complete answer to this question on the basis of the brief analysis provided here. I can, however, suggest a general approach to this question that is compatible with a restitutive justification.

If we accept restitution as the correct paradigm of criminal justice, then the most that can be required of an individual who has brought about a loss for another is that he make complete restitution for that loss. However, when we consider the number of persons affected by the secondary harm and the nature of the harm inflicted on them, it becomes apparent that we will not be able to exact full restitution for this harm.

When *A* brings about a loss for *B*, we believe, on an intuitive level, that there are limits to the sacrifices that can be justifiably imposed on *A* in order to obtain restitution. If *A* comes into *B*'s home and deliberately smashes *B*'s antique china collection, he certainly owes *B* some restitution. But if *A* would have to work fourteen hours a day seven days a week for the rest of his life in order to repay *B*, most of us would agree that *A* should not be required to pay the full amount.

We might support this intuition by appealing to the general principle of justice that each person ought to be treated with equal concern and respect. This principle dictates that, from the standpoint of the law, each person ought to be accorded an equal status with respect to fulfilling his life plans or pursuing his legitimate goals. If we were to require *A* to sacrifice the better part of his life in order to obtain restitution for *B* for a loss that is relatively inconsequential to him, it seems clear that we would not be treating these individuals with equal concern and respect. Here, *A* is required to forfeit most of his life plans so that *B* can be free of a minor hindrance in the pursuit of his. According each person equal concern and respect in this type of case requires some balancing of the interests that the individuals involved have at stake. It is beyond the scope of this paper to consider in depth how their interests ought to be balanced. However, if this general approach to the problem is valid, it is clear that the person who brings about the loss can justifiably be required to sacrifice more when the loss he has brought about is more serious.

When we determine the severity of the punishment, we must balance the extent of the criminal's sacrifice against the interest a representative member of the community has in receiving restitution for secondary harm he has suffered with respect to the type of violation in question. It is usually the case that some members of the community are more seriously affected than others by a particular type of secondary harm. For example, women are more likely to be raped than men and thus experience more secondary harm as a result of this crime. If we are to ensure that no individual is required to make a disproportionate sacrifice, we must compare the criminal's interests with the interests of the members of the community who are most affected by the secondary harm. It is important to emphasize that if we take this approach, we do not have to total up the interests of all of the members of the community who are affected by the secondary harm when we determine the severity of the punishment. We need only compare the criminal's interests with the interests of the worst-off representative citizen.

Let us now consider some of the more specific implications of this method of determining the severity of the punishment. Because the severity of the punishment depends on how seriously the worst-off representative member of the community is affected by the secondary harm, it varies with the following four factors.

First, the severity of the punishment varies directly with the seriousness of the primary harm that typically results from the type of violation in question. If there have been several murders in a community, the residents will be in a much worse position than they would have been in if the same number of minor thefts had occurred instead. It is more important for them to defend themselves against murder, and more sacrifices are warranted in maintaining such a defense; thus, they are more severely affected by the secondary harm in this case.

Second, the severity of the punishment varies directly with the probability that the worst-off representative member of the community will incur primary harm as a result of the type of violation in question. There are two important factors to be taken into account here. One is the probability that a person who commits the violation will harm another person. For example, it is very probable that someone who deliberately sets out to kill another person will succeed in doing so. But it is not as probable that someone who drives down a residential street at 80 miles per hour will kill someone, although there is some probability that he will. It is more important, then, for us to have a defense against the former crime, ceteris paribus, because it is more likely that we will be harmed as a result of this type of violation.

The other important factor to be taken into account is the number of violations that have occurred in relation to the population of the community that is vulnerable to the type of harm in question. If one murder occurs each year in a community of a given size, there is less need for any member of the community to defend himself than if one hundred murders occur each year in the same community. Thus, as the crime rate increases, the members of the community are more seriously affected by the secondary harm and an increase in the severity of the punishment is warranted.

Third, the severity of the punishment varies inversely with the probability that the victim of the crime will be adequately compensated for his primary loss. If there is a good chance that complete restitution will be made for the primary harm, then it is not as important to defend oneself as it would be if there were very little chance of receiving restitution.

Finally, the severity of the punishment depends on the nature of the steps one has to take to avoid becoming a victim of the crime. The more these steps interfere with the pursuit of one's life plans, the greater the interest of members of the community in receiving restitution for secondary harm suffered. If a device were invented that would make houses burglar-proof at a very low cost and with very little inconvenience, then no one would suffer serious secondary harm as a result of this crime. In this case, the punishment would not be severe. Thus the defenses of provocation, imperfect self-defense, and consent of the victim function to reduce the severity of the punishment. It is relatively easy to avoid becoming the victim of a crime involving any of these defenses.

The severity of the punishment also depends on the importance of the interest the criminal has at stake. Because this is the case, we cannot say that a given quantity of punishment will necessarily be appropriate for every person who commits a particular type of crime. One year in prison may constitute a moderate sacrifice for an individual who is physically strong and psychologically stable. But a small, emotionally disturbed adolescent who is likely to be gang-raped may suffer tremendously from such an experience. Thus we must consider the extent of the sacrifice that any given punishment imposes on an individual and make adjustments in the severity of the punishment accordingly.

In general, these implications of a restitutive theory of punishment correspond reasonably well with our convictions about the way in which a practice of legal punishment ought to be structured. The one notable exception is that in the context of the restitutive theory, the severity of the punishment varies with the crime rate. Because the severity of the punishment varies with the probability that the worst-off representative member of the community will become the victim of the type of crime in question, it depends on both the population of the community and the number of violations that have been committed. If criminal *A* commits a crime in a small community, ceteris paribus, he will be punished more severely than criminal *B* who commits the same crime in a larger community. And if criminal *A* commits a violation in a community in which there have been several violations of the same sort, ceteris paribus, he will be punished more severely than criminal B who commits the same crime in a community in which there have been very few violations of this sort. Further, it would be possible under some circumstances for a minor crime that is very prevalent to be punished more severely than an uncommon crime that is considered more serious.[14]

Thus the restitutive theory of punishment diverges significantly in this respect from retributivism, which demands that the criminal suffer in proportion to the gravity of his offense. This divergence points to an important difference between the paradigm of restitution and the traditional paradigm of retributive punishment. While the retributivist focuses on the moral gravity of the criminal's offense and attempts to "pay him back" for his wrongdoing, we have a different purpose in mind when we seek restitution for the losses persons inflict on others. The aim of this practice is to restore the persons who have been harmed to their base line positions, not to make the offender suffer in proportion to his wickedness. In many cases the two goals will not be compatible. When we exact restitution from an individual for the primary harm he has unjustly inflicted on another, we do not concern ourselves with the gravity of his offense. We simply concentrate on what is required to restore the victim to his base line position, making sure at the same time that the offender is not required to sacrifice too much in comparison with the loss his victim has suffered. The same is true in the context of a restitutive theory of punishment when we exact restitution from the criminal for the secondary harm. Thus, while it seems strange to say that the criminal's punishment should vary with the crime rate, it does not seem strange to say that the amount of restitution that the members of the community receive ought to depend on the extent of the secondary harm they have suffered.

The difference between these two paradigms warrants further consideration. On the one hand, we are reluctant to have the severity of the punishment vary with the crime rate. It seems that punishment should be retributive. But on the other hand, many persons want to say that punishment is justified because the criminal has harmed society, and if the arguments given in the first part of this paper are sound, then this claim is correct. In this case it would seem inconsistent to say that restitution is the appropriate framework for dealing with the unjust imposition of harm on an individual while retributive punishment is the appropriate framework for dealing with the unjust imposition of harm on the members of the community. Why should we use one model in the first case and a different model in the second?

In conclusion, I believe that this approach to the justification of punishment is plausible enough that it ought to be developed further and seriously considered as an alternative to the utilitarian and retributivist positions. In any case, if we cannot argue that we are justified in instituting a practice of punishment as a means of obtaining restitution for the secondary harm, then we should search for some other method of exacting restitution for this loss from those who are guilty of criminal violations.

NOTES

1. See Randy Barnett, "Restitution: A New Paradigm of Criminal Justice," *Ethics* 87 (1977): 279–301.
2. Stanley I. Benn, "Punishment," in *The Encyclopedia of Philosophy,* edited by Paul Edwards (New York: Macmillan Publishing Co., 1967), 7: 29.
3. Lawrence Becker and John Kleinig have each distinguished between criminal harm and non-criminal harm on the ground that a harm to society accompanies criminal violations. The analysis suggested here is based in part on the accounts they give, although it diverges from each of these accounts in important respects. Basically, this analysis of secondary harm differs from Becker's in that it does not depend on his notion of social volatility. On my analysis, secondary harm results from criminal violations even if each member of the community responds to these violations in a socially stable manner. My analysis diverges from Kleinig's account primarily in that it does not depend on any particular view of the relationship between the individual and society. See Lawrence Becker, "Criminal Attempts and the Theory of the Law of Crimes," *Philosophy and Public Affairs* 3 (1974); 262–294, and John Kleinig, "Crime and the Concept of Harm," *American Philosophical Quarterly* 15 (1978): 27–36, especially p. 36.
4. The terms *primary* harm and *secondary* harm are Jeremy Bentham's. I have drawn the distinction between these two types of harm in the same way he does, but I provide a different analysis of what secondary harm consists of. See Bentham's *Introduction to the Principles of Morals and Legislation* (1789), Chapter 12.
5. Bentham also argues that fear or alarm constitutes part of secondary harm, although he does not stipulate that secondary harm must be based on an accurate conception of the situation.
6. See Robert Nozick, *Anarchy, State, and Utopia* (New York: Basic Books, Inc., 1974), p. 194.
7. Henceforth, when I speak of the need for a defense against crime, I shall be referring to the projection we make on the basis of our past experience that we need this defense, and not to our actual need for it. A case can be made, I believe, that any justification of punishment that turns on the need for a defense against crime is based on the projected need rather than the actual need.
8. Herbert Morris, "Persons and Punishment," *Monist* 52 (1968), p. 478.
9. F. H. Bradley, *Ethical Studies* (Indianapolis: Bobbs-Merrill Co., Inc., 1951), pp. 26–27.
10. Jeffrie G. Murphy, ed., *Kant: The Philosophy of Right* (New York: St. Martin's Press, 1970), p. 143.
11. See especially T. M. Knox, trans., *Hegel's Philosophy of Right* (Oxford: Clarendon Press, 1958), pp. 69–70.
12. Becker reaches this conclusion in "Criminal Attempts and the Theory of the Law of Crimes."
13. Again, Becker points out that if criminal harm is associated with social harm, eventful and uneventful criminal negligence ought to be punished equally. This is one more implication of the line of argument I have just presented.
14. It is important to recognize that this result is not unique to the restitutive theory. Although the problem has not been generally recognized, it seems that this implication will arise in the context of any theory that justifies punishment by reference to the community's need for defense against crime. The need for a defense certainly depends on the probability that harm will materialize, and we must certainly calculate this probability on the basis of the number of crimes that have been committed in the past. Thus, given this type

of theory, the severity of the punishment would have to vary with the crime rate.

Study Questions

1. Are there any (uncontroversial) crimes for which Barnett's restitution theory seems inadequate?
2. Do you think Barnett's criticisms of what he terms "punitive" restitution are convincing?
3. Do you agree that punishment is a satisfactory way for the criminal to make restitution for what Holmgren terms "secondary" harms?
4. Do you think there would be any practical difficulties in implementing either of these proposals? If so, what would they be?

F Incapacitation

Prediction of Criminal Conduct and Preventive Confinement of Convicted Persons

Andrew von Hirsch

Von Hirsch defines *preventive confinement* as the practice of "incapacitating an allegedly dangerous individual in order to prevent him from engaging in predicted criminal conduct." He argues that, even if all feasible safeguards are observed, such a practice would be unjust since it would yield too many false positives, i.e., persons mistakenly predicted to be dangerous. Moreover, even if this problem could be overcome, preventive confinement would still be unacceptable because of its effects on individual freedom and because of the danger of serious abuses.

I. Introduction

Preventive confinement—incapacitating an allegedly dangerous individual in order to prevent him from engaging in predicted criminal conduct—is a concept that seems rather foreign to our traditions of justice. We would be prone to assert that a person may be deprived of his liberty, not on the basis of a prediction of criminal behavior, but only on the basis of a determination of guilt for a past offense. As the recent controversy over pretrial preventive detention in the District of Columbia illustrates,[1] it can arouse our concern or alarm when the state seeks to incarcerate preventively those suspected of criminal tendencies, even for brief periods. While predictions of dangerousness have historically been used to justify confining mentally ill persons, this practice also is beginning to generate criticism and doubts.[2]

Yet once a person has been convicted of a crime, our scruples about preventive confinement seem to disappear. Predictions of criminal conduct regularly enter into decisions concerning the disposition of convicted criminal offenders. With little public notice and few voiced objections, the state has been free to impose prolonged terms of confinement upon convicted persons predicted to be dangerous, for the express or implied purpose of incapacitating them from engaging in future criminal conduct; the duration of these individuals' confinement may far exceed what would ordinarily seem justified as punishment for their past offenses. Thus one is tempted to ask: "If we are so distrustful of preventive confinement in cases where there has been no conviction for a crime, why should we so readily accept it after there has been a conviction?" This paper will attempt to deal with that question.

A. Prevalence of the Practice of Preventive Confinement

Numerous examples could be cited in existing law involving essentially preventive confinement of convicted persons predicted to be dangerous. I shall mention just a few.

From the *Buffalo Law Review*, Vol. 21 (1972), pp. 717–758.

Canada has adopted a system explicitly termed "Preventive Detention," authorizing the imprisonment of convicted multiple offenders for an indeterminate term if:

> [T]he court is of the opinion that because the accused is an habitual criminal, it is expedient for the protection of the public to sentence him to preventive detention.[3]

England, having had a system of Preventive Detention similar to the Canadian one until 1967, still permits a judge to sentence an offender for a term well beyond the maximum term for his last offense, if, in the words of the statute, the court

> is satisfied, by reason of his previous conduct and of the likelihood of his committing further offences, that it is expedient to protect the public from him for substantial time . . .[4] .

One of the most overt schemes of preventive confinement in this country is the Maryland Defective Delinquent Law.[5] Under the Maryland statute, an individual who has been convicted for the first time of any of a wide variety of offenses (some rather minor), may be indefinitely confined if he is found by a court, on the basis of recommendations by a state medical board, to be a "defective delinquent." To be classified as such, the individual must meet two sets of criteria, one predictive and one quasi-psychiatric. The predictive criterion is that the individual

> by the demonstration of persistent aggravated anti-social or criminal behavior, evidences a propensity toward criminal activity . . . as to clearly demonstrate an actual danger to society so as to require such confinement and treatment, when appropriate, as may make it reasonably safe for society to terminate the confinement and treatment.[6]

The quasi-psychiatric criterion is that the individual, *though legally sane,* manifests "emotional unbalance" or "intellectual deficiency."[7] If the individual is found to meet these criteria, then he will be confined in a special institution for defective delinquents, Patuxent Institution. The term of his confinement is indeterminate, can exceed the maximum term of punishment for the offense of which he was convicted, and can even be for life.[8] He is entitled to release only when it is determined that he no longer meets the criteria for "defective delinquency" that justified his confinement.[9] During confinement, he is supposed to be subjected to an intensive program of rehabilitative treatment, although a Maryland court has recently found that such treatment is not being made available to the more recalcitrant prisoners.[10]

Colorado authorizes the preventive confinement of persons convicted for sexual offenses, if the court finds that such individuals constitute "a threat of bodily harm to members of the public."[11] Confinement is for an indeterminate term, up to the lifetime of the defendant.[12] According to a recent survey conducted under the auspices of the American Bar Foundation, seventeen other jurisdictions authorize the indeterminate confinement of sex offenders or so-called "sexual psychopaths," with or without a prior conviction.[13]

The Model Sentencing Act proposes that a felony offender convicted of certain serious crimes be sentenced for an extended term of up to thirty years (thrice the maximum term of confinement he otherwise could receive for such offenses) if the court, after ordering a psychiatric examination, finds that "because of the dangerousness of the defendant, such period of confined correctional treatment or custody is required for the protection of the public" and if it further finds that he "is suffering from a severe personality disorder indicating a propensity toward criminal activity."[14] The Model Penal Code provides that a trial judge, in sentencing a person convicted of a felony, may extend the term of his imprisonment well beyond the maximum provided for that category of felony, when "the defendant is a dangerous, mentally abnormal person whose commitment for an extended term is necessary for protection of the public."[15]

The California indeterminate sentence law gives an independent sentencing board—the Adult Authority—plenary discretion to determine release dates within the widest maximum and minimum statutory limits.[16] The

Adult Authority may—and apparently does—determine the duration of an offender's confinement in part upon the basis of informal estimates of his supposed individual dangerousness.[17]

Essentially predictive judgments are also frequently made in conventional parole situations. Since 1933, Illinois has made regular use of statistical prediction techniques in its parole system. An actuarial prediction table of parole outcomes has been prepared for each of the major institutions in the state. A sociologist-actuary at each institution prepares a routine prediction report based upon the tables for each inmate appearing at a parole hearing. He computes the prisoner's statistical chances for making a successful adjustment on parole; the final sentence in the report reads: "This inmate is in a class in which —% may be expected to violate the parole agreement." Together with sociological, psychiatric and psychological reports and interviews by the parole board, the predictive score is used to determine whether the prisoner is granted or denied parole.[18]

Based on the Illinois experience, several noted criminologists have advocated more extensive and systematic use of prediction tables in sentencing and parole decisions.[19] According to a nationwide survey conducted in 1962,[20] three other states—Ohio, California and Colorado—had developed formal prediction tables for application in individual parole decisions. While not using tables, parole boards in other states regularly make informal estimates of individual inmates' potential for future anti-social conduct in determining whether to grant or deny parole; a recent American Bar Foundation survey of sentencing and parole procedures found that "the principal consideration in the decision to grant or deny parole is the probability that the inmate will violate the criminal law if he is released."[21]

B. Scope of the Inquiry

Before proceeding, it is appropriate to define the scope of this inquiry more precisely. Imprisonment has or may have as one of its functions, the prevention of future crimes—even without any attempt at prediction of individual dangerousness. *Any* decision to confine a person convicted of a crime incapacitates him from committing, during his period of confinement, any criminal acts he might otherwise choose to commit against the outside community. That is true even if the decision to confine is made *solely* with reference to his past criminal conduct, and no effort is made to forecast his individual future behavior. So long as it is assumed that *some* convicted robbers (never mind which individual ones) would be inclined to commit further offenses if allowed to remain at large, imprisoning *all* convicted robbers for a specified period of time might prevent *some* future robberies from occurring. This kind of prevention is what might be called prevention in the *collective* sense. It raises some important questions, worthy of careful study.[22] However, it is outside the scope of the present article.

Instead, this article has a narrower scope. It is concerned with prevention in the *individual, predictive* sense—where decisions to confine persons turn upon official forecasts of their particular future conduct. More exactly, it focuses on this specific question: *Is it appropriate to decide whether and how long to confine a sane adult who has been convicted of a crime, on the basis that he is deemed likely to engage in certain criminal conduct in the future?*

This topic is of particular interest for two reasons. It raises questions of the reliability of predictions of individual dangerousness and of the policy consequences of erroneous predictions. It also raises questions of the propriety of confining an individual who is deemed of sound mind and full age for what he *will* do, not what he has done.

It is to this kind of prevention—in the individual, predictive sense—that I will be referring in this article when I use the term "preventive confinement."

C. Conceptual Nature of the Inquiry

Techniques for predicting criminal behavior are still relatively primitive, and existing schemes of preventive confinement generally lack even minimal legal safeguards, as the discussion below indicates. Thus it is easy enough to criticize preventive confinement in the state in which it exists today.

The more difficult question—and the one with which this article will primarily be concerned—is whether the *concept* of preventive confinement is a sound one, assuming that prediction techniques and legal safeguards are improved. If the *concept* is sound,[23] then preventive confinement may be an important and fruitful area for further innovation and development. If not, it may be a dangerous blind alley. In making this conceptual analysis, theoretical models have been found helpful and will be used.

II. Preventive Confinement—A Theoretical Model

We might start our analysis by examining the following theoretical model:

The Preventive Confinement Model. In an imaginary jurisdiction, a person convicted of a criminal offense would be subject to preventive confinement for an indeterminate term, if specified predictive criteria indicated a high probability of his committing a serious offense in the future. Following completion of his term in prison for the offense of which he was convicted, he would be transferred to and confined in a special facility designed solely for preventive purposes, in which living conditions would be made as "pleasant," i.e., as little punitive, as possible, consistent with the fact of incarceration itself. The individual would not be subjected to mandatory rehabilitative treatment during confinement in this special facility. The duration of confinement could substantially exceed the maximum statutory term of punishment prescribed for the offense of which he had been convicted. He would be released only at such time as he is found no longer to meet the predictive criteria for dangerousness.

In actual practice, preventive confinement frequently is mixed with other elements. The Maryland Defective Delinquent Law combines preventive confinement with mandatory treatment.[24] By giving the Adult Authority plenary discretion to determine an adult offender's release date, the California indeterminate sentence law allows preventive considerations to be mixed with judgments concerning punishment, treatment and institutional convenience.[25] In these contexts, it is difficult to isolate and analyze the preventive component of decisions to confine.

In our theoretical model, however, the preventive component is separately identified. The offender serves an indeterminate term in a special facility in which confinement is *for preventive purposes only*. The duration of confinement in that facility would be set *solely on the basis of a prediction of his individual future dangerousness, without regard to the nature of his past offense.*

Thus the model gives us the opportunity to evaluate preventive confinement in its more or less "pure state." Once we have done that, we will examine the effect of adding other components to the model, such as mandatory rehabilitative treatment.

A. Threshold Requirements: Explicit Legal Standards of Dangerousness; Validation of Prediction Method; Procedural Safeguards

To have any possible merit, the model should satisfy three important threshold requirements: 1. There must be reasonably precise legal standards of dangerousness; 2. The prediction methods used must be subjected to careful and continuous validation; and 3. The procedure for commitment must provide the defendant with certain minimal procedural safeguards. These requirements, however, are seldom met by current practices of preventive confinement.

1. Explicit Legal Standards of Dangerousness. As Dershowitz[26] and Goldstein and Katz[27] have pointed out in connection with the law of commitment of the insane, a supposedly "dangerous" person should never be preventively confined, unless the "danger" he poses is of sufficient gravity—and sufficient likelihood—to warrant deprivation of his freedom. That determination—of the seriousness and likelihood of the predicted misconduct required to justify confinement—is a value judgment the *law* should make: it is not a factual judgment within the professional competence of psychiatrists or other expert witnesses. Failure to provide explicit legal standards of "dangerousness" creates the unacceptable situation where, for example, one psychiatrist can decide that only those mental patients who are likely to perpetrate violent crimes ought to be confined, while another psychiatrist, depending upon his personal philosophy, can employ the concept of "dangerousness" to confine potential minor offenders, as well.

These considerations apply with equal force to the preventive incarceration of convicted persons. Yet existing preventive confinement schemes seldom, if ever, provide legal standards of dangerousness which have any definiteness. The Maryland Defective Delinquent Law, for example, authorizes commitment of individuals who demonstrate an "actual danger" to society.[28] No definition is supplied of what constitutes such a danger; nor is there even a statutory requirement that the supposed "dangerousness" be seriously criminal in character.

Unless "dangerousness" is defined by law with some minimal degree of precision, the entire preventive model may well be unconstitutional on grounds of vagueness.[29] Thus a threshold requirement for acceptability of the model would be a reasonably precise statutory definition of "dangerousness": one that specifies what kind of future criminal conduct, and what degree of likelihood of that conduct, warrants preventive confinement.

2. Validating the Predictive Method. In commitment proceedings for the mentally ill, there is rarely any effort made to check the accuracy of psychiatric predictions of dangerousness by following up and tabulating their results.[30] The same absence of validation pervades the existing preventive confinement practice for some offenders. No systematic follow-up is made, for example, of the predictions of dangerousness under the Maryland Defective Delinquent Law. Even among states that utilize prediction tables as an aid to parole decisions, validation is not always attempted.[31]

Not surprisingly under these circumstances, unverified predictions of dangerousness prove fallible, indeed, when their accuracy is subsequently examined by scholars. In his ongoing study of the accuracy of psychiatric prediction in commitment proceedings for the mentally ill, Dershowitz notes:

> [I] was able to discover fewer than a dozen studies which followed up psychiatric predictions of antisocial conduct. And even more surprisingly, these few studies strongly suggest that psychiatrists are rather inaccurate predictors; inaccurate in an absolute sense, and even less accurate when compared with other professionals, such as psychologists, social workers and correctional officials, and when compared to actuarial devices, such as prediction or experience tables. Even more significant for legal purposes: it seems that psychiatrists are particularly prone to one type of error—overprediction. In other words, they tend to predict antisocial conduct in many instances where it would not, in fact, occur. Indeed, our research suggests that for every correct psychiatric prediction of violence, there are numerous erroneous predictions.[32]

Predictions by supposedly "expert" correctional personnel show the same proneness to error, as a study by Hakeem suggests.[33] He requested ten trained parole officers and ten laymen with no correctional experience to make a series of predictions of parole survival on the basis of case summaries of 200 parolees, half of whom had been recommitted for parole violations and half of whom had not. He found that the laymen were substantially *more* accurate predictors than the parole officers. Moreover, both groups combined made fewer correct identifications of the nonviolators than would have been made by random selection.[34]

Aside from inaccuracy, hazards of class and racial discrimination inhere in giving psychiatrists, correctional officials or other supposed "experts" *carte blanche* powers to make predictive determinations of dangerousness—unless the predictive criteria used are first carefully validated. Psychiatrists or parole board members of middle-class backgrounds can and do, all too easily, misinterpret lower-class or nonconforming styles and attitudes as symptoms of supposed "dangerousness."[35]

If this kind of laxity is carried over to the model system of preventive confinement, that alone would be sufficient to condemn it.

Thus a second threshold requirement for acceptability of the model would be that its predictive method carefully be validated *in advance* of being applied in actual decisions to confine; and be subject to continual follow-up and review.

Adequate validation studies of the predictive technique in the model are required, regardless of whether the predictive method is purely statistical, purely clinical, or a mixture of the two.[36] Clinical evaluation avoids statistics in the projection itself, but the statistician must always have the last word in judging the accuracy and utility of the evaluation method; as Meehl points out in his *Clinical vs. Statistical Prediction*:

> All clinicians should make up their minds that of the two uses of statistics (structural and validating), the validating use is unavoidable. Regardless of one's theory about personality and regardless of one's choice of data . . . ; regardless of how these data are fused for predictive purposes—by intuition, table, equation, or rational hypotheses developed in a case conference—the honest clinician cannot avoid the question "Am I doing better than I could do by flipping pennies?" . . .
>
> Is any clinician infallible? No one claims to be. Hence, sometimes he is wrong. If he is sometimes wrong, why should we pay any attention to him? There is only one possible reply to this "silly" question. It is simply that he *tends* (read: "is likely") to be right. "Tending" to be right means just one thing—"being right in the long run." . . . [We thus] have no recourse except to record our predictions at the time, allow them to accumulate, and ultimately tally them up. . . . If the clinical utility is really established and not merely proclaimed, it will have been established by procedures which have all the earmarks of an acceptable validation study.[37]

3. Procedural Safeguards. Certain basic procedural safeguards—too often lacking today—should be built into the preventive model. At minimum, a full hearing should be required before any convicted individual is committed for preventive confinement. That hearing should be separate from the trial for his past offense, because the issues involved (for example, his supposed dangerousness) are distinct from the issues at trial. At this hearing, he must have the rights of counsel, confrontation and cross-examination of witnesses, and the right to call his own witnesses.[38] The Supreme Court has struck down a sexual psychopath law which denied such a hearing,[39] but many such state laws still abridge full implementation of these rights.[40] The Maryland Defective Delinquent Law, while providing a hearing and a right to counsel at the hearing, denies the defendant the right to confront and cross-examine staff psychiatrists whose reports are used in determining his status as a defective delinquent.[41]

A requirement more difficult to satisfy but equally important relates to indigents' right of representation. To conduct any kind of effective defense, an indigent defendant would not only need to have competent counsel provided for him but also to have access to competent expert witnesses able to challenge the state's prediction of his supposed dangerousness.[42] That would involve very considerable expense, which would have to be assumed by the state. The defendant's expert witnesses, to testify effectively on behalf of their client, would need, for example, to conduct extended psychiatric observations of the defendant, or run validation studies to check the accuracy of past predictions of dangerousness made by the state's expert witnesses. This will require a very much more ambitious and costly legal services program than is available today. But without it, indigent defendants will be virtually helpless to defend themselves, and the entire model would violate basic standards of procedural fairness.

A still more difficult question relates to the privilege against self-incrimination. If the privilege applies to preventive confinement under the model—and there are arguments to suggest that it should[43]—then the individual could be confined only if a prediction could be made on the basis of independently obtained data; the individual could not be compelled to cooperate with psychiatric investigations designed to determine whether he is dangerous. If that were so, the preventive model probably could not be implemented unless and until the predictive art had progressed to the point where it could rely safely upon "objective" data and dispose with psychiatric investigations in making predictions.

B. Theoretical Impediments to Prediction: The False Positive Problem

Even if these threshold requirements are satisfied, however, the preventive model will encounter a formidable theoretical impediment to prediction: the false positive problem.

1. The Significance of False Positives. Starting in the early 1920s with S. B. Warner's statistical study of recidivism among prisoners paroled from the Massachusetts State Reformatory and with the Gluecks' widely publicized prediction studies, an extensive literature has developed concerning the statistical prediction of parole recidivism and of delinquency.[44]

As Wilkins points out in his perceptive *Evaluation of Penal Measures,*[45] there has been a tendency in this predictive literature to adopt a rather one-sided criterion for success. A prediction table for delinquency or recidivism is thought effective if it can correctly forecast a relatively high proportion of those individuals who actually become delinquent or recidivist. The other side of the coin is less often considered: the so-called *false positives*—those mistakenly predicted to engage in such deviant conduct. There has been an inclination to overlook how many non-delinquents or non-recidivists a prediction table incorrectly classifies as potentially deviant.

In certain types of prediction, the criteria for success need not be too seriously concerned with false positives. If, for example, we develop a prediction table for recruitment into the army,[46] the table may well be useful if it successfully identifies a high percentage of individuals actually unsuitable for the service, who can then be screened out. If the manpower pool is ample, it does not really matter that the predictive index also yields a substantial number of false positives—individuals actually suitable for the service who are rejected as a result of a mistaken prediction of unsuitability. For the army does not need to recruit all suitable persons; and the impact upon affected individuals of a mistaken prediction of unsuitability generally is not damaging.

In predicting criminal conduct, however, the consequences of ignoring the false positives are much more serious. As Wilkins points out:

> Taking a sample of offenders and showing that a large proportion would have scored in the delinquent category does not validate the prediction. Yet claims of this kind are frequently found. If decisions are made upon the basis of prediction statements, it is to be expected that the consequences of errors in each class will be different. It may be more damaging to regard (predict) a person as delinquent or recidivist when this is incorrect, than to incorrectly regard a person as nondelinquent or nonrecidivist. Some recent writers have claimed that the first kind of error can lead to a self-fulfilling prophecy—the labeling process of classification as "likely delinquent" may change the perception of the person by others, and through this, his own self-image.[47]

In the context of our model system of preventive incarceration, we can afford little tolerance, indeed, of prediction methods that show a high yield of false positives. Here, mistakenly predicting nondangerous individuals to be dangerous is gravely damaging—for it can lead to their prolonged incarceration.

Because of the historical lack of concern with the question, the existing prediction indices for juvenile delinquency and parole recidivism seldom tabulate the actual rate of false positives. Yet where the false positive rate has been calculated for existing prediction tables, it turns out to be disturbingly high.[48]

It has sometimes been suggested that statistical predictive indices should be used only to identify the *risk category* in which offenders are located; and that selection of individuals within a given risk category for release or continued confinement should then be made by the parole board on the basis of clinical observation.[49] However, this suggestion does not solve the problem of false positives in the model. Given what we know of the fallibility of psychiatrists' and correctional officials' clinical forecasts,[50] there is no reason to expect that *their* predictive choices—even within statistically defined risk categories—will be dramatically free of false positives, where the prediction tables themselves are not. As Wilkins states:

> It is sometimes claimed that subjective judgment can help in regard to these kinds of error. Where the tables may fail to find the ten who will succeed in the 90 percent failure group, the human intelligence will be able to identify them. This is sometimes claimed by those who recognize that the human subjective intelligence is not adequate in any other part of the range of assessment. They want to cooperate with the tables, helping them when they fail. These kinds of claims for clinical supplementation of statistical tables have not been supported by any evidence. Their belief that something of this kind of supplementation *should* be possible seems again to originate in an inability to come to terms with uncertainty. For them, probability must be supplemented so that a deterministic model is provided—then a decision can be made![51] The false positive issue, therefore, must squarely be faced.

2. The Rare Event and False Positives: The Rosen Suicide Model. It might be hoped that with increased attention to the false positive problem and sufficient expenditure of time, money and effort, superior predictive indices could be developed which would be relatively free of false positives. That hope, however, may be misplaced—for there exist theoretical impediments to prediction of criminal conduct notwithstanding such efforts at improvement.

Generally speaking, criminal conduct tends to have two characteristics which make it resistant to accurate prediction: 1. It is comparatively rare. The more dangerous the conduct is, the rarer it is. Violent crime—perhaps the most dangerous of all—is the rarest of all; [and] 2. It has no known, clearly identifiable symptoms. Prediction therefore becomes a matter of developing statistical correlations between observed characteristics of offenders and subsequent criminal conduct. Where those two conditions obtain, false positives show a high degree of persistence, even in a theoretical predictive model.

In a valuable 1954 article, Albert Rosen[52] of the University of Minnesota developed a theoretical model for predicting suicide among mental patients, that illustrates this problem. Rosen constructed a hypothetical suicide detection index for an assumed population of 12,000 mental patients. On the basis of existing suicide statistics, he assumed that the rate of suicides was very low—one third of one percent of the total patient population. With this low rate, only 40 patients out of the initial population of 12,000 would actually commit suicide. Thus, without any test, *all* patients in this population could be predicted to be nonsuicidal, and the prediction would be right in 99⅔% of all cases. A hypothetical suicide detection index would have to perform better than this in identifying the potential suicides.

Rosen assumes such a hypothetical index is developed as follows: (a) the patient population is divided into two groups—patients who actually committed suicide during confinement (suicide population), and patients who did not (non-suicide population); (b) a random sample is selected and analyzed from each population; (c) a predictive index is developed, based upon the test data which significantly differentiate the two criterion samples; (d) a cutting line is established—that is, a differentiating score on the index, so that patients testing above that score would be classified as suicidal and patients testing below that score would be classified as non-suicidal; and (e) the cutting line is cross-validated—i.e., it is validated with new suicide and non-suicide samples, every psychiatric patient over a period of years being scored on the index.[53]

Such an index, Rosen finds, can identify a significant number of true positives only by mis-identifying a very much larger number of false positives. If an effort is made to reduce the false positives to a manageable number, only a tiny fraction of the true positives can be spotted—and even then, there are many more false positives than true positives.[54]

Suppose the cutting line is established at a point where, after cross-validation, the index will correctly identify 75% of the patients in both the suicide and the non-suicide populations, respectively. Using this cutting line, the index *will correctly identify 30 of the 40 actual suicides.* However, Rosen indicates, *it will also incorrectly identify 2,990 non-suicidal patients as potentially suicidal.*[55] The false positive rate here is so high as to make the prediction, in his words "[of] no appreciable value, for it would be impractical to treat as suicidal the prodigious number of misclassified cases."[56]

Suppose, then, a much higher cutting line is established—one which, when cross-validated, will correctly identify 90% of the non-suicide cases. It is assumed that the new cutting line reduces to 60% (regarded by Rosen as a liberal estimate) the proportion of correctly classified suicidal patients. Using this new cutting line, the index *will correctly identify 24 out of 40 actual suicides,* but still *will mis-identify as suicidal 1,196 false positives.* This is still "an impractical instrument because of the large number of false positives."[57]

With every elevation of the cutting line, Rosen shows, there would be some reduction in the number of false positives. However, there would be a corresponding shrinkage in the number of true positives. And the false positives will continue to greatly outnumber the true.

If the cutting line is raised to the point where it screens out 99.5% of the non-suicide cases, then, Rosen estimates, the predictive index will be able to spot only 2.5% of the actual suicides. Thus the problem remains unsolved. *Only 1 out of 40 actual suicides are correctly identified; and to achieve this meager result, 60 false positives will still have to be predicted.*

To achieve a better result, the experimenter might try to seek to develop a predictive index for a special diagnostic subgroup that has a substantially higher suicide rate than the general mental patient population. But, as Rosen points out,[58] there are inherent limitations in this approach. Any such diagnostic subgroup would be unlikely to have a suicide rate much higher than two percent, and that still would yield an excessive number of false positives. Moreover, a considerable proportion of the actual suicidal patients in the entire sample population would then be *excluded* from the diagnostic subgroup.

3. Violent Crimes and False Positives. Like suicide, crimes of violence are infrequent events. They are rare not only among the general population, but also (as will be discussed below) among previous offenders who have been released. The Rosen model thus has applicability to violent crimes, as well as to suicide. Predictions of violence tend to yield large numbers of false positives.

What makes violence so particularly difficult to predict is not merely its rarity, but its situational quality. Deterministic models to the contrary notwithstanding, violence generally is not a quality which inheres in certain "dangerous" individuals: it is an occurrence which may erupt—or may not—in certain crisis situations. Whether it does erupt, whether it is reported, whether the perpetrator is apprehended and punished, depend upon a wide variety of fortuitous circumstances, largely beyond the actor's control. Not only the actor's proclivities, but the decisions of other individuals—the victim, the bystanders, the police, the magistrate—may determine whether an act of violence occurs and whether it comes to be included in the criminal statistics. Trying to predict violence on the basis of information concerning only the supposedly violence-prone individual—

without taking these numerous external contingencies into account—is trying to solve a multi-variable problem by keeping track of only one variable. It is a hazardous undertaking, indeed.

The difficulty of predicting violent criminal behavior is strikingly illustrated by a recent study by Wenk and Robison of violent recidivism among California Youth Authority wards.[59] Wenk and Robison examined the records of all juvenile offenders who were processed during 1964–66 through the Deuel Reception-Guidance Center, a diagnostic unit that examines older juvenile offenders at the time they are committed to the Youth Authority. A follow-up study was made of their behavior on parole for a period of 15 months after release from confinement—with a view to determining how many were recommitted for a violent offense. As nearly one quarter of the sample had originally been committed for a violent offense or had a history of known violent behavior, the violence potential of the group might have been expected to be relatively high. Nevertheless, the investigators found that of this entire group, the incidence of violent recidivism during the 15-month follow-up period was only 2.4%.[60] As Rosen's analysis of his suicide model indicates, constructing a hypothetical predictive index upon a base rate as low as that—only 2.4%—would yield an unmanageable number of false positives.

Wenk and Robison's own tentative analysis supports this conclusion. They requested a psychologist and a statistician to project hypothetical predictive indices for violent recidivism, based upon the data in their sample. The *less* pessimistic projection—that of the psychologist—was that a multi-variable multiple regression equation could be developed from the data, which could identify about one-half of the true positives, *but in which the false positives would outnumber the true positives by a discouraging eight to one.*[61]

4. **Selection of High-Risk Subgroups.** One strategy mentioned by Rosen[62] for avoiding the false positive problem was to develop a predictive index only for narrowly defined subgroups of the original sample population, which manifest a considerably higher rate of the behavior to be tested. Applying this strategy to predictions of violent crime, we might try to construct a predictive instrument only for special subgroups of the convicted offender population, which manifest a substantially higher rate of violence.

The Wenk and Robison study suggests, however, that there may be serious obstacles to such a strategy. Their investigation identified five subgroups which manifested higher rates of violent recidivism than the general sample population.[63] The subgroups were: 1. Offenders with known histories of violence; 2. Offenders originally committed on a violent offense charge; 3. offenders committed to the Youth Authority for the fourth time or more (*i.e.*, multiple recidivists); 4. offenders with histories of "moderate to serious" opiate involvement; and 5. offenders referred to a psychiatrist for violence potential upon commitment to the Youth Authority.[64] The investigators' results indicated that *none* of these subgroups manifested a high enough incidence of violent recidivism to avoid the false positive problem. The highest rate (for category 5) was 6.2%; the other categories showed rates of about 5% or less.[65] These rates are well below the frequency needed for constructing an instrument relatively free of false positives—which, as Meehl and Rosen[66] estimate, should be closer to 50%.

Moreover, Wenk and Robison found that all these subgroups, except the first, account for a rather small fraction of the total incidence of violent recidivism in the sample population. For example, offenders in category five, which manifests the highest rate of violence, account for only 15% of the total incidence of violence on parole in the entire group. This creates another difficulty. If to construct an accurate predictive index, we are forced to limit its application to defined, high-risk subgroups that account for only a small fraction of the total occurrence of violence, then the public obtains little additional protection from preventive confinement so limited in scope.

5. Inclusion of Lesser Offenses. Another avoidance strategy might be to include non-violent offenses—since they are much more frequent. In the Wenk and Robison study, for example, if all parole violations are considered—which include not only violent crimes but also property crimes and other lesser offenses—then the recidivism rate climbs to a more statistically manageable 39.9%. Another serious objection is encountered here, however. To obtain the needed higher offense rates, we find ourselves fast descending the scale of seriousness toward the minor offenses. Then, it becomes increasingly difficult to demonstrate a need for societal protection of the degree of urgency that could conceivably warrant the kind of deprivation of liberty contemplated in the model. It should be recalled that the model involves incarceration for an indeterminate period that may be quite prolonged, perhaps lifelong.[67]

6. Concealing Overprediction. Even were we to extricate ourselves from this last difficulty we face another formidable theoretical problem: Any system of preventive incarceration *conceals erroneous confinements, while revealing erroneous releases.*[68] The individual who is wrongly identified as dangerous is confined, and thus has little or no opportunity to demonstrate that he would not have committed the crime had he been released. The individual who is wrongly identified as non-dangerous remains at large, so it comes to public attention if he later commits a crime. Thus, once a preventive system is established, it creates the illusion of generating only one kind of evidence: *evidence of erroneous release, that prompts decision-makers to expand the categories of persons who are preventively confined.* In short, a system of preventive confinement creates a self-fulfilling prophecy for the need of *more* preventive incarceration.[69]

Preventive confinement will also make it difficult to determine with any degree of confidence when a person ceases to be dangerous, and may be released. For the predictive criteria, in all likelihood, will largely rely upon the individual's behavior patterns in the relatively recent past. Incarceration itself will temporarily distort or suppress those behavior patterns, thus leaving few accurate clues concerning his probable behavior upon release.

Moreover, the problem of distortion of evidence would greatly be compounded by political-bureaucratic pressures. Under a system of preventive confinement, the public undoubtedly would hold officials responsible if they fail to incarcerate (or if they release) persons who subsequently do commit violent criminal acts. This would create overwhelming pressures upon officials to overpredict—since it would entail much less risk to the institution and to their own careers for them to confine (or fail to release) persons who actually are or have become harmless, than to release persons who are actually dangerous and do subsequently perpetrate crimes.

C. Evaluation of the Model—With False Positives

We are now ready to evaluate our model of preventive confinement. Let us begin by assuming that the technique of prediction used in the model manifests a relatively high incidence of false positives. More specifically, let us suppose that the prediction method *generates false positives at a rate which substantially exceeds the rate of erroneous convictions under the existing system of criminal justice for those categories of offenses.* (Since there is little available evidence concerning the rate of mistaken convictions, it is difficult to confirm that any given rate of false positives would, or would not, substantially exceed it. But if the rate of false positives is of the high order of magnitude discussed in the preceding analysis—say, the eight false positives to every one true positive suggested by the Wenk and Robison study—it is fairly safe to conjecture that, in Dershowitz' words, "any system of predicting future crimes would result in a vastly larger number of erroneous confinements"[70] than could be expected to occur under the present criminal justice system.) Later, we will go on to make an evaluation of the model in the context of a hypothetical "ideal" predictive technique that is relatively "free" of false positives.

1. Inappropriateness of Cost-Benefit Rationale. To sustain the model where false positives are present, a cost-benefit rationale must be assumed. Proponents of preventive confinement must argue in terms of "balancing" the individual's interest in not being mistakenly confined against society's need for protection from the actually dangerous person. It has to be contended that the "benefit" of preventing the really dangerous individual from committing future crimes exceeds, in the aggregate, the "cost" of mistakenly identifying and confining the nondangerous one.

Even if this kind of cost-benefit thinking were appropriate, it is highly questionable whether the preventive confinement model could be justified in its terms—once the magnitude of the "cost" of confining large numbers of false positives is fully taken into account. That is especially true because—for reasons just noted—strategies designed to minimize the number of false positives also sharply reduce the number of true positives that can be identified—and hence, minimize the social benefits of the system as a crime prevention device.

The more basic point, however, is that *cost-benefit thinking is wholly inappropriate here.* If a system of preventive incarceration is known systematically to generate mistaken confinements, then it is unacceptable in absolute terms because it violates the obligation of society to do *individual* justice. Such a system cannot be justified by arguing that its aggregate social benefits exceed the aggregate amount of injustice done to mistakenly confined individuals.

2. The Parallel of Conviction of the Innocent. In our criminal law, a whole variety of safeguards exist—most notably, the requirement of proof of guilt beyond a reasonable doubt—designed to assure that an innocent person is not convicted or punished. There, aggregate cost-benefit theories would definitely be inappropriate. Would reducing the standard of proof in criminal cases to a "preponderance of the evidence" yield favorable cost-benefit results—in terms of yielding a greater increase in numbers of convictions of the guilty than in numbers of additional convictions of the innocent? Perhaps so, perhaps not; but it does not really matter. A reduction in the standard of proof is absolutely unacceptable if it would materially increase convictions of the innocent. As Tribe states:

> Indeed, the very enterprise of formulating a tolerable ratio of false convictions to false acquittals puts an explicit price on an innocent man's liberty and defeats the concept of a human person as an entity with claims that cannot be extinguished, however great the payoff to society.
>
> This argument does not imply that we do or should insist on absolute certainty; we properly instruct juries to convict if they believe that guilt has been established "beyond a reasonable doubt" rather than "beyond all doubt." We do so, however, only because total certainty is incompatible with the human condition, and we do not wish to immobilize the system by demanding the impossible. Thus, guilt beyond a reasonable doubt represents not a lawyer's fumbling substitute for a specific percentage, but a standard that seeks to come as close to certainty as human knowledge allows—one that refuses to take a deliberate risk of punishing any innocent man.[71]

The Supreme Court has recently held that "the Due Process Clause protects the accused against conviction except upon proof beyond a reasonable doubt of every fact necessary to constitute the crime with which he is charged."[72] The Court cited three reasons for its decision. Its first reason was that of simple fairness (an individual should not be subjected to the deprivations of punishment if there is any reasonable doubt he deserved it):

> The accused during a criminal prosecution has at stake interests of immense importance, both because of the possibility that he may lose his liberty upon conviction and because of the certainty that he would be stigmatized by the conviction. Accordingly, a society that values the good name and freedom of every individual should not condemn a man for commission of

> a crime when there is reasonable doubt about his guilt . . . ;[73]

its second, the need to uphold the moral force of the law:

> Moreover, use of the reasonable-doubt standard is indispensable to command the respect and confidence of the community in applications of the criminal law. It is critical that the moral force of the criminal law not be diluted by a standard of proof which leaves people in doubt whether innocent men are being condemned . . . ;[74]

and its third, the need to preserve citizens' sense of security from wrongful state interference:

> It is also important in our free society that every individual going about his ordinary affairs have confidence that his government cannot adjudge him guilty of a criminal offense without convincing a proper factfinder of his guilt with utmost certainty.[75]

Assuming for the sake of argument that the state is entitled to confine *actually* dangerous individuals (an assumption to be examined below), the *mistaken* preventive confinement of actually non-dangerous persons can no more be tolerated than the conviction of the innocent. We are speaking here, of course, of persons who have already been convicted of crimes. But by hypothesis in our model, they have already served the full punishment for their past offense, and are being preventively confined for an additional time designed expressly and solely to incapacitate them from committing future crimes. Hence, the past conviction would not cure the unfairness inherent in preventively incarcerating nondangerous persons. After all, if a man is convicted of robbery and serves the maximum term in prison, we *still* would object to further imprisoning him for an alleged past murder of which he was wholly innocent. Why should we be more tolerant of taking a man who has been convicted and has served the full time for the robbery and confining him for more years to prevent a future murder which in fact he would never commit if given his freedom?

Even if preventive confinement is not officially labelled "punishment," the deprivations of prolonged preventive confinement would be much like those of prolonged imprisonment. The loss of liberty would be the same. So would many of the other unpleasant aspects of confinement, such as forced association with other persons, some of whom may well be actually dangerous. The social obloquy of confinement would be similar—since labeling someone a potential criminal would have much the same stigmatizing effect as labeling him a past offender.[76]

3. Reduced Trial Safeguards. If accused of a crime, an individual has recourse to various traditional trial safeguards that enable him to defend himself against a false charge. The prosecution has to meet a standard of proof beyond a reasonable doubt. It cannot show that the defendant had a propensity to commit criminal acts,[77] but must establish that he had the opportunity to commit, and did actually commit a specific crime. Thus the defendant, if he has effective counsel, can escape conviction by casting doubt upon the evidence connecting him with the offense.

These safeguards would not be available in a preventive proceeding. A standard of proof beyond a reasonable doubt would be virtually meaningless, and could not be applied. Given all the contingencies affecting future occurrences, how can any future event be predicted beyond a reasonable doubt? We can at least imagine what it would be like to be sure beyond reasonable question that *X* has committed a murder; but how could we imagine being so sure he *will* do so, since he could always change his mind, be arrested beforehand, be killed in an accident, etc.? How, particularly, could we be sure if we know our predictive method yields false positives and there is no way of ascertaining whether *he* is one of the false or one of the true positives? Moreover, evidence of a mere propensity to commit criminal acts would, necessarily, have to be sufficient to incarcerate. The defendant would have no way of challenging his actual connection with the crime—for the crime would be in the future. (How, for example, could he establish an alibi for an offense which has not yet occurred?)[78]

D. Evaluation of the Model—Minus the False Positives

Thus far, the objection to preventive confinement has centered upon the false positive issue—the injustice inflicted upon those wrongly confined on the basis of an erroneous prediction of dangerousness. Is this, however, the only objection? If it is, then it might be worthwhile to labor to overcome the obstacles to prediction, formidable as they are, with a view ultimately to establishing a system of preventive confinement when and if the accurate prediction of criminal conduct can be achieved.

Or do more fundamental evils inhere in the preventive concept—even if the false positive problem is assumed not to be present? If so, the entire concept deserves to be scrapped.

To answer these questions, we should inquire: how would we judge the preventive model described earlier, were we to assume that a predictive technique had been developed which is reasonably free of false positives? More specifically, let us hypothesize that the predictive technique mis-identifies false positives at a rate which is *no greater* than the rate of convictions of innocent persons for past crimes which are assumed to occur under the existing system of criminal justice.[79]

1. Universal Preventive Confinement. To evaluate the model assuming such a "foolproof" predictive technique, we might start by inquiring: "If our predictions are so accurate, why limit the model to previously convicted persons: why not preventively confine *anybody* found to be potentially dangerous?" If, as we shall find, there are serious objections to such a universal scheme of preventive confinement, then we should ask: "What, if anything, is there about a prior conviction that renders our preventive model any more acceptable?"

What are the objections, then, to a universal system of preventive confinement, assuming we can predict criminal conduct with a high degree of accuracy? Suppose a preventive system is established which is similar to our model in all major respects but one—it is not limited to persons who have already been convicted of crimes. If any individual meets specified standards of probable cause for being dangerous, the state could initiate commitment proceedings against him. After a full hearing, with maximum feasible procedural safeguards, he would be preventively confined for an indeterminate term if the predictive criteria indicate that he can be expected to commit a serious crime if permitted to remain at large.

Even with an accurate predictive technique, such an Orwellian scheme would be unacceptable, for two major reasons.

(1) Universal preventive confinement would run counter to basic concepts of individual liberty: it would deny individuals the fair opportunity to make their own decisions and order their own lives. A system of criminal justice which imposes specified punishments for specified crimes gives us some degree of assurance that we can, in Hart's words,

> predict and plan the future course of our lives within the coercive framework of the law. For the system which makes liability to the law's sanctions dependent upon a voluntary act not only maximizes the power of the individual to determine by his choice his future fate; it also maximizes his power to identify in advance the space which will be left open to him free from the law's interference.[80]

In a system of preventive confinement, this safeguard would be lost; an individual would have little choice as to whether he is confined or remains at large. His liberty would depend not upon his voluntary acts, but upon his *propensities* for future conduct as they are seen by the state. Far from being able "to identify in advance the space which would be left free to him from the law's interference," his liberty would depend upon predictive determinations which he would have little ability to foretell, let alone alter by his own choices.

Our constitutional scheme assigns a high value to the right of individual choice; this is reflected, for example, in the guarantees of free speech, free assembly and free association. It is likewise reflected in the basic rule of our criminal jurisprudence, that a sane adult may not be deprived of his liberty except as punishment for a crime of which he has been convicted.[81] The law thus warns that specified modes of anti-social conduct will be met by unpleasant consequences, including incarceration for a specified time. But the choice—whether to engage in such conduct and chance the punishment—is left up to the individual; the state will not intervene unless he has been found to have violated the law. By giving him that choice, society risks that the individual will make the wrong selection, to the community's detriment. Similar hazards are entailed by other constitutional guarantees. Free speech risks incitement to violence; free assembly risks riot; free association risks criminal conspiracy. Nevertheless, we choose to withhold the coercive power of the law until *after* the event. In so doing, we may incur the costs of certain anti-social conduct that might have been precluded by state preventive action. But that is felt to be well worth the assurance given to individual freedom.

Universal preventive confinement is inconsistent with this concept of individual choice. Because a prescient and paternalistic state is assumed to know that certain individuals will make the wrong choice, it confines them precisely for the purpose of depriving them of the opportunity of choosing at all. Even if the state's predictions are imagined to be highly accurate, such a scheme would entail undue sacrifice of individual freedom and dignity.

The force of this argument, it should be noted, does not depend upon any particular psychological or philosophical view of individual choice. Do individuals consciously weigh the risks when they decide whether or not to comply with the law—or do they act upon impulse, habit and social pressure? Are individuals really free to choose between legal and illegal conduct, or is their choice determined by their backgrounds and experiences? Interesting as these questions may be in themselves, they are of no relevance here. As Herbert Packer points out, we are not describing the process of individual choice, but expressing a value preference for limiting *state* intrusion into citizens' lives:

> Neither philosophic concepts nor psychological realities are actually at issue in the criminal law. The idea of free will in relation to conduct is not, in the legal system, a statement of fact, but rather a value preference having very little to do with the metaphysics of determinism and free will. The fallacy that legal values describe physical reality is a very common one. . . . But we need to dispose of it here, because it is a major impediment to rational thought about the criminal law. Very simply, the law treats man's conduct as autonomous and willed, not because it is, but because it is desirable to proceed as if it were. It is desirable because the capacity of the individual human being to live his life in reasonable freedom from socially imposed external constraints (the only kind with which the law is concerned) would be fatally impaired unless the law provided a locus *poenitentiae*, a point of no return beyond which external constraints may be imposed but before which the individual is free—not free of whatever compulsions determinists tell us he labors under but free of the very specific social compulsions of the law.[82]

(2) Preventive confinement also would entail unjustified risks of abuse. If the government had the power to designate any individual as dangerous and to confine him preventively regardless of any prior determination of guilt, it could misuse that power to incarcerate for racial, social or political ends. Granted, we are assuming here that a highly accurate predictive technique has been developed. However, the mere fact that such a technique is known to exist provides no guarantee that government—once it has the power of universal preventive confinement—will opt for that technique alone and will not resort to biased prediction devices. Prediction being such a highly technical matter, the difference between an accurate and a distort-

ing predictive instrument could depend upon subtle shifts in the data base, the sampling and validation methods, and the prediction variables and equations employed. It would be difficult, indeed, to develop workable constitutional or legal safeguards, that could effectively be administered by the courts, to assure that such distortions not be made. Nor could there be an effective popular check on abuses, given the arcane nature of the entire subject.

Of course, any human institution is susceptible to abuse. However, our tolerance for abuse diminishes as the institution's potential intrusiveness into citizens' lives increases. Universal preventive confinement has great potential intrusiveness. By abandoning the requirement of a prior criminal act, it reduces the protections and immunities available to individuals against state interference, and permits the state to confine a larger number of individuals, at an earlier time, and for a longer period than the criminal law would allow. Where the degree of intrusion can be so great, the risks of abuse implicit in a scheme of preventive confinement seem truly unacceptable.

2. Preventive Confinement for Those Convicted. If a scheme of universal preventive confinement is unacceptable, why is our model any better? If differs from the universal scheme in only one significant respect: it is applicable solely to persons who have been convicted of a crime. The fact of a prior conviction, however, gives no additional sustenance to the scheme.

It cannot be argued that the fact of the prior conviction justifies the preventive confinement in the model *as punishment*. For we are assuming in the model that the individual has already served the maximum statutory term of punishment for the past offense, and is now serving extra time that is expressly intended to be preventive, not punitive.

Nor can it be asserted that the supposed greater dangerousness of convicted persons justifies their preventive incarceration. A universal system of preventive confinement would not be rendered acceptable if its application were limited to the most dangerous individuals. With an accurate method of prediction—which we assume to be available—a finding of dangerousness would not have to depend upon the presence or absence of a prior conviction. Some persons who had never been convicted might well be found to be *more* dangerous than their convicted brethren.

The two major policy objections to universal preventive confinement, just described, would seem equally applicable to our model.

Objection (1)—the individual's loss of the fair opportunity "to identify in advance the space which will be left open to him free of the state's interference"—applies as well to the model. An individual who commits an offense will have no way of determining whether, in addition to being liable to punishment if he is apprehended, he will be subject to indeterminate and possibly lifelong confinement on the basis of a prediction of dangerousness. The possible result—the indeterminate confinement—is well beyond the reasonably foreseeable risk involved in committing an offense. True, he may be on notice that if he commits the offense, there is *some* possibility of his being subjected to indeterminate preventive confinement, whereas none exists if he complies with the law. However, the degree of likelihood of his being so confined if he commits an offense depends not upon the nature and quality of his chosen acts but upon the state's determination of his proclivities.

A violation of law may warrant punishment and punishment involves the temporary suspension of certain rights, including in some instances the right to liberty. In the model, however, we are speaking of the offender at a point in time where he has fully served his punishment; where he once again should be able to regain most, if not all of the ordinary rights of a citizen—including at least the right to remain free from seizure of his person by the state unless and until he has committed another offense.

Objection (2)—risk of abuse—applies *a fortiori* to the class of convicted offenders. Widely feared because of their past conduct[83] and drawn predominantly from the most under-privileged segments of society, convicted persons would have the most to fear from a deliberate "slanting" of the predictive criteria.

E. Preventive Confinement as "Punishment"

It is worth exploring more thoroughly whether a scheme of preventive confinement could be supported by resort to the concept of punishment. To do so, let us vary our original model slightly as follows:

> *Variation 1 of the Model. The legislature provides general maximum terms of imprisonment for various offenses. However, it provides that where any convicted offender meets specified predictive criteria for future dangerousness, he will be subject to an indeterminate term of confinement, possibly exceeding the normal maximum penalty, until he is adjudged no longer dangerous. The additional confinement would be classified by law as punishment and as an addition to the sentence for the crime of which he has been convicted; it would be served in a regular prison, rather than a special, less rigorous preventive facility.*

Thus in the revised model—unlike the original model—preventive confinement is officially labelled as *punishment* for the prior offense and is served under conventional punitive conditions, *i.e.*, in a regular prison. This change in the model is designed to enable us to focus squarely on the issue: can preventive confinement be *justified* as punishment for the prior offense?[84]

It is a basic principle of justice that the severity of punishment should not unduly exceed the gravity of the offense. While the legislature has wide discretion in defining the seriousness of offenses and determining the severity of punishments, it is subject to some moral and constitutional limits. The old English practice of hanging pick-pockets would now be regarded as repugnant. On at least one occasion, the Supreme Court has invalidated a criminal statute that imposed excessive fines and an extended prison term for a relatively minor crime. The Court in *Weems v. United States*[85] ruled the Eighth Amendment ban on cruel and unusual punishments extended not only to barbaric punishments, but also to prolonged punishments that were in no way proportional to the offense committed.

It is likewise a basic principle of justice—although one widely ignored in practice in our criminal justice system—that persons guilty of equally serious offenses should not be subjected to grossly unequal punishments.[86]

These are what Hart[87] calls principles of distribution—that is, principles limiting the way punishment may properly be distributed among individuals. As Hart points out, they should apply whether or not one adopts a retributive theory of the general aim of punishment.[88]

Suppose, for example, we reject the view that retribution for moral guilt is the main purpose of punishment, and hold instead that punishment serves the object of deterring the general public from engaging in criminal activity. Even with this deterrence philosophy, we should still—in fairness to the individuals affected—insist that punishment not be disproportionately severe in relation to the gravity of the offense. That being so, we should oppose the infliction of severe exemplary punishments upon certain individuals convicted of minor offenses, however useful that might be in deterring that type of offense.[89] If we consider prevention to be the main purpose of punishment, the same principles of justice still limit the manner in which we distribute punishment among individuals. Punishments of grossly disproportionate severity, and grossly unequal punishments for similar offenses, would still be objectionable.

Obviously, the application of these principles depends upon how we judge the seriousness of the offense. (Their application may also depend upon the extent to which we take into consideration the personal culpability of the offender. Should there, for example, be uniform penalties for each category of offense, disregarding the actor's state of mind except insofar as necessary to ascertain whether his conduct was intentional, negligent, accidental, etc., as some reformers have recently recommended?[90] Or should we continue to permit judges and parole boards to vary the punishment for an offense in order to reflect the actor's personal culpability, as indicated by his apparent motives, character or personal history?[91]) Without needing to resolve these difficult questions, it is fairly evident that the revised model violates the two principles of justice of which we are speaking. This is so because the revised model authorizes the imposition of indeterminate, even lifelong imprisonment, *without regard to the seriousness of the offender's past offense*—however such seriousness may be defined.

Consider the example of robbery. Under the revised model, the ordinary robber could be confined for no more than a specified number of years. But the robber who has the misfortune of being predicted to be dangerous would be subject to imprisonment for as much as his entire life. This would be objectionable for the two reasons just stated: 1. Confinement for as much as a lifetime for the crime of robbery would, by any humane standards, be disproportionately severe in relation to the character of the offense; and 2. Such prolonged confinement would be discriminatory against the robbers classified as dangerous, because their punishment would far exceed the penalty suffered by equally culpable robbers who happen not to be predicted to be dangerous.

Here, assuming the prediction of dangerousness to be accurate would not cure these objections. For the individual is, by hypothesis, serving the additional time as *punishment*, under punitive conditions. The punishment can be imposed only for the past offense—the robbery. If the extra time cannot be justified as punishment for the past robbery, then it cannot be justified with reference to the predicted crime, regardless of its prospective heinousness. For it likewise offends basic concepts of justice to *punish* someone—if confinement is seriously intended as punishment—except for a past offense.[92] Hence the revised version of the model would be unacceptable, whether one assumes false positives are involved or not.[93]

F. Addition of Rehabilitative Treatment

It has been suggested that the imposition of compulsory rehabilitative treatment gives justification to a scheme of preventive confinement.[94] This suggestion is worth critical examination. To do so, let us again vary our original model, this time to provide the additional element of compulsory individualized treatment.

> *Variation 2 of the Model. The legislature provides maximum terms of imprisonment for various criminal offenses. It prescribes, however, that where any convicted offender meets the predictive criteria for dangerousness, he will be subject to preventive confinement for an indeterminate period that may exceed the maximum statutory term of imprisonment for his offense. Preventive confinement would be served in a special facility under conditions of minimum rigorousness; there, he would be required to undergo psychological, educational and vocational rehabilitative treatment. Either the offender would first serve a prison term for his past offense and then be transferred to this special facility; or else he could be sent immediately to the special facility. In either case, he would not be released from the special facility until he no longer met the criteria for dangerousness.*[95]

Here, the individual's alleged need for treatment, alone, could not justify his being preventively confined—even were it supposed that he is suffering from an emotional or personality disturbance and could be genuinely helped by the treatment. For he is assumed to be an adult and—despite his psychological troubles—legally sane. Without the added elements of the prior conviction and the prediction of dangerousness, it could hardly be contended that the state had the right to confine *any* sane adult (even if he is somewhat disturbed) solely for therapeutic treatment, against his will.

Nor would the prior conviction alone justify his confinement. For we are assuming, again, that the period during which the individual is being confined for treatment exceeds the maximum statutory term of punishment for the offense of which he was convicted.

The justification of the mandatory treatment must depend, therefore, upon the prediction of dangerousness itself. The individual is being committed for treatment *because* he is thought to be dangerous, *precisely for the purpose of "curing" him of his dangerousness.* Were he not found dangerous he would not have to be treated.

The only functional difference between the original model of preventive confinement and this revised model of treatment-oriented confinement, is the manner by which they are designed to protect the community from individuals who are deemed dangerous. Pure preventive confinement operates only by incapacitating the individual; whatever his propensities for injuring the community, he is rendered incapable of exercising them because he is isolated. Treatment-oriented confinement operates by trying to eliminate these propensities in the individual, through a program of rehabilitative therapy: The individual is confined in order to assure his availability for the treatment program, and also in order to incapacitate him from doing harm during the interim period while the treatment is being administered and is supposedly taking effect.

Treatment could permit earlier release, assuming—and this assumption itself has been questioned[96]—that it can be effective. Under the preventive model, the individual simply remains in confinement until such a time as he changes sufficiently of his own accord so that he ceases to meet the criteria of dangerousness. Under the revised, treatment-oriented model, an effort would be made to hasten the process of change—and hence the prospects of his release—by application of the appropriate rehabilitative therapy. Despite these differences, however, both models have essentially the same purpose: to safeguard society against persons who have been identified by specified predictive criteria as individually dangerous if permitted to remain at large.

Thus the treatment-oriented model ultimately rests upon the same assumption as the purely preventive model: that society has the right to deprive persons of their freedom on the basis of individual predictions of future dangerousness. If for the reasons earlier explained, that assumption is unacceptable as applied to the original preventive model, it cannot sustain the treatment-oriented model either. (The false positive problem, for example, does not disappear merely because we choose to impose treatment upon the individuals who are mistakenly identified as dangerous.)

G. Implications for Current Practice

It is wise to be cautious in translating conclusions developed from a theoretical model to the real world; for the question can always be asked: "How do you know the real world is similar to the model in all the relevant respects?" In the field of preventive confinement, sufficient data concerning current practices is not available to enable us to answer this question with any certainty. However, some tentative conclusions might be ventured.

First, the foregoing analysis calls into serious doubt the rationality and fairness of overt schemes of preventive confinement in existing law—such as the Canadian Preventive Detention statute, the Maryland Defective Delinquent Law and the Colorado sexual offender statute, described at the beginning of this paper. Any such system—which takes legally sane individuals who have been convicted of crimes, makes predictions of their individual future dangerousness, and subjects them on the basis of such predictions to prolonged confinement, in excess of what could legally be imposed as punishment for their prior offenses—shares the essential defects of the models we have been analyzing. This conclusion holds also for the recommendations of the Model Sentencing Act and the Model Penal Code which would impose extended terms of confinement upon certain "dangerous" offenders.

Second, the analysis raises questions concerning the use of predictions of dangerousness in sentencing and parole decisions. Are sentencing judges and parole boards attempting to make individual assessments of the supposed dangerousness of convicted persons coming before them? To what extent do these assessments affect decisions concerning imposition and duration of confinement or grant or denial of parole? Is there evidence that individuals predicted to be dangerous receive materially *longer* sentences or serve materially *longer* terms of confinement than other offenders with similar offense histories not so predicted? Do individuals predicted to be dangerous receive terms of confinement of a duration that substantially exceeds what would ordinarily be regarded as appropriate as punishment for the past offense, if its seriousness alone is considered? A definitive answer to these questions would require a much more detailed investigation of existing law and practice than the scope of this theoretical analysis permits. However, if the answers to these questions are affirmative (as one might well suspect to be often the case) then the law is being used to create *de facto* preventive confinement—that would be subject to essentially the same objections as apply to the theoretical models discussed in this paper.

III. Conclusion

In this article, the following question was considered: "Is it appropriate to decide whether and how long to confine a person convicted of a crime on the basis of a prediction of his supposed individual dangerousness?"

To examine this question, we constructed a hypothetical model where a person convicted of a criminal offense is subjected to preventive confinement for an indeterminate term—possibly well in excess of the maximum statutory term of punishment for the crime of which he was convicted—if specified predictive criteria indicated a high probability of his committing a serious offense in the future. It was assumed that the model met certain threshold criteria, namely: that there would be a reasonably precise legal definition of "dangerousness"; that the predictive criteria would be adequately validated in advance; and that certain minimum procedural safeguards would be adopted.

Our analysis indicated that predictions of dangerousness would, because of the infrequency of the events to be predicted, generally yield a high incidence of false positives—that is, persons *mistakenly* predicted to be dangerous. Where numerous false positives are confined, the model was found to offend fundamental conceptions of individual justice.

Even if the predictive methods were assumed to be highly accurate, preventive confinement in the model was found not sustainable, because it infringed the right of individual choice and entailed significant risks of abuse. The preventive confinement could not, moreover, be justified by reference to concepts of punishment for the prior offense.

The addition of mandatory rehabilitative treatment, likewise, did not sustain the model, for the function of treatment itself was dependent upon the prior finding of individual dangerousness.

Thus, under our analysis, the model scheme of preventive confinement failed. The consequence of that failure for current practices has been examined.

Preventive confinement requires the assumption that conviction of a crime relegates the offender, even after he has completed the punishment for his prior offense, to *permanent* second-class status. The erroneous incarceration of false positives; the risk of abuse of prediction methods; and the abdication of concepts of personal choice which are inherent in such a scheme can be excused only if it is assumed that their infliction upon convicted persons does not matter—because, as a class, these persons are expendable. As Caleb Foote stated:

> It is a prerequisite for any system of preventive detention that you assume that those detained are going to be second-class citizens. The false positives are viewed as more expendable in the debates on preventive detention. Judges and

psychiatrists who support preventive detention assume that a mistaken identification of one actually safe person who is predicted to be dangerous is much less serious than the release of one actually dangerous person. The operating rationale, therefore, is much like that of a search-and-destroy mission. Some dangerous Viet Cong may be eliminated, and the civilians and children are expendable.[97]

NOTES

1. For a summary of arguments against pre-trial preventive detention, see Ervin, "Foreword: Preventive Detention—A Step Backward for Criminal Justice," 6 *Harv. Civ. Rights-Civ. Lib. L. Rev.* 291 (1971); Tribe, "An Ounce of Detention: Preventive Justice in the World of John Mitchell," 56 *Va. L. Rev.*, 371 (1970).
2. For critical analyses of the use of psychiatric predictions in civil commitment proceedings for the mentally ill, see Dershowitz, "The Law of Dangerousness: Some Fictions About Predictions," 23 *J. Legal Ed.* 24 (1970) [hereinafter cited as Dershowitz, "The Law of Dangerousness"]; Dershowitz, "Psychiatry in the Legal Process: A Knife That Cuts Both Ways," 4 *Trial* 29 (Feb.–Mar. 1968); Livermore, Malmquist & Meehl, "On the Justifications for Civil Commitment," 117 *U. Pa. L. Rev.* 75 (1968); Note, "Civil Commitment of the Mentally Ill: Theories and Procedures," 79 *Harv. L. Rev.* 1288 (1966).
3. *Can. Rev. Stat.* c. 34, § 688 (1970). According to the statute, an "habitual criminal" is one who has been previously convicted of three separate offenses punishable by five years or more of imprisonment, and who is "leading persistently a criminal life." For a description and history of the Canadian Preventive Detention law, see MacDonald, "A Critique of Habitual Criminal Legislation in Canada and England," 4 *U.B.C. L. Rev.* 87 (1969).
4. Gr. Brit., Criminal Justice Act of 1967, §§ 37–38. For a history of the British Preventive Detention law prior to 1967 see MacDonald, *supra* note 3.
5. Md. Ann Code art. 31B (Supp. 1971). For a useful analysis of the Maryland statute, see Note, " 'Defective Delinquent' and Habitual Criminal Offender Statutes—Required Constitutional Safeguards," 20 *Rutgers L. Rev.* 756 (1966) [hereinafter cited as *Rutgers Note*]. The Supreme Court has recently granted certiorari on a constitutional challenge to the Maryland law in Tippett v. Maryland, 436 F.2d 1153 (4th Cir. 1971), *cert. granted sub nom. Murel v. Baltimore City Court,* 92 S. Ct. 567 (1971).
6. Md. Ann Code art. 31B, § 5 (1971).
7. *Id.*
8. *Id.* § 9(b).
9. *Id.* § 9(a).
10. McCray v. Maryland, Misc. Pet. No. 4363 (Md. Cir. Ct., Montgomery County, Nov. 11, 1971).
11. *Colo. Rev. Stat. Ann.* § 39–1911(2) (Supp. 1969). This is the current version of the Colorado statute, revised since the U.S. Supreme Court held an earlier version unconstitutional, in Sprecht v. Patterson, 386 U.S. 605 (1967). For comment on the Colorado statute, see Note, "Indiana's Sexual Psychopath Law," 44 *Ind. L.J.* 242 (1969).
12. *Colo. Rev. Stat. Ann* § 39–19–3 (1969 Supp.).
13. S. Brakel & R. Rock, *The Mentally Disabled and the Law,* ch. 10 (American Bar Foundation rev. ed., 1971). According to this survey, these jurisdictions are Alabama, California, Florida, Illinois, Indiana, Iowa, Kansas, Massachusetts, Missouri, Nebraska, New Hampshire, Oregon, Pennsylvania, Tennessee, Washington, West Virginia, and the District of Columbia. The statutory definitions of "sexual psychopath," along with the statute citations, are set forth in this survey. Generally, the term "sexual psychopath" is used to refer to an individual who is not legally insane, is suffering from some kind of emotional or mental disturbance that makes him "disposed" to commit sex crimes, and is deemed to constitute a danger to the community if permitted to remain at large.
14. Advisory Council of Judges, National Council on Crime and Delinquency, Model Sentencing Act § 5 (1963); National Council on Crime and Delinquency, Guides to Sentencing the Dangerous Offender (1969).
15. Model Penal Code § 7.03(3) (Proposed Official Draft, 1962).
16. Cal. Penal Code §§ 1168, 3020 (West 1970).
17. *See* Johnson, "Multiple Punishment and Consecutive Sentences: Reflections on the Neal Doctrine," 58 *Calif. L. Rev.* 357, 379–83 (1970); Mitford "Kind and Usual Punishment in California," *The Atlantic,* March 1971, at 46.
18. Evjen, "Current Thinking on Parole Prediction Tables," 8 *Crime and Delin.* 215 (1962).
19. L. Ohlin, *Selection for Parole* (1951); Glaser, "Prediction Tables as Accounting Devices for Judges and Parole Boards," 8 *Crime and Delin.* 239 (1962). Ohlin and Glaser developed the prediction tables in use in Illinois. Evjen, *supra* note 18. For a valuable analysis and

summary of prediction studies, see, H. Mannheim & L. Wilkins, *Prediction Methods in Relation to Borstal Training* (1955).

20. Evjen, *supra* note 18, at 216–17.

21. R. Dawson, *Sentencing*, ch. 11, at 263 (American Bar Foundation, Administration of Criminal Justice Series, 1969).

22. If a specified term of confinement is imposed upon persons convicted of a criminal offense, without any attempt at predicting individual dangerousness, that will (by temporarily incapacitating such of those offenders as would otherwise be disposed to commit further offenses) prevent *some* crimes from occurring. The question remains, however, whether the use of imprisonment will prevent a sufficient number of offenses from occurring (considering only its incapacitating effect, and leaving general deterrence aside) to provide the public with a significant degree of net protection against crime. It also might be asked whether the public protection that is achieved is sufficient to warrant the costs and other negative side effects of the institution of imprisonment. Here, the following issues might be explored in further detail:

    (a) What percentage of the total number of actual offenders are apprehended, convicted and incarcerated for a given offense? For most types of crime—except, perhaps, murder, bank robbery and a few others—the percentage appears to be quite small. If this percentage is small, then the public may obtain little added protection from the incapacitating effect of incarceration upon confined criminals.

    (b) What is the average rate at which persons incarcerated for a specific crime could be expected to commit further offenses, if permitted to remain at large? If the rate is low, again, little public protection is achieved by incarceration. Generally, the rate is relatively low for the more serious offenses.

    (c) To what extent does the experience of imprisonment *increase* the propensity of those confined to commit criminal acts upon release? If imprisonment is criminogenic—as some studies suggest it might be—it may have a *counter-preventive* effect, by prompting more crimes after release than are prevented during confinement.

    (d) How cost-effective is imprisonment as a device for preventing crime by incapacitating criminals, in view of the high per prisoner cost of confinement?

    For a useful analysis of these issues, with some empirical data, see J. Robison, "The California Prison, Parole and Probation System" (Tech. Supp. 2, Cal. Assembly, "Preliminary Report on the Costs and Effects of the California Criminal Justice System," April 1969).

23. In evaluating the soundness of the concept of preventive confinement, I will be examining its broad implications for social policy, rather than the narrower question of its compliance with legal and constitutional standards under the present state of the law.

24. *See* text accompanying *supra* note 5.

25. *See supra* note 17.

26. Dershowitz, "The Law of Dangerousness," *supra* note 2.

27. Goldstein & Katz, "Dangerousness and Mental Illness: Some Observations on the Decision to Release Persons Acquitted by Reason of Insanity," 70 *Yale L.J.* 225 (1960).

28. *See* text accompanying *supra* note 6.

29. *See Rutgers Note, supra* note 5. This 1966 *Rutgers Law Review* Note argues that the Maryland Defective Delinquent Law is void for vagueness because the criterion for dangerousness—"actual danger to society"—is so imprecise as to leave the crucial decision of what kind of future conduct warrants incarceration wholly to the discretion of individual psychiatrists, without giving the courts any workable criteria for decision-making. The Note contends that the law's invalidity for vagueness does not depend upon whether it is classified as a civil or criminal statute. The vagueness question may be considered in the coming Supreme Court test of the constitutionality of the statute, Tippett v. Maryland, 436 F.2d 1153 (4th Cir. 1971), *cert. granted sub nom.* Murel v. Baltimore City Court, 92 S. Ct. 567 (1971) *See also* Schreiber, "Indeterminate Therapeutic Incarceration of Dangerous Criminals: Perspectives and Problems," 56 *Va. L. Rev.* 602 (1970).

30. Dershowitz, "The Law of Dangerousness," *supra* note 2.

31. Glaser, *supra* note 19, at 257.

32. Dershowitz, "The Law of Dangerousness," *supra* note 2, at 46. *See also,* J. Rappeport, *Clinical Evaluation of the Dangerousness of the Mentally Ill* (1967); Morris, "The Confusion of Confinement Syndrome: An Analysis of the Confinement of Mentally Ill Criminals and Ex-Criminals by the Department of Correction of the State of New York," 17 *Buffalo L. Rev.* 651 (1968).

33. Hakeem, "Prediction of Parole Outcome from Summaries of Case Histories," 52 *J. Crim. L.C. & P.S.* 145 (1961).

34. *Id.* at 149–50.

35. American Friends Service Committee, *Struggle for Justice,* ch. 5 (1971) [hereinafter cited as AFSC Report].
36. *See* text accompanying note 49, *infra.*
37. P. Meehl, *Clinical vs. Statistical Prediction,* 136–38 (1954).
38. *See* Specht v. Patterson, 386 U.S. 605 (1967).
39. *Id.*
40. For a summary of state court decisions concerning the applicability of procedural due process safeguards in sexual psychopath proceedings, see Annot., 34 A.L.R.3d 652 (1970).
41. Md. Ann. Code art. 31B (Supp. 1971); Tippett v. Maryland, 436 F.2d 1153 (4th Cir. 1971).
42. The Maryland Defective Delinquent Law provides an indigent defendant with a psychiatric witness at state expense, but no provision is made to enable the witness to conduct the kind of extended psychiatric observation needed to challenge the state's psychiatrists—who have had the defendant confined under prolonged observation. Md. Code Ann. art. 31B § 7(b) (Supp. 1971); *Rutgers Note, supra* note 5.
43. *See* S. Brakel & R. Rock, *supra* note 13, ch. 10, and Note, *Indiana's Sexual Psychopath Law, supra* note 11, arguing that the privilege against self-incrimination should apply in sexual psychopath proceedings; People v. Potter, 85 Ill. App. 2d 151, 228 N.E.2d 238 (1967), holding that, on the basis of the Supreme Court's reasoning in Specht v. Patterson, 386 U.S. 605 (1967), the privilege against self-incrimination should be applicable to proceedings under the Illinois Sexual Offender Act. *Contra, Rutgers Note, supra* note 5; Haskett v. Marion Criminal Court, 250 Ind. 229, 234 N.E.2d 636 (1968).
44. The Warner, Glueck, and other studies are summarized in H. Mannheim & L. Wilkins, *supra* note 19, ch. 1.
45. L. Wilkins, *Evaluation of Penal Measures,* ch. 5 (1969).
46. For an example of such a prediction study designed for Army recruitment purposes, see Danielson & Clark, "A Personality Inventory for Induction Screening," 10 *J. Clin. Psychol.* 137 (1954). The design of that study, however, was criticized in Meehl & Rosen, "Antecedent Probability and the Efficiency of Psychometric Signs, Patterns and Cutting Scores," 52 *Psychol. Bull.* 194 (1955).
47. L. Wilkins, *supra* note 45, at 69–70.
48. For example: Gottfredson developed a prediction table for parole recidivism, based upon California Base Expectancy scores, and applied it to a validation sample of 2,132 California male parolees. The lowest score category (Base Expectancy scores 0–4)—which indicated the highest expectancy of recidivism—correctly identified slightly under 10% of all violators in the sample; but 26% of those in this category were false positives. Those scoring in the lowest third of the sample (in percentile terms) constituted 46% of the actual violators; but 33% of those in this low scoring group were false positives. Gottfredson, "The Base Expectancy Approach," in *The Sociology of Punishment and Correction* 807–13 (N. Johnston, L. Savitz & M. Wolfgang eds. 1970). Wenk and Robison applied more elaborate prediction tables for parole recidivism, developed by Gough, Wenk and Rozynko and based upon the California Psychological Inventory and Minnesota Multiphasic Personality Inventory scores, to a large group of paroled California Youth Authority wards (the sample used in this study is described in the text accompanying note 59, *infra*). Again, the results were disappointing, with over 50% of those predicted to be violators being false positives, and with the incidence of correct predictions being lower than it would be by random selection. E. Wenk & J. Robison, Assaultive Experience and Assaultive Potential, May 1971 (unpublished paper, National Council on Crime and Delinquency Research Center, Davis, Cal.). *See also* Gough, Wenk & Rozynko, "Parole Outcome as Predicted from the CPI, the MMPI, and a Base Expectancy Table," 70 *J. Abnormal Psychol.* 432 (1965).
49. Glaser, *supra* note 19, at 247–48.
50. *See* text accompanying *supra* notes 32 and 33.
51. L. Wilkins, *supra* note 45, at 128–29.
52. Rosen, "Detection of Suicidal Patients: An Example of Some Limitations in the Prediction of Infrequent Events," 18 *J. Consulting Psych.* 397 (1954).
53. *Id.* at 398.
54. *Id.* at 399–400.
55. *Id.* at 399.
56. *Id.*
57. *Id.* at 400.
58. *Id.*
59. E. Wenk & J. Robison, "Assaultive Experience and Assaultive Potential." May 1971 (unpublished paper, National Council on Crime and Delinquency Research Center, Davis, Cal.)
60. *Id.* at 27.
61. *Id.* at 47.
62. *See* text accompanying *supra* note 58.
63. Wenk & Robison, *supra* note 59, at 27–38.
64. *Id.*
65. *Id.*
66. Meehl & Rosen, *supra* note 46.

67. As will be recalled, indeterminate terms of confinement are utilized in the model in order to assure that an individual predicted to be dangerous remains confined—and thus unable to harm the community—until he is found no longer dangerous.
68. Dershowitz, "On Preventive Detention," in *Crime, Law and Society* 307–19 (A. S. Goldstein & J. Goldstein eds. 1971); Tribe, *supra* note 1, 372–73.
69. To avoid this distortion of the evidence, it has been suggested that a random sample of the population of those preventively confined be released from time to time, and the accuracy of the prediction be tested upon that sample. That may get us involved, however, in the problem of infrequent events. If we are trying to predict violent crimes, where the offense rate is very low, a substantial number of persons would have to be released at random in order to be able to measure the effectiveness of the criteria. This would pose serious problems of fairness for those who remain subject to confinement. Also, any large-scale random release could reduce the effectiveness of the system as a measure of public protection—and rekindle much of the public anxiety that the preventive system is designed to alleviate. *But see* Dershowitz, "On Preventive Detention," *supra* note 68.
70. Dershowitz, *supra* note 68, at 313.
71. Tribe, *supra* note 1, at 387–88.
72. *In re* Winship, 397 U.S. 358, 364 (1970). The Court held that the requirement of proof beyond a reasonable doubt applied both to criminal and juvenile delinquency proceedings.
73. *Id.* at 363–64.
74. *Id.* at 364.
75. *Id.*ep
76. The force of this argument—that preventive confinement of the false positives is essentially unjust—does not, in fact, depend upon whether such confinement is classified as punishment. Even if it is regarded as a precautionary, rather than a punitive measure, the justification of preventively confining an individual would depend upon his *actually* being dangerous. The individual is being deprived of his liberty because, if he were to remain at large, he would interfere with the liberty of others by committing crimes. If he is *not* in fact dangerous, this justification simply collapses; and what we have left is gratuitous suffering imposed upon a harmless individual.

    See also In re Winship, 397 U.S. 358 (1970), where the Supreme Court ruled that the mere fact that juvenile delinquency proceedings were legislatively designated as civil, instead of criminal, did not obviate the need for criminal due process safeguards, including proof beyond reasonable doubt.

    For comment on reasons for the different treatment of the insane, see note 81 *infra.*
77. Generally, evidence of a defendant's propensity for criminal conduct is not even admissible in a criminal trial. *See* Comment, "Procedural Protections of the Criminal Defendant—A Reevaluation of the Privilege Against Self-Incrimination and the Rule Excluding Evidence of Propensity to Commit Crimes," 78 *Harv. L. Rev.* 426, 435–43 (1961).
78. Dershowitz has also pointed out that in a criminal trial, imperfect as it is, the judge and jurors have "some sense of what it means to decide whether a specifically charged act probably was or was not committed . . . some basis for sorting out the relevant from the irrelevant, the believable from the incredible, the significant from the trivial." Dershowitz, *supra* note 68, at 315. In a preventive proceeding, the regular participants in the judicial process would be ill-equipped to judge the validity of the prediction. In a traditional courtroom, one might imagine what predictive trials would become when they were contested; baffling arguments between prosecution and defense expert witnesses, each claiming superior expertise and offering contrasting clinical or statistical judgments. A lay judge and jury (if there is a jury) will find such evidence much harder to evaluate intelligently than evidence of past crimes.

    To provide greater expertise to the decision-makers, preventive confinement might be decided upon by specialists. That, however, would remove the traditional safeguard of lay control over the judicial process. If the experts decide, who chooses the experts and judges their performance?
79. *But see* Tribe, *supra* note 1, at 385–88.
80. H. L. A. Hart, *Punishment and Responsibility*, 181–82 (1968).
81. An exception has historically been made of the insane—who have been subjected to preventive confinement without the requirement of a prior conviction, if deemed to be "dangerous to themselves or others." Little concern has been shown with safeguarding mental patients' rights of individual choice—because, in part, they have been regarded as persons incapable of choosing: that is, so cognitively and emotionally deranged that, for them, choice has little or no meaning. As one commentary put it:

Another explanation might be found in the assumption that society's rules cannot deter the mentally ill from acting dangerously. Whether persons who are not mentally ill commit dangerous acts or avoid them is thought to depend on a process of choice. This process is respected and valued: only by not confining even those who can be accurately predicted to be dangerous can all persons be permitted to make the choice. On the other hand, whether mentally ill persons act dangerously is thought to depend not on their own choice but on the chance effects of their disease. Confining them hinders no respected process.

Note, "Civil Commitment of the Mentally Ill," *supra* note 2, at 1291. This view of mental illness has been questioned, *see* Livermore, Malmquist & Meehl, "On the Justifications for Civil Commitment," *supra* note 2. Whatever its merits, this justification points up the high value assigned to individual choice, in the case of persons not deemed insane.

82. H. Packer, *The Limits of the Criminal Sanction,* 74–75 (1968).
83. *See* Harris Poll on public attitudes toward convicted offenders in *Joint Commission on Correctional Manpower and Training, the Public Looks at Crime and Corrections* (1968).
84. *See* H. L. A. Hart, *supra* note 80, ch. 1, at 4–26.
85. 217 U.S. 349 (1910), invalidating a statute imposing a penalty of from 12 to 20 years imprisonment at hard and painful labor for the crime of falsifying official records. For a comment on this case, see *Rutgers Note, supra* note 5; Katkin, "Habitual Offender Laws: A Reconsideration," 21 *Buffalo L. Rev.* 99 (1971).
86. *See* H. L. A. Hart, *supra* note 80, ch. 1; AFSC Report, *supra* note 35, ch. 3, 9. *See also* United States v. Wiley, 278 F.2d 500 (7th Cir. 1960); President's Commission on Law Enforcement and Administration of Criminal Justice, Task Force Report: The Courts 23–24 (1967); S. Kadish & M. Paulsen, *Criminal Law and its Processes,* 1284–87 (1969).
87. H. L. A. Hart, *supra* note 80, ch. 1.
88. *Id.* at 11–13.
89. Hart explains this point as follows:

   The further principle that different kinds of offence of different gravity (however that is assessed) should not be punished with equal severity is one which like other principles of Distribution may qualify the pursuit of our General Aim and is not deducible from it. Long sentences of imprisonment might effectually stamp out car parking offences, yet we think it wrong to employ them; *not* because there is for each crime a penalty "naturally" fitted to its degree of iniquity (as some Retributionists in General Aim might think); not because we are convinced that the misery caused by such sentences (which might indeed be slight because they would rarely need to be applied) would be greater than that caused by the offences unchecked (as a Utilitarian might argue). The guiding principle is that of a proportion within a system of penalties between those imposed for different offences where these have a distinct place in a commonsense scale of gravity. This scale itself no doubt consists of very broad judgements both of relative moral iniquity and harmfulness of different types of offence: it draws rough distinctions like that between parking offences and homicide, or between "mercy killing" and murder for gain, but cannot cope with any precise assessment of an individual's wickedness in committing a crime (Who can?). Yet maintenance of proportion of this kind may be important: for where the legal gradation of crimes expressed in the relative severity of penalties diverges sharply from this rough scale, there is a risk of either confusing common morality or flouting it and bringing the law into contempt.

   H. L. A. Hart, *supra* note 80, ch. 1, at 25. *See also* American Bar Association, Project on Minimum Standards for Criminal Justice, "Standards Relating to Sentencing Alternatives and Procedures," 56–61 (1968).
90. *See* AFSC Report, *supra* note 35, ch. 9.
91. *See,* e.g., R. Dawson, *supra* note 21, at 79–93.
92. *See* H. L. A. Hart, *supra* note 80, ch. 7. *See also* H. Packer, *supra* note 82, at 73–79.
93. The concept of punishment might justify imposing longer sentences upon multiple offenders than upon first offenders—on the ground that a persistent course of criminal conduct evidences a greater degree of culpability. However, the model cannot be rescued by limiting its application to recidivists. Even for second robbery offenders, for example, an indeterminate and possible lifelong sentence would seem excessive; and selecting *some* second robbery offenders (namely, those predicted to be dangerous) and not others (namely, those not so predicted) for such harsh treatment would, again, be discriminatory. For a useful analysis of habitual offender laws, *see* Katkin, *supra* note 85.

94. *See,* e.g., Sas v. Maryland, 334 F.2d 506 (4th Cir. 1964), upholding the Maryland Defective Delinquent Law.
95. This revised model closely resembles Maryland's Defective Delinquent Law—described in the text accompanying *supra* notes 5–9—except that the procedures and predictive criteria would be improved to meet the threshold requirements described in part II-A of this article.
96. Several studies have shown that existing rehabilitative treatment programs have had little or no measurable success in reducing recidivism rates. *See* G. Kassebaum, D. Ward & D. Wilner, *Prison Treatment and Parole Survival* (1971); Robison & Smith, "The Effectiveness of Correctional Programs," 17 *Crime & Delin.* 67 (1971). The concept of mandatory rehabilitative treatment has also been attacked as having functioned almost exclusively as a pretext for widening the discretion of law enforcement and correctional officials, and having aggravated the repressive and discriminatory features of the correctional system. AFSC Report *supra* note 35, chs. 3, 6.
97. Foote, "Comments on Preventive Detention," 23 *J. Legal Ed.* 48, 52–53 (1970).

On Incapacitating the Dangerous

FERDINAND D. SCHOEMAN

Schoeman claims, in opposition to von Hirsch, that, at least in principle, a carefully monitored system of preventive detention may be no more objectionable morally than the analogous practice of quarantining people who have dangerous communicable diseases. He concedes, however, that at present there are serious legal and practical objections to legitimizing such a practice.

Given the extent and the intensity of public concern about violent crime, there is an ever-increasing willingness to consider deterring and incapacitating potential offenders by means that until recently would have been summarily rejected as violative of respect for the rights and dignity of free and equal persons. Indeed, it is not just willingness to consider options that is expanding; it is actual practices, which include use of aversive conditioning, token economies, electrical, physical and chemical manipulation of the brain,[1] indeterminate sentencing, and criminal commitment of the legally innocent. What will be of concern in this paper is a variant of this last option. Specifically, the discussion will center on arguments both for and against civil preventive detention—the incapacitating of individuals thought to be dangerous—as a potentially legitimate means of promoting social protection.

Some opposition to the use of civil preventive detention to effect this end has focused on the inadequacy of available predictive techniques for determining carefully enough who is dangerous. Other attacks have been directed at the vagueness of what is meant by the label "dangerous," or have stressed how inadequate present protections are for those civilly committed, whatever the rationale.[2] On the face of it, such particular objections seem directed to circumstances which appear in principle remediable, leaving open the possibility that under some future circumstances civil preventive detention of those deemed dangerous might be legitimate. Part I of this paper is devoted to an investigation of what such conditions might be.

Still other attacks on civil preventive detention have stemmed from more philosophical worries having to do with implications such a practice, however perfected, would have on our understanding of a person as an autonomous being deserving respect as well as on our appreciation of the role of the power—restraint aspect of the criminal law. Part II of this paper is devoted to gauging the moral weight of these more Olympian wor-

Reprinted from the *American Philosophical Quarterly,* vol. 16, no. 1 (1979) by permission of the publisher.

ries. A motif of the whole paper is a comparison of civil preventive detention with the presently accepted practice of quarantine, arguing that once certain conditions are met, it would not be consistent to countenance the use of quarantine and associated public health measures and reject civil preventive detention of the dangerous. The point of the paper then will not be to argue that civil preventive detention is not problematic, or that given available technology it is to be recommended. Rather, it is that assuming certain developments in both technology and law, no more serious problems arise in defending civil preventive detention, suitably qualified, than arise from the practice of quarantine as a measure for protecting public health. Civil preventive detention represents an assault on our notion of autonomous moral being only to the degree that quarantine does.

It is an important feature of gauging the legitimacy of the practice being considered here to be clear that the persons whose rights are to be transgressed for social protection need not be judged guilty of anything, need not be judged blameworthy, morally or legally, for any act they have committed. Furthermore, the reason such persons need not be thought blameworthy does not stem from any kind of general skepticism about the notions of praise or blame. Advocates of this practice may believe that those who commit crime are blameworthy and deserve punishment. The practice consists simply in incapacitating individuals predicted to be illegally violent, until such time as the potential for illegal violence diminishes to within tolerable levels. This practice of civil preventive detention involves restrictions on the liberty of persons who have not forfeited any rights by previous delinquent acts. For purposes of this paper, I shall include in the practice of civil preventive detention all interferences up to and including isolation of the dangerous person, with the presumption that the least restrictive means of accomplishing social protection is the maximum allowable under the practice.

I

As indicated, in this section I shall address the more practical and technical impediments to a morally legitimate system of preventive detention. Though, as I shall argue, some of the objections may prove decisive, I continue considering other objections and how a defender of civil preventive detention might be able to meet them. My justification for this procedure is first of all that we find out interesting things about our moral principles by continuing to address questions and press for answers. Second, since it could turn out that we are wrong in thinking that certain technical abilities are beyond human possibility, we should be prepared with contingency plans and contingency arguments just in case we find that we have been wrong. And third, as philosophers we might be interested in whether certain kinds of distinctions can be drawn, as well as whether theories can be defeated for certain kinds of reasons, even though we know that there may be practical objections which keep the issues from being pressing ones.

The first major source of opposition to civil preventive detention stems from skepticism about the adequacy of predictive techniques available or foreseeable on the basis of which mankind can be divided into two categories: the dangerous and the not-so-dangerous. The evidence on this predictability issue is reported to be as follows: There is no predictive technique available which does not include more false positives than true positives—which does not diagnose as future-guilty more persons who will not commit such crimes than persons who will. Furthermore, as one attempts to circumscribe a higher percentage of people who actually will commit crimes, the ratio of false positives to true positives increases.[3] (One does, after all, succeed in predicting all crimes that actually will be committed by claiming that everyone will commit every possible crime.)

It is worthwhile noting that some authorities on the issue of preventive detention treat this predictive problem as essentially the only problem with the practice, apparently conceding that if predictions improve sufficiently their opposition would vanish. No less an authority than Professor Alan Dershowitz expressed this view:

> What difference is there between imprisoning a man for past crimes on the basis of "statistical likelihood" and detaining him to prevent future crimes on the same kind of less-than-certain information? The important difference may not be one of principle; it may be, as Justice Holmes said all legal issues are, one of degree. The available evidence suggests that our system of determining past guilt results in the erroneous conviction of relatively few innocent people . . . But the indications are that any system of predicting future crimes would result in a vastly larger number of erroneous confinements—that is, confinements of persons predicted to engage in violent crimes who would not, in fact, do so.[4]

There are actually numerous problems which arise in working out solutions to this predictive problem. How accurate need the predictive techniques be before we can act on their basis? How invasive can the probing into the lives and thoughts of individuals be in order to achieve acceptable levels of accuracy? On what basis can an individual be required to submit to testing, the result of which might include civil confinement of that individual?

Perhaps the easiest question to deal with is the one relating to the standard of accuracy. If, following Dershowitz's suggestion, prediction of crime can be made as accurate as trials by juries, then we seem to have the problem of standards solved. In the legacy of the criminal law, the maxim that better that ten guilty men go free than that one innocent person be punished can be used to supply either qualitative or quantitative assistance here. Qualitatively what is asserted is the importance of not interfering with a person unless one is justifiably very confident that he did the wrong attributed to him. Quantitatively what is asserted is that the accuracy rate must be 90% or better. It cannot be interpreted as saying that the worst thing in the world is to find an innocent person guilty, for that interpretation would preclude all procedures for determining guilt we mortals know.

For our purposes, one can set the accuracy threshold as high as one desires, even at 100%, since the issues we want to address arise almost independently of the level of accuracy achievable. For the issue to be addressed is whether it would be legitimate to preventively detain someone when there is *moral certainty* that without such detention that person will perform some dangerous criminal act. In light of this requirement, it cannot be maintained that civil preventive detention must rest on "mere probabilities" while criminal conviction and quarantine are based on knowledge.

It is worth mentioning in passing that this moral certainty accuracy threshold is considerably higher than we would require in cases of serious danger from diseases. Suppose that someone has smallpox, and that the chance of being contagious at all is 50 percent and that the chance of dying from contagion is 50 percent. Under these conditions we would, I think, unhesitantly insist on the enforced isolation of the carrier, until such time as he no longer posed a threat to others.

With the level of accuracy set, we can now focus on the second question: how invasive can the information gathering process be? Given that accurate predictions of many natural phenomena involve acquiring as much information of details as possible, it would be rather startling if accurate predictions about people did not involve most extensive probing into every facet of persons' personalities and surroundings, both physical and social. Since so much of how a person responds to a situation depends on how he perceives or misperceives it, and since social situations will depend not only on how one perceives but how all involved do, the prospect of making accurate predictions seems negligible. The problems of interaction and interpretation seem to complicate the task of predicting what people will do beyond the point at which it can seem worthwhile even trying. It appears that we introduce problems of invasion of privacy as a result of our scruples about the minimization of false positives.

Granting this problem, it appears that we can and morally must dispense with civil preventive detention, not on grounds that isolating an individual for the protection of others is unjust, but on grounds that the process of finding out that someone is dangerous is itself so invasive of privacy that we are not entitled even to make the investigation into the threat potential of our citizenry. For purposes of this paper I am willing to grant the point that predictive techniques require such wholesale invasions of privacy that efforts at achieving this information might be prohibited on that score alone, depending on the stakes, without any reference to the fact that the practice involves the detention of the innocent for the well-being of others. But then I want to go on to ask if the information necessary for adequate predictions could be gathered or were available without invasion of privacy, would preventive detention then be legitimate? In the event that psychics could be used to predict what people would do, without paraphernalia like bugs or binoculars, and without interviews, would government use of their abilities be invasive of privacy? Is privacy invaded as a result of the means used for acquiring information or as a result of the state of knowing what another rightfully regards as his to conceal?[5]

How invasive can investigations be into the personal characteristics of individuals, and on what basis can such investigations be initiated? Besides the obvious point just made that the adequacy of data upon which to make predictions is directly proportional to the invasiveness of the means used to acquire it, another equally obvious point can be made. The fewer the number of people that can be legitimately screened, the smaller the percentage of would-be crime that can be arrested.

Again drawing attention to an analogy from public health, suppose that there is a deadly disease which spreads easily from carriers, who cannot contract the disease, to those who are susceptible. Next suppose that treatment for being a carrier requires months of confinement—a fact which affords people with a strong incentive not to undergo diagnostic test to discover whether they are indeed carriers. Finally suppose that 50,000 persons a year die from this disease. What would it be legitimate for the state to do in order to find and treat carriers of this disease, and thereby save 50,000 lives each year? In this context, I suspect that we would tend to demote in importance our concern over invasion of privacy, thinking that saving that many lives is so important as to be the decisive consideration. I am suggesting that under this circumstance mass mandatory screening would not seem out of the question, provided that such measures were prerequisite to preventing such an epidemic. If we may consider such measures for saving that many lives that otherwise would be lost because of disease, why not consider such measures to save that many lives otherwise lost because of fear, greed, jealousy, anger, love, etc.?

Some might be tempted to respond to this question by saying that it just is legitimate to isolate a person who is sick, something over which one has no control, but not for impending crime. But here the point must be made that even under quarantine, persons are not isolated because they are sick. Most sick persons are not quarantined. Persons quarantined are isolated *because they are dangerous to others,* the sickness being the cause of the danger. We shall return to this point of contention in Part II.

We must now ask ourselves, who can be screened and on what account? Using the strategy that we should try to stay within the bounds set by other acceptable social practices when setting limits on civil prevention detention, we shall not step beyond what the law seems to allow in cases of protecting the public health.

What we find in the area of public health law is that ". . . there are legally sanctioned compulsory examinations in which the subject may not be a willing participant because the examination primarily furthers the aim of public protection."[6] But still, with the exception of impending disaster, compulsory examination of individuals for communicable diseases must be based on more than mere suspicion.[7]

Two obvious questions arise in extrapolating this description of screening policy in the area of public health to screening for prevention of crime: What will count as reasonable grounds for examination, and when are situations dire enough to warrant loosening restrictions on barriers to screening? As suggested above, there is a certain parallel between epidemics and certain classes of crime—deadly consequences; similarities in terms of predictability and preventability via isolation may also emerge. Provided mass screening is thought legitimate in one case, why should it not be similarly conceived in the other?

The practice of preventive detention, to be justified, would not only have to be based on tests which had a very low rate of false positives, but would have to be administered on such a basis as to allow some rather significant reduction in the crime rate. Whether this can be done without overextensive invasion of privacy is something one can have grave doubts about. But the question here is: If effective screening can be done without unconscionable invasion of privacy, and if it could be shown that measures up to and including preventive detention would prevent high percentages of projected crimes, would such a practice of detaining the innocent but dangerous be legitimate? Would civil preventive detention be allowable provided our anxiety over the accuracy of predictions and over the invasiveness of screening could be calmed?

The next major line of criticism of practices of preventive detention focuses on the vagueness implicit in talk about detaining the "dangerous." Who will define what it is to be dangerous, and on what basis? Evidence from the field of civil commitment for the insane suggests widely varying practices, depending on not much more than the political and ethical biases of the examining doctors.[8] Such a disparity in the disposition of persons when based on individual value preferences rather than on clear standards represents the antithesis of a just system. On the other hand, there is no reason to think that the system of preventive detention which we have adumbrated thus far is differentially prey to this line of criticism. We can limit application of preventive measures to potential crimes which represent serious threat to life or bodily integrity, and we have specified already how accurate predictive devices must be before any interference is warranted, by indicating a moral certainty threshold.

There are, however, some related issues which must be addressed. Suppose that a person being tested for serious threat potential is found not to be dangerous, but is likely to violate a law of a less significant sort, like selling alcohol to minors. What should or can the government do with this information? Though it cannot detain the person to prevent such an act on the standards we have sketched, can it use this information to make eventual apprehension of the person inevitable by placing undercover officers in his bar? Can the government be asked, or expected and trusted not to give out information to businesses, which would have a great deal of interest in discovering whether potential employees are likely to embezzle, sell trade secrets, or do any of a large number of acts deleterious to the interests of the business?

In order to keep the practice of civil preventive detention a live option I shall distinguish between two types of tests. We shall distinguish between tests which indicate whether one specific crime type is likely and ones which give a read-out of a much more inclusive sort. Testing for dangerousness, we shall say, is only legitimate in case the tests devisable are of the specific sort and provide information only about behavior which is preventable according to the parameters already indicated.

The next major range of objections to systems of preventive detention, both civil and criminal, concentrates on issues falling under the heading of procedural safeguards. In this area of procedural safeguards, especially as it relates to civil commitment of the insane and the addicted, the fact that the infringements of liberties took place under a therapeutic rationale until recently blinded many people into thinking that talk of rights for such people interfered with acting on their behalf and in their interest.[9]

Recognizing the conflicts of interest involved in detention, we have not only demanded a very high level of predictive accuracy, but we here go on to recommend that the state supply those to be committed with resources to counteract state's expert testimony. Thus those in danger of being committed have a right to have the same accurate tests administered by non-state personnel, with differing results sufficient to preclude commitment.

There are other procedural safeguards which must be required. First of all, for those who are going to be committed, it has to be shown that nothing less invasive can be done feasibly. For instance, if a person "threatens" to seriously injure his child, supplying a guard or requiring counseling might do just as well as confining the parent. It is hard to conceive that for a high percentage of serious crimes such measures short of detention would not prove adequate.

What are the upper limits of confinement to prevent harm to others? Though it is not clear what the rationale would be for setting a limit, there is reason to require almost continual proof that the person confined is still dangerous. Here we find a similar situation to that of quarantine.

> The nature of quarantine as a species of physical confinement is borne out by the fact that the legality of keeping a person in quarantined premises, like the legality of other forms of detention, is tested by a *writ of habeas corpus*.[10]

What it is that has to be shown is that the likelihood of committing a certain kind of crime is still above the threshold mark, whatever it is. Once again the model of public health serves us well. We should keep a person with a contagious and deadly disease confined for as long as it takes to eliminate or reduce significantly the possibility of contagion. Since this can involve potentially lifelong confinement in the case of some diseases, mere duration of confinement cannot serve to distinguish quarantine from preventive detention. Depending on how time-consuming and expensive retesting is, perhaps every day or every week those necessarily confined could be reexamined for signs of dangerousness. It would not be unreasonable to assume that for different kinds of crimes and for different kinds of persons schedules would eventually be available about minimum, maximum and average times required before detainees prove less likely to commit the acts feared. Such schedules could then serve as a basis for what counts as a reasonable interval between tests and what grounds would constitute a valid *habeas corpus* action.

What kind of compensation for losses should be available to those who are detained, their families and their business associates? How will it be possible for persons once detained not to have their reputations besmirched and their job prospects unaffected? I ask these questions not because the answers are readily available but because they focus on serious difficulties with the proposal here considered. The most consoling point that can be made is that since the action is civil and not criminal, there is no reason why almost all of one's normal activities could not be carried out, either in a place of safety or under some kind of supervision, or during hours or on occasions on which the predicted crime is unlikely to transpire. As Professor Lionel Frankel has said about civil commitment, requiring compensation for those detained would not only provide the state with an incentive to minimize the number of those committed as well as their period of detention, but it would "also serve to vindicate the compensated individual's dignity and status as a person" and "it would serve to affirm his continuing membership in a society as an individual before the law."[11]

II

Thus far in this paper we have considered three general problem areas for a system of preventive detention—problems with predicting, vagueness of standards of dangerous ness, and inadequacy of procedural safeguards for persons civilly committed. We have shaped the practice when necessary to meet the major objections, elaborating a qualified version of civil preventive detention. On occasion the comparison has been made to the practices of quarantine and screening for contagious diseases to show the broad areas of similarity between measures designed to protect public health—measures which tend not to occasion much disagreement—and our practice of civil preventive detention.

But still someone might respond to the efforts so far made in favor of qualified preventive detention by saying: Besides the specific objections already mentioned, there is something more basic at stake in the issue of civil preventive detention. This more basic something has to do with our image of man as both autonomous and sacred, as entitled to a sphere of activity free from the interferences of others unless he intentionally interferes with another's sphere of freedom. To interfere preventively, this line of objection continues, even assuming the safeguards and provisions outlined, is to diminish the respect accorded to each individual's legitimate choices, to diminish one's sense of control over his own fate, and to impoverish the feeling for individual dignity protected by and encouraged through our present practices. The main issue that must be addressed is: does the very act of predicting and responding on the basis of a prediction to another person's behavior, when this response involves invoking nothing less than the police power of the state, violate something sacred in the human personality? Is it tantamount to denying that people are responsible? Does it involve seeing people as mere means to social ends? Does it presuppose a therapeutic and behavioristic, and not a moral and rights oriented, understanding of human activity? Is it an affront to human autonomy?[12]

Before responding to these challenges, it must be stressed that we are not saying about persons to be detained that they are as good as guilty and hence have no complaint against incapacitating efforts. Persons detained are detained not because they are guilty in any sense, but because they are dangerous—this danger being as real and as threatening if it results from free choice as if it results from involuntary spasm or microbe. But besides reiterating that the practice is to include numerous procedural safeguards, we emphasize that the practice in question involves no worse treatment of persons than does the practice of quarantine. In both practices persons are interfered with for the benefit of others.

Though civil preventive detention is not to be conceived as a cure for any disease—is not a therapeutic act—it does share with therapy several key features: both are imposed without any sense of moral outrage or resentment for those in its clutches, and the duration of detention is in both cases indeterminate. Perhaps it is thought that to deal with an individual's future conduct in this manner is tantamount to regarding his behavior in a medical-model and that such a perspective is what enervates our repeated claim that we are still looking on people as responsible. This allegation is made even more plausible by considering the perspective of a person about whom it is predicted that he will do some act unless detained in spite of his insistence that he won't, that he knows he won't, and that he is in the best position to know this, being the agent without whose intention the predicted behavior cannot take place. A person in this predicament will legitimately feel that his ability to control his conduct is questioned, if not denied outright. In the face of such a person's protests, our insistence that we are really still seeing him as free and responsible will surely seem disingenuous, if not self-deceptive.

So we have to show that we need not be denying a person's self-control just because we claim we have accurate predictive techniques which say he will do what he insists he won't. A number of alternatives present themselves. First of all, in disagreeing with a person about what he will do we might be saying that we know more about the circumstances than he does, our disagreement being attributed to his anticipation of circumstances different in significant ways from those he would actually confront. As an illustration of this, say we request of someone that he not use his telephone in the next few minutes to make a call. He responds saying that he will comply, at which point we know he is not going to adhere to his own decision. If we know that his wife will shortly run into the room and ask him to call the doctor quickly because their child stopped breathing, the person would have made a commitment he will not stick to. Here we shouldn't be tempted to think that the person couldn't control his behavior or that he wasn't acting as a responsible agent in acting in ways he just previously committed himself to avoiding.

Another way in which we might be successful in knowing more about what a person will do than the person himself knows is if we know more about how the agent will change than the agent himself does. If someone who just married maintained that he would never take an interest in pursuing extramarital relationships we might be skeptical, not on grounds that any such act is beyond the agent's control, but on the basis of our belief that the agent may not know very much about the natural history of human relationships, and hence is not in a favorable position to judge what he will eventually feel and what he will eventually find strong incentives for doing.

And finally, there are those cases in which we all act in ways we feel in cooler moments committed to avoiding. Though we usually do still want to regard ourselves as responsible for such behavior, it may well be predictable. And perhaps closely tied to such cases are those in which a person doesn't seem to lose control but still seems to be destined to act in ways he wants not to repeat. People who have bad eating, smoking, exercise or work habits fall into this category of persons who can be sincere in protesting that they will not do something which we have excellent inductive grounds for claiming that they will. Once again it would be probably too strong to say that they *cannot* act as they want, and hence are not responsible when they transgress their own resolutions. They just fail to muster the motivation at the crucial times or forget altogether that they are trying to do something different.

So without assuming compulsions or anything at all of a pathological nature, and without denying autonomy or choice to individuals, we can see how it is that we might come to discount people's own sincere assertions and resolutions about what they will do. Hence to make such predictions about people and deal with them on that basis does not necessarily involve us in changing our image of what it is to be a person, and does not force us to concede that we are implicitly using a medical model for interpreting people's behavior, for which issues of responsibility are inappropriate.

Of course some of the worries of those who oppose civil preventive detention are right on the mark: they worry that the basis of the preventive ideal involves denial of human dignity in the sense that it sanctions interfering with innocent people for the benefit of others. Though it is important for society not to coerce people for what they are, and we must all admit that, at times it *is* legitimate to coerce people though they have done nothing wrong. The issue cannot be over *whether* to coerce people in spite of no wrongdoing but over where to draw the line on thinking such coercion legitimate. We say this fully realizing that it involves considerably diminished capacity to avoid interferences of the state.[13] But it should be pointed out that, unlike quarantine, our practice of civil preventive detention is not invoked independent of a person's choices. It is after all, only because a person is likely to do what is proscribed or avoid what is required that confinement would be imposed. Still it is true in this case, as in the case of quarantine, that *given* a determination of future dangerousness to others there is little a person can then do to get himself reclassified.

One way of drawing this line as to when coercion prior to wrongdoing is justified is by distinguishing between controllable and uncontrollable harm, legitimizing preventive measures only in case the harm feared would be the product of some defective condition.

Deference to autonomy and freedom from prior restraint would be accorded to those who can be thought responsible for their behavior—desirable or undesirable. Making civil preventive detention dependent upon the incapacity to make one's conduct conform to the law or to incapacities of any sort does enhance the scope of individual freedom and does underscore the significance of respecting people as ends in themselves. Recognizing a policy of restricting preventive detention to such conditions of incapacity would surely suffice to preclude restraint on the type of grounds being considered here. It *would* distinguish how we could legitimately respond to the threat posed by the criminally insane on the one hand, and how we could respond to the threat posed by the ordinary person. Where responsible choices are possible, there would be no prior restraint. Such restraint would be legitimized only in case responsible choices were impossible.[14]

The problem with this criterion for distinguishing legitimate from illegitimate detention is that it will not distinguish quarantine from the practice of preventive detention we are considering. Responsible choices are not impossible for those who are either afflicted with, or mere carriers of, deadly contagious diseases. The person quarantined is dangerous, not just because he is ill, but because he might do something independent of his illness which would constitute a danger to others, like contaminate food at a restaurant or supermarket. Thus, such a person's disease is not sufficient to cause harm, except when conjoined with his choices and his actions. So, attractive as the present criterion is, it does not draw the distinction where most would like it drawn, between communicable diseases and ordinary kinds of dangerous conduct.

Someone might respond by saying that the line can still be drawn between quarantine and preventive detention in the way just now adumbrated if sufficient notice is taken of the following contrast: while the person quarantined is dangerous because of his illness—something over which he has no control—the person preventively detained is dangerous because of his choices, something over which a person does have control. So while carriers of a deadly contagious disease cannot lead a normal life without harming others, the criminally dangerous person apparently can but chooses not to. Consequently, if the government treated both of these cases in the same way, even though choice entered into one case in a way it did not enter into the other, it would represent an assault on respect for choice and a cheapening of the consideration paid to autonomy.[15]

Though this development of the criterion is powerful, it won't succeed. While it is true that the contagious person may not intend to endanger those with whom he comes into contact, it is clearly not true that the only things we can be said to control are those things we intend to do. The blind man who drives may not intend to kill pedestrians, or even to endanger them. But we would not call his dangerousness behind the wheel uncontrollable. Obviously, he can avoid getting behind the wheel in the first place. Though the person quarantined is restricted much further than is the case with the blind man, the situation is analogous. For though the sick man is dangerous because of a condition out of his control, the amount of actual harm that results is within his control. Hence it is just as significant an affront to autonomy and just as serious a limitation of choice to quarantine the sick as to detain the potential murderer.

Another tack one might take in trying to detach the practice of quarantine from that of civil preventive detention from a moral perspective might involve noting that while quarantine is clearly a response to an emergency, civil preventive detention would represent an everyday affair. And, after all, acts we tolerate during catastrophic episodes can hardly serve as a model for how we generally ought to behave. The fact that triage may be right in the midst of battle does not warrant its practice during less stressful periods.

Several points deserve mentioning in response to this distinction between emergency and nonemergency circumstances. First of all it is not clear that if plagues or other contagious diseases were with us most of the time, we would abandon belief in the legitimacy of quarantine and mandatory screening. It is not obvious that our concern for civil liberties overrides our concern with public health. The next point to be made in response to the distinction between emergency and non-emergency situations is that the rarity of an event can in itself hardly qualify as a legitimate moral basis for making distinctions. What excuses or legitimizes triage is not its rarity but its military necessity, its role in national defense. If it were not necessary for national defense, the rarity of the instance in which it would be practiced would hardly be a point in its favor.

Of course it is true that quarantine would be imposed in times of serious social threat, but so would preventive detention, each possibly being justified on the ground that tens of thousands of persons will otherwise die or suffer severely. I fail to see why if *x* number of people die from one cause it is an emergency, while if the same number die from some different cause, it is not an emergency situation, assuming everything else is left constant.

One could always try the response that making certain concessions in rare cases results in fewer abrogations of rights than does the same concession applied to frequently recurring situations. But this response is self-defeating since still fewer rights-abrogations would result if the concessions were never made.

If there is something worse about civil preventive detention, qualified in the ways indicated in Part I, than there is about quarantine, not only have we failed to locate it, but whatever it is that makes the distinction is nowhere to be found in the literature. Realizing this does not commit one to *actually* advocating civil preventive detention, for it must be remembered that there are grave practical and legal problems which keep our present world from being one in which the practice could be legitimized. In addition, the arguments throughout the paper relied on the reader's willingness to find quarantine morally acceptable. Those undisposed to think quarantine legitimate will find little in this paper to persuade them that preventive detention has virtues which outweigh its costs, even assuming the modifications in technology and law described above.[16]

NOTES

1. R. G. Spece, Jr., "Conditioning and Other Technologies Used to 'Treat?' 'Rehabilitate?' 'Demolish?' Prisoners and Mental Patients," *Southern California Law Review,* vol. 45 (1971), pp. 616–618.
2. Andrew von Hirsch, "Prediction of Criminal Conduct and Preventive Confinement of Convicted Persons," *Buffalo Law Review,* vol. 21 (1972), pp. 717–758 at Section 11, and "Civil Commitment of the Mentally Ill: Theories and Procedures," *Harvard Law Review,* vol. 79 (1966), pp. 1288–1298 at 1291.
3. A. R. Angel, E. D. Green, H. R. Kaufman, E. E. VanLoon, "Preventive Detention: An Empirical Analysis," *Harvard Civil Rights*–Civil Liberties Law Review, vol. 6 (1971), pp. 300–396 at 342.
4. Alan Dershowitz, "The Law of Dangerousness: Some Fictions About Predictions," *Journal of Legal Education,* vol. 23 (1970), pp. 24–47 at 31–32.
5. See *Olmstead* v. *U.S.,* 277 U.S. 438–474 (1927), Brandeis, J. dissenting.
6. Frank Grad, *Public Health Law Manual* (New York, 1970), p. 42.
7. Frank Grad, pp. 42–43.
8. Joseph Goldstein and Jay Katz, "Dangerousness and Mental Illness: Some Observations on the Decision to Release Persons Acquitted by Reason of Insanity," *Yale Law Journal,* vol. 70, pp. 225–239 at 235, and Alan Dershowitz, pp. 40, 41, and 43.
9. "Civil Commitment of Narcotics Addicts," *Yale Law Journal,* vol. 76 (1967), pp. 1160–1189 at 1181.
10. Frank Grad, pp. 47–48.
11. Lionel Frankel, "Preventive Restraints and Just Compensation: Toward a Sanction Law of the Future," *Yale Law Journal,* vol. 78 (1968), pp. 229–267 at 257–258.
12. Herbert Packer, *The Limits of the Criminal Sanction* (Stanford, 1968), pp. 74–77.
13. Andrew von Hirsch, Sect. 11 and H. L. A. Hart, "Punishment and the Elimination of Responsibility," *Punishment and Responsibility*

(Oxford, 1968) and Herbert Morris, "Persons and Punishment" *Monist*, vol. 52 (1968), pp. 475–501.

14. Lionel Frankel, pp. 247–250.
15. I am indebted to Professor Warner Wick for pressing this objection on my treatment of quarantine.
16. I wish to express my appreciation to Professors Joseph Goldstein, Alan Goldman, Kenneth Kipnis, Denis Nolan, Patrick Hubbard, Warner Wick, William McAninch, Herbert Fingarette and Barry Loewer for helpful comments on earlier versions of this paper.

Study Questions

1. What is the problem of *false positives?* Do you agree with von Hirsch that preventive confinement would be unacceptable even if this problem could be solved?
2. What sort of response do you think von Hirsch would make to Schoeman's arguments?
3. What would a utilitarian say about the practice of preventive confinement? What would a retributivist say?

G Mercy

Mercy and Legal Justice

Jeffrie G. Murphy

If a guilty criminal deserves a certain punishment, how can we justify showing *mercy* toward him by giving him a lesser one? Wouldn't such leniency itself be a form of injustice toward other offenders who are made to suffer the punishment that they deserve? Murphy suggests, very tentatively, that if we think of our moral views as the result of tacit bargains struck between the weak and the strong on the basis of self-interest, we can show why rational persons might adopt a principle that permits such *occasional* displays of mercy.

> I looked at him. Alive. His lap a puddle of blood. With the restoration of the normal order of matter and sensation, I felt I was seeing him for the first time as a person. The old human muddles and quirks were set flowing again. Compassion, remorse, mercy.
>
> Don DeLillo
> *White Noise*

Internal and External Questions

The most profound questions in ethics, social philosophy, and the philosophy of law are foundational; i.e., they are questions that call the entire framework of our ordinary evaluations into doubt in order to determine to what degree, if at all, that framework can be rationally defended. Such questions, called "external" by Rudolf Carnap, are currently dominating my own philosophical reflections and are forcing me to rethink a variety of positions I have in the past defended.[1]

Because my current thinking about external foundational questions is in such a state of flux, it is with some anxiety that I turn to the "internal" questions that motivate the present essay, i.e., questions that accept "our" ordinary framework of evaluation as a given and seek to explore certain tensions and puzzles within that framework in order to see to what degree that framework is internally coherent. The goal is to attain, if possible, that nirvana of moral epistemology that John Rawls calls "reflective equilibrium."[2] In spite of my increasing skepticism about the value of reflective equilibrium in foundational moral theory,[3] I am still inclined to believe (a) that internal coherence is relevant to external evaluation and (b) that questions of an internal nature, if properly explored with an appreciation of their limits, can be interesting and important in their own right.[4] Thus, I shall temporarily suppress my initial anxiety and plow ahead on the matter at hand.

Reprinted with permission from *Social Philosophy & Policy* 4:1, pp. 1–14. © 1986 by Blackwell Publishers, Oxford.

Several persons were kind enough to comment on earlier drafts of this paper, and I wish to thank them here: Lewis Beck, Ray Elugardo, Herbert Granger, Joshua Halberstam, Sterling Harwood, Margaret Holmgren, Lisa Isaacson, David Lyons, and Gareth Matthews. I learned a great deal from each of their comments—far more than the few changes I was able to make in the paper will indicate. Earlier versions of the paper were read at the 1985 Kraemer Lecture at the University of Arkansas, at the 1986 Conference on Law and

Mercy and Justice

We are ordinarily inclined to believe—or at least pay lip service to—the claim that justice and mercy are both moral virtues. We are also inclined to maintain that both of these virtues are characteristic of such lofty objects as God (as conceived in the Judeo-Christian tradition[5]) and of such human all too human objects as legal systems—where in literature and folklore we celebrate (perhaps without fully understanding what we are saying) those judges who can "temper their justice with mercy." As we expect God as cosmic judge to manifest both justice and mercy, so too do we expect this of secular judges. Or so we often say. Shakespeare's two important "comedies of mercy," for example, contain some of the most often quoted sentiments on mercy and justice in our civilization—so often quoted, indeed, that they have attained the status of clichés and may any day find their way onto Hallmark cards or table napkins:

The quality of mercy is not strain'd;
It droppeth as the gentle rain from heaven
Upon the place beneath: it is twice blessed;
It blesseth him that gives and him that takes:
'Tis mightiest in the mightiest; it becomes
The throned monarch better than his crown;
His sceptre shows the force of temporal power,
The attribute to awe and majesty,
Wherein doth sit the dread and fear of kings;
But mercy is above this scepter'd sway,—
It is enthroned in the heart of kings,
It is an attribute to God himself;
And earthly power doth then show likest God's
When mercy seasons justice.

(*Merchant of Venice*, IV, I; Portia speaks)

Continued from previous page. Philosophy held at the University of Michigan Law School and sponsored by the Bowling Green Social Philosophy and Policy Center, and at the 1986 meeting of the North American Society for Social Philosophy in conjunction with the American Philosophical Association, Central Division, in St. Louis. I am grateful for helpful comments I received from the audiences at these meetings and for helpful comments I received from the editors of *Social Philosophy and Policy*.

No ceremony that to great ones 'longs,
Not the king's crown, nor the deputed sword,
The marshall's truncheon, nor the judge's robe,
Become them with one half so good a grace
As mercy does.

(*Measure for Measure*, II, II; Isabella speaks)

These passages express some fairly widely held—and closely related—views about mercy: 1. It is an *autonomous* moral virtue (i.e., it is not reducible to some other virtue—especially justice). 2. It is a virtue that tempers or "seasons" justice, something that one adds to justice (the primary virtue) in order to dilute it and perhaps—if one takes the metallurgical metaphor of tempering seriously—to make it stronger. 3. It is never owed to anyone as a right or a matter of desert or justice. It always, therefore, transcends the realm of strict moral obligation and is best viewed as a free gift—an act of grace, love, or compassion that is beyond the claims of right, duty, and obligation. ("The quality of mercy is not [con]strained.") 4. As a moral virtue, it derives its value at least in part from the fact that it flows from a certain kind of *character*—a character disposed to perform merciful acts from love or compassion while not losing sight of the importance of justice. 5. It requires a generally retributive outlook on punishment and responsibility. Mercy is often regarded as found where a judge, out of compassion for the plight of a particular offender, imposes upon that offender a hardship less than his just deserts. This way of conceptualizing mercy requires, of course, that we be operating with a rich concept of "just desert"—something that is not easy to come by on a utilitarian/deterrence analysis.[6]

The foregoing suggests that there are certain other virtues or, at least, *desiderata* of moral and legal systems with which mercy often is but should not be confused: excuse, justification, and forgiveness. If a person has actually done the right thing (i.e., his conduct was justified), or if he was not responsible for what he did (i.e., he had a valid excuse), then it would simply be *unjust* to punish him, and no question of mercy need arise—for there is no responsible wrongdoing, and responsible wrongdoing is (it is commonly thought) the proper object of mercy.

Forgiveness is trickier. As I have argued elsewhere,[7] forgiveness is primarily a matter of changing how one *feels* with respect to a person who has done *oneself* an injury. It is particularly a matter of overcoming, on moral grounds, the *resentment* that a self-respecting person quite properly feels as a result of such an injury. Mercy, though related to forgiveness, is clearly different in at least these two respects. To be merciful to a person requires not merely that one change how one feels about that person but, also, requires a specific kind of action (or omission)—namely, treating that person less harshly than, in the absence of the mercy, one would have treated him. This explains how we can forgive in our heart of hearts but cannot show mercy in our heart of hearts, why we can forgive the dead but cannot show mercy to the dead, and so forth. Also, it is not a requirement of my showing mercy that I be an injured party. All that is required is that I stand in a certain relation to the potential beneficiary of mercy. This relation—typically established by legal or other institutional rules—makes it *fitting* (I purposely speak vaguely here for reasons that will later become clear) that I impose some hardship upon the potential beneficiary of mercy.

The Paradoxes of Mercy

All is not well with the above rosy picture. For the following pattern of argument seems tempting: If mercy requires a tempering of justice, than there is a sense in which mercy may require a departure from justice. (Temperings are tamperings.) Thus, to be merciful is, perhaps, to be *unjust*. But it is a vice, not a virtue, to manifest injustice. Thus, mercy must be not a virtue, but a vice—a product of morally dangerous sentimentality. This is particularly obvious in the case of a sentencing judge. We (society) hire this individual to enforce the rule of law under which we live. We think of this as "doing justice," and the doing of this is surely his sworn obligation. What business does he have, then, ignoring his obligations to justice while he pursues some private, idiosyncratic, and not publicly accountable virtue of love or compassion?[8] Shakespeare, always sensitive to both sides of complex moral issues, captures this thought well even in the midst of his dramatic sermons on mercy:

> I show [pity] most of all when I show justice,
> For then I pity those I do not know,
> Which a dismissed offense would after gall;
> And do him right that, answering one foul wrong,
> Lives not to act another.
>
> (*Measure for Measure,* II, II; Angelo speaks[9])

Perhaps the clearest statements of the paradoxes I want to develop on mercy come from St. Anselm. His worry is about the divine nature—how God can be both just and merciful—but the paradoxes he formulates can easily be adapted to secular and legal concerns. He writes:

> What justice is it that gives him who merits eternal death everlasting life? How, then, gracious Lord, good to the wicked, canst thou save the wicked if this is not just, and thou dost not aught that is not just? (*Proslogium* IX)
>
> But if it can be comprehended in any way why thou canst will to save the wicked, yet by no consideration can we comprehend why, of those who are alike wicked, thou savest some rather than others, through supreme goodness, and why thou dost condemn the latter, rather than the former, through supreme justice. (*Proslogium* XI)

Though Anselm's specific worry is about the divine nature (Are the divine attributes of perfect justice and perfect compassion coherently ascribable to the same being?), he raises a general worry about the concepts of justice and mercy themselves—namely, to what degree (if at all) are they consistent? More specifically: If we simply use the term "mercy" to refer to certain of the demands of justice (e.g., the demand for individuation), then mercy ceases to be an autonomous virtue and instead becomes a part of (is reducible to a part of) justice. It thus becomes obligatory, and all the talk about gifts, acts of grace, supererogation, and compassion becomes quite beside the point. If, on the other hand, mercy is totally different from justice and actually requires (or permits) that justice sometimes be set aside, it then counsels injustice.[10] In short: mercy is either a vice (injustice) or redundant (a part of justice). (This is a gloss on Anselm's first paradox—from IX. The second paradox—from XI—will be explored in a later section.)

Some Specific Cases and Some Good Journal Articles

Two of the most interesting articles on mercy are those by Alwynne Smart and Claudia Card.[11] Both seek to establish that there is indeed a place for mercy in a world that takes the value of justice seriously, and both (Smart especially) develop a discussion of this general issue in terms of specific cases—cases that are supposed to test and hone our intuitions so that we can be in "reflective equilibrium" about the issues of justice and mercy.

Smart asks that we consider the following pairs of cases—cases that might face a sentencing judge who, we may suppose, has some discretion and is not bound by mandatory sentencing rules:

A	*B*
(1) The defendant, convicted of vehicular homicide, had his own child—whom he loved deeply—as his victim.	The defendant has been convicted of killing another person in cold blood.
(2) The defendant is a young and inexperienced criminal.	The defendant is a hardened career criminal.

According to Smart, "we" would all agree that the judge should impose a lighter sentence on those persons under *A* than on those under *B* and that it would be proper, in a perfectly ordinary sense of the word "mercy," to express "our" conviction about what he should do by saying that he should show mercy in those cases.

Let us suppose that Smart is correct here. It is proper for the judge to go easy here, and such easing up would be called by many people (prior to reading this essay) an act of mercy. This still strikes me as philosophically confused and as an obstacle to philosophical clarity on the concept of mercy. If we feel that the judge should go easy in cases under *A*, this is surely because we believe that there is some morally relevant feature that distinguishes these cases from those under *B*. What might this feature be? In (1) it is no doubt our conviction that the criminal has already suffered a great deal—perhaps even that he has suffered enough—and that the infliction of any additional misery by the state would be gratuitous and cruel.[12] In (2) we are no doubt influenced by the idea that the character of a younger person is less mature and thus less responsible than that of a hardened criminal.[13] But, if this is our thinking, then why talk of mercy here and confuse what we are doing with some moral virtue that requires the tempering of justice? For to avoid inflicting upon persons more suffering than they deserve, or to avoid punishing the less responsible as much as the fully responsible, is a simple—indeed, obvious—demand of *justice*. A basic demand of justice is that like cases be treated alike, and that morally relevant differences between persons be noticed and our treatment of those persons be affected by those differences. This demand for individuation—a tailoring of our retributive response to the individual natures of the persons with whom we are dealing—is a part of what we mean by taking persons seriously as persons and is thus a basic demand of justice. One could introduce a sense of "mercy" that means "seeking to tailor our response to morally relevant individual differences." But this would be confusing and dangerous: confusing because it would make us think that the rich literature noted above (Shakespeare, Anselm) was somehow relevant to this; dangerous because it might lead us to suppose that individuation was not owed to persons as a right and was thus somehow optional as a free gift or act of grace. But this would be deeply wrong. The legal rules, if they are just, will base required penal treatment on morally relevant differences *or* they will give judges the discretion to so do; and criminal defendants surely have a *right* that it be this way.[14] One could talk of mercy here, but why? (One might as well protest strict criminal liability offenses by saying that they are unmerciful.) Judges or lawmakers who are unmindful of the importance of individuated response are not lacking in mercy; they lack a sense of justice.[15] Recall our earlier dilemma: mercy is either a vice or is redundant. The above cases illustrate redundancy.

Smart is sensitive to the fact that not everyone will find her initial cases representative of mercy in any deep or interesting sense, and she thus introduces some additional cases in an attempt to capture a different and more important kind of mercy. These are cases where (unlike the earlier cases) we agree that some punishment *P* is, *all* relevant things about Jones considered, the just punishment for what Jones has done. Still, on moral grounds, we argue that a punishment less than *P* should be inflicted. We now have a virtue that is not redundant—is not merely reducible to justice. These are the cases:

1. Jones's family, who need his support very much, would be harmed to an unacceptable degree if *P* is inflicted on Jones. Thus, we ought to show mercy to Jones and inflict less than *P*.
2. Adverse social consequences will result if *P* is inflicted on Jones. (Perhaps he is a popular leader of the political opposition, and his followers will riot or commit acts of terrorism if *P* is inflicted on Jones.) Thus, we should show mercy to Jones.
3. Jones has been in jail for a long time and has so reformed that he is, in a very real sense, a "new person." Thus, we should show him mercy and grant him an early release.

These cases strike me as unpersuasive. It strikes me as analytic that mercy is based on a concern for the *defendant's* plight, and this feature is absent in (1) and (2). If we are showing mercy to anyone in (1) it is to Jones's family, and he is simply the indirect beneficiary of the mercy. But even this seems a confusing way to talk. In (1) and (2) one is basically choosing to bring about a net gain in utility. This may be reasonable if a utilitarian moral outlook is reasonable. But these cases would not be interestingly unique given that outlook; and, for reasons sketched above, it is not an outlook in which a concern with mercy as a special virtue would arise.

Case (3) is, of course, very different. But it, like Smart's earlier cases, seems simply a matter of justice. I am suspicious of "new person" talk. However, if there really are cases where we should take it literally, then it is obviously a matter of justice that one not punish one person for the crime of another. Why talk of mercy here?

In summary: We have yet to find one case of genuine mercy as an autonomous virtue. The cases we have explored represent either virtuous behavior that is simply a matter of justice *or* they represent cases of unjustified sentimentality *or* they represent cases where the demands of justice are thought to be overridden by the demands of utility. Thus some skepticism about mercy seems in order. Judges in criminal cases are obligated to do justice.[16] So too, I would argue, are prosecutors and parole boards in their exercise of discretion.[17] There is thus simply no room for mercy as an autonomous virtue with which their justice should be tempered. Let them keep their sentimentality to themselves for use in their private lives with their families and pets.

A New Paradigm for Mercy[18]

But could all the rich and moving literature of mercy be totally worthless—nothing but propaganda for mindless sentimentality? I think not; and I shall spend the remainder of this essay attempting to think about mercy in a new way—one which may allow us to give it some meaningful life as an autonomous moral virtue.

Thus far we have been operating with what might be called the Criminal Law Paradigm of mercy—thinking of mercy as a virtue that most typically would be manifested by a sentencing judge in a criminal case. This is the paradigm represented in *Measure for Measure,* where Isabella begs that Angelo, a judge in a criminal case involving her brother, will show her brother mercy. It is this paradigm, I have suggested, that is probably a failure.

But there is another paradigm—that represented in *Merchant of Venice*—a paradigm that I will call the Private Law Paradigm. In that play, you will recall, the central focus is on a *civil* case—a contract dispute. Antonio has made a bad bargain with Shylock and, having defaulted, is contractually obligated to pay Shylock a pound of his flesh. Portia, acting as judge, asks that Shylock show mercy to Antonio by not demanding the harsh payment.[19]

Note how radically this case differs from the criminal law case. A judge in a criminal case has an *obligation* to do justice—which means, at a minimum, an obligation to uphold the rule of law. Thus, if he is moved, even by love or compassion, to act contrary to the rule of law—to the rules of justice—he acts wrongly (because he violates an obligation) and manifests a vice rather than a virtue. A criminal judge, in short, has an obligation to impose the just punishment; and all of his discretion within the rules is to be used to secure greater justice (e.g., more careful individuation). No rational society would write any other "job description" for such an important institutional role.

But a litigant in a civil suit is not the occupier—in anything like the same sense—of an institutional role. He occupies a private role. He does not have an antecedent obligation, required by the rules of justice, to impose harsh treatment. He rather has, in a case like Shylock's, a *right* to impose harsh treatment. Thus, if he chooses to show mercy, he is simply *waiving a right* that he could in justice claim—not violating an obligation demanded by justice.[20] (Consider here the analogy with the rules of chivalric combat. The fallen knight begs for mercy. He is not asking that the victor violate an obligation to kill him but is, rather, asking that the victor waive a right to kill him.) And there is no contradiction, paradox, or even tension here. I do not necessarily show a lack of respect for justice by waiving my justice-based rights as I would by ignoring my justice-derived obligations.[21] Thus, in the Private Law Paradigm, the virtue of mercy is revealed when a person, out of compassion for the hard position of the person who owes him an obligation, waives the right that generates the obligation and frees the individual of the burden of that obligation. People who are always standing on their rights, indifferent to the impact that this may have on others, are simply intolerable. Such persons cannot be faulted on grounds of justice, but they can certainly be faulted. And the disposition to mercy helps to check these narrow and self-involved tendencies present in each of us.[22] There is thus room for mercy as an important moral virtue with impact upon the law, but it is a virtue to be manifested by private persons using the law—*not* by officials enforcing the law.[23]

Note also that this Private Law Paradigm might help, by analogy, with Anselm's theological puzzle about mercy. Anselm sees a paradox in attributing both justice and mercy to God because he seems to see God as analogous to a judge in a criminal case—as someone with an obligation to enforce certain rules. But surely this is not the only model of God. God (at least on one fairly common view) is not bound by independent rules of obligation with respect to his creatures; for the rules of morality are, on this view, simply His commands. He does, however, have many *rights* with respect to His creatures. Thus, His mercy may be viewed as His deciding, out of love or compassion, to waive certain rights that He has—*not* to violate certain obligations that He has. Anselm's first paradox disappears.

Rationality and the Equal Protection Paradox

Is everything now coherent in the land of mercy? Is its status as an autonomous virtue, different from and tempering justice, intact, ready to be dispensed from our compassionate natures as a free gift or act of grace? Not quite. For Anselm's second paradox now appears to haunt us:

> But if it can be comprehended in any way why thou canst will to save the wicked, yet by no consideration can we comprehend why, of those who are alike wicked, thou savest some rather than others, through supreme goodness, and why thou dost condemn the latter, rather than the former, through supreme justice.(*Preoslogium* XI)

Anselm here seems to be raising a kind of "equal protection" paradox: If God (or any other rational being) shows mercy, then the mercy must not be arbitrary or capricious, but must rather rest upon some good reason—some morally relevant feature of the situation that made the mercy seem appropriate. Compassion and love are, after all, cognitively loaded emotions; they are not sensations like headaches or tickles. Thus, they are the sorts of reactions for which reasons may be given; and where reasons are given, it is possible to distinguish good from bad reasons, relevant from irrelevant ones. ("I showed him mercy because he was so sick" has a kind of sense lacking in "I showed him mercy because he was so handsome.") But once a reason, always a reason. And does not the Principle of Sufficient Reason require that if I, as a rational being, showed mercy to Jones because of characteristic *C*, then it is presumably required of me (rationally required, not morally required) that I show comparable mercy to *C*-bearing Smith?[24] But if so, then what becomes of all this grace/free gift talk when applied to mercy? (Of course, there can even be reasons for gifts: "It is your birthday.") Is it nothing more than this: I am not ever required to show mercy, but if I show it even once then I am rationally required to show it to all relevantly similar persons? But if I show mercy for a reason (which must be the case, if mercy is not simply capricious) does not that reason then *require* that I show mercy whenever I recognize the presence of that reason? The showing of mercy may not be an obligation in the strong sense (based on rights), but it may be something I *ought-for-a-reason* to do. In that case it cannot *totally* be a free act of grace. Some of Anselm's second paradox thus remains.

Internal and External Again[25]

Let me briefly return to the worry about foundations. It seems to be the case that "we" (all well brought up, educated, middle-class intellectuals?) see justice to be the primary value with respect to law, but that we also want to find some place for mercy as a secondary virtue to temper or otherwise have some effect on justice. It is interesting to inquire into why we think this and into whether our common pattern of thought is rationally justified.

Suppose that Gilbert Harman is right about ethics: our moral views are simply conventions that result from tacit bargains struck between the weak and poor and the rich and powerful—bargains where each attempts to maximize his self-interest while still securing the vital benefits of social cooperation.[26] This might be a start toward explaining some of our ordinary views about justice and mercy. Justice—the regular enforcement of the rules that make social stability (and thus social life) possible—will be a strong priority of all parties to the bargain—whether rich or poor, strong or weak. Not all will have the same stake in these rules, but all (or almost all) will have a high stake. Thus, it is not difficult to see why conventions of justice should have a very high priority. Mercy, however, is a different matter. It is more likely to be needed by the poor and weak than by the rich and powerful, and thus it is easy to see why it is present (some level of it is perhaps required to secure the cooperation and compliance of the disadvantaged) but also easy to see why it does not have the dominant role that justice has—why it only tempers justice but never replaces or supersedes it.

The bargaining model of moral conventions might also provide a start toward dealing with Anselm's second paradox—namely, if I show mercy to *C*-bearing Jones, how can I consistently (morally?) fail to show mercy to equally *C*-bearing Smith? If moral conventions are viewed as agreements based on rational self-interest, then the impact *on me* of my continued showings of mercy would become relevant. Thus, what relevantly distinguishes the Jones case from the Smith case will not be some feature that distinguishes Jones from Smith but, rather, some feature that distinguishes the impact on me of mercy to Jones from the impact on me of mercy to Smith. The mere fact that Jones got there first (or I noticed him first) might then make a great deal of difference. I show mercy to Jones, who is pitiful to degree *P*, and thus forgive his debt to me of five dollars. Smith, who is also pitiful to degree *P*, also owes me five dollars. I do not show him mercy, however, because, though I can afford the loss of five dollars, I cannot afford the loss of ten. Also, I may begin to fear—quite legitimately—that if I start to make a practice of showing mercy instead of simply showing it every now and then when the spirit moves me, I will be taken for an easy mark in future dealings with those who might attempt to exploit my perceived good will. Thus, if rational persons thought that once having shown mercy they would be stuck with making a regular practice of it, they might be inclined never to show it at all. But since, as I argued above, there are reasons why rational agents would agree to conventions establishing some level of mercy, they would not want to adopt a principle of mercy that would give rational persons incentives never to show it. And thus they would probably agree with the adoption of mercy as what Kant called an imperfect duty—a duty that admits of wide latitude in the time and manner of its fulfillment.[27]

And what does all this have to do with rational justification? I am not sure. But I suppose that, with respect to any bargain or convention, if it is the case that it represents, for each party, the best deal he could have struck for himself under the circumstances, then it may be called rational in some minimal sense. This may not be much (not what Kant, for example, would like the connection between morality and rationality to be), but it strikes me as a more impressive argument for a moral view than the argument that the view would put Mr. and Mrs. Front Porch in a state of reflective equilibrium with respect to their moral intuitions. But this is a very complex issue and should be—and will be—left to be pursued in another context.

NOTES

1. See Jeffrie G. Murphy and Jules L. Coleman, *The Philosophy of Law* (Totowa: Rowman and Allenheld, 1984) and Jeffrie G. Murphy, "Retributivism, Moral Education, and the Liberal State," *Criminal Justice Ethics*, vol. 4 (Winter/Spring 1985).
2. John Rawls, *A Theory of Justice* (Cambridge: Harvard University Press, 1971), pp. 48–51.
3. See my "Rationality and Constraints on Democratic Rule," J. Roland Pennock and John W. Chapman, eds., *Nomos XXVIII: Justification* (New York: New York University Press, 1986), pp. 141–164.
4. See, for example, Joel Feinberg, *Harm to Others* (Oxford: Oxford University Press, 1984). Feinberg explicitly refuses to address foundational issues (taking a kind of "liberalism" as a given) and still manages to enrich our thinking about morality and the criminal law to a profound degree.
5. "Even God prays. What Is His prayer? 'May it be My will that My love of compassion overwhelm My demand for strict justice.' " Mahzhor for Yom Kippur, The Rabbinical Assembly of New York, 439 (from Berakhot 7a).
6. Note that this is a list of commonly held views about mercy and its relation to justice. I shall later argue that some of these views—(5) in particular—are distorted or mistaken.
7. "Forgiveness and Resentment," Peter A. French, *et al.*, eds. *Midwest Studies In Philosophy, VII: Social and Political Philosophy* (Minneapolis: University of Minnesota Press, 1982) pp. 503–516.
8. Note that I describe the judge's job to be that of upholding the *rule of law*. I mean by this the upholding of legal rules that meet certain standards of justice, not the mechanical upholding of any legal rules at all no matter how unjust they may be. Of course, I do not

believe that judges should enforce legal rules in the absence of any reflection on the merits of those rules from the point of view of justice. If the rules are unjust, then if the judge has discretion, he should use that discretion to seek to do justice. (If the judge has no discretion and if the rules are terribly unjust, then such drastic acts as resignation or civil disobedience may be in order.) These complexities, however, do not show a need for a special virtue of mercy; and only a highly impoverished view of justice (i.e., that it is simply mechanical rule following) would make one think that these complexities could not be dealt with in terms of a sophisticated theory of justice.

9. The point here, I take it, is that the judge who is influenced by the plight of the offender before him may lose sight of the fact that his job is to uphold an entire system of justice that protects the rights and security of all citizens.

10. A critic has suggested that I am here confusing the unjust with the *non*-just—that I fail to notice that some acts (perhaps some acts of mercy) are non-just (neutral from the point of view of justice) in that they are neither unjust nor required by justice. What bearing might this observation have, even if correct, on the issue of mercy in a criminal law context? None that I can see. To be morally acceptable, a non-just act would at least have to be *permitted* by the rules of justice; but, on standard versions of retributive justice (e.g., Kant's), it is *not* permitted from the moral point of view that persons receive less punishment than, in justice, they deserve. To give them less punishment would be to do an injustice.

11. Alwynne Smart, "Mercy," H. B. Acton, ed., *The Philosophy Of Punishment* (New York: St. Martin's Press, 1969), pp. 212–227. (Smart's article originally appeared in *Philosophy,* October 1968). Claudia Card, "Mercy," *Philosophical Review,* vol. XI.III (April 1972), pp. 182–207. Since Smart's essay provides me with a useful starting point from which to develop what I want to say about mercy, I will focus my discussion primarily around her piece and will thus not give Card's rich essay the detailed discussion it deserves. I will comment on it only in passing. Card, like Smart, operates within what I will later call the Criminal Law Paradigm for mercy (a paradigm I will reject) and, also like Smart, she seems to offer a view of mercy that makes it a part of justice (on a sophisticated theory of justice) and not an autonomous moral virtue.

12. The idea that natural suffering can serve as a substitute for legally imposed suffering is complex and perhaps incoherent; see my "Forgiveness and Resentment," p. 509 and note 17.

13. Perhaps we also think that prison will be harder on them and thus that they may suffer more than they deserve. Perhaps we might also think that young people are more likely to be influenced by the bad environment that prison represents.

    The idea that it is immoral to impose a level of suffering out of proper proportion to a person's character is also central to Card's view of mercy. She writes: "Mercy ought to be shown to an offender when it is evident that otherwise (1) he would be made to suffer unusually more on the whole, owing to his peculiar misfortunes, than he deserves in view of his basic character and (2) he would be worse off in this respect than those who stand to benefit from the exercise of their right to punish him (or to have him punished). When the conditions of this principle are met, the offender deserves mercy." ("Mercy," p. 184) Card thus seems explicitly to classify merciful acts as a subcategory of just acts, and not as acts autonomous from justice. But then I fail to understand how she can say (also on p. 184) that "desert of mercy does not give rise to an obligation."

14. In commenting on an earlier draft of this paper, Lewis Beck raised the question of how the demand for individuation (which I suggest is a demand of justice) can be squared with the common and intuitively compelling metaphor that "justice is blind." The short answer, I think, is this: justice is not to be totally blind but is, rather, to be blind to all aspects of an individual that do not have a bearing on the question of what his just treatment or just deserts really are, e.g., race, sexual attractiveness and willingness, ability to bribe, etc.

15. Those who desire to talk about mercy in this context probably do so because they have an overly restricted and simplistic conception of justice and thus fail to appreciate all that would be involved in a sophisticated theory of retributive justice and the role of the judiciary in implementing such a theory. It might be worth noting, in this regard, that in our particular legal system most visible law-reforming judicial activism in the cause of greater individuation will take place at the level of a court of appeals. Trial judges (in giving instructions, for example) and trial juries (in refusing to convict, for example) may move toward greater justice in particular cases, but what they do does not become a public and permanent part of the law in the obvious way provided by written opinions of

a court of appeals (particularly the Supreme Court).

16. Recall that by this claim I do not mean that judges are always obligated to enforce any rule no matter how unjust that rule may be. My point is rather this: the focus of a judge, either in enforcing a rule *or* in seeking a way to modify or get around it, is to be on the question of what is required by justice—not on what he may be prompted out of compassion to do.
17. Special problems may arise for a chief executive or head of state in his exercise of the power of pardon. The "job description" for such an office may, to borrow some language from Aquinas, involve a concern for the common good or common welfare of the community in the executive's care. This might mean that, in deciding whether or not to pardon an individual, the chief executive (unlike a judge) might legitimately draw upon values other than the requirements of justice and thus might legitimately ignore the just deserts of an individual and pardon that individual if the good of the community requires it. This whole account, of course, presupposes a political theory of the various offices and roles required by society and a theory of the proper values and decision-making criteria proper to (and perhaps unique to) each of the offices and roles. Space does not allow the articulation, much less the defense, of such a theory here.
18. This section draws heavily on P. Twambley's important article "Mercy and Forgiveness," *Analysis*, vol. 36 (January 1976), pp. 84–90.
19. Portia serves a complex role in the play. She does not simply represent the virtue of mercy but also stands as a representative of hypocrisy, unjust manipulation, and anti-Semitism.
20. There may be special problems in cases (defamation?) where tort suits aid in upholding certain socially important rules and protections. In this sense they are not purely private legal matters even though they are handled in the private law rather than in the criminal law. Thus, there may be cases where an individual might feel a public responsibility to proceed with a private lawsuit.
21. I say "not necessarily" because there are cases where a refusal to stand on one's rights and demand just treatment would reveal a lack of self-respect and a lack of respect for oneself as a morally relevant object (and thus a lack of respect for the rules of morality themselves). Of course, not every case of standing on one's rights (no matter how trivial) is of this nature.
22. Sterling Harwood has suggested to me in correspondence that the tempering metaphor might illuminate if applied to persons and their dispositions rather than to the rules of justice themselves. A person, on this view, should temper his just personality (a dominant disposition to see that justice is done) by developing (if possible) a disposition to be merciful (an openness to being moved by the plight of others to the degree that one will not always demand one's just rights from them). This suggestion seems correct to me. Bishop Butler, in his classic sermons "Upon Resentment" and "Upon the Forgiveness of Injuries" is, of course, brilliant on such topics.
23. Should judges in civil cases follow Portia's lead and encourage litigants in some cases to show mercy? Perhaps; but there are problems here. The desire to settle cases and avoid the human and financial costs of litigation is certainly a reasonable one; but, as Jules Coleman and Charles Silver have argued elsewhere in this volume, there are serious social costs involved in settlement as well, e.g., the cost of not having the law clarified in the way that actual litigation makes possible.
24. For a discussion of the Principle of Sufficient Reason (a rational being will not prefer one thing over another without basing that preference upon some relevant difference between the things) and equal protection, see my "Justifying Departures from Equal Treatment," *Journal of Philosophy* (October 1984), pp. 587–593.
25. This section of the paper was greatly improved by some comments and suggestions of Ray Elugardo.
26. Gilbert Harman, "Justice and Moral Bargaining," *Social Philosophy and Policy*, vol. I (Autumn 1983), pp. 114–131. Similar views may also be found in such otherwise diverse thinkers as Hume, Marx, and Nietzsche.
27. For a stimulating argument that Kantian conclusions can be generated from egoistic premisis and that central Kantian doctrines can be rationally reconstructed on the basis of models that initially seem anti-Kantian, see David Gauthier, "The Unity of Reason: A Subversive Reinterpretation of Kant," *Ethics*, vol. 96 (October 1985), pp. 74–88. As Lisa Isaacson has pointed out to me, the analysis presented in this final section of the paper will probably not help with the paradoxes of divine mercy, for it is probably not reasonable to view God's morality as a result of a bargain He strikes with humanity in order to advance His interests.

Is Mercy Inherently Unjust?

Sterling Harwood

Harwood, a co-editor of this book, argues that mercy is not inherently unjust. Justice requires a judge to give a criminal the punishment the criminal deserves. But mercy is a virtue and a supererogatory trait leading a merciful judge to give a criminal less punishment than the criminal deserves. So is mercy unjust? But how can injustice be a virtue? Since justice concerns requirements, while mercy is supererogatory (i.e., above and beyond the call of duty) and thus cannot be required, how can mercy even be on a par with justice, much less override it? Harwood considers these questions and argues that the conflict between justice and mercy seems caused by the retributivist view that we have a duty to punish criminals fully. Harwood tries to deny that mercy is inherently unjust by showing how justice need not require us to give a criminal all the punishment that, in justice, the criminal deserves. He tries to reconcile mercy with the retributivism of Immanual Kant (1724–1804).

> The law concerning punishment is a categorical imperative, and woe to him who rummages around in the winding paths of a theory of happiness looking for some advantage to be gained by releasing the criminal from punishment or by reducing the amount of it—in keeping with the Pharisaic motto: "It is better that one man should die than that the whole people should perish." If legal justice perishes, then it is no longer worth while for men to remain alive on this earth.[1]
>
> —Immanuel Kant

I wish to thank Phil Davis, J. L. A. Garcia, Mike Gorr, Bruce Russell, Bill Shaw, and Michael Wreen for their comments.

> The right to pardon a criminal . . . is certainly the most slippery of all the rights of the sovereign. By exercising it he can demonstrate the splendor of his majesty and yet thereby wreak a great injustice.[2]
>
> —Immanuel Kant

1 Introduction

Justice requires a judge to give a criminal the punishment he deserves. But mercy is a virtue and a supererogatory trait leading a merciful judge to give a criminal less punishment than he deserves. So is mercy unjust? Is mercy a sentimental emotion leading one to be unjustly preoccupied with a criminal's happiness or plight? But how can injustice be a virtue? How can anything be unjust *and* above and beyond the call of duty?[3] Similarly, Jeffrie Murphy poses this paradox:

> If mercy requires a tempering of justice, than [sic: then] there is a sense in which mercy may require a departure from justice. (Temperings are tamperings.) Thus, to be merciful is, perhaps, to be *unjust*. But it is a vice, not a virtue to manifest injustice. Thus, mercy must be not a virtue, but a vice—a product of morally dangerous sentimentality.[4]

Murphy also poses the dilemma as: either mercy is redundant—a mere part of justice—or a vice—a departure from justice.[5] And since justice concerns requirements, while mercy is supererogatory and thus cannot be required, it is hard to see how even an ethical pluralist could put mercy on a par with justice, much less override justice with mercy.

The paradoxical conflict between justice and mercy seems caused by the assumption that we have a duty always *requiring* us fully to punish criminals. Kantian retributivism seems committed to such a view. I will argue that despite the apparent conflict there are plausible principles supporting the view that mercy is not unjust. I will proceed in part by showing the plausibility of the view that justice does not strictly require us to give a criminal all the punishment that, in justice, he deserves. I will try to reconcile mercy with Kantian retributivist justice, making as few modifications of Kantian retributivism as possible. I shall also briefly argue that refocusing on mercy and justice as virtues (i.e., dispositions to do good; or good dispositions or traits) also reveals a plausible reconciliation. I agree with other philosophers that mercy conceptually cannot be both supererogatory and wrong (unjust).[6] For all supererogatory acts must be morally permissible while all morally wrong acts must be impermissible.

2 Hestevold on Justice and Mercy

So how can we reconcile mercy and justice? H. Hestevold responds that mercy is possible only when a disjunction describes what the criminal deserves. For example, the law may provide only two punishments—(1) two years in jail, or (2) only one year in jail—each of which is well deserved by a criminal. Mercy, then, is manifested in sentencing the criminal to the more lenient of the punishments (i.e., the punishment that is less severe, harsh or harmful to the criminal) described in the disjuncts.

Steven Sverdlik criticizes Hestevold's response, arguing:

> Suppose that it is obligatory that I either call my mother on her birthday or send her a card three days before that date. Given that I must do one or the other to discharge my obligation to my mother, how could it be that, say, calling my mother was supererogatory? . . . Given that each disjunct fully discharges the obligation (for each is "*sufficient*") it cannot be that one disjunct also does more than discharge the obligation. Hestevold's position is similar to saying that a glass holds *just* enough water to slake my thrist and more than enought [sic: enough] water to do so.[7]

Sverdlik's criticism fails, since he jumps to the conclusion that what is *sufficient* to discharge an obligation is *just enough* to discharge it. Further, as Sverdlik asks, how can calling be supererogatory when it is also sufficient to discharge the obligation to one's mother? First, one's mother might understandably prefer a call much more than a card. Second, a call may well cost much more than a card, and thus involve a significantly greater sacrifice by the caller. Thus the mother's preference for a call can easily explain why a call is better than a card, and the difference in cost can easily explain why the call is supererogatory while the card is not.

But I agree with Sverdlik that Hestevold's view is flawed. For I agree with J. L. A. Garcia that Hestevold's view involves errors of omission. Garcia says "If, for instance, you deserve to go to jail for a year or two for your crimes, then sending you for [only] one year is merciful but, according to Hestevold, suspending your sentence is immoral [unjust]."[8] Hestevold's view is underinclusive, clearly covering too few cases of mercy. Consider a governmental official who by law can only (1) suspend a criminal's sentence or completely pardon a criminal; or else (2) let the criminal's sentence stand. It seems clear that a governor can in at least *some* cases issue to a guilty criminal a full pardon and be merciful and not unjust, yet in no sense was a full pardon deserved or treatment to which the criminal, in justice, was entitled (or to which he had a right). For example, the governor may be forced to pardon to alleviate overcrowded prisons. And so he starts pardoning the "hard luck cases" (i.e., those who have suffered most in prison, or who have the most dependents, etc.). But those pardoned had no right to demand pardon, since it was merely the fortuitous overcrowding (rather than any earned entitlement) which even raised the issue of pardoning in the first place.

Hestevold says "suspending the wrongdoer's sentence is immoral [i.e. ceteris paribus unjust] only if suspending the sentence fails to belong to the disjunctive desert for the misdeed in question."[9] But a full pardon or complete suspension of sentence is almost never in the disjunction describing what the criminal deserves. Further, Garcia says, *ex hypothesi,* that the alleged counterexample does not have suspension of sentence in the disjunction of desert, for he says the criminal deserves to go to jail for a year or two. Furthermore, Hestevold's response merely restates the problem and simply gives *no* argument at all to support his claim that mercy would be unjust in such cases. He cannot evade the issue. *Complete* forgiveness is not only mercy, but it is the *most* merciful (and most clearly merciful) act possible, since it is the most lenient and least harsh option. So Hestevold cannot account for even the *clearest* cases of mercy.

3 The Prima Facie Duty to Punish

The paradoxical conflict between justice and mercy seems caused by the assumption that we have a duty *requiring* us always to punish criminals. Retributivism seems committed to such a view. For example, the retributivist Kant says: "A judge who pardons is quite unthinkable. A judge must rather weigh all conduct strictly according to the laws of holiness and allow to each only that measure of happiness which is proportionate to his worthiness."[10]

One way to reconcile justice and mercy is to argue that instead of such a duty, what we have is a *right* (i.e., a liberty, in Hohfeldian terms) and also a moral *reason* to punish. This moral reason can be called a duty, but it is only a *prima facie* duty. And Hestevold says that punishment is prima facie obligatory.[11] So we might conclude that there is no unoverridable duty absolutely requiring us always to punish. But the prima facie duty to punish can be extremely strong, as can our moral reason to punish. But when other moral factors provide reasons for mercy, they can outweigh and override our reason and prima facie duty to punish. So mercy can then be not unjust. Indeed, the great strength of our prima facie duty and reason to punish can explain why the countervailing considerations of mercy can never be more than supererogatory.

Hestevold's analysis does help explain how the nature of mercy allows criminals to make better and worse cases (i.e., rational arguments, not purely emotional pleas) for mercy. Some criminals are more deserving of mercy than others. Yet, since mercy is supererogatory, no criminal can claim mercy to be *only* his just deserts (i.e., his claim right or entitlement). The cases can never *require* mercy of us (as his right), since mercy is supererogatory. But the cases can often provide excellent reasons to be merciful. We say that some criminals are more deserving of mercy than are others. But what we mean here is that some criminals are more *nearly* deserving of mercy. For many of the factors which counsel mercy are relevant for determining the just course as well. Mercy can be deserved in the sense of being not undeserved (i.e., permissible). But mercy can never be *merely* one's just deserts. For mercy is supererogatory and must therefore involve a greater sacrifice or favor than the other punitive option, which would also be the criminal's just deserts.

A plausible reconciliation of justice and mercy is that punitive justice can tie cosmic justice (i.e., that the good should fare well and the bad should fare badly), and then mercy can break the tie in favor of the criminal. For example, suppose an innocent man pleads not guilty but is falsely convicted and jailed. After he serves his jail term, his innocence is proven by new evidence, but he receives no compensation for his false imprisonment. Then he commits a crime carrying a mandatory jail term for an amount of time similar to the amount he already served. But the governor can fully pardon the man (but not merely commute the sentence). The governor has good reason to be merciful and pardon the man, but there could be an equally good case for not doing so. So, as on Hestevold's view, there is a disjunction describing what is deserved. And there is no absolute obligation to give someone what he most deserves. To say a person, *A1*, is deserving of *X* is to imply that giving *A1* is permissible (and reasonable). But it does not imply that giving *A1 X* is absolutely required. For someone else may be equally deserving (or even more deserving). (We might suppose, for example, that a legal system, or public opinion, limits the number of pardons a governor can grant.)

Kant and other retributivists, however, believe we have more than a prima facie duty to punish.[12] What are the standard arguments for Kantian retributivism which requires punishment? As Stuart Brown, Jr. observes, Kant "argues that *lex talionis* [i.e., an eye for an eye; a tooth for a tooth] is just and that any departure from it is a perversion of justice."[13] This creates for Kantians the paradoxical conflict between justice and mercy, for Kant's conception of justice is so strict or narrow that it apparently allows no room in which one can rightly temper justice with mercy. But, of course, Kant also gives charitable benevolence (which would include mercy) as a prime example of moral action according to the categorical imperative.[14] I agree with Hillel Steiner's interpretation that in distinguishing justice from virtue Kant is not denying the compatibility of just conduct and virtue.[15] So Kant is faced with a problem of reconciling justice and mercy.

Kant argues for *lex talionis,* saying:

> the principle of equality (illustrated by the pointer on the scales of justice) . . . is . . . the principle of not treating one side more favorably than the other. Accordingly, any undeserved evil that you inflict on someone else . . . is one that you do to yourself. If you vilify him, you vilify yourself; if you steal from him, you steal from yourself; if you kill him; you kill yourself. Only the Law of retribution . . . can determine exactly the kind and degree of punishment. . . ."[16]

Brown interprets this principle as "weakly suggestive of the first formulation of the Categorical Imperative: act on that maxim which you can at the same time will to be a universal law."[17]

Note that Hestevold's proposed reconciliation of justice and mercy, which views mercy operating only within a *range* of just punishments, seems inapplicable to Kant's *strictly proportional* punishment. Even where Kant says retribution should not or cannot be applied by the letter (e.g., in cases of rape or pederasty) Kant's view of the required punishment still is not a range but a determinate (and unmerciful) act, namely, castration.[18]

Brown proposes a counterexample to Kant's argument for *lex talionis.* Brown persuasively argues:

> on Kant's own theory, if I kill in anger, my decision to kill is determined by the anger and not by reason. To say that I killed out of anger logically contradicts the contention that I acted on a maxim which I at the same time willed to be a universal law. Killing in anger, I logically could not be acting on a purely rational motive. Therefore, from the fact that I have killed another man, it does not follow that I have authorized anyone to kill me.[19]

Brown is not questioning whether the angry killer should be punished at all. Rather, Brown's point is that, as far as Kant has shown, "the question as to what is proper punishment is completely open."[20] Thus, there is ample room in which mercy can operate, even on Kant's view. Brown's argument lends support to Steiner's interpretation that in Kant's views there is "fairly firm support" for the view that "rationality in normative willing does not necessitate a regard for the requirements of justice" (at least the justice of *lex talionis*).[21] So, since rationality in normative willing is, for Kant, more fundamental than *lex talionis,* mercy departing from *lex talionis* is compatible with the more fundamental justice of the categorical imperative itself.

One might recast everything that supports Kant's arguments for *lex talionis* as reasons for a strong prima facie duty to punish rather than an absolute duty always to punish. Murphy says retributivism standardly claims that giving criminals less punishment than they deserve would be unjust. But *to whom* would it be unjust? If no one objects, and everyone—even the victim of the crime—would benefit from the mercy, then there seems to be no room for injustice. If what is pareto optimal is not wrong, or if J. S. Mill's celebrated harm principle is sound, then mercy cannot be wrong, and thus cannot be unjust.

For injustice is wrong. The harm principle states:

> the sole end for which mankind are warranted, individually or collectively, in interfering with the liberty of action of any of their number, is self-protection. That [is,] the only purpose for which power can be rightfully exercised over any member of a civilized community, against his will, is to prevent harm to others.[22]

One may object that Mill's harm principle is based on utilitarianism and is thus fundamentally incompatible with Kantianism. And Kant famously insists we must, to avoid the blood guilt of being murder conspirators after the fact, execute a murderer even if doing so has no benefit because the society is about to end.[23] I have three replies. First, Brown's foregoing counterexample of killing in anger seems to counter Kant's insistence on execution. Second, some philosophers have raised serious doubts about whether Mill could possibly base the harm principle on utilitarianism (as opposed to, say, autonomy, which would be more Kantian).[24] Further, Mill seems to have a retributivist streak, making reconciliation of his view with Kant's more likely. As David Lyons observes, Mill "claims that calling an act wrong, or the breach of a moral obligation, implies that there is some justification for punishing a person who performs it, 'if not by law, by the opinion of his fellow creatures; if not by opinion, by the reproaches of his own conscience. . . . Duty is a thing which may be *exacted* from a person, as one exacts a debt.' "[25]

Third, and most important, Kant's definition of justice is remarkably similar to Mill's harm principle. Kant says "Every action is just which in itself or in its maxim is such that the freedom of the will of each can coexist with the freedom of everyone in accordance with a universal law."[26] As Brown observes, Kant says "there is but one innate right, the right to be free in so far as one's own freedom is compatible with the freedom of others in accordance with a universal law . . . ; and he defines justice in terms of this principle."[27] Kant says:

> Freedom (independence from the constraint of another's will), insofar as it is compatible with the freedom of everyone else in accordance with a universal law, is the one sole and original right that belongs to every human being by virtue of his humanity.[28]

I suggest that Mill's harm principle is a plausible universal law that fits Kant's description, though it plausibly allows mercy in many more cases than Kant does. But Kant's only exception allowing a pardon falls squarely within the scope of the harm principle, which also seems to account for the exception. Kant says the sovereign "can make use of this right of pardon only in connection with an injury committed against himself. . . . But, even in these cases, he cannot allow a crime to go unpunished if the safety of the people might be endangered thereby."[29] And since Kant says the right to equal freedom is the sole innate (or human) right, if my view takes account of that right, then there is no other innate right to contend with that can require punishment rather than mercy.

One may object that John Rawls, whose theory of justice seems Kantian in several respects, argues for his well-known difference principle, which implies that even pareto optimal moves are unjust when they do not benefit the class worst off in society. The difference principle states that "inequalities are to be arranged so that they are . . . to the greatest benefit of the least advantaged."[30] Much can be, and has been, said of Rawls' argument—too much to reexamine here. But his argument does not vanquish all plausible alternatives. Rawls' claim is too extreme to succeed to the exclusion of all plausible alternatives. His claim is so extreme just because pareto optimality is so extremely good—involving *no* harm at all and having *no* state that is pareto superior to it. Moreover, Kant's definition of justice, and Mill's harm principle are, as Rawls himself recognizes, remarkably similar to Rawls' principle of equal maximum liberty, which states: "each person is to have an equal right to the most extensive basic liberty compatible with a similar liberty for others."[31] So even a Rawlsian must grant that a reconciliation of mercy and justice based on the harm principle would at least be based on a plausible principle.

4 Conclusion

I conclude that my view of mercy and justice, which blends elements in the views of Hestevold and Garcia with new elements of my own, provides a plausible account and reconciliation of the interrelations and functions of mercy and justice. Hestevold moves to a prima facie obligation to punish not in order to reconcile justice and mercy (since he thinks disjunctive desert already does that adequately), but only as a purely defensive move against Garcia in order to deny Garcia's claim that there is no initial tension to reconcile. I use a prima facie duty to punish to help reconcile mercy and justice. And I can use it in precisely those cases which Garcia rightly notes as counterexamples to Hestevold's view, namely, the cases where the merciful acts are not in the disjunction describing what is deserved (e.g., full pardon or complete suspension of sentence). The theory I outlined granting a right to punish (perhaps even an absolute right, as Kant might demand) and a duty to punish (but not an absolute duty) can still embrace retributivism, as Kant did, though only a form of retributivism milder than *lex talionis*.[32] Even a Kantian retributivist should respect Mill's harm principle (or perhaps alternatively, using pareto optimality as an exception to punishment) as a standard plausibly providing room for tempering justice with mercy.

There is one final possibility whose plausibility is worth noting. Switching the focus to an agent's dispositions helps show how mercy and justice are compatible, since the dispositions are clearly compatible, involving weighing factors in the agent's deliberations. Two opposing dispositions can be present and felt without any cognitive defect resembling a contradiction.[33] This switch of focus is marked by discussing the duty to *be* just (rather than merely act justly) and the (imperfect) duty to *be* merciful (rather than merely act mercifully).[34] As Murphy reckons, mercy is fundamentally motivated by an agent's concern for the criminal's plight.[35]

Even if the specifics of Kant's arguments here are, as others have claimed, all too often ad hoc, I conclude that there is a retributivist view of justice, generally Kantian in spirit, that is plausibly reconciled with mercy.[36]

NOTES

1. Immanuel Kant, *Metaphysical Elements of Justice* 100 (tr. John Ladd 1965, original published 1797).
2. Id. at 107–08.
3. For this framing of the issue, see H. Scott Hestevold, "On the Moral Status of Punishment," 6 *Law & Philosophy* 249, 249 (1987); and Steven Sverdlik, "Justice and Mercy," 16 *Journal of Social Philosophy* 36 (1985): 36.
4. Jeffrie G. Murphy, "Mercy and Legal Justice," 4 *Social Philosophy & Policy* 1, 4 (1986) (emphasis in original).
5. Id. at 8.
6. H. Scott Hestevold, "Disjunctive Desert," 20 *American Philosophical Quarterly* 357 (1983); and Sverdlik, *supra* note 3, at 36.
7. Sverdlik, *supra* note 3, at 39 (emphasis added).
8. J. L. A. Garcia, "Two Concepts of Desert," 5 *Law & Philosophy* 219, 229 (1986).
9. Hestevold, *supra* note 3, at 252.
10. Immanuel Kant, *Lectures on Philosophical Theology* 127 (tr. Allen W. Wood and Gertrude M. Clark 1978, original published 1830).
11. Hestevold, *supra* note 3, at 249.
12. See, e.g., Murphy, *supra* note 4, at 5 n. 10.
13. Stuart M. Brown, Jr., "Has Kant a Philosophy of Law?" 71 *Philosophical Review* 33, 36 (1962).
14. See Immanuel Kant, *Foundations of the Metaphysics of Morals* 47 ff. (ed. Robert Paul Wolff 1969, original published 1785).
15. Hillel Steiner, "Kant's Kelsenianism," in Richard Tur and William Twining, eds., *Essays on Kelsen* 68 ff. (1986)
16. Kant, *supra* note 1, at 101.
17. Brown, *supra* note 13, at 36.
18. Kant, *supra* note 1, at 132–33.
19. Brown, *supra* note 13, at 37 (citation omitted).
20. Id. at 38.
21. Steiner, *supra* note 15, at 69–70 and 72–74.

22. John Stuart Mill, *On Liberty*, Ch. 1 (1859).
23. Immanuel Kant, "The Right To Punish," in Jeffrie G. Murphy, ed., *Punishment and Rehabilitation* (Belmont 1973), p. 37 (originally in *supra* note 1).
24. See, e.g., Gerald Dworkin, "Paternalism," in Richard A. Wasserstrom, ed., *Morality and the Law* 107–26 (Wadsworth 1971), Fred R. Berger, *Happiness, Justice & Freedom: The Moral & Political Philosophy of John Stuart Mill* (University of California Press 1984), Ch. 5 and pp. 292–96, and David Lyons, "Liberty and Harm to Others," in Wesley E. Cooper, Kai Nielsen, and Steven C. Patten, eds., *New Essays on John Stuart Mill and Utilitarianism* (1979).
25. David Lyons, *Ethics and The Rule of Law* (Cambridge University Press 1984), p. 180, quoting Mill, *Utilitarianism*, Ch. V, para. 14.
26. Kant, *supra* note 1, at 35.
27. Brown, *supra* note 13, at 40.
28. Kant (1797), pp. 43–44.
29. Id. at 108.
30. John Rawls, *A Theory of Justice* 302 (1971).
31. Id. at 60. Rawls recognizes the similarity. Id. at 205 n. 6.
32. See James B. Brady, "A 'Rights-based' Theory of Punishment," 97 *Ethics* 792, 792 (1987).
33. See Murphy, *supra* note 4, at 11 n. 22.
34. See, e.g., Allen Buchanan, "Justice and Charity," 97 *Ethics*, 558, 569 n. 22 (1987).
35. Murphy, *supra* note 4, at 8. For more complexities in the relationship between benevolence and justice, see my "Is Inheritance Immoral?", 1 *The Barrister* 11 (1989).
36. See Brown, *supra* note 13; and Buchanan, supra note 33, at 569 n. 22.

Study Questions

1. How satisfactory is Murphy's attempt to resolve the paradoxes of mercy?

2. Does Harwood succeed in his attempt to reconcile the positions of J. S. Mill, a utilitarian, and Immanuel Kant, a retributivist?

H Execution

Furman v. *Georgia*

United States Supreme Court, 1972

The Eighth Amendment to the United States Constitution forbids the infliction of "cruel and unusual" punishment. In this landmark case, the majority of the Court ruled that the death penalty as it was then administered was a violation of this amendment. In the excerpt from his concurring opinion that is included here, Justice Douglas argues that since, under existing Georgia law, the imposition of the death penalty was left entirely to the discretion of the jury, it was unconstitutional because it was administered in an arbitrary and capricious manner. Justice Brennan, in his concurrence, takes the even stronger position (which the majority of the Court did not endorse) that the death penalty is unconstitutional by its very nature, primarily because it is "uniquely degrading to human dignity."

Mr. Justice Douglas, concurring.

In these three cases the death penalty was imposed, one of them for murder, and two for rape. In each the determination of whether the penalty should be death or a lighter punishment was left by the State to the discretion of the judge or of the jury. In each of the three cases the trial was to a jury. They are here on petitions for certiorari which we granted limited to the questions whether the imposition and execution of the death penalty constitutes "cruel and unusual punishment" within the meaning of the Eighth Amendment as applied to the States by the Fourteenth. I vote to vacate each judgment, believing that the exaction of the death penalty does violate the Eighth and Fourteenth Amendments.

. . . We cannot say from facts disclosed in these records that these defendants were sentenced to death because they were black. Yet our task is not restricted to an effort to divine what motives impelled these death penalties. Rather, we deal with a system of law and of justice that leaves to the uncontrolled discretion of judges or juries the determination whether defendants committing these crimes should die or be imprisoned. Under these laws no standards govern the selection of the penalty. People live or die, dependent on the whim of one man or of 12.

. . . In a Nation committed to equal protection of the laws there is no permissible "caste" aspect of law enforcement. Yet we know that the discretion of judges and juries in imposing the death penalty enables the penalty to be selectively applied, feeding prejudices against the accused if he is poor despised, and lacking political clout, or if he is a member of a suspect or unpopular minority, and saving those who by social position may be in a more protected position. In ancient Hindu law a Brahman was exempt from capital punishment, and in those days, "[g]enerally, in the law books, punishment increased in severity as social status diminished." We have, I fear, taken in practice the same position, partially as a result of making the death penalty discretionary and partially as a result of the ability of the rich to purchase the services of the most respected and most resourceful legal talent in the Nation.

The high service rendered by the "cruel and unusual" punishment clause of the Eighth Amendment is to require legislatures to write penal laws that are evenhanded, nonselective, and nonarbitrary, and to require judges to see to it that general laws are not applied sparsely, selectively, and spottily to unpopular groups.

A law that stated that anyone making more than $50,000 would be exempt from the death penalty would plainly fall, as would a law that in terms said that blacks, those who never went beyond the fifth grade in school, those who made less than $3,000 a year, or those who were unpopular or unstable should be the only people executed. A law which in the overall view reaches that result in practice has no more sanctity than a law which in terms provides the same.

Thus, these discretionary statutes are unconstitutional in their operation. They are pregnant with discrimination and discrimination is an ingredient not compatible with the idea of equal protection of the laws that is implicit in the ban on "cruel and unusual" punishments. . . .

Mr. Justice Brennan, concurring.

. . . There are, then, four principles by which we may determine whether a particular punishment is "cruel and unusual." The primary principle, which I believe supplies the essential predicate for the application of the others, is that a punishment must not by its severity be degrading to human dignity. The paradigm violation of this principle would be the infliction of a torturous punishment of the type that the Clause has always prohibited. Yet "[i]t is unlikely that any State at this moment in history," *Robinson v. California*, 370 U.S., at 666, would pass a law providing for the infliction of such a punishment. Indeed, no such punishment has ever been before this Court. The same may be said of the other principles. It is unlikely that this Court will confront a severe punishment that is obviously inflicted in wholly arbitrary fashion; no State would engage in a reign of blind terror. Nor is it likely that this Court will be called upon to review a severe punishment that is clearly and totally rejected throughout society; no legislature would be able even to authorize the infliction of such a punishment. Nor, finally, it is likely that this Court will have to consider a severe punishment that is patently unnecessary; no State today would inflict a severe punishment knowing that there was no reason whatever for doing so. In short, we are unlikely to have occasion to determine that a punishment is fatally offensive under any one principle.

Since the Bill of Rights was adopted, this Court has adjudged only three punishments to be within the prohibition of the Clause. See *Weems* v. *United States,* 217 U.S. 349 (1910) (12 years in chains at hard and painful labor); *Trop* v. *Dulles,* 356 U.S. 86 (1958) (expatriation); *Robinson* v. *California,* 370 U.S. 660 (1962) (imprisonment for narcotics addiction). Each punishment, of course, was degrading to human dignity, but of none could it be said conclusively that it was fatally offensive under one or the other of the principles. Rather, these "cruel and unusual punishments" seriously implicated several of the principles, and it was the application of the principles in combination that supported the judgment. That, indeed, is not surprising. The function of these principles, after all, is simply to provide means by which a court can determine whether a challenged punishment comports with human dignity. They are, therefore, interrelated, and in most cases it will be their convergence that will justify the conclusion that a punishment is "cruel and unusual." The test, then, will ordinarily be a cumulative one: If a punishment is unusually severe, if there is a strong probability that it is inflicted arbitrarily, if it is substantially rejected by contemporary society, and if there is no reason to believe that it serves any penal purpose more effectively than some less severe punishment, then the continued infliction of that punishment violates the command of the Clause that the State may not inflict inhuman and uncivilized punishments upon those convicted of crimes.

. . . The question, then, is whether the deliberate infliction of death is today consistent with the command of the Clause that the State may not inflict punishments that do not comport with human dignity. I will analyze the punishment of death in terms of the principles set out above and the cumulative test to which they lead: It is a denial of human dignity for the State arbitrarily to subject a person to an unusually severe punishment that society has indicated it does not regard as acceptable, and that cannot be shown to serve any penal purpose more effectively than a significantly less drastic punishment. Under these principles and this test, death is today a "cruel and unusual" punishment.

Death is a unique punishment in the United States. In a society that so strongly affirms the sanctity of life, not surprisingly the common view is that death is the ultimate sanction. This natural human feeling appears all about us. There has been no national debate about punishment, in general or by imprisonment, comparable to the debate about the punishment of death. No other punishment has been so continuously restricted, see *infra*, at 296–298, nor has any State yet abolished prisons, as some have abolished this punishment. And those States that still inflict death reserve it for the most heinous crimes. Juries, of course, have always treated death cases differently, as have governors exercising their communication powers. Criminal defendants are of the same view. "As all practicing lawyers know, who have defended persons charged with capital offenses, often the only goal possible is to avoid the death penalty." *Griffin* v. *Illinois,* 351 U.S. 12, 28 (1956) (Burton and Minton, 33., dissenting). Some legislatures have required particular procedures, such as two-stage trials and automatic appeals, applicable only in death cases. "It is the universal experience in the administration of criminal justice that those charged with capital offenses are granted special considerations." *Abid.* See *Williams* v. *Florida,* 399 U.S. 78, 103 (1970) (all States require juries of 12 in death cases). This Court, too, almost always treats death cases as a class apart. And the unfortunate effect of this punishment upon the functioning of the judicial process is well known; no other punishment has a similar effect.

The only explanation for the uniqueness of death is its extreme severity. Death is today an unusually severe punishment, unusual in its pain, in its finality, and in its enormity. No other existing punishment is comparable to death in terms of physical and mental suffering. Although our information is not conclusive, it appears that there is no method available that guarantees an immediate and painless death. Since the discontinuance of flogging as a constitutionally permissible punishment, *Jackson* v. *Bishop,* 404 F. 2d 571 (CA8 1968), death remains as the only punishment that may involve the conscious infliction of physical pain. In addition, we know that mental pain is an inseparable part of our practice of punishing criminals by death for the prospect of pending execution exacts a frightful toll during the inevitable long wait between the imposition of sentence and the actual infliction of death. Cf *Ex parte Medley,* 134 U.S. 160, 172 (1890). As the California Supreme Court pointed out, "the process of carrying out a verdict of death is often so degrading and brutalizing to the human spirit as to constitute psychological torture." *People* v. *Anderson, 6 Cal. 3d 628, 649, 493 P. 2d 880, 894 (1972). Indeed, as Mr. Justice Frankfurter noted, "the onset of insanity while awaiting execution of a death sentence is not a rare phenomenon." Solesbee* v. *Balkcom,* 339 U.S. 9, 14 (1950) (dissenting opinion). The "fate of ever-increasing fear and distress" to which the expatriate is subjected, *Trop* v. *Dulles,* 356 U.S., at 102, can only exist to a greater degree for a person confined in prison awaiting death.

The unusual severity of death is manifested most clearly in its finality and enormity. Death, in these respects, is in a class by itself. Expatriation, for example, is a punishment that "destroys for the individual the political existence that was centuries in the development," that "strips the citizen of his status in the national and international political community," and that puts "[h]is very existence" in jeopardy. Expatriation thus inherently entails "the total destruction of the individual's status in organized society." *Id.,* at 101. "In short, the expatriate has lost the right to have rights." *Id.,* at 102. Yet, demonstrably, expatriation is not "a fate worse than death." *Id.*, at 125 (Frankfurther, J., dissenting). Although death, like expatriation, destroys the individual's "political existence" and his "status in organized society," it does more, for unlike expatriation, death also destroys "[h]is very existence." There is, too at least the possibility that the expatriate will in the future regain "the right to have rights." Death forecloses even that possibility.

Death is truly an awesome punishment. The calculated killing of a human being by the State involves, by its very nature, a denial of the executed person's humanity. The contrast with the plight of a person punished by imprisonment is evident. An individual in prison does not lose "the right to have rights." A prisoner retains, for example, the constitutional rights to the free exercise of religion, to be free of cruel and unusual punishments, and to treatment as a "person" for purposes of due process of law and the equal protection of the laws. A prisoner remains a member of the human family. Moreover, he retains the right of access to the courts. His punishment is not irrevocable. Apart from the common charge, grounded upon the recognition of human fallibility, that the punishment of death must inevitably be inflicted upon innocent men, we know that death has been the lot of men whose convictions were unconstitutionally secured in view of later, retroactively applied, holdings of this Court. The punishment itself may have been unconstitutionally inflicted, see *Witherspoon* v. *Illinois,* 391 U.S. 510 (1968), yet the finality of death precludes relief. An executed person has indeed "lost the right to have rights." As one 19-century proponent of punishing criminals by death declared, "When a man is hung, there is an end of our relations with him. His execution is a way of saying, 'You are not fit for this world, take your chance elsewhere.' "

In comparison to all other punishments today, then, the deliberate extinguishment of human life by the State is uniquely degrading to human dignity. I would not hesitate to hold, on that ground alone, that death is today a "cruel and unusual" punishment, were it not that death is a punishment of longstanding usage and acceptance in this country. I therefore turn to the second principle—that the State may not arbitrarily inflict an unusually severe punishment.

. . . When the punishment of death is inflicted in a trivial number of the cases in which it is legally available, the conclusion is virtually inescapable that it is being inflicted arbitrarily. Indeed, it smacks of little more than a lottery system. The States claim, however, that this rarity is evidence not of arbitrariness, but of informed selectivity. Death is indicated, they say, only in "extreme" cases.

Informed selectivity, of course, is a value not to be denigrated. Yet presumably the States could make precisely the same claim if there were 10 executions per year, or five, or even if there were but one. That there may be as many as 50 per year does not strengthen the claim. When the rate of infliction is at this low level, it is highly implausible that only the worst criminals or the criminals who commit the worst crimes are selected for this punishment. No one has yet suggested a rational basis that could differentiate in those terms the few who die from the many who go to prison. Crimes and criminals simply do not admit of a distinction that can be drawn so finely as to explain, on that ground, the execution of such a tiny sample of those eligible. Certainly the laws that provide for this punishment do not attempt to draw the distinction; all cases to which the laws apply are necessarily "extreme." Nor is the distinction credible in fact. If, for example, petitioner Furman or his crime illustrates the "extreme," then nearly all murderers and their murders are also "extreme." Furthermore, our procedures in death cases, rather than resulting in the selection of "extreme" cases for this punishment, actually sanction an arbitrary selection. For this Court has held that juries may, as they do, make the decision whether to impose a death sentence wholly unguided by standards governing that decision. *McGautha* v. *California,* 402 U.S. 183, 196–208 (1971). In other words, our procedures are not constructed to guard against the totally capricious selection of criminals for the punishment of death.

Although it is difficult to imagine what further facts would be necessary in order to prove that death is, as my Brother Stewart puts it, "wantonly and . . . freakishly" inflicted. I need not conclude that arbitrary infliction is patently obvious. I am not considering this punishment by the isolated light of one principle. The probability of arbitrariness is sufficiently substantial that it can be relied upon, in combination with the other principles, in reaching a judgment on the constitutionality of this punishment.

When there is a strong probability that an unusually severe and degrading punishment is being inflicted arbitrarily, we may well expect that society will disapprove of its infliction. I turn, therefore, to the third principle. An examination of the history and present operation of the American practice of punishing criminals by death reveals that this punishment has been almost totally rejected by contemporary society.

. . . The progressive decline in, and the current rarity of, the infliction of death demonstrate that our society seriously questions the appropriateness of this punishment today. The States point out that many legislatures authorize death as the punishment for certain crimes and that substantial segments of the public, as reflected in opinion polls and referendum votes, continue to support it. Yet the availability of this punishment through statutory authorization, as well as the polls and referenda, which amount simply to approval of that authorization, simply underscores the extent to which our society has in fact rejected this punishment. When an uneasily severe punishment is authorized for wide-scale application but not, because of society's refusal, indicted save in a few instances, the inference is compelling that there is a deep-seated reluctance to inflict it. Indeed, the likelihood is great that the punishment is tolerated only because of its disuse. The objective indicator of society's view of an unusually severe punishment is what society does with it, and today society will inflict death upon only a small sample of the eligible criminals. Rejection could hardly be more complete without becoming absolute. At the very least, I must conclude that contemporary society views this punishment with substantial doubt.

The final principle to be considered is that an unusually severe and degrading punishment may not be excessive in view of the purposes for which it is inflicted. This principle, too, is related to the others. When there is a strong probability that the State is arbitrarily inflicting an unusually severe punishment that is subject to grave societal doubts, it is likely also that the punishment cannot be shown to be serving any penal purpose that could not be served equally well by some less severe punishment.

The States' primary claim is that death is a necessary punishment because it prevents the commission of capital crimes more effectively than any less severe punishment. The first part of this claim is that the infliction of death is necessary to stop the individuals executed from committing further crimes. The sufficient answer to this is that if a criminal convicted of a capital crime poses a danger to society, effective administration of the State's pardon and parole laws can delay or deny his release from prison, and techniques of isolation can eliminate or minimize the danger while he remains confined.

The more significant argument is that the threat of death prevents the commission of capital crimes because it deters potential criminals who would not be deterred by the threat of imprisonment. The argument is not based upon evidence that the threat of death is a superior deterrent. Indeed, as my Brother Marshall establishes, the available evidence uniformly indicates, although it does not conclusively prove, that the threat of death has no greater deterrent effect than the threat of imprisonment. The States argue, however, that they are entitled to rely upon common human experience, and that experience, they say, supports the conclusion that death must be a more effective deterrent than any less severe punishment. Because people fear death the most, the argument runs, the threat of death must be the greatest deterrent.

It is important to focus upon the precise import of this argument. It is not denied that many, and probably most, capital crimes cannot be deterred by the threat of punishment. Thus the argument can apply only to those who think rationally about the commission of capital crimes. Particularly is that true when the potential criminal, under this argument, must not only consider the risk of punishment, but also distinguish between two possible punishments. The concern, then, is with a particular type of potential criminal, the rational person who will commit a capital crime knowing that the punishment is long-term imprisonment, which may well be for the rest of his life, but will not commit the crime knowing that the punishment is death. On the face of it, the assumption that such persons exist is implausible.

In any event, this argument cannot be appraised in the abstract. We are not presented with the theoretical question whether under any imaginable circumstances the threat of death might be a greater deterrent to the commission of capital crimes than the threat of imprisonment. We are concerned with the practice of punishing criminals by death as it exists in the United States today. Proponents of this argument necessarily admit that its validity depends upon the existence of a system in which the punishment of death is invariably and swiftly imposed. Our system, of course, satisfied neither condition. A rational person contemplating a murder or rape is confronted, not with the certainty of a speedy death, but with the slightest possibility that he will be executed in the distant future. The risk of death is remote and improbable; in contrast, the risk of long-term imprisonment is near and great. In short, whatever the speculative validity of the assumption that the threat of death is a superior deterrent, there is no reason to believe that as currently administered the punishment of death is necessary to deter the commission of capital crimes. Whatever might be the case were all or substantially all eligible criminals quickly put to death, unverifiable possibilities are an insufficient basis upon which to conclude that the threat of death today has any greater deterrent efficacy than the threat of imprisonment.

There is, however, another aspect to the argument that the punishment of death is necessary for the protection of society. The infliction of death, the States urge, serves to manifest the community's outrage at the commission of the crime. It is, they say, a concrete public expression of moral indignation that inculcates respect for the law and helps assure a more peaceful community. Moreover, we are told, not only does the punishment of death exert this widespread moralizing influence upon community values, it also satisfies the popular demand for grievous condemnation of abhorrent crimes and thus prevents disorder, lynching, and attempts by private citizens to take the law into their own hands.

The question, however, is not whether death serves these supposed purposes of punishment, but whether death serves them more effectively than imprisonment. There is no evidence whatever that utilization of imprisonment rather than death encourages private blood feuds and other disorders. Surely if there were such a danger, the execution of a handful of criminals each year would not prevent it. The assertion that death alone is a sufficiently emphatic denunciation for capital crimes suffers from the same defect. If capital crimes require the punishment of death in order to provide moral reinforcement for the basic values of the community, those values can only be undermined when death is so rarely inflicted upon the criminals who commit the crimes. Furthermore, it is certainly doubtful that the infliction of death by the State does in fact strengthen the community's moral code; if the deliberate extinguishment of human life has any effect at all, it more likely tends to lower our respect for life and brutalize our values. That, after all, is why we no longer carry out public executions. In any event, this claim simply means that one purpose of punishment is indicate social disapproval of crime. To serve that purpose our laws distribute punishments according to the gravity of crimes and punish more severely the crimes society regards as more serious. That purpose cannot justify any particular punishment as the upper limit of severity.

McCleskey v. *Kemp* (1987)

UNITED STATES SUPREME COURT

This case concerned a black male who was sentenced to death for the murder of a police officer. Part of his defense was that statistical evidence demonstrated that the process by which people in Georgia are sentenced to death was administered in a racially discriminatory manner. Hence McCleskey claimed that his execution would violate both the Eighth Amendment and the Fourteenth Amendment (which guarantees all citizens due process of law). The majority of the Court upheld McCleskey's conviction, arguing that discretion was an inevitable part of the trial process and that, if McCleskey's conviction were overturned, there would be dire implications for the entire system of criminal justice. Justice Brennan, in a vigorous dissenting opinion (part of which is also included here), argued that the majority's view was unsatisfactory since "preventing the arbitrary administration of punishment is a basic ideal of any society that purports to be governed by the rule of law."

Justice Powell delivered the opinion of the court.

This case presents the question whether a complex statistical study that indicates a risk that racial considerations enter into capital sentencing determinations proves that petitioner McCleskey's capital sentence is unconstitutional under the Eighth or Fourteenth Amendment.

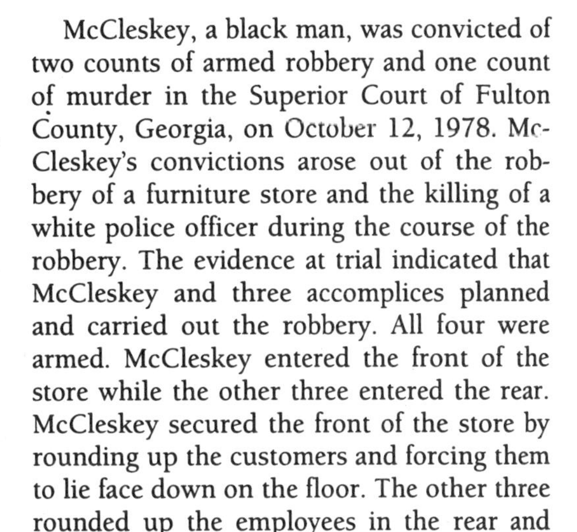

✦ ✦ ✦

McCleskey, a black man, was convicted of two counts of armed robbery and one count of murder in the Superior Court of Fulton County, Georgia, on October 12, 1978. McCleskey's convictions arose out of the robbery of a furniture store and the killing of a white police officer during the course of the robbery. The evidence at trial indicated that McCleskey and three accomplices planned and carried out the robbery. All four were armed. McCleskey entered the front of the store while the other three entered the rear. McCleskey secured the front of the store by rounding up the customers and forcing them to lie face down on the floor. The other three rounded up the employees in the rear and tied them up with tape. The manager was forced at gunpoint to turn over the store receipts, his watch, and $6.00. During the course of the robbery, a police officer, answering a silent alarm, entered the store through the front door. As he was walking down the center aisle of the store, two shots were fired. Both struck the officer. One hit him in the face and killed him.

Several weeks later, McCleskey was arrested in connection with an unrelated offense. He confessed that he had participated in the furniture store robbery, but denied that he had shot the police officer. At trial, the State introduced evidence that at least one of the bullets that struck the officer was fired from a .38 caliber Rossi revolver. This description matched the description of the gun that McCleskey had carried during the robbery. The State also introduced the testimony of two witnesses who had heard McCleskey admit to the shooting.

The jury convicted McCleskey of murder. At the penalty hearing, the jury heard arguments as to the appropriate sentence. Under Georgia law, the jury could not consider imposing the death penalty unless it found beyond a reasonable doubt that the murder was accompanied by one of the statutory aggravating circumstances.

. . . The jury in this case found two aggravating circumstances to exist beyond a reasonable doubt: the murder was committed during the course of an armed robbery, and the murder was committed upon a peace officer engaged in the performance of his duties. In making its decision whether to impose the death sentence, the jury considered the mitigating and aggravating circumstances of McCleskey's conduct. McCleskey offered no mitigating evidence. The jury recommended that he be sentenced to death on the murder charge and to consecutive life sentences on the armed robbery charges. The court followed the jury's recommendation and sentenced McCleskey to death.

McCleskey next filed a petition for a writ of habeas corpus in the federal District Court for the Northern District of Georgia. His petition raised 18 claims, one of which was that the Georgia capital sentencing process is administered in a racially discriminatory manner in violation of the Eighth and Fourteenth Amendments to the United States Constitution. In support of his claim, McCleskey proffered a statistical study performed by Professors David C. Baldus, George Woodworth, and Charles Pulaski (the Baldus study) that purports to show a disparity in the imposition of the death sentence in Georgia based on the race of the murder victim and, to a lesser extent, the race of the defendant. The Baldus study is actually two sophisticated statistical studies that examine over 2,000 murder cases that occurred in Georgia during the 1970s. The raw numbers collected by Professor Baldus indicate that defendants charged with killing white persons received the death penalty in 11% of the cases, but defendants charged with killing blacks received the death penalty in only 1% of the cases. The raw numbers also indicate a reverse racial disparity according to the race of the defendant: 4% of the black defendants received the death penalty, as opposed to 7% of the white defendants.

Baldus also divided the cases according to the combination of the race of the defendant and the race of the victim. He found that the death penalty was assessed in 22% of the cases involving black defendants and white victims: 8% of the cases involving white defendants and white victims: 1% of the cases involving black defendants and black victims: and 3% of the cases involving white defendants and black victims. Similarly, Baldus found that prosecutors sought the death penalty in 70% of the cases involving black defendants and white victims: 32% of the cases involving white defendants and white victims: 15% of the cases involving black defendants and black victims: and 19% of the cases involving white defendants and black victims.

Baldus subjected his data to an extensive analysis, taking account of 230 variables that could have explained the disparities on nonracial grounds. One of his models concludes that, even after taking account of 39 nonracial variables, defendants charged with killing white victims were 4.3 times as likely to receive a death sentence as defendants charged with killing blacks. According to this model, black defendants were 1.1 times as likely to receive a death sentence as other defendants. Thus, the Baldus study indicates that black defendants, such as McCleskey, who kill white victims have the greatest likelihood of receiving the death penalty.

In light of our precedents under the Eighth Amendment, McCleskey cannot argue successfully that his sentence is "disproportionate to the crime in the traditional sense." He does not deny that he committed a murder in the course of a planned robbery, a crime for which this Court has determined that the death penalty constitutionally may be imposed. *Gregg* v. *Georgia*. His disproportionality claim "is of a different sort." McCleskey argues that the sentence in his case is disproportionate to the sentences in other murder cases.

On the one hand, he cannot base a constitutional claim on an argument that his case differs from other cases in which defendants *did* receive the death penalty. On automatic appeal, the Georgia Supreme Court found that McCleskey's death sentence was not disproportionate to other death sentences imposed in the State. The court supported this conclusion with an appendix containing citations to 13 cases involving generally similar murders. Moreover, where the statutory procedures adequately channel the sentencer's discretion, such proportionality review is not constitutionally required.

On the other hand, absent a showing that the Georgia capital punishment system operates in an arbitrary and capricious manner, McCleskey cannot prove a constitutional violation by demonstrating that other defendants who may be similarly situated did *not* receive the death penalty. In *Gregg*, the Court confronted the argument that "the opportunities for discretionary action that are inherent in the processing of any murder case under Georgia law," *Gregg* v. *Georgia*, specifically the opportunities for discretionary leniency, rendered the capital sentences imposed arbitrary and capricious. We rejected this contention:

> The existence of these discretionary stages is not determinative of the issues before us. At each of these stages an actor in the criminal justice system makes a decision which may remove a defendant from consideration as a candidate for the death penalty. *Furman*, in contrast, dealt with the decision to impose the death sentence on a specific individual who had been convicted of a capital offense. Nothing in any of our cases suggests that the decision to afford an individual defendant mercy violates the Constitution. *Furman* held only that, in order to minimize the risk that the death penalty would be imposed on a capriciously selected group of offenders, the decision to impose it had to be guided by standards so that the sentencing authority would focus on the particularized circumstances of the crime and the defendant.

Because McCleskey's sentence was imposed under Georgia sentencing procedures that focus discretion "on the particularized nature of the crime and the particularized characteristics of the individual defendant," we lawfully may presume that McCleskey's death sentence was not "wantonly and freakishly" imposed, and thus that the sentence is not disproportionate within any recognized meaning under the Eighth Amendment.

Although our decision in *Gregg* as to the facial validity of the Georgia capital punishment statute appears to foreclose McCleskey's disproportionality argument, he further contends that the Georgia capital punishment system is arbitrary and capricious in *application*, and therefore his sentence is excessive, because racial considerations may influence capital sentencing decisions in Georgia. We now address this claim.

To evaluate McCleskey's challenge, we must examine exactly what the Baldus study may show. Even Professor Baldus does not contend that his statistics *prove* that race enters into any capital sentencing decisions or that race was a factor in McCleskey's particular case. Statistics at most may show only a likelihood that a particular factor entered into some decisions. There is, of course, some risk of racial prejudice influencing a jury's decision in a criminal case. There are similar risks that other kinds of prejudice will influence other criminal trials. The question "is at what point that risk becomes constitutionally unacceptable." McCleskey asks us to accept the likelihood allegedly shown by the Baldus study as the constitutional measure of an unacceptable risk of racial prejudice influencing capital sentencing decisions. This we decline to do.

Because of the risk that the factor of race may enter the criminal justice process, we have engaged in "unceasing efforts" to eradicate racial prejudice from our criminal justice system. Our efforts have been guided by our recognition that "the inestimable privilege of trial by jury . . . is a vital principle, underlying the whole administration of criminal justice." Thus, it is the jury that is a criminal defendant's fundamental "protection of life and liberty against race or color prejudice." Specifically, a capital sentencing jury representative of a criminal defendant's community assures a " 'diffused impartiality,' " in the jury's task of "express[ing] the conscience of the community on the ultimate question of life or death."

Individual jurors bring to their deliberations "qualities of human nature and varieties of human experience, the range of which is unknown and perhaps unknowable." The capital sentencing decision requires the individual jurors to focus their collective judgment on the unique characteristics of a particular criminal defendant. It is not surprising that such collective judgments often are difficult to explain. But the inherent lack of predictability of jury decisions does not justify their condemnation. On the contrary, it is the jury's function to make the difficult and uniquely human judgments that defy codification and that "buil[d] discretion, equity, and flexibility into a legal system."

McCleskey's argument that the Constitution condemns the discretion allowed decisionmakers in the Georgia capital sentencing system is antithetical to the fundamental role of discretion in our criminal justice system. Discretion in the criminal justice system offers substantial benefits to the criminal defendant. Not only can a jury decline to impose the death sentence, it can decline to convict, or choose to convict of a lesser offense. Whereas decisions against a defendant's interest may be reversed by the trial judge or on appeal, these discretionary exercises of leniency are final and unreviewable. Similarly, the capacity of prosecutorial discretion to provide individualized justice is "firmly entrenched in American law." As we have noted, a prosecutor can decline to charge, offer a plea bargain, or decline to seek a death sentence in any particular case. Of course, "the power to be lenient [also] is the power to discriminate," but a capital-punishment system that did not allow for discretionary acts of leniency "would be totally alien to our notions of criminal justice." *Gregg* v. *Georgia.*

✦ ✦ ✦

At most, the Baldus study indicates a discrepancy that appears to correlate with race. Apparent disparities in sentencing are an inevitable part of our criminal justice system. The discrepancy indicated by the Baldus study is "a far cry from the major systemic defects identified in *Furman.*" As this Court has recognized, any mode for determining guilt or punishment "has its weaknesses and the potential for misuse." Specifically, "there can be 'no perfect procedure for deciding in which cases governmental authority should be used to impose death.' " Despite these imperfections, our consistent rule has been that constitutional guarantees are met when "the mode [for determining guilt or punishment] itself has been surrounded with safeguards to make it as fair as possible." Where the discretion that is fundamental to our criminal process is involved, we decline to assume that what is unexplained is invidious. In light of the safeguards designed to minimize racial bias in the process, the fundamental value of jury trial in our criminal justice system, and the benefits that discretion provides to criminal defendants, we hold that the Baldus study does not demonstrate a constitutionally significant risk of racial bias affecting the Georgia capital-sentencing process.

Two additional concerns inform our decision in this case. First, McCleskey's claim, taken to its logical conclusion, throws into serious question the principles that underlie our entire criminal justice system. The Eighth Amendment is not limited in application to capital punishment, but applies to all penalties. Thus, if we accepted McCleskey's claim that racial bias has impermissibly tainted the capital sentencing decision, we could soon be faced with similar claims as to other types of penalty. Moreover, the claim that his sentence rests on the irrelevant factor of race easily could be extended to apply to claims based on unexplained discrepancies that correlate to membership in other minority groups, and even to gender. Similarly, since McCleskey's claim relates to the race of his victim, other claims could apply with equally logical force to statistical disparities that correlate with the race or sex of other actors in the criminal justice system, such as defense attorneys, or judges. Also, there is no logical reason that such a claim need be limited to racial or sexual bias. If arbitrary and capricious punishment is the touchstone under the Eighth Amendment, such a claim could—at least in theory—be based upon any arbitrary variable, such as the defendant's facial characteristics, or the physical attractiveness of the defendant or the victim, that some statistical study indicates may be influential in jury decisionmaking. As these examples illustrate, there is no limiting principle to the type of challenge brought by McCleskey. The Constitution does not require that a State eliminate any demonstrable disparity that correlates with a potentially irrelevant factor in order to operate a criminal justice system that includes capital punishment. As we have stated specifically in the context of capital punishment, the Constitution does not "plac[e] totally unrealistic conditions on its use."

Second, McCleskey's arguments are best presented to the legislative bodies. It is not the responsibility—or indeed even the right—of this Court to determine the appropriate punishment for particular crimes. It is the legislatures, the elected representatives of the people, that are "constituted to respond to the will and consequently the moral values of the people." *Furman* v. *Georgia* (Burger, C. J., dissenting). Legislatures also are better qualified to weigh and "evaluate the results of statistical studies in terms of their own local conditions and with a flexibility of approach that is not available to the courts," *Gregg* v. *Georgia*. Capital punishment is now the law in more than two thirds of our States. It is the ultimate duty of courts to determine on a case-by-case basis whether these laws are applied consistently with the Constitution. Despite McCleskey's wide ranging arguments that basically challenge the validity of capital punishment in our multi-racial society, the only question before us is whether in his case the law of Georgia was properly applied. We agree with the District Court and the Court of Appeals for the Eleventh Circuit that this was carefully and correctly done in this case.

Accordingly, we affirm the judgment of the Court of Appeals for the Eleventh Circuit.

It is so ordered.

Justice Brennan, with whom Justice Marshall joins, and with whom Justice Blackmun and Justice Stevens join. . . .

The Court assumes the statistical validity of the Baldus study, and acknowledges that McCleskey has demonstrated a risk that racial prejudice plays a role in capital sentencing in Georgia. Nonetheless, it finds the probability of prejudice insufficient to create constitutional concern. Close analysis of the Baldus study, however, in light of both statistical principles and human experience, reveals that the risk that race influenced McCleskey's sentence is intolerable by any imaginable standard.

The Baldus study indicates that, after taking into account some 230 nonracial factors that might legitimately influence a sentencer, the jury *more likely than not* would have spared McCleskey's life had his victim been black. The study distinguishes between those cases in which (1) the jury exercises virtually no discretion because the strength or weakness of aggravating factors usually suggests that only one out come is appropriate; and (2) cases reflecting an "intermediate" level of aggravation, in which the jury has considerable discretion in choosing a sentence. McCleskey's case falls into the intermediate range. In such cases, death is imposed in 34% of white-victim crimes and 14% of black-victim crimes, a difference of 139% in the rate of imposition of the death penalty. In other words, just under 59%—almost 6 in 10—defendants comparable to McCleskey would not have received the death penalty if their victims had been black.

Furthermore, even examination of the sentencing system as a whole, factoring in those cases in which the jury exercises little discretion, indicates the influence of race on capital sentencing. For the Georgia system as a whole, race accounts for a six percentage point difference in the rate at which capital punishment is imposed. Since death is imposed in 11% of all white-victim cases, the rate in comparably aggravated black-victim cases is 5%. The rate of capital sentencing in a white-victim case is thus 120% greater than the rate in a black-victim case. Put another way, over half—55%—of defendants in white-victim crimes in Georgia would not have been sentenced to die if their victims had been black. Of the more than 200 variables potentially relevant to a sentencing decision, race of the victim is a powerful explanation for variation in death sentence rates—as powerful as nonracial aggravating factors such as a prior murder conviction or acting as the principal planner of the homicide.

These adjusted figures are only the most conservative indication of the risk that race will influence the death sentences of defendants in Georgia. Data unadjusted for the mitigating or aggravating effect of other factors show an even more pronounced disparity by race. The capital sentencing rate for all white-victim cases was almost *11 times* greater than the rate for black-victim cases. Furthermore, blacks who kill whites are sentenced to death at nearly *22 times* the rate of blacks who kill blacks, and more than *7 times* the rate of whites who kill blacks. In addition, prosecutors seek the death penalty for 70% of black defendants with white victims, but for only 15% of black defendants with black victims, and only 19% of white defendants with black victims. Since our decision upholding the Georgia capital-sentencing system in *Gregg*, the State has executed 7 persons. All of the 7 were convicted of killing whites, and 6 of the 7 executed were black. Such execution figures are especially striking in light of the fact that, during the period encompassed by the Baldus study, only 9.2% of Georgia homicides involved black defendants and white victims, while 60.7% involved black victims.

McCleskey's statistics have particular force because most of them are the product of sophisticated multiple-regression analysis. Such analysis is designed precisely to identify patterns in the aggregate, even though we may not be able to reconstitute with certainty any individual decision that goes to make up that pattern. Multiple-regression analysis is particularly well-suited to identify the influence of impermissible considerations in sentencing, since it is able to control for permissible factors that may explain an apparent arbitrary pattern. While the decision-making process of body such as a jury may be complex, the Baldus study provides a massive compilation of the details that are most relevant to that decision. As we held in the Title VII context last term in *Bazemore* v. *Friday* (1986), a multiple-regression analysis need not include every conceivable variable to establish a party's case, as long as it includes those variables that account for the major factors that are likely to influence decisions. In this case, Professor Baldus in fact conducted additional regression analyses in response to criticisms and suggestions by the District Court, all of which confirmed, and some of which even strengthened, the study's original conclusions.

The statistical evidence in this case thus relentlessly documents the risk that McCleskey's sentence was influenced by racial considerations. This evidence shows that there is a better than even chance in Georgia that race will influence the decision to impose the death penalty: a majority of defendants in white-victim crimes would not have been sentenced to die if their victims had been black. In determining whether this risk is acceptable, our judgment must be shaped by the awareness that "[t]he risk of racial prejudice infecting a capital sentencing proceeding is especially serious in light of the complete finality of the death sentence" . . . and that "[i]t is of vital importance to the defendant and to the community that any decision to impose the death sentence be, and appear to be, based on reason rather than caprice or emotion." In determining the guilt of a defendant, a state must prove its case beyond a reasonable doubt. That is, we refuse to convict if the chance of error is simply less likely than not. Surely, we should not be willing to take a person's life if the chance that his death sentence was irrationally imposed is *more* likely than not. In light of the gravity of the interest at stake, petitioner's statistics on their face are a powerful demonstration of the type of risk that our Eighth Amendment jurisprudence has consistently condemned.

The Court cites four reasons for shrinking from the implications of McCleskey's evidence: the desirability of discretion for actors in the criminal-justice system, the existence of statutory safeguards against abuse of that discretion, the potential consequences for broader challenges to criminal sentencing, and an understanding of the contours of the judicial role. While these concerns underscore the need for sober deliberation, they do not justify rejecting evidence as convincing as McCleskey has presented.

The Court maintains that petitioner's claim "is antithetical to the fundamental role of discretion in our criminal justice system." It states that "[w]here the discretion that is fundamental to our criminal process is involved, we decline to assume that what is unexplained is invidious."

Reliance on race in imposing capital punishment, however, is antithetical to the very rationale for granting sentencing discretion. Discretion is a means, not an end. It is bestowed in order to permit the sentencer to "trea[t] each defendant in a capital case with that degree of respect due the uniqueness of the individual." The decision to impose the punishment of death must be based on a "particularized consideration of relevant aspects of the character and record of each convicted defendant." Failure to conduct such an individualized moral inquiry "treats all persons convicted of a designated offense not as unique individual human beings, but as members of a faceless, undifferentiated mass to be subjected to the blind infliction of the penalty of death."

Considering the race of a defendant or victim in deciding if the death penalty should be imposed is completely at odds with this concern that an individual be evaluated as a unique human being. Decisions influenced by race rest in part on a categorical assessment of the worth of human beings according to color, insensitive to whatever qualities the individuals in question may possess. Enhanced willingness to impose the death sentence on black defendants, or diminished willingness to render such a sentence when blacks are victims, reflects a devaluation of the lives of black persons. When confronted with evidence that race more likely than not plays such a role in a capital-sentencing system, it is plainly insufficient to say that the importance of discretion demands that the risk be higher before we will act—for in such a case the very end that discretion is designed to serve is being undermined.

Our desire for individualized moral judgments may lead us to accept some inconsistencies in sentencing outcomes. Since such decisions are not reducible to mathematical formulae, we are willing to assume that a certain degree of variation reflects the fact that no two defendants are completely alike. There is thus a presumption that actors in the criminal-justice system exercise their discretion in responsible fashion, and we do not automatically infer that sentencing patterns that do not comport with ideal rationality are suspect.

As we made clear in *Batson* v. *Kentucky* (1986), however, that presumption is rebuttable. *Batson* dealt with another arena in which considerable discretion traditionally has been afforded, the exercise of peremptory challenges. Those challenges are normally exercised without any indication whatsoever of the grounds for doing so. The rationale for this deference has been a belief that the unique characteristics of particular prospective jurors may raise concern on the part of the prosecution or defense, despite the fact that counsel may not be able to articulate that concern in a manner sufficient to support exclusion for cause. As with sentencing, therefore, peremptory challenges are justified as an occasion for particularized determinations related to specific individuals, and, as with sentencing, we presume that such challenges normally are not made on the basis of a factor such as race. As we said in *Batson,* however, such features do not justify imposing a "crippling burden of proof" in order to rebut that presumption. The Court in this case apparently seeks to do just that. On the basis of the need for individualized decisions, it rejects evidence, drawn from the most sophisticated capital-sentencing analysis ever performed, that reveals that race more likely than not infects capital-sentencing decisions. The Court's position converts a rebuttable presumption into a virtually conclusive one.

The Court also declines to find McCleskey's evidence sufficient in view of "the safeguards designed to minimize racial bias in the [capital sentencing] process." In *Gregg* v. *Georgia*, the Court rejected a facial challenge to the Georgia capital sentencing statute, describing such a challenge as based on "simply an assertion of lack of faith" that the system could operate in a fair manner." (White, J., concurring.) Justice White observed that the claim that prosecutors might act in an arbitrary fashion was "unsupported by any facts," and that prosecutors must be assumed to exercise their charging duties properly "[a]bsent facts to the contrary." It is clear that *Gregg* bestowed no permanent approval on the Georgia system. It simply held that the State's statutory safeguards were assumed sufficient to channel discretion without evidence otherwise.

It has now been over 13 years since Georgia adopted the provisions upheld in *Gregg*. Professor Baldus and his colleagues have compiled data on almost 2,500 homicides committed during the period 1973–1979. They have taken into account the influence of 230 nonracial variables, using a multitude of data from the State itself, and have produced striking evidence that the odds of being sentenced to death are significantly greater than average if a defendant is black or his or her victim is white. The challenge to the Georgia system is not speculative or theoretical; it is empirical. As a result, the Court cannot rely on the statutory safeguards in discounting McCleskey's evidence, for it is the very effectiveness of those safeguards that such evidence calls into question. While we may hope that a model of procedural fairness will curb the influence of race on sentencing, "we cannot simply assume that the model works as intended; we must critique its performance in terms of its results."

The Court next states that its unwillingness to regard the petitioner's evidence as sufficient is based in part on the fear that recognition of McCleskey's claim would open the door to widespread challenges to all aspects of criminal sentencing. Taken on its face, such a statement seems to suggest a fear of too much justice. Yet surely the majority would acknowledge that if striking evidence indicated that other minority groups, or women, or even persons with blond hair, were disproportionately sentenced to death, such a state of affairs would be repugnant to deeply rooted conceptions of fairness. The prospect that there may be more widespread abuse than McCleskey documents may be dismaying, but it does not justify complete abdication of our judicial role. The Constitution was framed fundamentally as a bulwark against governmental power, and preventing the arbitrary administration of punishment is a basic ideal of any society that purports to be governed by the rule of law.

In fairness, the Court's fear that McCleskey's claim is an invitation to descend a slippery slope also rests on the realization that any humanly imposed system of penalties will exhibit some imperfection. Yet to reject McCleskey's powerful evidence on this basis is to ignore both the qualitatively different character of the death penalty and the particular repugnance of racial discrimination, considerations which may properly be taken into account in determining whether various punishments are "cruel and unusual." Furthermore, it fails to take account of the unprecedented refinement and strength of the Baldus study.

It hardly needs reiteration that this Court has consistently acknowledged the uniqueness of the punishment of death. "Death, in its finality, differs more from life imprisonment than a 100-year prison term differs from one of only a year or two. Because of that qualitative difference, there is a corresponding difference in the need for reliability in the determination that death is the appropriate punishment." Furthermore, the relative interests of the state and the defendant differ dramatically in the death penalty context. The marginal benefits accruing to the state from obtaining the death penalty rather than life imprisonment are considerably less than the marginal difference to the defendant between death and life in prison. Such a disparity is an additional reason for tolerating scant arbitrariness in capital sentencing. Even those who believe that society can impose the death penalty in a manner sufficiently rational to justify its continuation must acknowledge that the level of rationality that is considered satisfactory must be *uniquely* high. As a result, the degree of arbitrariness that may be adequate to render the death penalty "cruel and unusual" punishment may not be adequate to invalidate lesser penalties. What these relative degrees of arbitrariness might be in other cases need not concern us here; the point is that majority's fear of wholesale invalidation of criminal sentences is unfounded.

The Court also maintains that accepting McCleskey's claim would pose a threat to all sentencing because of the prospect that a correlation might be demonstrated between sentencing outcomes and other personal characteristics. Again, such a view is indifferent to the considerations that enter into a determination of whether punishment is "cruel and unusual." Race is a consideration whose influence is expressly constitutionally proscribed. We have expressed a moral commitment, as embodied in our fundamental law, that this specific characteristic should not be the basis for allotting burdens and benefits. Three constitutional amendments, and numerous statutes, have been prompted specifically by the desire to address the effects of racism. "Over the years, this Court has consistently repudiated '[d]istinctions between citizens solely because of their ancestry' as being 'odious to a free people whose institutions are founded upon the doctrine of equality.' " Furthermore, we have explicitly acknowledged the illegitimacy of race as a consideration in capital sentencing. That a decision to impose the death penalty could be influenced by *race* is thus a particularly repugnant prospect, and evidence that race may play even a modest role in levying a death sentence should be enough to characterize that sentence as "cruel and unusual."

Certainly, a factor that we would regard as morally irrelevant, such as hair color, at least theoretically could be associated with sentencing results to such an extent that we would regard as arbitrary a system in which that factor played a significant role. As I have said above, however, the evaluation of evidence suggesting such a correlation must be informed not merely by statistics, but by history and experience. One could hardly contend that this nation has on the basis of hair color inflicted upon persons deprivation comparable to that imposed on the basis of race. Recognition of this fact would necessarily influence the evaluation of data suggesting the influence of hair color on sentencing, and would require evidence of statistical correlation even more powerful than that presented by the Baldus study.

Furthermore, the Court's fear of the expansive ramifications of a holding for McCleskey in this case is unfounded because it fails to recognize the uniquely sophisticated nature of the Baldus study. McCleskey presents evidence that is far and away the most refined data ever assembled on any system of punishment, data not readily replicated through casual effort. Moreover, that evidence depicts not merely arguable tendencies, but striking correlations, all the more powerful because nonracial explanations have been eliminated. Acceptance of petitioner's evidence would therefore establish a remarkably stringent standard of statistical evidence unlikely to be satisfied with any frequency.

The Court's projection of apocalyptic consequences for criminal sentencing is thus greatly exaggerated. The Court can indulge in such speculation only by ignoring its own jurisprudence demanding the highest scrutiny on issues of death and race. As a result, it fails to do justice to a claim in which both those elements are intertwined—an occasion calling for the most sensitive inquiry a court can conduct. Despite its acceptance of the validity of Warren McCleskey's evidence, the Court is willing to let his death sentence stand because it fears that we cannot successfully define a different standard for lesser punishments. This fear is baseless.

Finally, the Court justifies its rejection of McCleskey's claim by cautioning against usurpation of the legislatures' role in devising and monitoring criminal punishment. The Court is, of course, correct to emphasize the gravity of constitutional intervention and the importance that it be sparingly employed. The fact that "[c]apital punishment is now the law in more than two thirds of our States," however, does not diminish the fact that capital punishment is the most awesome act that a State can perform. The judiciary's role in this society counts for little if the use of governmental power to extinguish life does not elicit close scrutiny. It is true that society has a legitimate interest in punishment. Yet, as Alexander Bickel wrote:

> It is a premise we deduce not merely from the fact of a written constitution but from the history of the race, and ultimately as a moral judgment of the good society, that government should serve not only what we conceive from time to time to be our immediate material needs but also certain enduring values. This in part is what is meant by government under law.—A. Bickel, *The Least Dangerous Branch* (1962).

Our commitment to these values requires fidelity to them even when there is temptation to ignore them. Such temptation is especially apt to arise in criminal matters, for those granted constitutional protection in this context are those whom society finds most menacing and opprobious. Even less sympathetic are those we consider for the sentence of death, for execution "is a way of saying, 'You are not fit for this world, take your chance elsewhere.' " *Furman,* (Brennan, J., concurring).

For these reasons, "[t]he methods we employ in the enforcement of our criminal law have aptly been called the measures by which the quality of our civilization may be judged." Those whom we would banish from society or from the human community itself often speak in too faint a voice to be heard above society's demand for punishment. It is the particular role of courts to hear these voices, for the Constitution declares that the majoritarian chorus may not alone dictate the conditions of social life. The Court thus fulfills, rather than disrupts, the scheme of separation of powers by closely scrutinizing the imposition of the death penalty, for no decision of a society is more deserving of the "sober second thought."

At the time our Constitution was framed 200 years ago this year, blacks "had for more than a century before been regarded as beings of an inferior order, and altogether unfit to associate with the white race, either in social or political relations: and so far inferior, that they had no rights which the white man was bound to respect." *Dred Scott* v. *Sandford* (1857). Only 130 years ago, this Court relied on these observations to deny American citizenship to blacks. A mere three generations ago, this Court sanctioned racial segregation, stating that "[i]f one race be inferior to the other socially, the Constitution of the United States cannot put them upon the same plane." *Plessy* v. *Ferguson* (1896).

In more recent times, we have sought to free ourselves from the burden of this history. Yet is has been scarcely a generation since this Court's first decision striking down racial segregation, and barely two decades since the legislative prohibition of racial discrimination in major domains of national life. These have been honorable steps, but we cannot pretend that in three decades we have completely escaped the grip of an historical legacy spanning centuries. Warren McCleskey's evidence confronts us with the subtle and persistent influence of the past. His message is a disturbing one to a society that has formally repudiated racism, and a frustrating one to a Nation accustomed to regarding its destiny as the product of its own will. Nonetheless, we ignore him at our peril, for we remain imprisoned by the past as long as we deny its influence in the present.

It is tempting to pretend that minorities on death row share a fate in no way connected to our own, that our treatment of them sounds no echoes beyond the chambers in which they die. Such an illusion is ultimately corrosive, for the reverberations of injustice are not so easily confined. "The destinies of the two races in this country are indissolubly linked together," and the way in which we choose those who will die reveals the depth of moral commitment among the living.

The Court's decision today will not change what attorneys in Georgia tell other Warren McCleskeys about their chances of execution. Nothing will soften the harsh message they must convey, nor alter the prospect that race undoubtedly will continue to be a topic of discussion. McCleskey's evidence will not have obtained judicial acceptance, but that will not affect what is said on death row. However many criticisms of today's decision may be rendered, these painful conversations will serve as the most eloquent dissents of all.

In Defense of Capital Punishment

ERNEST VAN DEN HAAG

Van den Haag defends the death penalty on both legal and moral grounds. He argues, first, that there are no valid constitutional reasons for prohibiting its use in the case of serious crimes such as murder. He then attempts to show that, even if the death penalty is sometimes administered in an arbitrary manner, considerations of both utility and justice strongly support its continued use.

Three questions about the death penalty so overlap that they must each be answered. I shall ask seriatim: Is the death penalty constitutional? Is it useful? Is it morally justifiable?

This is a greatly revised version of a paper first delivered at a symposium sponsored by the Graduate School of Criminal Justice and the Criminal Justice Research Center of Albany, N.Y., in April 1977. Reprinted by permission of the author.

I. The Constitutional Question

The Fifth Amendment states that no one shall be "deprived of life, liberty, or property without due process of law," implying a "due process of law" to deprive persons of life. The Eighth Amendment prohibits "cruel and unusual punishment." It is unlikely that this prohibition was meant to supersede the Fifth Amendment, since the amendments were simultaneously enacted in 1791.[1]

The Fourteenth Amendment, enacted in 1868, reasserted and explicitly extended to the states the implied authority to "deprive of life, liberty, or property" by "due process of law." Thus, to regard the death penalty as unconstitutional one must believe that the standards which determine what is "cruel and unusual" have so evolved since 1868 as to prohibit now what was authorized then, and that the Constitution authorizes the courts to overrule laws in the light of *new* moral standards. What might these standards be? And what shape must their evolution take to be constitutionally decisive?

Consensus

A moral consensus, intellectual or popular, could have evolved to find execution "cruel and unusual." It did not. Intellectual opinion is divided. Polls suggest that most people would vote for the death penalty. Congress recently has legislated the death penalty for skyjacking under certain conditions. The representative assemblies of two-thirds of the states did re-enact capital punishment when previous laws were found constitutionally defective.[2]

If, however, there were a consensus against the death penalty, the Constitution expects the political process, rather than judicial decisions, to reflect it. Courts are meant to interpret the laws made by the political process and to set constitutional limits to it—not to replace it by responding to a presumed moral consensus. Surely the "cruel and unusual" phrase was not meant to authorize the courts to become legislatures.[3] Thus, neither a consensus of moral opinion nor a moral discovery by judges is meant to be disguised as a constitutional interpretation. Even when revealed by a burning bush, new moral norms were not meant to become constitutional norms by means of court decisions.[4] To be sure, the courts in the past have occasionally done away with obsolete kinds of punishment—but never in the face of legislative and popular opposition and reenactment. Abolitionists constantly press the courts now to create rather than to confirm obsolescence. That courts are urged to do what so clearly is for voters and lawmakers to decide suggests that the absence of consensus for abolition is recognized by the opponents of capital punishment. What then can the phrase "cruel and unusual punishment" mean today?

Cruel may be understood to mean excessive—punishment without, or beyond, a rational-utilitarian purpose. Since capital punishment excludes rehabilitation and is not needed for incapacitation, the remaining rational-utilitarian purpose would be deterrence, the reduction of the rate at which the crime punished is committed by others. I shall consider this reduction below. Here I wish to note that, if the criterion for the constitutionality of any punishment were an actual demonstration of its rational-utilitarian effectiveness, all legal punishments would be in as much constitutional jeopardy as the death penalty. Are fines for corporations deterrent? rehabilitative? incapacitative? Is a jail term for marijuana possession? Has it ever been established that ten years in prison are doubly as deterrent as five, or at least sufficiently more deterrent? (I don't pretend to know what "sufficiently" might mean; whether 10 percent or 80 percent added deterrence would warrant 100 percent added severity.)

The Constitution certainly does not require a demonstration of rational-utilitarian effects for any punishment. Such a demonstration so far has not been available. To demand it for one penalty—however grave—and not for others, when it is known that no such demonstration is available, or has been required hitherto for any punishment, seems unjustified. Penalties have always been regarded as constitutional if they can be plausibly intended (rather than demonstrated) to be effective (useful), and if they are not grossly excessive, i.e., unjust.

Justice, a rational but non-utilitarian purpose of punishment, requires that it be proportioned to the felt gravity of the crime. Thus, constitutional justice authorizes, even calls for, a higher penalty the graver the crime. One cannot demand that this constitutionally required escalation stop short of the death penalty unless one furnishes positive proof of its irrationality by showing injustice, i.e., disproportionality (to the felt gravity of the crime punished or to other punishments of similar crimes), as well as ineffectiveness, i.e., uselessness in reducing the crime rate. There is no proof of cruelty here in either sense.

"Unusual" is generally interpreted to mean either randomly capricious and therefore unconstitutional, or capricious in a biased, discriminatory way, so as particularly to burden specifiable groups, and therefore unconstitutional. (Random arbitrariness might violate the Eighth, biased arbitrariness the Fourteenth Amendment, which promises "the equal protection of the laws.") Apart from the historical interpretation noted above (note 1), "unusual" seems to mean "unequal" then. The dictionary equivalent—"rare"—seems to be regarded as relevant only inasmuch as it implies "unequal." Indeed it is hard to see why rarity should be objectionable otherwise.

For the sake of argument, let me grant that either or both forms of capriciousness prevail[5] and that they are less tolerable with respect to the death penalty than with respect to milder penalties—which certainly are not meted out less capriciously. However prevalent, neither form of capriciousness would argue for abolishing the death penalty. Capriciousness is not inherent in that penalty, or in any penalty, but occurs in its distribution. Therefore, the remedy lies in changing the laws and procedures which distribute the penalty. It is the process of distribution which is capable of discriminating, not that which it distributes.

Unavoidable Capriciousness

If capricious distribution places some convicts, or groups of convicts, at an unwarranted disadvantage,[6] can it be remedied enough to satisfy the Eighth and Fourteenth Amendments? Some capriciousness is unavoidable because decisions of the criminal justice system necessarily rest on accidental factors at many points, such as the presence or absence of witnesses to an act; or the cleverness or clumsiness of police officers who exercise their discretion in arresting suspects and seizing evidence. All court decisions must rest on the available and admissible evidence for, rather than the actuality of, guilt. Availability of evidence is necessarily accidental to the actuality of whatever it is that the evidence is needed for. Accident is the capriciousness of fate.

Now, if possible without loss of other desiderata, accident and human capriciousness should be minimized. But, obviously, discretionary judgments cannot be avoided altogether. The Framers of the Constitution were certainly aware of the unavoidable elements of discretion which affect all human decisions, including those of police officers, of prosecutors, and of the courts. Because it always was unavoidable, discretion no more speaks against the constitutionality of the criminal justice system or of any of its penalties now than it did when the Constitution was written—unless something has evolved since, to make unavoidable discretion, tolerable before, intolerable now, at least for the death penalty. I know of no such evolution; and I would think it was up to the legislative branch of government to register it had it occurred.

The Constitution, though it enjoins us to minimize capriciousness, does not enjoin a standard of unattainable perfection or exclude penalties because that standard has not been attained.[7] Actually, modern legislative trends hitherto have favored enlargement of discretion in the judicial process. I have always thought that enlargement to be excessive, immoral, irrational, and possibly unconstitutional—even when not abused for purposes of discrimination. Yet, though we should not enlarge it *praeter necessitatem,* some discretion is unavoidable and even desirable, and no reason for giving up any punishment.

Avoidable Capriciousness

Capriciousness should be prevented by abolishing penalties capriciously distributed only in one case: when it is so unavoidable and so excessive that penalties are randomly distributed between the guilty and the innocent. When that is not the case, the abuses of discretion which lead to discrimination against particular groups of defendants or convicts certainly require correction, but not abolition of the penalty abused by maldistribution.

II. Preliminary Moral Issues

Justice and Equality

Regardless of constitutional interpretation, the morality and legitimacy of the abolitionist argument from capriciousness, or discretion, or discrimination, would be more persuasive if it were alleged that those selectively executed are not guilty. But the argument merely maintains that some other guilty but more favored persons, or groups, escape the death penalty. This is hardly sufficient for letting anyone else found guilty escape the penalty. On the contrary, that some guilty persons or groups elude it argues for extending the death penalty to them. Surely "due process of law" is meant to do justice; and "the equal protection of the law" is meant to extend justice equally to all. Nor do I read the Constitution to command us to prefer equality to justice. When we clamor for "equal justice for all" it is justice which is to be equalized and extended, and which therefore is the prior desideratum, not to be forsaken and replaced by equality but rather to be extended.

Justice requires punishing the guilty—as many of the guilty as possible, even if only some can be punished—and sparing the innocent—as many of the innocent as possible, even if not all are spared. Morally, justice must always be preferred to equality. It would surely be wrong to treat everybody with equal injustice in preference to meting out justice at least to some. Justice then cannot ever permit sparing some guilty persons, or punishing some innocent ones, for the sake of equality—because others have been unjustly spared or punished. In practice, penalties never could be applied if we insisted that they cannot be inflicted on any guilty person unless we can make sure that they are equally applied to all other guilty persons. Anyone familiar with law enforcement knows that punishments can be inflicted only on an unavoidably capricious, at best a random, selection of the guilty. I see no more merit in the attempt to persuade the courts to let all capital-crime defendants go free of capital punishment because some have wrongly escaped it than I see in an attempt to persuade the courts to let all burglars go because some have wrongly escaped imprisonment.

Although it hardly warrants serious discussion, the argument from capriciousness looms large in briefs and decisions because for the last seventy years courts have tried—unproductively—to prevent errors of procedure, or of evidence collection, or of decision-making, by the paradoxical method of letting defendants go free as a punishment, or warning, or deterrent, to errant law enforcers. The strategy admittedly never has prevented the errors it was designed to prevent—although it has released countless guilty persons. But however ineffective it be, the strategy had a rational purpose. The rationality, on the other hand, of arguing that a penalty must be abolished because of allegations that some guilty persons escape it, is hard to fathom—even though the argument was accepted by some Justices of the Supreme Court.

The Essential Moral Question

Is the death penalty morally just and/or useful? This is the essential moral, as distinguished from constitutional, question. Discrimination is irrelevant to this moral question. If the death penalty were distributed quite equally and uncapriciously and with superhuman perfection to all the guilty, but was morally unjust, it would remain unjust in each case. Contrariwise, if the death penalty is morally just, however discriminatorily applied to only some of the guilty, it does remain just in each case in which it is applied. Thus, if it were applied exclusively to guilty males, and never to guilty females, the death penalty, though unequally applied, would remain just. For justice consists in punishing the guilty and sparing the innocent, and its equal extension, though desirable, is not part of it. It is part of equality, not of justice (or injustice), which is what equality equalizes. The same consideration would apply if some benefit were distributed only to males but not equally to deserving females. The inequality would not argue against the benefit, or against distribution to deserving males, but rather for distribution to equally deserving females. Analogously, the nondistribution of the death penalty to guilty females would argue for applying it to them as well, and not against applying it to guilty males.

The utilitarian (political) effects of unequal justice may well be detrimental to the social fabric because they outrage our passion for equality, particularly for equality before the law. Unequal justice is also morally repellent. Nonetheless unequal justice is justice still. What is repellent is the incompleteness, the inequality, not the justice. The guilty do not become innocent or less deserving of punishment because others escaped it. Nor does any innocent deserve punishment because others suffer it. Justice remains just, however unequal, while injustice remains unjust, however equal. However much each is desired, justice and equality are not identical. Equality before the law should be extended and enforced, then—but not at the expense of justice.

Maldistribution Among the Guilty: A Sham Argument

Capriciousness, at any rate, is used as a sham argument against capital punishment by all abolitionists I have ever known. They would oppose the death penalty if it could be meted out without any discretion whatsoever. They would oppose the death penalty in a homogeneous country without racial discrimination. And they would oppose the death penalty if the incomes of those executed and of those spared were the same. Abolitionists oppose the death penalty, not its possible maldistribution. They should have the courage of their convictions.

Maldistribution Between the Guilty and the Innocent: Another Sham Argument

What about persons executed in error? The objection here is not that some of the guilty get away, but that some of the innocent do not—a matter far more serious than discrimination among the guilty. Yet, when urged by abolitionists, this too is a sham argument, as are all distributional arguments. For abolitionists are opposed to the death penalty for the guilty as much as for the innocent. Hence, the question of guilt, if at all relevant to their position, cannot be decisive for them. Guilt is decisive only to those who urge the death penalty for the guilty. They must worry about distribution—part of the justice they seek.

Miscarriages of Justice

The execution of innocents believed guilty is a miscarriage of justice which must be opposed whenever detected. But such miscarriages of justice do not warrant abolition of the death penalty. Unless the moral drawbacks of an activity or practice, which include the possible death of innocent bystanders, outweigh the moral advantages, which include the innocent lives that might be saved by it, the activity is warranted. Most human activities—construction, manufacturing, automobile and air traffic, sports, not to speak of wars and revolutions—cause the death of some innocent bystanders. Nevertheless, if the advantages sufficiently outweigh the disadvantages, human activities, including those of the penal system with all its punishments, are morally justified. Consider now the advantages in question.

III. Deterrence

New Evidence

Is there evidence for the usefulness of the death penalty in securing the life of the citizens? Researchers in the past found no statistical evidence for the effects sought: i.e., marginal deterrent effects; deterrent effects over and above those of alternative sanctions. However, in the last few years new and more sophisticated research has led, for instance, Professor Isaac Ehrlich to conclude that over the period 1933–1969, "an additional execution per year . . . may have resulted on the average in seven or eight fewer murders."[8] Other investigators have confirmed Ehrlich's tentative results. Not surprisingly, refutations have been attempted, and Professor Ehrlich has answered them. He has also published a new cross-sectional analysis of the data which confirms the conclusions of his original (time-series) study.[9] The matter will remain controversial for some time,[10] but two tentative conclusions can be drawn with some confidence by now. First, Ehrlich has shown that previous investigations, which did not find deterrent effects of the death penalty, suffer from fatal defects. Second, there is now some likelihood—much more than hitherto—of demonstrating marginal deterrent effects statistically.

The Choice

Thus, with respect to deterrence, we must choose (1) to trade the certain shortening of the life of a convicted murderer for the survival of between seven and eight innocent victims whose future murder by others may be less likely if the convicted murderer is executed. Or (2) to trade the certain lengthening of the life of a convicted murderer for the possible loss of the lives of between seven and eight innocent victims, who may be more likely to be murdered by others because of our failure to execute the convicted murderer.[11]

If we were certain that executions have a zero marginal effect, they could not be justified in deterrent terms. But even the pre-Ehrlich investigations never did demonstrate this. They merely found that an above-zero effect cannot be demonstrated statistically. While we do now know at present the degree of confidence with which we can assign an above-zero marginal deterrent effect to executions, we can be more confident than in the past. It seems morally indefensible to let convicted murderers survive at the probable—even at the merely possible—expense of the lives of innocent victims who might have been spared had the murderers been executed.

Non-Deterrence as a Sham Argument

Most of the studies purporting to show that capital punishment produces no added deterrence, or that it cannot be shown to do so, were made by abolitionists, such as Professor Thorsten Sellin. They were used to show the futility of the death penalty. Relying on their intuition as well as on these studies, many abolitionists still are convinced that the death penalty is no more deterrent than life imprisonment. And they sincerely believe that the failure of capital punishment to produce additional deterrence argues for abolishing it. However, the more passionate and committed abolitionists use the asserted ineffectiveness of the death penalty as a deterrent as a sham argument—just as they use alleged capriciousness and maldistribution in application. They use the argument for debating purposes—but actually would abolish the death penalty even if it were an effective deterrent, just as they would abolish the death penalty if it were neither discriminatorily nor otherwise maldistributed.

Professors Charles Black (Yale Law School) and Hugo Adam Bedau (Tufts, Philosophy) are both well known for their public commitment to abolition of the death penalty, attested to by numerous writings. At a symposium held on October 15, 1977 at the Arizona State University at Tempe, Arizona, they were asked to entertain the hypothesis—whether or not contrary to fact—that the death penalty is strongly deterrent over and above alternative penalties: Would they favor abolition in the face of conclusive proof of a strong deterrent effect over and above that of alternative penalties? Both gentlemen answered affirmatively. They were asked whether they would still abolish the death penalty if they knew that abolition (and replacement by life imprisonment) would increase the homicide rate by 10 percent, 20 percent, 50 percent, 100 percent, or 1,000 percent. Both gentlemen continued to answer affirmatively.

I am forced to conclude that Professors Black and Bedau think the lives of convicted murderers (however small their number) are more worth preserving than the lives of an indefinite number of innocent victims (however great their number). Or, the principle of abolition is more important to them than the lives of any number of innocent murder victims who would be spared if convicted murderers were executed.

I have had occasion subsequently to ask former Attorney General Ramsey Clark the same questions; he answered as Professors Black and Bedau did, stressing that nothing could persuade him to favor the death penalty—however deterrent it might be. (Mr. Clark has kindly permitted me to quote his view here.)

Now, Professors Black and Bedau and Mr. Clark do *not* believe that the death penalty adds deterrence. They do not believe therefore—regardless of the evidence—that abolition would cause an increase in the homicide rate. But the question they were asked, and which—after some dodging—they answered forthrightly, had nothing to do with the acceptance or rejection of the deterrent effect of the death penalty. It was a hypothetical question: If it were deterrent, would you still abolish the death penalty? Would you still abolish it if it were very deterrent, so that abolition would lead to a quantum jump in the murder rate? They answered affirmatively.

These totally committed abolitionists, then, are not interested in deterrence. They claim that the death penalty does not add to deterrence only as a sham argument. Actually, whether or not the death penalty deters is, to them, irrelevant. The intransigence of these committed humanitarians is puzzling as well as inhumane. Passionate ideological commitments have been known to have such effects. These otherwise kind and occasionally reasonable persons do not want to see murderers executed ever—however many innocent lives can be saved thereby. *Fiat injustitia, pereat humanitas.*

Experiments?

In principle one could experiment to test the deterrent effect of capital punishment. The most direct way would be to legislate the death penalty for certain kinds of murder if committed on weekdays, but never on Sunday. Or, on Monday, Wednesday, and Friday, and not on other days; on other days, life imprisonment would be the maximum sentence. (The days could be changed around every few years to avoid possible bias.) I am convinced there will be fewer murders on death-penalty than on life-imprisonment days. Unfortunately the experiment faces formidable obstacles.[12]

The Burden of Proof of Usefulness

Let me add a common-sense remark. Our penal system rests on the proposition that more severe penalties are more deterrent than less sever penalties. We assume, rightly, I believe, that a $5 fine deters rape less than a $500 fine, and that the threat of five years in prison will deter more than either fine.[13] This assumption of the penal system rests on the common experience that, once aware of them, people learn to avoid natural dangers the more likely these are to be injurious and the more severe the likely injuries. Else the survival of the human race would be hard to explain. People endowed with ordinary common sense (a class that includes a modest but significant number of sociologists) have found no reason why behavior with respect to legal dangers should differ from behavior with respect to natural dangers. Indeed, it doesn't. Hence, all legal systems proportion threatened penalties to the gravity of crimes, both to do justice and to achieve deterrence in proportion to that gravity.

But if, *ceteris paribus,* the more severe the penalty the greater the deterrent effect, then the most severe available penalty—the death penalty—would have the greatest deterrent effect. Arguments to the contrary assume either than capital crimes never are deterrable (sometimes merely because not all capital crimes have been deterred), or that, beyond life imprisonment, the deterrent effect of added severity is necessarily zero. Perhaps. But the burden of proof must be borne by those who presume to have located the point of zero marginal returns before the death penalty.

The Threat of Death Needed in Special Circumstances

Another common-sense observation. Without the death penalty, we necessarily confer immunity on just those persons most likely to be in need of deterrent threats: thus, prisoners serving life sentences can kill fellow prisoners or guards with impunity. Prison wardens are unlikely to be able to prevent violence in prisons as long as they give humane treatment to inmates and have no serious threats of additional punishment available for the murderers among them who are already serving life sentences. I cannot see the moral or utilitarian reasons for giving permanent immunity to homicidal life prisoners, thereby endangering the other prisoners and the guards, in effect preferring the life prisoners to their victims who *could* be punished if they murdered.

Outside prison an offender who expects a

life sentence for his offense may murder his victim or witnesses, or the arresting officer, to improve his chances of escaping. He could not be threatened with an additional penalty for his additional crime—an open invitation. Only the death penalty could deter in such cases.[14] If there is but a possibility that it will, we should retain it. But I believe there is a *probability* that the threat of the death penalty will deter.

Reserved for the Worst Crimes

However, effective deterrence requires that the threat of the ultimate penalty be reserved for the worst crime from which the offender may be deterred by that threat. Hence, the extreme punishment should not be prescribed when the offender, because already threatened by it, might feel he can add further crimes with impunity. Thus, rape, or kidnapping, should not incur the death penalty, while killing the victim of either crime should.[15] (The death penalty for rape may actually function as an incentive to murder the victim/witness.) This may not stop an Eichmann after his first murder; but it will stop most people before. To be sure, an offender not deterred from murdering one victim by the threat of execution is unlikely to be deterred from additional murders by further threats. The range of effective punishments is not infinite; on the contrary, it is necessarily more restricted than the range of possible crimes. Some offenders cannot be deterred by any threat. But most people can be; and most people respond to the size of the threat addressed to them. Since death is the ultimate penalty—the greatest threat available—it must be reserved for the ultimate crime even though it cannot always prevent it.

IV. Some Popular Arguments

Consider now some popular arguments against capital punishment.

Barbarization

According to Beccaria, with the death penalty the "laws which punish homicide . . . themselves commit it," thus giving "an example ofbarbarity." Those who speak of "legalized murder" use an oxymoronic phrase to echo this allegation. However, punishments—fines, incarcerations, or executions—although often physically identical to the crimes punished, are neither crimes, nor their moral equivalent. The difference between crimes and lawful acts, including punishments, is not physical, but legal: crimes differ from other acts by being unlawful. Driving a stolen car is a crime, though not physically distinguishable from driving a car lawfully owned. Unlawful imprisonment and kidnapping need not differ physically from the lawful arrest and incarceration used to punish unlawful imprisonment and kidnapping. Finally, whether a lawful punishment gives an "example of barbarity" depends on how the moral difference between crime and punishment is perceived. To suggest that its physical quality, *ipso facto,* morally disqualifies the punishment is to assume what is to be shown.

It is quite possible that all displays of violence, criminal or punitive, influence people to engage in unlawful imitations. This seems one good reason not to have public executions. But it does not argue against executions. Objections to displaying on TV the process of violently subduing a resistant offender do not argue against actually subduing him.[16] Arguments against the public display of vivisections, or of the effects of painful medications, do not argue against either. Arguments against the public display of sexual activity do not argue against sexual activity. Arguments against public executions, then, do not argue against executions.[17] The deterrent effect of punishments depends on their being known. But it does not depend on punishments' being carried out publicly. The threat of imprisonment deters, but incarcerated persons are not on public display.

Crimes of Passion

Abolitionists often maintain that most capital crimes are "acts of passion" which (a) could not be restrained by the threat of the death penalty, and (b) do not deserve it morally even if other crimes might. It is not clear to me why a crime motivated by, say, sexual passion is morally less deserving of punishment than one motivated by passion for money. Is the sexual passion morally more respectable than others? or more gripping? or just more popular? Generally, is violence in personal conflicts morally more excusable than violence among people who do not know each other? A precarious case might be made for such a view, but I shall not attempt to make it.

Perhaps it is true, however, that many murders are irrational "acts of passion" which cannot be deterred by the threat of the death penalty. Either for this reason or because "crimes of passion" are thought less blameworthy than other homicides, most "crimes of passion" are not punishable by death now.[18]

But if most murders are irrational acts, it would therefore seem that the traditional threat of the death penalty has succeeded in deterring most rational people, or most people when rational, from committing murder, and that the fear of the penalty continues to deter all but those who are so irrational that they cannot be deterred by any threat. Hardly a reason for abolishing the death penalty. Indeed, that capital crimes are committed mostly by irrational persons and only by some rational ones would suggest that more rational persons might commit these crimes if the penalty were lower. This hardly argues against capital punishment. Else we would have to abolish penalties whenever they succeed in deterring people. Yet abolitionists urge that capital punishment be abolished because capital crimes are most often committed by the irrational—as though deterring the rational is not quite enough.

Samuel Johnson

Finally, some observations on an anecdote reported by Boswell and repeated ever since *ad nauseam*. Dr. Johnson found pickpockets active in a crowd assembled to see one of their number hanged. He concluded that executions do not deter. His conclusion does not follow from his observation.

1. Since the penalty Johnson witnessed was what pickpockets had expected all along, they had no reason to reduce their activities. Deterrence is expected to increase (i.e., crime is expected to decrease) only when penalties do. It is unreasonable to expect people who entered a criminal occupation—e.g., that of pickpocket—fully aware of the risks, to be subsequently deterred by those risks if they are not increased. They will not be deterred unless the penalty becomes more severe, or is inflicted more often.
2. At most, a public execution could have had the deterrent effect on pickpockets expected by Dr. Johnson because of its visibility. But visibility may also have had a contrary effect: the spectacle of execution was probably more fascinating to the crowd than other spectacles; it distracted attention from the activities of pickpockets and thereby increased their opportunities more than other spectacles would. Hence, an execution crowd might have been more inviting to pickpockets than other crowds. (As mentioned before, deterrence depends on knowledge, but does not require visibility.)
3. Even when the penalty is greatly increased, let alone when it is unchanged, the deterrent effect of penalties is usually slight with respect to those already engaged in criminal activities.[19] Deterrence is effective in the main by restraining people not as yet committed to a criminal occupation from entering it. This point bears some expansion.

The risk of penalty is the cost of crime offenders expect. When this cost (the penalty multiplied by the risk of suffering it) is high enough, relative to the benefit the crime is expected to yield, the cost will deter a considerable number of people who would have entered a criminal occupation had the cost been lower. When the net benefit is very low, only those who have no other opportunities at all, or are irrationally attracted to it, will want to engage in an illegal activity such as picking pockets. In this respect the effects of the cost of crimes are not different from the effects of the cost of automobiles or movie tickets, or from the effects of the cost (effort, risks, and other disadvantages) of any activity relative to its benefits. When (comparative) net benefits decrease because of cost increases, so does the flow of new entrants. But those already in the occupation usually continue. *Habits, law-abiding or criminal, are less influenced by costs than habit formation is.* That is as true for the risk of penalties as for any other cost.

Most deterrence studies disregard the fact that the major effect of the legal threat system is on habit formation rather than on habits formed. It is a long- rather than a short-run effect. By measuring only the short-run effects (on habits already formed) rather than the far more important long-run (habit-forming) effects of the threat system, such studies underrate the effectiveness of the deterrence.

4. Finally, Dr. Johnson did not actually address the question of the deterrent effect of execution in any respect whatever. To do so would have had to compare the number of pocket-picking episodes in the crowd assembled to witness the execution with the number of such episodes in a similar crowd assembled for some other purpose. He did not do so, probably because he thought that a deterrent effect occurs only if the crime is altogether eliminated. That is a common misunderstanding. But crime can only be reduced, not eliminated. However harsh the penalties there are always non-deterrables. Many, perhaps most, people can be deterred, but never all.

V. Final Moral Considerations

The Motive of Revenge

One objection to capital punishment is that it gratifies the desire for revenge, regarded as morally unworthy. The Bible has the Lord declare: "Vengeance is mine" (Romans 12:19). He thus legitimized vengeance and reserved it to Himself, probably because it would otherwise be disruptive. But He did not deprecate the desire for vengeance.

Indeed Romans 12:19 barely precedes Romans 13:4, which tells us that the ruler "beareth not the sword in vain: for he is the minister of God, a revenger to execute wrath upon him that doeth evil." It is not unreasonable to interpret Romans 12:19 to suggest that revenge is to be delegated by the injured to the ruler, "the minister of God" who is "to execute wrath." The Bible also enjoins, "the murderer shall surely be put to death" (Numbers 35:16–18), recognizing that the death penalty can be warranted—whatever the motive. Religious tradition certainly suggests no less. However, since religion expects justice and vengeance in the world to come, the faithful may dispense with either in this world, and with any particular penalties—though they seldom have. But a secular state must do justice here and now—it cannot assume that another power, elsewhere, will do justice where its courts did not.

The motives for the death penalty may indeed include vengeance. Vengeance is a compensatory and psychologically reparatory satisfaction for an injured party, group, or society. I do not see wherein it is morally blameworthy. When regulated and controlled by law, vengeance is also socially useful: legal vengeance solidifies social solidarity against lawbreakers and probably is the only alternative to the disruptive private revenge of those who feel harmed. Abolitionists want to promise murderers that what they did to their victims will never be done to them. That promise strikes most people as psychologically incongruous. It is.

At any rate, vengeance is irrelevant to the function of the death penalty. It must be justified independently, by its purpose, whatever the motive. An action, a rule, or a penalty cannot be justified or discredited by the motive for it. No rule should be discarded or regarded as morally wrong (or right) because of the motive of those who support it. Actions, rules, or penalties are justified not by the motives of supporters but by their purpose and by their effectiveness in achieving it without excessively impairing other objectives.[20] Capital punishment is warranted if it achieves its purpose—doing justice and deterring crime—regardless of whether or not it is motivated by vengeful feelings.

Characteristics

Before turning to its purely moral aspects, we must examine some specific characteristics of capital punishment. It is feared above all punishments because (1) it is not merely irreversible, as most other penalties are, but also irrevocable; (2) it hastens an event which, unlike pain, deprivation, or injury, is unique in every life and never has been reported on by anyone. Death is an experience that cannot actually be experienced and that ends all experience. Actually, being dead is no different from not being born—a (non)experience we all had before being born. But death is not so perceived. The process of dying, a quite different matter, is confused with it. In turn, dying is feared mainly because death is anticipated—even though death is feared because confused with dying. At any rate, the fear of death is universal and is often attached to the penalty that hastens it—as though without that penalty death would not come. (3) However, the penalty is feared for another reason as well. When death is imposed as a deliberate punishment by one's fellow men, it signifies a complete severing of human solidarity. The convict is explicitly and dramatically rejected by his fellow humans, found unworthy of their society, of sharing life with them. The rejection exacerbates the natural separation anxiety of those who expect imminent death, the fear of final annihilation. Inchoate as these characteristics are in most minds, the specific deterrent effect of executions depends on them, and the moral justification of the death penalty, above and beyond the deterrent effect, does no less.

Methodological Aside

Hitherto I have relied on logic and fact. Without relinquishing either, I must appeal to plausibility as well, as I turn to questions of morality unalloyed by other issues. For, whatever ancillary service facts and logic can render, what one is persuaded to accept as morally right or wrong depends on what appears to be plausible in the end. Outside the realm of morals one relies on plausibility only in the beginning.

The Value of Life

If there is nothing for the sake of which one may be put to death, can there ever be anything worth risking one's life for? If there is nothing worth dying for, is there any moral value worth living for? Is a life that cannot be transcended by—and given up, or taken, for—anything beyond itself more valuable than one that can be transcended? Can it be that existence, life itself, is the highest moral value, never to be given up, or taken, for the sake of anything? And, psychologically, does a social value system in which life itself, however it is lived, becomes the highest of goods enhance the value of human life or cheapen it? I shall content myself here with raising these questions.[21]

Homo Homini Res Sacra

"The life of each man should be sacred to each other man," the ancients tell us. They unflinchingly executed murderers.[22] They realized it is not enough to proclaim the sacredness and inviolability of human life. It must be secured as well, by threatening with the loss of their own life those who violate what has been proclaimed as inviolable—the right of innocents to live. Else the inviolability of human life is neither credibly proclaimed nor actually protected. No society can profess that the lives of its members are secure if those who did not allow innocent others to continue living are themselves allowed to continue living—at the expense of the community. To punish a murderer by incarcerating him as one does a pickpocket cannot but cheapen human life. Murder differs in quality from other crimes and deserves, therefore, a punishment that differs in quality from other punishments. There is a discontinuity. It should be underlined, not blurred.

If it were shown that no punishment is more deterrent than a trivial fine, capital punishment for murder would remain just, even if not useful. For murder is not a trifling offense. Punishment must be proportioned to the gravity of the crime, if only to denounce it and to vindicate the importance of the norm violated. Wherefore all penal systems proportion punishments to crimes. The worse the crime the higher the penalty deserved. Why not then the highest penalty—death—for the worst crime—wanton murder? Those rejecting the death penalty have the burden of showing that no crime ever deserves capital punishment[23]—a burden which they have not so far been willing to bear.

Abolitionists insist that we all have an imprescriptible right to live to our natural term: if the innocent victim had a right to live, so does the murderer. That takes egalitarianism too far for my taste. The crime sets victim and murderer apart; if the victim did, the murderer does not deserve to live. If innocents are to be secure in their lives murderers cannot be. The thought that murderers are to be given as much right to live as their victims oppresses me. So does the thought that a Stalin, a Hitler, an Idi Amin should have as much right to live as their victims did.

Failure of Nerve

Never to execute a wrongdoer, regardless of how depraved his acts, is to proclaim that no act can be so irredeemably vicious as to deserve death—that no human being can be wicked enough to be deprived of life. Who actually can believe that? I find it easier to believe that those who affect such a view suffer from a failure of nerve. They do not think themselves—and therefore anyone else—competent to decide questions of life and death. Aware of human frailty, they shudder at the gravity of the decision and refuse to make it. The irrevocability of a verdict of death is contrary to the modern spirit that likes to pretend that nothing ever is definitive, that everything is open-ended, that doubts must always be entertained and revisions must always remain possible. Such an attitude may be helpful to the reflections of inquiring philosophers and scientists; but it is not proper for courts. They must make final judgments beyond a reasonable doubt. They must decide. They can evade decisions on life and death only by giving up their paramount duties: to do justice, to secure the lives of the citizens, and to vindicate the norms society holds inviolable.

One may object that the death penalty either cannot actually achieve the vindication of violated norms, or is not needed for it. If so, failure to inflict death on the criminal does not belittle the crime, or imply that the life of the criminal is of greater importance than the moral value he violated or the harm he did to his victim. But it is not so. In all societies the degree of social disapproval of wicked acts is expressed in the degree of punishment threatened.[24] Thus, punishments both proclaim and enforce social values according to the importance given to them. There is no other way for society to affirm its values. There is no other effective way of denouncing socially disapproved acts. To refuse to punish any crime with death is to suggest that the negative value of a crime can never exceed the positive value of the life of the person who committed it. I find that proposition quite implausible.

NOTES

1. Apparently the punishment must be both—else cruel *or* unusual would have done. Historically it appears that punishments were prohibited if unusual in 1791 *and* cruel: the

Framers did want to prohibit punishments, even cruel ones, only if already unusual in 1791; they did prohibit new (unusual) punishments if cruel. The Eighth Amendment was not meant to apply to the death penalty in 1791 since it was not unusual then; nor was the Eighth Amendment intended to be used against capital punishment in the future, regardless of whether it may have come to be considered cruel: it is neither a new penalty nor one unusual in 1791.

2. There may be a consensus against the death penalty among the college educated. If so, it demonstrates (a) the power of indoctrination wielded by sociologists; (b) the fact that those who are least threatened by violence are most inclined to do without the death penalty. College graduates are less often threatened by murder than the uneducated.
3. See Chief Justice Burger dissenting in *Furman:* "In a democratic society legislatures not courts are constituted to respond to the will and consequently the moral values of the people."
4. The First Amendment might be invoked against such sources of revelation. When specific laws do not suffice to decide a case, courts, to be sure, make decisions based on general legal principles. But the death penalty (as distinguished from applications) raises no serious legal problem.
5. Attention should be drawn to John Hagan's "Extralegal Attributes and Criminal Sentencing" (*Law and Society Review,* Spring 1974), which throws doubt on much of the discrimination which sociologists have found.
6. I am referring throughout to discrimination among those already convicted of capital crimes. That discrimination can be tested. However, the fact that a higher proportion of blacks, or poor people, than of whites, or rich people, are found guilty of capital crimes does not *ipso facto* indicate discrimination, any more than does the fact that a comparatively high proportion of blacks or poor people become professional baseball players or boxers.
7. Although this is the burden of Charles Black's *Capital Punishment: The Inevitability of Caprice and Mistake* (Norton, 1974). *Codex ipsus loquitur.*
8. "The Deterrent Effect of Capital Punishment: A Question of Life and Death." *American Economic Review,* June 1975. In the period studied capital punishment was already infrequent and uncertain. Its deterrent effect might be greater when more frequently imposed for capital crimes, so that a prospective offender would feel more certain of it.
9. See *Journal of Legal Studies,* January 1977; *Journal of Political Economy,* June 1977; and (this is the cross-sectional analysis), *American Economic Review,* June 1977.
10. *Per contra* see Brian Forst in *Minnesota Law Review,* May 1977, and *Deterrence and Incapacitation* (National Academy of Sciences, Washington, D.C., 1978). By now statistical analyses of the effects of the death penalty have become a veritable cottage industry. This has happened since Ehrlich found deterrent effects. No one much bothered when Thorsten Sellin found none. Still, it is too early for more than tentative conclusions. The two papers mentioned above are replied to, more than adequately in my view, in Isaac Ehrlich's "Fear of Deterrence," *Journal of Legal Studies,* June 1977.
11. I thought that prudence as well as morality commanded us to choose the first alternative even when I believed that the degree of probability and the extent of deterrent effects might remain unknown. (See my "On Deterrence and the Death Penalty," *Journal of Criminal Law, Criminology, and Police Science,* June 1969.) That probability is more likely to become known now and to be greater than was apparent a few years ago.
12. Though it would isolate deterrent effects of the punishment from incapacitating effects, and also from the effect of Durkheimian "normative validation" when it does not depend on threats. Still, it is not acceptable to our sense of justice that people guilty of the same crime would deliberately get different punishments and that the difference would be made to depend deliberately on a factor irrelevant to the nature of the crime or of the criminal.
13. As indicated before, demonstrations are not available for the exact addition to deterrence of each added degree of severity in various circumstances, and with respect to various acts. We have coasted so far on a sea of plausible assumptions. (It is not contended, of course, that the degree of severity alone determines deterrent effects. Other factors may reinforce or offset the effect of severity, be it on the motivational [incentive] side, or as added costs and risks.)
14. Particularly since he, unlike the person already in custody, may have much to gain from his additional crime (see note 18).
15. The Supreme Court has decided that capital punishment for rape (at least of adults) is "cruel and unusual" (*Coker* v. *Georgia,* 1977). For the reasons stated in the text, I welcome the decision—but not the justification given by the Supreme Court. The penalty may

indeed be as excessive as the court feels it is, but not in the constitutional sense of being irrationally or extravagantly so, and thus contrary to the Eighth Amendment. The seriousness of the crime of rape and the appropriateness of the death penalty for it are matters for political rather than judicial institutions to decide. I should vote against the death penalty for rape—and not only for the reasons stated in the text above; but the Court should have left the matter to the vote of the citizens.

The charge of racially discriminatory application was most often justified when the penalty was inflicted for rape. Yet I doubt that the charge will be dropped, or that the agitation against the death penalty will stop, once it is no longer inflicted for rape. Discrimination never was more than a pretext used by abolitionists.

16. There is a good argument here against unnecessary public displays of violence. (See my "What to Do about TV Violence," *The Alternative*, August/September 1976).
17. It may be noted that in Beccaria's time executions were regarded as public entertainments. *Tempora mutantur et nos mutamur in illis.*
18. I have reservations on both these counts, being convinced that many crimes among relatives, friends, and associates are as blameworthy and as deterrable as crimes among strangers. Thus, major heroin dealers in New York are threatened with life imprisonment. In the absence of the death penalty they find it advantageous to have witnesses killed. Such murders surely are not acts of passion in the classical sense, though they occur among associates. They are, in practice, encouraged by the present penal law in New York.
19. The high degree of uncertainty and arbitrariness of penalization in Johnson's time may also have weakened deterrent effects. Witnessing an execution cannot correct this defect.
20. Different motives (the reason why something is done) may generate the same action (what is done), purpose, or intent, just as the same motive may lead to different actions.
21. Insofar as these questions are psychological, empirical evidence would not be irrelevant. But it is likely to be evaluated in terms depending on moral views.
22. Not always. On the disastrous consequences of periodic failure to do so, Sir Henry Maine waxes eloquent with sorrow in his *Ancient Law* (pp. 408–9).
23. One may argue that some crimes deserve more than execution and that the above reasoning would justify punitive torture as well. Perhaps. But torture, unlike death, is generally rejected. Therefore penalties have been reduced to a few kinds—fines, confinement, and execution. The issue is academic because, unlike the death penalty, torture has become repulsive to us. (Some reasons for this public revulsion are listed in Chapter 17 of my *Punishing Criminals*, Basic Books, 1975). As was noted above (p. 404) the range of punishments is bound to be more limited than the range of crimes. We do not accept some punishments, however much deserved they may be.
24. Social approval is usually not unanimous, and the system of rewards reflects it less.

A Matter of Life and Death

HUGO ADAM BEDAU

Bedau argues that, at present, there is no good reason to suppose that a utilitarian cost-benefit analysis would support retention of the death penalty. He also claims that the retributive case for its retention is similarly inconclusive. Since death is clearly a more severe punishment than imprisonment, he supports abolition of the death penalty on the basis of the following moral principle: "Unless there is a good reason for choosing a more rather than a less severe punishment for a crime, the less severe penalty is to be preferred."

I noted . . . that there is an important tie between the religious idea of the sanctity of human life and the secular ideas of the right to life and the dignity of man. Their common factor is the way each of these ideas rules out as immoral the taking of a person's life on grounds of social usefulness and nothing more. From the standpoint of moral theory, this amounts to the claim that when the moral principle of overall social welfare conflicts with the moral principle of the individual's right to life, the latter shall prevail. We have also seen how the right to life and the dignity of man generate the requirement that society must forbid and punish severely the crime of murder. From the standpoint of moral theory, this is an instance where a moral ideal is the source of a social or legal rule.

With a little reflection it is possible to connect several other moral principles with the idea of the worth of human life. We may regard these principles as corollaries or theorems of that ideal taken as an axiom or first principle of morality. Each of these principles bears on the moral desirability or permissibility of the death penalty. Some of these subsidiary principles we have already encountered; others will emerge in the discussions that follow. The full set looks like this:

1. Deliberately taking the life of anyone is not justified unless it is necessary, that is, as long as there is a feasible alternative.
2. Unless there is a good reason to punish a crime severely, a less severe penalty is to be preferred.
3. The more severe a penalty is, the more important it is to inflict it fairly and equally, that is, on all and only those who deserve it.
4. If human lives are to be risked, risking the life of the guilty is morally preferable to risking the life of the innocent.

All of the above principles can be seen, in one way or another, as expressive of ideas that have their origin in the worth of human life. In addition, two other principles have emerged that express aspects of the idea of retribution, or justice in punishment. These are:

5. Crimes should be punished.
6. Punishments should be graded in their severity according to the gravity of the crimes for which they are imposed.

The task I have set is to determine the scope and application of these several principles in order to render a judgment on capital punishment from the moral point of view. These six principles are not, of course, of equal weight or scope. Whether utilitarianism or Kantianism, for example, would give the better defense of these principles is not immediately obvious. Nothing short of a full-scale moral theory could incorporate each of these principles to the extent that is proper, and this is not the place for the development of such a theory. Instead, I will attempt to show how each of these principles enters into a line of reasoning relevant to the morality of capital punishment and thus how each can be accorded something like its proper weight. By the time I am finished, a plausible role for each principle will have been found. None of these principles has any specific reference to the morality of capital punishment. That should not be surprising, and it is certainly no defect. In general, one prefers a moral principle of broader rather than narrower application, one that covers many different kinds of cases and situations. If such broad generalizations can withstand criticism and counterexamples that test their plausibility, then they are likely to be sound principles.

Some critics of opposition to capital punishment have complained that such opposition involves an overestimation of the value of human life: It tends to ignore the fact that we are all bound to die eventually. According to these critics, all that capital punishment does it to schedule a person's death at a definite time and place, by a definite mode and for a definite reason. This raises a new question for us, namely, whether the ideas of the value, worth, dignity, or sanctity of human life can be made consistent with the fact of human mortality.

Even though death is a fact of life, emphasizing the worth of human life is a way of giving sense to the familiar notions of an "untimely" death and of an "undignified" death. These terms are admittedly vague, and have application in a wide variety of settings, but they also have a place where crime and punishment are concerned. Other things being equal, if a death is brought about by one person killing another, as in murder, then it is an untimely death. If a death is brought about in a way that causes terror during the dying and disfigurement of the body, then it is an undignified death. This, of course, is exactly what murder and capital punishment both typically do. (The French film "We Are All Murderers" [1956] rendered this theme vividly.)

Historically, however, the most brutal methods of execution have been practiced in public, despite any objection that might be brought on these grounds. Such brutality was thought necessary to enhance the deterrent effect of the execution and to pay back the guilty offender, with interest, for the crime that had been committed. Stoning, crucifixion, impalement, beheading, even hanging and shooting, have often been hideously painful and terrifying to anticipate and experience. They have also left the executed person in various degrees of bodily disfigurement. In principle, of course, there is no medical or technical barrier to the development of modes of inflicting the death penalty that do not conspicuously affront human dignity. The gas chamber was introduced in this country in the 1920s as just such an "improvement" on the electric chair, much as the electric chair itself had been introduced in the 1890s in the belief that electrocution was more humane than hanging. During the 1970s, several state legislatures enacted laws to impose the death penalty by painless lethal injection.[1]

Confronted by these considerations, what should be the reply of the defender of the death penalty? One could argue that (1) neither retribution nor social defense, each of which does require brutal methods or administering the death penalty, is part of the purpose or justification of capital punishment. Or one could argue that (2) neither retribution nor social defense really requires any of the brutalities still characteristic of capital punishment. Or one could even argue that (3) the idea that death should be neither untimely nor undignified is a moral consideration of little weight, easily outweighed by other moral principles favoring the death penalty. No defender of the death penalty is likely to rest content with the first alternative. The second alternative is more promising, but for reasons suggested above and to be examined below, it really will not withstand close scrutiny. More likely, the defender of capital punishment would prefer to stand on the third alternative. If so, the dispute between defenders and critics of the morality of capital punishment will turn on how that punishment fares when measured by the requirements of just retribution and social defense. Accordingly, most of the remaining discussion will need to be devoted to resolving this dispute.

The most common punishments can be plausibly graded into three categories of relative severity: Fining (loss of property) is the least severe, imprisonment (loss of liberty) is much more severe, and death (loss of life) is the most severe of all. Fines, as we noted earlier, are often like a mere tax on conduct, and relatively little social disgrace is attached to illegal conduct if the main consequence for the offender is incurring a fine. Loss of liberty, however, not only curtails freedom of association and movement; it is also a stigma, as well as a reminder hour by hour to the offender that he or she is undergoing punishment in a form that makes one (at least for the time being) literally a social outcast. As for the death penalty, most of those who oppose it as well as those who favor it believe it is far more severe than imprisonment. In what way it is more severe, however, is often in dispute. Because opposition to the death penalty rests largely on the belief that this unusual severity is unnecessary and unjustified, it is important to examine this issue with some care.

Prolonged imprisonment without hope of release except by natural death has figured in dozens of novels and stories as the ultimate horror. Especially if the incarceration is compounded by wretched living conditions and solitary confinement, this is hardly surprising. Thus life imprisonment without the possibility of parole can verge on the borderline that normally divides imprisonment from death as the lesser from the greater punishment. Occasionally, prisoners under life sentence will commit suicide rather than face a bleak future any longer. "Lifers" also occasionally report that if they had known what it would be like to serve thirty or forty years in prison, they would have made no effort at their trial to avoid a death sentence.[2] For those of us with just enough exposure to prison life to be appalled by the thought of being imprisoned, and with imaginations vivid enough to realize what we would be deprived of once we were locked behind bars, it is understandable that some reach the sober conclusion that they would rather die than be imprisoned for life.

But do these considerations really show that death is not the more severe punishment? Do they indicate that life imprisonment can be as great or even a greater affront to the dignity of a person than the death penalty? The answer has to be negative. Personal preference of one penalty over another does not show that the latter is more severe than the former. First of all, it is not really possible to tell which of two penalties one prefers, where the one is death and the other life, the way it is possible to tell whether one prefers a week at the seashore or a week in the mountains. One can try each of the vacations and then, on the basis of actual experience, decide which is the preferable. But where a future punishment of death or life imprisonment is concerned, at most one can hope to *imagine* which of the two would be liked least. Any comparative judgment, in the nature of the case, must be based on no experience of the one (death) and very incomplete experience of the other (life imprisonment). If the severity of these alternative punishments must be judged in this way, we will never be able to tell which is the more severe. Or we will have to conclude that severity of punishments is a matter not for objective evaluation, but only of individual preference or arbitrary decision.

Further reflection on the matter makes clear that the idea of the severity of a punishment is complex and contains identifiable factors that permit clear comparison between modes of punishment. Roughly, of two punishments, one is more severe than the other depending on its duration and on its interference with things a person so punished might otherwise do. Death is interminable, whereas it is always possible to revoke or interrupt a life sentence. Death also makes compensation impossible, whereas it is possible to compensate a prisoner in some way for wrongful confinement even if it is not possible to give back any of the liberty that was taken away. Of most importance, death permits of no concurrent experiences or activities, whereas even a life-term prisoner can read a book, watch television, perhaps even write a book or repair a television set, and experience social relations of some variety with other people. Death eliminates the presupposition of all experience and activity: life itself. For these reasons, the death penalty is unquestionably the more severe punishment, no matter what a few despondent life-term prisoners or sentimental observers may think they prefer, and no matter how painless and dignified the mode of execution might be.

Of course it is possible to make even short-term imprisonment a living hell for prisoners. No doubt methods of imprisonment have been designed that would make death a blessed relief. Opponents of the death penalty, however, need favor no such brutal alternatives. To be sure, Europe's first outspoken opponent of the death penalty, the young Italian nobleman Cesare Beccaria, recommended imprisonment over the death penalty because of "the perpetual example" that life-term prisoners afforded the public of what could happen to those who committed a felony. Beccaria thought this would make long imprisonment a better deterrent than death because of the "much stronger impression" on the imagination of a whole life in prison as opposed to a few moment on the gallows.[3]

Today most opponents of the death penalty would favor as an alternative punishment a prison term of relatively brief duration (say, ten years) and then eligibility for parole release, with actual release depending upon the likelihood of further violent offenses and upon the public acceptability of the offender's release. Thus, a Charles Manson might never be released,[4] whereas an armed robber who shot a gas station attendant during a holdup might be released in fifteen years or less (as, in fact, happens today in some such cases). The day-to-day prison regimen, while it need not approximate a country club—as it is cynically said to do by some of those who have never been to prison—also need not involve mistreatment, neglect, and brutality of a sort to delight the Spanish Inquisition, either.

We should also not forget that, as history shows, it is possible to aggravate the severity of the death penalty by any of several well-known techniques. Burning at the stake, for instance, would do very nicely as a more severe mode of execution than the electric chair. However, even if it could be established that such severe methods accomplished a marvelous improvement in the deterrent effect over less brutal methods, or that they were superbly fitted to repay a particular criminal for the kind of murder he committed, the indignity of such cruelties should prohibit their use. They would be widely if not universally seen as a dangerous throwback to more savage times. Our understanding of and respect for our common humanity has grown, and so we see that even retribution and deterrence have their moral limits, limits imposed in the name of human dignity.

In addition to the severity of the death penalty, killing persons as punishment shares certain important features with other modes of corporal punishment once widely practiced in our society—maiming, flogging, branding—but now abandoned. All these other methods of corporal punishment have been prohibited in part because they are now seen to violate the dignity of the person being punished. We accept today that it is undignified to have to carry for the rest of one's life the visible stigma of having been convicted of a crime. But this is exactly what branding and maiming (such as cutting off the hand of a thief) did. Since the Freudian revolution earlier in this century, informed and reflective persons have become uneasy whenever violent physical abuse is deliberately inflicted by one person upon another who is helpless to do anything about it. Yet this is exactly what flogging involves. (By "flogging" I do not mean the paddling a parent might administer to the bottom of a wayward child. I mean tying a person to a post or a railing and then beating him raw on the naked back so that bloody welts are raised that leave scars for life, a standard form of punishment only a few decades ago and still used within prisons until fairly recently.) Any attempt by the authorities to revive such modes of punishment would be denounced as an unacceptable return to primitive techniques, and as needless physical violence that only hardens both those who undergo it and those who inflict it.[5]

Why has death as a punishment escaped the nearly universal social and moral condemnation visited on all these other punishments with which it is historically and naturally associated? In part, it may be owing to a failure of imagination. Whereas we all know or can easily and vividly imagine the pain and humiliation involved in other corporal punishments, executions today are carried out away from public view, they are quickly over, and the person punished by death is no longer in our midst as a constant reminder. Other factors come into play, too. One is the belief that in some cases there is truly no alternative, because if the criminal were not killed there would be too much risk that he or she would repeat the crime. If so, then neither retribution nor deterrence, but rather prevention, turns out to be the last line of defense. I shall examine this line of reasoning more closely below.

Capital punishment, it is sometimes said, is to the body politic what self-defense is to the individual. If the latter is not morally wrong, how can the former be? In order to assess the strength of this analogy, I will first review the morality of self-defense.

Except for absolute pacifists, who believe it is morally wrong to use violence even to defend themselves or others from unprovoked and undeserved aggression, most of us believe that it is not morally wrong and may even be our moral duty to use violence to prevent aggression directed either against us or against innocent third parties. The law has long granted persons the right to defend themselves against the unjust aggressions of others, even to the extent of using lethal force to kill an assailant.[6] To think of any convincing argument that would show it is never rational to risk the death of another in order to prevent death or grave injury to oneself is very difficult. Certainly self-interest dictates the legitimacy of self-defense. So does concern for the well-being of others, in at least some circumstances. So also does justice. If it is unfair for one person to inflict undeserved violence on another, then it is hard to see how morality could require the victim to acquiesce in the attempt by another to do so, even if resistance risks or involves injury to the assailant.

The foregoing account assumes that the person acting in self-defense is innocent of any provocation of the assailant, and that there is no alternative to victimization except resistance. In actual life, both assumptions—especially the second—are often false, because there may be a third alternative: escape, or removing oneself from the scene of imminent aggression. Hence, the law imposes on us the "duty to retreat." Before we use violence to resist aggression, we must try to get out of the way, lest unnecessary violence be used. Now suppose that unjust aggression is imminent, and there is no path open for escape. How much violence may justifiably be used to ward off aggression? The answer is: No more violence than is necessary to prevent the aggressive assault. Violence beyond that is unnecessary and therefore unjustified. We may restate the principle governing the use of violence in self-defense by reference to the concept of "deadly force" by the police in the discharge of their duties. The rule is this: Use of deadly force is justified only to prevent loss of life in immediate jeopardy where a lesser use of force cannot reasonably be expected to save the life that is threatened.

In real life, violence in self-defense in excess of the minimum necessary to prevent aggression, even though it is not justifiable, is often excusable. One cannot always tell what will suffice to deter an aggressor or to avoid becoming a victim; thus the law looks with a certain tolerance on the frightened and innocent victim who in self-defense turns upon a vicious assailant and inflicts a fatal injury even though a lesser injury would have been sufficient. What is not justified is deliberately using far more violence than is necessary to avoid becoming a victim. It is the deliberate, not the impulsive or the unintentional, use of violence that is relevant to the death penalty controversy, since the death penalty is enacted into law and carried out in each case deliberately—with ample time to weigh alternatives. Notice that I am assuming that the fact of self-defense is to protect one's person of that of a third party. The reasoning outlined here does not extend to the defense of one's property. Shooting a thief to prevent one's automobile from being stolen cannot be excused or justified in the way that shooting an assailant charging with a knife pointed at one's face can be. Our criterion must be that deadly force is never justified to prevent crimes against property or other violent crimes not immediately threatening the life of an innocent person.

The rationale for self-defense as set out above illustrates two moral principles of great importance to this discussion. One is that if a life is to be risked, then it is better that it be the life of someone who is guilty (in this context, the initial assailant) rather than the life of someone who is not (the innocent potential victim). To expect the innocent prospective victim to run the added risk of severe injury or death in order to avoid using violence in self-defense that might kill the assailant is not fair. Rather, fairness dictates that the guilty aggressor should be the one to run the risk.

The other principle is that taking life deliberately is not justified so long as there is any feasible alternative. One does not expect miracles, of course, but in theory, if shooting a burglar through the foot will stop the burglary and enable one to call the police for help, then there is no reason to shoot to kill. Likewise, if the burglar is unarmed, there is no reason to shoot at all. In actual life, of course, a burglar is likely to be shot at by an aroused householder who does not know whether the burglar is armed; prudence may seem to dictate the assumption that he is. Even so, although the burglar has no right to commit a felony against a person or a person's property, the attempt does not give the chosen victim the right to respond in whatever way he pleases, and then to excuse or justify such conduct on the ground that he was "acting only in self-defense." In these ways, the law shows a tacit regard for the life even of a felon and discourages the use of unnecessary violence even by the innocent. Morality can hardly do less.

The analogy between capital punishment and self-defense requires us to face squarely the empirical questions surrounding the preventive and deterrent effects of the death penalty. Executing a murderer in the name of punishment can be seen as a crime-*preventive* measure just to the extent it is reasonable to believe that if the murderer had not been executed he or she would have committed other crimes (including, but not necessarily confined to, murder). Executing a murderer can be seen as a crime *deterrent* just to the extent it is reasonable to believe that by the example of the execution other persons would be frightened off from committing murder. Any punishment can be a crime preventive without being a crime deterrent, just as it can be a deterrent without being a preventive. It can also be both or neither. Prevention and deterrence are theoretically independent because they operate by different methods. Crimes can be prevented by taking guns out of the hands of criminals, by putting criminals behind bars, by alerting the public to be less careless and less prone to victimization, and so forth. Crimes can be deterred only by making would-be criminals so frightened of being arrested, convicted, and punished for crimes that they overcome any desire to commit crimes with a stronger desire to avoid the risk of being caught and punished.

Capital punishment is unusual among penalties because its preventive effects limit its deterrent effects. The death penalty can never deter an executed person from further crimes. At most, it prevents the executed person from committing them. (Popular discussions of the death penalty are frequently confused in that they often assume the death penalty is a perfect and infallible deterrent so far as the executed criminal is concerned.) Even more important, it is also wrong to think that in every execution the death penalty proves itself to be an infallible crime preventive. True, once an offender has been executed, it is physically impossible for that person to commit any further crimes, since the punishment is totally incapacitative. But incapacitation is not identical with prevention. Prevention by means of incapacitation occurs only if the executed criminal would have committed other crimes if he or she had not been executed and had been punished only in some less incapacitative way (e.g., by imprisonment).

What evidence is there that the incapacitative results of the death penalty are an effective crime preventive?[7] From the study of imprisonment, parole, release records, this much is clear: If the murderers and other criminals who have been executed are like the murderers who were convicted but *not* executed, then (1) executing all convicted murderers would have prevented many crimes, but not many murders (about one convicted murderer in five hundred commits another murder); and (2) convicted murderers, whether inside prison or outside after release, have at least as good a record of no further criminal activity as any other class of convicted felon.

These facts show that the general public tends to overrate the danger and threat to public safety constituted by the failure to execute every murderer who is caught and convicted. While it would be quite wrong to say that there is no risk such criminals will repeat their crimes—or similar ones—if they are not executed, it would be nearly as erroneous to say that executing every convicted murderer would prevent many horrible crimes. All we know is that such executions would prevent a few such crimes from being committed; we do not know how many or by whom they would have been committed. (Obviously, if we did know we would try to prevent them!) This is the nub of the problem. There is no way to know in advance which if any of the incarcerated or released murderers will kill again. In this connection it is useful to remember that the only way to guarantee that no horrible crimes ever occur is to execute *everyone* who might conceivably commit such a crime. Similarly, the only way to guarantee that no convicted murderer ever commits another murder is to execute them all. No modern society has ever done this, and for two hundred years ours has been moving steadily in the direction of a more civilized and individuated system of justice.

These considerations show that our society has implicitly adopted an attitude toward the risk of murder rather like the attitude it has adopted toward the risk of fatality from other sources, such as automobile accidents, lung cancer, or drowning. Since no one knows when or where or upon whom any of these lethal events will fall, it would be too great an invasion of freedom to undertake the severe restrictions that alone would suffice to prevent any such deaths from occurring. We agree it is better to take the risks and keep our freedom than to try to eliminate the risks altogether and lose our freedom in the process. Hence, we have lifeguards at the beach, but swimming is not totally prohibited; smokers are warned, but cigarettes are still legally sold; pedestrians may have the right of way in marked crosswalks, but marginally competent drivers are still allowed to operate motor vehicles. Some risk is thereby imposed on the innocent. In the name of our right to freedom, we do not insist on having society protect our rights at all costs.

Determining whether the death penalty is an effective deterrent is even more difficult than determining its effectiveness as a crime preventive. In general, our knowledge about how penalties deter crimes and whether in fact they do—whom they deter, from which crimes, and under what conditions—is distressingly inexact.[8] Most people nevertheless are convinced that punishments do deter, and that the more severe a punishment is the better it will deter. For half a century, social scientists have studied the questions whether the death penalty is a deterrent and whether it is a better deterrent than the alternative of imprisonment. Their verdict, while not unanimous, is nearly so. Whatever may be true about the deterrence of lesser crimes by other penalties, the deterrence achieved by the death penalty for murder is not measurably any greater than the deterrence achieved by long-term imprisonment. In the nature of the case, the evidence is quite indirect. No one can identify for certain any crimes that did not occur because the would-be offender was deterred by the threat of the death penalty and could not have been deterred by a less severe threat. Likewise, no one can identify any crimes that did occur because the offender was not deterred by the threat of prison even though he would have been deterred by the threat of death. Nevertheless, such evidence as we have fails to show that the more severe penalty (death) is really a better deterrent than the less severe penalty (imprisonment) for such crimes as murder.

If the death penalty and long-term imprisonment really are equally effective (or ineffective) as deterrents to murder, then the argument for the death penalty on grounds of deterrence is seriously weakened. One of the moral principles identified earlier now comes into play: Unless there is a good reason for choosing a more rather than a less severe punishment for a crime, the less severe penalty is to be preferred. This principle obviously comments itself to anyone who values human life and who concedes that, all other things being equal, less pain and suffering is always better than more. Human life is valued in part to the degree that it is free of pain, suffering, misery, and frustration, and in particular to the extent that it is free of such experiences when they serve no known purpose. If the death penalty is not a more effective deterrent than imprisonment, then its greater severity is gratuitous, purposeless suffering and deprivation. Accordingly, we must reject it in favor of some less severe alternative, unless we can identify some other and more weighty moral principle that the death penalty protects and that an alternative mode of punishment violates. Whether there is any such principle is unclear.

A full study of the costs and benefits involved in the practice of capital punishment would not be confined solely to the question of whether it is a better deterrent or preventive of murder than imprisonment. Any thorough-going utilitarian approach to the death penalty controversy would need to examine carefully other costs and benefits as well, because maximizing the balance of all the social benefits over all the social costs is the sole criterion of right and wrong according to utilitarianism. Let us consider, therefore, some of the other costs and benefits to be calculated. Clinical psychologists have presented evidence to suggest that the death penalty actually incites some persons of unstable mind to murder others, either because they are afraid to take their own lives and hope that society will punish them for murder by putting them to death, or because they fancy that they are also killing with justification analogously to the lawful and presumably justified killing involved in capital punishment. If such evidence is sound, capital punishment can serve as a counter-preventive or even an incitement to murder; such incited murders become part of its social cost. Imprisonment, however, has not been known to incite any murders or other crimes of violence in a comparable fashion. (A possible exception might be found in the imprisonment of terrorists, which has inspired other terrorists to take hostages as part of a scheme to force the authorities to release their imprisoned comrades.)

The risks of executing the innocent are also part of the social cost. The historical record is replete with innocent persons arrested, indicted, convicted, sentenced, and occasionally legally executed for crimes they did not commit.[9] This is quite apart from the guilty persons unfairly convicted, sentenced to death, and executed on the strength of perjured testimony, fraudulent evidence, subordination of jurors, and other violations of the civil rights and liberties of the accused. Nor is this all. The high costs of a capital trial and of the inevitable appeals, the costly methods of custody most prisons adopt for convicts on death row, are among the straightforward economic costs that the death penalty incurs.[10] Conducting a valid cost/benefit analysis of capital punishment would be extremely difficult, and it is impossible to predict exactly what such a study would show. Nevertheless, given the evidence we do have, it is quite possible that a study of this sort would favor abolition of all death penalties rather than their retention.

From the moral point of view, it is quite important to determine what one should think about capital punishment if the evidence were clearly to show that the death penalty is a distinctly superior method of social defense by comparison with less severe alternatives. Kantian moralists, as we have seen, would have no use for such knowledge, because their entire case for the morality of the death penalty rests on the way it is thought to provide just retribution, not on the way it is thought to provide social defense. For a utilitarian, however, such knowledge would be conclusive. Those who follow Locke's reasoning would be gratified, because they defend the morality of the death penalty both on the ground that it is retributively just and on the ground that it provides needed social defense.

What about the opponents of the death penalty, however? To oppose the death penalty in the face of incontestable evidence that it is an effective method of social defense violates the moral principle that where grave risks are to be run it is better that they be run by the guilty than by the innocent. Consider in this connection an imaginary world in which executing the murderer would invariably restore the murder victim to life, whole and intact, as though no homicide had occurred. In such a miraculous world, it is hard to see how anyone could oppose the death penalty, on moral or other grounds. Why shouldn't a murderer die if that will infallibly bring the victim back to life? What could possibly be wrong with taking the murderer's life under such conditions? The death penalty would be an instrument of perfect restitution, and it would give a new and better meaning to *lex talionis*. The whole idea is fanciful, of course, but it shows as nothing else can how opposition to the death penalty cannot be both moral and wholly unconditional. If opposition to the death penalty is to be morally responsible, then it must be conceded that there are conditions (however unlikely) under which that opposition should cease.

But even if the death penalty were known to be a uniquely effective social defense, we could still imagine conditions under which it would be reasonable to oppose it. Suppose that in addition to being a slightly better preventive and deterrent than imprisonment, executions also has a slight incitive effect (so that for every ten murders that an execution prevented or deterred, another murder was incited). Suppose also that the administration of criminal justice in capital cases were inefficient and unequal, and tended to secure convictions and death sentences only for murderers who least "deserved" to be sentenced to death (including some death sentences and a few executions of the innocent). Under such conditions, it would be reasonable to oppose the death penalty, because on the facts supposed more (or not fewer) innocent lives would be threatened and lost by using the death penalty than would be risked by abolishing it. It is important to remember throughout our evaluation of the deterrence controversy that we cannot ever apply the principle that advises us to risk the lives of the guilty in order to save the lives of the innocent. Instead, the most we can do is weigh the risk for the general public against the execution of those who are *found* guilty by an imperfect system of criminal justice. These hypothetical factual assumptions illustrate the contingencies upon which the morality of opposition to the death penalty rests. And not only the morality of opposition. The morality of any defense of the death penalty rests on the same contingencies. This should help us understand why, in resolving the morality of capital punishment one way or the other, it is so important to know as well as we can whether the death penalty really does deter, prevent, or incite crime; whether the innocent really are ever executed; and how likely the occurrence of these things in the future is.

The great unanswered question that utilitarians must face concerns the level of social defense that executions should be expected to achieve before it is justifiable to carry them out. Consider three possible situations: (1) At the level of a hundred executions per year, each additional execution of a convicted murderer reduced the number of murder victims by ten. (2) Executing every convicted murderer reduced the number of murders to 5,000 victims annually, whereas executing only one out of ten murderers reduces the number of victims to 5,001. (3) Executing every convicted murderer reduces the murder rate no more than does executing one in a hundred and no more than does a random pattern of executions.

Many people contemplating situation (1) would regard this as a reasonable trade-off: The execution of each additional guilty person saves the lives of ten innocent ones. In fact, situation (1) or something like it may be taken as a description of what most of those who defend the death penalty on grounds of social defense believe is true. But suppose that, instead of saving ten lives, the number dropped to 0.5, that is, one victim avoided for each two additional executions. Would that be a reasonable price to pay? We are on the road toward the situation described in (2), where a drastic 90 percent reduction in the number of persons executed causes the level of social defense to drop by only 0.0002 percent. Would it be worth it to execute so many more murderers to secure such a slight increase in social defense? How many guilty lives is one innocent life worth? (Only those who think that guilty lives are *worthless* can avoid facing this problem.) In situation (3), of course, there is no basis for executing all convicted murderers, since there is no gain in social defense to show for each additional execution after the first out of each hundred has been executed. How, then, should we determine which out of each hundred convicted murderers is the one to be put to death?

If a complete and thoroughgoing cost/benefit analysis of the death penalty were possible, we might be able to answer such questions. But an appeal merely to the moral principle that if lives are to be risked it should be the lives of the guilty rather than of the innocent will not suffice. (I noted above that this abstract principle is of little use in the actual administration of criminal justice, because the police and the courts do not deal with the guilty as such but only with those *judged* guilty.) Nor will it suffice to agree that society deserves all the crime prevention and deterrence it can get as a result of inflicting severe punishments. These principles are consistent with too many different policies. They are too vague by themselves to resolve the choice on the grounds of social defense when confronted with hypothetical situations like those proposed above.

Since no adequate cost/benefit analysis of the death penalty exists, there is no way to resolve these questions from that standpoint at this time. Moreover, it can be argued that we cannot have such an analysis without already establishing in some way or other the relative value of innocent lives versus guilty lives. Far from being a product of cost/benefit analysis, a comparative evaluation of lives would have to be available to us before we undertook any such analysis. (And no one has yet come up with a satisfactory means of doing this.) Without it, no adequate cost/benefit analysis of this problem can get off the ground. Finally, it must be noted that our knowledge at present does not indicate that we are in anything like the situation described above in (1). On the contrary, from the evidence we do have it seems we achieve about the same deterrent and preventive effects whether we punish murder by death or by imprisonment. Something like the situation in (2) or in (3) may therefore be correct. If so, this shows that the choice between the two policies of capital punishment and life imprisonment for murder will probably have to be made on some basis other than social defense; on that basis alone, the two policies appear to be virtually equivalent and therefore equally acceptable.

No discussion of the morality of punishment would be complete without taking into account the two leading principles of retributive justice relevant to the capital punishment controversy. I have made reference to them several times. One is the principle that crimes should be punished; the other is the principle that the severity of a punishment should be proportional to the gravity of the offense. These are moral principles of recognized weight. Leaving aside all questions of social defense, how strong a case for capital punishment can be made on their basis? How reliable and persuasive are these principles themselves?

Given the general rationale for punishment sketched earlier, there cannot be any dispute over the principle that crime must be punished. In embracing it, of course, we are not automatically making a fetish of "law and order," in the sense that we would be if we thought that the most important single thing to do with social resources is to punish crimes. In addition, the principle that crime must be punished need not be in dispute between proponents and opponents of the death penalty. Even defenders of the death penalty must admit that putting a convicted murderer in prison for years is a punishment of that criminal. The principle that crime must be punished is neutral to our controversy, because both sides acknowledge it.

The other principle of retributive justice is the one that seems to be decisive. Under *lex talionis,* it must always have seemed that murderers ought to be put to death. Proponents of the death penalty, with rare exceptions, have insisted on this point; and even opponents of the death penalty must give grudging assent to the logic of demanding capital punishment for murder. The strategy for opponents of the death penalty is to argue either that (1) this principle is not really a principle of justice after all, or that (2) to the extent it is, it does not require death for murderers, or that (3) in any case it is not the only principle of punitive justice. As we shall see, each of these objections has merit.

Let us recall, first, that not even the biblical world limited the death penalty to the punishment of murder. Many other nonhomicidal crimes also carried this penalty (e.g., kidnapping, witchcraft, cursing one's parents).[11] In our own nation's recent history, persons have been executed for aggravated assault, rape, kidnapping, armed robbery, sabotage, and espionage.[12] We cannot defend *any* of these executions (not to mention some of the more bizarre capital statutes, like the one in Georgia that not so long ago provided an optional death penalty for desecration of a grave[13]) on grounds of just retribution. This entails either that such executions are not justified or that they are justified on some ground other than retribution. In actual practice, few defenders of the death penalty have ever been willing to rest their case entirely on the moral principle of just retribution as formulated in terms of "a life for a life." (Kant was a conspicuous exception.) Most defenders of the death penalty have implied, by their willingness to use executions to defend not only life but limb and property as well, that they did not place much value on the lives of criminals when compared to the value of either lives or things belonging to innocent citizens.

European civilization for several centuries has tended to limit the criminal homicides punishable by death. Even Kant took a casual attitude toward a mother's killing of her illegitimate child. ("A child born into the world outside marriage is outside the law . . . , and consequently it is also outside the protection of the law."[14]) In our society, the development nearly two hundred years ago of the distinction between first- and second-degree murder was an attempt to narrow the class of criminal homicides deserving the death penalty.[15] Yet those dead owing to manslaughter, or to any kind of unintentional, accidental, unpremeditated, unavoidable, unmalicious killing, are just as dead as the victims of the most ghastly murder. Both moral reflection and the law in practice show how difficult it is to identify all and only the criminal homicides that are appropriately punished by death (assuming that any are). Individual judges and juries differ in the conclusions they reach. The history of capital punishment for homicides reveals continual efforts, uniformly unsuccessful, to specify the criteria defining those homicides for which the slayer should die.

Similar skepticism has been expressed on the reliability and rationality of death penalty statutes that give the trial court the discretion to sentence to prison or to death. As Justice John Marshall Harlan of the Supreme Court observed more than a decade ago,

> Those who have come to grips with the hard task of actually attempting to draft means of channeling capital sentencing discretion have confirmed the lesson taught by history. . . . To identify before the fact those characteristics of criminal homicide and the perpetrators which call for the death penalty, and to express these characteristics in language which can be fairly understood and applied by the sentencing au-

> thority, appear to be tasks which are beyond present human ability.[16]

The abstract principle that the punishment of death best fits the crime of murder turns out to be extremely difficult to interpret and apply.

If we look at the matter from the standpoint of the actual practice of criminal justice, we can only conclude that "a life for a life" plays little or no role whatever. Plea bargaining, even where murder is concerned, is widespread. Studies of criminal justice . . . reveal that what trial or appellate courts in a given jurisdiction decide on a given day is first-degree murder suitably punished by death could just as well have been decided in a neighboring jurisdiction on another death either as second-degree murder or as first-degree murder but without the death penalty. The factors that influence prosecutors in determining the charge under which they will prosecute go far beyond the simple principle of "a life for a life." Cynics, of course, will say that these facts show that our society does not care about justice. I would reply that either justice in punishment does not consist of retribution, because there are other principles of justice; or there are other moral considerations besides justice that must be honored; or retributive justice is not adequately expressed in the idea of "a life for a life"; or justice in the criminal justice system is beyond our reach.

Those who advocate capital punishment for murder on retributive grounds must face the objection that, on their own principles, the death penalty in some cases is morally inadequate. How could death in the electric chair or the gas chamber or before a firing squad or on a gallows suffice as just retribution, given the savage, brutal, wanton character of so many murders? How can retributive justice be served by anything less than equally savage methods of execution? From a retributive point of view, the oft-heard exclamation, "Death is too good for him!" has a certain truth. Are defenders of the death penalty willing to embrace this consequence of their own doctrine?

If they were, they would be stooping to the squalor of the murderer and denying the very tenets of civilized behavior they claim to be defending. Where the quality of the crime sets the limits of just methods of punishment, as it will if we attempt to give exact and literal implementation to *lex talionis,* society as a whole will find itself descending to the cruelties and savagery that criminals employ. What is worse, society would be deliberately authorizing such acts, in the cool light of reason, and not (as is usually true of criminals) impulsively or in hatred or anger or with an insane or unbalanced mind. Well-established and universally recognized moral constraints, in short, prohibit us from trying to make executions perfectly retributive. Once we grant that such constraints are proper, it is unreasonable to insist that the principle of "a life for a life" nevertheless by itself justifies the execution of murderers.

Other considerations take us in a different direction. Few murders, outside television and movie scripts, involve anything like an execution. An execution, after all, begins with a solemn pronouncement of the death sentence from a judge, is followed by detention in maximum security awaiting the date of execution (during which various complex and protected appeals will be pursued, followed by a clemency hearing before the governor), and culminates in the condemned prisoner walking "the last mile" to the execution chamber itself. As Albert Camus once remarked,

> For there to be an equivalence, the death penalty would have to punish a criminal who had warned his victim of the date at which he would inflict a horrible death on him and who, from that moment onward, had confined him at his mercy for months. Such a monster is not encountered in private life.[17]

What, then, emerges from our examination of retributive justice and the death penalty? If retributive justice is thought to consist in *lex talionis,* all one can say is that this principle has never exercised more than a crude and indirect effect on the actual punishments meted out by society. Other moral principles simply do interfere with a literal and single-minded application of this one. Some homicides seem improperly punished by death at all; others would require methods of execution too horrible to inflict. In any case, proponents of the death penalty rarely confine themselves to reliance on nothing but this principle of just retribution, since they rarely confine themselves to supporting the death penalty only for murder.

Retributive justice need not be identified with *lex talionis*. One may reject that principle as too crude and still embrace the retributive principle that the severity of punishments should be graded according to the gravity of the offense. Even though one need not claim that life imprisonment (or any kind of punishment other than death) "fits" the crime of murder, one can claim that this punishment is the proper one for murder. To do this, one must accept a schedule of punishments arranged so that this mode of imprisonment is the most severe penalty used. Opponents of the death penalty can embrace this principle of retributive justice, even though they must reject a literal *lex talionis*.

Despite the past generation, the strongest practical objection to the death penalty has been the inequity with which it has been applied.[18] As the late Supreme Court Justice William O. Douglas once observed, "One searches our chronicles in vain for the execution of any member of the affluent strata of this society."[19] One does not search our chronicles in vain for the crime of murder committed by the affluent. Every study of the death penalty for rape (unconstitutional only since 1977) has confirmed that black male rapists (especially where the victim is a white female) are far more likely to be sentenced to death and executed than white male rapists.[20] Convicted black murders are more likely to end up on death row than are others, and the killers of whites (whether white or nonwhite) are more likely to be sentenced to death than are the killers of nonwhites.[21] All the sociological evidence points to the conclusion that the death penalty is the poor man's justice; hence the epigram "Those without the capital get the punishment."

Let us suppose that the factual basis for such a criticism is sound. What follows for the morality of capital punishment? Many defenders of the death penalty have been quick to point out that since there is nothing intrinsic about the crime of murder or rape dictating that only the poor or only racial-minority males will commit it, and since there is nothing overtly racist about the statutes that authorize the death penalty for murder or rape, capital punishment itself is hardly at fault if in practice it falls with unfair impact on the poor and the black. There is, in short, nothing in the death penalty that requires it to be applied unfairly and with arbitrary or discriminatory results. At worst, such results stem from a fault in the system of administering criminal justice. (Some, who dispute the facts cited above, would deny even this.) There is an adequate remedy—execute more whites, women, and affluent murderers.

Presumably both proponents and opponents of capital punishment would concede that it is a fundamental dictate of justice that a punishment should not be unfairly—inequitably or unevenly—enforced and applied. They should also be able to agree that when the punishment in question is the extremely severe one of death, then the requirement to be fair in using such a punishment becomes even more stringent. There should be no dispute in the death penalty controversy over these principles of justice. The dispute begins as soon as one attempts to connect these principles with the actual use of this punishment.

In this country, many critics of the death penalty have argued, we would long ago have got rid of capital punishment entirely if equal and fair application had been a condition of its use. In the words of the attorneys who argued against the death penalty in the Supreme Court during 1972, "It is a freakish aberration, a random extreme act of violence, visibly arbitrary and discriminatory—a penalty reserved for unusual application because, if it were usually used, it would affront universally shared standards of public decency."[22] It is difficult to dispute this judgment, when one considers that there have been in the United States during the past fifty years about half a million criminal homicides, about a third of a million persons arrested for these crimes, but fewer than four thousand executions (all but thirty-three of which were of men).[23]

We can look at these statistics in another way to illustrate the same point. If we could be assured that the nearly four thousand persons who have been executed were the worst of the bad, repeat offenders impossible to incarcerate safely (much less to rehabilitate), the most dangerous murderers in captivity—the ones who had killed more than once and were likely to kill again, and the least likely to be confined in prison without chronic danger to other inmates and the staff—then one might accept half a million murders and a few thousand executions with a sense that rough justice had been done. But the truth is otherwise. Persons are sentenced to death and executed not because they have been found to be uncontrollably violent or hopelessly poor confinement and release risks. Instead they are executed because at trial they have a poor defense (inexperienced or overworked counsel), they have no funds to bring witnesses to court, they are transients or strangers in the community where they are tried, the prosecuting attorney wants the publicity that does with "sending a killer to the chair," there are no funds for an appeal or for a transcript of the trial record, they are members of a despised racial or political minority. In short, the actual study of why particular persons have been sentenced to death and executed does not show any careful winnowing of the worst from the bad; it shows that those executed were usually the unlucky victims of prejudice and discrimination, the losers in an arbitrary lottery that could just as well have spared them, the victims of the disadvantages that almost always go with poverty. A system like this does not enhance human life; it cheapens and degrades it. However heinous murder and other crimes are, the system of capital punishment does not compensate for or erase those crimes. It tends only to add new injuries of its own to the catalogue of human brutality.

✦ ✦ ✦

My discussion of the death penalty from the moral point of view shows that there is no one moral principle that has paramount validity and that decisively favors one side of the controversy. Rather, I have shown how it is possible to argue either for or against the death penalty, and in each case to be appealing to moral principles that derive from the worth, value, or dignity of human life. I have also shown how it is impossible to connect any of these abstract principles with the actual practice of capital punishment without a close study of sociological, psychological, and economic factors. By themselves, the moral principles that are relevant are too abstract and uncertain in application to be of much help. Without the guidance of such principles, of course, the facts (who gets executed, and why) are of little use, either.

My own view of the controversy is that, given the moral principles identified in the course of this discussion (including the overriding value of human life), and given all the facts about capital punishment, the balance of reasons favors abolition of the death penalty. The alternative to capital punishment that I favor, as things currently stand, is long-term imprisonment. Such a punishment is retributive and can be made more (or less) severe to reflect the gravity of the crime. Adequate (though hardly perfect) protection can be given to the public. It is free of the worst defect to which the death penalty is liable: execution of the innocent. It tacitly acknowledges that there is no way for a criminal, alive or dead, to make complete amends for murder or other grave crimes against the person. Last but not least, long-term imprisonment has symbolic significance. The death penalty, more than any other kind of killing, is done by officials in the name of society and on its behalf. Yet each of us has a hand in such killings. Unless they are absolutely necessary they cannot be justified. Thus abolishing the death penalty represents extending the hand of life even to those who by their crimes may have "forfeited" any right to live. A penal policy limiting the severity of punishment to long-term imprisonment is one way of admitting that we must abandon the folly and pretense of attempting to secure perfect justice in an imperfect world.

Searching for an epigram suitable for our times, in which governments have waged war and suppressed internal dissent by using methods that can be described only as savage and criminal, Camus was prompted to admonish: "Let us be neither victims nor executioners." Perhaps better than any other, this exhortation points the way between unacceptable extremes if we are to respect the humanity in each of us.

NOTES

1. See Bedau, ed., *The Death Penalty in America*, 3d ed. (1982), pp. 17–18, 33–34; and Scott Christianson, "Corrections Law Developments: Execution by Lethal Injection," *Criminal Law Bulletin* 15 (1979):69–78.
2. See, e.g., Bedau, ed., *The Death Penalty in America*, rev. ed. (1967), pp. 402–04.
3. Cesare Beccaria, *On Crimes and Punishments* (1764), trans. Henry Paolucci (1963), p. 50.
4. See George Bishop, *Witness to Evil* (1971).
5. For a recent argument that attempts to meet such objections, see Graeme Newman, *Just and Painful: A Case for the Corporal Punishment of Criminals* (1983).
6. For a thoughtful historical and critical discussion, see George P. Fletcher, *Rethinking Criminal Law* (1978), pp. 237, 352–53, 956–75.
7. The best theoretical discussion of deterrence and related issues is Jack P. Gibbs, *Crime, Punishment, and Deterrence* (1975).
8. See Bernard L. Diamond, "Murder and the Death Penalty," and George F. Solomon, "Capital Punishment as Suicide and as Murder," reprinted in Bedau and Pierce, eds., *Capital Punishment in the United States* (1976).
9. See Bedau and Radelet, "Miscarriages of Justice in Potentially Capital Cases," *Stanford Law Review* 39 (1987).
10. See Comment, "The Cost of Taking a Life: Dollars and Sense of the Death Penalty." *U. C. Davis Law Review* 18 (1985): 1221–74; New York State Defenders Association, Inc., *Capital Losses: The Price of the Death Penalty for New York State* (1982); and Barry Nakell, "The Cost of the Death Penalty" (1978), reprinted in Bedau, *The Death Penalty in America*, 3d ed. (1982).
11. The relevant biblical texts and ancient Jewish law are discussed in Haim Cohen, "Capital Punishment," *Encyclopedia Judaica* (1971) 5:142–45. See also Edna Erez, "Thou Shalt Not Execute: Hebrew Law Perspective on Capital Punishment," *Criminology* 19 (1981):25–43; and Thorsten Sellin, *The Penalty of Death* (1980), pp. 9–15.
12. See United States, Department of Justice, Bureau of Justice Statistics, *Capital Punishment 1982* (1984), p. 14 (Table 1).
13. Code of Georgia Annotated, §26–8117 (repealed 1963).
14. Kant, *The Metaphysical Elements of Justice*, p. 101.
15. Edwin R. Keedy, "History of the Pennsylvania Statute Creating Degrees of Murder," *University of Pennsylvania Law Review* 97 (1949):759–77.
16. *McGautha* v. *California*, 402 U.S. 183 (1971), at 204 (Harlan, J.).
17. Albert Camus, *Resistance, Rebellion, and Death* (1961), p. 199.
18. See especially Charles L. Black, Jr., *Capital Punishment: The Inevitability of Caprice and Mistake*, 2d ed. (1981).
19. *Furman* v. *Georgia*, 408 U.S. 238 (1972), at 251–52 (Douglas, J., concurring).
20. Marvin E. Wolfgang and Marc Riedel, "Race, Judicial Discretion, and the Death Penalty," *The Annals* 407 (May 1973):119–33.
21. Samuel R. Gross and Robert Mauro, "Patterns of Death: An Analysis of Racial Disparities in Capital Sentencing and Homicide Victimization," *Stanford Law Review* 37 (1984):27–153.
22. NAACP Legal Defense and Educational Fund, Inc., Brief for Petitioner, *Aikens* v. *California*, reprinted in part in Philip English Mackey, ed., *Voices Against Death* (1976), p. 288.
23. These figures are estimates based on execution data reported in the United States Department of Justice bulletin, *Capital Punishment*, and on data reported annually since 1930 by the F.B.I. in *Uniform Crime Reports* on the volume of murder and nonnegligent manslaughter and the clearance (arrest) rates for those crimes.

Study Question #1

Which of the following pros (that is, arguments) for capital punishment is the strongest, and which of the pros is the weakest? Explain your answer fully.

The Pros (Arguments for Capital Punishment)

Pro #1

Lex talionis says capital punishment fits the crime of murder. Justice requires an eye for an eye and a tooth for a tooth. Proportionality should govern. As Senator Orrin Hatch says, "Capital punishment is our society's recognition of the sanctity of human life."

Rebuttals

1. *Lex talionis* is unnecessarily harsh, since it uses force unnecessary to give reasonable protection, and since it is exclusively backward-looking, ignoring consequences. Don't be cruel. See Con #1.
2. "Killin's too good for 'em!" Make murderers toil long and hard to help compensate society for their crimes.
3. Why ape murderers? *Lex talionis* means monkey see, monkey do. This sends a confusing message to the people on the moral distinction between the government and murderers. Ghouls gather outside prisons to celebrate executions (for example, the crowd at Ted Bundy's execution). Hugo Bedau (p. 115 in Narveson, 1983) notes that clinical psychologists have presented evidence that executions incite some murders by those who fancy that they, too, are killing with justification analogous to the allegedly justified executions by the state.
4. Capital punishment fails to recognize the sanctity of human life, since executing innocent people is inevitable.

Pro #2

Capital punishment incapacitates with 100% effectiveness. Unlike life imprisonment or any other alternative, no more innocent people will be murdered by escapees or prisoners.

Rebuttals

1. Pro #2 is an argument for beefed-up security, not executions. No one escapes from the best brig the U.S. Marines have to offer, for example. Indeed, our military could use the practice of guarding murderers, in preparation for guarding prisoners of war, who are often similarly dangerous.
2. Hugo Bedau (Narveson, 1983, p. 114) notes that murderers do not commit additional murders at a rate any greater than that of many other felons we refuse to execute. So justice condemns singling out murderers solely on the basis of incapacitation.
3. Hugo Bedau (Narveson, 1983, p. 114) notes that only one in 100 murderers murders again. So to incapacitate that one, we execute 99 others who would not have killed at all. That's very wasteful of lives and manpower. See Con #1. And some of the 99 will be innocent. See Con #6.
4. The average time on death row before execution is almost six years. Murders occur on death row—two in 1993 of the inmates themselves. Security or other innocent people can be killed under capital punishment too. So execution is not a 100 percent success at incapacitation. See Con #2 on reducing the period on death row by reducing rights of appeal.
5. Irreparable mistakes occur in executing innocent people. Thirteen-thousand per year will inevitably involve mistakes that can never be corrected. See Con #6.
6. Innocent family members and friends, who often believe the convict is innocent, will often be severely hurt by executing their loved one. The harm to them almost always exceeds life imprisonment without parole. See Con #3.
7. The death of a few innocent people is not decisive. We routinely make decisions (for example, whether to open freeways or use air bags in cars) that gain sufficient benefits to justify actions involving the accidental deaths of innocents. See Con #1 to see if the benefits outweigh the cost.

Pro #3

Capital punishment is a greater deterrent than is life imprisonment without parole. The fear of death is the ultimate fear. It stands to reason.

Rebuttals

1. Murderers are not known for their powers of reason. Many murderers murder only when they are drunk or drugged. There is a "high correlation between murders and emotional disturbance" in the murderer. [Irwin Isenberg, ed., *The Death Penalty* (1977), p. 119] Some (for example, Gary Gilmore) are even fanatics, or suicidal or would-be martyrs who accept or even prefer an execution and its publicity. Many (for example, Gilmore) attempt suicide before capture or conviction. Someone who is willing to risk life imprisonment without parole is such a risktaker that the extra risk of capital punishment has little or no effect. Murderers are often desperate characters. Since they don't think they'll get caught, the difference in severity between death and the extremely severe punishment of life imprisonment without parole will have only a negligible impact on criminal behavior. Adjacent states, one that employs capital punishment and the other that does not, show no significant long-term differences in the murder rate. [L.L. Bram, *Funk & Wagnalls New Encyclopedia,* Vol. 5, p. 282 (1983)] Thomas Hurka (Narveson, 1983, p. 128) concludes that "Extensive criminological studies have failed to produce any evidence that capital punishment is a more effective deterrent to murder than life imprisonment" (much less, life imprisonment without parole). Bedau (Narveson, 1983, p. 114) concludes that "the deterrence achieved by the death penalty for murder is not measurably greater than the deterrence achieved by long-term imprisonment" (much less, the deterrence achieved by life imprisonment without parole, the long*est*-term imprisonment). Bedau (Narveson, 1983, p. 115) notes evidence from clinical psychiatrists that capital punishment actually incites murder and increases the incidence of murder. C.L. Black argues (pp. 26–27) that, since suicide is one of the half-dozen chief killers in the U.S., ranking near automobile accidents, and since therefore tens of thousands of people want to die, it is very likely that a significant number of them—disturbed as most of them are—will, consciously or unconsciously, pick the commission of a capital crime as a means of suicide.
2. Statistics show that there is no extra deterrence to capital punishment. Studies in Philadelphia by Leonard Savitz and in California in the late 1950s by William F. Graves show that capital punishment had no extra deterrence. Ernest van den Haag, a staunch and famous supporter of capital punishment, says the death penalty "has not been, and perhaps cannot be shown statistically, to be a deterrent over and above other penalties." [*Journal of Criminal Law* #2 (1969), p. 600] van den Haag says consideration for innocent life (see Con #6) puts the burden of proof on advocates of capital punishment. Justice Marshall, in *Furman v. Georgia,* presents an exhaustive analysis that shows capital punishment has no extra deterrent effect over life imprisonment. The incidence of crime seems to fluctuate with the age, sex, poverty and economic prospects of the population. Poor, young men with bleak economic prospects commit a greatly disproportionate share of violent crimes.
3. Those executed spend an average of almost six years on death row waiting to die. Since the desperation of death row tends to lead them to feel they have nothing to lose, and since they are under intense anxiety or fear of death, they tend to lash out at innocent guards or other inmates. If they were assured of life without parole, then the stable and less

drastic sentence would promote a safer place for those in prison, including those who, due to prison overcrowding or whatever, have committed lesser crimes but are imprisoned with murderers.

Pro #4

Murderers sentenced to life imprisonment should at least be given the option of execution.

Rebuttals

1. Many people falsely confess to crimes, especially famous crimes. Such disturbed people don't deserve death. And executing them covers up the fact that the real murderer is still at large.
2. Hugo Bedau (Narveson, 1983, p. 115) notes evidence from clinical psychologists that the option of execution incites murders that otherwise would not have happened.
3. "Killin's too good for 'em!" Make them feel their punishment, and toil long and hard to help compensate society for their crimes.

Pro #5

Execution will eventually be needed to prevent those sentenced to life imprisonment without parole from being above the law. Justice requires that no one be above the law, and that the ladder of law has no top and no bottom. An incorrigible criminal who can escape like Houdini and who is imprisoned for life without parole (and deprived of recreational and entertainment privileges, etc.) must be incapacitated or deterred from escape or other crimes. Execution is the last resort to avoid having such menaces beyond the reach of the law, to commit further crimes with impunity.

Rebuttal:

1. Solitary confinement is an adequate last resort.

First reply to rebuttal: Some will escape from solitary confinement and commit crimes.
Second reply to rebuttal: Solitary confinement for life is cruel and unusual. Humans are by nature social beings.

Pro #6

Capital punishment is a symbolic sign of safety that boosts public confidence in the protection of the criminal law.

Rebuttal

1. Capital punishment provides no extra deterrence over life imprisonment. So any confidence it fosters would be false confidence, which should be avoided. We shouldn't dupe the people in a democracy.

Pro #7

Capital punishment is permissible if it is democratically legislated. Give the people what they want. Long live majority rule.

Rebuttals

1. Law and morality condemn the tyranny of the majority. Ours is rightly a system, not of simple majority rule, but of a balance of majority rule with minority rights and individual rights. One such legal and moral right is the right not to be subject to unnecessarily cruel punishment. (8th Amendment) Since capital punishment has no deterrent or other penal purpose unserved by life imprisonment, executions are unnecessary and, combined with their greater severity, therefore cruel.
2. Bedau (p. 113) says, "Facts show that the general public tends to overrate the danger and threat to public safety constituted by the failure to execute every murderer who is caught and convicted." The public's ignorance should not decide matters of life and death.

3. Pro #7 can't be, by itself, decisive; for that would commit the *ad populum* fallacy.

Pro #8

Prisons are overcrowded, as the facts above show. Execution will relieve overcrowding.

Rebuttal

1. Give no relief for murderers in particular (or for prisoners in general). "Killin's too good for 'em!" Let 'em live in overcrowded prisons and feel their punishment for years.

Study Question #2

Which of the following cons (that is, arguments) against capital punishment is the strongest, and which of the cons is the weakest? Explain your answer fully.

The Cons (Arguments Against Capital Punishment)

Con #1

Thirteen-thousand people each year (in their healthy median age of 32) is a tremendous amount of manpower to waste. Lost benefits are enormous. Examples of murderers becoming productive members of society include the examples in Grant S. McClellan, *Capital Punishment* (1961), p. 38.

Con #2

Costs of capital punishment include lengthy appeals as desperate prisoners try to save their lives. Publicly provided defense attorneys are expensive. For example, Ted Bundy's execution cost $6 million. (*Time*, Feb. 6, 1989, p. 34) Thirteen-thousand executions and burials is a net loss with not even the slightest gross gain economically.

Rebuttals

1. Save economic costs of food, shelter, clothing, medicine and security.

Reply: The manpower of 13,000 a year is so great that, if efficiently managed, it would be not only self-sufficient but also profitable. The 13th Amendment allows slavery for punishment.

2. Significantly or drastically reduce rights of appeal.

Reply to rebuttals: If we follow the rebuttals' suggestions, then too many more innocents will be executed. See Con #6.

Con #3

The lives of convicts have value to the prisoners themselves and to their friends and family. Convicts can still love their families and friends, practice religion, and lead lives worth living. Convicts' families (and even close friends) are almost always innocent of the convicts' crime. So they should not be hurt by killing their relative. We should not make innocent people suffer due to another's crime.

Con #4

Capital punishment is cruel and unusual, and hence unconstitutional, since it involves force exceeding the amount necessary to protect society from murderers. Death row is stressful due to the Sword of Damacles hanging over inmates' heads. The days before scheduled execution are filled with anxiety triggered by hearing any rumor of commutation or even hearing a phone ring, which could be the governor calling with a commutation. Here are cases of especially cruel executions:

1. Willie Francis didn't die the first time he was electrocuted. He was taken back to his cell to wait for the second attempt, which killed him.
2. A case in the 1980s took three attempts to kill. Before the fatal attempt, sparks flew out of the prisoner's cheek and one

of his eyes popped completely out of its socket.

Con #5

Capital punishment is discriminatory. Fifty-four percent of the 3,859 persons executed between 1930 and 1980 were members of racial minorities. Almost half (over 48.8%) of those on death row are minorities. Minorities compose about only 16 percent of the general population of Americans. Eight-hundred-eighty-one minorities are on death row, compared to 903 whites (and 21 women). In some states (for example, Georgia) a murderer of a white is eleven times more likely to be sentenced to capital punishment than is a murderer of a black. This strongly suggests that juries value white lives more than black lives. And given that most murders are intraracial, this fact shows how discriminatory the other statistics above are. Poorer defendants cannot afford the same quality of legal defense as richer defendants. And many are poor through no fault of their own, born into poor families in depressed areas and atrocious schools. Justice Thurgood Marshall reported that one searches the record in vain to find a rich man executed. Since we began keeping records in 1930, there have been 2,066 blacks and only 1,751 whites put to death, while only 11.7 percent of our population is black. [Isenberg, 1977, p. 123] Similarly, though women commit nearly 20 percent of all murders, they are very rarely sentenced to death or executed. (Bram, 1983, p. 282) See generally, C.L. Black, *Capital Punishment: The Inevitability of Caprice and Mistake.*

Con #6

Capital punishment will inevitably kill innocent people. Executing 13,000 people a year will inevitably lead to mistakes which are irreversible and the most extreme sort of mistake—a fatal mistake. Innocent but poor defendants cannot afford the defense the rich can afford. See generally, C.L. Black, Jr., *Capital Punishment: The Inevitability of Caprice and Mistake.* Remember that Socrates and Jesus were capitally punished.

Suggestions for Further Reading

Acton, H. B., ed. *The Philosophy of Punishment: A Collection of Papers.* (London: Macmillan Press, 1969).

Andenaes, Johannes. *Punishment and Deterrence* (Ann Arbor: University of Michigan Press, 1974).

Bedau, Hugo Adam, Ed. *The Death Penalty in America,* 3rd ed. (Oxford: Oxford University Press, 1982).

Black, Charles L. Jr. *Capital Punishment: The Inevitability of Caprice and Mistake* (New York: Norton and Co., 1974).

Davis, Michael, "Is the Death Penalty Irrevocable?" *Social Theory and Practice* 10 (1984): 143–156.

Fletcher, George, P., *Rethinking Criminal Law* (Boston: Little, Brown and Co., 1978).

Gross, Hyman. *A Theory of Criminal Justice* (New York: Oxford University Press, 1979).

Hart, H. L. A. *Punishment and Responsibility* (New York: Oxford University Press, 1968).

Honderich, Ted. *Punishment: The Supposed Justification* (New York: Penguin, 1984).

Husak, Douglas. *Philosophy of Criminal Law* (Totowa, N. J.: Rowman & Littlefield, 1987).

Moore, Kathleen Dean. *Pardons: Justice, Mercy, and the Public Interest* (New York: Oxford University Press, 1989).

Murphy, Jeffrie G., and Hampton, Jean. *Forgiveness and Mercy* (Cambridge: Cambridge University Press, 1988).

Schulhofer, Stephen J. "The Gender Question in Criminal Law," *Social Philosophy and Policy* 7 (1990):105.

Van den Haag, Ernest. *Punishing Criminals: Concerning a Very Old and Painful Questions* (New York: Basic Books, 1975).

Von Hirsch, Andrew. *Doing Justice: The Choice of Punishments* (New York: Hill and Wang, 1976).

Zimring, Franklin E., and Hawkins, Gordon J. *Deterrence* (Chicago: University of Chicago Press, 1972).

Epilogue: Can We All Get Along?

THE *LOS ANGELES TIMES*

This article scrutinizes the background conditions leading to the explosion of riots—what some call a rebellion—that rocked Los Angeles, America's second largest city, for almost a solid week in the Spring of 1992. The riots were the most costly in American history. At least sixty died, thousands were wounded, and more than a billion dollars' worth of property was destroyed. The aftermath of the riots is of course still felt keenly. The pending trials of some of those arrested for crimes during the riots are making many especially fearful of a return to rioting. The article also debates the question, "How will the events of April and May 1992 shape the future?" The article helps us answer the famous question posed by Rodney King, the motorist beaten repeatedly by police officers Laurence M. Powell, Theordore J. Briseno, and Timothy E. Wind under the supervision of Stacey C. Koon. The question is "Can We All Get Along?" Powell and Koon were convicted of federal crimes and were each sentenced to thirty months in prison.

"Let us please not go back to normal."

—Distressed caller to a radio show during the riots

After the last flames were snuffed out, Los Angeles simultaneously confronted its past and future while grappling with the present. The traumatic days of upheaval left people throughout the region—and across the nation—asking: Why did thousands of residents take to the street in rage? What conditions led to the explosion? What lessons will the city carry forward? And how will the events of April and May, 1992, shape the future?

Even as the charred, twisted remains of buildings awaited demolition, aftershocks rippled along fault lines in the social mosaic, threatening to undermine whatever fragile peace had settled uneasily over the city. Two-thirds of Los Angeles residents surveyed shortly after the riots said they believed that the city had not seen the end of the violence, that another outbreak was likely within a few years.

Pending legal actions posed perhaps the greatest threats. The Justice Department continued the civil rights investigation that could result in federal charges against the four officers in the King case. In addition, Officer Powell faced retrial on a state assault charge in the King beating, while three alleged gang members were charged with beating Reginald Denny. Some people argued that anything less than conviction for the white police officers and acquittal for the black men would be an injustice. Without justice, they warned, there would be no peace.

As the city took its first tentative steps toward healing, Chief Gate's long-awaited autobiography was released. Filled with the brashness and venom that had become his trademark, it rose quickly on best-seller lists.

Then Sgt. Stacy Koon's unpublished manuscript surfaced, laced with racial references. Philadelphia Police Commissioner Willie Williams, poised to succeed Gates, said such "disgraceful" comments would not be tolerated under his leadership.

Just days after voters approved historic police reforms prompted by the King beating, Gates threatened to stay on the job long enough to invalidate Williams' selection as chief. His action, which he later called a bluff, threw city government into turmoil once again.

On the streets, meanwhile, police kept a wary eye on the truce between the Crips and the Bloods—and clashed violently with gang members as officers broke up "unity" meetings and parties.

From *Los Angeles Times*, 22 November 1992.

But none of these aftershocks had sufficient force to knock the city off the course toward recovery. Reaching out was the first step in bridging racial, ethnic and economic chasms. People gave food, clothing, money. Some traveled across the city, some across the state, to extend a hand. And many of them rediscovered that cultural diversity is more than a concept, that a population is not synonymous with a community. In some unlikely quarters, one-time antagonists haltingly sought to close the fissures keeping them apart. The truce between rival black street gangs held at least for several weeks, despite the doubts of police and other skeptics. Leaders of a Korean grocers group met with gang members, hoping to develop a rapprochement and to discuss a jobs proposal. The grocers faced withering criticism from some of their members for negotiating with "extortionists," especially while some Koreans faced bankruptcy or struggled to rebuild following the violence.

Their task, like that facing the city at large, is enormously more complex than the situation following the Watts riots of 1965. The fire this time left bigger and deeper scars. It directly touched a much larger area of the city—virtually all ethnic groups—and the impact resonated in cities across the nation. The challenge is not only to rebuild structures, but to reshape attitudes and to see whether, as Rodney King asked, "Can we all get along?" Hope itself needs to be rekindled. In the seven years since Peter Ueberroth helped organize the Los Angeles Olympics, the percentage of residents saying that things are going badly in the city rose to 85% from 25%.

Now as Ueberroth's Rebuild L.A. begins the work of helping businesses recover, several companies have demonstrated their confidence in the city by committing to rebuild quickly in areas hardest hit by the rioting, including Koreatown and Pico-Union. Sears announced that it would redesign and expand its Hollywood store, which was damaged by looters. Fedco restocked and reopened its La Cienega store in a mere 18 days, announcing, "We're here to stay." The Wherehouse record store hung a huge banner across the burned-out remains of its store on La Brea Avenue, saying, "We will be back." Other firms—Payless shoes, Taco Bell and Broadway Federal Savings among them—showed equally strong commitments to the area. And hundreds of small businesses applied for low-interest government loans to rebuild.

Despite the hopeful early signs, questions remained about the rebuilding effort: Would it produce significant numbers of jobs for residents of the most devastated areas? Would the rebuilding effort reflect the wishes of residents? For instance, would the rebuilt neighborhoods in South Los Angeles be saturated with liquor stores, as they were before the riots? And if liquor store owners were denied permission to rebuild, how would they be compensated?

The questions went on. With the city's schools and the state university system facing budget crises, would plans emerge for investing in the future of young people? Would there be more recreational opportunities and summer jobs for inner-city youth? Could government, particularly the Police Department, become more responsive? Accountable? Would voters regain interest in civic life and challenge their elected leaders to find new ways to confront Los Angeles' problems?

Just as rebuilding was getting under way, nearly two-thirds of the city's voters passed Charter Amendment F, the measure incorporating some of the Christopher Commission's key reforms of the LAPD.

Gates' successor, Williams, won high marks in Philadelphia as a reformer who restored trust in a department long accused of brutality and racism. Williams had publicly supported community-based policing, another key Christopher Commission reform designed to make the LAPD more accountable to the public. But in the sobering days after the riot, he cautioned, "Willie Williams is not a miracle worker. The work we have to do . . . is going to take time."

Time—and commitment. "Can we all get along?" That, the riots showed, would require new attitudes, new priorities. And hard work.

Appendix A

Guidelines for Writing Papers on Philosophical Issues

Concentrate primarily on guidelines 1 through 6 when writing your first draft, but follow *all* 18 guidelines before submitting your paper. Points with an asterisk (*) are especially important. The numerical order does not indicate any order of importance.

1. Number *all* your pages (except the title page) and *don't* use any covers for your paper. Just staple your paper in the upper left-hand corner. Create an imaginative title for your paper that clearly indicates your paper's main question and that summarizes your answer to that question.

*2. Announce in your first paragraph what conclusion you will argue for in your paper and what moral principles you will use to support your conclusions. State your moral evaluations of each morally questionable action in your case clearly and early in your first paragraph on page 1. You must argue from at least one moral principle. Clearly identify which arguments are yours. Take a stand on the main issues early on, and continue to take stands on issues throughout your paper.

*3. Anticipate and fully present all significant counterarguments to your view, and respond to them. You may respond by modifying your position or by arguing against them. In your first paragraph on page 1 announce what moral principles your opponents will use. You will find counterarguments in the assigned readings. The better the argument, whether it favors your side or not, the more space you should devote to it in your paper.

*4. Avoid extreme moral relativism and extreme moral skepticism.

*5. Show that you have read and mastered all the assigned readings. You must always use endnotes to indicate what readings you are discussing. See guideline no. 15. Carefully present and evaluate *all* the arguments in the assigned readings that are relevant to your paper topic. *Don't* view the paper as a mere exercise that must be completed; the paper is one of the few chances you will have to show what you know. View the paper as a great opportunity to show *all* of the *relevant* information you know. Your paper should be an analytical paper rather than a research paper. You might find some outside research helpful *after* mastering and analyzing the readings assigned. But you *must* document *any* factual claims you make that are not obvious. If you have any doubt about whether your factual claims are obvious, document them. See guideline no. 15. Philosophy papers are not history or psychology papers. Morally evaluate and argue; don't just describe.

*6. Give the *full* and *complete* definition of any principle or concept when you first use it. After you have given the definition, you should just repeat the element in the definition that you intend to apply to evaluate an action in your case. Since this course involves applying principles and concepts, define your terms and then *show how* they *apply* to the case or argument in question. Show, *by argument*, that the moral principles make the facts of the case morally relevant. Argue that the facts favor one side rather than the other(s). The more principles you can use (without distorting the moral principles or the facts of your case) to support your moral evaluations, the better your paper will be.

7. Use topic sentences. Use words to show the relationships between sentences in your arguments (e.g., "In other words," "That is," "For example," "But," "However," "Still," "And," "Besides," "Indeed," "So," "Therefore," "Further," "Furthermore," "Moreover," "Similarly," "Likewise," "Contrariwise," "On the contrary," "Rather," "Instead," "In sum," "Finally," "In conclusion,").

*8. Minimize assumptions, especially key, controversial, or unstated assumptions. *Clearly* and *explicitly argue* for every moral evaluation you make. Morally evaluate every morally questionable action in your case. The number will vary from case to case.

*9. Be specific.

*10. Use *extreme* words (e.g., "any," "all," "always," "whenever," "never," "no," "none," "every," "solely," "only," "must," "absolutely," "unquestionable") only with *extreme caution*. Avoid hyperbole. Don't overstate arguments. Avoid slanted rhetoric.

11. Avoid using rhetorical questions as substitutes for arguments. Try to answer any questions you pose in your paper. Consider the following exchange from Gore Vidal's novel *Lincoln:*

> Seward: "Never end a speech with a question."
> Lincoln smiled, "For fear you'll get the wrong answer?"
> Seward nodded, "People are perverse."

12. Be brief. Eliminate unnecessary words, but use any words needed to make your argument clear and forceful.

*13. If a paragraph consists of only one or two brief sentences, check to see whether the paragraph is best incorporated into another paragraph of your paper. If a paragraph runs for much over a page, check to see that you are neither rambling, merely drifting down a stream of consciousness, nor being verbose.

14. Avoid using scarequotes (i.e., inverted commas).

*15. Use an endnote precisely citing the *page* and the source to credit others whenever you use their ideas. Follow the same method of using endnotes that is used in one of our required books. Avoid quote-quilting (that is, overusing others' arguments and merely weaving them together into a position).

*16. Avoid understating your point. Probabilities are usually crucial. Showing a mere possibility is helpful only when rebutting a claim that something is impossible.

*17. Expose the commission of any fallacies others commit, but don't oversimplify or distort others' views or the definitions of fallacies just to rebut your opponents. Don't commit any fallacies yourself.

*18. *Proofread your paper carefully!* At best, typographical or grammatical errors distract your reader; and dividing your reader's attention risks misinterpretation. At worst, such errors obscure thoughts you wish to convey, and convince your reader that his or her wisdom is no match for your ignorance. Here are some words often misspelled or misused: (1) it's "argument," not "arguement"; (2) "it's" means "it is"; (3) "its" is the possessive of "it"; (4) "criterion" is singular and "criteria" is plural; (5) it's "solely," not "soley" or "soly"; (6) "occurrence," not "occurence"; (7) "likelihood," not "likelyhood."

Basic Definitions of Five Major Moral Principles

Egalitarianism (also called Fairness or Justice).

The basic value of egalitarianism is equality (also called fairness or justice). The basic idea of egalitarianism is that good people should fare well and bad people should fare badly.

The definition of egalitarianism includes the following principles:

1. Treat relevantly similar cases similarly, and relevantly different cases differently.
2. Discrimination (e.g., racism and sexism) is wrong. Discrimination is failing to treat relevantly similar cases similarly or failing to treat relevantly different cases differently.
3. We should prevent innocent people from suffering through no fault of their own.
4. Exploitation—taking unfair advantage of an innocent person's predicament—is wrong.
5. We should regularly give significant amounts to charity.
6. No one should profit from his or her own wrong.
7. The punishment should fit (be proportional to) the crime.
8. Promises should be kept.
9. Merit should be rewarded.
10. Reciprocity is important.
11. Gratitude is important.

Libertarianism

The basic value of libertarianism is liberty (also called freedom). But libertarianism does *not* support always maximizing liberty, since it generally does not allow violating one person's liberty to increase the liberty of others. The definition of libertarianism includes the following principles:

1. Anything between consenting adults is morally permissible. (Note that this does not mean that doing some things to an adult without his consent (e.g., punishment) is immoral.)
2. Laissez-faire capitalism is morally required. This includes *caveat emptor* (let the buyer beware) rather than government safety or health regulations. There would be no welfare state or government food stamps to save the poor.
3. Coercion (the deprivation of liberty) is wrong except to punish criminals, to defend against an immoral attack, and to supervise the mentally incompetent (e.g., children, the senile, the retarded, and the insane).
4. Promises must be kept and fraud is wrong.
5. Government should be minimal; it should be as a nightwatchperson limited to peacekeeping functions (the police and the military) enforcing principles 1–4 above with as little force as possible.

Utilitarianism

The basic and only value of utilitarianism is utility (also called happiness, welfare, well-being or flourishing). Since this is the only value utilitarianism has, utilitarianism has only one principle in its definition, namely, to maximize net happiness for all in the long run. Utilitarianism has two slogans: (1) Promote the greatest happiness for the greatest number of people; and (2) Each person counts for one and only one in calculating the maximum amount of happiness. Note that (1) does *not* mean that we should do whatever most people want to do. The minority might be made so unhappy, for example, that the majority's happiness cannot outweigh it. Utilitarianism also does *not* require merely that you produce some more happiness than unhappiness. It requires each person to produce the *greatest* net balance of happiness over unhappiness for everyone in the long run. Slogan (2) means that each person's happiness counts the same, so it would be wrong, for example, to count a particular amount of happiness for a white person as more important (or less important) than the same amount of happiness for a black person.

Prima Facie Moral Principles

The basic idea of these principles is that there is more than one basic moral value. The principles below will often conflict, and so some will outweigh others depending on the circumstances. We cannot say in advance which ones will outweigh which others. We must take each moral situation as it comes and judge, based on its particular circumstances, which principle is more important in that case. *Prima facie* moral principles are moral factors that can be outweighed by other moral factors (i.e., by other *prima facie* moral principles). The main *prima facie* moral principles are:

1. Fidelity: Avoid breaking promises.
2. Veracity: Avoid telling lies.
3. Fair play: Avoid exploiting, cheating, or freeloading.
4. Gratitude: Return favors and appreciate the good others do for you.
5. Nonmaleficence: Avoid causing pain or suffering. (Note this is not the same as nonmalevolence, which concerns only motivation rather than causation.)
6. Beneficence: Benefit others and cause them to be happier. (Note this is not the same as benevolence, which concerns only motivation rather than causation.)
7. Reparation: Right your wrongs; repair the damage that's your fault.
8. Avoid killing except when necessary to defend against an immoral attack.
9. Avoid stealing.
10. Oppose injustices at least when this involves no great sacrifice.
11. Promote just institutions and work for their establishment, maintenance, and improvement.

Perfectionism (also called Virtue Ethics)

The basic value of perfectionism is having a good character. The following are the main character traits which are good, or bad:

1. Being courageous is good and being uncourageous (a coward) is bad.
2. Being honest is good and being dishonest is bad.
3. Being kind is good and being unkind is bad.
4. Being loyal is good and being disloyal is bad.
5. Being grateful is good and being ungrateful is bad.
6. Being charitable is good and being uncharitable is bad.
7. Being forgiving is good and being unforgiving is bad.

Taking Morality Seriously: The Pros and Cons of Moral Relativism

A. Key Definitions

Many students already have adopted an extreme philosophy about morality even before they enter their first college course in philosophy or morality. This extreme philosophy is moral relativism. The point of this Appendix is to give students reasons to take morality more seriously and reasons to doubt moral relativism. Students who accept moral relativism tend not to take morality as seriously as they should, since they tend to think that any moral argument is just as good as any other moral argument because morality is all purely subjective opinion. Students who think that all moral arguments are created equal will tend not to strive in developing and pursuing moral arguments in philosophy papers or in classroom discussions. Following are key definitions of moral relativism and its alternative, moral realism. Examples of views in moral realism include ones where facts such as how much suffering and death an alternative would probably cause help determine that alternative's rightness or wrongness, regardless of what a group or individual deemed relevant merely believes about that alternative's rightness or wrongness. The doctrine is named *moral realism* because it emphasizes reality over mere belief, and because it emphasizes the real properties actions have in fact rather than mere opinion. Moral realism insists that, when it comes to morality, merely believing it does not make it so.

Moral relativism: What is right (or wrong) is determined exclusively by what the relevant entity (group or individual) believes is right (or wrong).

Moral realism: What is right (or wrong) is not determined exclusively by what any relevant entity (group or individual) believes is right (or wrong).

B. Four Arguments for Moral Relativism

1. Comment: There is a suspiciously large amount of moral disagreement. Reasonable people disagree about moral issues. So there's no right answer to questions of morality. Morality seems more like a matter of taste, and there's no disputing matters of taste.

Reply: There is much transcultural moral agreement about the basic particular evils of rape, murder, theft, and lying. And there's even much transcultural agreement on such general moral principles as The Golden Rule. There is much more agreement about political ethics now that communism has fallen in the Soviet bloc, South Africa has made major reforms moving toward a multiracial democracy, and Israel and the Palestine Liberation Organization have signed a historic peace treaty.

2. Comment: Relativism promotes tolerance, which is good.

Reply: Argument 2 is self-contradictory because it accepts relativism and the idea that tolerance is good transculturally or independent of culture.

3. Comment: Relativism is fairer to historical figures, which is good. For example, Lincoln wanted to repatriate all American blacks to Africa. We now think this would be immoral, but Lincoln was a great man and it is unfair to judge him as immoral and require The Great Emancipator to be further ahead of his time than he already was.

Reply: Argument 3 is self-contradictory because it accepts relativism and the idea that fairness is good transculturally or independent of culture. Also, one need not be ahead of one's time to see the contradictions in racism, sexism, etc. As an example, racists inconsistently believe blacks are filthy, lazy, and untrustworthy yet believe blacks are naturally suited to cook, clean, and handle the children while white parents are away. Sexists believe women are dull, passive, and poor entrepreneurs yet believe women are scheming manipulators with great verbal skills. Puritans believe sex is a dirty, disgusting, degrading act we share only with someone we love. Nazis believed Jews are generally bankers or rich and that Jews were generally revolutionary communists. Nazis believed that Jews are mentally and physically inferior yet controlled Germany.

4. Comment: Relativity is true even in hard, objective science. So it must be true in squishy-soft subjects like art and morality.

Reply: First, not everything goes in art. Beauty is not in the eye of the beholder. For example, two computer-generated paintings identical in microscopic detail cannot rationally be judged to have different aesthetic value by the naked eye. Second, Pro 4 equivocates on 'relativity,' since 'relativity' does not mean the same thing in physics and in morality.

C. Four Arguments Against Moral Relativism

1. Relativism cannot rationally specify which group's beliefs determine right and wrong. Each of us is a member of many different groups (an age group, an ethnic group, a family, a nation, a gender). And these groups will, as relativists admit in Pro 1 above, disagree about what we should do. So it is relativism's burden to argue that one.

2. If relativists try to specify the majority of people in a group as the relevant entity whose beliefs determine right and wrong, then relativism will be too intolerant since it will then dismiss moral reformers, minorities, and dissidents within that group as hopelessly and automatically wrong.

3. Relativism commits the *ad populum* fallacy. Most believe *X* is moral. Therefore, *X* is moral.

4. Relativism commits the fallacy of equivocation by ignoring the distinction between critical morality and conventional morality. For example, consider "What is right for America?" The question has two different meanings. One meaning involves what Americans happens to believe to be right. The other involves what really is right for America independently of what Americans happens to believe to be right. The first meaning of moral rightness is called conventional, customary, or prevailing morality. The second meaning of moral rightness is called critical, reflective, or enlightened morality. Philosophy requires us to go beyond conventional morality to critical morality, since philosophy requires us to think critically about moral customs and traditions.

Appendix D

Is Abuse an Excuse?

Announcer: This is a Nightline Friday Night Special.

Lorena Bobbitt: He hurt me.

Ted Koppel: *[voice-over]* The Lorena Bobbitt trial.

Menendez Brother *[?]*: I just told him that I didn't want to do this, and that it hurt me.

Koppel: *[voice-over]* The Menendez trial.

Mr. Menendez *[?]*: And he said that he didn't mean to hurt me.

Koppel: *[voice-over]* It seems to have become a part of our national character, pointing the finger, shifting the blame, blaming the past.

Charles Krauthammer, Essayist/Journalist: Is there a living soul who doesn't have psychological traumas in their past? The answer is no.

Woman *[?]*: Yes, I did shoot and kill my husband, who was also my abuser. It was never my intention to shoot and kill him.

Koppel: *[voice-over]* But what about the principle that people ought to be responsible for their own actions?

Wendy Kaminer, Attorney/Author: When we think about victims, we think about innocent victims, but in fact there are a lot of guilty victims in this world.

Jeffrey Weiner, Defense Attorney: We cannot view acts in a vacuum. We've got to understand the context that they come in.

Koppel: *[voice-over]* High-profile trials, and a national debate about whether compassion and justice are compatible.

Announcer: This is an ABC News Special, a Nightline Town Meeting, Is Abuse an Excuse? Now, reporting from ABC News in Washington, Ted Koppel.

Koppel: Consider this fair warning. Before this program is over tonight, someone on the distinguished panel joining me will have said something to drive you up the wall. Among the lawyers, psychologists and talk show hosts who have been nice enough to join us here is a sufficient diversity of opinion on the subject of the abuse excuse to make the finding of common ground unlikely.

Whatever happened to the time when Americans stoically accepted responsibility for their actions, no matter what excuse might be at hand? Are we on the verge of substituting a talk-show empathy for our criminal code? America seems trapped between a wistful recollection of a past that never was and a future we should desperately avoid. If anything neatly symbolizes our national confusion on the subject, it is the hung juries in the recent cases of Lyle and Erik Menendez, a triumph of compassionate justice, or as cynical a piece of jury manipulation as you're ever likely to see? No matter which opinion you pick, you'll find roughly half the country arrayed in angry opposition. Here's some background from Jeff Greenfield.

Jeff Greenfield, ABC News: *[voice-over]* Thirty-five years ago it was a joke. "They're depraved on account of they're deprived" *["West Side Story," MGM United]*

Greenfield: *[voice-over]* A joke? Not anymore. Why did two grown young men shotgun their parents to death and then lie about it? Years of abuse made them do it.

> **Leslie Abramson, Defense Attorney:** There is a point, if you have been traumatized most of your life, when you go over the edge, period, and that is what happened that Sunday night to Erik Menendez.

Greenfield: *[voice-over]* Why did Lorena Bobbitt mutilate her sleeping husband? Years of physical abuse had rendered her temporarily insane.

> **Lisa Kemler, Defense Attorney:** At the time when Lorena Bobbitt cut off her husband's penis, she was a battered woman in the classic sense.

Greenfield: *[voice-over]* Why did Damian Williams savagely beat trucker Reginald Denny during the Los Angeles riots? He couldn't help it.

> **Edi Faal, Defense Attorney:** Frustration could bring about agitation, and of course, agitation could bring about a situation where people gather together in a mob situation and start acting out in a thoughtless and impulsive manner.

Charles Sykes, Author, "Nation of Victims": Basically, they all sent the message that you can say, "It's not my fault." We've basically turned being a victim into being an excuse for not taking responsibility for your actions. In a sense, we've sanctioned revenge for people who can claim to be victims.

Greenfield: Are these cases typical? No. One recent study showed that fewer than 1 percent of all felony suspects even claim an insanity defense, and only a quarter of those actually succeed. Moreover, the average murder suspect who's acquitted by reason of insanity spends just about as much time in confinement as those convicted. So, what's the problem?

Charles Krauthammer, Essayist/Journalist: These are extremely important cases. These are the ones that everyone sees, everyone hears about, and that set the tone, not only for other cases in the future, but also for a sense that people have of what constitutes justice in today's society.

Greenfield: *[voice-over]* By this standard, the trouble can be traced at least as far back as 1978, when San Francisco ex-supervisor Dan White killed Mayor Mosconi and a fellow supervisor, then avoided a murder conviction with a claim of diminished mental capacity, triggered in part by junk foods. They called that the "Twinkie defense."

And it flourished after John Hinckley was acquitted of trying to kill Ronald Reagan in 1981, after a regiment of psychiatrists battled over whether Hinckley was, in fact, insane. Essayist Charles Krauthammer, who was trained as a psychiatrist, rejects the whole idea of excusing today's conduct because of yesterday's traumas.

Mr. Krauthammer: Is there a living soul who doesn't have psychological traumas in their past? The answer is no. And if the answer is no, then who is going to be found guilty of any offense if they can trace it to that psychiatric hurt in the past and say, "Look, I was driven to it"?

Greenfield: *[voice-over]* It looks very different to Jeffrey Weiner, who's spent 20 years defending criminal suspects.

Jeffrey Weiner, Defense Attorney: Jurors reflect the public, and I think the public has become more sophisticated in understanding that the mind is very complex, and that we cannot view acts in a vacuum. And that's not bad, that's not someone not taking responsibility for their actions, that's not anything to be ashamed of or anything to regret.

Greenfield: But why would juries be more willing to extend sympathy to criminal defendants in a time when the public is supposedly so tough on crime? One answer may be found not in the courtroom, but out there, in the court of public opinion and the mass media.

> *[voice-over]* For years, the American culture has been heavily influenced by the language of therapy, of recovery, the language that defines millions of us as victims

of one sort or another. And it's language that has come to dominate the surrogate salons of the American talk show.

"Donahue" Guest: I was abused for eight years in north New Jersey by my abuser, who is a police officer, still is a police officer.

Ms. Kaminer: The talk shows have helped promote the celebration of victimization that you see at work in the culture and that you see reflected in some of these cases. I mean, the other thing that's going on in these cases is that people tend to confuse the claims of victimization with claims of innocence.

Greenfield: *[voice-over]* This is precisely what worries the critics of the recent high-profile cases.

Mr. Sykes: Not only do you start to say that people aren't going to be held responsible, not only do you sanction revenge, but that we no longer will have a standard of law that says you will be responsible for your actions.

Mr. Weiner: Jurors don't fall for people trying to get out of responsibility for their acts with an illegitimate defense. The jurors are intelligent people that have the right and a duty to analyze the evidence that's presented to them, to listen to the arguments, and then to make their decisions.

Greenfield: But maybe our real concern about these cases has less to do with the law than with the larger society. Maybe what we're really worried about is that a culture that seems more comfortable with explanations than with judgments is a culture that's losing its sense of what is right and what is wrong. I'm Jeff Greenfield in New York.

Koppel: In a few minutes or so, we will come back to two of the most prominent practitioners of the talk show mentality, Sally Jessy Raphael and Montel Williams, and we'll be talking about the degree to which the kind of programs that they put on every afternoon has created a climate in this country, but I want to get the blood boiling here a little bit first, and therefore I'm going to turn to a colleague, a journalist who has spent much—you spent the whole trial, did you not, Dominick Dunne?

Dominick Dunne, "Vanity Fair" Magazine: All six months I was there.

Koppel: All six months, covering the Menendez trial, and I've just read a piece that's going to be coming out in *Vanity Fair* shortly that you've written. You think the thing was a bit of a farce, don't you?

Mr. Dunne: I do. I do.

Koppel: Tell me why.

Mr. Dunne: I found that it was a—I felt that the—that the molestation abuse defense was a fabrication. I found it impossible, utterly impossible, that two men, young men, could go to a psychologist, who was later discredited, but at the time that they went to him, they trusted him, even thought of him as a friend, and confessed to the murder of their mother and their father, they blew their mother's face off, they blew their father's brains out, and describe it in graphic detail, and how they had to go outside, reload, come back in, reshoot Mom, who wasn't dead yet, with a contact wound to the side of her face, how they could tell all this and fail to mention, "Oh, by the way, my father was molesting us," and I just find that impossible to accept.

Koppel: Alan Dershowitz, you're one of the most prominent defense attorneys in the country. I can imagine you doing exactly what the Menendez brothers' attorney did, and doing it very skillfully, but you have been surprisingly critical of the abuse excuse. In fact, I think you even lay claim to having coined the phrase. Why?

Alan Dershowitz, Harvard Law Professor: Well, first of all, I would never manufacture a defense if the facts didn't justify it, and I agree with Dominick that the defense here was manufactured. I do not believe that the Menendez brothers were molested, I don't think they were in imminent fear of their parents, who were sitting and eating ice cream when they came in there, blew their heads off. As a criminal defense lawyer, I'm very tough on making sure that the prosecution proves beyond any doubt that the person did it. But once it's proved that the person did it, I'm not so easy on allowing excuses to come in. Remember, these are not cases of self-defense, these are not traditional self-defense cases. These are cases where the alleged abuser is either sleeping, like in the Bobbitt case, or is eating ice cream and not posing an imminent danger. I worry about vigilante justice, I worry about the message that this sends to abused or alleged abused people, that if you can come up with an abuse excuse, you can literally get away with murder, and I worry about the message it sends to jurors.

Koppel: Let me ask you one very quick question, and then we're going to take a break and we will broaden things out a little bit further. Do you think that these kinds of defense tactics would have been successful 10 or 20 years ago?

Mr. Dershowitz: I do not, I do not. I do think that jurors are confusing their roles as social workers. I think they're becoming very much attuned to the talk show mentality during the day, that everybody is becoming an abuse victim. I do think that the split along gender lines does reflect a little bit the dominance of people who stay home and watch these talk shows. I think Court TV has had an influence. And I think we are changing as a people. We are becoming hard on crime on the one hand, and very, very soft on people who allege victimization, on the other hand.

Koppel: Lorena Bobbitt's attorney, to your left, is already cracking her knuckles, waiting for us to come back, which we will do, in just a moment.

[Commercial break]

Announcer: This Nightline Town Meeting, Is Abuse an Excuse?, now continues.

> **Leslie Abramson, Menendez Attorney:** When the jurors and the public got to see what Lyle was like, it all began to fall into place. He was what he is, a very sincere, full of pain, very troubled, tortured, abused kid.
>
> **Robert, Menendez Juror:** I think that when they use that as an excuse that they're taking the law into their own hands. They're getting revenge. They're taking the job away from the court system, the judicial system.
>
> **Linda, Menendez Juror:** It was harder, sitting there listening to him have to tell us with everybody in the world listening and watching, to know that your father could do this, like—something like this to you.

Koppel: And we are back once again. I hope I [introduced] you before. This is Lisa Kemler. Ms. Kemler was Lorena Bobbitt's attorney and very successful in her defense of Lorena Bobbitt. And I know I was accurate in saying you were cracking your knuckles while Alan Dershowitz was speaking before, though, so why don't you put those cracked knuckles into words?

Lisa Kemler, Criminal Defense Attorney *[Lorena Bobbitt defense: sexual abuse, self-defense & temporary insanity]*: Well, I think that the views just—that we just heard from Professor Dershowitz are quite a retreat from his earlier well-published and well-publicized positions. I know, I think, from his book, *The Best Defense*—and I know he'll correct me if I'm wrong—and he expressed the notion that he, when he represents a client, his job is to win, and that he will do whatever is necessary, as long as it's fair and legal, regardless of the consequences, to get that client off. And I would suggest, that at least with respect to Lorena Bobbitt, the defense that was presented, in terms of insanity, is a defense that has existed since, at least in the commonwealth of Virginia, since the early 1800s. We presented the classic form of insanity defense. And I think that we as a society, as a civilized society, have made the conscious choice to accept that if a person, because of a mental disease or illness, commits a crime and the crime is a product of that, whether it's caused by abuse or because you were born with a mental illness, or because of a tragic accident you developed a mental illness, we're not going to hold that person legally responsible. And this is not some new, newfangled defense. I mean, this has been on the books dating back to the common law in England.

Koppel: Let me introduce Lenore Walker, who is a clinical psychologist and an expert on the subject of battered women. I think where some of us who are laypeople in this look at a case like this and say, "I have a little bit of trouble with it," is not with the notion that someone could be abused and therefore mentally impaired as a consequence of that, but that the legal argument is she was mentally impaired for that one moment. She may have been okay before, she's probably okay again now, but at just that moment when, it could be argued, it was legally convenient to be mentally impaired, that was it. How do you pinpoint that?

Lenore Walker, Clinical & Forensic Psychologist *[Principal investigator for a study that identified the "Battered Woman Syndrome." Executive director, Domestic Violence Institute]*: Well, for most of the cases that I work on, we don't use a mental impairment defense. Most battered women are not mentally impaired, or battered children are not mentally impaired.

Koppel: But in this case.

Ms. Walker: Most of them—well, I'm not sure I would have used an insanity defense in this case. I think you could have made just as good an argument that this was self-defense. And the difficulty is that we've been doing this now since 1977, and the difference is not because we've become a soft culture, but because we have become a culture that now understands the impact of abuse on victims and what that does to their state of mind. It changes their perception of danger. Just like animals in a forest fire, the next time you light a match, those animals are going to be more sensitive to the smell of fire and danger.

Mr. Dershowitz: But people aren't animals.

Ms. Walker: Well, people are animals. But they have the cognitive ability to understand that indeed, they can be hurt, and they are in danger, and most abuse victims, when they get to tell their story before reasonable people, those people make a decision. And I think the jury system, if it's selected properly, is the best system, not law professors who come up with the kinds of ideas that simply say, "They're not abused," without really being there, understanding, researching, and learning about the impact of abuse on a human being.

Koppel: There is, of course, more than one view on this. Syd Brown is also a clinical psychologist. Variation?

Syd Brown, Clinical Psychologist *[More than 15 years experience as a child and forensic psychologist. Assesses mental state of children at juvenile detention facilities]*: I'm not quite as sold in these two cases, in particular on the Menendez case. I was more struck by the outcome of some of the evaluations in the Bobbitt case, in particular the psychologist who had a more neutral stance and came down, basically, in favor of your client. I would make the point that I would prefer to see, rather than the hired gun approach of experts coming in from one side, and then the other side, and the battle of the hired guns, I would prefer to see panels of psychologists and psychiatrists brought in to conduct court-ordered evaluations and hammer out a stance on the basis of the data, which would include interviews, which would include testing, which would include background investigations of the people, which would include interviewing people who know them in various situations. When we conduct a thorough forensic evaluation, compared to a clinical one that we might do, we've very careful to include as many sources of data as possible, so that we're not basing our impressions, our conclusions, on one source of data, be it testing or interviews or whatever. We want to know as much about the person as we can.

And there is a precedent for this in custody work, in that most people who do child custody work will not go into court as a hired gun. I've turned down far more work than I've accepted because I won't go in as the father's shrink or the mother's shrink. I will only go in if both sides agree to use me to conduct an independent evaluation.

Koppel: Let me bring in one of the jurors—you were actually the foreman—Clay Cogalis was the foreman of the Bobbitt jury. You had to make head or tail of the battling clinical psychologists.

Clay Cogalis, Lorena Bobbitt Jury Foreman: And that's why I think the jury system is actually a very good system, in the fact that although we have the benefit of expert testimony, we're still a body of 12 people who have common sense and can take the bits and pieces of both sides' testimonies and try to distinguish for yourself, you know, where you think the ultimate outcome should come from. So I don't think that any of us were bound by either side's expert witnesses, although in this case I think it was unique for the fact that three out of the four doctors were pretty much—had a consensus opinion, and that's from both sides.

Koppel: What, ultimately, when you reached your decision, swayed you—I don't mean you individually—but you as a group?

Mr. Cogalis: I think there were several factors. I think that the abuse certainly was a part of it, but not as a separate part, only to the fact that abuse led up to, you know, the situation that night, and I think the prior abuse made it easier to believe that someone could snap after four years of being, you know, terribly abused, and then to be savagely raped. I think that just leads to the credibility that she did, in fact, snap that night.

Ms. Kemler: If I might just interrupt for a second?

Koppel: Please.

Ms. Kemler: I think that, if we take this out of the context of a battered woman and talk about abuse victims, I don't think anybody sitting around here would have any trouble with a death camp inmate who reacted, finally, and struck out at his guard and killed him, saying that that person—I don't think Professor Dershowitz would even have problems defending that—

Mr. Dershowitz: Well, I've actually had that experience, and I'll talk to it in a minute.

Ms. Kemler: —excuse me one second, let me finish—defending that person either on self-defense claim or that that person had snapped, as Mr. Cogalis said, And I think that, you know, we need to look at the abuse and what that does to people.

Mr. Dershowitz: A few years ago, a guy came to me, he was a Holocaust survivor from Auschwitz, and he came in with a psychiatrist who said he has the Holocaust syndrome, that is, he was abused in the concentration camp, and that explained why he did what he did. My response to the psychiatrist was, "I know thousands of Holocaust survivors who don't violate the law. It wasn't the Auschwitz experience alone which distinguished this man from all the other law-abiding Holocaust survivors."

Koppel: Well, let me just take it—*[crosstalk]*—let me take it one tiny step further, but it's a huge step. Why don't we just have someone validated as being a victim, and then let him go out and kill afterwards?

Mr. Dershowitz: Well, you know, the point is, most victims don't kill.

Koppel: I mean, you understand my point.

Mr. Dershowitz: Yes, and that's—what's wrong with the battered woman syndrome is it doesn't explain why a teeny, teeny, tiny percentage of battered women decide to kill, or why almost no one ever cuts her husband's penis off except Lorena Bobbitt. What made her do that when other equally abused people don't, and that's what's missing from this debate.

Ms. Walker: Well, it's the desperation, and the belief—

Mr. Dershowitz: Circular.

Ms. Walker: —that somebody is actually going to die that is created. It's not circular, because what you leave out is the first part of it, and that is the part of somebody who is continuously being abused, being threatened. Four thousand women in this country are killed by batterers. One thousand women have been killing men. When we give battered women safety, when we provide them some protection, they don't kill. That number has decreased in the 10 years we've used this.

Koppel: Let me stop you just for one moment, because otherwise we're going to have another short segment when we come back, and I'd rather that we even it out a little bit. We're going to take a break, and we're also going to introduce the subject of the talk show programs in the afternoon, when we come back.

[ABC News Nightline poll: Women who kill their abusers should get lighter sentences. Agree, 64%; Disagree, 30%]
[Commercial break]

Announcer: This Nightline Town Meeting, Is Abuse an Excuse?, now continues.

Dwight Jackson, Prosecutor: Now, what happens is, jurors, because now we live in a popular culture, people watch TV more than they read, and they hear these defenses, and when they come up in a criminal trial, you're fighting against their preconceived notions that they have about specific things.

Mr. Sykes: As a society, Americans have become much more comfortable with saying that someone is sick, or they suffer from this complex or this syndrome, than with saying that someone has done something bad or evil. We've abolished sin, we've medicalized it.

Koppel: Sally Jessy Raphael is a professional, therefore she seethes quietly, but she is seething nevertheless. Go ahead. It's—

Sally Jessy Raphael, Talk Show Host: I wonder, with Alan, when did talk show mentality become a pejorative? In other words, what is he doing here now, if he's not on a talk show? And he goes on them quite regularly.

Mr. Dershowitz: Good talk shows.

Ms. Raphael: Why damn the arena in which he's arguing?

Koppel: No, no, no, and he does it very well, but that's not the point. The point is whether we have changed the mentality of the American public—and I say "we," all of us, those of us who, you know—

Ms. Raphael: We have.

Koppel: —that we have created, you know, a bunch of—

Ms. Raphael: We have.

Koppel: —what in legal terms would be called Philadelphia lawyers, right? We've created a bunch of amateur psychologists out there.

Ms. Raphael: No.

Koppel: Everyone thinks they know a lot more than they really do.

Ms. Raphael: I don't think that's the case. I think we have sensitized and, to some degree, educated people about things that have remained in the closet, such as spousal abuse and child abuse. That's what I think we've done. I think we've enlightened. I don't think that— I think— I agree that the jury system is excellent. I don't think they're sitting there trying to pretend they're either lawyers or psychologists. And by the way, the idea that six psychologists instead of 12 jurors, that would be just as bad as six lawyers instead of 12 jurors.

Dr. Brown: Probably worse.

Ms. Raphael: Yeah. I'll go with the common man.

Koppel: Montel Williams.

Montel Williams, Talk Show Host: *["The Montel Williams Show" is seen by nearly 4 million people in 117 markets each day]* Ted, I've got to jump in, because, let me tell you something. In 1835 there were no talk shows on television, matter of fact, there was no television, and back then that defense was utilized, temporary insanity, for a man who attempted to murder the president of the United States. And he was set free, got off.

Mr. Dershowitz: He wasn't set free, he spent the rest of his life in prison. It was Richard Lawrence, who shot at the—

Mr. Williams: Doesn't matter. But he got off, he was not convicted of murder. Am I right or wrong, 1835, right?

Mr. Dershowitz: Spent the rest of his life in prison, never saw— 1832.

Mr. Williams: Nineteen-twelve, it happened again, another president was attempted to be assassinated by a man. He didn't get off, he was not found guilty of murder, he was let off for reason of insanity. There were no talk shows on television then. To say that talk shows are leading society down some path is absolutely ludicrous. I will tell you something, I don't know one talk show host who has gone in to defend a client and come up with this defense. It is lawyers who come up with this defense. You guys have to be held accountable for what you do, and our justice system has to be held accountable for what it has done so far.

Wendy Kaminer, Attorney/Social Critic: Lawyers come up with defenses that will appeal to people, based on what the culture is telling them. And the talk show culture, in conjunction with the recovery movement, is making these defenses believable.

Mr. Williams: Was there a talk show in 1835? No.
Ms. Kaminer: We're not talking about insanity defenses.
Mr. Williams: Okay.
Ms. Kaminer: Insanity defenses, we know, date back to the mid-19th century. We understand that.
Mr. Williams: And before that.
Ms. Kaminer: We're talking about the specific kinds of claims that are being raised, claims of abuse, abuse very broadly defined, and I think we're also talking about a kind of moral relativism that's promoted by the talk shows and by the recovery movement in general, with this relentless emphasis on self-esteem. Feeling good about yourself becomes the primary moral imperative, so that feeling good becomes the equivalent of being good or doing good.
Koppel: Let me just—
Ms. Kaminer: And I can tell you that when you're on a talk show— let me just finish—
Koppel: I just wanted to introduce you.
Ms. Kaminer: Okay.
Koppel: Wendy Kaminer, author of—
Ms. Kaminer: Oh, please introduce me.
Koppel: *I'm Dysfunctional, You're Dysfunctional*. Go ahead. There you go.
Ms. Kaminer: Thank you. When you're on a talk show, on the daytime talk shows, it is almost impossible to talk about an issue without making reference to some personal experience or personal feeling, so that instead of struggling to develop some kind of objective ethical standard of behavior, we're always falling back on personal experiences, our own or somebody else's.
Ms. Raphael: That's not our job.
Ms. Kaminer: And what's remarkable—
Mr. Williams: That is an *[crosstalk]* the American public—
Ms. Kaminer: no, let me—
Mr. Williams: —that says the American public is not smart enough to understand what they see.
Ms. Kaminer: —what is remarkable about these cases—
Ms. Raphael: Yeah.
Mr. Williams: And for you to say that about the people who are viewing this show is absolutely ludicrous. These people can tell the difference between theatrics and non-theatrics. What you see in the Menendez trial, I wish I had that lawyer as one of my producers.
Ms. Kaminer: Oh, if people could so easily—
Mr. Williams: One of the best producers in the world, because what she did was produce a facade, preparing it for the motion picture that's going to come out. That's what's going on there.
Ms. Kaminer: If people could so easily tell the difference between theatrics and reality, you guys would be out of business.
Mr. Williams: And so would you, with a book like the one you have out saying that we're all crazy. I'm telling you right now, that the bottom line clearly is—
Ms. Raphael: Yours is an extremely elitist attitude. What you're saying is that the public culture, that is, everybody—
Mr. Williams: Is too stupid.
Ms. Kaminer: I think you're much more elitist, because I think that you assume that people are stupider than they are.
Ms. Raphael: No.
Ms. Kaminer: I think you pander to them. I think people are capable of much more than you give them.
Ms. Raphael: Montel and I are tired of people saying that talk show hosts pander. It's authors who pander, it's lawyers who pander.
Mr. Williams: She really believes that.
Ms. Raphael: All we do is run the arena.
Koppel: Folks, I'll tell you what. It's anchormen who try to keep, you know, one person talking at a time, simply so that we can appreciate everything that you have to say. Go ahead and finish your point, Sally, and—
Ms. Raphael: She is espousing the— which is, one would expect the printed press to espouse that attitude, right—I rarely have trouble with other— with electronic journalists—and that is, make television, especially talk shows, the whipping boy for everything that goes wrong in the society. The one thing they can't pin on us is violence, because except for— in one instance, we don't have very much violence. But it's ludicrous to assume

that with really genuine problems that women face today, that it is the responsibility of talk show hosts, we're the ones *[crosstalk]*—

Ms. Kaminer: No one has suggested that, and no one is suggesting that talk shows are solely responsible for all this. Talk shows are a small piece of it. Talk shows are a part of the larger culture. And one of the things that's going on, that's being— that talk shows are a part of is, I think, a confusion of law and therapy. What is remarkable about these cases, the Menendez case and the Bobbitt case, is that the defendant's feelings become the facts of the case.

Mr. Cogalis: Wait a minute. *[crosstalk]* I mean, I take offense to that. I mean—

Koppel: All right. Go ahead, you've got the last word in this segment, we're going to take a quick break after you, and then introduce the rest of our guests.

Mr. Cogalis: I think that that's absurd. I think that everybody is trying to make too many parallel conclusions based on this case, and I think they're giving the jurors too little credit. I mean, we don't sit around daytime television, we're all gainfully employed and work very hard for our livings, nor do we go home and read books on psychology or, you know, on medicine. It just really came down to the basic facts of the case, and I think to read anymore into it is a disservice to the justice system.

Koppel: We also have a law professor and a judge here. When we come back, I'd like to ask the question of whether juries, in fact, are taking too much upon themselves, whether perhaps what they ought to be doing is finding these folks guilty so that the judges, then, can show a little discretion in sentencing. We'll raise that issue when we come back.

[ABC News Nightline poll: Too many blame their behavior on prior abuse: Agree, 76%; Disagree, 21%]
[Commercial break]

Announcer: This Nightline Friday Night Special, Is Abuse an Excuse?, now continues.

Mr. Jackson: There'll always be designer defenses, because defense attorneys, prosecutors, lawyers, it's our job to be creative and to come up with whatever you need to have an edge.

Judge Vincent Femia: I remember back in the early '70s, we had— the popular defense back then was the double Y chromosome, "I am genetically required to kill you." That didn't last too long, but it was the defense of the moment.

Joseph Niland, Defense Attorney: They're not something that I, the defense, invents. They're something that's recognized by authorities in the field, mental health field. So the same thing is true with the battered spouse syndrome. This is not something that defense attorneys invented.

Koppel: Let me introduce Circuit Court Judge Lynn Tepper of Florida. It's your fault. You don't instruct the juries appropriately.

Judge Lynn Tepper, Florida Circuit Court *[Member of the Florida Governor's Battered Women's Clemency Review Panel. Created county task force on domestic violence]*: That's right.

Koppel: You sort of leave it up to them to do it, you leave all this wishy-washy stuff out there and so juries end up doing what they feel they ought to be doing.

Judge Tepper: Well, of course, that's not true. We have very specific instructions on the law that we give, but it varies from state to state as to what law can be given to the jury, and yes, in some cases it depends on what a creative attorney submits to the court as a new instruction that may or may not be given. Obviously, we have the standard instructions on self-defense and on insanity, but the battered women's syndrome is different, and there are different tests to assist a jury. That is an evolving area of the law. The judges give it and the juries then have to determine what the facts are. Do they believe the Menendez brothers, number one? Is it relevant to the defense that the judge has structured for them? Did it impact on the outcome of the case? Has it any impact upon the commission of the crime?

That is separate and apart from the judge's job in sentencing, assuming that the defense either was not utilized or was not successful. Then the judge could choose to mitigate and say, "Gee, what a terrible childhood you had. Because of that I'm going to give you a lighter sentence." I'm not suggesting that that happens a lot, but that's a different area.

Mr. Dershowitz: But judges don't speak English. They don't speak to juries. Judges are much more concerned about not being reversed on appeal, and so they give these gobbledy-gook instructions. I have to tell you, I read parts of the Menendez instruction. I've been teaching criminal law for 30 years. I didn't understand a word the judge was saying. The juries threw their arms up in that case and they said, "Look, the judge won't talk to us in English, he won't tell us what to do, he won't let us read the instructions, we might as well take the law into our own hands." It is largely the judge's fault, and in the Menendez and Bobbitt cases, it was the prosecutors' fault. Why in the Menendez case?

Ms. Kemler: So now you have juries taking the law into their own hands?

Koppel: Let me just bring in Professor Pat King of Georgetown University, Georgetown Law School. You're shaking your head. Why?

Patricia King, Georgetown Law Professor *[Teaches family law and torts at Georgetown University]*: This really is driving me crazy . . . we're all looking for somebody to point the finger at. It is our fault, if it's fault, is this society's fault, that once we understand that battering exists, abuse of children exists, we're not doing about anything about it[?]. That is what the problem is. We are in the criminal justice system, where juries are responding to this kind of testimony because jurors know that spousal abuse exists, jurors know that child abuse exists, and they also know if you're a battered woman and you call the police, the police [officer] comes and looks and leaves, if he does anything. There is no protection in the broader society. One has to worry about being afraid and taking care of oneself. What we ought to be talking about is taking this out of the criminal justice system, looking at the social, economic and other problems raised with abuse and battering, and doing something about it so the criminal justice system could do its job, which is to [not] allow people to use this necessarily as an excuse, but to retain our traditional excuses.

I don't want to send a message that it is all right to kill because I was abused as a child, or because I was abused as a woman. That's a bad message to send. I don't want my child growing up thinking that's acceptable. But it's not going to change, because jurors know what's going on in the broader community, and they understand that abuse and battering is not narcissism, it is real.

Koppel: Now, let me just introduce Jeff Weiner, who is a criminal defense attorney, or a defense attorney who defends criminals, I guess, would be a nicer way of putting it.

Jeffrey Weiner, Criminal Defense Attorney *[Past president of the National Association of Criminal Defense Lawyers. Handled 15 murder cases. Only one found guilty of first degree murder. None went to the electric chair.]*: You know, in this day and age, until people need a criminal defense attorney, sometimes they confuse things, and that's unfortunate, because I keep hearing talk about fault. I don't understand why there's any fault. When I hear Mr. Cogalis, who is a foreperson of a jury, say what he did and that he used the common sense that the judge told him to use, and that that jury came back with the appropriate verdict, I salute him, and I salute everyone on that jury. There's no reason to blame you or anyone on that jury, and the same way in the Menendez case and every other case that has been spotlighted here today. Those jurors used common sense, those jurors sort out the expert testimony on both sides. They do what their oath calls them to do.

Guest: Oh, but that's *[crosstalk]*—

Koppel: Well, wait— well, wait, one second. Wait one second, if you would. Let's separate the Bobbitt case from the Menendez case.

Mr. Weiner: Okay.

Koppel: Because in the Menendez case, what you had, clearly, is total confusion, in both trials, and what's interesting about the way the jury broke down is that it seemed to break down along gender lines. Would anyone like to address why they think that happened?

Mr. Weiner: I'm not so sure it was confusion, if I might just respond to that. You see, the fact that the jurors could not reach a unanimous verdict doesn't mean that there was confusion or a problem. It means that the prosecution did not prove their case beyond and to the exclusion of every reasonable doubt, and they weren't entitled to a conviction. Had they brought a proper charge, let's say a lesser degree of murder, they might well have gotten a conviction. But what they did is what prosecutors do around the country, and that is they typically overcharge, and as a result, the jurors have trouble believing in the sincerity of the prosecutors and they compromise very often, which is exactly what they should do, because juries are the conscience of the community, and that's just what we want them to do.

Mr. Dershowitz: But every argument you're making could have been made about the racist southern jurors who, in the 1950s, acquitted white Ku Klux Klanners for [attacking] blacks. They, too, reflected the conscience of the community. They, too, had clever lawyers making racist arguments that they knew would appeal to them. Would you sit opposite a jury in one of those cases and say, "I commend you for having done that?" You wouldn't do that—

Mr. Weiner: But Alan, you know what bothers me?

Mr. Dershowitz: —because jurors can be wrong and they can be right.

Mr. Weiner: Well, I don't know of a better system.

Mr. Dershowitz: I agree with you.

Mr. Weiner: And when you commented that the lawyers in Menendez made up that defense, I was insulted and repulsed, because how dare you call all of those jurors fools? They had a chance to hear—

Mr. Dershowitz: Oh, not all of them, only the ones who voted to acquit.

Mr. Weiner: —Alan, that's so unfair. They had a chance to hear both sides, to sort out the evidence. They had good lawyers on both sides—

Mr. Dershowitz: They were fools.

Mr. Weiner: —and they did what was right.

Mr. Dershowitz: And they were fools.

Mr. Weiner: You know better than the jurors? I don't buy that.

Ms. Kaminer: Why do you assume that jurors are smarter than the rest of us? *[crosstalk]*

Koppel: Hold on just one second, if you would. We can take numbers, if you want to. Montel Williams, go ahead.

Mr. Williams: I mean, this is a point that I've heard talked about all over the nation, in both cases. We were not talking about whether or not a person was guilty or not, and most people in this country have to understand this. The Menendez brothers, they admitted that they walked in a room with a shotgun and shot their parents. That is the guilt, that is what we're talking about. Lorena Bobbitt *[crosstalk]*—wait, just let me finish—said that she sliced off her husband's penis. She is guilty. Now, if a court can decide the guilt in that case, like the judge said, why not decide guilt and then let's talk about all the mitigating circumstances—

Mr. Weiner: The guilt of what offense?

Mr. Williams: She cut off his penis. It's called—it's mutilation.

Ms. Kemler: Well, are you going to get rid of self-defense as a defense? Are you going to get rid of alibi as a defense?

Mr. Williams: No. I'll tell you why—because—

Ms. Kemler: Where do you draw the line?

Mr. Williams: We draw the line when we only do this for cases that people know down the road there's a lot of money in, and I'll tell you what, if this was a gang member in L.A. who walked down the street tomorrow and shoots up four white people and robs them, and then walks into a court of law and says, "The reason why I did that is because for the last 300 years I have been under mental oppression by white people, I was enslaved by white people, and so in my genes I carry that for the rest of my life"—let me finish—and they say that, they make that point—

Koppel: Careful, Montel, because you've got Damian Williams, who did, in fact, say, or who had a smart lawyer who said, "Wait a second, it wasn't his fault, he got caught up in the excitement of the moment."

Ms. Kaminer: He said he got caught up in the rapture, in the rapture.

Koppel: In the rapture of the moment.

Mr. Williams: But he didn't say that he was temporarily insane because of all the abuse. If a black person uses that—

Koppel: Whatever works, right?

Mr. Williams: —would we buy that?

Mr. Weiner: But those are the laws. Those are the laws. If you've got a problem, you've got to take it to the legislature. But those are the laws that we have to—

Ms. Raphael: These are two bad cases.

Koppel: I'm delighted that you're all this interested in the subject, but if we could just go one at a time.

Ms. Raphael: I'm sorry.

Koppel: Sally.

Ms. Raphael: I think these are two— these are two cases, what we're doing is discussing two cases which are really not good cases, if you're teaching law—

Guest: Right.

Ms. Raphael: —to prove a point. The point is, should an abused person have the right to tell the jury or prove to the jury about that abuse?

Mr. Dershowitz: No.

Ms. Raphael: Okay.

Koppel: Why not?

Mr. Dershowitz: But why? Why should they be able to tell the jury that they were abused, if the vast majority of people who are abused don't kill? Of what relevance is the abuse—

Mr. Weiner: That's totally irrelevant, to make that argument.

Mr. Dershowitz: —if in fact most people who are abused don't kill? *[crosstalk]*

Mr. Cogalis: But you think that you're more intelligent than any juror, and I take exception to that.

Mr. Weiner: Good for you, because you're right. Because this is the elitist thinking that I don't buy, being a trial lawyer.

Mr. Cogalis: I don't have to be a lawyer to sit there and listen to two weeks' worth of testimony and decide for myself, and try to ferret out the truth from what I hear.

Mr. Dershowitz: You voted that a woman who cut somebody's penis off and with no real evidence of preexisting mental illness, who will be out on the street in a couple of weeks was insane. You fell for it.

Mr. Cogalis: I didn't fall for it. I don't know how you can say that, I mean, I don't—

Ms. Walker: As a psychologist, when I testify in a case, I testify to three things. One, was the person abused? Two, did that abuse affect that person in some psychological way? And I use all the psychology that I've learned and that other psychologists who are trained that way can use. And then, three, did that affect that person's state of mind at the time they committed the act? And I believe that every person has the right to present that evidence to a jury, and the jury can make up their mind and sort it out.

Koppel: Lisa Kemler.

Prof. King: Every person doesn't get a chance to present that kind of evidence.

Guest: That's correct.

Prof. King: We are not being realistic about the way our criminal justice system operates. There are people, the prisons are full of people who are abused, who have suffered deprived conditions, because people who get a chance to elaborate on this kind of testimony are indeed people who have very good lawyers.

Mr. Weiner: That's the problem, though, you see. There's enough funding for indigent defense, which is the primary, the overwhelming majority of people, Ted, that are charged with crimes.

Guest: True.

Mr. Weiner: And we don't want to give the money to public defenders and to lawyers who dedicate their lives to upholding the presumption of innocence, to going into court and letting jurors like Mr. Cogalis decide. They don't have money for investigators, they don't have money for psychologists or other expert witnesses, and that's why they don't often get a fair shot, and his point is well-taken.

Prof. King: No, the problem is we don't put money in battered women's shelters—

Mr. Weiner: You're right.
Guest: You're right.
Guest: That's right.
Prof. King: The problem is that we don't put money in making therapy available to people who could use it, so they in fact live in fear, and then we expect the criminal justice system to rescue us.
Mr. Weiner: And that's why Janet Reno is so good, because she sees the big picture, and if she gets a chance to effectuate some of the things she's trying to do, there will be more money to stop crime before it starts and then to deal with it, because most offenders get out of prison—
Koppel: Let me just raise one other issue, and then we've got to take a quick break, and I'd like you to address it when we come back. We also have so much public pressure being put on our legal system right now that says, particularly as it relates to drugs, send them away. And we have so many cases being funneled through—I assume it's the same down in Florida—every courtroom in the country, that ultimately what we have to do is, we have to plea bargain all these things away because there simply isn't time.
Mr. Weiner: Doesn't happen. Doesn't happen, Ted.
Koppel: You can't spend six months on every case that goes through the system.
Mr. Weiner: But Ted, with these sentencing guidelines, the judges can't be judges, the judges hate the guidelines—
Koppel: That's what I'm saying.
Mr. Weiner: And so there aren't plea bargains, there are trials with people getting 40-, 50-, 60-year sentences that, by all—most judges would probably give them a lesser and fairer sentence. The guidelines strip the judges of the ability to be judges, and thank God we have juries under those circumstances.
Koppel: We'll pick up on that theme in just a moment. We'll be back with all of our guests in just a couple of minutes.
[Commercial break]
Announcer: This Nightline Town Meeting, Is Abuse an Excuse?, now continues.

Joe Haran, Friend of Tonya Harding, on Jeff Gillooly: He has sought to control Tonya and dominate her for the entire course of their relationship, which goes back several years. He has battered her. I have seen the bruises, bruises which were not there the evening before, yet are there in the morning. I've seen the fear and despair in her eyes when she's known that I've known what's gone on, and I've felt helpless to be able to help her out of this situation.

Koppel: Don't say this program isn't on the cutting edge. The woman hasn't even been charged yet and we're already hearing the defense. Alan?
Mr. Dershowitz: It's not surprising they're setting up an abuse defense here. Here is a woman who has money, who has access to 911, and I wish that you folks would spend more time teaching women to call 911—
Ms. Walker: It doesn't do any good.
Ms. Raphael: You know how much good that does?
Ms. Kemler: It doesn't do any good.
Mr. Dershowitz: Lorena Bobbitt went down to the police, they told her to go back and file a report, and she slept in that day and didn't file a report, and then she sees her husband sleeping in bed, and instead of leaving the house—she's an adult without any children—the Menendezes, instead of leaving the house and leaving their money behind—kill not only their father, but their mother. That's where the prosecutor screwed up.
Mr. Cogalis: I heard different evidence.
Ms. Walker: Alan, you really ought to go to a battered woman's shelter and spend about four hours.
Koppel: Go ahead, please.
Ms. Kemler: It's unfortunate, you know. When you sit in your ivory tower, it's real easy to pontificate from a distance, because you weren't there, and the evidence in the Bobbitt case, Professor Dershowitz, was that when she called 911 in the past, they came, they took pictures of her, he was charged, he gets out the next day, he then swears out a warrant as to her. Then they go to court, the warrant against her is dismissed, and he's given a slap on the wrist, he's told, "Well, if you admit your guilt we won't find you

guilty, and if you go for some counseling, you know, all's well and good." When she reported him to the Marines, he went and she never even found out because—

Mr. Dershowitz: Why didn't she leave? Why didn't she leave?

Ms. Kemler: She can't leave.

Mr. Dershowitz: Most people leave.

Mr. Weiner: Yeah, why is the onus on her? *[crosstalk]*

Mr. Dershowitz: I think he should have been convicted. Both juries in Virginia were wrong.

Ms. Raphael: Alan, now you known yourself that a woman is 75 percent more likely to be killed if she leaves than if she stays.

Ms. Walker: That's correct.

Mr. Dershowitz: That's statistic babble. That's not true. If a woman goes back, she's 75 percent more likely to be killed.

Koppel: Folks, hold on.

Mr. Dershowitz: You're sending a terrible message. You're telling women not to leave. They should leave.

Koppel: Please. Please— I need— I need to hear the clear, clarion voice of another journalist. Dominick?

Mr. Dunne: Well, you see, I think— I can only talk about the Lyle and Erik Menendez [case], but they should have left, there's no excuse. These were not eight- and 10-year-old kids. These were men with money in their pockets, and anytime they could have bailed out of that house. There was no— there was nothing holding them there.

Mr. Williams: When you're looking at this defense, and you're looking at both cases, these are two cases where people have a lot of money. Now, I'm not just saying that Lorena Bobbitt has a lot of money now, but the potential for her money is there.

Ms. Kemler: And you think she thought about that when she took the action she took?

Mr. Williams: The Menendez brothers have the opportunity to hire and pay $5,000 a whack for psychologists that come into a courtroom, testify, and leave. Think about all those kids across this country who are in prison right now, who went to jail for drug cases, who were abused and beaten and don't have that kind of money to pay $5,000 a whack to get attorneys to step up and just have people just flow through a courtroom like water testifying that they're insane. And when you stop and think—

Dr. Brown: But that's like anything else in our society, where people who have a lot of money can buy a whole lot more things than people who can't.

Mr. Williams: —or the potential for a lot of money. I just had John Bobbitt on our show, he's going to air next week. I didn't pay him. But I know that several other talk shows have paid him big money to be on, and they're already talking about his book, they're already talking about the next thing. They're talking about the same thing with Lorena.

Koppel: You're making a couple of very interesting points, but let me just extract from what you've said one point that I think needs to be emphasized tonight, and that is for all that the Bobbitt case and the Menendez case have gotten a tremendous amount of publicity, everyone in the country is talking about it—we wouldn't be here tonight if it weren't for those cases.

Mr. Dershowitz: That's right.

Koppel: We somehow have created an illusion that this kind of defense is being used all over the country in every courtroom, and the fact of the matter is?

Mr. Weiner: Well, the fact of the matter is that it's used very rarely. There are rules of evidence which determine what evidence can come in. And so it's very tightly regulated. Juries sort out phony defenses in an instant, and I have a lot of faith in them for that. And the fact of the matter is that when— when— nobody is suggesting that abuse is an excuse, the title of this show. The fact is, abuse is a factor which often needs to be considered by the triors *[sic]* of fact, which are the juries, and that's the way it should be. There's nothing wrong with that. We should hold our heads up high when a jury comes back with a verdict of not guilty or a hung jury. That means that there was not proof beyond a reasonable doubt, and that is what the Bill of Rights is all about.

Koppel: Ms. Kaminer.

Ms. Kaminer: What troubles me about these cases is what it says about the double standard in the criminal justice system, and the inconsistencies between these cases and the kinds of cases that you see in the criminal courts every day. We seem to be veering between two extremes of excessive leniency, people wanting to acquit Lorena Bobbitt, wanting to acquit the Menendez boys, because there are these claims of abuse, and excessive harshness—

Ms. Kemler: Excuse me, claims of abuse? What about the— this wasn't Lorena Bobbitt's word against John Bobbitt. *[crosstalk]* a ton of witnesses.

Ms. Kaminer: I believe that Lorena Bobbitt— can I please finish? I believe that Lorena Bobbitt was abused.

Ms. Kemler: No, I just want to say that to say "these claims of abuse," this was not one woman's word against one man's word.

Ms. Kaminer: I believe that Lorena Bobbitt was abused. I don't believe that the Menendez boys were abused, but that's not really the point. The point is that we go— we're very inconsistent about our standards of accountability, you know? At the same time that a lot of people wanted to see Lorena Bobbitt acquitted and wanted to see the Menendez boys acquitted, Bill Clinton, during the presidential campaign, flew down to Arkansas to execute a retarded person to make sure that he'd be elected.

Guest: Absolutely.

Ms. Kaminer: We have 2,600 people on Death Row with terrible histories of abuse.

Judge Tepper: I wanted to address the issue of that this is not a common defense. We have so many individuals in prison that are there because they never had the opportunity to present this defense, either because their attorneys were not schooled in it, they didn't know how to uncover by asking the questions of their defendant, or these women were incapable of revealing this information, they had blacked it out, for many of them, and they couldn't even begin to explain what they had survived day after day after day.

You know, we talk about the impact that rape has on a woman, a stranger rapes a woman and we recognize that there is significant psychological impact. What about the woman who's raped every day for two years? And perhaps she's been raped by her father, and perhaps she's gone on and then she's been raped subsequently by a boyfriend. A person that's mugged once by a stranger is afraid to walk down that street at night. And yet somebody that's being mugged in her household every day of their life, of their relationship with that individual, they in essence are suffering from—and this has been diagnosed—with post-traumatic stress disorder. We are talking about valid defenses that haven't been revealed.

So how do we deal with them? Well, we have nine states now, like Florida is one of the states that's taken a lead. Governor Chiles has created battered women's syndrome review panels, and we have three three-person panels that are made up of alleged experts—I happen to be on one of the panels—and we go through the extensive process that Dr. Brown was suggesting. We read trial transcripts, if there was a trial. Many of these women don't have trials, because they're too afraid to go to court, because their attorney tells them the truth. That defense attorney knows they're not going to succeed in getting it into court, so they plead it down and they take life, or they have a history of chemical dependency, they have some convictions for prostitution because of the dismal lives that they've led, they don't want to take a chance as a habitual offender. They plead it out. They go to prison.

We review their records, we review whatever depositions exist. We have input from the prosecutor, we have input from the victim's family, and there's a public hearing, we make our recommendation to the parole commission, they do an extensive study, and then the cabinet and the governor decides. And we have a number of women who have cases pending. Some have been granted, some have been denied. Some I've recommended, some I haven't. That's a valid process. That only *[crosstalk]*.

Koppel: Dr. Brown, please.
Dr. Brown: That's a rational way of attempting to utilize a great deal of information, and I salute that kind of thing. I think the issue with Menendez and with Bobbitt is that they've become sideshows, and that in fact the defendants, who should be the main figures, almost become— you know, they're kind of pictures there, they're puppets.
Ms. Kemler: Well, maybe they become sideshows because of the media.
Dr. Brown: The main actors become the lawyers and the supporting cast becomes the experts, and it's really the lawyers who battle it out, so that Leslie Abramson and the— I don't know, the prosecutor in that case, I don't know her name—
Mr. Weiner: Pamela Bazonich *[sp?]*.
Dr. Brown: Thank you— are the ones who become the main warriors, and they come riding in on their horses, you know, and you can just see them coming into the site of battle each morning, and they become the actors. And instead of the defendants and the victims becoming the central figures, I think it gets put aside on the lawyers. That's why taking it out of that arena so that it's away from some of the publicity—
Ms. Walker: I've worked on 300 of these cases before Lorena Bobbitt and before the Menendez boys, and I say the media is responsible for making this a circus right now. These cases have been going on since 1977. This is nothing new. And the issue that we should be dealing with—I agree with what Pat is saying . . . we ought to be dealing with what is the criminal justice system doing to prosecute abusers before a woman has to get to cut off his penis.
Ms. Raphael: Ted, you said that the prisons are too full of people, in there for using drugs. Why? Because we've said using drugs is not acceptable. I want us to say being violent is not acceptable behavior.
Guest: That's right.
Guest: Exactly.
Ms. Raphael: And we have a law up in front of Congress, and they're dragging their feet, and that's the violence against—
Ms. Walker: The Domestic Violence *[crosstalk]*
Ms. Raphael: —the domestic violence against women law, that has to be enacted. So if I say nothing else on this panel, that's very important.
Mr. Weiner: Ted, you know, you mentioned drug cases. Her prisons are full of people serving life sentences for drugs when murderers and rapists and other violent criminals are out. That's how messed up the federal and state systems are around the country. We put our priority on drugs, and not on protecting the public. People are afraid to walk out on the streets because our priorities are so messed up. We're learning more about how the mind works. Jurors are entitled to the benefit of that knowledge, and there are no simple solutions. There are many that need to be employed.
Koppel: Let me ask the clinical psychologists here, why is it that, as you and your colleagues seem to be moving further and further away from any confidence in Freudian psychology, the courts seem to be moving—and, indeed, we in the media seem to be moving—more and more toward an acceptance of it?
Ms. Walker: Well, we're not. It's not Freudian psychology that most of us are presenting. It's really learning theory, it's psychology that's based on very firm research. I mean, I spent three years researching—
Koppel: Says who?
Ms. Walker: Well, I mean, I had a panel of 12—
Koppel: Let me just stop here—one second—let me just stop here for one second. In reading my research before, you seemed to be perfectly confident that the Menendez brothers were abused by their parents.
Ms. Walker: That's correct.
Koppel: Based on what?
Ms. Walker: Based on my knowledge of what happens to children when they are abused, based on my review of the psychologists who work on the case. They are really very competent psychologists who I've worked with before—
Mr. Dershowitz: These aren't psychologists, these are advocates, and this is advocacy psychobabble. What we're hearing is

people who are politicians, who have a political agenda, it's not that we're learning more about the mind, we're learning more about the politics of certain movements, and these politics are giving us false statistics, they're giving us false psychology, they're giving us false information, and we're falling for it because they are part of a political movement.

Ms. Walker: And what is that political movement, to end violence?

Mr. Dershowitz: No, we have to start—no, selectively ending violence of a particular kind. We have to start subjecting these analyses to double-blind experiments, to see whether you can predict on a basis of data which abused women will and won't kill, which you can't do, to see if you can satisfy any kind of scientific rigor———

Dr. Brown: That's not a valid test of scientific———

Ms. Walker: What do you want to do, put them in one group and say, "You kill and you don't?"

Koppel: Let me—

Mr. Dershowitz: —no scientific basis for this advocacy psychobabble that we're hearing today.

Ms. Walker: Well, scientists say that there is. Scientists say that there is, Alan.

Koppel: We just— you guys keep on talking, we have to take a break.

[ABC News Nightline poll: What should the Menendez verdicts have been? Murder, 45%; Manslaughter, 42%; Not guilty, 5%]

[Commercial break]

Koppel: Pat King, come on into this and give me your sense of the degree to which we are becoming a society of, in the legal sense, of excusemakers, among those who can afford it.

Prof. King: Ted, I have to be like a good law professor. I don't like that question, because I think it's the wrong question.

Koppel: Rephrase it, that's all.

Prof. King: I think that we are a society that has started to pay more attention to the fact that there are victims out there. There are people that— we've ignored abuse, we've ignored battering. It always existed. We're just beginning to pay attention to it. I think, as a society, it is right for us to do that, and I don't think that means that we are creating excuses. I personally am appalled at the message we're sending in these cases. I'm a hardliner. You commit a crime, you kill somebody, you mutilate them, you go to prison. Maybe you get mitigation in the sentencing. I think that's the message I want to send the society, so I'm clear about that. But—

Koppel: But that is not the message that society is getting.

Prof. King: —I agree with you, and what I've been trying to suggest is that is because we are expecting the criminal— we are putting the weight on the criminal justice system to take care of what are really other conditions in the society.

Guest: That's right.

Prof. King: Listening to this discussion has been all about—and in this I agree with Alan—it's all about the fact that the criminal justice system has to bear the weight. The jury is stuck with the fact that we have not dealt, up until that point, with any of these issues, at any other place in our system, effectively. I applaud the jury because they have a hard job, and as far as I'm concerned, if I were on a jury I'd probably act exactly the way they've been acting. The issue is, should they get the case? In my ideal world, they would not, because I don't want to send these kinds of messages in the society I live in. This is not an ideal world. We are in a peculiar transition—

Koppel: But you're looking— I mean, forgive me for saying this, you're looking for an ideal solution. You're saying somehow society has an obligation to resolve the cases of spousal abuse, for example, before it gets to a point that a woman feels that she has to mutilate her husband just to be heard.

Prof. King: Well, I'll start with this show. I'll start with this show. We shouldn't be sitting here talking about is abuse an excuse.

Koppel: Why not?

Prof. King: We should have been sitting here talking about why is it that people who batter and are abusers escape? Why is it that people grow up in fear? Why is it that they're so fearful that they don't leave home?

Mr. Dershowitz: Well, Jeff would applaud the juries that acquit them. Jeff would sit there and say juries that acquitted John Bobbitt of rape, way, terrific, and the juries that acquit these batterers, terrific, because all he likes is acquittals.

Mr. Weiner: No, that's not true, Alan. Juries follow the rules of court. They judge cases on evidence—

Mr. Dershowitz: But juries acquit batterers.

Mr. Weiner: —or lack of evidence.

Mr. Dershowitz: But they acquit batterers, don't they?

Mr. Weiner: Sometimes they do, and if there isn't enough proof—

Guest: Jurors also go into the jury box with their own prejudices.

Mr. Weiner: —those people should be accused *[?]*. They're not batterers if the jury says they're not batterers.

Mr. Dershowitz: Yes, they are. Juries can be wrong.

Mr. Weiner: I don't convict people as being guilty.

Mr. Dershowitz: People can be batterers and be acquitted.

Ms. Kemler: You know, the problem here—

Mr. Weiner: It happens, yes, but— but we have a presumption of innocence in the United States.

Ms. Kemler: The problem here is you can't just focus on the event that the person is on trial for, because it's like—like discussing *War and Peace* after reading one chapter. I mean, the person is there, I mean, you've got to look at the entire book. And the crime that Lorena Bobbitt was on trial for, as well as the trial that the Menendez brothers were on trial for, were specific intent crimes, and traditionally and historically, evidence that relates to that person's state of mind at the time that they committed the offense is relevant and material to the jury's determination, and we have to make a decision in this society as to whether we're going to trust the jury.

Koppel: But answer the point that we heard Charles Krauthammer make at the beginning of this program. Every one of us has something in his or her past that could be interpreted, under certain circumstances, as giving us cause, at some later time in our lives, for committing one crime or another.

Mr. Williams: I have the answer to that question.

Koppel: Go ahead, Montel.

Mr. Williams: Whatever happened in the American society for responsibility, and I'll tell you what. I interviewed a gentleman by the name of Wesley Andive *[sp?]*, serial child molester and murderer in Washington State. I asked him the question, I said, "Wesley, were you ever abused or sexually molested as a child?" And he said, "You know what, Montel? I'm not even going to tell you that. The answer to that question is I am responsible for what I did, therefore I should hang." And Wesley Andive hung in upstate Washington for abusing and murdering children, he did that. It's called responsibility in America, and I'm sorry, maybe I'm the person out on the outer edge here, but I'm going to tell you the truth. We have to be responsible for the action. The responsible thing for the Menendez brothers is, they murdered their parents. Being responsible.

Let's talk about the mitigation in sentencing. For Lorena Bobbitt, she cut off— she mutilated her husband. Let's be responsible for your action and then we'll talk about mitigating circumstances. If we don't do that, Ted, there are over 800,000 people in state penitentiaries right now, and if 400,000 of them have an excuse of some sort of mental incapacity, someone in this society has to pay for that, and we are not willing to pay for that.

Ms. Kemler: Well, then we might as all live in China. *[crosstalk]* We might as well all live in China.

Koppel: Judge Tepper.

Judge Tepper: I think we need to distinguish between the abuse history of an individual that they may have suffered in general and how it may play into mitigation in sentencing for a criminal act that they may have committed against somebody other than their abuser, and then look at a case in which, for instance, you have an individual who has been involved in an abusive relationship, be it a child and parent or two spouses. That is entirely different, and those are the cases that I believe should go forward in a court of law, for a jury to determine whether or not what happened on that occasion was the result of triggering not just what was happening an hour earlier, or 15 minutes earlier, but what was triggering what they knew was going to happen, for instance, if they turned their back and walked out the door. They knew, from past experience with that particular abuser, that the likelihood was that they would be punished for leaving, there would be severe retribution if they called the law, that the law was likely to do little.

Mr. Dershowitz: You're sending a terrible message. You're sending a terrible message to women, you're telling women not to leave.

Judge Tepper: It is absolutely true and for years—

Ms. Raphael: But she is telling the truth. Surviving is important.

Judge Tepper: Surviving is important.

Ms. Walker: She's telling the truth.

Mr. Dershowitz: I'd want to tell women to leave, to call 911, to get out of the house.

Ms. Raphael: Let me ask you a question. Judge, what happens when she goes to the police?

Mr. Dershowitz: And not to believe these phony statistics that you're more likely to get killed if you leave than you stay. Those are phony statistics.

Ms. Raphael: Mr. Dershowitz—

Koppel: Sally.

Mr. Dershowitz: Leave, get out, call 911.

Mr. Weiner: Alan, that's not true.

Judge Tepper: That's definitely not true.

Koppel: Ladies and gentlemen, if you all talk at once, it's really pointless. Go ahead, Sally.

Ms. Raphael: Is there any way to change the laws, is there any way to make it so that when that person goes in and says, "I have been abused and can prove it," that immediately we get some kind of trial, immediately we get some kind of action?

Ms. Walker: As a matter of fact, I just testified this week before the Colorado state legislature, which is considering a bill which about 10 other states now have considered and passed, that says if a person is abused and they raise the issue of abuse, they have the right to present that evidence at their trial.

Guest: How does that help? How does that help *[crosstalk]*

Ms. Raphael: Can't we get trial immediately? Can't we get—

Judge Tepper: You mean trial of the batterer immediately?

Koppel: Let me just interrupt—while you're considering that, let me just interrupt for one moment. We're going to have to take another break, and when we come back, I would like each of you just to address very quickly, because we're going to be down to about our last five or six minutes, the issue of whether, as legitimate as some of these excuses may be in many cases, whether they are not being misused in some of the more prominent cases that are before us right now because, precisely because, they're getting the kind of publicity that they're getting. Let's address that when we come back, and we will wrap up in just a minute.

[Commercial break]

Koppel: Let me raise two quick points about the Tonya Harding case. Number one, I think until she's found guilty of anything in an appropriate court of law, she ought to be able to skate. Number two, I don't think any—I don't think any kind of abuse had anything to do with what happened to Nancy Kerrigan. Now, with that as a starting point, does any of what we have been talking about here—sort of pull it all together, if you would.

Ms. Walker: I think it's important for us to understand that abuse is a really serious problem. For those people who doubt whether it occurs or not, I'd suggest going to a local battered women's shelter or a child abuse center, and spend a little time just listening to what the victims have to say. It's a better context within which to judge it.

Koppel: What kind of application should it have in the legal cases that come before our courts?
Mr. Dunne: Well, what I think is, in the case that I am interested in, the reason I do not believe in the molestation and the abuse is that it was so planned and premeditated, they drove three hours to buy the guns, they bought it with a fake thing. If they had picked up the kitchen knife and killed their parents, I could have believed it a lot more.
Koppel: Montel Williams.
Mr. Williams: In 1994, I think we need to make sure that we bring the judicial system into this era, and we have to account for things like this, but they should be accounted for after the fact. Let's try the case on its merits. If you are guilty, you are guilty. Present everything else in mitigation. And if a judge decides yes, you have a problem, yes, there was this problem, then I think we should make sure the judge does the right thing when he sentences, but we should try the case.
Koppel: Wendy Kaminer.
Ms. Kaminer: I think we should stop spending so much time talking about these sensational cases and think about the thousands of more ordinary cases that are being processed every day, and think about what rational sentence policies might be, and not be hoodwinked by things like "three-time loser" statutes.
Koppel: Jeff Weiner.
Mr. Weiner: Ted, I believe that juries use common sense, they sort out the evidence, they do what's right. They are the—liberty's last champions, along with the lawyers that present the evidence from all sides, and let the juries decide. That's what America is all about.
Koppel: And the appropriateness of these—if you don't want to call it abuse excuse, call it whatever you want?
Mr. Weiner: It's part of life, it's part of the evidence in the case. The jurors should consider everything, not consider a case with blinders or in a vacuum. They need to have all the facts. I trust the jurors to be fair.
Koppel: But should it be the determining factor, Judge Tepper, as it appears to have been in the two cases that we've been discussing for most of this evening?
Judge Tepper: I think if the alleged abuser is the victim, it should be introduced and should be considered and focused upon by the attorneys and the juries. My concern is these cases are distracting us from where our focus should be, and that is we should be asking not why she stayed. We should be asking why he's battering, and what we as a society should be doing about it. Should we be enforcing our laws? Should we be improving our laws? Should we be mandating better education for our judges, for our law enforcement officers, for the attorneys in the system? That's where we should be looking, so that we don't get to the point, as Professor King was suggesting, where somebody feels that their only way to preserve their life is to take the law into their own hands.
Koppel: The juror's perspective.
Mr. Cogalis: I think the message that this should send is that we read too much into these cases. Each case has individual facts that need to be decided upon, and I feel very comfortable that that's the beauty of our justice system, that you have 12 good people from any community who get to sit there and listen to the facts and come to their conclusion. And I think that's the only message that should be interpreted from these cases, because I think it's ludicrous to come to some other type of conclusion.
Koppel: Professor King.
Prof. King: I think that the message we should draw is that we should not dump all of society's problems in the criminal justice system, which is where they end up if we don't tackle them in other places. I'd also suggest that the proper focus is really to look at those who do the battering. And there are legitimate reforms that we can make in our criminal justice system that will make it easier to prosecute batterers, for example, than it is today.
Koppel: Dr. Brown
Dr. Brown: I think that a lot of the focus on these two cases is a matter of voyeurism and a

way for everyone to have something to talk about, and I think that the more important work is the ongoing setting up of systems, such as Florida is talking about, to make this available in a rational way, rather than in a sensationalistic way in which no one is really served, and certainly justice in some general sense is not served. We need to be able to draw on all points of information so that we can really understand what happened. And I am attracted to the point of view of finding of facts, and then using the other information for mitigation.

Koppel: Sally.

Ms. Raphael: Abuse needs exposure. I'm grateful to the case. I think it's wonderful that it's gotten all— these two cases that have gotten all this media exposure, because that's allowed us to talk about abuse and allowed us to shine a light on violence.

Koppel: Lisa Kemler.

Ms. Kemler: I think that there are a variety of reasons why a person commits a crime, and some of those reasons provide a defense, and some don't. And the day that you have to walk into a courtroom, a person who's charged with a crime, and say, "I'm guilty, now punish me," is the day we might as well all pack up our bags and move to China.

Koppel: End of summation.

Mr. Dershowitz: To understand is not necessarily to forgive, and the one message I'd like to send to women who are battered is do something about it, leave, call 911, don't get yourself in a position where you kill a spouse or hurt somebody, because then you will become a victim, too. The women who respond in that way don't come out the better. Leave, call the cops. Improve our system of dealing with battery, I agree with that. I agree with Professor King.

Koppel: Ladies and gentlemen, I thank all of you very much for being with us. I appreciate the courtesy of your taking the time.

That's our report for tonight. I'm Ted Koppel in Washington. For all of us here at ABC News, good night.

Index